The Official *SCRABBLE*® Players Dictionary

Third Edition

MERRIAM-WEBSTER, INCORPORATED
Springfield, Massachusetts, U.S.A.

Copyright © 1995 by Milton Bradley Company, a division of
Hasbro, Inc.

Library of Congress Cataloging in Publication Data
Main entry under title:

The Official Scrabble® players dictionary. — 3rd ed.

       p.   cm.
  ISBN 0-87779-220-8
  1. Scrabble® (Game) — Glossaries, vocabularies, etc.
GV1507.S3036   1995
793.73—dc20   95-20437
                                              CIP

The game board shown on the dust jacket is copyright © 1948
by Milton Bradley Company, a division of Hasbro, Inc.

Made in the United States of America

11 12 13 14 UG:RRD 01 00

P₃ **REFACE** ● This is the third edition of the enormously popular Official SCRABBLE® Players Dictionary, and it includes more than 1,000 words not included in the previous edition. This dictionary has been prepared especially for lovers of SCRABBLE® Brand crossword games and is endorsed by the National SCRABBLE® Association for recreational and school use.

It is important to remember that The Official SCRABBLE® Players Dictionary was edited solely with this limited purpose in mind. It is not intended to serve as a general dictionary of English; thus, such important features of general dictionaries as definitions of multiple senses, pronunciation respellings, etymologies, and usage labels are omitted.

It is the intention of the makers of SCRABBLE® Brand crossword games that they be enjoyed by children and adults alike. With this consideration in mind, words likely to offend players of the game have been omitted from this edition. The words omitted are those that would qualify for a warning usage note on the basis of standards applied in other Merriam-Webster dictionaries.

The detailed organization and special features of the dictionary are explained in the Introduction which follows. It should be read with care by all who use the dictionary. Now that this new updated work is available, we are confident that it will afford satisfaction and enjoyment to SCRABBLE® Brand crossword game players everywhere.

I NTRODUCTION ● MAIN ENTRIES ● Main entries are listed in boldface type and are set flush with the left-hand margin of each column. Except for an occasional cross-reference (such as **MISSPOKEN** past participle of misspeak), main entries contain from two to eight letters, since words within this range are considered to be most useful to SCRABBLE® crossword game players. Words that are not permissible in SCRABBLE® crossword games have not been included in this dictionary. Thus, proper names, words requiring hyphens or apostrophes, words considered foreign, and abbreviations have been omitted. Because dictionaries have different standards for selecting entries, several desk dictionaries were consulted in preparing the list of main entries for this book. Obsolete, archaic, slang, and nonstandard words are included because they are permitted by the rules of the game. All variant forms of a main entry are shown at their own alphabetical places and defined in terms of the principal form. Words that exceed eight letters in length and are not inflected forms of words entered in this dictionary should be looked up in a desk dictionary. The National SCRABBLE® Association recommends Merriam-Webster's Collegiate Dictionary, Tenth Edition, as a source of additional words.

RUN-ON ENTRIES ● A main entry may be followed by one or more derivatives in boldface type with a different part-of-speech label. These are run-on entries. Run-on entries are not defined since their meanings are readily derivable from the meaning of the root word.

FENDER   *n* pl. -S a metal guard over the wheel of a motor vehicle
FENDERED *adj*
HAMULUS   *n* pl. -LI a small hook
HAMULAR, HAMULATE, HAMULOSE, HAMULOUS *adj*

No entry has been run on at another if it would fall alphabetically more than three places from the entry. **When you do not find a word at its own place, it is always wise to check several entries above and below to see if it is run on.**

CROSS-REFERENCES ● A cross-reference is a main entry that is an inflected form (such as the plural form of a noun, the past tense form of a verb, or the comparative form of an adjective) of another word. An inflected form is entered as a main entry if it undergoes a spelling change in addition to or instead of suffixation *and* if it falls alphabetically more than three places away from the root word.

For example, in the entries reproduced below, **DICING** is a main entry because it involves a spelling change (the final -*e* of *dice* is dropped) besides the addition of the -ING ending and because it falls more than three places from the entry **DICE.** On the other hand, *dices* is not a main entry because it involves no spelling change beyond the addition of the ending -S. The word *diced,* although involving a spelling change (the final -*e* of *dice* is dropped), is not a main entry because it does not fall more than three places from **DICE. DICIER** and **DICIEST** are main entries because they involve a spelling change (the -*e*- is dropped and the final -*y* is changed to -*i*-) besides the addition of the -ER, -EST endings and they fall more than three places from the entry **DICEY.**

DICE	*v* DICED, DICING, DICES to cut into small cubes
DICENTRA	*n* pl. -S a perennial herb
DICER	*n* pl. -S a device that dices food
DICEY	*adj* DICIER, DICIEST dangerous
DICHASIA	*n/pl* flower clusters
DICHOTIC	*adj* affecting the two ears differently
DICHROIC	*adj* having two colors
DICIER	comparative of dicey
DICIEST	superlative of dicey
DICING	present participle of dice

This policy is intended to make the word desired as easy to find as possible without wasting space. Nevertheless, many inflected forms will appear only at the main entry.

You should always look at several entries above and below the expected place if you do not find the desired word as a main entry.

Cross-reference entries for present tense third person singular forms of verbs use the abbreviation "sing."

PARTS OF SPEECH ● An italic label indicating a part of speech follows each main entry except cross-references (such as **DICIER, DICIEST, DICING**), for which the label is given at the root word. The eight traditional parts of speech are indicated as follows:

n	noun	*pron*	pronoun
v	verb	*prep*	preposition
adj	adjective	*conj*	conjunction
adv	adverb	*interj*	interjection

The label *n/pl* is given to two kinds of nouns. One is the plural noun that has no singular form.

KINETICS	*n/pl* a branch of science dealing with motion

The other is the plural noun of which the singular is not entered in this dictionary. Singular forms are omitted if they contain more than eight letters.

NUCLEOLI   *n/pl* nucleoles

Nucleolus, the singular form, has nine letters and is not entered.

When a word can be used as more than one part of speech, each part of speech is entered separately if the inflected forms are not spelled alike. For example, both the adjective *pale* and the verb *pale* are entered because the inflected forms vary.

PALE   *adj* PALER, PALEST lacking intensity of color

PALE   *v* PALED, PALING, PALES to make or become pale

On the other hand, the verb *leg* is entered while the noun *leg* is not because the inflected form *legs* at the verb is spelled the same as the plural form of the noun. In a dictionary for SCRABBLE® crossword game players, entry of the noun is therefore redundant. Homographs (words spelled alike) which may be used as the same part of speech are treated in the same way. For example, *gin* is entered as a verb twice because the inflected forms are spelled differently.

GIN   *v* GINNED, GINNING, GINS to remove seeds from cotton

GIN   *v* GAN, GUNNEN, GINNING, GINS to begin

If both set of inflected forms were spelled alike, only one *gin* would be entered in this dictionary. In this way the dictionary includes as many different spellings as possible yet avoids wasting space with repeated entry of words spelled in the same way. The SCRABBLE® crossword game player, after all, needs only one entry to justify a play.

INFLECTED FORMS   ●   Inflected forms include the past tense, past participle, present participle, and present tense third person singular of verbs, the plural of nouns, and the comparative and superlative of adjectives and adverbs. They are shown in capital letters immediately following the part-of-speech label. Irregular inflected forms are listed as main entries when they fall four or more alphabetical places away from the root word (see **Cross-References** above). All inflected forms are allowable for play in SCRABBLE® crossword games.

The principal parts of the majority of verbs are shown as -ED, -ING, -S (or -ES when applicable). This indicates that the past tense and past participle are formed simply by adding -*ed* to the entry word, that the present participle is formed simply by adding -*ing* to the entry word, and that the present third person singular is formed simply by adding -*s* (or -*es*) to the entry word.

NEATEN   *v* -ED, -ING, -S to make neat

When inflection of an entry word involves any spelling change in addition to the suffixal ending (such as the dropping of a final -*e,* the doubling of a final consonant, or the changing of a final -*y* to -*i*-) or when the inflection is irregular, the inflected forms given indicate such changes.

MOVE   *v* MOVED, MOVING, MOVES to change from one position to another

SUP   *v* SUPPED, SUPPING, SUPS to eat supper

PLY   *v* PLIED, PLYING, PLIES to supply with or offer repeatedly PLYINGLY *adv*

EAT   *v* ATE or ET, EATEN, EATING, EATS to consume food

For verbs of more than one syllable, either the last syllable or the last two syllables are shown.

MUMBLE   *v* -BLED, -BLING, -BLES to speak unclearly

BENEFIT   *v* -FITED, -FITING, -FITS or -FITTED, -FITTING, -FITS to be helpful or useful to

The plurals of nouns are preceded by the abbreviation "pl." Most plurals are shown as -S (or -ES when applicable) to indicate that the plural is formed simply by adding the given suffix to the entry word.

ACID   *n* pl. -S a type of chemical compound

When pluralizing a noun involves any spelling change in addition to the suffixal ending (such as the changing of a final -*y* to -*i*- or a final -*f* to -*v*-) or when the plural is irregular, the plural form shown indicates such change.

CITY   *n* pl. CITIES a large town

BEEF   *n* pl. BEEFS or BEEVES a steer or cow fattened for food

ORNIS   *n* pl. ORNITHES avifauna

In such cases involving polysyllabic nouns at least the last syllable is shown.

EULOGY   *n* pl. -GIES a formal expression of high praise

For the sake of clarity, two groups of nouns that are confusing to many, those ending in -*o* and those ending in -*y,* are always indicated in this dictionary by showing at least the last syllable, even though no spelling change is involved.

MUNGO *n* pl. -GOS a low-quality wool

NAY *n* pl. NAYS a negative vote

Variant plurals are shown wherever they add another word permissible in SCRABBLE® crossword games.

CELLO *n* pl. -LOS or -LI a stringed musical instrument

Plurals which have the same form as the singular are shown only when they are the only plural for that entry. This is done to show that for the entry in question it is not permissible to add -*s* (or -*es*) to the singular to create a plural.

TAKA *n* pl. TAKA a monetary unit of Bangladesh

VEG *n* pl. VEG a vegetable

Otherwise, they are omitted and only the plural with the inflection is shown.

DEER *n* pl. -S a ruminant mammal

The comparative and superlative forms of adjectives and adverbs are shown, when applicable, immediately following the part-of-speech label. Any spelling changes are indicated in the forms shown.

JUST *adj* JUSTER, JUSTEST acting in conformity with what is morally good

FAR *adv* FARTHER, FARTHEST or FURTHER, FURTHEST at or to a great distance

LACEY *adj* LACIER, LACIEST lacy

Not all adjectives or adverbs can be inflected, and only those inflected forms shown are acceptable. None of the adjectives and adverbs listed as run-on entries in this dictionary have inflected forms.

DEFINITIONS ● In most cases, only one very brief definition is given for each main entry since definitions do not play a significant role in the SCRABBLE® crossword game. This definition serves only to orient the player in a general way to a single meaning of the word. It is not intended to have all the precision and detail of a definition in a good general dictionary.

When a word consisting of eight letters or less appears in a definition but is not an entry in this dictionary, it is glossed in parentheses. For example, at the entry for the verb *hand,* the noun "hand" is used in the definition and is glossed because the noun *hand* is not a separate entry.

HAND   *v* -ED, -ING, -S to present with the hand (the end of the forearm)

A main entry that is a variant form of another entry is defined in terms of the most common form, which is entered and defined at its own alphabetical place.

MATZA   *n* pl. -S matzo
MATZAH   *n* pl. -S matzo
MATZO   *n* pl. -ZOS, -ZOT, or -ZOTH an unleavened bread

SCRABBLE® crossword game players in Canada will be pleased to learn that variant forms such as *honour, centre,* and *cheque,* which are often omitted from general dictionaries, have also been included in this book.

LISTS OF UNDEFINED WORDS   ●   Lists of undefined words appear after the entries of the prefixes **RE-** and **UN-.** These words are not defined because they are self-explanatory: their meanings are simply the sum of a meaning of the prefix combined with a meaning of the root word. All of their inflected forms are given, however.

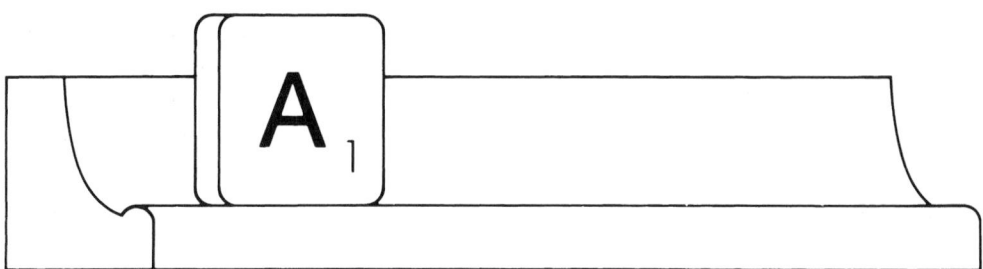

AA   *n* pl. -S rough, cindery lava

AAH   *v* -ED, -ING, -S to exclaim in amazement, joy, or surprise

AAL   *n* pl. -S an East Indian shrub

AALII   *n* pl. -S a tropical tree

AARDVARK   *n* pl. -S an African mammal

AARDWOLF   *n* pl. -WOLVES an African mammal

AARGH   *interj* — used to express disgust

AARRGH   *interj* aargh

AARRGHH   *interj* aargh

AASVOGEL   *n* pl. -S a vulture

AB   *n* pl. -S an abdominal muscle

ABA   *n* pl. -S a sleeveless garment worn by Arabs

ABACA   *n* pl. -S a Philippine plant

ABACK   *adv* toward the back

ABACUS   *n* pl. -CI or -CUSES a calculating device

ABAFT   *adv* toward the stern

ABAKA   *n* pl. -S abaca

ABALONE   *n* pl. -S an edible shellfish

ABAMP   *n* pl. -S abampere

ABAMPERE   *n* pl. -S a unit of electric current

ABANDON   *v* -ED, -ING, -S to leave or give up completely

ABAPICAL   *adj* directed away from the apex

ABASE   *v* ABASED, ABASING, ABASES to lower in rank, prestige, or esteem **ABASEDLY** *adv*

ABASER   *n* pl. -S one that abases

ABASH   *v* -ED, -ING, -ES to make ashamed or embarrassed

ABASIA   *n* pl. -S a defect in muscular coordination in walking

ABASING   present participle of abase

ABATE   *v* ABATED, ABATING, ABATES to reduce in degree or intensity **ABATABLE** *adj*

ABATER   *n* pl. -S one that abates

ABATIS   *n* pl. -TISES a barrier made of felled trees

ABATOR   *n* pl. -S one that unlawfully seizes an inheritance

ABATTIS   *n* pl. -TISES abatis

ABATTOIR   *n* pl. -S a slaughterhouse

ABAXIAL   *adj* situated away from the axis

ABAXILE   *adj* abaxial

ABBA   *n* pl. -S father — used as a title of honor

ABBACY   *n* pl. -CIES the office of an abbot

ABBATIAL   *adj* pertaining to an abbot

ABBE   *n* pl. -S an abbot

ABBESS   *n* pl. -ES the female superior of a convent of nuns

ABBEY   *n* pl. -BEYS a monastery or convent

ABBOT   *n* pl. -S the superior of a monastery

ABBOTCY   *n* pl. -CIES abbacy

ABDICATE   *v* -CATED, -CATING, -CATES to give up formally

ABDOMEN   *n* pl. -MENS or -MINA the body cavity containing the viscera

ABDUCE   *v* -DUCED, -DUCING, -DUCES to abduct

ABDUCENS   *n* pl. -CENTES a cranial nerve

ABDUCENT   *adj* serving to abduct

ABDUCING   present participle of abduce

ABDUCT   *v* -ED, -ING, -S to draw away from the original position

ABDUCTOR   *n* pl. -ES or -S an abducent muscle

ABEAM   *adv* at right angles to the keel of a ship

ABED *adv* in bed

ABELE *n* pl. -S a Eurasian tree

ABELIA *n* pl. -S an Asian or Mexican shrub

ABELIAN *adj* being a commutative group in mathematics

ABELMOSK *n* pl. -S a tropical herb

ABERRANT *n* pl. -S a deviant

ABET *v* ABETTED, ABETTING, ABETS to encourage and support

ABETMENT *n* pl. -S the act of abetting

ABETTAL *n* pl. -S abetment

ABETTED past tense of abet

ABETTER *n* pl. -S abettor

ABETTING present participle of abet

ABETTOR *n* pl. -S one that abets

ABEYANCE *n* pl. -S temporary inactivity

ABEYANCY *n* pl. -CIES abeyance

ABEYANT *adj* marked by abeyance

ABFARAD *n* pl. -S a unit of capacitance

ABHENRY *n* pl. -RIES or -RYS a unit of inductance

ABHOR *v* -HORRED, -HORRING, -HORS to loathe

ABHORRER *n* pl. -S one that abhors

ABIDANCE *n* pl. -S the act of abiding

ABIDE *v* ABODE or ABIDED, ABIDING, ABIDES to accept without objection

ABIDER *n* pl. -S one that abides

ABIGAIL *n* pl. -S a lady's maid

ABILITY *n* pl. -TIES the quality of being able to do something

ABIOSIS *n* pl. -OSES absence of life **ABIOTIC** *adj*

ABJECT *adj* sunk to a low condition **ABJECTLY** *adv*

ABJURE *v* -JURED, -JURING, -JURES to renounce under oath

ABJURER *n* pl. -S one that abjures

ABLATE *v* -LATED, -LATING, -LATES to remove by cutting

ABLATION *n* pl. -S surgical removal of a bodily part

ABLATIVE *n* pl. -S a grammatical case

ABLAUT *n* pl. -S a patterned change in root vowels of verb forms

ABLAZE *adj* being on fire

ABLE *adj* ABLER, ABLEST having sufficient power, skill, or resources

ABLE *n* pl. -S a communications code word for the letter A

ABLEGATE *n* pl. -S a papal envoy

ABLER comparative of able

ABLEST superlative of able

ABLINGS *adv* ablins

ABLINS *adv* perhaps

ABLOOM *adj* blooming

ABLUENT *n* pl. -S a cleansing agent

ABLUSH *adj* blushing

ABLUTED *adj* washed clean

ABLUTION *n* pl. -S a washing

ABLY *adv* in an able manner

ABMHO *n* pl. -MHOS a unit of electrical conductance

ABNEGATE *v* -GATED, -GATING, -GATES to deny to oneself

ABNORMAL *n* pl. -S a mentally deficient person

ABOARD *adv* into, in, or on a ship, train, or airplane

ABODE *v* ABODED, ABODING, ABODES to forebode

ABOHM *n* pl. -S a unit of electrical resistance

ABOIDEAU *n* pl. -DEAUS or -DEAUX a type of dike

ABOIL *adj* boiling

ABOITEAU *n* pl. -TEAUS or -TEAUX aboideau

ABOLISH *v* -ED, -ING, -ES to do away with

ABOLLA *n* pl. -LAE a cloak worn in ancient Rome

ABOMA *n* pl. -S a South American snake

ABOMASAL *adj* pertaining to the abomasum

ABOMASUM *n* pl. -SA the fourth stomach of a ruminant

ABOMASUS *n* pl. -MASI abomasum

ABOON *adv* above

ABORAL *adj* situated away from the mouth **ABORALLY** *adv*

ABORNING *adv* while being born

ABORT *v* -ED, -ING, -S to bring forth a fetus prematurely

ABORTER *n* pl. -S one that aborts

ABORTION   *n* pl. -S induced expulsion of a nonviable fetus

ABORTIVE   *adj* failing to succeed

ABOUGHT   past tense of aby and abye

ABOULIA   *n* pl. -S abulia **ABOULIC** *adj*

ABOUND   *v* -ED, -ING, -S to have a large number or amount

ABOUT   *adv* approximately

ABOVE   *n* pl. -S something that is above (in a higher place)

ABRACHIA   *n* pl. -S a lack of arms

ABRADANT   *n* pl. -S an abrasive

ABRADE   *v* ABRADED, ABRADING, ABRADES to wear away by friction

ABRADER   *n* pl. -S a tool for abrading

ABRASION   *n* pl. -S the act of abrading

ABRASIVE   *n* pl. -S an abrading substance

ABREACT   *v* -ED, -ING, -S to release repressed emotions by reliving the original traumatic experience

ABREAST   *adv* side by side

ABRI   *n* pl. -S a bomb shelter

ABRIDGE   *v* ABRIDGED, ABRIDGING, ABRIDGES to reduce the length of

ABRIDGER   *n* pl. -S one that abridges

ABROACH   *adj* astir

ABROAD   *adv* out of one's own country

ABROGATE   *v* -GATED, -GATING, -GATES to abolish by authoritative action

ABROSIA   *n* pl. -S a fasting from food

ABRUPT   *adj* -RUPTER, -RUPTEST rudely brief **ABRUPTLY** *adv*

ABSCESS   *v* -ED, -ING, -ES to form an abscess (a localized collection of pus surrounded by inflamed tissue)

ABSCISE   *v* -SCISED, -SCISING, -SCISES to cut off

ABSCISIN   *n* pl. -S a regulatory substance found in plants

ABSCISSA   *n* pl. -SAS or -SAE a particular geometric coordinate

ABSCOND   *v* -ED, -ING, -S to depart suddenly and secretly

ABSEIL   *v* -ED, -ING, -S to rappel

ABSENCE   *n* pl. -S the state of being away

ABSENT   *v* -ED, -ING, -S to take or keep away

ABSENTEE   *n* pl. -S one that is not present

ABSENTER   *n* pl. -S one that absents himself

ABSENTLY   *adv* in an inattentive manner

ABSINTH   *n* pl. -S absinthe

ABSINTHE   *n* pl. -S a bitter liqueur

ABSOLUTE   *adj* -LUTER, -LUTEST free from restriction

ABSOLUTE   *n* pl. -S something that is absolute

ABSOLVE   *v* -SOLVED, -SOLVING, -SOLVES to free from the consequences of an action

ABSOLVER   *n* pl. -S one that absolves

ABSONANT   *adj* unreasonable

ABSORB   *v* -ED, -ING, -S to take up or in

ABSORBER   *n* pl. -S one that absorbs

ABSTAIN   *v* -ED, -ING, -S to refrain voluntarily

ABSTERGE   *v* -STERGED, -STERGING, -STERGES to cleanse by wiping

ABSTRACT   *adj* -STRACTER, -STRACTEST difficult to understand

ABSTRACT   *v* -ED, -ING, -S to take away

ABSTRICT   *v* -ED, -ING, -S to form by cutting off

ABSTRUSE   *adj* -STRUSER, -STRUSEST difficult to understand

ABSURD   *adj* -SURDER, -SURDEST ridiculously incongruous or unreasonable **ABSURDLY** *adv*

ABSURD   *n* pl. -S the condition in which man exists in an irrational and meaningless universe

ABUBBLE   *adj* bubbling

ABULIA   *n* pl. -S loss of will power **ABULIC** *adj*

ABUNDANT   *adj* present in great quantity

ABUSE   *v* ABUSED, ABUSING, ABUSES to use wrongly or improperly **ABUSABLE** *adj*

ABUSER   *n* pl. -S one that abuses

ABUSIVE   *adj* characterized by wrong or improper use

ABUT   *v* ABUTTED, ABUTTING, ABUTS to touch along a border

ABUTILON   *n* pl. -S a flowering plant

ABUTMENT   *n* pl. -S something that abuts

ABUTTAL   *n* pl. -S an abutment

ABUTTED   past tense of abut

ABUTTER   *n* pl. -S one that abuts

ABUTTING	present participle of abut
ABUZZ	*adj* buzzing
ABVOLT	*n* pl. -S a unit of electromotive force
ABWATT	*n* pl. -S a unit of power
ABY	*v* ABOUGHT, ABYING, ABYS to pay the penalty for
ABYE	*v* ABOUGHT, ABYING, ABYES to aby
ABYSM	*n* pl. -S an abyss
ABYSMAL	*adj* immeasurably deep
ABYSS	*n* pl. -ES a bottomless chasm **ABYSSAL** *adj*
ACACIA	*n* pl. -S a flowering tree or shrub
ACADEME	*n* pl. -S a place of instruction
ACADEMIA	*n* pl. -S scholastic life or environment
ACADEMIC	*n* pl. -S a college student or teacher
ACADEMY	*n* pl. -MIES a secondary school
ACAJOU	*n* pl. -S a tropical tree
ACALEPH	*n* pl. -LEPHAE or -LEPHS a jellyfish
ACALEPHE	*n* pl. -S acaleph
ACANTHUS	*n* pl. -THI or -THUSES a prickly herb
ACAPNIA	*n* pl. -S a lack of carbon dioxide in blood and tissues
ACARI	pl. of acarus
ACARID	*n* pl. -S a type of arachnid
ACARIDAN	*n* pl. -S acarid
ACARINE	*n* pl. -S acarid
ACAROID	*adj* resembling an acarid
ACARPOUS	*adj* not producing fruit
ACARUS	*n* pl. -RI a mite
ACAUDAL	*adj* having no tail
ACAUDATE	*adj* acaudal
ACAULINE	*adj* having no stem
ACAULOSE	*adj* acauline
ACAULOUS	*adj* acauline
ACCEDE	*v* -CEDED, -CEDING, -CEDES to consent
ACCEDER	*n* pl. -S one that accedes
ACCENT	*v* -ED, -ING, -S to pronounce with prominence
ACCENTOR	*n* pl. -S a songbird
ACCEPT	*v* -ED, -ING, -S to receive willingly
ACCEPTEE	*n* pl. -S one that is accepted
ACCEPTER	*n* pl. -S one that accepts
ACCEPTOR	*n* pl. -S accepter
ACCESS	*v* -ED, -ING, -ES to get at
ACCIDENT	*n* pl. -S an unexpected or unintentional occurrence
ACCIDIA	*n* pl. -S acedia
ACCIDIE	*n* pl. -S acedia
ACCLAIM	*v* -ED, -ING, -S to shout approval of
ACCOLADE	*n* pl. -S an expression of praise
ACCORD	*v* -ED, -ING, -S to bring into agreement
ACCORDER	*n* pl. -S one that accords
ACCOST	*v* -ED, -ING, -S to approach and speak to first
ACCOUNT	*v* -ED, -ING, -S to give an explanation
ACCOUTER	*v* -ED, -ING, -S to equip
ACCOUTRE	*v* -TRED, -TRING, -TRES to accouter
ACCREDIT	*v* -ED, -ING, -S to give official authorization to
ACCRETE	*v* -CRETED, -CRETING, -CRETES to grow together
ACCRUAL	*n* pl. -S the act of accruing
ACCRUE	*v* -CRUED, -CRUING, -CRUES to come as an increase or addition
ACCURACY	*n* pl. -CIES the quality of being accurate
ACCURATE	*adj* free from error
ACCURSED	*adj* damnable
ACCURST	*adj* accursed
ACCUSAL	*n* pl. -S the act of accusing
ACCUSANT	*n* pl. -S an accuser
ACCUSE	*v* -CUSED, -CUSING, -CUSES to make an assertion against
ACCUSER	*n* pl. -S one that accuses
ACCUSTOM	*v* -ED, -ING, -S to make familiar
ACE	*v* ACED, ACING, ACES to score a point against in a single stroke
ACEDIA	*n* pl. -S apathy
ACELDAMA	*n* pl. -S a place of bloodshed
ACENTRIC	*adj* having no center
ACEQUIA	*n* pl. -S an irrigation ditch or canal
ACERATE	*adj* acerose
ACERATED	*adj* acerose

ACERB   *adj* ACERBER, ACERBEST sour

ACERBATE   *v* -BATED, -BATING, -BATES to make sour

ACERBIC   *adj* acerb

ACERBITY   *n* pl. -TIES sourness

ACEROLA   *n* pl. -S a West Indian shrub

ACEROSE   *adj* needle-shaped

ACEROUS   *adj* acerose

ACERVATE   *adj* growing in compact clusters

ACERVULI   *n/pl* spore-producing organs of certain fungi

ACESCENT   *n* pl. -S something that is slightly sour

ACETA   pl. of acetum

ACETAL   *n* pl. -S a flammable liquid

ACETAMID   *n* pl. -S an amide of acetic acid

ACETATE   *n* pl. -S a salt of acetic acid **ACETATED** *adj*

ACETIC   *adj* pertaining to vinegar

ACETIFY   *v* -FIED, -FYING, -FIES to convert into vinegar

ACETIN   *n* pl. -S a chemical compound

ACETONE   *n* pl. -S a flammable liquid **ACETONIC** *adj*

ACETOSE   *adj* acetous

ACETOUS   *adj* tasting like vinegar

ACETOXYL   *n* pl. -S a univalent radical

ACETUM   *n* pl. -TA vinegar

ACETYL   *n* pl. -S a univalent radical **ACETYLIC** *adj*

ACHE   *v* ACHED, ACHING, ACHES to suffer a dull, continuous pain

ACHENE   *n* pl. -S a type of fruit **ACHENIAL** *adj*

ACHIER   comparative of achy

ACHIEST   superlative of achy

ACHIEVE   *v* ACHIEVED, ACHIEVING, ACHIEVES to carry out successfully

ACHIEVER   *n* pl. -S one that achieves

ACHILLEA   *n* pl. -S yarrow

ACHINESS   *n* pl. -ES the state of being achy

ACHING   present participle of ache

ACHINGLY   *adv* in an aching manner

ACHIOTE   *n* pl. -S a yellowish red dye

ACHOLIA   *n* pl. -S a lack of bile

ACHOO   *interj* ahchoo

ACHROMAT   *n* pl. -S a type of lens

ACHROMIC   *adj* having no color

ACHY   *adj* ACHIER, ACHIEST aching

ACICULA   *n* pl. -LAE or -LAS a needlelike part or process **ACICULAR** *adj*

ACICULUM   *n* pl. -LA or -LUMS a bristlelike part

ACID   *n* pl. -S a type of chemical compound

ACIDEMIA   *n* pl. -S a condition of increased acidity of the blood

ACIDHEAD   *n* pl. -S one who uses LSD

ACIDIC   *adj* sour

ACIDIFY   *v* -FIED, -FYING, -FIES to convert into an acid

ACIDITY   *n* pl. -TIES sourness

ACIDLY   *adv* sourly

ACIDNESS   *n* pl. -ES acidity

ACIDOSIS   *n* pl. -DOSES an abnormal condition of the blood **ACIDOTIC** *adj*

ACIDURIA   *n* pl. -S a condition of having excessive amounts of acid in the urine

ACIDY   *adj* sour

ACIERATE   *v* -ATED, -ATING, -ATES to turn into steel

ACIFORM   *adj* needle-shaped

ACING   present participle of ace

ACINUS   *n* pl. -NI a small, saclike division of a gland **ACINAR, ACINIC, ACINOSE, ACINOUS** *adj*

ACKEE   *n* pl. -S akee

ACLINIC   *adj* having no inclination

ACME   *n* pl. -S the highest point **ACMATIC, ACMIC** *adj*

ACNE   *n* pl. -S a skin disease **ACNED** *adj*

ACNODE   *n* pl. -S an element of a mathematical set that is isolated from the other elements

ACOCK   *adj* cocked

ACOLD   *adj* cold

ACOLYTE   *n* pl. -S an assistant

ACONITE   *n* pl. -S a poisonous herb **ACONITIC** *adj*

ACONITUM   *n* pl. -S aconite

ACORN   *n* pl. -S the fruit of the oak tree

ACOUSTIC   *n* pl. -S a hearing aid

ACQUAINT   *v* -ED, -ING, -S to cause to know

ACQUEST   *n* pl. -S something acquired

ACQUIRE	*v* -QUIRED, -QUIRING, -QUIRES to come into possession of
ACQUIRER	*n* pl. -S one that acquires
ACQUIT	*v* -QUITTED, -QUITTING, -QUITS to free or clear from a charge of fault or crime
ACRASIA	*n* pl. -S a lack of self-control
ACRASIN	*n* pl. -S a substance secreted by the cells of a slime mold
ACRE	*n* pl. -S a unit of area
ACREAGE	*n* pl. -S area in acres
ACRED	*adj* owning many acres
ACRID	*adj* -RIDER, -RIDEST sharp and harsh to the taste or smell
ACRIDINE	*n* pl. -S a chemical compound
ACRIDITY	*n* pl. -TIES the state of being acrid
ACRIDLY	*adv* in an acrid manner
ACRIMONY	*n* pl. -NIES sharpness or bitterness of speech or temper
ACROBAT	*n* pl. -S one skilled in feats of agility and balance
ACRODONT	*n* pl. -S an animal having rootless teeth
ACROGEN	*n* pl. -S a plant growing at the apex only
ACROLECT	*n* pl. -S a high form of a language
ACROLEIN	*n* pl. -S a flammable liquid
ACROLITH	*n* pl. -S a type of statue
ACROMION	*n* pl. -MIA the outward end of the shoulder blade **ACROMIAL** *adj*
ACRONIC	*adj* occurring at sunset
ACRONYM	*n* pl. -S a word formed from the initials of a compound term or series of words
ACROSOME	*n* pl. -S a thin sac at the head of a sperm
ACROSS	*prep* from one side of to the other
ACROSTIC	*n* pl. -S a poem in which certain letters taken in order form a word or phrase
ACROTISM	*n* pl. -S weakness of the pulse **ACROTIC** *adj*
ACRYLATE	*n* pl. -S an acrylic
ACRYLIC	*n* pl. -S a type of resin
ACT	*v* -ED, -ING, -S to do something
ACTA	*n/pl* recorded proceedings
ACTABLE	*adj* suitable for performance on the stage
ACTIN	*n* pl. -S a protein in muscle tissue
ACTINAL	*adj* having tentacles
ACTING	*n* pl. -S the occupation of an actor
ACTINIA	*n* pl. -IAE or -IAS a marine animal
ACTINIAN	*n* pl. -S actinia
ACTINIC	*adj* pertaining to actinism
ACTINIDE	*n* pl. -S any of a series of radioactive elements
ACTINISM	*n* pl. -S the property of radiant energy that effects chemical changes
ACTINIUM	*n* pl. -S a radioactive element
ACTINOID	*n* pl. -S an actinide
ACTINON	*n* pl. -S an isotope of radon
ACTION	*n* pl. -S the process of acting
ACTIVATE	*v* -VATED, -VATING, -VATES to set in motion
ACTIVE	*n* pl. -S a participating member of an organization
ACTIVELY	*adv* with activity
ACTIVISM	*n* pl. -S a doctrine that emphasizes direct and decisive action
ACTIVIST	*n* pl. -S an advocate of activism
ACTIVITY	*n* pl. -TIES brisk action or movement
ACTIVIZE	*v* -IZED, -IZING, -IZES to activate
ACTOR	*n* pl. -S a theatrical performer **ACTORISH** *adj*
ACTRESS	*n* pl. -ES a female actor **ACTRESSY** *adj*
ACTUAL	*adj* existing in fact **ACTUALLY** *adv*
ACTUARY	*n* pl. -ARIES a statistician who computes insurance risks and premiums
ACTUATE	*v* -ATED, -ATING, -ATES to set into action or motion
ACTUATOR	*n* pl. -S one that actuates
ACUATE	*adj* sharp
ACUITY	*n* pl. -ITIES sharpness
ACULEATE	*adj* having a sting
ACULEUS	*n* pl. -LEI a sharp-pointed part
ACUMEN	*n* pl. -S mental keenness
ACUTANCE	*n* pl. -S a measure of photographic clarity

ACUTE — *adj* ACUTER, ACUTEST marked by sharpness or severity **ACUTELY** *adv*

ACUTE — *n* pl. -S a type of accent mark

ACYCLIC — *adj* not cyclic

ACYL — *n* pl. -S a univalent radical

ACYLATE — *v* -ATED, -ATING, -ATES to introduce acyl into

ACYLOIN — *n* pl. -S a type of chemical compound

AD — *n* pl. -S an advertisement

ADAGE — *n* pl. -S a traditional saying expressing a common observation **ADAGIAL** *adj*

ADAGIO — *n* pl. -GIOS a musical composition or movement played in a slow tempo

ADAMANCE — *n* pl. -S adamancy

ADAMANCY — *n* pl. -CIES unyielding hardness

ADAMANT — *n* pl. -S an extremely hard substance

ADAMSITE — *n* pl. -S a lung-irritating gas

ADAPT — *v* -ED, -ING, -S to make suitable

ADAPTER — *n* pl. -S one that adapts

ADAPTION — *n* pl. -S the act of adapting **ADAPTIVE** *adj*

ADAPTOR — *n* pl. -S adapter

ADAXIAL — *adj* situated on the same side as

ADD — *v* -ED, -ING, -S to combine or join so as to bring about an increase **ADDABLE** *adj*

ADDAX — *n* pl. -ES a large antelope

ADDEDLY — *adv* additionally

ADDEND — *n* pl. -S a number to be added to another

ADDENDUM — *n* pl. -DA something added or to be added

ADDER — *n* pl. -S a venomous snake

ADDIBLE — *adj* capable of being added

ADDICT — *v* -ED, -ING, -S to devote or surrender to something habitually or compulsively

ADDITION — *n* pl. -S something added

ADDITIVE — *n* pl. -S a substance added to another to impart desirable qualities

ADDITORY — *adj* making an addition

ADDLE — *v* -DLED, -DLING, -DLES to confuse

ADDRESS — *v* -DRESSED or -DREST, -DRESSING, -DRESSES to speak to

ADDUCE — *v* -DUCED, -DUCING, -DUCES to bring forward as evidence

ADDUCENT — *adj* serving to adduct

ADDUCER — *n* pl. -S one that adduces

ADDUCING — present participle of adduce

ADDUCT — *v* -ED, -ING, -S to draw toward the main axis

ADDUCTOR — *n* pl. -S an adducent muscle

ADEEM — *v* -ED, -ING, -S to take away

ADENINE — *n* pl. -S an alkaloid

ADENITIS — *n* pl. -TISES inflammation of a lymph node

ADENOID — *n* pl. -S an enlarged lymphoid growth behind the pharynx

ADENOMA — *n* pl. -MAS or -MATA a tumor of glandular origin

ADENOSIS — *n* pl. -NOSES abnormal growth of glandular tissue

ADENYL — *n* pl. -S a univalent radical

ADEPT — *adj* ADEPTER, ADEPTEST highly skilled **ADEPTLY** *adv*

ADEPT — *n* pl. -S an adept person

ADEQUACY — *n* pl. -CIES the state of being adequate

ADEQUATE — *adj* sufficient for a specific requirement

ADHERE — *v* -HERED, -HERING, -HERES to become or remain attached or close to something

ADHEREND — *n* pl. -S the surface to which an adhesive adheres

ADHERENT — *n* pl. -S a supporter

ADHERER — *n* pl. -S one that adheres

ADHERING — present participle of adhere

ADHESION — *n* pl. -S the act of adhering

ADHESIVE — *n* pl. -S a substance that causes adhesion

ADHIBIT — *v* -ED, -ING, -S to take or let in

ADIEU — *n* pl. ADIEUS or ADIEUX a farewell

ADIOS — *interj* — used to express farewell

ADIPOSE — *n* pl. -S animal fat **ADIPIC** *adj*

ADIPOSIS — *n* pl. -POSES obesity

ADIPOUS — *adj* pertaining to adipose

ADIT — *n* pl. -S an entrance

ADJACENT — *adj* next to

ADJOIN *v* -ED, -ING, -S to lie next to

ADJOINT *n* pl. -S a type of mathematical matrix

ADJOURN *v* -ED, -ING, -S to suspend until a later time

ADJUDGE *v* -JUDGED, -JUDGING, -JUDGES to determine judicially

ADJUNCT *n* pl. -S something attached in a subordinate position

ADJURE *v* -JURED, -JURING, -JURES to command solemnly

ADJURER *n* pl. -S one that adjures

ADJUROR *n* pl. -S adjurer

ADJUST *v* -ED, -ING, -S to bring to a more satisfactory state

ADJUSTER *n* pl. -S one that adjusts

ADJUSTOR *n* pl. -S adjuster

ADJUTANT *n* pl. -S an assistant

ADJUVANT *n* pl. -S an assistant

ADMAN *n* pl. -MEN a man employed in the advertising business

ADMASS *adj* pertaining to a society strongly influenced by advertising

ADMIRAL *n* pl. -S a high-ranking naval officer

ADMIRE *v* -MIRED, -MIRING, -MIRES to regard with wonder, pleasure, and approval

ADMIRER *n* pl. -S one that admires

ADMIT *v* -MITTED, -MITTING, -MITS to allow to enter

ADMITTER *n* pl. -S one that admits

ADMIX *v* -MIXED or -MIXT, -MIXING, -MIXES to mix

ADMONISH *v* -ED, -ING, -ES to reprove mildly or kindly

ADNATE *adj* joined to another part or organ

ADNATION *n* pl. -S the state of being adnate

ADNEXA *n/pl* conjoined anatomical parts **ADNEXAL** *adj*

ADNOUN *n* pl. -S an adjective when used as a noun

ADO *n* pl. ADOS bustling excitement

ADOBE *n* pl. -S an unburnt, sun-dried brick

ADOBO *n* pl. -BOS a Philippine dish of fish or meat

ADONIS *n* pl. -ISES a handsome young man

ADOPT *v* -ED, -ING, -S to take into one's family by legal means

ADOPTEE *n* pl. -S one that is adopted

ADOPTER *n* pl. -S one that adopts

ADOPTION *n* pl. -S the act of adopting **ADOPTIVE** *adj*

ADORABLE *adj* worthy of being adored **ADORABLY** *adv*

ADORE *v* ADORED, ADORING, ADORES to love deeply

ADORER *n* pl. -S one that adores

ADORN *v* -ED, -ING, -S to add something to for the purpose of making more attractive

ADORNER *n* pl. -S one that adorns

ADOWN *adv* downward

ADOZE *adj* dozing

ADRENAL *n* pl. -S an endocrine gland

ADRIFT *adj* drifting

ADROIT *adj* ADROITER, ADROITEST skillful **ADROITLY** *adv*

ADSCRIPT *n* pl. -S a distinguishing symbol written after another character

ADSORB *v* -ED, -ING, -S to gather on a surface in a condensed layer

ADSORBER *n* pl. -S one that adsorbs

ADULARIA *n* pl. -S a mineral

ADULATE *v* -LATED, -LATING, -LATES to praise excessively

ADULATOR *n* pl. -S one that adulates

ADULT *n* pl. -S a fully developed individual

ADULTERY *n* pl. -TERIES voluntary sexual intercourse between a married person and someone other than his or her spouse

ADULTLY *adv* in a manner typical of an adult

ADUMBRAL *adj* shadowy

ADUNC *adj* bent inward

ADUNCATE *adj* adunc

ADUNCOUS *adj* adunc

ADUST *adj* scorched

ADVANCE *v* -VANCED, -VANCING, -VANCES to move or cause to move ahead

ADVANCER *n* pl. -S one that advances

ADVECT *v* -ED, -ING, -S to convey or transport by the flow of a fluid

ADVENT *n* pl. -S arrival

ADVERB	*n* pl. -S a word used to modify a verb, adjective, or other adverb
ADVERSE	*adj* acting in opposition
ADVERT	*v* -ED, -ING, -S to call attention
ADVICE	*n* pl. -S recommendation regarding a decision or action
ADVISE	*v* -VISED, -VISING, -VISES to give advice to
ADVISEE	*n* pl. -S one that is advised
ADVISER	*n* pl. -S one that advises
ADVISING	present participle of advise
ADVISOR	*n* pl. -S adviser
ADVISORY	*n* pl. -RIES a report giving information
ADVOCACY	*n* pl. -CIES the act of advocating
ADVOCATE	*v* -CATED, -CATING, -CATES to speak in favor of
ADVOWSON	*n* pl. -S the right of presenting a nominee to a vacant church office
ADYNAMIA	*n* pl. -S lack of physical strength **ADYNAMIC** *adj*
ADYTUM	*n* pl. -TA an inner sanctuary in an ancient temple
ADZ	*n* pl. -ES a cutting tool
ADZE	*n* pl. -S adz
ADZUKI	*n* pl. -S the edible seed of an Asian plant
AE	*adj* one
AECIA	pl. of aecium
AECIAL	*adj* pertaining to an aecium
AECIDIAL	*adj* pertaining to an aecium
AECIDIUM	*n* pl. -IA an aecium
AECIUM	*n* pl. -IA a spore-producing organ of certain fungi
AEDES	*n* pl. AEDES any of a genus of mosquitoes
AEDILE	*n* pl. -S a magistrate of ancient Rome
AEDINE	*adj* pertaining to an aedes
AEGIS	*n* pl. -GISES protection
AENEOUS	*adj* having a greenish gold color
AENEUS	*adj* aeneous
AEOLIAN	*adj* eolian
AEON	*n* pl. -S eon
AEONIAN	*adj* eonian
AEONIC	*adj* eonian
AEQUORIN	*n* pl. -S a protein secreted by jellyfish

AERATE	*v* -ATED, -ATING, -ATES to supply with air
AERATION	*n* pl. -S the act of aerating
AERATOR	*n* pl. -S one that aerates
AERIAL	*n* pl. -S an antenna
AERIALLY	*adv* in a manner pertaining to the air
AERIE	*n* pl. -S a bird's nest built high on a mountain or cliff **AERIED** *adj*
AERIER	comparative of aery
AERIES	pl. of aery
AERIEST	superlative of aery
AERIFORM	*adj* having the form of air
AERIFY	*v* -FIED, -FYING, -FIES to aerate
AERILY	*adv* in an aery manner
AERO	*adj* pertaining to aircraft
AEROBE	*n* pl. -S an organism that requires oxygen to live **AEROBIC** *adj*
AEROBICS	*n/pl* exercises for conditioning the heart and lungs by increasing oxygen consumption
AEROBIUM	*n* pl. -BIA aerobe
AERODUCT	*n* pl. -S a type of jet engine
AERODYNE	*n* pl. -S an aircraft that is heavier than air
AEROFOIL	*n* pl. -S airfoil
AEROGEL	*n* pl. -S a highly porous solid
AEROGRAM	*n* pl. -S an airmail letter
AEROLITE	*n* pl. -S a meteorite containing more stone than iron
AEROLITH	*n* pl. -S aerolite
AEROLOGY	*n* pl. -GIES the study of the atmosphere
AERONAUT	*n* pl. -S one who operates an airship
AERONOMY	*n* pl. -MIES the study of the upper atmosphere
AEROSAT	*n* pl. -S a satellite for use in air-traffic control
AEROSOL	*n* pl. -S a gaseous suspension of fine solid or liquid particles
AEROSTAT	*n* pl. -S an aircraft that is lighter than air
AERUGO	*n* pl. -GOS a green film that forms on copper
AERY	*adj* AERIER, AERIEST airy
AERY	*n* pl. AERIES aerie
AESTHETE	*n* pl. -S esthete

AESTIVAL	*adj* estival
AETHER	*n* pl. -S the upper region of the atmosphere **AETHERIC** *adj*
AFAR	*n* pl. -S a great distance
AFEARD	*adj* afraid
AFEARED	*adj* afeard
AFEBRILE	*adj* having no fever
AFF	*adv* off
AFFABLE	*adj* easy to talk to **AFFABLY** *adv*
AFFAIR	*n* pl. -S anything done or to be done
AFFAIRE	*n* pl. -S a brief amorous relationship
AFFECT	*v* -ED, -ING, -S to give a false appearance of
AFFECTER	*n* pl. -S one that affects
AFFERENT	*n* pl. -S a nerve that conveys impulses toward a nerve center
AFFIANCE	*v* -ANCED, -ANCING, -ANCES to betroth
AFFIANT	*n* pl. -S one who makes a written declaration under oath
AFFICHE	*n* pl. -S a poster
AFFINAL	*adj* related by marriage
AFFINE	*n* pl. -S a relative by marriage
AFFINED	*adj* closely related
AFFINELY	*adv* in the manner of a type of mathematical mapping
AFFINITY	*n* pl. -TIES a natural attraction or inclination
AFFIRM	*v* -ED, -ING, -S to state positively
AFFIRMER	*n* pl. -S one that affirms
AFFIX	*v* -ED, -ING, -ES to attach
AFFIXAL	*adj* pertaining to a prefix or suffix
AFFIXER	*n* pl. -S one that affixes
AFFIXIAL	*adj* affixal
AFFLATUS	*n* pl. -ES a creative inspiration
AFFLICT	*v* -ED, -ING, -S to distress with mental or physical pain
AFFLUENT	*n* pl. -S a stream that flows into another
AFFLUX	*n* pl. -ES a flowing toward a point
AFFORD	*v* -ED, -ING, -S to have sufficient means for
AFFOREST	*v* -ED, -ING, -S to convert into forest
AFFRAY	*v* -ED, -ING, -S to frighten
AFFRAYER	*n* pl. -S one that affrays
AFFRIGHT	*v* -ED, -ING, -S to frighten
AFFRONT	*v* -ED, -ING, -S to insult openly
AFFUSION	*n* pl. -S an act of pouring a liquid on
AFGHAN	*n* pl. -S a woolen blanket or shawl
AFGHANI	*n* pl. -S a monetary unit of Afghanistan
AFIELD	*adv* in the field
AFIRE	*adj* being on fire
AFLAME	*adj* flaming
AFLOAT	*adj* floating
AFLUTTER	*adj* nervously excited
AFOOT	*adv* on foot
AFORE	*adv* before
AFOUL	*adj* entangled
AFRAID	*adj* filled with apprehension
AFREET	*n* pl. -S an evil spirit in Arabic mythology
AFRESH	*adv* anew
AFRIT	*n* pl. -S afreet
AFT	*adv* toward the stern
AFTER	*prep* behind in place or order
AFTERS	*n/pl* dessert
AFTERTAX	*adj* remaining after payment of taxes
AFTMOST	*adj* nearest the stern
AFTOSA	*n* pl. -S a disease of hoofed mammals
AG	*adj* pertaining to agriculture
AGA	*n* pl. -S a high-ranking Turkish military officer
AGAIN	*adv* once more
AGAINST	*prep* in opposition to
AGALLOCH	*n* pl. -S the fragrant wood of a tropical tree
AGALWOOD	*n* pl. -S agalloch
AGAMA	*n* pl. -S a tropical lizard
AGAMETE	*n* pl. -S an asexual reproductive cell
AGAMIC	*adj* asexual
AGAMOUS	*adj* agamic
AGAPE	*n* pl. -PAE or -PAI the love of God for mankind **AGAPEIC** *adj*
AGAR	*n* pl. -S a viscous substance obtained from certain seaweeds
AGARIC	*n* pl. -S any of a family of fungi

AGAROSE   *n* pl. -S a sugar obtained from agar

AGATE   *n* pl. -S a variety of quartz **AGATOID** *adj*

AGATIZE   *v* -IZED, -IZING, -IZES to cause to resemble agate

AGAVE   *n* pl. -S a tropical plant

AGAZE   *adj* gazing

AGE   *v* AGED, AGING or AGEING, AGES to grow old

AGEDLY   *adv* oldly

AGEDNESS   *n* pl. -ES oldness

AGEE   *adv* to one side

AGEING   *n* pl. -S aging

AGEISM   *n* pl. -S discrimination based on age

AGEIST   *n* pl. -S an advocate of ageism

AGELESS   *adj* never growing old

AGELONG   *adj* lasting for a long time

AGENCY   *n* pl. -CIES an organization that does business for others

AGENDA   *n* pl. -S a list of things to be done

AGENDUM   *n* pl. -S an item on an agenda

AGENE   *n* pl. -S a chemical compound used in bleaching flour

AGENESIA   *n* pl. -S agenesis

AGENESIS   *n* pl. AGENESES absence or imperfect development of a bodily part **AGENETIC** *adj*

AGENIZE   *v* -NIZED, -NIZING, -NIZES to treat with agene

AGENT   *n* pl. -S one who is authorized to act for another **AGENTIAL** *adj*

AGENTING   *n* pl. -S the business or activities of an agent

AGENTIVE   *n* pl. -S a word part that denotes the doer of an action

AGENTRY   *n* pl. -RIES the office or duties of an agent

AGER   *n* pl. -S one that ages

AGERATUM   *n* pl. -S a flowering plant

AGGADIC   *adj* haggadic

AGGER   *n* pl. -S a mound of earth used as a fortification

AGGIE   *n* pl. -S a type of playing marble

AGGRADE   *v* -GRADED, -GRADING, -GRADES to fill with detrital material

AGGRESS   *v* -ED, -ING, -ES to commit the first act of hostility

AGGRIEVE   *v* -GRIEVED, -GRIEVING, -GRIEVES to distress

AGGRO   *n* pl. -GROS a rivalry or grievance

AGHA   *n* pl. -S aga

AGHAST   *adj* shocked by something horrible

AGILE   *adj* able to move quickly and easily **AGILELY** *adv*

AGILITY   *n* pl. -TIES the quality of being agile

AGIN   *prep* against

AGING   *n* pl. -S the process of growing old

AGINNER   *n* pl. -S one that is against change

AGIO   *n* pl. AGIOS a premium paid for the exchange of one currency for another

AGIOTAGE   *n* pl. -S the business of a broker

AGISM   *n* pl. -S ageism

AGIST   *v* -ED, -ING, -S to feed and take care of for a fee, as livestock

AGITATE   *v* -TATED, -TATING, -TATES to move with a violent, irregular action **AGITABLE** *adj*

AGITATO   *adj* fast and stirring — used as a musical direction

AGITATOR   *n* pl. -S one that agitates

AGITPROP   *n* pl. -S pro-Communist propaganda

AGLARE   *adj* glaring

AGLEAM   *adj* gleaming

AGLEE   *adv* agley

AGLET   *n* pl. -S a metal sheath at the end of a lace

AGLEY   *adv* awry

AGLIMMER   *adj* glimmering

AGLITTER   *adj* glittering

AGLOW   *adj* glowing

AGLY   *adv* agley

AGLYCON   *n* pl. -S a type of chemical compound

AGLYCONE   *n* pl. -S aglycon

AGMA   *n* pl. -S eng

AGMINATE   *adj* clustered together

AGNAIL   *n* pl. -S a piece of loose skin at the base of a fingernail

AGNATE   *n* pl. -S a relative on the father's side **AGNATIC** *adj*

AGNATION   *n* pl. -S the relationship of agnates

AGNIZE   *v* -NIZED, -NIZING, -NIZES to acknowledge

AGNOMEN   *n* pl. -MINA or -MENS an additional name given to an ancient Roman

AGNOSIA   *n* pl. -S loss of ability to recognize familiar objects

AGNOSTIC   *n* pl. -S one who disclaims any knowledge of God

AGO   *adv* in the past

AGOG   *adv* in a state of eager curiosity

AGON   *n* pl. -S or -ES the dramatic conflict between the main characters in a Greek play

AGONAL   *adj* pertaining to agony

AGONE   *adv* ago

AGONES   a pl. of agon

AGONIC   *adj* not forming an angle

AGONIES   pl. of agony

AGONISE   *v* -NISED, -NISING, -NISES to agonize

AGONIST   *n* pl. -S one that is engaged in a struggle

AGONIZE   *v* -NIZED, -NIZING, -NIZES to suffer extreme pain

AGONY   *n* pl. -NIES extreme pain

AGORA   *n* pl. -RAS or -RAE a marketplace in ancient Greece

AGORA   *n* pl. AGOROT or AGOROTH a monetary unit of Israel

AGOUTI   *n* pl. -S or -ES a burrowing rodent

AGOUTY   *n* pl. -TIES agouti

AGRAFE   *n* pl. -S agraffe

AGRAFFE   *n* pl. -S an ornamental clasp

AGRAPHA   *n/pl* the sayings of Jesus not found in the Bible

AGRAPHIA   *n* pl. -S a mental disorder marked by inability to write **AGRAPHIC** *adj*

AGRARIAN   *n* pl. -S one who favors equal distribution of land

AGRAVIC   *adj* pertaining to a condition of no gravitation

AGREE   *v* AGREED, AGREEING, AGREES to have the same opinion

AGRESTAL   *adj* growing wild

AGRESTIC   *adj* rural

AGRIA   *n* pl. -S severe pustular eruption

AGRIMONY   *n* pl. -NIES a perennial herb

AGROLOGY   *n* pl. -GIES the science of soils in relation to crops

AGRONOMY   *n* pl. -MIES the application of scientific principles to the cultivation of land

AGROUND   *adv* on the ground

AGRYPNIA   *n* pl. -S insomnia

AGUE   *n* pl. -S a malarial fever **AGUELIKE, AGUISH** *adj* **AGUISHLY** *adv*

AGUEWEED   *n* pl. -S a flowering plant

AH   *interj* — used to express delight, relief, or contempt

AHA   *interj* — used to express surprise, triumph, or derision

AHCHOO   *interj* — used to represent the sound of a sneeze

AHEAD   *adv* at or to the front

AHEM   *interj* — used to attract attention

AHIMSA   *n* pl. -S the Hindu principle of nonviolence

AHOLD   *n* pl. -S a hold or grasp of something

AHORSE   *adv* on a horse

AHOY   *interj* — used in hailing a ship or person

AHULL   *adj* abandoned and flooded, as a ship

AI   *n* pl. -S a three-toed sloth

AIBLINS   *adv* ablins

AID   *v* -ED, -ING, -S to help

AIDE   *n* pl. -S an assistant

AIDER   *n* pl. -S one that aids

AIDFUL   *adj* helpful

AIDLESS   *adj* helpless

AIDMAN   *n* pl. -MEN a corpsman

AIGLET   *n* pl. -S aglet

AIGRET   *n* pl. -S aigrette

AIGRETTE   *n* pl. -S a tuft of feathers worn as a head ornament

AIGUILLE   *n* pl. -S a sharp, pointed mountain peak

AIKIDO   *n* pl. -DOS a Japanese art of self-defense

AIL   *v* -ED, -ING, -S to cause pain or discomfort to

AILERON   *n* pl. -S a movable control surface on an airplane wing

AILMENT   *n* pl. -S a physical or mental disorder

AIM   *v* -ED, -ING, -S to direct toward a specified object or goal

AIMER   *n* pl. -S one that aims

AIMFUL   *adj* full of purpose **AIMFULLY** *adv*

AIMLESS   *adj* lacking direction or purpose

AIN   *n* pl. -S ayin

AINSELL   *n* pl. -S own self

AIOLI   *n* pl. -S garlic mayonnaise

AIR   *v* -ED, -ING, -S to expose to the air (the mixture of gases that surrounds the earth)

AIR   *adv* AIRER, AIREST early

AIRBOAT   *n* pl. -S a boat used in swampy areas

AIRBORNE   *adj* flying

AIRBOUND   *adj* stopped up by air

AIRBRUSH   *v* -ED, -ING, -ES to apply in a fine spray by compressed air, as paint

AIRBURST   *n* pl. -S an explosion in the air

AIRBUS   *n* pl. -BUSES or -BUSSES a passenger airplane

AIRCHECK   *n* pl. -S a recording made from a radio broadcast

AIRCOACH   *n* pl. -ES the cheaper class of accommodations in commercial aircraft

AIRCRAFT   *n* pl. AIRCRAFT any machine or device capable of flying

AIRCREW   *n* pl. -S the crew of an aircraft

AIRDATE   *n* pl. -S the scheduled date of a broadcast

AIRDROME   *n* pl. -S an airport

AIRDROP   *v* -DROPPED, -DROPPING, -DROPS to drop from an aircraft

AIRER   *n* pl. -S a frame on which to dry clothes

AIRFARE   *n* pl. -S payment for travel by airplane

AIRFIELD   *n* pl. -S an airport

AIRFLOW   *n* pl. -S a flow of air

AIRFOIL   *n* pl. -S a part of an aircraft designed to provide lift or control

AIRFRAME   *n* pl. -S the framework and external covering of an airplane

AIRGLOW   *n* pl. -S a glow in the upper atmosphere

AIRHEAD   *n* pl. -S a stupid person

AIRHOLE   *n* pl. -S a hole to let air in or out

AIRIER   comparative of airy

AIRIEST   superlative of airy

AIRILY   *adv* in an airy manner

AIRINESS   *n* pl. -ES the state of being airy

AIRING   *n* pl. -S an exposure to the air

AIRLESS   *adj* having no air

AIRLIFT   *v* -ED, -ING, -S to transport by airplane

AIRLIKE   *adj* resembling air

AIRLINE   *n* pl. -S an air transportation system

AIRLINER   *n* pl. -S a large passenger aircraft

AIRMAIL   *v* -ED, -ING, -S to send mail by airplane

AIRMAN   *n* pl. -MEN an aviator

AIRN   *n* pl. -S iron

AIRPARK   *n* pl. -S a small airport

AIRPLANE   *n* pl. -S a winged aircraft propelled by jet engines or propellers

AIRPLAY   *n* pl. -PLAYS the playing of a record on a radio program

AIRPORT   *n* pl. -S a tract of land maintained for the landing and takeoff of aircraft

AIRPOST   *n* pl. -S a system of conveying mail by airplane

AIRPOWER   *n* pl. -S the military strength of a nation's air force

AIRPROOF   *v* -ED, -ING, -S to make impermeable to air

AIRSCAPE   *n* pl. -S a view of the earth from an aircraft or a high position

AIRSCREW   *n* pl. -S an airplane propeller

AIRSHED   *n* pl. -S the air supply of a given region

AIRSHIP   *n* pl. -S a lighter-than-air aircraft having propulsion and steering systems

AIRSICK   *adj* nauseated from flying in an airplane

AIRSPACE   *n* pl. -S the portion of the atmosphere above a particular land area

AIRSPEED   *n* pl. -S the speed of an aircraft with relation to the air

AIRSTRIP   *n* pl. -S a runway

AIRT   *v* -ED, -ING, -S to guide

AIRTH   *v* -ED, -ING, -S to airt

AIRTIGHT *adj* not allowing air to escape or enter

AIRTIME *n* pl. -S the time when a broadcast begins

AIRWARD *adv* toward the sky

AIRWAVE *n* pl. -S the medium of radio and television transmission

AIRWAY *n* pl. -WAYS a passageway in which air circulates

AIRWISE *adj* skillful in aviation

AIRWOMAN *n* pl. -WOMEN a female aviator

AIRY *adj* AIRIER, AIRIEST having the nature of air

AISLE *n* pl. -S a passageway between sections of seats **AISLED** *adj*

AISLEWAY *n* pl. -WAYS an aisle

AIT *n* pl. -S a small island

AITCH *n* pl. -ES the letter H

AIVER *n* pl. -S a draft horse

AJAR *adj* partly open

AJEE *adv* agee

AJIVA *n* pl. -S inanimate matter

AJOWAN *n* pl. -S the fruit of an Egyptian plant

AJUGA *n* pl. -S a flowering plant

AKEE *n* pl. -S a tropical tree

AKELA *n* pl. -S a leader of a cub scout pack

AKENE *n* pl. -S achene

AKIMBO *adj* having hands on hips and elbows bent outward

AKIN *adj* related by blood

AKVAVIT *n* pl. -S aquavit

AL *n* pl. -S an East Indian tree

ALA *n* pl. ALAE a wing or winglike part

ALACK *interj* — used to express sorrow or regret

ALACRITY *n* pl. -TIES cheerful promptness

ALAE pl. of ala

ALAMEDA *n* pl. -S a shaded walkway

ALAMO *n* pl. -MOS a softwood tree

ALAMODE *n* pl. -S a silk fabric

ALAN *n* pl. -S a large hunting dog

ALAND *n* pl. -S alan

ALANE *adj* alone

ALANG *adv* along

ALANIN *n* pl. -S alanine

ALANINE *n* pl. -S an amino acid

ALANT *n* pl. -S alan

ALANYL *n* pl. -S a univalent radical

ALAR *adj* pertaining to wings

ALARM *v* -ED, -ING, -S to frighten by a sudden revelation of danger

ALARMISM *n* pl. -S the practice of alarming others needlessly

ALARMIST *n* pl. -S one who alarms others needlessly

ALARUM *v* -ED, -ING, -S to alarm

ALARY *adj* alar

ALAS *interj* — used to express sorrow or regret

ALASKA *n* pl. -S a heavy fabric

ALASTOR *n* pl. -S an avenging deity in Greek tragedy

ALATE *n* pl. -S a winged insect

ALATED *adj* having wings

ALATION *n* pl. -S the state of having wings

ALB *n* pl. -S a long-sleeved vestment

ALBA *n* pl. -S the white substance of the brain

ALBACORE *n* pl. -S a marine food fish

ALBATA *n* pl. -S an alloy of copper, nickel, and zinc

ALBEDO *n* pl. -DOS or -DOES the ratio of the light reflected by a planet to that received by it

ALBEIT *conj* although

ALBICORE *n* pl. -S albacore

ALBINAL *adj* albinic

ALBINIC *adj* pertaining to albinism

ALBINISM *n* pl. -S the condition of being an albino

ALBINO *n* pl. -NOS an organism lacking normal pigmentation

ALBITE *n* pl. -S a mineral **ALBITIC** *adj*

ALBIZIA *n* pl. -S a tropical tree

ALBIZZIA *n* pl. -S albizia

ALBUM *n* pl. -S a book for preserving photographs or stamps

ALBUMEN *n* pl. -S the white of an egg

ALBUMIN *n* pl. -S a simple protein

ALBUMOSE *n* pl. -S a proteose

ALBURNUM *n* pl. -S sapwood

ALCADE *n* pl. -S alcalde

ALCAHEST *n* pl. -S alkahest

ALCAIC	n pl. -S a type of verse form
ALCAIDE	n pl. -S the commander of a Spanish fortress
ALCALDE	n pl. -S the mayor of a Spanish town
ALCAYDE	n pl. -S alcaide
ALCAZAR	n pl. -S a Spanish fortress or palace
ALCHEMY	n pl. -MIES a medieval form of chemistry **ALCHEMIC** adj
ALCHYMY	n pl. -MIES alchemy
ALCID	n pl. -S a diving seabird
ALCIDINE	adj pertaining to a family of seabirds
ALCOHOL	n pl. -S a flammable liquid
ALCOVE	n pl. -S a recessed section of a room **ALCOVED** adj
ALDEHYDE	n pl. -S a type of chemical compound
ALDER	n pl. -S a shrub or small tree
ALDERFLY	n pl. -FLIES a winged insect
ALDERMAN	n pl. -MEN a member of a municipal legislative body
ALDOL	n pl. -S a chemical compound
ALDOLASE	n pl. -S an enzyme
ALDOSE	n pl. -S a type of sugar
ALDRIN	n pl. -S an insecticide
ALE	n pl. -S an alcoholic beverage
ALEATORY	adj pertaining to luck
ALEC	n pl. -S a herring
ALEE	adv toward the side of a vessel sheltered from the wind
ALEF	n pl. -S aleph
ALEGAR	n pl. -S sour ale
ALEHOUSE	n pl. -S a tavern where ale is sold
ALEMBIC	n pl. -S an apparatus formerly used in distilling
ALENCON	n pl. -S a needlepoint lace
ALEPH	n pl. -S a Hebrew letter
ALERT	adj ALERTER, ALERTEST ready for sudden action **ALERTLY** adv
ALERT	v -ED, -ING, -S to warn
ALEURON	n pl. -S aleurone
ALEURONE	n pl. -S protein matter found in the seeds of certain plants
ALEVIN	n pl. -S a young fish
ALEWIFE	n pl. -WIVES a marine fish
ALEXIA	n pl. -S a cerebral disorder marked by the loss of the ability to read
ALEXIN	n pl. -S a substance in the blood that aids in the destruction of bacteria
ALEXINE	n pl. -S alexin
ALFA	n pl. -S a communications code word for the letter A
ALFAKI	n pl. -S alfaqui
ALFALFA	n pl. -S a plant cultivated for use as hay and forage
ALFAQUI	n pl. -S a teacher of Muslim law
ALFAQUIN	n pl. -S alfaqui
ALFORJA	n pl. -S a leather bag
ALFRESCO	adv outdoors
ALGA	n pl. -GAE or -GAS any of a group of primitive aquatic plants **ALGAL** adj
ALGAROBA	n pl. -S the mesquite
ALGEBRA	n pl. -S a branch of mathematics
ALGERINE	n pl. -S a woolen fabric
ALGICIDE	n pl. -S a substance used to kill algae
ALGID	adj cold
ALGIDITY	n pl. -TIES coldness
ALGIN	n pl. -S a viscous substance obtained from certain algae
ALGINATE	n pl. -S a chemical salt
ALGOID	adj resembling algae
ALGOLOGY	n pl. -GIES the study of algae
ALGOR	n pl. -S coldness
ALGORISM	n pl. -S the Arabic system of arithmetic notation
ALGUM	n pl. -S almug
ALIAS	n pl. -ES an assumed name
ALIBI	v -BIED, -BIING, -BIES or -BIS to make excuses for oneself
ALIBLE	adj nourishing
ALIDAD	n pl. -S alidade
ALIDADE	n pl. -S a device used in angular measurement
ALIEN	v -ED, -ING, -S to transfer to another, as property
ALIENAGE	n pl. -S the state of being foreign
ALIENATE	v -ATED, -ATING, -ATES to make indifferent or unfriendly
ALIENEE	n pl. -S one to whom property is transferred

ALIENER *n* pl. -S alienor

ALIENISM *n* pl. -S alienage

ALIENIST *n* pl. -S a physician who treats mental disorders

ALIENLY *adv* in a foreign manner

ALIENOR *n* pl. -S one that transfers property

ALIF *n* pl. -S an Arabic letter

ALIFORM *adj* shaped like a wing

ALIGHT *v* ALIGHTED or ALIT, ALIGHTING, ALIGHTS to come down from something

ALIGN *v* -ED, -ING, -S to arrange in a straight line

ALIGNER *n* pl. -S one that aligns

ALIKE *adj* having close resemblance

ALIMENT *v* -ED, -ING, -S to nourish

ALIMONY *n* pl. -NIES an allowance paid to a woman by her divorced husband

ALINE *v* ALINED, ALINING, ALINES to align

ALINER *n* pl. -S aligner

ALIPED *n* pl. -S an animal having a membrane connecting the toes

ALIQUANT *adj* not dividing evenly into another number

ALIQUOT *n* pl. -S a number that divides evenly into another

ALIST *adj* leaning to one side

ALIT a past tense of alight

ALIUNDE *adv* from a source extrinsic to the matter at hand

ALIVE *adj* having life

ALIYA *n* pl. -S aliyah

ALIYAH *n* pl. -YAHS or -YOS or -YOT the immigration of Jews to Israel

ALIZARIN *n* pl. -S a red dye

ALKAHEST *n* pl. -S the hypothetical universal solvent sought by alchemists

ALKALI *n* pl. -LIES or -LIS a type of chemical compound **ALKALIC** *adj*

ALKALIFY *v* -FIED, -FYING, -FIES to alkalize

ALKALIN *adj* alkaline

ALKALINE *adj* containing an alkali

ALKALISE *v* -LISED, -LISING, -LISES to alkalize

ALKALIZE *v* -LIZED, -LIZING, -LIZES to convert into an alkali

ALKALOID *n* pl. -S a type of chemical compound

ALKANE *n* pl. -S a type of chemical compound

ALKANET *n* pl. -S a European plant

ALKENE *n* pl. -S a type of chemical compound

ALKIES pl. of alky

ALKINE *n* pl. -S alkyne

ALKOXIDE *n* pl. -S a type of chemical salt

ALKOXY *adj* containing a univalent radical composed of alkyl united with oxygen

ALKY *n* pl. -KIES one who is habitually drunk

ALKYD *n* pl. -S a synthetic resin

ALKYL *n* pl. -S a univalent radical **ALKYLIC** *adj*

ALKYLATE *v* -ATED, -ATING, -ATES to combine with alkyl

ALKYNE *n* pl. -S a type of chemical compound

ALL *n* pl. -S everything that one has

ALLANITE *n* pl. -S a mineral

ALLAY *v* -ED, -ING, -S to reduce in intensity or severity

ALLAYER *n* pl. -S one that allays

ALLEE *n* pl. -S a tree-lined walkway

ALLEGE *v* -LEGED, -LEGING, -LEGES to assert without proof or before proving

ALLEGER *n* pl. -S one that alleges

ALLEGORY *n* pl. -RIES a story presenting a moral principle

ALLEGRO *n* pl. -GROS a musical passage played in rapid tempo

ALLELE *n* pl. -S any of several forms of a gene **ALLELIC** *adj*

ALLELISM *n* pl. -S the state of possessing alleles

ALLELUIA *n* pl. -S a song of praise to God

ALLERGEN *n* pl. -S a substance capable of inducing an allergy

ALLERGIC *adj* pertaining to allergy

ALLERGIN *n* pl. -S allergen

ALLERGY *n* pl. -GIES a state of hypersensitive reaction to certain things

ALLEY *n* pl. -LEYS a narrow passageway

ALLEYWAY *n* pl. -WAYS an alley

ALLHEAL *n* pl. -S a medicinal herb

ALLIABLE *adj* capable of being allied

ALLIANCE *n* pl. -S an association formed to further the common interests of its members

ALLICIN *n* pl. -S a liquid compound

ALLIED past tense of ally

ALLIES present 3d person sing. of ally

ALLIUM *n* pl. -S a bulbous herb

ALLOBAR *n* pl. -S a change in barometric pressure

ALLOCATE *v* -CATED, -CATING, -CATES to set apart for a particular purpose

ALLOD *n* pl. -S allodium

ALLODIUM *n* pl. -DIA land held in absolute ownership **ALLODIAL** *adj*

ALLOGAMY *n* pl. -MIES fertilization of a flower by pollen from another

ALLONGE *n* pl. -S an addition to a document

ALLONYM *n* pl. -S the name of one person assumed by another

ALLOPATH *n* pl. -S one who treats diseases by producing effects incompatible with those of the disease

ALLOT *v* -LOTTED, -LOTTING, -LOTS to give as a share or portion

ALLOTTEE *n* pl. -S one to whom something is allotted

ALLOTTER *n* pl. -S one that allots

ALLOTTING present participle of allot

ALLOTYPE *n* pl. -S a type of antibody

ALLOTYPY *n* pl. -TYPIES the condition of being an allotype

ALLOVER *n* pl. -S a fabric having a pattern extending over the entire surface

ALLOW *v* -ED, -ING, -S to put no obstacle in the way of

ALLOXAN *n* pl. -S a chemical compound

ALLOY *v* -ED, -ING, -S to combine to form an alloy (a homogenous mixture of metals)

ALLSEED *n* pl. -S a plant having many seeds

ALLSPICE *n* pl. -S a tropical tree

ALLUDE *v* -LUDED, -LUDING, -LUDES to make an indirect reference

ALLURE *v* -LURED, -LURING, -LURES to attract with something desirable

ALLURER *n* pl. -S one that allures

ALLUSION *n* pl. -S the act of alluding **ALLUSIVE** *adj*

ALLUVIA a pl. of alluvium

ALLUVIAL *n* pl. -S soil composed of alluvium

ALLUVION *n* pl. -S alluvium

ALLUVIUM *n* pl. -VIA or -VIUMS detrital material deposited by running water

ALLY *v* -LIED, -LYING, -LIES to unite in a formal relationship

ALLYL *n* pl. -S a univalent radical **ALLYLIC** *adj*

ALMA *n* pl. -S almah

ALMAGEST *n* pl. -S a medieval treatise on astrology or alchemy

ALMAH *n* pl. -S an Egyptian girl who sings and dances professionally

ALMANAC *n* pl. -S an annual publication containing general information

ALME *n* pl. -S almah

ALMEH *n* pl. -S almah

ALMEMAR *n* pl. -S a bema

ALMIGHTY *adj* having absolute power over all

ALMNER *n* pl. -S almoner

ALMOND *n* pl. -S the edible nut of a small tree

ALMONER *n* pl. -S one that distributes alms

ALMONRY *n* pl. -RIES a place where alms are distributed

ALMOST *adv* very nearly

ALMS *n* pl. ALMS money or goods given to the poor

ALMSMAN *n* pl. -MEN one who receives alms

ALMUCE *n* pl. -S a hooded cape

ALMUD *n* pl. -S a Spanish unit of capacity

ALMUDE *n* pl. -S almud

ALMUG *n* pl. -S a precious wood mentioned in the Bible

ALNICO *n* pl. -COES a magnetic alloy

ALODIUM *n* pl. -DIA allodium **ALODIAL** *adj*

ALOE *n* pl. -S an African plant **ALOETIC** *adj*

ALOFT *adv* in or into the air

ALOGICAL *adj* being outside the bounds of that to which logic can apply

ALOHA *n* pl. -S love — used as a greeting or farewell

ALOIN *n* pl. -S a laxative

ALONE *adj* apart from others

ALONG *adv* onward

ALOOF *adj* distant in interest or feeling **ALOOFLY** *adv*

ALOPECIA *n* pl. -S baldness **ALOPECIC** *adj*

ALOUD *adv* audibly

ALOW *adv* in or to a lower position

ALP *n* pl. -S a high mountain

ALPACA *n* pl. -S a ruminant mammal

ALPHA *n* pl. -S a Greek letter

ALPHABET *v* -ED, -ING, -S to arrange in the customary order of the letters of a language

ALPHORN *n* pl. -S a wooden horn used by Swiss herdsmen

ALPHOSIS *n* pl. -SISES lack of skin pigmentation

ALPHYL *n* pl. -S a univalent radical

ALPINE *n* pl. -S a plant native to high mountain regions

ALPINELY *adv* in a lofty manner

ALPINISM *n* pl. -S mountain climbing

ALPINIST *n* pl. -S a mountain climber

ALREADY *adv* by this time

ALRIGHT *adj* satisfactory

ALSIKE *n* pl. -S a European clover

ALSO *adv* in addition

ALT *n* pl. -S a high-pitched musical note

ALTAR *n* pl. -S a raised structure used in worship

ALTER *v* -ED, -ING, -S to make different

ALTERANT *n* pl. -S something that alters

ALTERER *n* pl. -S one that alters

ALTHAEA *n* pl. -S althea

ALTHEA *n* pl. -S a flowering plant

ALTHO *conj* although

ALTHORN *n* pl. -S a brass wind instrument

ALTHOUGH *conj* despite the fact that

ALTITUDE *n* pl. -S the vertical elevation of an object above a given level

ALTO *n* pl. -TOS a low female singing voice

ALTOIST *n* pl. -S one who plays the alto saxophone

ALTRUISM *n* pl. -S selfless devotion to the welfare of others

ALTRUIST *n* pl. -S one that practices altruism

ALUDEL *n* pl. -S a pear-shaped vessel

ALULA *n* pl. -LAE a tuft of feathers on the first digit of a bird's wing **ALULAR** *adj*

ALUM *n* pl. -S a chemical compound

ALUMIN *n* pl. -S alumina

ALUMINA *n* pl. -S an oxide of aluminum

ALUMINE *n* pl. -S alumina

ALUMINUM *n* pl. -S a metallic element **ALUMINIC** *adj*

ALUMNA *n* pl. -NAE a female graduate

ALUMNUS *n* pl. -NI a male graduate

ALUMROOT *n* pl. -S a flowering plant

ALUNITE *n* pl. -S a mineral

ALVEOLAR *n* pl. -S a sound produced with the tongue touching a place just behind the front teeth

ALVEOLUS *n* pl. -LI a small anatomical cavity

ALVINE *adj* pertaining to the abdomen and lower intestines

ALWAY *adv* always

ALWAYS *adv* at all times

ALYSSUM *n* pl. -S a flowering plant

AM present 1st person sing. of be

AMA *n* pl. -S amah

AMADAVAT *n* pl. -S an Asian songbird

AMADOU *n* pl. -S a substance prepared from fungi for use as tinder

AMAH *n* pl. -S an Oriental nurse

AMAIN *adv* with full strength

AMALGAM *n* pl. -S an alloy of mercury with another metal

AMANDINE *adj* prepared with almonds

AMANITA *n* pl. -S any of a genus of poisonous fungi

AMANITIN *n* pl. -S a chemical compound

AMARANTH *n* pl. -S a flowering plant

AMARELLE *n* pl. -S a variety of sour cherry

AMARETTI *n/pl* macaroons made with bitter almonds

AMARETTO *n* pl. -TOS a kind of liqueur

AMARNA *adj* pertaining to a certain historical period of ancient Egypt

AMASS *v* -ED, -ING, -ES to gather

AMASSER *n* pl. -S one that amasses

AMATEUR *n* pl. -S one that engages in an activity for pleasure

AMATIVE *adj* amorous

AMATOL *n* pl. -S a powerful explosive

AMATORY *adj* pertaining to sexual love

AMAZE *v* AMAZED, AMAZING, AMAZES to overwhelm with surprise or wonder **AMAZEDLY** *adv*

AMAZON *n* pl. -S a tall, powerful woman

AMBAGE *n* pl. -S a winding path

AMBARI *n* pl. -S ambary

AMBARY *n* pl. -RIES an East Indian plant

AMBEER *n* pl. -S tobacco juice

AMBER *n* pl. -S a fossil resin

AMBERINA *n* pl. -S a type of glassware

AMBEROID *n* pl. -S ambroid

AMBERY *n* pl. -BERIES ambry

AMBIANCE *n* pl. -S ambience

AMBIENCE *n* pl. -S the character, mood, or atmosphere of a place or situation

AMBIENT *n* pl. -S ambience

AMBIT *n* pl. -S the external boundary of something

AMBITION *v* -ED, -ING, -S to seek with eagerness

AMBIVERT *n* pl. -S a person whose personality type is intermediate between introvert and extravert

AMBLE *v* -BLED, -BLING, -BLES to saunter

AMBLER *n* pl. -S one that ambles

AMBO *n* pl. AMBOS or AMBONES a pulpit in an early Christian church

AMBOINA *n* pl. -S amboyna

AMBOYNA *n* pl. -S the mottled wood of an Indonesian tree

AMBRIES pl. of ambry

AMBROID *n* pl. -S a synthetic amber

AMBROSIA *n* pl. -S the food of the Greek and Roman gods

AMBRY *n* pl. -BRIES a recess in a church wall for sacred vessels

AMBSACE *n* pl. -S bad luck

AMBULANT *adj* ambulating

AMBULATE *v* -LATED, -LATING, -LATES to move or walk about

AMBUSH *v* -ED, -ING, -ES to attack from a concealed place

AMBUSHER *n* pl. -S one that ambushes

AMEBA *n* pl. -BAS or -BAE amoeba **AMEBAN, AMEBIC, AMEBOID** *adj*

AMEBEAN *adj* alternately responding

AMEER *n* pl. -S amir

AMEERATE *n* pl. -S amirate

AMELCORN *n* pl. -S a variety of wheat

AMEN *n* pl. -S a word used at the end of a prayer to express agreement

AMENABLE *adj* capable of being persuaded **AMENABLY** *adv*

AMEND *v* -ED, -ING, -S to improve

AMENDER *n* pl. -S one that amends

AMENITY *n* pl. -TIES the quality of being pleasant or agreeable

AMENT *n* pl. -S a mentally deficient person

AMENTIA *n* pl. -S mental deficiency

AMERCE *v* AMERCED, AMERCING, AMERCES to punish by imposing an arbitrary fine

AMERCER *n* pl. -S one that amerces

AMESACE *n* pl. -S ambsace

AMETHYST *n* pl. -S a variety of quartz

AMI *n* pl. -S a friend

AMIA *n* pl. -S a freshwater fish

AMIABLE *adj* having a pleasant disposition **AMIABLY** *adv*

AMIANTUS *n* pl. -ES a variety of asbestos

AMICABLE *adj* friendly **AMICABLY** *adv*

AMICE *n* pl. -S a vestment worn about the neck and shoulders

AMICUS *n* pl. AMICI one not party to a lawsuit but permitted by the court to advise it

AMID *n* pl. -S amide

AMIDASE *n* pl. -S an enzyme

AMIDE *n* pl. -S a type of chemical compound **AMIDIC** *adj*

AMIDIN *n* pl. -S the soluble matter of starch

AMIDINE *n* pl. -S a type of chemical compound

AMIDO *adj* containing an amide united with an acid radical

AMIDOGEN *n* pl. -S a univalent chemical radical

AMIDOL   *n* pl. -S a chemical compound

AMIDONE   *n* pl. -S a chemical compound

AMIDSHIP   *adv* toward the middle of a ship

AMIDST   *prep* in the midst of

AMIE   *n* pl. -S a female friend

AMIGA   *n* pl. -S a female friend

AMIGO   *n* pl. -GOS a friend

AMIN   *n* pl. -S amine

AMINE   *n* pl. -S a type of chemical compound **AMINIC** *adj*

AMINITY   *n* pl. -TIES the state of being an amine

AMINO   *adj* containing an amine united with a nonacid radical

AMIR   *n* pl. -S a Muslim prince or governor

AMIRATE   *n* pl. -S the rank of an amir

AMISS   *adj* being out of proper order

AMITIES   pl. of amity

AMITOSIS   *n* pl. -TOSES a type of cell division **AMITOTIC** *adj*

AMITROLE   *n* pl. -S an herbicide

AMITY   *n* pl. -TIES friendship

AMMETER   *n* pl. -S an instrument for measuring amperage

AMMINE   *n* pl. -S a type of chemical compound

AMMINO   *adj* pertaining to an ammine

AMMO   *n* pl. -MOS ammunition

AMMOCETE   *n* pl. -S the larva of a lamprey

AMMONAL   *n* pl. -S a powerful explosive

AMMONIA   *n* pl. -S a pungent gas

AMMONIAC   *n* pl. -S a gum resin

AMMONIC   *adj* pertaining to ammonia

AMMONIFY   *v* -FIED, -FYING, -FIES to treat with ammonia

AMMONITE   *n* pl. -S the coiled shell of an extinct mollusk

AMMONIUM   *n* pl. -S a univalent chemical radical

AMMONO   *adj* containing ammonia

AMMONOID   *n* pl. -S ammonite

AMNESIA   *n* pl. -S loss of memory

AMNESIAC   *n* pl. -S one suffering from amnesia

AMNESIC   *n* pl. -S amnesiac

AMNESTIC   *adj* pertaining to amnesia

AMNESTY   *v* -TIED, -TYING, -TIES to pardon

AMNION   *n* pl. -NIONS or -NIA a membranous sac enclosing an embryo **AMNIC, AMNIONIC, AMNIOTIC** *adj*

AMNIOTE   *n* pl. -S a vertebrate that develops an amnion during the embryonic stage

AMOEBA   *n* pl. -BAS or -BAE a unicellular microscopic organism **AMOEBAN, AMOEBIC, AMOEBOID** *adj*

AMOEBEAN   *adj* amebean

AMOK   *n* pl. -S a murderous frenzy

AMOLE   *n* pl. -S a plant root used as a substitute for soap

AMONG   *prep* in the midst of

AMONGST   *prep* among

AMORAL   *adj* lacking a sense of right and wrong **AMORALLY** *adv*

AMORETTO   *n* pl. -TI or -TOS a cupid

AMORINO   *n* pl. -NI an amoretto

AMORIST   *n* pl. -S a lover

AMOROSO   *adv* tenderly — used as a musical direction

AMOROUS   *adj* pertaining to love

AMORT   *adj* being without life

AMORTISE   *v* -TISED, -TISING, -TISES to amortize

AMORTIZE   *v* -TIZED, -TIZING, -TIZES to liquidate gradually, as a debt

AMOSITE   *n* pl. -S a type of asbestos

AMOTION   *n* pl. -S the removal of a corporate officer from his office

AMOUNT   *v* -ED, -ING, -S to combine to yield a sum

AMOUR   *n* pl. -S a love affair

AMP   *n* pl. -S ampere

AMPERAGE   *n* pl. -S the strength of an electric current expressed in amperes

AMPERE   *n* pl. -S a unit of electric current strength

AMPHIBIA   *n/pl* organisms adapted for life both on land and in water

AMPHIOXI   *n/pl* lancelets

AMPHIPOD   *n* pl. -S a small crustacean

AMPHORA   *n* pl. -RAE or -RAS a narrow-necked jar used in ancient Greece **AMPHORAL** *adj*

AMPLE   *adj* -PLER, -PLEST abundant **AMPLY** *adv*

AMPLEXUS   *n* pl. -ES the mating embrace of frogs

AMPLIFY   *v* -FIED, -FYING, -FIES to make larger or more powerful

AMPOULE   *n* pl. -S ampule

AMPUL   *n* pl. -S ampule

AMPULE   *n* pl. -S a small glass vial

AMPULLA   *n* pl. -LAE a globular bottle used in ancient Rome **AMPULLAR** *adj*

AMPUTATE   *v* -TATED, -TATING, -TATES to cut off by surgical means

AMPUTEE   *n* pl. -S one that has had a limb amputated

AMREETA   *n* pl. -S amrita

AMRITA   *n* pl. -S a beverage that bestows immortality in Hindu mythology

AMTRAC   *n* pl. -S a military vehicle equipped to move on land and water

AMTRACK   *n* pl. -S amtrac

AMU   *n* pl. -S a unit of mass

AMUCK   *n* pl. -S amok

AMULET   *n* pl. -S an object worn to protect against evil or injury

AMUSE   *v* AMUSED, AMUSING, AMUSES to occupy pleasingly **AMUSABLE** *adj* **AMUSEDLY** *adv*

AMUSER   *n* pl. -S one that amuses

AMUSIA   *n* pl. -S the inability to recognize musical sounds

AMUSIVE   *adj* amusing

AMYGDALA   *n* pl. -LAE an almond-shaped anatomical part

AMYGDALE   *n* pl. -S amygdule

AMYGDULE   *n* pl. -S a small gas bubble in lava

AMYL   *n* pl. -S a univalent radical

AMYLASE   *n* pl. -S an enzyme

AMYLENE   *n* pl. -S a flammable liquid

AMYLIC   *adj* pertaining to amyl

AMYLOGEN   *n* pl. -S amylose

AMYLOID   *n* pl. -S a hard protein deposit resulting from degeneration of tissue

AMYLOSE   *n* pl. -S the relatively soluble component of starch

AMYLUM   *n* pl. -S starch

AN   *indefinite article* — used before words beginning with a vowel sound

ANA   *n* pl. -S a collection of miscellaneous information about a particular subject

ANABAENA   *n* pl. -S a freshwater alga

ANABAS   *n* pl. -ES a freshwater fish

ANABASIS   *n* pl. -ASES a military advance

ANABATIC   *adj* pertaining to rising wind currents

ANABLEPS   *n* pl. -ES a freshwater fish

ANABOLIC   *adj* pertaining to a process by which food is built up into protoplasm

ANACONDA   *n* pl. -S a large snake

ANADEM   *n* pl. -S a wreath for the head

ANAEMIA   *n* pl. -S anemia **ANAEMIC** *adj*

ANAEROBE   *n* pl. -S an organism that does not require oxygen to live

ANAGLYPH   *n* pl. -S a type of carved ornament

ANAGOGE   *n* pl. -S a spiritual interpretation of words **ANAGOGIC** *adj*

ANAGOGY   *n* pl. -GIES anagoge

ANAGRAM   *v* -GRAMMED, -GRAMMING, -GRAMS to transpose the letters of a word or phrase to form a new one

ANAL   *adj* pertaining to the anus

ANALCIME   *n* pl. -S analcite

ANALCITE   *n* pl. -S a mineral

ANALECTA   *n/pl* analects

ANALECTS   *n/pl* selections from a literary work or group of works

ANALEMMA   *n* pl. -MAS or -MATA a type of graduated scale

ANALGIA   *n* pl. -S inability to feel pain

ANALITY   *n* pl. -TIES a type of psychological state

ANALLY   *adv* at or through the anus

ANALOG   *n* pl. -S analogue

ANALOGIC   *adj* pertaining to an analogy

ANALOGUE   *n* pl. -S something that bears an analogy to something else

ANALOGY   *n* pl. -GIES resemblance in some respects between things otherwise unlike

ANALYSE   *v* -LYSED, -LYSING, -LYSES to analyze

ANALYSER   *n* pl. -S analyzer

ANALYSIS	*n* pl. -YSES the separation of a whole into its parts
ANALYST	*n* pl. -S one that analyzes
ANALYTIC	*adj* pertaining to analysis
ANALYZE	*v* -LYZED, -LYZING, -LYZES to subject to analysis
ANALYZER	*n* pl. -S one that analyzes
ANANKE	*n* pl. -S a compelling necessity in ancient Greek religion
ANAPAEST	*n* pl. -S anapest
ANAPEST	*n* pl. -S a type of metrical foot
ANAPHASE	*n* pl. -S a stage of mitosis
ANAPHOR	*n* pl. -S a word or phrase that takes reference from a preceding word or phrase
ANAPHORA	*n* pl. -S the repetition of a word or phrase at the beginning of several successive verses or sentences
ANARCH	*n* pl. -S an advocate of anarchy
ANARCHY	*n* pl. -CHIES absence of government **ANARCHIC** *adj*
ANASARCA	*n* pl. -S a form of dropsy
ANATASE	*n* pl. -S a mineral
ANATHEMA	*n* pl. -MAS or -MATA a formal ecclesiastical ban or curse
ANATOMY	*n* pl. -MIES the structure of an organism **ANATOMIC** *adj*
ANATOXIN	*n* pl. -S a toxoid
ANATTO	*n* pl. -TOS annatto
ANCESTOR	*v* -ED, -ING, -S to be an ancestor (a person from whom one is descended) of
ANCESTRY	*n* pl. -TRIES a line or body of ancestors
ANCHOR	*v* -ED, -ING, -S to secure by means of an anchor (a device for holding a floating vessel in place)
ANCHORET	*n* pl. -S a recluse
ANCHOVY	*n* pl. -VIES a small food fish
ANCHUSA	*n* pl. -S a hairy-stemmed plant
ANCHUSIN	*n* pl. -S a red dye
ANCIENT	*adj* -CIENTER, -CIENTEST of or pertaining to time long past
ANCIENT	*n* pl. -S one who lived in ancient times
ANCILLA	*n* pl. -LAE or -LAS a helper
ANCON	*n* pl. -ES the elbow **ANCONAL, ANCONEAL, ANCONOID** *adj*
ANCONE	*n* pl. -S ancon
ANCRESS	*n* pl. -ES a female recluse
AND	*n* pl. -S an added condition or stipulation
ANDANTE	*n* pl. -S a moderately slow musical passage
ANDESITE	*n* pl. -S a volcanic rock
ANDESYTE	*n* pl. -S andesite
ANDIRON	*n* pl. -S a metal support for holding wood in a fireplace
ANDROGEN	*n* pl. -S a male sex hormone
ANDROID	*n* pl. -S a synthetic man
ANE	*n* pl. -S one
ANEAR	*v* -ED, -ING, -S to approach
ANECDOTE	*n* pl. -DOTES or -DOTA a brief story
ANECHOIC	*adj* neither having nor producing echoes
ANELE	*v* ANELED, ANELING, ANELES to anoint
ANEMIA	*n* pl. -S a disorder of the blood **ANEMIC** *adj*
ANEMONE	*n* pl. -S a flowering plant
ANEMOSIS	*n* pl. -MOSES separation of rings of growth in timber due to wind
ANENST	*prep* anent
ANENT	*prep* in regard to
ANERGIA	*n* pl. -S anergy
ANERGY	*n* pl. -GIES lack of energy **ANERGIC** *adj*
ANEROID	*n* pl. -S a type of barometer
ANESTRUS	*n* pl. -TRI a period of sexual dormancy
ANETHOL	*n* pl. -S anethole
ANETHOLE	*n* pl. -S a chemical compound
ANEURIN	*n* pl. -S thiamine
ANEURISM	*n* pl. -S aneurysm
ANEURYSM	*n* pl. -S an abnormal blood-filled dilation of a blood vessel
ANEW	*adv* once more
ANGA	*n* pl. -S any of the eight practices of yoga
ANGAKOK	*n* pl. -S an Eskimo medicine man
ANGARIA	*n* pl. -S angary
ANGARY	*n* pl. -RIES the right of a warring state to seize neutral property
ANGEL	*v* -ED, -ING, -S to support financially
ANGELIC	*adj* pertaining to an angel (a winged celestial being)

ANGELICA	*n* pl. -S an aromatic herb
ANGELUS	*n* pl. -ES a Roman Catholic prayer
ANGER	*v* -ED, -ING, -S to make angry
ANGERLY	*adv* in an angry manner
ANGINA	*n* pl. -S a disease marked by spasmodic attacks of intense pain **ANGINAL, ANGINOSE, ANGINOUS** *adj*
ANGIOMA	*n* pl. -MAS or -MATA a tumor composed of blood or lymph vessels
ANGLE	*v* -GLED, -GLING, -GLES to fish with a hook and line
ANGLEPOD	*n* pl. -S a flowering plant
ANGLER	*n* pl. -S one that angles
ANGLICE	*adv* in readily understood English
ANGLING	*n* pl. -S the sport of fishing
ANGORA	*n* pl. -S the long, silky hair of a domestic goat
ANGRY	*adj* -GRIER, -GRIEST feeling strong displeasure or hostility **ANGRILY** *adv*
ANGST	*n* pl. -S a feeling of anxiety or dread
ANGSTROM	*n* pl. -S a unit of length
ANGUINE	*adj* resembling a snake
ANGUISH	*v* -ED, -ING, -ES to suffer extreme pain
ANGULAR	*adj* having sharp corners
ANGULATE	*v* -LATED, -LATING, -LATES to make angular
ANGULOSE	*adj* angular
ANGULOUS	*adj* angular
ANHINGA	*n* pl. -S an aquatic bird
ANI	*n* pl. -S a tropical American bird
ANIL	*n* pl. -S a West Indian shrub
ANILE	*adj* resembling an old woman
ANILIN	*n* pl. -S aniline
ANILINE	*n* pl. -S a chemical compound
ANILITY	*n* pl. -TIES the state of being anile
ANIMA	*n* pl. -S the soul
ANIMAL	*n* pl. -S a living organism typically capable of voluntary motion and sensation **ANIMALIC** *adj*
ANIMALLY	*adv* physically
ANIMATE	*v* -MATED, -MATING, -MATES to give life to
ANIMATER	*n* pl. -S animator
ANIMATO	*adv* in a lively manner — used as a musical direction
ANIMATOR	*n* pl. -S one that animates
ANIME	*n* pl. -S a resin obtained from a tropical tree
ANIMI	*n* pl. -S anime
ANIMISM	*n* pl. -S the belief that souls may exist apart from bodies
ANIMIST	*n* pl. -S an adherent of animism
ANIMUS	*n* pl. -ES a feeling of hostility
ANION	*n* pl. -S a negatively charged ion **ANIONIC** *adj*
ANISE	*n* pl. -S a North African plant
ANISEED	*n* pl. -S the seed of the anise used as a flavoring
ANISETTE	*n* pl. -S a liqueur flavored with aniseed
ANISIC	*adj* pertaining to an anise
ANISOLE	*n* pl. -S a chemical compound
ANKERITE	*n* pl. -S a mineral
ANKH	*n* pl. -S an Egyptian symbol of enduring life
ANKLE	*v* -KLED, -KLING, -KLES to walk
ANKLET	*n* pl. -S an ornament for the ankle
ANKUS	*n* pl. -ES an elephant goad
ANKUSH	*n* pl. -ES ankus
ANKYLOSE	*v* -LOSED, -LOSING, -LOSES to unite or grow together, as the bones of a joint
ANLACE	*n* pl. -S a medieval dagger
ANLAGE	*n* pl. -GEN or -GES the initial cell structure from which an embryonic organ develops
ANLAS	*n* pl. -ES anlace
ANNA	*n* pl. -S a former coin of India and Pakistan
ANNAL	*n* pl. -S a record of a single year
ANNALIST	*n* pl. -S a historian
ANNATES	*n/pl* the first year's revenue of a bishop paid to the pope
ANNATTO	*n* pl. -TOS a yellowish-red dye
ANNEAL	*v* -ED, -ING, -S to toughen
ANNEALER	*n* pl. -S one that anneals
ANNELID	*n* pl. -S any of a phylum of segmented worms
ANNEX	*v* -ED, -ING, -ES to add or attach

ANNEXE   *n* pl. -S something added or attached

ANNOTATE   *v* -TATED, -TATING, -TATES to furnish with critical or explanatory notes

ANNOUNCE   *v* -NOUNCED, -NOUNCING, -NOUNCES to make known publicly

ANNOY   *v* -ED, -ING, -S to be troublesome to

ANNOYER   *n* pl. -S one that annoys

ANNUAL   *n* pl. -S a publication issued once a year

ANNUALLY   *adv* once a year

ANNUITY   *n* pl. -TIES an allowance or income paid at regular intervals

ANNUL   *v* -NULLED, -NULLING, -NULS to make or declare void or invalid

ANNULAR   *adj* shaped like a ring

ANNULATE   *adj* composed of or furnished with rings

ANNULET   *n* pl. -S a small ring

ANNULI   a pl. of annulus

ANNULLED   past tense of annul

ANNULLING   present participle of annul

ANNULUS   *n* pl. -LI or -LUSES a ring or ringlike part **ANNULOSE** *adj*

ANOA   *n* pl. -S a wild ox

ANODE   *n* pl. -S a positively charged electrode **ANODAL, ANODIC** *adj* **ANODALLY** *adv*

ANODIZE   *v* -IZED, -IZING, -IZES to coat with a protective film by chemical means

ANODYNE   *n* pl. -S a medicine that relieves pain **ANODYNIC** *adj*

ANOINT   *v* -ED, -ING, -S to apply oil to as a sacred rite

ANOINTER   *n* pl. -S one that anoints

ANOLE   *n* pl. -S a tropical lizard

ANOLYTE   *n* pl. -S the part of an electricity-conducting solution nearest the anode

ANOMALY   *n* pl. -LIES a deviation from the common rule, type, or form

ANOMIE   *n* pl. -S a collapse of the social structures governing a given society **ANOMIC** *adj*

ANOMY   *n* pl. -MIES anomie

ANON   *adv* at another time

ANONYM   *n* pl. -S a false or assumed name

ANOOPSIA   *n* pl. -S a visual defect

ANOPIA   *n* pl. -S anoopsia

ANOPSIA   *n* pl. -S anoopsia

ANORAK   *n* pl. -S a parka

ANORETIC   *n* pl. -S anorexic

ANOREXIA   *n* pl. -S loss of appetite

ANOREXIC   *n* pl. -S one affected with anorexia

ANOREXY   *n* pl. -OREXIES anorexia

ANORTHIC   *adj* denoting a certain type of crystal system

ANOSMIA   *n* pl. -S loss of the sense of smell **ANOSMIC** *adj*

ANOTHER   *adj* one more

ANOVULAR   *adj* not involving ovulation

ANOXEMIA   *n* pl. -S a disorder of the blood **ANOXEMIC** *adj*

ANOXIA   *n* pl. -S absence of oxygen **ANOXIC** *adj*

ANSA   *n* pl. -SAE the projecting part of Saturn's rings

ANSATE   *adj* having a handle

ANSATED   *adj* ansate

ANSERINE   *n* pl. -S a chemical compound

ANSEROUS   *adj* silly

ANSWER   *v* -ED, -ING, -S to say, write, or act in return

ANSWERER   *n* pl. -S one that answers

ANT   *n* pl. -S a small insect

ANTA   *n* pl. -TAE or -TAS a pilaster formed at the termination of a wall

ANTACID   *n* pl. -S a substance that neutralizes acid

ANTALGIC   *n* pl. -S an anodyne

ANTBEAR   *n* pl. -S an aardvark

ANTE   *v* ANTED or ANTEED, ANTEING, ANTES to put a fixed stake into the pot before the cards are dealt in poker

ANTEATER   *n* pl. -S any of several mammals that feed on ants

ANTECEDE   *v* -CEDED, -CEDING, -CEDES to precede

ANTED   a past tense of ante

ANTEDATE   *v* -DATED, -DATING, -DATES to be of an earlier date than

ANTEFIX   *n* pl. -FIXES or -FIXA an upright ornament at the eaves of a tiled roof

ANTELOPE   *n* pl. -S a ruminant mammal

ANTENNA   *n* pl. -NAE or -NAS a metallic device for sending or receiving radio waves **ANTENNAL** *adj*

ANTEPAST   *n* pl. -S an appetizer

ANTERIOR   *adj* situated in or toward the front

ANTEROOM   *n* pl. -S a waiting room

ANTETYPE   *n* pl. -S an earlier form

ANTEVERT   *v* -ED, -ING, -S to displace by tipping forward

ANTHELIA   *n/pl* halolike areas seen in the sky opposite the sun

ANTHELIX   *n* pl. -LICES or -LIXES the inner curved ridge on the cartilage of the external ear

ANTHEM   *v* -ED, -ING, -S to praise in a song

ANTHEMIA   *n/pl* decorative floral patterns used in Greek art

ANTHER   *n* pl. -S the pollen-bearing part of a stamen **ANTHERAL** *adj*

ANTHERID   *n* pl. -S a male reproductive organ of certain plants

ANTHESIS   *n* pl. -THESES the full bloom of a flower

ANTHILL   *n* pl. -S a mound formed by ants in building their nest

ANTHODIA   *n/pl* flower heads of certain plants

ANTHOID   *adj* resembling a flower

ANTHRAX   *n* pl. -THRACES an infectious disease

ANTI   *n* pl. -S one that is opposed

ANTIAIR   *adj* directed against attacking aircraft

ANTIAR   *n* pl. -S an arrow poison

ANTIARIN   *n* pl. -S antiar

ANTIATOM   *n* pl. -S an atom comprised of antiparticles

ANTIBIAS   *adj* opposed to bias

ANTIBODY   *n* pl. -BODIES a body protein that produces immunity against certain microorganisms or toxins

ANTIBOSS   *adj* opposed to bosses

ANTIBUG   *adj* effective against bugs

ANTIC   *v* -TICKED, -TICKING, -TICS to act in a clownish manner

ANTICAR   *adj* opposed to cars

ANTICITY   *adj* opposed to cities

ANTICK   *v* -ED, -ING, -S to antic

ANTICLY   *adv* in a clownish manner

ANTICOLD   *adj* effective against the common cold

ANTICULT   *adj* opposed to cults

ANTIDORA   *n/pl* holy breads

ANTIDOTE   *v* -DOTED, -DOTING, -DOTES to counteract the effects of a poison with a remedy

ANTIDRUG   *adj* opposed to illicit drugs

ANTIFAT   *adj* preventing the formation of fat

ANTIFLU   *adj* combating the flu

ANTIFOAM   *adj* reducing or preventing foam

ANTIFUR   *adj* opposed to the wearing of animal furs

ANTIGAY   *adj* opposed to homosexuals

ANTIGEN   *n* pl. -S a substance that stimulates the production of antibodies

ANTIGENE   *n* pl. -S antigen

ANTIGUN   *adj* opposed to guns

ANTIHERO   *n* pl. -ROES a protagonist who is notably lacking in heroic qualities

ANTIJAM   *adj* blocking interfering signals

ANTIKING   *n* pl. -S a usurping king

ANTILEAK   *adj* preventing leaks

ANTILEFT   *adj* opposed to leftism

ANTILIFE   *adj* opposed to life

ANTILOCK   *adj* designed to prevent the wheels of a vehicle from locking

ANTILOG   *n* pl. -S the number corresponding to a given logarithm

ANTILOGY   *n* pl. -GIES a contradiction in terms or ideas

ANTIMALE   *adj* opposed to men

ANTIMAN   *adj* antimale

ANTIMASK   *n* pl. -S a comic performance between the acts of a masque

ANTIMERE   *n* pl. -S a part of an organism symmetrical with a part on the opposite side of the main axis

ANTIMONY   *n* pl. -NIES a metallic element

ANTING   *n* pl. -S the deliberate placing, by certain birds, of living ants among the feathers

ANTINODE   *n* pl. -S a region between adjacent nodes

ANTINOMY   *n* pl. -MIES a contradiction between two seemingly valid principles

ANTINUKE *adj* opposing the use of nuclear power plants or nuclear weapons

ANTIPHON *n* pl. -S a psalm or hymn sung responsively

ANTIPILL *adj* opposing the use of contraceptive pills

ANTIPODE *n* pl. -S an exact opposite

ANTIPOLE *n* pl. -S the opposite pole

ANTIPOPE *n* pl. -S one claiming to be pope in opposition to the one chosen by church law

ANTIPORN *adj* opposed to pornography

ANTIPOT *adj* opposing the use of pot (marijuana)

ANTIPYIC *n* pl. -S a medicine that prevents the formation of pus

ANTIQUE *v* -TIQUED, -TIQUING, -TIQUES to give an appearance of age to

ANTIQUER *n* pl. -S one that antiques

ANTIRAPE *adj* concerned with preventing rape

ANTIRED *adj* opposed to communism

ANTIRIOT *adj* designed to prevent or end riots

ANTIROCK *adj* opposed to rock music

ANTIROLL *adj* designed to reduce roll

ANTIRUST *n* pl. -S something that prevents rust

ANTISAG *adj* designed to prevent sagging

ANTISERA *n/pl* serums that contain antibodies

ANTISEX *adj* opposed to sexual activity

ANTISHIP *adj* designed for use against ships

ANTISKID *adj* designed to prevent skidding

ANTISLIP *adj* designed to prevent slipping

ANTISMOG *adj* designed to reduce pollutants that cause smog

ANTISMUT *adj* opposed to pornography

ANTISNOB *adj* opposed to snobbery

ANTISTAT *adj* designed to prevent the buildup of static electricity

ANTITANK *adj* designed to combat tanks

ANTITAX *adj* opposing taxes

ANTITYPE *n* pl. -S an opposite type

ANTIWAR *adj* opposing war

ANTIWEAR *adj* designed to reduce the effects of long or hard use

ANTIWEED *adj* concerned with the destruction of weeds

ANTLER *n* pl. -S the horn of an animal of the deer family **ANTLERED** *adj*

ANTLIKE *adj* resembling an ant

ANTLION *n* pl. -S a predatory insect

ANTONYM *n* pl. -S a word opposite in meaning to another

ANTONYMY *n* pl. -MIES the state of being an antonym

ANTRA a pl. of antrum

ANTRAL *adj* pertaining to an antrum

ANTRE *n* pl. -S a cave

ANTRORSE *adj* directed forward or upward

ANTRUM *n* pl. -TRA or -TRUMS a cavity in a bone

ANTSY *adj* -SIER, -SIEST fidgety

ANURAL *adj* anurous

ANURAN *n* pl. -S a frog or toad

ANURESIS *n* pl. -RESES inability to urinate **ANURETIC** *adj*

ANURIA *n* pl. -S absence of urine **ANURIC** *adj*

ANUROUS *adj* having no tail

ANUS *n* pl. -ES the excretory opening at the end of the alimentary canal

ANVIL *v* -VILED, -VILING, -VILS or -VILLED, -VILLING, -VILS to shape on an anvil (a heavy iron block)

ANVILTOP *n* pl. -S an anvil-shaped cloud mass

ANXIETY *n* pl. -ETIES painful or apprehensive uneasiness of mind

ANXIOUS *adj* full of anxiety

ANY *adj* one, no matter which

ANYBODY *n* pl. -BODIES a person of some importance

ANYHOW *adv* in any way

ANYMORE *adv* at the present time

ANYONE *pron* any person

ANYPLACE *adv* in any place

ANYTHING *n* pl. -S a thing of any kind

ANYTIME *adv* at any time

ANYWAY *adv* in any way

ANYWAYS *adv* anyway

ANYWHERE *n* pl. -S any place

ANYWISE *adv* in any way

AORIST *n* pl. -S a verb tense **AORISTIC** *adj*

AORTA *n* pl. -TAS or -TAE a main artery **AORTAL, AORTIC** *adj*

AOUDAD *n* pl. -S a wild sheep

APACE *adv* swiftly

APACHE *n* pl. -S a Parisian gangster

APAGOGE *n* pl. -S establishment of a thesis by showing its contrary to be absurd **APAGOGIC** *adj*

APANAGE *n* pl. -S appanage

APAREJO *n* pl. -JOS a type of saddle

APART *adv* not together

APATETIC *adj* having coloration serving as natural camouflage

APATHY *n* pl. -THIES lack of emotion

APATITE *n* pl. -S a mineral

APE *v* APED, APING, APES to mimic

APEAK *adv* in a vertical position

APEEK *adv* apeak

APELIKE *adj* resembling an ape (a large, tailless primate)

APER *n* pl. -S one that apes

APERCU *n* pl. -S a brief summary

APERIENT *n* pl. -S a mild laxative

APERITIF *n* pl. -S an alcoholic drink taken before a meal

APERTURE *n* pl. -S an opening

APERY *n* pl. -ERIES the act of aping

APETALY *n* pl. -ALIES the state of having no petals

APEX *n* pl. APEXES or APICES the highest point

APHAGIA *n* pl. -S inability to swallow

APHANITE *n* pl. -S an igneous rock

APHASIA *n* pl. -S loss of the ability to use words

APHASIAC *n* pl. -S one suffering from aphasia

APHASIC *n* pl. -S aphasiac

APHELION *n* pl. -ELIA or -ELIONS the point in a planetary orbit farthest from the sun **APHELIAN** *adj*

APHESIS *n* pl. -ESES the loss of an unstressed vowel from the beginning of a word **APHETIC** *adj*

APHID *n* pl. -S any of a family of small, soft-bodied insects

APHIDIAN *n* pl. -S an aphid

APHIS *n* pl. APHIDES an aphid

APHOLATE *n* pl. -S a chemical used to control houseflies

APHONIA *n* pl. -S loss of voice

APHONIC *n* pl. -S one affected with aphonia

APHORISE *v* -RISED, -RISING, -RISES to aphorize

APHORISM *n* pl. -S a brief statement of a truth or principle

APHORIST *n* pl. -S one that aphorizes

APHORIZE *v* -RIZED, -RIZING, -RIZES to write or speak in aphorisms

APHOTIC *adj* lacking light

APHTHA *n* pl. -THAE a small blister in the mouth or stomach **APHTHOUS** *adj*

APHYLLY *n* pl. -LIES the state of being leafless

APIAN *adj* pertaining to bees

APIARIAN *n* pl. -S an apiarist

APIARIST *n* pl. -S a person who raises bees

APIARY *n* pl. -ARIES a place where bees are kept

APICAL *n* pl. -S a sound articulated with the apex (tip) of the tongue

APICALLY *adv* at or toward the apex

APICES a pl. of apex

APICULUS *n* pl. -LI a sharp point at the end of a leaf

APIECE *adv* for each one

APIMANIA *n* pl. -S an excessive interest in bees

APING present participle of ape

APIOLOGY *n* pl. -GIES the study of bees

APISH *adj* slavishly or foolishly imitative **APISHLY** *adv*

APLASIA *n* pl. -S defective development of an organ or part

APLASTIC *adj* not plastic

APLENTY *adj* being in sufficient quantity

APLITE *n* pl. -S a fine-grained rock **APLITIC** *adj*

APLOMB *n* pl. -S self-confidence

APNEA *n* pl. -S temporary cessation of respiration **APNEAL, APNEIC** *adj*

APNOEA *n* pl. -S apnea **APNOEAL, APNOEIC** *adj*

APOAPSIS *n* pl. -APSIDES the high point in an orbit

APOCARP   *n* pl. -S a fruit having separated carpels

APOCARPY   *n* pl. -PIES the state of being an apocarp

APOCOPE   *n* pl. -S an omission of the last sound of a word **APOCOPIC** *adj*

APOCRINE   *adj* pertaining to a type of gland

APOD   *n* pl. -S an apodal animal

APODAL   *adj* having no feet or footlike appendages

APODOSIS   *n* pl. -OSES the main clause of a conditional sentence

APODOUS   *adj* apodal

APOGAMY   *n* pl. -MIES a form of plant reproduction **APOGAMIC** *adj*

APOGEE   *n* pl. -S the point in the orbit of a body which is farthest from the earth **APOGEAL, APOGEAN, APOGEIC** *adj*

APOLLO   *n* pl. -LOS a handsome young man

APOLOG   *n* pl. -S apologue

APOLOGAL   *adj* pertaining to an apologue

APOLOGIA   *n* pl. -GIAS or -GIAE a formal justification or defense

APOLOGUE   *n* pl. -S an allegory

APOLOGY   *n* pl. -GIES an expression of regret for some error or offense

APOLUNE   *n* pl. -S the point in the orbit of a body which is farthest from the moon

APOMICT   *n* pl. -S an organism produced by apomixis

APOMIXIS   *n* pl. -MIXES a type of reproductive process

APOPHONY   *n* pl. -NIES ablaut

APOPHYGE   *n* pl. -S a concave curve in a column

APOPLEXY   *n* pl. -PLEXIES a sudden loss of sensation and muscular control

APORT   *adv* on or toward the left side of a ship

APOSPORY   *n* pl. -RIES a type of reproduction without spore formation

APOSTACY   *n* pl. -CIES apostasy

APOSTASY   *n* pl. -SIES an abandonment of one's faith or principles

APOSTATE   *n* pl. -S one who commits apostasy

APOSTIL   *n* pl. -S a marginal note

APOSTLE   *n* pl. -S a disciple sent forth by Christ to preach the gospel

APOTHECE   *n* pl. -S a spore-producing organ of certain fungi

APOTHEGM   *n* pl. -S a maxim

APOTHEM   *n* pl. -S the perpendicular from the center to any side of a regular polygon

APPAL   *v* -PALLED, -PALLING, -PALS to appall

APPALL   *v* -ED, -ING, -S to fill with horror or dismay

APPANAGE   *n* pl. -S land or revenue granted to a member of a royal family

APPARAT   *n* pl. -S a political organization

APPAREL   *v* -ELED, -ELING, -ELS or -ELLED, -ELLING, -ELS to provide with outer garments

APPARENT   *adj* easily seen

APPEAL   *v* -ED, -ING, -S to make an earnest request

APPEALER   *n* pl. -S one that appeals

APPEAR   *v* -ED, -ING, -S to come into view

APPEASE   *v* -PEASED, -PEASING, -PEASES to bring to a state of peace or contentment

APPEASER   *n* pl. -S one that appeases

APPEL   *n* pl. -S a feint in fencing

APPELLEE   *n* pl. -S the defendant in a type of judicial proceeding

APPELLOR   *n* pl. -S a confessed criminal who accuses an accomplice

APPEND   *v* -ED, -ING, -S to add as a supplement

APPENDIX   *n* pl. -DIXES or -DICES a collection of supplementary material at the end of a book

APPESTAT   *n* pl. -S the mechanism in the central nervous system that regulates appetite

APPETENT   *adj* marked by strong desire

APPETITE   *n* pl. -S a desire for food or drink

APPLAUD   *v* -ED, -ING, -S to express approval by clapping the hands

APPLAUSE   *n* pl. -S the sound made by persons applauding

APPLE   *n* pl. -S an edible fruit

APPLIED   past tense of apply

APPLIER   *n* pl. -S one that applies

APPLIQUE   *v* -QUED, -QUEING, -QUES to apply as a decoration to a larger surface

APPLY   *v* -PLIED, -PLYING, -PLIES to bring into contact with something

APPOINT   *v* -ED, -ING, -S to name or assign to a position or office

APPOSE   *v* -POSED, -POSING, -POSES to place side by side

APPOSER   *n* pl. -S one that apposes

APPOSITE   *adj* relevant

APPRAISE   *v* -PRAISED, -PRAISING, -PRAISES to set a value on

APPRISE   *v* -PRISED, -PRISING, -PRISES to notify

APPRISER   *n* pl. -S one that apprises

APPRIZE   *v* -PRIZED, -PRIZING, -PRIZES to appraise

APPRIZER   *n* pl. -S one that apprizes

APPROACH   *v* -ED, -ING, -ES to come near or nearer to

APPROVAL   *n* pl. -S the act of approving

APPROVE   *v* -PROVED, -PROVING, -PROVES to regard favorably

APPROVER   *n* pl. -S one that approves

APPULSE   *n* pl. -S the approach of one moving body toward another

APRAXIA   *n* pl. -S loss of the ability to perform coordinated movements **APRACTIC, APRAXIC** *adj*

APRES   *prep* after

APRICOT   *n* pl. -S an edible fruit

APRON   *v* -ED, -ING, -S to provide with an apron (a garment worn to protect one's clothing)

APROPOS   *adj* relevant

APROTIC   *adj* being a type of solvent

APSE   *n* pl. -S a domed, semicircular projection of a building **APSIDAL** *adj*

APSIS   *n* pl. -SIDES an apse

APT   *adj* APTER, APTEST suitable

APTERAL   *adj* apterous

APTERIUM   *n* pl. -RIA a bare area of skin between feathers

APTEROUS   *adj* having no wings

APTERYX   *n* pl. -ES the kiwi

APTITUDE   *n* pl. -S an ability

APTLY   *adv* in an apt manner

APTNESS   *n* pl. -ES the quality of being apt

APYRASE   *n* pl. -S an enzyme

APYRETIC   *adj* having no fever

AQUA   *n* pl. AQUAE or AQUAS water

AQUACADE   *n* pl. -S a swimming and diving exhibition

AQUANAUT   *n* pl. -S a scuba diver trained to live in underwater installations

AQUARIA   a pl. of aquarium

AQUARIAL   *adj* pertaining to an aquarium

AQUARIAN   *n* pl. -S a member of the old sects that used water rather than wine in religious ceremonies

AQUARIST   *n* pl. -S one who keeps an aquarium

AQUARIUM   *n* pl. -IUMS or -IA a water-filled enclosure in which aquatic animals are kept

AQUATIC   *n* pl. -S an organism living or growing in or near water

AQUATINT   *v* -ED, -ING, -S to etch, using a certain process

AQUATONE   *n* pl. -S a type of printing process

AQUAVIT   *n* pl. -S a Scandinavian liquor

AQUEDUCT   *n* pl. -S a water conduit

AQUEOUS   *adj* pertaining to water

AQUIFER   *n* pl. -S a water-bearing rock formation

AQUILINE   *adj* curving like an eagle's beak

AQUIVER   *adj* quivering

AR   *n* pl. -S the letter R

ARABESK   *n* pl. -S a design of intertwined floral figures

ARABIC   *adj* derived from gum arabic

ARABICA   *n* pl. -S an evergreen shrub that produces coffee beans

ARABIZE   *v* -IZED, -IZING, -IZES to cause to acquire Arabic customs

ARABLE   *n* pl. -S land suitable for cultivation

ARACEOUS   *adj* belonging to the arum family of plants

ARACHNID   *n* pl. -S any of a class of segmented invertebrate animals

ARAK   *n* pl. -S arrack

ARAMID   *n* pl. -S a type of chemical compound

ARANEID   *n* pl. -S a spider

ARAPAIMA   *n* pl. -S a large food fish

ARAROBA   *n* pl. -S a Brazilian tree

ARB   *n* pl. -S a type of stock trader

ARBALEST   *n* pl. -S a type of crossbow

ARBALIST   *n* pl. -S arbalest

ARBELEST *n* pl. -S arbalest

ARBITER *n* pl. -S one chosen or appointed to judge a disputed issue **ARBITRAL** *adj*

ARBOR *n* pl. -S a shady garden shelter

ARBOR *n* pl. -ES a tree

ARBOREAL *adj* living in trees

ARBORED *adj* having trees

ARBORETA *n/pl* places for the study and exhibition of trees

ARBORIST *n* pl. -S a tree specialist

ARBORIZE *v* -IZED, -IZING, -IZES to form many branches

ARBOROUS *adj* pertaining to trees

ARBOUR *n* pl. -S a shady garden shelter **ARBOURED** *adj*

ARBUSCLE *n* pl. -S a dwarf tree

ARBUTE *n* pl. -S an evergreen tree **ARBUTEAN** *adj*

ARBUTUS *n* pl. -ES an evergreen tree

ARC *v* ARCED, ARCING, ARCS or ARCKED, ARCKING, ARCS to move in a curved course

ARCADE *v* -CADED, -CADING, -CADES to provide with an arcade (a series of arches)

ARCADIA *n* pl. -S a region of simple pleasure and quiet

ARCADIAN *n* pl. -S one who lives in an arcadia

ARCADING *n* pl. -S an arcade

ARCANE *adj* mysterious

ARCANUM *n* pl. -NA or -NUMS a mystery

ARCATURE *n* pl. -S a small arcade

ARCH *v* -ED, -ING, -ES to bend like an arch (a curved structure spanning an opening)

ARCHAIC *adj* pertaining to an earlier time

ARCHAISE *v* -ISED, -ISING, -ISES to archaize

ARCHAISM *n* pl. -S an archaic word, idiom, or expression

ARCHAIST *n* pl. -S one that archaizes

ARCHAIZE *v* -IZED, -IZING, -IZES to use archaisms

ARCHDUKE *n* pl. -S an Austrian prince

ARCHER *n* pl. -S one that shoots with a bow and arrow

ARCHERY *n* pl. -CHERIES the sport of shooting with a bow and arrow

ARCHIL *n* pl. -S orchil

ARCHINE *n* pl. -S a Russian unit of linear measure

ARCHING *n* pl. -S a series of arches

ARCHIVE *v* -CHIVED, -CHIVING, -CHIVES to file in an archive (a place where records are kept) **ARCHIVAL** *adj*

ARCHLY *adv* slyly

ARCHNESS *n* pl. -ES slyness

ARCHON *n* pl. -S a magistrate of ancient Athens

ARCHWAY *n* pl. -WAYS a passageway under an arch

ARCIFORM *adj* having the form of an arch

ARCKED a past tense of arc

ARCKING a present participle of arc

ARCO *adv* with the bow — used as a direction to players of stringed instruments

ARCSINE *n* pl. -S the inverse function to the sine

ARCTIC *n* pl. -S a warm, waterproof overshoe

ARCUATE *adj* curved like a bow

ARCUATED *adj* arcuate

ARCUS *n* pl. -ES an arch-shaped cloud

ARDEB *n* pl. -S an Egyptian unit of capacity

ARDENCY *n* pl. -CIES ardor

ARDENT *adj* characterized by intense emotion **ARDENTLY** *adv*

ARDOR *n* pl. -S intensity of emotion

ARDOUR *n* pl. -S ardor

ARDUOUS *adj* involving great labor or hardship

ARE *n* pl. -S a unit of surface measure

AREA *n* pl. AREAE a section of the cerebral cortex having a specific function

AREA *n* pl. -S a particular extent of space or surface **AREAL** *adj* **AREALLY** *adv*

AREAWAY *n* pl. -WAYS a sunken area leading to a basement entrance

ARECA *n* pl. -S a tropical tree

AREIC *adj* pertaining to a region of the earth contributing little surface drainage

ARENA *n* pl. -S an enclosed area for contests

ARENITE	n pl. -S rock made up chiefly of sand grains
ARENOSE	adj sandy
ARENOUS	adj arenose
AREOLA	n pl. -LAE or -LAS a small space in a network of leaf veins **AREOLAR, AREOLATE** adj
AREOLE	n pl. -S areola
AREOLOGY	n pl. -GIES the study of the planet Mars
ARETE	n pl. -S a sharp mountain ridge
ARETHUSA	n pl. -S a flowering plant
ARF	n pl. -S a barking sound
ARGAL	n pl. -S argol
ARGALA	n pl. -S a type of stork
ARGALI	n pl. -S a wild sheep
ARGENT	n pl. -S silver **ARGENTAL, ARGENTIC** adj
ARGENTUM	n pl. -S silver
ARGIL	n pl. -S a white clay
ARGINASE	n pl. -S an enzyme
ARGININE	n pl. -S an amino acid
ARGLE	v -GLED, -GLING, -GLES to argue
ARGOL	n pl. -S a crust deposited in wine casks during aging
ARGON	n pl. -S a gaseous element
ARGONAUT	n pl. -S a marine mollusk
ARGOSY	n pl. -SIES a large merchant ship
ARGOT	n pl. -S a specialized vocabulary **ARGOTIC** adj
ARGUABLE	adj capable of being argued about **ARGUABLY** adv
ARGUE	v -GUED, -GUING, -GUES to present reasons for or against
ARGUER	n pl. -S one that argues
ARGUFIER	n pl. -S one that argufies
ARGUFY	v -FIED, -FYING, -FIES to argue stubbornly
ARGUING	present participle of argue
ARGUMENT	n pl. -S a discussion involving differing points of view
ARGUS	n pl. -ES an East Indian pheasant
ARGYLE	n pl. -S a knitting pattern
ARGYLL	n pl. -S argyle
ARHAT	n pl. -S a Buddhist who has attained nirvana
ARIA	n pl. -S an elaborate melody for a single voice
ARID	adj -IDER, -IDEST extremely dry **ARIDLY** adv
ARIDITY	n pl. -TIES the state of being arid
ARIDNESS	n pl. -ES aridity
ARIEL	n pl. -S an African gazelle
ARIETTA	n pl. -S a short aria
ARIETTE	n pl. -S arietta
ARIGHT	adv rightly; correctly
ARIL	n pl. -S an outer covering of certain seeds **ARILED, ARILLATE, ARILLOID** adj
ARILLODE	n pl. -S a type of aril
ARIOSE	adj characterized by melody
ARIOSO	n pl. -SOS or -SI a musical passage resembling an aria
ARISE	v AROSE, ARISEN, ARISING, ARISES to get up
ARISTA	n pl. -TAE or -TAS a bristlelike structure or appendage **ARISTATE** adj
ARISTO	n pl. -TOS an aristocrat
ARK	n pl. -S a large boat
ARKOSE	n pl. -S a type of sandstone **ARKOSIC** adj
ARLES	n/pl money paid to bind a bargain
ARM	v -ED, -ING, -S to supply with weapons
ARMADA	n pl. -S a fleet of warships
ARMAGNAC	n pl. -S a French brandy
ARMAMENT	n pl. -S a military force equipped for war
ARMATURE	v -TURED, -TURING, -TURES to furnish with armor
ARMBAND	n pl. -S a band worn around an arm (an upper appendage of the human body)
ARMCHAIR	n pl. -S a chair with armrests
ARMER	n pl. -S one that arms
ARMET	n pl. -S a medieval helmet
ARMFUL	n pl. ARMFULS or ARMSFUL as much as the arm can hold
ARMHOLE	n pl. -S an opening for the arm in a garment
ARMIES	pl. of army
ARMIGER	n pl. -S one who carries the armor of a knight
ARMIGERO	n pl. -GEROS armiger

ARMILLA	n pl. -LAE or -LAS a thin membrane around the stem of certain fungi	**ARPENT**	n pl. -S an old French unit of area
ARMING	n pl. -S the act of one that arms	**ARQUEBUS**	n pl. -ES an early portable firearm
ARMLESS	adj having no arms	**ARRACK**	n pl. -S an Oriental liquor
ARMLET	n pl. -S an armband	**ARRAIGN**	v -ED, -ING, -S to call before a court of law to answer an indictment
ARMLIKE	adj resembling an arm		
ARMLOAD	n pl. -S an armful	**ARRANGE**	v -RANGED, -RANGING, -RANGES to put in definite or proper order
ARMLOCK	n pl. -S a hold in wrestling		
ARMOIRE	n pl. -S a large, ornate cabinet		
ARMONICA	n pl. -S a type of musical instrument	**ARRANGER**	n pl. -S one that arranges
		ARRANT	adj outright **ARRANTLY** adv
ARMOR	v -ED, -ING, -S to furnish with armor (a defensive covering)	**ARRAS**	n pl. ARRAS a tapestry **ARRASED** adj
ARMORER	n pl. -S one that makes or repairs armor	**ARRAY**	v -ED, -ING, -S to place in proper or desired order
ARMORIAL	n pl. -S a treatise on heraldry	**ARRAYAL**	n pl. -S the act of arraying
ARMORY	n pl. -MORIES a place where weapons are stored	**ARRAYER**	n pl. -S one that arrays
		ARREAR	n pl. -S an unpaid and overdue debt
ARMOUR	v -ED, -ING, -S to armor		
ARMOURER	n pl. -S armorer	**ARREST**	v -ED, -ING, -S to seize and hold by legal authority
ARMOURY	n pl. -MOURIES armory		
ARMPIT	n pl. -S the hollow under the arm at the shoulder	**ARRESTEE**	n pl. -S one that is arrested
		ARRESTER	n pl. -S one that arrests
ARMREST	n pl. -S a support for the arm	**ARRESTOR**	n pl. -S arrester
ARMSFUL	a pl. of armful	**ARRHIZAL**	adj rootless
ARMURE	n pl. -S a woven fabric	**ARRIS**	n pl. -RISES a ridge formed by the meeting of two surfaces
ARMY	n pl. -MIES a large body of men trained and armed for war		
		ARRIVAL	n pl. -S the act of arriving
ARMYWORM	n pl. -S a destructive moth larva	**ARRIVE**	v -RIVED, -RIVING, -RIVES to reach a destination
ARNATTO	n pl. -TOS annatto		
ARNICA	n pl. -S a perennial herb	**ARRIVER**	n pl. -S one that arrives
ARNOTTO	n pl. -TOS a tropical tree	**ARROBA**	n pl. -S a Spanish unit of weight
AROID	n pl. -S a flowering plant	**ARROGANT**	adj overly convinced of one's own worth or importance
AROINT	v -ED, -ING, -S to drive away		
AROMA	n pl. -S a pleasant odor	**ARROGATE**	v -GATED, -GATING, -GATES to claim or take without right
AROMATIC	n pl. -S a fragrant plant or substance		
		ARROW	v -ED, -ING, -S to indicate the proper position of with an arrow (a linear figure with a wedge-shaped end)
AROSE	past tense of arise		
AROUND	prep on all sides of		
AROUSAL	n pl. -S the act of arousing	**ARROWY**	adj moving swiftly
AROUSE	v AROUSED, AROUSING, AROUSES to stimulate	**ARROYO**	n pl. -ROYOS a brook or creek
		ARSENAL	n pl. -S a collection or supply of weapons
AROUSER	n pl. -S one that arouses		
AROYNT	v -ED, -ING, -S to aroint	**ARSENATE**	n pl. -S a chemical salt
ARPEGGIO	n pl. -GIOS a technique of playing a musical chord	**ARSENIC**	n pl. -S a metallic element
		ARSENIDE	n pl. -S an arsenic compound
ARPEN	n pl. -S arpent	**ARSENITE**	n pl. -S a chemical salt

ARSENO	*adj* containing a certain bivalent chemical radical	**ARUM**	*n* pl. -S a flowering plant
ARSENOUS	*adj* pertaining to arsenic	**ARUSPEX**	*n* pl. -PICES haruspex
ARSES	pl. of arsis	**ARVAL**	*adj* pertaining to plowed land
ARSHIN	*n* pl. -S archine	**ARVO**	*n* pl. -VOS afternoon
ARSINE	*n* pl. -S a poisonous gas	**ARYL**	*n* pl. -S a univalent radical
ARSINO	*adj* containing a certain univalent chemical radical	**ARYTHMIA**	*n* pl. -S an irregularity in the rhythm of the heartbeat **ARYTHMIC** *adj*
ARSIS	*n* pl. ARSES the unaccented part of a musical measure	**AS**	*adv* to the same degree
ARSON	*n* pl. -S the malicious or fraudulent burning of property **ARSONOUS** *adj*	**ASANA**	*n* pl. -S a posture in yoga
		ASARUM	*n* pl. -S a perennial herb
ARSONIST	*n* pl. -S one that commits arson	**ASBESTOS**	*n* pl. -ES a mineral **ASBESTIC** *adj*
ART	*n* pl. -S an esthetically pleasing and meaningful arrangement of elements	**ASBESTUS**	*n* pl. -ES asbestos
		ASCARID	*n* pl. -S a parasitic worm
ARTAL	a pl. of rotl	**ASCARIS**	*n* pl. -RIDES ascarid
ARTEFACT	*n* pl. -S artifact	**ASCEND**	*v* -ED, -ING, -S to go or move upward
ARTEL	*n* pl. -S a collective farm in Russia	**ASCENDER**	*n* pl. -S one that ascends
ARTERIAL	*n* pl. -S a type of highway	**ASCENT**	*n* pl. -S the act of ascending
ARTERY	*n* pl. -TERIES a vessel that carries blood away from the heart	**ASCESIS**	*n* pl. -CESES the conduct of an ascetic
ARTFUL	*adj* crafty **ARTFULLY** *adv*	**ASCETIC**	*n* pl. -S one who practices extreme self-denial for religious reasons
ARTICLE	*v* -CLED, -CLING, -CLES to charge with specific offenses	
ARTIER	comparative of arty	**ASCI**	pl. of ascus
ARTIEST	superlative of arty	**ASCIDIAN**	*n* pl. -S a small marine animal
ARTIFACT	*n* pl. -S an object made by man	**ASCIDIUM**	*n* pl. -DIA a flask-shaped plant appendage
ARTIFICE	*n* pl. -S a clever stratagem	**ASCITES**	*n* pl. ASCITES accumulation of serous fluid in the abdomen **ASCITIC** *adj*
ARTILY	*adv* in an arty manner	
ARTINESS	*n* pl. -ES the quality of being arty	
ARTISAN	*n* pl. -S a trained or skilled workman	**ASCOCARP**	*n* pl. -S a spore-producing organ of certain fungi
ARTIST	*n* pl. -S one who practices one of the fine arts	**ASCORBIC**	*adj* relieving scurvy
		ASCOT	*n* pl. -S a broad neck scarf
ARTISTE	*n* pl. -S a skilled public performer	**ASCRIBE**	*v* -CRIBED, -CRIBING, -CRIBES to attribute to a specified cause, source, or origin
ARTISTIC	*adj* characteristic of art	
ARTISTRY	*n* pl. -RIES artistic quality or workmanship	**ASCUS**	*n* pl. ASCI a spore sac in certain fungi
ARTLESS	*adj* lacking cunning or guile	**ASDIC**	*n* pl. -S sonar
ARTSY	*adj* -SIER, -SIEST arty	**ASEA**	*adv* at sea
ARTWORK	*n* pl. -S illustrative or decorative work in printed matter	**ASEPSIS**	*n* pl. -SEPSES the condition of being aseptic
ARTY	*adj* ARTIER, ARTIEST showily or pretentiously artistic	**ASEPTIC**	*adj* free from germs
ARUGOLA	*n* pl. -S arugula	**ASEXUAL**	*adj* occurring or performed without sexual action
ARUGULA	*n* pl. -S a European annual herb	

ASH	v -ED, -ING, -ES to convert into ash (the residue of a substance that has been burned)
ASHAMED	adj feeling shame, guilt, or disgrace
ASHCAN	n pl. -S a metal receptacle for garbage
ASHEN	adj consisting of ashes
ASHFALL	n pl. -S a deposit of volcanic ash
ASHIER	comparative of ashy
ASHIEST	superlative of ashy
ASHINESS	n pl. -ES the condition of being ashy
ASHLAR	v -ED, -ING, -S to build with squared stones
ASHLER	v -ED, -ING, -S to ashlar
ASHLESS	adj having no ashes
ASHMAN	n pl. -MEN one who collects and removes ashes
ASHORE	adv toward or on the shore
ASHPLANT	n pl. -S a walking stick
ASHRAM	n pl. -S a secluded dwelling of a Hindu sage
ASHTRAY	n pl. -TRAYS a receptacle for tobacco ashes
ASHY	adj ASHIER, ASHIEST covered with ashes
ASIDE	n pl. -S a comment by an actor intended to be heard by the audience but not the other actors
ASININE	adj obstinately stupid or silly
ASK	v -ED, -ING, -S to put a question to
ASKANCE	adv with a side glance
ASKANT	adv askance
ASKER	n pl. -S one that asks
ASKESIS	n pl. ASKESES ascesis
ASKEW	adv to one side
ASKING	n pl. -S the act of one who asks
ASKOS	n pl. ASKOI an oil jar used in ancient Greece
ASLANT	adj slanting
ASLEEP	adj sleeping
ASLOPE	adj sloping
ASOCIAL	adj avoiding the company of others
ASP	n pl. -S a venomous snake
ASPARKLE	adj sparkling

ASPECT	n pl. -S appearance of something to the eye or mind
ASPEN	n pl. -S any of several poplars
ASPER	n pl. -S a Turkish money of account
ASPERATE	v -ATED, -ATING, -ATES to make uneven
ASPERGES	n pl. ASPERGES a Roman Catholic rite
ASPERITY	n pl. -TIES acrimony
ASPERSE	v -PERSED, -PERSING, -PERSES to spread false charges against
ASPERSER	n pl. -S one that asperses
ASPERSOR	n pl. -S asperser
ASPHALT	v -ED, -ING, -S to coat with asphalt (a substance used for paving and roofing)
ASPHERIC	adj varying slightly from an exactly spherical shape
ASPHODEL	n pl. -S a flowering plant
ASPHYXIA	n pl. -S unconsciousness caused by lack of oxygen
ASPHYXY	n pl. -PHYXIES asphyxia
ASPIC	n pl. -S the asp
ASPIRANT	n pl. -S one that aspires
ASPIRATA	n pl. -TAE a type of plosive
ASPIRATE	v -RATED, -RATING, -RATES to pronounce with an initial release of breath
ASPIRE	v -PIRED, -PIRING, -PIRES to have an earnest desire or ambition
ASPIRER	n pl. -S an aspirant
ASPIRIN	n pl. -S a pain reliever
ASPIRING	present participle of aspire
ASPIS	n pl. -PISES aspic
ASPISH	adj resembling an asp
ASQUINT	adv with a sidelong glance
ASRAMA	n pl. -S ashram
ASS	n pl. -ES a hoofed mammal
ASSAGAI	v -GAIED, -GAIING, -GAIS to pierce with a light spear
ASSAI	n pl. -S a tropical tree
ASSAIL	v -ED, -ING, -S to attack
ASSAILER	n pl. -S one that assails
ASSASSIN	n pl. -S a murderer
ASSAULT	v -ED, -ING, -S to attack
ASSAY	v -ED, -ING, -S to attempt

ASSAYER	*n* pl. -S one that assays
ASSEGAI	*v* -GAIED, -GAIING, -GAIS to assagai
ASSEMBLE	*v* -BLED, -BLING, -BLES to come or bring together
ASSEMBLY	*n* pl. -BLIES the act of assembling
ASSENT	*v* -ED, -ING, -S to express agreement
ASSENTER	*n* pl. -S one that assents
ASSENTOR	*n* pl. -S assenter
ASSERT	*v* -ED, -ING, -S to state positively
ASSERTER	*n* pl. -S one that asserts
ASSERTOR	*n* pl. -S asserter
ASSESS	*v* -ED, -ING, -ES to estimate the value of for taxation
ASSESSOR	*n* pl. -S one that assesses
ASSET	*n* pl. -S a useful quality or thing
ASSIGN	*v* -ED, -ING, -S to set apart for a particular purpose
ASSIGNAT	*n* pl. -S one of the notes issued as currency by the French revolutionary government
ASSIGNEE	*n* pl. -S one to whom property or right is legally transferred
ASSIGNER	*n* pl. -S one that assigns
ASSIGNOR	*n* pl. -S one who legally transfers property or right
ASSIST	*v* -ED, -ING, -S to give aid or support to
ASSISTER	*n* pl. -S one that assists
ASSISTOR	*n* pl. -S assister
ASSIZE	*n* pl. -S a session of a legislative or judicial body
ASSLIKE	*adj* resembling an ass
ASSOIL	*v* -ED, -ING, -S to pardon
ASSONANT	*n* pl. -S a word or syllable that resembles another in sound
ASSORT	*v* -ED, -ING, -S to distribute into groups according to kind or class
ASSORTER	*n* pl. -S one that assorts
ASSUAGE	*v* -SUAGED, -SUAGING, -SUAGES to make less severe
ASSUME	*v* -SUMED, -SUMING, -SUMES to take on
ASSUMER	*n* pl. -S one that assumes
ASSURE	*v* -SURED, -SURING, -SURES to insure
ASSURED	*n* pl. -S an insured person
ASSURER	*n* pl. -S one that assures
ASSURING	present participle of assure
ASSUROR	*n* pl. -S assurer
ASSWAGE	*v* -SWAGED, -SWAGING, -SWAGES to assuage
ASTASIA	*n* pl. -S inability to stand resulting from muscular incoordination
ASTATIC	*adj* unstable
ASTATINE	*n* pl. -S a radioactive element
ASTER	*n* pl. -S a flowering plant
ASTERIA	*n* pl. -S a gemstone cut to exhibit asterism
ASTERISK	*v* -ED, -ING, -S to mark with an asterisk (a star-shaped printing mark)
ASTERISM	*n* pl. -S a property of certain minerals of showing a starlike luminous figure
ASTERN	*adv* at or toward the rear of a ship
ASTERNAL	*adj* not connected to the sternum
ASTEROID	*n* pl. -S a type of celestial body
ASTHENIA	*n* pl. -S lack of strength
ASTHENIC	*n* pl. -S a slender, lightly muscled person
ASTHENY	*n* pl. -NIES asthenia
ASTHMA	*n* pl. -S a respiratory disease
ASTIGMIA	*n* pl. -S a visual defect
ASTILBE	*n* pl. -S an Asian perennial
ASTIR	*adj* moving about
ASTOMOUS	*adj* having no stomata
ASTONISH	*v* -ED, -ING, -ES to fill with sudden wonder or surprise
ASTONY	*v* -TONIED, -TONYING, -TONIES to astonish
ASTOUND	*v* -ED, -ING, -S to amaze
ASTRAGAL	*n* pl. -S a convex molding
ASTRAL	*n* pl. -S a type of oil lamp
ASTRALLY	*adv* in a stellar manner
ASTRAY	*adv* off the right course
ASTRICT	*v* -ED, -ING, -S to restrict
ASTRIDE	*adv* with one leg on each side
ASTRINGE	*v* -TRINGED, -TRINGING, -TRINGES to bind or draw together
ASTUTE	*adj* shrewd **ASTUTELY** *adv*
ASTYLAR	*adj* having no columns
ASUNDER	*adv* into pieces
ASWARM	*adj* swarming

ASWIRL *adj* swirling

ASWOON *adj* swooning

ASYLUM *n* pl. -LUMS or -LA an institution for the care of the mentally ill

ASYNDETA *n/pl* omissions of certain conjunctions

AT *prep* in the position of

ATABAL *n* pl. -S a type of drum

ATACTIC *adj* showing no regularity of structure

ATAGHAN *n* pl. -S yataghan

ATALAYA *n* pl. -S a watchtower

ATAMAN *n* pl. -S a hetman

ATAMASCO *n* pl. -COS a flowering plant

ATAP *n* pl. -S the nipa palm tree

ATARAXIA *n* pl. -S peace of mind

ATARAXIC *n* pl. -S a tranquilizing drug

ATARAXY *n* pl. -RAXIES ataraxia

ATAVIC *adj* pertaining to a remote ancestor

ATAVISM *n* pl. -S the reappearance of a genetic characteristic after several generations of absence

ATAVIST *n* pl. -S an individual displaying atavism

ATAXIA *n* pl. -S loss of muscular coordination

ATAXIC *n* pl. -S one suffering from ataxia

ATAXY *n* pl. ATAXIES ataxia

ATE *n* pl. -S blind impulse or reckless ambition that drives one to ruin

ATECHNIC *adj* lacking technical knowledge

ATELIC *adj* pertaining to a type of verb form

ATELIER *n* pl. -S a workshop or studio

ATEMOYA *n* pl. -S a fruit of a hybrid tropical tree

ATHANASY *n* pl. -SIES immortality

ATHEISM *n* pl. -S the belief that there is no God

ATHEIST *n* pl. -S a believer in atheism

ATHELING *n* pl. -S an Anglo-Saxon prince or nobleman

ATHENEUM *n* pl. -S a literary institution

ATHEROMA *n* pl. -MAS or -MATA a disease of the arteries

ATHETOID *adj* affected with a type of nervous disorder

ATHIRST *adj* having a strong desire

ATHLETE *n* pl. -S one skilled in feats of physical strength and agility **ATHLETIC** *adj*

ATHODYD *n* pl. -S a type of jet engine

ATHWART *adv* from side to side

ATILT *adj* being in a tilted position

ATINGLE *adj* tingling

ATLAS *n* pl. ATLANTES or ATLASES a male figure used as a supporting column

ATLATL *n* pl. -S a device for throwing a spear or dart

ATMA *n* pl. -S atman

ATMAN *n* pl. -S the individual soul in Hinduism

ATOLL *n* pl. -S a coral island

ATOM *n* pl. -S the smallest unit of an element **ATOMIC, ATOMICAL** *adj*

ATOMICS *n/pl* the science dealing with atoms

ATOMIES pl. of atomy

ATOMISE *v* -ISED, -ISING, -ISES to atomize

ATOMISER *n* pl. -S atomizer

ATOMISM *n* pl. -S the theory that the universe is composed of simple, indivisible, minute particles

ATOMIST *n* pl. -S an adherent of atomism

ATOMIZE *v* -IZED, -IZING, -IZES to reduce to a fine spray

ATOMIZER *n* pl. -S a device for atomizing liquids

ATOMY *n* pl. -MIES a tiny particle

ATONAL *adj* lacking tonality **ATONALLY** *adv*

ATONE *v* ATONED, ATONING, ATONES to make amends or reparation **ATONABLE** *adj*

ATONER *n* pl. -S one that atones

ATONIC *n* pl. -S an unaccented syllable or word

ATONING present participle of atone

ATONY *n* pl. -NIES muscular weakness

ATOP *adj* being on or at the top

ATOPY *n* pl. -PIES a type of allergy **ATOPIC** *adj*

ATRAZINE *n* pl. -S an herbicide

ATREMBLE *adj* trembling

ATRESIA *n* pl. -S absence or closure of a natural bodily passage

ATRIA	a pl. of atrium	**ATTIRE**	v -TIRED, -TIRING, -TIRES to clothe
ATRIAL	adj pertaining to an atrium	**ATTITUDE**	n pl. -S a state of mind with regard to some matter
ATRIP	adj aweigh		
ATRIUM	n pl. ATRIA or ATRIUMS the main room of an ancient Roman house	**ATTORN**	v -ED, -ING, -S to acknowledge a new owner as one's landlord
ATROCITY	n pl. -TIES a heinous act	**ATTORNEY**	n pl. -NEYS a lawyer
ATROPHIA	n pl. -S a wasting away of the body or any of its parts **ATROPHIC** adj	**ATTRACT**	v -ED, -ING, -S to cause to approach or adhere
		ATTRITE	adj attrited
ATROPHY	v -PHIED, -PHYING, -PHIES to waste away	**ATTRITED**	adj worn down by rubbing
		ATTUNE	v -TUNED, -TUNING, -TUNES to bring into harmony
ATROPIN	n pl. -S atropine		
ATROPINE	n pl. -S a poisonous alkaloid	**ATWAIN**	adv in two
ATROPISM	n pl. -S atropine poisoning	**ATWEEN**	prep between
ATT	n pl. ATT a monetary unit of Laos	**ATWITTER**	adj twittering
ATTABOY	interj —used to express encouragement or approval	**ATYPIC**	adj atypical
		ATYPICAL	adj not typical
ATTACH	v -ED, -ING, -ES to connect as an associated part	**AUBADE**	n pl. -S a morning song
		AUBERGE	n pl. -S an inn
ATTACHE	n pl. -S a diplomatic official	**AUBRETIA**	n pl. -S aubrieta
ATTACHER	n pl. -S one that attaches	**AUBRIETA**	n pl. -S a flowering plant
ATTACK	v -ED, -ING, -S to set upon violently	**AUBURN**	n pl. -S a reddish brown color
ATTACKER	n pl. -S one that attacks	**AUCTION**	v -ED, -ING, -S to sell publicly to the highest bidder
ATTAIN	v -ED, -ING, -S to gain or achieve by mental or physical effort	**AUCUBA**	n pl. -S a shrub of the dogwood family
ATTAINER	n pl. -S one that attains	**AUDACITY**	n pl. -TIES boldness
ATTAINT	v -ED, -ING, -S to disgrace	**AUDAD**	n pl. -S aoudad
ATTAR	n pl. -S a fragrant oil	**AUDIAL**	adj aural
ATTEMPER	v -ED, -ING, -S to modify the temperature of	**AUDIBLE**	n pl. -S a type of play in football
		AUDIBLY	adv in a way so as to be heard
ATTEMPT	v -ED, -ING, -S to make an effort to do or accomplish	**AUDIENCE**	n pl. -S a group of listeners or spectators
ATTEND	v -ED, -ING, -S to be present at	**AUDIENT**	n pl. -S one that hears
ATTENDEE	n pl. -S an attender	**AUDILE**	n pl. -S one whose mental imagery is chiefly auditory
ATTENDER	n pl. -S one that attends		
ATTENT	adj heedful	**AUDING**	n pl. -S the process of hearing, recognizing, and interpreting a spoken language
ATTEST	v -ED, -ING, -S to affirm to be true or genuine		
		AUDIO	n pl. -DIOS sound reception or transmission
ATTESTER	n pl. -S one that attests		
ATTESTOR	n pl. -S attester	**AUDIT**	v -ED, -ING, -S to examine with intent to verify
ATTIC	n pl. -S a story or room directly below the roof of a house	**AUDITION**	v -ED, -ING, -S to give a trial performance
ATTICISM	n pl. -S a concise and elegant expression	**AUDITIVE**	n pl. -S an auditory
		AUDITOR	n pl. -S one that audits
ATTICIST	n pl. -S one who uses atticisms	**AUDITORY**	n pl. -RIES a group of listeners

AUGEND	*n* pl. -S a number to which another is to be added
AUGER	*n* pl. -S a tool for boring
AUGHT	*n* pl. -S a zero
AUGITE	*n* pl. -S a mineral **AUGITIC** *adj*
AUGMENT	*v* -ED, -ING, -S to increase
AUGUR	*v* -ED, -ING, -S to foretell from omens
AUGURAL	*adj* pertaining to augury
AUGURER	*n* pl. -S one that augurs
AUGURY	*n* pl. -RIES the practice of auguring
AUGUST	*adj* -GUSTER, -GUSTEST inspiring reverence or admiration **AUGUSTLY** *adv*
AUK	*n* pl. -S a diving seabird
AUKLET	*n* pl. -S a small auk
AULD	*adj* AULDER, AULDEST old
AULIC	*adj* pertaining to a royal court
AUNT	*n* pl. -S the sister of one's father or mother
AUNTHOOD	*n* pl. -S the state of being an aunt
AUNTIE	*n* pl. -S aunt
AUNTIES	pl. of aunty
AUNTLIKE	*adj* resembling an aunt
AUNTLY	*adj* -LIER, -LIEST of or suggesting an aunt
AUNTY	*n* pl. AUNTIES aunt
AURA	*n* pl. -RAS or -RAE an invisible emanation
AURAL	*adj* pertaining to the sense of hearing **AURALLY** *adv*
AURAR	pl. of eyrir
AURATE	*adj* having ears
AURATED	*adj* aurate
AUREATE	*adj* golden
AUREI	pl. of aureus
AUREOLA	*n* pl. -LAS or -LAE a halo
AUREOLE	*v* -OLED, -OLING, -OLES to surround with a halo
AURES	pl. of auris
AUREUS	*n* pl. -REI a gold coin of ancient Rome
AURIC	*adj* pertaining to gold
AURICLE	*n* pl. -S an ear or ear-shaped part **AURICLED** *adj*
AURICULA	*n* pl. -LAS or -LAE an auricle
AURIFORM	*adj* ear-shaped

AURIS	*n* pl. AURES the ear
AURIST	*n* pl. -S a specialist in diseases of the ear
AUROCHS	*n* pl. -ES an extinct European ox
AURORA	*n* pl. -RAS or -RAE the rising light of the morning **AURORAL, AUROREAN** *adj*
AUROUS	*adj* pertaining to gold
AURUM	*n* pl. -S gold
AUSFORM	*v* -ED, -ING, -S to subject steel to a strengthening process
AUSPEX	*n* pl. -PICES a soothsayer of ancient Rome
AUSPICE	*n* pl. -S a favorable omen
AUSTERE	*adj* -TERER, -TEREST grave in disposition or appearance
AUSTRAL	*n* pl. -ES or -S a former monetary unit of Argentina
AUSUBO	*n* pl. -BOS a tropical tree
AUTACOID	*n* pl. -S a hormone
AUTARCHY	*n* pl. -CHIES absolute rule
AUTARKY	*n* pl. -KIES national economic self-sufficiency **AUTARKIC** *adj*
AUTECISM	*n* pl. -S the development of the entire life cycle of a parasitic fungus on a single host
AUTEUR	*n* pl. -S the creator of a film
AUTHOR	*v* -ED, -ING, -S to write
AUTISM	*n* pl. -S extreme withdrawal into fantasy
AUTISTIC	*n* pl. -S one who is affected with autism
AUTO	*v* -ED, -ING, -S to ride in an automobile
AUTOBAHN	*n* pl. -BAHNS or -BAHNEN a German superhighway
AUTOBUS	*n* pl. -BUSES or -BUSSES a bus
AUTOCADE	*n* pl. -S a parade of automobiles
AUTOCOID	*n* pl. -S autacoid
AUTOCRAT	*n* pl. -S an absolute ruler
AUTODYNE	*n* pl. -S a type of electrical circuit
AUTOGAMY	*n* pl. -MIES fertilization of a flower by its own pollen
AUTOGENY	*n* pl. -NIES the production of living organisms from inanimate matter
AUTOGIRO	*n* pl. -ROS a type of airplane
AUTOGYRO	*n* pl. -ROS autogiro
AUTOLYSE	*v* -LYSED, -LYSING, -LYSES to autolyze

AUTOLYZE   *v* -LYZED, -LYZING, -LYZES to break down tissue by the action of self-contained enzymes

AUTOMAN   *n* pl. -MEN an automobile maker

AUTOMATA   *n/pl* robots

AUTOMATE   *v* -MATED, -MATING, -MATES to convert to a system of automatic control

AUTOMEN   *n* pl. of automan

AUTONOMY   *n* pl. -MIES the state of being self-governing

AUTOPSIC   *adj* pertaining to an autopsy

AUTOPSY   *v* -SIED, -SYING, -SIES to examine a dead body to determine the cause of death

AUTOSOME   *n* pl. -S a type of chromosome

AUTOTOMY   *n* pl. -MIES the shedding of a damaged body part

AUTOTYPE   *n* pl. -S a type of photographic process

AUTOTYPY   *n* pl. -TYPIES autotype

AUTUMN   *n* pl. -S a season of the year **AUTUMNAL** *adj*

AUTUNITE   *n* pl. -S a mineral

AUXESIS   *n* pl. AUXESES an increase in cell size without cell division

AUXETIC   *n* pl. -S a substance that promotes auxesis

AUXIN   *n* pl. -S a substance used to regulate plant growth **AUXINIC** *adj*

AVA   *adv* at all

AVADAVAT   *n* pl. -S a small songbird

AVAIL   *v* -ED, -ING, -S to be of use or advantage to

AVANT   *adj* culturally or stylistically new

AVARICE   *n* pl. -S greed

AVAST   *interj* — used as a command to stop

AVATAR   *n* pl. -S the incarnation of a Hindu deity

AVAUNT   *interj* — used as an order of dismissal

AVE   *n* pl. -S an expression of greeting or farewell

AVELLAN   *adj* having the four arms shaped like filberts — used of a heraldic cross

AVELLANE   *adj* avellan

AVENGE   *v* AVENGED, AVENGING, AVENGES to exact retribution for

AVENGER   *n* pl. -S one that avenges

AVENS   *n* pl. -ES a perennial herb

AVENTAIL   *n* pl. -S ventail

AVENUE   *n* pl. -S a wide street

AVER   *v* AVERRED, AVERRING, AVERS to declare positively

AVERAGE   *v* -AGED, -AGING, -AGES to calculate the arithmetic mean of

AVERMENT   *n* pl. -S the act of averring

AVERRED   past tense of aver

AVERRING   present participle of aver

AVERSE   *adj* opposed; reluctant **AVERSELY** *adv*

AVERSION   *n* pl. -S a feeling of repugnance **AVERSIVE** *adj*

AVERT   *v* -ED, -ING, -S to turn away

AVGAS   *n* pl. -GASES or -GASSES gasoline for airplanes

AVIAN   *n* pl. -S a bird

AVIANIZE   *v* -IZED, -IZING, -IZES to make less severe by repeated culture in a chick embryo, as a virus

AVIARIST   *n* pl. -S the keeper of an aviary

AVIARY   *n* pl. -ARIES a large enclosure for live birds

AVIATE   *v* -ATED, -ATING, -ATES to fly an aircraft

AVIATION   *n* pl. -S the act of aviating

AVIATOR   *n* pl. -S one that aviates

AVIATRIX   *n* pl. -TRICES or -TRIXES a female aviator

AVICULAR   *adj* pertaining to birds

AVID   *adj* eager

AVIDIN   *n* pl. -S a protein found in egg white

AVIDITY   *n* pl. -TIES the state of being avid

AVIDLY   *adv* in an avid manner

AVIDNESS   *n* pl. -ES avidity

AVIFAUNA   *n* pl. -NAS or -NAE the bird life of a particular region

AVIGATOR   *n* pl. -S one that navigates aircraft

AVION   *n* pl. -S an airplane

AVIONICS   *n/pl* the science of electronics applied to aviation **AVIONIC** *adj*

AVISO   *n* pl. -SOS advice

AVO   *n* pl. AVOS a monetary unit of Macao

AVOCADO   *n* pl. -DOS or -DOES the edible fruit of a tropical tree

AVOCET   *n* pl. -S a shore bird

AVODIRE   *n* pl. -S an African tree

AVOID   *v* -ED, -ING, -S to keep away from

AVOIDER   *n* pl. -S one that avoids

AVOSET   *n* pl. -S avocet

AVOUCH   *v* -ED, -ING, -ES to affirm

AVOUCHER   *n* pl. -S one that avouches

AVOW   *v* -ED, -ING, -S to declare openly **AVOWABLE** *adj* **AVOWABLY, AVOWEDLY** *adv*

AVOWAL   *n* pl. -S an open declaration

AVOWER   *n* pl. -S one that avows

AVULSE   *v* AVULSED, AVULSING, AVULSES to tear off forcibly

AVULSION   *n* pl. -S the act of avulsing

AW   *interj* — used to express protest, disgust, or disbelief

AWA   *adv* away

AWAIT   *v* -ED, -ING, -S to wait for

AWAITER   *n* pl. -S one that awaits

AWAKE   *v* AWAKED or AWOKE, AWOKEN, AWAKING, AWAKES to wake up

AWAKEN   *v* -ED, -ING, -S to awake

AWAKENER   *n* pl. -S one that awakens

AWAKING   present participle of awake

AWARD   *v* -ED, -ING, -S to grant as due or merited

AWARDEE   *n* pl. -S one that is awarded something

AWARDER   *n* pl. -S one that awards

AWARE   *adj* having perception or knowledge

AWASH   *adj* covered with water

AWAY   *adv* from a certain place

AWAYNESS   *n* pl. -ES the state of being distant

AWE   *v* AWED, AWING or AWEING, AWES to inspire with awe (reverential fear)

AWEARY   *adj* weary

AWEATHER   *adv* toward the windward side of a vessel

AWED   past tense of awe

AWEE   *adv* awhile

AWEIGH   *adj* hanging just clear of the bottom — used of an anchor

AWELESS   *adj* lacking awe

AWESOME   *adj* inspiring awe

AWFUL   *adj* -FULLER, -FULLEST extremely bad or unpleasant **AWFULLY** *adv*

AWHILE   *adv* for a short time

AWHIRL   *adj* whirling

AWING   a present participle of awe

AWKWARD   *adj* -WARDER, -WARDEST lacking skill, dexterity, or grace

AWL   *n* pl. -S a pointed tool for making small holes

AWLESS   *adj* aweless

AWLWORT   *n* pl. -S an aquatic plant

AWMOUS   *n* pl. AWMOUS alms

AWN   *n* pl. -S a bristlelike appendage of certain grasses **AWNED, AWNLESS, AWNY** *adj*

AWNING   *n* pl. -S a rooflike canvas cover **AWNINGED** *adj*

AWOKE   a past tense of awake

AWOKEN   a past participle of awake

AWOL   *n* pl. -S one who is absent without leave

AWRY   *adv* with a turn or twist to one side

AX   *v* -ED, -ING, -ES to work on with an ax (a type of cutting tool)

AXAL   *adj* axial

AXE   *v* AXED, AXING, AXES to ax

AXEL   *n* pl. -S a jump in figure skating

AXEMAN   *n* pl. -MEN axman

AXENIC   *adj* free from germs

AXES   pl. of axis

AXIAL   *adj* pertaining to or forming an axis **AXIALLY** *adv*

AXIALITY   *n* pl. -TIES the state of being axial

AXIL   *n* pl. -S the angle between the upper side of a leaf and its supporting stem

AXILE   *adj* axial

AXILLA   *n* pl. -LAE or -LAS the armpit

AXILLAR   *n* pl. -S a feather on the undersurface of a bird's wing

AXILLARY   *n* pl. -LARIES an axillar

AXING   present participle of axe

AXIOLOGY   *n* pl. -GIES the study of values and value judgments

AXIOM   *n* pl. -S a self-evident truth

AXION   *n* pl. -S a hypothetical subatomic particle

AXIS   *n* pl. AXES a straight line about which a body rotates **AXISED** *adj*

AXIS   *n* pl. AXISES an Asian deer

AXITE   *n* pl. -S a fiber of an axon

AXLE   *n* pl. -S a shaft upon which a wheel revolves **AXLED** *adj*

AXLETREE   *n* pl. -S a type of axle

AXLIKE   *adj* resembling an ax

AXMAN   *n* pl. -MEN one who wields an ax

AXOLOTL   *n* pl. -S a salamander of Mexico and western United States

AXON   *n* pl. -S the central process of a neuron **AXONAL** *adj*

AXONE   *n* pl. -S axon

AXONEMAL   *adj* pertaining to an axoneme

AXONEME   *n* pl. -S a part of a cilium

AXONIC   *adj* pertaining to an axon

AXOPLASM   *n* pl. -S the protoplasm of an axon

AXSEED   *n* pl. -S a European herb

AY   *n* pl. AYS aye

AYAH   *n* pl. -S a native maid or nurse in India

AYE   *n* pl. -S an affirmative vote

AYIN   *n* pl. -S a Hebrew letter

AYURVEDA   *n* pl. -S a Hindu system of medicine

AZALEA   *n* pl. -S a flowering shrub

AZAN   *n* pl. -S a Muslim call to prayer

AZIDE   *n* pl. -S a type of chemical compound **AZIDO** *adj*

AZIMUTH   *n* pl. -S an angle of horizontal deviation

AZINE   *n* pl. -S a type of chemical compound

AZLON   *n* pl. -S a textile fiber

AZO   *adj* containing nitrogen

AZOIC   *adj* pertaining to geologic time before the appearance of life

AZOLE   *n* pl. -S a type of chemical compound

AZON   *n* pl. -S a radio-controlled aerial bomb

AZONAL   *adj* pertaining to a type of a soil group

AZONIC   *adj* not restricted to any particular zone

AZOTE   *n* pl. -S nitrogen **AZOTED** *adj*

AZOTEMIA   *n* pl. -S an excess of nitrogenous substances in the blood **AZOTEMIC** *adj*

AZOTH   *n* pl. -S mercury

AZOTIC   *adj* pertaining to azote

AZOTISE   *v* -TISED, -TISING, -TISES to azotize

AZOTIZE   *v* -TIZED, -TIZING, -TIZES to treat with nitrogen

AZOTURIA   *n* pl. -S an excess of nitrogenous substances in the urine

AZURE   *n* pl. -S a blue color

AZURITE   *n* pl. -S a mineral

AZYGOS   *n* pl. -ES an azygous anatomical part

AZYGOUS   *adj* not being one of a pair

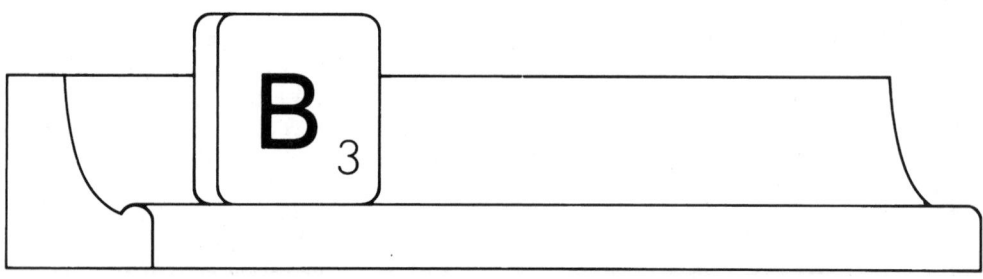

BA	*n* pl. -S the eternal soul, in Egyptian mythology	**BACCA**	*n* pl. -CAE a berry
BAA	*v* -ED, -ING, -S to bleat	**BACCARA**	*n* pl. -S baccarat
BAAL	*n* pl. -S or -IM a false god	**BACCARAT**	*n* pl. -S a card game
BAALISM	*n* pl. -S the worship of a baal	**BACCATE**	*adj* pulpy like a berry
BAAS	*n* pl. -ES master; boss	**BACCATED**	*adj* baccate
BAASKAAP	*n* pl. -S the policy of domination by white people in South Africa	**BACCHANT**	*n* pl. -S or -ES a carouser
		BACCHIC	*adj* riotous
BABA	*n* pl. -S a rum cake	**BACCHIUS**	*n* pl. -CHII a type of metrical foot
BABASSU	*n* pl. -S a palm tree	**BACH**	*v* -ED, -ING, -ES to live as a bachelor
BABBITT	*v* -ED, -ING, -S to line with babbitt (an alloy of tin, copper, and antimony)	**BACHELOR**	*n* pl. -S an unmarried man
		BACILLAR	*adj* rod-shaped
BABBLE	*v* -BLED, -BLING, -BLES to talk idly or excessively	**BACILLUS**	*n* pl. -LI any of a class of rod-shaped bacteria
BABBLER	*n* pl. -S one that babbles	**BACK**	*v* -ED, -ING, -S to support
BABBLING	*n* pl. -S idle talk	**BACKACHE**	*n* pl. -S a pain in the back
BABE	*n* pl. -S a baby	**BACKBEAT**	*n* pl. -S a type of rhythm in music
BABEL	*n* pl. -S confusion	**BACKBEND**	*n* pl. -S an acrobatic feat
BABESIA	*n* pl. -S a parasitic protozoan	**BACKBITE**	*v* -BIT, -BITTEN, -BITING, -BITES to slander
BABICHE	*n* pl. -S rawhide thongs		
BABIED	past tense of baby	**BACKBONE**	*n* pl. -S the spine
BABIES	present 3d person sing. of baby	**BACKCAST**	*n* pl. -S a backward movement in casting a fishing line
BABIRUSA	*n* pl. -S a wild pig		
BABKA	*n* pl. -S a coffee cake	**BACKCHAT**	*n* pl. -S repartee
BABOO	*n* pl. -BOOS a Hindu gentleman	**BACKDATE**	*v* -DATED, -DATING, -DATES to predate
BABOOL	*n* pl. -S babul		
BABOON	*n* pl. -S a large ape	**BACKDOOR**	*adj* secretive
BABU	*n* pl. -S baboo	**BACKDROP**	*v* -DROPPED or -DROPT, -DROPPING, -DROPS to provide with a scenic background
BABUL	*n* pl. -S a North African tree		
BABUSHKA	*n* pl. -S a woman's scarf	**BACKER**	*n* pl. -S a supporter
BABY	*v* -BIED, -BYING, -BIES to coddle	**BACKFILL**	*v* -ED, -ING, -S to refill
		BACKFIRE	*v* -FIRED, -FIRING, -FIRES to produce undesirable effects
BABYHOOD	*n* pl. -S the state of being a baby (an infant)		
		BACKFIT	*v* -FITTED, -FITTING, -FITS to retrofit
BABYISH	*adj* resembling a baby		
BACALAO	*n* pl. -LAOS codfish	**BACKFLOW**	*n* pl. -S a flowing back toward a source

BACKHAND   *v* -ED, -ING, -S to strike with the back of the hand

BACKHAUL   *v* -ED, -ING, -S to return after delivering a load

BACKHOE   *n* pl. -S an excavating machine

BACKING   *n* pl. -S support

BACKLAND   *n* pl. -S a region remote from cities

BACKLASH   *v* -ED, -ING, -ES to cause a reaction

BACKLESS   *adj* having no back

BACKLIST   *v* -ED, -ING, -S to include in a publisher's list of older book titles

BACKLIT   *adj* illuminated from behind

BACKLOG   *v* -LOGGED, -LOGGING, -LOGS to accumulate

BACKMOST   *adj* hindmost

BACKOUT   *n* pl. -S a reversal of launching procedures

BACKPACK   *v* -ED, -ING, -S to hike with a pack on one's back

BACKREST   *n* pl. -S a back support

BACKROOM   *adj* made or operating inconspicuously

BACKRUSH   *n* pl. -ES the seaward return of water from a wave

BACKSAW   *n* pl. -S a type of saw

BACKSEAT   *n* pl. -S a rear seat

BACKSET   *n* pl. -S a setback

BACKSIDE   *n* pl. -S the hind part

BACKSLAP   *v* -SLAPPED, -SLAPPING, -SLAPS to show much approval

BACKSLID   past tense of backslide (to revert to sin)

BACKSPIN   *n* pl. -S a backward rotation

BACKSTAY   *n* pl. -STAYS a support for a mast

BACKSTOP   *v* -STOPPED, -STOPPING, -STOPS to bolster

BACKUP   *n* pl. -S a substitute

BACKWARD   *adv* toward the back

BACKWASH   *v* -ED, -ING, -ES to spray water backward

BACKWOOD   *adj* uncouth

BACKWRAP   *n* pl. -S a wraparound garment that fastens in the back

BACKYARD   *n* pl. -S an area at the rear of a house

BACON   *n* pl. -S a side of a pig cured and smoked

BACTERIA   *n* pl. -S a group of microscopic organisms

BACTERIN   *n* pl. -S a vaccine prepared from dead bacteria

BACULINE   *adj* pertaining to a rod

BACULUM   *n* pl. -LA or -LUMS a bone in the penis of many mammals

BAD   *adj* BADDER, BADDEST very good

BAD   *adj* WORSE, WORST not good

BAD   *n* pl. -S something that is bad

BADDIE   *n* pl. -S a bad person

BADDY   *n* pl. -DIES baddie

BADE   past tense of bid

BADGE   *v* BADGED, BADGING, BADGES to supply with an insignia

BADGER   *v* -ED, -ING, -S to harass

BADGERLY   *adj* bothersome

BADGING   present participle of badge

BADINAGE   *v* -NAGED, -NAGING, -NAGES to banter

BADLAND   *n* pl. -S a barren, hilly area

BADLY   *adv* in a bad manner

BADMAN   *n* pl. -MEN an outlaw

BADMOUTH   *v* -ED, -ING, -S to criticize

BADNESS   *n* pl. -ES the state of being bad

BAFF   *v* -ED, -ING, -S to strike under a golf ball

BAFFIES   pl. of baffy

BAFFLE   *v* -FLED, -FLING, -FLES to confuse

BAFFLER   *n* pl. -S one that baffles

BAFFY   *n* pl. -FIES a wooden golf club

BAG   *v* BAGGED, BAGGING, BAGS to put into a bag (a flexible container)

BAGASS   *n* pl. -ES bagasse

BAGASSE   *n* pl. -S crushed sugarcane

BAGEL   *n* pl. -S a ring-shaped roll

BAGFUL   *n* pl. BAGFULS or BAGSFUL as much as a bag can hold

BAGGAGE   *n* pl. -S luggage

BAGGED   past tense of bag

BAGGER   *n* pl. -S one that bags

BAGGIE   *n* pl. -S the stomach

BAGGING   *n* pl. -S material for making bags

BAGGY   *adj* -GIER, -GIEST loose-fitting **BAGGILY** *adv*

BAGHOUSE	*n pl.* -S a facility for removing particulates from exhaust gases
BAGMAN	*n pl.* -MEN a traveling salesman
BAGNIO	*n pl.* -NIOS a brothel
BAGPIPE	*n pl.* -S a wind instrument
BAGPIPER	*n pl.* -S one that plays bagpipes
BAGSFUL	a *pl.* of bagful
BAGUET	*n pl.* -S baguette
BAGUETTE	*n pl.* -S a rectangular gem
BAGWIG	*n pl.* -S a type of wig
BAGWORM	*n pl.* -S the larva of certain moths
BAH	*interj* — an exclamation of disgust
BAHADUR	*n pl.* -S a Hindu title of respect
BAHT	*n pl.* -S a monetary unit of Thailand
BAIDARKA	*n pl.* -S bidarka
BAIL	*v* -ED, -ING, -S to transfer property temporarily **BAILABLE** *adj*
BAILEE	*n pl.* -S a person to whom property is bailed
BAILER	*n pl.* -S bailor
BAILEY	*n pl.* -LEYS an outer castle wall
BAILIE	*n pl.* -S a Scottish magistrate
BAILIFF	*n pl.* -S a court officer
BAILMENT	*n pl.* -S the act of bailing
BAILOR	*n pl.* -S a person who bails property to another
BAILOUT	*n pl.* -S the act of parachuting from an aircraft
BAILSMAN	*n pl.* -MEN one who provides security for another
BAIRN	*n pl.* -S a child **BAIRNISH** *adj*
BAIRNLY	*adj* -LIER, -LIEST childish
BAIT	*v* -ED, -ING, -S to lure
BAITER	*n pl.* -S one that baits
BAITH	*adj* both
BAIZA	*n pl.* -S a monetary unit of Oman
BAIZE	*n pl.* -S a green, woolen fabric
BAKE	*v* BAKED, BAKING, BAKES to prepare food in an oven
BAKEMEAT	*n pl.* -S a pastry
BAKER	*n pl.* -S one that bakes
BAKERY	*n pl.* -ERIES a place where baked goods are sold
BAKESHOP	*n pl.* -S a bakery
BAKING	*n pl.* -S a quantity baked

BAKLAVA	*n pl.* -S a Turkish pastry
BAKLAWA	*n pl.* -S baklava
BAKSHISH	*v* -ED, -ING, -ES to give a tip
BAL	*n pl.* -S a balmoral
BALANCE	*v* -ANCED, -ANCING, -ANCES to weigh
BALANCER	*n pl.* -S one that balances
BALAS	*n pl.* -ES a red variety of spinel
BALATA	*n pl.* -S a tropical tree
BALBOA	*n pl.* -S a monetary unit of Panama
BALCONY	*n pl.* -NIES an elevated platform
BALD	*adj* BALDER, BALDEST lacking hair
BALD	*v* -ED, -ING, -S to become bald
BALDHEAD	*n pl.* -S a bald person
BALDIES	*pl.* of baldy
BALDISH	*adj* somewhat bald
BALDLY	*adv* in a plain and blunt manner
BALDNESS	*n pl.* -ES the state of being bald
BALDPATE	*n pl.* -S a baldhead
BALDRIC	*n pl.* -S a shoulder belt
BALDRICK	*n pl.* -S baldric
BALDY	*n pl.* BALDIES a bald person
BALE	*v* BALED, BALING, BALES to form into tightly compressed bundles
BALEEN	*n pl.* -S whalebone
BALEFIRE	*n pl.* -S a bonfire
BALEFUL	*adj* menacing
BALER	*n pl.* -S one that bales
BALING	present participle of bale
BALISAUR	*n pl.* -S a long-tailed badger
BALK	*v* -ED, -ING, -S to stop short and refuse to proceed
BALKER	*n pl.* -S one that balks
BALKLINE	*n pl.* -S the starting line in track events
BALKY	*adj* BALKIER, BALKIEST stubborn **BALKILY** *adv*
BALL	*v* -ED, -ING, -S to form into a ball (a spherical object)
BALLAD	*n pl.* -S a narrative poem or song **BALLADIC** *adj*
BALLADE	*n pl.* -S a type of poem
BALLADRY	*n pl.* -RIES ballad poetry
BALLAST	*v* -ED, -ING, -S to stabilize
BALLER	*n pl.* -S one that balls

BALLET *n* pl. -S a classical dance form **BALLETIC** *adj*

BALLGAME *n* pl. -S a game played with a ball

BALLHAWK *n* pl. -S a very good defensive ballplayer

BALLIES pl. of bally

BALLISTA *n* pl. -TAE an ancient weapon

BALLON *n* pl. -S lightness of movement

BALLONET *n* pl. -S a small balloon

BALLONNE *n* pl. -S a ballet jump

BALLOON *v* -ED, -ING, -S to swell out

BALLOT *v* -ED, -ING, -S to vote

BALLOTER *n* pl. -S one that ballots

BALLPARK *n* pl. -S a facility in which ballgames are played

BALLROOM *n* pl. -S a large room for dancing

BALLUTE *n* pl. -S a small inflatable parachute

BALLY *n* pl. -LIES a noisy uproar

BALLYHOO *v* -ED, -ING, -S to promote by uproar

BALLYRAG *v* -RAGGED, -RAGGING, -RAGS to bullyrag

BALM *n* pl. -S a fragrant resin **BALMLIKE** *adj*

BALMORAL *n* pl. -S a type of shoe

BALMY *adj* BALMIER, BALMIEST mild **BALMILY** *adv*

BALNEAL *adj* pertaining to baths

BALONEY *n* pl. -NEYS bologna

BALSA *n* pl. -S a tropical tree

BALSAM *v* -ED, -ING, -S to anoint with balsam (an aromatic, resinous substance)

BALSAMIC *adj* containing balsam

BALUSTER *n* pl. -S a railing support

BAM *v* BAMMED, BAMMING, BAMS to strike with a dull resounding noise

BAMBINO *n* pl. -NOS or -NI a baby

BAMBOO *n* pl. -BOOS a tropical grass

BAN *v* BANNED, BANNING, BANS to prohibit

BAN *n* pl. BANI a monetary unit of Romania

BANAL *adj* ordinary **BANALLY** *adv*

BANALITY *n* pl. -TIES something banal

BANALIZE *v* -IZED, -IZING, -IZES to make banal

BANANA *n* pl. -S an edible fruit

BANAUSIC *adj* practical

BANCO *n* pl. -COS a bet in certain gambling games

BAND *v* -ED, -ING, -S to decorate with flexible strips of material

BANDAGE *v* -DAGED, -DAGING, -DAGES to cover a wound with a strip of cloth

BANDAGER *n* pl. -S one that bandages

BANDANA *n* pl. -S bandanna

BANDANNA *n* pl. -S a large, colored handkerchief

BANDBOX *n* pl. -ES a lightweight box

BANDEAU *n* pl. -DEAUX or -DEAUS a headband

BANDER *n* pl. -S one that bands

BANDEROL *n* pl. -S a streamer

BANDIED past tense of bandy

BANDIES present 3d person sing. of bandy

BANDIT *n* pl. -DITS or -DITTI a robber

BANDITRY *n* pl. -TRIES robbery by bandits

BANDOG *n* pl. -S a watchdog

BANDORA *n* pl. -S bandore

BANDORE *n* pl. -S an ancient lute

BANDSMAN *n* pl. -MEN a member of a musical band

BANDY *v* -DIED, -DYING, -DIES to throw to and fro

BANE *v* BANED, BANING, BANES to kill with poison

BANEFUL *adj* poisonous

BANG *v* -ED, -ING, -S to hit sharply

BANGER *n* pl. -S a sausage

BANGKOK *n* pl. -S a straw hat

BANGLE *n* pl. -S a bracelet

BANGTAIL *n* pl. -S a racehorse

BANI pl. of ban

BANIAN *n* pl. -S a Hindu merchant

BANING present participle of bane

BANISH *v* -ED, -ING, -ES to expel

BANISHER *n* pl. -S one that banishes

BANISTER *n* pl. -S a handrail

BANJAX *v* -ED, -ING, -ES to damage or ruin

BANJO *n* pl. -JOS or -JOES a musical instrument

BANJOIST *n* pl. -S one who plays the banjo

BANK	*v* -ED, -ING, -S to keep money in a bank (an institution dealing in money matters) **BANKABLE** *adj*
BANKBOOK	*n* pl. -S a depositor's book
BANKCARD	*n* pl. -S a credit card issued by a bank
BANKER	*n* pl. -S one who works in a bank **BANKERLY** *adj*
BANKING	*n* pl. -S the business of a bank
BANKNOTE	*n* pl. -S a promissory note
BANKROLL	*v* -ED, -ING, -S to fund
BANKRUPT	*v* -ED, -ING, -S to impoverish
BANKSIA	*n* pl. -S an Australian plant
BANKSIDE	*n* pl. -S the slope of a river bank
BANNED	past tense of ban
BANNER	*v* -ED, -ING, -S to furnish with a flag
BANNERET	*n* pl. -S a small flag
BANNEROL	*n* pl. -S a banderol
BANNET	*n* pl. -S a bonnet
BANNING	present participle of ban
BANNOCK	*n* pl. -S a type of cake
BANNS	*n/pl* a marriage notice
BANQUET	*v* -ED, -ING, -S to feast
BANSHEE	*n* pl. -S a female spirit
BANSHIE	*n* pl. -S banshee
BANTAM	*n* pl. -S a small fowl
BANTENG	*n* pl. -S a wild ox
BANTER	*v* -ED, -ING, -S to exchange mildly teasing remarks
BANTERER	*n* pl. -S one that banters
BANTLING	*n* pl. -S a very young child
BANTY	*n* pl. -TIES a bantam
BANYAN	*n* pl. -S an East Indian tree
BANZAI	*n* pl. -S a Japanese battle cry
BAOBAB	*n* pl. -S a tropical tree
BAP	*n* pl. -S a small bun or roll
BAPTISE	*v* -TISED, -TISING, -TISES to baptize
BAPTISIA	*n* pl. -S a flowering plant
BAPTISM	*n* pl. -S a Christian ceremony
BAPTIST	*n* pl. -S one who baptizes
BAPTIZE	*v* -TIZED, -TIZING, -TIZES to administer baptism to
BAPTIZER	*n* pl. -S a baptist
BAR	*v* BARRED, BARRING, BARS to exclude
BARATHEA	*n* pl. -S a silk fabric
BARB	*v* -ED, -ING, -S to furnish with a barb (a sharp projection)
BARBAL	*adj* pertaining to the beard
BARBARIC	*adj* uncivilized
BARBASCO	*n* pl. -COS or -COES a tropical tree
BARBATE	*adj* bearded
BARBE	*n* pl. -S a medieval cloth headdress
BARBECUE	*v* -CUED, -CUING, -CUES to cook over live coals or an open fire
BARBEL	*n* pl. -S an organ of a fish
BARBELL	*n* pl. -S an exercise apparatus
BARBEQUE	*v* -QUED, -QUING, -QUES barbecue
BARBER	*v* -ED, -ING, -S to cut hair
BARBERRY	*n* pl. -RIES a shrub
BARBET	*n* pl. -S a tropical bird
BARBETTE	*n* pl. -S a platform
BARBICAN	*n* pl. -S an outer fortification
BARBICEL	*n* pl. -S a part of a feather
BARBITAL	*n* pl. -S a sedative
BARBLESS	*adj* having no barbs
BARBULE	*n* pl. -S a small barb
BARBUT	*n* pl. -S a type of helmet
BARBWIRE	*n* pl. -S barbed wire
BARCHAN	*n* pl. -S a type of sand dune
BARD	*v* -ED, -ING, -S to armor a horse
BARDE	*v* BARDED, BARDING, BARDES to bard
BARDIC	*adj* poetic
BARE	*adj* BARER, BAREST naked
BARE	*v* BARED, BARING, BARES to expose
BAREBACK	*adv* without a saddle
BAREBOAT	*n* pl. -S a pleasure boat rented without personnel
BAREFIT	*adj* barefoot
BAREFOOT	*adj* being without shoes
BAREGE	*n* pl. -S a sheer fabric
BAREHEAD	*adv* without a hat
BARELY	*adv* scarcely
BARENESS	*n* pl. -ES the state of being bare
BARER	comparative of bare
BARESARK	*n* pl. -S an ancient warrior

BAREST	superlative of bare
BARF	v -ED, -ING, -S to vomit
BARFLY	n pl. -FLIES a drinker who frequents bars
BARGAIN	v -ED, -ING, -S to discuss terms for selling or buying
BARGE	v BARGED, BARGING, BARGES to move by barge (a long, large boat)
BARGEE	n pl. -S a bargeman
BARGELLO	n pl. -LOS a needlepoint stitch that makes a zigzag pattern
BARGEMAN	n pl. -MEN the master or a crew member of a barge
BARGHEST	n pl. -S a goblin
BARGING	present participle of barge
BARGUEST	n pl. -S barghest
BARHOP	v -HOPPED, -HOPPING, -HOPS to visit a number of bars during an evening
BARIC	adj pertaining to barium
BARILLA	n pl. -S a chemical compound
BARING	present participle of bare
BARITE	n pl. -S a mineral
BARITONE	n pl. -S a male singing voice
BARIUM	n pl. -S a metallic element
BARK	v -ED, -ING, -S to cry like a dog
BARKEEP	n pl. -S a bartender
BARKER	n pl. -S one that barks
BARKLESS	adj having no bark; unable to bark
BARKY	adj BARKIER, BARKIEST covered with bark (tough outer covering of a root or stem)
BARLEDUC	n pl. -S a fruit jam
BARLESS	adj having no restraints
BARLEY	n pl. -LEYS a cereal grass
BARLOW	n pl. -S a jackknife
BARM	n pl. -S the foam on malt liquors
BARMAID	n pl. -S a female bartender
BARMAN	n pl. -MEN a male bartender
BARMIE	adj barmy
BARMY	adj BARMIER, BARMIEST full of barm; frothy
BARN	n pl. -S a large storage building
BARNACLE	n pl. -S a shellfish
BARNLIKE	adj resembling a barn
BARNY	adj BARNIER, BARNIEST resembling a barn in size, shape, or smell
BARNYARD	n pl. -S a yard near a barn
BAROGRAM	n pl. -S a barometric reading
BARON	n pl. -S a lower member of nobility
BARONAGE	n pl. -S the rank of a baron
BARONESS	n pl. -ES the wife of a baron
BARONET	n pl. -S the holder of a rank below that of a baron
BARONG	n pl. -S a broad knife
BARONIAL	adj pertaining to a baron
BARONNE	n pl. -S a baroness
BARONY	n pl. -ONIES the domain of a baron
BAROQUE	n pl. -S an ornate object
BAROUCHE	n pl. -S a type of carriage
BARQUE	n pl. -S a sailing vessel
BARRABLE	adj capable of being barred
BARRACK	v -ED, -ING, -S to shout boisterously
BARRAGE	v -RAGED, -RAGING, -RAGES to subject to a massive attack
BARRANCA	n pl. -S a steep ravine
BARRANCO	n pl. -COS barranca
BARRATER	n pl. -S barrator
BARRATOR	n pl. -S one who commits barratry
BARRATRY	n pl. -TRIES fraud committed by a master or crew of a ship
BARRE	v BARRED, BARRING, BARRES to play a type of guitar chord
BARRED	past tense of bar
BARREL	v -RELED, -RELING, -RELS or -RELLED, -RELLING, -RELS to move fast
BARREN	adj -RENER, -RENEST unproductive **BARRENLY** adv
BARREN	n pl. -S a tract of barren land
BARRET	n pl. -S a flat cap
BARRETOR	n pl. -S barrator
BARRETRY	n pl. -TRIES barratry
BARRETTE	n pl. -S a hair clip
BARRIER	n pl. -S an obstacle
BARRING	present participle of bar and barre
BARRIO	n pl. -RIOS a district
BARROOM	n pl. -S a room where liquor is sold

BARROW	*n* pl. -S a type of cart
BARSTOOL	*n* pl. -S a stool in a barroom
BARTEND	*v* -ED, -ING, -S to tend a barroom
BARTER	*v* -ED, -ING, -S to trade
BARTERER	*n* pl. -S one that barters
BARTISAN	*n* pl. -S bartizan
BARTIZAN	*n* pl. -S a small turret
BARWARE	*n* pl. -S barroom equipment
BARYE	*n* pl. -S a unit of pressure
BARYON	*n* pl. -S a type of subatomic particle **BARYONIC** *adj*
BARYTA	*n* pl. -S a compound of barium **BARYTIC** *adj*
BARYTE	*n* pl. -S barite
BARYTONE	*n* pl. -S baritone
BASAL	*adj* pertaining to the foundation **BASALLY** *adv*
BASALT	*n* pl. -S a volcanic rock **BASALTIC** *adj*
BASALTES	*n* pl. BASALTES unglazed stoneware
BASCULE	*n* pl. -S a type of seesaw
BASE	*adj* BASER, BASEST morally low
BASE	*v* BASED, BASING, BASES to found
BASEBALL	*n* pl. -S a type of ball
BASEBORN	*adj* of low birth
BASED	past tense of base
BASELESS	*adj* having no foundation
BASELINE	*n* pl. -S a line at either end of a court in certain sports
BASELY	*adv* in a base manner
BASEMAN	*n* pl. -MEN a certain player in baseball
BASEMENT	*n* pl. -S the part of a building below ground level
BASENESS	*n* pl. -ES the state of being base
BASENJI	*n* pl. -S a barkless dog
BASER	comparative of base
BASES	pl. of basis
BASEST	superlative of base
BASH	*v* -ED, -ING, -ES to smash
BASHAW	*n* pl. -S a pasha
BASHER	*n* pl. -S one that bashes
BASHFUL	*adj* shy; timid
BASHLYK	*n* pl. -S a cloth hood

BASIC	*n* pl. -S a fundamental
BASICITY	*n* pl. -TIES the state of being alkaline
BASIDIUM	*n* pl. -IA a structure on a fungus **BASIDIAL** *adj*
BASIFIER	*n* pl. -S one that basifies
BASIFY	*v* -FIED, -FYING, -FIES to alkalize
BASIL	*n* pl. -S an aromatic herb
BASILAR	*adj* basal
BASILARY	*adj* basilar
BASILIC	*adj* pertaining to a basilica
BASILICA	*n* pl. -CAS or -CAE an ancient Roman building
BASILISK	*n* pl. -S a fabled serpent
BASIN	*n* pl. -S a large bowl **BASINAL, BASINED** *adj*
BASINET	*n* pl. -S a medieval helmet
BASINFUL	*n* pl. -S as much as a basin can hold
BASING	present participle of base
BASION	*n* pl. -S a part of the skull
BASIS	*n* pl. BASES the foundation of something
BASK	*v* -ED, -ING, -S to lie in a pleasant warmth
BASKET	*n* pl. -S a wooden container
BASKETRY	*n* pl. -RIES basket weaving
BASMATI	*n* pl. -S a long-grain rice
BASOPHIL	*n* pl. -S a type of cell
BASQUE	*n* pl. -S a bodice
BASS	*n* pl. -ES an edible fish
BASSET	*v* -SETED, -SETING, -SETS or -SETTED, -SETTING, -SETS to outcrop
BASSI	a pl. of basso
BASSINET	*n* pl. -S a basket used as a baby's crib
BASSIST	*n* pl. -S a person who plays a double bass
BASSLY	*adv* in a low-pitched manner
BASSNESS	*n* pl. -ES lowness in pitch
BASSO	*n* pl. -SOS or -SI a low-pitched singer
BASSOON	*n* pl. -S a low-pitched instrument
BASSWOOD	*n* pl. -S a linden tree
BASSY	*adj* low in pitch
BAST	*n* pl. -S a woody fiber
BASTARD	*n* pl. -S an illegitimate child

BASTARDY   *n* pl. -TARDIES the state of being a bastard

BASTE   *v* BASTED, BASTING, BASTES to sew loosely together

BASTER   *n* pl. -S one that bastes

BASTILE   *n* pl. -S bastille

BASTILLE   *n* pl. -S a prison

BASTING   *n* pl. -S the thread used by a baster

BASTION   *n* pl. -S a fortified place

BAT   *v* BATTED, BATTING, BATS to hit a baseball

BATBOY   *n* pl. -BOYS a boy who minds baseball equipment

BATCH   *v* -ED, -ING, -ES to bring together

BATCHER   *n* pl. -S one that batches

BATE   *v* BATED, BATING, BATES to reduce the force of

BATEAU   *n* pl. -TEAUX a flat-bottomed boat

BATFISH   *n* pl. -ES a batlike fish

BATFOWL   *v* -ED, -ING, -S to catch birds at night

BATH   *n* pl. -S a washing

BATHE   *v* BATHED, BATHING, BATHES to wash

BATHER   *n* pl. -S one that bathes

BATHETIC   *adj* trite

BATHING   present participle of bathe

BATHLESS   *adj* not having had a bath

BATHMAT   *n* pl. -S a mat used in a bathroom

BATHOS   *n* pl. -ES triteness

BATHROBE   *n* pl. -S a housecoat

BATHROOM   *n* pl. -S a room in which to bathe

BATHTUB   *n* pl. -S a tub in which to bathe

BATHYAL   *adj* pertaining to deep water

BATIK   *n* pl. -S a dyeing process

BATING   present participle of bate

BATISTE   *n* pl. -S a sheer fabric

BATLIKE   *adj* resembling a bat (a flying mammal)

BATMAN   *n* pl. -MEN an orderly

BATON   *n* pl. -S a short rod

BATSMAN   *n* pl. -MEN one who bats

BATT   *n* pl. -S a sheet of cotton

BATTALIA   *n* pl. -S a military unit

BATTEAU   *n* pl. -TEAUX bateau

BATTED   past tense of bat

BATTEN   *v* -ED, -ING, -S to fasten with strips of wood

BATTENER   *n* pl. -S one that battens

BATTER   *v* -ED, -ING, -S to beat repeatedly

BATTERIE   *n* pl. -S a ballet movement

BATTERY   *n* pl. -TERIES a device for generating an electric current

BATTIER   comparative of batty

BATTIEST   superlative of batty

BATTIK   *n* pl. -S batik

BATTING   *n* pl. -S a batt

BATTLE   *v* -TLED, -TLING, -TLES to fight

BATTLER   *n* pl. -S one that battles

BATTU   *adj* pertaining to a ballet movement

BATTUE   *n* pl. -S a type of hunt

BATTY   *adj* -TIER, -TIEST crazy

BATWING   *adj* shaped like a bat's wing

BAUBEE   *n* pl. -S bawbee

BAUBLE   *n* pl. -S a cheap trinket

BAUD   *n* pl. -S a unit of data transmission speed

BAUDEKIN   *n* pl. -S a brocaded fabric

BAUDRONS   *n* pl. -ES a cat

BAUHINIA   *n* pl. -S a small tropical tree

BAULK   *v* -ED, -ING, -S to balk

BAULKY   *adj* BAULKIER, BAULKIEST balky

BAUSOND   *adj* having white marks

BAUXITE   *n* pl. -S an ore of aluminum **BAUXITIC** *adj*

BAWBEE   *n* pl. -S a Scottish coin

BAWCOCK   *n* pl. -S a fine fellow

BAWD   *n* pl. -S a madam

BAWDIER   comparative of bawdy

BAWDIES   pl. of bawdy

BAWDIEST   superlative of bawdy

BAWDILY   *adv* in a bawdy manner

BAWDRIC   *n* pl. -S baldric

BAWDRY   *n* pl. -RIES obscenity

BAWDY   *adj* BAWDIER, BAWDIEST obscene

BAWDY   *n* pl. BAWDIES obscene language

BAWL   *v* -ED, -ING, -S to cry loudly

BAWLER	*n* pl. -S one that bawls
BAWSUNT	*adj* bausond
BAWTIE	*n* pl. -S a dog
BAWTY	*n* pl. -TIES bawtie
BAY	*v* -ED, -ING, -S to howl
BAYADEER	*n* pl. -S bayadere
BAYADERE	*n* pl. -S a dancing girl
BAYAMO	*n* pl. -MOS a strong wind
BAYARD	*n* pl. -S a horse
BAYBERRY	*n* pl. -RIES a berry tree
BAYMAN	*n* pl. -MEN a person who fishes on a bay
BAYONET	*v* -NETED, -NETING, -NETS or -NETTED, -NETTING, -NETS to stab with a dagger-like weapon
BAYOU	*n* pl. -S a marshy body of water
BAYWOOD	*n* pl. -S a coarse mahogany
BAZAAR	*n* pl. -S a marketplace
BAZAR	*n* pl. -S bazaar
BAZOO	*n* pl. -ZOOS the mouth
BAZOOKA	*n* pl. -S a small rocket launcher
BDELLIUM	*n* pl. -S a gum resin
BE	*v* present sing. 1st person AM, 2d ARE or ART, 3d IS, past sing. 1st and 3d persons WAS, 2d WERE or WAST or WERT, past participle BEEN, present participle BEING to have actuality
BEACH	*v* -ED, -ING, -ES to drive ashore
BEACHBOY	*n* pl. -BOYS a male beach attendant
BEACHY	*adj* BEACHIER, BEACHIEST sandy or pebbly
BEACON	*v* -ED, -ING, -S to warn or guide
BEAD	*v* -ED, -ING, -S to adorn with beads (round pieces of glass)
BEADIER	comparative of beady
BEADIEST	superlative of beady
BEADILY	*adv* in a beady manner
BEADING	*n* pl. -S beaded material
BEADLE	*n* pl. -S a parish official
BEADLIKE	*adj* beady
BEADMAN	*n* pl. -MEN beadsman
BEADROLL	*n* pl. -S a list of names
BEADSMAN	*n* pl. -MEN one who prays for another
BEADWORK	*n* pl. -S beading
BEADY	*adj* BEADIER, BEADIEST resembling beads
BEAGLE	*n* pl. -S a small hound
BEAK	*n* pl. -S a bird's bill **BEAKED, BEAKLESS, BEAKLIKE** *adj*
BEAKER	*n* pl. -S a large cup
BEAKY	*adj* BEAKIER, BEAKIEST resembling a beak
BEAM	*v* -ED, -ING, -S to emit in beams (rays of light)
BEAMIER	comparative of beamy
BEAMIEST	superlative of beamy
BEAMILY	*adv* in a beamy manner
BEAMISH	*adj* cheerful
BEAMLESS	*adj* having no beam
BEAMLIKE	*adj* resembling a beam
BEAMY	*adj* BEAMIER, BEAMIEST beaming
BEAN	*v* -ED, -ING, -S to hit on the head
BEANBAG	*n* pl. -S a small cloth bag
BEANBALL	*n* pl. -S a baseball thrown at the head
BEANERY	*n* pl. -ERIES a cheap restaurant
BEANIE	*n* pl. -S a small cap
BEANLIKE	*adj* resembling a bean
BEANO	*n* pl. BEANOS a form of bingo
BEANPOLE	*n* pl. -S a thin pole
BEAR	*v* BORE, BORNE or BORN, BEARING, BEARS to endure **BEARABLE** *adj* **BEARABLY** *adv*
BEARCAT	*n* pl. -S a small mammal
BEARD	*v* -ED, -ING, -S to oppose boldly
BEARER	*n* pl. -S one that bears
BEARHUG	*n* pl. -S a rough tight embrace
BEARING	*n* pl. -S demeanor
BEARISH	*adj* resembling a bear (a large mammal)
BEARLIKE	*adj* bearish
BEARSKIN	*n* pl. -S the skin of a bear
BEARWOOD	*n* pl. -S a small tree of the buckthorn family
BEAST	*n* pl. -S an animal
BEASTIE	*n* pl. -S a tiny animal
BEASTLY	*adj* -LIER, -LIEST resembling a beast
BEAT	*v* BEAT, BEATEN, BEATING, BEATS to strike repeatedly **BEATABLE** *adj*

BEATER	*n* pl. -S one that beats	**BECLOUD**	*v* -ED, -ING, -S to make cloudy
BEATIFIC	*adj* blissful	**BECLOWN**	*v* -ED, -ING, -S to cause to appear ridiculous
BEATIFY	*v* -FIED, -FYING, -FIES to make happy	**BECOME**	*v* -CAME, -COMING, -COMES to come to be
BEATING	*n* pl. -S a defeat	**BECOMING**	*n* pl. -S a process of change
BEATLESS	*adj* having no rhythm	**BECOWARD**	*v* -ED, -ING, -S to accuse of cowardice
BEATNIK	*n* pl. -S a nonconformist		
BEAU	*n* pl. BEAUX or BEAUS a boyfriend **BEAUISH** *adj*	**BECRAWL**	*v* -ED, -ING, -S to crawl over
		BECRIME	*v* -CRIMED, -CRIMING, -CRIMES to make guilty of a crime
BEAUCOUP	*adj* many or much		
BEAUT	*n* pl. -S something beautiful	**BECROWD**	*v* -ED, -ING, -S to crowd closely
BEAUTIFY	*v* -FIED, -FYING, -FIES to make beautiful	**BECRUST**	*v* -ED, -ING, -S to cover with a crust
BEAUTY	*n* pl. -TIES one that is lovely	**BECUDGEL**	*v* -GELLED, -GELLING, -GELS or -GELED, -GELING, -GELS to cudgel thoroughly
BEAUX	a pl. of beau		
BEAVER	*v* -ED, -ING, -S to work hard	**BECURSE**	*v* -CURSED or -CURST, -CURSING, -CURSES to curse severely
BEBEERU	*n* pl. -S a tropical tree		
BEBLOOD	*v* -ED, -ING, -S to cover with blood		
		BED	*v* BEDDED, BEDDING, BEDS to provide with a bed (a piece of furniture used for sleeping)
BEBOP	*n* pl. -S a type of jazz		
BEBOPPER	*n* pl. -S one that likes bebop	**BEDABBLE**	*v* -BLED, -BLING, -BLES to soil
BECALM	*v* -ED, -ING, -S to make calm	**BEDAMN**	*v* -ED, -ING, -S to swear at
BECAME	past tense of become	**BEDARKEN**	*v* -ED, -ING, -S to darken
BECAP	*v* -CAPPED, -CAPPING, -CAPS to put a cap on	**BEDAUB**	*v* -ED, -ING, -S to besmear
		BEDAZZLE	*v* -ZLED, -ZLING, -ZLES to confuse
BECARPET	*v* -ED, -ING, -S to cover with a carpet		
		BEDBUG	*n* pl. -S a bloodsucking insect
BECAUSE	*conj* for the reason that	**BEDCHAIR**	*n* pl. -S a chair near a bed
BECHALK	*v* -ED, -ING, -S to cover with chalk	**BEDCOVER**	*n* pl. -S a cover for a bed
		BEDDABLE	*adj* suitable for taking to bed
BECHAMEL	*n* pl. -S a white sauce	**BEDDED**	past tense of bed
BECHANCE	*v* -CHANCED, -CHANCING, -CHANCES to befall	**BEDDER**	*n* pl. -S one that makes up beds
		BEDDING	*n* pl. -S material for making up a bed
BECHARM	*v* -ED, -ING, -S to hold under a spell		
		BEDEAFEN	*v* -ED, -ING, -S to deafen
BECK	*v* -ED, -ING, -S to beckon	**BEDECK**	*v* -ED, -ING, -S to clothe with finery
BECKET	*n* pl. -S a securing rope		
BECKON	*v* -ED, -ING, -S to signal by sign or gesture	**BEDEL**	*n* pl. -S an English university officer
BECKONER	*n* pl. -S one that beckons	**BEDELL**	*n* pl. -S bedel
BECLAMOR	*v* -ED, -ING, -S to clamor loudly	**BEDEMAN**	*n* pl. -MEN beadsman
BECLASP	*v* -ED, -ING, -S to embrace	**BEDESMAN**	*n* pl. -MEN beadsman
BECLOAK	*v* -ED, -ING, -S to place a cloak on	**BEDEVIL**	*v* -ILED, -ILING, -ILS or -ILLED, -ILLING, -ILS to harass
BECLOG	*v* -CLOGGED, -CLOGGING, -CLOGS to clog thoroughly	**BEDEW**	*v* -ED, -ING, -S to wet with dew
BECLOTHE	*v* -CLOTHED, -CLOTHING, -CLOTHES to clothe	**BEDFAST**	*adj* confined to bed

BEDFRAME *n* pl. -S the frame of a bed

BEDGOWN *n* pl. -S a dressing gown

BEDIAPER *v* -ED, -ING, -S to ornament with a kind of design

BEDIGHT *v* -ED, -ING, -S to bedeck

BEDIM *v* -DIMMED, -DIMMING, -DIMS to make dim

BEDIMPLE *v* -PLED, -PLING, -PLES to dimple

BEDIRTY *v* -DIRTIED, -DIRTYING, -DIRTIES to make dirty

BEDIZEN *v* -ED, -ING, -S to dress gaudily

BEDLAM *n* pl. -S confusion

BEDLAMP *n* pl. -S a lamp near a bed

BEDLESS *adj* having no bed

BEDLIKE *adj* resembling a bed

BEDMAKER *n* pl. -S one that makes beds

BEDMATE *n* pl. -S a bed companion

BEDOTTED *adj* covered with dots

BEDOUIN *n* pl. -S a nomadic Arab

BEDPAN *n* pl. -S a toilet pan

BEDPLATE *n* pl. -S a frame support

BEDPOST *n* pl. -S a post of a bed

BEDQUILT *n* pl. -S a quilt for a bed

BEDRAIL *n* pl. -S a board at bedside

BEDRAPE *v* -DRAPED, -DRAPING, -DRAPES to drape

BEDRENCH *v* -ED, -ING, -ES to drench thoroughly

BEDRID *adj* bedfast

BEDRIVEL *v* -ELLED, -ELLING, -ELS or -ELED, -ELING, -ELS to cover with saliva

BEDROCK *n* pl. -S the rock under soil

BEDROLL *n* pl. -S a portable roll of bedding

BEDROOM *n* pl. -S a room for sleeping

BEDRUG *v* -DRUGGED, -DRUGGING, -DRUGS to make sleepy

BEDSHEET *n* pl. -S a sheet for a bed

BEDSIDE *n* pl. -S the side of a bed

BEDSIT *n* pl. -S a one-room apartment

BEDSONIA *n* pl. -S a virus

BEDSORE *n* pl. -S a type of sore

BEDSTAND *n* pl. -S a table next to a bed

BEDSTEAD *n* pl. -S a support for a bed

BEDSTRAW *n* pl. -S a woody herb

BEDTICK *n* pl. -S the cloth case of a mattress

BEDTIME *n* pl. -S a time for going to bed

BEDU *n* pl. BEDU a bedouin

BEDUIN *n* pl. -S bedouin

BEDUMB *v* -ED, -ING, -S to render speechless

BEDUNCE *v* -DUNCED, -DUNCING, -DUNCES to make a dunce of

BEDWARD *adv* toward bed

BEDWARDS *adv* bedward

BEDWARF *v* -ED, -ING, -S to cause to appear small by comparison

BEE *n* pl. -S a winged insect

BEEBEE *n* pl. -S a pellet

BEEBREAD *n* pl. -S a pollen mixture

BEECH *n* pl. -ES a type of tree **BEECHEN** *adj*

BEECHNUT *n* pl. -S the nut of a beech

BEECHY *adj* BEECHIER, BEECHIEST abounding in beeches

BEEF *n* pl. BEEFS or BEEVES a steer or cow fattened for food

BEEF *v* -ED, -ING, -S to add bulk to

BEEFALO *n* pl. -LOS or -LOES the offspring of an American buffalo and domestic cattle

BEEFCAKE *n* pl. -S pictures of male physiques

BEEFIER comparative of beefy

BEEFIEST superlative of beefy

BEEFILY *adv* in a beefy manner

BEEFLESS *adj* being without beef

BEEFWOOD *n* pl. -S a hardwood tree

BEEFY *adj* BEEFIER, BEEFIEST brawny

BEEHIVE *n* pl. -S a hive for bees

BEELIKE *adj* resembling a bee

BEELINE *v* -LINED, -LINING, -LINES to go in a straight direct course

BEEN past participle of be

BEEP *v* -ED, -ING, -S to honk a horn

BEEPER *n* pl. -S a signaling device

BEER *n* pl. -S an alcoholic beverage

BEERY *adj* BEERIER, BEERIEST affected by beer

BEESWAX *n* pl. -ES a type of wax

BEESWING *n* pl. -S a crust that forms on wines

BEET *n* pl. -S a garden plant

BEETLE *v* -TLED, -TLING, -TLES to jut out

BEETLER	*n* pl. -S one that operates a cloth-finishing machine
BEETROOT	*n* pl. -S the root of the beet
BEEVES	a pl. of beef
BEEYARD	*n* pl. -S an apiary
BEEZER	*n* pl. -S the nose
BEFALL	*v* -FELL, -FALLEN, -FALLING, -FALLS to happen to
BEFINGER	*v* -ED, -ING, -S to touch all over
BEFIT	*v* -FITTED, -FITTING, -FITS to be suitable to
BEFLAG	*v* -FLAGGED, -FLAGGING, -FLAGS to deck with flags
BEFLEA	*v* -ED, -ING, -S to infest with fleas
BEFLECK	*v* -ED, -ING, -S to fleck
BEFLOWER	*v* -ED, -ING, -S to cover with flowers
BEFOG	*v* -FOGGED, -FOGGING, -FOGS to envelop in fog
BEFOOL	*v* -ED, -ING, -S to deceive
BEFORE	*adv* previously
BEFOUL	*v* -ED, -ING, -S to foul
BEFOULER	*n* pl. -S one that befouls
BEFRET	*v* -FRETTED, -FRETTING, -FRETS to gnaw
BEFRIEND	*v* -ED, -ING, -S to act as a friend to
BEFRINGE	*v* -FRINGED, -FRINGING, -FRINGES to border with a fringe
BEFUDDLE	*v* -DLED, -DLING, -DLES to confuse
BEG	*v* BEGGED, BEGGING, BEGS to plead
BEGALL	*v* -ED, -ING, -S to make sore by rubbing
BEGAN	past tense of begin
BEGAZE	*v* -GAZED, -GAZING, -GAZES to gaze at
BEGET	*v* -GOT or -GAT, -GOTTEN, -GETTING, -GETS to cause to exist
BEGETTER	*n* pl. -S one that begets
BEGGAR	*v* -ED, -ING, -S to impoverish
BEGGARLY	*adj* very poor
BEGGARY	*n* pl. -GARIES extreme poverty
BEGGED	past tense of beg
BEGGING	present participle of beg
BEGIN	*v* -GAN, -GUN, -GINNING, -GINS to start
BEGINNER	*n* pl. -S one that begins
BEGIRD	*v* -GIRT or -GIRDED, -GIRDING, -GIRDS to surround
BEGIRDLE	*v* -DLED, -DLING, -DLES to surround
BEGLAD	*v* -GLADDED, -GLADDING, -GLADS to gladden
BEGLAMOR	*v* -ED, -ING, -S to dazzle with glamor
BEGLOOM	*v* -ED, -ING, -S to make gloomy
BEGONE	*interj* — used as an order of dismissal
BEGONIA	*n* pl. -S a tropical herb
BEGORAH	*interj* begorra
BEGORRA	*interj* — used as a mild oath
BEGORRAH	*interj* begorra
BEGOT	a past tense of beget
BEGOTTEN	past participle of beget
BEGRIM	*v* -GRIMMED, -GRIMMING, -GRIMS to begrime
BEGRIME	*v* -GRIMED, -GRIMING, -GRIMES to dirty
BEGROAN	*v* -ED, -ING, -S to groan at
BEGRUDGE	*v* -GRUDGED, -GRUDGING, -GRUDGES to concede reluctantly
BEGUILE	*v* -GUILED, -GUILING, -GUILES to deceive
BEGUILER	*n* pl. -S one that beguiles
BEGUINE	*n* pl. -S a lively dance
BEGULF	*v* -ED, -ING, -S to engulf
BEGUM	*n* pl. -S a Muslim lady of high rank
BEGUN	past participle of begin
BEHALF	*n* pl. -HALVES interest, support, or benefit
BEHAVE	*v* -HAVED, -HAVING, -HAVES to act properly
BEHAVER	*n* pl. -S one that behaves
BEHAVIOR	*n* pl. -S demeanor
BEHEAD	*v* -ED, -ING, -S to cut off the head of
BEHELD	past tense of behold
BEHEMOTH	*n* pl. -S a large beast
BEHEST	*n* pl. -S a command
BEHIND	*n* pl. -S the buttocks
BEHOLD	*v* -HELD, -HOLDING, -HOLDS to view
BEHOLDEN	*adj* indebted

BEHOLDER	*n* pl. -S one that beholds
BEHOOF	*n* pl. -HOOVES use, advantage, or benefit
BEHOOVE	*v* -HOOVED, -HOOVING, -HOOVES to be proper for
BEHOVE	*v* -HOVED, -HOVING, -HOVES to behoove
BEHOWL	*v* -ED, -ING, -S to howl at
BEIGE	*n* pl. -S a tan color
BEIGNET	*n* pl. -S a type of fritter or doughnut
BEIGY	*adj* of the color beige
BEING	*n* pl. -S something that exists
BEJABERS	*interj* bejesus
BEJEEZUS	*interj* bejesus
BEJESUS	*interj* — used as a mild oath
BEJEWEL	*v* -ELED, -ELING, -ELS or -ELLED, -ELLING, -ELS to adorn with jewels
BEJUMBLE	*v* -BLED, -BLING, -BLES to jumble
BEKISS	*v* -ED, -ING, -ES to cover with kisses
BEKNIGHT	*v* -ED, -ING, -S to raise to knighthood
BEKNOT	*v* -KNOTTED, -KNOTTING, -KNOTS to tie in knots
BEL	*n* pl. -S a unit of power
BELABOR	*v* -ED, -ING, -S to discuss for an absurd amount of time
BELABOUR	*v* -ED, -ING, -S to belabor
BELACED	*adj* adorned with lace
BELADY	*v* -DIED, -DYING, -DIES to apply the title of lady to
BELATED	*adj* late or too late
BELAUD	*v* -ED, -ING, -S to praise
BELAY	*v* -ED, -ING, -S to fasten a rope
BELCH	*v* -ED, -ING, -ES to expel gas through the mouth
BELCHER	*n* pl. -S one that belches
BELDAM	*n* pl. -S an old woman
BELDAME	*n* pl. -S beldam
BELEAP	*v* -LEAPT or -LEAPED, -LEAPING, -LEAPS to leap upon
BELFRY	*n* pl. -FRIES a bell tower **BELFRIED** *adj*
BELGA	*n* pl. -S a former Belgian monetary unit
BELIE	*v* -LIED, -LYING, -LIES to misrepresent

BELIEF	*n* pl. -S acceptance of the truth or actuality of something
BELIER	*n* pl. -S one that belies
BELIEVE	*v* -LIEVED, -LIEVING, -LIEVES to accept as true or real
BELIEVER	*n* pl. -S one that believes
BELIKE	*adv* perhaps
BELIQUOR	*v* -ED, -ING, -S to soak with liquor
BELITTLE	*v* -TLED, -TLING, -TLES to disparage
BELIVE	*adv* in due time
BELL	*v* -ED, -ING, -S to provide with a bell (a ringing device)
BELLBIRD	*n* pl. -S a tropical bird
BELLBOY	*n* pl. -BOYS a hotel's errand boy
BELLE	*n* pl. -S an attractive woman
BELLEEK	*n* pl. -S a very thin translucent porcelain
BELLHOP	*n* pl. -S a bellboy
BELLIED	past tense of belly
BELLIES	present 3d person sing. of belly
BELLMAN	*n* pl. -MEN a town crier
BELLOW	*v* -ED, -ING, -S to shout in a deep voice
BELLOWER	*n* pl. -S one that bellows
BELLPULL	*n* pl. -S a cord pulled to ring a bell
BELLWORT	*n* pl. -S a flowering plant
BELLY	*v* -LIED, -LYING, -LIES to swell out
BELLYFUL	*n* pl. -S an excessive amount
BELONG	*v* -ED, -ING, -S to be a member of
BELOVED	*n* pl. -S one who is loved
BELOW	*n* pl. -S something that is beneath
BELT	*v* -ED, -ING, -S to fasten with a belt (a strap or band worn around the waist)
BELTER	*n* pl. -S one that belts
BELTING	*n* pl. -S material for belts
BELTLESS	*adj* having no belt
BELTLINE	*n* pl. -S the waistline
BELTWAY	*n* pl. -WAYS a highway around an urban area
BELUGA	*n* pl. -S a white sturgeon
BELYING	present participle of belie

BEMA	*n* pl. -MATA or -MAS a platform in a synagogue
BEMADAM	*v* -ED, -ING, -S to call by the title of madam
BEMADDEN	*v* -ED, -ING, -S to madden
BEMATA	a pl. of bema
BEMEAN	*v* -ED, -ING, -S to debase
BEMINGLE	*v* -GLED, -GLING, -GLES to mix together
BEMIRE	*v* -MIRED, -MIRING, -MIRES to soil with mud
BEMIST	*v* -ED, -ING, -S to envelop in a mist
BEMIX	*v* -MIXED or -MIXT, -MIXING, -MIXES to mix thoroughly
BEMOAN	*v* -ED, -ING, -S to lament
BEMOCK	*v* -ED, -ING, -S to mock
BEMUDDLE	*v* -DLED, -DLING, -DLES to confuse completely
BEMURMUR	*v* -ED, -ING, -S to murmur at
BEMUSE	*v* -MUSED, -MUSING, -MUSES to confuse
BEMUZZLE	*v* -ZLED, -ZLING, -ZLES to muzzle
BEN	*n* pl. -S an inner room
BENAME	*v* -NAMED, -NEMPT or -NEMPTED, -NAMING, -NAMES to name
BENCH	*v* -ED, -ING, -ES to take a player out of a game
BENCHER	*n* pl. -S a magistrate
BEND	*v* BENT or BENDED, BENDING, BENDS to curve **BENDABLE** *adj*
BENDAY	*v* -ED, -ING, -S to reproduce using a certain process
BENDEE	*n* pl. -S bendy
BENDER	*n* pl. -S one that bends
BENDWAYS	*adv* bendwise
BENDWISE	*adv* diagonally
BENDY	*n* pl. -DYS okra
BENE	*n* pl. -S benne
BENEATH	*prep* under
BENEDICK	*n* pl. -S benedict
BENEDICT	*n* pl. -S a newly married man
BENEFIC	*adj* kindly
BENEFICE	*v* -FICED, -FICING, -FICES to endow with land
BENEFIT	*v* -FITED, -FITING, -FITS or -FITTED, -FITTING, -FITS to be helpful or useful to

BENEMPT	a past participle of bename
BENEMPTED	a past participle of bename
BENIGN	*adj* kind **BENIGNLY** *adv*
BENISON	*n* pl. -S a blessing
BENJAMIN	*n* pl. -S benzoin
BENNE	*n* pl. -S the sesame plant
BENNET	*n* pl. -S a perennial herb
BENNI	*n* pl. -S benne
BENNY	*n* pl. -NIES an amphetamine tablet
BENOMYL	*n* pl. -S a chemical compound
BENT	*n* pl. -S an inclination
BENTHAL	*adj* benthic
BENTHIC	*adj* pertaining to oceanic depths
BENTHOS	*n* pl. -ES benthic sea life
BENTWOOD	*n* pl. -S wood bent for use in furniture
BENUMB	*v* -ED, -ING, -S to make numb
BENZAL	*adj* pertaining to a certain chemical group
BENZENE	*n* pl. -S a volatile liquid
BENZIDIN	*n* pl. -S a hydrocarbon
BENZIN	*n* pl. -S benzine
BENZINE	*n* pl. -S a volatile liquid
BENZOATE	*n* pl. -S a chemical salt
BENZOIN	*n* pl. -S a gum resin **BENZOIC** *adj*
BENZOL	*n* pl. -S a benzene
BENZOLE	*n* pl. -S benzol
BENZOYL	*n* pl. -S a univalent chemical radical
BENZYL	*n* pl. -S a univalent chemical radical **BENZYLIC** *adj*
BEPAINT	*v* -ED, -ING, -S to tinge
BEPIMPLE	*v* -PLED, -PLING, -PLES to cover with pimples
BEQUEATH	*v* -ED, -ING, -S to grant by testament
BEQUEST	*n* pl. -S a legacy
BERAKE	*v* -RAKED, -RAKING, -RAKES to rake all over
BERASCAL	*v* -ED, -ING, -S to accuse of being a rascal
BERATE	*v* -RATED, -RATING, -RATES to scold severely
BERBERIN	*n* pl. -S a medicinal alkaloid
BERBERIS	*n* pl. -ES a barberry
BERCEUSE	*n* pl. -S a lullaby

BERDACHE *n* pl. -S an American Indian male transvestite

BEREAVE *v* -REAVED or -REFT, -REAVING, -REAVES to deprive

BEREAVER *n* pl. -S one that bereaves

BERET *n* pl. -S a soft, flat cap

BERETTA *n* pl. -S biretta

BERG *n* pl. -S an iceberg

BERGAMOT *n* pl. -S a citrus tree

BERGERE *n* pl. -S an upholstered armchair

BERHYME *v* -RHYMED, -RHYMING, -RHYMES to compose in rhyme

BERIBERI *n* pl. -S a thiamine deficiency disease

BERIME *v* -RIMED, -RIMING, -RIMES to berhyme

BERINGED *adj* adorned with rings

BERLIN *n* pl. -S a type of carriage

BERLINE *n* pl. -S a limousine

BERM *n* pl. -S a ledge

BERME *n* pl. -S berm

BERMUDAS *n/pl* knee-length walking shorts

BERNICLE *n* pl. -S a wild goose

BEROBED *adj* wearing a robe

BEROUGED *adj* obviously or thickly rouged

BERRETTA *n* pl. -S biretta

BERRY *v* -RIED, -RYING, -RIES to produce berries (fleshy fruits)

BERSEEM *n* pl. -S a clover

BERSERK *n* pl. -S a fierce warrior

BERTH *v* -ED, -ING, -S to provide with a mooring

BERTHA *n* pl. -S a wide collar

BERYL *n* pl. -S a green mineral
BERYLINE *adj*

BESCORCH *v* -ED, -ING, -ES to scorch

BESCOUR *v* -ED, -ING, -S to scour thoroughly

BESCREEN *v* -ED, -ING, -S to screen

BESEECH *v* -SOUGHT or -SEECHED, -SEECHING, -SEECHES to implore

BESEEM *v* -ED, -ING, -S to be suitable

BESET *v* -SET, -SETTING, -SETS to assail

BESETTER *n* pl. -S one that besets

BESHADOW *v* -ED, -ING, -S to cast a shadow on

BESHAME *v* -SHAMED, -SHAMING, -SHAMES to put to shame

BESHIVER *v* -ED, -ING, -S to break into small pieces

BESHOUT *v* -ED, -ING, -S to shout at

BESHREW *v* -ED, -ING, -S to curse

BESHROUD *v* -ED, -ING, -S to cover

BESIDE *prep* next to

BESIDES *adv* in addition

BESIEGE *v* -SIEGED, -SIEGING, -SIEGES to surround

BESIEGER *n* pl. -S one that besieges

BESLAVED *adj* filled with slaves

BESLIME *v* -SLIMED, -SLIMING, -SLIMES to cover with slime

BESMEAR *v* -ED, -ING, -S to smear over

BESMILE *v* -SMILED, -SMILING, -SMILES to smile on

BESMIRCH *v* -ED, -ING, -ES to dirty

BESMOKE *v* -SMOKED, -SMOKING, -SMOKES to soil with smoke

BESMOOTH *v* -ED, -ING, -S to smooth

BESMUDGE *v* -SMUDGED, -SMUDGING, -SMUDGES to smudge

BESMUT *v* -SMUTTED, -SMUTTING, -SMUTS to blacken with smut

BESNOW *v* -ED, -ING, -S to cover with snow

BESOM *n* pl. -S a broom

BESOOTHE *v* -SOOTHED, -SOOTHING -SOOTHES to soothe

BESOT *v* -SOTTED, -SOTTING, -SOTS to stupefy

BESOUGHT a past tense of beseech

BESPEAK *v* -SPOKE or -SPAKE, -SPOKEN, -SPEAKING, -SPEAKS to claim in advance

BESPOUSE *v* -SPOUSED, -SPOUSING, -SPOUSES to marry

BESPREAD *v* -SPREAD, -SPREADING, -SPREADS to spread over

BESPRENT *adj* sprinkled over

BEST *v* -ED, -ING, -S to outdo

BESTEAD *v* -ED, -ING, -S to help

BESTIAL *adj* pertaining to beasts

BESTIARY *n* pl. -ARIES a collection of animal fables

BESTIR *v* -STIRRED, -STIRRING, -STIRS to rouse

BESTOW *v* -ED, -ING, -S to present as a gift

BESTOWAL *n* pl. -S a gift

BESTREW *v* -STREWED, -STREWN, -STREWING, -STREWS to scatter

BESTRIDE *v* -STRODE or -STRID, -STRIDDEN, -STRIDING, -STRIDES to straddle

BESTROW *v* -STROWED, -STROWN, -STROWING, -STROWS to bestrew

BESTUD *v* -STUDDED, -STUDDING, -STUDS to dot

BESWARM *v* -ED, -ING, -S to swarm all over

BET *v* BET or BETTED, BETTING, BETS to wager

BETA *n* pl. -S a Greek letter

BETAINE *n* pl. -S an alkaloid

BETAKE *v* -TOOK, -TAKEN, -TAKING, -TAKES to cause to go

BETATRON *n* pl. -S an electron accelerator

BETATTER *v* -ED, -ING, -S to tatter

BETAXED *adj* burdened with taxes

BETEL *n* pl. -S a climbing plant

BETELNUT *n* pl. -S a seed chewed as a stimulant

BETH *n* pl. -S a Hebrew letter

BETHANK *v* -ED, -ING, -S to thank

BETHEL *n* pl. -S a holy place

BETHESDA *n* pl. -S a chapel

BETHINK *v* -THOUGHT, -THINKING, -THINKS to consider

BETHORN *v* -ED, -ING, -S to fill with thorns

BETHUMP *v* -ED, -ING, -S to thump soundly

BETIDE *v* -TIDED, -TIDING, -TIDES to befall

BETIME *adv* betimes

BETIMES *adv* soon

BETISE *n* pl. -S stupidity

BETOKEN *v* -ED, -ING, -S to indicate

BETON *n* pl. -S a type of concrete

BETONY *n* pl. -NIES a European herb

BETOOK past tense of betake

BETRAY *v* -ED, -ING, -S to aid an enemy of

BETRAYAL *n* pl. -S the act of betraying

BETRAYER *n* pl. -S one that betrays

BETROTH *v* -ED, -ING, -S to engage to marry

BETTA *n* pl. -S a freshwater fish

BETTED a past tense of bet

BETTER *v* -ED, -ING, -S to improve

BETTING present participle of bet

BETTOR *n* pl. -S one that bets

BETWEEN *prep* in the space that separates

BETWIXT *prep* between

BEUNCLED *adj* having many uncles

BEVATRON *n* pl. -S a proton accelerator

BEVEL *v* -ELED, -ELING, -ELS or -ELLED, -ELLING, -ELS to cut at an angle

BEVELER *n* pl. -S one that bevels

BEVELLER *n* pl. -S beveler

BEVELLING a present participle of bevel

BEVERAGE *n* pl. -S a liquid for drinking

BEVIES pl. of bevy

BEVOMIT *v* -ED, -ING, -S to vomit all over

BEVOR *n* pl. -S a piece of armor for the lower face

BEVY *n* pl. BEVIES a group

BEWAIL *v* -ED, -ING, -S to lament

BEWAILER *n* pl. -S one that bewails

BEWARE *v* -WARED, -WARING, -WARES to be careful

BEWEARY *v* -WEARIED, -WEARYING, -WEARIES to make weary

BEWEEP *v* -WEPT, -WEEPING, -WEEPS to lament

BEWIG *v* -WIGGED, -WIGGING, -WIGS to adorn with a wig

BEWILDER *v* -ED, -ING, -S to confuse

BEWINGED *adj* having wings

BEWITCH *v* -ED, -ING, -ES to affect by witchcraft or magic

BEWORM *v* -ED, -ING, -S to infest with worms

BEWORRY *v* -RIED, -RYING, -RIES to worry

BEWRAP *v* -WRAPPED or -WRAPT, -WRAPPING, -WRAPS to wrap completely

BEWRAY *v* -ED, -ING, -S to divulge

BEWRAYER *n* pl. -S one that bewrays

BEY *n* pl. BEYS a Turkish ruler

BEYLIC *n* pl. -S the domain of a bey

BEYLIK *n* pl. -S beylic

BEYOND   *n* pl. -S something that lies farther ahead

BEZANT   *n* pl. -S a coin of ancient Rome

BEZAZZ   *n* pl. -ES pizazz

BEZEL   *n* pl. -S a slanted surface

BEZIL   *n* pl. -S bezel

BEZIQUE   *n* pl. -S a card game

BEZOAR   *n* pl. -S a gastric mass

BEZZANT   *n* pl. -S bezant

BHAKTA   *n* pl. -S one who practices bhakti

BHAKTI   *n* pl. -S a selfless devotion to a deity in Hinduism

BHANG   *n* pl. -S the hemp plant

BHARAL   *n* pl. -S a goatlike Asian mammal

BHEESTIE   *n* pl. -S bheesty

BHEESTY   *n* pl. -TIES a water carrier

BHISTIE   *n* pl. -S bheesty

BHOOT   *n* pl. -S bhut

BHUT   *n* pl. -S a small whirlwind

BI   *n* pl. -S a bisexual

BIACETYL   *n* pl. -S a chemical flavor enhancer

BIALI   *n* pl. -S bialy

BIALY   *n* pl. -ALYS an onion roll

BIANNUAL   *adj* occurring twice a year

BIAS   *v* -ASED, -ASING, -ASES or -ASSED, -ASSING, -ASSES to prejudice **BIASEDLY** *adv*

BIASNESS   *n* pl. -ES the state of being slanted

BIATHLON   *n* pl. -S an athletic contest

BIAXAL   *adj* biaxial

BIAXIAL   *adj* having two axes

BIB   *v* BIBBED, BIBBING, BIBS to tipple

BIBASIC   *adj* dibasic

BIBB   *n* pl. -S a mast support

BIBBED   past tense of bib

BIBBER   *n* pl. -S a tippler

BIBBERY   *n* pl. -BERIES the act of bibbing

BIBBING   present participle of bib

BIBCOCK   *n* pl. -S a type of faucet

BIBELOT   *n* pl. -S a trinket

BIBLE   *n* pl. -S an authoritative publication **BIBLICAL** *adj*

BIBLESS   *adj* having no bib (a cloth covering)

BIBLIKE   *adj* resembling a bib

BIBLIST   *n* pl. -S one who takes the words of the Bible literally

BIBULOUS   *adj* given to drinking

BICARB   *n* pl. -S sodium bicarbonate

BICAUDAL   *adj* having two tails

BICE   *n* pl. -S a blue or green pigment

BICEPS   *n* pl. -ES an arm muscle

BICHROME   *adj* two-colored

BICKER   *v* -ED, -ING, -S to argue

BICKERER   *n* pl. -S one that bickers

BICOLOR   *n* pl. -S something having two colors

BICOLOUR   *n* pl. -S bicolor

BICONVEX   *adj* convex on both sides

BICORN   *adj* having two horns

BICORNE   *n* pl. -S a type of hat

BICRON   *n* pl. -S one billionth of a meter

BICUSPID   *n* pl. -S a tooth

BICYCLE   *v* -CLED, -CLING, -CLES to ride a bicycle (a two-wheeled vehicle)

BICYCLER   *n* pl. -S one that bicycles

BICYCLIC   *adj* having two cycles

BICYCLING   present participle of bicycle

BID   *v* BADE, BIDDEN, BIDDING, BIDS to make a bid (an offer of a price)

BIDARKA   *n* pl. -S an Eskimo canoe

BIDARKEE   *n* pl. -S bidarka

BIDDABLE   *adj* obedient **BIDDABLY** *adv*

BIDDEN   past participle of bid

BIDDER   *n* pl. -S one that bids

BIDDING   *n* pl. -S a command

BIDDY   *n* pl. -DIES a hen

BIDE   *v* BIDED or BODE, BIDING, BIDES to wait

BIDENTAL   *adj* having two teeth

BIDER   *n* pl. -S one that bides

BIDET   *n* pl. -S a low basin used for washing

BIDING   present participle of bide

BIELD   *v* -ED, -ING, -S to shelter

BIENNALE   *n* pl. -S a biennial show

BIENNIAL   *n* pl. -S an event that occurs every two years

BIENNIUM   *n* pl. -NIA or -NIUMS a period of two years

BIER	*n* pl. -S a coffin stand
BIFACE	*n* pl. -S a stone tool having a cutting edge
BIFACIAL	*adj* having two faces
BIFF	*v* -ED, -ING, -S to hit
BIFFIN	*n* pl. -S a cooking apple
BIFFY	*n* pl. -FIES a toilet
BIFID	*adj* divided into two parts **BIFIDLY** *adv*
BIFIDITY	*n* pl. -TIES the state of being bifid
BIFILAR	*adj* having two threads
BIFLEX	*adj* bent in two places
BIFOCAL	*n* pl. -S a type of lens
BIFOLD	*adj* twofold
BIFORATE	*adj* having two perforations
BIFORKED	*adj* divided into two branches
BIFORM	*adj* having two forms
BIFORMED	*adj* biform
BIG	*adj* BIGGER, BIGGEST of considerable size
BIG	*n* pl. -S one of great importance
BIGAMIES	pl. of bigamy
BIGAMIST	*n* pl. -S one who commits bigamy
BIGAMOUS	*adj* guilty of bigamy
BIGAMY	*n* pl. -MIES the crime of being married to two people at once
BIGARADE	*n* pl. -S a citrus tree
BIGAROON	*n* pl. -S a type of cherry
BIGEMINY	*n* pl. -NIES the state of having a double pulse
BIGEYE	*n* pl. -S a marine fish
BIGFOOT	*n* pl. -FEET or -FOOTS a large hairy humanlike creature
BIGGER	comparative of big
BIGGEST	superlative of big
BIGGETY	*adj* biggity
BIGGIE	*n* pl. -S one that is big
BIGGIN	*n* pl. -S a house
BIGGING	*n* pl. -S biggin
BIGGISH	*adj* somewhat big
BIGGITY	*adj* conceited
BIGHEAD	*n* pl. -S a disease of animals
BIGHORN	*n* pl. -S a wild sheep
BIGHT	*v* -ED, -ING, -S to fasten with a loop of rope
BIGLY	*adv* in a big manner
BIGMOUTH	*n* pl. -S a talkative person
BIGNESS	*n* pl. -ES the state of being big
BIGNONIA	*n* pl. -S a climbing plant
BIGOT	*n* pl. -S a prejudiced person
BIGOTED	*adj* intolerant
BIGOTRY	*n* pl. -RIES prejudice
BIGWIG	*n* pl. -S an important person
BIHOURLY	*adj* occurring every two hours
BIJOU	*n* pl. -JOUX or -JOUS a jewel
BIJUGATE	*adj* two-paired
BIJUGOUS	*adj* bijugate
BIKE	*v* BIKED, BIKING, BIKES to bicycle
BIKER	*n* pl. -S one that bikes
BIKEWAY	*n* pl. -WAYS a route for bikes
BIKIE	*n* pl. -S biker
BIKING	present participle of bike
BIKINI	*n* pl. -S a type of bathing suit **BIKINIED** *adj*
BILABIAL	*n* pl. -S a sound articulated with both lips
BILANDER	*n* pl. -S a small ship
BILAYER	*n* pl. -S a film with two molecular layers
BILBERRY	*n* pl. -RIES an edible berry
BILBO	*n* pl. -BOS or -BOES a finely tempered sword
BILBOA	*n* pl. -S bilbo
BILE	*n* pl. -S a fluid secreted by the liver
BILGE	*v* BILGED, BILGING, BILGES to spring a leak
BILGY	*adj* BILGIER, BILGIEST smelling like seepage
BILIARY	*adj* pertaining to bile
BILINEAR	*adj* pertaining to two lines
BILIOUS	*adj* pertaining to bile
BILK	*v* -ED, -ING, -S to cheat
BILKER	*n* pl. -S one that bilks
BILL	*v* -ED, -ING, -S to present a statement of costs to **BILLABLE** *adj*
BILLBUG	*n* pl. -S a weevil
BILLER	*n* pl. -S one that bills
BILLET	*v* -ED, -ING, -S to lodge soldiers
BILLETER	*n* pl. -S one that billets
BILLFISH	*n* pl. -ES a fish with long, slender jaws

BILLFOLD	*n* pl. -S a wallet
BILLHEAD	*n* pl. -S a letterhead
BILLHOOK	*n* pl. -S a cutting tool
BILLIARD	*n* pl. -S a carom shot in billiards (a table game)
BILLIE	*n* pl. -S a comrade
BILLIES	pl. of billy
BILLING	*n* pl. -S the relative position in which a performer is listed
BILLION	*n* pl. -S a number
BILLON	*n* pl. -S an alloy of silver and copper
BILLOW	*v* -ED, -ING, -S to swell
BILLOWY	*adj* -LOWIER, -LOWIEST swelling; surging
BILLY	*n* pl. -LIES a short club
BILLYCAN	*n* pl. -S a pot for heating water
BILOBATE	*adj* having two lobes
BILOBED	*adj* bilobate
BILSTED	*n* pl. -S a hardwood tree
BILTONG	*n* pl. -S dried and cured meat
BIMA	*n* pl. -S bema
BIMAH	*n* pl. -S bema
BIMANOUS	*adj* two-handed
BIMANUAL	*adj* done with two hands
BIMBO	*n* pl. -BOS or -BOES a disreputable person
BIMENSAL	*adj* occurring every two months
BIMESTER	*n* pl. -S a two-month period
BIMETAL	*n* pl. -S something composed of two metals
BIMETHYL	*n* pl. -S ethane
BIMODAL	*adj* having two statistical modes
BIMORPH	*n* pl. -S a device consisting of two crystals cemented together
BIN	*v* BINNED, BINNING, BINS to store in a large receptacle
BINAL	*adj* twofold
BINARY	*n* pl. -RIES a combination of two things
BINATE	*adj* growing in pairs **BINATELY** *adv*
BINAURAL	*adj* hearing with both ears
BIND	*v* BOUND, BINDING, BINDS to tie or secure **BINDABLE** *adj*
BINDER	*n* pl. -S one that binds
BINDERY	*n* pl. -ERIES a place where books are bound
BINDI	*n* pl. -S a dot worn on the forehead by women in India
BINDING	*n* pl. -S the cover and fastenings of a book
BINDLE	*n* pl. -S a bundle
BINDWEED	*n* pl. -S a twining plant
BINE	*n* pl. -S a twining plant stem
BINGE	*v* BINGED, BINGEING or BINGING, BINGES to indulge in something without restraint
BINGER	*n* pl. -S one that binges
BINGO	*n* pl. -GOS a game of chance
BINIT	*n* pl. -S a unit of computer information
BINNACLE	*n* pl. -S a compass stand
BINNED	past tense of bin
BINNING	present participle of bin
BINOCLE	*n* pl. -S a binocular
BINOCS	*n/pl* binoculars
BINOMIAL	*n* pl. -S an algebraic expression
BINT	*n* pl. -S a woman
BIO	*n* pl. BIOS a biography
BIOASSAY	*v* -ED, -ING, -S to test a substance (as a drug)
BIOCHIP	*n* pl. -S a hypothetical computer component that uses proteins to store or process data
BIOCIDE	*n* pl. -S a substance destructive to living organisms **BIOCIDAL** *adj*
BIOCLEAN	*adj* free of harmful organisms
BIOCYCLE	*n* pl. -S a life-supporting region
BIOETHIC	*adj* pertaining to ethical questions arising from advances in biology
BIOGAS	*n* pl. -GASES or -GASSES fuel gas produced by organic waste
BIOGEN	*n* pl. -S a hypothetical protein molecule
BIOGENIC	*adj* produced by living organisms
BIOGENY	*n* pl. -NIES the development of life from preexisting life
BIOHERM	*n* pl. -S a mass of marine fossils
BIOLOGIC	*n* pl. -S a drug obtained from an organic source
BIOLOGY	*n* pl. -GIES the science of life
BIOLYSIS	*n* pl. -YSES death **BIOLYTIC** *adj*
BIOMASS	*n* pl. -ES an amount of living matter
BIOME	*n* pl. -S an ecological community

BIOMETRY *n* pl. -TRIES the statistical study of biological data

BIONICS *n/pl* a science joining biology and electronics **BIONIC** *adj*

BIONOMY *n* pl. -MIES ecology **BIONOMIC** *adj*

BIONT *n* pl. -S a living organism **BIONTIC** *adj*

BIOPIC *n* pl. -S a biographical movie

BIOPLASM *n* pl. -S living matter

BIOPSIC *adj* pertaining to the examination of living tissue

BIOPSY *v* -SIED, -SYING, -SIES to examine living tissue

BIOPTIC *adj* biopsic

BIOSCOPE *n* pl. -S an early movie projector

BIOSCOPY *n* pl. -PIES a type of medical examination

BIOTA *n* pl. -S flora and fauna

BIOTECH *n* pl. -S applied biology

BIOTIC *adj* pertaining to life

BIOTICAL *adj* biotic

BIOTICS *n/pl* a life science

BIOTIN *n* pl. -S a B vitamin

BIOTITE *n* pl. -S a form of mica **BIOTITIC** *adj*

BIOTOPE *n* pl. -S a stable habitat

BIOTOXIN *n* pl. -S poison made by a plant or animal

BIOTRON *n* pl. -S a climate control chamber

BIOTYPE *n* pl. -S a group of genetically similar organisms **BIOTYPIC** *adj*

BIOVULAR *adj* derived from two ova

BIPACK *n* pl. -S a pair of films

BIPAROUS *adj* producing offspring in pairs

BIPARTED *adj* having two parts

BIPARTY *adj* of two parties

BIPED *n* pl. -S a two-footed animal **BIPEDAL** *adj*

BIPHASIC *adj* having two phases

BIPHENYL *n* pl. -S a hydrocarbon

BIPLANE *n/pl* a type of airplane

BIPOD *n* pl. -S a two-legged support

BIPOLAR *adj* having two poles

BIRACIAL *adj* having members of two races

BIRADIAL *adj* having dual symmetry

BIRAMOSE *adj* biramous

BIRAMOUS *adj* divided into two branches

BIRCH *v* -ED, -ING, -ES to whip

BIRCHEN *adj* made of birch wood

BIRD *v* -ED, -ING, -S to hunt birds (winged, warm-blooded vertebrates)

BIRDBATH *n* pl. -S a bath for birds

BIRDCAGE *n* pl. -S a cage for birds

BIRDCALL *n* pl. -S the call of a bird

BIRDER *n* pl. -S a bird hunter

BIRDFARM *n* pl. -S an aircraft carrier

BIRDIE *v* BIRDIED, BIRDIEING, BIRDIES to shoot in one stroke under par in golf

BIRDING *n* pl. -S bird-watching

BIRDLIKE *adj* resembling a bird

BIRDLIME *v* -LIMED, -LIMING, -LIMES to trap small birds

BIRDMAN *n* pl. -MEN one who keeps birds

BIRDSEED *n* pl. -S a mixture of seeds used for feeding birds

BIRDSEYE *n* pl. -S a flowering plant

BIRDSHOT *n* pl. -S small shot for shooting birds

BIRDSONG *n* pl. -S the song of a bird

BIREME *n* pl. -S an ancient galley

BIRETTA *n* pl. -S a cap worn by clergymen

BIRK *n* pl. -S a birch tree

BIRKIE *n* pl. -S a lively person

BIRL *v* -ED, -ING, -S to rotate a floating log

BIRLE *v* BIRLED, BIRLING, BIRLES to carouse

BIRLER *n* pl. -S one that birls

BIRLING *n* pl. -S a lumberjack's game

BIRR *v* -ED, -ING, -S to make a whirring noise

BIRR *n* pl. BIRROTCH a monetary unit of Ethiopia

BIRRETTA *n* pl. -S biretta

BIRSE *n* pl. -S a bristle

BIRTH *v* -ED, -ING, -S to originate

BIRTHDAY *n* pl. -DAYS an anniversary of a birth

BIS *adv* twice

BISCUIT *n* pl. -S a small cake of shortened bread

BISE *n* pl. -S a cold wind

BISECT *v* -ED, -ING, -S to cut into two parts

BISECTOR	*n* pl. -S something that bisects
BISEXUAL	*n* pl. -S one who is attracted to both sexes
BISHOP	*v* -ED, -ING, -S to appoint as a bishop (the head of a diocese)
BISK	*n* pl. -S bisque
BISMUTH	*n* pl. -S a metallic element
BISNAGA	*n* pl. -S a type of cactus
BISON	*n* pl. -S an ox-like animal
BISQUE	*n* pl. -S a thick soup
BISTATE	*adj* pertaining to two states
BISTER	*n* pl. -S a brown pigment **BISTERED** *adj*
BISTORT	*n* pl. -S a perennial herb with roots used as astringents
BISTOURY	*n* pl. -RIES a surgical knife
BISTRE	*n* pl. -S bister **BISTRED** *adj*
BISTRO	*n* pl. -TROS a small tavern **BISTROIC** *adj*
BIT	*v* BITTED, BITTING, BITS to restrain
BITABLE	*adj* capable of being bitten
BITCH	*v* -ED, -ING, -ES to complain
BITCHERY	*n* pl. -ERIES bitchy behavior
BITCHY	*adj* BITCHIER, BITCHIEST malicious **BITCHILY** *adv*
BITE	*v* BIT, BITTEN, BITING, BITES to seize with the teeth **BITEABLE** *adj*
BITER	*n* pl. -S one that bites
BITEWING	*n* pl. -S a dental X-ray film
BITING	present participle of bite
BITINGLY	*adv* sarcastically
BITSTOCK	*n* pl. -S a brace on a drill
BITSY	*adj* tiny
BITT	*v* -ED, -ING, -S to secure a cable
BITTED	past tense of bit
BITTEN	a past participle of bite
BITTER	*adj* -TERER, -TEREST having a disagreeable taste **BITTERLY** *adv*
BITTER	*v* -ED, -ING, -S to make bitter
BITTERN	*n* pl. -S a wading bird
BITTIER	comparative of bitty
BITTIEST	superlative of bitty
BITTING	*n* pl. -S an indentation in a key
BITTOCK	*n* pl. -S a small amount
BITTY	*adj* -TIER, -TIEST fragmented

BITUMEN	*n* pl. -S an asphalt
BIUNIQUE	*adj* being a type of correspondence between two sets
BIVALENT	*n* pl. -S a pair of chromosomes
BIVALVE	*n* pl. -S a bivalved mollusk
BIVALVED	*adj* having a two-valved shell
BIVINYL	*n* pl. -S a flammable gas used in making synthetic rubber
BIVOUAC	*v* -OUACKED, -OUACKING, -OUACKS or -OUACS to make a camp
BIWEEKLY	*n* pl. -LIES a publication issued every two weeks
BIYEARLY	*adj* occurring every two years
BIZ	*n* pl. BIZZES business
BIZARRE	*n* pl. -S a strangely striped flower
BIZE	*n* pl. -S bise
BIZNAGA	*n* pl. -S bisnaga
BIZONE	*n* pl. -S two combined zones **BIZONAL** *adj*
BLAB	*v* BLABBED, BLABBING, BLABS to talk idly
BLABBER	*v* -ED, -ING, -S to blab
BLABBY	*adj* talkative
BLACK	*adj* BLACKER, BLACKEST being of the darkest color
BLACK	*v* -ED, -ING, -S to make black
BLACKBOY	*n* pl. -BOYS an Australian plant
BLACKCAP	*n* pl. -S a small European bird
BLACKEN	*v* -ED, -ING, -S to make black
BLACKFIN	*n* pl. -S a food fish
BLACKFLY	*n* pl. -FLIES a biting fly
BLACKGUM	*n* pl. -S a tupelo
BLACKING	*n* pl. -S black shoe polish
BLACKISH	*adj* somewhat black
BLACKLEG	*n* pl. -S a cattle disease
BLACKLY	*adv* in a black manner
BLACKOUT	*n* pl. -S a power failure
BLACKTOP	*v* -TOPPED, -TOPPING, -TOPS to pave with asphalt
BLADDER	*n* pl. -S a saclike receptacle **BLADDERY** *adj*
BLADE	*n* pl. -S a cutting edge **BLADED** *adj*
BLAE	*adj* bluish-black
BLAH	*n* pl. -S nonsense
BLAIN	*n* pl. -S a blister

BLAM	*n* pl. -S the sound of a gunshot	**BLATTING**	present participle of blat
BLAMABLE	*adj* being at fault **BLAMABLY** *adv*	**BLAUBOK**	*n* pl. -S an extinct antelope
BLAME	*v* BLAMED, BLAMING, BLAMES to find fault with	**BLAW**	*v* BLAWED, BLAWN, BLAWING, BLAWS to blow
BLAMEFUL	*adj* blamable	**BLAZE**	*v* BLAZED, BLAZING, BLAZES to burn brightly
BLAMER	*n* pl. -S one that blames	**BLAZER**	*n* pl. -S a lightweight jacket
BLAMING	present participle of blame	**BLAZON**	*v* -ED, -ING, -S to proclaim
BLANCH	*v* -ED, -ING, -ES to whiten	**BLAZONER**	*n* pl. -S one that blazons
BLANCHER	*n* pl. -S a whitener	**BLAZONRY**	*n* pl. -RIES a great display
BLAND	*adj* BLANDER, BLANDEST soothing **BLANDLY** *adv*	**BLEACH**	*v* -ED, -ING, -ES to whiten
BLANDISH	*v* -ED, -ING, -ES to coax by flattery	**BLEACHER**	*n* pl. -S one that bleaches
BLANK	*adj* BLANKER, BLANKEST empty	**BLEAK**	*adj* BLEAKER, BLEAKEST dreary
BLANK	*v* -ED, -ING, -S to delete	**BLEAK**	*n* pl. -S a freshwater fish
BLANKET	*v* -ED, -ING, -S to cover uniformly	**BLEAKISH**	*adj* somewhat bleak
BLANKLY	*adv* in a blank manner	**BLEAKLY**	*adv* in a bleak manner
BLARE	*v* BLARED, BLARING, BLARES to sound loudly	**BLEAR**	*v* -ED, -ING, -S to dim
BLARNEY	*v* -NEYED, -NEYING, -NEYS to beguile with flattery	**BLEARY**	*adj* BLEARIER, BLEARIEST dimmed **BLEARILY** *adv*
BLASE	*adj* indifferent	**BLEAT**	*v* -ED, -ING, -S to utter the cry of a sheep
BLAST	*v* -ED, -ING, -S to use an explosive	**BLEATER**	*n* pl. -S one that bleats
BLASTEMA	*n* pl. -MAS or -MATA a region of embryonic cells	**BLEB**	*n* pl. -S a blister **BLEBBY** *adj*
BLASTER	*n* pl. -S one that blasts	**BLEED**	*v* BLED, BLEEDING, BLEEDS to lose blood
BLASTIE	*n* pl. -S a dwarf	**BLEEDER**	*n* pl. -S one that bleeds
BLASTIER	comparative of blasty	**BLEEDING**	*n* pl. -S the act of losing blood
BLASTIEST	superlative of blasty	**BLEEP**	*v* -ED, -ING, -S to blip
BLASTING	*n* pl. -S the act of one that blasts	**BLELLUM**	*n* pl. -S a babbler
BLASTOFF	*n* pl. -S the launching of a rocket	**BLEMISH**	*v* -ED, -ING, -ES to mar
BLASTOMA	*n* pl. -MAS or -MATA a type of tumor	**BLENCH**	*v* -ED, -ING, -ES to flinch
		BLENCHER	*n* pl. -S one that blenches
BLASTULA	*n* pl. -LAS or -LAE an early embryo	**BLEND**	*v* BLENDED or BLENT, BLENDING, BLENDS to mix smoothly and inseparably together
BLASTY	*adj* BLASTIER, BLASTIEST gusty		
BLAT	*v* BLATTED, BLATTING, BLATS to bleat	**BLENDE**	*n* pl. -S a shiny mineral
		BLENDER	*n* pl. -S one that blends
BLATANCY	*n* pl. -CIES something blatant	**BLENNY**	*n* pl. -NIES a marine fish
BLATANT	*adj* obvious	**BLENT**	a past tense of blend
BLATE	*adj* timid	**BLESBOK**	*n* pl. -S a large antelope
BLATHER	*v* -ED, -ING, -S to talk foolishly	**BLESBUCK**	*n* pl. -S blesbok
BLATTED	past tense of blat	**BLESS**	*v* BLESSED or BLEST, BLESSING, BLESSES to sanctify
BLATTER	*v* -ED, -ING, -S to chatter	**BLESSED**	*adj* -EDER, -EDEST holy
		BLESSER	*n* pl. -S one that blesses

BLESSING	*n* pl. -S a prayer
BLEST	a past tense of bless
BLET	*n* pl. -S a decay of fruit
BLETHER	*v* -ED, -ING, -S to blather
BLEW	past tense of blow
BLIGHT	*v* -ED, -ING, -S to cause decay
BLIGHTER	*n* pl. -S one that blights
BLIGHTY	*n* pl. BLIGHTIES a wound causing one to be sent home to England
BLIMEY	*interj* — used as an expression of surprise
BLIMP	*n* pl. -S a nonrigid aircraft **BLIMPISH** *adj*
BLIMY	*interj* blimey
BLIN	*n* pl. BLINI or BLINIS a blintze
BLIND	*adj* BLINDER, BLINDEST sightless
BLIND	*v* -ED, -ING, -S to make sightless
BLINDAGE	*n* pl. -S a protective screen
BLINDER	*n* pl. -S an obstruction to sight
BLINDLY	*adv* in a blind manner
BLINI	a pl. of blin
BLINIS	a pl. of blin
BLINK	*v* -ED, -ING, -S to open and shut the eyes
BLINKARD	*n* pl. -S one who habitually blinks
BLINKER	*v* -ED, -ING, -S to put blinders on
BLINTZ	*n* pl. -ES blintze
BLINTZE	*n* pl. -S a thin pancake
BLIP	*v* BLIPPED, BLIPPING, BLIPS to remove sound from a recording
BLISS	*v* -ED, -ING, -ES to experience or produce ecstasy
BLISSFUL	*adj* very happy
BLISTER	*v* -ED, -ING, -S to cause blisters (skin swellings)
BLISTERY	*adj* having blisters
BLITE	*n* pl. -S an annual herb
BLITHE	*adj* BLITHER, BLITHEST merry **BLITHELY** *adv*
BLITHER	*v* -ED, -ING, -S to blather
BLITZ	*v* -ED, -ING, -ES to subject to a sudden attack
BLIZZARD	*n* pl. -S a heavy snowstorm
BLOAT	*v* -ED, -ING, -S to swell
BLOATER	*n* pl. -S a smoked herring
BLOB	*v* BLOBBED, BLOBBING, BLOBS to splotch
BLOC	*n* pl. -S a coalition
BLOCK	*v* -ED, -ING, -S to obstruct
BLOCKADE	*v* -ADED, -ADING, -ADES to block
BLOCKAGE	*n* pl. -S the act of blocking
BLOCKER	*n* pl. -S one that blocks
BLOCKISH	*adj* blocky
BLOCKY	*adj* BLOCKIER, BLOCKIEST short and stout
BLOKE	*n* pl. -S a fellow
BLOND	*adj* BLONDER, BLONDEST light-colored
BLOND	*n* pl. -S a blond person
BLONDE	*n* pl. -S blond
BLONDISH	*adj* somewhat blond
BLOOD	*v* -ED, -ING, -S to stain with blood (the fluid circulated by the heart)
BLOODFIN	*n* pl. -S a freshwater fish
BLOODIED	past tense of bloody
BLOODIER	comparative of bloody
BLOODIES	present 3d person sing. of bloody
BLOODIEST	superlative of bloody
BLOODILY	*adv* in a bloody manner
BLOODING	*n* pl. -S a fox hunting ceremony
BLOODRED	*adj* of the color of blood
BLOODY	*adj* BLOODIER, BLOODIEST stained with blood
BLOODY	*v* BLOODIED, BLOODYING, BLOODIES to make bloody
BLOOEY	*adj* being out of order
BLOOIE	*adj* blooey
BLOOM	*v* -ED, -ING, -S to bear flowers
BLOOMER	*n* pl. -S a blooming plant
BLOOMERY	*n* pl. -ERIES a furnace for smelting iron
BLOOMY	*adj* BLOOMIER, BLOOMIEST covered with flowers
BLOOP	*v* -ED, -ING, -S to hit a short fly ball
BLOOPER	*n* pl. -S a public blunder
BLOSSOM	*v* -ED, -ING, -S to bloom
BLOSSOMY	*adj* having blossoms
BLOT	*v* BLOTTED, BLOTTING, BLOTS to spot or stain

BLOTCH	*v* -ED, -ING, -ES to mark with large spots	**BLOWUP**	*n* pl. -S an explosion
BLOTCHY	*adj* BLOTCHIER, BLOTCHIEST blotched	**BLOWY**	*adj* BLOWIER, BLOWIEST windy
		BLOWZED	*adj* blowzy
BLOTLESS	*adj* spotless	**BLOWZY**	*adj* -ZIER, -ZIEST blowsy **BLOWZILY** *adv*
BLOTTED	past tense of blot		
BLOTTER	*n* pl. -S a piece of ink-absorbing paper	**BLUB**	*v* BLUBBED, BLUBBING, BLUBS to blubber
BLOTTIER	comparative of blotty	**BLUBBER**	*v* -ED, -ING, -S to weep noisily
BLOTTIEST	superlative of blotty	**BLUBBERY**	*adj* fat; swollen
BLOTTING	present participle of blot	**BLUCHER**	*n* pl. -S a half boot
BLOTTO	*adj* drunk	**BLUDGEON**	*v* -ED, -ING, -S to hit with a club
BLOTTY	*adj* -TIER, -TIEST spotty	**BLUDGER**	*n* pl. -S a loafer or shirker
BLOUSE	*v* BLOUSED, BLOUSING, BLOUSES to hang loosely	**BLUE**	*adj* BLUER, BLUEST having the color of the clear sky
BLOUSON	*n* pl. -S a woman's garment	**BLUE**	*v* BLUED, BLUEING or BLUING, BLUES to make blue
BLOUSY	*adj* BLOUSIER, BLOUSIEST blowsy **BLOUSILY** *adv*	**BLUEBALL**	*n* pl. -S a medicinal herb
BLOVIATE	*v* -ATED, -ATING, -ATES to speak pompously	**BLUEBELL**	*n* pl. -S a flowering plant
		BLUEBILL	*n* pl. -S the scaup duck
BLOW	*v* BLEW, BLOWN, BLOWING, BLOWS to drive or impel by a current of air	**BLUEBIRD**	*n* pl. -S a songbird
		BLUEBOOK	*n* pl. -S an examination booklet
BLOW	*v* BLEW, BLOWED, BLOWING, BLOWS to damn	**BLUECAP**	*n* pl. -S a flowering plant
		BLUECOAT	*n* pl. -S a police officer
BLOWBACK	*n* pl. -S an escape of gases	**BLUED**	past tense of blue
BLOWBALL	*n* pl. -S a fluffy seed ball	**BLUEFIN**	*n* pl. -S a large tuna
BLOWBY	*n* pl. -BYS leakage of exhaust fumes	**BLUEFISH**	*n* pl. -ES a marine fish
		BLUEGILL	*n* pl. -S an edible sunfish
BLOWDOWN	*n* pl. -S a tree blown down by the wind	**BLUEGUM**	*n* pl. -S a timber tree
		BLUEHEAD	*n* pl. -S a marine fish
BLOWER	*n* pl. -S one that blows	**BLUEING**	*n* pl. -S bluing
BLOWFISH	*n* pl. -ES a marine fish	**BLUEISH**	*adj* bluish
BLOWFLY	*n* pl. -FLIES a type of fly	**BLUEJACK**	*n* pl. -S an oak tree
BLOWGUN	*n* pl. -S a tube through which darts may be blown	**BLUEJAY**	*n* pl. -JAYS a corvine bird
		BLUELINE	*n* pl. -S a line that divides a hockey rink
BLOWHARD	*n* pl. -S a braggart		
BLOWHOLE	*n* pl. -S an air or gas vent	**BLUELY**	*adv* in a blue manner
BLOWIER	comparative of blowy	**BLUENESS**	*n* pl. -ES the state of being blue
BLOWIEST	superlative of blowy	**BLUENOSE**	*n* pl. -S a puritanical person
BLOWN	past participle of blow	**BLUER**	comparative of blue
BLOWOFF	*n* pl. -S the expelling of gas	**BLUESIER**	comparative of bluesy
BLOWOUT	*n* pl. -S a sudden rupture	**BLUESIEST**	superlative of bluesy
BLOWPIPE	*n* pl. -S a blowgun	**BLUESMAN**	*n* pl. -MEN one who plays the blues
BLOWSED	*adj* blowsy		
BLOWSY	*adj* -SIER, -SIEST slovenly **BLOWSILY** *adv*	**BLUEST**	superlative of blue
BLOWTUBE	*n* pl. -S a blowgun	**BLUESTEM**	*n* pl. -S a prairie grass

BLUESY	*adj* BLUESIER, BLUESIEST resembling the blues (a musical form)
BLUET	*n* pl. -S a meadow flower
BLUETICK	*n* pl. -S a hunting dog
BLUEWEED	*n* pl. -S a bristly weed
BLUEWOOD	*n* pl. -S a shrub
BLUEY	*n* pl. BLUEYS a bag of clothing carried in travel
BLUFF	*v* -ED, -ING, -S to mislead
BLUFF	*adj* BLUFFER, BLUFFEST having a broad front **BLUFFLY** *adv*
BLUFFER	*n* pl. -S one that bluffs
BLUING	*n* pl. -S a fabric coloring
BLUISH	*adj* somewhat blue
BLUME	*v* BLUMED, BLUMING, BLUMES to blossom
BLUNDER	*v* -ED, -ING, -S to make a mistake
BLUNGE	*v* BLUNGED, BLUNGING, BLUNGES to mix clay with water
BLUNGER	*n* pl. -S one that blunges
BLUNT	*adj* BLUNTER, BLUNTEST not sharp or pointed **BLUNTLY** *adv*
BLUNT	*v* -ED, -ING, -S to make blunt
BLUR	*v* BLURRED, BLURRING, BLURS to make unclear
BLURB	*v* -ED, -ING, -S to praise in a publicity notice
BLURRY	*adj* -RIER, -RIEST unclear **BLURRILY** *adv*
BLURT	*v* -ED, -ING, -S to speak abruptly
BLURTER	*n* pl. -S one that blurts
BLUSH	*v* -ED, -ING, -ES to become red
BLUSHER	*n* pl. -S one that blushes
BLUSHFUL	*adj* of a red color
BLUSTER	*v* -ED, -ING, -S to blow violently
BLUSTERY	*adj* windy
BLYPE	*n* pl. -S a shred
BO	*n* pl. BOS a pal
BOA	*n* pl. -S a large snake
BOAR	*n* pl. -S a male pig
BOARD	*v* -ED, -ING, -S to take meals for a fixed price
BOARDER	*n* pl. -S one that boards
BOARDING	*n* pl. -S a surface of wooden boards
BOARDMAN	*n* pl. -MEN a board member

BOARFISH	*n* pl. -ES a marine fish
BOARISH	*adj* swinish; coarse
BOART	*n* pl. -S bort
BOAST	*v* -ED, -ING, -S to brag
BOASTER	*n* pl. -S one that boasts
BOASTFUL	*adj* given to boasting
BOAT	*v* -ED, -ING, -S to travel by boat (watercraft) **BOATABLE** *adj*
BOATBILL	*n* pl. -S a wading bird
BOATEL	*n* pl. -S a waterside hotel
BOATER	*n* pl. -S one that boats
BOATFUL	*n* pl. -S as much as a boat can hold
BOATHOOK	*n* pl. -S a pole with a metal hook for use aboard a boat
BOATING	*n* pl. -S the sport of traveling by boat
BOATLIKE	*adj* resembling a boat
BOATLOAD	*n* pl. -S the amount that a boat holds
BOATMAN	*n* pl. -MEN one who works on boats
BOATSMAN	*n* pl. -MEN boatman
BOATYARD	*n* pl. -S a marina
BOB	*v* BOBBED, BOBBING, BOBS to move up and down
BOBBER	*n* pl. -S one that bobs
BOBBERY	*n* pl. -BERIES a disturbance
BOBBIES	pl. of bobby
BOBBIN	*n* pl. -S a thread holder
BOBBINET	*n* pl. -S a machine-made net
BOBBING	present participle of bob
BOBBLE	*v* -BLED, -BLING, -BLES to fumble
BOBBY	*n* pl. -BIES a police officer
BOBCAT	*n* pl. -S a lynx
BOBECHE	*n* pl. -S a glass collar on a candle holder
BOBOLINK	*n* pl. -S a songbird
BOBSLED	*v* -SLEDDED, -SLEDDING, -SLEDS to ride on a bobsled (a racing sled)
BOBSTAY	*n* pl. -STAYS a steadying rope
BOBTAIL	*v* -ED, -ING, -S to cut short
BOBWHITE	*n* pl. -S a game bird
BOCACCIO	*n* pl. -CIOS a rockfish
BOCCE	*n* pl. -S boccie
BOCCI	*n* pl. -S boccie

BOCCIA   *n* pl. -S boccie

BOCCIE   *n* pl. -S an Italian bowling game

BOCK   *n* pl. -S a dark beer

BOD   *n* pl. -S a body

BODE   *v* BODED, BODING, BODES to be an omen of

BODEGA   *n* pl. -S a grocery store

BODEMENT   *n* pl. -S an omen

BODHRAN   *n* pl. -S an Irish drum

BODICE   *n* pl. -S a corset

BODIED   past tense of body

BODIES   present 3d person sing. of body

BODILESS   *adj* lacking material form

BODILY   *adj* of the body

BODING   *n* pl. -S an omen

BODINGLY   *adv* ominously

BODKIN   *n* pl. -S a sharp instrument

BODY   *v* BODIED, BODYING, BODIES to give form to

BODYSUIT   *n* pl. -S a one-piece garment for the torso

BODYSURF   *v* -ED, -ING, -S to ride a wave without a surfboard

BODYWORK   *n* pl. -S a vehicle body

BOEHMITE   *n* pl. -S a mineral

BOFF   *n* pl. -S a hearty laugh

BOFFIN   *n* pl. -S a scientific expert

BOFFO   *n* pl. -FOS a boff

BOFFOLA   *n* pl. -S a boff

BOG   *v* BOGGED, BOGGING, BOGS to impede

BOGAN   *n* pl. -S a backwater or tributary

BOGBEAN   *n* pl. -S a marsh plant

BOGEY   *v* -GEYED, -GEYING, -GEYS to shoot in one stroke over par in golf

BOGEYMAN   *n* pl. -MEN a terrifying creature

BOGGED   past tense of bog

BOGGIER   comparative of boggy

BOGGIEST   superlative of boggy

BOGGING   present participle of bog

BOGGISH   *adj* boggy

BOGGLE   *v* -GLED, -GLING, -GLES to hesitate

BOGGLER   *n* pl. -S one that causes another to boggle

BOGGY   *adj* -GIER, -GIEST marshy

BOGIE   *n* pl. -S bogy

BOGIES   pl. of bogy

BOGLE   *n* pl. -S a bogy

BOGUS   *adj* not genuine; fake

BOGWOOD   *n* pl. -S preserved tree wood

BOGY   *n* pl. -GIES a goblin

BOGYISM   *n* pl. -S behavior characteristic of a bogy

BOGYMAN   *n* pl. -MEN bogeyman

BOHEA   *n* pl. -S a black tea

BOHEMIA   *n* pl. -S a community of bohemians

BOHEMIAN   *n* pl. -S an unconventional person

BOHUNK   *n* pl. -S an unskilled laborer

BOIL   *v* -ED, -ING, -S to vaporize liquid
BOILABLE *adj*

BOILER   *n* pl. -S a vessel for boiling

BOILOFF   *n* pl. -S the vaporization of liquid

BOING   *interj* — used to express the sound of reverberation or vibration

BOISERIE   *n* pl. -S wood paneling on a wall

BOITE   *n* pl. -S a nightclub

BOLA   *n* pl. -S a throwing weapon

BOLAR   *adj* pertaining to bole

BOLAS   *n* pl. -ES bola

BOLD   *adj* BOLDER, BOLDEST daring
BOLDLY *adv*

BOLD   *n* pl. -S a thick type

BOLDFACE   *v* -FACED, -FACING, -FACES to print in thick type

BOLDNESS   *n* pl. -ES the quality of being bold

BOLE   *n* pl. -S a fine clay

BOLERO   *n* pl. -ROS a lively Spanish dance

BOLETE   *n* pl. -S boletus

BOLETUS   *n* pl. -TUSES or -TI a fungus

BOLIDE   *n* pl. -S an exploding meteor

BOLIVAR   *n* pl. -S or -ES a monetary unit of Venezuela

BOLIVIA   *n* pl. -S a soft fabric

BOLL   *v* -ED, -ING, -S to form pods

BOLLARD   *n* pl. -S a thick post on a ship or wharf

BOLLIX   *v* -ED, -ING, -ES to bungle

BOLLOX   *v* -ED, -ING, -ES to bollix

BOLLWORM *n* pl. -S the larva of a certain moth

BOLO *n* pl. -LOS a machete

BOLOGNA *n* pl. -S a seasoned sausage

BOLONEY *n* pl. -NEYS bologna

BOLSHIE *n* pl. -S a Bolshevik

BOLSHY *n* pl. -SHIES bolshie

BOLSON *n* pl. -S a flat arid valley

BOLSTER *v* -ED, -ING, -S to support

BOLT *v* -ED, -ING, -S to sift

BOLTER *n* pl. -S a sifting machine

BOLTHEAD *n* pl. -S a matrass

BOLTHOLE *n* pl. -S a place or way of escape

BOLTONIA *n* pl. -S a perennial herb

BOLTROPE *n* pl. -S a rope sewn to a sail

BOLUS *n* pl. -ES a large pill

BOMB *v* -ED, -ING, -S to attack with bombs (explosive projectiles)

BOMBARD *v* -ED, -ING, -S to bomb

BOMBAST *n* pl. -S pompous language

BOMBAX *adj* pertaining to a family of tropical trees

BOMBE *n* pl. -S a frozen dessert

BOMBER *n* pl. -S one that bombs

BOMBESIN *n* pl. -S a combination of amino acids

BOMBING *n* pl. -S an attack with bombs

BOMBLOAD *n* pl. -S the quantity of bombs being carried

BOMBYCID *n* pl. -S a moth

BOMBYX *n* pl. -ES a silkworm

BONACI *n* pl. -S an edible fish

BONANZA *n* pl. -S a rich mine

BONBON *n* pl. -S a sugared candy

BOND *v* -ED, -ING, -S to join together **BONDABLE** *adj*

BONDAGE *n* pl. -S slavery

BONDER *n* pl. -S one that bonds

BONDING *n* pl. -S the formation of a close personal relationship

BONDMAID *n* pl. -S a female slave

BONDMAN *n* pl. -MEN a male slave

BONDSMAN *n* pl. -MEN bondman

BONDUC *n* pl. -S a prickly seed

BONE *v* BONED, BONING, BONES to debone

BONEFISH *n* pl. -ES a slender marine fish

BONEHEAD *n* pl. -S a stupid person

BONELESS *adj* having no bones (hard connective tissue)

BONEMEAL *n* pl. -S fertilizer or feed made from crushed bone

BONER *n* pl. -S a blunder

BONESET *n* pl. -S a perennial herb

BONEY *adj* BONIER, BONIEST bony

BONEYARD *n* pl. -S a junkyard

BONFIRE *n* pl. -S an open fire

BONG *v* -ED, -ING, -S to make a deep, ringing sound

BONGO *n* pl. -GOS or -GOES a small drum

BONGOIST *n* pl. -S a bongo player

BONHOMIE *n* pl. -S friendliness

BONIER comparative of bony or boney

BONIEST superlative of bony or boney

BONIFACE *n* pl. -S an innkeeper

BONINESS *n* pl. -ES the state of being bony

BONING present participle of bone

BONITA *n* pl. -S bonito

BONITO *n* pl. -TOS or -TOES a marine food fish

BONK *v* -ED, -ING, -S to hit on the head with a hollow blow

BONKERS *adj* crazy

BONNE *n* pl. -S a housemaid

BONNET *v* -ED, -ING, -S to provide with a bonnet (a type of hat)

BONNIE *adj* bonny

BONNOCK *n* pl. -S bannock

BONNY *adj* -NIER, -NIEST pretty **BONNILY** *adv*

BONSAI *n* pl. BONSAI a potted shrub that has been dwarfed

BONSPELL *n* pl. -S bonspiel

BONSPIEL *n* pl. -S a curling match or tournament

BONTEBOK *n* pl. -S an antelope

BONUS *n* pl. -ES an additional payment

BONY *adj* BONIER, BONIEST full of bones

BONZE *n* pl. -S a Buddhist monk

BONZER *adj* very good

BOO *v* -ED, -ING, -S to cry "boo"

BOOB *v* -ED, -ING, -S to make a foolish mistake

BOOBISH	*adj* doltish
BOOBOO	*n* pl. -BOOS a mistake
BOOBY	*n* pl. -BIES a dolt
BOODLE	*v* -DLED, -DLING, -DLES to take bribes
BOODLER	*n* pl. -S one that boodles
BOOGER	*n* pl. -S a bogeyman
BOOGEY	*v* -GEYED, -GEYING, -GEYS boogie
BOOGIE	*v* -GIED, -GYING, -GIES to dance to rock music
BOOGY	*v* -GIED, -GYING, -GIES boogie
BOOGYMAN	*n* pl. -MEN bogeyman
BOOHOO	*v* -ED, -ING, -S to weep noisily
BOOK	*v* -ED, -ING, -S to engage services **BOOKABLE** *adj*
BOOKCASE	*n* pl. -S a case which holds books (literary volumes)
BOOKEND	*n* pl. -S a support for a row of books
BOOKER	*n* pl. -S one that books
BOOKFUL	*n* pl. -S as much as a book can hold
BOOKIE	*n* pl. -S a bet taker
BOOKING	*n* pl. -S an engagement
BOOKISH	*adj* pertaining to books
BOOKLET	*n* pl. -S a small book
BOOKLICE	*n/pl* wingless insects that damage books
BOOKLORE	*n* pl. -S book learning
BOOKMAN	*n* pl. -MEN a scholar
BOOKMARK	*n* pl. -S a marker for finding a place in a book
BOOKRACK	*n* pl. -S a support for an open book
BOOKREST	*n* pl. -S a bookrack
BOOKSHOP	*n* pl. -S a store where books are sold
BOOKWORM	*n* pl. -S an avid book reader
BOOM	*v* -ED, -ING, -S to make a deep, resonant sound
BOOMBOX	*n* pl. -ES a portable radio and tape or compact disc player
BOOMER	*n* pl. -S one that booms
BOOMIER	comparative of boomy
BOOMIEST	superlative of boomy
BOOMKIN	*n* pl. -S a bumkin
BOOMLET	*n* pl. -S a small increase in prosperity
BOOMTOWN	*n* pl. -S a prospering town
BOOMY	*adj* BOOMIER, BOOMIEST prospering
BOON	*n* pl. -S a timely benefit
BOONDOCK	*adj* pertaining to a backwoods area
BOONIES	*n/pl* a backwoods area
BOOR	*n* pl. -S a rude person
BOORISH	*adj* rude
BOOST	*v* -ED, -ING, -S to support
BOOSTER	*n* pl. -S one that boosts
BOOT	*v* -ED, -ING, -S to load a program into a computer **BOOTABLE** *adj*
BOOTEE	*n* pl. -S a baby's sock
BOOTERY	*n* pl. -ERIES a shoe store
BOOTH	*n* pl. -S a small enclosure
BOOTIE	*n* pl. -S bootee
BOOTIES	pl. of booty
BOOTJACK	*n* pl. -S a device for pulling off boots
BOOTLACE	*n* pl. -S a shoelace
BOOTLEG	*v* -LEGGED, -LEGGING, -LEGS to smuggle
BOOTLESS	*adj* useless
BOOTLICK	*v* -ED, -ING, -S to flatter servilely
BOOTY	*n* pl. -TIES a rich gain or prize
BOOZE	*v* BOOZED, BOOZING, BOOZES to drink liquor excessively
BOOZER	*n* pl. -S one that boozes
BOOZY	*adj* BOOZIER, BOOZIEST drunken **BOOZILY** *adv*
BOP	*v* BOPPED, BOPPING, BOPS to hit or strike
BOPEEP	*n* pl. -S a game of peekaboo
BOPPER	*n* pl. -S a bebopper
BORA	*n* pl. -S a cold wind
BORACES	a pl. of borax
BORACIC	*adj* boric
BORACITE	*n* pl. -S a mineral
BORAGE	*n* pl. -S a medicinal herb
BORAL	*n* pl. -S a mixture of boron carbide and aluminum
BORANE	*n* pl. -S a chemical compound
BORATE	*v* -RATED, -RATING, -RATES to mix with borax or boric acid
BORAX	*n* pl. -RAXES or -RACES a white crystalline compound

BORDEAUX *n* pl. BORDEAUX a red or white wine

BORDEL *n* pl. -S a brothel

BORDELLO *n* pl. -LOS a brothel

BORDER *v* -ED, -ING, -S to put a border (an edge) on

BORDERER *n* pl. -S one that borders

BORDURE *n* pl. -S a border around a shield

BORE *v* BORED, BORING, BORES to pierce with a rotary tool

BOREAL *adj* pertaining to the north

BORECOLE *n* pl. -S kale

BORED past tense of bore

BOREDOM *n* pl. -S tedium

BOREEN *n* pl. -S a lane in Ireland

BOREHOLE *n* pl. -S a hole bored in the earth

BORER *n* pl. -S one that bores

BORESOME *adj* tedious

BORIC *adj* pertaining to boron

BORIDE *n* pl. -S a boron compound

BORING *n* pl. -S an inner cavity

BORINGLY *adv* tediously

BORN *adj* having particular qualities from birth

BORNE a past participle of bear

BORNEOL *n* pl. -S an alcohol

BORNITE *n* pl. -S an ore of copper

BORON *n* pl. -S a nonmetallic element **BORONIC** *adj*

BOROUGH *n* pl. -S an incorporated town

BORROW *v* -ED, -ING, -S to take on loan

BORROWER *n* pl. -S one that borrows

BORSCH *n* pl. -ES borscht

BORSCHT *n* pl. -S a beet soup

BORSHT *n* pl. -S borscht

BORSTAL *n* pl. -S a reformatory

BORT *n* pl. -S a low-quality diamond **BORTY** *adj*

BORTZ *n* pl. -ES bort

BORZOI *n* pl. -S a Russian hound

BOSCAGE *n* pl. -S a thicket

BOSCHBOK *n* pl. -S bushbuck

BOSH *n* pl. -ES nonsense

BOSHBOK *n* pl. -S bushbuck

BOSHVARK *n* pl. -S a wild hog

BOSK *n* pl. -S a small wooded area

BOSKAGE *n* pl. -S boscage

BOSKER *adj* fine; very good

BOSKET *n* pl. -S a thicket

BOSKY *adj* BOSKIER, BOSKIEST wooded; bushy

BOSOM *v* -ED, -ING, -S to embrace

BOSOMY *adj* swelling outward

BOSON *n* pl. -S a subatomic particle

BOSQUE *n* pl. -S bosk

BOSQUET *n* pl. -S bosket

BOSS *v* -ED, -ING, -ES to supervise

BOSSDOM *n* pl. -S the domain of a political boss

BOSSIER comparative of bossy

BOSSIES pl. of bossy

BOSSISM *n* pl. -S control by political bosses

BOSSY *adj* BOSSIER, BOSSIEST domineering **BOSSILY** *adv*

BOSSY *n* pl. BOSSIES a cow

BOSTON *n* pl. -S a card game

BOSUN *n* pl. -S a boatswain

BOT *n* pl. -S the larva of a botfly

BOTA *n* pl. -S a leather bottle

BOTANIC *adj* pertaining to botany

BOTANICA *n* pl. -S a shop that sells herbs and magic charms

BOTANIES pl. of botany

BOTANISE *v* -NISED, -NISING, -NISES to botanize

BOTANIST *n* pl. -S one skilled in botany

BOTANIZE *v* -NIZED, -NIZING, -NIZES to study plants

BOTANY *n* pl. -NIES the science of plants

BOTCH *v* -ED, -ING, -ES to bungle

BOTCHER *n* pl. -S one that botches

BOTCHERY *n* pl. -ERIES something botched

BOTCHY *adj* BOTCHIER, BOTCHIEST badly done **BOTCHILY** *adv*

BOTEL *n* pl. -S boatel

BOTFLY *n* pl. -FLIES a type of fly

BOTH *adj* being the two

BOTHER *v* -ED, -ING, -S to annoy

BOTHRIUM *n* pl. -RIA or -RIUMS a groove on a tapeworm

BOTHY *n* pl. BOTHIES a hut in Scotland

BOTONEE *adj* having arms ending in a trefoil — used of a heraldic cross

BOTONNEE *adj* botonee

BOTRYOID *adj* resembling a cluster of grapes

BOTRYOSE *adj* botryoid

BOTRYTIS *n* pl. -TISES a plant disease

BOTT *n* pl. -S bot

BOTTLE *v* -TLED, -TLING, -TLES to put into a bottle (a rigid container)

BOTTLER *n* pl. -S one that bottles

BOTTLING *n* pl. -S a bottled beverage

BOTTOM *v* -ED, -ING, -S to comprehend

BOTTOMER *n* pl. -S one that bottoms

BOTTOMRY *n* pl. -RIES a maritime contract

BOTULIN *n* pl. -S a nerve poison

BOTULISM *n* pl. -S botulin poisoning

BOUBOU *n* pl. -S a long flowing garment

BOUCHEE *n* pl. -S a small patty shell

BOUCLE *n* pl. -S a knitted fabric

BOUDOIR *n* pl. -S a woman's bedroom

BOUFFANT *n* pl. -S a woman's hairdo

BOUFFE *n* pl. -S a comic opera

BOUGH *n* pl. -S a tree branch **BOUGHED** *adj*

BOUGHPOT *n* pl. -S a large vase

BOUGHT past tense of buy

BOUGHTEN *adj* purchased

BOUGIE *n* pl. -S a wax candle

BOUILLON *n* pl. -S a clear broth

BOULDER *n* pl. -S a large rock **BOULDERY** *adj*

BOULE *n* pl. -S buhl

BOULLE *n* pl. -S buhl

BOUNCE *v* BOUNCED, BOUNCING, BOUNCES to spring back

BOUNCER *n* pl. -S one that bounces

BOUNCY *adj* BOUNCIER, BOUNCIEST tending to bounce **BOUNCILY** *adv*

BOUND *v* -ED, -ING, -S to leap

BOUNDARY *n* pl. -ARIES a dividing line

BOUNDEN *adj* obliged

BOUNDER *n* pl. -S one that bounds

BOUNTY *n* pl. -TIES a reward **BOUNTIED** *adj*

BOUQUET *n* pl. -S a bunch of flowers

BOURBON *n* pl. -S a whiskey

BOURDON *n* pl. -S a part of a bagpipe

BOURG *n* pl. -S a medieval town

BOURGEON *v* -ED, -ING, -S to burgeon

BOURN *n* pl. -S a stream

BOURNE *n* pl. -S bourn

BOURREE *n* pl. -S an old French dance

BOURRIDE *n* pl. -S a fish stew

BOURSE *n* pl. -S a stock exchange

BOURTREE *n* pl. -S a European tree

BOUSE *v* BOUSED, BOUSING, BOUSES to haul by means of a tackle

BOUSOUKI *n* pl. -KIA or -KIS bouzouki

BOUSY *adj* boozy

BOUT *n* pl. -S a contest

BOUTIQUE *n* pl. -S a small shop

BOUTON *n* pl. -S an enlarged end of a nerve fiber

BOUVIER *n* pl. -S a large dog

BOUZOUKI *n* pl. -KIA or -KIS a stringed musical instrument

BOVID *n* pl. -S a bovine

BOVINE *n* pl. -S an ox-like animal

BOVINELY *adv* stolidly

BOVINITY *n* pl. -TIES the state of being a bovine

BOW *v* -ED, -ING, -S to bend forward

BOWEL *v* -ELED, -ELING, -ELS or -ELLED, -ELLING, -ELS to disbowel

BOWER *v* -ED, -ING, -S to embower

BOWERY *n* pl. -ERIES a colonial Dutch farm

BOWFIN *n* pl. -S a freshwater fish

BOWFRONT *adj* having a curved front

BOWHEAD *n* pl. -S an arctic whale

BOWING *n* pl. -S the technique of managing the bow of a stringed instrument

BOWINGLY *adv* in a bowing manner

BOWKNOT *n* pl. -S a type of knot

BOWL *v* -ED, -ING, -S to play at bowling

BOWLDER *n* pl. -S boulder

BOWLEG *n* pl. -S an outwardly curved leg

BOWLER *n* pl. -S one that bowls

BOWLESS *adj* being without an archery bow

BOWLFUL *n* pl. -S as much as a bowl can hold

BOWLIKE	*adj* curved
BOWLINE	*n* pl. -S a type of knot
BOWLING	*n* pl. -S a game in which balls are rolled at objects
BOWLLIKE	*adj* concave
BOWMAN	*n* pl. -MEN an archer
BOWPOT	*n* pl. -S boughpot
BOWSE	*v* BOWSED, BOWSING, BOWSES to bouse
BOWSHOT	*n* pl. -S the distance an arrow is shot
BOWSPRIT	*n* pl. -S a ship's spar
BOWWOW	*v* -ED, -ING, -S to bark like a dog
BOWYER	*n* pl. -S a maker of archery bows
BOX	*v* -ED, -ING, -ES to put in a box (a rectangular container)
BOXBERRY	*n* pl. -RIES an evergreen plant
BOXBOARD	*n* pl. -S stiff paperboard
BOXCAR	*n* pl. -S a roofed freight car
BOXER	*n* pl. -S one that packs boxes
BOXFISH	*n* pl. -ES a marine fish
BOXFUL	*n* pl. -S as much as a box can hold
BOXHAUL	*v* -ED, -ING, -S to veer a ship around
BOXIER	comparative of boxy
BOXIEST	superlative of boxy
BOXINESS	*n* pl. -ES the state of being boxy
BOXING	*n* pl. -S a casing
BOXLIKE	*adj* resembling a box
BOXTHORN	*n* pl. -S a thorny shrub
BOXWOOD	*n* pl. -S an evergreen shrub
BOXY	*adj* BOXIER, BOXIEST resembling a box
BOY	*n* pl. BOYS a male child
BOYAR	*n* pl. -S a former Russian aristocrat
BOYARD	*n* pl. -S boyar
BOYARISM	*n* pl. -S the rule of boyars
BOYCHICK	*n* pl. -S boychik
BOYCHIK	*n* pl. -S a young man
BOYCOTT	*v* -ED, -ING, -S to refuse to buy
BOYHOOD	*n* pl. -S the state of being a boy
BOYISH	*adj* resembling a boy **BOYISHLY** *adv*
BOYLA	*n* pl. -S a witch doctor
BOYO	*n* pl. BOYOS a boy
BOZO	*n* pl. -ZOS a fellow
BRA	*n* pl. -S a brassiere
BRABBLE	*v* -BLED, -BLING, -BLES to quarrel noisily
BRABBLER	*n* pl. -S one that brabbles
BRACE	*v* BRACED, BRACING, BRACES to support
BRACELET	*n* pl. -S a wrist ornament
BRACER	*n* pl. -S one that braces
BRACERO	*n* pl. -ROS a Mexican laborer
BRACH	*n* pl. -ES or -S a hound bitch
BRACHET	*n* pl. -S a brach
BRACHIAL	*n* pl. -S a part of the arm
BRACHIUM	*n* pl. -IA the upper part of arm
BRACING	*n* pl. -S a brace or reinforcement
BRACIOLA	*n* pl. -S a thin slice of meat
BRACIOLE	*n* pl. -S braciola
BRACKEN	*n* pl. -S a large fern
BRACKET	*v* -ED, -ING, -S to classify
BRACKISH	*adj* salty
BRACONID	*n* pl. -S any of a family of flies
BRACT	*n* pl. -S a leaflike plant part **BRACTEAL, BRACTED** *adj*
BRACTLET	*n* pl. -S a small bract
BRAD	*v* BRADDED, BRADDING, BRADS to fasten with thin nails
BRADAWL	*n* pl. -S a type of awl
BRADOON	*n* pl. -S bridoon
BRAE	*n* pl. -S a hillside
BRAG	*adj* BRAGGER, BRAGGEST first-rate
BRAG	*v* BRAGGED, BRAGGING, BRAGS to speak vainly of one's deeds
BRAGGART	*n* pl. -S one who brags
BRAGGER	*n* pl. -S a braggart
BRAGGEST	superlative of brag
BRAGGING	present participle of brag
BRAGGY	*adj* -GIER, -GIEST tending to brag
BRAHMA	*n* pl. -S a large domestic fowl
BRAID	*v* -ED, -ING, -S to weave together
BRAIDER	*n* pl. -S one that braids
BRAIDING	*n* pl. -S something made of braided material
BRAIL	*v* -ED, -ING, -S to haul in a sail

BRAILLE	*v* BRAILLED, BRAILLING, BRAILLES to write in braille (raised writing for the blind)
BRAIN	*v* -ED, -ING, -S to hit on the head
BRAINIER	comparative of brainy
BRAINIEST	superlative of brainy
BRAINILY	*adv* in a brainy manner
BRAINISH	*adj* impetuous
BRAINPAN	*n* pl. -S the skull
BRAINY	*adj* BRAINIER, BRAINIEST smart
BRAISE	*v* BRAISED, BRAISING, BRAISES to cook in fat
BRAIZE	*n* pl. -S a marine fish
BRAKE	*v* BRAKED, BRAKING, BRAKES to slow down or stop
BRAKEAGE	*n* pl. -S the act of braking
BRAKEMAN	*n* pl. -MEN a trainman
BRAKING	present participle of brake
BRAKY	*adj* BRAKIER, BRAKIEST abounding in shrubs or ferns
BRALESS	*adj* wearing no bra
BRAMBLE	*v* -BLED, -BLING, -BLES to gather berries
BRAMBLY	*adj* -BLIER, -BLIEST prickly
BRAN	*v* BRANNED, BRANNING, BRANS to soak in water mixed with bran (the outer coat of cereals)
BRANCH	*v* -ED, -ING, -ES to form branches (offshoots)
BRANCHIA	*n* pl. -CHIAE a respiratory organ of aquatic animals
BRANCHY	*adj* BRANCHIER, BRANCHIEST having many branches
BRAND	*v* -ED, -ING, -S to mark with a hot iron
BRANDER	*n* pl. -S one that brands
BRANDISH	*v* -ED, -ING, -ES to wave menacingly
BRANDY	*v* -DIED, -DYING, -DIES to mix with brandy (a liquor)
BRANK	*n* pl. -S a device used to restrain the tongue
BRANNED	past tense of bran
BRANNER	*n* pl. -S one that brans
BRANNING	present participle of bran
BRANNY	*adj* -NIER, -NIEST containing bran
BRANT	*n* pl. -S a wild goose
BRANTAIL	*n* pl. -S a singing bird
BRASH	*adj* BRASHER, BRASHEST rash; hasty **BRASHLY** *adv*
BRASH	*n* pl. -ES a mass of fragments
BRASHY	*adj* BRASHIER, BRASHIEST brash
BRASIER	*n* pl. -S brazier
BRASIL	*n* pl. -S brazil
BRASILIN	*n* pl. -S brazilin
BRASS	*v* -ED, -ING, -ES to coat with brass (an alloy of copper and zinc)
BRASSAGE	*n* pl. -S a fee for coining money
BRASSARD	*n* pl. -S an insignia
BRASSART	*n* pl. -S brassard
BRASSICA	*n* pl. -S a tall herb
BRASSIE	*n* pl. -S a golf club
BRASSISH	*adj* resembling brass
BRASSY	*adj* BRASSIER, BRASSIEST resembling brass **BRASSILY** *adv*
BRAT	*n* pl. -S a spoiled child **BRATTISH** *adj*
BRATTICE	*v* -TICED, -TICING, -TICES to partition
BRATTLE	*v* -TLED, -TLING, -TLES to clatter
BRATTY	*adj* -TIER, -TIEST resembling a brat
BRAUNITE	*n* pl. -S a mineral
BRAVA	*n* pl. -S a shout of approval
BRAVADO	*n* pl. -DOS or -DOES false bravery
BRAVE	*adj* BRAVER, BRAVEST showing courage **BRAVELY** *adv*
BRAVE	*v* BRAVED, BRAVING, BRAVES to face with courage
BRAVER	*n* pl. -S one that braves
BRAVERY	*n* pl. -ERIES courage
BRAVEST	superlative of brave
BRAVI	a pl. of bravo
BRAVING	present participle of brave
BRAVO	*n* pl. -VOS or -VOES or -VI a hired killer
BRAVO	*v* -ED, -ING, -ES to applaud by shouting "bravo"
BRAVURA	*n* pl. -RAS or -RE fine musical technique
BRAW	*adj* BRAWER, BRAWEST splendid

BRAWL	v -ED, -ING, -S to fight
BRAWLER	n pl. -S a fighter
BRAWLIE	adv splendidly
BRAWLY	adj BRAWLIER, BRAWLIEST inclined to brawl
BRAWN	n pl. -S muscular strength
BRAWNY	adj BRAWNIER, BRAWNIEST muscular **BRAWNILY** adv
BRAWS	n/pl fine clothes
BRAXY	n pl. BRAXIES a fever of sheep
BRAY	v BRAYED, BRAYING, BRAYS to utter a harsh cry
BRAYER	n pl. -S a roller used to spread ink
BRAZA	n pl. -S a Spanish unit of length
BRAZE	v BRAZED, BRAZING, BRAZES to solder together
BRAZEN	v -ED, -ING, -S to face boldly
BRAZENLY	adv boldly
BRAZER	n pl. -S one that brazes
BRAZIER	n pl. -S one who works in brass
BRAZIL	n pl. -S a dyewood
BRAZILIN	n pl. -S a chemical compound
BRAZING	present participle of braze
BREACH	v -ED, -ING, -ES to break through
BREACHER	n pl. -S one that breaches
BREAD	v -ED, -ING, -S to cover with crumbs of bread (a baked foodstuff made from flour)
BREADBOX	n pl. -ES a container for bread
BREADNUT	n pl. -S a tropical fruit
BREADTH	n pl. -S width
BREADY	adj resembling or characteristic of bread
BREAK	v BROKE, BROKEN, BREAKING, BREAKS to reduce to fragments
BREAKAGE	n pl. -S the act of breaking
BREAKER	n pl. -S one that breaks
BREAKING	n pl. -S the change of a pure vowel to a diphthong
BREAKOUT	n pl. -S an escape
BREAKUP	n pl. -S the act of breaking up
BREAM	v -ED, -ING, -S to clean a ship's bottom
BREAST	v -ED, -ING, -S to confront boldly
BREATH	n pl. -S air inhaled and exhaled
BREATHE	v BREATHED, BREATHING, BREATHES to inhale and exhale air
BREATHER	n pl. -S one that breathes
BREATHY	adj BREATHIER, BREATHIEST marked by loud breathing
BRECCIA	n pl. -S a type of rock **BRECCIAL** adj
BRECHAM	n pl. -S a collar for a horse
BRECHAN	n pl. -S brecham
BRED	past tense of breed
BREDE	n pl. -S a braid
BREE	n pl. -S broth
BREECH	v -ED, -ING, -ES to clothe with breeches (trousers)
BREED	v BRED, BREEDING, BREEDS to cause to give birth
BREEDER	n pl. -S one that breeds
BREEDING	n pl. -S upbringing
BREEKS	n/pl breeches
BREEZE	v BREEZED, BREEZING, BREEZES to move swiftly
BREEZY	adj BREEZIER, BREEZIEST windy **BREEZILY** adv
BREGMA	n pl. -MATA a junction point of the skull **BREGMATE** adj
BREN	n pl. -S a submachine gun
BRENT	n pl. -S brant
BRETHREN	a pl. of brother
BREVE	n pl. -S a symbol used to indicate a short vowel
BREVET	v -VETED, -VETING, -VETS or -VETTED, -VETTING, -VETS to confer an honorary rank upon
BREVETCY	n pl. -CIES an honorary rank
BREVIARY	n pl. -RIES a prayer book
BREVIER	n pl. -S a size of type
BREVITY	n pl. -TIES shortness of duration
BREW	v -ED, -ING, -S to make beer or the like
BREWAGE	n pl. -S a brewed beverage
BREWER	n pl. -S one that brews
BREWERY	n pl. -ERIES a place for brewing
BREWING	n pl. -S a quantity brewed at one time
BREWIS	n pl. BREWISES broth
BRIAR	n pl. -S brier **BRIARY** adj
BRIARD	n pl. -S a large dog

BRIBE	*v* BRIBED, BRIBING, BRIBES to practice bribery **BRIBABLE** *adj*	**BRIMLESS**	*adj* having no brim (an upper edge)
BRIBEE	*n* pl. -S one that is bribed	**BRIMMED**	past tense of brim
BRIBER	*n* pl. -S one that bribes	**BRIMMER**	*n* pl. -S a brimming cup or glass
BRIBERY	*n* pl. -ERIES an act of influencing corruptly	**BRIMMING**	present participle of brim
BRIBING	present participle of bribe	**BRIN**	*n* pl. -S a rib of a fan
BRICK	*v* -ED, -ING, -S to build with bricks (blocks of clay)	**BRINDED**	*adj* brindled
BRICKBAT	*n* pl. -S a piece of brick	**BRINDLE**	*n* pl. -S a brindled color
BRICKLE	*n* pl. -S a brittle candy	**BRINDLED**	*adj* streaked
BRICKY	*adj* BRICKIER, BRICKIEST made of bricks	**BRINE**	*v* BRINED, BRINING, BRINES to treat with brine (salted water)
BRICOLE	*n* pl. -S a cushion shot in billiards	**BRINER**	*n* pl. -S one that brines
BRIDAL	*n* pl. -S a wedding	**BRING**	*v* BROUGHT, BRINGING, BRINGS to take with oneself to a place
BRIDALLY	*adv* in a manner befitting a bride	**BRINGER**	*n* pl. -S one that brings
BRIDE	*n* pl. -S a woman just married or about to be married	**BRINIER**	comparative of briny
BRIDGE	*v* BRIDGED, BRIDGING, BRIDGES to connect	**BRINIES**	pl. of briny
BRIDGING	*n* pl. -S a bracing	**BRINIEST**	superlative of briny
BRIDLE	*v* -DLED, -DLING, -DLES to control with a restraint	**BRINING**	present participle of brine
BRIDLER	*n* pl. -S one that bridles	**BRINISH**	*adj* resembling brine
BRIDOON	*n* pl. -S a device used to control a horse	**BRINK**	*n* pl. -S an extreme edge
BRIE	*n* pl. -S bree	**BRINY**	*n* pl. BRINIES the sea
BRIEF	*adj* BRIEFER, BRIEFEST short	**BRINY**	*adj* BRINIER, BRINIEST salty
BRIEF	*v* -ED, -ING, -S to summarize	**BRIO**	*n* pl. BRIOS liveliness
BRIEFER	*n* pl. -S one that briefs	**BRIOCHE**	*n* pl. -S a rich roll
BRIEFING	*n* pl. -S a short lecture	**BRIONY**	*n* pl. -NIES bryony
BRIEFLY	*adv* in a brief manner	**BRIQUET**	*v* -QUETTED, -QUETTING, -QUETS to mold into small bricks
BRIER	*n* pl. -S a thorny shrub **BRIERY** *adj*	**BRIS**	*n* pl. BRISSES a Jewish circumcision rite
BRIG	*n* pl. -S a two-masted ship	**BRISANCE**	*n* pl. -S the shattering effect of an explosive **BRISANT** *adj*
BRIGADE	*v* -GADED, -GADING, -GADES to group together	**BRISK**	*adj* BRISKER, BRISKEST lively
BRIGAND	*n* pl. -S a bandit	**BRISK**	*v* -ED, -ING, -S to make brisk
BRIGHT	*adj* BRIGHTER, BRIGHTEST emitting much light **BRIGHTLY** *adv*	**BRISKET**	*n* pl. -S the breast of an animal
BRIGHT	*n* pl. -S a light-hued tobacco	**BRISKLY**	*adv* in a brisk manner
BRIGHTEN	*v* -ED, -ING, -S to make bright	**BRISLING**	*n* pl. -S a small herring
BRILL	*n* pl. -S an edible flatfish	**BRISSES**	pl. of bris
BRIM	*v* BRIMMED, BRIMMING, BRIMS to fill to the top	**BRISTLE**	*v* -TLED, -TLING, -TLES to rise stiffly
BRIMFUL	*adj* ready to overflow	**BRISTLY**	*adj* -TLIER, -TLIEST stiffly erect
BRIMFULL	*adj* brimful	**BRISTOL**	*n* pl. -S a smooth cardboard
		BRIT	*n* pl. -S a young herring
		BRITCHES	*n/pl* breeches; trousers
		BRITSKA	*n* pl. -S an open carriage
		BRITT	*n* pl. -S brit

BRITTLE *adj* -TLER, -TLEST likely to break

BRITTLE *v* -TLED, -TLING, -TLES to become brittle

BRITTLY *adv* in a brittle manner

BRITZKA *n* pl. -S britska

BRITZSKA *n* pl. -S britska

BRO *n* pl. BROS a brother

BROACH *v* -ED, -ING, -ES to pierce so as to withdraw a liquid

BROACHER *n* pl. -S one that broaches

BROAD *adj* BROADER, BROADEST wide

BROAD *n* pl. -S an expansion of a river

BROADAX *n* pl. -ES a broad-edged ax

BROADAXE *n* pl. -S broadax

BROADEN *v* -ED, -ING, -S to make broad

BROADISH *adj* somewhat broad

BROADLY *adv* in a broad manner

BROCADE *v* -CADED, -CADING, -CADES to weave with a raised design

BROCATEL *n* pl. -S a heavy fabric

BROCCOLI *n* pl. -S a vegetable related to the cabbage

BROCHE *adj* brocaded

BROCHURE *n* pl. -S a pamphlet

BROCK *n* pl. -S a badger

BROCKAGE *n* pl. -S an imperfectly minted coin

BROCKET *n* pl. -S a small, red deer

BROCOLI *n* pl. -S broccoli

BROGAN *n* pl. -S a heavy shoe

BROGUE *n* pl. -S an Irish accent

BROGUERY *n* pl. -ERIES the use of an Irish accent

BROGUISH *adj* resembling a brogue

BROIDER *v* -ED, -ING, -S to adorn with needlework

BROIDERY *n* pl. -DERIES the act of broidering

BROIL *v* -ED, -ING, -S to cook by direct heat

BROILER *n* pl. -S a device for broiling

BROKAGE *n* pl. -S the business of a broker

BROKE past tense of break

BROKEN *adj* shattered **BROKENLY** *adv*

BROKER *v* -ED, -ING, -S to act as a broker (an agent who buys and sells stocks)

BROKING *n* pl. -S the business of a broker

BROLLY *n* pl. -LIES an umbrella

BROMAL *n* pl. -S a medicinal liquid

BROMATE *v* -MATED, -MATING, -MATES to combine with bromine

BROME *n* pl. -S a tall grass

BROMELIN *n* pl. -S an enzyme

BROMIC *adj* containing bromine

BROMID *n* pl. -S bromide

BROMIDE *n* pl. -S a bromine compound

BROMIDIC *adj* commonplace; trite

BROMIN *n* pl. -S bromine

BROMINE *n* pl. -S a volatile liquid element

BROMISM *n* pl. -S a diseased condition of the skin

BROMIZE *v* -MIZED, -MIZING, -MIZES to treat with bromine or a bromide

BROMO *n* pl. -MOS a medicinal compound

BRONC *n* pl. -S bronco

BRONCHI pl. of bronchus

BRONCHIA *n/pl* the main air passages of the lungs

BRONCHO *n* pl. -CHOS bronco

BRONCHUS *n* pl. -CHI a tracheal branch

BRONCO *n* pl. -COS a wild horse

BRONZE *v* BRONZED, BRONZING, BRONZES to make brown or tan

BRONZER *n* pl. -S one that bronzes

BRONZING *n* pl. -S a brownish coloring

BRONZY *adj* BRONZIER, BRONZIEST of a brownish color

BROO *n* pl. BROOS a bree

BROOCH *n* pl. -ES a decorative pin

BROOD *v* -ED, -ING, -S to ponder deeply

BROODER *n* pl. -S one that broods

BROODY *adj* BROODIER, BROODIEST tending to brood **BROODILY** *adv*

BROOK *v* -ED, -ING, -S to tolerate

BROOKIE *n* pl. -S a brook trout

BROOKITE *n* pl. -S a mineral

BROOKLET *n* pl. -S a small brook or creek

BROOM *v* -ED, -ING, -S to sweep

BROOMY   *adj* BROOMIER, BROOMIEST abounding in broom (a type of shrub)

BROS   pl. of bro

BROSE   *n* pl. -S a porridge

BROSY   *adj* smeared with brose

BROTH   *n* pl. -S a thin clear soup

BROTHEL   *n* pl. -S a house of prostitution

BROTHER   *n* pl. -S or BRETHREN a male sibling

BROTHER   *v* -ED, -ING, -S to treat like a brother

BROTHY   *adj* resembling broth

BROUGHAM   *n* pl. -S a type of carriage

BROUGHT   past tense of bring

BROUHAHA   *n* pl. -S an uproar

BROW   *n* pl. -S the forehead **BROWED** *adj*

BROWBAND   *n* pl. -S a band designed to cross the forehead

BROWBEAT   *v* -BEAT, -BEATEN, -BEATING, -BEATS to intimidate

BROWLESS   *adj* lacking eyebrows

BROWN   *adj* BROWNER, BROWNEST of a dark color

BROWN   *v* -ED, -ING, -S to make brown

BROWNIE   *n* pl. -S a small sprite

BROWNIER   comparative of browny

BROWNIEST   superlative of browny

BROWNISH   *adj* somewhat brown

BROWNOUT   *n* pl. -S a power reduction

BROWNY   *adj* BROWNIER, BROWNIEST somewhat brown

BROWSE   *v* BROWSED, BROWSING, BROWSES to look at casually

BROWSER   *n* pl. -S one that browses

BRR   *interj* brrr

BRRR   *interj* — used to indicate that one feels cold

BRUCELLA   *n* pl. -LAE or -LAS any of a genus of harmful bacteria

BRUCIN   *n* pl. -S brucine

BRUCINE   *n* pl. -S a poisonous alkaloid

BRUGH   *n* pl. -S a borough

BRUIN   *n* pl. -S a bear

BRUISE   *v* BRUISED, BRUISING, BRUISES to injure without breaking the surface of the skin

BRUISER   *n* pl. -S a big, husky man

BRUIT   *v* -ED, -ING, -S to spread news of

BRUITER   *n* pl. -S one that bruits

BRULOT   *n* pl. -S a biting fly

BRULYIE   *n* pl. -S a noisy quarrel

BRULZIE   *n* pl. -S brulyie

BRUMAL   *adj* wintry

BRUMBY   *n* pl. -BIES a wild horse

BRUME   *n* pl. -S fog **BRUMOUS** *adj*

BRUNCH   *v* -ED, -ING, -ES to eat a late morning meal

BRUNET   *n* pl. -S a dark-haired male

BRUNETTE   *n* pl. -S a dark-haired female

BRUNIZEM   *n* pl. -S a prairie soil

BRUNT   *n* pl. -S the main impact

BRUSH   *v* -ED, -ING, -ES to touch lightly

BRUSHER   *n* pl. -S one that brushes

BRUSHIER   comparative of brushy

BRUSHIEST   superlative of brushy

BRUSHOFF   *n* pl. -S an abrupt dismissal

BRUSHUP   *n* pl. -S a quick review

BRUSHY   *adj* BRUSHIER, BRUSHIEST shaggy; rough

BRUSK   *adj* BRUSKER, BRUSKEST brusque

BRUSQUE   *adj* BRUSQUER, BRUSQUEST abrupt in manner

BRUT   *adj* very dry

BRUTAL   *adj* cruel; savage **BRUTALLY** *adv*

BRUTE   *v* BRUTED, BRUTING, BRUTES to shape a diamond by rubbing it with another diamond

BRUTELY   *adv* in a brutal manner

BRUTIFY   *v* -FIED, -FYING, -FIES to make brutal

BRUTING   present participle of brute

BRUTISH   *adj* brutal

BRUTISM   *n* pl. -S the state of being brutal

BRUXISM   *n* pl. -S a nervous grinding of the teeth

BRYOLOGY   *n* pl. -GIES the study of mosses

BRYONY   *n* pl. -NIES a climbing plant

BRYOZOAN   *n* pl. -S a type of small aquatic animal

BUB   *n* pl. -S young fellow

BUBAL   *n* pl. -S a large antelope

BUBALE   *n* pl. -S bubal

BUBALINE *adj* pertaining to the bubal

BUBALIS *n* pl. -LISES bubal

BUBBLE *v* -BLED, -BLING, -BLES to form bubbles (bodies of gas contained within a liquid)

BUBBLER *n* pl. -S a drinking fountain

BUBBLY *n* pl. -BLIES champagne

BUBBLY *adj* -BLIER, -BLIEST full of bubbles

BUBINGA *n* pl. -S an African tree

BUBO *n* pl. -BOES a swelling of a lymph gland **BUBOED** *adj*

BUBONIC *adj* pertaining to a bubo

BUCCAL *adj* pertaining to the cheek **BUCCALLY** *adv*

BUCK *v* -ED, -ING, -S to leap forward and upward suddenly

BUCKAROO *n* pl. -ROOS a cowboy

BUCKAYRO *n* pl. -ROS buckaroo

BUCKBEAN *n* pl. -S a marsh plant

BUCKEEN *n* pl. -S a poor man who acts as if wealthy

BUCKER *n* pl. -S a bucking horse

BUCKEROO *n* pl. -ROOS buckaroo

BUCKET *v* -ED, -ING, -S to hurry

BUCKEYE *n* pl. -S a nut-bearing tree

BUCKISH *adj* foppish

BUCKLE *v* -LED, -LING, -LES to bend under pressure

BUCKLER *v* -ED, -ING, -S to shield

BUCKO *n* pl. BUCKOES a bully

BUCKRAM *v* -ED, -ING, -S to stiffen

BUCKSAW *n* pl. -S a wood-cutting saw

BUCKSHEE *n* pl. -S something extra obtained free

BUCKSHOT *n* pl. -S a large lead shot

BUCKSKIN *n* pl. -S the skin of a male deer

BUCKTAIL *n* pl. -S a fishing lure

BUCOLIC *n* pl. -S a pastoral poem

BUD *v* BUDDED, BUDDING, BUDS to put forth buds (undeveloped plant parts)

BUDDER *n* pl. -S one that buds

BUDDIED past tense of buddy

BUDDIES present 3d person sing. of buddy

BUDDING *n* pl. -S a type of asexual reproduction

BUDDLE *n* pl. -S an apparatus on which crushed ore is washed

BUDDLEIA *n* pl. -S a tropical shrub

BUDDY *v* -DIED, -DYING, -DIES to become close friends

BUDGE *v* BUDGED, BUDGING, BUDGES to move slightly

BUDGER *n* pl. -S one that budges

BUDGET *v* -ED, -ING, -S to estimate expenditures

BUDGETER *n* pl. -S one that budgets

BUDGIE *n* pl. -S a small parrot

BUDGING present participle of budge

BUDLESS *adj* being without buds

BUDLIKE *adj* resembling a bud

BUDWORM *n* pl. -S a caterpillar that eats buds

BUFF *v* -ED, -ING, -S to polish **BUFFABLE** *adj*

BUFFALO *n* pl. -LOES or -LOS an ox-like animal

BUFFALO *v* -ED, -ING, -ES to intimidate

BUFFER *v* -ED, -ING, -S to cushion

BUFFET *v* -ED, -ING, -S to hit sharply

BUFFETER *n* pl. -S one that buffets

BUFFI a pl. of buffo

BUFFIER comparative of buffy

BUFFIEST superlative of buffy

BUFFO *n* pl. -FI or -FOS an operatic clown

BUFFOON *n* pl. -S a clown

BUFFY *adj* BUFFIER, BUFFIEST of a yellowish-brown color

BUG *v* BUGGED, BUGGING, BUGS to annoy

BUGABOO *n* pl. -BOOS a bugbear

BUGBANE *n* pl. -S a perennial herb

BUGBEAR *n* pl. -S an object or source of dread

BUGEYE *n* pl. -S a small boat

BUGGED past tense of bug

BUGGER *v* -ED, -ING, -S to damn

BUGGERY *n* pl. -GERIES sodomy

BUGGING present participle of bug

BUGGY *n* pl. -GIES a light carriage

BUGGY *adj* -GIER, -GIEST infested with bugs

BUGHOUSE *n* pl. -S an insane asylum

BUGLE	*v* -GLED, -GLING, -GLES to play a bugle (a brass wind instrument)	**BULLDOZE**	*v* -DOZED, -DOZING, -DOZES to bully
BUGLER	*n* pl. -S one that plays a bugle	**BULLET**	*v* -ED, -ING, -S to move swiftly
BUGLOSS	*n* pl. -ES a coarse plant	**BULLETIN**	*v* -ED, -ING, -S to issue a news item
BUGSEED	*n* pl. -S an annual herb	**BULLFROG**	*n* pl. -S a large frog
BUGSHA	*n* pl. -S buqsha	**BULLHEAD**	*n* pl. -S a freshwater catfish
BUHL	*n* pl. -S a style of furniture decoration	**BULLHORN**	*n* pl. -S an electric megaphone
BUHLWORK	*n* pl. -S buhl	**BULLIED**	past tense of bully
BUHR	*n* pl. -S a heavy stone	**BULLIER**	comparative of bully
BUILD	*v* BUILT or BUILDED, BUILDING, BUILDS to construct	**BULLIES**	present 3d person sing. of bully
BUILDER	*n* pl. -S one that builds	**BULLIEST**	superlative of bully
BUILDING	*n* pl. -S something that is built	**BULLION**	*n* pl. -S uncoined gold or silver
BUILDUP	*n* pl. -S an accumulation	**BULLISH**	*adj* stubborn
BUILT	a past tense of build	**BULLNECK**	*n* pl. -S a thick neck
BUIRDLY	*adj* burly	**BULLNOSE**	*n* pl. -S a disease of swine
BULB	*n* pl. -S an underground bud **BULBAR, BULBED** *adj*	**BULLOCK**	*n* pl. -S a castrated bull **BULLOCKY** *adj*
BULBEL	*n* pl. -S bulbil	**BULLOUS**	*adj* resembling bullae
BULBIL	*n* pl. -S a small bulb	**BULLPEN**	*n* pl. -S an enclosure for bulls
BULBLET	*n* pl. -S a small bulb	**BULLPOUT**	*n* pl. -S a bullhead
BULBOUS	*adj* bulb-shaped; bulging	**BULLRING**	*n* pl. -S a bullfight arena
BULBUL	*n* pl. -S a songbird	**BULLRUSH**	*n* pl. -ES bulrush
BULGE	*v* BULGED, BULGING, BULGES to swell out	**BULLSHOT**	*n* pl. -S a drink made of vodka and bouillon
BULGER	*n* pl. -S a golf club	**BULLWEED**	*n* pl. -S knapweed
BULGUR	*n* pl. -S crushed wheat	**BULLWHIP**	*v* -WHIPPED, -WHIPPING, -WHIPS to strike with a long whip
BULGY	*adj* BULGIER, BULGIEST bulging	**BULLY**	*v* -LIED, -LYING, -LIES to treat abusively
BULIMIA	*n* pl. -S insatiable appetite **BULIMIAC** *adj*	**BULLY**	*adj* -LIER, -LIEST wonderful
BULIMIC	*n* pl. -S one who is affected with bulimia	**BULLYBOY**	*n* pl. -BOYS a ruffian
		BULLYRAG	*v* -RAGGED, -RAGGING, -RAGS to bully
BULK	*v* -ED, -ING, -S to gather into a mass	**BULRUSH**	*n* pl. -ES a tall marsh plant
BULKAGE	*n* pl. -S a peristaltic stimulant	**BULWARK**	*v* -ED, -ING, -S to fortify with a defensive wall
BULKHEAD	*n* pl. -S a partition in a ship	**BUM**	*v* BUMMED, BUMMING, BUMS to live idly
BULKY	*adj* BULKIER, BULKIEST massive **BULKILY** *adv*	**BUM**	*adj* BUMMER, BUMMEST of little value; worthless
BULL	*v* -ED, -ING, -S to push ahead	**BUMBLE**	*v* -BLED, -BLING, -BLES to bungle
BULLA	*n* pl. -LAE a large blister	**BUMBLER**	*n* pl. -S one that bumbles
BULLACE	*n* pl. -S a purple plum	**BUMBLING**	*n* pl. -S an instance of clumsiness
BULLATE	*adj* blistered in appearance		
BULLBAT	*n* pl. -S a nocturnal bird	**BUMBOAT**	*n* pl. -S a boat used to peddle wares to larger ships
BULLDOG	*v* -DOGGED, -DOGGING, -DOGS to throw a steer		

BUMF	*n* pl. -S paperwork	**BUNTER**	*n* pl. -S one that bunts
BUMKIN	*n* pl. -S a ship's spar	**BUNTING**	*n* pl. -S a fabric used for flags
BUMMED	past tense of bum	**BUNTLINE**	*n* pl. -S a rope used to haul up a sail
BUMMER	*n* pl. -S one that bums		
BUMMEST	superlative of bum	**BUNYA**	*n* pl. -S an evergreen tree
BUMMING	present participle of bum	**BUOY**	*v* -ED, -ING, -S to mark with a buoy (a warning float)
BUMP	*v* -ED, -ING, -S to knock against		
BUMPER	*v* -ED, -ING, -S to fill to the brim	**BUOYAGE**	*n* pl. -S a group of buoys
BUMPH	*n* pl. -S bumf	**BUOYANCE**	*n* pl. -S buoyancy
BUMPKIN	*n* pl. -S an unsophisticated rustic	**BUOYANCY**	*n* pl. -CIES the tendency to float
BUMPY	*adj* BUMPIER, BUMPIEST of uneven surface **BUMPILY** *adv*	**BUOYANT**	*adj* having buoyancy
		BUPPIE	*n* pl. -S a black professional person working in a city
BUN	*n* pl. -S a small bread roll		
BUNCH	*v* -ED, -ING, -ES to group together	**BUQSHA**	*n* pl. -S a monetary unit of Yemen
BUNCHY	*adj* BUNCHIER, BUNCHIEST clustered **BUNCHILY** *adv*	**BUR**	*v* BURRED, BURRING, BURS to burr
BUNCO	*v* -ED, -ING, -S to swindle	**BURA**	*n* pl. -S buran
BUNCOMBE	*n* pl. -S nonsense	**BURAN**	*n* pl. -S a violent windstorm
BUND	*n* pl. -S a political association	**BURBLE**	*v* -BLED, -BLING, -BLES to speak quickly and excitedly
BUNDIST	*n* pl. -S a member of a bund		
BUNDLE	*v* -DLED, -DLING, -DLES to fasten a group of objects together	**BURBLER**	*n* pl. -S one that burbles
		BURBLY	*adj* -BLIER, -BLIEST burbling
BUNDLER	*n* pl. -S one that bundles	**BURBOT**	*n* pl. -S a freshwater fish
BUNDLING	*n* pl. -S a former courtship custom	**BURBS**	*n/pl* the suburbs
		BURD	*n* pl. -S a maiden
BUNDT	*n* pl. -S a type of cake pan	**BURDEN**	*v* -ED, -ING, -S to load heavily
BUNG	*v* -ED, -ING, -S to plug with a cork or stopper	**BURDENER**	*n* pl. -S one that burdens
		BURDIE	*n* pl. -S burd
BUNGALOW	*n* pl. -S a small cottage	**BURDOCK**	*n* pl. -S a coarse weed
BUNGEE	*n* pl. -S an elasticized cord	**BUREAU**	*n* pl. -REAUS or -REAUX a chest of drawers
BUNGHOLE	*n* pl. -S a hole in a keg or barrel		
BUNGLE	*v* -GLED, -GLING, -GLES to work, make, or do clumsily	**BURET**	*n* pl. -S burette
		BURETTE	*n* pl. -S a measuring tube
BUNGLER	*n* pl. -S one that bungles	**BURG**	*n* pl. -S a city or town
BUNGLING	*n* pl. -S something done clumsily	**BURGAGE**	*n* pl. -S a feudal tenure
BUNION	*n* pl. -S a painful swelling of the foot	**BURGEE**	*n* pl. -S a small flag
		BURGEON	*v* -ED, -ING, -S to develop rapidly
BUNK	*v* -ED, -ING, -S to go to bed		
BUNKER	*v* -ED, -ING, -S to store in a large bin	**BURGER**	*n* pl. -S a hamburger
		BURGESS	*n* pl. -ES a citizen of an English borough
BUNKMATE	*n* pl. -S a person with whom sleeping quarters are shared		
		BURGH	*n* pl. -S a Scottish borough **BURGHAL** *adj*
BUNKO	*v* -ED, -ING, -S to bunco		
BUNKUM	*n* pl. -S nonsense	**BURGHER**	*n* pl. -S a citizen of a borough
BUNN	*n* pl. -S bun	**BURGLAR**	*n* pl. -S one who commits burglary
BUNNY	*n* pl. -NIES a rabbit		
BUNRAKU	*n* pl. -S a Japanese puppet show	**BURGLARY**	*n* pl. -GLARIES a felonious theft
BUNT	*v* -ED, -ING, -S to butt		

BURGLE	*v* -GLED, -GLING, -GLES to commit burglary
BURGONET	*n* pl. -S an open helmet
BURGOO	*n* pl. -GOOS a thick oatmeal
BURGOUT	*n* pl. -S burgoo
BURGRAVE	*n* pl. -S a German nobleman
BURGUNDY	*n* pl. -DIES a red wine
BURIAL	*n* pl. -S the act of burying
BURIED	past tense of bury
BURIER	*n* pl. -S one that buries
BURIES	present 3d person sing. of bury
BURIN	*n* pl. -S an engraving tool
BURKE	*v* BURKED, BURKING, BURKES to murder by suffocation
BURKER	*n* pl. -S one that burkes
BURKITE	*n* pl. -S a burker
BURL	*v* -ED, -ING, -S to finish cloth by removing lumps
BURLAP	*n* pl. -S a coarse fabric
BURLER	*n* pl. -S one that burls
BURLESK	*n* pl. -S a type of stage show
BURLEY	*n* pl. -LEYS a light tobacco
BURLY	*adj* -LIER, -LIEST heavy and muscular **BURLILY** *adv*
BURN	*v* BURNED or BURNT, BURNING, BURNS to destroy by fire
BURNABLE	*n* pl. -S something that can be burned
BURNER	*n* pl. -S one that burns
BURNET	*n* pl. -S a perennial herb
BURNIE	*n* pl. -S a brooklet
BURNING	*n* pl. -S the firing of ceramic materials
BURNISH	*v* -ED, -ING, -ES to polish
BURNOOSE	*n* pl. -S a hooded cloak
BURNOUS	*n* pl. -ES burnoose
BURNOUT	*n* pl. -S a destructive fire
BURNT	a past tense of burn
BURP	*v* -ED, -ING, -S to belch
BURR	*v* -ED, -ING, -S to remove a rough edge from
BURRED	past tense of bur
BURRER	*n* pl. -S one that burrs
BURRIER	comparative of burry
BURRIEST	superlative of burry
BURRING	present participle of bur

BURRITO	*n* pl. -TOS a tortilla rolled around a filling
BURRO	*n* pl. -ROS a small donkey
BURROW	*v* -ED, -ING, -S to dig a hole or tunnel in the ground
BURROWER	*n* pl. -S one that burrows
BURRY	*adj* -RIER, -RIEST prickly
BURSA	*n* pl. -SAS or -SAE a bodily pouch **BURSAL** *adj*
BURSAR	*n* pl. -S a college treasurer
BURSARY	*n* pl. -RIES a college treasury
BURSATE	*adj* pertaining to a bursa
BURSE	*n* pl. -S a small bag or pouch
BURSEED	*n* pl. -S a coarse weed
BURSERA	*adj* designating a family of shrubs and trees
BURSITIS	*n* pl. -TISES inflammation of a bursa
BURST	*v* BURST or BURSTED, BURSTING, BURSTS to break open suddenly or violently
BURSTER	*n* pl. -S one that bursts
BURSTONE	*n* pl. -S a heavy stone
BURTHEN	*v* -ED, -ING, -S to burden
BURTON	*n* pl. -S a hoisting tackle
BURWEED	*n* pl. -S a coarse weed
BURY	*v* BURIED, BURYING, BURIES to put in the ground and cover with earth
BUS	*v* BUSED, BUSING, BUSES or BUSSED, BUSSING, BUSSES to transport by bus (a large motor vehicle)
BUSBAR	*n* pl. -S a type of electrical conductor
BUSBOY	*n* pl. -BOYS a waiter's assistant
BUSBY	*n* pl. -BIES a tall fur hat
BUSH	*v* -ED, -ING, -ES to cover with bushes (shrubs)
BUSHBUCK	*n* pl. -S a small antelope
BUSHEL	*v* -ELED, -ELING, -ELS or -ELLED, -ELLING, -ELS to mend clothing
BUSHELER	*n* pl. -S one that bushels
BUSHER	*n* pl. -S a minor league baseball player
BUSHFIRE	*n* pl. -S a fire in a wooded area
BUSHGOAT	*n* pl. -S a bushbuck
BUSHIDO	*n* pl. -DOS the code of the samurai

BUSHIER	comparative of bushy
BUSHIEST	superlative of bushy
BUSHILY	*adv* in a bushy manner
BUSHING	*n* pl. -S a lining for a hole
BUSHLAND	*n* pl. -S unsettled forest land
BUSHLESS	*adj* having no bushes
BUSHLIKE	*adj* resembling a bush
BUSHMAN	*n* pl. -MEN a woodsman
BUSHPIG	*n* pl. -S a wild African pig
BUSHTIT	*n* pl. -S a titmouse
BUSHWA	*n* pl. -S nonsense
BUSHWAH	*n* pl. -S bushwa
BUSHY	*adj* BUSHIER, BUSHIEST covered with bushes
BUSIED	past tense of busy
BUSIER	comparative of busy
BUSIES	present 3d person sing. of busy
BUSIEST	superlative of busy
BUSILY	*adv* in a busy manner
BUSINESS	*n* pl. -ES an occupation, profession, or trade
BUSING	*n* pl. -S the act of transporting by bus
BUSK	*v* -ED, -ING, -S to prepare
BUSKER	*n* pl. -S a roaming entertainer
BUSKIN	*n* pl. -S a high shoe **BUSKINED** *adj*
BUSLOAD	*n* pl. -S a load that fills a bus
BUSMAN	*n* pl. -MEN a bus operator
BUSS	*v* -ED, -ING, -ES to kiss
BUSSED	a past tense of bus
BUSSES	a present 3d person sing. of bus
BUSSING	*n* pl. -S busing
BUST	*v* -ED, -ING, -S to burst
BUSTARD	*n* pl. -S a game bird
BUSTER	*n* pl. -S one that breaks up something
BUSTIC	*n* pl. -S a tropical tree
BUSTIER	*n* pl. -S a woman's undergarment
BUSTLE	*v* -TLED, -TLING, -TLES to move energetically
BUSTLINE	*n* pl. -S the distance around the bust (the upper torso of a woman)
BUSTY	*adj* BUSTIER, BUSTIEST full-bosomed
BUSULFAN	*n* pl. -S a medicine
BUSY	*adj* BUSIER, BUSIEST occupied

BUSY	*v* BUSIED, BUSYING, BUSIES to make busy
BUSYBODY	*n* pl. -BODIES a nosy person
BUSYNESS	*n* pl. -ES the state of being busy
BUSYWORK	*n* pl. -S active but valueless work
BUT	*n* pl. -S a flatfish
BUTANE	*n* pl. -S a flammable gas
BUTANOL	*n* pl. -S a flammable alcohol
BUTANONE	*n* pl. -S a flammable ketone
BUTCH	*n* pl. -ES a lesbian with mannish traits
BUTCHER	*v* -ED, -ING, -S to slaughter
BUTCHERY	*n* pl. -ERIES wanton or cruel killing
BUTE	*n* pl. BUTE a pain-relieving drug
BUTENE	*n* pl. -S butylene
BUTEO	*n* pl. -TEOS a hawk
BUTLE	*v* -LED, -LING, -LES to serve as a butler
BUTLER	*n* pl. -S a male servant
BUTLERY	*n* pl. -LERIES a storage room
BUTLES	present 3d person sing. of butle
BUTLING	present participle of butle
BUTT	*v* -ED, -ING, -S to hit with the head
BUTTALS	*n/pl* boundary lines
BUTTE	*n* pl. -S an isolated hill
BUTTER	*v* -ED, -ING, -S to spread with butter (a milk product)
BUTTERY	*adj* -TERIER, -TERIEST containing butter
BUTTERY	*n* pl. -TERIES a wine cellar
BUTTIES	pl. of butty
BUTTOCK	*n* pl. -S either of the two rounded parts of the rump
BUTTON	*v* -ED, -ING, -S to fasten with a button (a small disk)
BUTTONER	*n* pl. -S one that buttons
BUTTONY	*adj* resembling a button
BUTTRESS	*v* -ED, -ING, -ES to prop up
BUTTY	*n* pl. -TIES a fellow workman
BUTUT	*n* pl. -S a monetary unit of Gambia
BUTYL	*n* pl. -S a hydrocarbon radical
BUTYLATE	*v* -ATED, -ATING, -ATES to add a butyl to
BUTYLENE	*n* pl. -S a gaseous hydrocarbon
BUTYRAL	*n* pl. -S a chemical compound

BUTYRATE   *n* pl. -S a chemical salt

BUTYRIC   *adj* derived from butter

BUTYRIN   *n* pl. -S a chemical compound

BUTYROUS   *adj* resembling butter

BUTYRYL   *n* pl. -S a radical of butyric acid

BUXOM   *adj* -OMER, -OMEST healthily plump **BUXOMLY** *adv*

BUY   *v* BOUGHT, BUYING, BUYS to purchase **BUYABLE** *adj*

BUYBACK   *n* pl. -S the repurchase by a corporation of its own stock

BUYER   *n* pl. -S one that buys

BUYOUT   *n* pl. -S the purchase of a business

BUZUKI   *n* pl. -KIA or -KIS bouzouki

BUZZ   *v* -ED, -ING, -ES to make a vibrating sound

BUZZARD   *n* pl. -S a large bird of prey

BUZZER   *n* pl. -S a signaling device

BUZZWIG   *n* pl. -S a large, thick wig

BUZZWORD   *n* pl. -S a word used to impress someone

BWANA   *n* pl. -S master; boss

BY   *n* pl. BYS a pass in certain card games

BYE   *n* pl. -S a side issue

BYELAW   *n* pl. -S bylaw

BYGONE   *n* pl. -S a past occurrence

BYLAW   *n* pl. -S a secondary law

BYLINE   *v* -LINED, -LINING, -LINES to write under a byline (a line giving the author's name)

BYLINER   *n* pl. -S one that writes under a byline

BYNAME   *n* pl. -S a secondary name

BYPASS   *v* -ED, -ING, -ES to avoid by going around

BYPAST   *adj* past; gone by

BYPATH   *n* pl. -S an indirect road

BYPLAY   *n* pl. -PLAYS secondary action

BYRE   *n* pl. -S a cowshed

BYRL   *v* -ED, -ING, -S to birle

BYRNIE   *n* pl. -S an armored shirt

BYROAD   *n* pl. -S a side road

BYSSUS   *n* pl. BYSSUSES or BYSSI a fine linen

BYSTREET   *n* pl. -S a side street

BYTALK   *n* pl. -S small talk

BYTE   *n* pl. -S a group of adjacent binary digits

BYWAY   *n* pl. -WAYS a side road

BYWORD   *n* pl. -S a well-known saying

BYWORK   *n* pl. -S work done during leisure time

BYZANT   *n* pl. -S bezant

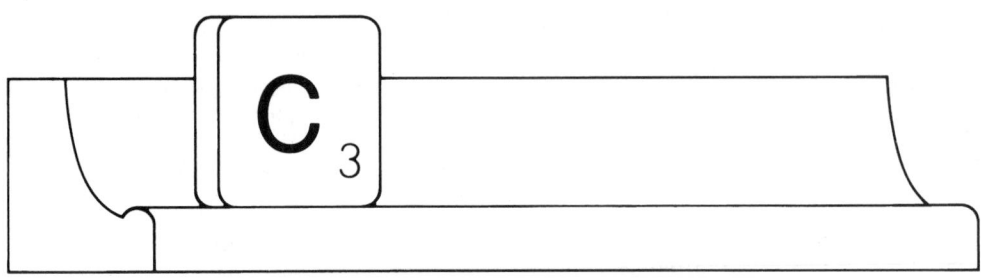

CAB	*v* CABBED, CABBING, CABS to take or drive a taxicab
CABAL	*v* -BALLED, -BALLING, -BALS to conspire
CABALA	*n* pl. -S an occult or secret doctrine
CABALISM	*n* pl. -S adherence to a cabala
CABALIST	*n* pl. -S one who practices cabalism
CABALLED	past tense of cabal
CABALLING	present participle of cabal
CABANA	*n* pl. -S a small cabin
CABARET	*n* pl. -S a music hall
CABBAGE	*v* -BAGED, -BAGING, -BAGES to steal
CABBALA	*n* pl. -S cabala
CABBALAH	*n* pl. -S cabala
CABBED	past tense of cab
CABBIE	*n* pl. -S cabby
CABBING	present participle of cab
CABBY	*n* pl. -BIES a driver of a cab
CABER	*n* pl. -S a heavy pole thrown as a trial of strength
CABERNET	*n* pl. -S a dry red wine
CABESTRO	*n* pl. -TROS a lasso
CABEZON	*n* pl. -S a large, edible fish
CABEZONE	*n* pl. -S cabezon
CABILDO	*n* pl. -DOS a town council
CABIN	*v* -ED, -ING, -S to live in a cabin (a roughly built house)
CABINET	*n* pl. -S a piece of furniture with shelves and drawers
CABLE	*v* -BLED, -BLING, -BLES to fasten with a cable (a heavy rope)
CABLET	*n* pl. -S a small cable
CABLEWAY	*n* pl. -WAYS a suspended cable
CABLING	present participle of cable
CABMAN	*n* pl. -MEN a driver of a cab
CABOB	*n* pl. -S kabob
CABOCHED	*adj* full-faced — used of an animal's head in heraldry
CABOCHON	*n* pl. -S a precious stone
CABOMBA	*n* pl. -S an aquatic plant
CABOODLE	*n* pl. -S a collection
CABOOSE	*n* pl. -S the last car of a freight train
CABOSHED	*adj* caboched
CABOTAGE	*n* pl. -S coastal trade
CABRESTA	*n* pl. -S cabestro
CABRESTO	*n* pl. -TOS cabestro
CABRETTA	*n* pl. -S a soft leather
CABRILLA	*n* pl. -S a sea bass
CABRIOLE	*n* pl. -S a curved furniture leg
CABSTAND	*n* pl. -S a place where cabs await hire
CACA	*n* pl. -S excrement
CACAO	*n* pl. -CAOS a tropical tree
CACHALOT	*n* pl. -S a large whale
CACHE	*v* CACHED, CACHING, CACHES to store in a hiding place
CACHEPOT	*n* pl. -S an ornamental container for a flowerpot
CACHET	*v* -ED, -ING, -S to print a design on an envelope
CACHEXIA	*n* pl. -S general ill health **CACHEXIC** *adj*
CACHEXY	*n* pl. -CHEXIES cachexia
CACHING	present participle of cache
CACHOU	*n* pl. -S catechu
CACHUCHA	*n* pl. -S a Spanish dance
CACIQUE	*n* pl. -S a tropical oriole
CACKLE	*v* -LED, -LING, -LES to make the sound of a hen
CACKLER	*n* pl. -S one that cackles

CACODYL	*n* pl. -S a poisonous liquid
CACOMIXL	*n* pl. -S a raccoon-like mammal
CACTUS	*n* pl. -TI or -TUSES a plant native to arid regions **CACTOID** *adj*
CAD	*n* pl. -S an ungentlemanly man
CADASTER	*n* pl. -S a public record of land ownership
CADASTRE	*n* pl. -S cadaster
CADAVER	*n* pl. -S a corpse
CADDICE	*n* pl. -S caddis
CADDIE	*v* -DIED, -DYING, -DIES to serve as a golfer's assistant
CADDIS	*n* pl. -DISES a coarse woolen fabric
CADDISH	*adj* resembling a cad
CADDY	*v* -DIED, -DYING, -DIES to caddie
CADE	*n* pl. -S a European shrub
CADELLE	*n* pl. -S a small, black beetle
CADENCE	*v* -DENCED, -DENCING, -DENCES to make rhythmic
CADENCY	*n* pl. -CIES a rhythm
CADENT	*adj* having rhythm
CADENZA	*n* pl. -S an elaborate musical passage
CADET	*n* pl. -S a student at a military school
CADGE	*v* CADGED, CADGING, CADGES to get by begging
CADGER	*n* pl. -S one that cadges
CADGY	*adj* cheerful
CADI	*n* pl. -S a Muslim judge
CADMIUM	*n* pl. -S a metallic element **CADMIC** *adj*
CADRE	*n* pl. -S a nucleus of trained personnel
CADUCEUS	*n* pl. -CEI a heraldic wand or staff **CADUCEAN** *adj*
CADUCITY	*n* pl. -TIES senility
CADUCOUS	*adj* transitory; perishable
CAECUM	*n* pl. -CA cecum **CAECAL** *adj* **CAECALLY** *adv*
CAEOMA	*n* pl. -S a spore-forming organ of a fungus
CAESAR	*n* pl. -S an emperor
CAESIUM	*n* pl. -S cesium
CAESTUS	*n* pl. -ES cestus
CAESURA	*n* pl. -RAS or -RAE a pause in a line of verse **CAESURAL, CAESURIC** *adj*
CAFE	*n* pl. -S a small restaurant
CAFF	*n* pl. -S a cafe
CAFFEIN	*n* pl. -S caffeine
CAFFEINE	*n* pl. -S a bitter alkaloid used as a stimulant
CAFTAN	*n* pl. -S a full-length tunic
CAGE	*v* CAGED, CAGING, CAGES to confine
CAGEFUL	*n* pl. -S the number held in a cage (an enclosure)
CAGELING	*n* pl. -S a caged bird
CAGER	*n* pl. -S a basketball player
CAGEY	*adj* CAGIER, CAGIEST shrewd
CAGIER	comparative of cagy
CAGIEST	superlative of cagy
CAGILY	*adv* in a cagey manner
CAGINESS	*n* pl. -ES the quality of being cagey
CAGING	present participle of cage
CAGY	*adj* CAGIER, CAGIEST cagey
CAHIER	*n* pl. -S a notebook
CAHOOT	*n* pl. -S partnership
CAHOW	*n* pl. -S a sea bird
CAID	*n* pl. -S a Muslim leader
CAIMAN	*n* pl. -S a tropical reptile
CAIN	*n* pl. -S kain
CAIQUE	*n* pl. -S a long, narrow rowboat
CAIRD	*n* pl. -S a gypsy
CAIRN	*n* pl. -S a mound of stones set up as a memorial **CAIRNED, CAIRNY** *adj*
CAISSON	*n* pl. -S a watertight chamber
CAITIFF	*n* pl. -S a despicable person
CAJAPUT	*n* pl. -S cajeput
CAJEPUT	*n* pl. -S an Australian tree
CAJOLE	*v* -JOLED, -JOLING, -JOLES to persuade by flattery
CAJOLER	*n* pl. -S one that cajoles
CAJOLERY	*n* pl. -ERIES persuasion by flattery
CAJOLING	present participle of cajole
CAJON	*n* pl. -ES a steep-sided canyon
CAJUPUT	*n* pl. -S cajeput
CAKE	*v* CAKED, CAKING, CAKES to form into a hardened mass

CAKEWALK *v* -ED, -ING, -S to step stylishly

CAKEY *adj* CAKIER, CAKIEST tending to form lumps

CAKY *adj* CAKIER, CAKIEST cakey

CALABASH *n* pl. -ES a gourd

CALADIUM *n* pl. -S a tropical plant

CALAMAR *n* pl. -S calamary

CALAMARI *n* pl. -S squid used as food

CALAMARY *n* pl. -MARIES a squid

CALAMI pl. of calamus

CALAMINE *v* -MINED, -MINING, -MINES to apply an ointment for skin ailments

CALAMINT *n* pl. -S a perennial herb

CALAMITE *n* pl. -S an extinct treelike plant

CALAMITY *n* pl. -TIES a grievous misfortune

CALAMUS *n* pl. -MI a marsh plant

CALANDO *adj* gradually diminishing

CALASH *n* pl. -ES a light carriage

CALATHOS *n* pl. -THI a fruit basket

CALATHUS *n* pl. -THI calathos

CALCANEA *n/pl* calcanei

CALCANEI *n/pl* bones of the heel

CALCAR *n* pl. -CARIA an anatomical projection

CALCAR *n* pl. -S a type of oven

CALCEATE *adj* wearing shoes

CALCES a pl. of calx

CALCIC *adj* pertaining to lime or calcium

CALCIFIC *adj* containing salts of calcium

CALCIFY *v* -FIED, -FYING, -FIES to harden

CALCINE *v* -CINED, -CINING, -CINES to reduce to a calx by heat

CALCITE *n* pl. -S a mineral **CALCITIC** *adj*

CALCIUM *n* pl. -S a metallic element

CALCSPAR *n* pl. -S a calcite

CALCTUFA *n* pl. -S a mineral deposit

CALCTUFF *n* pl. -S calctufa

CALCULUS *n* pl. -LI or -LUSES a branch of mathematics

CALDARIA *n/pl* rooms for taking hot baths

CALDERA *n* pl. -S a large crater

CALDRON *n* pl. -S a large kettle or boiler

CALECHE *n* pl. -S calash

CALENDAL *adj* pertaining to calends

CALENDAR *v* -ED, -ING, -S to schedule

CALENDER *v* -ED, -ING, -S to smooth by pressing between rollers

CALENDS *n* pl. CALENDS the first day of the Roman month

CALESA *n* pl. -S a calash

CALF *n* pl. CALVES or CALFS a young cow or bull **CALFLIKE** *adj*

CALFSKIN *n* pl. -S the skin of a calf

CALIBER *n* pl. -S the diameter of a gun barrel

CALIBRE *n* pl. -S caliber **CALIBRED** *adj*

CALICES pl. of calix

CALICHE *n* pl. -S a mineral deposit

CALICLE *n* pl. -S a cup-shaped, anatomical structure

CALICO *n* pl. -COES or -COS a cotton fabric

CALIF *n* pl. -S caliph

CALIFATE *n* pl. -S the domain of a calif

CALIPASH *n* pl. -ES an edible part of a turtle

CALIPEE *n* pl. -S an edible part of a turtle

CALIPER *v* -ED, -ING, -S to use a type of measuring device

CALIPH *n* pl. -S a Muslim leader **CALIPHAL** *adj*

CALISAYA *n* pl. -S the medicinal bark of the cinchona

CALIX *n* pl. -LICES a cup

CALK *v* -ED, -ING, -S to caulk

CALKER *n* pl. -S one that calks

CALKIN *n* pl. -S a gripping projection on a horseshoe

CALL *v* -ED, -ING, -S to summon **CALLABLE** *adj*

CALLA *n* pl. -S a tropical plant

CALLALOO *n* pl. -LOOS a crabmeat soup

CALLAN *n* pl. -S callant

CALLANT *n* pl. -S a lad

CALLBACK *n* pl. -S a recall of a defective product

CALLBOY *n* pl. -BOYS a bellboy

CALLER *n* pl. -S one that calls

CALLET *n* pl. -S a prostitute

CALLING *n* pl. -S a vocation or profession

CALLIOPE *n* pl. -S a keyboard musical instrument

CALLIPEE *n* pl. -S calipee

CALLIPER	*v* -ED, -ING, -S to caliper
CALLOSE	*n* pl. -S a part of a plant cell wall
CALLOUS	*v* -ED, -ING, -ES to make or become hard
CALLOW	*adj* -LOWER, -LOWEST immature
CALLUS	*v* -ED, -ING, -ES to form a hard growth
CALM	*adj* CALMER, CALMEST free from agitation **CALMLY** *adv*
CALM	*v* -ED, -ING, -S to make calm
CALMNESS	*n* pl. -ES the state of being calm
CALO	*n* pl. CALO a Spanish argot used by Chicano youths
CALOMEL	*n* pl. -S a chemical compound used as a purgative
CALORIC	*n* pl. -S heat
CALORIE	*n* pl. -S a unit of heat
CALORIZE	*v* -RIZED, -RIZING, -RIZES to coat steel with aluminum
CALORY	*n* pl. -RIES calorie
CALOTTE	*n* pl. -S a skullcap
CALOTYPE	*n* pl. -S a kind of photograph
CALOYER	*n* pl. -S a monk of the Eastern Church
CALPAC	*n* pl. -S a sheepskin hat
CALPACK	*n* pl. -S calpac
CALQUE	*v* CALQUED, CALQUING, CALQUES to model a word's meaning upon that of an analogous word in another language
CALTHROP	*n* pl. -S caltrop
CALTRAP	*n* pl. -S caltrop
CALTROP	*n* pl. -S a spiny plant
CALUMET	*n* pl. -S a ceremonial pipe
CALUMNY	*n* pl. -NIES a false and malicious accusation
CALUTRON	*n* pl. -S a device used for separating isotopes
CALVADOS	*n* pl. -ES a dry apple brandy
CALVARIA	*n* pl. -S the dome of the skull
CALVARY	*n* pl. -RIES a representation of the Crucifixion
CALVE	*v* CALVED, CALVING, CALVES to give birth to a calf
CALVES	a pl. of calf
CALX	*n* pl. -ES or CALCES a mineral residue
CALYCATE	*adj* calycine
CALYCEAL	*adj* calycine
CALYCES	a pl. of calyx
CALYCINE	*adj* pertaining to a calyx
CALYCLE	*n* pl. -S an outer calyx
CALYCULI	*n/pl* small, cup-shaped structures
CALYPSO	*n* pl. -SOS or -SOES an improvised song
CALYPTER	*n* pl. -S calyptra
CALYPTRA	*n* pl. -S a hood-shaped organ of flowers
CALYX	*n* pl. -LYXES or -LYCES the outer protective covering of a flower
CALZONE	*n* pl. -S a turnover with a savory filling
CAM	*n* pl. -S a rotating or sliding piece of machinery
CAMAIL	*n* pl. -S a piece of armor for the neck **CAMAILED** *adj*
CAMAS	*n* pl. -ES camass
CAMASS	*n* pl. -ES a perennial herb
CAMBER	*v* -ED, -ING, -S to arch slightly
CAMBIA	a pl. of cambium
CAMBIAL	*adj* pertaining to cambium
CAMBISM	*n* pl. -S the theory and practice of exchange in commerce
CAMBIST	*n* pl. -S a dealer in bills of exchange
CAMBIUM	*n* pl. -BIUMS or -BIA a layer of plant tissue
CAMBOGIA	*n* pl. -S a gum resin
CAMBRIC	*n* pl. -S a fine linen
CAME	*n* pl. -S a leaden window rod
CAMEL	*n* pl. -S a large, humped mammal
CAMELEER	*n* pl. -S a camel driver
CAMELIA	*n* pl. -S camellia
CAMELLIA	*n* pl. -S a tropical shrub
CAMEO	*v* -ED, -ING, -S to portray in sharp, delicate relief
CAMERA	*n* pl. -ERAS or -ERAE a judge's chamber **CAMERAL** *adj*
CAMION	*n* pl. -S a military truck
CAMISA	*n* pl. -S a shirt or chemise
CAMISADE	*n* pl. -S camisado
CAMISADO	*n* pl. -DOS or -DOES an attack made at night
CAMISE	*n* pl. -S a loose shirt or gown
CAMISIA	*n* pl. -S camise

CAMISOLE *n* pl. -S a brief negligee

CAMLET *n* pl. -S a durable fabric

CAMOMILE *n* pl. -S a medicinal herb

CAMORRA *n* pl. -S an unscrupulous secret society

CAMP *v* -ED, -ING, -S to live in the open

CAMPAGNA *n* pl. -PAGNE a flat, open plain

CAMPAIGN *v* -ED, -ING, -S to conduct a series of operations to reach a specific goal

CAMPER *n* pl. -S one that camps

CAMPFIRE *n* pl. -S an outdoor fire

CAMPHENE *n* pl. -S camphine

CAMPHINE *n* pl. -S an explosive liquid

CAMPHIRE *n* pl. -S a flowering plant

CAMPHOL *n* pl. -S borneol

CAMPHOR *n* pl. -S a volatile compound

CAMPI pl. of campo

CAMPIER comparative of campy

CAMPIEST superlative of campy

CAMPILY *adv* in a campy manner

CAMPING *n* pl. -S the act of living outdoors

CAMPION *n* pl. -S an herb

CAMPO *n* pl. -PI an open space in a town

CAMPO *n* pl. -POS a level, grassy plain

CAMPONG *n* pl. -S kampong

CAMPOREE *n* pl. -S a gathering of Boy Scouts

CAMPSITE *n* pl. -S an area suitable for camping

CAMPUS *v* -ED, -ING, -ES to restrict a student to the school grounds

CAMPY *adj* CAMPIER, CAMPIEST comically exaggerated

CAMSHAFT *n* pl. -S a shaft fitted with cams

CAN *v* CANNED, CANNING, CANS to put in a can (a cylindrical container)

CAN *v* present sing. 2d person CAN or CANST, past sing. 2d person COULD, COULDEST, or COULDST — used as an auxiliary to express ability

CANAILLE *n* pl. -S the common people

CANAKIN *n* pl. -S cannikin

CANAL *v* -NALLED, -NALLING, -NALS or -NALED, -NALING, -NALS to dig an artificial waterway through

CANALISE *v* -ISED, -ISING, -ISES to canalize

CANALIZE *v* -IZED, -IZING, -IZES to canal

CANALLED a past tense of canal

CANALLER *n* pl. -S a freight boat

CANALLING a present participle of canal

CANAPE *n* pl. -S a food served before a meal

CANARD *n* pl. -S a false story

CANARY *n* pl. -NARIES a songbird

CANASTA *n* pl. -S a card game

CANCAN *n* pl. -S a dance marked by high kicking

CANCEL *v* -CELED, -CELING, -CELS or -CELLED, -CELLING, -CELS to annul

CANCELER *n* pl. -S one that cancels

CANCER *n* pl. -S a malignant growth

CANCHA *n* pl. -S a jai alai court

CANCROID *n* pl. -S a skin cancer

CANDELA *n* pl. -S a unit of light intensity

CANDENT *adj* glowing

CANDID *adj* -DIDER, -DIDEST frank and sincere

CANDID *n* pl. -S an unposed photograph

CANDIDA *n* pl. -S a parasitic fungus

CANDIDLY *adv* in a candid manner

CANDIED past tense of candy

CANDIES present 3d person sing. of candy

CANDLE *v* -DLED, -DLING, -DLES to examine eggs in front of a light

CANDLER *n* pl. -S one that candles

CANDOR *n* pl. -S frankness; sincerity

CANDOUR *n* pl. -S candor

CANDY *v* -DIED, -DYING, -DIES to coat with sugar

CANE *v* CANED, CANING, CANES to weave or furnish with cane (hollow woody stems)

CANELLA *n* pl. -S a medicinal tree bark

CANEPHOR *n* pl. -S a Greek maiden bearing a basket on her head

CANER *n* pl. -S one that canes

CANEWARE *n* pl. -S a yellowish stoneware

CANFIELD *n* pl. -S a card game

CANFUL *n* pl. CANFULS or CANSFUL as much as a can holds

CANGUE *n* pl. -S an ancient Chinese punishing device

CANID *n* pl. -S a dog

CANIKIN *n* pl. -S cannikin

CANINE *n* pl. -S a dog

CANING present participle of cane

CANINITY *n* pl. -TIES the state of being a canine

CANISTER *n* pl. -S a small, metal box

CANITIES *n* pl. CANITIES the turning gray of the hair

CANKER *v* -ED, -ING, -S to affect with ulcerous sores

CANNA *n* pl. -S a tropical plant

CANNABIC *adj* pertaining to cannabis

CANNABIN *n* pl. -S a resin extracted from cannabis

CANNABIS *n* pl. -BISES hemp

CANNED past tense of can

CANNEL *n* pl. -S an oily, compact coal

CANNELON *n* pl. -S a stuffed roll

CANNER *n* pl. -S one that cans food

CANNERY *n* pl. -NERIES a place where food is canned

CANNIBAL *n* pl. -S one who eats his own kind

CANNIE *adj* -NIER, -NIEST canny

CANNIER comparative of canny

CANNIEST superlative of canny

CANNIKIN *n* pl. -S a small can or cup

CANNILY *adv* in a canny manner

CANNING *n* pl. -S the business of preserving food in airtight containers

CANNOLI *n/pl* a tube of pastry

CANNON *v* -ED, -ING, -S to fire a cannon (a heavy firearm)

CANNONRY *n* pl. -RIES artillery

CANNOT the negative form of can

CANNULA *n* pl. -LAS or -LAE a tube inserted into a bodily cavity **CANNULAR** *adj*

CANNY *adj* -NIER, -NIEST prudent

CANOE *v* -NOED, -NOEING, -NOES to paddle a canoe (a light, slender boat)

CANOEIST *n* pl. -S one who canoes

CANOLA *n* pl. CANOLA an oil from the seeds of a kind of herb

CANON *n* pl. -S a law decreed by a church council **CANONIC** *adj*

CANONESS *n* pl. -ES a woman who lives according to a canon

CANONISE *v* -ISED, -ISING, -ISES to canonize

CANONIST *n* pl. -S a specialist in canon law

CANONIZE *v* -IZED, -IZING, -IZES to declare to be a saint

CANONRY *n* pl. -RIES a clerical office

CANOODLE *v* -DLED, -DLING, -DLES to caress

CANOPY *v* -PIED, -PYING, -PIES to cover from above

CANOROUS *adj* melodic

CANSFUL a pl. of canful

CANSO *n* pl. -SOS a love song

CANST a present 2d person sing. of can

CANT *v* -ED, -ING, -S to tilt or slant

CANTALA *n* pl. -S a tropical plant

CANTATA *n* pl. -S a vocal composition

CANTDOG *n* pl. -S a device used to move logs

CANTEEN *n* pl. -S a small container for carrying water

CANTER *v* -ED, -ING, -S to ride a horse at a moderate pace

CANTHUS *n* pl. -THI a corner of the eye **CANTHAL** *adj*

CANTIC *adj* slanted

CANTICLE *n* pl. -S a hymn

CANTINA *n* pl. -S a saloon

CANTLE *n* pl. -S the rear part of a saddle

CANTO *n* pl. -TOS a division of a long poem

CANTON *v* -ED, -ING, -S to divide into cantons (districts)

CANTONAL *adj* pertaining to a canton

CANTOR *n* pl. -S a religious singer

CANTRAIP *n* pl. -S cantrip

CANTRAP *n* pl. -S cantrip

CANTRIP *n* pl. -S a magic spell

CANTUS *n* pl. CANTUS a style of church music

CANTY *adj* cheerful

CANULA *n* pl. -LAS or -LAE cannula

CANULATE *v* -LATED, -LATING, -LATES to insert a canula into

CANVAS *v* -ED, -ING, -ES to canvass

CANVASER	*n* pl. -S one that canvases
CANVASS	*v* -ED, -ING, -ES to examine thoroughly
CANYON	*n* pl. -S a deep valley with steep sides
CANZONA	*n* pl. -S canzone
CANZONE	*n* pl. -NI or -NES a form of lyric poetry
CANZONET	*n* pl. -S a short song
CAP	*v* CAPPED, CAPPING, CAPS to provide with a cap (a type of head covering)
CAPABLE	*adj* -BLER, -BLEST having ability **CAPABLY** *adv*
CAPACITY	*n* pl. -TIES the ability to receive or contain
CAPE	*n* pl. -S a sleeveless garment **CAPED** *adj*
CAPELAN	*n* pl. -S capelin
CAPELET	*n* pl. -S a small cape
CAPELIN	*n* pl. -S a small, edible fish
CAPER	*v* -ED, -ING, -S to frolic
CAPERER	*n* pl. -S one that capers
CAPESKIN	*n* pl. -S a soft leather
CAPEWORK	*n* pl. -S a bullfighting technique
CAPFUL	*n* pl. -S as much as a cap can hold
CAPH	*n* pl. -S kaph
CAPIAS	*n* pl. -ES a judicial writ
CAPITA	pl. of caput
CAPITAL	*n* pl. -S the upper part of a column
CAPITATE	*adj* head-shaped
CAPITOL	*n* pl. -S a building occupied by a state legislature
CAPITULA	*n/pl* flower clusters
CAPLESS	*adj* being without a cap
CAPLET	*n* pl. -S a coated tablet
CAPLIN	*n* pl. -S capelin
CAPMAKER	*n* pl. -S one that makes caps
CAPO	*n* pl. -POS a pitch-raising device for fretted instruments
CAPON	*n* pl. -S a gelded rooster
CAPONATA	*n* pl. -S a relish made with eggplant
CAPONIER	*n* pl. -S a type of defense
CAPONIZE	*v* -IZED, -IZING, -IZES to geld a rooster
CAPORAL	*n* pl. -S a coarse tobacco
CAPOTE	*n* pl. -S a hooded cloak or overcoat
CAPOUCH	*n* pl. -ES capuche
CAPPED	past tense of cap
CAPPER	*n* pl. -S a capmaker
CAPPING	*n* pl. -S a wax covering in a honeycomb
CAPRIC	*adj* pertaining to a goat
CAPRICCI	*n/pl* caprices
CAPRICE	*n* pl. -S a whim
CAPRIFIG	*n* pl. -S a European tree
CAPRINE	*adj* capric
CAPRIOLE	*v* -OLED, -OLING, -OLES to leap
CAPRIS	*n/pl* pants for women
CAPROCK	*n* pl. -S an overlying rock layer
CAPSICIN	*n* pl. -S a liquid used as a flavoring
CAPSICUM	*n* pl. -S a tropical herb
CAPSID	*n* pl. -S the outer shell of a virus particle **CAPSIDAL** *adj*
CAPSIZE	*v* -SIZED, -SIZING, -SIZES to overturn
CAPSOMER	*n* pl. -S a protein forming the capsid
CAPSTAN	*n* pl. -S a machine used to hoist weights
CAPSTONE	*n* pl. -S the top stone of a structure
CAPSULAR	*adj* enclosed and compact
CAPSULE	*v* -SULED, -SULING, -SULES to condense into a brief form
CAPTAIN	*v* -ED, -ING, -S to lead or command
CAPTAN	*n* pl. -S a fungicide
CAPTION	*v* -ED, -ING, -S to provide with a title
CAPTIOUS	*adj* tending to find fault
CAPTIVE	*n* pl. -S a prisoner
CAPTOR	*n* pl. -S one who takes or holds a captive
CAPTURE	*v* -TURED, -TURING, -TURES to take by force or cunning
CAPTURER	*n* pl. -S one that captures
CAPUCHE	*n* pl. -S a hood or cowl **CAPUCHED** *adj*
CAPUCHIN	*n* pl. -S a long-tailed monkey
CAPUT	*n* pl. CAPITA a head or head-like part
CAPYBARA	*n* pl. -S a large rodent

CAR *n* pl. -S an automobile

CARABAO *n* pl. -BAOS a water buffalo

CARABID *n* pl. -S a predatory beetle

CARABIN *n* pl. -S carbine

CARABINE *n* pl. -S carbine

CARACAL *n* pl. -S an African lynx

CARACARA *n* pl. -S a large hawk

CARACK *n* pl. -S carrack

CARACOL *v* -COLLED, -COLLING, -COLS to caracole

CARACOLE *v* -COLED, -COLING, -COLES to perform a half turn on a horse

CARACUL *n* pl. -S karakul

CARAFE *n* pl. -S a glass bottle

CARAGANA *n* pl. -S an Asian shrub

CARAGEEN *n* pl. -S an edible seaweed

CARAMBA *interj* — used to express surprise or dismay

CARAMEL *n* pl. -S a chewy candy

CARANGID *n* pl. -S a marine fish

CARAPACE *n* pl. -S a hard, protective outer covering

CARAPAX *n* pl. -ES carapace

CARASSOW *n* pl. -S curassow

CARAT *n* pl. -S a unit of weight for gems

CARATE *n* pl. -S a tropical skin disease

CARAVAN *v* -VANED, -VANING, -VANS or -VANNED, -VANNING, -VANS to travel in a group

CARAVEL *n* pl. -S a small sailing ship

CARAWAY *n* pl. -WAYS an herb used in cooking

CARB *n* pl. -S a carburetor

CARBAMIC *adj* pertaining to a type of acid

CARBAMYL *n* pl. -S a chemical radical

CARBARN *n* pl. -S a garage for buses

CARBARYL *n* pl. -S an insecticide

CARBIDE *n* pl. -S a carbon compound

CARBINE *n* pl. -S a light rifle

CARBINOL *n* pl. -S an alcohol

CARBO *n* pl. -S a carbohydrate

CARBOLIC *n* pl. -S an acidic compound

CARBON *n* pl. -S a nonmetallic element **CARBONIC** *adj*

CARBONYL *n* pl. -S a chemical compound

CARBORA *n* pl. -S a wood-boring worm

CARBOXYL *n* pl. -S a univalent acid radical

CARBOY *n* pl. -BOYS a large bottle **CARBOYED** *adj*

CARBURET *v* -RETED, -RETING, -RETS or -RETTED, -RETTING, -RETS to combine chemically with carbon

CARCAJOU *n* pl. -S a carnivorous mammal

CARCANET *n* pl. -S a jeweled necklace

CARCASE *n* pl. -S carcass

CARCASS *n* pl. -ES the body of a dead animal

CARCEL *n* pl. -S a unit of illumination

CARD *v* -ED, -ING, -S to provide with a card (a stiff piece of paper)

CARDAMOM *n* pl. -S a tropical herb

CARDAMON *n* pl. -S cardamom

CARDAMUM *n* pl. -S cardamom

CARDCASE *n* pl. -S a case for holding cards

CARDER *n* pl. -S one that does carding

CARDIA *n* pl. -DIAS or -DIAE an opening of the esophagus

CARDIAC *n* pl. -S a person with a heart disorder

CARDIGAN *n* pl. -S a type of sweater

CARDINAL *n* pl. -S a bright red bird

CARDING *n* pl. -S the process of combing and cleaning cotton fibers; cleaned and combed fibers

CARDIOID *n* pl. -S a heart-shaped curve

CARDITIS *n* pl. -TISES inflammation of the heart **CARDITIC** *adj*

CARDOON *n* pl. -S a perennial plant

CARE *v* CARED, CARING, CARES to be concerned or interested

CAREEN *v* -ED, -ING, -S to lurch while moving

CAREENER *n* pl. -S one that careens

CAREER *v* -ED, -ING, -S to go at full speed

CAREERER *n* pl. -S one that careers

CAREFREE *adj* being without worry or anxiety

CAREFUL *adj* -FULLER, -FULLEST cautious

CARELESS *adj* inattentive; negligent

CARER *n* pl. -S one that cares

CARESS *v* -ED, -ING, -ES to touch lovingly

CARESSER *n* pl. -S one that caresses

CARET *n* pl. -S a proofreaders' symbol

CARETAKE *v* -TOOK, -TAKEN, -TAKING, -TAKES to take care of someone else's house or land

CAREWORN *adj* haggard

CAREX *n* pl. CARICES a marsh plant

CARFARE *n* pl. -S payment for a bus or car ride

CARFUL *n* pl. -S as much as a car can hold

CARGO *n* pl. -GOS or -GOES conveyed merchandise

CARHOP *n* pl. -S a waitress at a drive-in restaurant

CARIBE *n* pl. -S the piranha

CARIBOU *n* pl. -S a large deer

CARICES pl. of carex

CARIES *n* pl. CARIES tooth decay **CARIED** *adj*

CARILLON *v* -LONNED, -LONNING, -LONS to play a set of bells

CARINA *n* pl. -NAS or -NAE a carinate anatomical part **CARINAL** *adj*

CARINATE *adj* shaped like the keel of a ship

CARING present participle of care

CARIOCA *n* pl. -S a South American dance

CARIOLE *n* pl. -S a small, open carriage

CARIOUS *adj* decayed

CARITAS *n* pl. -ES love for all people

CARK *v* -ED, -ING, -S to worry

CARL *n* pl. -S a peasant

CARLE *n* pl. -S carl

CARLESS *adj* being without a car

CARLIN *n* pl. -S an old woman

CARLINE *n* pl. -S carling

CARLING *n* pl. -S a beam supporting a ship's deck

CARLISH *adj* resembling a carl

CARLOAD *n* pl. -S as much as a car can hold

CARMAKER *n* pl. -S an automobile manufacturer

CARMAN *n* pl. -MEN a streetcar driver

CARMINE *n* pl. -S a vivid red color

CARN *n* pl. -S cairn

CARNAGE *n* pl. -S great and bloody slaughter

CARNAL *adj* pertaining to bodily appetites **CARNALLY** *adv*

CARNAUBA *n* pl. -S a palm tree

CARNET *n* pl. -S an official permit

CARNEY *n* pl. -NEYS carny

CARNIE *n* pl. -S carny

CARNIES pl. of carny

CARNIFY *v* -FIED, -FYING, -FIES to form into flesh

CARNIVAL *n* pl. -S a traveling amusement show

CARNY *n* pl. -NIES a carnival

CAROACH *n* pl. -ES caroche

CAROB *n* pl. -S an evergreen tree

CAROCH *n* pl. -ES caroche

CAROCHE *n* pl. -S a stately carriage

CAROL *v* -OLED, -OLING, -OLS or -OLLED, -OLLING, -OLS to sing joyously

CAROLER *n* pl. -S one that carols

CAROLI a pl. of carolus

CAROLLED a past tense of carol

CAROLLER *n* pl. -S caroler

CAROLLING a present participle of carol

CAROLUS *n* pl. -LUSES or -LI an old English coin

CAROM *v* -ED, -ING, -S to collide with and rebound

CAROTENE *n* pl. -S a plant pigment

CAROTID *n* pl. -S an artery in the neck

CAROTIN *n* pl. -S carotene

CAROUSAL *n* pl. -S a boisterous drinking party

CAROUSE *v* -ROUSED, -ROUSING, -ROUSES to engage in a carousal

CAROUSEL *n* pl. -S an amusement park ride

CAROUSER *n* pl. -S one that carouses

CAROUSING present participle of carouse

CARP *v* -ED, -ING, -S to find fault unreasonably

CARPAL *n* pl. -S carpale

CARPALE *n* pl. -LIA a bone of the wrist

CARPEL *n* pl. -S a simple pistil

CARPER *n* pl. -S one that carps

CARPET *v* -ED, -ING, -S to cover a floor with a heavy fabric

CARPI pl. of carpus

CARPING *n* pl. -S the act of one who carps

CARPOOL *v* -ED, -ING, -S to take turns driving a group of commuters

CARPORT *n* pl. -S a shelter for a car

CARPUS *n* pl. -PI the wrist

CARR *n* pl. -S a marsh

CARRACK *n* pl. -S a type of merchant ship

CARREL *n* pl. -S a desk in a library stack for solitary study

CARRELL *n* pl. -S carrel

CARRIAGE *n* pl. -S a wheeled, horse-drawn vehicle

CARRIED past tense of carry

CARRIER *n* pl. -S one that carries

CARRIES present 3d person sing. of carry

CARRIOLE *n* pl. -S cariole

CARRION *n* pl. -S dead and putrefying flesh

CARRITCH *n* pl. -ES a religious handbook

CARROCH *n* pl. -ES caroche

CARROM *v* -ED, -ING, -S to carom

CARROT *n* pl. -S an edible orange root

CARROTIN *n* pl. -S carotene

CARROTY *adj* -ROTIER, -ROTIEST resembling a carrot in color

CARRY *v* -RIED, -RYING, -RIES to convey from one place to another

CARRYALL *n* pl. -S a light covered carriage

CARRYON *n* pl. -S a small piece of luggage

CARRYOUT *n* pl. -S a take-out order of food

CARSE *n* pl. -S low, fertile land along a river

CARSICK *adj* nauseated from riding in a car

CART *v* -ED, -ING, -S to convey in a cart (a two-wheeled vehicle) **CARTABLE** *adj*

CARTAGE *n* pl. -S the act of carting

CARTE *n* pl. -S a menu

CARTEL *n* pl. -S a business organization

CARTER *n* pl. -S one that carts

CARTLOAD *n* pl. -S as much as a cart can hold

CARTON *v* -ED, -ING, -S to pack in a cardboard box

CARTOON *v* -ED, -ING, -S to sketch a cartoon (a humorous representation) of

CARTOONY *adj* resembling a cartoon

CARTOP *adj* able to fit on top of a car

CARTOUCH *n* pl. -ES a scroll-like tablet

CARUNCLE *n* pl. -S a fleshy outgrowth

CARVE *v* CARVED, CARVING, CARVES to form by cutting

CARVEL *n* pl. -S caravel

CARVEN *adj* carved

CARVER *n* pl. -S one that carves

CARVING *n* pl. -S a carved figure or design

CARWASH *n* pl. -ES an establishment equipped to wash automobiles

CARYATIC *adj* resembling a caryatid

CARYATID *n* pl. -S or -ES a sculptured female figure used as a column

CARYOTIN *n* pl. -S karyotin

CASA *n* pl. -S a dwelling

CASABA *n* pl. -S a variety of melon

CASAVA *n* pl. -S cassava

CASBAH *n* pl. -S the old section of a North African city

CASCABEL *n* pl. -S the rear part of a cannon

CASCABLE *n* pl. -S cascabel

CASCADE *v* -CADED, -CADING, -CADES to fall like a waterfall

CASCARA *n* pl. -S a medicinal tree bark

CASE *v* CASED, CASING, CASES to put in a case (a container or receptacle)

CASEASE *n* pl. -S an enzyme

CASEATE *v* -ATED, -ATING, -ATES to become cheesy

CASEBOOK *n* pl. -S a law textbook

CASED past tense of case

CASEFY *v* -FIED, -FYING, -FIES to caseate

CASEIN *n* pl. -S a milk protein **CASEIC** *adj*

CASELOAD *n* pl. -S the number of cases being handled

CASEMATE *n* pl. -S a bombproof shelter

CASEMENT *n* pl. -S a type of window

CASEOSE *n* pl. -S a proteose

CASEOUS *adj* cheesy

CASERN *n* pl. -S a barracks for soldiers

CASERNE *n* pl. -S casern

CASETTE *n* pl. -S cassette

CASEWORK *n* pl. -S a form of social work

CASEWORM *n* pl. -S an insect larva

CASH *v* -ED, -ING, -ES to convert into cash (ready money) **CASHABLE** *adj*

CASHAW	*n* pl. -S cushaw
CASHBOOK	*n* pl. -S a book of monetary records
CASHBOX	*n* pl. -ES a container for money
CASHEW	*n* pl. -S a nut-bearing tree
CASHIER	*v* -ED, -ING, -S to dismiss in disgrace
CASHLESS	*adj* having no cash
CASHMERE	*n* pl. -S a fine wool
CASHOO	*n* pl. -SHOOS catechu
CASIMERE	*n* pl. -S a woolen fabric
CASIMIRE	*n* pl. -S casimere
CASING	*n* pl. -S a protective outer covering
CASINO	*n* pl. -NOS or -NI a gambling room
CASITA	*n* pl. -S a small house
CASK	*v* -ED, -ING, -S to store in a cask (a strong barrel)
CASKET	*v* -ED, -ING, -S to place in a casket (a burial case)
CASKY	*adj* resembling a cask
CASQUE	*n* pl. -S a helmet **CASQUED** *adj*
CASSABA	*n* pl. -S casaba
CASSATA	*n* pl. -S an Italian ice cream
CASSAVA	*n* pl. -S a tropical plant
CASSETTE	*n* pl. -S a small case containing audiotape or videotape
CASSIA	*n* pl. -S a variety of cinnamon
CASSINO	*n* pl. -NOS a card game
CASSIS	*n* pl. -SISES a European bush
CASSOCK	*n* pl. -S a long garment worn by clergymen
CAST	*v* CAST, CASTING, CASTS to throw with force **CASTABLE** *adj*
CASTANET	*n* pl. -S a rhythm instrument
CASTAWAY	*n* pl. -WAYS an outcast
CASTE	*n* pl. -S a system of distinct social classes
CASTEISM	*n* pl. -S the use of a caste system
CASTER	*n* pl. -S a small, swiveling wheel
CASTING	*n* pl. -S something made in a mold
CASTLE	*v* -TLED, -TLING, -TLES to make a certain move in chess
CASTOFF	*n* pl. -S a discarded person or thing
CASTOR	*n* pl. -S caster
CASTRATE	*v* -TRATED, -TRATING, -TRATES to remove the testes of
CASTRATO	*n* pl. -TI a singer castrated in boyhood
CASUAL	*n* pl. -S one who works occasionally
CASUALLY	*adv* informally
CASUALTY	*n* pl. -TIES a victim of war or disaster
CASUIST	*n* pl. -S one who resolves ethical problems
CASUS	*n* pl. CASUS a legal occurrence or event
CAT	*v* CATTED, CATTING, CATS to hoist an anchor to the cathead
CATACOMB	*n* pl. -S an underground cemetery
CATALASE	*n* pl. -S an enzyme
CATALO	*n* pl. -LOS or -LOES a hybrid between a buffalo and a cow
CATALOG	*v* -ED, -ING, -S to classify information descriptively
CATALPA	*n* pl. -S a tree
CATALYST	*n* pl. -S a substance that accelerates a chemical reaction
CATALYZE	*v* -LYZED, -LYZING, -LYZES to act as a catalyst
CATAMITE	*n* pl. -S a boy used in sodomy
CATAPULT	*v* -ED, -ING, -S to hurl through the air
CATARACT	*n* pl. -S a tremendous waterfall
CATARRH	*n* pl. -S inflammation of a mucous membrane
CATAWBA	*n* pl. -S a variety of fox grape
CATBIRD	*n* pl. -S a songbird
CATBOAT	*n* pl. -S a small sailboat
CATBRIER	*n* pl. -S a thorny vine
CATCALL	*v* -ED, -ING, -S to deride by making shrill sounds
CATCH	*v* CAUGHT, CATCHING, CATCHES to capture after pursuit
CATCHALL	*n* pl. -S a container for odds and ends
CATCHER	*n* pl. -S one that catches
CATCHFLY	*n* pl. -FLIES an insect-catching plant
CATCHUP	*n* pl. -S ketchup
CATCHY	*adj* CATCHIER, CATCHIEST pleasing and easily remembered
CATCLAW	*n* pl. -S a flowering shrub

CATE	*n* pl. -S a choice food
CATECHIN	*n* pl. -S a chemical used in dyeing
CATECHOL	*n* pl. -S a chemical used in photography
CATECHU	*n* pl. -S a resin used in tanning
CATEGORY	*n* pl. -RIES a division in any system of classification
CATENA	*n* pl. -NAS or -NAE a closely linked series
CATENARY	*n* pl. -NARIES a mathematical curve
CATENATE	*v* -NATED, -NATING, -NATES to link together
CATENOID	*n* pl. -S a geometric surface
CATER	*v* -ED, -ING, -S to provide food and service for
CATERAN	*n* pl. -S a brigand
CATERER	*n* pl. -S one that caters
CATERESS	*n* pl. -ES a woman who caters
CATFACE	*n* pl. -S a deformity of fruit
CATFALL	*n* pl. -S an anchor line
CATFIGHT	*n* pl. -S a fight between two women
CATFISH	*n* pl. -ES a scaleless, large-headed fish
CATGUT	*n* pl. -S a strong cord
CATHEAD	*n* pl. -S a beam projecting from a ship's bow
CATHECT	*v* -ED, -ING, -S to invest with psychic energy
CATHEDRA	*n* pl. -DRAS or -DRAE a bishop's throne
CATHETER	*n* pl. -S a medical instrument
CATHEXIS	*n* pl. -THEXES the concentration of psychic energy on a person or idea
CATHODE	*n* pl. -S a negatively charged electrode **CATHODAL, CATHODIC** *adj*
CATHOLIC	*n* pl. -S a member of the early Christian church
CATHOUSE	*n* pl. -S a brothel
CATION	*n* pl. -S a positively charged ion **CATIONIC** *adj*
CATKIN	*n* pl. -S a flower cluster
CATLIKE	*adj* resembling a cat; stealthy; silent
CATLIN	*n* pl. -S catling
CATLING	*n* pl. -S a surgical knife
CATMINT	*n* pl. -S catnip
CATNAP	*v* -NAPPED, -NAPPING, -NAPS to doze
CATNAPER	*n* pl. -S one that steals cats
CATNIP	*n* pl. -S an aromatic herb
CATSPAW	*n* pl. -S a light wind
CATSUP	*n* pl. -S ketchup
CATTAIL	*n* pl. -S a marsh plant
CATTALO	*n* pl. -LOS or -LOES catalo
CATTED	past tense of cat
CATTERY	*n* pl. -TERIES an establishment for breeding cats
CATTIE	*n* pl. -S an Asian unit of weight
CATTIER	comparative of catty
CATTIEST	superlative of catty
CATTILY	*adv* in a catty manner
CATTING	present participle of cat
CATTISH	*adj* catty
CATTLE	*n/pl* domesticated bovines
CATTLEYA	*n* pl. -S a tropical orchid
CATTY	*adj* -TIER, -TIEST catlike; spiteful
CATWALK	*n* pl. -S a narrow walkway
CAUCUS	*v* -CUSED, -CUSING, -CUSES or -CUSSED, -CUSSING, -CUSSES to hold a political meeting
CAUDAD	*adv* toward the tail
CAUDAL	*adj* taillike **CAUDALLY** *adv*
CAUDATE	*n* pl. -S a basal ganglion of the brain
CAUDATED	*adj* having a tail
CAUDEX	*n* pl. -DICES or -DEXES the woody base of some plants
CAUDILLO	*n* pl. -DILLOS a military dictator
CAUDLE	*n* pl. -S a warm beverage
CAUGHT	past tense of catch
CAUL	*n* pl. -S a fetal membrane
CAULD	*n* pl. -S cold
CAULDRON	*n* pl. -S caldron
CAULES	pl. of caulis
CAULICLE	*n* pl. -S a small stem
CAULINE	*adj* pertaining to a stem
CAULIS	*n* pl. -LES a plant stem
CAULK	*v* -ED, -ING, -S to make the seams of a ship watertight
CAULKER	*n* pl. -S one that caulks

CAULKING *n* pl. -S the material used to caulk

CAUSABLE *adj* capable of being caused

CAUSAL *n* pl. -S a word expressing cause or reason

CAUSALLY *adv* by way of causing

CAUSE *v* CAUSED, CAUSING, CAUSES to bring about

CAUSER *n* pl. -S one that causes

CAUSERIE *n* pl. -S an informal conversation

CAUSEWAY *v* -ED, -ING, -S to build a causeway (a raised roadway) over

CAUSEY *n* pl. -SEYS a paved road

CAUSING present participle of cause

CAUSTIC *n* pl. -S a corrosive substance

CAUTERY *n* pl. -TERIES something used to destroy tissue

CAUTION *v* -ED, -ING, -S to warn

CAUTIOUS *adj* exercising prudence to avoid danger

CAVALERO *n* pl. -ROS a horseman

CAVALIER *v* -ED, -ING, -S to behave haughtily

CAVALLA *n* pl. -S a large food fish

CAVALLY *n* pl. -LIES cavalla

CAVALRY *n* pl. -RIES a mobile army unit

CAVATINA *n* pl. -NAS or -NE a simple song

CAVE *v* CAVED, CAVING, CAVES to hollow out

CAVEAT *v* -ED, -ING, -S to enter a type of legal notice

CAVEATOR *n* pl. -S one that files a caveat

CAVED past tense of cave

CAVEFISH *n* pl. -ES a sightless fish

CAVELIKE *adj* resembling a cave (an underground chamber)

CAVEMAN *n* pl. -MEN a cave dweller

CAVER *n* pl. -S one that caves

CAVERN *v* -ED, -ING, -S to hollow out

CAVETTO *n* pl. -TOS or -TI a concave molding

CAVIAR *n* pl. -S the roe of sturgeon

CAVIARE *n* pl. -S caviar

CAVICORN *adj* having hollow horns

CAVIE *n* pl. -S a hencoop

CAVIES pl. of cavy

CAVIL *v* -ILED, -ILING, -ILS or -ILLED, -ILLING, -ILS to carp

CAVILER *n* pl. -S one that cavils

CAVILLER *n* pl. -S caviler

CAVILLING a present participle of cavil

CAVING *n* pl. -S the sport of exploring caves

CAVITARY *adj* pertaining to the formation of cavities in tissue

CAVITATE *v* -TATED, -TATING, -TATES to form cavities

CAVITY *n* pl. -TIES an unfilled space within a mass **CAVITIED** *adj*

CAVORT *v* -ED, -ING, -S to frolic

CAVORTER *n* pl. -S one that cavorts

CAVY *n* pl. -VIES a short-tailed rodent

CAW *v* -ED, -ING, -S to utter the sound of a crow

CAY *n* pl. CAYS a small low island

CAYENNE *n* pl. -S a hot seasoning **CAYENNED** *adj*

CAYMAN *n* pl. -S caiman

CAYUSE *n* pl. -S an Indian pony

CAZIQUE *n* pl. -S cacique

CEASE *v* CEASED, CEASING, CEASES to stop

CEBID *n* pl. -S ceboid

CEBOID *n* pl. -S one of a family of monkeys

CECUM *n* pl. CECA a bodily cavity with one opening **CECAL** *adj* **CECALLY** *adv*

CEDAR *n* pl. -S an evergreen tree **CEDARN** *adj*

CEDE *v* CEDED, CEDING, CEDES to yield

CEDER *n* pl. -S one that cedes

CEDI *n* pl. -S a monetary unit of Ghana

CEDILLA *n* pl. -S a pronunciation mark

CEDING present participle of cede

CEDULA *n* pl. -S a Philippine tax

CEE *n* pl. -S the letter C

CEIBA *n* pl. -S a tropical tree

CEIL *v* -ED, -ING, -S to furnish with a ceiling

CEILER *n* pl. -S one that ceils

CEILING *n* pl. -S the overhead lining of a room

CEINTURE *n* pl. -S a belt for the waist

CEL *n* pl. -S a sheet of celluloid used in animation

CELADON *n* pl. -S a pale green color

CELEB *n* pl. -S a celebrity; a famous person

CELERIAC *n* pl. -S a variety of celery

CELERITY *n* pl. -TIES swiftness

CELERY *n* pl. -ERIES a plant with edible stalks

CELESTA *n* pl. -S a keyboard instrument

CELESTE *n* pl. -S celesta

CELIAC *n* pl. -S one that has a chronic nutritional disturbance

CELIBACY *n* pl. -CIES abstention from sexual intercourse

CELIBATE *n* pl. -S one who lives a life of celibacy

CELL *v* -ED, -ING, -S to store in a honeycomb

CELLA *n* pl. -LAE the interior of an ancient temple

CELLAR *v* -ED, -ING, -S to store in an underground room

CELLARER *n* pl. -S the steward of a monastery

CELLARET *n* pl. -S a cabinet for wine bottles

CELLIST *n* pl. -S one who plays the cello

CELLMATE *n* pl. -S one of two or more prisoners sharing a cell

CELLO *n* pl. -LOS or -LI a stringed musical instrument

CELLULAR *adj* pertaining to a cell (a basic unit of life)

CELLULE *n* pl. -S a small cell

CELOM *n* pl. -LOMS or -LOMATA coelom

CELOSIA *n* pl. -S a flowering plant

CELT *n* pl. -S a primitive ax

CEMBALO *n* pl. -LI or -LOS a harpsichord

CEMENT *v* -ED, -ING, -S to bind firmly

CEMENTER *n* pl. -S one that cements

CEMENTUM *n* pl. -TA the hard tissue covering the roots of the teeth

CEMETERY *n* pl. -TERIES a burial ground

CENACLE *n* pl. -S a small dining room

CENOBITE *n* pl. -S a member of a religious order

CENOTAPH *n* pl. -S an empty tomb

CENOTE *n* pl. -S a sinkhole in limestone

CENSE *v* CENSED, CENSING, CENSES to perfume with incense

CENSER *n* pl. -S a vessel for burning incense

CENSOR *v* -ED, -ING, -S to delete an objectionable word or passage

CENSUAL *adj* pertaining to the act of censusing

CENSURE *v* -SURED, -SURING, -SURES to criticize severely

CENSURER *n* pl. -S one that censures

CENSUS *v* -ED, -ING, -ES to take an official count of

CENT *n* pl. -S the 100th part of a dollar

CENTAL *n* pl. -S a unit of weight

CENTARE *n* pl. -S a measure of land area

CENTAUR *n* pl. -S a mythological creature

CENTAURY *n* pl. -RIES a medicinal herb

CENTAVO *n* pl. -VOS a coin of various Spanish-American nations

CENTER *v* -ED, -ING, -S to place at the center (the midpoint)

CENTESIS *n* pl. -TESES a surgical puncture

CENTIARE *n* pl. -S centare

CENTILE *n* pl. -S a value of a statistical variable

CENTIME *n* pl. -S the 100th part of a franc

CENTIMO *n* pl. -MOS any of various small coins

CENTNER *n* pl. -S a unit of weight

CENTO *n* pl. -TONES or -TOS a literary work made up of parts from other works

CENTRA a pl. of centrum

CENTRAL *n* pl. -S a telephone exchange

CENTRAL *adj* -TRALER, -TRALEST situated at, in, or near the center

CENTRE *v* -TRED, -TRING, -TRES to center

CENTRIC *adj* situated at the center

CENTRING *n* pl. -S a temporary framework for an arch

CENTRISM *n* pl. -S moderate political philosophy

CENTRIST *n* pl. -S an advocate of centrism

CENTROID *n* pl. -S the center of mass of an object

CENTRUM *n* pl. -TRUMS or -TRA the body of a vertebra

CENTUM *n* pl. -S one hundred

CENTUPLE	*v* -PLED, -PLING, -PLES to increase a hundredfold	**CEROTYPE**	*n* pl. -S a process of engraving using wax
CENTURY	*n* pl. -RIES a period of 100 years	**CEROUS**	*adj* pertaining to cerium
CEORL	*n* pl. -S a freeman of low birth **CEORLISH** *adj*	**CERTAIN**	*adj* -TAINER, -TAINEST absolutely confident
CEP	*n* pl. -S cepe	**CERTES**	*adv* in truth
CEPE	*n* pl. -S a large mushroom	**CERTIFY**	*v* -FIED, -FYING, -FIES to confirm
CEPHALAD	*adv* toward the head	**CERULEAN**	*n* pl. -S a blue color
CEPHALIC	*adj* pertaining to the head	**CERUMEN**	*n* pl. -S a waxy secretion of the ear
CEPHALIN	*n* pl. -S a bodily chemical		
CEPHEID	*n* pl. -S a giant star	**CERUSE**	*n* pl. -S a lead compound
CERAMAL	*n* pl. -S a heat-resistant alloy	**CERUSITE**	*n* pl. -S a lead ore
CERAMIC	*n* pl. -S an item made of baked clay	**CERVELAS**	*n* pl. -ES cervelat
		CERVELAT	*n* pl. -S a smoked sausage
CERAMIST	*n* pl. -S one who makes ceramics	**CERVICAL**	*adj* pertaining to the cervix
CERASTES	*n* pl. CERASTES a venomous snake	**CERVID**	*adj* of the deer family
		CERVINE	*adj* pertaining to deer
CERATE	*n* pl. -S a medicated ointment	**CERVIX**	*n* pl. -VICES or -VIXES the neck
CERATED	*adj* covered with wax	**CESAREAN**	*n* pl. -S a method of child delivery
CERATIN	*n* pl. -S keratin		
CERATOID	*adj* hornlike	**CESARIAN**	*n* pl. -S cesarean
CERCARIA	*n* pl. -IAE or -IAS a parasitic worm	**CESIUM**	*n* pl. -S a metallic element
		CESS	*v* -ED, -ING, -ES to tax or assess
CERCIS	*n* pl. -CISES a shrub	**CESSION**	*n* pl. -S the act of ceding
CERCUS	*n* pl. CERCI a sensory appendage of an insect	**CESSPIT**	*n* pl. -S a cesspool
		CESSPOOL	*n* pl. -S a covered well or pit for sewage
CERE	*v* CERED, CERING, CERES to wrap in a waxy cloth		
CEREAL	*n* pl. -S a food made from grain	**CESTA**	*n* pl. -S a basket used in jai alai
CEREBRAL	*n* pl. -S a kind of consonant	**CESTI**	pl. of cestus
CEREBRUM	*n* pl. -BRUMS or -BRA a part of the brain **CEREBRIC** *adj*	**CESTODE**	*n* pl. -S a tapeworm
		CESTOID	*n* pl. -S cestode
CERED	past tense of cere	**CESTOS**	*n* pl. -TOI cestus
CEREMENT	*n* pl. -S a waxy cloth	**CESTUS**	*n* pl. -TI a belt or girdle
CEREMONY	*n* pl. -NIES a formal observance	**CESTUS**	*n* pl. -ES a hand covering for ancient Roman boxers
CEREUS	*n* pl. -ES a tall cactus		
CERIA	*n* pl. -S a chemical compound	**CESURA**	*n* pl. -RAS or -RAE caesura
CERIC	*adj* containing cerium	**CETACEAN**	*n* pl. -S an aquatic mammal
CERING	present participle of cere	**CETANE**	*n* pl. -S a diesel fuel
CERIPH	*n* pl. -S serif	**CETE**	*n* pl. -S a group of badgers
CERISE	*n* pl. -S a red color	**CETOLOGY**	*n* pl. -GIES the study of whales
CERITE	*n* pl. -S a mineral	**CEVICHE**	*n* pl. -S seviche
CERIUM	*n* pl. -S a metallic element	**CHABLIS**	*n* pl. CHABLIS a dry white wine
CERMET	*n* pl. -S ceramal	**CHABOUK**	*n* pl. -S a type of whip
CERNUOUS	*adj* drooping or nodding	**CHABUK**	*n* pl. -S chabouk
CERO	*n* pl. CEROS a large food fish	**CHACMA**	*n* pl. -S a large baboon
CEROTIC	*adj* pertaining to beeswax		

CHACONNE	*n* pl. -S an ancient dance	**CHALKY**	*adj* CHALKIER, CHALKIEST resembling chalk
CHAD	*n* pl. -S a scrap of paper **CHADLESS** *adj*	**CHALLA**	*n* pl. -S challah
CHADAR	*n* pl. -DARS or -DRI chador	**CHALLAH**	*n* pl. -LAHS, -LOTH, or -LOT a kind of bread
CHADARIM	a pl. of cheder	**CHALLIE**	*n* pl. -S challis
CHADOR	*n* pl. -DORS or -DRI a large shawl	**CHALLIES**	pl. of chally
CHAETA	*n* pl. -TAE a bristle or seta **CHAETAL** *adj*	**CHALLIS**	*n* pl. -LISES a light fabric
		CHALLOT	a pl. of challah
CHAFE	*v* CHAFED, CHAFING, CHAFES to warm by rubbing	**CHALLOTH**	a pl. of challah
		CHALLY	*n* pl. -LIES challis
CHAFER	*n* pl. -S a large beetle	**CHALONE**	*n* pl. -S a hormone
CHAFF	*v* -ED, -ING, -S to poke fun at	**CHALOT**	a pl. of chalah
CHAFFER	*v* -ED, -ING, -S to bargain or haggle	**CHALOTH**	a pl. of chalah
		CHALUTZ	*n* pl. -LUTZIM halutz
CHAFFY	*adj* CHAFFIER, CHAFFIEST worthless	**CHAM**	*n* pl. -S a khan
CHAFING	present participle of chafe	**CHAMADE**	*n* pl. -S a signal made with a drum
CHAGRIN	*v* -GRINED, -GRINING, -GRINS or -GRINNED, -GRINNING, -GRINS to humiliate	**CHAMBER**	*v* -ED, -ING, -S to put in a chamber (a room)
		CHAMBRAY	*n* pl. -BRAYS a fine fabric
CHAIN	*v* -ED, -ING, -S to bind with a chain (a series of connected rings)	**CHAMFER**	*v* -ED, -ING, -S to groove
		CHAMFRON	*n* pl. -S armor for a horse's head
CHAINE	*n* pl. -S a series of ballet turns	**CHAMISE**	*n* pl. -S chamiso
CHAINMAN	*n* pl. -MEN a surveyor's assistant who uses a measuring chain	**CHAMISO**	*n* pl. -SOS a flowering shrub
		CHAMMY	*v* -MIED, -MYING, -MIES to chamois
CHAINSAW	*v* -SAWED, -SAWING, -SAWS to cut with a chain saw	**CHAMOIS**	*n* pl. -OIX a soft leather
CHAIR	*v* -ED, -ING, -S to install in office	**CHAMOIS**	*v* -ED, -ING, -ES to prepare leather like chamois
CHAIRMAN	*n* pl. -MEN the presiding officer of a meeting	**CHAMP**	*v* -ED, -ING, -S to chew noisily
		CHAMPAC	*n* pl. -S champak
CHAIRMAN	*v* -MANED, -MANING, -MANS or -MANNED, -MANNING, -MANS to act as chairman of	**CHAMPAK**	*n* pl. -S an East Indian tree
		CHAMPER	*n* pl. -S one that champs
		CHAMPION	*v* -ED, -ING, -S to defend or support
CHAISE	*n* pl. -S a light carriage	**CHAMPY**	*adj* broken up by the trampling of beasts
CHAKRA	*n* pl. -S a body center in yoga		
CHALAH	*n* pl. -LAHS, -LOTH or -LOT challah	**CHANCE**	*v* CHANCED, CHANCING, CHANCES to risk
CHALAZA	*n* pl. -ZAS or -ZAE a band of tissue in an egg **CHALAZAL** *adj*	**CHANCEL**	*n* pl. -S an area around a church altar
CHALAZIA	*n/pl* tumors of the eyelid	**CHANCERY**	*n* pl. -CERIES a court of public record
CHALCID	*n* pl. -S a tiny fly	**CHANCIER**	comparative of chancy
CHALDRON	*n* pl. -S a unit of dry measure	**CHANCIEST**	superlative of chancy
CHALEH	*n* pl. -S challah	**CHANCILY**	*adv* in a chancy manner
CHALET	*n* pl. -S a Swiss cottage	**CHANCING**	present participle of chance
CHALICE	*n* pl. -S a drinking cup **CHALICED** *adj*		
CHALK	*v* -ED, -ING, -S to mark with chalk (a soft limestone)		

CHANCRE *n* pl. -S a hard-based sore

CHANCY *adj* CHANCIER, CHANCIEST risky

CHANDLER *n* pl. -S a dealer in provisions

CHANFRON *n* pl. -S chamfron

CHANG *n* pl. -S a cattie

CHANGE *v* CHANGED, CHANGING, CHANGES to make different

CHANGER *n* pl. -S one that changes

CHANNEL *v* -NELED, -NELING, -NELS or -NELLED, -NELLING, -NELS to direct along some desired course

CHANSON *n* pl. -S a song

CHANT *v* -ED, -ING, -S to sing

CHANTAGE *n* pl. -S blackmail

CHANTER *n* pl. -S one that chants

CHANTEY *n* pl. -TEYS a sailor's song

CHANTIES pl. of chanty

CHANTOR *n* pl. -S chanter

CHANTRY *n* pl. -TRIES an endowment given to a church

CHANTY *n* pl. -TIES chantey

CHAO *n* pl. CHAO a monetary unit of Vietnam

CHAOS *n* pl. -ES a state of total disorder; a confused mass **CHAOTIC** *adj*

CHAP *v* CHAPPED or CHAPT, CHAPPING, CHAPS to split, crack, or redden

CHAPATI *n* pl. -S an unleavened bread of India

CHAPATTI *n* pl. -S chapati

CHAPBOOK *n* pl. -S a small book of popular tales

CHAPE *n* pl. -S a part of a scabbard

CHAPEAU *n* pl. -PEAUX or -PEAUS a hat

CHAPEL *n* pl. -S a place of worship

CHAPERON *v* -ED, -ING, -S to accompany

CHAPITER *n* pl. -S the capital of a column

CHAPLAIN *n* pl. -S a clergyman for a chapel

CHAPLET *n* pl. -S a wreath for the head

CHAPMAN *n* pl. -MEN a peddler

CHAPPATI *n* pl. -S chapati

CHAPPED a past tense of chap

CHAPPING present participle of chap

CHAPT a past tense of chap

CHAPTER *v* -ED, -ING, -S to divide a book into chapters (main sections)

CHAQUETA *n* pl. -S a jacket worn by cowboys

CHAR *v* CHARRED, CHARRING, CHARS to burn slightly

CHARACID *n* pl. -S characin

CHARACIN *n* pl. -S a tropical fish

CHARADE *n* pl. -S a word represented by pantomime

CHARAS *n* pl. -ES hashish

CHARCOAL *v* -ED, -ING, -S to blacken with charcoal (a dark, porous carbon)

CHARD *n* pl. -S a variety of beet

CHARE *v* CHARED, CHARING, CHARES to do small jobs

CHARGE *v* CHARGED, CHARGING, CHARGES to accuse formally

CHARGER *n* pl. -S one that charges

CHARIER comparative of chary

CHARIEST superlative of chary

CHARILY *adv* in a chary manner

CHARING present participle of chare

CHARIOT *v* -ED, -ING, -S to ride in a chariot (a type of cart)

CHARISM *n* pl. -S charisma

CHARISMA *n* pl. -MATA a special magnetic appeal

CHARITY *n* pl. -TIES something given to the needy

CHARK *v* -ED, -ING, -S to char

CHARKA *n* pl. -S charkha

CHARKHA *n* pl. -S a spinning wheel

CHARLADY *n* pl. -DIES a cleaning woman

CHARLEY *n* pl. -LEYS charlie

CHARLIE *n* pl. -LIES a fool

CHARLOCK *n* pl. -S a troublesome weed

CHARM *v* -ED, -ING, -S to attract irresistibly

CHARMER *n* pl. -S one that charms

CHARMING *adj* -INGER, -INGEST pleasing

CHARNEL *n* pl. -S a room where corpses are placed

CHARPAI *n* pl. -S charpoy

CHARPOY *n* pl. -POYS a bed used in India

CHARQUI *n* pl. -S a type of meat **CHARQUID** *adj*

CHARR *n* pl. -S a small-scaled trout

CHARRED past tense of char

CHARRIER comparative of charry

CHARRIEST superlative of charry

CHARRING present participle of char

CHARRO n pl. -ROS a cowboy

CHARRY adj -RIER, -RIEST resembling charcoal

CHART v -ED, -ING, -S to map out

CHARTER v -ED, -ING, -S to lease or hire

CHARTIST n pl. -S a stock market specialist

CHARY adj CHARIER, CHARIEST cautious

CHASE v CHASED, CHASING, CHASES to pursue

CHASER n pl. -S one that chases

CHASING n pl. -S a design engraved on metal

CHASM n pl. -S a deep cleft in the earth **CHASMAL, CHASMED, CHASMIC, CHASMY** adj

CHASSE v CHASSED, CHASSEING, CHASSES to perform a dance movement

CHASSEUR n pl. -S a cavalry soldier

CHASSIS n pl. CHASSIS the frame of a car

CHASTE adj CHASTER, CHASTEST morally pure **CHASTELY** adv

CHASTEN v -ED, -ING, -S to chastise

CHASTISE v -TISED, -TISING, -TISES to discipline by punishment

CHASTITY n pl. -TIES moral purity

CHASUBLE n pl. -S a sleeveless vestment

CHAT v CHATTED, CHATTING, CHATS to converse informally

CHATCHKA n pl. -S a knickknack

CHATCHKE n pl. -S chatchka

CHATEAU n pl. -TEAUX or -TEAUS a large country house

CHATTED past tense of chat

CHATTEL n pl. -S a slave

CHATTER v -ED, -ING, -S to talk rapidly and trivially **CHATTERY** adj

CHATTING present participle of chat

CHATTY adj -TIER, -TIEST talkative **CHATTILY** adv

CHAUFER n pl. -S chauffer

CHAUFFER n pl. -S a small furnace

CHAUNT v -ED, -ING, -S to chant

CHAUNTER n pl. -S one that chaunts

CHAUSSES n/pl medieval armor

CHAW v -ED, -ING, -S to chew

CHAWER n pl. -S one that chaws

CHAY n pl. CHAYS the root of an East Indian herb

CHAYOTE n pl. -S a tropical vine

CHAZAN n pl. -ZANS or -ZANIM a cantor

CHAZZAN n pl. -ZANS or -ZANIM chazan

CHAZZEN n pl. -ZENS or -ZENIM chazan

CHEAP adj CHEAPER, CHEAPEST inexpensive

CHEAP n pl. -S a market

CHEAPEN v -ED, -ING, -S to make cheap

CHEAPIE n pl. -S one that is cheap

CHEAPISH adj somewhat cheap

CHEAPLY adv in a cheap manner

CHEAPO n pl. CHEAPOS a cheapie

CHEAT v -ED, -ING, -S to defraud

CHEATER n pl. -S one that cheats

CHEBEC n pl. -S a small bird

CHECHAKO n pl. -KOS a newcomer

CHECK v -ED, -ING, -S to inspect

CHECKER v -ED, -ING, -S to mark with squares

CHECKOFF n pl. -S a method of collecting union dues

CHECKOUT n pl. -S a test of a machine

CHECKROW v -ED, -ING, -S to plant in rows which divide the land into squares

CHECKUP n pl. -S an examination

CHEDDAR n pl. -S a type of cheese

CHEDDITE n pl. -S chedite

CHEDER n pl. CHADARIM or CHEDERS heder

CHEDITE n pl. -S an explosive

CHEEK v -ED, -ING, -S to speak impudently to

CHEEKFUL n pl. -S the amount held in one's cheek

CHEEKY adj CHEEKIER, CHEEKIEST impudent **CHEEKILY** adv

CHEEP v -ED, -ING, -S to chirp

CHEEPER n pl. -S one that cheeps

CHEER v -ED, -ING, -S to applaud with shouts of approval

CHEERER n pl. -S one that cheers

CHEERFUL adj -FULLER, -FULLEST full of spirits

CHEERIER comparative of cheery

CHEERIEST superlative of cheery

CHEERILY	*adv* in a cheery manner	**CHESSMAN**	*n* pl. -MEN one of the pieces used in chess (a board game for two players)
CHEERIO	*n* pl. -IOS a greeting		
CHEERLED	past tense of cheerlead	**CHEST**	*n* pl. -S a part of the body **CHESTED** *adj*
CHEERLY	*adv* cheerily		
CHEERO	*n* pl. CHEEROS cheerio	**CHESTFUL**	*n* pl. -S as much as a chest or box can hold
CHEERY	*adj* CHEERIER, CHEERIEST cheerful		
		CHESTNUT	*n* pl. -S an edible nut
CHEESE	*v* CHEESED, CHEESING, CHEESES to stop	**CHESTY**	*adj* CHESTIER, CHESTIEST proud
CHEESY	*adj* CHEESIER, CHEESIEST resembling cheese (a food made from milk curds) **CHEESILY** *adv*	**CHETAH**	*n* pl. -S cheetah
		CHETH	*n* pl. -S heth
		CHETRUM	*n* pl. -S a monetary unit of Bhutan
CHEETAH	*n* pl. -S a swift-running wildcat		
CHEF	*v* CHEFFED, CHEFFING, CHEFS to work as a chef (a chief cook)	**CHEVALET**	*n* pl. -S a part of a stringed instrument
		CHEVERON	*n* pl. -S chevron
CHEFDOM	*n* pl. -S the status of a chef	**CHEVIED**	past tense of chevy
CHEGOE	*n* pl. -S chigoe	**CHEVIES**	present 3d person sing. of chevy
CHELA	*n* pl. -LAE a pincerlike claw	**CHEVIOT**	*n* pl. -S a coarse fabric
CHELA	*n* pl. -S a pupil of a guru	**CHEVRE**	*n* pl. -S a cheese made from goat's milk
CHELATE	*v* -LATED, -LATING, -LATES to combine a metal ion with a compound		
		CHEVRON	*n* pl. -S a V-shaped pattern
CHELATOR	*n* pl. -S one that chelates	**CHEVY**	*v* CHEVIED, CHEVYING, CHEVIES to chase about
CHELIPED	*n* pl. -S a claw-bearing leg		
CHELOID	*n* pl. -S keloid	**CHEW**	*v* -ED, -ING, -S to crush or grind with the teeth **CHEWABLE** *adj*
CHEMIC	*n* pl. -S a chemist		
CHEMICAL	*n* pl. -S a substance obtained by a process of chemistry	**CHEWER**	*n* pl. -S one that chews
		CHEWINK	*n* pl. -S a common finch
CHEMISE	*n* pl. -S a loose dress	**CHEWY**	*adj* CHEWIER, CHEWIEST not easily chewed
CHEMISM	*n* pl. -S chemical attraction		
CHEMIST	*n* pl. -S one versed in chemistry	**CHEZ**	*prep* at the home of
CHEMURGY	*n* pl. -GIES a branch of applied chemistry	**CHI**	*n* pl. -S a Greek letter
		CHIA	*n* pl. -S a Mexican herb
CHENILLE	*n* pl. -S a soft fabric	**CHIAO**	*n* pl. CHIAO a monetary unit of China
CHENOPOD	*n* pl. -S a flowering plant		
CHEQUE	*n* pl. -S a written order directing a bank to pay money	**CHIASM**	*n* pl. -S chiasma
		CHIASMA	*n* pl. -MATA or -MAS an anatomical junction **CHIASMAL, CHIASMIC** *adj*
CHEQUER	*v* -ED, -ING, -S to checker		
CHERISH	*v* -ED, -ING, -ES to hold dear		
CHEROOT	*n* pl. -S a square-cut cigar	**CHIASMUS**	*n* pl. -MI a reversal of word order between parallel phrases **CHIASTIC** *adj*
CHERRY	*n* pl. -RIES a fruit		
CHERT	*n* pl. -S a compact rock	**CHIAUS**	*n* pl. -ES a Turkish messenger
CHERTY	*adj* CHERTIER, CHERTIEST resembling chert	**CHIBOUK**	*n* pl. -S a tobacco pipe
		CHIC	*n* pl. -S elegance
CHERUB	*n* pl. -UBS or -UBIM or -UBIMS an angel **CHERUBIC** *adj*	**CHIC**	*adj* CHICER, CHICEST smartly stylish
CHERVIL	*n* pl. -S an aromatic herb	**CHICANE**	*v* -CANED, -CANING, -CANES to trick
CHESS	*n* pl. -ES a weed		

CHICANER	n pl. -S one that chicanes	**CHILIDOG**	n pl. -S a hot dog topped with chili
CHICANO	n pl. -NOS an American of Mexican descent	**CHILL**	v -ED, -ING, -S to make cold
CHICCORY	n pl. -RIES chicory	**CHILL**	adj CHILLER, CHILLEST cool
CHICHI	n pl. -S elaborate ornamentation	**CHILLER**	n pl. -S one that chills
CHICK	n pl. -S a young bird	**CHILLI**	n pl. -ES chili
CHICKEE	n pl. -S a stilt house of the Seminole Indians	**CHILLUM**	n pl. -S a part of a water pipe
CHICKEN	v -ED, -ING, -S to lose one's nerve	**CHILLY**	adj CHILLIER, CHILLIEST cool **CHILLILY** adv
CHICKORY	n pl. -RIES chicory	**CHILOPOD**	n pl. -S a multi-legged insect
CHICKPEA	n pl. -S an Asian herb	**CHIMAERA**	n pl. -S a marine fish
CHICLE	n pl. -S a tree gum	**CHIMAR**	n pl. -S chimere
CHICLY	adv in an elegant manner	**CHIMB**	n pl. -S the rim of a cask
CHICNESS	n pl. -ES elegance	**CHIMBLEY**	n pl. -BLEYS chimley
CHICO	n pl. -COS a prickly shrub	**CHIMBLY**	n pl. -BLIES chimley
CHICORY	n pl. -RIES a perennial herb	**CHIME**	v CHIMED, CHIMING, CHIMES to ring harmoniously
CHIDE	v CHIDED or CHID, CHIDDEN, CHIDING, CHIDES to scold	**CHIMER**	n pl. -S one that chimes
CHIDER	n pl. -S one that chides	**CHIMERA**	n pl. -S an imaginary monster
CHIEF	adj CHIEFER, CHIEFEST highest in authority	**CHIMERE**	n pl. -S a bishop's robe
		CHIMERIC	adj imaginary; unreal
CHIEF	n pl. -S the person highest in authority	**CHIMING**	present participle of chime
		CHIMLA	n pl. -S chimley
CHIEFDOM	n pl. -S the domain of a chief	**CHIMLEY**	n pl. -LEYS a chimney
CHIEFLY	adv above all	**CHIMNEY**	n pl. -NEYS a flue
CHIEL	n pl. -S chield	**CHIMP**	n pl. -S a chimpanzee
CHIELD	n pl. -S a young man	**CHIN**	v CHINNED, CHINNING, CHINS to hold with the chin (the lower part of the face)
CHIFFON	n pl. -S a sheer fabric		
CHIGETAI	n pl. -S a wild ass	**CHINA**	n pl. -S fine porcelain ware
CHIGGER	n pl. -S a parasitic mite	**CHINBONE**	n pl. -S the lower jaw
CHIGNON	n pl. -S a woman's hairdo	**CHINCH**	n pl. -ES a bedbug
CHIGOE	n pl. -S a tropical flea	**CHINCHY**	adj CHINCHIER, CHINCHIEST stingy
CHILD	n pl. CHILDREN a young person		
CHILDBED	n pl. -S the state of a woman giving birth	**CHINE**	v CHINED, CHINING, CHINES to cut through the backbone of
CHILDE	n pl. -S a youth of noble birth	**CHINK**	v -ED, -ING, -S to fill cracks or fissures in
CHILDING	adj pregnant		
CHILDISH	adj resembling a child	**CHINKY**	adj CHINKIER, CHINKIEST full of cracks
CHILDLY	adj -LIER, -LIEST resembling a child	**CHINLESS**	adj lacking a chin
CHILDREN	pl. of child	**CHINNED**	past tense of chin
CHILE	n pl. -S chili	**CHINNING**	present participle of chin
CHILI	n pl. -ES a hot pepper	**CHINO**	n pl. -NOS a strong fabric
CHILIAD	n pl. -S a group of one thousand	**CHINONE**	n pl. -S quinone
CHILIASM	n pl. -S a religious doctrine	**CHINOOK**	n pl. -S a warm wind
CHILIAST	n pl. -S a supporter of chiliasm	**CHINTS**	n pl. -ES chintz

CHINTZ   *n* pl. -ES a cotton fabric

CHINTZY   *adj* CHINTZIER, CHINTZIEST gaudy; cheap

CHIP   *v* CHIPPED, CHIPPING, CHIPS to break a small piece from

CHIPMUCK   *n* pl. -S a chipmunk

CHIPMUNK   *n* pl. -S a small rodent

CHIPPED   past tense of chip

CHIPPER   *v* -ED, -ING, -S to chirp

CHIPPIE   *n* pl. -S chippy

CHIPPING   present participle of chip

CHIPPY   *n* pl. -PIES a prostitute

CHIPPY   *adj* -PIER, -PIEST belligerent

CHIRAL   *adj* pertaining to an asymmetrical molecule

CHIRK   *v* -ED, -ING, -S to make a shrill noise

CHIRK   *adj* CHIRKER, CHIRKEST cheerful

CHIRM   *v* -ED, -ING, -S to chirp

CHIRO   *n* pl. -ROS a marine fish

CHIRP   *v* -ED, -ING, -S to utter a short, shrill sound

CHIRPER   *n* pl. -S one that chirps

CHIRPY   *adj* CHIRPIER, CHIRPIEST cheerful **CHIRPILY** *adv*

CHIRR   *v* -ED, -ING, -S to make a harsh, vibrant sound

CHIRRE   *v* CHIRRED, CHIRRING, CHIRRES to chirr

CHIRRUP   *v* -ED, -ING, -S to chirp repeatedly **CHIRRUPY** *adj*

CHISEL   *v* -ELED, -ELING, -ELS or -ELLED, -ELLING, -ELS to use a chisel (a cutting tool)

CHISELER   *n* pl. -S one that chisels

CHIT   *n* pl. -S a short letter

CHITAL   *n* pl. CHITAL an Asian deer

CHITCHAT   *v* -CHATTED, -CHATTING, -CHATS to indulge in small talk

CHITIN   *n* pl. -S the main component of insect shells

CHITLIN   *n* pl. -S chitling

CHITLING   *n* pl. -S a part of the small intestine of swine

CHITON   *n* pl. -S a tunic worn in ancient Greece

CHITOSAN   *n* pl. -S a compound derived from chitin

CHITTER   *v* -ED, -ING, -S to twitter

CHITTY   *n* pl. -TIES a chit

CHIVALRY   *n* pl. -RIES knightly behavior and skill

CHIVAREE   *v* -REED, -REEING, -REES to perform a mock serenade

CHIVARI   *v* -RIED, -RIING, -RIES to chivaree

CHIVE   *n* pl. -S an herb used as a seasoning

CHIVVY   *v* -VIED, -VYING, -VIES to chevy

CHIVY   *v* CHIVIED, CHIVYING, CHIVIES to chevy

CHLAMYS   *n* pl. -MYSES or -MYDES a garment worn in ancient Greece

CHLOASMA   *n* pl. -MATA a skin discoloration

CHLORAL   *n* pl. -S a chemical compound

CHLORATE   *n* pl. -S a chemical salt

CHLORDAN   *n* pl. -S a toxic compound of chlorine

CHLORIC   *adj* pertaining to chlorine

CHLORID   *n* pl. -S chloride

CHLORIDE   *n* pl. -S a chlorine compound

CHLORIN   *n* pl. -S chlorine

CHLORINE   *n* pl. -S a gaseous element

CHLORITE   *n* pl. -S a mineral group

CHLOROUS   *adj* pertaining to chlorine

CHOANA   *n* pl. -NAE a funnel-shaped opening

CHOCK   *v* -ED, -ING, -S to secure with a wedge of wood or metal

CHOCKFUL   *adj* full to the limit

CHOICE   *n* pl. -S one that is chosen

CHOICE   *adj* CHOICER, CHOICEST of fine quality **CHOICELY** *adv*

CHOIR   *v* -ED, -ING, -S to sing in unison

CHOIRBOY   *n* pl. -BOYS a boy who sings in a choir (a body of church singers)

CHOKE   *v* CHOKED, CHOKING, CHOKES to impede the breathing of

CHOKER   *n* pl. -S one that chokes

CHOKEY   *adj* CHOKIER, CHOKIEST choky

CHOKING   present participle of choke

CHOKY   *adj* CHOKIER, CHOKIEST tending to cause choking

CHOLATE   *n* pl. -S a chemical salt

CHOLENT   *n* pl. -S a traditional Jewish stew

CHOLER   *n* pl. -S anger

CHOLERA   *n* pl. -S an acute disease

CHOLERIC	*adj* bad-tempered	**CHORIAMB**	*n* pl. -S a type of metrical foot
CHOLINE	*n* pl. -S a B vitamin	**CHORIC**	*adj* pertaining to a chorus
CHOLLA	*n* pl. -S a treelike cactus	**CHORINE**	*n* pl. -S a chorus girl
CHOLO	*n* pl. -LOS a pachuco	**CHORING**	present participle of chore
CHOMP	*v* -ED, -ING, -S to champ	**CHORIOID**	*n* pl. -S choroid
CHOMPER	*n* pl. -S one that chomps	**CHORION**	*n* pl. -S an embryonic membrane
CHON	*n* pl. CHON a monetary unit of South Korea	**CHORIZO**	*n* pl. -ZOS a highly seasoned sausage
CHOOK	*n* pl. -S a chicken	**CHOROID**	*n* pl. -S a membrane of the eye
CHOOSE	*v* CHOSE, CHOSEN, CHOOSING, CHOOSES to take by preference	**CHORTLE**	*v* -TLED, -TLING, -TLES to chuckle with glee
CHOOSER	*n* pl. -S one that chooses	**CHORTLER**	*n* pl. -S one that chortles
CHOOSEY	*adj* CHOOSIER, CHOOSIEST choosy	**CHORUS**	*v* -RUSED, -RUSING, -RUSES or -RUSSED, -RUSSING, -RUSSES to sing in unison
CHOOSING	present participle of choose	**CHOSE**	*n* pl. -S an item of personal property
CHOOSY	*adj* CHOOSIER, CHOOSIEST hard to please	**CHOSEN**	past participle of choose
CHOP	*v* CHOPPED, CHOPPING, CHOPS to sever with a sharp tool	**CHOTT**	*n* pl. -S a saline lake
		CHOUGH	*n* pl. -S a crow-like bird
CHOPIN	*n* pl. -S chopine	**CHOUSE**	*v* CHOUSED, CHOUSING, CHOUSES to swindle
CHOPINE	*n* pl. -S a type of shoe		
CHOPPED	past tense of chop	**CHOUSER**	*n* pl. -S one that chouses
CHOPPER	*v* -ED, -ING, -S to travel by helicopter	**CHOUSH**	*n* pl. -ES chiaus
CHOPPING	present participle of chop	**CHOUSING**	present participle of chouse
CHOPPY	*adj* CHOPPIER, CHOPPIEST full of short, rough waves **CHOPPILY** *adv*	**CHOW**	*v* -ED, -ING, -S to eat
		CHOWCHOW	*n* pl. -S a relish of mixed pickles in mustard
CHORAGUS	*n* pl. -GI or -GUSES the leader of a chorus or choir **CHORAGIC** *adj*	**CHOWDER**	*v* -ED, -ING, -S to make a thick soup of
CHORAL	*n* pl. -S chorale	**CHOWSE**	*v* CHOWSED, CHOWSING, CHOWSES to chouse
CHORALE	*n* pl. -S a hymn that is sung in unison		
		CHOWTIME	*n* pl. -S mealtime
CHORALLY	*adv* harmoniously	**CHRESARD**	*n* pl. -S the available water of the soil
CHORD	*v* -ED, -ING, -S to play a chord (a combination of three or more musical tones)	**CHRISM**	*n* pl. -S a consecrated oil **CHRISMAL** *adj*
CHORDAL	*adj* pertaining to a chord	**CHRISMON**	*n* pl. -MA or -MONS a Christian monogram
CHORDATE	*n* pl. -S any of a large phylum of animals		
		CHRISOM	*n* pl. -S chrism
CHORE	*v* CHORED, CHORING, CHORES to do small jobs	**CHRISTEN**	*v* -ED, -ING, -S to baptise
		CHRISTIE	*n* pl. -S christy
CHOREA	*n* pl. -S a nervous disorder **CHOREAL, CHOREIC** *adj*	**CHRISTY**	*n* pl. -TIES a skiing turn
		CHROMA	*n* pl. -S the purity of a color
CHOREGUS	*n* pl. -GI or -GUSES choragus	**CHROMATE**	*n* pl. -S a chemical salt
CHOREMAN	*n* pl. -MEN a menial worker	**CHROME**	*v* CHROMED, CHROMING, CHROMES to plate with chromium
CHOREOID	*adj* resembling chorea		
CHORIAL	*adj* pertaining to the chorion	**CHROMIC**	*adj* pertaining to chromium

CHROMIDE *n* pl. -S a tropical fish

CHROMING *n* pl. -S a chromium ore

CHROMITE *n* pl. -S a chromium ore

CHROMIUM *n* pl. -S a metallic element

CHROMIZE *v* -MIZED, -MIZING, -MIZES to chrome

CHROMO *n* pl. -MOS a type of color picture

CHROMOUS *adj* pertaining to chromium

CHROMYL *n* pl. -S a bivalent radical

CHRONAXY *n* pl. -AXIES the time required to excite a nerve cell electrically

CHRONIC *n* pl. -S one that suffers from a long-lasting disease

CHRONON *n* pl. -S a hypothetical unit of time

CHTHONIC *adj* pertaining to the gods of the underworld

CHUB *n* pl. -S a freshwater fish

CHUBASCO *n* pl. -COS a violent thunderstorm

CHUBBY *adj* -BIER, -BIEST plump **CHUBBILY** *adv*

CHUCK *v* -ED, -ING, -S to throw

CHUCKIES pl. of chucky

CHUCKLE *v* -LED, -LING, -LES to laugh quietly

CHUCKLER *n* pl. -S one that chuckles

CHUCKY *n* pl. CHUCKIES a little chick

CHUDDAH *n* pl. -S chuddar

CHUDDAR *n* pl. -S a large, square shawl

CHUDDER *n* pl. -S chuddar

CHUFA *n* pl. -S a European sedge

CHUFF *adj* CHUFFER, CHUFFEST gruff

CHUFF *v* -ED, -ING, -S to chug

CHUFFY *adj* -FIER, -FIEST plump

CHUG *v* CHUGGED, CHUGGING, CHUGS to move with a dull explosive sound

CHUGALUG *v* -LUGGED, -LUGGING, -LUGS to drink without pause

CHUGGER *n* pl. -S one that chugs

CHUKAR *n* pl. -S a game bird

CHUKKA *n* pl. -S a type of boot

CHUKKAR *n* pl. -S a chukker

CHUKKER *n* pl. -S a period of play in polo

CHUM *v* CHUMMED, CHUMMING, CHUMS to be close friends with someone

CHUMMY *adj* -MIER, -MIEST friendly **CHUMMILY** *adv*

CHUMP *v* -ED, -ING, -S to munch

CHUMSHIP *n* pl. -S friendship

CHUNK *v* -ED, -ING, -S to make a dull explosive sound

CHUNKY *adj* CHUNKIER, CHUNKIEST stocky **CHUNKILY** *adv*

CHUNTER *v* -ED, -ING, -S to mutter

CHURCH *v* -ED, -ING, -ES to bring to church (a building for Christian worship)

CHURCHLY *adj* -LIER, -LIEST pertaining to a church

CHURCHY *adj* CHURCHIER, CHURCHIEST churchly

CHURL *n* pl. -S a rude person **CHURLISH** *adj*

CHURN *v* -ED, -ING, -S to stir briskly in order to make butter

CHURNER *n* pl. -S one that churns

CHURNING *n* pl. -S the butter churned at one time

CHURR *v* -ED, -ING, -S to make a vibrant sound

CHUTE *v* CHUTED, CHUTING, CHUTES to convey by chute (a vertical passage)

CHUTIST *n* pl. -S a parachutist

CHUTNEE *n* pl. -S chutney

CHUTNEY *n* pl. -NEYS a sweet and sour sauce

CHUTZPA *n* pl. -S chutzpah

CHUTZPAH *n* pl. -S supreme self-confidence

CHYLE *n* pl. -S a digestive fluid **CHYLOUS** *adj*

CHYME *n* pl. -S semi-digested food

CHYMIC *n* pl. -S chemic

CHYMIST *n* pl. -S chemist

CHYMOSIN *n* pl. -S rennin

CHYMOUS *adj* pertaining to chyme

CIAO *interj* — used as an expression of greeting and farewell

CIBOL *n* pl. -S a variety of onion

CIBORIUM *n* pl. -RIA a vessel for holding holy bread

CIBOULE *n* pl. -S cibol

CICADA *n* pl. -DAS or -DAE a winged insect

CICALA *n* pl. -LAS or -LE cicada

CICATRIX *n* pl. -TRICES or -TRIXES scar tissue

CICELY *n* pl. -LIES a fragrant herb

CICERO *n* pl. -ROS a unit of measure in printing

CICERONE *n* pl. -NES or -NI a tour guide

CICHLID *n* pl. -LIDS or -LIDAE a tropical fish

CICISBEO *n* pl. -BEI or -BEOS a lover of a married woman

CICOREE *n* pl. -S a perennial herb

CIDER *n* pl. -S the juice pressed from apples

CIGAR *n* pl. -S a roll of tobacco leaf for smoking

CIGARET *n* pl. -S a narrow roll of finely cut tobacco for smoking

CILANTRO *n* pl. -TROS an herb used in cooking

CILIA pl. of cilium

CILIARY *adj* pertaining to cilia

CILIATE *n* pl. -S one of a class of ciliated protozoans

CILIATED *adj* having cilia

CILICE *n* pl. -S a coarse cloth

CILIUM *n* pl. CILIA a short, hairlike projection

CIMBALOM *n* pl. -S a Hungarian dulcimer

CIMEX *n* pl. -MICES a bedbug

CINCH *v* -ED, -ING, -ES to girth

CINCHONA *n* pl. -S a Peruvian tree

CINCTURE *v* -TURED, -TURING, -TURES to gird or encircle

CINDER *v* -ED, -ING, -S to reduce to cinders (ashes)

CINDERY *adj* containing cinders

CINE *n* pl. -S a motion picture

CINEAST *n* pl. -S a devotee of motion pictures

CINEASTE *n* pl. -S cineast

CINEMA *n* pl. -S a motion-picture theater

CINEOL *n* pl. -S a liquid used as an antiseptic

CINEOLE *n* pl. -S cineol

CINERARY *adj* used for cremated ashes

CINERIN *n* pl. -S a compound used in insecticides

CINGULUM *n* pl. -LA an anatomical band or girdle

CINNABAR *n* pl. -S the principal ore of mercury

CINNAMON *n* pl. -S a spice obtained from tree bark **CINNAMIC** *adj*

CINNAMYL *n* pl. -S a chemical used to make soap

CINQUAIN *n* pl. -S a stanza of five lines

CINQUE *n* pl. -S the number five

CION *n* pl. -S a cutting from a plant or tree

CIOPPINO *n* pl. -NOS a spicy fish stew

CIPHER *v* -ED, -ING, -S to solve problems in arithmetic

CIPHONY *n* pl. -NIES the electronic scrambling of voice transmissions

CIPOLIN *n* pl. -S a type of marble

CIRCA *prep* about; around

CIRCLE *v* -CLED, -CLING, -CLES to move or revolve around

CIRCLER *n* pl. -S one that circles

CIRCLET *n* pl. -S a small ring or ring-shaped object

CIRCLING present participle of circle

CIRCUIT *v* -ED, -ING, -S to move around

CIRCUITY *n* pl. -ITIES lack of straightforwardness

CIRCULAR *n* pl. -S a leaflet intended for wide distribution

CIRCUS *n* pl. -ES a public entertainment **CIRCUSY** *adj*

CIRE *n* pl. -S a highly glazed finish for fabrics

CIRQUE *n* pl. -S a deep, steep-walled basin on a mountain

CIRRATE *adj* having cirri

CIRRI pl. of cirrus

CIRRIPED *n* pl. -S any of an order of crustaceans

CIRROSE *adj* cirrous

CIRROUS *adj* having cirri

CIRRUS *n* pl. -RI a tendril or similar part

CIRSOID *adj* varicose

CIS *adj* having certain atoms on the same side of the molecule

CISCO *n* pl. -COS or -COES a freshwater fish

CISLUNAR *adj* situated between the earth and the moon

CISSOID *n* pl. -S a type of geometric curve

CISSY *n* pl. -SIES sissy

CIST   *n* pl. -S a prehistoric stone coffin

CISTERN   *n* pl. -S a water tank

CISTERNA   *n* pl. -NAE a fluid-containing sac

CISTRON   *n* pl. -S a segment of DNA

CISTUS   *n* pl. -ES a flowering shrub

CITABLE   *adj* citeable

CITADEL   *n* pl. -S a fortress or stronghold

CITATION   *n* pl. -S the act of citing **CITATORY** *adj*

CITATOR   *n* pl. -S one that cites

CITE   *v* CITED, CITING, CITES to quote as an authority or example

CITEABLE   *adj* suitable for citation

CITER   *n* pl. -S one that cites

CITHARA   *n* pl. -S an ancient stringed instrument

CITHER   *n* pl. -S cittern

CITHERN   *n* pl. -S cittern

CITHREN   *n* pl. -S cittern

CITIED   *adj* having cities

CITIES   pl. of city

CITIFY   *v* -FIED, -FYING, -FIES to urbanize

CITING   present participle of cite

CITIZEN   *n* pl. -S a resident of a city or town

CITOLA   *n* pl. -S a cittern

CITOLE   *n* pl. -S citola

CITRAL   *n* pl. -S a lemon flavoring

CITRATE   *n* pl. -S a salt of citric acid **CITRATED** *adj*

CITREOUS   *adj* having a lemonlike color

CITRIC   *adj* derived from citrus fruits

CITRIN   *n* pl. -S a citric vitamin

CITRINE   *n* pl. -S a variety of quartz

CITRININ   *n* pl. -S an antibiotic

CITRON   *n* pl. -S a lemonlike fruit

CITROUS   *adj* pertaining to a citrus tree

CITRUS   *n* pl. -ES any of a genus of tropical, fruit-bearing trees **CITRUSY** *adj*

CITTERN   *n* pl. -S a pear-shaped guitar

CITY   *n* pl. CITIES a large town

CITYFIED   *adj* having the customs and manners of city people

CITYWARD   *adv* toward the city

CITYWIDE   *adj* including all parts of a city

CIVET   *n* pl. -S a catlike mammal

CIVIC   *adj* pertaining to a city

CIVICISM   *n* pl. -S a system of government based upon individual rights

CIVICS   *n/pl* the science of civic affairs

CIVIE   *n* pl. -S civvy

CIVIL   *adj* pertaining to citizens

CIVILIAN   *n* pl. -S a nonmilitary person

CIVILISE   *v* -LISED, -LISING, -LISES to civilize

CIVILITY   *n* pl. -TIES courtesy; politeness

CIVILIZE   *v* -LIZED, -LIZING, -LIZES to bring out of savagery

CIVILLY   *adv* politely

CIVISM   *n* pl. -S good citizenship

CIVVY   *n* pl. -VIES a civilian

CLABBER   *v* -ED, -ING, -S to curdle

CLACH   *n* pl. -S clachan

CLACHAN   *n* pl. -S a hamlet

CLACK   *v* -ED, -ING, -S to make an abrupt, dry sound

CLACKER   *n* pl. -S one that clacks

CLAD   *v* CLAD, CLADDING, CLADS to coat one metal over another

CLADDING   *n* pl. -S something that overlays

CLADE   *n* pl. -S a group of biological taxa

CLADIST   *n* pl. -S a taxonomist who uses clades in classifying life-forms

CLADODE   *n* pl. -S a leaflike part of a stem

CLAG   *v* CLAGGED, CLAGGING, CLAGS to clog

CLAIM   *v* -ED, -ING, -S to demand as one's due

CLAIMANT   *n* pl. -S one that asserts a right or title

CLAIMER   *n* pl. -S one that claims

CLAM   *v* CLAMMED, CLAMMING, CLAMS to dig for clams (bivalve mollusks)

CLAMANT   *adj* noisy

CLAMBAKE   *n* pl. -S a beach picnic

CLAMBER   *v* -ED, -ING, -S to climb awkwardly

CLAMMED   past tense of clam

CLAMMER   *n* pl. -S one that clams

CLAMMING   present particple of clam

CLAMMY   *adj* CLAMMIER, CLAMMIEST cold and damp **CLAMMILY** *adv*

CLAMOR *v* -ED, -ING, -S to make loud outcries

CLAMORER *n* pl. -S one that clamors

CLAMOUR *v* -ED, -ING, -S to clamor

CLAMP *v* -ED, -ING, -S to fasten with a clamp (a securing device)

CLAMPER *n* pl. -S a device worn on shoes to prevent slipping on ice

CLAMWORM *n* pl. -S a marine worm

CLAN *n* pl. -S a united group of families

CLANG *v* -ED, -ING, -S to ring loudly

CLANGER *n* pl. -S a blunder

CLANGOR *v* -ED, -ING, -S to clang repeatedly

CLANGOUR *v* -ED, -ING, -S to clangor

CLANK *v* -ED, -ING, -S to make a sharp, metallic sound

CLANNISH *adj* characteristic of a clan

CLANSMAN *n* pl. -MEN a member of a clan

CLAP *v* CLAPPED or CLAPT, CLAPPING, CLAPS to strike one palm against the other

CLAPPER *n* pl. -S one that claps

CLAPTRAP *n* pl. -S pretentious language

CLAQUE *n* pl. -S a group of hired applauders

CLAQUER *n* pl. -S claqueur

CLAQUEUR *n* pl. -S a member of a claque

CLARENCE *n* pl. -S a closed carriage

CLARET *n* pl. -S a dry red wine

CLARIES pl. of clary

CLARIFY *v* -FIED, -FYING, -FIES to make clear

CLARINET *n* pl. -S a woodwind instrument

CLARION *v* -ED, -ING, -S to proclaim by blowing a medieval trumpet

CLARITY *n* pl. -TIES the state of being clear

CLARKIA *n* pl. -S an annual herb

CLARO *n* pl. -ROS or -ROES a mild cigar

CLARY *n* pl. CLARIES an aromatic herb

CLASH *v* -ED, -ING, -ES to conflict or disagree

CLASHER *n* pl. -S one that clashes

CLASP *v* CLASPED or CLASPT, CLASPING, CLASPS to embrace tightly

CLASPER *n* pl. -S one that clasps

CLASS *v* -ED, -ING, -ES to classify

CLASSER *n* pl. -S one that classes

CLASSES pl. of classis

CLASSIC *n* pl. -S a work of enduring excellence

CLASSICO *adj* made from grapes grown in a certain part of Italy

CLASSIER comparative of classy

CLASSIEST superlative of classy

CLASSIFY *v* -FIED, -FYING, -FIES to arrange according to characteristics

CLASSILY *adj* in a classy manner

CLASSIS *n* pl. CLASSES a governing body in certain churches

CLASSISM *n* pl. -S discrimination based on social class

CLASSIST *n* pl. -S an advocate of classism

CLASSY *adj* CLASSIER, CLASSIEST stylish; elegant

CLAST *n* pl. -S a fragment of rock

CLASTIC *n* pl. -S a rock made up of other rocks

CLATTER *v* -ED, -ING, -S to move with a rattling noise

CLATTERY *adj* having a rattling noise

CLAUCHT a past tense of cleek

CLAUGHT *v* -ED, -ING, -S to clutch

CLAUSE *n* pl. -S a distinct part of a composition **CLAUSAL** *adj*

CLAUSTRA *n/pl* basal ganglia in the brain

CLAVATE *adj* shaped like a club

CLAVE *n* pl. -S one of a pair of percussion sticks

CLAVER *v* -ED, -ING, -S to gossip

CLAVI pl. of clavus

CLAVICLE *n* pl. -S a bone of the shoulder

CLAVIER *n* pl. -S a keyboard instrument

CLAVUS *n* pl. -VI a horny thickening of the skin

CLAW *v* -ED, -ING, -S to scratch with claws (sharp, curved toenails)

CLAWER *n* pl. -S one that claws

CLAWLESS *adj* having no claws

CLAWLIKE *adj* resembling a claw

CLAXON *n* pl. -S klaxon

CLAY *v* -ED, -ING, -S to treat with clay (a fine-grained, earthy material)

CLAYBANK *n* pl. -S a yellow-brown color

CLAYEY *adj* CLAYIER, CLAYIEST resembling clay

CLAYISH	*adj* resembling or containing clay
CLAYLIKE	*adj* resembling clay
CLAYMORE	*n* pl. -S a type of sword
CLAYPAN	*n* pl. -S a shallow natural depression
CLAYWARE	*n* pl. -S pottery
CLEAN	*adj* CLEANER, CLEANEST free from dirt or stain
CLEAN	*v* -ED, -ING, -S to rid of dirt or stain
CLEANER	*n* pl. -S one that cleans
CLEANLY	*adj* -LIER, -LIEST habitually clean
CLEANSE	*v* CLEANSED, CLEANSING, CLEANSES to clean
CLEANSER	*n* pl. -S one that cleanses
CLEANUP	*n* pl. -S an act of cleaning
CLEAR	*adj* CLEARER, CLEAREST clean and pure
CLEAR	*v* -ED, -ING, -S to remove obstructions
CLEARER	*n* pl. -S one that clears
CLEARING	*n* pl. -S an open space
CLEARLY	*adv* in a clear manner
CLEAT	*v* -ED, -ING, -S to strengthen with a strip of wood or iron
CLEAVAGE	*n* pl. -S the act of cleaving
CLEAVE	*v* CLEAVED, CLEFT, CLOVE or CLAVE, CLOVEN, CLEAVING, CLEAVES to split or divide
CLEAVER	*n* pl. -S a heavy knife
CLEEK	*v* CLAUCHT or CLEEKED, CLEEKING, CLEEKS to clutch
CLEF	*n* pl. -S a musical symbol
CLEFT	*v* -ED, -ING, -S to insert a scion into the stock of a plant
CLEIDOIC	*adj* enclosed in a shell
CLEMATIS	*n* pl. -TISES a flowering vine
CLEMENCY	*n* pl. -CIES mercy
CLEMENT	*adj* merciful
CLENCH	*v* -ED, -ING, -ES to grasp firmly
CLENCHER	*n* pl. -S one that clenches
CLEOME	*n* pl. -S a tropical plant
CLEPE	*v* CLEPED or CLEPT, CLEPING, CLEPES to call by name
CLERGY	*n* pl. -GIES the body of persons ordained for religious service
CLERIC	*n* pl. -S a member of the clergy
CLERICAL	*n* pl. -S a cleric
CLERID	*n* pl. -S a predatory beetle
CLERIHEW	*n* pl. -S a humorous poem
CLERISY	*n* pl. -SIES the well-educated class
CLERK	*v* -ED, -ING, -S to serve as a clerk (an office worker)
CLERKDOM	*n* pl. -S the status or function of a clerk
CLERKISH	*adj* resembling or suitable to a clerk
CLERKLY	*adj* -LIER, -LIEST pertaining to a clerk
CLEVEITE	*n* pl. -S a radioactive mineral
CLEVER	*adj* -ERER, -EREST mentally keen **CLEVERLY** *adv*
CLEVIS	*n* pl. -ISES a metal fastening device
CLEW	*v* -ED, -ING, -S to roll into a ball
CLICHE	*n* pl. -S a trite expression **CLICHED** *adj*
CLICK	*v* -ED, -ING, -S to make a short, sharp sound
CLICKER	*n* pl. -S one that clicks
CLIENT	*n* pl. -S a customer **CLIENTAL** *adj*
CLIFF	*n* pl. -S a high, steep face of rock
CLIFFY	*adj* CLIFFIER, CLIFFIEST abounding in cliffs
CLIFT	*n* pl. -S cliff
CLIMATE	*n* pl. -S the weather conditions characteristic of an area **CLIMATAL, CLIMATIC** *adj*
CLIMAX	*v* -ED, -ING, -ES to reach a high or dramatic point
CLIMB	*v* CLIMBED or CLOMB, CLIMBING, CLIMBS to ascend
CLIMBER	*n* pl. -S one that climbs
CLIME	*n* pl. -S climate
CLINAL	*adj* pertaining to a cline
CLINALLY	*adv* in a clinal manner
CLINCH	*v* -ED, -ING, -ES to settle a matter decisively
CLINCHER	*n* pl. -S a decisive fact or remark
CLINE	*n* pl. -S a series of changes within a species
CLING	*v* CLUNG, CLINGING, CLINGS to adhere closely
CLING	*v* -ED, -ING, -S to make a high-pitched ringing sound
CLINGER	*n* pl. -S one that clings

CLINGY	*adj* CLINGIER, CLINGIEST adhesive
CLINIC	*n* pl. -S a medical facility **CLINICAL** *adj*
CLINK	*v* -ED, -ING, -S to make a soft, sharp, ringing sound
CLINKER	*v* -ED, -ING, -S to form fused residue in burning
CLIP	*v* CLIPPED or CLIPT, CLIPPING, CLIPS to trim by cutting
CLIPPER	*n* pl. -S one that clips
CLIPPING	*n* pl. -S something that is clipped out or off
CLIPT	a past participle of clip
CLIQUE	*v* CLIQUED, CLIQUING, CLIQUES to form a clique (an exclusive group of persons)
CLIQUEY	*adj* CLIQUIER, CLIQUIEST inclined to form cliques
CLIQUISH	*adj* cliquey
CLIQUY	*adj* CLIQUIER, CLIQUIEST cliquey
CLITELLA	*n/pl* regions in the body walls of certain annelids
CLITIC	*n* pl. -S a word pronounced as part of a neighboring word
CLITORIS	*n* pl. -RISES or -RIDES a sex organ **CLITORAL, CLITORIC** *adj*
CLIVERS	*n* pl. CLIVERS an annual herb
CLIVIA	*n* pl. -S a flowering plant
CLOACA	*n* pl. -ACAE or -ACAS a sewer **CLOACAL** *adj*
CLOAK	*v* -ED, -ING, -S to conceal
CLOBBER	*v* -ED, -ING, -S to trounce
CLOCHARD	*n* pl. -S a vagrant
CLOCHE	*n* pl. -S a bell-shaped hat
CLOCK	*v* -ED, -ING, -S to time with a stopwatch
CLOCKER	*n* pl. -S one that clocks
CLOD	*n* pl. -S a dolt **CLODDISH** *adj*
CLODDY	*adj* -DIER, -DIEST lumpy
CLODPATE	*n* pl. -S a stupid person
CLODPOLE	*n* pl. -S clodpate
CLODPOLL	*n* pl. -S clodpate
CLOG	*v* CLOGGED, CLOGGING, CLOGS to block up or obstruct
CLOGGER	*n* pl. -S one that clogs
CLOGGY	*adj* -GIER, -GIEST clogging or able to clog
CLOISTER	*v* -ED, -ING, -S to seclude
CLOMB	a past tense of climb
CLOMP	*v* -ED, -ING, -S to walk heavily and clumsily
CLON	*n* pl. -S a group of asexually derived organisms **CLONAL** *adj* **CLONALLY** *adv*
CLONE	*v* CLONED, CLONING, CLONES to reproduce by asexual means
CLONER	*n* pl. -S one that clones
CLONIC	*adj* pertaining to clonus
CLONING	*n* pl. -S a technique for reproducing by asexual means
CLONISM	*n* pl. -S the condition of having clonus
CLONK	*v* -ED, -ING, -S to make a dull thumping sound
CLONUS	*n* pl. -ES a form of muscular spasm
CLOOT	*n* pl. -S a cloven hoof
CLOP	*v* CLOPPED, CLOPPING, CLOPS to make the sound of a hoof striking pavement
CLOQUE	*n* pl. -S a fabric with an embossed design
CLOSE	*adj* CLOSER, CLOSEST near **CLOSELY** *adv*
CLOSE	*v* CLOSED, CLOSING, CLOSES to block against entry or passage **CLOSABLE** *adj*
CLOSEOUT	*n* pl. -S a clearance sale
CLOSER	*n* pl. -S one that closes
CLOSEST	superlative of close
CLOSET	*v* -ED, -ING, -S to enclose in a private room
CLOSING	*n* pl. -S a concluding part
CLOSURE	*v* -SURED, -SURING, -SURES to cloture
CLOT	*v* CLOTTED, CLOTTING, CLOTS to form into a clot (a thick mass)
CLOTH	*n* pl. -S fabric
CLOTHE	*v* CLOTHED or CLAD, CLOTHING, CLOTHES to provide with clothing
CLOTHIER	*n* pl. -S one who makes or sells clothing
CLOTHING	*n* pl. -S wearing apparel
CLOTTED	past tense of clot
CLOTTING	present participle of clot
CLOTTY	*adj* tending to clot

CLOTURE *v* -TURED, -TURING, -TURES to end a debate by calling for a vote

CLOUD *v* -ED, -ING, -S to cover with clouds (masses of visible vapor)

CLOUDLET *n* pl. -S a small cloud

CLOUDY *adj* CLOUDIER, CLOUDIEST overcast with clouds **CLOUDILY** *adv*

CLOUGH *n* pl. -S a ravine

CLOUR *v* -ED, -ING, -S to knock or bump

CLOUT *v* -ED, -ING, -S to hit with the hand

CLOUTER *n* pl. -S one that clouts

CLOVE *n* pl. -S a spice

CLOVEN *adj* split; divided

CLOVER *n* pl. -S a plant

CLOWDER *n* pl. -S a group of cats

CLOWN *v* -ED, -ING, -S to act like a clown (a humorous performer)

CLOWNERY *n* pl. -ERIES clownish behavior

CLOWNISH *adj* resembling or befitting a clown

CLOY *v* -ED, -ING, -S to gratify beyond desire

CLOZE *n* pl. -S a test of reading comprehension

CLUB *v* CLUBBED, CLUBBING, CLUBS to form a club (an organized group of persons)

CLUBABLE *adj* sociable

CLUBBER *n* pl. -S a member of a club

CLUBBING present participle of club

CLUBBISH *adj* clubby

CLUBBY *adj* -BIER, -BIEST characteristic of a club

CLUBFOOT *n* pl. -FEET a deformed foot

CLUBHAND *n* pl. -S a deformed hand

CLUBHAUL *v* -ED, -ING, -S to put a vessel about

CLUBMAN *n* pl. -MEN a male member of a club

CLUBROOM *n* pl. -S a room for a club's meetings

CLUBROOT *n* pl. -S a plant disease

CLUCK *v* -ED, -ING, -S to make the sound of a hen

CLUE *v* CLUED, CLUEING or CLUING, CLUES to give guiding information

CLUELESS *adj* hopelessly confused or ignorant

CLUMBER *n* pl. -S a stocky spaniel

CLUMP *v* -ED, -ING, -S to form into a thick mass

CLUMPISH *adj* resembling a clump (a thick mass)

CLUMPY *adj* CLUMPIER, CLUMPIEST lumpy

CLUMSY *adj* -SIER, -SIEST awkward **CLUMSILY** *adv*

CLUNG past tense of cling

CLUNK *v* -ED, -ING, -S to thump

CLUNKER *n* pl. -S a jalopy

CLUNKY *adj* CLUNKIER, CLUNKIEST clumsy in style

CLUPEID *n* pl. -S a fish of the herring family

CLUPEOID *n* pl. -S a clupeid

CLUSTER *v* -ED, -ING, -S to form into a cluster (a group of similar objects)

CLUSTERY *adj* pertaining to a cluster

CLUTCH *v* -ED, -ING, -ES to grasp and hold tightly

CLUTCHY *adj* tending to clutch

CLUTTER *v* -ED, -ING, -S to pile in a disorderly state

CLUTTERY *adj* characterized by disorder

CLYPEUS *n* pl. CLYPEI a shield-like structure **CLYPEAL, CLYPEATE** *adj*

CLYSTER *n* pl. -S an enema

COACH *v* -ED, -ING, -ES to tutor or train

COACHER *n* pl. -S one that coaches

COACHMAN *n* pl. -MEN one who drives a coach or carriage

COACT *v* -ED, -ING, -S to act together

COACTION *n* pl. -S joint action

COACTIVE *adj* mutually active

COACTOR *n* pl. -S a fellow actor in a production

COADMIRE *v* -MIRED, -MIRING, -MIRES to admire together

COADMIT *v* -MITTED, -MITTING, -MITS to admit several things equally

COAEVAL *n* pl. -S coeval

COAGENCY *n* pl. -CIES a joint agency

COAGENT *n* pl. -S a person, force, or other agent working together with another

COAGULUM *n* pl. -LA or -LUMS a clot

COAL *v* -ED, -ING, -S to supply with coal (a carbon fuel)

COALA *n* pl. -S koala

COALBIN *n* pl. -S a bin for storing coal

COALBOX *n* pl. -ES a box for storing coal

COALER *n* pl. -S one that supplies coal

COALESCE *v* -ALESCED, -ALESCING, -ALESCES to blend

COALFISH *n* pl. -ES a blackish fish

COALHOLE *n* pl. -S a compartment for storing coal

COALIER comparative of coaly

COALIEST superlative of coaly

COALIFY *v* -FIED, -FYING, -FIES to convert into coal

COALLESS *adj* lacking coal

COALPIT *n* pl. -S a pit from which coal is obtained

COALSACK *n* pl. -S a dark region of the Milky Way

COALSHED *n* pl. -S a shed for storing coal

COALY *adj* COALIER, COALIEST containing coal

COALYARD *n* pl. -S a yard for storing coal

COAMING *n* pl. -S a raised border

COANCHOR *v* -ED, -ING, -S to present televised news reports jointly

COANNEX *v* -ED, -ING, -ES to annex jointly

COAPPEAR *v* -ED, -ING, -S to appear together or at the same time

COAPT *v* -ED, -ING, -S to fit together and make fast

COARSE *adj* COARSER, COARSEST rough **COARSELY** *adv*

COARSEN *v* -ED, -ING, -S to make coarse

COASSIST *v* -ED, -ING, -S to assist jointly

COASSUME *v* -SUMED, -SUMING, -SUMES to assume together

COAST *v* -ED, -ING, -S to slide down a hill

COASTAL *adj* pertaining to or located near a seashore

COASTER *n* pl. -S a sled

COASTING *n* pl. -S coastal trade

COAT *v* -ED, -ING, -S to cover with a coat (an outer garment)

COATEE *n* pl. -S a small coat

COATER *n* pl. -S one that coats

COATI *n* pl. -S a tropical mammal

COATING *n* pl. -S a covering layer

COATLESS *adj* lacking a coat

COATRACK *n* pl. -S a rack or stand for coats

COATROOM *n* pl. -S a room for storing coats

COATTAIL *n* pl. -S the back lower portion of a coat

COATTEND *v* -ED, -ING, -S to attend together

COATTEST *v* -ED, -ING, -S to attest jointly

COAUTHOR *v* -ED, -ING, -S to write together

COAX *v* -ED, -ING, -ES to cajole

COAXAL *adj* coaxial

COAXER *n* pl. -S one that coaxes

COAXIAL *adj* having a common axis

COB *n* pl. -S a corncob

COBALT *n* pl. -S a metallic element **COBALTIC** *adj*

COBB *n* pl. -S a sea gull

COBBER *n* pl. -S a comrade

COBBIER comparative of cobby

COBBIEST superlative of cobby

COBBLE *v* -BLED, -BLING, -BLES to mend

COBBLER *n* pl. -S a mender of shoes

COBBY *adj* -BIER, -BIEST stocky

COBIA *n* pl. -S a large game fish

COBLE *n* pl. -S a small fishing boat

COBNUT *n* pl. -S an edible nut

COBRA *n* pl. -S a venomous snake

COBWEB *v* -WEBBED, -WEBBING, -WEBS to cover with cobwebs (spider webs)

COBWEBBY *adj* -BIER, -BIEST covered with cobwebs

COCA *n* pl. -S a South American shrub

COCAIN *n* pl. -S cocaine

COCAINE *n* pl. -S a narcotic alkaloid

COCCAL *adj* pertaining to a coccus

COCCI pl. of coccus

COCCIC *adj* coccal

COCCID *n* pl. -S an insect

COCCIDIA *n/pl* parasitic protozoans

COCCOID *n* pl. -S a spherical cell or body

COCCUS	*n* pl. COCCI a spherical bacterium **COCCOUS** *adj*
COCCYX	*n* pl. -CYGES or -CYXES a bone of the spine
COCHAIR	*v* -ED, -ING, -S to serve jointly as chairman of
COCHIN	*n* pl. -S a large domestic chicken
COCHLEA	*n* pl. -CHLEAE or -CHLEAS a part of the ear **COCHLEAR** *adj*
COCINERA	*n* pl. -S a cook
COCK	*v* -ED, -ING, -S to tilt to one side
COCKADE	*n* pl. -S an ornament worn on a hat **COCKADED** *adj*
COCKAPOO	*n* pl. -POOS a hybrid between a cocker spaniel and a poodle
COCKATOO	*n* pl. -TOOS a parrot
COCKBILL	*v* -ED, -ING, -S to raise the yardarm on a ship
COCKBOAT	*n* pl. -S a small boat
COCKCROW	*n* pl. -S daybreak
COCKER	*v* -ED, -ING, -S to pamper
COCKEREL	*n* pl. -S a young rooster
COCKEYE	*n* pl. -S a squinting eye **COCKEYED** *adj*
COCKIER	comparative of cocky
COCKIEST	superlative of cocky
COCKILY	*adv* in a cocky manner
COCKISH	*adj* cocky
COCKLE	*v* -LED, -LING, -LES to wrinkle or pucker
COCKLIKE	*adj* resembling a rooster
COCKLOFT	*n* pl. -S a small attic
COCKNEY	*n* pl. -NEYS a resident of the East End of London
COCKPIT	*n* pl. -S a pilot's compartment in certain airplanes
COCKSHUT	*n* pl. -S the close of day
COCKSHY	*n* pl. -SHIES a target in a throwing contest
COCKSPUR	*n* pl. -S a thorny plant
COCKSURE	*adj* certain
COCKTAIL	*v* -ED, -ING, -S to drink alcoholic beverages
COCKUP	*n* pl. -S a turned-up part of something
COCKY	*adj* COCKIER, COCKIEST arrogantly self-confident
COCO	*n* pl. -COS a tall palm tree
COCOA	*n* pl. -S chocolate
COCOANUT	*n* pl. -S coconut
COCOBOLA	*n* pl. -S cocobolo
COCOBOLO	*n* pl. -LOS a tropical tree
COCOMAT	*n* pl. -S a matting made from coir
COCONUT	*n* pl. -S the fruit of the coco
COCOON	*v* -ED, -ING, -S to wrap or envelop tightly
COCOTTE	*n* pl. -S a prostitute
COCOYAM	*n* pl. -S a tropical plant having edible rootstocks
COCREATE	*v* -ATED, -ATING, -ATES to create together
COD	*v* CODDED, CODDING, CODS to fool
CODA	*n* pl. -S a passage at the end of a musical composition
CODABLE	*adj* capable of being coded
CODDED	past tense of cod
CODDER	*n* pl. -S a cod fisherman
CODDING	present participle of cod
CODDLE	*v* -DLED, -DLING, -DLES to pamper
CODDLER	*n* pl. -S one that coddles
CODE	*v* CODED, CODING, CODES to convert into symbols
CODEBOOK	*n* pl. -S a book listing words and their coded equivalents
CODEBTOR	*n* pl. -S one that shares a debt
CODEC	*n* pl. -S an integrated circuit
CODED	past tense of code
CODEIA	*n* pl. -S codeine
CODEIN	*n* pl. -S codeine
CODEINA	*n* pl. -S codeine
CODEINE	*n* pl. -S a narcotic alkaloid
CODELESS	*adj* being without a set of laws
CODEN	*n* pl. -S a coding classification
CODER	*n* pl. -S one that codes
CODERIVE	*v* -RIVED, -RIVING, -RIVES to derive jointly
CODESIGN	*v* -ED, -ING, -S to design jointly
CODEX	*n* pl. -DICES an ancient manuscript
CODFISH	*n* pl. -ES a marine food fish
CODGER	*n* pl. -S an old man
CODICES	pl. of codex
CODICIL	*n* pl. -S a supplement to a will
CODIFIER	*n* pl. -S one that codifies
CODIFY	*v* -FIED, -FYING, -FIES to arrange or systematize

CODING	present participle of code	**COESITE**	*n* pl. -S a type of silica
CODIRECT	*v* -ED, -ING, -S to direct jointly	**COEVAL**	*n* pl. -S one of the same era or period as another
CODLIN	*n* pl. -S codling	**COEVALLY**	*adv* contemporarily
CODLING	*n* pl. -S an unripe apple	**COEVOLVE**	*v* -VOLVED, -VOLVING, -VOLVES to evolve together
CODON	*n* pl. -S a triplet of nucleotides (basic components of DNA)	**COEXERT**	*v* -ED, -ING, -S to exert jointly
CODPIECE	*n* pl. -S a cover for the crotch in men's breeches	**COEXIST**	*v* -ED, -ING, -S to exist together
CODRIVE	*v* -DROVE, -DRIVEN, -DRIVING, -DRIVES to work as a codriver	**COEXTEND**	*v* -ED, -ING, -S to extend through the same space or time as another
CODRIVER	*n* pl. -S one who takes turns driving a vehicle	**COFACTOR**	*n* pl. -S a coenzyme
COED	*n* pl. -S a female student	**COFF**	*v* COFT, COFFING, COFFS to buy
COEDIT	*v* -ED, -ING, -S to edit with another person	**COFFEE**	*n* pl. -S an aromatic, mildly stimulating beverage
COEDITOR	*n* pl. -S one that coedits	**COFFER**	*v* -ED, -ING, -S to put in a strongbox
COEFFECT	*n* pl. -S an accompanying effect	**COFFIN**	*v* -ED, -ING, -S to put in a coffin (a burial case)
COELIAC	*adj* celiac	**COFFLE**	*v* -FLED, -FLING, -FLES to chain slaves together
COELOM	*n* pl. -LOMS or -LOMATA a body cavity in some animals **COELOMIC** *adj*	**COFFRET**	*n* pl. -S a small strongbox
COELOME	*n* pl. -S coelom	**COFOUND**	*v* -ED, -ING, -S to found jointly
COEMBODY	*v* -BODIED, -BODYING, -BODIES to embody jointly	**COFT**	past tense of coff
COEMPLOY	*v* -ED, -ING, -S to employ together	**COG**	*v* COGGED, COGGING, COGS to cheat at dice
COEMPT	*v* -ED, -ING, -S to buy up the entire supply of a product	**COGENCY**	*n* pl. -CIES the state of being cogent
COENACT	*v* -ED, -ING, -S to enact jointly or at the same time	**COGENT**	*adj* convincing **COGENTLY** *adv*
COENAMOR	*v* -ED, -ING, -S to inflame with mutual love	**COGGED**	past tense of cog
COENDURE	*v* -DURED, -DURING, -DURES to endure together	**COGGING**	present participle of cog
COENURE	*n* pl. -S coenurus	**COGITATE**	*v* -TATED, -TATING, -TATES to ponder
COENURUS	*n* pl. -RI a tapeworm larva	**COGITO**	*n* pl. -TOS a philosophical principle
COENZYME	*n* pl. -S a substance necessary for the functioning of certain enzymes	**COGNAC**	*n* pl. -S a brandy
COEQUAL	*n* pl. -S one who is equal with another	**COGNATE**	*n* pl. -S one that is related to another
COEQUATE	*v* -QUATED, -QUATING, -QUATES to equate with something else	**COGNISE**	*v* -NISED, -NISING, -NISES to cognize
COERCE	*v* -ERCED, -ERCING, -ERCES to compel by force or threat	**COGNIZE**	*v* -NIZED, -NIZING, -NIZES to become aware of in one's mind
COERCER	*n* pl. -S one that coerces	**COGNIZER**	*n* pl. -S one that cognizes
COERCION	*n* pl. -S the act of coercing	**COGNOMEN**	*n* pl. -MENS or -MINA a family name
COERCIVE	*adj* serving to coerce	**COGNOVIT**	*n* pl. -S a written admission of liability
COERECT	*v* -ED, -ING, -S to erect together	**COGON**	*n* pl. -S a tall tropical grass

COGWAY *n* pl. -WAYS a railway operating on steep slopes

COGWHEEL *n* pl. -S a toothed wheel

COHABIT *v* -ED, -ING, -S to live together as man and wife while unmarried

COHEAD *v* -ED, -ING, -S to head jointly

COHEIR *n* pl. -S a joint heir

COHERE *v* -HERED, -HERING, -HERES to stick together

COHERENT *adj* sticking together

COHERER *n* pl. -S a device used to detect radio waves

COHERING present participle of cohere

COHESION *n* pl. -S the act or state of cohering **COHESIVE** *adj*

COHO *n* pl. -HOS a small salmon

COHOBATE *v* -BATED, -BATING, -BATES to distill again

COHOG *n* pl. -S a quahog

COHOLDER *n* pl. -S an athlete who holds a record with another

COHORT *n* pl. -S a companion or associate

COHOSH *n* pl. -ES a medicinal plant

COHOST *v* -ED, -ING, -S to host jointly

COHUNE *n* pl. -S a palm tree

COIF *v* -ED, -ING, -S to style the hair

COIFFE *v* COIFFED, COIFFING, COIFFES to coif

COIFFEUR *n* pl. -S a male hairdresser

COIFFURE *v* -FURED, -FURING, -FURES to coif

COIGN *v* -ED, -ING, -S to quoin

COIGNE *v* COIGNED, COIGNING, COIGNES to quoin

COIL *v* -ED, -ING, -S to wind in even rings

COILER *n* pl. -S one that coils

COIN *v* -ED, -ING, -S to make coins (metal currency) **COINABLE** *adj*

COINAGE *n* pl. -S the act of making coins

COINCIDE *v* -CIDED, -CIDING, -CIDES to be in the same place

COINER *n* pl. -S one that coins

COINFER *v* -FERRED, -FERRING, -FERS to infer jointly

COINHERE *v* -HERED, -HERING, -HERES to inhere jointly

COINMATE *n* pl. -S a fellow inmate

COINSURE *v* -SURED, -SURING, -SURES to insure with another

COINTER *v* -TERRED, -TERRING, -TERS to bury together

COINVENT *v* -ED, -ING, -S to invent together

COIR *n* pl. -S a fiber obtained from coconut husks

COISTREL *n* pl. -S a knave

COISTRIL *n* pl. -S coistrel

COITION *n* pl. -S coitus

COITUS *n* pl. -ES sexual intercourse **COITAL** *adj* **COITALLY** *adv*

COJOIN *v* -ED, -ING, -S to join together

COKE *v* COKED, COKING, COKES to change into a carbon fuel

COKEHEAD *n* pl. -S a cocaine addict

COL *n* pl. -S a depression between two mountains

COLA *n* pl. -S a carbonated beverage

COLANDER *n* pl. -S a kitchen utensil for draining off liquids

COLD *adj* COLDER, COLDEST having little or no warmth

COLD *n* pl. -S the relative lack of heat; a chill

COLDCOCK *v* -ED, -ING, -S to knock unconscious

COLDISH *adj* somewhat cold

COLDLY *adv* in a cold manner

COLDNESS *n* pl. -ES the state of being cold

COLE *n* pl. -S a plant of the cabbage family

COLEAD *v* -LED, -LEADING, -LEADS to lead jointly

COLEADER *n* pl. -S one that coleads

COLESEED *n* pl. -S colza

COLESLAW *n* pl. -S a salad made of shredded raw cabbage

COLESSEE *n* pl. -S a joint lessee

COLESSOR *n* pl. -S a joint lessor

COLEUS *n* pl. -ES a tropical plant

COLEWORT *n* pl. -S cole

COLIC *n* pl. -S acute abdominal pain

COLICIN *n* pl. -S an antibacterial substance

COLICINE *n* pl. -S colicin

COLICKY *adj* pertaining to or associated with colic

COLIES pl. of coly

COLIFORM *n* pl. -S a bacillus of the colon

COLIN *n* pl. -S the bobwhite

COLINEAR *adj* lying in the same straight line

COLISEUM *n* pl. -S a large structure for public entertainment

COLISTIN *n* pl. -S an antibiotic

COLITIS *n* pl. -TISES inflammation of the colon **COLITIC** *adj*

COLLAGE *v* -LAGED, -LAGING, -LAGES to arrange materials in a collage (a kind of artistic composition)

COLLAGEN *n* pl. -S a protein

COLLAPSE *v* -LAPSED, -LAPSING, -LAPSES to crumble suddenly

COLLAR *v* -ED, -ING, -S to provide with a collar (something worn around the neck)

COLLARD *n* pl. -S a variety of kale

COLLARET *n* pl. -S a small collar

COLLATE *v* -LATED, -LATING, -LATES to compare critically

COLLATOR *n* pl. -S one that collates

COLLECT *v* -ED, -ING, -S to bring together in a group

COLLEEN *n* pl. -S an Irish girl

COLLEGE *n* pl. -S a school of higher learning

COLLEGER *n* pl. -S a student supported by funds from his college

COLLEGIA *n/pl* soviet executive councils

COLLET *v* -ED, -ING, -S to set a gem in a rim or ring

COLLIDE *v* -LIDED, -LIDING, -LIDES to come together with violent impact

COLLIDER *n* pl. -S a type of particle accelerator

COLLIE *n* pl. -S a large dog

COLLIED past tense of colly

COLLIER *n* pl. -S a coal miner

COLLIERY *n* pl. -LIERIES a coal mine

COLLIES present 3d person sing. of colly

COLLINS *n* pl. -ES an alcoholic beverage

COLLOGUE *v* -LOGUED, -LOGUING, -LOGUES to conspire

COLLOID *n* pl. -S a type of chemical suspension

COLLOP *n* pl. -S a small portion of meat

COLLOQUY *n* pl. -QUIES a conversation

COLLUDE *v* -LUDED, -LUDING, -LUDES to conspire

COLLUDER *n* pl. -S one that colludes

COLLUVIA *n/pl* rock debris

COLLY *v* -LIED, -LYING, -LIES to blacken with coal dust

COLLYRIA *n/pl* medicinal lotions

COLOBOMA *n* pl. -MATA a lesion of the eye

COLOBUS *n* pl. -BI a long-tailed monkey

COLOCATE *v* -CATED, -CATING, -CATES to place two or more housing units in close proximity

COLOG *n* pl. -S the logarithm of the reciprocal of a number

COLOGNE *n* pl. -S a scented liquid **COLOGNED** *adj*

COLON *n* pl. -S a section of the large intestine

COLON *n* pl. -ES a monetary unit of Costa Rica

COLONE *n* pl. -S colon

COLONEL *n* pl. -S a military officer

COLONI pl. of colonus

COLONIAL *n* pl. -S a citizen of a colony

COLONIC *n* pl. -S irrigation of the colon

COLONIES pl. of colony

COLONISE *v* -NISED, -NISING, -NISES to colonize

COLONIST *n* pl. -S one who settles a colony

COLONIZE *v* -NIZED, -NIZING, -NIZES to establish a colony

COLONUS *n* pl. -NI a freeborn serf

COLONY *n* pl. -NIES a group of emigrants living in a new land

COLOPHON *n* pl. -S an inscription placed at the end of a book

COLOR *v* -ED, -ING, -S to give color (a visual attribute of objects) to

COLORADO *adj* of medium strength and color — used of cigars

COLORANT *n* pl. -S a pigment or dye

COLORED *adj* having color

COLORER *n* pl. -S one that colors

COLORFUL *adj* full of color

COLORING *n* pl. -S appearance in regard to color

COLORISM *n* pl. -S coloring

COLORIST *n* pl. -S a person skilled in the use of color

COLORIZE *v* -IZED, -IZING, -IZES to give color to a black-and-white film

COLORMAN *n* pl. -MEN a sportscaster who provides commentary during a game

COLOSSAL *adj* gigantic

COLOSSUS *n* pl. -LOSSI or -LOSSUSES a gigantic statue

COLOTOMY *n* pl. -MIES a surgical incision of the colon

COLOUR *v* -ED, -ING, -S to color

COLOURER *n* pl. -S colorer

COLPITIS *n* pl. -TISES a vaginal inflammation

COLT *n* pl. -S a young male horse **COLTISH** *adj*

COLTER *n* pl. -S a blade on a plow

COLUBRID *n* pl. -S any of a large family of snakes

COLUGO *n* pl. -GOS a small mammal

COLUMBIC *adj* pertaining to niobium

COLUMEL *n* pl. -S a small column-like anatomical part

COLUMN *n* pl. -S a vertical cylindrical support **COLUMNAL, COLUMNAR, COLUMNED** *adj*

COLURE *n* pl. -S an astronomical circle

COLY *n* pl. COLIES an African bird

COLZA *n* pl. -S a plant of the cabbage family

COMA *n* pl. -S a condition of prolonged unconsciousness

COMA *n* pl. -MAE a tuft of silky hairs

COMAKE *v* -MADE, -MAKING, -MAKES to serve as comaker for another's loan

COMAKER *n* pl. -S one who assumes financial responsibility for another's default

COMAL *adj* comose

COMANAGE *v* -AGED, -AGING, -AGES to manage jointly

COMATE *n* pl. -S a companion

COMATIC *adj* having blurred vision as a result of coma

COMATIK *n* pl. -S komatik

COMATOSE *adj* affected with coma

COMATULA *n* pl. -LAE a marine animal

COMB *v* -ED, -ING, -S to arrange or clean with a comb (a toothed instrument)

COMBAT *v* -BATED, -BATING, -BATS or -BATTED, -BATTING, -BATS to fight against

COMBATER *n* pl. -S one that combats

COMBE *n* pl. -S a narrow valley

COMBER *n* pl. -S one that combs

COMBINE *v* -BINED, -BINING, -BINES to blend

COMBINER *n* pl. -S one that combines

COMBINGS *n/pl* hair removed by a comb

COMBINING present participle of combine

COMBLIKE *adj* resembling a comb

COMBO *n* pl. -BOS a small jazz band

COMBUST *v* -ED, -ING, -S to burn

COME *v* CAME, COMING, COMES or COMETH to move toward something or someone

COMEBACK *n* pl. -S a return to former prosperity

COMEDIAN *n* pl. -S a humorous entertainer

COMEDIC *adj* pertaining to comedy

COMEDIES pl. of comedy

COMEDO *n* pl. -DOS or -DONES a skin blemish

COMEDOWN *n* pl. -S a drop in status

COMEDY *n* pl. -DIES a humorous play, movie, or other work

COMELY *adj* -LIER, -LIEST pleasing to look at **COMELILY** *adv*

COMEMBER *n* pl. -S one that shares membership

COMER *n* pl. -S one showing great promise

COMET *n* pl. -S a celestial body **COMETARY** *adj*

COMETH a present 3d person sing. of come

COMETHER *n* pl. -S an affair or matter

COMETIC *adj* pertaining to a comet

COMFIER comparative of comfy

COMFIEST superlative of comfy

COMFIT *n* pl. -S a candy

COMFORT *v* -ED, -ING, -S to soothe in time of grief

COMFREY *n* pl. -FREYS a coarse herb

COMFY *adj* -FIER, -FIEST comfortable

COMIC *n* pl. -S a comedian

COMICAL *adj* funny

COMING *n* pl. -S arrival

COMINGLE *v* -GLED, -GLING, -GLES to blend thoroughly

COMITIA *n* pl. COMITIA a public assembly in ancient Rome **COMITIAL** *adj*

COMITY *n* pl. -TIES civility

COMIX *n/pl* comic books or strips

COMMA *n* pl. -MAS or -MATA a fragment of a few words or feet in ancient prosody

COMMAND *v* -ED, -ING, -S to direct with authority

COMMANDO *n* pl. -DOES or -DOS a military unit

COMMATA a pl. of comma

COMMENCE *v* -MENCED, -MENCING, -MENCES to begin

COMMEND *v* -ED, -ING, -S to praise

COMMENT *v* -ED, -ING, -S to remark

COMMERCE *v* -MERCED, -MERCING, -MERCES to commune

COMMIE *n* pl. -S a Communist

COMMIES pl. of commy

COMMIT *v* -MITTED, -MITTING, -MITS to do, perform, or perpetrate

COMMIX *v* -MIXED or -MIXT, -MIXING, -MIXES to mix together

COMMODE *n* pl. -S a cabinet

COMMON *adj* -MONER, -MONEST ordinary

COMMON *n* pl. -S a tract of publicly used land

COMMONER *n* pl. -S one of the common people

COMMONLY *adv* in a common manner

COMMOVE *v* -MOVED, -MOVING, -MOVES to move violently

COMMUNAL *adj* belonging to a community; public

COMMUNE *v* -MUNED, -MUNING, -MUNES to converse intimately

COMMUTE *v* -MUTED, -MUTING, -MUTES to exchange

COMMUTER *n* pl. -S one that commutes

COMMY *n* pl. -MIES commie

COMOSE *adj* bearing a tuft of silky hairs

COMOUS *adj* comose

COMP *v* -ED, -ING, -S to play a jazz accompaniment

COMPACT *adj* -PACTER, -PACTEST closely and firmly united

COMPACT *v* -ED, -ING, -S to pack closely together

COMPADRE *n* pl. -S a close friend

COMPANY *v* -NIED, -NYING, -NIES to associate with

COMPARE *v* -PARED, -PARING, -PARES to represent as similar

COMPARER *n* pl. -S one that compares

COMPART *v* -ED, -ING, -S to divide into parts

COMPASS *v* -ED, -ING, -ES to go around

COMPEER *v* -ED, -ING, -S to equal or match

COMPEL *v* -PELLED, -PELLING, -PELS to urge forcefully

COMPEND *n* pl. -S a brief summary

COMPERE *v* -PERED, -PERING, -PERES to act as master of ceremonies

COMPETE *v* -PETED, -PETING, -PETES to vie

COMPILE *v* -PILED, -PILING, -PILES to collect into a volume

COMPILER *n* pl. -S one that compiles

COMPLAIN *v* -ED, -ING, -S to express discontent

COMPLEAT *adj* highly skilled

COMPLECT *v* -ED, -ING, -S to weave together

COMPLETE *adj* -PLETER, -PLETEST having all necessary parts

COMPLETE *v* -PLETED, -PLETING, -PLETES to bring to an end

COMPLEX *adj* -PLEXER, -PLEXEST complicated

COMPLEX *v* -ED, -ING, -ES to make complex

COMPLICE *n* pl. -S an associate

COMPLIED past tense of comply

COMPLIER *n* pl. -S one that complies

COMPLIES present 3d person sing. of comply

COMPLIN *n* pl. -S compline

COMPLINE *n* pl. -S the last liturgical prayer of the day

COMPLOT *v* -PLOTTED, -PLOTTING, -PLOTS to conspire

COMPLY *v* -PLIED, -PLYING, -PLIES to obey

COMPO *n* pl. -POS a mixed substance

COMPONE *adj* compony

COMPONY *adj* composed of squares of alternating colors

COMPORT v -ED, -ING, -S to conduct oneself in a certain way

COMPOSE v -POSED, -POSING, -POSES to form the substance of

COMPOSER n pl. -S one that writes music

COMPOST v -ED, -ING, -S to fertilize

COMPOTE n pl. -S fruit stewed in syrup

COMPOUND v -ED, -ING, -S to add to

COMPRESS v -ED, -ING, -ES to compact

COMPRISE v -PRISED, -PRISING, -PRISES to include or contain

COMPRIZE v -PRIZED, -PRIZING, -PRIZES to comprise

COMPT v -ED, -ING, -S to count

COMPUTE v -PUTED, -PUTING, -PUTES to calculate

COMPUTER n pl. -S a machine that computes automatically

COMRADE n pl. -S a close friend

COMTE n pl. -S a French nobleman

CON v CONNED, CONNING, CONS to study carefully

CONATION n pl. -S the inclination to act purposefully **CONATIVE** adj

CONATUS n pl. CONATUS an effort

CONCAVE v -CAVED, -CAVING, -CAVES to make concave (curving inward)

CONCEAL v -ED, -ING, -S to keep from sight or discovery

CONCEDE v -CEDED, -CEDING, -CEDES to acknowledge as true

CONCEDER n pl. -S one that concedes

CONCEIT v -ED, -ING, -S to imagine

CONCEIVE v -CEIVED, -CEIVING, -CEIVES to understand

CONCENT n pl. -S harmony

CONCEPT n pl. -S a general idea

CONCERN v -ED, -ING, -S to be of interest to

CONCERT v -ED, -ING, -S to plan

CONCERTO n pl. -TOS or -TI a musical composition

CONCH n pl. -S or -ES a marine mollusk

CONCHA n pl. -CHAE an anatomical shell-like structure **CONCHAL** adj

CONCHIE n pl. -S conchy

CONCHOID n pl. -S a type of geometric curve

CONCHY n pl. -CHIES a conscientious objector

CONCISE adj -CISER, -CISEST succinct

CONCLAVE n pl. -S a secret meeting

CONCLUDE v -CLUDED, -CLUDING, -CLUDES to finish

CONCOCT v -ED, -ING, -S to prepare by combining ingredients

CONCORD n pl. -S a state of agreement

CONCRETE v -CRETED, -CRETING, -CRETES to solidify

CONCUR v -CURRED, -CURRING, -CURS to agree

CONCUSS v -ED, -ING, -ES to injure the brain by a violent blow

CONDEMN v -ED, -ING, -S to criticize severely

CONDENSE v -DENSED, -DENSING, -DENSES to compress

CONDIGN adj deserved; appropriate

CONDO n pl. -DOS or -DOES an individually owned unit in a multiunit structure

CONDOLE v -DOLED, -DOLING, -DOLES to mourn

CONDOLER n pl. -S one that condoles

CONDOM n pl. -S a prophylactic

CONDONE v -DONED, -DONING, -DONES to forgive or overlook

CONDONER n pl. -S one that condones

CONDOR n pl. -S or -ES a coin of Chile

CONDUCE v -DUCED, -DUCING, -DUCES to contribute to a result

CONDUCER n pl. -S one that conduces

CONDUCT v -ED, -ING, -S to lead or guide

CONDUIT n pl. -S a channel or pipe for conveying fluids

CONDYLE n pl. -S a protuberance on a bone **CONDYLAR** adj

CONE v CONED, CONING, CONES to shape like a cone (a geometric solid)

CONELRAD n pl. -S a system of defense in the event of air attack

CONENOSE n pl. -S a bloodsucking insect

CONEPATE n pl. -S a skunk

CONEPATL n pl. -S conepate

CONEY n pl. -NEYS cony

CONFAB v -FABBED, -FABBING, -FABS to chat

CONFECT v -ED, -ING, -S to prepare from various ingredients

CONFER   *v* -FERRED, -FERRING, -FERS to bestow

CONFEREE   *n* pl. -S one upon whom something is conferred

CONFERVA   *n* pl. -VAE or -VAS a freshwater alga

CONFESS   *v* -ED, -ING, -ES to acknowledge or disclose

CONFETTO   *n* pl. -TI a bonbon

CONFIDE   *v* -FIDED, -FIDING, -FIDES to reveal in trust or confidence

CONFIDER   *n* pl. -S one that confides

CONFINE   *v* -FINED, -FINING, -FINES to shut within an enclosure

CONFINER   *n* pl. -S one that confines

CONFIRM   *v* -ED, -ING, -S to assure the validity of

CONFIT   *n* pl. -S meat cooked and preserved in its own fat

CONFLATE   *v* -FLATED, -FLATING, -FLATES to blend

CONFLICT   *v* -ED, -ING, -S to come into opposition

CONFLUX   *n* pl. -ES a flowing together of streams

CONFOCAL   *adj* having the same focus or foci

CONFORM   *v* -ED, -ING, -S to become the same or similar

CONFOUND   *v* -ED, -ING, -S to confuse

CONFRERE   *n* pl. -S a colleague

CONFRONT   *v* -ED, -ING, -S to face defiantly

CONFUSE   *v* -FUSED, -FUSING, -FUSES to mix up mentally

CONFUTE   *v* -FUTED, -FUTING, -FUTES to disprove

CONFUTER   *n* pl. -S one that confutes

CONGA   *v* -ED, -ING, -S to perform a conga (Latin American dance)

CONGE   *n* pl. -S permission to depart

CONGEAL   *v* -ED, -ING, -S to change from a fluid to a solid

CONGEE   *v* -GEED, -GEEING, -GEES to bow politely

CONGENER   *n* pl. -S one of the same kind or class

CONGER   *n* pl. -S a marine eel

CONGEST   *v* -ED, -ING, -S to fill to excess

CONGIUS   *n* pl. -GII an ancient unit of measure

CONGLOBE   *v* -GLOBED, -GLOBING, -GLOBES to become a globule

CONGO   *n* pl. -GOS congou

CONGO   *n* pl. -GOES an eellike amphibian

CONGOU   *n* pl. -S a Chinese tea

CONGRATS   *n/pl* congratulations

CONGRESS   *v* -ED, -ING, -ES to assemble together

CONI   pl. of conus

CONIC   *n* pl. -S a geometric curve

CONICAL   *adj* shaped like a cone

CONICITY   *n* pl. -TIES the state of being conical

CONIDIUM   *n* pl. -NIDIA a fungus spore **CONIDIAL, CONIDIAN** *adj*

CONIES   pl. of cony

CONIFER   *n* pl. -S an evergreen tree

CONIINE   *n* pl. -S a poisonous alkaloid

CONIN   *n* pl. -S coniine

CONINE   *n* pl. -S coniine

CONING   present participle of cone

CONIOSIS   *n* pl. -OSES an infection caused by the inhalation of dust

CONIUM   *n* pl. -S a poisonous herb

CONJOIN   *v* -ED, -ING, -S to join together **CONJOINT** *adj*

CONJUGAL   *adj* pertaining to marriage

CONJUNCT   *n* pl. -S one that is joined with another

CONJURE   *v* -JURED, -JURING, -JURES to summon a spirit

CONJURER   *n* pl. -S a sorcerer

CONJUROR   *n* pl. -S conjurer

CONK   *v* -ED, -ING, -S to hit on the head

CONKER   *n* pl. -S a chestnut used in a British game

CONKY   *adj* full of a tree fungus

CONN   *v* -ED, -ING, -S to direct the steering of a ship

CONNATE   *adj* innate

CONNECT   *v* -ED, -ING, -S to join together

CONNED   past tense of con

CONNER   *n* pl. -S one that cons

CONNING   present participle of con

CONNIVE   *v* -NIVED, -NIVING, -NIVES to feign ignorance of wrongdoing

CONNIVER   *n* pl. -S one that connives

CONNOTE   *v* -NOTED, -NOTING, -NOTES to imply another meaning besides the literal one

CONODONT *n* pl. -S a fossil

CONOID *n* pl. -S a geometric solid
CONOIDAL *adj*

CONQUER *v* -ED, -ING, -S to overcome by force

CONQUEST *n* pl. -S the act of conquering

CONQUIAN *n* pl. -S a card game

CONSENT *v* -ED, -ING, -S to permit or approve

CONSERVE *v* -SERVED, -SERVING, -SERVES to protect from loss or depletion

CONSIDER *v* -ED, -ING, -S to think about

CONSIGN *v* -ED, -ING, -S to give over to another's care

CONSIST *v* -ED, -ING, -S to be made up or composed

CONSOL *n* pl. -S a government bond

CONSOLE *v* -SOLED, -SOLING, -SOLES to comfort

CONSOLER *n* pl. -S one that consoles

CONSOMME *n* pl. -S a clear soup

CONSORT *v* -ED, -ING, -S to keep company

CONSPIRE *v* -SPIRED, -SPIRING, -SPIRES to plan secretly with another

CONSTANT *n* pl. -S something that does not vary

CONSTRUE *v* -STRUED, -STRUING, -STRUES to interpret

CONSUL *n* pl. -S an official serving abroad
CONSULAR *adj*

CONSULT *v* -ED, -ING, -S to ask an opinion of

CONSUME *v* -SUMED, -SUMING, -SUMES to use up

CONSUMER *n* pl. -S one that consumes

CONTACT *v* -ED, -ING, -S to communicate with

CONTAGIA *n/pl* causative agents of infectious diseases

CONTAIN *v* -ED, -ING, -S to hold within

CONTE *n* pl. -S a short story

CONTEMN *v* -ED, -ING, -S to scorn

CONTEMPT *n* pl. -S the feeling of one who views something as mean, vile, or worthless

CONTEND *v* -ED, -ING, -S to vie

CONTENT *v* -ED, -ING, -S to satisfy

CONTEST *v* -ED, -ING, -S to compete for

CONTEXT *n* pl. -S the part of a discourse in which a particular word or phrase appears

CONTINUA *n/pl* mathematical sets

CONTINUE *v* -UED, -UING, -UES to go on with

CONTINUO *n* pl. -UOS a type of instrumental part

CONTO *n* pl. -TOS a Portuguese money of account

CONTORT *v* -ED, -ING, -S to twist out of shape

CONTOUR *v* -ED, -ING, -S to make the outline of

CONTRA *n* pl. -S a Nicaraguan revolutionary

CONTRACT *v* -ED, -ING, -S to decrease in size or volume

CONTRAIL *n* pl. -S a visible trail of water vapor from an aircraft

CONTRARY *n* pl. -TRARIES an opposite

CONTRAST *v* -ED, -ING, -S to place in opposition to set off differences

CONTRITE *adj* deeply sorry for one's sins

CONTRIVE *v* -TRIVED, -TRIVING, -TRIVES to devise

CONTROL *v* -TROLLED, -TROLLING, -TROLS to exercise authority over

CONTUSE *v* -TUSED, -TUSING, -TUSES to bruise

CONUS *n* pl. CONI an anatomical part in mammals

CONVECT *v* -ED, -ING, -S to transfer heat by a process of circulation

CONVENE *v* -VENED, -VENING, -VENES to assemble

CONVENER *n* pl. -S one that convenes

CONVENOR *n* pl. -S convener

CONVENT *v* -ED, -ING, -S to convene

CONVERGE *v* -VERGED, -VERGING, -VERGES to come together

CONVERSE *v* -VERSED, -VERSING, -VERSES to speak together

CONVERT *v* -ED, -ING, -S to change into another form

CONVEX *n* pl. -ES a surface or body that is convex (curving outward)

CONVEXLY *adv* in a convex manner

CONVEY *v* -ED, -ING, -S to transport

CONVEYER *n* pl. -S one that conveys

CONVEYOR   *n* pl. -S conveyer

CONVICT   *v* -ED, -ING, -S to prove guilty

CONVINCE   *v* -VINCED, -VINCING, -VINCES to cause to believe something

CONVOKE   *v* -VOKED, -VOKING, -VOKES to cause to assemble

CONVOKER   *n* pl. -S one that convokes

CONVOLVE   *v* -VOLVED, -VOLVING, -VOLVES to roll together

CONVOY   *v* -ED, -ING, -S to escort

CONVULSE   *v* -VULSED, -VULSING, -VULSES to shake violently

CONY   *n* pl. CONIES a rabbit

COO   *v* COOED, COOING, COOS to make the sound of a dove

COOCH   *n* pl. -ES a sinuous dance

COOCOO   *adj* crazy

COOEE   *v* COOEED, COOEEING, COOEES to cry out shrilly

COOER   *n* pl. -S one that coos

COOEY   *v* -EYED, -EYING, -EYS to cooee

COOF   *n* pl. -S a dolt

COOINGLY   *adv* in the manner of cooing doves; affectionately

COOK   *v* -ED, -ING, -S to prepare food by heating **COOKABLE** *adj*

COOKBOOK   *n* pl. -S a book of recipes

COOKER   *n* pl. -S one that cooks

COOKERY   *n* pl. -ERIES the art of cooking

COOKEY   *n* pl. -EYS cookie

COOKIE   *n* pl. -S a small, flat cake

COOKING   *n* pl. -S the act of one that cooks

COOKLESS   *adj* having no person that cooks

COOKOUT   *n* pl. -S a meal eaten and prepared outdoors

COOKSHOP   *n* pl. -S a shop that sells cooked food

COOKTOP   *n* pl. -S a counter-top cooking apparatus

COOKWARE   *n* pl. -S utensils used in cooking

COOKY   *n* pl. COOKIES cookie

COOL   *adj* COOLER, COOLEST moderately cold

COOL   *v* -ED, -ING, -S to make less warm

COOLANT   *n* pl. -S a fluid used to cool engines

COOLDOWN   *n* pl. -S a gradual return of physiological functions to normal levels after strenuous exercise

COOLER   *n* pl. -S something that cools

COOLIE   *n* pl. -S an Oriental laborer

COOLIES   pl. of cooly

COOLISH   *adj* somewhat cool

COOLLY   *adv* in a cool manner

COOLNESS   *n* pl. -ES the state of being cool

COOLTH   *n* pl. -S coolness

COOLY   *n* pl. COOLIES coolie

COOMB   *n* pl. -S combe

COOMBE   *n* pl. -S combe

COON   *n* pl. -S a raccoon

COONCAN   *n* pl. -S conquian

COONSKIN   *n* pl. -S the pelt of a raccoon

COONTIE   *n* pl. -S a tropical plant

COOP   *v* -ED, -ING, -S to confine

COOPER   *v* -ED, -ING, -S to make or mend barrels

COOPERY   *n* pl. -ERIES the trade of coopering

COOPT   *v* -ED, -ING, -S to elect or appoint

COOPTION   *n* pl. -S the act of coopting

COOT   *n* pl. -S an aquatic bird

COOTER   *n* pl. -S a turtle

COOTIE   *n* pl. -S a body louse

COP   *v* COPPED, COPPING, COPS to steal

COPAIBA   *n* pl. -S a resin

COPAL   *n* pl. -S a resin

COPALM   *n* pl. -S a hardwood tree

COPARENT   *n* pl. -S a fellow parent

COPASTOR   *n* pl. -S one that shares the duties of a pastor

COPATRON   *n* pl. -S a fellow patron

COPE   *v* COPED, COPING, COPES to contend or strive

COPECK   *n* pl. -S kopeck

COPEMATE   *n* pl. -S an antagonist

COPEN   *n* pl. -S a blue color

COPEPOD   *n* pl. -S a minute crustacean

COPER   *n* pl. -S a horse dealer

COPIED   past tense of copy

COPIER   *n* pl. -S one that copies

COPIES   present 3d person sing. of copy

COPIHUE   *n* pl. -S a climbing vine

COPILOT   *n* pl. -S an assistant pilot

COPING   *n* pl. -S the top part of a wall

COPIOUS   *adj* abundant

COPLANAR   *adj* lying in the same plane

COPLOT   *v* -PLOTTED, -PLOTTING, -PLOTS to plot together

COPPED   past tense of cop

COPPER   *v* -ED, -ING, -S to cover with copper (a metallic element)

COPPERAH   *n* pl. -S copra

COPPERAS   *n* pl. -ES a compound used in making inks

COPPERY   *adj* resembling copper

COPPICE   *v* -PICED, -PICING, -PICES to cause to grow in the form of a coppice (a thicket)

COPPING   present participle of cop

COPPRA   *n* pl. -S copra

COPRA   *n* pl. -S dried coconut meat

COPRAH   *n* pl. -S copra

COPREMIA   *n* pl. -S a form of blood poisoning **COPREMIC** *adj*

COPRINCE   *n* pl. -S one of two princes ruling jointly

COPSE   *n* pl. -S a coppice

COPTER   *n* pl. -S a helicopter

COPULA   *n* pl. -LAS or -LAE something that links **COPULAR** *adj*

COPULATE   *v* -LATED, -LATING, -LATES to engage in coitus

COPURIFY   *v* -FIED, -FYING, -FIES to become purified with another substance

COPY   *v* COPIED, COPYING, COPIES to imitate

COPYBOOK   *n* pl. -S a book used in teaching penmanship

COPYBOY   *n* pl. -BOYS an office boy

COPYCAT   *v* -CATTED, -CATTING, -CATS to imitate

COPYDESK   *n* pl. -S an editor's desk in a newspaper office

COPYEDIT   *v* -ED, -ING, -S to prepare copy for the printer

COPYHOLD   *n* pl. -S a type of ownership of land

COPYIST   *n* pl. -S an imitator

COPYREAD   *v* -READ, -READING, -READS to copyedit

COQUET   *v* -QUETTED, -QUETTING, -QUETS to flirt

COQUETRY   *n* pl. -TRIES flirtatious behavior

COQUETTE   *v* -QUETTED, -QUETTING, -QUETTES to coquet

COQUILLE   *n* pl. -S a cooking utensil

COQUINA   *n* pl. -S a small marine clam

COQUITO   *n* pl. -TOS a palm tree

COR   *interj* — used to express surprise, admiration, or irritation

CORACLE   *n* pl. -S a small boat

CORACOID   *n* pl. -S a bone of the shoulder girdle

CORAL   *n* pl. -S a mass of marine animal skeletons

CORANTO   *n* pl. -TOS or -TOES courante

CORBAN   *n* pl. -S an offering to God

CORBEIL   *n* pl. -S a sculptured fruit basket

CORBEL   *v* -BELED, -BELING, -BELS or -BELLED, -BELLING, -BELS to provide a wall with a bracket

CORBIE   *n* pl. -S a raven or crow

CORBINA   *n* pl. -S a food and game fish

CORBY   *n* pl. CORBIES corbie

CORD   *v* -ED, -ING, -S to fasten with a cord (a thin rope)

CORDAGE   *n* pl. -S the amount of wood in an area

CORDATE   *adj* heart-shaped

CORDELLE   *v* -DELLED, -DELLING, -DELLES to tow a boat with a cordelle (a towrope)

CORDER   *n* pl. -S one that cords

CORDIAL   *n* pl. -S a liqueur

CORDING   *n* pl. -S the ribbed surface of cloth

CORDITE   *n* pl. -S an explosive powder

CORDLESS   *adj* having no cord

CORDLIKE   *adj* resembling a cord

CORDOBA   *n* pl. -S a monetary unit of Nicaragua

CORDON   *v* -ED, -ING, -S to form a barrier around

CORDOVAN   *n* pl. -S a fine leather

CORDUROY   *v* -ED, -ING, -S to build a type of road

CORDWAIN   *n* pl. -S cordovan

CORDWOOD   *n* pl. -S wood used for fuel

CORE   v CORED, CORING, CORES to remove the core (the central part) of

COREDEEM   v -ED, -ING, -S to redeem jointly

COREIGN   n pl. -S a joint reign

CORELATE   v -LATED, -LATING, -LATES to place into mutual or reciprocal relation

CORELESS   adj having no core

COREMIUM   n pl. -MIA an organ of certain fungi

CORER   n pl. -S a utensil for coring apples

CORF   n pl. CORVES a wagon used in a mine

CORGI   n pl. -S a short-legged dog

CORING   present participle of core

CORIUM   n pl. -RIA a skin layer

CORK   v -ED, -ING, -S to stop up

CORKAGE   n pl. -S a charge for wine in a restaurant

CORKER   n pl. -S one that corks

CORKIER   comparative of corky

CORKIEST   superlative of corky

CORKLIKE   adj resembling cork (a porous tree bark)

CORKWOOD   n pl. -S a small tree

CORKY   adj CORKIER, CORKIEST corklike

CORM   n pl. -S a stem of certain plants **CORMLIKE, CORMOID, CORMOUS** adj

CORMEL   n pl. -S a small corm

CORN   v -ED, -ING, -S to preserve with salt

CORNBALL   n pl. -S a hick

CORNCAKE   n pl. -S a cake made of cornmeal

CORNCOB   n pl. -S the woody core of an ear of corn

CORNCRIB   n pl. -S a building in which corn is stored

CORNEA   n pl. -S a part of the eye **CORNEAL** adj

CORNEL   n pl. -S a hardwood tree or shrub

CORNEOUS   adj of a hornlike texture

CORNER   v -ED, -ING, -S to gain control of

CORNET   n pl. -S a trumpetlike instrument

CORNETCY   n -CIES a rank in the British cavalry

CORNFED   adj fed on corn

CORNHUSK   n pl. -S the husk covering an ear of corn

CORNICE   v -NICED, -NICING, -NICES to decorate with a molding

CORNICHE   n pl. -S a road built along a cliff

CORNICLE   n pl. -S a part of an aphid

CORNIER   comparative of corny

CORNIEST   superlative of corny

CORNILY   adv in a corny manner

CORNMEAL   n pl. -S meal made from corn

CORNPONE   n pl. -S a bread made with cornmeal

CORNROW   v -ED, -ING, -S to braid hair tightly in rows close to the scalp

CORNU   n pl. -NUA a hornlike bone formation **CORNUAL** adj

CORNUS   n pl. -ES a cornel

CORNUTE   adj horn-shaped

CORNUTED   adj cornute

CORNUTO   n pl. -TOS the husband of an unfaithful wife

CORNY   adj CORNIER, CORNIEST trite

CORODY   n pl. -DIES an allowance of food or clothes

COROLLA   n pl. -S a protective covering of a flower

CORONA   n pl. -NAS or -NAE a luminous circle around a celestial body

CORONACH   n pl. -S a dirge

CORONAL   n pl. -S a wreath worn on the head

CORONARY   n -NARIES an artery supplying blood to the heart

CORONATE   v -NATED, -NATING, -NATES to crown

CORONEL   n pl. -S coronal

CORONER   n pl. -S an officer who investigates questionable deaths

CORONET   n pl. -S a small crown

CORONOID   adj crown-shaped

COROTATE   v -TATED, -TATING, -TATES to rotate together

CORPORA   pl. of corpus

CORPORAL   n pl. -S a military rank

CORPS   n pl. CORPS a military unit

CORPSE   n pl. -S a dead body

CORPSMAN   n pl. -MEN an enlisted man trained in first aid

CORPUS *n* pl. -PORA a human or animal body

CORRADE *v* -RADED, -RADING, -RADES to erode

CORRAL *v* -RALLED, -RALLING, -RALS to place livestock in a corral (an enclosure)

CORRECT *v* -ED, -ING, -S to make free from error

CORRECT *adj* -RECTER, -RECTEST free from error

CORRIDA *n* pl. -S a bullfight

CORRIDOR *n* pl. -S a narrow hallway

CORRIE *n* pl. -S a cirque

CORRIVAL *n* pl. -S a rival or opponent

CORRODE *v* -RODED, -RODING, -RODES to eat away gradually

CORRODY *n* pl. -DIES corody

CORRUPT *adj* -RUPTER, -RUPTEST dishonest and venal

CORRUPT *v* -ED, -ING, -S to subvert the honesty or integrity of

CORSAC *n* pl. -S an Asian fox

CORSAGE *n* pl. -S a small bouquet of flowers

CORSAIR *n* pl. -S a pirate

CORSE *n* pl. -S a corpse

CORSELET *n* pl. -S a piece of body armor

CORSET *v* -ED, -ING, -S to fit with a corset (a supporting undergarment)

CORSETRY *n* pl. -RIES the work of making corsets

CORSLET *n* pl. -S corselet

CORTEGE *n* pl. -S a retinue

CORTEX *n* pl. -TICES or -TEXES the outer layer of an organ **CORTICAL** *adj*

CORTIN *n* pl. -S a hormone

CORTISOL *n* pl. -S a hormone

CORULER *n* pl. -S one that rules jointly

CORUNDUM *n* pl. -S a hard mineral

CORVEE *n* pl. -S an obligation to perform feudal service

CORVES pl. of corf

CORVET *n* pl. -S corvette

CORVETTE *n* pl. -S a small, swift warship

CORVINA *n* pl. -S corbina

CORVINE *adj* pertaining or belonging to the crow family of birds

CORY *n* pl. CORY a former monetary unit of Guinea

CORYBANT *n* pl. -BANTS or -BANTES a reveler

CORYMB *n* pl. -S a flower cluster **CORYMBED** *adj*

CORYPHEE *n* pl. -S a ballet dancer

CORYZA *n* pl. -S a head cold **CORYZAL** *adj*

COS *n* pl. -ES a variety of lettuce

COSCRIPT *v* -ED, -ING, -S to collaborate in preparing a script for

COSEC *n* pl. -S cosecant

COSECANT *n* pl. -S a trigonometric function of an angle

COSET *n* pl. -S a mathematical subset

COSEY *n* pl. -SEYS a cozy

COSH *v* -ED, -ING, -ES to bludgeon

COSHER *v* -ED, -ING, -S to coddle

COSIE *n* pl. -S a cozy

COSIED past tense of cosy

COSIER comparative of cosy

COSIES present 3d person sing. of cosy

COSIEST superlative of cosy

COSIGN *v* -ED, -ING, -S to sign jointly

COSIGNER *n* pl. -S one that cosigns

COSILY *adv* in a cosy manner

COSINE *n* pl. -S a trigonometric function of an angle

COSINESS *n* pl. -ES coziness

COSMETIC *n* pl. -S a beauty preparation

COSMIC *adj* pertaining to the cosmos

COSMICAL *adj* cosmic

COSMISM *n* pl. -S a philosophical theory

COSMIST *n* pl. -S a supporter of cosmism

COSMOS *n* pl. -ES the universe regarded as an orderly system

COSS *n* pl. COSS kos

COSSACK *n* pl. -S a Russian cavalryman

COSSET *v* -ED, -ING, -S to fondle

COST *v* COST or COSTED, COSTING, COSTS to estimate a price for production of

COSTA *n* pl. -TAE a rib **COSTAL** *adj*

COSTAR *v* -STARRED, -STARRING, -STARS to star with another actor

COSTARD *n* pl. -S a large cooking apple

COSTATE *adj* having a rib or ribs

COSTER *n* pl. -S a hawker of fruit or vegetables

COSTIVE *adj* constipated

COSTLESS *adj* free of charge

COSTLY *adj* -LIER, -LIEST expensive

COSTMARY *n* pl. -MARIES an herb used in salads

COSTREL *n* pl. -S a flask

COSTUME *v* -TUMED, -TUMING, -TUMES to supply with a costume (a style of dress)

COSTUMER *n* pl. -S one that costumes

COSTUMEY *adj* of or pertaining to a costume

COSTUMING present participle of costume

COSY *v* COSIED, COSYING, COSIES cozy

COSY *adj* COSIER, COSIEST cozy

COT *n* pl. -S a light, narrow bed

COTAN *n* pl. -S a trigonometric function of an angle

COTE *v* COTED, COTING, COTES to pass by

COTEAU *n* pl. -TEAUX the higher ground of a region

COTENANT *n* pl. -S one who is a tenant with another in the same place

COTERIE *n* pl. -S a clique

COTHURN *n* pl. -S a buskin worn by ancient Roman actors

COTHURNI *n/pl* cothurns

COTIDAL *adj* indicating coincidence of the tides

COTILLON *n* pl. -S a ballroom dance

COTING present participle of cote

COTQUEAN *n* pl. -S a vulgar woman

COTTA *n* pl. -TAE or -TAS a short surplice

COTTAGE *n* pl. -S a small house **COTTAGEY** *adj*

COTTAGER *n* pl. -S one that lives in a cottage

COTTAR *n* pl. -S a tenant farmer

COTTER *n* pl. -S a pin or wedge used for fastening parts together **COTTERED** *adj*

COTTIER *n* pl. -S cottar

COTTON *v* -ED, -ING, -S to take a liking

COTTONY *adj* resembling cotton (a soft, fibrous material)

COTYLOID *adj* cup-shaped

COTYPE *n* pl. -S a taxonomic type

COUCH *v* -ED, -ING, -ES to put into words

COUCHANT *adj* lying down

COUCHER *n* pl. -S one that couches

COUCHING *n* pl. -S a form of embroidery

COUDE *adj* pertaining to a type of telescope

COUGAR *n* pl. -S a mountain lion

COUGH *v* -ED, -ING, -S to expel air from the lungs noisily

COUGHER *n* pl. -S one that coughs

COULD past tense of can

COULDEST a past 2d person sing. of can

COULDST a past 2d person sing. of can

COULEE *n* pl. -S a small ravine

COULIS *n* pl. -LISES a thick sauce of pureed vegetable or fruit

COULISSE *n* pl. -S a side scene of a theatre stage

COULOIR *n* pl. -S a deep gorge or gully

COULOMB *n* pl. -S an electrical measure

COULTER *n* pl. -S colter

COUMARIN *n* pl. -S a chemical compound **COUMARIC** *adj*

COUMAROU *n* pl. -S the seed of a tropical tree

COUNCIL *n* pl. -S a group of persons appointed for a certain function

COUNSEL *v* -SELED, -SELING, -SELS or -SELLED, -SELLING, -SELS to advise

COUNT *v* -ED, -ING, -S to list or mention the units of one by one to ascertain the total

COUNTER *v* -ED, -ING, -S to oppose

COUNTESS *n* pl. -ES a noblewoman

COUNTIAN *n* pl. -S a resident of a county

COUNTRY *n* pl. -TRIES the territory of a nation

COUNTY *n* pl. -TIES an administrative division of a state

COUP *v* -ED, -ING, -S to overturn

COUPE *n* pl. -S an automobile with two doors

COUPLE *v* -PLED, -PLING, -PLES to unite in pairs

COUPLER *n* pl. -S one that couples

COUPLET *n* pl. -S a pair of successive lines of verse

COUPLING *n* pl. -S a joining device

COUPON *n* pl. -S a certificate entitling the holder to certain benefits

COURAGE *n* pl. -S the quality that enables one to face danger fearlessly; spirit

COURANT *n* pl. -S courante

COURANTE *n* pl. -S an old, lively dance

COURANTO *n* pl. -TOS or -TOES courante

COURIER *n* pl. -S a messenger

COURLAN *n* pl. -S a wading bird

COURSE *v* COURSED, COURSING, COURSES to cause hounds to chase game

COURSER *n* pl. -S one that courses

COURSING *n* pl. -S the pursuit of game by hounds

COURT *v* -ED, -ING, -S to woo

COURTER *n* pl. -S one that courts

COURTESY *v* -SIED, -SYING, -SIES to curtsy

COURTIER *n* pl. -S one who attends a royal court

COURTLY *adj* -LIER, -LIEST stately

COUSCOUS *n* pl. -ES a North African cereal

COUSIN *n* pl. -S a child of one's aunt or uncle **COUSINLY** *adj*

COUSINRY *n* pl. -RIES cousins collectively

COUTEAU *n* pl. -TEAUX a knife

COUTER *n* pl. -S a piece of armor for the elbow

COUTH *adj* COUTHER, COUTHEST sophisticated

COUTH *n* pl. -S refinement

COUTHIE *adj* COUTHIER, COUTHIEST friendly

COUTURE *n* pl. -S the business of dressmaking

COUVADE *n* pl. -S a primitive birth ritual

COVALENT *adj* sharing electron pairs

COVE *v* COVED, COVING, COVES to curve over or inward

COVEN *n* pl. -S a group of witches

COVENANT *v* -ED, -ING, -S to enter into a binding agreement

COVER *v* -ED, -ING, -S to place something over or upon

COVERAGE *n* pl. -S the extent to which something is covered

COVERALL *n* pl. -S a one-piece work garment

COVERER *n* pl. -S one that covers

COVERING *n* pl. -S something that covers

COVERLET *n* pl. -S a bed covering

COVERLID *n* pl. -S a coverlet

COVERT *n* pl. -S a hiding place

COVERTLY *adv* secretly

COVERUP *n* pl. -S something used to conceal improper activity

COVET *v* -ED, -ING, -S to desire greatly

COVETER *n* pl. -S one that covets

COVETOUS *adj* excessively desirous

COVEY *n* pl. -EYS a flock of birds

COVIN *n* pl. -S a conspiracy to defraud

COVING *n* pl. -S a concave molding

COW *n* pl. -S or KINE a farm animal

COW *v* -ED, -ING, -S to intimidate

COWAGE *n* pl. -S a tropical vine

COWARD *n* pl. -S one who lacks courage

COWARDLY *adj* lacking courage

COWBANE *n* pl. -S a poisonous plant

COWBELL *n* pl. -S a bell around a cow's neck

COWBERRY *n* pl. -RIES a pasture shrub

COWBIND *n* pl. -S a species of bryony

COWBIRD *n* pl. -S a blackbird

COWBOY *n* pl. -BOYS a ranch worker

COWEDLY *adv* in a cowed manner

COWER *v* -ED, -ING, -S to cringe

COWFISH *n* pl. -ES an aquatic mammal

COWFLAP *n* pl. -S cowflop

COWFLOP *n* pl. -S a cowpat

COWGIRL *n* pl. -S a female ranch worker

COWHAGE *n* pl. -S cowage

COWHAND *n* pl. -S a cowboy

COWHERB *n* pl. -S an annual herb

COWHERD *n* pl. -S one who tends cattle

COWHIDE *v* -HIDED, -HIDING, -HIDES to flog with a leather whip

COWIER comparative of cowy

COWIEST superlative of cowy

COWINNER *n* pl. -S one of two or more winners

COWL *v* -ED, -ING, -S to cover with a hood

COWLICK *n* pl. -S a lock of unruly hair

COWLING   *n* pl. -S a covering for an aircraft engine

COWMAN   *n* pl. -MEN one who owns cattle

COWORKER   *n* pl. -S a fellow worker

COWPAT   *n* pl. -S a dropping of cow dung

COWPEA   *n* pl. -S a black-eyed pea

COWPIE   *n* pl. -S a cowpat

COWPLOP   *n* pl. -S a cowpat

COWPOKE   *n* pl. -S a cowboy

COWPOX   *n* pl. -ES a cattle disease

COWRIE   *n* pl. -S cowry

COWRITE   *v* -WROTE, -WRITTEN, -WRITING, -WRITES to collaborate in writing

COWRY   *n* pl. -RIES a glossy seashell

COWSHED   *n* pl. -S a shelter for cows

COWSKIN   *n* pl. -S the hide of a cow

COWSLIP   *n* pl. -S a flowering plant

COWY   *adj* COWIER, COWIEST suggestive of a cow

COX   *v* -ED, -ING, -ES to coxswain

COXA   *n* pl. COXAE the hip or hip joint **COXAL** *adj*

COXALGIA   *n* pl. -S pain in the hip **COXALGIC** *adj*

COXALGY   *n* pl. -GIES coxalgia

COXCOMB   *n* pl. -S a conceited dandy

COXITIS   *n* pl. COXITIDES inflammation of the hip joint

COXSWAIN   *v* -ED, -ING, -S to steer a racing rowboat

COY   *adj* COYER, COYEST shy

COY   *v* -ED, -ING, -S to caress

COYDOG   *n* pl. -S a hybrid between a coyote and a wild dog

COYISH   *adj* somewhat coy

COYLY   *adv* in a coy manner

COYNESS   *n* pl. -ES the state of being coy

COYOTE   *n* pl. -S a small wolf

COYPOU   *n* pl. -S a coypu

COYPU   *n* pl. -S an aquatic rodent

COZ   *n* pl. COZES or COZZES a cousin

COZEN   *v* -ED, -ING, -S to deceive

COZENAGE   *n* pl. -S the practice of cozening

COZENER   *n* pl. -S one that cozens

COZEY   *n* pl. -ZEYS a cover for a teapot

COZIE   *n* pl. -S a cozey

COZIED   past tense of cozy

COZIER   comparative of cozy

COZIES   present 3d person sing. of cozy

COZIEST   superlative of cozy

COZINESS   *n* pl. -ES the state of being cozy

COZY   *v* COZIED, COZYING, COZIES to attempt to get on friendly terms

COZY   *adj* COZIER, COZIEST snug and comfortable **COZILY** *adv*

COZZES   a pl. of coz

CRAAL   *v* -ED, -ING, -S to kraal

CRAB   *v* CRABBED, CRABBING, CRABS to complain

CRABBER   *n* pl. -S one that crabs

CRABBY   *adj* -BIER, -BIEST grumpy **CRABBILY** *adv*

CRABMEAT   *n* pl. -S the edible part of a crab

CRABWISE   *adv* sideways

CRACK   *v* -ED, -ING, -S to break without dividing into parts

CRACKER   *n* pl. -S a thin, crisp biscuit

CRACKING   *n* pl. -S a chemical process

CRACKLE   *v* -LED, -LING, -LES to make a succession of snapping sounds

CRACKLY   *adj* -LIER, -LIEST brittle

CRACKNEL   *n* pl. -S a hard, crisp biscuit

CRACKPOT   *n* pl. -S an eccentric person

CRACKUP   *n* pl. -S a collision

CRACKY   *interj* — used to express surprise

CRADLE   *v* -DLED, -DLING, -DLES to nurture during infancy

CRADLER   *n* pl. -S one that cradles

CRAFT   *v* -ED, -ING, -S to make by hand

CRAFTY   *adj* CRAFTIER, CRAFTIEST skillful in deceiving **CRAFTILY** *adv*

CRAG   *n* pl. -S a large jagged rock **CRAGGED** *adj*

CRAGGY   *adj* -GIER, -GIEST full of crags **CRAGGILY** *adv*

CRAGSMAN   *n* pl. -MEN one who climbs crags

CRAKE   *n* pl. -S a small, harsh-voiced bird

CRAM   *v* CRAMMED, CRAMMING, CRAMS to fill or pack tightly

CRAMBE   *n* pl. -S an annual herb

CRAMBO   *n* pl. -BOS or -BOES a word game

CRAMMED	past tense of cram	**CRASES**	pl. of crasis
CRAMMER	*n* pl. -S one that crams	**CRASH**	*v* -ED, -ING, -ES to collide noisily
CRAMMING	present participle of cram	**CRASHER**	*n* pl. -S one that crashes
CRAMOISY	*n* pl. -SIES crimson cloth	**CRASIS**	*n* pl. CRASES a vowel contraction
CRAMP	*v* -ED, -ING, -S to restrain or confine	**CRASS**	*adj* CRASSER, CRASSEST grossly vulgar or stupid **CRASSLY** *adv*
CRAMPIT	*n* pl. -S a piece of equipment used in curling	**CRATCH**	*n* pl. -ES a manger
CRAMPON	*n* pl. -S a device for raising heavy objects	**CRATE**	*v* CRATED, CRATING, CRATES to put in a packing box
CRAMPOON	*n* pl. -S crampon	**CRATER**	*v* -ED, -ING, -S to form cavities in a surface
CRANCH	*v* -ED, -ING, -ES to craunch	**CRATON**	*n* pl. -S a part of the earth's crust **CRATONIC** *adj*
CRANE	*v* CRANED, CRANING, CRANES to stretch out one's neck	**CRAUNCH**	*v* -ED, -ING, -ES to crunch
CRANIA	a pl. of cranium	**CRAVAT**	*n* pl. -S a necktie
CRANIAL	*adj* pertaining to the skull	**CRAVE**	*v* CRAVED, CRAVING, CRAVES to desire greatly
CRANIATE	*n* pl. -S one that has a skull		
CRANING	present participle of crane	**CRAVEN**	*v* -ED, -ING, -S to make cowardly
CRANIUM	*n* pl. -NIUMS or -NIA the skull	**CRAVENLY**	*adv* in a cowardly manner
CRANK	*v* -ED, -ING, -S to start manually	**CRAVER**	*n* pl. -S one that craves
CRANK	*adj* CRANKER, CRANKEST lively	**CRAVING**	*n* pl. -S a great desire
CRANKIER	comparative of cranky	**CRAW**	*n* pl. -S the stomach of an animal
CRANKIEST	superlative of cranky	**CRAWDAD**	*n* pl. -S a crayfish
CRANKILY	*adv* in a cranky manner	**CRAWFISH**	*v* -ED, -ING, -ES to back out or retreat
CRANKISH	*adj* eccentric		
CRANKLE	*v* -KLED, -KLING, -KLES to crinkle	**CRAWL**	*v* -ED, -ING, -S to move with the body on or near the ground
CRANKLY	*adv* in a crank manner	**CRAWLER**	*n* pl. -S one that crawls
CRANKOUS	*adj* cranky	**CRAWLWAY**	*n* pl. -WAYS a small, low tunnel
CRANKPIN	*n* pl. -S the handle of a crank	**CRAWLY**	*adj* CRAWLIER, CRAWLIEST creepy
CRANKY	*adj* CRANKIER, CRANKIEST grumpy		
CRANNIED	*adj* having crannies	**CRAYFISH**	*n* pl. -ES a crustacean
CRANNIES	pl. of cranny	**CRAYON**	*v* -ED, -ING, -S to use a drawing implement
CRANNOG	*n* pl. -S an artificial island		
CRANNOGE	*n* pl. -S crannog	**CRAZE**	*v* CRAZED, CRAZING, CRAZES to make insane
CRANNY	*n* pl. -NIES a crevice **CRANNIED** *adj*	**CRAZY**	*adj* -ZIER, -ZIEST insane **CRAZILY** *adv*
CRAP	*v* CRAPPED, CRAPPING, CRAPS to throw a 2, 3, or 12 in a dice game	**CRAZY**	*n* pl. -ZIES a crazy person
		CREAK	*v* -ED, -ING, -S to squeak
CRAPE	*v* CRAPED, CRAPING, CRAPES to crepe	**CREAKY**	*adj* CREAKIER, CREAKIEST creaking **CREAKILY** *adv*
CRAPPIE	*n* pl. -S an edible fish	**CREAM**	*v* -ED, -ING, -S to form cream (a part of milk)
CRAPPING	present participle of crap		
CRAPPY	*adj* -PIER, -PIEST markedly inferior in quality	**CREAMER**	*n* pl. -S a cream pitcher
		CREAMERY	*n* pl. -ERIES a dairy

CREAMY *adj* CREAMIER, CREAMIEST rich in cream **CREAMILY** *adv*

CREASE *v* CREASED, CREASING, CREASES to make a fold or wrinkle in

CREASER *n* pl. -S one that creases

CREASY *adj* CREASIER, CREASIEST having folds or wrinkles

CREATE *v* -ATED, -ATING, -ATES to cause to exist

CREATIN *n* pl. -S creatine

CREATINE *n* pl. -S a chemical compound

CREATION *n* pl. -S something created

CREATIVE *adj* having the ability to create

CREATOR *n* pl. -S one that creates

CREATURE *n* pl. -S a living being

CRECHE *n* pl. -S a day nursery

CREDAL *adj* pertaining to a creed

CREDENCE *n* pl. -S belief

CREDENDA *n/pl* articles of faith

CREDENT *adj* believing

CREDENZA *n* pl. -S a piece of furniture

CREDIBLE *adj* believable **CREDIBLY** *adv*

CREDIT *v* -ED, -ING, -S to accept as true

CREDITOR *n* pl. -S one to whom money is owed

CREDO *n* pl. -DOS a creed

CREED *n* pl. -S a statement of belief **CREEDAL** *adj*

CREEK *n* pl. -S a watercourse smaller than a river

CREEL *v* -ED, -ING, -S to put fish in a creel (a fish basket)

CREEP *v* CREPT, CREEPING, CREEPS to crawl

CREEPAGE *n* pl. -S gradual movement

CREEPER *n* pl. -S one that creeps

CREEPIE *n* pl. -S a low stool

CREEPY *adj* CREEPIER, CREEPIEST repugnant **CREEPILY** *adv*

CREESE *n* pl. -S kris

CREESH *v* -ED, -ING, -ES to grease

CREMAINS *n/pl* the ashes of a cremated body

CREMATE *v* -MATED, -MATING, -MATES to reduce to ashes by burning

CREMATOR *n* pl. -S one that cremates

CREME *n* pl. -S cream

CRENATE *adj* having an edge with rounded projections

CRENATED *adj* crenate

CRENEL *v* -ELED, -ELING, -ELS or -ELLED, -ELLING, -ELS to provide with crenelles

CRENELLE *n* pl. -S a rounded projection

CREODONT *n* pl. -S an extinct carnivore

CREOLE *n* pl. -S a type of mixed language

CREOLISE *v* -ISED, -ISING, -ISES to creolize

CREOLIZE *v* -IZED, -IZING, -IZES to cause a language to become a creole

CREOSOL *n* pl. -S a chemical compound

CREOSOTE *v* -SOTED, -SOTING, -SOTES to treat with a wood preservative

CREPE *v* CREPED, CREPING, CREPES to frizz the hair

CREPEY *adj* CREPIER, CREPIEST crinkly

CREPON *n* pl. -S a crinkled fabric

CREPT past tense of creep

CREPY *adj* CREPIER, CREPIEST crepey

CRESCENT *n* pl. -S the figure of the moon in its first or last quarter

CRESCIVE *adj* increasing

CRESOL *n* pl. -S a chemical disinfectant

CRESS *n* pl. -ES a plant used in salads

CRESSET *n* pl. -S a metal cup for burning oil

CREST *v* -ED, -ING, -S to reach a crest (a peak)

CRESTAL *adj* pertaining to a crest (a peak)

CRESTING *n* pl. -S a decorative coping

CRESYL *n* pl. -S tolyl

CRESYLIC *adj* pertaining to cresol

CRETIC *n* pl. -S a type of metrical foot

CRETIN *n* pl. -S an idiot

CRETONNE *n* pl. -S a heavy fabric

CREVALLE *n* pl. -S a food and game fish

CREVASSE *v* -VASSED, -VASSING, -VASSES to fissure

CREVICE *n* pl. -S a cleft **CREVICED** *adj*

CREW *v* -ED, -ING, -S to serve aboard a ship

CREWEL *n* pl. -S a woolen yarn

CREWLESS *adj* without any crewmen

CREWMAN *n* pl. -MEN one who serves on a ship

CREWMATE *n* pl. -S a fellow crewman

CREWNECK *n* pl. -S a sweater with a collarless neckline

CRIB *v* CRIBBED, CRIBBING, CRIBS to confine closely

CRIBBAGE *n* pl. -S a card game

CRIBBER *n* pl. -S one that cribs

CRIBBING *n* pl. -S a supporting framework

CRIBBLED *adj* covered with dots

CRIBROUS *adj* pierced with small holes

CRIBWORK *n* pl. -S a framework of logs

CRICETID *n* pl. -S a small rodent

CRICK *v* -ED, -ING, -S to cause a spasm of the neck

CRICKET *v* -ED, -ING, -S to play cricket (a ball game)

CRICKEY *interj* — used as a mild oath

CRICOID *n* pl. -S a cartilage of the larynx

CRIED past tense of cry

CRIER *n* pl. -S one that cries

CRIES present 3d person sing. of cry

CRIKEY *interj* — used as a mild oath

CRIME *n* pl. -S a violation of the law

CRIMINAL *n* pl. -S one who has committed a crime

CRIMMER *n* pl. -S krimmer

CRIMP *v* -ED, -ING, -S to pleat

CRIMPER *n* pl. -S one that crimps

CRIMPLE *v* -PLED, -PLING, -PLES to wrinkle

CRIMPY *adj* CRIMPIER, CRIMPIEST wavy

CRIMSON *v* -ED, -ING, -S to make crimson (a red color)

CRINGE *v* CRINGED, CRINGING, CRINGES to shrink in fear

CRINGER *n* pl. -S one that cringes

CRINGLE *n* pl. -S a small loop of rope

CRINITE *n* pl. -S a fossil crinoid

CRINKLE *v* -KLED, -KLING, -KLES to wrinkle

CRINKLY *adj* -KLIER, -KLIEST crinkled

CRINOID *n* pl. -S a marine animal

CRINUM *n* pl. -S a tropical herb

CRIOLLO *n* pl. -LLOS a person of Spanish ancestry

CRIPE *interj* — used as a mild oath

CRIPES *interj* — used as a mild oath

CRIPPLE *v* -PLED, -PLING, -PLES to disable or impair

CRIPPLER *n* pl. -S one that cripples

CRIS *n* pl. -ES kris

CRISIS *n* pl. CRISES a crucial turning point **CRISIC** *adj*

CRISP *adj* CRISPER, CRISPEST brittle

CRISP *v* -ED, -ING, -S to make crisp

CRISPATE *adj* curled

CRISPEN *v* -ED, -ING, -S to make crisp

CRISPER *n* pl. -S one that crisps

CRISPLY *adv* in a crisp manner

CRISPY *adj* CRISPIER, CRISPIEST crisp **CRISPILY** *adv*

CRISSUM *n* pl. CRISSA a region of feathers on a bird **CRISSAL** *adj*

CRISTA *n* pl. -TAE a part of a cell

CRISTATE *adj* having a projection on the head

CRITERIA *n/pl* standards of judgment

CRITIC *n* pl. -S one who judges the merits of something **CRITICAL** *adj*

CRITIQUE *v* -TIQUED, -TIQUING, -TIQUES to judge as a critic

CRITTER *n* pl. -S a creature

CRITTUR *n* pl. -S critter

CROAK *v* -ED, -ING, -S to utter a low, hoarse sound

CROAKER *n* pl. -S one that croaks

CROAKY *adj* CROAKIER, CROAKIEST low and hoarse **CROAKILY** *adv*

CROC *n* pl. -S a crocodile

CROCEIN *n* pl. -S a red dye

CROCEINE *n* pl. -S crocein

CROCHET *v* -ED, -ING, -S to do a type of needlework

CROCI a pl. of crocus

CROCINE *adj* pertaining to the crocus

CROCK *v* -ED, -ING, -S to stain or soil

CROCKERY *n* pl. -ERIES pottery

CROCKET *n* pl. -S an architectural ornament

CROCOITE *n* pl. -S a mineral

CROCUS *n* pl. -CUSES or -CI a flowering plant

CROFT *n* pl. -S a small tenant farm

CROFTER *n* pl. -S a tenant farmer

CROJIK *n* pl. -S a triangular sail

CROMLECH *n* pl. -S a dolmen

CRONE *n* pl. -S a withered old woman

CRONY *n* pl. CRONIES a close friend

CRONYISM *n* pl. -S a kind of political favoritism

CROOK *v* -ED, -ING, -S to bend

CROOKED *adj* -EDER, -EDEST dishonest

CROOKERY *n* pl. -ERIES crooked activity

CROON *v* -ED, -ING, -S to sing softly

CROONER *n* pl. -S one that croons

CROP *v* CROPPED, CROPPING, CROPS to cut off short

CROPLAND *n* pl. -S farmland

CROPLESS *adj* being without crops (agricultural produce)

CROPPED past tense of crop

CROPPER *n* pl. -S one that crops

CROPPIE *n* pl. -S crappie

CROPPING present participle of crop

CROQUET *v* -ED, -ING, -S to drive a ball away in a certain game

CROQUIS *n* pl. CROQUIS a sketch

CRORE *n* pl. -S a monetary unit of India

CROSIER *n* pl. -S a bishop's staff

CROSS *v* -ED, -ING, -ES to intersect

CROSS *adj* CROSSER, CROSSEST ill-tempered

CROSSARM *n* pl. -S a horizontal bar

CROSSBAR *v* -BARRED, -BARRING, -BARS to fasten with crossarms

CROSSBOW *n* pl. -S a kind of weapon

CROSSCUT *v* -CUT, -CUTTING, -CUTS to cut across

CROSSE *n* pl. -S a lacrosse stick

CROSSER *n* pl. -S one that crosses

CROSSING *n* pl. -S an intersection

CROSSLET *n* pl. -S a heraldic symbol

CROSSLY *adv* in a cross manner

CROSSTIE *n* pl. -S a transverse beam

CROSSWAY *n* pl. -WAYS a road that crosses another road

CROTCH *n* pl. -ES an angle formed by two diverging parts **CROTCHED** *adj*

CROTCHET *n* pl. -S a small hook

CROTON *n* pl. -S a tropical plant

CROUCH *v* -ED, -ING, -ES to stoop

CROUP *n* pl. -S a disease of the throat

CROUPE *n* pl. -S the rump of certain animals

CROUPIER *n* pl. -S an attendant in a casino

CROUPOUS *adj* pertaining to croup

CROUPY *adj* CROUPIER, CROUPIEST affected with croup **CROUPILY** *adv*

CROUSE *adj* lively **CROUSELY** *adv*

CROUTON *n* pl. -S a small cube of toasted bread

CROW *v* -ED, -ING, -S to boast

CROWBAR *v* -BARRED, -BARRING, -BARS to use a steel bar as a lever

CROWD *v* -ED, -ING, -S to press into an insufficient space

CROWDER *n* pl. -S one that crowds

CROWDIE *n* pl. -S crowdy

CROWDY *n* pl. -DIES porridge

CROWER *n* pl. -S one that crows

CROWFOOT *n* pl. -FOOTS or -FEET a flowering plant

CROWN *v* -ED, -ING, -S to supply with a crown (a royal headpiece)

CROWNER *n* pl. -S a coroner

CROWNET *n* pl. -S a coronet

CROWSTEP *n* pl. -S a step on top of a wall

CROZE *n* pl. -S a tool used in barrel-making

CROZER *n* pl. -S a croze

CROZIER *n* pl. -S crosier

CRUCES a pl. of crux

CRUCIAL *adj* of supreme importance

CRUCIAN *n* pl. -S a European fish

CRUCIATE *adj* cross-shaped

CRUCIBLE *n* pl. -S a heat-resistant vessel

CRUCIFER *n* pl. -S one who carries a cross

CRUCIFIX *n* pl. -ES a cross bearing an image of Christ

CRUCIFY *v* -FIED, -FYING, -FIES to put to death on a cross

CRUCK *n* pl. -S a curved roof timber

CRUD *v* CRUDDED, CRUDDING, CRUDS to curd

CRUDDY *adj* -DIER, -DIEST filthy; contemptible

CRUDE *adj* CRUDER, CRUDEST unrefined **CRUDELY** *adv*

CRUDE *n* pl. -S unrefined petroleum

CRUDITES	*n/pl* pieces of raw vegetables served with a dip
CRUDITY	*n* pl. -TIES the state of being crude
CRUEL	*adj* CRUELER, CRUELEST or CRUELLER, CRUELLEST indifferent to the pain of others **CRUELLY** *adv*
CRUELTY	*n* pl. -TIES a cruel act
CRUET	*n* pl. -S a glass bottle
CRUISE	*v* CRUISED, CRUISING, CRUISES to sail about touching at several ports
CRUISER	*n* pl. -S a boat that cruises
CRUISING	*n* pl. -S the act of driving around in search of fun
CRULLER	*n* pl. -S a small sweet cake
CRUMB	*v* -ED, -ING, -S to break into crumbs (small pieces)
CRUMBER	*n* pl. -S one that crumbs
CRUMBIER	comparative of crumby
CRUMBIEST	superlative of crumby
CRUMBLE	*v* -BLED, -BLING, -BLES to break into small pieces
CRUMBLY	*adj* -BLIER, -BLIEST easily crumbled
CRUMBUM	*n* pl. -S a despicable person
CRUMBY	*adj* CRUMBIER, CRUMBIEST full of crumbs
CRUMHORN	*n* pl. -S a double-reed woodwind instrument
CRUMMIE	*n* pl. -S a cow with crooked horns
CRUMMY	*adj* -MIER, -MIEST of little or no value
CRUMP	*v* -ED, -ING, -S to crunch
CRUMPET	*n* pl. -S a small cake cooked on a griddle
CRUMPLE	*v* -PLED, -PLING, -PLES to wrinkle
CRUMPLY	*adj* -PLIER, -PLIEST easily wrinkled
CRUNCH	*v* -ED, -ING, -ES to chew with a crackling sound
CRUNCHER	*n* pl. -S one that crunches
CRUNCHY	*adj* CRUNCHIER, CRUNCHIEST crisp
CRUNODE	*n* pl. -S a point at which a curve crosses itself **CRUNODAL** *adj*
CRUOR	*n* pl. -S clotted blood
CRUPPER	*n* pl. -S the rump of a horse
CRURAL	*adj* pertaining to the thigh or leg
CRUS	*n* pl. CRURA a part of the leg
CRUSADE	*v* -SADED, -SADING, -SADES to engage in a holy war
CRUSADER	*n* pl. -S one that crusades
CRUSADO	*n* pl. -DOES or -DOS an old Portuguese coin
CRUSE	*n* pl. -S a small bottle
CRUSET	*n* pl. -S a melting pot
CRUSH	*v* -ED, -ING, -ES to press or squeeze out of shape
CRUSHER	*n* pl. -S one that crushes
CRUSILY	*adj* covered with crosslets
CRUST	*v* -ED, -ING, -S to form a crust (a hardened outer surface)
CRUSTAL	*adj* pertaining to the earth's crust
CRUSTOSE	*adj* forming a thin, brittle crust
CRUSTY	*adj* CRUSTIER, CRUSTIEST surly **CRUSTILY** *adv*
CRUTCH	*v* -ED, -ING, -ES to prop up or support
CRUX	*n* pl. CRUXES or CRUCES a basic or decisive point
CRUZADO	*n* pl. -DOES or -DOS crusado
CRUZEIRO	*n* pl. -ROS a monetary unit of Brazil
CRWTH	*n* pl. -S an ancient stringed musical instrument
CRY	*v* CRIED, CRYING, CRIES to weep **CRYINGLY** *adv*
CRYBABY	*n* pl. -BIES a person who cries easily
CRYOGEN	*n* pl. -S a substance for producing low temperatures
CRYOGENY	*n* pl. -NIES a branch of physics
CRYOLITE	*n* pl. -S a mineral
CRYONICS	*n/pl* the practice of freezing dead bodies for future revival **CRYONIC** *adj*
CRYOSTAT	*n* pl. -S a refrigerating device
CRYOTRON	*n* pl. -S an electronic device
CRYPT	*n* pl. -S a burial vault **CRYPTAL** *adj*
CRYPTIC	*adj* mysterious
CRYPTO	*n* pl. -TOS one who belongs secretly to a group
CRYSTAL	*n* pl. -S a transparent mineral
CTENIDIA	*n/pl* comblike anatomical structures
CTENOID	*adj* comblike

CUB n pl. -S the young of certain animals

CUBAGE n pl. -S cubature

CUBATURE n pl. -S cubical content

CUBBISH adj resembling a cub

CUBBY n pl. -BIES a small, enclosed space

CUBE v CUBED, CUBING, CUBES to form into a cube (a regular solid)

CUBEB n pl. -S a woody vine

CUBER n pl. -S one that cubes

CUBIC n pl. -S a mathematical equation or expression

CUBICAL adj shaped like a cube

CUBICITY n pl. -TIES the state of being cubical

CUBICLE n pl. -S a small chamber

CUBICLY adv in the form of a cube

CUBICULA n/pl burial chambers

CUBIFORM adj shaped like a cube

CUBING present participle of cube

CUBISM n pl. -S a style of art **CUBISTIC** adj

CUBIST n pl. -S an adherent of cubism

CUBIT n pl. -S an ancient measure of length **CUBITAL** adj

CUBOID n pl. -S a bone of the foot **CUBOIDAL** adj

CUCKOLD v -ED, -ING, -S to make a cuckold (a cornuto) of

CUCKOO v -ED, -ING, -S to repeat monotonously

CUCUMBER n pl. -S a garden vegetable

CUCURBIT n pl. -S a gourd

CUD n pl. -S a portion of food to be chewed again

CUDBEAR n pl. -S a red dye

CUDDIE n pl. -S cuddy

CUDDIES pl. of cuddy

CUDDLE v -DLED, -DLING, -DLES to hug tenderly

CUDDLER n pl. -S one that cuddles

CUDDLY adj -DLIER, -DLIEST fit for cuddling

CUDDY n pl. -DIES a donkey

CUDGEL v -ELED, -ELING, -ELS or -ELLED, -ELLING, -ELS to beat with a heavy club

CUDGELER n pl. -S one that cudgels

CUDWEED n pl. -S a perennial herb

CUE v CUED, CUING or CUEING, CUES to give a signal to an actor

CUESTA n pl. -S a type of land elevation

CUFF v -ED, -ING, -S to furnish with a cuff (a part of a sleeve)

CUFFLESS adj having no cuff

CUIF n pl. -S coof

CUING a present participle of cue

CUIRASS v -ED, -ING, -ES to cover with a type of armor

CUISH n pl. -ES cuisse

CUISINE n pl. -S a style of cooking

CUISSE n pl. -S a piece of armor for the thigh

CUITTLE v -TLED, -TLING, -TLES to coax

CUKE n pl. -S a cucumber

CULCH n pl. -ES an oyster bed

CULET n pl. -S a piece of armor for the lower back

CULEX n pl. CULICES a mosquito

CULICID n pl. -S a culicine

CULICINE n pl. -S a mosquito

CULINARY adj pertaining to cookery

CULL v -ED, -ING, -S to select from others

CULLAY n pl. -LAYS quillai

CULLER n pl. -S one that culls

CULLET n pl. -S broken glass gathered for remelting

CULLIED past tense of cully

CULLIES present 3d person sing. of cully

CULLION n pl. -S a vile fellow

CULLIS n pl. -LISES a gutter in a roof

CULLY v -LIED, -LYING, -LIES to trick

CULM v -ED, -ING, -S to form a hollow stem

CULOTTE n pl. -S a divided skirt

CULPA n pl. -PAE negligence for which one is liable

CULPABLE adj deserving blame or censure **CULPABLY** adv

CULPRIT n pl. -S one that is guilty

CULT n pl. -S a group of zealous devotees

CULTCH n pl. -ES culch

CULTI a pl. of cultus

CULTIC adj pertaining to a cult

CULTIGEN	*n* pl. -S a cultivar
CULTISH	*adj* pertaining to a cult
CULTISM	*n* pl. -S devotion to a cult
CULTIST	*n* pl. -S a member of a cult
CULTIVAR	*n* pl. -S a variety of plant originating under cultivation
CULTLIKE	*adj* resembling a cult
CULTRATE	*adj* sharp-edged and pointed
CULTURAL	*adj* produced by breeding
CULTURE	*v* -TURED, -TURING, -TURES to make fit for raising crops
CULTUS	*n* pl. -TUSES or -TI a cult
CULVER	*n* pl. -S a pigeon
CULVERIN	*n* pl. -S a medieval musket
CULVERT	*n* pl. -S a conduit
CUM	*prep* together with
CUMARIN	*n* pl. -S coumarin
CUMBER	*v* -ED, -ING, -S to hinder
CUMBERER	*n* pl. -S one that cumbers
CUMBROUS	*adj* unwieldy
CUMIN	*n* pl. -S a plant used in cooking
CUMMER	*n* pl. -S a godmother
CUMMIN	*n* pl. -S cumin
CUMQUAT	*n* pl. -S kumquat
CUMSHAW	*n* pl. -S a gift
CUMULATE	*v* -LATED, -LATING, -LATES to heap
CUMULUS	*n* pl. -LI a type of cloud **CUMULOUS** *adj*
CUNDUM	*n* pl. -S condom
CUNEAL	*adj* cuneate
CUNEATE	*adj* wedge-shaped; triangular
CUNEATED	*adj* cuneate
CUNEATIC	*adj* cuneate
CUNIFORM	*n* pl. -S wedge-shaped writing characters
CUNNER	*n* pl. -S a marine fish
CUNNING	*adj* -NINGER, -NINGEST crafty
CUNNING	*n* pl. -S skill in deception
CUP	*v* CUPPED, CUPPING, CUPS to place in a cup (a small, open container)
CUPBOARD	*n* pl. -S a cabinet
CUPCAKE	*n* pl. -S a small cake
CUPEL	*v* -PELED, -PELING, -PELS or -PELLED, -PELLING, -PELS to refine gold or silver in a cuplike vessel
CUPELER	*n* pl. -S cupeller
CUPELLER	*n* pl. -S one that cupels
CUPFUL	*n* pl. CUPFULS or CUPSFUL as much as a cup can hold
CUPID	*n* pl. -S a naked, winged representation of the Roman god of love
CUPIDITY	*n* pl. -TIES greed; lust
CUPLIKE	*adj* resembling a cup
CUPOLA	*v* -ED, -ING, -S to shape like a dome
CUPPA	*n* pl. -S a cup of tea
CUPPED	past tense of cup
CUPPER	*n* pl. -S one that performs cupping
CUPPING	*n* pl. -S an archaic medical process
CUPPY	*adj* -PIER, -PIEST cuplike
CUPREOUS	*adj* containing copper
CUPRIC	*adj* containing copper
CUPRITE	*n* pl. -S an ore of copper
CUPROUS	*adj* containing copper
CUPRUM	*n* pl. -S copper
CUPSFUL	a pl. of cupful
CUPULA	*n* pl. -LAE a cup-shaped anatomical structure
CUPULAR	*adj* cupulate
CUPULATE	*adj* cup-shaped
CUPULE	*n* pl. -S a cup-shaped anatomical structure
CUR	*n* pl. -S a mongrel dog
CURABLE	*adj* capable of being cured **CURABLY** *adv*
CURACAO	*n* pl. -S a type of liqueur
CURACOA	*n* pl. -S curacao
CURACY	*n* pl. -CIES the office of a curate
CURAGH	*n* pl. -S currach
CURARA	*n* pl. -S curare
CURARE	*n* pl. -S an arrow poison
CURARI	*n* pl. -S curare
CURARINE	*n* pl. -S a poisonous alkaloid
CURARIZE	*v* -RIZED, -RIZING, -RIZES to poison with curare
CURASSOW	*n* pl. -S a turkey-like bird

CURATE   v -RATED, -RATING, -RATES to act as curator of

CURATIVE   n pl. -S something that cures

CURATOR   n pl. -S a museum manager

CURB   v -ED, -ING, -S to restrain **CURBABLE** adj

CURBER   n pl. -S one that curbs

CURBING   n pl. -S a concrete border along a street

CURBSIDE   n pl. -S the side of a pavement bordered by a curbing

CURCH   n pl. -ES a kerchief

CURCULIO   n pl. -LIOS a weevil

CURCUMA   n pl. -S a tropical plant

CURD   v -ED, -ING, -S to curdle

CURDIER   comparative of curdy

CURDIEST   superlative of curdy

CURDLE   v -DLED, -DLING, -DLES to congeal

CURDLER   n pl. -S one that curdles

CURDY   adj CURDIER, CURDIEST curdled

CURE   v CURED, CURING, CURES to restore to health

CURELESS   adj not curable

CURER   n pl. -S one that cures

CURET   n pl. -S a surgical instrument

CURETTE   v -RETTED, -RETTING, -RETTES to treat with a curet

CURF   n pl. -S an incision made by a cutting tool

CURFEW   n pl. -S a regulation concerning the hours which one may keep

CURIA   n pl. -RIAE a court of justice **CURIAL** adj

CURIE   n pl. -S a unit of radioactivity

CURING   present participle of cure

CURIO   n pl. -RIOS an unusual art object

CURIOSA   n/pl pornographic books

CURIOUS   adj -OUSER, -OUSEST eager for information

CURITE   n pl. -S a radioactive mineral

CURIUM   n pl. -S a radioactive element

CURL   v -ED, -ING, -S to form into ringlets

CURLER   n pl. -S one that curls

CURLEW   n pl. -S a shore bird

CURLICUE   v -CUED, -CUING, -CUES to decorate with curlicues (fancy spiral figures)

CURLING   n pl. -S a game played on ice

CURLY   adj CURLIER, CURLIEST tending to curl **CURLILY** adv

CURLYCUE   n pl. -S curlicue

CURN   n pl. -S grain

CURR   v -ED, -ING, -S to purr

CURRACH   n pl. -S a coracle

CURRAGH   n pl. -S currach

CURRAN   n pl. -S curn

CURRANT   n pl. -S an edible berry

CURRENCY   n pl. -CIES money

CURRENT   n pl. -S a continuous flow

CURRICLE   n pl. -S a light carriage

CURRIE   v -RIED, -RYING, -RIES to prepare food a certain way

CURRIED   past tense of curry

CURRIER   n pl. -S one that curries leather

CURRIERY   n pl. -ERIES the shop of a currier

CURRISH   adj resembling a cur

CURRY   v -RIED, -RYING, -RIES to prepare leather for use or sale

CURRYING   present participle of currie

CURSE   v CURSED or CURST, CURSING, CURSES to wish evil upon

CURSED   adj CURSEDER, CURSEDEST wicked **CURSEDLY** adv

CURSER   n pl. -S one that curses

CURSING   present participle of curse

CURSIVE   n pl. -S a style of print

CURSOR   n pl. -S a light indicator on a computer display

CURSORY   adj hasty and superficial

CURST   a past tense of curse

CURT   adj CURTER, CURTEST abrupt

CURTAIL   v -ED, -ING, -S to cut short

CURTAIN   v -ED, -ING, -S to provide with a hanging piece of fabric

CURTAL   n pl. -S an animal with a clipped tail

CURTALAX   n pl. -ES a cutlass

CURTATE   adj shortened

CURTESY   n pl. -SIES a type of legal tenure

CURTLY   adv in a curt manner

CURTNESS   n pl. -ES the quality of being curt

CURTSEY	*v* -ED, -ING, -S to curtsy
CURTSY	*v* -SIED, -SYING, -SIES to bow politely
CURULE	*adj* of the highest rank
CURVE	*v* CURVED, CURVING, CURVES to deviate from straightness **CURVEDLY** *adv*
CURVET	*v* -VETED, -VETING, -VETS or -VETTED, -VETTING, -VETS to prance
CURVEY	*adj* CURVIER, CURVIEST curvy
CURVING	present participle of curve
CURVY	*adj* CURVIER, CURVIEST curved
CUSCUS	*n* pl. -ES an arboreal mammal
CUSEC	*n* pl. -S a volumetric unit of flow of liquids
CUSHAT	*n* pl. -S a pigeon
CUSHAW	*n* pl. -S a variety of squash
CUSHIER	comparative of cushy
CUSHIEST	superlative of cushy
CUSHILY	*adv* in a cushy manner
CUSHION	*v* -ED, -ING, -S to pad with soft material
CUSHIONY	*adj* soft
CUSHY	*adj* CUSHIER, CUSHIEST easy
CUSK	*n* pl. -S a marine food fish
CUSP	*n* pl. -S a pointed end **CUSPATE, CUSPATED, CUSPED** *adj*
CUSPID	*n* pl. -S a pointed tooth
CUSPIDAL	*adj* having a cusp
CUSPIDOR	*n* pl. -S a spittoon
CUSPIS	*n* pl. -PIDES a cusp
CUSS	*v* -ED, -ING, -ES to curse
CUSSEDLY	*adv* in a cranky manner
CUSSER	*n* pl. -S one that cusses
CUSSO	*n* pl. -SOS an Ethiopian tree
CUSSWORD	*n* pl. -S a profane or obscene word
CUSTARD	*n* pl. -S a thick, soft dessert **CUSTARDY** *adj*
CUSTODES	pl. of custos
CUSTODY	*n* pl. -DIES guardianship
CUSTOM	*n* pl. -S a habitual practice
CUSTOMER	*n* pl. -S one who buys something
CUSTOS	*n* pl. -TODES a guardian or keeper
CUSTUMAL	*n* pl. -S a written record of laws and customs
CUT	*v* CUT, CUTTING, CUTS to divide into parts with a sharp-edged instrument
CUTAWAY	*n* pl. -AWAYS a type of coat
CUTBACK	*n* pl. -S a reduction
CUTBANK	*n* pl. -S a steep stream bank
CUTCH	*n* pl. -ES catechu
CUTCHERY	*n* pl. -CHERIES a judicial office in India
CUTDOWN	*n* pl. -S a reduction
CUTE	*adj* CUTER, CUTEST pleasingly attractive **CUTELY** *adv*
CUTENESS	*n* pl. -ES the quality of being cute
CUTES	a pl. of cutis
CUTESIE	*adj* -SIER, -SIEST cutesy
CUTEST	superlative of cute
CUTESY	*adj* -SIER, -SIEST self-consciously cute
CUTEY	*n* pl. -TEYS cutie
CUTGRASS	*n* pl. -ES a swamp grass
CUTICLE	*n* pl. -S the epidermis
CUTICULA	*n* pl. -LAE the outer hard covering of an insect
CUTIE	*n* pl. -S a cute person
CUTIN	*n* pl. -S a waxy substance found on plants
CUTINISE	*v* -ISED, -ISING, -ISES to cutinize
CUTINIZE	*v* -IZED, -IZING, -IZES to become coated with cutin
CUTIS	*n* pl. -TES or -TISES the corium
CUTLAS	*n* pl. -ES cutlass
CUTLASS	*n* pl. -ES a short sword
CUTLER	*n* pl. -S one who sells and repairs cutting tools
CUTLERY	*n* pl. -LERIES the occupation of a cutler
CUTLET	*n* pl. -S a slice of meat
CUTLINE	*n* pl. -S a caption
CUTOFF	*n* pl. -S the point at which something terminates
CUTOUT	*n* pl. -S something cut out
CUTOVER	*n* pl. -S land cleared of trees
CUTPURSE	*n* pl. -S a pickpocket
CUTTABLE	*adj* capable of being cut
CUTTAGE	*n* pl. -S a means of plant propagation

CUTTER *n* pl. -S one that cuts

CUTTIES pl. of cutty

CUTTING *n* pl. -S a section cut from a plant

CUTTLE *v* -TLED, -TLING, -TLES to fold cloth in a particular fashion

CUTTY *n* pl. -TIES a thickset girl

CUTUP *n* pl. -S a mischievous person

CUTWATER *n* pl. -S the front part of a ship's prow

CUTWORK *n* pl. -S a type of embroidery

CUTWORM *n* pl. -S a caterpillar

CUVETTE *n* pl. -S a small tube or vessel

CWM *n* pl. -S a cirque

CYAN *n* pl. -S a blue color

CYANAMID *n* pl. -S a chemical compound

CYANATE *n* pl. -S a chemical salt

CYANIC *adj* blue or bluish

CYANID *n* pl. -S a compound of cyanogen

CYANIDE *v* -NIDED, -NIDING, -NIDES to treat an ore with cyanid

CYANIN *n* pl. -S cyanine

CYANINE *n* pl. -S a blue dye

CYANITE *n* pl. -S a mineral **CYANITIC** *adj*

CYANO *adj* pertaining to cyanogen

CYANOGEN *n* pl. -S a reactive compound of carbon and nitrogen

CYANOSIS *n* pl. -NOSES bluish discoloration of the skin **CYANOSED, CYANOTIC** *adj*

CYBORG *n* pl. -S a human linked to a mechanical device for life support

CYCAD *n* pl. -S a tropical plant

CYCAS *n* pl. -ES a tropical plant

CYCASIN *n* pl. -S a sugar derivative

CYCLAMEN *n* pl. -S a flowering plant

CYCLASE *n* pl. -S an enzyme

CYCLE *v* -CLED, -CLING, -CLES to ride a bicycle

CYCLECAR *n* pl. -S a type of motor vehicle

CYCLER *n* pl. -S a cyclist

CYCLERY *n* pl. -RIES a bicycle shop

CYCLIC *adj* moving in complete circles **CYCLICLY** *adv*

CYCLICAL *n* pl. -S a stock whose earnings fluctuate widely with variations in the economy

CYCLING *n* pl. -S the act of riding a bicycle

CYCLIST *n* pl. -S one who rides a bicycle

CYCLITOL *n* pl. -S a chemical compound

CYCLIZE *v* -CLIZED, -CLIZING, -CLIZES to form one or more rings in a chemical compound

CYCLO *n* pl. -CLOS a three-wheeled motor vehicle

CYCLOID *n* pl. -S a geometric curve

CYCLONE *n* pl. -S a rotating system of winds **CYCLONAL, CYCLONIC** *adj*

CYCLOPS *n* pl. CYCLOPS a freshwater animal

CYCLOSIS *n* pl. -CLOSES the circulation of protoplasm within a cell

CYDER *n* pl. -S cider

CYESIS *n* pl. CYESES pregnancy

CYGNET *n* pl. -S a young swan

CYLINDER *v* -ED, -ING, -S to furnish with a cylinder (a chamber in an engine)

CYLIX *n* pl. CYLICES kylix

CYMA *n* pl. -MAS or -MAE a curved molding

CYMAR *n* pl. -S simar

CYMATIUM *n* pl. -TIA a cyma

CYMBAL *n* pl. -S a percussion instrument

CYMBALER *n* pl. -S one that plays the cymbals

CYMBALOM *n* pl. -S cimbalom

CYMBIDIA *n/pl* tropical orchids

CYMBLING *n* pl. -S cymling

CYME *n* pl. -S a flower cluster

CYMENE *n* pl. -S a hydrocarbon

CYMLIN *n* pl. -S cymling

CYMLING *n* pl. -S a variety of squash

CYMOGENE *n* pl. -S a volatile compound

CYMOID *adj* resembling a cyma

CYMOL *n* pl. -S cymene

CYMOSE *adj* resembling a cyme **CYMOSELY** *adv*

CYMOUS *adj* cymose

CYNIC *n* pl. -S a cynical person

CYNICAL *adj* distrusting the motives of others

CYNICISM *n* pl. -S cynical quality

CYNOSURE *n* pl. -S a center of attraction

CYPHER *v* -ED, -ING, -S to cipher

CYPRES *n* pl. -ES a legal doctrine

CYPRESS *n* pl. -ES a thin fabric

CYPRIAN   *n* pl. -S a prostitute

CYPRINID   *n* pl. -S a small freshwater fish

CYPRUS   *n* pl. -ES cypress

CYPSELA   *n* pl. -LAE an achene in certain plants

CYST   *n* pl. -S a sac

CYSTEIN   *n* pl. -S cysteine

CYSTEINE   *n* pl. -S an amino acid

CYSTIC   *adj* pertaining to a cyst

CYSTINE   *n* pl. -S an amino acid

CYSTITIS   *n* pl. -TITIDES inflammation of the urinary bladder

CYSTOID   *n* pl. -S a cyst-like structure

CYTASTER   *n* pl. -S a structure formed in a cell during mitosis

CYTIDINE   *n* pl. -S a compound containing cytosine

CYTOGENY   *n* pl. -NIES the formation of cells

CYTOKINE   *n* pl. -S a kind of substance secreted by cells of the immune system

CYTOLOGY   *n* pl. -GIES a study of cells

CYTON   *n* pl. -S the body of a nerve cell

CYTOSINE   *n* pl. -S a component of DNA and RNA

CYTOSOL   *n* pl. -S the fluid portion of cell material

CZAR   *n* pl. -S an emperor or king

CZARDAS   *n* pl. CZARDAS a Hungarian dance

CZARDOM   *n* pl. -S the domain of a czar

CZAREVNA   *n* pl. -S the daughter of a czar

CZARINA   *n* pl. -S the wife of a czar

CZARISM   *n* pl. -S autocratic government

CZARIST   *n* pl. -S a supporter of czarism

CZARITZA   *n* pl. -S a czarina

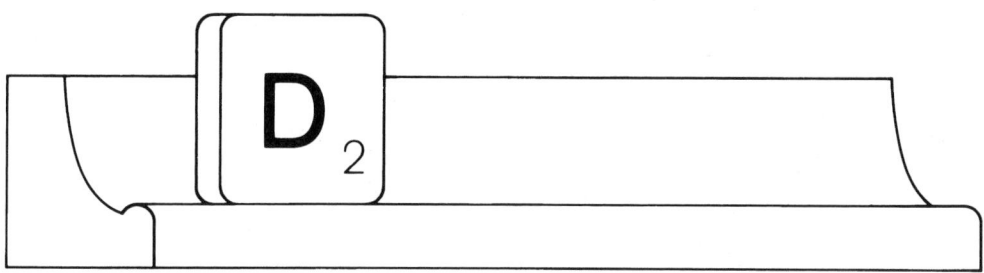

DAB	v DABBED, DABBING, DABS to touch lightly	**DAFT**	adj DAFTER, DAFTEST insane **DAFTLY** adv
DABBER	n pl. -S one that dabs	**DAFTNESS**	n pl. -ES the quality of being daft
DABBLE	v -BLED, -BLING, -BLES to involve oneself in a superficial interest	**DAG**	n pl. -S a hanging end or shred
		DAGGA	n pl. -S marijuana
DABBLER	n pl. -S one that dabbles	**DAGGER**	v -ED, -ING, -S to stab with a small knife
DABBLING	n pl. -S a superficial interest	**DAGGLE**	v -GLED, -GLING, -GLES to drag in mud
DABCHICK	n pl. -S a small grebe		
DABSTER	n pl. -S a dabbler	**DAGLOCK**	n pl. -S a dirty or tangled lock of wool
DACE	n pl. -S a freshwater fish		
DACHA	n pl. -S a Russian cottage	**DAGOBA**	n pl. -S a Buddhist shrine
DACKER	v -ED, -ING, -S to waver	**DAGWOOD**	n pl. -S a large sandwich
DACOIT	n pl. -S a bandit in India	**DAH**	n pl. -S a dash in Morse code
DACOITY	n pl. -COITIES robbery by dacoits	**DAHABEAH**	n pl. -S a large passenger boat
		DAHABIAH	n pl. -S dahabeah
DACTYL	n pl. -S a type of metrical foot	**DAHABIEH**	n pl. -S dahabeah
DACTYLIC	n pl. -S a verse consisting of dactyls	**DAHABIYA**	n pl. -S dahabeah
		DAHL	n pl. -S dal
DACTYLUS	n pl. -LI a leg joint of certain insects	**DAHLIA**	n pl. -S a flowering plant
		DAHOON	n pl. -S an evergreen tree
DAD	n pl. -S father	**DAIKER**	v -ED, -ING, -S to dacker
DADA	n pl. -S an artistic and literary movement	**DAIKON**	n pl. -S a Japanese radish
		DAILY	n pl. -LIES a newspaper published every weekday
DADAISM	n pl. -S the dada movement		
DADAIST	n pl. -S a follower of dadaism	**DAIMEN**	adj occasional
DADDLE	v -DLED, -DLING, -DLES to diddle	**DAIMIO**	n pl. -MIOS a former Japanese nobleman
DADDY	n pl. -DIES father	**DAIMON**	n pl. -S or -ES an attendant spirit **DAIMONIC** adj
DADO	v -ED, -ING, -ES or -S to set into a groove		
		DAIMYO	n pl. -MYOS daimio
DAEDAL	adj skillful	**DAINTY**	n pl. -TIES something delicious
DAEMON	n pl. -S demon **DAEMONIC** adj	**DAINTY**	adj -TIER, -TIEST delicately pretty **DAINTILY** adv
DAFF	v -ED, -ING, -S to thrust aside	**DAIQUIRI**	n pl. -S a cocktail
DAFFODIL	n pl. -S a flowering plant	**DAIRY**	n pl. DAIRIES an establishment dealing in milk products
DAFFY	adj -FIER, -FIEST silly **DAFFILY** adv		
		DAIRYING	n pl. -S the business of a dairy

DAIRYMAN   *n* pl. -MEN a man who works in or owns a dairy

DAIS   *n* pl. -ISES a raised platform

DAISHIKI   *n* pl. -S dashiki

DAISY   *n* pl. -SIES a flowering plant **DAISIED** *adj*

DAK   *n* pl. -S transportation by relays of men and horses

DAKERHEN   *n* pl. -S a European bird

DAKOIT   *n* pl. -S dacoit

DAKOITY   *n* pl. -TIES dacoity

DAL   *n* pl. -S a dish of lentils and spices in India

DALAPON   *n* pl. -S an herbicide used on unwanted grasses

DALASI   *n* pl. DALASI or DALASIS a unit of Gambian currency

DALE   *n* pl. -S a valley

DALEDH   *n* pl. -S daleth

DALESMAN   *n* pl. -MEN one living in a dale

DALETH   *n* pl. -S a Hebrew letter

DALLES   *n/pl* rapids

DALLIER   *n* pl. -S one that dallies

DALLY   *v* -LIED, -LYING, -LIES to waste time

DALMATIC   *n* pl. -S a wide-sleeved vestment

DALTON   *n* pl. -S a unit of atomic mass

DALTONIC   *adj* pertaining to a form of color blindness

DAM   *v* DAMMED, DAMMING, DAMS to build a barrier to obstruct the flow of water

DAMAGE   *v* -AGED, -AGING, -AGES to injure

DAMAGER   *n* pl. -S one that damages

DAMAN   *n* pl. -S a small mammal

DAMAR   *n* pl. -S dammar

DAMASK   *v* -ED, -ING, -S to weave with elaborate design

DAME   *n* pl. -S a matron

DAMEWORT   *n* pl. -S a flowering plant

DAMMAR   *n* pl. -S a hard resin

DAMMED   past tense of dam

DAMMER   *n* pl. -S dammar

DAMMING   present participle of dam

DAMN   *v* -ED, -ING, -S to curse

DAMNABLE   *adj* detestable **DAMNABLY** *adv*

DAMNDEST   *n* pl. -S utmost

DAMNED   *adj* DAMNEDER, DAMNEDEST or DAMNDEST damnable

DAMNER   *n* pl. -S one that damns

DAMNIFY   *v* -FIED, -FYING, -FIES to cause loss or damage to

DAMOSEL   *n* pl. -S damsel

DAMOZEL   *n* pl. -S damsel

DAMP   *adj* DAMPER, DAMPEST moist

DAMP   *v* -ED, -ING, -S to lessen in intensity

DAMPEN   *v* -ED, -ING, -S to moisten

DAMPENER   *n* pl. -S one that dampens

DAMPER   *n* pl. -S one that damps

DAMPING   *n* pl. -S the ability of a device to prevent instability

DAMPISH   *adj* somewhat damp

DAMPLY   *adv* in a damp manner

DAMPNESS   *n* pl. -ES the state of being damp

DAMSEL   *n* pl. -S a maiden

DAMSON   *n* pl. -S a small purple plum

DANCE   *v* DANCED, DANCING, DANCES to move rhythmically to music

DANCER   *n* pl. -S one that dances

DANDER   *v* -ED, -ING, -S to stroll

DANDIER   comparative of dandy

DANDIES   pl. of dandy

DANDIEST   superlative of dandy

DANDIFY   *v* -FIED, -FYING, -FIES to cause to resemble a dandy

DANDILY   *adv* in a dandy manner

DANDLE   *v* -DLED, -DLING, -DLES to fondle

DANDLER   *n* pl. -S one that dandles

DANDRIFF   *n* pl. -S dandruff

DANDRUFF   *n* pl. -S a scurf that forms on the scalp

DANDY   *adj* -DIER, -DIEST fine

DANDY   *n* pl. -DIES a man who is overly concerned about his appearance

DANDYISH   *adj* suggestive of a dandy

DANDYISM   *n* pl. -S the style or conduct of a dandy

DANEGELD   *n* pl. -S an annual tax in medieval England

DANEWEED   *n* pl. -S a danewort

DANEWORT   *n* pl. -S a flowering plant

DANG   *v* -ED, -ING, -S to damn

DANGER   *v* -ED, -ING, -S to endanger

DANGLE *v* -GLED, -GLING, -GLES to hang loosely

DANGLER *n* pl. -S one that dangles

DANIO *n* pl. -NIOS an aquarium fish

DANISH *n* pl. DANISH a pastry of raised dough

DANK *adj* DANKER, DANKEST unpleasantly damp **DANKLY** *adv*

DANKNESS *n* pl. -ES the state of being dank

DANSEUR *n* pl. -S a male ballet dancer

DANSEUSE *n* pl. -S a female ballet dancer

DAP *v* DAPPED, DAPPING, DAPS to dip lightly or quickly into water

DAPHNE *n* pl. -S a flowering shrub

DAPHNIA *n* pl. -S a minute crustacean

DAPPED past tense of dap

DAPPER *adj* -PERER, -PEREST looking neat and trim **DAPPERLY** *adv*

DAPPING present participle of dap

DAPPLE *v* -PLED, -PLING, -PLES to mark with spots

DAPSONE *n* pl. -S a medicinal substance

DARB *n* pl. -S something considered extraordinary

DARBIES *n/pl* handcuffs

DARE *v* DARED or DURST, DARING, DARES to have the necessary courage

DAREFUL *adj* brave

DARER *n* pl. -S one that dares

DARESAY *v* to venture to say — DARESAY is the only form of this verb; it is not conjugated

DARIC *n* pl. -S an ancient Persian coin

DARING *n* pl. -S bravery

DARINGLY *adv* in a brave manner

DARIOLE *n* pl. -S a type of pastry filled with cream, custard, or jelly

DARK *adj* DARKER, DARKEST having little or no light

DARK *v* -ED, -ING, -S to darken

DARKEN *v* -ED, -ING, -S to make dark

DARKENER *n* pl. -S one that darkens

DARKISH *adj* somewhat dark

DARKLE *v* -KLED, -KLING, -KLES to become dark

DARKLY *adv* -LIER, -LIEST in a dark manner

DARKNESS *n* pl. -ES the state of being dark

DARKROOM *n* pl. -S a room in which film is processed

DARKSOME *adj* dark

DARLING *n* pl. -S a much-loved person

DARN *v* -ED, -ING, -S to mend with interlacing stitches

DARNDEST *n* pl. -S damndest

DARNED *adj* DARNEDER, DARNEDEST or DARNDEST damned

DARNEL *n* pl. -S an annual grass

DARNER *n* pl. -S one that darns

DARNING *n* pl. -S things to be darned

DARSHAN *n* pl. -S a Hindu blessing

DART *v* -ED, -ING, -S to move suddenly or swiftly

DARTER *n* pl. -S one that darts

DARTLE *v* -TLED, -TLING, -TLES to dart repeatedly

DASH *v* -ED, -ING, -ES to strike violently

DASHEEN *n* pl. -S a tropical plant

DASHER *n* pl. -S one that dashes

DASHI *n* pl. -S a fish broth

DASHIER comparative of dashy

DASHIEST superlative of dashy

DASHIKI *n* pl. -S an African tunic

DASHPOT *n* pl. -S a shock absorber

DASHY *adj* DASHIER, DASHIEST stylish

DASSIE *n* pl. -S a hyrax

DASTARD *n* pl. -S a base coward

DASYURE *n* pl. -S a flesh-eating mammal

DATA a pl. of datum

DATABANK *n* pl. -S a database

DATABASE *n* pl. -S a collection of data in a computer

DATABLE *adj* capable of being dated

DATARY *n* pl. -RIES a cardinal in the Roman Catholic Church

DATCHA *n* pl. -S dacha

DATE *v* DATED, DATING, DATES to determine or record the date of **DATEABLE** *adj*

DATEDLY *adv* in an old-fashioned manner

DATELESS *adj* having no date

DATELINE *v* -LINED, -LINING, -LINES to provide a news story with its date and place of origin

DATER *n* pl. -S one that dates

DATING	present participle of date
DATIVE	*n* pl. -S a grammatical case **DATIVAL** *adj* **DATIVELY** *adv*
DATO	*n* pl. -TOS datto
DATTO	*n* pl. -TOS a Philippine tribal chief
DATUM	*n* pl. -TA or -TUMS something used as a basis for calculating
DATURA	*n* pl. -S a flowering plant **DATURIC** *adj*
DAUB	*v* -ED, -ING, -S to smear
DAUBE	*n* pl. -S a braised meat stew
DAUBER	*n* pl. -S one that daubs
DAUBERY	*n* pl. -ERIES a bad or inexpert painting
DAUBRY	*n* pl. -RIES daubery
DAUBY	*adj* **DAUBIER, DAUBIEST** smeary
DAUGHTER	*n* pl. -S a female child
DAUNDER	*v* -ED, -ING, -S to dander
DAUNT	*v* -ED, -ING, -S to intimidate
DAUNTER	*n* pl. -S one that daunts
DAUPHIN	*n* pl. -S the eldest son of a French king
DAUPHINE	*n* pl. -S the wife of a dauphin
DAUT	*v* -ED, -ING, -S to fondle
DAUTIE	*n* pl. -S a small pet
DAVEN	*v* -ED, -ING, -S to utter Jewish prayers
DAVIT	*n* pl. -S a hoisting device on a ship
DAVY	*n* pl. -VIES a safety lamp
DAW	*v* DAWED, DAWEN, DAWING, DAWS to dawn
DAWDLE	*v* -DLED, -DLING, -DLES to waste time
DAWDLER	*n* pl. -S one that dawdles
DAWEN	past participle of daw
DAWK	*n* pl. -S dak
DAWN	*v* -ED, -ING, -S to begin to grow light in the morning
DAWNLIKE	*adj* suggestive of daybreak
DAWT	*v* -ED, -ING, -S to daut
DAWTIE	*n* pl. -S dautie
DAY	*n* pl. DAYS the time between sunrise and sunset
DAYBED	*n* pl. -S a couch that can be converted into a bed
DAYBOOK	*n* pl. -S a diary

DAYBREAK	*n* pl. -S the first appearance of light in the morning
DAYDREAM	*v* -DREAMED or -DREAMT, -DREAMING, -DREAMS to fantasize
DAYFLY	*n* pl. -FLIES a mayfly
DAYGLOW	*n* pl. -S airglow seen during the day
DAYLIGHT	*v* -LIGHTED or -LIT, -LIGHTING, -LIGHTS to illuminate with the light of day
DAYLILY	*n* pl. -LILIES a flowering plant
DAYLONG	*adj* lasting all day
DAYMARE	*n* pl. -S a nightmarish fantasy experienced while awake
DAYROOM	*n* pl. -S a room for reading and recreation
DAYSIDE	*n* pl. -S the sun side of a planet or the moon
DAYSMAN	*n* pl. -MEN an arbiter
DAYSTAR	*n* pl. -S a planet visible in the east just before sunrise
DAYTIME	*n* pl. -S day
DAYWORK	*n* pl. -S work done on a daily basis
DAZE	*v* DAZED, DAZING, DAZES to stun **DAZEDLY** *adv*
DAZZLE	*v* -ZLED, -ZLING, -ZLES to blind by bright light
DAZZLER	*n* pl. -S one that dazzles
DE	*prep* of; from — used in names
DEACON	*v* -ED, -ING, -S to read a hymn aloud
DEACONRY	*n* pl. -RIES a clerical office
DEAD	*adj* **DEADER, DEADEST** deprived of life
DEAD	*n* pl. -S the period of greatest intensity
DEADBEAT	*n* pl. -S a loafer
DEADBOLT	*n* pl. -S a lock for a door
DEADEN	*v* -ED, -ING, -S to diminish the sensitivity or vigor of
DEADENER	*n* pl. -S one that deadens
DEADEYE	*n* pl. -S an expert marksman
DEADFALL	*n* pl. -S a type of animal trap
DEADHEAD	*v* -ED, -ING, -S to travel without freight
DEADLIER	comparative of deadly
DEADLIEST	superlative of deadly

DEADLIFT   *v* -ED, -ING, -S to execute a type of lift in weight lifting

DEADLINE   *n* pl. -S a time limit

DEADLOCK   *v* -ED, -ING, -S to come to a standstill

DEADLY   *adj* -LIER, -LIEST fatal

DEADNESS   *n* pl. -ES the state of being dead

DEADPAN   *v* -PANNED, -PANNING, -PANS to act without emotion

DEADWOOD   *n* pl. -S a reinforcement in a ship's keel

DEAERATE   *v* -ATED, -ATING, -ATES to remove air or gas from

DEAF   *adj* DEAFER, DEAFEST lacking the sense of hearing

DEAFEN   *v* -ED, -ING, -S to make deaf

DEAFISH   *adj* somewhat deaf

DEAFLY   *adv* in a deaf manner

DEAFNESS   *n* pl. -ES the state of being deaf

DEAIR   *v* -ED, -ING, -S to remove air from

DEAL   *v* DEALT, DEALING, DEALS to trade or do business

DEALATE   *n* pl. -S an insect divested of its wings **DEALATED** *adj*

DEALER   *n* pl. -S one that deals

DEALFISH   *n* pl. -ES a marine fish

DEALING   *n* pl. -S a business transaction

DEALT   past tense of deal

DEAN   *v* -ED, -ING, -S to serve as dean (the head of a faculty)

DEANERY   *n* pl. -ERIES the office of a dean

DEANSHIP   *n* pl. -S deanery

DEAR   *adj* DEARER, DEAREST greatly loved

DEAR   *n* pl. -S a loved one

DEARIE   *n* pl. -S deary

DEARIES   pl. of deary

DEARLY   *adv* in a dear manner

DEARNESS   *n* pl. -ES the state of being dear

DEARTH   *n* pl. -S scarcity

DEARY   *n* pl. DEARIES darling

DEASH   *v* -ED, -ING, -ES to remove ash from

DEASIL   *adv* clockwise

DEATH   *n* pl. -S the end of life

DEATHBED   *n* pl. -S the bed on which a person dies

DEATHCUP   *n* pl. -S a poisonous mushroom

DEATHFUL   *adj* fatal

DEATHLY   *adj* fatal

DEATHY   *adj* deathly

DEAVE   *v* DEAVED, DEAVING, DEAVES to deafen

DEB   *n* pl. -S a debutante

DEBACLE   *n* pl. -S a sudden collapse

DEBAR   *v* -BARRED, -BARRING, -BARS to exclude

DEBARK   *v* -ED, -ING, -S to unload from a ship

DEBASE   *v* -BASED, -BASING, -BASES to lower in character, quality, or value

DEBASER   *n* pl. -S one that debases

DEBATE   *v* -BATED, -BATING, -BATES to argue about

DEBATER   *n* pl. -S one that debates

DEBAUCH   *v* -ED, -ING, -ES to corrupt

DEBEAK   *v* -ED, -ING, -S to remove the tip of the upper beak of

DEBILITY   *n* pl. -TIES weakness

DEBIT   *v* -ED, -ING, -S to charge with a debt

DEBONAIR   *adj* suave

DEBONE   *v* -BONED, -BONING, -BONES to remove the bones from

DEBONER   *n* pl. -S a bone remover

DEBOUCH   *v* -ED, -ING, -ES to march into the open

DEBOUCHE   *n* pl. -S an opening for the passage of troops

DEBRIDE   *v* -BRIDED, -BRIDING, -BRIDES to remove dead tissue surgically

DEBRIEF   *v* -ED, -ING, -S to question after a mission

DEBRIS   *n* pl. DEBRIS fragments or scattered remains

DEBRUISE   *v* -BRUISED, -BRUISING, -BRUISES to cross a coat of arms

DEBT   *n* pl. -S something that is owed **DEBTLESS** *adj*

DEBTOR   *n* pl. -S one who owes something to another

DEBUG   *v* -BUGGED, -BUGGING, -BUGS to remove bugs from

DEBUGGER   *n* pl. -S one that debugs

DEBUNK   *v* -ED, -ING, -S to expose the sham or falseness of

DEBUNKER *n pl.* -S one that debunks

DEBUT *v* -ED, -ING, -S to make one's first public appearance

DEBUTANT *n pl.* -S one who is debuting

DEBYE *n pl.* -S a unit of measure for electric dipole moments

DECADE *n pl.* -S a period of ten years **DECADAL** *adj*

DECADENT *n pl.* -S one in a state of mental or moral decay

DECAF *n pl.* -S decaffeinated coffee

DECAGON *n pl.* -S a ten-sided polygon

DECAGRAM *n pl.* -S dekagram

DECAL *n pl.* -S a picture or design made to be transferred from specially prepared paper

DECALOG *n pl.* -S the Ten Commandments

DECAMP *v* -ED, -ING, -S to depart from a camping ground

DECANAL *adj* pertaining to a dean

DECANE *n pl.* -S a hydrocarbon

DECANT *v* -ED, -ING, -S to pour from one container into another

DECANTER *n pl.* -S a decorative bottle

DECAPOD *n pl.* -S a ten-legged crustacean

DECARE *n pl.* -S dekare

DECAY *v* -ED, -ING, -S to decompose

DECAYER *n pl.* -S one that decays

DECEASE *v* -CEASED, -CEASING, -CEASES to die

DECEDENT *n pl.* -S a deceased person

DECEIT *n pl.* -S the act of deceiving

DECEIVE *v* -CEIVED, -CEIVING, -CEIVES to mislead by falsehood

DECEIVER *n pl.* -S one that deceives

DECEMVIR *n pl.* -VIRS or -VIRI one of a body of ten Roman magistrates

DECENARY *n pl.* -RIES a tithing

DECENCY *n pl.* -CIES the state of being decent

DECENNIA *n/pl* decades

DECENT *adj* -CENTER, -CENTEST conforming to recognized standards of propriety **DECENTLY** *adv*

DECENTER *v* -ED, -ING, -S to put out of center

DECENTRE *v* -TRED, -TRING, -TRES to decenter

DECERN *v* -ED, -ING, -S to decree by judicial sentence

DECIARE *n pl.* -S a metric unit of area

DECIBEL *n pl.* -S a unit of sound intensity

DECIDE *v* -CIDED, -CIDING, -CIDES to make a choice or judgment

DECIDER *n pl.* -S one that decides

DECIDUA *n pl.* -UAS or -UAE a mucous membrane of the uterus **DECIDUAL** *adj*

DECIGRAM *n pl.* -S one tenth of a gram

DECILE *n pl.* -S a statistical interval

DECIMAL *n pl.* -S a fraction whose denominator is some power of ten

DECIMATE *v* -MATED, -MATING, -MATES to destroy a large part of

DECIPHER *v* -ED, -ING, -S to decode

DECISION *v* -ED, -ING, -S to win a victory over a boxing opponent on points

DECISIVE *adj* conclusive

DECK *v* -ED, -ING, -S to adorn

DECKEL *n pl.* -S deckle

DECKER *n pl.* -S something having a specified number of levels, floors, or layers

DECKHAND *n pl.* -S a seaman who performs manual duties

DECKING *n pl.* -S material for a ship's deck

DECKLE *n pl.* -S a frame used in making paper by hand

DECLAIM *v* -ED, -ING, -S to speak formally

DECLARE *v* -CLARED, -CLARING, -CLARES to make known clearly

DECLARER *n pl.* -S one that declares

DECLASS *v* -ED, -ING, -ES to lower in status

DECLASSE *adj* lowered in status

DECLINE *v* -CLINED, -CLINING, -CLINES to refuse

DECLINER *n pl.* -S one that declines

DECO *n pl.* DECOS a decorative style

DECOCT *v* -ED, -ING, -S to extract the flavor of by boiling

DECODE *v* -CODED, -CODING, -CODES to convert a coded message into plain language

DECODER *n pl.* -S one that decodes

DECOLOR *v* -ED, -ING, -S to deprive of color

DECOLOUR *v* -ED, -ING, -S to decolor

DECOR *n* pl. -S style or mode of decoration

DECORATE *v* -RATED, -RATING, -RATES to adorn

DECOROUS *adj* proper

DECORUM *n* pl. -S conformity to social conventions

DECOUPLE *v* -PLED, -PLING, -PLES to disconnect

DECOY *v* -ED, -ING, -S to lure into a trap

DECOYER *n* pl. -S one that decoys

DECREASE *v* -CREASED, -CREASING, -CREASES to diminish

DECREE *v* -CREED, -CREEING, -CREES to order or establish by law or edict

DECREER *n* pl. -S one that decrees

DECREPIT *adj* worn out by long use

DECRETAL *n* pl. -S a papal edict

DECRIAL *n* pl. -S the act of decrying

DECRIED past tense of decry

DECRIER *n* pl. -S one that decries

DECROWN *v* -ED, -ING, -S to deprive of a crown; depose

DECRY *v* -CRIED, -CRYING, -CRIES to denounce

DECRYPT *v* -ED, -ING, -S to decode

DECUMAN *adj* extremely large

DECUPLE *v* -PLED, -PLING, -PLES to increase tenfold

DECURIES pl. of decury

DECURION *n* pl. -S a commander of a decury

DECURVE *v* -CURVED, -CURVING, -CURVES to curve downward

DECURY *n* pl. -RIES a group of ten soldiers in ancient Rome

DEDAL *adj* daedal

DEDANS *n* pl. DEDANS a gallery for tennis spectators

DEDICATE *v* -CATED, -CATING, -CATES to set apart for some special use

DEDUCE *v* -DUCED, -DUCING, -DUCES to infer

DEDUCT *v* -ED, -ING, -S to subtract

DEE *n* pl. -S the letter D

DEED *v* -ED, -ING, -S to transfer by deed (a legal document)

DEEDLESS *adj* being without deeds

DEEDY *adj* DEEDIER, DEEDIEST industrious

DEEJAY *n* pl. -JAYS a disc jockey

DEEM *v* -ED, -ING, -S to hold as an opinion

DEEMSTER *n* pl. -S a judicial officer of the Isle of Man

DEEP *adj* DEEPER, DEEPEST extending far down from a surface

DEEP *n* pl. -S a place or thing of great depth

DEEPEN *v* -ED, -ING, -S to make deep

DEEPENER *n* pl. -S one that deepens

DEEPLY *adv* at or to a great depth

DEEPNESS *n* pl. -ES the quality of being deep

DEER *n* pl. -S a ruminant mammal **DEERLIKE** *adj*

DEERFLY *n* pl. -FLIES a bloodsucking fly

DEERSKIN *n* pl. -S the skin of a deer

DEERWEED *n* pl. -S a bushlike herb

DEERYARD *n* pl. -S an area where deer herd in winter

DEET *n* pl. -S an insect repellent

DEEWAN *n* pl. -S dewan

DEFACE *v* -FACED, -FACING, -FACES to mar the appearance of

DEFACER *n* pl. -S one that defaces

DEFAME *v* -FAMED, -FAMING, -FAMES to attack the good name of

DEFAMER *n* pl. -S one that defames

DEFANG *v* -ED, -ING, -S to make harmless

DEFAT *v* -FATTED, -FATTING, -FATS to remove fat from

DEFAULT *v* -ED, -ING, -S to fail to do something required

DEFEAT *v* -ED, -ING, -S to win victory over

DEFEATER *n* pl. -S one that defeats

DEFECATE *v* -CATED, -CATING, -CATES to discharge feces

DEFECT *v* -ED, -ING, -S to desert an allegiance

DEFECTOR *n* pl. -S one that defects

DEFENCE *n* pl. -S something that defends

DEFEND *v* -ED, -ING, -S to protect

DEFENDER *n* pl. -S one that defends

DEFENSE *v* -FENSED, -FENSING, -FENSES to guard against a specific attack

DEFER *v* -FERRED, -FERRING, -FERS to postpone

DEFERENT *n* pl. -S an imaginary circle around the earth

DEFERRAL *n* pl. -S the act of deferring

DEFERRED past tense of defer

DEFERRER *n* pl. -S one that defers

DEFERRING present participle of defer

DEFI *n* pl. -S a challenge

DEFIANCE *n* pl. -S bold opposition

DEFIANT *adj* showing defiance

DEFICIT *n* pl. -S a shortage

DEFIED past tense of defy

DEFIER *n* pl. -S one that defies

DEFIES present 3d person sing. of defy

DEFILADE *v* -LADED, -LADING, -LADES to shield from enemy fire

DEFILE *v* -FILED, -FILING, -FILES to make dirty

DEFILER *n* pl. -S one that defiles

DEFINE *v* -FINED, -FINING, -FINES to state the meaning of

DEFINER *n* pl. -S one that defines

DEFINITE *adj* known for certain

DEFLATE *v* -FLATED, -FLATING, -FLATES to release the air or gas from

DEFLATER *n* pl. -S one that deflates

DEFLATOR *n* pl. -S one that deflates

DEFLEA *v* -ED, -ING, -S to rid of fleas

DEFLECT *v* -ED, -ING, -S to turn aside

DEFLEXED *adj* bent downward

DEFLOWER *v* -ED, -ING, -S to deprive of flowers

DEFOAM *v* -ED, -ING, -S to remove foam from

DEFOAMER *n* pl. -S one that defoams

DEFOCUS *v* -CUSED, -CUSING, -CUSES or -CUSSED, -CUSSING, -CUSSES to cause to go out of focus

DEFOG *v* -FOGGED, -FOGGING, -FOGS to remove fog from

DEFOGGER *n* pl. -S one that defogs

DEFORCE *v* -FORCED, -FORCING, -FORCES to withhold by force

DEFOREST *v* -ED, -ING, -S to clear of forests

DEFORM *v* -ED, -ING, -S to spoil the form of

DEFORMER *n* pl. -S one that deforms

DEFRAUD *v* -ED, -ING, -S to swindle

DEFRAY *v* -ED, -ING, -S to pay

DEFRAYAL *n* pl. -S the act of defraying

DEFRAYER *n* pl. -S one that defrays

DEFROCK *v* -ED, -ING, -S to unfrock

DEFROST *v* -ED, -ING, -S to remove frost from

DEFT *adj* DEFTER, DEFTEST skillful **DEFTLY** *adv*

DEFTNESS *n* pl. -ES the quality of being deft

DEFUNCT *adj* deceased

DEFUND *v* -ED, -ING, -S to withdraw funding from

DEFUSE *v* -FUSED, -FUSING, -FUSES to remove the fuse from

DEFUZE *v* -FUZED, -FUZING, -FUZES to defuse

DEFY *v* -FIED, -FYING, -FIES to resist openly and boldly

DEGAGE *adj* free and relaxed in manner

DEGAME *n* pl. -S a tropical tree

DEGAMI *n* pl. -S degame

DEGAS *v* -GASSED, -GASSING, -GASSES or -GASES to remove gas from

DEGASSER *n* pl. -S one that degasses

DEGAUSS *v* -ED, -ING, -ES to demagnetize

DEGERM *v* -ED, -ING, -S to remove germs from

DEGLAZE *v* -GLAZED, -GLAZING, -GLAZES to remove the glaze from

DEGRADE *v* -GRADED, -GRADING, -GRADES to debase

DEGRADER *n* pl. -S one that degrades

DEGREASE *v* -GREASED, -GREASING, -GREASES to remove the grease from

DEGREE *n* pl. -S one of a series of stages **DEGREED** *adj*

DEGUM *v* -GUMMED, -GUMMING, -GUMS to free from gum

DEGUST *v* -ED, -ING, -S to taste with pleasure

DEHISCE *v* -HISCED, -HISCING, -HISCES to split open

DEHORN *v* -ED, -ING, -S to deprive of horns

DEHORNER *n* pl. -S one that dehorns

DEHORT *v* -ED, -ING, -S to try to dissuade

DEICE   v -ICED, -ICING, -ICES to free from ice

DEICER   n pl. -S one that deices

DEICIDE   n pl. -S the killing of a god **DEICIDAL** adj

DEICING   present participle of deice

DEICTIC   adj proving directly

DEIFIC   adj godlike

DEIFICAL   adj deific

DEIFIED   past tense of deify

DEIFIER   n pl. -S one that deifies

DEIFORM   adj having the form of a god

DEIFY   v -FIED, -FYING, -FIES to make a god of

DEIGN   v -ED, -ING, -S to lower oneself to do something

DEIL   n pl. -S the devil

DEIONIZE   v -IZED, -IZING, -IZES to remove ions from

DEISM   n pl. -S a religious philosophy

DEIST   n pl. -S an adherent of deism **DEISTIC** adj

DEITY   n pl. -TIES a god or goddess

DEIXIS   n pl. DEIXISES the specifying function of some words

DEJECT   v -ED, -ING, -S to depress or discourage

DEJECTA   n/pl excrements

DEJEUNER   n pl. -S a late breakfast

DEKAGRAM   n pl. -S a measure equal to ten grams

DEKARE   n pl. -S a measure equal to ten ares

DEKE   v DEKED, DEKING, DEKES to feint in hockey

DEKKO   n pl. -KOS a look

DEL   n pl. -S an operator in differential calculus

DELAINE   n pl. -S a wool fabric

DELATE   v -LATED, -LATING, -LATES to accuse

DELATION   n pl. -S the act of delating

DELATOR   n pl. -S one that delates

DELAY   v -ED, -ING, -S to put off to a later time

DELAYER   n pl. -S one that delays

DELE   v DELED, DELEING, DELES to delete

DELEAD   v -ED, -ING, -S to remove lead from

DELEAVE   v -LEAVED, -LEAVING, -LEAVES to separate the copies of

DELEGACY   n pl. -CIES the act of delegating

DELEGATE   v -GATED, -GATING, -GATES to appoint as one's representative

DELETE   v -LETED, -LETING, -LETES to remove written or printed matter

DELETION   n pl. -S the act of deleting

DELF   n pl. -S delft

DELFT   n pl. -S an earthenware

DELI   n pl. DELIS a delicatessen

DELICACY   n pl. -CIES a choice food

DELICATE   n pl. -S a delicacy

DELICT   n pl. -S an offense against civil law

DELIGHT   v -ED, -ING, -S to give great pleasure to

DELIME   v -LIMED, -LIMING, -LIMES to free from lime

DELIMIT   v -ED, -ING, -S to mark the boundaries of

DELIRIUM   n pl. -IUMS or -IA wild frenzy

DELIST   v -ED, -ING, -S to remove from a list

DELIVER   v -ED, -ING, -S to take to the intended recipient

DELIVERY   n pl. -ERIES the act of delivering

DELL   n pl. -S a small, wooded valley

DELLY   n pl. DELLIES deli

DELOUSE   v -LOUSED, -LOUSING, -LOUSES to remove lice from

DELOUSER   n pl. -S one that gets rid of lice

DELPHIC   adj ambiguous

DELTA   n pl. -S an alluvial deposit at the mouth of a river **DELTAIC, DELTIC** adj

DELTOID   n pl. -S a shoulder muscle

DELUDE   v -LUDED, -LUDING, -LUDES to mislead the mind or judgment of

DELUDER   n pl. -S one that deludes

DELUGE   v -UGED, -UGING, -UGES to flood

DELUSION   n pl. -S the act of deluding

DELUSIVE   adj tending to delude

DELUSORY   adj delusive

DELUSTER   v -ED, -ING, -S to lessen the sheen of

DELUXE	*adj* of special elegance or luxury	**DEMOB**	*v* -MOBBED, -MOBBING, -MOBS to discharge from military service
DELVE	*v* DELVED, DELVING, DELVES to search in depth	**DEMOCRAT**	*n* pl. -S one who believes in political and social equality
DELVER	*n* pl. -S one that delves	**DEMODE**	*adj* demoded
DEMAGOG	*v* -ED, -ING, -S to behave like a demagog (a leader who appeals to emotions and prejudices)	**DEMODED**	*adj* out-of-date
		DEMOLISH	*v* -ED, -ING, -ES to destroy
		DEMON	*n* pl. -S an evil spirit
DEMAGOGY	*n* pl. -GOGIES the rule of a demagog	**DEMONESS**	*n* pl. -ES a female demon
DEMAND	*v* -ED, -ING, -S to ask for with authority	**DEMONIAC**	*n* pl. -S one regarded as possessed by a demon
DEMANDER	*n* pl. -S one that demands	**DEMONIAN**	*adj* demonic
DEMARCHE	*n* pl. -S a procedure	**DEMONIC**	*adj* characteristic of a demon
DEMARK	*v* -ED, -ING, -S to delimit	**DEMONISE**	*v* -ISED, -ISING, -ISES to demonize
DEMAST	*v* -ED, -ING, -S to strip masts from	**DEMONISM**	*n* pl. -S belief in demons
DEME	*n* pl. -S a Greek district	**DEMONIST**	*n* pl. -S one who believes in demons
DEMEAN	*v* -ED, -ING, -S to conduct oneself in a particular manner	**DEMONIZE**	*v* -IZED, -IZING, -IZES to make a demon of
DEMEANOR	*n* pl. -S the manner in which one conducts oneself	**DEMOS**	*n* pl. -ES the people of an ancient Greek state
DEMENT	*v* -ED, -ING, -S to make insane	**DEMOTE**	*v* -MOTED, -MOTING, -MOTES to lower in rank or grade
DEMENTIA	*n* pl. -S mental illness		
DEMERARA	*n* pl. -S a coarse light-brown sugar	**DEMOTIC**	*adj* pertaining to a simplified form of ancient Egyptian writing
DEMERGE	*v* -MERGED, -MERGING, -MERGES to remove a division from a corporation	**DEMOTICS**	*n/pl* the study of people in society
		DEMOTING	present participle of demote
DEMERGER	*v* -ED, -ING, -S to demerge	**DEMOTION**	*n* pl. -S the act of demoting
DEMERIT	*v* -ED, -ING, -S to lower in rank or status	**DEMOTIST**	*n* pl. -S a student of demotic writings
DEMERSAL	*adj* found at the bottom of the sea	**DEMOUNT**	*v* -ED, -ING, -S to remove from a mounting
DEMESNE	*n* pl. -S the legal possession of land as one's own	**DEMPSTER**	*n* pl. -S a deemster
DEMETON	*n* pl. -S an insecticide	**DEMUR**	*v* -MURRED, -MURRING, -MURS to object
DEMIES	pl. of demy	**DEMURE**	*adj* -MURER, -MUREST shy and modest **DEMURELY** *adv*
DEMIGOD	*n* pl. -S a lesser god		
DEMIJOHN	*n* pl. -S a narrow-necked jug	**DEMURRAL**	*n* pl. -S the act of demurring
DEMILUNE	*n* pl. -S a half-moon	**DEMURRED**	past tense of demur
DEMIREP	*n* pl. -S a prostitute	**DEMURRER**	*n* pl. -S one that demurs
DEMISE	*v* -MISED, -MISING, -MISES to bequeath	**DEMURRING**	present participle of demur
DEMIT	*v* -MITTED, -MITTING, -MITS to resign	**DEMY**	*n* pl. -MIES a size of paper
		DEN	*v* DENNED, DENNING, DENS to live in a lair
DEMIURGE	*n* pl. -S a magistrate of ancient Greece	**DENARIUS**	*n* pl. DENARII a coin of ancient Rome
DEMIVOLT	*n* pl. -S a half turn made by a horse		
DEMO	*n* pl. DEMOS a demonstration	**DENARY**	*adj* containing ten

DENATURE *v* -TURED, -TURING, -TURES to deprive of natural qualities

DENAZIFY *v* -FIED, -FYING, -FIES to rid of Nazism

DENDRITE *n* pl. -S a branched part of a nerve cell

DENDROID *adj* shaped like a tree

DENDRON *n* pl. -S a dendrite

DENE *n* pl. -S a valley

DENGUE *n* pl. -S a tropical disease

DENIABLE *adj* capable of being denied **DENIABLY** *adv*

DENIAL *n* pl. -S the act of denying

DENIED past tense of deny

DENIER *n* pl. -S one that denies

DENIES present 3d person sing. of deny

DENIM *n* pl. -S a durable fabric

DENIZEN *v* -ED, -ING, -S to make a citizen of

DENNED past tense of den

DENNING present participle of den

DENOTE *v* -NOTED, -NOTING, -NOTES to indicate **DENOTIVE** *adj*

DENOUNCE *v* -NOUNCED, -NOUNCING, -NOUNCES to condemn openly

DENSE *adj* DENSER, DENSEST compact **DENSELY** *adv*

DENSIFY *v* -FIED, -FYING, -FIES to make denser

DENSITY *n* pl. -TIES the state of being dense

DENT *v* -ED, -ING, -S to make a depression in

DENTAL *n* pl. -S a dentally produced sound

DENTALIA *n/pl* mollusks with long, tapering shells

DENTALLY *adv* with the tip of the tongue against the upper front teeth

DENTATE *adj* having teeth

DENTATED *adj* dentate

DENTICLE *n* pl. -S a small tooth

DENTIL *n* pl. -S a small rectangular block **DENTILED** *adj*

DENTIN *n* pl. -S the hard substance forming the body of a tooth **DENTINAL** *adj*

DENTINE *n* pl. -S dentin

DENTIST *n* pl. -S one who treats the teeth

DENTOID *adj* resembling a tooth

DENTURE *n* pl. -S a set of teeth **DENTURAL** *adj*

DENUDATE *v* -DATED, -DATING, -DATES to denude

DENUDE *v* -NUDED, -NUDING, -NUDES to strip of all covering

DENUDER *n* pl. -S one that denudes

DENY *v* -NIED, -NYING, -NIES to declare to be untrue

DEODAND *n* pl. -S property forfeited to the crown under a former English law

DEODAR *n* pl. -S an East Indian cedar

DEODARA *n* pl. -S deodar

DEONTIC *adj* pertaining to moral obligation

DEORBIT *v* -ED, -ING, -S to come out of an orbit

DEOXY *adj* having less oxygen than the compound from which it is derived

DEPAINT *v* -ED, -ING, -S to depict

DEPART *v* -ED, -ING, -S to go away

DEPARTEE *n* pl. -S one that departs

DEPEND *v* -ED, -ING, -S to rely

DEPERM *v* -ED, -ING, -S to demagnetize

DEPICT *v* -ED, -ING, -S to portray

DEPICTER *n* pl. -S one that depicts

DEPICTOR *n* pl. -S depicter

DEPILATE *v* -LATED, -LATING, -LATES to remove hair from

DEPLANE *v* -PLANED, -PLANING, -PLANES to get off an airplane

DEPLETE *v* -PLETED, -PLETING, -PLETES to lessen or exhaust the supply of

DEPLORE *v* -PLORED, -PLORING, -PLORES to regret strongly

DEPLORER *n* pl. -S one that deplores

DEPLOY *v* -ED, -ING, -S to position troops for battle

DEPLUME *v* -PLUMED, -PLUMING, -PLUMES to deprive of feathers

DEPOLISH *v* -ED, -ING, -ES to remove the gloss or polish of

DEPONE *v* -PONED, -PONING, -PONES to testify under oath

DEPONENT *n* pl. -S one that depones

DEPORT *v* -ED, -ING, -S to expel from a country

DEPORTEE *n* pl. -S one who is deported

DEPOSAL *n* pl. -S the act of deposing

DEPOSE	v -POSED, -POSING, -POSES to remove from office
DEPOSER	n pl. -S one that deposes
DEPOSIT	v -ED, -ING, -S to place
DEPOT	n pl. -S a railroad or bus station
DEPRAVE	v -PRAVED, -PRAVING, -PRAVES to corrupt in morals
DEPRAVER	n pl. -S one that depraves
DEPRESS	v -ED, -ING, -ES to make sad
DEPRIVAL	n pl. -S the act of depriving
DEPRIVE	v -PRIVED, -PRIVING, -PRIVES to take something away from
DEPRIVER	n pl. -S one that deprives
DEPSIDE	n pl. -S an aromatic compound
DEPTH	n pl. -S deepness
DEPURATE	v -RATED, -RATING, -RATES to free from impurities
DEPUTE	v -PUTED, -PUTING, -PUTES to delegate
DEPUTIZE	v -TIZED, -TIZING, -TIZES to appoint as a deputy
DEPUTY	n pl. -TIES one appointed to act for another
DERAIGN	v -ED, -ING, -S to dispute a claim
DERAIL	v -ED, -ING, -S to run off the rails of a track
DERANGE	v -RANGED, -RANGING, -RANGES to disorder
DERAT	v -RATTED, -RATTING, -RATS to rid of rats
DERATE	v -RATED, -RATING, -RATES to lower the rated capability of
DERAY	n pl. -RAYS disorderly revelry
DERBY	n pl. -BIES a type of hat
DERE	adj dire
DERELICT	n pl. -S something abandoned
DERIDE	v -RIDED, -RIDING, -RIDES to ridicule
DERIDER	n pl. -S one that derides
DERINGER	n pl. -S a short-barreled pistol
DERISION	n pl. -S the act of deriding
DERISIVE	adj expressing derision
DERISORY	adj derisive
DERIVATE	n pl. -S something derived
DERIVE	v -RIVED, -RIVING, -RIVES to obtain or receive from a source
DERIVER	n pl. -S one that derives
DERM	n pl. -S derma
DERMA	n pl. -S a layer of the skin **DERMAL** adj
DERMIS	n pl. -MISES derma **DERMIC** adj
DERMOID	n pl. -S a cystic tumor
DERNIER	adj last
DEROGATE	v -GATED, -GATING, -GATES to detract
DERRICK	n pl. -S a hoisting apparatus
DERRIERE	n pl. -S the buttocks
DERRIS	n pl. -RISES a climbing plant
DERRY	n pl. -RIES a meaningless word used in the chorus of old songs
DERVISH	n pl. -ES a member of a Muslim religious order
DESALT	v -ED, -ING, -S to remove the salt from
DESALTER	n pl. -S one that desalts
DESAND	v -ED, -ING, -S to remove sand from
DESCANT	v -ED, -ING, -S to sing a counterpoint to a melody
DESCEND	v -ED, -ING, -S to come or go down
DESCENT	n pl. -S the act of descending
DESCRIBE	v -SCRIBED, -SCRIBING, -SCRIBES to give a verbal account of
DESCRIER	n pl. -S one that descries
DESCRY	v -SCRIED, -SCRYING, -SCRIES to discern
DESELECT	v -ED, -ING, -S to dismiss from a training program
DESERT	v -ED, -ING, -S to abandon
DESERTER	n pl. -S one that deserts
DESERTIC	adj arid and barren
DESERVE	v -SERVED, -SERVING, -SERVES to be entitled to or worthy of
DESERVER	n pl. -S one that deserves
DESEX	v -ED, -ING, -ES to castrate or spay
DESIGN	v -ED, -ING, -S to conceive and plan out
DESIGNEE	n pl. -S one who is designated
DESIGNER	n pl. -S one that designs
DESILVER	v -ED, -ING, -S to remove the silver from
DESINENT	adj terminating
DESIRE	v -SIRED, -SIRING, -SIRES to wish for

DESIRER	*n* pl. -S one that desires
DESIROUS	*adj* desiring
DESIST	*v* -ED, -ING, -S to cease doing something
DESK	*n* pl. -S a writing table
DESKMAN	*n* pl. -MEN one who works at a desk
DESKTOP	*n* pl. -S the top of a desk
DESMAN	*n* pl. -S an aquatic mammal
DESMID	*n* pl. -S a freshwater alga
DESMOID	*n* pl. -S a very hard tumor
DESOLATE	*v* -LATED, -LATING, -LATES to lay waste
DESORB	*v* -ED, -ING, -S to remove by the reverse of absorption
DESOXY	*adj* deoxy
DESPAIR	*v* -ED, -ING, -S to lose all hope
DESPATCH	*v* -ED, -ING, -ES to dispatch
DESPISE	*v* -SPISED, -SPISING, -SPISES to loathe
DESPISER	*n* pl. -S one that despises
DESPITE	*v* -SPITED, -SPITING, -SPITES to treat with contempt
DESPOIL	*v* -ED, -ING, -S to plunder
DESPOND	*v* -ED, -ING, -S to lose spirit or hope
DESPOT	*n* pl. -S a tyrant **DESPOTIC** *adj*
DESSERT	*n* pl. -S something served as the last course of a meal
DESTAIN	*v* -ED, -ING, -S to remove stain from
DESTINE	*v* -TINED, -TINING, -TINES to determine beforehand
DESTINY	*n* pl. -NIES the fate or fortune to which one is destined
DESTRIER	*n* pl. -S a war horse
DESTROY	*v* -ED, -ING, -S to damage beyond repair or renewal
DESTRUCT	*v* -ED, -ING, -S to destroy
DESUGAR	*v* -ED, -ING, -S to remove sugar from
DESULFUR	*v* -ED, -ING, -S to free from sulfur
DETACH	*v* -ED, -ING, -ES to unfasten and separate
DETACHER	*n* pl. -S one that detaches
DETAIL	*v* -ED, -ING, -S to report with complete particulars
DETAILER	*n* pl. -S one that details

DETAIN	*v* -ED, -ING, -S to hold in custody
DETAINEE	*n* pl. -S one who is detained
DETAINER	*n* pl. -S the unlawful withholding of another's property
DETASSEL	*v* -SELED, -SELING, -SELS or -SELLED, -SELLING, -SELS to remove tassels from
DETECT	*v* -ED, -ING, -S to discover or perceive
DETECTER	*n* pl. -S detector
DETECTOR	*n* pl. -S one that detects
DETENT	*n* pl. -S a locking or unlocking mechanism
DETENTE	*n* pl. -S an easing of international tension
DETER	*v* -TERRED, -TERRING, -TERS to stop from proceeding
DETERGE	*v* -TERGED, -TERGING, -TERGES to cleanse
DETERGER	*n* pl. -S one that deterges
DETERRED	past tense of deter
DETERRER	*n* pl. -S one that deters
DETERRING	present participle of deter
DETEST	*v* -ED, -ING, -S to dislike intensely
DETESTER	*n* pl. -S one that detests
DETHRONE	*v* -THRONED, -THRONING, -THRONES to remove from a throne
DETICK	*v* -ED, -ING, -S to remove ticks from
DETICKER	*n* pl. -S one that deticks
DETINUE	*n* pl. -S an action to recover property wrongfully detained
DETONATE	*v* -NATED, -NATING, -NATES to cause to explode
DETOUR	*v* -ED, -ING, -S to take an indirect route
DETOX	*v* -ED, -ING, -ES to detoxify
DETOXIFY	*v* -FIED, -FYING, -FIES to remove a toxin from
DETRACT	*v* -ED, -ING, -S to take away
DETRAIN	*v* -ED, -ING, -S to get off a railroad train
DETRITUS	*n* pl. DETRITUS particles of rock **DETRITAL** *adj*
DETRUDE	*v* -TRUDED, -TRUDING, -TRUDES to thrust out
DEUCE	*v* DEUCED, DEUCING, DEUCES to bring a tennis score to a tie

DEUCEDLY	*adv* extremely
DEUTERIC	*adj* pertaining to heavy hydrogen
DEUTERON	*n* pl. -S an atomic particle
DEUTZIA	*n* pl. -S an ornamental shrub
DEV	*n* pl. -S deva
DEVA	*n* pl. -S a Hindu god
DEVALUE	*v* -UED, -UING, -UES to lessen the worth of
DEVEIN	*v* -ED, -ING, -S to remove the dorsal vein from
DEVEL	*v* -ED, -ING, -S to strike forcibly
DEVELOP	*v* -ED, -ING, -S to bring to a more advanced or effective state
DEVELOPE	*v* -OPED, -OPING, -OPES to develop
DEVERBAL	*adj* derived from a verb
DEVEST	*v* -ED, -ING, -S to divest
DEVIANCE	*n* pl. -S the behavior of a deviant
DEVIANCY	*n* pl. -CIES deviance
DEVIANT	*n* pl. -S one that deviates from a norm
DEVIATE	*v* -ATED, -ATING, -ATES to turn aside from a course or norm
DEVIATOR	*n* pl. -S one that deviates
DEVICE	*n* pl. -S something devised or constructed for a specific purpose
DEVIL	*v* -ILED, -ILING, -ILS or -ILLED, -ILLING, -ILS to prepare food with pungent seasoning
DEVILISH	*adj* fiendish
DEVILKIN	*n* pl. -S a small demon
DEVILLED	a past tense of devil
DEVILLING	a present participle of devil
DEVILRY	*n* pl. -RIES deviltry
DEVILTRY	*n* pl. -TRIES mischief
DEVIOUS	*adj* indirect
DEVISAL	*n* pl. -S the act of devising
DEVISE	*v* -VISED, -VISING, -VISES to form in the mind
DEVISEE	*n* pl. -S one to whom a will is made
DEVISER	*n* pl. -S one that devises
DEVISING	present participle of devise
DEVISOR	*n* pl. -S one who makes a will
DEVOICE	*v* -VOICED, -VOICING, -VOICES to unvoice
DEVOID	*adj* completely lacking
DEVOIR	*n* pl. -S an act of civility or respect
DEVOLVE	*v* -VOLVED, -VOLVING, -VOLVES to transfer from one person to another
DEVON	*n* pl. -S one of a breed of small, hardy cattle
DEVOTE	*v* -VOTED, -VOTING, -VOTES to give oneself wholly to
DEVOTEE	*n* pl. -S an ardent follower or supporter
DEVOTION	*n* pl. -S the act of devoting
DEVOUR	*v* -ED, -ING, -S to eat up voraciously
DEVOURER	*n* pl. -S one that devours
DEVOUT	*adj* -VOUTER, -VOUTEST pious **DEVOUTLY** *adv*
DEW	*v* -ED, -ING, -S to wet with dew (condensed moisture)
DEWAN	*n* pl. -S an official in India
DEWAR	*n* pl. -S a double-walled flask
DEWATER	*v* -ED, -ING, -S to remove water from
DEWAX	*v* -ED, -ING, -ES to remove wax from
DEWBERRY	*n* pl. -RIES an edible berry
DEWCLAW	*n* pl. -S a vestigial toe
DEWDROP	*n* pl. -S a drop of dew
DEWFALL	*n* pl. -S the formation of dew
DEWIER	comparative of dewy
DEWIEST	superlative of dewy
DEWILY	*adv* in a dewy manner
DEWINESS	*n* pl. -ES the state of being dewy
DEWLAP	*n* pl. -S a fold of loose skin under the neck
DEWLESS	*adj* having no dew
DEWOOL	*v* -ED, -ING, -S to remove the wool from
DEWORM	*v* -ED, -ING, -S to rid of worms
DEWORMER	*n* pl. -S one that deworms
DEWY	*adj* DEWIER, DEWIEST moist with dew
DEX	*n* pl. -ES a sulfate used as a central nervous system stimulant
DEXIE	*n* pl. -S a tablet of dex
DEXIES	pl. of dexy
DEXTER	*adj* situated on the right
DEXTRAL	*adj* pertaining to the right
DEXTRAN	*n* pl. -S a substance used as a blood plasma substitute

DEXTRIN	*n* pl. -S a substance used as an adhesive
DEXTRINE	*n* pl. -S dextrin
DEXTRO	*adj* turning to the right
DEXTROSE	*n* pl. -S a form of glucose
DEXTROUS	*adj* adroit
DEXY	*n* pl. DEXIES dexie
DEY	*n* pl. DEYS a former North African ruler
DEZINC	*v* -ZINCKED, -ZINCKING, -ZINCS or -ZINCED, -ZINCING, -ZINCS to remove zinc from
DHAK	*n* pl. -S an Asian tree
DHAL	*n* pl. -S dal
DHARMA	*n* pl. -S conformity to Hindu law **DHARMIC** *adj*
DHARNA	*n* pl. -S a form of protest in India
DHOBI	*n* pl. -S a person who does laundry in India
DHOLE	*n* pl. -S a wild dog of India
DHOOLY	*n* pl. -LIES dooly
DHOORA	*n* pl. -S durra
DHOOTI	*n* pl. -S dhoti
DHOOTIE	*n* pl. -S dhoti
DHOTI	*n* pl. -S a loincloth worn by Hindu men
DHOURRA	*n* pl. -S durra
DHOW	*n* pl. -S an Arabian sailing vessel
DHURNA	*n* pl. -S dharna
DHURRIE	*n* pl. -S a cotton rug made in India
DHUTI	*n* pl. -S dhoti
DIABASE	*n* pl. -S an igneous rock **DIABASIC** *adj*
DIABETES	*n* pl. DIABETES a metabolic disorder
DIABETIC	*n* pl. -S one who has diabetes
DIABLERY	*n* pl. -RIES sorcery
DIABOLIC	*adj* devilish
DIABOLO	*n* pl. -LOS a game requiring manual dexterity
DIACETYL	*n* pl. -S biacetyl
DIACID	*n* pl. -S a type of acid **DIACIDIC** *adj*
DIACONAL	*adj* pertaining to a deacon
DIADEM	*v* -ED, -ING, -S to adorn with a crown
DIAGNOSE	*v* -NOSED, -NOSING, -NOSES to recognize a disease by its signs and symptoms
DIAGONAL	*n* pl. -S an oblique line
DIAGRAM	*v* -GRAMED, -GRAMING, -GRAMS or -GRAMMED, -GRAMMING, -GRAMS to illustrate by a diagram (a graphic design)
DIAGRAPH	*n* pl. -S a drawing device
DIAL	*v* DIALED, DIALING, DIALS or DIALLED, DIALLING, DIALS to manipulate a calibrated disk
DIALECT	*n* pl. -S a regional variety of a language
DIALER	*n* pl. -S one that dials
DIALING	*n* pl. -S the measurement of time by sundials
DIALIST	*n* pl. -S a dialer
DIALLAGE	*n* pl. -S a mineral
DIALLED	a past tense of dial
DIALLEL	*adj* pertaining to a genetic crossing
DIALLER	*n* pl. -S dialer
DIALLING	*n* pl. -S dialing
DIALLIST	*n* pl. -S dialist
DIALOG	*v* -ED, -ING, -S to dialogue
DIALOGER	*n* pl. -S one that dialogs
DIALOGIC	*adj* conversational
DIALOGUE	*v* -LOGUED, -LOGUING, -LOGUES to carry on a conversation
DIALYSE	*v* -LYSED, -LYSING, -LYSES to dialyze
DIALYSER	*n* pl. -S dialyzer
DIALYSIS	*n* pl. -YSES the separation of substances in a solution by diffusion through a membrane
DIALYTIC	*adj* pertaining to dialysis
DIALYZE	*v* -LYZED, -LYZING, -LYZES to subject to dialysis
DIALYZER	*n* pl. -S an apparatus used for dialysis
DIAMANTE	*n* pl. -S a sparkling decoration
DIAMETER	*n* pl. -S a straight line passing through the center of a circle and ending at the periphery
DIAMIDE	*n* pl. -S a chemical compound
DIAMIN	*n* pl. -S diamine
DIAMINE	*n* pl. -S a chemical compound

DIAMOND   *v* -ED, -ING, -S to adorn with diamonds (precious gems)

DIANTHUS   *n* pl. -ES an ornamental herb

DIAPASON   *n* pl. -S a burst of harmonious sound

DIAPAUSE   *v* -PAUSED, -PAUSING, -PAUSES to undergo dormancy

DIAPER   *v* -ED, -ING, -S to put a diaper (a baby's breechcloth) on

DIAPHONE   *n* pl. -S a low-pitched foghorn

DIAPHONY   *n* pl. -NIES organum

DIAPIR   *n* pl. -S a bend in a layer of rock **DIAPIRIC** *adj*

DIAPSID   *adj* pertaining to a type of reptile

DIARCHY   *n* pl. -CHIES a government with two rulers **DIARCHIC** *adj*

DIARIES   pl. of diary

DIARIST   *n* pl. -S one who keeps a diary

DIARRHEA   *n* pl. -S an intestinal disorder

DIARY   *n* pl. -RIES a personal journal

DIASPORA   *n* pl. -S migration

DIASPORE   *n* pl. -S a mineral

DIASTASE   *n* pl. -S an enzyme

DIASTEM   *n* pl. -S an interruption in the deposition of sediment

DIASTEMA   *n* pl. -MATA a space between teeth

DIASTER   *n* pl. -S a stage in mitosis **DIASTRAL** *adj*

DIASTOLE   *n* pl. -S the normal rhythmical dilation of the heart

DIATOM   *n* pl. -S any of a class of algae

DIATOMIC   *adj* composed of two atoms

DIATONIC   *adj* pertaining to a type of musical scale

DIATRIBE   *n* pl. -S a bitter and abusive criticism

DIATRON   *n* pl. -S a circuitry design that uses diodes

DIAZEPAM   *n* pl. -S a tranquilizer

DIAZIN   *n* pl. -S diazine

DIAZINE   *n* pl. -S a chemical compound

DIAZINON   *n* pl. -S an insecticide

DIAZO   *adj* containing a certain chemical group

DIAZOLE   *n* pl. -S a chemical compound

DIB   *v* DIBBED, DIBBING, DIBS to fish by letting the bait bob lightly on the water

DIBASIC   *adj* having two replaceable hydrogen atoms

DIBBER   *n* pl. -S a planting implement

DIBBING   present participle of dib

DIBBLE   *v* -BLED, -BLING, -BLES to dib

DIBBLER   *n* pl. -S one that dibbles

DIBBUK   *n* pl. -BUKS or -BUKIM dybbuk

DICAST   *n* pl. -S a judge of ancient Athens **DICASTIC** *adj*

DICE   *v* DICED, DICING, DICES to cut into small cubes

DICENTRA   *n* pl. -S a perennial herb

DICER   *n* pl. -S a device that dices food

DICEY   *adj* DICIER, DICIEST dangerous

DICHASIA   *n/pl* flower clusters

DICHOTIC   *adj* affecting the two ears differently

DICHROIC   *adj* having two colors

DICIER   comparative of dicey

DICIEST   superlative of dicey

DICING   present participle of dice

DICK   *n* pl. -S a detective

DICKENS   *n* pl. -ES devil

DICKER   *v* -ED, -ING, -S to bargain

DICKEY   *n* pl. -EYS a blouse front

DICKIE   *n* pl. -S dickey

DICKY   *n* pl. DICKIES dickey

DICKY   *adj* DICKIER, DICKIEST poor in condition

DICLINY   *n* pl. -NIES the state of having stamens and pistils in separate flowers

DICOT   *n* pl. -S a plant with two seed leaves

DICOTYL   *n* pl. -S dicot

DICROTAL   *adj* dicrotic

DICROTIC   *adj* having a double pulse beat

DICTA   a pl. of dictum

DICTATE   *v* -TATED, -TATING, -TATES to read aloud for recording

DICTATOR   *n* pl. -S one that dictates

DICTIER   comparative of dicty

DICTIEST   superlative of dicty

DICTION   *n* pl. -S choice and use of words in speech or writing

DICTUM   *n* pl. -TA or -TUMS an authoritative statement

DICTY   *adj* -TIER, -TIEST snobbish

DICYCLIC *adj* having two maxima of population each year

DICYCLY *n* pl. -CLIES the state of being dicyclic

DID a past tense of do

DIDACT *n* pl. -S a didactic person

DIDACTIC *adj* instructive

DIDACTYL *adj* having two digits at the end of each limb

DIDAPPER *n* pl. -S a dabchick

DIDDLE *v* -DLED, -DLING, -DLES to swindle

DIDDLER *n* pl. -S one that diddles

DIDDLEY *n* pl. -DLEYS diddly

DIDDLY *n* pl. -DLIES the least amount

DIDIE *n* pl. -S didy

DIDIES pl. of didy

DIDO *n* pl. -DOS or -DOES a mischievous act

DIDST a past tense of do

DIDY *n* pl. -DIES a diaper

DIDYMIUM *n* pl. -S a mixture of rare-earth elements

DIDYMOUS *adj* occurring in pairs

DIDYNAMY *n* pl. -MIES the state of having four stamens in pairs of unequal length

DIE *v* DIED, DYING, DIES to cease living

DIE *v* DIED, DIEING, DIES to cut with a die (a device for shaping material)

DIEBACK *n* pl. -S a gradual dying of plant shoots

DIECIOUS *adj* dioicous

DIED past tense of die

DIEHARD *n* pl. -S a stubborn person

DIEL *adj* involving a full day

DIELDRIN *n* pl. -S an insecticide

DIEMAKER *n* pl. -S one that makes dies

DIENE *n* pl. -S a chemical compound

DIERESIS *n* pl. DIERESES the separation of two vowels into two syllables **DIERETIC** *adj*

DIESEL *v* -ED, -ING, -S to continue running after the ignition is turned off

DIESIS *n* pl. DIESES a reference mark in printing

DIESTER *n* pl. -S a type of chemical compound

DIESTOCK *n* pl. -S a frame for holding dies

DIESTRUM *n* pl. -S diestrus

DIESTRUS *n* pl. -ES a period of sexual inactivity

DIET *v* -ED, -ING, -S to regulate one's daily sustenance

DIETARY *n* pl. -ETARIES a system of dieting

DIETER *n* pl. -S one that diets

DIETETIC *adj* pertaining to diet

DIETHER *n* pl. -S a chemical compound

DIFFER *v* -ED, -ING, -S to be unlike

DIFFRACT *v* -ED, -ING, -S to separate into parts

DIFFUSE *v* -FUSED, -FUSING, -FUSES to spread widely or thinly

DIFFUSER *n* pl. -S one that diffuses

DIFFUSOR *n* pl. -S diffuser

DIG *v* DUG or DIGGED, DIGGING, DIGS to break up, turn over, or remove earth

DIGAMIES pl. of digamy

DIGAMIST *n* pl. -S one who practices digamy

DIGAMMA *n* pl. -S a Greek letter

DIGAMY *n* pl. -MIES a second legal marriage **DIGAMOUS** *adj*

DIGEST *v* -ED, -ING, -S to render food usable for the body

DIGESTER *n* pl. -S an apparatus in which substances are softened or decomposed

DIGESTOR *n* pl. -S digester

DIGGED a past tense of dig

DIGGER *n* pl. -S one that digs

DIGGING present participle of dig

DIGGINGS *n/pl* an excavation site

DIGHT *v* -ED, -ING, -S to adorn

DIGIT *n* pl. -S a finger or toe

DIGITAL *n* pl. -S a piano key

DIGITATE *adj* having digits

DIGITIZE *v* -TIZED, -TIZING, -TIZES to put data into digital notation

DIGLOT *n* pl. -S a bilingual book or edition

DIGNIFY *v* -FIED, -FYING, -FIES to add dignity to

DIGNITY	*n* pl. -TIES stateliness and nobility of manner
DIGOXIN	*n* pl. -S a drug to improve heart function
DIGRAPH	*n* pl. -S a pair of letters representing a single speech sound
DIGRESS	*v* -ED, -ING, -ES to stray from the main topic
DIHEDRAL	*n* pl. -S a dihedron
DIHEDRON	*n* pl. -S a figure formed by two intersecting planes
DIHYBRID	*n* pl. -S an offspring of parents differing in two pairs of genes
DIHYDRIC	*adj* containing two hydroxyl radicals
DIKDIK	*n* pl. -S a small antelope
DIKE	*v* DIKED, DIKING, DIKES to furnish with an embankment
DIKER	*n* pl. -S one that dikes
DIKTAT	*n* pl. -S a harsh settlement imposed on a defeated nation
DILATANT	*n* pl. -S a dilator
DILATATE	*adj* dilated
DILATE	*v* -LATED, -LATING, -LATES to make wider or larger
DILATER	*n* pl. -S dilator
DILATION	*n* pl. -S the act of dilating
DILATIVE	*adj* tending to dilate
DILATOR	*n* pl. -S one that dilates
DILATORY	*adj* tending to delay
DILDO	*n* pl. -DOS an object used as a penis substitute
DILDOE	*n* pl. -S dildo
DILEMMA	*n* pl. -S a perplexing situation **DILEMMIC** *adj*
DILIGENT	*adj* persevering
DILL	*n* pl. -S an annual herb
DILLED	*adj* flavored with dill
DILLY	*n* pl. DILLIES something remarkable
DILUENT	*n* pl. -S a diluting substance
DILUTE	*v* -LUTED, -LUTING, -LUTES to thin or reduce the concentration of
DILUTER	*n* pl. -S one that dilutes
DILUTION	*n* pl. -S the act of diluting
DILUTIVE	*adj* tending to dilute
DILUTOR	*n* pl. -S diluter
DILUVIA	a pl. of diluvium
DILUVIAL	*adj* pertaining to a flood
DILUVIAN	*adj* diluvial
DILUVION	*n* pl. -S diluvium
DILUVIUM	*n* pl. -VIA or -VIUMS coarse rock material deposited by glaciers
DIM	*adj* DIMMER, DIMMEST obscure
DIM	*v* DIMMED, DIMMING, DIMS to make dim
DIME	*n* pl. -S a coin of the United States
DIMER	*n* pl. -S a molecule composed of two identical molecules
DIMERIC	*adj* dimerous
DIMERISM	*n* pl. -S the state of being dimerous
DIMERIZE	*v* -IZED, -IZING, -IZES to form a dimer
DIMEROUS	*adj* composed of two parts
DIMETER	*n* pl. -S a verse of two metrical feet
DIMETHYL	*n* pl. -S ethane
DIMETRIC	*adj* pertaining to a type of crystal system
DIMINISH	*v* -ED, -ING, -ES to lessen
DIMITY	*n* pl. -TIES a cotton fabric
DIMLY	*adv* in a dim manner
DIMMABLE	*adj* capable of being dimmed
DIMMED	past tense of dim
DIMMER	*n* pl. -S a device for varying the intensity of illumination
DIMMEST	superlative of dim
DIMMING	present participle of dim
DIMNESS	*n* pl. -ES the state of being dim
DIMORPH	*n* pl. -S either of two distinct forms
DIMOUT	*n* pl. -S a condition of partial darkness
DIMPLE	*v* -PLED, -PLING, -PLES to mark with indentations
DIMPLY	*adj* -PLIER, -PLIEST dimpled
DIMWIT	*n* pl. -S a dunce
DIN	*v* DINNED, DINNING, DINS to make a loud noise
DINAR	*n* pl. -S an ancient gold coin of Muslim areas
DINDLE	*v* -DLED, -DLING, -DLES to tingle

DINE	*v* DINED, DINING, DINES to eat dinner
DINER	*n* pl. -S one that dines
DINERIC	*adj* pertaining to the interface between two immiscible liquids
DINERO	*n* pl. -ROS a former silver coin of Peru
DINETTE	*n* pl. -S a small dining room
DING	*v* -ED, -ING, -S to ring
DINGBAT	*n* pl. -S a typographical ornament
DINGDONG	*v* -ED, -ING, -S to make a ringing sound
DINGE	*n* pl. -S the condition of being dingy
DINGER	*n* pl. -S a home run
DINGEY	*n* pl. -GEYS dinghy
DINGHY	*n* pl. -GHIES a small boat
DINGIER	comparative of dingy
DINGIES	pl. of dingy
DINGIEST	superlative of dingy
DINGILY	*adv* in a dingy manner
DINGLE	*n* pl. -S a dell
DINGO	*n* pl. -GOES a wild dog of Australia
DINGUS	*n* pl. -ES a doodad
DINGY	*n* pl. -GIES dinghy
DINGY	*adj* -GIER, -GIEST grimy
DINING	present participle of dine
DINITRO	*adj* containing two nitro groups
DINK	*v* -ED, -ING, -S to adorn
DINKEY	*n* pl. -KEYS a small locomotive
DINKIER	comparative of dinky
DINKIES	pl. of dinky
DINKIEST	superlative of dinky
DINKLY	*adv* neatly
DINKUM	*n* pl. -S the truth
DINKY	*n* pl. -KIES dinkey
DINKY	*adj* -KIER, -KIEST small
DINNED	past tense of din
DINNER	*n* pl. -S the main meal of the day
DINNING	present participle of din
DINOSAUR	*n* pl. -S one of a group of extinct reptiles
DINT	*v* -ED, -ING, -S to dent
DIOBOL	*n* pl. -S a coin of ancient Greece
DIOBOLON	*n* pl. -S diobol
DIOCESAN	*n* pl. -S a bishop
DIOCESE	*n* pl. -S an ecclesiastical district
DIODE	*n* pl. -S a type of electron tube
DIOECISM	*n* pl. -S the state of being dioicous
DIOECY	*n* pl. DIOECIES dioecism
DIOICOUS	*adj* unisexual
DIOL	*n* pl. -S a chemical compound
DIOLEFIN	*n* pl. -S a hydrocarbon
DIOPSIDE	*n* pl. -S a mineral
DIOPTASE	*n* pl. -S a mineral
DIOPTER	*n* pl. -S a measure of refractive power **DIOPTRAL** *adj*
DIOPTRE	*n* pl. -S diopter
DIOPTRIC	*adj* aiding the vision by refraction
DIORAMA	*n* pl. -S a three-dimensional exhibit **DIORAMIC** *adj*
DIORITE	*n* pl. -S an igneous rock **DIORITIC** *adj*
DIOXAN	*n* pl. -S dioxane
DIOXANE	*n* pl. -S a flammable liquid
DIOXID	*n* pl. -S dioxide
DIOXIDE	*n* pl. -S a type of oxide
DIOXIN	*n* pl. -S a toxic solid hydrocarbon
DIP	*v* DIPPED or DIPT, DIPPING, DIPS to immerse briefly
DIPHASE	*adj* having two phases
DIPHASIC	*adj* diphase
DIPHENYL	*n* pl. -S biphenyl
DIPLEGIA	*n* pl. -S paralysis of the same part on both sides of the body
DIPLEX	*adj* pertaining to the simultaneous transmission or reception of two radio signals
DIPLEXER	*n* pl. -S a coupling device
DIPLOE	*n* pl. -S a bony tissue of the cranium **DIPLOIC** *adj*
DIPLOID	*n* pl. -S a cell having the basic chromosome number doubled
DIPLOIDY	*n* pl. -DIES the condition of being a diploid
DIPLOMA	*n* pl. -MAS or -MATA a certificate of an academic degree
DIPLOMA	*v* -ED, -ING, -S to furnish with a diploma
DIPLOMAT	*n* pl. -S a governmental official
DIPLONT	*n* pl. -S an organism having a particular chromosomal structure

DIPLOPIA	*n* pl. -S double vision **DIPLOPIC** *adj*
DIPLOPOD	*n* pl. -S a multi-legged insect
DIPLOSIS	*n* pl. -LOSES a method of chromosome formation
DIPNET	*v* -NETTED, -NETTING, -NETS to scoop fish with a type of net
DIPNOAN	*n* pl. -S a lungfish
DIPODY	*n* pl. -DIES a dimeter **DIPODIC** *adj*
DIPOLE	*n* pl. -S a pair of equal and opposite electric charges **DIPOLAR** *adj*
DIPPABLE	*adj* capable of being dipped
DIPPED	a past tense of dip
DIPPER	*n* pl. -S one that dips
DIPPING	present participle of dip
DIPPY	*adj* -PIER, -PIEST foolish
DIPSAS	*n* pl. DIPSADES a fabled serpent
DIPSO	*n* pl. -SOS a person who craves alcoholic liquors
DIPSTICK	*n* pl. -S a measuring rod
DIPT	a past tense of dip
DIPTERA	pl. of dipteron
DIPTERAL	*adj* having two rows or columns
DIPTERAN	*n* pl. -S a two-winged fly
DIPTERON	*n* pl. -TERA dipteran
DIPTYCA	*n* pl. -S diptych
DIPTYCH	*n* pl. -S an ancient writing tablet
DIQUAT	*n* pl. -S an herbicide
DIRDUM	*n* pl. -S blame
DIRE	*adj* DIRER, DIREST disastrous
DIRECT	*v* -ED, -ING, -S to control or conduct the affairs of
DIRECT	*adj* -RECTER, -RECTEST straightforward **DIRECTLY** *adv*
DIRECTOR	*n* pl. -S one that directs
DIREFUL	*adj* dreadful
DIRELY	*adv* in a dire manner
DIRENESS	*n* pl. -ES the state of being dire
DIRER	comparative of dire
DIREST	superlative of dire
DIRGE	*n* pl. -S a funeral song **DIRGEFUL** *adj*
DIRHAM	*n* pl. -S a monetary unit of Morocco
DIRIMENT	*adj* nullifying
DIRK	*v* -ED, -ING, -S to stab with a small knife
DIRL	*v* -ED, -ING, -S to tremble
DIRNDL	*n* pl. -S a woman's dress
DIRT	*n* pl. -S earth or soil
DIRTBAG	*n* pl. -S a dirty or contemptible person
DIRTY	*adj* DIRTIER, DIRTIEST unclean **DIRTILY** *adv*
DIRTY	*v* DIRTIED, DIRTYING, DIRTIES to make dirty
DIS	*v* DISSED, DISSING, DISSES to insult or criticize
DISABLE	*v* -ABLED, -ABLING, -ABLES to render incapable or unable
DISABUSE	*v* -ABUSED, -ABUSING, -ABUSES to free from false or mistaken ideas
DISAGREE	*v* -AGREED, -AGREEING, -AGREES to differ in opinion
DISALLOW	*v* -ED, -ING, -S to refuse to allow
DISANNUL	*v* -NULLED, -NULLING, -NULS to annul
DISARM	*v* -ED, -ING, -S to deprive of weapons
DISARMER	*n* pl. -S one that disarms
DISARRAY	*v* -ED, -ING, -S to disorder
DISASTER	*n* pl. -S a calamity
DISAVOW	*v* -ED, -ING, -S to disclaim responsibility for
DISBAND	*v* -ED, -ING, -S to break up
DISBAR	*v* -BARRED, -BARRING, -BARS to expel from the legal profession
DISBOSOM	*v* -ED, -ING, -S to confess
DISBOUND	*adj* not having a binding
DISBOWEL	*v* -ELED, -ELING, -ELS or -ELLED, -ELLING, -ELS to remove the intestines of
DISBUD	*v* -BUDDED, -BUDDING, -BUDS to remove buds from
DISBURSE	*v* -BURSED, -BURSING, -BURSES to pay out
DISC	*v* -ED, -ING, -S to disk
DISCANT	*v* -ED, -ING, -S to descant
DISCARD	*v* -ED, -ING, -S to throw away
DISCASE	*v* -CASED, -CASING, -CASES to remove the case of
DISCEPT	*v* -ED, -ING, -S to debate
DISCERN	*v* -ED, -ING, -S to perceive
DISCI	a pl. of discus

DISCIPLE   *v* -PLED, -PLING, -PLES to cause to become a follower

DISCLAIM   *v* -ED, -ING, -S to renounce any claim to or connection with

DISCLIKE   *adj* disklike

DISCLOSE   *v* -CLOSED, -CLOSING, -CLOSES to reveal

DISCO   *v* -ED, -ING, -S to dance at a discotheque

DISCOID   *n* pl. -S a disk

DISCOLOR   *v* -ED, -ING, -S to alter the color of

DISCORD   *v* -ED, -ING, -S to disagree

DISCOUNT   *v* -ED, -ING, -S to reduce the price of

DISCOVER   *v* -ED, -ING, -S to gain sight or knowledge of

DISCREET   *adj* -CREETER, -CREETEST tactful

DISCRETE   *adj* separate

DISCROWN   *v* -ED, -ING, -S to deprive of a crown

DISCUS   *n* pl. -CUSES or -CI a disk hurled in athletic competition

DISCUSS   *v* -ED, -ING, -ES to talk over or write about

DISDAIN   *v* -ED, -ING, -S to scorn

DISEASE   *v* -EASED, -EASING, -EASES to make unhealthy

DISENDOW   *v* -ED, -ING, -S to deprive of endowment

DISEUSE   *n* pl. -S a female entertainer

DISFAVOR   *v* -ED, -ING, -S to regard with disapproval

DISFROCK   *v* -ED, -ING, -S to unfrock

DISGORGE   *v* -GORGED, -GORGING, -GORGES to vomit

DISGRACE   *v* -GRACED, -GRACING, -GRACES to bring shame or discredit upon

DISGUISE   *v* -GUISED, -GUISING, -GUISES to alter the appearance of

DISGUST   *v* -ED, -ING, -S to cause nausea or loathing in

DISH   *v* -ED, -ING, -ES to put into a dish (a concave vessel)

DISHELM   *v* -ED, -ING, -S to deprive of a helmet

DISHERIT   *v* -ED, -ING, -S to deprive of an inheritance

DISHEVEL   *v* -ELED, -ELING, -ELS or -ELLED, -ELLING, -ELS to make messy

DISHFUL   *n* pl. -S as much as a dish can hold

DISHIER   comparative of dishy

DISHIEST   superlative of dishy

DISHLIKE   *adj* resembling a dish

DISHONOR   *v* -ED, -ING, -S to deprive of honor

DISHPAN   *n* pl. -S a pan for washing dishes

DISHRAG   *n* pl. -S a cloth for washing dishes

DISHWARE   *n* pl. -S tableware used in serving food

DISHY   *adj* DISHIER, DISHIEST attractive

DISINTER   *v* -TERRED, -TERRING, -TERS to exhume

DISJECT   *v* -ED, -ING, -S to disperse

DISJOIN   *v* -ED, -ING, -S to separate

DISJOINT   *v* -ED, -ING, -S to put out of order

DISJUNCT   *n* pl. -S an alternative in a logical disjunction

DISK   *v* -ED, -ING, -S to break up land with a type of farm implement

DISKETTE   *n* pl. -S a floppy disk for a computer

DISKLIKE   *adj* resembling a disk (a flat, circular plate)

DISLIKE   *v* -LIKED, -LIKING, -LIKES to regard with aversion

DISLIKER   *n* pl. -S one that dislikes

DISLIMN   *v* -ED, -ING, -S to make dim

DISLODGE   *v* -LODGED, -LODGING, -LODGES to remove from a firm position

DISLOYAL   *adj* not loyal

DISMAL   *n* pl. -S a track of swampy land

DISMAL   *adj* -MALER, -MALEST cheerless and depressing **DISMALLY** *adv*

DISMAST   *v* -ED, -ING, -S to remove the mast of

DISMAY   *v* -ED, -ING, -S to deprive of courage or resolution

DISME   *n* pl. -S a former coin of the United States

DISMISS   *v* -ED, -ING, -ES to permit or cause to leave

DISMOUNT *v* -ED, -ING, -S to get down from an elevated position

DISOBEY *v* -ED, -ING, -S to fail to obey

DISOMIC *adj* having a number of chromosomes duplicated

DISORDER *v* -ED, -ING, -S to put out of order

DISOWN *v* -ED, -ING, -S to deny the ownership of

DISPART *v* -ED, -ING, -S to separate

DISPATCH *v* -ED, -ING, -ES to send off with speed

DISPEL *v* -PELLED, -PELLING, -PELS to drive off in various directions

DISPEND *v* -ED, -ING, -S to squander

DISPENSE *v* -PENSED, -PENSING, -PENSES to distribute

DISPERSE *v* -PERSED, -PERSING, -PERSES to scatter

DISPIRIT *v* -ED, -ING, -S to lower in spirit

DISPLACE *v* -PLACED, -PLACING, -PLACES to remove from the usual or proper place

DISPLANT *v* -ED, -ING, -S to dislodge

DISPLAY *v* -ED, -ING, -S to make evident or obvious

DISPLODE *v* -PLODED, -PLODING, -PLODES to explode

DISPLUME *v* -PLUMED, -PLUMING, -PLUMES to deplume

DISPORT *v* -ED, -ING, -S to amuse oneself

DISPOSAL *n* pl. -S the act of disposing

DISPOSE *v* -POSED, -POSING, -POSES to put in place

DISPOSER *n* pl. -S one that disposes

DISPREAD *v* -SPREAD, -SPREADING, -SPREADS to spread out

DISPRIZE *v* -PRIZED, -PRIZING, -PRIZES to disdain

DISPROOF *n* pl. -S the act of disproving

DISPROVE *v* -PROVED, -PROVEN, -PROVING, -PROVES to refute

DISPUTE *v* -PUTED, -PUTING, -PUTES to argue about

DISPUTER *n* pl. -S one that disputes

DISQUIET *v* -ED, -ING, -S to deprive of quiet, rest, or peace

DISRATE *v* -RATED, -RATING, -RATES to lower in rating or rank

DISROBE *v* -ROBED, -ROBING, -ROBES to undress

DISROBER *n* pl. -S one that disrobes

DISROOT *v* -ED, -ING, -S to uproot

DISRUPT *v* -ED, -ING, -S to throw into confusion

DISS *v* -ED, -ING, -ES to dis

DISSAVE *v* -SAVED, -SAVING, -SAVES to use savings for current expenses

DISSEAT *v* -ED, -ING, -S to unseat

DISSECT *v* -ED, -ING, -S to cut apart for scientific examination

DISSED past tense of dis

DISSEISE *v* -SEISED, -SEISING, -SEISES to deprive

DISSEIZE *v* -SEIZED, -SEIZING, -SEIZES to disseise

DISSENT *v* -ED, -ING, -S to disagree

DISSERT *v* -ED, -ING, -S to discuss in a learned or formal manner

DISSERVE *v* -SERVED, -SERVING, -SERVES to treat badly

DISSES present 3d person sing. of dis

DISSEVER *v* -ED, -ING, -S to sever

DISSING present participle of dis

DISSOLVE *v* -SOLVED, -SOLVING, -SOLVES to make into a solution

DISSUADE *v* -SUADED, -SUADING, -SUADES to persuade not to do something

DISTAFF *n* pl. -TAFFS or -TAVES a type of staff

DISTAIN *v* -ED, -ING, -S to stain

DISTAL *adj* located far from the point of origin **DISTALLY** *adv*

DISTANCE *v* -TANCED, -TANCING, -TANCES to leave behind

DISTANT *adj* far off or apart

DISTASTE *v* -TASTED, -TASTING, -TASTES to dislike

DISTAVES a pl. of distaff

DISTEND *v* -ED, -ING, -S to swell

DISTENT *adj* distended

DISTICH *n* pl. -S a couplet

DISTIL *v* -TILLED, -TILLING, -TILS to distill

DISTILL *v* -ED, -ING, -S to extract by vaporization and condensation

DISTINCT *adj* -TINCTER, -TINCTEST clearly different

DISTOME *n* pl. -S a parasitic flatworm

DISTORT *v* -ED, -ING, -S to put out of shape

DISTRACT   *v* -ED, -ING, -S to divert the attention of

DISTRAIN   *v* -ED, -ING, -S to seize and hold property as security

DISTRAIT   *adj* absentminded

DISTRESS   *v* -ED, -ING, -ES to cause anxiety or suffering to

DISTRICT   *v* -ED, -ING, -S to divide into localities

DISTRUST   *v* -ED, -ING, -S to have no trust in

DISTURB   *v* -ED, -ING, -S to interrupt the quiet, rest, or peace of

DISULFID   *n* pl. -S a chemical compound

DISUNION   *n* pl. -S the state of being disunited

DISUNITE   *v* -UNITED, -UNITING, -UNITES to separate

DISUNITY   *n* pl. -TIES lack of unity

DISUSE   *v* -USED, -USING, -USES to stop using

DISVALUE   *v* -UED, -UING, -UES to treat as of little value

DISYOKE   *v* -YOKED, -YOKING, -YOKES to free from a yoke

DIT   *n* pl. -S a dot in Morse code

DITA   *n* pl. -S a Philippine tree

DITCH   *v* -ED, -ING, -ES to dig a long, narrow excavation in the ground

DITCHER   *n* pl. -S one that ditches

DITE   *n* pl. -S a small amount

DITHEISM   *n* pl. -S belief in two coequal gods

DITHEIST   *n* pl. -S an adherent of ditheism

DITHER   *v* -ED, -ING, -S to act nervously or indecisively

DITHERER   *n* pl. -S one that dithers

DITHERY   *adj* nervously excited

DITHIOL   *adj* containing two chemical groups both of which include sulfur and hydrogen

DITSY   *adj* -SIER, -SIEST silly, eccentric

DITTANY   *n* pl. -NIES a perennial herb

DITTO   *v* -ED, -ING, -S to repeat

DITTY   *n* pl. -TIES a short, simple song

DITZ   *n* pl. -ES a ditsy person

DITZY   *adj* -ZIER, -ZIEST ditsy

DIURESIS   *n* pl. DIURESES excessive discharge of urine

DIURETIC   *n* pl. -S a drug which increases urinary discharge

DIURNAL   *n* pl. -S a diary

DIURON   *n* pl. -S an herbicide

DIVA   *n* pl. -S a distinguished female operatic singer

DIVAGATE   *v* -GATED, -GATING, -GATES to wander

DIVALENT   *adj* having a valence of two

DIVAN   *n* pl. -S a sofa or couch

DIVE   *v* DIVED or DOVE, DIVING, DIVES to plunge headfirst into water

DIVEBOMB   *v* -ED, -ING, -S to drop bombs on a target from a diving airplane

DIVER   *n* pl. -S one that dives

DIVERGE   *v* -VERGED, -VERGING, -VERGES to move in different directions from a common point

DIVERSE   *adj* different

DIVERT   *v* -ED, -ING, -S to turn aside

DIVERTER   *n* pl. -S one that diverts

DIVEST   *v* -ED, -ING, -S to strip or deprive of anything

DIVIDE   *v* -VIDED, -VIDING, -VIDES to separate into parts, areas, or groups

DIVIDEND   *n* pl. -S a quantity to be divided

DIVIDER   *n* pl. -S one that divides

DIVIDING   present participle of divide

DIVIDUAL   *adj* capable of being divided

DIVINE   *v* -VINED, -VINING, -VINES to foretell by occult means

DIVINE   *adj* -VINER, -VINEST pertaining to or characteristic of a god **DIVINELY** *adv*

DIVINER   *n* pl. -S one that divines

DIVING   present participle of dive

DIVINING   present participle of divine

DIVINISE   *v* -NISED, -NISING, -NISES to divinize

DIVINITY   *n* pl. -TIES the state of being divine

DIVINIZE   *v* -NIZED, -NIZING, -NIZES to make divine

DIVISION   *n* pl. -S the act of dividing

DIVISIVE   *adj* causing disunity or dissension

DIVISOR   *n* pl. -S a number by which a dividend is divided

DIVORCE   *v* -VORCED, -VORCING, -VORCES to terminate the marriage contract between

DIVORCEE   *n* pl. -S a divorced woman

DIVORCER   *n* pl. -S one that divorces

DIVORCING   present participle of divorce

DIVOT   *n* pl. -S a piece of turf

DIVULGE   *v* -VULGED, -VULGING, -VULGES to reveal

DIVULGER   *n* pl. -S one that divulges

DIVVY   *v* -VIED, -VYING, -VIES to divide

DIWAN   *n* pl. -S dewan

DIXIT   *n* pl. -S a statement

DIZEN   *v* -ED, -ING, -S to dress in fine clothes

DIZYGOUS   *adj* developed from two fertilized ova

DIZZY   *adj* -ZIER, -ZIEST having a sensation of whirling **DIZZILY** *adv*

DIZZY   *v* -ZIED, -ZYING, -ZIES to make dizzy

DJEBEL   *n* pl. -S jebel

DJELLABA   *n* pl. -S a long hooded garment

DJIN   *n* pl. -S jinni

DJINN   *n* pl. -S jinni

DJINNI   *n* pl. DJINN jinni

DJINNY   *n* pl. DJINN jinni

DO   *v* DID or DIDST, DONE, DOING, present sing. 2d person DO, DOEST or DOST, 3d person DOES, DOETH or DOTH to begin and carry through to completion

DO   *n* pl. DOS the first tone of the diatonic musical scale

DOABLE   *adj* able to be done

DOAT   *v* -ED, -ING, -S to dote

DOBBER   *n* pl. -S a float for a fishing line

DOBBIN   *n* pl. -S a farm horse

DOBBY   *n* pl. -BIES a fool

DOBIE   *n* pl. -S adobe

DOBIES   pl. of doby

DOBLA   *n* pl. -S a former gold coin of Spain

DOBLON   *n* pl. -S or -ES a former gold coin of Spain and Spanish America

DOBRA   *n* pl. -S a former gold coin of Portugal

DOBSON   *n* pl. -S an aquatic insect larva

DOBY   *n* pl. -BIES dobie

DOC   *n* pl. -S doctor

DOCENT   *n* pl. -S a college or university lecturer

DOCETIC   *adj* pertaining to a religious doctrine

DOCILE   *adj* easily trained **DOCILELY** *adv*

DOCILITY   *n* pl. -TIES the quality of being docile

DOCK   *v* -ED, -ING, -S to bring into a dock (a wharf)

DOCKAGE   *n* pl. -S a charge for the use of a dock

DOCKER   *n* pl. -S a dock worker

DOCKET   *v* -ED, -ING, -S to supply with an identifying statement

DOCKHAND   *n* pl. -S a docker

DOCKLAND   *n* pl. -S the part of a port occupied by docks

DOCKSIDE   *n* pl. -S the area adjacent to a dock

DOCKYARD   *n* pl. -S a shipyard

DOCTOR   *v* -ED, -ING, -S to treat medically

DOCTORAL   *adj* pertaining to a doctor

DOCTRINE   *n* pl. -S a belief or set of beliefs taught or advocated

DOCUMENT   *v* -ED, -ING, -S to support by conclusive information or evidence

DODDER   *v* -ED, -ING, -S to totter

DODDERER   *n* pl. -S one that dodders

DODDERY   *adj* feeble

DODGE   *v* DODGED, DODGING, DODGES to evade

DODGEM   *n* pl. -S an amusement park ride

DODGER   *n* pl. -S one that dodges

DODGERY   *n* pl. -ERIES evasion

DODGING   present participle of dodge

DODGY   *adj* DODGIER, DODGIEST evasive

DODO   *n* pl. -DOES or -DOS an extinct flightless bird

DODOISM   *n* pl. -S a stupid remark

DOE   *n* pl. -S a female deer

DOER   *n* pl. -S one that does something

DOES   a present 3d person sing. of do

DOESKIN   *n* pl. -S the skin of a doe

DOEST   a present 2d person sing. of do

DOETH   a present 3d person sing. of do

DOFF   *v* -ED, -ING, -S to take off

DOFFER *n* pl. -S one that doffs

DOG *v* DOGGED, DOGGING, DOGS to follow after like a dog (a domesticated, carnivorous mammal)

DOGBANE *n* pl. -S a perennial herb

DOGBERRY *n* pl. -RIES a wild berry

DOGCART *n* pl. -S a one-horse carriage

DOGDOM *n* pl. -S the world of dogs

DOGE *n* pl. -S the chief magistrate in the former republics of Venice and Genoa

DOGEAR *v* -ED, -ING, -S to turn down a corner of a page

DOGEDOM *n* pl. -S the domain of a doge

DOGESHIP *n* pl. -S the office of a doge

DOGEY *n* pl. -GEYS dogie

DOGFACE *n* pl. -S a soldier in the U.S. Army

DOGFIGHT *v* -FOUGHT, -FIGHTING, -FIGHTS to engage in an aerial battle

DOGFISH *n* pl. -ES a small shark

DOGGED past tense of dog

DOGGEDLY *adv* stubbornly

DOGGER *n* pl. -S a fishing vessel

DOGGEREL *n* pl. -S trivial, awkwardly written verse

DOGGERY *n* pl. -GERIES surly behavior

DOGGIE *n* pl. -S doggy

DOGGIER comparative of doggy

DOGGIES pl. of doggy

DOGGIEST superlative of doggy

DOGGING present participle of dog

DOGGISH *adj* doglike

DOGGO *adv* in hiding

DOGGONE *v* -GONED, -GONING, -GONES to damn

DOGGONE *adj* -GONER, -GONEST damned

DOGGONED *adj* -GONEDER, -GONEDEST damned

DOGGONING present participle of doggone

DOGGREL *n* pl. -S doggerel

DOGGY *n* pl. -GIES a small dog

DOGGY *adj* -GIER, -GIEST resembling or suggestive of a dog

DOGHOUSE *n* pl. -S a shelter for a dog

DOGIE *n* pl. -S a stray calf

DOGIES pl. of dogy

DOGLEG *v* -LEGGED, -LEGGING, -LEGS to move along a bent course

DOGLIKE *adj* resembling a dog

DOGMA *n* pl. -MAS or -MATA a principle or belief put forth as authoritative **DOGMATIC** *adj*

DOGNAP *v* -NAPED, -NAPING, -NAPS or -NAPPED, -NAPPING, -NAPS to steal a dog

DOGNAPER *n* pl. -S one that dognaps

DOGSBODY *n* pl. -BODIES a menial worker

DOGSLED *v* -SLEDDED, -SLEDDING, -SLEDS to move on a sled drawn by dogs

DOGTOOTH *n* pl. -TEETH a cuspid

DOGTROT *v* -TROTTED, -TROTTING, -TROTS to move at a steady trot

DOGVANE *n* pl. -S a small vane

DOGWATCH *n* pl. -ES a short period of watch duty on a ship

DOGWOOD *n* pl. -S a tree

DOGY *n* pl. -GIES dogie

DOILED *adj* dazed

DOILY *n* pl. -LIES a small napkin

DOING *n* pl. -S an action

DOIT *n* pl. -S a former Dutch coin

DOITED *adj* old and feeble

DOJO *n* pl. -JOS a school that teaches judo or karate

DOL *n* pl. -S a unit of pain intensity

DOLCE *n* pl. -CI a soft-toned organ stop

DOLDRUMS *n/pl* a slump or slack period

DOLE *v* DOLED, DOLING, DOLES to distribute in small portions

DOLEFUL *adj* -FULLER, -FULLEST mournful

DOLERITE *n* pl. -S a variety of basalt

DOLESOME *adj* doleful

DOLING present participle of dole

DOLL *v* -ED, -ING, -S to dress stylishly

DOLLAR *n* pl. -S a monetary unit of the United States

DOLLIED past tense of dolly

DOLLIES present 3d person sing. of dolly

DOLLISH *adj* pretty

DOLLOP *v* -ED, -ING, -S to dispense in small amounts

DOLLY *v* -LIED, -LYING, -LIES to move on a wheeled platform

DOLMA *n* pl. -MAS or -MADES a stuffed grape leaf

DOLMAN *n* pl. -S a Turkish robe

DOLMEN *n* pl. -S a prehistoric monument

DOLOMITE *n* pl. -S a mineral

DOLOR *n* pl. -S grief

DOLOROSO *adj* having a mournful musical quality

DOLOROUS *adj* mournful

DOLOUR *n* pl. -S dolor

DOLPHIN *n* pl. -S a marine mammal

DOLT *n* pl. -S a stupid person **DOLTISH** *adj*

DOM *n* pl. -S a title given to certain monks

DOMAIN *n* pl. -S an area of control

DOMAL *adj* domical

DOME *v* DOMED, DOMING, DOMES to cover with a dome (a rounded roof)

DOMELIKE *adj* resembling a dome

DOMESDAY *n* pl. -DAYS doomsday

DOMESTIC *n* pl. -S a household servant

DOMIC *adj* domical

DOMICAL *adj* shaped like a dome

DOMICIL *v* -ED, -ING, -S to domicile

DOMICILE *v* -CILED, -CILING, -CILES to establish in a residence

DOMINANT *n* pl. -S a controlling genetic character

DOMINATE *v* -NATED, -NATING, -NATES to control

DOMINE *n* pl. -S master

DOMINEER *v* -ED, -ING, -S to tyrannize

DOMING present participle of dome

DOMINICK *n* pl. -S one of an American breed of chickens

DOMINIE *n* pl. -S a clergyman

DOMINION *n* pl. -S supreme authority

DOMINIUM *n* pl. -S the right of ownership and control of property

DOMINO *n* pl. -NOES or -NOS a small mask

DON *v* DONNED, DONNING, DONS to put on

DONA *n* pl. -S a Spanish lady

DONATE *v* -NATED, -NATING, -NATES to contribute

DONATION *n* pl. -S something donated

DONATIVE *n* pl. -S a donation

DONATOR *n* pl. -S a donor

DONE past participle of do

DONEE *n* pl. -S a recipient of a gift

DONENESS *n* pl. -ES the state of being cooked enough

DONG *n* pl. -S a deep sound like that of a large bell

DONGA *n* pl. -S a gully in a veldt

DONGOLA *n* pl. -S a type of leather

DONJON *n* pl. -S the main tower of a castle

DONKEY *n* pl. -KEYS the domestic ass

DONNA *n* pl. DONNAS or DONNE an Italian lady

DONNED past tense of don

DONNEE *n* pl. -S the set of assumptions upon which a story proceeds

DONNERD *adj* donnered

DONNERED *adj* dazed

DONNERT *adj* donnered

DONNIKER *n* pl. -S a bathroom or privy

DONNING present participle of don

DONNISH *adj* scholarly

DONOR *n* pl. -S one that donates

DONSIE *adj* unlucky

DONSY *adj* donsie

DONUT *n* pl. -S doughnut

DONZEL *n* pl. -S a young squire

DOODAD *n* pl. -S an article whose name is unknown or forgotten

DOODLE *v* -DLED, -DLING, -DLES to draw or scribble aimlessly

DOODLER *n* pl. -S one that doodles

DOOFUS *n* pl. -ES a stupid or foolish person

DOOLEE *n* pl. -S a stretcher for the sick or wounded

DOOLIE *n* pl. -S doolee

DOOLY *n* pl. -LIES doolee

DOOM *v* -ED, -ING, -S to destine to an unhappy fate

DOOMFUL *adj* ominous

DOOMSDAY *n* pl. -DAYS judgment day

DOOMSTER *n* pl. -S a judge

DOOMY *adj* doomful **DOOMILY** *adv*

DOOR *n* pl. -S a movable barrier at an entranceway

DOORBELL	*n* pl. -S a bell at a door	**DORK**	*n* pl. -S a stupid or foolish person
DOORJAMB	*n* pl. -S a vertical piece at the side of a doorway	**DORKY**	*adj* DORKIER, DORKIEST stupid, foolish
DOORKNOB	*n* pl. -S a handle for opening a door	**DORM**	*n* pl. -S a dormitory
DOORLESS	*adj* having no door	**DORMANCY**	*n* pl. -CIES the state of being dormant
DOORMAN	*n* pl. -MEN the door attendant of a building	**DORMANT**	*adj* lying asleep
DOORMAT	*n* pl. -S a mat placed in front of a door	**DORMER**	*n* pl. -S a type of window
		DORMICE	pl. of dormouse
DOORNAIL	*n* pl. -S a large-headed nail	**DORMIE**	*adj* being ahead by as many holes in golf as remain to be played
DOORPOST	*n* pl. -S a doorjamb		
DOORSILL	*n* pl. -S the sill of a door		
DOORSTEP	*n* pl. -S a step leading to a door	**DORMIENT**	*adj* dormant
DOORSTOP	*n* pl. -S an object used for holding a door open	**DORMIN**	*n* pl. -S a plant hormone
		DORMOUSE	*n* pl. -MICE a small rodent
DOORWAY	*n* pl. -WAYS the entranceway to a room or building	**DORMY**	*adj* dormie
		DORNECK	*n* pl. -S dornick
DOORYARD	*n* pl. -S a yard in front of a house	**DORNICK**	*n* pl. -S a heavy linen fabric
DOOZER	*n* pl. -S an extraordinary one of its kind	**DORNOCK**	*n* pl. -S dornick
		DORP	*n* pl. -S a village
DOOZIE	*n* pl. -S doozy	**DORPER**	*n* pl. -S one of a breed of mutton-producing sheep
DOOZY	*n* pl. -ZIES doozer		
DOPA	*n* pl. -S a drug to treat Parkinson's disease	**DORR**	*n* pl. -S dor
		DORSA	pl. of dorsum
DOPAMINE	*n* pl. -S a form of dopa used to stimulate the heart	**DORSAD**	*adv* dorsally
DOPANT	*n* pl. -S an impurity added to a pure substance	**DORSAL**	*n* pl. -S a dorsally located anatomical part
DOPE	*v* DOPED, DOPING, DOPES to give a narcotic to	**DORSALLY**	*adv* toward the back
		DORSEL	*n* pl. -S a dossal
DOPEHEAD	*n* pl. -S a drug addict	**DORSER**	*n* pl. -S dosser
DOPER	*n* pl. -S one that dopes	**DORSUM**	*n* pl. -SA the back
DOPESTER	*n* pl. -S one who predicts the outcomes of contests	**DORTY**	*adj* sullen
		DORY	*n* pl. -RIES a flat-bottomed boat
DOPEY	*adj* DOPIER, DOPIEST lethargic; stupid	**DOSAGE**	*n* pl. -S the amount of medicine to be given
DOPIER	comparative of dopy	**DOSE**	*v* DOSED, DOSING, DOSES to give a specified quantity of medicine to
DOPIEST	superlative of dopy		
DOPINESS	*n* pl. -ES the state of being dopey		
		DOSER	*n* pl. -S one that doses
DOPING	present participle of dope	**DOSS**	*v* -ED, -ING, -ES to sleep in any convenient place
DOPY	*adj* DOPIER, DOPIEST dopey		
DOR	*n* pl. -S a black European beetle	**DOSSAL**	*n* pl. -S an ornamental cloth hung behind an altar
DORADO	*n* pl. -DOS a marine fish		
DORBUG	*n* pl. -S a dor	**DOSSEL**	*n* pl. -S dossal
DORE	*adj* gilded	**DOSSER**	*n* pl. -S a basket carried on the back
DORHAWK	*n* pl. -S a nocturnal bird		
DORIES	pl. of dory	**DOSSERET**	*n* pl. -S a block resting on the capital of a column

DOSSIER *n* pl. -S a file of papers on a single subject

DOSSIL *n* pl. -S a cloth roll for wiping ink

DOST a present 2d person sing. of do

DOT *v* DOTTED, DOTTING, DOTS to cover with dots (tiny round marks)

DOTAGE *n* pl. -S a state of senility

DOTAL *adj* pertaining to a dowry

DOTARD *n* pl. -S a senile person **DOTARDLY** *adj*

DOTATION *n* pl. -S an endowment

DOTE *v* DOTED, DOTING, DOTES to show excessive affection

DOTER *n* pl. -S one that dotes

DOTH a present 3d person sing. of do

DOTIER comparative of doty

DOTIEST superlative of doty

DOTING present participle of dote

DOTINGLY *adv* in an excessively affectionate manner

DOTTED past tense of dot

DOTTEL *n* pl. -S dottle

DOTTER *n* pl. -S one that dots

DOTTEREL *n* pl. -S a shore bird

DOTTIER comparative of dotty

DOTTIEST superlative of dotty

DOTTILY *adv* in a dotty manner

DOTTING present participle of dot

DOTTLE *n* pl. -S a mass of half-burnt pipe tobacco

DOTTREL *n* pl. -S dotterel

DOTTY *adj* -TIER, -TIEST crazy

DOTY *adj* DOTIER, DOTIEST stained by decay

DOUBLE *v* -BLED, -BLING, -BLES to make twice as great

DOUBLER *n* pl. -S one that doubles

DOUBLET *n* pl. -S a close-fitting jacket

DOUBLING present participle of double

DOUBLOON *n* pl. -S a former Spanish gold coin

DOUBLURE *n* pl. -S the lining of a book cover

DOUBLY *adv* to twice the degree

DOUBT *v* -ED, -ING, -S to be uncertain about

DOUBTER *n* pl. -S one that doubts

DOUBTFUL *adj* uncertain

DOUCE *adj* sedate **DOUCELY** *adv*

DOUCEUR *n* pl. -S a gratuity

DOUCHE *v* DOUCHED, DOUCHING, DOUCHES to cleanse with a jet of water

DOUGH *n* pl. -S a flour mixture

DOUGHBOY *n* pl. -BOYS an infantryman

DOUGHIER comparative of doughy

DOUGHIEST superlative of doughy

DOUGHNUT *n* pl. -S a ring-shaped cake

DOUGHT a past tense of dow

DOUGHTY *adj* -TIER, -TIEST courageous

DOUGHY *adj* DOUGHIER, DOUGHIEST resembling dough

DOUM *n* pl. -S an African palm tree

DOUMA *n* pl. -S duma

DOUPIONI *n* pl. -S a silk yarn

DOUR *adj* DOURER, DOUREST sullen

DOURA *n* pl. -S durra

DOURAH *n* pl. -S durra

DOURINE *n* pl. -S a disease of horses

DOURLY *adv* in a dour manner

DOURNESS *n* pl. -ES the state of being dour

DOUSE *v* DOUSED, DOUSING, DOUSES to plunge into water

DOUSER *n* pl. -S one that douses

DOUX *adj* very sweet — used of champagne

DOUZEPER *n* pl. -S one of twelve legendary knights

DOVE *n* pl. -S a bird of the pigeon family

DOVECOT *n* pl. -S dovecote

DOVECOTE *n* pl. -S a roost for domesticated pigeons

DOVEKEY *n* pl. -KEYS dovekie

DOVEKIE *n* pl. -S a seabird

DOVELIKE *adj* resembling or suggestive of a dove

DOVEN *v* -ED, -ING, -S to daven

DOVETAIL *v* -ED, -ING, -S to fit together closely

DOVISH *adj* not warlike

DOW *v* DOWED or DOUGHT, DOWING, DOWS to prosper

DOWABLE *adj* entitled to an endowment

DOWAGER *n* pl. -S a dignified elderly woman

DOWDY	*adj* DOWDIER, DOWDIEST lacking in stylishness or neatness **DOWDILY** *adv* **DOWDYISH** *adj*
DOWDY	*n* pl. DOWDIES a dowdy woman
DOWEL	*v* -ELED, -ELING, -ELS or -ELLED, -ELLING, -ELS to fasten with wooden pins
DOWER	*v* -ED, -ING, -S to provide with a dowry
DOWERY	*n* pl. -ERIES dowry
DOWIE	*adj* dreary
DOWN	*v* -ED, -ING, -S to cause to fall
DOWNBEAT	*n* pl. -S the first beat of a musical measure
DOWNCAST	*n* pl. -S an overthrow or ruin
DOWNCOME	*n* pl. -S downfall
DOWNER	*n* pl. -S a depressant drug
DOWNFALL	*n* pl. -S a sudden fall
DOWNHAUL	*n* pl. -S a rope for hauling down sails
DOWNHILL	*n* pl. -S a downward slope
DOWNIER	comparative of downy
DOWNIEST	superlative of downy
DOWNLAND	*n* pl. -S a rolling treeless upland
DOWNLINK	*n* pl. -S a communications channel from a spacecraft
DOWNLOAD	*v* -ED, -ING, -S to transfer data from a large computer to a smaller one
DOWNPIPE	*n* pl. -S a pipe for draining water from a roof
DOWNPLAY	*v* -ED, -ING, -S to de-emphasize
DOWNPOUR	*n* pl. -S a heavy rain
DOWNSIDE	*n* pl. -S a negative aspect
DOWNSIZE	*v* -SIZED, -SIZING, -SIZES to produce in a smaller size
DOWNTICK	*n* pl. -S a stock market transaction
DOWNTIME	*n* pl. -S the time when a machine or factory is inactive
DOWNTOWN	*n* pl. -S the business district of a city
DOWNTROD	*adj* oppressed
DOWNTURN	*n* pl. -S a downward turn
DOWNWARD	*adv* from a higher to a lower place
DOWNWASH	*n* pl. -ES a downward deflection of air
DOWNWIND	*adv* in the direction that the wind blows
DOWNY	*adj* DOWNIER, DOWNIEST soft
DOWRY	*n* pl. -RIES the money or property a wife brings to her husband at marriage
DOWSABEL	*n* pl. -S a sweetheart
DOWSE	*v* DOWSED, DOWSING, DOWSES to search for underground water with a divining rod
DOWSER	*n* pl. -S one that dowses
DOXIE	*n* pl. -S doxy
DOXOLOGY	*n* pl. -GIES a hymn or verse of praise to God
DOXY	*n* pl. DOXIES a doctrine
DOYEN	*n* pl. -S the senior member of a group
DOYENNE	*n* pl. -S a female doyen
DOYLEY	*n* pl. -LEYS doily
DOYLY	*n* pl. -LIES doily
DOZE	*v* DOZED, DOZING, DOZES to sleep lightly
DOZEN	*v* -ED, -ING, -S to stun
DOZENTH	*n* pl. -S twelfth
DOZER	*n* pl. -S one that dozes
DOZIER	comparative of dozy
DOZIEST	superlative of dozy
DOZILY	*adv* in a dozy manner
DOZINESS	*n* pl. -ES the state of being dozy
DOZING	present participle of doze
DOZY	*adj* DOZIER, DOZIEST drowsy
DRAB	*adj* DRABBER, DRABBEST cheerless
DRAB	*v* DRABBED, DRABBING, DRABS to consort with prostitutes
DRABBET	*n* pl. -S a coarse linen fabric
DRABBLE	*v* -BLED, -BLING, -BLES to draggle
DRABLY	*adv* in a drab manner
DRABNESS	*n* pl. -ES the quality of being drab
DRACAENA	*n* pl. -S a tropical plant
DRACHM	*n* pl. -S a unit of weight
DRACHMA	*n* pl. -MAS, -MAE or -MAI a monetary unit of Greece
DRACONIC	*adj* pertaining to a dragon
DRAFF	*n* pl. -S the damp remains of malt after brewing
DRAFFISH	*adj* draffy

DRAFFY *adj* DRAFFIER, DRAFFIEST worthless

DRAFT *v* -ED, -ING, -S to conscript for military service

DRAFTEE *n* pl. -S one that is drafted

DRAFTER *n* pl. -S one that drafts

DRAFTING *n* pl. -S mechanical drawing

DRAFTY *adj* DRAFTIER, DRAFTIEST having or exposed to currents of air **DRAFTILY** *adv*

DRAG *v* DRAGGED, DRAGGING, DRAGS to pull along the ground

DRAGEE *n* pl. -S a sugarcoated candy

DRAGGER *n* pl. -S one that drags

DRAGGIER comparative of draggy

DRAGGIEST superlative of draggy

DRAGGING present participle of drag

DRAGGLE *v* -GLED, -GLING, -GLES to make wet and dirty

DRAGGY *adj* -GIER, -GIEST sluggish

DRAGLINE *n* pl. -S a line used for dragging

DRAGNET *n* pl. -S a net for trawling

DRAGOMAN *n* pl. -MANS or -MEN an interpreter in Near Eastern countries

DRAGON *n* pl. -S a mythical, serpentlike monster

DRAGONET *n* pl. -S a marine fish

DRAGOON *v* -ED, -ING, -S to harass by the use of troops

DRAGROPE *n* pl. -S a rope used for dragging

DRAGSTER *n* pl. -S a vehicle used in drag racing

DRAIL *n* pl. -S a heavy fishhook

DRAIN *v* -ED, -ING, -S to draw off a liquid

DRAINAGE *n* pl. -S the act of draining

DRAINER *n* pl. -S one that drains

DRAKE *n* pl. -S a male duck

DRAM *v* DRAMMED, DRAMMING, DRAMS to tipple

DRAMA *n* pl. -S a composition written for theatrical performance

DRAMATIC *adj* pertaining to drama

DRAMEDY *n* pl. -DIES a sitcom having dramatic scenes

DRAMMED past tense of dram

DRAMMING present participle of dram

DRAMMOCK *n* pl. -S raw oatmeal mixed with cold water

DRAMSHOP *n* pl. -S a barroom

DRANK past tense of drink

DRAPE *v* DRAPED, DRAPING, DRAPES to arrange in graceful folds **DRAPABLE** *adj*

DRAPER *n* pl. -S a dealer in cloth

DRAPERY *n* pl. -ERIES cloth arranged in graceful folds

DRAPEY *adj* characterized by graceful folds

DRAPING present participle of drape

DRASTIC *adj* extremely severe

DRAT *v* DRATTED, DRATTING, DRATS to damn

DRAUGHT *v* -ED, -ING, -S to draft

DRAUGHTY *adj* DRAUGHTIER, DRAUGHTIEST drafty

DRAVE a past tense of drive

DRAW *v* DREW, DRAWN, DRAWING, DRAWS to move by pulling **DRAWABLE** *adj*

DRAWBACK *n* pl. -S a hindrance

DRAWBAR *n* pl. -S a railroad coupler

DRAWBORE *n* pl. -S a hole for joining a mortise and tenon

DRAWDOWN *n* pl. -S a lowering of a water level

DRAWEE *n* pl. -S the person on whom a bill of exchange is drawn

DRAWER *n* pl. -S one that draws

DRAWING *n* pl. -S a portrayal in lines of a form or figure

DRAWL *v* -ED, -ING, -S to speak slowly with vowels greatly prolonged

DRAWLER *n* pl. -S one that drawls

DRAWLY *adj* DRAWLIER, DRAWLIEST marked by drawling

DRAWN past participle of draw

DRAWTUBE *n* pl. -S a tube that slides within another tube

DRAY *v* -ED, -ING, -S to transport by dray (a low, strong cart)

DRAYAGE *n* pl. -S transportation by dray

DRAYMAN *n* pl. -MEN one who drives a dray

DREAD *v* -ED, -ING, -S to fear greatly

DREADFUL *n* pl. -S a publication containing sensational material

DREAM	*v* DREAMED or DREAMT, DREAMING, DREAMS to have a dream (a series of images occurring during sleep)	**DRIBBLING**	present participle of dribble
		DRIBBLY	*adj* tending to dribble
		DRIBLET	*n* pl. -S a small drop of liquid
DREAMER	*n* pl. -S one that dreams	**DRIED**	past tense of dry
DREAMFUL	*adj* dreamy	**DRIEGH**	*adj* dreary
DREAMT	a past tense of dream	**DRIER**	*n* pl. -S one that dries
DREAMY	*adj* DREAMIER, DREAMIEST full of dreams **DREAMILY** *adv*	**DRIES**	present 3d person sing. of dry
DREAR	*n* pl. -S the state of being dreary	**DRIEST**	a superlative of dry
DREARY	*adj* DREARIER, DREARIEST dismal **DREARILY** *adv*	**DRIFT**	*v* -ED, -ING, -S to move along in a current
DREARY	*n* pl. DREARIES a dismal person	**DRIFTAGE**	*n* pl. -S the act of drifting
DRECK	*n* pl. -S rubbish **DRECKY** *adj*	**DRIFTER**	*n* pl. -S one that drifts
DREDGE	*v* DREDGED, DREDGING, DREDGES to clear with a dredge (a machine for scooping mud)	**DRIFTPIN**	*n* pl. -S a metal rod for securing timbers
		DRIFTY	*adj* DRIFTIER, DRIFTIEST full of drifts (masses of wind-driven snow)
DREDGER	*n* pl. -S one that dredges		
DREDGING	*n* pl. -S matter that is dredged up	**DRILL**	*v* -ED, -ING, -S to bore a hole in
DREE	*v* DREED, DREEING, DREES to suffer	**DRILLER**	*n* pl. -S one that drills
		DRILLING	*n* pl. -S a heavy twilled cotton fabric
DREG	*n* pl. -S the sediment of liquors **DREGGISH** *adj*		
		DRILY	*adv* dryly
DREGGY	*adj* -GIER, -GIEST full of dregs	**DRINK**	*v* DRANK, DRUNK, DRINKING, DRINKS to swallow liquid
DREICH	*adj* dreary		
DREIDEL	*n* pl. -S a spinning toy	**DRINKER**	*n* pl. -S one that drinks
DREIDL	*n* pl. -S dreidel	**DRIP**	*v* DRIPPED or DRIPT, DRIPPING, DRIPS to fall in drops
DREIGH	*adj* dreich		
DREK	*n* pl. -S dreck	**DRIPLESS**	*adj* designed not to drip
DRENCH	*v* -ED, -ING, -ES to wet thoroughly	**DRIPPER**	*n* pl. -S something from which a liquid drips
DRENCHER	*n* pl. -S one that drenches	**DRIPPING**	*n* pl. -S juice drawn from meat during cooking
DRESS	*v* DRESSED or DREST, DRESSING, DRESSES to put clothes on	**DRIPPY**	*adj* -PIER, -PIEST very wet
		DRIPT	a past tense of drip
DRESSAGE	*n* pl. -S the training of a horse in obedience and deportment	**DRIVE**	*v* DROVE or DRAVE, DRIVEN, DRIVING, DRIVES to urge or propel forward **DRIVABLE** *adj*
DRESSER	*n* pl. -S one that dresses		
DRESSING	*n* pl. -S material applied to cover a wound	**DRIVEL**	*v* -ELED, -ELING, -ELS or -ELLED, -ELLING, -ELS to let saliva flow from the mouth
DRESSY	*adj* DRESSIER, DRESSIEST stylish **DRESSILY** *adv*		
		DRIVELER	*n* pl. -S one that drivels
DREST	a past tense of dress	**DRIVEN**	past participle of drive
DREW	past tense of draw	**DRIVER**	*n* pl. -S one that drives
DRIB	*v* DRIBBED, DRIBBING, DRIBS to drip	**DRIVEWAY**	*n* pl. -WAYS a private road providing access to a building
DRIBBLE	*v* -BLED, -BLING, -BLES to drivel	**DRIVING**	*n* pl. -S management of a motor vehicle
DRIBBLER	*n* pl. -S one that dribbles	**DRIZZLE**	*v* -ZLED, -ZLING, -ZLES to rain lightly
DRIBBLET	*n* pl. -S driblet		

DRIZZLY   *adj* -ZLIER, -ZLIEST characterized by light rain

DROGUE   *n* pl. -S a sea anchor

DROIT   *n* pl. -S a legal right

DROLL   *adj* DROLLER, DROLLEST comical

DROLL   *v* -ED, -ING, -S to jest

DROLLERY   *n* pl. -ERIES something droll

DROLLY   *adv* in a droll manner

DROMON   *n* pl. -S dromond

DROMOND   *n* pl. -S a large fast-sailing medieval galley

DRONE   *v* DRONED, DRONING, DRONES to make a continuous low sound

DRONER   *n* pl. -S one that drones

DRONGO   *n* pl. -GOS a tropical bird

DRONING   present participle of drone

DRONISH   *adj* habitually lazy

DROOL   *v* -ED, -ING, -S to drivel

DROOP   *v* -ED, -ING, -S to hang downward

DROOPY   *adj* DROOPIER, DROOPIEST drooping **DROOPILY** *adv*

DROP   *v* DROPPED or DROPT, DROPPING, DROPS to fall in drops (globules)

DROPHEAD   *n* pl. -S a convertible car

DROPKICK   *n* pl. -S a type of kick in football

DROPLET   *n* pl. -S a tiny drop

DROPOUT   *n* pl. -S one who quits school prematurely

DROPPED   a past tense of drop

DROPPER   *n* pl. -S a tube for dispensing liquid in drops

DROPPING   *n* pl. -S something that has been dropped

DROPSHOT   *n* pl. -S a type of shot in tennis

DROPSY   *n* pl. -SIES an excessive accumulation of serous fluid **DROPSIED** *adj*

DROPT   a past tense of drop

DROPWORT   *n* pl. -S a perennial herb

DROSERA   *n* pl. -S a sundew

DROSHKY   *n* pl. -KIES an open carriage

DROSKY   *n* pl. -KIES droshky

DROSS   *n* pl. -ES waste matter

DROSSY   *adj* DROSSIER, DROSSIEST worthless

DROUGHT   *n* pl. -S a dry period

DROUGHTY   *adj* DROUGHTIER, DROUGHTIEST dry

DROUK   *v* -ED, -ING, -S to drench

DROUTH   *n* pl. -S drought

DROUTHY   *adj* DROUTHIER, DROUTHIEST droughty

DROVE   *v* DROVED, DROVING, DROVES to drive cattle or sheep

DROVER   *n* pl. -S a driver of cattle or sheep

DROWN   *v* -ED, -ING, -S to suffocate in water

DROWND   *v* -ED, -ING, -S to drown

DROWNER   *n* pl. -S one that drowns

DROWSE   *v* DROWSED, DROWSING, DROWSES to doze

DROWSY   *adj* DROWSIER, DROWSIEST sleepy **DROWSILY** *adv*

DRUB   *v* DRUBBED, DRUBBING, DRUBS to beat severely

DRUBBER   *n* pl. -S one that drubs

DRUBBING   *n* pl. -S a severe beating

DRUDGE   *v* DRUDGED, DRUDGING, DRUDGES to do hard, menial, or tedious work

DRUDGER   *n* pl. -S one that drudges

DRUDGERY   *n* pl. -ERIES hard, menial, or tedious work

DRUDGING   present participle of drudge

DRUG   *v* DRUGGED, DRUGGING, DRUGS to affect with a drug (a medicinal substance)

DRUGGET   *n* pl. -S a coarse woolen fabric

DRUGGIE   *n* pl. -S a drug addict

DRUGGIST   *n* pl. -S a pharmacist

DRUGGY   *adj* -GIER, -GIEST affected by drugs

DRUID   *n* pl. -S one of an ancient Celtic order of priests **DRUIDIC** *adj*

DRUIDESS   *n* pl. -ES a female druid

DRUIDISM   *n* pl. -S the religious system of the druids

DRUM   *v* DRUMMED, DRUMMING, DRUMS to beat a drum (a percussion instrument)

DRUMBEAT   *n* pl. -S the sound of a drum

DRUMBLE   *v* -BLED, -BLING, -BLES to move slowly

DRUMFIRE   *n* pl. -S heavy, continuous gunfire

DRUMFISH	*n* pl. -ES a fish that makes a drumming sound	**DUALITY**	*n* pl. -TIES the state of being twofold
DRUMHEAD	*n* pl. -S the material stretched over the end of a drum	**DUALIZE**	*v* -IZED, -IZING, -IZES to make twofold
DRUMLIER	comparative of drumly	**DUALLY**	*adv* in two ways
DRUMLIEST	superlative of drumly	**DUB**	*v* DUBBED, DUBBING, DUBS to confer knighthood on
DRUMLIKE	*adj* resembling the head of a drum	**DUBBER**	*n* pl. -S one that dubs
DRUMLIN	*n* pl. -S a long hill of glacial drift	**DUBBIN**	*n* pl. -S material for softening and waterproofing leather
DRUMLY	*adj* -LIER, -LIEST dark and gloomy	**DUBBING**	*n* pl. -S dubbin
DRUMMED	past tense of drum	**DUBIETY**	*n* pl. -ETIES the state of being dubious
DRUMMER	*n* pl. -S one that drums	**DUBIOUS**	*adj* doubtful
DRUMMING	present participle of drum	**DUBONNET**	*n* pl. -S a red color
DRUMROLL	*n* pl. -S a roll played on a drum	**DUCAL**	*adj* pertaining to a duke (a high-ranking nobleman) **DUCALLY** *adv*
DRUNK	*adj* DRUNKER, DRUNKEST intoxicated	**DUCAT**	*n* pl. -S any of several gold coins formerly used in Europe
DRUNK	*n* pl. -S a drunken person	**DUCE**	*n* pl. DUCES or DUCI a leader
DRUNKARD	*n* pl. -S one who is habitually drunk	**DUCHESS**	*n* pl. -ES the wife or widow of a duke
DRUNKEN	*adj* drunk	**DUCHY**	*n* pl. DUCHIES the domain of a duke
DRUPE	*n* pl. -S a fleshy fruit		
DRUPELET	*n* pl. -S a small drupe	**DUCI**	a pl. of duce
DRUSE	*n* pl. -S a crust of small crystals lining a rock cavity	**DUCK**	*v* -ED, -ING, -S to lower quickly
		DUCKBILL	*n* pl. -S a platypus
DRUTHERS	*n/pl* one's preference	**DUCKER**	*n* pl. -S one that ducks
DRY	*adj* DRIER, DRIEST or DRYER, DRYEST having no moisture	**DUCKIE**	*adj* ducky
		DUCKIER	comparative of ducky
DRY	*v* DRIED, DRYING, DRIES to make dry **DRYABLE** *adj*	**DUCKIES**	pl. of ducky
		DUCKIEST	superlative of ducky
DRY	*n* pl. DRYS a prohibitionist	**DUCKLING**	*n* pl. -S a young duck
DRYAD	*n* pl. -S or -ES a nymph of the woods **DRYADIC** *adj*	**DUCKPIN**	*n* pl. -S a type of bowling pin
		DUCKTAIL	*n* pl. -S a style of haircut
DRYER	*n* pl. -S drier	**DUCKWALK**	*v* -ED, -ING, -S to walk in a squatting position
DRYISH	*adj* somewhat dry		
DRYLAND	*adj* relating to an arid region	**DUCKWEED**	*n* pl. -S an aquatic plant
DRYLOT	*n* pl. -S an enclosure for livestock	**DUCKY**	*adj* DUCKIER, DUCKIEST excellent
DRYLY	*adv* in a dry manner		
DRYNESS	*n* pl. -ES the state of being dry	**DUCKY**	*n* pl. DUCKIES a darling
DRYPOINT	*n* pl. -S a method of engraving	**DUCT**	*v* -ED, -ING, -S to convey through a duct (a tubular passage)
DRYSTONE	*adj* constructed of stone without mortar		
DRYWALL	*n* pl. -S board used instead of plaster in walls	**DUCTAL**	*adj* made up of ducts
		DUCTILE	*adj* easily molded or shaped
DUAD	*n* pl. -S a pair	**DUCTING**	*n* pl. -S a system of ducts
DUAL	*n* pl. -S a linguistic form	**DUCTLESS**	*adj* being without a duct
DUALISM	*n* pl. -S a philosophical theory		
DUALIST	*n* pl. -S an adherent of dualism		

DUCTULE	*n* pl. -S a small duct
DUCTWORK	*n* pl. -S a system of ducts
DUD	*n* pl. -S a bomb that fails to explode
DUDDIE	*adj* ragged
DUDDY	*adj* duddie
DUDE	*v* DUDED, DUDING, DUDES to dress up in flashy clothes
DUDEEN	*n* pl. -S a short tobacco pipe
DUDGEON	*n* pl. -S a feeling of resentment
DUDING	present participle of dude
DUDISH	*adj* resembling a dude (a dandy)
DUDISHLY	*adv* in the manner of a dude
DUE	*n* pl. -S something that is owed
DUECENTO	*n* pl. -TOS the thirteenth century
DUEL	*v* DUELED, DUELING, DUELS or DUELLED, DUELLING, DUELS to fight formally
DUELER	*n* pl. -S one that duels
DUELIST	*n* pl. -S a dueler
DUELLED	a past tense of duel
DUELLER	*n* pl. -S dueler
DUELLI	a pl. of duello
DUELLING	a present participle of duel
DUELLIST	*n* pl. -S duelist
DUELLO	*n* pl. -LOS or -LI the art of dueling; a duel
DUENDE	*n* pl. -S charisma
DUENESS	*n* pl. -ES the state of being owed
DUENNA	*n* pl. -S a governess
DUET	*v* DUETTED, DUETTING, DUETS to perform a duet (a musical composition for two)
DUETTIST	*n* pl. -S a participant in a duet
DUFF	*n* pl. -S a thick pudding
DUFFEL	*n* pl. -S a coarse woolen fabric
DUFFER	*n* pl. -S a clumsy person
DUFFLE	*n* pl. -S duffel
DUG	*n* pl. -S the teat or udder of a female mammal
DUGONG	*n* pl. -S an aquatic mammal
DUGOUT	*n* pl. -S a canoe made by hollowing out a log
DUI	a pl. of duo
DUIKER	*n* pl. -S a small antelope
DUIT	*n* pl. -S doit

DUKE	*v* DUKED, DUKING, DUKES to fight
DUKEDOM	*n* pl. -S a duchy
DULCET	*n* pl. -S a soft-toned organ stop
DULCETLY	*adv* melodiously
DULCIANA	*n* pl. -S a soft-toned organ stop
DULCIFY	*v* -FIED, -FYING, -FIES to sweeten
DULCIMER	*n* pl. -S a stringed instrument
DULCINEA	*n* pl. -S a sweetheart
DULIA	*n* pl. -S veneration of saints
DULL	*adj* DULLER, DULLEST mentally slow
DULL	*v* -ED, -ING, -S to make less sharp
DULLARD	*n* pl. -S a dolt
DULLISH	*adj* somewhat dull
DULLNESS	*n* pl. -ES the state of being dull
DULLY	*adv* in a dull manner
DULNESS	*n* pl. -ES dullness
DULSE	*n* pl. -S an edible seaweed
DULY	*adv* rightfully
DUMA	*n* pl. -S a Russian council
DUMB	*adj* DUMBER, DUMBEST incapable of speech
DUMB	*v* -ED, -ING, -S to make silent
DUMBBELL	*n* pl. -S a weight lifted for muscular exercise
DUMBCANE	*n* pl. -S a tropical plant
DUMBHEAD	*n* pl. -S a stupid person
DUMBLY	*adv* in a dumb manner
DUMBNESS	*n* pl. -ES the state of being dumb
DUMDUM	*n* pl. -S a type of bullet
DUMFOUND	*v* -ED, -ING, -S to astonish
DUMKA	*n* pl. -KY a Slavic folk ballad
DUMMKOPF	*n* pl. -S a dolt
DUMMY	*v* -MIED, -MYING, -MIES to make a representation of
DUMP	*v* -ED, -ING, -S to let fall heavily
DUMPCART	*n* pl. -S a type of cart
DUMPER	*n* pl. -S one that dumps
DUMPIER	comparative of dumpy
DUMPIEST	superlative of dumpy
DUMPILY	*adv* in a dumpy manner
DUMPING	*n* pl. -S the selling of large quantities of goods at below the market price

DUMPISH	*adj* sad	**DUOPOLY**	*n* pl. -LIES the market condition existing when there are two sellers only
DUMPLING	*n* pl. -S a ball of dough cooked with stew or soup		
DUMPY	*adj* DUMPIER, DUMPIEST short and thick	**DUOPSONY**	*n* pl. -NIES the market condition existing when there are two buyers only
DUN	*v* DUNNED, DUNNING, DUNS to make demands upon for payment of a debt	**DUOTONE**	*n* pl. -S an illustration in two tones
		DUP	*v* DUPPED, DUPPING, DUPS to open
DUN	*adj* DUNNER, DUNNEST of a dull brown color	**DUPE**	*v* DUPED, DUPING, DUPES to deceive **DUPABLE** *adj*
DUNAM	*n* pl. -S a unit of land measure in Israel	**DUPER**	*n* pl. -S one that dupes
DUNCE	*n* pl. -S a stupid person **DUNCICAL, DUNCISH** *adj*	**DUPERY**	*n* pl. -ERIES the act of duping
		DUPING	present participle of dupe
DUNCH	*n* pl. -ES a push	**DUPLE**	*adj* having two parts or elements
DUNE	*n* pl. -S a hill of sand **DUNELIKE** *adj*	**DUPLEX**	*v* -ED, -ING, -ES to make duple
DUNELAND	*n* pl. -S an area having many dunes	**DUPLEXER**	*n* pl. -S an electronic switching device
DUNG	*v* -ED, -ING, -S to fertilize with manure	**DUPPED**	past tense of dup
		DUPPING	present participle of dup
DUNGAREE	*n* pl. -S a coarse cotton fabric	**DURA**	*n* pl. -S durra
DUNGEON	*v* -ED, -ING, -S to confine in a dungeon (an underground prison)	**DURABLE**	*adj* able to withstand wear or decay **DURABLY** *adv*
DUNGHILL	*n* pl. -S a heap of manure	**DURABLES**	*n/pl* durable goods
DUNGY	*adj* DUNGIER, DUNGIEST filthy	**DURAL**	*adj* of the dura mater (a brain membrane)
DUNITE	*n* pl. -S an igneous rock **DUNITIC** *adj*	**DURAMEN**	*n* pl. -S the central wood of a tree
DUNK	*v* -ED, -ING, -S to dip into liquid	**DURANCE**	*n* pl. -S restraint by or as if by physical force
DUNKER	*n* pl. -S one that dunks		
DUNLIN	*n* pl. -S a wading bird	**DURATION**	*n* pl. -S continuance in time
DUNNAGE	*n* pl. -S packing material used to protect cargo	**DURATIVE**	*n* pl. -S a type of verb
		DURBAR	*n* pl. -S the court of a native ruler in India
DUNNED	past tense of dun		
DUNNER	comparative of dun	**DURE**	*v* DURED, DURING, DURES to endure
DUNNESS	*n* pl. -ES the state of being dun		
DUNNEST	superlative of dun	**DURESS**	*n* pl. -ES compulsion by threat
DUNNING	present participle of dun	**DURIAN**	*n* pl. -S an East Indian tree
DUNNITE	*n* pl. -S an explosive	**DURING**	*prep* throughout the duration of
DUNT	*v* -ED, -ING, -S to strike with a heavy blow	**DURION**	*n* pl. -S durian
		DURMAST	*n* pl. -S a European oak
DUO	*n* pl. DUOS or DUI an instrumental duet	**DURN**	*v* -ED, -ING, -S to damn
DUODENUM	*n* pl. -DENA or -DENUMS the first portion of the small intestine **DUODENAL** *adj*	**DURNED**	*adj* DURNEDER, DURNEDEST or DURNDEST damned
		DURO	*n* pl. -ROS a Spanish silver dollar
DUOLOG	*n* pl. -S duologue	**DUROC**	*n* pl. -S a large red hog
DUOLOGUE	*n* pl. -S a conversation between two persons	**DURR**	*n* pl. -S durra
		DURRA	*n* pl. -S a cereal grain
DUOMO	*n* pl. -MOS or -MI a cathedral	**DURRIE**	*n* pl. -S dhurrie

DURST	a past tense of dare
DURUM	n pl. -S a kind of wheat
DUSK	v -ED, -ING, -S to become dark
DUSKISH	adj dusky
DUSKY	adj DUSKIER, DUSKIEST somewhat dark **DUSKILY** adv
DUST	v -ED, -ING, -S to make free of dust (minute particles of matter)
DUSTBIN	n pl. -S a trash can
DUSTER	n pl. -S one that dusts
DUSTHEAP	n pl. -S a pile of trash
DUSTIER	comparative of dusty
DUSTIEST	superative of dusty
DUSTILY	adv in a dusty manner
DUSTLESS	adj being without dust
DUSTLIKE	adj resembling dust
DUSTMAN	n pl. -MEN a trashman
DUSTOFF	n pl. -S a military helicopter for evacuating the wounded
DUSTPAN	n pl. -S a pan for holding swept dust
DUSTRAG	n pl. -S a rag used for dusting
DUSTUP	n pl. -S an argument
DUSTY	adj DUSTIER, DUSTIEST full of dust
DUTCH	adv with each person paying for himself
DUTCHMAN	n pl. -MEN something used to hide structural defects
DUTEOUS	adj dutiful
DUTIABLE	adj subject to import tax
DUTIFUL	adj obedient
DUTY	n pl. -TIES a moral or legal obligation
DUUMVIR	n pl. -VIRS or -VIRI a magistrate of ancient Rome
DUVET	n pl. -S a down-filled bed covering
DUVETINE	n pl. -S duvetyn
DUVETYN	n pl. -S a soft fabric
DUVETYNE	n pl. -S duvetyn
DUXELLES	n pl. DUXELLES a garnish or sauce with minced mushrooms
DWARF	adj DWARFER, DWARFEST extremely small
DWARF	n pl. DWARFS or DWARVES an extremely small person
DWARF	v -ED, -ING, -S to cause to appear small
DWARFISH	adj resembling a dwarf
DWARFISM	n pl. -S a condition of stunted growth
DWARVES	a pl. of dwarf
DWEEB	n pl. -S an unattractive or inept person
DWELL	v DWELT or DWELLED, DWELLING, DWELLS to reside
DWELLER	n pl. -S one that dwells
DWELLING	n pl. -S a place of residence
DWELT	a past tense of dwell
DWINDLE	v -DLED, -DLING, -DLES to decrease steadily
DWINE	v DWINED, DWINING, DWINES to pine or waste away
DYABLE	adj dyeable
DYAD	n pl. -S a pair of units
DYADIC	n pl. -S a sum of mathematical dyads
DYARCHY	n pl. -CHIES diarchy **DYARCHIC** adj
DYBBUK	n pl. -BUKS or -BUKIM a wandering soul in Jewish folklore
DYE	v DYED, DYEING, DYES to treat with a dye (a coloring matter)
DYEABLE	adj capable of being dyed
DYEING	n pl. -S something colored with a dye
DYER	n pl. -S one that dyes
DYESTUFF	n pl. -S a dye
DYEWEED	n pl. -S a shrub that yields a yellow dye
DYEWOOD	n pl. -S a wood from which a dye is extracted
DYING	n pl. -S a passing out of existence
DYKE	v DYKED, DYKING, DYKES to dike
DYNAMIC	n pl. -S a physical force
DYNAMISM	n pl. -S a theory that explains the universe in terms of force or energy
DYNAMIST	n pl. -S an adherent of dynamism
DYNAMITE	v -MITED, -MITING, -MITES to blow up with a powerful explosive
DYNAMO	n pl. -MOS a generator
DYNAST	n pl. -S a ruler
DYNASTY	n pl. -TIES a succession of rulers from the same line of descent **DYNASTIC** adj

DYNATRON	*n* pl. -S a type of electron tube
DYNE	*n* pl. -S a unit of force
DYNEIN	*n* pl. DYNEIN an enzyme involved in cell movement
DYNEL	*n* pl. -S a synthetic fiber
DYNODE	*n* pl. -S a type of electrode
DYSGENIC	*adj* causing the deterioration of hereditary qualities
DYSLEXIA	*n* pl. -S impairment of the ability to read
DYSLEXIC	*n* pl. -S one who is affected with dyslexia
DYSPEPSY	*n* pl. -SIES indigestion
DYSPNEA	*n* pl. -S labored breathing **DYSPNEAL, DYSPNEIC** *adj*
DYSPNOEA	*n* pl. -S dyspnea **DYSPNOIC** *adj*
DYSTAXIA	*n* pl. -S a form of muscular tremor
DYSTOCIA	*n* pl. -S difficult labor and delivery in childbirth
DYSTONIA	*n* pl. -S a condition of disordered tonicity of muscle tissue **DYSTONIC** *adj*
DYSTOPIA	*n* pl. -S a wretched place
DYSURIA	*n* pl. -S painful urination **DYSURIC** *adj*
DYVOUR	*n* pl. -S one who is bankrupt

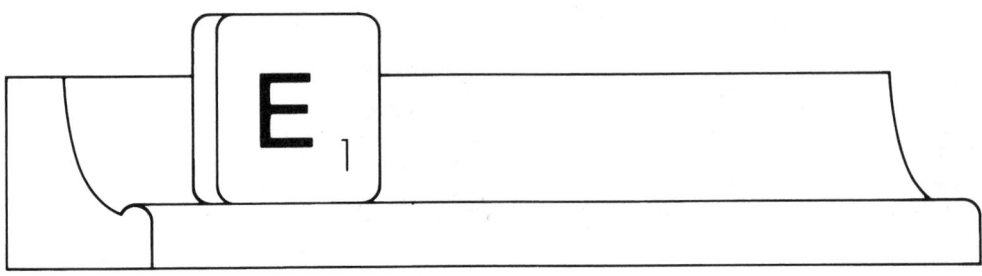

EACH   *adj* being one of two or more distinct individuals

EAGER   *adj* -GERER, -GEREST impatiently longing **EAGERLY** *adv*

EAGER   *n* pl. -S eagre

EAGLE   *n* pl. -S a large bird of prey

EAGLET   *n* pl. -S a young eagle

EAGRE   *n* pl. -S a tidal flood

EANLING   *n* pl. -S yeanling

EAR   *v* -ED, -ING, -S to form the fruiting head of a cereal

EARACHE   *n* pl. -S a pain in the ear (an organ of hearing)

EARDROP   *n* pl. -S an earring

EARDRUM   *n* pl. -S the tympanic membrane

EARED   *adj* having ears

EARFLAP   *n* pl. -S a part of a cap designed to cover the ears

EARFUL   *n* pl. -S a flow of information

EARING   *n* pl. -S a line on a ship

EARL   *n* pl. -S a British nobleman

EARLAP   *n* pl. -S an earflap

EARLDOM   *n* pl. -S the rank of an earl

EARLESS   *adj* lacking ears

EARLIER   comparative of early

EARLIEST   superlative of early

EARLOBE   *n* pl. -S a part of the ear

EARLOCK   *n* pl. -S a curl of hair by the ear

EARLSHIP   *n* pl. -S earldom

EARLY   *adv* -LIER, -LIEST near the beginning of a period of time or a series of events

EARMARK   *v* -ED, -ING, -S to designate for a specific use

EARMUFF   *n* pl. -S one of a pair of ear coverings

EARN   *v* -ED, -ING, -S to gain or deserve for one's labor or service

EARNER   *n* pl. -S one that earns

EARNEST   *n* pl. -S a down payment

EARNINGS   *n/pl* something earned

EARPHONE   *n* pl. -S a listening device worn over the ear

EARPIECE   *n* pl. -S an earphone

EARPLUG   *n* pl. -S a plug for the ear

EARRING   *n* pl. -S an ornament for the earlobe

EARSHOT   *n* pl. -S the range within which sound can be heard

EARSTONE   *n* pl. -S an otolith

EARTH   *v* -ED, -ING, -S to cover with earth (soil)

EARTHEN   *adj* made of earth

EARTHIER   comparative of earthy

EARTHIEST   superlative of earthy

EARTHILY   *adv* in an earthy manner

EARTHLY   *adj* -LIER, -LIEST worldly

EARTHMAN   *n* pl. -MEN a person from the planet earth

EARTHNUT   *n* pl. -S a European herb

EARTHPEA   *n* pl. -S a twining plant

EARTHSET   *n* pl. -S the setting of the earth as seen from the moon

EARTHY   *adj* EARTHIER, EARTHIEST composed of, resembling, or suggestive of earth

EARWAX   *n* pl. -ES cerumen

EARWIG   *v* -WIGGED, -WIGGING, -WIGS to insinuate against in secret

EARWORM   *n* pl. -S a bollworm

EASE   *v* EASED, EASING, EASES to give rest or relief to

EASEFUL   *adj* restful

EASEL   *n* pl. -S a three-legged frame

EASEMENT   *n* pl. -S relief

EASIER   comparative of easy

EASIES	pl. of easy
EASIEST	superlative of easy
EASILY	*adv* without difficulty
EASINESS	*n* pl. -ES the state of being easy
EASING	present participle of ease
EAST	*n* pl. -S a cardinal point of the compass
EASTER	*n* pl. -S a wind or storm from the east
EASTERLY	*n* pl. -LIES a wind from the east
EASTERN	*adj* being to, toward, or in the east
EASTING	*n* pl. -S a movement toward the east
EASTWARD	*n* pl. -S a direction toward the east
EASY	*adj* EASIER, EASIEST not difficult
EASY	*n* pl. EASIES a communications code word for the letter E
EAT	*v* ATE or ET, EATEN, EATING, EATS to consume food
EATABLE	*n* pl. -S an edible
EATER	*n* pl. -S one that eats
EATERY	*n* pl. -ERIES a lunchroom
EATH	*adj* easy
EATING	*n* pl. -S the act of consuming food
EAU	*n* pl. EAUX water
EAVE	*n* pl. -S the lower projecting edge of a roof **EAVED** *adj*
EBB	*v* -ED, -ING, -S to recede
EBBET	*n* pl. -S a common green newt
EBON	*n* pl. -S ebony
EBONIES	pl. of ebony
EBONISE	*v* -ISED, -ISING, -ISES to ebonize
EBONITE	*n* pl. -S a hard rubber
EBONIZE	*v* -IZED, -IZING, -IZES to stain black in imitation of ebony
EBONY	*n* pl. -NIES a hard, heavy wood
ECARTE	*n* pl. -S a card game
ECAUDATE	*adj* having no tail
ECBOLIC	*n* pl. -S a type of drug
ECCLESIA	*n* pl. -SIAE an assembly in ancient Greece
ECCRINE	*adj* producing secretions externally

ECDYSIS	*n* pl. -DYSES the shedding of an outer layer of skin **ECDYSIAL** *adj*
ECDYSON	*n* pl. -S ecdysone
ECDYSONE	*n* pl. -S an insect hormone
ECESIS	*n* pl. -SISES the establishment of a plant or animal in a new environment
ECHARD	*n* pl. -S the water in the soil not available to plants
ECHE	*v* ECHED, ECHING, ECHES to increase
ECHELLE	*n* pl. -S a device for spreading light into its component colors
ECHELON	*v* -ED, -ING, -S to group in a particular formation
ECHIDNA	*n* pl. -NAS or -NAE a spiny anteater
ECHINATE	*adj* spiny
ECHING	present participle of eche
ECHINOID	*n* pl. -S a spiny marine animal
ECHINUS	*n* pl. -NI echinoid
ECHO	*v* -ED, -ING, -ES to produce an echo
ECHO	*n* pl. ECHOES or ECHOS a repetition of sound by reflection of sound waves
ECHOER	*n* pl. -S one that echoes
ECHOEY	*adj* full of echoes
ECHOGRAM	*n* pl. -S a record produced by a device that uses ultrasonic waves
ECHOIC	*adj* resembling an echo
ECHOISM	*n* pl. -S the formation of words in imitation of sounds
ECHOLESS	*adj* producing no echo
ECLAIR	*n* pl. -S a type of pastry
ECLAT	*n* pl. -S brilliance
ECLECTIC	*n* pl. -S one who draws his beliefs from various sources
ECLIPSE	*v* ECLIPSED, ECLIPSING, ECLIPSES to obscure
ECLIPSIS	*n* pl. ECLIPSES or ECLIPSISES an ellipsis
ECLIPTIC	*n* pl. -S an astronomical plane
ECLOGITE	*n* pl. -S a type of rock
ECLOGUE	*n* pl. -S a pastoral poem
ECLOSION	*n* pl. -S the emergence of an insect larva from an egg
ECOCIDE	*n* pl. -S the destruction of the natural environment **ECOCIDAL** *adj*

ECOFREAK	*n* pl. -S a zealous environmentalist
ECOLOGY	*n* pl. -GIES an environmental science **ECOLOGIC** *adj*
ECONOBOX	*n* pl. -ES a small economical car
ECONOMIC	*adj* pertaining to financial matters
ECONOMY	*n* pl. -MIES thrift
ECOTONE	*n* pl. -S a type of ecological zone **ECOTONAL** *adj*
ECOTYPE	*n* pl. -S a subspecies adapted to specific environmental conditions **ECOTYPIC** *adj*
ECRASEUR	*n* pl. -S a surgical instrument
ECRU	*n* pl. -S a yellowish brown color
ECSTASY	*n* pl. -SIES a state of exaltation
ECSTATIC	*n* pl. -S one that is subject to ecstasies
ECTASIS	*n* pl. -TASES the lengthening of a usually short syllable **ECTATIC** *adj*
ECTHYMA	*n* pl. -MATA a virus disease
ECTODERM	*n* pl. -S the outermost germ layer of an embryo
ECTOMERE	*n* pl. -S a cell that develops into ectoderm
ECTOPIA	*n* pl. -S congenital displacement of parts or organs **ECTOPIC** *adj*
ECTOSARC	*n* pl. -S the outermost layer of protoplasm of certain protozoans
ECTOZOAN	*n* pl. -S ectozoon
ECTOZOON	*n* pl. -ZOA a parasite on the body of an animal
ECTYPE	*n* pl. -S a copy **ECTYPAL** *adj*
ECU	*n* pl. -S an old French coin
ECUMENIC	*adj* universal
ECZEMA	*n* pl. -S a skin disease
ED	*n* pl. ED education
EDACIOUS	*adj* voracious
EDACITY	*n* pl. -TIES gluttony
EDAPHIC	*adj* pertaining to the soil
EDDO	*n* pl. -DOES a tropical plant
EDDY	*v* -DIED, -DYING, -DIES to move against the main current
EDEMA	*n* pl. -MAS or -MATA an excessive accumulation of serous fluid
EDENIC	*adj* pertaining to a paradise
EDENTATE	*n* pl. -S a toothless mammal

EDGE	*v* EDGED, EDGING, EDGES to provide with an edge (a bounding or dividing line)
EDGELESS	*adj* lacking an edge
EDGER	*n* pl. -S a tool used to trim a lawn's edge
EDGEWAYS	*adv* edgewise
EDGEWISE	*adv* sideways
EDGIER	comparative of edgy
EDGIEST	superlative of edgy
EDGILY	*adv* in an edgy manner
EDGINESS	*n* pl. -ES the state of being edgy
EDGING	*n* pl. -S something that forms or serves as an edge
EDGY	*adj* EDGIER, EDGIEST tense, nervous, or irritable
EDH	*n* pl. -S an Old English letter
EDIBLE	*n* pl. -S something fit to be eaten
EDICT	*n* pl. -S an authoritative order having the force of law **EDICTAL** *adj*
EDIFICE	*n* pl. -S a building
EDIFIER	*n* pl. -S one that edifies
EDIFY	*v* -FIED, -FYING, -FIES to enlighten
EDILE	*n* pl. -S aedile
EDIT	*v* -ED, -ING, -S to correct and prepare for publication **EDITABLE** *adj*
EDITION	*n* pl. -S a particular series of printed material
EDITOR	*n* pl. -S one that edits
EDITRESS	*n* pl. -ES a female editor
EDUCABLE	*n* pl. -S a mildly retarded person
EDUCATE	*v* -CATED, -CATING, -CATES to teach
EDUCATOR	*n* pl. -S one that educates
EDUCE	*v* EDUCED, EDUCING, EDUCES to draw forth or bring out **EDUCIBLE** *adj*
EDUCT	*n* pl. -S something educed
EDUCTION	*n* pl. -S the act of educing **EDUCTIVE** *adj*
EDUCTOR	*n* pl. -S one that educes
EEL	*n* pl. -S a snakelike fish
EELGRASS	*n* pl. -ES an aquatic plant
EELIER	comparative of eely
EELIEST	superlative of eely
EELLIKE	*adj* resembling an eel

EELPOUT   *n* pl. -S a marine fish

EELWORM   *n* pl. -S a small roundworm

EELY   *adj* EELIER, EELIEST resembling an eel

EERIE   *adj* -RIER, -RIEST weird **EERILY** *adv*

EERINESS   *n* pl. -ES the state of being eerie

EERY   *adj* -RIER, -RIEST eerie

EF   *n* pl. -S the letter F

EFF   *n* pl. -S ef

EFFABLE   *adj* capable of being uttered or expressed

EFFACE   *v* -FACED, -FACING, -FACES to rub or wipe out

EFFACER   *n* pl. -S one that effaces

EFFECT   *v* -ED, -ING, -S to bring about

EFFECTER   *n* pl. -S effector

EFFECTOR   *n* pl. -S a bodily organ that responds to a nerve impulse

EFFENDI   *n* pl. -S a Turkish title of respect

EFFERENT   *n* pl. -S an organ or part conveying nervous impulses to an effector

EFFETE   *adj* exhausted of vigor or energy **EFFETELY** *adv*

EFFICACY   *n* pl. -CIES effectiveness

EFFIGIAL   *adj* resembling an effigy

EFFIGY   *n* pl. -GIES a likeness or representation

EFFLUENT   *n* pl. -S an outflow

EFFLUVIA   *n/pl* byproducts in the form of waste

EFFLUX   *n* pl. -ES an outflow

EFFORT   *n* pl. -S a deliberate exertion

EFFULGE   *v* -FULGED, -FULGING, -FULGES to shine forth

EFFUSE   *v* -FUSED, -FUSING, -FUSES to pour forth

EFFUSION   *n* pl. -S an outpouring of emotion

EFFUSIVE   *adj* pouring forth

EFT   *n* pl. -S a newt

EFTSOON   *adv* soon afterward

EFTSOONS   *adv* eftsoon

EGAD   *interj* — used as a mild oath

EGADS   *interj* egad

EGAL   *adj* equal

EGALITE   *n* pl. -S equality

EGER   *n* pl. -S eagre

EGEST   *v* -ED, -ING, -S to discharge from the body

EGESTA   *n/pl* egested matter

EGESTION   *n* pl. -S the act of egesting **EGESTIVE** *adj*

EGG   *v* -ED, -ING, -S to incite or urge

EGGAR   *n* pl. -S egger

EGGCUP   *n* pl. -S a cup from which an egg is eaten

EGGER   *n* pl. -S a kind of moth

EGGHEAD   *n* pl. -S an intellectual

EGGLESS   *adj* lacking eggs

EGGNOG   *n* pl. -S a beverage

EGGPLANT   *n* pl. -S a perennial herb yielding edible fruit

EGGSHELL   *n* pl. -S the hard exterior of a bird's egg

EGGY   *adj* containing eggs

EGIS   *n* pl. EGISES aegis

EGLATERE   *n* pl. -S a wild rose

EGLOMISE   *adj* made of glass with a painted picture on the back

EGO   *n* pl. EGOS the conscious self

EGOISM   *n* pl. -S extreme devotion to self-interest

EGOIST   *n* pl. -S one who practices egoism **EGOISTIC** *adj*

EGOLESS   *adj* not characterized by egoism

EGOMANIA   *n* pl. -S extreme egotism

EGOTISM   *n* pl. -S self-conceit

EGOTIST   *n* pl. -S a conceited person

EGRESS   *v* -ED, -ING, -ES to go out

EGRET   *n* pl. -S a wading bird

EGYPTIAN   *n* pl. -S a typeface with squared serifs

EH   *interj* — used to express doubt or surprise

EIDE   pl. of eidos

EIDER   *n* pl. -S a large sea duck

EIDETIC   *adj* pertaining to vivid recall

EIDOLIC   *adj* pertaining to an eidolon

EIDOLON   *n* pl. -LONS or -LA a phantom

EIDOS   *n* pl. EIDE an essence

EIGHT   *n* pl. -S a number

EIGHTEEN   *n* pl. -S a number

EIGHTH   *n* pl. -S one of eight equal parts

EIGHTHLY   *adv* in the eighth place

EIGHTVO   *n* pl. -VOS octavo

EIGHTY   *n* pl. EIGHTIES a number

EIKON   *n* pl. -S or -ES icon

EINKORN   *n* pl. -S a variety of wheat

EINSTEIN   *n* pl. -S a very intelligent person

EIRENIC   *adj* irenic

EISWEIN   *n* pl. -S a sweet German wine

EITHER   *adj* being one or the other

EJECT   *v* -ED, -ING, -S to throw out forcibly

EJECTA   *n/pl* ejected material

EJECTION   *n* pl. -S the act of ejecting

EJECTIVE   *n* pl. -S a sound produced with air compressed above the closed glottis

EJECTOR   *n* pl. -S one that ejects

EKE   *v* EKED, EKING, EKES to supplement with great effort

EKISTICS   *n/pl* a science dealing with human habitats **EKISTIC** *adj*

EKPWELE   *n* pl. -S a former monetary unit of Equatorial Guinea

EKTEXINE   *n* pl. -S an outer layer of the exine

EKUELE   *n* pl. EKUELE ekpwele

EL   *n* pl. -S an elevated railroad or train

ELAIN   *n* pl. -S olein

ELAN   *n* pl. -S enthusiasm

ELAND   *n* pl. -S a large antelope

ELAPHINE   *adj* pertaining to a genus of deer

ELAPID   *n* pl. -S a venomous snake

ELAPINE   *adj* pertaining to a family of snakes

ELAPSE   *v* ELAPSED, ELAPSING, ELAPSES to pass away

ELASTASE   *n* pl. -S an enzyme

ELASTIC   *n* pl. -S a stretchable material

ELASTIN   *n* pl. -S a bodily protein

ELATE   *v* ELATED, ELATING, ELATES to raise the spirits of **ELATEDLY** *adv*

ELATER   *n* pl. -S a click beetle

ELATERID   *n* pl. -S an elater

ELATERIN   *n* pl. -S a chemical compound

ELATING   present participle of elate

ELATION   *n* pl. -S a feeling of great joy

ELATIVE   *n* pl. -S an adjectival form in some languages

ELBOW   *v* -ED, -ING, -S to jostle

ELD   *n* pl. -S old age

ELDER   *n* pl. -S an older person

ELDERLY   *n* pl. -LIES a rather old person

ELDEST   *adj* oldest

ELDRESS   *n* pl. -ES a female elder (a church officer)

ELDRICH   *adj* eldritch

ELDRITCH   *adj* weird

ELECT   *v* -ED, -ING, -S to select by vote for an office

ELECTEE   *n* pl. -S a person who has been elected

ELECTION   *n* pl. -S the act of electing

ELECTIVE   *n* pl. -S an optional course of study

ELECTOR   *n* pl. -S one that elects

ELECTRET   *n* pl. -S a type of nonconductor

ELECTRIC   *n* pl. -S something run by electricity

ELECTRO   *v* -ED, -ING, -S to make a metallic copy of a page of type for printing

ELECTRON   *n* pl. -S an elementary particle

ELECTRUM   *n* pl. -S an alloy of gold and silver

ELEGANCE   *n* pl. -S tasteful opulence

ELEGANCY   *n* pl. -CIES elegance

ELEGANT   *adj* tastefully opulent

ELEGIAC   *n* pl. -S a type of verse

ELEGIES   pl. of elegy

ELEGISE   *v* -GISED, -GISING, -GISES to elegize

ELEGIST   *n* pl. -S one that writes elegies

ELEGIT   *n* pl. -S a type of judicial writ

ELEGIZE   *v* -GIZED, -GIZING, -GIZES to write an elegy

ELEGY   *n* pl. -GIES a mournful poem for one who is dead

ELEMENT   *n* pl. -S a substance that cannot be separated into simpler substances by chemical means

ELEMI   *n* pl. -S a fragrant resin

ELENCHUS   *n* pl. -CHI a logical refutation **ELENCHIC, ELENCTIC** *adj*

ELEPHANT   *n* pl. -S a large mammal

ELEVATE   *v* -VATED, -VATING, -VATES to raise

ELEVATED	*n* pl. -S a railway that operates on a raised structure	**ELOPE**	*v* ELOPED, ELOPING, ELOPES to run off secretly to be married
ELEVATOR	*n* pl. -S one that elevates	**ELOPER**	*n* pl. -S one that elopes
ELEVEN	*n* pl. -S a number	**ELOQUENT**	*adj* fluent and convincing in speech
ELEVENTH	*n* pl. -S one of eleven equal parts		
ELEVON	*n* pl. -S a type of airplane control surface	**ELSE**	*adv* in a different place, time, or way
ELF	*n* pl. ELVES a small, often mischievous fairy **ELFLIKE** *adj*	**ELUANT**	*n* pl. -S a solvent
		ELUATE	*n* pl. -S the material obtained by eluting
ELFIN	*n* pl. -S an elf		
ELFISH	*adj* resembling an elf **ELFISHLY** *adv*	**ELUDE**	*v* ELUDED, ELUDING, ELUDES to evade
ELFLOCK	*n* pl. -S a lock of tangled hair	**ELUDER**	*n* pl. -S one that eludes
ELHI	*adj* pertaining to school grades 1 through 12	**ELUENT**	*n* pl. -S eluant
		ELUSION	*n* pl. -S the act of eluding
ELICIT	*v* -ED, -ING, -S to educe	**ELUSIVE**	*adj* tending to elude
ELICITOR	*n* pl. -S one that elicits	**ELUSORY**	*adj* elusive
ELIDE	*v* ELIDED, ELIDING, ELIDES to omit **ELIDIBLE** *adj*	**ELUTE**	*v* ELUTED, ELUTING, ELUTES to remove by means of a solvent
ELIGIBLE	*n* pl. -S one that is qualified to be chosen	**ELUTION**	*n* pl. -S the act of eluting
		ELUVIA	a pl. of eluvium
ELIGIBLY	*adv* in a qualified manner	**ELUVIAL**	*adj* pertaining to an eluvium
ELINT	*n* pl. -S the gathering of intelligence by electronic devices	**ELUVIATE**	*v* -ATED, -ATING, -ATES to undergo a transfer of materials in the soil
ELISION	*n* pl. -S the act of eliding		
ELITE	*n* pl. -S a socially superior group	**ELUVIUM**	*n* pl. -VIA or -VIUMS a soil deposit .
ELITISM	*n* pl. -S belief in rule by an elite		
ELITIST	*n* pl. -S an adherent of elitism	**ELVER**	*n* pl. -S a young eel
ELIXIR	*n* pl. -S a medicinal beverage	**ELVES**	pl. of elf
ELK	*n* pl. -S a large deer	**ELVISH**	*adj* elfish **ELVISHLY** *adv*
ELKHOUND	*n* pl. -S a hunting dog	**ELYSIAN**	*adj* delightful
ELL	*n* pl. -S the letter L	**ELYTRON**	*n* pl. -TRA a hardened forewing of certain insects **ELYTROID, ELYTROUS** *adj*
ELLIPSE	*n* pl. -S a type of plane curve		
ELLIPSIS	*n* pl. -LIPSES an omission of a word or words in a sentence	**ELYTRUM**	*n* pl. -TRA elytron
		EM	*n* pl. -S the letter M
ELLIPTIC	*adj* having the shape of an ellipse	**EMACIATE**	*v* -ATED, -ATING, -ATES to make thin
ELM	*n* pl. -S a deciduous tree	**EMANATE**	*v* -NATED, -NATING, -NATES to send forth
ELMY	*adj* -MIER, -MIEST abounding in elms		
		EMANATOR	*n* pl. -S one that emanates
ELODEA	*n* pl. -S an aquatic herb	**EMBALM**	*v* -ED, -ING, -S to treat so as to protect from decay
ELOIGN	*v* -ED, -ING, -S to remove to a distant place		
		EMBALMER	*n* pl. -S one that embalms
ELOIGNER	*n* pl. -S one that eloigns	**EMBANK**	*v* -ED, -ING, -S to confine or protect with a raised structure
ELOIN	*v* -ED, -ING, -S to eloign		
ELOINER	*n* pl. -S one that eloins	**EMBAR**	*v* -BARRED, -BARRING, -BARS to imprison
ELONGATE	*v* -GATED, -GATING, -GATES to lengthen	**EMBARGO**	*v* -ED, -ING, -ES to restrain trade by a governmental order

EMBARK v -ED, -ING, -S to make a start

EMBARRED past tense of embar

EMBARRING present participle of embar

EMBASSY n pl. -SIES the headquarters of an ambassador

EMBATTLE v -TLED, -TLING, -TLES to prepare for battle

EMBAY v -ED, -ING, -S to enclose in a bay

EMBED v -BEDDED, -BEDDING, -BEDS to fix firmly into a surrounding mass

EMBER n pl. -S a glowing fragment from a fire

EMBEZZLE v -ZLED, -ZLING, -ZLES to appropriate fraudulently to one's own use

EMBITTER v -ED, -ING, -S to make bitter

EMBLAZE v -BLAZED, -BLAZING, -BLAZES to set on fire

EMBLAZER n pl. -S one that emblazes

EMBLAZON v -ED, -ING, -S to decorate with brilliant colors

EMBLEM v -ED, -ING, -S to represent with an emblem (a graphical symbol)

EMBODIER n pl. -S one that embodies

EMBODY v -BODIED, -BODYING, -BODIES to provide with a body

EMBOLDEN v -ED, -ING, -S to instill with courage

EMBOLI pl. of embolus

EMBOLIES pl. of emboly

EMBOLISM n pl. -S the obstruction of a blood vessel by an embolus **EMBOLIC** adj

EMBOLUS n pl. -LI an abnormal particle circulating in the blood

EMBOLY n pl. -LIES a phase of embryonic growth

EMBORDER v -ED, -ING, -S to provide with a border

EMBOSK v -ED, -ING, -S to conceal with foliage

EMBOSOM v -ED, -ING, -S to embrace

EMBOSS v -ED, -ING, -ES to decorate with raised designs

EMBOSSER n pl. -S one that embosses

EMBOW v -ED, -ING, -S to arch

EMBOWEL v -ELED, -ELING, -ELS or -ELLED, -ELLING, -ELS to disbowel

EMBOWER v -ED, -ING, -S to surround with foliage

EMBRACE v -BRACED, -BRACING, -BRACES to hug

EMBRACER n pl. -S one that embraces

EMBROIL v -ED, -ING, -S to involve in conflict

EMBROWN v -ED, -ING, -S to make brown

EMBRUE v -BRUED, -BRUING, -BRUES to imbrue

EMBRUTE v -BRUTED, -BRUTING, -BRUTES to imbrute

EMBRYO n pl. -BRYOS an organism in its early stages of development

EMBRYOID n pl. -S a mass of tissue that resembles an embryo

EMBRYON n pl. -S an embryo

EMCEE v -CEED, -CEEING, -CEES to serve as master of ceremonies

EME n pl. -S an uncle

EMEER n pl. -S emir

EMEERATE n pl. -S emirate

EMEND v -ED, -ING, -S to correct

EMENDATE v -DATED, -DATING, -DATES to emend

EMENDER n pl. -S one that emends

EMERALD n pl. -S a green gem

EMERGE v EMERGED, EMERGING, EMERGES to come out into view

EMERGENT n pl. -S a type of aquatic plant

EMERIES pl. of emery

EMERITA n pl. -TAE a retired woman who retains an honorary title

EMERITUS n pl. -TI a retired person who retains an honorary title

EMEROD n pl. -S a tumor

EMEROID n pl. -S emerod

EMERSED adj standing out of water

EMERSION n pl. -S the act of emerging

EMERY n pl. -ERIES a granular corundum

EMESIS n pl. EMESES the act of vomiting

EMETIC n pl. -S a substance which induces vomiting

EMETIN n pl. -S emetine

EMETINE n pl. -S an alkaloid

EMEU n pl. -S emu

EMEUTE n pl. -S a riot

EMF	*n* pl. -S a difference in electric potential
EMIC	*adj* relating to a type of linguistic analysis
EMIGRANT	*n* pl. -S one that emigrates
EMIGRATE	*v* -GRATED, -GRATING, -GRATES to leave one country or region to settle in another
EMIGRE	*n* pl. -S an emigrant
EMINENCE	*n* pl. -S high station or rank
EMINENCY	*n* pl. -CIES eminence
EMINENT	*adj* of high station or rank
EMIR	*n* pl. -S an Arab chieftain or prince
EMIRATE	*n* pl. -S the rank of an emir
EMISSARY	*n* pl. -SARIES a person sent on a mission
EMISSION	*n* pl. -S the act of emitting **EMISSIVE** *adj*
EMIT	*v* EMITTED, EMITTING, EMITS to send forth
EMITTER	*n* pl. -S one that emits
EMMER	*n* pl. -S a type of wheat
EMMET	*n* pl. -S an ant
EMODIN	*n* pl. -S a chemical compound
EMOTE	*v* EMOTED, EMOTING, EMOTES to express emotion in an exaggerated manner
EMOTER	*n* pl. -S one that emotes
EMOTION	*n* pl. -S an affective state of consciousness
EMOTIVE	*adj* pertaining to emotion
EMPALE	*v* -PALED, -PALING, -PALES to impale
EMPALER	*n* pl. -S one that empales
EMPANADA	*n* pl. -S a pastry turnover
EMPANEL	*v* -ELED, -ELING, -ELS or -ELLED, -ELLING, -ELS to impanel
EMPATHY	*n* pl. -THIES imaginative identification with another's thoughts and feelings **EMPATHIC** *adj*
EMPEROR	*n* pl. -S the ruler of an empire
EMPERY	*n* pl. -PERIES absolute dominion
EMPHASIS	*n* pl. -PHASES special significance imparted to something
EMPHATIC	*adj* strongly expressive
EMPIRE	*n* pl. -S a major political unit
EMPIRIC	*n* pl. -S one who relies on practical experience
EMPLACE	*v* -PLACED, -PLACING, -PLACES to position
EMPLANE	*v* -PLANED, -PLANING, -PLANES to enplane
EMPLOY	*v* -ED -ING, -S to hire
EMPLOYE	*n* pl. -S employee
EMPLOYEE	*n* pl. -S a person who is employed
EMPLOYER	*n* pl. -S one that employs
EMPOISON	*v* -ED, -ING, -S to embitter
EMPORIUM	*n* pl. -RIUMS or -RIA a trading or market center
EMPOWER	*v* -ED, -ING, -S to give legal power to
EMPRESS	*n* pl. -ES a female ruler of an empire
EMPRISE	*n* pl. -S an adventurous undertaking
EMPRIZE	*n* pl. -S emprise
EMPTIED	past tense of empty
EMPTIER	*n* pl. -S one that empties
EMPTIES	present 3d person sing. of empty
EMPTIEST	superlative of empty
EMPTILY	*adv* in an empty manner
EMPTINGS	*n/pl* emptins
EMPTINS	*n/pl* a liquid leavening
EMPTY	*adj* -TIER, -TIEST containing nothing
EMPTY	*v* -TIED, -TYING, -TIES to remove the contents of
EMPURPLE	*v* -PLED, -PLING, -PLES to tinge with purple
EMPYEMA	*n* pl. -EMATA or -EMAS a collection of pus in a body cavity **EMPYEMIC** *adj*
EMPYREAL	*adj* pertaining to the sky
EMPYREAN	*n* pl. -S the highest heaven
EMU	*n* pl. -S a large, flightless bird
EMULATE	*v* -LATED, -LATING, -LATES to try to equal or surpass
EMULATOR	*n* pl. -S one that emulates
EMULOUS	*adj* eager to equal or surpass another
EMULSIFY	*v* -FIED, -FYING, -FIES to make into an emulsion
EMULSION	*n* pl. -S a type of liquid mixture **EMULSIVE** *adj*

EMULSOID *n* pl. -S a liquid dispersed in another liquid

EMYD *n* pl. -S a freshwater tortoise

EMYDE *n* pl. -S emyd

EN *n* pl. -S the letter N

ENABLE *v* -BLED, -BLING, -BLES to make possible

ENABLER *n* pl. -S one that enables

ENACT *v* -ED, -ING, -S to make into a law

ENACTIVE *adj* having the power to enact

ENACTOR *n* pl. -S one that enacts

ENACTORY *adj* pertaining to the enactment of law

ENAMEL *v* -ELED, -ELING, -ELS or -ELLED, -ELLING, -ELS to cover with a hard, glossy surface

ENAMELER *n* pl. -S one that enamels

ENAMINE *n* pl. -S a type of amine

ENAMOR *v* -ED, -ING, -S to inspire with love

ENAMOUR *v* -ED, -ING, -S to enamor

ENATE *n* pl. -S a relative on the mother's side **ENATIC** *adj*

ENATION *n* pl. -S an outgrowth from the surface of an organ

ENCAENIA *n/pl* annual university ceremonies

ENCAGE *v* -CAGED, -CAGING, -CAGES to confine in a cage

ENCAMP *v* -ED, -ING, -S to set up a camp

ENCASE *v* -CASED, -CASING, -CASES to enclose in a case

ENCASH *v* -ED, -ING, -ES to cash

ENCEINTE *n* pl. -S an encircling fortification

ENCHAIN *v* -ED, -ING, -S to bind with chains

ENCHANT *v* -ED, -ING, -S to delight

ENCHASE *v* -CHASED, -CHASING, -CHASES to place in an ornamental setting

ENCHASER *n* pl. -S one that enchases

ENCHORIC *adj* belonging to a particular country

ENCINA *n* pl. -S an evergreen oak **ENCINAL** *adj*

ENCIPHER *v* -ED, -ING, -S to write in characters of hidden meaning

ENCIRCLE *v* -CLED, -CLING, -CLES to form a circle around

ENCLASP *v* -ED, -ING, -S to embrace

ENCLAVE *n* pl. -S a territorial unit enclosed within foreign territory

ENCLITIC *n* pl. -S a word pronounced as part of the preceding word

ENCLOSE *v* -CLOSED, -CLOSING, -CLOSES to close in on all sides

ENCLOSER *n* pl. -S one that encloses

ENCODE *v* -CODED, -CODING, -CODES to put into code

ENCODER *n* pl. -S one that encodes

ENCOMIUM *n* pl. -MIUMS or -MIA a eulogy

ENCORE *v* -CORED, -CORING, -CORES to call for the reappearance of a performer

ENCROACH *v* -ED, -ING, -ES to advance beyond the proper limits

ENCRUST *v* -ED, -ING, -S to cover with a crust

ENCRYPT *v* -ED, -ING, -S to encipher

ENCUMBER *v* -ED, -ING, -S to hinder in action or movement

ENCYCLIC *n* pl. -S a letter addressed by the pope to the bishops of the world

ENCYST *v* -ED, -ING, -S to enclose in a cyst

END *v* -ED, -ING, -S to terminate

ENDAMAGE *v* -AGED, -AGING, -AGES to damage

ENDAMEBA *n* pl. -BAS or -BAE a parasitic ameba

ENDANGER *v* -ED, -ING, -S to imperil

ENDARCH *adj* formed from the center outward

ENDARCHY *n* pl. -CHIES the condition of being endarch

ENDBRAIN *n* pl. -S a part of the brain

ENDEAR *v* -ED, -ING, -S to make dear or beloved

ENDEAVOR *v* -ED, -ING, -S to make an effort

ENDEMIAL *adj* peculiar to a country or people

ENDEMIC *n* pl. -S an endemial disease

ENDEMISM *n* pl. -S the state of being endemial

ENDER *n* pl. -S one that ends something

ENDERMIC *adj* acting by absorption through the skin

ENDEXINE *n* pl. -S an inner layer of the exine

ENDGAME *n* pl. -S the last stage of a chess game

ENDING *n* pl. -S a termination

ENDITE *v* -DITED, -DITING, -DITES to indite

ENDIVE *n* pl. -S an herb cultivated as a salad plant

ENDLEAF *n* pl. -LEAVES an endpaper

ENDLESS *adj* enduring forever

ENDLONG *adv* lengthwise

ENDMOST *adj* farthest

ENDNOTE *n* pl. -S a note placed at the end of the text

ENDOCARP *n* pl. -S the inner layer of a pericarp

ENDOCAST *n* pl. -S a cast of the cranial cavity

ENDODERM *n* pl. -S the innermost germ layer of an embryo

ENDOGAMY *n* pl. -MIES marriage within a particular group

ENDOGEN *n* pl. -S a type of plant

ENDOGENY *n* pl. -NIES growth from within

ENDOPOD *n* pl. -S a branch of a crustacean limb

ENDORSE *v* -DORSED, -DORSING, -DORSES to sign the back of a negotiable document

ENDORSEE *n* pl. -S one to whom a document is transferred by endorsement

ENDORSER *n* pl. -S one that endorses

ENDORSING present participle of endorse

ENDORSOR *n* pl. -S endorser

ENDOSARC *n* pl. -S a portion of a cell

ENDOSMOS *n* pl. -ES a form of osmosis

ENDOSOME *n* pl. -S a cellular particle

ENDOSTEA *n/pl* bone membranes

ENDOW *v* -ED, -ING, -S to provide with something

ENDOWER *n* pl. -S one that endows

ENDOZOIC *adj* involving passage through an animal

ENDPAPER *n* pl. -S a sheet of paper used in bookbinding

ENDPLATE *n* pl. -S a type of nerve terminal

ENDPOINT *n* pl. -S either of two points that mark the end of a line segment

ENDRIN *n* pl. -S an insecticide

ENDUE *v* -DUED, -DUING, -DUES to provide with some quality or gift

ENDURE *v* -DURED, -DURING, -DURES to last

ENDURO *n* pl. -DUROS a long race

ENDWAYS *adv* endwise

ENDWISE *adv* lengthwise

ENEMA *n* pl. -MAS or -MATA a liquid injected into the rectum

ENEMY *n* pl. -MIES one that is antagonistic toward another

ENERGID *n* pl. -S a nucleus and the body of cytoplasm with which it interacts

ENERGIES pl. of energy

ENERGISE *v* -GISED, -GISING, -GISES to energize

ENERGIZE *v* -GIZED, -GIZING, -GIZES to give energy to

ENERGY *n* -GIES the capacity for vigorous activity

ENERVATE *v* -VATED, -VATING, -VATES to deprive of strength or vitality

ENFACE *v* -FACED, -FACING, -FACES to write on the front of

ENFEEBLE *v* -BLED, -BLING, -BLES to make feeble

ENFEOFF *v* -ED, -ING, -S to invest with a feudal estate

ENFETTER *v* -ED, -ING, -S to enchain

ENFEVER *v* -ED, -ING, -S to fever

ENFILADE *v* -LADED, -LADING, -LADES to direct heavy gunfire along the length of

ENFLAME *v* -FLAMED, -FLAMING, -FLAMES to inflame

ENFOLD *v* -ED, -ING, -S to envelop

ENFOLDER *n* pl. -S one that enfolds

ENFORCE *v* -FORCED, -FORCING, -FORCES to compel obedience to

ENFORCER *n* pl. -S one that enforces

ENFRAME *v* -FRAMED, -FRAMING, -FRAMES to frame

ENG *n* pl. -S a phonetic symbol

ENGAGE *v* -GAGED, -GAGING, -GAGES to employ

ENGAGER *n* pl. -S one that engages

ENGENDER *v* -ED, -ING, -S to bring into existence

ENGILD *v* -ED, -ING, -S to brighten

ENGINE *v* -GINED, -GINING, -GINES to equip with machinery

ENGINEER v -ED, -ING, -S to carry through or manage by contrivance

ENGINERY n pl. -RIES machinery

ENGINING present participle of engine

ENGINOUS adj ingenious

ENGIRD v -GIRT or -GIRDED, -GIRDING, -GIRDS to gird

ENGIRDLE v -DLED, -DLING, -DLES to engird

ENGLISH v -ED, -ING, -ES to cause a billiard ball to spin around its vertical axis

ENGLUT v -GLUTTED, -GLUTTING, -GLUTS to gulp down

ENGORGE v -GORGED, -GORGING, -GORGES to fill with blood

ENGRAFT v -ED, -ING, -S to graft for propagation

ENGRAIL v -ED, -ING, -S to ornament the edge of with curved indentations

ENGRAIN v -ED, -ING, -S to ingrain

ENGRAM n pl. -S the durable mark caused by a stimulus upon protoplasm

ENGRAMME n pl. -S engram

ENGRAVE v -GRAVED, -GRAVING, -GRAVES to form by incision

ENGRAVER n pl. -S one that engraves

ENGROSS v -ED, -ING, -ES to occupy completely

ENGULF v -ED, -ING, -S to surround completely

ENHALO v -ED, -ING, -ES or -S to surround with a halo

ENHANCE v -HANCED, -HANCING, -HANCES to raise to a higher degree

ENHANCER n pl. -S one that enhances

ENIGMA n pl. -MAS or -MATA something that is hard to understand or explain

ENISLE v -ISLED, -ISLING, -ISLES to isolate

ENJAMBED adj marked by the continuation of a sentence from one line of a poem to the next

ENJOIN v -ED, -ING, -S to command

ENJOINER n pl. -S one that enjoins

ENJOY v -ED, -ING, -S to receive pleasure from

ENJOYER n pl. -S one that enjoys

ENKINDLE v -DLED, -DLING, -DLES to set on fire

ENLACE v -LACED, -LACING, -LACES to bind with laces

ENLARGE v -LARGED, -LARGING, -LARGES to make or become larger

ENLARGER n pl. -S a device used to enlarge photographs

ENLIST v -ED, -ING, -S to engage for military service

ENLISTEE n pl. -S one that is enlisted

ENLISTER n pl. -S one that enlists

ENLIVEN v -ED, -ING, -S to make lively

ENMESH v -ED, -ING, -ES to ensnare or entangle in a net

ENMITY n pl. -TIES hostility

ENNEAD n pl. -S a group of nine **ENNEADIC** adj

ENNEAGON n pl. -S a nonagon

ENNOBLE v -BLED, -BLING, -BLES to make noble

ENNOBLER n pl. -S one that ennobles

ENNUI n pl. -S a feeling of weariness and discontent

ENNUYE adj oppressed with ennui

ENNUYEE adj ennuye

ENOKI n pl. -S a small mushroom

ENOL n pl. -S a chemical compound **ENOLIC** adj

ENOLASE n pl. -S an enzyme

ENOLOGY n pl. -GIES oenology

ENORM adj enormous

ENORMITY n pl. -TIES great wickedness

ENORMOUS adj huge

ENOSIS n pl. -SISES union

ENOUGH n pl. -S a sufficient supply

ENOUNCE v ENOUNCED, ENOUNCING, ENOUNCES to announce

ENOW n pl. -S enough

ENPLANE v -PLANED, -PLANING, -PLANES to board an airplane

ENQUIRE v -QUIRED, -QUIRING, -QUIRES to inquire

ENQUIRY n pl. -RIES inquiry

ENRAGE v -RAGED, -RAGING, -RAGES to make very angry

ENRAPT adj rapt

ENRAVISH v -ED, -ING, -ES to delight greatly

ENRICH v -ED, -ING, -ES to add desirable elements to

ENRICHER *n* pl. -S one that enriches

ENROBE *v* -ROBED, -ROBING, -ROBES to dress

ENROBER *n* pl. -S one that enrobes

ENROL *v* -ROLLED, -ROLLING, -ROLS to enroll

ENROLL *v* -ED, -ING, -S to enter the name of in a register, record, or roll

ENROLLEE *n* pl. -S one that is enrolled

ENROLLER *n* pl. -S one that enrolls

ENROLLING present participle of enrol

ENROOT *v* -ED, -ING, -S to implant

ENS *n* pl. ENTIA an entity

ENSAMPLE *n* pl. -S an example

ENSCONCE *v* -SCONCED, -SCONCING, -SCONCES to settle securely or comfortably

ENSCROLL *v* -ED, -ING, -S to write on a scroll

ENSEMBLE *n* pl. -S a group of complementary parts

ENSERF *v* -ED, -ING, -S to make a serf of

ENSHEATH *v* -ED, -ING, -S to enclose in a sheath

ENSHRINE *v* -SHRINED, -SHRINING, -SHRINES to place in a shrine

ENSHROUD *v* -ED, -ING, -S to conceal

ENSIFORM *adj* sword-shaped

ENSIGN *n* pl. -S a navy officer

ENSIGNCY *n* pl. -CIES the rank of an ensign

ENSILAGE *v* -LAGED, -LAGING, -LAGES to ensile

ENSILE *v* -SILED, -SILING, -SILES to store in a silo

ENSKY *v* -SKIED or -SKYED, -SKYING, -SKIES to raise to the skies

ENSLAVE *v* -SLAVED, -SLAVING, -SLAVES to make a slave of

ENSLAVER *n* pl. -S one that enslaves

ENSNARE *v* -SNARED, -SNARING, -SNARES to trap

ENSNARER *n* pl. -S one that ensnares

ENSNARL *v* -ED, -ING, -S to tangle

ENSORCEL *v* -ED, -ING, -S to bewitch

ENSOUL *v* -ED, -ING, -S to endow with a soul

ENSPHERE *v* -SPHERED, -SPHERING, -SPHERES to enclose in a sphere

ENSUE *v* -SUED, -SUING, -SUES to occur afterward or as a result

ENSURE *v* -SURED, -SURING, -SURES to make certain

ENSURER *n* pl. -S one that ensures

ENSWATHE *v* -SWATHED, -SWATHING, -SWATHES to swathe

ENTAIL *v* -ED, -ING, -S to restrict the inheritance of to a specified line of heirs

ENTAILER *n* pl. -S one that entails

ENTAMEBA *n* pl. -BAE or -BAS endameba

ENTANGLE *v* -TANGLED, -TANGLING, -TANGLES to tangle

ENTASIA *n* pl. -S spasmodic contraction of a muscle

ENTASIS *n* pl. -TASES a slight convexity in a column **ENTASTIC** *adj*

ENTELLUS *n* pl. -ES a hanuman

ENTENTE *n* pl. -S an agreement between nations

ENTER *v* -ED, -ING, -S to come or go into

ENTERA a pl. of enteron

ENTERAL *adj* enteric

ENTERER *n* pl. -S one that enters

ENTERIC *adj* pertaining to the enteron

ENTERON *n* pl. -TERONS or -TERA the alimentary canal

ENTHALPY *n* pl. -PIES a thermodynamic measure of heat

ENTHETIC *adj* introduced from outside

ENTHRAL *v* -THRALLED, -THRALLING, -THRALS to enthrall

ENTHRALL *v* -ED, -ING, -S to charm

ENTHRONE *v* -THRONED, -THRONING, -THRONES to place on a throne

ENTHUSE *v* -THUSED, -THUSING, -THUSES to show enthusiasm

ENTIA pl. of ens

ENTICE *v* -TICED, -TICING, -TICES to allure

ENTICER *n* pl. -S one that entices

ENTIRE *n* pl. -S the whole of something

ENTIRELY *adv* completely

ENTIRETY *n* pl. -TIES completeness

ENTITLE *v* -TLED, -TLING, -TLES to give a title to

ENTITY *n* pl. -TIES something that has a real existence

ENTODERM   *n* pl. -S endoderm

ENTOIL   *v* -ED, -ING, -S to entrap

ENTOMB   *v* -ED, -ING, -S to place in a tomb

ENTOPIC   *adj* situated in the normal place

ENTOZOA   a pl. of entozoan and pl. of entozoon

ENTOZOAL   *adj* entozoic

ENTOZOAN   *n* pl. -ZOANS or -ZOA an entozoic parasite

ENTOZOIC   *adj* living within an animal

ENTOZOON   *n* pl. -ZOA entozoan

ENTRAILS   *n/pl* the internal organs

ENTRAIN   *v* -ED, -ING, -S to board a train

ENTRANCE   *v* -TRANCED, -TRANCING, -TRANCES to fill with delight or wonder

ENTRANT   *n* pl. -S one that enters

ENTRAP   *v* -TRAPPED, -TRAPPING, -TRAPS to trap

ENTREAT   *v* -ED, -ING, -S to ask for earnestly

ENTREATY   *n* pl. -TREATIES an earnest request

ENTREE   *n* pl. -S the principal dish of a meal

ENTRENCH   *v* -ED, -ING, -ES to establish firmly

ENTREPOT   *n* pl. -S a warehouse

ENTRESOL   *n* pl. -S a mezzanine

ENTRIES   pl. of entry

ENTROPY   *n* pl. -PIES a thermodynamic measure of disorder **ENTROPIC** *adj*

ENTRUST   *v* -ED, -ING, -S to give over for safekeeping

ENTRY   *n* pl. -TRIES a place of entrance

ENTRYWAY   *n* pl. -WAYS a passage serving as an entrance

ENTWINE   *v* -TWINED, -TWINING, -TWINES to twine around

ENTWIST   *v* -ED, -ING, -S to twist together

ENURE   *v* -URED, -URING, -URES to inure

ENURESIS   *n* pl. -SISES involuntary urination

ENURETIC   *n* pl. -S one who is affected with enuresis

ENVELOP   *v* -ED, -ING, -S to cover completely

ENVELOPE   *n* pl. -S a paper container

ENVENOM   *v* -ED, -ING, -S to put venom into

ENVIABLE   *adj* desirable **ENVIABLY** *adv*

ENVIED   past tense of envy

ENVIER   *n* pl. -S one that envies

ENVIES   present 3d person sing. of envy

ENVIOUS   *adj* resentful and desirous of another's possessions or qualities

ENVIRON   *v* -ED, -ING, -S to encircle

ENVISAGE   *v* -AGED, -AGING, -AGES to form a mental image of

ENVISION   *v* -ED, -ING, -S to envisage

ENVOI   *n* pl. -S the closing of a poem or prose work

ENVOY   *n* pl. -VOYS a representative

ENVY   *v* -VIED, -VYING, -VIES to be envious of

ENWHEEL   *v* -ED, -ING, -S to encircle

ENWIND   *v* -WOUND, -WINDING, -WINDS to wind around

ENWOMB   *v* -ED, -ING, -S to enclose as if in a womb

ENWRAP   *v* -WRAPPED, -WRAPPING, -WRAPS to envelop

ENZOOTIC   *n* pl. -S a type of animal disease

ENZYM   *n* pl. -S enzyme

ENZYME   *n* pl. -S a complex protein **ENZYMIC** *adj*

EOBIONT   *n* pl. -S a type of basic organism

EOHIPPUS   *n* pl. -ES an extinct horse

EOLIAN   *adj* pertaining to the wind

EOLIPILE   *n* pl. -S a type of engine

EOLITH   *n* pl. -S a prehistoric stone tool **EOLITHIC** *adj*

EOLOPILE   *n* pl. -S eolipile

EON   *n* pl. -S an indefinitely long period of time

EONIAN   *adj* everlasting

EONISM   *n* pl. -S adoption of the dress and mannerisms of the opposite sex

EOSIN   *n* pl. -S a red dye **EOSINIC** *adj*

EOSINE   *n* pl. -S eosin

EPACT   *n* pl. -S the difference between the lengths of the solar and lunar years

EPARCH   *n* pl. -S the head of an eparchy

EPARCHY   *n* pl. -CHIES a district of modern Greece

EPAULET   *n* pl. -S a shoulder ornament

EPAZOTE *n* pl. -S an herb of the goosefoot family

EPEE *n* pl. -S a type of sword

EPEEIST *n* pl. -S one who fences with an epee

EPEIRIC *adj* pertaining to vertical movement of the earth's crust

EPENDYMA *n* pl. -S a membrane lining certain body cavities

EPERGNE *n* pl. -S an ornamental dish

EPHA *n* pl. -S ephah

EPHAH *n* pl. -S a Hebrew unit of dry measure

EPHEBE *n* pl. -S ephebus **EPHEBIC** *adj*

EPHEBOS *n* pl. -BOI ephebus

EPHEBUS *n* pl. -BI a young man of ancient Greece

EPHEDRA *n* pl. -S a desert shrub

EPHEDRIN *n* pl. -S an alkaloid used to treat allergies

EPHEMERA *n* pl. -ERAS or -ERAE something of very short life or duration

EPHOD *n* pl. -S an ancient Hebrew vestment

EPHOR *n* pl. -ORS or -ORI a magistrate of ancient Greece **EPHORAL** *adj*

EPHORATE *n* pl. -S the office of ephor

EPIBLAST *n* pl. -S the ectoderm

EPIBOLY *n* pl. -LIES the growth of one part around another **EPIBOLIC** *adj*

EPIC *n* pl. -S a long narrative poem **EPICAL** *adj* **EPICALLY** *adv*

EPICALYX *n* pl. -LYXES or -LYCES a set of bracts close to and resembling a calyx

EPICARP *n* pl. -S the outer layer of a pericarp

EPICEDIA *n/pl* funeral songs

EPICENE *n* pl. -S one having both male and female characteristics

EPICLIKE *adj* resembling an epic

EPICOTYL *n* pl. -S a part of a plant embryo

EPICURE *n* pl. -S a gourmet

EPICYCLE *n* pl. -S a circle that rolls on the circumference of another circle

EPIDEMIC *n* pl. -S a rapid spread of a disease

EPIDERM *n* pl. -S the outer layer of skin

EPIDOTE *n* pl. -S a mineral **EPIDOTIC** *adj*

EPIDURAL *adj* situated on the membrane that encloses the brain

EPIFAUNA *n* pl. -FAUNAE or -FAUNAS fauna living on a hard sea floor

EPIFOCAL *adj* pertaining to the point of origin of an earthquake

EPIGEAL *adj* epigeous

EPIGEAN *adj* epigeous

EPIGEIC *adj* epigeous

EPIGENE *adj* occurring near the surface of the earth

EPIGENIC *adj* pertaining to change in the mineral character of a rock

EPIGEOUS *adj* growing on or close to the ground

EPIGON *n* pl. -S epigone

EPIGONE *n* pl. -S an inferior imitator **EPIGONIC** *adj*

EPIGONUS *n* pl. -NI epigone

EPIGRAM *n* pl. -S a brief, witty remark

EPIGRAPH *n* pl. -S an engraved inscription

EPIGYNY *n* pl. -NIES the state of having floral organs near the top of the ovary

EPILEPSY *n* pl. -SIES a disorder of the nervous system

EPILOG *n* pl. -S a concluding section

EPILOGUE *v* -LOGUED, -LOGUING, -LOGUES to provide with a concluding section

EPIMER *n* pl. -S a type of sugar compound **EPIMERIC** *adj*

EPIMERE *n* pl. -S a part of an embryo

EPIMYSIA *n/pl* muscle sheaths

EPINAOS *n* pl. -NAOI a rear vestibule

EPINASTY *n* pl. -TIES a downward bending of plant parts

EPIPHANY *n* pl. -NIES an appearance of a deity

EPIPHYTE *n* pl. -S a plant growing upon another plant

EPISCIA *n* pl. -S a tropical herb

EPISCOPE *n* pl. -S a type of projector

EPISODE *n* pl. -S an incident in the course of a continuous experience **EPISODIC** *adj*

EPISOME *n* pl. -S a genetic determinant **EPISOMAL** *adj*

EPISTASY *n* pl. -SIES a suppression of genetic effect

EPISTLE *n* pl. -S a long or formal letter

EPISTLER *n* pl. -S one that writes epistles

EPISTOME *n* pl. -S a structure covering the mouth of various invertebrates

EPISTYLE *n* pl. -S a part of a classical building

EPITAPH *n* pl. -S an inscription on a tomb

EPITASIS *n* pl. -ASES the main part of a classical drama

EPITAXY *n* pl. -TAXIES a type of crystalline growth **EPITAXIC** *adj*

EPITHET *n* pl. -S a term used to characterize a person or thing

EPITOME *n* pl. -S a typical or ideal example **EPITOMIC** *adj*

EPITOPE *n* pl. -S a region on the surface of an antigen

EPIZOA pl. of epizoon

EPIZOIC *adj* living on the body of an animal

EPIZOISM *n* pl. -S the state of being epizoic

EPIZOITE *n* pl. -S an epizoic organism

EPIZOON *n* pl. -ZOA an epizoic parasite

EPIZOOTY *n* pl. -TIES a type of animal disease

EPOCH *n* pl. -S a particular period of time **EPOCHAL** *adj*

EPODE *n* pl. -S a type of poem

EPONYM *n* pl. -S the person for whom something is named **EPONYMIC** *adj*

EPONYMY *n* pl. -MIES the derivation of an eponymic name

EPOPEE *n* pl. -S an epic poem

EPOPOEIA *n* pl. -S epopee

EPOS *n* pl. -ES an epic poem

EPOXIDE *n* pl. -S an epoxy compound

EPOXY *v* EPOXIED or EPOXYED, EPOXYING, EPOXIES to glue with epoxy (a type of resin)

EPSILON *n* pl. -S a Greek letter

EQUABLE *adj* not changing or varying greatly **EQUABLY** *adv*

EQUAL *adj* having the same capability, quantity, or effect as another

EQUAL *v* EQUALED, EQUALING, EQUALS or EQUALLED, EQUALLING, EQUALS to be equal to

EQUALISE *v* -ISED, -ISING, -ISES to equalize

EQUALITY *n* pl. -TIES the state of being equal

EQUALIZE *v* -IZED, -IZING, -IZES to make equal

EQUALLED a past tense of equal

EQUALLING a past participle of equal

EQUALLY *adv* in an equal manner

EQUATE *v* EQUATED, EQUATING, EQUATES to make equal

EQUATION *n* pl. -S the act of equating

EQUATOR *n* pl. -S a great circle of spherical celestial bodies

EQUERRY *n* pl. -RIES an officer in charge of the care of horses

EQUID *n* pl. -S an animal of the horse family

EQUINE *n* pl. -S a horse

EQUINELY *adv* in a horselike manner

EQUINITY *n* pl. -TIES the state of being like a horse

EQUINOX *n* pl. -ES a point on the celestial sphere

EQUIP *v* EQUIPPED, EQUIPPING, EQUIPS to provide with whatever is needed

EQUIPAGE *n* pl. -S a carriage

EQUIPPER *n* pl. -S one that equips

EQUIPPING present participle of equip

EQUISETA *n/pl* rushlike plants

EQUITANT *adj* overlapping

EQUITES *n/pl* a privileged military class of ancient Rome

EQUITY *n* pl. -TIES fairness or impartiality

EQUIVOKE *n* pl. -S a play on words

ER *interj* — used to express hesitation

ERA *n* pl. -S an epoch

ERADIATE *v* -ATED, -ATING, -ATES to radiate

ERASE *v* ERASED, ERASING, ERASES to rub or scrape out **ERASABLE** *adj*

ERASER *n* pl. -S one that erases

ERASION *n* pl. -S an erasure

ERASURE *n* pl. -S the act of erasing

ERBIUM *n* pl. -S a metallic element

ERE *prep* previous to; before

ERECT *v* -ED, -ING, -S to build

ERECTER *n* pl. -S erector

ERECTILE *adj* capable of being raised upright

ERECTION *n* pl. -S the act of erecting

ERECTIVE *adj* tending to erect

ERECTLY *adv* in an upright manner

ERECTOR *n* pl. -S one that erects

ERELONG *adv* soon

EREMITE *n* pl. -S a hermit **EREMITIC** *adj*

EREMURUS *n* pl. -URI a perennial herb

ERENOW *adv* before this time

EREPSIN *n* pl. -S a mixture of enzymes in the small intestine

ERETHISM *n* pl. -S abnormal irritability **ERETHIC** *adj*

EREWHILE *adv* some time ago

ERG *n* pl. -S a unit of work or energy

ERGASTIC *adj* constituting the nonliving by-products of protoplasmic activity

ERGATE *n* pl. -S a worker ant

ERGATIVE *adj* pertaining to a type of language

ERGO *conj* therefore

ERGODIC *adj* pertaining to the probability that any state will recur

ERGOT *n* pl. -S a fungus **ERGOTIC** *adj*

ERGOTISM *n* pl. -S poisoning produced by eating ergot-infected grain

ERICA *n* pl. -S a shrub of the heath family

ERICOID *adj* resembling heath

ERIGERON *n* pl. -S an herb

ERINGO *n* pl. -GOES or -GOS eryngo

ERISTIC *n* pl. -S an expert in debate

ERLKING *n* pl. -S an evil spirit of Germanic folklore

ERMINE *n* pl. -S the fur of certain weasels **ERMINED** *adj*

ERN *n* pl. -S erne

ERNE *n* pl. -S a sea eagle

ERODE *v* ERODED, ERODING, ERODES to wear away by constant friction

ERODENT *adj* erosive

ERODIBLE *adj* erosible

ERODING present participle of erode

EROGENIC *adj* arousing sexual desire

EROS *n* pl. -ES sexual desire

EROSE *adj* uneven **EROSELY** *adv*

EROSIBLE *adj* capable of being eroded

EROSION *n* pl. -S the act of eroding

EROSIVE *adj* causing erosion

EROTIC *n* pl. -S an amatory poem **EROTICAL** *adj*

EROTICA *n/pl* literature or art dealing with sexual love

EROTISM *n* pl. -S sexual excitement

EROTIZE *v* -TIZED, -TIZING, -TIZES to give a sexual meaning to

ERR *v* -ED, -ING, -S to make a mistake

ERRANCY *n* pl. -CIES an instance of erring

ERRAND *n* pl. -S a short trip made for a particular purpose

ERRANT *n* pl. -S a wanderer

ERRANTLY *adv* in a wandering manner

ERRANTRY *n* pl. -RIES the state of wandering

ERRATA *n* pl. -S a list of printing errors

ERRATIC *n* pl. -S an eccentric person

ERRATUM *n* pl. -TA a printing error

ERRHINE *n* pl. -S a substance that promotes nasal discharge

ERRINGLY *adv* in a mistaken manner

ERROR *n* pl. -S a mistake

ERS *n* pl. -ES ervil

ERSATZ *n* pl. -ES a substitute

ERST *adv* formerly

ERUCT *v* -ED, -ING, -S to belch

ERUCTATE *v* -TATED, -TATING, -TATES to eruct

ERUDITE *adj* scholarly

ERUGO *n* pl. -GOS aerugo

ERUMPENT *adj* bursting forth

ERUPT *v* -ED, -ING, -S to burst forth

ERUPTION *n* pl. -S the act of erupting

ERUPTIVE *n* pl. -S a type of rock

ERVIL *n* pl. -S a European vetch

ERYNGO *n* pl. -GOES or -GOS a medicinal herb

ERYTHEMA *n* pl. -S a redness of the skin

ERYTHRON *n* pl. -S a bodily organ consisting of the red blood cells

ES *n* pl. ESES ess

ESCALADE *v* -LADED, -LADING, -LADES to enter by means of ladders

ESCALATE   v -LATED, -LATING, -LATES to increase

ESCALLOP   v -ED, -ING, -S to scallop

ESCALOP   v -ED, -ING, -S to escallop

ESCAPADE   n pl. -S a reckless adventure

ESCAPE   v -CAPED, -CAPING, -CAPES to get away

ESCAPEE   n pl. -S one that has escaped

ESCAPER   n pl. -S one that escapes

ESCAPING   present participle of escape

ESCAPISM   n pl. -S the avoidance of reality by diversion of the mind

ESCAPIST   n pl. -S one given to escapism

ESCAR   n pl. -S esker

ESCARGOT   n pl. -S an edible snail

ESCAROLE   n pl. -S a variety of endive

ESCARP   v -ED, -ING, -S to cause to slope steeply

ESCHALOT   n pl. -S a shallot

ESCHAR   n pl. -S a hard, dry scab

ESCHEAT   v -ED, -ING, -S to confiscate

ESCHEW   v -ED, -ING, -S to avoid

ESCHEWAL   n pl. -S the act of eschewing

ESCOLAR   n pl. -S a food fish

ESCORT   v -ED, -ING, -S to accompany

ESCOT   v -ED, -ING, -S to provide support for

ESCROW   v -ED, -ING, -S to place in the custody of a third party

ESCUAGE   n pl. -S scutage

ESCUDO   n pl. -DOS a monetary unit of Portugal

ESCULENT   n pl. -S something that is edible

ESERINE   n pl. -S a toxic alkaloid

ESKAR   n pl. -S esker

ESKER   n pl. -S a narrow ridge of gravel and sand

ESOPHAGI   n/pl tubes connecting the mouth to the stomach

ESOTERIC   adj designed for a select few

ESPALIER   v -ED, -ING, -S to furnish with a trellis

ESPANOL   n pl. -ES a native of Spain

ESPARTO   n pl. -TOS a perennial grass

ESPECIAL   adj special

ESPIAL   n pl. -S the act of espying

ESPIED   past tense of espy

ESPIEGLE   adj playful

ESPIES   present 3d person sing. of espy

ESPOUSAL   n pl. -S a marriage ceremony

ESPOUSE   v -POUSED, -POUSING, -POUSES to marry

ESPOUSER   n pl. -S one that espouses

ESPRESSO   n pl. -SOS a strong coffee

ESPRIT   n pl. -S spirit

ESPY   v -PIED, -PYING, -PIES to catch sight of

ESQUIRE   v -QUIRED, -QUIRING, -QUIRES to escort

ESS   n pl. -ES the letter S

ESSAY   v -ED, -ING, -S to try

ESSAYER   n pl. -S one that essays

ESSAYIST   n pl. -S a writer of essays (prose compositions)

ESSENCE   n pl. -S a fundamental nature or quality

ESSOIN   n pl. -S an excuse

ESSONITE   n pl. -S a variety of garnet

ESTANCIA   n pl. -S a cattle ranch

ESTATE   v -TATED, -TATING, -TATES to provide with landed property

ESTEEM   v -ED, -ING, -S to have a high opinion of

ESTER   n pl. -S a type of chemical compound

ESTERASE   n pl. -S a type of enzyme

ESTERIFY   v -FIED, -FYING, -FIES to convert into an ester

ESTHESIA   n pl. -S the ability to receive sensation

ESTHESIS   n pl. -THESISES or -THESES esthesia

ESTHETE   n pl. -S an esthetic person

ESTHETIC   adj keenly appreciative of the beautiful

ESTIMATE   v -MATED, -MATING, -MATES to make an approximate judgment of

ESTIVAL   adj pertaining to summer

ESTIVATE   v -VATED, -VATING, -VATES to spend the summer

ESTOP   v -TOPPED, -TOPPING, -TOPS to impede by estoppel

ESTOPPEL   n pl. -S a legal restraint preventing a person from contradicting his own previous statement

ESTOVERS	*n/pl* necessities allowed by law	**ETH**	*n* pl. -S edh
ESTRAGON	*n* pl. -S tarragon	**ETHANE**	*n* pl. -S a gaseous hydrocarbon
ESTRAL	*adj* estrous	**ETHANOL**	*n* pl. -S an alcohol
ESTRANGE	*v* -TRANGED, -TRANGING, -TRANGES to alienate	**ETHENE**	*n* pl. -S ethylene
ESTRAY	*v* -ED, -ING, -S to stray	**ETHEPHON**	*n* pl. -S a synthetic plant growth regulator
ESTREAT	*v* -ED, -ING, -S to copy from court records for use in prosecution	**ETHER**	*n* pl. -S a volatile liquid used as an anesthetic **ETHERIC** *adj*
ESTRIN	*n* pl. -S estrone	**ETHEREAL**	*adj* airy
ESTRIOL	*n* pl. -S an estrogen	**ETHERIFY**	*v* -FIED, -FYING, -FIES to convert into ether
ESTROGEN	*n* pl. -S a female sex hormone promoting or producing estrus	**ETHERISH**	*adj* resembling ether
ESTRONE	*n* pl. -S an estrogen	**ETHERIZE**	*v* -IZED, -IZING, -IZES to treat with ether
ESTROUS	*adj* pertaining to estrus	**ETHIC**	*n* pl. -S a body of moral principles
ESTRUAL	*adj* estrous		
ESTRUM	*n* pl. -S estrus	**ETHICAL**	*n* pl. -S a drug sold by prescription only
ESTRUS	*n* pl. -ES the period of heat in female mammals	**ETHICIAN**	*n* pl. -S an ethicist
ESTUARY	*n* pl. -ARIES an inlet of the sea at a river's lower end	**ETHICIST**	*n* pl. -S a specialist in ethics
ESURIENT	*adj* greedy	**ETHICIZE**	*v* -CIZED, -CIZING, -CIZES to make ethical
ET	a past tense of eat	**ETHINYL**	*n* pl. -S ethynyl
ETA	*n* pl. -S a Greek letter	**ETHION**	*n* pl. -S a pesticide
ETAGERE	*n* pl. -S an ornamental stand	**ETHMOID**	*n* pl. -S a bone of the nasal cavity
ETALON	*n* pl. -S an optical instrument		
ETAMIN	*n* pl. -S etamine	**ETHNARCH**	*n* pl. -S the ruler of a people or province
ETAMINE	*n* pl. -S a loosely woven fabric	**ETHNIC**	*n* pl. -S a member of a particular ethnos **ETHNICAL** *adj*
ETAPE	*n* pl. -S a warehouse		
ETATISM	*n* pl. -S state socialism **ETATIST** *adj*	**ETHNOS**	*n* pl. -ES a group of people who share a common and distinctive culture
ETCETERA	*n* pl. -S a number of additional items	**ETHOLOGY**	*n* pl. -GIES the study of animal behavior
ETCH	*v* -ED, -ING, -ES to engrave with acid	**ETHOS**	*n* pl. -ES the fundamental character of a culture
ETCHANT	*n* pl. -S a substance used in etching	**ETHOXY**	*n* pl. -OXIES ethoxyl
ETCHER	*n* pl. -S one that etches	**ETHOXYL**	*n* pl. -S a univalent chemical radical
ETCHING	*n* pl. -S an etched design	**ETHYL**	*n* pl. -S a univalent chemical radical
ETERNAL	*n* pl. -S something lasting forever		
ETERNE	*adj* everlasting	**ETHYLATE**	*v* -ATED, -ATING, -ATES to introduce the ethyl group into
ETERNISE	*v* -NISED, -NISING, -NISES to eternize	**ETHYLENE**	*n* pl. -S a flammable gas
ETERNITY	*n* pl. -TIES infinite time	**ETHYLIC**	*adj* pertaining to ethyl
ETERNIZE	*v* -NIZED, -NIZING, -NIZES to make everlasting	**ETHYNE**	*n* pl. -S a flammable gas
ETESIAN	*n* pl. -S an annually recurring wind	**ETHYNYL**	*n* pl. -S a univalent chemical radical

ETIC *adj* relating to a type of linguistic analysis

ETIOLATE *v* -LATED, -LATING, -LATES to whiten

ETIOLOGY *n* pl. -GIES the study of the causes of diseases

ETNA *n* pl. -S a container for heating liquids

ETOILE *n* pl. -S a star

ETOUFFEE *n* pl. -S a Cajun stew

ETUDE *n* pl. -S a piece of music for the practice of a point of technique

ETUI *n* pl. -S a case for holding small articles

ETWEE *n* pl. -S etui

ETYMON *n* pl. -MA or -MONS the earliest known form of a word

EUCAINE *n* pl. -S an anesthetic

EUCALYPT *n* pl. -S an evergreen tree

EUCHARIS *n* pl. -RISES a flowering plant

EUCHRE *v* -CHRED, -CHRING, -CHRES to prevent from winning three tricks in euchre (a card game)

EUCLASE *n* pl. -S a mineral

EUCRITE *n* pl. -S a type of meteorite **EUCRITIC** *adj*

EUDAEMON *n* pl. -S eudemon

EUDEMON *n* pl. -S a good spirit

EUGENIA *n* pl. -S a tropical evergreen tree

EUGENICS *n/pl* the science of hereditary improvement **EUGENIC** *adj*

EUGENIST *n* pl. -S a student of eugenics

EUGENOL *n* pl. -S an aromatic liquid

EUGLENA *n* pl. -S a freshwater protozoan

EULACHAN *n* pl. -S eulachon

EULACHON *n* pl. -S a marine food fish

EULOGIA *n* pl. -GIAE holy bread

EULOGIA *n* pl. -S a blessing

EULOGIES pl. of eulogy

EULOGISE *v* -GISED, -GISING, -GISES to eulogize

EULOGIST *n* pl. -S one that eulogizes

EULOGIUM *n* pl. -GIA or -GIUMS a eulogy

EULOGIZE *v* -GIZED, -GIZING, -GIZES to praise highly

EULOGY *n* pl. -GIES a formal expression of high praise

EUNUCH *n* pl. -S a castrated man

EUONYMUS *n* pl. -ES any of a genus of shrubs or small trees

EUPATRID *n* pl. -RIDS or -RIDAE an aristocrat of ancient Athens

EUPEPSIA *n* pl. -S good digestion **EUPEPTIC** *adj*

EUPEPSY *n* pl. -SIES eupepsia

EUPHENIC *adj* dealing with biological improvement

EUPHONY *n* pl. -NIES pleasant sound **EUPHONIC** *adj*

EUPHORIA *n* pl. -S a feeling of well-being **EUPHORIC** *adj*

EUPHOTIC *adj* pertaining to the upper layer of a body of water

EUPHRASY *n* pl. -SIES an annual herb

EUPHROE *n* pl. -S a device used to adjust a shipboard awning

EUPHUISM *n* pl. -S an artificially elegant style of speech or writing

EUPHUIST *n* pl. -S one given to euphuism

EUPLOID *n* pl. -S a cell having three or more identical genomes

EUPLOIDY *n* pl. -DIES the state of being a euploid

EUPNEA *n* pl. -S normal breathing **EUPNEIC** *adj*

EUPNOEA *n* pl. -S eupnea **EUPNOEIC** *adj*

EUREKA *interj* — used to express triumph upon discovering something

EURIPUS *n* pl. -PI a swift sea channel

EURO *n* pl. EUROS a large kangaroo

EUROKY *n* pl. -KIES the ability of an organism to live under variable conditions **EUROKOUS** *adj*

EUROPIUM *n* pl. -S a metallic element

EURYBATH *n* pl. -S an organism that can live in a wide range of water depths

EURYOKY *n* pl. -KIES euroky

EURYTHMY *n* pl. -MIES harmony of movement or structure

EUSTACY *n* pl. -CIES a worldwide change in sea level **EUSTATIC** *adj*

EUSTELE *n* pl. -S a plant part

EUTAXY *n* pl. -TAXIES good order

EUTECTIC *n* pl. -S an alloy that has the lowest possible melting point

EUTROPHY *n* pl. -PHIES healthful nutrition

EUXENITE *n* pl. -S a mineral

EVACUANT *n* pl. -S a cathartic medicine

EVACUATE   v -ATED, -ATING, -ATES to remove from a dangerous area

EVACUEE   n pl. -S one that is evacuated

EVADE   v EVADED, EVADING, EVADES to escape or avoid by cleverness or deceit **EVADABLE, EVADIBLE** adj

EVADER   n pl. -S one that evades

EVALUATE   v -ATED, -ATING, -ATES to determine the value of

EVANESCE   v -NESCED, -NESCING, -NESCES to fade away

EVANGEL   n pl. -S a preacher of the gospel

EVANISH   v -ED, -ING, -ES to vanish

EVASION   n pl. -S the act of evading

EVASIVE   adj tending to evade

EVE   n pl. -S evening

EVECTION   n pl. -S irregularity in the moon's motion

EVEN   adj EVENER, EVENEST flat and smooth

EVEN   v -ED, -ING, -S to make even

EVENER   n pl. -S one that evens

EVENFALL   n pl. -S twilight

EVENING   n pl. -S the latter part of the day and early part of the night

EVENLY   adv in an even manner

EVENNESS   n pl. -ES the state of being even

EVENSONG   n pl. -S an evening prayer service

EVENT   n pl. -S something that occurs

EVENTFUL   adj momentous

EVENTIDE   n pl. -S evening

EVENTUAL   adj occurring at a later time

EVER   adv at all times

EVERMORE   adv forever

EVERSION   n pl -S the act of everting

EVERT   v -ED, -ING, -S to turn outward or inside out

EVERTOR   n pl. -S a muscle that turns a part outward

EVERY   adj each without exception

EVERYDAY   adj ordinary

EVERYMAN   n pl. -MEN the typical or ordinary man

EVERYONE   pron every person

EVERYWAY   adv in every way

EVICT   v -ED, -ING, -S to expel by legal process

EVICTEE   n pl. -S one that is evicted

EVICTION   n pl. -S the act of evicting

EVICTOR   n pl. -S one that evicts

EVIDENCE   v -DENCED, -DENCING, -DENCES to indicate clearly

EVIDENT   adj clear to the vision or understanding

EVIL   adj EVILER, EVILEST or EVILLER, EVILLEST morally bad

EVIL   n pl. -S something that is evil

EVILDOER   n pl. -S one that does evil

EVILLER   a comparative of evil

EVILLEST   a superlative of evil

EVILLY   adv in an evil manner

EVILNESS   n pl. -ES the quality of being evil

EVINCE   v EVINCED, EVINCING, EVINCES to show clearly **EVINCIVE** adj

EVITE   v EVITED, EVITING, EVITES to avoid **EVITABLE** adj

EVOCABLE   adj capable of being evoked

EVOCATOR   n pl. -S one that evokes

EVOKE   v EVOKED, EVOKING, EVOKES to call forth

EVOKER   n pl. -S an evocator

EVOLUTE   n pl. -S a type of geometric curve

EVOLVE   v EVOLVED, EVOLVING, EVOLVES to develop

EVOLVER   n pl. -S one that evolves

EVONYMUS   n pl. -ES euonymus

EVULSION   n pl. -S the act of pulling out

EVZONE   n pl. -S a Greek soldier

EWE   n pl. -S a female sheep

EWER   n pl. -S a large pitcher

EX   n pl. -ES the letter X

EXACT   adj -ACTER, -ACTEST precise

EXACT   v -ED, -ING, -S to force the payment or yielding of

EXACTA   n pl. -S a type of horse racing bet

EXACTER   n pl. -S one that exacts

EXACTION   n pl. -S the act of exacting

EXACTLY   adv in an exact manner

EXACTOR   n pl. -S exacter

EXALT   v -ED, -ING, -S to raise

EXALTER   n pl. -S one that exalts

EXAM   n pl. -S an examination

EXAMEN   n pl. -S a critical study

EXAMINE   *v* -INED, -INING, -INES to inspect

EXAMINEE   *n* pl. -S one that is taking an examination

EXAMINER   *n* pl. -S one that examines

EXAMINING   present participle of examine

EXAMPLE   *v* -PLED, -PLING, -PLES to show by representation

EXANTHEM   *n* pl. -S a skin eruption

EXARCH   *n* pl. -S the ruler of a province in the Byzantine Empire **EXARCHAL** *adj*

EXARCHY   *n* pl. -CHIES the domain of an exarch

EXCAVATE   *v* -VATED, -VATING, -VATES to dig out

EXCEED   *v* -ED, -ING, -S to go beyond

EXCEEDER   *n* pl. -S one that exceeds

EXCEL   *v* -CELLED, -CELLING, -CELS to surpass others

EXCEPT   *v* -ED, -ING, -S to leave out

EXCERPT   *v* -ED, -ING, -S to pick out a passage from for quoting

EXCESS   *v* -ED, -ING, -ES to eliminate the position of

EXCHANGE   *v* -CHANGED, -CHANGING, -CHANGES to give and receive reciprocally

EXCIDE   *v* -CIDED, -CIDING, -CIDES to excise

EXCIMER   *n* pl. -S a dimer that exists in an excited state

EXCIPLE   *n* pl. -S a rim around the hymenium of various lichens

EXCISE   *v* -CISED, -CISING, -CISES to remove by cutting out

EXCISION   *n* pl. -S the act of excising

EXCITANT   *n* pl. -S a stimulant

EXCITE   *v* -CITED, -CITING, -CITES to arouse the emotions of

EXCITER   *n* pl. -S one that excites

EXCITON   *n* pl. -S a phenomenon occurring in an excited crystal

EXCITOR   *n* pl. -S exciter

EXCLAIM   *v* -ED, -ING, -S to cry out suddenly

EXCLAVE   *n* pl. -S a portion of a country which is isolated in foreign territory

EXCLUDE   *v* -CLUDED, -CLUDING, -CLUDES to shut out

EXCLUDER   *n* pl. -S one that excludes

EXCRETA   *n/pl* excreted matter **EXCRETAL** *adj*

EXCRETE   *v* -CRETED, -CRETING, -CRETES to separate and eliminate from an organic body

EXCRETER   *n* pl. -S one that excretes

EXCURSUS   *n* pl. -ES a long appended exposition of a topic

EXCUSE   *v* -CUSED, -CUSING, -CUSES to apologize for

EXCUSER   *n* pl. -S one that excuses

EXEC   *n* pl. -S an executive officer

EXECRATE   *v* -CRATED, -CRATING, -CRATES to curse

EXECUTE   *v* -CUTED, -CUTING, -CUTES to carry out

EXECUTER   *n* pl. -S executor

EXECUTOR   *n* pl. -S one that executes

EXEDRA   *n* pl. -DRAE a curved outdoor bench

EXEGESIS   *n* pl. -GESES critical explanation or analysis **EXEGETIC** *adj*

EXEGETE   *n* pl. -S one skilled in exegesis

EXEMPLAR   *n* pl. -S one that is worthy of being copied

EXEMPLUM   *n* pl. -PLA an example

EXEMPT   *v* -ED, -ING, -S to free from an obligation required of others

EXEQUY   *n* pl. -QUIES a funeral procession **EXEQUIAL** *adj*

EXERCISE   *v* -CISED, -CISING, -CISES to make use of

EXERGUE   *n* pl. -S a space on a coin **EXERGUAL** *adj*

EXERT   *v* -ED, -ING, -S to put into action

EXERTION   *n* pl. -S the act of exerting

EXERTIVE   *adj* tending to exert

EXEUNT   *v* they leave the stage — used as a stage direction

EXHALANT   *n* pl. -S something that exhales

EXHALE   *v* -HALED, -HALING, -HALES to expel air or vapor

EXHALENT   *n* pl. -S exhalant

EXHAUST   *v* -ED, -ING, -S to use up

EXHIBIT   *v* -ED, -ING, -S to present for public viewing

EXHORT   *v* -ED, -ING, -S to advise urgently

EXHORTER   *n* pl. -S one that exhorts

EXHUME   *v* -HUMED, -HUMING, -HUMES to dig out of the earth

EXHUMER   *n* pl. -S one that exhumes

EXIGENCE   *n* pl. -S exigency

EXIGENCY   *n* pl. -CIES urgency

EXIGENT   *adj* urgent

EXIGIBLE   *adj* liable to be demanded

EXIGUITY   *n* pl. -ITIES the state of being exiguous

EXIGUOUS   *adj* meager

EXILE   *v* -ILED, -ILING, -ILES to banish from one's own country

EXILIAN   *adj* exilic

EXILIC   *adj* pertaining to exile (banishment from one's own country)

EXILING   present participle of exile

EXIMIOUS   *adj* excellent

EXINE   *n* pl. -S the outer layer of certain spores

EXIST   *v* -ED, -ING, -S to be

EXISTENT   *n* pl. -S something that exists

EXIT   *v* -ED, -ING, -S to go out

EXITLESS   *adj* lacking a way out

EXOCARP   *n* pl. -S the epicarp

EXOCRINE   *n* pl. -S an external secretion

EXODERM   *n* pl. -S the ectoderm

EXODOS   *n* pl. -DOI a concluding dramatic scene

EXODUS   *n* pl. -ES a movement away

EXOERGIC   *adj* releasing energy

EXOGAMY   *n* pl. -MIES marriage outside of a particular group **EXOGAMIC** *adj*

EXOGEN   *n* pl. -S a type of plant

EXON   *n* pl. -S a sequence in the genetic code **EXONIC** *adj*

EXONUMIA   *n/pl* numismatic items other than coins or paper money

EXORABLE   *adj* persuadable

EXORCISE   *v* -CISED, -CISING, -CISES to free of an evil spirit

EXORCISM   *n* pl. -S the act of exorcising

EXORCIST   *n* pl. -S one who practices exorcism

EXORCIZE   *v* -CIZED, -CIZING, -CIZES to exorcise

EXORDIUM   *n* pl. -DIUMS or -DIA a beginning **EXORDIAL** *adj*

EXOSMOSE   *n* pl. -S a form of osmosis **EXOSMIC** *adj*

EXOSPORE   *n* pl. -S the outer coat of a spore

EXOTERIC   *adj* suitable for the public

EXOTIC   *n* pl. -S something from another part of the world

EXOTICA   *n/pl* things excitingly different or unusual

EXOTISM   *n* pl. -S an exotic

EXOTOXIN   *n* pl. -S an excreted toxin **EXOTOXIC** *adj*

EXPAND   *v* -ED, -ING, -S to increase in size or volume

EXPANDER   *n* pl. -S one that expands

EXPANDOR   *n* pl. -S a type of transducer

EXPANSE   *n* pl. -S a wide, continuous area

EXPAT   *n* pl. -S an expatriate person

EXPECT   *v* -ED, -ING, -S to anticipate

EXPEDITE   *v* -DITED, -DITING, -DITES to speed up the progress of

EXPEL   *v* -PELLED, -PELLING, -PELS to force out

EXPELLEE   *n* pl. -S a deportee

EXPELLER   *n* pl. -S one that expels

EXPELLING   present participle of expel

EXPEND   *v* -ED, -ING, -S to use up

EXPENDER   *n* pl. -S one that expends

EXPENSE   *v* -PENSED, -PENSING, -PENSES to charge with costs

EXPERT   *v* -ED, -ING, -S to serve as an authority

EXPERTLY   *adv* skillfully

EXPIABLE   *adj* capable of being expiated

EXPIATE   *v* -ATED, -ATING, -ATES to atone for

EXPIATOR   *n* pl. -S one that expiates

EXPIRE   *v* -PIRED, -PIRING, -PIRES to come to an end

EXPIRER   *n* pl. -S one that expires

EXPIRY   *n* pl. -RIES a termination

EXPLAIN   *v* -ED, -ING, -S to make plain or understandable

EXPLANT   *v* -ED, -ING, -S to remove from the natural site of growth and place in a medium

EXPLICIT   *n* pl. -S a statement formerly used at the close of a book

EXPLODE   *v* -PLODED, -PLODING, -PLODES to blow up

EXPLODER *n* pl. -S one that explodes

EXPLOIT *v* -ED, -ING, -S to take advantage of

EXPLORE *v* -PLORED, -PLORING, -PLORES to travel through for the purpose of discovery

EXPLORER *n* pl. -S one that explores

EXPO *n* pl. -POS a public exhibition

EXPONENT *n* pl. -S one who expounds

EXPORT *v* -ED, -ING, -S to send to other countries for commercial purposes

EXPORTER *n* pl. -S one that exports

EXPOSAL *n* pl. -S an exposure

EXPOSE *v* -POSED, -POSING, -POSES to lay open to view

EXPOSER *n* pl. -S one that exposes

EXPOSIT *v* -ED, -ING, -S to expound

EXPOSURE *n* pl. -S the act of exposing

EXPOUND *v* -ED, -ING, -S to explain in detail

EXPRESS *v* -ED, -ING, -ES to set forth in words

EXPRESSO *n* pl. -SOS espresso

EXPULSE *v* -PULSED, -PULSING, -PULSES to expel

EXPUNGE *v* -PUNGED, -PUNGING, -PUNGES to delete

EXPUNGER *n* pl. -S one that expunges

EXSCIND *v* -ED, -ING, -S to cut out

EXSECANT *n* pl. -S a trigonometric function of an angle

EXSECT *v* -ED, -ING, -S to cut out

EXSERT *v* -ED, -ING, -S to thrust out

EXTANT *adj* still in existence

EXTEND *v* -ED, -ING, -S to stretch out to full length

EXTENDER *n* pl. -S a substance added to another substance

EXTENSOR *n* pl. -S a muscle that extends a limb

EXTENT *n* pl. -S the range over which something extends

EXTERIOR *n* pl. -S a part or surface that is outside

EXTERN *n* pl. -S a nonresident of an institution

EXTERNAL *n* pl. -S an exterior

EXTERNE *n* pl. -S extern

EXTINCT *v* -ED, -ING, -S to extinguish

EXTOL *v* -TOLLED, -TOLLING, -TOLS to praise highly

EXTOLL *v* -ED, -ING, -S to extol

EXTOLLER *n* pl. -S one that extols

EXTOLLING present participle of extol

EXTORT *v* -ED, -ING, -S to obtain from a person by violence or intimidation

EXTORTER *n* pl. -S one that extorts

EXTRA *n* pl. -S something additional

EXTRACT *v* -ED, -ING, -S to pull or draw out

EXTRADOS *n* pl. -ES the outer curve of an arch

EXTREMA pl. of extremum

EXTREME *adj* -TREMER, -TREMEST existing in a very high degree

EXTREME *n* pl. -S the highest degree

EXTREMUM *n* pl. -MA a maximum or a minimum of a mathematical function

EXTRORSE *adj* facing outward

EXTRUDE *v* -TRUDED, -TRUDING, -TRUDES to force, thrust, or push out

EXTRUDER *n* pl. -S one that extrudes

EXTUBATE *v* -BATED, -BATING, -BATES to remove a tube from

EXUDATE *n* pl. -S an exuded substance

EXUDE *v* -UDED, -UDING, -UDES to ooze forth

EXULT *v* -ED, -ING, -S to rejoice greatly

EXULTANT *adj* exulting

EXURB *n* pl. -S a residential area lying beyond the suburbs of a city **EXURBAN** *adj*

EXURBIA *n* pl. -S an exurb

EXUVIATE *v* -ATED, -ATING, -ATES to molt

EXUVIUM *n* pl. -VIAE or -VIA the molted covering of an animal **EXUVIAL** *adj*

EYAS *n* pl. -ES a young hawk

EYE *v* EYED, EYING or EYEING, EYES to watch closely **EYEABLE** *adj*

EYE *n* pl. EYES, EYEN or EYNE the organ of sight

EYEBALL *v* -ED, -ING, -S to eye

EYEBAR *n* pl. -S a metal bar with a loop at one or both ends

EYEBEAM *n* pl. -S a glance

EYEBOLT	*n* pl. -S a type of bolt or screw
EYEBROW	*n* pl. -S the ridge over the eye
EYECUP	*n* pl. -S a cup used for applying lotions to the eyes
EYED	past tense of eye
EYEDNESS	*n* pl. -ES preference for the use of one eye over the other
EYEDROPS	*n/pl* a medicated solution for the eyes applied in drops
EYEFUL	*n* pl. -S a complete view
EYEGLASS	*n* pl. -ES a lens used to aid vision
EYEHOLE	*n* pl. -S a small opening
EYEHOOK	*n* pl. -S a type of hook
EYELASH	*n* pl. -ES a hair growing on the edge of an eyelid
EYELESS	*adj* lacking eyes
EYELET	*v* -LETTED, -LETTING, -LETS to make a small hole in
EYELID	*n* pl. -S the lid of skin that can be closed over an eyeball
EYELIKE	*adj* resembling an eye
EYELINER	*n* pl. -S makeup for the eyes
EYEN	a pl. of eye
EYEPIECE	*n* pl. -S the lens or lens group nearest the eye in an optical instrument
EYEPOINT	*n* pl. -S the point at which an eye is placed in using an optical instrument
EYER	*n* pl. -S one that eyes
EYESHADE	*n* pl. -S a visor for shading the eyes
EYESHOT	*n* pl. -S the range of vision
EYESIGHT	*n* pl. -S the ability to see
EYESOME	*adj* pleasant to look at
EYESORE	*n* pl. -S something offensive to the sight
EYESPOT	*n* pl. -S a simple visual organ of lower animals
EYESTALK	*n* pl. -S a stalklike structure with an eye at its tip
EYESTONE	*n* pl. -S a disk used to remove foreign matter from the eye
EYETOOTH	*n* pl. -TEETH a cuspid
EYEWASH	*n* pl. -ES an eye lotion
EYEWATER	*n* pl. -S an eyewash
EYEWEAR	*n* pl. EYEWEAR a device worn on or over the eyes
EYEWINK	*n* pl. -S a wink of the eye
EYING	a present participle of eye
EYNE	a pl. of eye
EYRA	*n* pl. -S a wild cat of tropical America
EYRE	*n* pl. -S a journey
EYRIE	*n* pl. -S aerie
EYRIR	*n* pl. AURAR a monetary unit of Iceland
EYRY	*n* pl. -RIES aerie

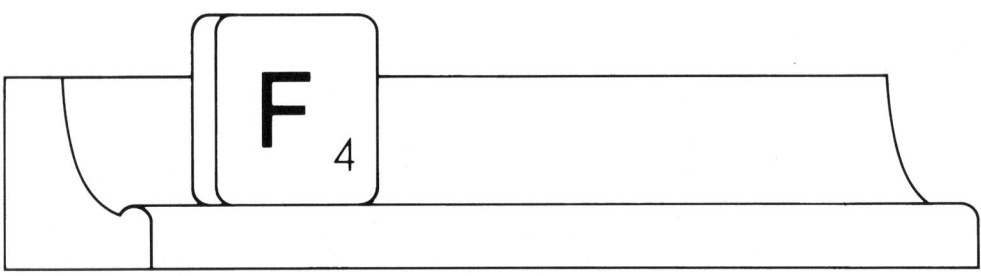

FA	*n* pl. -S the fourth tone of the diatonic musical scale
FABLE	*v* -BLED, -BLING, -BLES to compose or tell fictitious tales
FABLER	*n* pl. -S one that fables
FABLIAU	*n* pl. -AUX a short metrical tale popular in medieval France
FABLING	present participle of fable
FABRIC	*n* pl. -S a woven, felted, or knitted material
FABULAR	*adj* legendary
FABULIST	*n* pl. -S a liar
FABULOUS	*adj* almost unbelievable
FACADE	*n* pl. -S the front of a building
FACE	*v* FACED, FACING, FACES to oppose or meet defiantly **FACEABLE** *adj*
FACEDOWN	*adv* with the front part down
FACELESS	*adj* lacking personal distinction or identity
FACER	*n* pl. -S one that faces
FACET	*v* -ETED, -ETING, -ETS or -ETTED, -ETTING, -ETS to cut small plane surfaces on
FACETE	*adj* witty **FACETELY** *adv*
FACETIAE	*n/pl* witty sayings or writings
FACETTED	a past tense of facet
FACETTING	a present participle of facet
FACEUP	*adv* with the front part up
FACIA	*n* pl. -S fascia
FACIAL	*n* pl. -S a treatment for the face
FACIALLY	*adv* with respect to the face
FACIEND	*n* pl. -S a number to be multiplied by another
FACIES	*n* pl. FACIES general appearance
FACILE	*adj* easily achieved or performed **FACILELY** *adv*
FACILITY	*n* pl. -TIES the quality of being facile
FACING	*n* pl. -S a lining at the edge of a garment
FACT	*n* pl. -S something known with certainty **FACTFUL** *adj*
FACTION	*n* pl. -S a clique within a larger group
FACTIOUS	*adj* promoting dissension
FACTOID	*n* pl. -S a brief news item
FACTOR	*v* -ED, -ING, -S to express as a product of two or more quantities
FACTORY	*n* pl. -RIES a building or group of buildings in which goods are manufactured
FACTOTUM	*n* pl. -S a person employed to do many kinds of work
FACTUAL	*adj* pertaining to facts
FACTURE	*n* pl. -S the act of making something
FACULA	*n* pl. -LAE an unusually bright spot on the sun's surface **FACULAR** *adj*
FACULTY	*n* pl. -TIES an inherent power or ability
FAD	*n* pl. -S a practice or interest that enjoys brief popularity
FADABLE	*adj* capable of fading
FADDIER	comparative of faddy
FADDIEST	superlative of faddy
FADDISH	*adj* inclined to take up fads
FADDISM	*n* pl. -S inclination to take up fads
FADDIST	*n* pl. -S a faddish person
FADDY	*adj* -DIER, -DIEST faddish
FADE	*v* FADED, FADING, FADES to lose color or brightness **FADEDLY** *adv*
FADEAWAY	*n* pl. -AWAYS a type of pitch in baseball
FADELESS	*adj* not fading

FADER	*n* pl. -S one that fades
FADGE	*v* FADGED, FADGING, FADGES to succeed
FADING	*n* pl. -S an Irish dance
FADO	*n* pl. -DOS a Portuguese folk song
FAECES	*n/pl* feces **FAECAL** *adj*
FAENA	*n* pl. -S a series of passes made by a matador in a bullfight
FAERIE	*n* pl. -S a fairy
FAERY	*n* pl. -ERIES faerie
FAG	*v* FAGGED, FAGGING, FAGS to make weary by hard work
FAGGOT	*v* -ED, -ING, -S to fagot
FAGIN	*n* pl. -S a person who instructs others in crime
FAGOT	*v* -ED, -ING, -S to bind together into a bundle
FAGOTER	*n* pl. -S one that fagots
FAGOTING	*n* pl. -S a type of embroidery
FAHLBAND	*n* pl. -S a band or stratum of rock impregnated with metallic sulfides
FAIENCE	*n* pl. -S a variety of glazed pottery
FAIL	*v* -ED, -ING, -S to be unsuccessful in an attempt
FAILING	*n* pl. -S a minor fault or weakness
FAILLE	*n* pl. -S a woven fabric
FAILURE	*n* pl. -S the act of failing
FAIN	*adj* FAINER, FAINEST glad
FAINEANT	*n* pl. -S a lazy person
FAINT	*v* -ED, -ING, -S to lose consciousness
FAINT	*adj* FAINTER, FAINTEST lacking strength or vigor
FAINTER	*n* pl. -S one that faints
FAINTISH	*adj* somewhat faint
FAINTLY	*adv* in a faint manner
FAIR	*adj* FAIRER, FAIREST free from bias, dishonesty, or injustice
FAIR	*v* -ED, -ING, -S to make smooth
FAIRIES	pl. of fairy
FAIRING	*n* pl. -S a structure on an aircraft serving to reduce drag
FAIRISH	*adj* moderately good
FAIRLEAD	*n* pl. -S a device used to hold a ship's rigging in place
FAIRLY	*adv* in a fair manner
FAIRNESS	*n* pl. -ES the quality of being fair
FAIRWAY	*n* pl. -WAYS the mowed part of a golf course between tee and green
FAIRY	*n* pl. FAIRIES an imaginary supernatural being
FAIRYISM	*n* pl. -S the quality of being like a fairy
FAITH	*v* -ED, -ING, -S to believe or trust
FAITHFUL	*n* pl. -S a loyal follower or member
FAITOUR	*n* pl. -S an impostor
FAJITA	*n* pl. -S marinated and grilled beef, chicken, or shrimp served with a flour tortilla
FAKE	*v* FAKED, FAKING, FAKES to contrive and present as genuine
FAKEER	*n* pl. -S fakir
FAKER	*n* pl. -S one that fakes
FAKERY	*n* pl. -ERIES the practice of faking
FAKEY	*adj* not genuine; phony
FAKING	present participle of fake
FAKIR	*n* pl. -S a Hindu ascetic
FALAFEL	*n* pl. FALAFEL ground spiced vegetables formed into patties
FALBALA	*n* pl. -S a trimming for a woman's garment
FALCATE	*adj* curved and tapering to a point
FALCATED	*adj* falcate
FALCES	pl. of falx
FALCHION	*n* pl. -S a broad-bladed sword
FALCON	*n* pl. -S a bird of prey
FALCONER	*n* pl. -S one that hunts with hawks
FALCONET	*n* pl. -S a small falcon
FALCONRY	*n* pl. -RIES the sport of hunting with falcons
FALDERAL	*n* pl. -S nonsense
FALDEROL	*n* pl. -S falderal
FALL	*v* FELL, FALLEN, FALLING, FALLS to descend under the force of gravity
FALLACY	*n* pl. -CIES a false idea
FALLAL	*n* pl. -S a showy article of dress
FALLAWAY	*n* pl. -AWAYS a shot in basketball
FALLBACK	*n* pl. -S an act of retreating
FALLEN	past participle of fall

FALLER *n* pl. -S one that falls

FALLFISH *n* pl. -ES a freshwater fish

FALLIBLE *adj* capable of erring **FALLIBLY** *adv*

FALLOFF *n* pl. -S a decline in quantity or quality

FALLOUT *n* pl. -S radioactive debris resulting from a nuclear explosion

FALLOW *v* -ED, -ING, -S to plow and leave unseeded

FALSE *adj* FALSER, FALSEST contrary to truth or fact **FALSELY** *adv*

FALSETTO *n* pl. -TOS an artificially high voice

FALSIE *n* pl. -S a pad worn within a brassiere

FALSIFY *v* -FIED, -FYING, -FIES to represent falsely

FALSITY *n* pl. -TIES something false

FALTBOAT *n* pl. -S a collapsible boat resembling a kayak

FALTER *v* -ED, -ING, -S to hesitate

FALTERER *n* pl. -S one that falters

FALX *n* pl. FALCES a sickle-shaped structure

FAME *v* FAMED, FAMING, FAMES to make famous

FAMELESS *adj* not famous

FAMILIAL *adj* pertaining to a family

FAMILIAR *n* pl. -S a close friend or associate

FAMILISM *n* pl. -S a social structure in which the family takes precedence over the individual

FAMILY *n* pl. -LIES a group of persons related by blood or marriage

FAMINE *n* pl. -S a widespread scarcity of food

FAMING present participle of fame

FAMISH *v* -ED, -ING, -ES to suffer extreme hunger

FAMOUS *adj* well-known **FAMOUSLY** *adv*

FAMULUS *n* pl. -LI a servant or attendant

FAN *v* FANNED, FANNING, FANS to cool or refresh with a fan (a device for putting air into motion)

FANATIC *n* pl. -S a zealot

FANCIED past tense of fancy

FANCIER *n* pl. -S one that has a special liking for something

FANCIES present 3d person sing. of fancy

FANCIFUL *adj* unrealistic

FANCIFY *v* -FIED, -FYING, -FIES to make fancy

FANCY *adj* -CIER, -CIEST ornamental **FANCILY** *adv*

FANCY *v* -CIED, -CYING, -CIES to take a liking to

FANDANGO *n* pl. -GOS a lively Spanish dance

FANDOM *n* pl. -S an aggregate of enthusiastic devotees

FANE *n* pl. -S a temple

FANEGA *n* pl. -S a Spanish unit of dry measure

FANEGADA *n* pl. -S a Spanish unit of area

FANFARE *n* pl. -S a short, lively musical flourish

FANFARON *n* pl. -S a braggart

FANFOLD *v* -ED, -ING, -S to fold paper like a fan

FANG *n* pl. -S a long, pointed tooth **FANGED, FANGLESS, FANGLIKE** *adj*

FANGA *n* pl. -S fanega

FANION *n* pl. -S a small flag

FANJET *n* pl. -S a type of jet engine

FANLIGHT *n* pl. -S a type of window

FANLIKE *adj* resembling a fan

FANNED past tense of fan

FANNER *n* pl. -S one that fans

FANNING present participle of fan

FANNY *n* pl. -NIES the buttocks

FANO *n* pl. FANOS a fanon

FANON *n* pl. -S a cape worn by the pope

FANTAIL *n* pl. -S a fan-shaped tail or end

FANTASIA *n* pl. -S a free-form musical composition

FANTASIE *n* pl. -S a fantasia

FANTASIED past tense of fantasy

FANTASIES present 3d person sing. of fantasy

FANTASM *n* pl. -S phantasm

FANTAST *n* pl. -S an impractical person

FANTASY *v* -SIED, -SYING, -SIES to imagine

FANTOD *n* pl. -S an emotional outburst

FANTOM *n* pl. -S phantom

FANUM *n* pl. -S fanon

FANWISE	*adj* spread out like an open fan
FANWORT	*n* pl. -S an aquatic plant
FANZINE	*n* pl. -S a magazine written by and for enthusiastic devotees
FAQIR	*n* pl. -S fakir
FAQUIR	*n* pl. -S fakir
FAR	*adv* FARTHER, FARTHEST or FURTHER, FURTHEST at or to a great distance
FARAD	*n* pl. -S a unit of electrical capacitance
FARADAIC	*adj* faradic
FARADAY	*n* pl. -DAYS a unit of electricity
FARADIC	*adj* pertaining to a type of electric current
FARADISE	*v* -DISED, -DISING, -DISES to faradize
FARADISM	*n* pl. -S the use of faradic current for therapeutic purposes
FARADIZE	*v* -DIZED, -DIZING, -DIZES to treat by faradism
FARAWAY	*adj* distant
FARCE	*v* FARCED, FARCING, FARCES to fill out with witty material
FARCER	*n* pl. -S farceur
FARCEUR	*n* pl. -S a joker
FARCI	*adj* stuffed with finely chopped meat
FARCICAL	*adj* absurd
FARCIE	*adj* farci
FARCING	present participle of farce
FARCY	*n* pl. -CIES a disease of horses
FARD	*v* -ED, -ING, -S to apply cosmetics to
FARDEL	*n* pl. -S a bundle
FARE	*v* FARED, FARING, FARES to get along
FARER	*n* pl. -S a traveler
FAREWELL	*v* -ED, -ING, -S to say goodby
FARFAL	*n* pl. -S farfel
FARFEL	*n* pl. -S noodles in the form of small pellets or granules
FARINA	*n* pl. -S a fine meal made from cereal grain
FARING	present participle of fare
FARINHA	*n* pl. -S a meal made from the root of the cassava
FARINOSE	*adj* resembling farina
FARL	*n* pl. -S a thin oatmeal cake
FARLE	*n* pl. -S farl
FARM	*v* -ED, -ING, -S to manage and cultivate as a farm (a tract of land devoted to agriculture) **FARMABLE** *adj*
FARMER	*n* pl. -S one that farms
FARMHAND	*n* pl. -S a farm laborer
FARMING	*n* pl. -S the business of operating a farm
FARMLAND	*n* pl. -S cultivated land
FARMWIFE	*n* pl. -WIVES a farmer's wife
FARMWORK	*n* pl. -S labor done on a farm
FARMYARD	*n* pl. -S an area surrounded by farm buildings
FARNESOL	*n* pl. -S an alcohol used in perfumes
FARNESS	*n* pl. -ES the state of being far off or apart
FARO	*n* pl. FAROS a card game
FAROUCHE	*adj* sullenly shy
FARRAGO	*n* pl. -GOES a confused mixture
FARRIER	*n* pl. -S one that shoes horses
FARRIERY	*n* pl. -ERIES the trade of a farrier
FARROW	*v* -ED, -ING, -S to give birth to a litter of pigs
FARSIDE	*n* pl. -S the farther side
FARTHER	a comparative of far
FARTHEST	a superlative of far
FARTHING	*n* pl. -S a former British coin
FASCES	*n* pl. FASCES an ancient Roman symbol of power
FASCIA	*n* pl. -CIAE or -CIAS a broad and distinct band of color **FASCIAL, FASCIATE** *adj*
FASCICLE	*n* pl. -S a small bundle
FASCINE	*n* pl. -S a bundle of sticks used in building fortifications
FASCISM	*n* pl. -S an oppressive political system
FASCIST	*n* pl. -S an advocate of fascism
FASH	*v* -ED, -ING, -ES to annoy
FASHION	*v* -ED, -ING, -S to give a particular shape or form to
FASHIOUS	*adj* annoying
FAST	*adj* FASTER, FASTEST moving or able to move quickly
FAST	*v* -ED, -ING, -S to abstain from eating
FASTBACK	*n* pl. -S a type of automobile roof

FASTBALL	*n* pl. -S a type of pitch in baseball
FASTEN	*v* -ED, -ING, -S to secure
FASTENER	*n* pl. -S one that fastens
FASTING	*n* pl. -S abstention from eating
FASTNESS	*n* pl. -ES the quality of being fast
FASTUOUS	*adj* arrogant
FAT	*adj* FATTER, FATTEST having an abundance of flesh
FAT	*v* FATTED, FATTING, FATS to make fat
FATAL	*adj* causing or capable of causing death
FATALISM	*n* pl. -S the doctrine that all events are predetermined
FATALIST	*n* pl. -S a believer in fatalism
FATALITY	*n* pl. -TIES a death resulting from an unexpected occurrence
FATALLY	*adv* in a fatal manner
FATBACK	*n* pl. -S a marine fish
FATBIRD	*n* pl. -S a wading bird
FATE	*v* FATED, FATING, FATES to destine
FATEFUL	*adj* decisively important
FATHEAD	*n* pl. -S a dolt
FATHER	*v* -ED, -ING, -S to cause to exist
FATHERLY	*adj* paternal
FATHOM	*v* -ED, -ING, -S to understand
FATIDIC	*adj* pertaining to prophecy
FATIGUE	*v* -TIGUED, -TIGUING, -TIGUES to weary
FATING	present participle of fate
FATLESS	*adj* having no fat
FATLIKE	*adj* resembling fat
FATLING	*n* pl. -S a young animal fattened for slaughter
FATLY	*adv* in the manner of one that is fat
FATNESS	*n* pl. -ES the state of being fat
FATSTOCK	*n* pl. -S livestock that is fat and ready for market
FATTED	past tense of fat
FATTEN	*v* -ED, -ING, -S to make fat
FATTENER	*n* pl. -S one that fattens
FATTER	comparative of fat
FATTEST	superlative of fat
FATTIER	comparative of fatty
FATTIES	pl. of fatty
FATTIEST	superlative of fatty
FATTILY	*adv* in a fatty manner
FATTING	present participle of fat
FATTISH	*adj* somewhat fat
FATTY	*adj* -TIER, -TIEST greasy; oily
FATTY	*n* pl. -TIES one that is fat
FATUITY	*n* pl. -ITIES something foolish or stupid
FATUOUS	*adj* smugly stupid
FATWA	*n* pl. -S an Islamic legal decree
FATWOOD	*n* pl. -S wood used for kindling
FAUBOURG	*n* pl. -S a suburb
FAUCAL	*n* pl. -S a sound produced in the fauces
FAUCES	*n/pl* the passage from the mouth to the pharynx
FAUCET	*n* pl. -S a device for controlling the flow of liquid from a pipe
FAUCIAL	*adj* pertaining to the fauces
FAUGH	*interj* — used to express disgust
FAULD	*n* pl. -S a piece of armor below the breastplate
FAULT	*v* -ED, -ING, -S to criticize
FAULTY	*adj* FAULTIER, FAULTIEST imperfect **FAULTILY** *adv*
FAUN	*n* pl. -S a woodland deity of Roman mythology **FAUNLIKE** *adj*
FAUNA	*n* pl. -NAS or -NAE the animal life of a particular region **FAUNAL** *adj* **FAUNALLY** *adv*
FAUTEUIL	*n* pl. -S an armchair
FAUVE	*n* pl. -S a fauvist
FAUVISM	*n* pl. -S a movement in painting
FAUVIST	*n* pl. -S an advocate of fauvism
FAUX	*adj* not genuine; fake
FAVA	*n* pl. -S the edible seed of a climbing vine
FAVE	*n* pl. -S a favorite
FAVELA	*n* pl. -S a slum area
FAVELLA	*n* pl. -S favela
FAVISM	*n* pl. -S an acute anemia
FAVONIAN	*adj* pertaining to the west wind
FAVOR	*v* -ED, -ING, -S to regard with approval
FAVORER	*n* pl. -S one that favors
FAVORITE	*n* pl. -S a person or thing preferred above all others
FAVOUR	*v* -ED, -ING, -S to favor

FAVOURER   *n* pl. -S favorer

FAVUS   *n* pl. -ES a skin disease

FAWN   *v* -ED, -ING, -S to seek notice or favor by servile demeanor

FAWNER   *n* pl. -S one that fawns

FAWNLIKE   *adj* resembling a young deer

FAWNY   *adj* FAWNIER, FAWNIEST of a yellowish-brown color

FAX   *v* -ED, -ING, -ES to transmit and reproduce by electronic means

FAY   *v* -ED, -ING, -S to join closely

FAYALITE   *n* pl. -S a mineral

FAZE   *v* FAZED, FAZING, FAZES to disturb the composure of

FAZENDA   *n* pl. -S a Brazilian plantation

FEAL   *adj* loyal

FEALTY   *n* pl. -TIES loyalty

FEAR   *v* -ED, -ING, -S to be afraid of

FEARER   *n* pl. -S one that fears

FEARFUL   *adj* -FULLER, -FULLEST afraid

FEARLESS   *adj* unafraid

FEARSOME   *adj* frightening

FEASANCE   *n* pl. -S the performance of a condition, obligation, or duty

FEASE   *v* FEASED, FEASING, FEASES to faze

FEASIBLE   *adj* capable of being done **FEASIBLY** *adv*

FEAST   *v* -ED, -ING, -S to eat sumptuously

FEASTER   *n* pl. -S one that feasts

FEASTFUL   *adj* festive

FEAT   *n* pl. -S a notable act or achievement

FEAT   *adj* FEATER, FEATEST skillful

FEATHER   *v* -ED, -ING, -S to cover with feathers (horny structures that form the principal covering of birds)

FEATHERY   *adj* -ERIER, -ERIEST resembling feathers

FEATLY   *adj* -LIER, -LIEST graceful

FEATURE   *v* -TURED, -TURING, -TURES to give special prominence to

FEAZE   *v* FEAZED, FEAZING, FEAZES to faze

FEBRIFIC   *adj* feverish

FEBRILE   *adj* feverish

FECAL   *adj* pertaining to feces

FECES   *n/pl* bodily waste discharged through the anus

FECIAL   *n* pl. -S fetial

FECK   *n* pl. -S value

FECKLESS   *adj* worthless

FECKLY   *adv* almost

FECULA   *n* pl. -LAE fecal matter

FECULENT   *adj* foul with impurities

FECUND   *adj* fruitful

FED   *n* pl. -S a federal agent

FEDAYEE   *n* pl. -YEEN an Arab commando

FEDERACY   *n* pl. -CIES an alliance

FEDERAL   *n* pl. -S a supporter of a type of central government

FEDERATE   *v* -ATED, -ATING, -ATES to unite in an alliance

FEDORA   *n* pl. -S a type of hat

FEE   *v* FEED, FEEING, FEES to pay a fee (a fixed charge) to

FEEBLE   *adj* -BLER, -BLEST weak **FEEBLY** *adv*

FEEBLISH   *adj* somewhat feeble

FEED   *v* FED, FEEDING, FEEDS to give food to **FEEDABLE** *adj*

FEEDBACK   *n* pl. -S the return of a portion of the output to the input

FEEDBAG   *n* pl. -S a bag for feeding horses

FEEDBOX   *n* pl. -ES a box for animal feed

FEEDER   *n* pl. -S one that feeds

FEEDHOLE   *n* pl. -S one of a series of holes in paper tape

FEEDLOT   *n* pl. -S a plot of land on which livestock is fattened

FEEL   *v* FELT, FEELING, FEELS to perceive through the sense of touch

FEELER   *n* pl. -S a tactile organ

FEELESS   *adj* requiring no fee

FEELING   *n* pl. -S the function or power of perceiving by touch

FEET   pl. of foot **FEETLESS** *adj*

FEEZE   *v* FEEZED, FEEZING, FEEZES to faze

FEH   *n* pl. -S peh

FEIGN   *v* -ED, -ING, -S to pretend

FEIGNER   *n* pl. -S one that feigns

FEIJOA   *n* pl. -S a green edible fruit

FEINT   *v* -ED, -ING, -S to make a deceptive movement

FEIRIE   *adj* nimble

FEIST   *n* pl. -S a small dog of mixed breed

FEISTY   *adj* FEISTIER, FEISTIEST full of nervous energy

FELAFEL   *n* pl. FELAFEL falafel

FELDSHER   *n* pl. -S a medical worker in Russia

FELDSPAR   *n* pl. -S a mineral

FELICITY   *n* pl. -TIES happiness

FELID   *n* pl. -S a feline

FELINE   *n* pl. -S an animal of the cat family

FELINELY   *adv* in a catlike manner

FELINITY   *n* pl. -TIES the quality of being catlike

FELL   *v* -ED, -ING, -S to cause to fall

FELL   *adj* FELLER, FELLEST cruel

FELLA   *n* pl. -S a man or boy

FELLABLE   *adj* capable of being felled

FELLAH   *n* pl. -LAHS, -LAHIN, or -LAHEEN a peasant or laborer in Arab countries

FELLATE   *v* -LATED, -LATING, -LATES to perform fellatio

FELLATIO   *n* pl. -TIOS oral stimulation of the penis

FELLATOR   *n* pl. -S one that fellates

FELLER   *n* pl. -S one that fells

FELLIES   pl. of felly

FELLNESS   *n* pl. -ES extreme cruelty

FELLOE   *n* pl. -S the rim of a wheel

FELLOW   *v* -ED, -ING, -S to produce an equal to

FELLOWLY   *adj* friendly

FELLY   *n* pl. -LIES a felloe

FELON   *n* pl. -S a person who has committed a felony

FELONRY   *n* pl. -RIES the whole class of felons

FELONY   *n* pl. -NIES a grave crime

FELSITE   *n* pl. -S an igneous rock
FELSITIC *adj*

FELSPAR   *n* pl. -S feldspar

FELSTONE   *n* pl. -S felsite

FELT   *v* -ED, -ING, -S to mat together

FELTING   *n* pl. -S felted material

FELTLIKE   *adj* like a cloth made from wool

FELUCCA   *n* pl. -S a swift sailing vessel

FELWORT   *n* pl. -S a flowering plant

FEM   *n* pl. -S a passive homosexual

FEMALE   *n* pl. -S an individual that bears young or produces ova

FEME   *n* pl. -S a wife

FEMINACY   *n* pl. -CIES the state of being a female

FEMINIE   *n/pl* women collectively

FEMININE   *n* pl. -S a word or form having feminine gender

FEMINISE   *v* -NISED, -NISING, -NISES to feminize

FEMINISM   *n* pl. -S a doctrine advocating rights for women equal to those of men

FEMINIST   *n* pl. -S a supporter of feminism

FEMINITY   *n* pl. -TIES the quality of being womanly

FEMINIZE   *v* -NIZED, -NIZING, -NIZES to make womanly

FEMME   *n* pl. -S a woman

FEMORAL   *adj* pertaining to the femur

FEMUR   *n* pl. -MURS or -MORA a bone of the leg

FEN   *n* pl. -S a marsh

FENAGLE   *v* -GLED, -GLING, -GLES to finagle

FENCE   *v* FENCED, FENCING, FENCES to practice the art of fencing

FENCER   *n* pl. -S one that fences

FENCEROW   *n* pl. -S the land occupied by a fence

FENCIBLE   *n* pl. -S a soldier enlisted for home service only

FENCING   *n* pl. -S the art of using a sword in attack and defense

FEND   *v* -ED, -ING, -S to ward off

FENDER   *n* pl. -S a metal guard over the wheel of a motor vehicle
FENDERED *adj*

FENESTRA   *n* pl. -TRAE a small anatomical opening

FENLAND   *n* pl. -S marshy ground

FENNEC   *n* pl. -S an African fox

FENNEL   *n* pl. -S a perennial herb

FENNY   *adj* marshy

FENTHION   *n* pl. -S an insecticide

FENURON   *n* pl. -S an herbicide

FEOD   *n* pl. -S a fief

FEODARY	*n* pl. -RIES a vassal
FEOFF	*v* -ED, -ING, -S to grant a fief to
FEOFFEE	*n* pl. -S one to whom a fief is granted
FEOFFER	*n* pl. -S one that grants a fief to another
FEOFFOR	*n* pl. -S feoffer
FER	*prep* for
FERACITY	*n* pl. -TIES the state of being fruitful
FERAL	*adj* wild
FERBAM	*n* pl. -S a fungicide
FERE	*n* pl. -S a companion
FERETORY	*n* pl. -RIES a receptacle in which sacred relics are kept
FERIA	*n* pl. -RIAS or -RIAE a weekday of a church calendar on which no feast is celebrated **FERIAL** *adj*
FERINE	*adj* feral
FERITY	*n* pl. -TIES wildness
FERLIE	*n* pl. -S a strange sight
FERLY	*n* pl. -LIES ferlie
FERMATA	*n* pl. -TAS or -TE the sustaining of a musical note, chord, or rest beyond its written time value
FERMENT	*v* -ED, -ING, -S to undergo a type of chemical reaction
FERMI	*n* pl. -S a unit of length
FERMION	*n* pl. -S a type of atomic particle
FERMIUM	*n* pl. -S a radioactive element
FERN	*n* pl. -S a flowerless vascular plant **FERNLESS, FERNLIKE** *adj*
FERNERY	*n* pl. -ERIES a place in which ferns are grown
FERNY	*adj* FERNIER, FERNIEST abounding in ferns
FEROCITY	*n* pl. -TIES fierceness
FERRATE	*n* pl. -S a chemical salt
FERREL	*v* -RELED, -RELING, -RELS or -RELLED, -RELLING, -RELS ferrule
FERREOUS	*adj* containing iron
FERRET	*v* -ED, -ING, -S to search out by careful investigation
FERRETER	*n* pl. -S one that ferrets
FERRETY	*adj* suggestive of a ferret (a polecat)
FERRIAGE	*n* pl. -S transportation by ferry
FERRIC	*adj* pertaining to iron
FERRIED	past tense of ferry
FERRIES	present 3d person sing. of ferry
FERRITE	*n* pl. -S a magnetic substance **FERRITIC** *adj*
FERRITIN	*n* pl. -S a protein that contains iron
FERROUS	*adj* pertaining to iron
FERRULE	*v* -RULED, -RULING, -RULES to furnish with a metal ring or cap to prevent splitting
FERRUM	*n* pl. -S iron
FERRY	*v* -RIED, -RYING, -RIES to transport by ferry (a type of boat)
FERRYMAN	*n* pl. -MEN one who operates a ferry
FERTILE	*adj* capable of reproducing
FERULA	*n* pl. -LAE or -LAS a flat piece of wood
FERULE	*v* -ULED, -ULING, -ULES to ferrule
FERVENCY	*n* pl. -CIES fervor
FERVENT	*adj* marked by fervor
FERVID	*adj* fervent **FERVIDLY** *adv*
FERVOR	*n* pl. -S great warmth or intensity
FERVOUR	*n* pl. -S fervor
FESCUE	*n* pl. -S a perennial grass
FESS	*v* -ED, -ING, -ES to confess
FESSE	*n* pl. -S a horizontal band across the middle of a heraldic shield
FESSWISE	*adv* horizontally
FESTAL	*adj* festive **FESTALLY** *adv*
FESTER	*v* -ED, -ING, -S to generate pus
FESTIVAL	*n* pl. -S a day or time of celebration
FESTIVE	*adj* of or befitting a festival
FESTOON	*v* -ED, -ING, -S to hang decorative chains or strips on
FET	*v* FETTED, FETTING, FETS to fetch
FETA	*n* pl. -S a Greek cheese
FETAL	*adj* pertaining to a fetus
FETATION	*n* pl. -S the development of a fetus
FETCH	*v* -ED, -ING, -ES to go after and bring back
FETCHER	*n* pl. -S one that fetches
FETE	*v* FETED, FETING, FETES to honor with a celebration
FETERITA	*n* pl. -S a cereal grass

FETIAL	*n* pl. -S a priest of ancient Rome
FETIALIS	*n* pl. -LES fetial
FETICH	*n* pl. -ES fetish
FETICIDE	*n* pl. -S the killing of a fetus
FETID	*adj* having an offensive odor **FETIDLY** *adv*
FETING	present participle of fete
FETISH	*n* pl. -ES an object believed to have magical power
FETLOCK	*n* pl. -S a joint of a horse's leg
FETOLOGY	*n* pl. -GIES the branch of medicine dealing with the fetus
FETOR	*n* pl. -S an offensive odor
FETTED	past tense of fet
FETTER	*v* -ED, -ING, -S to shackle
FETTERER	*n* pl. -S one that fetters
FETTING	present participle of fet
FETTLE	*v* -TLED, -TLING, -TLES to cover the hearth of with fettling
FETTLING	*n* pl. -S loose material thrown on the hearth of a furnace to protect it
FETUS	*n* pl. -ES the unborn organism carried within the womb in the later stages of its development
FEU	*v* -ED, -ING, -S to grant land to under Scottish feudal law
FEUAR	*n* pl. -S one granted land under Scottish feudal law
FEUD	*v* -ED, -ING, -S to engage in a feud (a bitter, continuous hostility)
FEUDAL	*adj* pertaining to a political and economic system of medieval Europe **FEUDALLY** *adv*
FEUDARY	*n* pl. -RIES a vassal
FEUDIST	*n* pl. -S one that feuds
FEVER	*v* -ED, -ING, -S to affect with fever (abnormal elevation of the body temperature)
FEVERFEW	*n* pl. -S a perennial herb
FEVERISH	*adj* having a fever
FEVEROUS	*adj* feverish
FEW	*adj* FEWER, FEWEST amounting to or consisting of a small number
FEWNESS	*n* pl. -ES the state of being few
FEWTRILS	*n/pl* things of little value
FEY	*adj* FEYER, FEYEST crazy **FEYLY** *adv*
FEYNESS	*n* pl. -ES the state of being fey
FEZ	*n* pl. FEZZES or FEZES a brimless cap worn by men in the Near East **FEZZED** *adj*
FIACRE	*n* pl. -S a small carriage
FIANCE	*n* pl. -S a man engaged to be married
FIANCEE	*n* pl. -S a woman engaged to be married
FIAR	*n* pl. -S the holder of a type of absolute ownership of land under Scottish law
FIASCO	*n* pl. -COES or -CHI a wine bottle
FIASCO	*n* pl. -COES or -COS a complete failure
FIAT	*n* pl. -S an authoritative order
FIB	*v* FIBBED, FIBBING, FIBS to tell a trivial lie
FIBBER	*n* pl. -S one that fibs
FIBER	*n* pl. -S a thread or threadlike object or structure **FIBERED** *adj*
FIBERIZE	*v* -IZED, -IZING, -IZES to break into fibers
FIBRANNE	*n* pl. -S a fabric made of spun-rayon yarn
FIBRE	*n* pl. -S fiber
FIBRIL	*n* pl. -S a small fiber
FIBRILLA	*n* pl. -LAE a fibril
FIBRIN	*n* pl. -S an insoluble protein
FIBROID	*n* pl. -S a fibroma
FIBROIN	*n* pl. -S an insoluble protein
FIBROMA	*n* pl. -MAS or -MATA a benign tumor composed of fibrous tissue
FIBROSIS	*n* pl. -BROSES the development of excess fibrous tissue in a bodily organ **FIBROTIC** *adj*
FIBROUS	*adj* containing, consisting of, or resembling fibers
FIBULA	*n* pl. -LAE or -LAS a bone of the leg **FIBULAR** *adj*
FICE	*n* pl. -S a feist
FICHE	*n* pl. -S a sheet of microfilm
FICHU	*n* pl. -S a woman's scarf
FICIN	*n* pl. -S an enzyme
FICKLE	*adj* -LER, -LEST not constant or loyal **FICKLY** *adv*
FICO	*n* pl. -COES something of little worth
FICTILE	*adj* moldable
FICTION	*n* pl. -S a literary work whose content is produced by the imagination

FICTIVE	*adj* imaginary
FICUS	*n* pl. -ES a tropical tree
FID	*n* pl. -S a square bar used as a support for a topmast
FIDDLE	*v* -DLED, -DLING, -DLES to play a violin
FIDDLER	*n* pl. -S one that fiddles
FIDDLY	*adj* intricately difficult to handle
FIDEISM	*n* pl. -S reliance on faith rather than reason
FIDEIST	*n* pl. -S a believer in fideism
FIDELITY	*n* pl. -TIES loyalty
FIDGE	*v* FIDGED, FIDGING, FIDGES to fidget
FIDGET	*v* -ED, -ING, -S to move nervously or restlessly
FIDGETER	*n* pl. -S one that fidgets
FIDGETY	*adj* nervously restless
FIDGING	present participle of fidge
FIDO	*n* pl. -DOS a defective coin
FIDUCIAL	*adj* based on faith or trust
FIE	*interj* — used to express disapproval
FIEF	*n* pl. -S a feudal estate
FIEFDOM	*n* pl. -S a fief
FIELD	*v* -ED, -ING, -S to play as a fielder
FIELDER	*n* pl. -S one that catches or picks up a ball in play
FIEND	*n* pl. -S a demon
FIENDISH	*adj* extremely wicked or cruel
FIERCE	*adj* FIERCER, FIERCEST violently hostile or aggressive **FIERCELY** *adv*
FIERY	*adj* -ERIER, -ERIEST intensely hot **FIERILY** *adv*
FIESTA	*n* pl. -S a festival
FIFE	*v* FIFED, FIFING, FIFES to play a fife (a high-pitched flute)
FIFER	*n* pl. -S one that plays a fife
FIFTEEN	*n* pl. -S a number
FIFTH	*n* pl. -S one of five equal parts
FIFTHLY	*adv* in the fifth place
FIFTIETH	*n* pl. -S one of fifty equal parts
FIFTY	*n* pl. -TIES a number
FIFTYISH	*adj* being about fifty years old
FIG	*v* FIGGED, FIGGING, FIGS to adorn
FIGEATER	*n* pl. -S a large beetle
FIGHT	*v* FOUGHT, FIGHTING, FIGHTS to attempt to defeat an adversary
FIGHTER	*n* pl. -S one that fights
FIGHTING	*n* pl. -S the act of one that fights
FIGMENT	*n* pl. -S a product of mental invention
FIGULINE	*n* pl. -S a piece of pottery
FIGURAL	*adj* consisting of human or animal form
FIGURANT	*n* pl. -S a ballet dancer who dances only in groups
FIGURATE	*adj* having a definite shape
FIGURE	*v* -URED, -URING, -URES to compute
FIGURER	*n* pl. -S one that figures
FIGURINE	*n* pl. -S a small statue
FIGURING	present participle of figure
FIGWORT	*n* pl. -S a flowering plant
FIL	*n* pl. -S a coin of Iraq and Jordan
FILA	pl. of filum
FILAGREE	*v* -GREED, -GREEING, -GREES to filigree
FILAMENT	*n* pl. -S a very thin thread or threadlike structure
FILAR	*adj* pertaining to a thread
FILAREE	*n* pl. -S a European weed
FILARIA	*n* pl. -IAE a parasitic worm **FILARIAL, FILARIAN** *adj*
FILARIID	*n* pl. -S filaria
FILATURE	*n* pl. -S the reeling of silk from cocoons
FILBERT	*n* pl. -S the edible nut of a European shrub
FILCH	*v* -ED, -ING, -ES to steal
FILCHER	*n* pl. -S one that filches
FILE	*v* FILED, FILING, FILES to arrange in order for future reference **FILEABLE** *adj*
FILEFISH	*n* pl. -ES a marine fish
FILEMOT	*adj* of a brownish yellow color
FILER	*n* pl. -S one that files
FILET	*v* -ED, -ING, -S to fillet
FILIAL	*adj* pertaining to a son or daughter **FILIALLY** *adv*
FILIATE	*v* -ATED, -ATING, -ATES to bring into close association
FILIBEG	*n* pl. -S a pleated skirt worn by Scottish Highlanders

FILICIDE	*n* pl. -S the killing of one's child
FILIFORM	*adj* shaped like a filament
FILIGREE	*v* -GREED, -GREEING, -GREES to adorn with intricate ornamental work
FILING	*n* pl. -S a particle removed by a file
FILISTER	*n* pl. -S a groove on a window frame
FILL	*v* -ED, -ING, -S to put as much as can be held into
FILLE	*n* pl. -S a girl
FILLER	*n* pl. -S one that fills
FILLET	*v* -ED, -ING, -S to cut boneless slices from
FILLIES	pl. of filly
FILLING	*n* pl. -S that which is used to fill something
FILLIP	*v* -ED, -ING, -S to strike sharply
FILLO	*n* pl. -LOS phyllo
FILLY	*n* pl. -LIES a young female horse
FILM	*v* -ED, -ING, -S to make a motion picture **FILMABLE** *adj*
FILMCARD	*n* pl. -S a fiche
FILMDOM	*n* pl. -S the motion-picture industry
FILMER	*n* pl. -S one that films
FILMGOER	*n* pl. -S one that goes to see motion pictures
FILMIC	*adj* pertaining to motion pictures
FILMIER	comparative of filmy
FILMIEST	superlative of filmy
FILMILY	*adv* in a filmy manner
FILMLAND	*n* pl. -S filmdom
FILMSET	*v* -SET, -SETTING, -SETS to photoset
FILMY	*adj* FILMIER, FILMIEST resembling or covered with film; hazy
FILO	*n* pl. -LOS phyllo
FILOSE	*adj* resembling a thread
FILTER	*v* -ED, -ING, -S to pass through a filter (a device for removing suspended matter)
FILTERER	*n* pl. -S one that filters
FILTH	*n* pl. -S foul or dirty matter
FILTHY	*adj* FILTHIER, FILTHIEST offensively dirty **FILTHILY** *adv*
FILTRATE	*v* -TRATED, -TRATING, -TRATES to filter
FILUM	*n* pl. -LA a threadlike anatomical structure
FIMBLE	*n* pl. -S the male hemp plant
FIMBRIA	*n* pl. -BRIAE a fringe or fringe-like structure **FIMBRIAL** *adj*
FIN	*v* FINNED, FINNING, FINS to equip with fins (external paddle-like structures)
FINABLE	*adj* subject to the payment of a fine
FINAGLE	*v* -GLED, -GLING, -GLES to obtain by trickery
FINAGLER	*n* pl. -S one that finagles
FINAL	*n* pl. -S the last examination of an academic course
FINALE	*n* pl. -S a close or termination of something
FINALIS	*n* pl. -LES a type of tone in medieval music
FINALISE	*v* -ISED, -ISING, -ISES finalize
FINALISM	*n* pl. -S the doctrine that all events are determined by ultimate purposes
FINALIST	*n* pl. -S a contestant who reaches the last part of a competition
FINALITY	*n* pl. -TIES the state of being conclusive
FINALIZE	*v* -IZED, -IZING, -IZES to put into finished form
FINALLY	*adv* at the end
FINANCE	*v* -NANCED, -NANCING, -NANCES to supply the money for
FINBACK	*n* pl. -S the rorqual
FINCH	*n* pl. -ES a small bird
FIND	*v* FOUND, FINDING, FINDS to come upon after a search **FINDABLE** *adj*
FINDER	*n* pl. -S one that finds
FINDING	*n* pl. -S something that is found
FINE	*adj* FINER, FINEST excellent
FINE	*v* FINED, FINING, FINES to subject to a fine (a monetary penalty)
FINEABLE	*adj* finable
FINELY	*adv* in a fine manner
FINENESS	*n* pl. -ES the quality of being fine
FINER	comparative of fine
FINERY	*n* pl. -ERIES elaborate adornment
FINESPUN	*adj* developed with extreme care

FINESSE	*v* -NESSED, -NESSING, -NESSES to bring about by adroit maneuvering	**FIRE**	*v* FIRED, FIRING, FIRES to project by discharging from a gun **FIREABLE** *adj*
FINEST	superlative of fine	**FIREARM**	*n* pl. -S a weapon from which a shot is discharged by gunpowder
FINFISH	*n* pl. -ES a true fish		
FINFOOT	*n* pl. -S an aquatic bird	**FIREBACK**	*n* pl. -S a cast-iron plate along the back of a fireplace
FINGER	*v* -ED, -ING, -S to touch with the fingers (the terminating members of the hand)	**FIREBALL**	*n* pl. -S a luminous meteor
		FIREBASE	*n* pl. -S a military base from which fire is directed against the enemy
FINGERER	*n* pl. -S one that fingers		
FINIAL	*n* pl. -S a crowning ornament **FINIALED** *adj*	**FIREBIRD**	*n* pl. -S a brightly colored bird
FINICAL	*adj* finicky	**FIREBOAT**	*n* pl. -S a boat equipped with fire-fighting apparatus
FINICKIN	*adj* finicky		
FINICKY	*adj* -ICKIER, -ICKIEST difficult to please	**FIREBOMB**	*v* -ED, -ING, -S to attack with incendiary bombs
FINIKIN	*adj* finicky	**FIREBOX**	*n* pl. -ES a chamber in which fuel is burned
FINIKING	*adj* finicky		
FINING	*n* pl. -S the clarifying of wines	**FIREBRAT**	*n* pl. -S a small, wingless insect
FINIS	*n* pl. -NISES the end	**FIREBUG**	*n* pl. -S an arsonist
FINISH	*v* -ED, -ING, -ES to bring to an end	**FIRECLAY**	*n* pl. -CLAYS a heat-resistant clay
FINISHER	*n* pl. -S one that finishes	**FIRED**	past tense of fire
FINITE	*n* pl. -S something that is finite (having definite limits)	**FIREDAMP**	*n* pl. -S a combustible gas
		FIREDOG	*n* pl. -S an andiron
FINITELY	*adv* to a finite extent	**FIREFANG**	*v* -ED, -ING, -S to decompose by oxidation
FINITUDE	*n* pl. -S the state of being finite		
FINK	*v* -ED, -ING, -S to inform to the police	**FIREFLY**	*n* pl. -FLIES a luminous insect
		FIREHALL	*n* pl. -S a fire station
FINLESS	*adj* having no fins	**FIRELESS**	*adj* having no fire
FINLIKE	*adj* resembling a fin	**FIRELIT**	*adj* lighted by firelight
FINMARK	*n* pl. -S a monetary unit of Finland	**FIRELOCK**	*n* pl. -S a type of gun
		FIREMAN	*n* pl. -MEN a man employed to extinguish fires
FINNED	past tense of fin		
FINNICKY	*adj* -NICKIER, -NICKIEST finicky	**FIREPAN**	*n* pl. -S an open pan for holding live coals
FINNIER	comparative of finny		
FINNIEST	superlative of finny	**FIREPINK**	*n* pl. -S a flowering plant
FINNING	present participle of fin	**FIREPLUG**	*n* pl. -S a hydrant
FINNMARK	*n* pl. -S finmark	**FIREPOT**	*n* pl. -S a clay pot filled with burning items
FINNY	*adj* -NIER, -NIEST having or characterized by fins	**FIRER**	*n* pl. -S one that fires
FINO	*n* pl. -NOS a very dry sherry	**FIREROOM**	*n* pl. -S a room containing a ship's boilers
FINOCHIO	*n* pl. -CHIOS a perennial herb		
FIORD	*n* pl. -S fjord	**FIRESIDE**	*n* pl. -S the area immediately surrounding a fireplace
FIPPLE	*n* pl. -S a plug of wood at the mouth of certain wind instruments	**FIRETRAP**	*n* pl. -S a building that is likely to catch on fire
FIQUE	*n* pl. -S a tropical plant	**FIREWEED**	*n* pl. -S a perennial herb
FIR	*n* pl. -S an evergreen tree	**FIREWOOD**	*n* pl. -S wood used as fuel

FIREWORK *n* pl. -S a device for producing a striking display of light or a loud noise

FIREWORM *n* pl. -S a glowworm

FIRING *n* pl. -S the process of maturing ceramic products by heat

FIRKIN *n* pl. -S a British unit of capacity

FIRM *adj* FIRMER, FIRMEST unyielding to pressure

FIRM *v* -ED, -ING, -S to make firm

FIRMAN *n* pl. -S an edict issued by a Middle Eastern sovereign

FIRMER *n* pl. -S a woodworking tool

FIRMLY *adv* in a firm manner

FIRMNESS *n* pl. -ES the state of being firm

FIRMWARE *n* pl. -S computer programs permanently stored on a microchip

FIRN *n* pl. -S neve

FIRRY *adj* abounding in firs

FIRST *n* pl. -S something that precedes all others

FIRSTLY *adv* before all others

FIRTH *n* pl. -S an inlet of the sea

FISC *n* pl. -S a state or royal treasury

FISCAL *n* pl. -S a public prosecutor

FISCALLY *adv* with regard to financial matters

FISH *v* -ED, -ING, -ES to catch or try to catch fish (cold-blooded aquatic vertebrates)

FISHABLE *adj* suitable for fishing

FISHBOLT *n* pl. -S a type of bolt

FISHBONE *n* pl. -S a bone of a fish

FISHBOWL *n* pl. -S a bowl in which live fish are kept

FISHER *n* pl. -S one that fishes

FISHERY *n* pl. -ERIES a place for catching fish

FISHEYE *n* pl. -S a suspicious stare

FISHGIG *n* pl. -S a pronged implement for spearing fish

FISHHOOK *n* pl. -S a barbed hook for catching fish

FISHIER comparative of fishy

FISHIEST superlative of fishy

FISHILY *adv* in a fishy manner

FISHING *n* pl. -S the occupation or pastime of catching fish

FISHLESS *adj* having no fish

FISHLIKE *adj* resembling a fish

FISHLINE *n* pl. -S a line used in fishing

FISHMEAL *n* pl. -S ground dried fish

FISHNET *n* pl. -S a net for catching fish

FISHPOLE *n* pl. -S a fishing rod

FISHPOND *n* pl. -S a pond abounding in edible fish

FISHTAIL *v* -ED, -ING, -S to have the rear end of a moving vehicle slide from side to side

FISHWAY *n* pl. -WAYS a device for enabling fish to pass around a dam

FISHWIFE *n* pl. -WIVES a woman who sells fish

FISHWORM *n* pl. -S a worm used as bait

FISHY *adj* FISHIER, FISHIEST of or resembling fish

FISSATE *adj* deeply split

FISSILE *adj* capable of being split

FISSION *v* -ED, -ING, -S to split into parts

FISSIPED *n* pl. -S a mammal that has separated toes

FISSURE *v* -SURED, -SURING, -SURES to split

FIST *v* -ED, -ING, -S to strike with the fist (the hand closed tightly)

FISTFUL *n* pl. -S a handful

FISTIC *adj* pertaining to pugilism

FISTNOTE *n* pl. -S a part of a text to which attention is drawn by an index mark

FISTULA *n* pl. -LAE or -LAS a duct formed by the imperfect closing of a wound **FISTULAR** *adj*

FIT *adj* FITTER, FITTEST healthy

FIT *v* FITTED, FITTING, FITS to bring to a required form and size

FITCH *n* pl. -ES a polecat

FITCHEE *adj* fitchy

FITCHET *n* pl. -S a fitch

FITCHEW *n* pl. -S a fitch

FITCHY *adj* having the arms ending in a point — used of a heraldic cross

FITFUL *adj* recurring irregularly **FITFULLY** *adv*

FITLY *adv* in a fit manner

FITMENT *n* pl. -S equipment

FITNESS *n* pl. -ES the state of being fit

FITTABLE	*adj* capable of being fitted
FITTED	past tense of fit
FITTER	*n* pl. -S one that fits
FITTEST	superlative of fit
FITTING	*n* pl. -S a small often standardized accessory part
FIVE	*n* pl. -S a number
FIVEFOLD	*adj* five times as great
FIVEPINS	*n/pl* a bowling game
FIVER	*n* pl. -S a five-dollar bill
FIX	*v* FIXED or FIXT, FIXING, FIXES to repair **FIXABLE** *adj*
FIXATE	*v* -ATED, -ATING, -ATES to make stable or stationary
FIXATIF	*n* pl. -S fixative
FIXATION	*n* pl. -S the act of fixating
FIXATIVE	*n* pl. -S a substance for preserving paintings or drawings
FIXEDLY	*adv* firmly
FIXER	*n* pl. -S one that fixes
FIXINGS	*n/pl* accompaniments to the main dish of a meal
FIXIT	*adj* involved with fixing things
FIXITY	*n* pl. -TIES stability
FIXT	a past tense of fix
FIXTURE	*n* pl. -S a permanent part or appendage of a house
FIXURE	*n* pl. -S firmness
FIZ	*n* pl. FIZZES a hissing or sputtering sound
FIZGIG	*n* pl. -S fishgig
FIZZ	*v* -ED, -ING, -ES to make a hissing or sputtering sound
FIZZER	*n* pl. -S one that fizzes
FIZZES	pl. of fiz
FIZZLE	*v* -ZLED, -ZLING, -ZLES to fizz
FIZZY	*adj* FIZZIER, FIZZIEST fizzing
FJELD	*n* pl. -S a high, barren plateau
FJORD	*n* pl. -S a narrow inlet of the sea between steep cliffs
FLAB	*n* pl. -S flabby body tissue
FLABBY	*adj* -BIER, -BIEST flaccid **FLABBILY** *adv*
FLABELLA	*n/pl* fan-shaped anatomical structures
FLACCID	*adj* lacking firmness
FLACK	*v* -ED, -ING, -S to work as a press agent

FLACKERY	*n* pl. -ERIES publicity
FLACON	*n* pl. -S a small stoppered bottle
FLAG	*v* FLAGGED, FLAGGING, FLAGS to mark with a flag (a piece of cloth used as a symbol)
FLAGELLA	*n/pl* long, slender plant shoots
FLAGGER	*n* pl. -S one that flags
FLAGGING	*n* pl. -S a type of pavement
FLAGGY	*adj* -GIER, -GIEST drooping
FLAGLESS	*adj* having no flag
FLAGMAN	*n* pl. -MEN one who carries a flag
FLAGON	*n* pl. -S a large bulging bottle
FLAGPOLE	*n* pl. -S a pole on which a flag is displayed
FLAGRANT	*adj* extremely conspicuous
FLAGSHIP	*n* pl. -S a ship bearing the flag of a fleet
FLAIL	*v* -ED, -ING, -S to swing freely
FLAIR	*n* pl. -S a natural aptitude
FLAK	*n* pl. FLAK antiaircraft fire
FLAKE	*v* FLAKED, FLAKING, FLAKES to peel off in flakes (flat, thin pieces)
FLAKER	*n* pl. -S one that flakes
FLAKEY	*adj* FLAKIER, FLAKIEST flaky
FLAKY	*adj* FLAKIER, FLAKIEST resembling flakes **FLAKILY** *adv*
FLAM	*v* FLAMMED, FLAMMING, FLAMS to deceive
FLAMBE	*v* -BEED, -BEING, -BES to douse with a liqueur and ignite
FLAMBEAU	*n* pl. -BEAUX or -BEAUS a flaming torch
FLAMBEE	*adj* flaming
FLAME	*v* FLAMED, FLAMING, FLAMES to burn brightly
FLAMEN	*n* pl. -MENS or -MINES a priest of ancient Rome
FLAMENCO	*n* pl. -COS a strongly rhythmic style of dancing
FLAMEOUT	*n* pl. -S a failure of a jet engine in flight
FLAMER	*n* pl. -S one that flames
FLAMIER	comparative of flamy
FLAMIEST	superlative of flamy
FLAMINES	a pl. of flamen
FLAMING	present participle of flame
FLAMINGO	*n* pl. -GOS or -GOES a wading bird

FLAMMED	past tense of flam
FLAMMING	present participle of flam
FLAMY	*adj* FLAMIER, FLAMIEST flaming
FLAN	*n* pl. -S or -ES a type of custard
FLANCARD	*n* pl. -S a piece of armor for the side of a horse
FLANERIE	*n* pl. -S idleness
FLANEUR	*n* pl. -S an idler
FLANGE	*v* FLANGED, FLANGING, FLANGES to provide with a protecting rim
FLANGER	*n* pl. -S one that flanges
FLANK	*v* -ED, -ING, -S to be located at the side of
FLANKEN	*n/pl* beef cut from the sides that is boiled with vegetables
FLANKER	*n* pl. -S one that flanks
FLANNEL	*v* -NELED, -NELING, -NELS or -NELLED, -NELLING, -NELS to cover with flannel (a soft fabric)
FLAP	*v* FLAPPED, FLAPPING, FLAPS to wave up and down
FLAPJACK	*n* pl. -S a pancake
FLAPLESS	*adj* having no flap (a flat appendage)
FLAPPED	past tense of flap
FLAPPER	*n* pl. -S one that flaps
FLAPPING	present participle of flap
FLAPPY	*adj* -PIER, -PIEST flapping
FLARE	*v* FLARED, FLARING, FLARES to burn with a bright, wavering light
FLASH	*v* -ED, -ING, -ES to send forth a sudden burst of light
FLASHER	*n* pl. -S one that flashes
FLASHGUN	*n* pl. -S a photographic apparatus
FLASHING	*n* pl. -S sheet metal used in waterproofing a roof
FLASHY	*adj* FLASHIER, FLASHIEST gaudy **FLASHILY** *adv*
FLASK	*n* pl. -S a narrow-necked container
FLASKET	*n* pl. -S a small flask
FLAT	*adj* FLATTER, FLATTEST having a smooth or even surface
FLAT	*v* FLATTED, FLATTING, FLATS to flatten
FLATBED	*n* pl. -S a type of truck or trailer
FLATBOAT	*n* pl. -S a flat-bottomed boat
FLATCAP	*n* pl. -S a type of hat

FLATCAR	*n* pl. -S a railroad car without sides or roof
FLATFISH	*n* pl. -ES any of an order of marine fishes
FLATFOOT	*n* pl. -FEET a foot condition
FLATFOOT	*v* -ED, -ING, -S to walk with a dragging gait
FLATHEAD	*n* pl. -S a marine food fish
FLATIRON	*n* pl. -S a device for pressing clothes
FLATLAND	*n* pl. -S land lacking significant variation in elevation
FLATLET	*n* pl. -S a type of apartment
FLATLING	*adv* with a flat side or edge
FLATLONG	*adv* flatling
FLATLY	*adv* in a flat manner
FLATMATE	*n* pl. -S one with whom an apartment is shared
FLATNESS	*n* pl. -ES the state of being flat
FLATTED	past tense of flat
FLATTEN	*v* -ED, -ING, -S to make or become flat
FLATTER	*v* -ED, -ING, -S to praise excessively
FLATTERY	*n* pl. -TERIES the act of flattering
FLATTEST	superlative of flat
FLATTING	present participle of flat
FLATTISH	*adj* somewhat flat
FLATTOP	*n* pl. -S an aircraft carrier
FLATUS	*n* pl. -ES intestinal gas
FLATWARE	*n* pl. -S tableware that is fairly flat
FLATWASH	*n* pl. -ES flatwork
FLATWAYS	*adv* flatwise
FLATWISE	*adv* with the flat side in a particular position
FLATWORK	*n* pl. -S laundry that can be ironed mechanically
FLATWORM	*n* pl. -S a flat-bodied worm
FLAUNT	*v* -ED, -ING, -S to exhibit in a gaudy manner
FLAUNTER	*n* pl. -S one that flaunts
FLAUNTY	*adj* FLAUNTIER, FLAUNTIEST gaudy
FLAUTIST	*n* pl. -S flutist
FLAVANOL	*n* pl. -S flavonol
FLAVIN	*n* pl. -S a yellow pigment
FLAVINE	*n* pl. -S flavin

FLAVONE	*n* pl. -S a chemical compound
FLAVONOL	*n* pl. -S a derivative of flavone
FLAVOR	*v* -ED, -ING, -S to give flavor (distinctive taste) to
FLAVORER	*n* pl. -S one that flavors
FLAVORY	*adj* full of flavor
FLAVOUR	*v* -ED, -ING, -S to flavor
FLAVOURY	*adj* flavory
FLAW	*v* -ED, -ING, -S to produce a flaw (an imperfection) in
FLAWLESS	*adj* having no flaw
FLAWY	*adj* FLAWIER, FLAWIEST full of flaws
FLAX	*n* pl. -ES an annual herb
FLAXEN	*adj* of a pale yellow color
FLAXSEED	*n* pl. -S the seed of flax
FLAXY	*adj* FLAXIER, FLAXIEST flaxen
FLAY	*v* -ED, -ING, -S to strip off the skin of
FLAYER	*n* pl. -S one that flays
FLEA	*n* pl. -S a parasitic insect
FLEABAG	*n* pl. -S an inferior hotel
FLEABANE	*n* pl. -S a flowering plant
FLEABITE	*n* pl. -S the bite of a flea
FLEAM	*n* pl. -S a surgical instrument
FLEAPIT	*n* pl. -S a run-down movie theater
FLEAWORT	*n* pl. -S a European herb
FLECHE	*n* pl. -S a steeple
FLECK	*v* -ED, -ING, -S to mark with flecks (tiny streaks or spots)
FLECKY	*adj* flecked
FLECTION	*n* pl. -S the act of bending
FLED	past tense of flee
FLEDGE	*v* FLEDGED, FLEDGING, FLEDGES to furnish with feathers
FLEDGY	*adj* FLEDGIER, FLEDGIEST covered with feathers
FLEE	*v* FLED, FLEEING, FLEES to run away
FLEECE	*v* FLEECED, FLEECING, FLEECES to remove the coat of wool from
FLEECER	*n* pl. -S one that fleeces
FLEECH	*v* -ED, -ING, -ES to coax
FLEECING	present participle of fleece
FLEECY	*adj* FLEECIER, FLEECIEST woolly **FLEECILY** *adv*
FLEER	*v* -ED, -ING, -S to deride
FLEET	*adj* FLEETER, FLEETEST swift **FLEETLY** *adv*
FLEET	*v* -ED, -ING, -S to move swiftly
FLEISHIG	*adj* made of meat or meat products
FLEMISH	*v* -ED, -ING, -ES to coil rope in a certain manner
FLENCH	*v* -ED, -ING, -ES to flense
FLENSE	*v* FLENSED, FLENSING, FLENSES to strip the blubber or skin from
FLENSER	*n* pl. -S one that flenses
FLESH	*v* -ED, -ING, -ES to plunge into the flesh (soft body tissue)
FLESHER	*n* pl. -S one that removes flesh from animal hides
FLESHIER	comparative of fleshy
FLESHIEST	superlative of fleshy
FLESHING	*n* pl. -S the distribution of the lean and fat on an animal
FLESHLY	*adj* -LIER, -LIEST pertaining to the body
FLESHPOT	*n* pl. -S a pot for cooking meat
FLESHY	*adj* FLESHIER, FLESHIEST having much flesh
FLETCH	*v* -ED, -ING, -ES to fledge
FLETCHER	*n* pl. -S one that makes arrows
FLEURY	*adj* having the arms terminating in three leaves — used of a heraldic cross
FLEW	*n* pl. -S a fishing net
FLEX	*v* -ED, -ING, -ES to bend
FLEXAGON	*n* pl. -S a folded paper construction
FLEXIBLE	*adj* capable of being bent **FLEXIBLY** *adv*
FLEXILE	*adj* flexible
FLEXION	*n* pl. -S flection
FLEXOR	*n* pl. -S a muscle that serves to bend a bodily part
FLEXTIME	*n* pl. -S a system that allows flexible working hours
FLEXUOSE	*adj* flexuous
FLEXUOUS	*adj* winding
FLEXURE	*n* pl. -S the act of bending **FLEXURAL** *adj*
FLEY	*v* -ED, -ING, -S to frighten
FLIC	*n* pl. -S a Parisian policeman
FLICHTER	*v* -ED, -ING, -S to flicker

FLICK   v -ED, -ING, -S to strike with a quick, light blow

FLICKER   v -ED, -ING, -S to move waveringly

FLICKERY   adj flickering

FLIED   a past tense of fly

FLIER   n pl. -S one that flies

FLIES   present 3d person sing. of fly

FLIEST   superlative of fly

FLIGHT   v -ED, -ING, -S to fly in a flock

FLIGHTY   adj FLIGHTIER, FLIGHTIEST fickle

FLIMFLAM   v -FLAMMED, -FLAMMING, -FLAMS to swindle

FLIMSY   adj -SIER, -SIEST lacking solidity or strength **FLIMSILY** adv

FLIMSY   n pl. -SIES a thin paper

FLINCH   v -ED, -ING, -ES to shrink back involuntarily

FLINCHER   n pl. -S one that flinches

FLINDER   n pl. -S a small fragment

FLING   v FLUNG, FLINGING, FLINGS to throw with force

FLINGER   n pl. -S one that flings

FLINKITE   n pl. -S a mineral

FLINT   v -ED, -ING, -S to provide with flint (a spark-producing rock)

FLINTY   adj FLINTIER, FLINTIEST resembling flint **FLINTILY** adv

FLIP   v FLIPPED, FLIPPING, FLIPS to throw with a brisk motion

FLIP   adj FLIPPER, FLIPPEST flippant

FLIPPANT   adj impudent

FLIPPED   past tense of flip

FLIPPER   n pl. -S a broad, flat limb adapted for swimming

FLIPPEST   superlative of flip

FLIPPING   present participle of flip

FLIPPY   adj flaring at the bottom

FLIRT   v -ED, -ING, -S to behave amorously without serious intent

FLIRTER   n pl. -S one that flirts

FLIRTY   adj FLIRTIER, FLIRTIEST given to flirting

FLIT   v FLITTED, FLITTING, FLITS to move lightly and swiftly

FLITCH   v -ED, -ING, -ES to cut into strips

FLITE   v FLITED, FLITING, FLITES to quarrel

FLITTED   past tense of flit

FLITTER   v -ED, -ING, -S to flutter

FLITTING   present participle of flit

FLIVVER   n pl. -S an old, battered car

FLOAT   v -ED, -ING, -S to rest or remain on the surface of a liquid

FLOATAGE   n pl. -S flotage

FLOATEL   n pl. -S a houseboat used as a hotel

FLOATER   n pl. -S one that floats

FLOATY   adj FLOATIER, FLOATIEST tending to float

FLOC   v FLOCCED, FLOCCING, FLOCS to aggregate into floccules

FLOCCI   pl. of floccus

FLOCCOSE   adj having woolly tufts

FLOCCULE   n pl. -S a tuft-like mass

FLOCCULI   n/pl small, loosely aggregated masses

FLOCCUS   n pl. FLOCCI a floccule

FLOCK   v -ED, -ING, -S to gather or move in a crowd

FLOCKING   n pl. -S a velvety design in short fibers on cloth or paper

FLOCKY   adj FLOCKIER, FLOCKIEST woolly

FLOE   n pl. -S a large mass of floating ice

FLOG   v FLOGGED, FLOGGING, FLOGS to beat with a whip or rod

FLOGGER   n pl. -S one that flogs

FLOGGING   n pl. -S a whipping

FLOKATI   n pl. -S a Greek handwoven rug

FLONG   n pl. -S a sheet of a certain type of paper

FLOOD   v -ED, -ING, -S to inundate

FLOODER   n pl. -S one that floods

FLOODLIT   adj illuminated by floodlights

FLOODWAY   n pl. -WAYS an overflow channel

FLOOEY   adj awry

FLOOIE   adj flooey

FLOOR   v -ED, -ING, -S to provide with a floor (the level base of a room)

FLOORAGE   n pl. -S floor space

FLOORER   n pl. -S one that floors

FLOORING   n pl. -S a floor

FLOOSIE   n pl. -S floozy

FLOOSY	*n* pl. -SIES floozy	**FLOUT**	*v* -ED, -ING, -S to treat with contempt
FLOOZIE	*n* pl. -S floozy	**FLOUTER**	*n* pl. -S one that flouts
FLOOZY	*n* pl. -ZIES a prostitute	**FLOW**	*v* -ED, -ING, -S to move steadily and smoothly along
FLOP	*v* FLOPPED, FLOPPING, FLOPS to fall heavily and noisily	**FLOWAGE**	*n* pl. -S the act of flowing
FLOPOVER	*n* pl. -S a defect in television reception	**FLOWER**	*v* -ED, -ING, -S to put forth flowers (reproductive structures of seed-bearing plants)
FLOPPER	*n* pl. -S one that flops	**FLOWERER**	*n* pl. -S a plant that flowers at a certain time
FLOPPING	present participle of flop		
FLOPPY	*n* pl. -PIES a type of computer disk	**FLOWERET**	*n* pl. -S a floret
FLOPPY	*adj* -PIER, -PIEST soft and flexible **FLOPPILY** *adv*	**FLOWERY**	*adj* -ERIER, -ERIEST abounding in flowers
FLORA	*n* pl. -RAS or -RAE the plant life of a particular region	**FLOWN**	a past participle of fly
		FLU	*n* pl. -S a virus disease
FLORAL	*n* pl. -S a design having flowers	**FLUB**	*v* FLUBBED, FLUBBING, FLUBS to bungle
FLORALLY	*adv* in a manner like that of a flower	**FLUBBER**	*n* pl. -S one that flubs
FLORENCE	*n* pl. -S florin	**FLUBDUB**	*n* pl. -S pretentious nonsense
FLORET	*n* pl. -S a small flower	**FLUE**	*n* pl. -S an enclosed passageway for directing a current **FLUED** *adj*
FLORID	*adj* ruddy **FLORIDLY** *adv*		
FLORIGEN	*n* pl. -S a plant hormone	**FLUENCY**	*n* pl. -CIES the quality of being fluent
FLORIN	*n* pl. -S a former gold coin of Europe	**FLUENT**	*adj* spoken or written with effortless ease **FLUENTLY** *adv*
FLORIST	*n* pl. -S a grower or seller of flowers	**FLUERICS**	*n/pl* fluidics **FLUERIC** *adj*
FLORUIT	*n* pl. -S a period of flourishing	**FLUFF**	*v* -ED, -ING, -S to make fluffy
FLOSS	*v* -ED, -ING, -ES to clean between the teeth with a thread	**FLUFFY**	*adj* FLUFFIER, FLUFFIEST light and soft **FLUFFILY** *adv*
FLOSSIE	*n* pl. -S a floozy	**FLUID**	*n* pl. -S a substance that tends to flow **FLUIDAL** *adj*
FLOSSY	*adj* FLOSSIER, FLOSSIEST resembling floss (a soft, light fiber) **FLOSSILY** *adv*	**FLUIDICS**	*n/pl* a branch of mechanical engineering **FLUIDIC** *adj*
FLOTA	*n* pl. -S a fleet of Spanish ships	**FLUIDISE**	*v* -ISED, -ISING, -ISES to fluidize
FLOTAGE	*n* pl. -S the act of floating	**FLUIDITY**	*n* pl. -TIES the quality of being able to flow
FLOTILLA	*n* pl. -S a fleet of ships		
FLOTSAM	*n* pl. -S floating wreckage of a ship or its cargo	**FLUIDIZE**	*v* -IZED, -IZING, -IZES to cause to flow like a fluid
FLOUNCE	*v* FLOUNCED, FLOUNCING, FLOUNCES to move with exaggerated motions	**FLUIDLY**	*adv* with fluidity
		FLUIDRAM	*n* pl. -S a unit of liquid capacity
		FLUKE	*v* FLUKED, FLUKING, FLUKES to obtain by chance
FLOUNCY	*adj* FLOUNCIER, FLOUNCIEST flouncing	**FLUKEY**	*adj* FLUKIER, FLUKIEST fluky
FLOUNDER	*v* -ED, -ING, -S to struggle clumsily	**FLUKY**	*adj* FLUKIER, FLUKIEST happening by or depending on chance
FLOUR	*v* -ED, -ING, -S to cover with flour (a finely ground meal of grain)	**FLUME**	*v* FLUMED, FLUMING, FLUMES to convey by means of an artificial water channel
FLOURISH	*v* -ED, -ING, -ES to thrive		
FLOURY	*adj* resembling flour	**FLUMMERY**	*n* pl. -MERIES a sweet dessert

FLUMMOX	*v* -ED, -ING, -ES to confuse	**FLYABLE**	*adj* suitable for flying
FLUMP	*v* -ED, -ING, -S to fall heavily	**FLYAWAY**	*n pl.* -AWAYS one that is elusive
FLUNG	past tense of fling	**FLYBELT**	*n pl.* -S an area infested with tsetse flies
FLUNK	*v* -ED, -ING, -S to fail an examination or course	**FLYBLOW**	*v* -BLEW, -BLOWN, -BLOWING, -BLOWS to taint
FLUNKER	*n pl.* -S one that flunks	**FLYBOAT**	*n pl.* -S a small, fast boat
FLUNKEY	*n pl.* -KEYS flunky	**FLYBOY**	*n pl.* -BOYS a pilot in an air force
FLUNKY	*n pl.* -KIES a servile follower	**FLYBY**	*n pl.* -BYS a flight of aircraft close to a specified place
FLUOR	*n pl.* -S fluorite **FLUORIC** *adj*		
FLUORENE	*n pl.* -S a chemical compound	**FLYER**	*n pl.* -S flier
FLUORID	*n pl.* -S fluoride	**FLYING**	*n pl.* -S the operation of an aircraft
FLUORIDE	*n pl.* -S a compound of fluorine	**FLYLEAF**	*n pl.* -LEAVES a blank leaf at the beginning or end of a book
FLUORIN	*n pl.* -S fluorine		
FLUORINE	*n pl.* -S a gaseous element	**FLYLESS**	*adj* free of flies (winged insects)
FLUORITE	*n pl.* -S a mineral	**FLYMAN**	*n pl.* -MEN a stage worker in a theater
FLURRY	*v* -RIED, -RYING, -RIES to confuse	**FLYOFF**	*n pl.* -S a competitive testing of model aircraft
FLUSH	*adj* FLUSHER, FLUSHEST ruddy		
FLUSH	*v* -ED, -ING, -ES to blush	**FLYOVER**	*n pl.* -S a flight of aircraft over a specific location
FLUSHER	*n pl.* -S one that flushes		
FLUSTER	*v* -ED, -ING, -S to put into a state of nervous confusion	**FLYPAPER**	*n pl.* -S paper designed to catch or kill flies
FLUTE	*v* FLUTED, FLUTING, FLUTES to play on a flute (a woodwind instrument)	**FLYPAST**	*n pl.* -S a flyby
		FLYSCH	*n pl.* -ES a sandstone deposit
		FLYSPECK	*v* -ED, -ING, -S to mark with minute spots
FLUTER	*n pl.* -S a flutist		
FLUTEY	*adj* FLUTIER, FLUTIEST fluty	**FLYTE**	*v* FLYTED, FLYTING, FLYTES to flite
FLUTIER	comparative of fluty		
FLUTIEST	superlative of fluty	**FLYTIER**	*n pl.* -S a maker of fishing flies
FLUTING	*n pl.* -S a series of parallel grooves	**FLYTING**	*n pl.* -S a dispute in verse form
		FLYTRAP	*n pl.* -S a trap for catching flies
FLUTIST	*n pl.* -S one who plays the flute	**FLYWAY**	*n pl.* -WAYS an established air route of migratory birds
FLUTTER	*v* -ED, -ING, -S to wave rapidly and irregularly		
FLUTTERY	*adj* marked by fluttering	**FLYWHEEL**	*n pl.* -S a heavy disk used in machinery
FLUTY	*adj* FLUTIER, FLUTIEST resembling a flute in sound	**FOAL**	*v* -ED, -ING, -S to give birth to a horse
FLUVIAL	*adj* pertaining to a river	**FOAM**	*v* -ED, -ING, -S to form foam (a light, bubbly, gas and liquid mass) **FOAMABLE** *adj*
FLUX	*v* -ED, -ING, -ES to melt		
FLUXGATE	*n pl.* -S a device to measure a magnetic field		
		FOAMER	*n pl.* -S one that foams
FLUXION	*n pl.* -S the act of flowing	**FOAMIER**	comparative of foamy
FLUYT	*n pl.* -S a type of ship	**FOAMIEST**	superlative of foamy
FLY	*v* FLEW, FLOWN, FLYING, FLIES to move through the air	**FOAMILY**	*adv* in a foamy manner
		FOAMLESS	*adj* being without foam
FLY	*v* FLIED, FLYING, FLIES to hit a ball high into the air in baseball	**FOAMLIKE**	*adj* resembling foam
		FOAMY	*adj* FOAMIER, FOAMIEST covered with foam
FLY	*adj* FLIER, FLIEST clever		

FOB	*v* FOBBED, FOBBING, FOBS to deceive
FOCACCIA	*n* pl. -S a flat Italian bread
FOCAL	*adj* pertaining to a focus
FOCALISE	*v* -ISED, -ISING, -ISES to focalize
FOCALIZE	*v* -IZED, -IZING, -IZES to focus
FOCALLY	*adv* with regard to focus
FOCUS	*n* pl. -CUSES or -CI a point at which rays converge or from which they diverge
FOCUS	*v* -CUSED, -CUSING, -CUSES or -CUSSED, -CUSSING, -CUSSES to bring to a focus
FOCUSER	*n* pl. -S one that focuses
FODDER	*v* -ED, -ING, -S to feed with coarse food
FODGEL	*adj* plump
FOE	*n* pl. -S an enemy
FOEHN	*n* pl. -S a warm, dry wind
FOEMAN	*n* pl. -MEN an enemy in war
FOETAL	*adj* fetal
FOETID	*adj* fetid
FOETOR	*n* pl. -S fetor
FOETUS	*n* pl. -ES fetus
FOG	*v* FOGGED, FOGGING, FOGS to cover with fog (condensed water vapor near the earth's surface)
FOGBOUND	*adj* surrounded by fog
FOGBOW	*n* pl. -S a nebulous arc of light sometimes seen in a fog
FOGDOG	*n* pl. -S a fogbow
FOGEY	*n* pl. -GEYS fogy
FOGFRUIT	*n* pl. -S a flowering plant
FOGGAGE	*n* pl. -S a second growth of grass
FOGGED	past tense of fog
FOGGER	*n* pl. -S one that fogs
FOGGING	present participle of fog
FOGGY	*adj* -GIER, -GIEST filled with fog **FOGGILY** *adv*
FOGHORN	*n* pl. -S a horn sounded in a fog
FOGIE	*n* pl. -S fogy
FOGLESS	*adj* having no fog
FOGY	*n* pl. -GIES an old-fashioned person **FOGYISH** *adj*
FOGYISM	*n* pl. -S old-fashioned behavior
FOH	*interj* faugh
FOHN	*n* pl. -S foehn
FOIBLE	*n* pl. -S a minor weakness
FOIL	*v* -ED, -ING, -S to prevent the success of **FOILABLE** *adj*
FOILSMAN	*n* pl. -MEN a fencer
FOIN	*v* -ED, -ING, -S to thrust with a pointed weapon
FOISON	*n* pl. -S strength
FOIST	*v* -ED, -ING, -S to force upon slyly
FOLACIN	*n* pl. -S a B vitamin
FOLATE	*n* pl. -S folacin
FOLD	*v* -ED, -ING, -S to lay one part over another part of **FOLDABLE** *adj*
FOLDAWAY	*adj* designed to fold out of the way
FOLDBOAT	*n* pl. -S a faltboat
FOLDER	*n* pl. -S one that folds
FOLDEROL	*n* pl. -S falderal
FOLDOUT	*n* pl. -S a gatefold
FOLIA	a pl. of folium
FOLIAGE	*n* pl. -S the growth of leaves of a plant **FOLIAGED** *adj*
FOLIAR	*adj* pertaining to a leaf
FOLIATE	*v* -ATED, -ATING, -ATES to hammer into thin plates
FOLIO	*v* -ED, -ING, -S to number the pages of
FOLIOSE	*adj* having leaves
FOLIOUS	*adj* foliose
FOLIUM	*n* pl. -LIA or -LIUMS a thin layer
FOLK	*n* pl. -S a people or tribe
FOLKIE	*n* pl. -S a performer of folk music
FOLKISH	*adj* characteristic of the common people
FOLKLIFE	*n* pl. -LIVES the traditions, skills, and products of a people
FOLKLIKE	*adj* folkish
FOLKLORE	*n* pl. -S the lore of a people
FOLKMOOT	*n* pl. -S a general assembly of the people in early England
FOLKMOT	*n* pl. -S folkmoot
FOLKMOTE	*n* pl. -S folkmoot
FOLKSY	*adj* FOLKSIER, FOLKSIEST friendly **FOLKSILY** *adv*
FOLKTALE	*n* pl. -S a tale forming part of the oral tradition of a people
FOLKWAY	*n* pl. -WAYS a traditional custom of a people

FOLKY	*n* pl. FOLKIES folkie
FOLLES	pl. of follis
FOLLICLE	*n* pl. -S a small bodily cavity
FOLLIES	pl. of folly
FOLLIS	*n* pl. -LES a coin of ancient Rome
FOLLOW	*v* -ED, -ING, -S to come or go after
FOLLOWER	*n* pl. -S one that follows
FOLLY	*n* pl. -LIES a foolish idea or action
FOMENT	*v* -ED, -ING, -S to promote the development of
FOMENTER	*n* pl. -S one that foments
FOMITE	*n* pl. -S an inanimate object that serves to transmit infectious organisms
FON	*n* pl. -S foehn
FOND	*adj* FONDER, FONDEST having an affection
FOND	*v* -ED, -ING, -S to display affection
FONDANT	*n* pl. -S a soft, creamy candy
FONDLE	*v* -DLED, -DLING, -DLES to caress
FONDLER	*n* pl. -S one that fondles
FONDLING	*n* pl. -S one that is fondled
FONDLY	*adv* in a fond manner
FONDNESS	*n* pl. -ES affection
FONDU	*n* pl. -S fondue
FONDUE	*n* pl. -S a dish of melted cheese
FONT	*n* pl. -S a receptacle for the water used in baptism **FONTAL** *adj*
FONTANEL	*n* pl. -S a space in the fetal and infantile skull
FONTINA	*n* pl. -S an Italian cheese
FOOD	*n* pl. -S a substance taken into the body to maintain life and growth **FOODLESS** *adj*
FOODIE	*n* pl. -S an enthusiast of foods and their preparation
FOODWAYS	*n/pl* the eating habits of a people
FOOFARAW	*n* pl. -S excessive ornamentation
FOOL	*v* -ED, -ING, -S to deceive
FOOLERY	*n* pl. -ERIES foolish behavior or speech
FOOLFISH	*n* pl. -ES a marine fish
FOOLISH	*adj* -ISHER, -ISHEST lacking good sense or judgment

FOOLSCAP	*n* pl. -S a paper size
FOOT	*n* pl. FEET the terminal part of the leg on which the body stands and moves
FOOT	*v* -ED, -ING, -S to walk
FOOTAGE	*n* pl. -S a length or quantity expressed in feet
FOOTBALL	*n* pl. -S a type of ball
FOOTBATH	*n* pl. -S a bath for the feet
FOOTBOY	*n* pl. -BOYS a serving boy
FOOTER	*n* pl. -S one that walks
FOOTFALL	*n* pl. -S the sound of a footstep
FOOTGEAR	*n* pl. -S footwear
FOOTHILL	*n* pl. -S a low hill at the foot of higher hills
FOOTHOLD	*n* pl. -S a secure support for the feet
FOOTIE	*n* pl. -S footsie
FOOTIER	comparative of footy
FOOTIEST	superlative of footy
FOOTING	*n* pl. -S a foothold
FOOTLE	*v* -TLED, -TLING, -TLES to waste time
FOOTLER	*n* pl. -S one that footles
FOOTLESS	*adj* having no feet
FOOTLIKE	*adj* resembling a foot
FOOTLING	present participle of footle
FOOTMAN	*n* pl. -MEN a male servant
FOOTMARK	*n* pl. -S a mark left by the foot on a surface
FOOTNOTE	*v* -NOTED, -NOTING, -NOTES to furnish with explanatory notes
FOOTPACE	*n* pl. -S a walking pace
FOOTPAD	*n* pl. -S one who robs a pedestrian
FOOTPATH	*n* pl. -S a path for pedestrians
FOOTRACE	*n* pl. -S a race run on foot
FOOTREST	*n* pl. -S a support for the feet
FOOTROPE	*n* pl. -S a rope used in sailing
FOOTSIE	*n* pl. -S a flirting game played with the feet
FOOTSLOG	*v* -SLOGGED, -SLOGGING, -SLOGS to march through mud
FOOTSORE	*adj* having sore or tired feet
FOOTSTEP	*n* pl. -S a step with the foot
FOOTSY	*n* pl. -SIES footsie
FOOTWALL	*n* pl. -S the layer of rock beneath a vein of ore

FOOTWAY *n* pl. -WAYS a footpath

FOOTWEAR *n* pl. FOOTWEAR wearing apparel for the feet

FOOTWORK *n* pl. -S the use of the feet

FOOTWORN *adj* footsore

FOOTY *adj* -TIER, -TIEST paltry

FOOZLE *v* -ZLED, -ZLING, -ZLES to bungle

FOOZLER *n* pl. -S one that foozles

FOP *v* FOPPED, FOPPING, FOPS to deceive

FOPPERY *n* pl. -PERIES foppish behavior

FOPPISH *adj* characteristic of a dandy

FOR *prep* directed or sent to

FORA a pl. of forum

FORAGE *v* -AGED, -AGING, -AGES to search about

FORAGER *n* pl. -S one that forages

FORAM *n* pl. -S a marine rhizopod

FORAMEN *n* pl. -MINA or -MENS a small anatomical opening

FORAY *v* -ED, -ING, -S to raid

FORAYER *n* pl. -S one that forays

FORB *n* pl. -S an herb other than grass

FORBAD a past tense of forbid

FORBADE a past tense of forbid

FORBEAR *v* -BORE, -BORNE, -BEARING, -BEARS to refrain from

FORBID *v* -BADE or -BAD, -BIDDEN, -BIDDING, -BIDS to command not to do something

FORBIDAL *n* pl. -S the act of forbidding

FORBODE *v* -BODED, -BODING, -BODES to forebode

FORBORE past tense of forbear

FORBORNE past participle of forbear

FORBY *prep* close by

FORBYE *prep* forby

FORCE *v* FORCED, FORCING, FORCES to overcome resistance by the exertion of strength **FORCEDLY** *adv*

FORCEFUL *adj* strong

FORCEPS *n* pl. -CIPES an instrument for seizing and holding objects

FORCER *n* pl. -S one that forces

FORCIBLE *adj* effected by force **FORCIBLY**

FORCING present participle of force

FORCIPES pl. of forceps

FORD *v* -ED, -ING, -S to cross by wading **FORDABLE** *adj*

FORDLESS *adj* unable to be forded

FORDO *v* -DID, -DONE, -DOING, -DOES to destroy

FORE *n* pl. -S the front part of something

FOREARM *v* -ED, -ING, -S to arm in advance

FOREBAY *n* pl. -BAYS a reservoir from which water is taken to run equipment

FOREBEAR *n* pl. -S an ancestor

FOREBODE *v* -BODED, -BODING, -BODES to indicate in advance

FOREBODY *n* pl. -BODIES the forward part of a ship

FOREBOOM *n* pl. -S the boom of a ship's foremast

FOREBY *prep* forby

FOREBYE *prep* forby

FORECAST *v* -ED, -ING, -S to estimate or calculate in advance

FOREDATE *v* -DATED, -DATING, -DATES to antedate

FOREDECK *n* pl. -S the forward part of a ship's deck

FOREDO *v* -DID, -DONE, -DOING, -DOES to fordo

FOREDOOM *v* -ED, -ING, -S to doom in advance

FOREFACE *n* pl. -S the front part of the head of a quadruped

FOREFEEL *v* -FELT, -FEELING, -FEELS to have a premonition of

FOREFEND *v* -ED, -ING, -S to forfend

FOREFOOT *n* pl. -FEET one of the front feet of an animal

FOREGO *v* -WENT, -GONE, -GOING, -GOES to go before

FOREGOER *n* pl. -S one that foregoes

FOREGUT *n* pl. -S the front part of the embryonic alimentary canal

FOREHAND *n* pl. -S a type of tennis stroke

FOREHEAD *n* pl. -S the part of the face above the eyes

FOREHOOF *n* pl. -HOOFS or -HOOVES the hoof of a forefoot

FOREIGN *adj* situated outside a place or country

FOREKNOW v -KNEW, -KNOWN, -KNOWING, -KNOWS to know in advance

FORELADY n pl. -DIES a woman who supervises workers

FORELAND n pl. -S a projecting mass of land

FORELEG n pl. -S one of the front legs of an animal

FORELIMB n pl. -S a foreleg

FORELOCK v -ED, -ING, -S to fasten with a linchpin

FOREMAN n pl. -MEN a man who supervises workers

FOREMAST n pl. -S the forward mast of a ship

FOREMILK n pl. -S the milk secreted immediately after childbirth

FOREMOST adj first in position

FORENAME n pl. -S a first name

FORENOON n pl. -S the period of daylight before noon

FORENSIC n pl -S an argumentative exercise

FOREPART n pl. -S the front part

FOREPAST adj already in the past

FOREPAW n pl. -S the paw of a foreleg

FOREPEAK n pl. -S the forward part of a ship's hold

FOREPLAY n pl. -PLAYS erotic stimulation preceding sexual intercourse

FORERANK n pl. -S the first rank

FORERUN v -RAN, -RUNNING, -RUNS to run in advance of

FORESAID adj previously said

FORESAIL n pl. -S the lowest sail on a foremast

FORESEE v -SAW, -SEEN, -SEEING, -SEES to see in advance

FORESEER n pl. -S one that foresees

FORESHOW v -SHOWED, -SHOWN, -SHOWING, -SHOWS to show in advance

FORESIDE n pl. -S the front side

FORESKIN n pl. -S the prepuce

FOREST v -ED, -ING, -S to convert into a forest (a densely wooded area)

FORESTAL adj of or pertaining to a forest

FORESTAY n pl. -STAYS a wire or rope used to support a foremast

FORESTER n pl. -S one skilled in forestry

FORESTRY n pl. -RIES the science of planting and managing forests

FORETELL v -TOLD, -TELLING, -TELLS to tell of or about in advance

FORETIME n pl. -S the past

FORETOP n pl. -S a forelock

FOREVER n pl. -S an indefinite length of time

FOREWARN v -ED, -ING, -S to warn in advance

FOREWENT past tense of forego

FOREWING n pl. -S an anterior wing of an insect

FOREWORD n pl. -S an introductory statement

FOREWORN adj forworn

FOREYARD n pl. -S the lowest yard on a foremast

FORFEIT v -ED, -ING, -S to lose as a penalty

FORFEND v -ED, -ING, -S to protect

FORGAT a past tense of forget

FORGAVE past tense of forgive

FORGE v FORGED, FORGING, FORGES to fashion or reproduce for fraudulent purposes

FORGER n pl. -S one that forges

FORGERY n pl. -ERIES the act of forging

FORGET v -GOT or -GAT, -GOTTEN, -GETTING, -GETS to fail to remember

FORGING n pl. -S a forgery

FORGIVE v -GAVE, -GIVEN, -GIVING, -GIVES to pardon

FORGIVER n pl. -S one that forgives

FORGO v -WENT, -GONE, -GOING, -GOES to refrain from

FORGOER n pl. -S one that forgoes

FORGOT a past tense of forget

FORGOTTEN past participle of forget

FORINT n pl. -S a monetary unit of Hungary

FORJUDGE v -JUDGED, -JUDGING, -JUDGES to deprive by judgment of a court

FORK v -ED, -ING, -S to work with a fork (a pronged implement) **FORKEDLY** adv

FORKBALL n pl. -S a breaking pitch in baseball

FORKER n pl. -S one that forks

FORKFUL	*n* pl. FORKFULS or FORKSFUL as much as a fork will hold
FORKIER	comparative of forky
FORKIEST	superlative of forky
FORKLESS	*adj* having no fork
FORKLIFT	*v* -ED, -ING, -S to raise or transport by means of a forklift (a machine with projecting prongs)
FORKLIKE	*adj* resembling a fork
FORKSFUL	a pl. of forkful
FORKY	*adj* FORKIER, FORKIEST resembling a fork
FORLORN	*adj* -LORNER, -LORNEST dreary
FORM	*v* -ED, -ING, -S to produce **FORMABLE** *adj*
FORMAL	*n* pl. -S a social event that requires evening dress
FORMALIN	*n* pl. -S an aqueous solution of formaldehyde
FORMALLY	*adv* in a prescribed or customary manner
FORMANT	*n* pl. -S a characteristic component of the quality of a speech sound
FORMAT	*v* -MATTED, -MATTING, -MATS to produce in a specified style
FORMATE	*n* pl. -S a chemical salt
FORME	*n* pl. -S an assemblage of printing type secured in a metal frame
FORMEE	*adj* having the arms narrow at the center and expanding toward the ends — used of a heraldic cross
FORMER	*n* pl. -S one that forms
FORMERLY	*adv* previously
FORMFUL	*adj* exhibiting good form
FORMIC	*adj* pertaining to ants
FORMLESS	*adj* lacking structure
FORMOL	*n* pl. -S formalin
FORMULA	*n* pl. -LAS or -LAE an exact method for doing something
FORMWORK	*n* pl. -S a set of forms to hold concrete until it sets
FORMYL	*n* pl. -S a univalent chemical radical
FORNIX	*n* pl. -NICES an arched anatomical structure **FORNICAL** *adj*
FORRADER	*adv* further ahead
FORRIT	*adv* toward the front
FORSAKE	*v* -SOOK, -SAKEN, -SAKING, -SAKES to quit or leave entirely
FORSAKER	*n* pl. -S one that forsakes
FORSOOTH	*adv* in truth
FORSPENT	*adj* worn out
FORSWEAR	*v* -SWORE, -SWORN, -SWEARING, -SWEARS to deny under oath
FORT	*n* pl. -S a fortified enclosure or structure
FORTE	*n* pl. -S a strong point
FORTES	pl. of fortis
FORTH	*adv* onward in time, place, or order
FORTIES	pl. of forty
FORTIETH	*n* pl. -S one of forty equal parts
FORTIFY	*v* -FIED, -FYING, -FIES to strengthen against attack
FORTIS	*n* pl. -TES a consonant pronounced with relatively strong release of breath
FORTRESS	*v* -ED, -ING, -ES to fortify
FORTUITY	*n* pl. -ITIES an accidental occurrence
FORTUNE	*v* -TUNED, -TUNING, -TUNES to endow with wealth
FORTY	*n* pl. -TIES a number
FORTYISH	*adj* being about forty years old
FORUM	*n* pl. -RUMS or -RA a public meeting place
FORWARD	*adj* -WARDER, -WARDEST being at a point in advance
FORWARD	*v* -ED, -ING, -S to help onward
FORWENT	past tense of forgo
FORWHY	*adv* for what reason
FORWORN	*adj* worn out
FORZANDO	*n* pl. -DOS sforzato
FOSS	*n* pl. -ES fosse
FOSSA	*n* pl. -SAE an anatomical depression **FOSSATE** *adj*
FOSSA	*n* pl. -S a catlike mammal
FOSSE	*n* pl. -S a ditch
FOSSETTE	*n* pl. -S a small fossa
FOSSICK	*v* -ED, -ING, -S to search for gold
FOSSIL	*n* pl. -S the remains of an animal or plant preserved in the earth's crust
FOSTER	*v* -ED, -ING, -S to promote the growth of
FOSTERER	*n* pl. -S one that fosters

FOU	*adj* drunk
FOUETTE	*n* pl. -S a movement in ballet
FOUGHT	past tense of fight
FOUGHTEN	*adj* exhausted especially from fighting
FOUL	*adj* FOULER, FOULEST offensive to the senses
FOUL	*v* -ED, -ING, -S to make foul
FOULARD	*n* pl. -S a soft fabric
FOULING	*n* pl. -S a deposit or crust
FOULLY	*adv* in a foul manner
FOULNESS	*n* pl. -ES the state of being foul
FOUND	*v* -ED, -ING, -S to establish
FOUNDER	*v* -ED, -ING, -S to become disabled
FOUNDRY	*n* pl. -RIES an establishment in which metal is cast
FOUNT	*n* pl. -S a fountain
FOUNTAIN	*v* -ED, -ING, -S to flow like a fountain (a spring of water)
FOUR	*n* pl. -S a number
FOURCHEE	*adj* having the end of each arm forked — used of a heraldic cross
FOURFOLD	*adj* four times as great
FOURGON	*n* pl. -S a wagon for carrying baggage
FOURPLEX	*n* pl. -ES quadplex
FOURSOME	*n* pl. -S a group of four
FOURTEEN	*n* pl. -S a number
FOURTH	*n* pl. -S one of four equal parts
FOURTHLY	*adv* in the fourth place
FOVEA	*n* pl. -VEAE or -VEAS a shallow anatomical depression **FOVEAL, FOVEATE, FOVEATED** *adj*
FOVEOLA	*n* pl. -LAE or -LAS a small fovea **FOVEOLAR** *adj*
FOVEOLE	*n* pl. -S a foveola
FOVEOLET	*n* pl. -S a foveola
FOWL	*v* -ED, -ING, -S to hunt birds
FOWLER	*n* pl. -S one that fowls
FOWLING	*n* pl. -S the hunting of birds
FOWLPOX	*n* pl. -ES a virus disease of poultry
FOX	*v* -ED, -ING, -ES to outwit
FOXFIRE	*n* pl. -S a glow produced by certain fungi on decaying wood
FOXFISH	*n* pl. -ES a large shark
FOXGLOVE	*n* pl. -S a flowering plant
FOXHOLE	*n* pl. -S a small pit used for cover in a battle area
FOXHOUND	*n* pl. -S a hunting dog
FOXHUNT	*v* -ED, -ING, -S to hunt with hounds for a fox
FOXIER	comparative of foxy
FOXIEST	superlative of foxy
FOXILY	*adv* in a foxy manner
FOXINESS	*n* pl. -ES the state of being foxy
FOXING	*n* pl. -S a piece of material used to cover the upper portion of a shoe
FOXLIKE	*adj* resembling a fox (a carnivorous mammal)
FOXSKIN	*n* pl. -S the skin of a fox
FOXTAIL	*n* pl. -S the tail of a fox
FOXTROT	*v* -TROTTED, -TROTTING, -TROTS to dance the fox trot (a dance for couples)
FOXY	*adj* FOXIER, FOXIEST crafty
FOY	*n* pl. FOYS a farewell feast or gift
FOYER	*n* pl. -S an entrance room or hall
FOZINESS	*n* pl. -ES the state of being fozy
FOZY	*adj* -ZIER, -ZIEST too ripe
FRABJOUS	*adj* splendid
FRACAS	*n* pl. -ES a brawl
FRACTAL	*n* pl. -S a complex geometric curve
FRACTED	*adj* broken
FRACTI	pl. of fractus
FRACTION	*v* -ED, -ING, -S to divide into portions
FRACTUR	*n* pl. -S fraktur
FRACTURE	*v* -TURED, -TURING, -TURES to break
FRACTUS	*n* pl. -TI a ragged cloud
FRAE	*prep* from
FRAENUM	*n* pl. -NA or -NUMS frenum
FRAG	*v* FRAGGED, FRAGGING, FRAGS to injure with a type of grenade
FRAGGING	*n* pl. -S the act of one that frags
FRAGILE	*adj* easily broken or damaged
FRAGMENT	*v* -ED, -ING, -S to break into pieces
FRAGRANT	*adj* having a pleasant odor
FRAIL	*adj* FRAILER, FRAILEST fragile **FRAILLY** *adv*

FRAIL	*n* pl. -S a basket for holding dried fruits
FRAILTY	*n* pl. -TIES a weakness of character
FRAISE	*n* pl. -S a barrier of pointed stakes
FRAKTUR	*n* pl. -S a style of type
FRAME	*v* FRAMED, FRAMING, FRAMES to construct by putting together the various parts **FRAMABLE** *adj*
FRAMER	*n* pl. -S one that frames
FRAMING	*n* pl. -S framework
FRANC	*n* pl. -S a monetary unit of France
FRANCIUM	*n* pl. -S a radioactive element
FRANK	*adj* FRANKER, FRANKEST honest and unreserved in speech
FRANK	*v* -ED, -ING, -S to mark (a piece of mail) for free delivery
FRANKER	*n* pl. -S one that franks
FRANKLIN	*n* pl. -S a medieval English landowner
FRANKLY	*adv* in a frank manner
FRANTIC	*adj* wildly excited
FRAP	*v* FRAPPED, FRAPPING, FRAPS to bind firmly
FRAPPE	*n* pl. -S a partly frozen drink
FRASS	*n* pl. -ES debris made by insects
FRAT	*n* pl. -S a college fraternity
FRATER	*n* pl. -S a comrade
FRAUD	*n* pl. -S trickery
FRAUGHT	*v* -ED, -ING, -S to load down
FRAULEIN	*n* pl. -S a German governess
FRAY	*v* -ED, -ING, -S to wear off by rubbing
FRAYING	*n* pl. -S something worn off by rubbing
FRAZIL	*n* pl. -S tiny ice crystals formed in supercooled waters
FRAZZLE	*v* -ZLED, -ZLING, -ZLES to fray
FREAK	*v* -ED, -ING, -S to streak with color
FREAKIER	comparative of freaky
FREAKIEST	superlative of freaky
FREAKILY	*adv* in a freaky manner
FREAKISH	*adj* unusual
FREAKOUT	*n* pl. -S an event marked by wild excitement
FREAKY	*adj* FREAKIER, FREAKIEST freakish
FRECKLE	*v* -LED, -LING, -LES to mark with freckles (small, brownish spots)
FRECKLY	*adj* -LIER, -LIEST marked with freckles
FREE	*adj* FREER, FREEST not subject to restriction or control
FREE	*v* FREED, FREEING, FREES to make free
FREEBASE	*v* -BASED, -BASING, -BASES to use a form of cocaine that is inhaled
FREEBEE	*n* pl. -S freebie
FREEBIE	*n* pl. -S something given or received without charge
FREEBOOT	*v* -ED, -ING, -S to plunder
FREEBORN	*adj* born free
FREED	past tense of free
FREEDMAN	*n* pl. -MEN a man who has been freed from slavery
FREEDOM	*n* pl. -S the state of being free
FREEFORM	*adj* having a free flowing design or shape
FREEHAND	*adj* drawn by hand without mechanical aids
FREEHOLD	*n* pl. -S a form of tenure of real property
FREELOAD	*v* -ED, -ING, -S to live at the expense of others
FREELY	*adv* in a free manner
FREEMAN	*n* pl. -MEN one who is free
FREENESS	*n* pl. -ES freedom
FREER	*n* pl. -S one that frees
FREESIA	*n* pl. -S an African herb
FREEST	superlative of free
FREEWAY	*n* pl. -WAYS an express highway
FREEWILL	*adj* voluntary
FREEZE	*v* FROZE, FROZEN, FREEZING, FREEZES to become hardened into a solid body by loss of heat
FREEZER	*n* pl. -S an apparatus for freezing food
FREIGHT	*v* -ED, -ING, -S to load with goods for transportation
FREMD	*adj* strange
FREMITUS	*n* pl. -ES a palpable vibration
FRENA	a pl. of frenum
FRENCH	*v* -ED, -ING, -ES to cut into thin strips before cooking

FRENETIC   *n* pl. -S a frantic person

FRENULUM   *n* pl. -LA or -LUMS a frenum

FRENUM   *n* pl. -NA or -NUMS a connecting fold of membrane

FRENZILY   *adv* in a frantic manner

FRENZY   *v* -ZIED, -ZYING, -ZIES to make frantic

FREQUENT   *adj* -QUENTER, -QUENTEST occurring again and again

FREQUENT   *v* -ED, -ING, -S to be in or at often

FRERE   *n* pl. -S brother

FRESCO   *v* -ED, -ING, -ES or -S to paint on a surface of plaster

FRESCOER   *n* pl. -S one that frescoes

FRESH   *adj* FRESHER, FRESHEST new

FRESH   *v* -ED, -ING, -ES to freshen

FRESHEN   *v* -ED, -ING, -S to make or become fresh

FRESHET   *n* pl. -S a sudden overflow of a stream

FRESHLY   *adv* in a fresh manner

FRESHMAN   *n* pl. -MEN a first-year student

FRESNEL   *n* pl. -S a unit of frequency

FRET   *v* FRETTED, FRETTING, FRETS to worry

FRETFUL   *adj* inclined to fret

FRETLESS   *adj* having no fretwork

FRETSAW   *n* pl. -S a narrow-bladed saw

FRETSOME   *adj* fretful

FRETTED   past tense of fret

FRETTER   *n* pl. -S one that frets

FRETTING   present participle of fret

FRETTY   *adj* -TIER, -TIEST fretful

FRETWORK   *n* pl. -S ornamental work consisting of interlacing parts

FRIABLE   *adj* easily crumbled

FRIAR   *n* pl. -S a member of a religious order **FRIARLY** *adj*

FRIARY   *n* pl. -ARIES a monastery of friars

FRIBBLE   *v* -BLED, -BLING, -BLES to act foolishly

FRIBBLER   *n* pl. -S one that fribbles

FRICANDO   *n* pl. -DOES a roasted loin of veal

FRICTION   *n* pl. -S the rubbing of one body against another

FRIDGE   *n* pl. -S a refrigerator

FRIED   past tense of fry

FRIEND   *v* -ED, -ING, -S to enter into a warm association with

FRIENDLY   *adj* -LIER, -LIEST inclined to approve, help, or support

FRIENDLY   *n* pl. -LIES one who is friendly

FRIER   *n* pl. -S fryer

FRIES   present 3d person sing. of fry

FRIEZE   *n* pl. -S a coarse woolen fabric

FRIGATE   *n* pl. -S a sailing vessel

FRIGHT   *v* -ED, -ING, -S to frighten

FRIGHTEN   *v* -ED, -ING, -S to make afraid

FRIGID   *adj* very cold **FRIGIDLY** *adv*

FRIJOL   *n* pl. -ES a bean used as food

FRIJOLE   *n* pl. -S frijol

FRILL   *v* -ED, -ING, -S to provide with a frill (an ornamental ruffled edge)

FRILLER   *n* pl. -S one that frills

FRILLING   *n* pl. -S an arrangement of frills

FRILLY   *adj* FRILLIER, FRILLIEST having frills

FRINGE   *v* FRINGED, FRINGING, FRINGES to provide with a fringe (an ornamental border)

FRINGY   *adj* FRINGIER, FRINGIEST resembling a fringe

FRIPPERY   *n* pl. -PERIES excessive ornamentation

FRISE   *n* pl. -S frieze

FRISETTE   *n* pl. -S frizette

FRISEUR   *n* pl. -S a hairdresser

FRISK   *v* -ED, -ING, -S to move or leap about playfully

FRISKER   *n* pl. -S one that frisks

FRISKET   *n* pl. -S a frame used to protect paper in a printing press

FRISKY   *adj* FRISKIER, FRISKIEST lively and playful **FRISKILY** *adv*

FRISSON   *n* pl. -S a shudder

FRIT   *v* FRITTED, FRITTING, FRITS to fuse into a vitreous substance

FRITH   *n* pl. -S firth

FRITT   *v* -ED, -ING, -S to frit

FRITTATA   *n* pl. -S an unfolded omelet with chopped vegetables or meat

FRITTED   past tense of frit

FRITTER   *v* -ED, -ING, -S to squander little by little

FRITTING   present participle of frit

FRITZ	*n* pl. -ES a nonfunctioning state
FRIVOL	*v* -OLED, -OLING, -OLS or -OLLED, -OLLING, -OLS to behave playfully
FRIVOLER	*n* pl. -S one that frivols
FRIZ	*v* -ED, -ING, -ES to frizz
FRIZER	*n* pl. -S frizzer
FRIZETTE	*n* pl. -S a frizzed fringe of hair
FRIZZ	*v* -ED, -ING, -ES to form into small, tight curls
FRIZZER	*n* pl. -S one that frizzes
FRIZZIER	comparative of frizzy
FRIZZIEST	superlative of frizzy
FRIZZILY	*adv* in a frizzy manner
FRIZZLE	*v* -ZLED, -ZLING, -ZLES to frizz
FRIZZLER	*n* pl. -S one that frizzles
FRIZZLY	*adj* -ZLIER, -ZLIEST frizzy
FRIZZY	*adj* FRIZZIER, FRIZZIEST tightly curled
FRO	*adv* away
FROCK	*v* -ED, -ING, -S to clothe in a long, loose outer garment
FROE	*n* pl. -S a cleaving tool
FROG	*v* FROGGED, FROGGING, FROGS to hunt frogs (web-footed, tailless amphibians)
FROGEYE	*n* pl. -S a plant disease **FROGEYED** *adj*
FROGFISH	*n* pl. -ES a marine fish
FROGGED	past tense of frog
FROGGING	present participle of frog
FROGGY	*adj* -GIER, -GIEST abounding in frogs
FROGLIKE	*adj* resembling a frog
FROGMAN	*n* pl. -MEN a person equipped for extended periods of underwater swimming
FROLIC	*v* -ICKED, -ICKING, -ICS to play and run about merrily **FROLICKY** *adj*
FROM	*prep* starting at
FROMAGE	*n* pl. -S cheese
FROMENTY	*n* pl. -TIES frumenty
FROND	*n* pl. -S a type of leaf **FRONDED, FRONDOSE** *adj*
FRONDEUR	*n* pl. -S a rebel
FRONS	*n* pl. FRONTES the upper anterior portion of an insect's head
FRONT	*v* -ED, -ING, -S to provide with a front (a forward part)
FRONT	*adj* FRONTER articulated at the front of the oral passage
FRONTAGE	*n* pl. -S the front of a building or lot
FRONTAL	*n* pl. -S a bone of the skull
FRONTES	pl. of frons
FRONTIER	*n* pl. -S a border between two countries
FRONTLET	*n* pl. -S a decorative band worn across the forehead
FRONTON	*n* pl. -S a jai alai arena
FRORE	*adj* frozen
FROSH	*n* pl. FROSH a freshman
FROST	*v* -ED, -ING, -S to cover with frost (a deposit of minute ice crystals)
FROSTBIT	*adj* injured by extreme cold
FROSTED	*n* pl. -S a type of milk shake
FROSTING	*n* pl. -S icing
FROSTY	*adj* FROSTIER, FROSTIEST covered with frost **FROSTILY** *adv*
FROTH	*v* -ED, -ING, -S to foam
FROTHY	*adj* FROTHIER, FROTHIEST foamy **FROTHILY** *adv*
FROTTAGE	*n* pl. -S masturbation by rubbing against another person
FROTTEUR	*n* pl. -S one who practices frottage
FROUFROU	*n* pl. -S a rustling sound
FROUNCE	*v* FROUNCED, FROUNCING, FROUNCES to pleat
FROUZY	*adj* -ZIER, -ZIEST frowzy
FROW	*n* pl. -S froe
FROWARD	*adj* disobedient
FROWN	*v* -ED, -ING, -S to contract the brow in displeasure
FROWNER	*n* pl. -S one that frowns
FROWST	*v* -ED, -ING, -S to lounge in a stuffy room
FROWSTY	*adj* -TIER, -TIEST musty
FROWSY	*adj* -SIER, -SIEST frowzy
FROWZY	*adj* -ZIER, -ZIEST unkempt **FROWZILY** *adv*
FROZE	past tense of freeze
FROZEN	*adj* very cold **FROZENLY** *adv*
FRUCTIFY	*v* -FIED, -FYING, -FIES to bear fruit

FRUCTOSE *n* pl. -S a sugar found in various fruits

FRUG *v* FRUGGED, FRUGGING, FRUGS to perform a type of vigorous dance

FRUGAL *adj* thrifty **FRUGALLY** *adv*

FRUIT *v* -ED, -ING, -S to bear fruit (usually edible reproductive bodies of a seed plant)

FRUITAGE *n* pl. -S the process of bearing fruit

FRUITER *n* pl. -S one that grows or sells fruit

FRUITFUL *adj* -FULLER, -FULLEST producing abundantly

FRUITIER comparative of fruity

FRUITIEST superlative of fruity

FRUITION *n* pl. -S the accomplishment of something desired

FRUITLET *n* pl. -S a small fruit

FRUITY *adj* FRUITIER, FRUITIEST suggestive of fruit **FRUITILY** *adv*

FRUMENTY *n* pl. -TIES a dish of wheat boiled in milk and sweetened with sugar

FRUMP *n* pl. -S a dowdy woman **FRUMPISH** *adj*

FRUMPY *adj* FRUMPIER, FRUMPIEST dowdy **FRUMPILY** *adv*

FRUSTULE *n* pl. -S the shell of a diatom

FRUSTUM *n* pl. -TA or -TUMS a part of a conical solid

FRY *v* FRIED, FRYING, FRIES to cook over direct heat in hot fat or oil

FRYER *n* pl. -S one that fries

FRYPAN *n* pl. -S a pan for frying food

FUB *v* FUBBED, FUBBING, FUBS to fob

FUBSY *adj* FUBSIER, FUBSIEST chubby and somewhat squat

FUCHSIA *n* pl. -S a flowering shrub

FUCHSIN *n* pl. -S a red dye

FUCHSINE *n* pl. -S fuchsin

FUCI a pl. of fucus

FUCOID *n* pl. -S a brown seaweed **FUCOIDAL** *adj*

FUCOSE *n* pl. -S a type of sugar

FUCOUS *adj* of or pertaining to fucoids

FUCUS *n* pl. -CI or -CUSES any of a genus of brown algae

FUD *n* pl. -S an old-fashioned person

FUDDLE *v* -DLED, -DLING, -DLES to confuse

FUDGE *v* FUDGED, FUDGING, FUDGES to falsify

FUEHRER *n* pl. -S fuhrer

FUEL *v* -ELED, -ELING, -ELS or -ELLED, -ELLING, -ELS to provide with fuel (material used to produce energy)

FUELER *n* pl. -S one that fuels

FUELLER *n* pl. -S fueler

FUELLING a present participle of fuel

FUELWOOD *n* pl. -S firewood

FUG *v* FUGGED, FUGGING, FUGS to make stuffy and odorous

FUGACITY *n* pl. -TIES lack of enduring qualities

FUGAL *adj* being in the style of a fugue **FUGALLY** *adv*

FUGATO *n* pl. -TOS a fugal composition

FUGGED past tense of fug

FUGGING present participle of fug

FUGGY *adj* -GIER, -GIEST stuffy and odorous **FUGGILY** *adv*

FUGIO *n* pl. -GIOS a former coin of the United States

FUGITIVE *n* pl. -S one who flees

FUGLE *v* -GLED, -GLING, -GLES to lead

FUGLEMAN *n* pl. -MEN a leader

FUGU *n* pl. -S a toxin-containing fish

FUGUE *v* FUGUED, FUGUING, FUGUES to compose a fugue (a type of musical composition)

FUGUIST *n* pl. -S one who composes fugues

FUHRER *n* pl. -S a leader

FUJI *n* pl. -S a silk fabric

FULCRUM *n* pl. -CRUMS or -CRA a support for a lever

FULFIL *v* -FILLED, -FILLING, -FILS to fulfill

FULFILL *v* -ED, -ING, -S to bring about the accomplishment of

FULGENT *adj* shining brightly

FULGID *adj* fulgent

FULHAM *n* pl. -S a loaded die

FULL *adj* FULLER, FULLEST filled completely

FULL *v* -ED, -ING, -S to shrink and thicken, as cloth

FULLAM   *n* pl. -S fulham

FULLBACK   *n* pl. -S an offensive back in football

FULLER   *v* -ED, -ING, -S to groove with a type of hammer

FULLERY   *n* pl. -ERIES a place for fulling cloth

FULLFACE   *n* pl. -S a heavy-faced type

FULLNESS   *n* pl. -ES the state of being full

FULLY   *adv* in a full manner

FULMAR   *n* pl. -S an arctic seabird

FULMINE   *v* -MINED, -MINING, -MINES to explode loudly

FULMINIC   *adj* highly explosive

FULNESS   *n* pl. -ES fullness

FULSOME   *adj* repulsive

FULVOUS   *adj* of a brownish yellow color

FUMARASE   *n* pl. -S an enzyme

FUMARATE   *n* pl. -S a chemical salt

FUMARIC   *adj* pertaining to a certain acid

FUMAROLE   *n* pl. -S a hole from which volcanic vapors issue

FUMATORY   *n* pl. -RIES a fumigation chamber

FUMBLE   *v* -BLED, -BLING, -BLES to handle clumsily

FUMBLER   *n* pl. -S one that fumbles

FUME   *v* FUMED, FUMING, FUMES to give off fumes (gaseous exhalations)

FUMELESS   *adj* having no fumes

FUMELIKE   *adj* resembling fumes

FUMER   *n* pl. -S one that fumes

FUMET   *n* pl. -S the odor of meat while cooking

FUMETTE   *n* pl. -S fumet

FUMIER   comparative of fumy

FUMIEST   superlative of fumy

FUMIGANT   *n* pl. -S a substance used in fumigating

FUMIGATE   *v* -GATED, -GATING, -GATES to subject to fumes in order to destroy pests

FUMING   present participle of fume

FUMINGLY   *adv* angrily

FUMITORY   *n* pl. -RIES a climbing plant

FUMULUS   *n* pl. -LI a thin cloud

FUMY   *adj* FUMIER, FUMIEST producing or full of fumes

FUN   *v* FUNNED, FUNNING, FUNS to act playfully

FUN   *adj* FUNNER, FUNNEST providing enjoyment

FUNCTION   *v* -ED, -ING, -S to be in action

FUNCTOR   *n* pl. -S one that functions

FUND   *v* -ED, -ING, -S to provide money for

FUNDUS   *n* pl. -DI the inner basal surface of a bodily organ **FUNDIC** *adj*

FUNERAL   *n* pl. -S a ceremony held for a dead person

FUNERARY   *adj* pertaining to a funeral

FUNEREAL   *adj* funerary

FUNEST   *adj* portending death or evil

FUNFAIR   *n* pl. -S an amusement park

FUNGAL   *n* pl. -S a fungus

FUNGI   a pl. of fungus

FUNGIBLE   *n* pl. -S something that may be exchanged for an equivalent unit of the same class

FUNGIC   *adj* fungous

FUNGO   *n* pl. -GOES a fly ball hit to a fielder for practice in baseball

FUNGOID   *n* pl. -S a growth resembling a fungus

FUNGOUS   *adj* pertaining to a fungus

FUNGUS   *n* pl. -GI or -GUSES any of a major group of lower plants

FUNICLE   *n* pl. -S a cordlike anatomical structure

FUNICULI   *n/pl* funicles

FUNK   *v* -ED, -ING, -S to shrink back in fear

FUNKER   *n* pl. -S one that funks

FUNKIA   *n* pl. -S a flowering plant

FUNKY   *adj* FUNKIER, FUNKIEST having an offensive odor

FUNNED   past tense of fun

FUNNEL   *v* -NELED, -NELING, -NELS or -NELLED, -NELLING, -NELS to pass through a funnel (a cone-shaped utensil)

FUNNER   comparative of fun

FUNNEST   superlative of fun

FUNNING   present participle of fun

FUNNY   *adj* -NIER, -NIEST causing laughter or amusement **FUNNILY** *adv*

FUNNY   *n* pl. -NIES a comic strip

FUNNYMAN *n* pl. -MEN a comedian

FUR *v* FURRED, FURRING, FURS to cover with fur (a dressed animal pelt)

FURAN *n* pl. -S a flammable liquid

FURANE *n* pl. -S furan

FURANOSE *n* pl. -S a type of sugar

FURBELOW *v* -ED, -ING, -S to decorate with ruffles

FURBISH *v* -ED, -ING, -ES to polish

FURCATE *v* -CATED, -CATING, -CATES to divide into branches

FURCRAEA *n* pl. -S a tropical plant

FURCULA *n* pl. -LAE a forked bone
FURCULAR *adj*

FURCULUM *n* pl. -LA a furcula

FURFUR *n* pl. -ES dandruff

FURFURAL *n* pl. -S a chemical compound

FURFURAN *n* pl. -S furan

FURIBUND *adj* furious

FURIES pl. of fury

FURIOSO *adv* with great force — used as a musical direction

FURIOUS *adj* extremely angry

FURL *v* -ED, -ING, -S to roll up
FURLABLE *adj*

FURLER *n* pl. -S one that furls

FURLESS *adj* having no fur

FURLONG *n* pl. -S a unit of distance

FURLOUGH *v* -ED, -ING, -S to grant a leave of absence to

FURMENTY *n* pl. -TIES frumenty

FURMETY *n* pl. -TIES frumenty

FURMITY *n* pl. -TIES frumenty

FURNACE *v* -NACED, -NACING, -NACES to subject to heat

FURNISH *v* -ED, -ING, -ES to equip

FUROR *n* pl. -S an uproar

FURORE *n* pl. -S furor

FURRED past tense of fur

FURRIER *n* pl. -S one that deals in furs

FURRIERY *n* pl. -ERIES the business of a furrier

FURRIEST superlative of furry

FURRILY *adv* in a furry manner

FURRINER *n* pl. -S a foreigner

FURRING *n* pl. -S a trimming or lining of fur

FURROW *v* -ED, -ING, -S to make furrows (narrow depressions) in

FURROWER *n* pl. -S one that furrows

FURROWY *adj* marked by furrows

FURRY *adj* -RIER, -RIEST covered with fur

FURTHER *v* -ED, -ING, -S to help forward

FURTHEST a superlative of far

FURTIVE *adj* stealthy

FURUNCLE *n* pl. -S a painful swelling of the skin

FURY *n* pl. -RIES violent anger

FURZE *n* pl. -S a spiny shrub

FURZY *adj* FURZIER, FURZIEST abounding in furze

FUSAIN *n* pl. -S a fine charcoal used in drawing

FUSCOUS *adj* of a dusky color

FUSE *v* FUSED, FUSING, FUSES to equip with a fuse (a detonating device)

FUSEE *n* pl. -S a large-headed friction match

FUSEL *n* pl. -S an oily liquid

FUSELAGE *n* pl. -S the body of an airplane

FUSELESS *adj* lacking a fuse

FUSIBLE *adj* capable of being melted
FUSIBLY *adv*

FUSIFORM *adj* tapering toward each end

FUSIL *n* pl. -S a type of musket

FUSILE *adj* formed by melting

FUSILEER *n* pl. -S fusilier

FUSILIER *n* pl. -S a soldier armed with a fusil

FUSILLI *n* pl. -S spiral-shaped pasta

FUSING present participle of fuse

FUSION *n* pl. -S the act of melting together

FUSS *v* -ED, -ING, -ES to be overly concerned with small details

FUSSER *n* pl. -S one that fusses

FUSSPOT *n* pl. -S a fusser

FUSSY *adj* FUSSIER, FUSSIEST overly concerned with small details
FUSSILY *adv*

FUSTIAN *n* pl. -S a cotton fabric

FUSTIC *n* pl. -S a tropical tree

FUSTY *adj* -TIER, -TIEST musty
FUSTILY *adv*

FUTHARC   *n* pl. -S futhark

FUTHARK   *n* pl. -S an ancient alphabet

FUTHORC   *n* pl. -S futhark

FUTHORK   *n* pl. -S futhark

FUTILE   *adj* having no useful result **FUTILELY** *adv*

FUTILITY   *n* pl. -TIES the quality of being futile

FUTON   *n* pl. -S a cotton filled mattress for use as a bed

FUTTOCK   *n* pl. -S a curved timber in the frame of a wooden ship

FUTURE   *n* pl. -S the time yet to come **FUTURAL** *adj*

FUTURISM   *n* pl. -S an artistic and literary movement

FUTURIST   *n* pl. -S an advocate of futurism

FUTURITY   *n* pl. -TIES the future

FUTZ   *v* -ED, -ING, -ES to spend time aimlessly

FUZE   *v* FUZED, FUZING, FUZES to fuse

FUZEE   *n* pl. -S fusee

FUZIL   *n* pl. -S fusil

FUZING   present participle of fuze

FUZZ   *v* -ED, -ING, -ES to become fuzzy

FUZZY   *adj* FUZZIER, FUZZIEST blurry **FUZZILY** *adv*

FYCE   *n* pl. -S feist

FYKE   *n* pl. -S a bag-shaped fishnet

FYLFOT   *n* pl. -S a swastika

FYTTE   *n* pl. -S a division of a poem or song

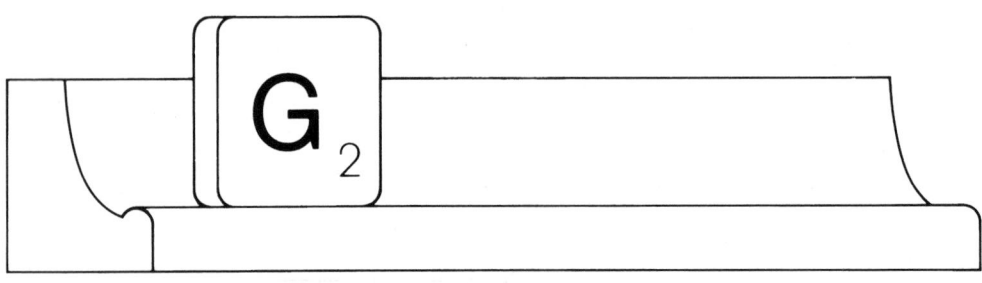

GAB   *v* GABBED, GABBING, GABS to chatter

GABBARD   *n* pl. -S a barge

GABBART   *n* pl. -S gabbard

GABBED   past tense of gab

GABBER   *n* pl. -S one that gabs

GABBIER   comparative of gabby

GABBIEST   superlative of gabby

GABBING   present participle of gab

GABBLE   *v* -BLED, -BLING, -BLES to jabber

GABBLER   *n* pl. -S one that gabbles

GABBRO   *n* pl. -BROS a type of rock **GABBROIC, GABBROID** *adj*

GABBY   *adj* -BIER, -BIEST talkative

GABELLE   *n* pl. -S a tax on salt **GABELLED** *adj*

GABFEST   *n* pl. -S an informal gathering for general talk

GABIES   pl. of gaby

GABION   *n* pl. -S a type of basket

GABLE   *v* -BLED, -BLING, -BLES to form a triangular section of a wall

GABOON   *n* pl. -S a spittoon

GABY   *n* pl. -BIES a dolt

GAD   *v* GADDED, GADDING, GADS to roam about restlessly

GADABOUT   *n* pl. -S one that gads about

GADARENE   *adj* headlong

GADDED   past tense of gad

GADDER   *n* pl. -S one that gads about

GADDI   *n* pl. -S a hassock

GADDING   present participle of gad

GADFLY   *n* pl. -FLIES a biting fly

GADGET   *n* pl. -S a mechanical device **GADGETY** *adj*

GADGETRY   *n* pl. -RIES the devising or constructing of gadgets

GADI   *n* pl. -S gaddi

GADID   *n* pl. -S gadoid

GADOID   *n* pl. -S a type of fish

GADROON   *v* -ED, -ING, -S to decorate with bands of fluted or reeded molding

GADWALL   *n* pl. -S a wild duck

GADZOOKS   *interj* — used as a mild oath

GAE   *v* GAED, GANE or GAEN, GAEING or GAUN, GAES to go

GAFF   *v* -ED, -ING, -S to catch a fish with a sharp hook

GAFFE   *n* pl. -S a social blunder

GAFFER   *n* pl. -S an old man

GAG   *v* GAGGED, GAGGING, GAGS to stop up the mouth

GAGA   *adj* crazy

GAGAKU   *n* pl. -S ancient court music of Japan

GAGE   *v* GAGED, GAGING, GAGES to pledge as security

GAGER   *n* pl. -S gauger

GAGGED   past tense of gag

GAGGER   *n* pl. -S one that gags

GAGGING   present participle of gag

GAGGLE   *v* -GLED, -GLING, -GLES to cackle

GAGING   present participle of gage

GAGMAN   *n* pl. -MEN one who writes jokes

GAGSTER   *n* pl. -S a gagman

GAHNITE   *n* pl. -S a mineral

GAIETY   *n* pl. -ETIES festive activity

GAIJIN   *n* pl. GAIJIN a foreigner in Japan

GAILY   *adv* in a gay manner

GAIN   *v* -ED, -ING, -S to acquire **GAINABLE** *adj*

GAINER   *n* pl. -S one that gains

GAINFUL   *adj* profitable

GAINLESS *adj* profitless

GAINLY *adj* -LIER, -LIEST graceful

GAINSAY *v* -SAID, -SAYING, -SAYS to deny

GAINST *prep* against

GAIT *v* -ED, -ING, -S to train a horse to move in a particular way

GAITER *n* pl. -S a covering for the lower leg

GAL *n* pl. -S a girl

GALA *n* pl. -S a celebration

GALABIA *n* pl. -S djellaba

GALABIEH *n* pl. -S djellaba

GALABIYA *n* pl. -S djellaba

GALACTIC *adj* pertaining to a galaxy

GALAGO *n* pl. -GOS a small primate

GALAH *n* pl. -S a cockatoo

GALANGAL *n* pl. -S a medicinal plant

GALATEA *n* pl. -S a strong cotton fabric

GALAVANT *v* -ED, -ING, -S to gad about

GALAX *n* pl. -ES an evergreen herb

GALAXY *n* pl. -AXIES a large system of celestial bodies

GALBANUM *n* pl. -S a gum resin

GALE *n* pl. -S a strong wind

GALEA *n* pl. -LEAE or -LEAS a helmet-shaped anatomical part **GALEATE, GALEATED** *adj*

GALENA *n* pl. -S the principal ore of lead **GALENIC** *adj*

GALENITE *n* pl. -S galena

GALERE *n* pl. -S a group of people having a common quality

GALILEE *n* pl. -S a type of porch

GALIOT *n* pl. -S galliot

GALIPOT *n* pl. -S a type of turpentine

GALIVANT *v* -ED, -ING, -S to gad about

GALL *v* -ED, -ING, -S to vex or irritate

GALLANT *v* -ED, -ING, -S to court a woman

GALLATE *n* pl. -S a chemical salt

GALLEASS *n* pl. -ES a large war galley

GALLEIN *n* pl. -S a green dye

GALLEON *n* pl. -S a large sailing vessel

GALLERIA *n* pl. -S a roofed promenade or court

GALLERY *v* -LERIED, -LERYING, -LERIES to provide with a long covered area

GALLET *v* -ED, -ING, -S to fill in mortar joints with stone chips

GALLETA *n* pl. -S a perennial grass

GALLEY *n* pl. -LEYS a long, low medieval ship

GALLFLY *n* pl. -FLIES a small insect

GALLIARD *n* pl. -S a lively dance

GALLIASS *n* pl. -ES galleass

GALLIC *adj* containing gallium

GALLICAN *adj* pertaining to a French religious movement

GALLIED past tense of gally

GALLIES present 3d person sing. of gally

GALLIOT *n* pl. -S a small galley

GALLIPOT *n* pl. -S a small earthen jar

GALLIUM *n* pl. -S a metallic element

GALLNUT *n* pl. -S an abnormal swelling of plant tissue

GALLON *n* pl. -S a unit of liquid measure

GALLOON *n* pl. -S an ornamental braid

GALLOOT *n* pl. -S galoot

GALLOP *v* -ED, -ING, -S to ride a horse at full speed

GALLOPER *n* pl. -S one that gallops

GALLOUS *adj* containing gallium

GALLOWS *n* pl. -ES a structure used for hanging a condemned person

GALLUS *n* pl. -ES a suspender for trousers **GALLUSED** *adj*

GALLY *v* -LIED, -LYING, -LIES to frighten

GALOOT *n* pl. -S an awkward or uncouth person

GALOP *v* -ED, -ING, -S to dance a galop (a lively round dance)

GALOPADE *n* pl. -S a lively round dance

GALORE *n* pl. -S abundance

GALOSH *n* pl. -ES an overshoe **GALOSHED** *adj*

GALOSHE *n* pl. -S galosh

GALUMPH *v* -ED, -ING, -S to move clumsily

GALVANIC *adj* pertaining to a direct electric current

GALYAC *n* pl. -S galyak

GALYAK *n* pl. -S a fur made from lambskin

GAM *v* GAMMED, GAMMING, GAMS to visit socially

GAMA *n* pl. -S a pasture grass

GAMASHES *n/pl* boots worn by horseback riders

GAMAY *n* pl. -MAYS a red grape

GAMB *n* pl. -S a leg

GAMBA *n* pl. -S a bass viol

GAMBADE *n* pl. -S a gambado

GAMBADO *n* pl. -DOES or -DOS a leap made by a horse

GAMBE *n* pl. -S gamb

GAMBESON *n* pl. -S a medieval coat

GAMBIA *n* pl. -S gambier

GAMBIER *n* pl. -S an extract obtained from an Asian vine

GAMBIR *n* pl. -S gambier

GAMBIT *n* pl. -S a type of chess opening

GAMBLE *v* -BLED, -BLING, -BLES to play a game of chance for money or valuables

GAMBLER *n* pl. -S one that gambles

GAMBOGE *n* pl. -S a gum resin

GAMBOL *v* -BOLED, -BOLING, -BOLS or -BOLLED, -BOLLING, -BOLS to leap about playfully

GAMBREL *n* pl. -S a part of a horse's leg

GAMBUSIA *n* pl. -S a small fish

GAME *adj* GAMER, GAMEST plucky

GAME *v* GAMED, GAMING, GAMES to gamble

GAMECOCK *n* pl. -S a rooster trained for fighting

GAMELAN *n* pl. -S a type of orchestra

GAMELIKE *adj* similar to a game (a contest governed by a set of rules)

GAMELY *adv* in a game manner

GAMENESS *n* pl. -ES the quality of being game

GAMER *n* pl. -S an avid game player

GAMESMAN *n* pl. -MEN one who plays games

GAMESOME *adj* playful

GAMEST superlative of game

GAMESTER *n* pl. -S a gambler

GAMETE *n* pl. -S a mature reproductive cell **GAMETIC** *adj*

GAMEY *adj* GAMIER, GAMIEST gamy

GAMIC *adj* requiring fertilization

GAMIER comparative of gamy

GAMIEST superlative of gamy

GAMILY *adv* in a game manner

GAMIN *n* pl. -S an urchin

GAMINE *n* pl. -S a tomboy

GAMINESS *n* pl. -ES the quality of being gamy

GAMING *n* pl. -S the practice of gambling

GAMMA *n* pl. -S a Greek letter

GAMMADIA *n/pl* Greek ornamental designs

GAMMED past tense of gam

GAMMER *n* pl. -S an old woman

GAMMIER comparative of gammy

GAMMIEST superlative of gammy

GAMMING present participle of gam

GAMMON *v* -ED, -ING, -S to mislead by deceptive talk

GAMMONER *n* pl. -S one that gammons

GAMMY *adj* -MIER, -MIEST lame

GAMODEME *n* pl. -S a somewhat isolated breeding community of organisms

GAMP *n* pl. -S a large umbrella

GAMUT *n* pl. -S an entire range

GAMY *adj* GAMIER, GAMIEST plucky

GAN past tense of gin

GANACHE *n* pl. -S creamy chocolate mixture

GANDER *v* -ED, -ING, -S to wander

GANE a past participle of gae

GANEF *n* pl. -S a thief

GANEV *n* pl. -S ganef

GANG *v* -ED, -ING, -S to form into a gang (a group)

GANGER *n* pl. -S a foreman of a gang of laborers

GANGLAND *n* pl. -S the criminal underworld

GANGLIA a pl. of ganglion

GANGLIAL *adj* gangliar

GANGLIAR *adj* pertaining to a ganglion

GANGLIER comparative of gangly

GANGLIEST superlative of gangly

GANGLING *adj* awkwardly tall and lanky

GANGLION *n* pl. -GLIA or -GLIONS a group of nerve cells

GANGLY *adj* -GLIER, -GLIEST gangling

GANGPLOW *n* pl. -S an agricultural implement

GANGREL *n* pl. -S a vagabond

GANGRENE *v* -GRENED, -GRENING, -GRENES to suffer the loss of tissue in part of the body

GANGSTER *n* pl. -S a member of a criminal gang

GANGUE *n* pl. -S the worthless rock in which valuable minerals are found

GANGWAY *n* pl. -WAYS a passageway

GANISTER *n* pl. -S a type of rock

GANJA *n* pl. -S cannabis used for smoking

GANJAH *n* pl. -S ganja

GANNET *n* pl. -S a large seabird

GANOF *n* pl. -S ganef

GANOID *n* pl. -S a type of fish

GANTLET *v* -ED, -ING, -S to overlap railroad tracks

GANTLINE *n* pl. -S a rope on a ship

GANTLOPE *n* pl. -S a former military punishment

GANTRY *n* pl. -TRIES a structure for supporting railroad signals

GANYMEDE *n* pl. -S a youth who serves liquors

GAOL *v* -ED, -ING, -S to jail

GAOLER *n* pl. -S jailer

GAP *v* GAPPED, GAPPING, GAPS to make an opening in

GAPE *v* GAPED, GAPING, GAPES to stare with open mouth

GAPER *n* pl. -S one that gapes

GAPESEED *n* pl. -S something that causes wonder

GAPEWORM *n* pl. -S a worm that causes a disease of young birds

GAPING present participle of gape

GAPINGLY *adv* in a gaping manner

GAPOSIS *n* pl. -SISES a gap in a row of buttons or snaps

GAPPED past tense of gap

GAPPING present participle of gap

GAPPY *adj* -PIER, -PIEST having openings

GAPY *adj* infested with gapeworms

GAR *v* GARRED, GARRING, GARS to cause or compel

GARAGE *v* -RAGED, -RAGING, -RAGES to put in a garage (a car shelter)

GARB *v* -ED, -ING, -S to clothe

GARBAGE *n* pl. -S food waste

GARBANZO *n* pl. -ZOS a chickpea

GARBLE *v* -BLED, -BLING, -BLES to distort the meaning of

GARBLER *n* pl. -S one that garbles

GARBLESS *adj* being without clothing

GARBOARD *n* pl. -S a plank on a ship's bottom

GARBOIL *n* pl. -S turmoil

GARCON *n* pl. -S a waiter

GARDANT *adj* turned directly toward the observer — used of a heraldic animal

GARDEN *v* -ED, -ING, -S to cultivate a plot of ground

GARDENER *n* pl. -S one that gardens

GARDENIA *n* pl. -S a tropical shrub or tree

GARDYLOO *interj* — used as a warning cry

GARFISH *n* pl. -ES a freshwater fish

GARGANEY *n* pl. -NEYS a small duck

GARGET *n* pl. -S mastitis of domestic animals **GARGETY** *adj*

GARGLE *v* -GLED, -GLING, -GLES to rinse the mouth or throat

GARGLER *n* pl. -S one that gargles

GARGOYLE *n* pl. -S an ornamental figure

GARIGUE *n* pl. -S a low scrubland

GARISH *adj* gaudy **GARISHLY** *adv*

GARLAND *v* -ED, -ING, -S to deck with wreaths of flowers

GARLIC *n* pl. -S an herb used in cooking **GARLICKY** *adj*

GARMENT *v* -ED, -ING, -S to clothe

GARNER *v* -ED, -ING, -S to gather and store

GARNET *n* pl. -S a mineral

GARNI *adj* garnished

GARNISH *v* -ED, -ING, -ES to decorate

GAROTE *v* -ROTED, -ROTING, -ROTES to garrote

GAROTTE *v* -ROTTED, -ROTTING, -ROTTES to garrote

GAROTTER *n* pl. -S one that garottes

GARPIKE *n* pl. -S a garfish

GARRED past tense of gar

GARRET *n* pl. -S an attic

GARRING present participle of gar

GARRISON *v* -ED, -ING, -S to assign to a military post

GARRON *n* pl. -S a small, sturdy horse

GARROTE _v_ -ROTED, -ROTING, -ROTES to execute by strangling

GARROTER _n_ pl. -S one that garrotes

GARROTTE _v_ -ROTTED, -ROTTING, -ROTTES to garrote

GARTER _v_ -ED, -ING, -S to fasten with an elastic band

GARTH _n_ pl. -S a yard or garden

GARVEY _n_ pl. -VEYS a small scow

GAS _v_ GASSED, GASSING, GASES or GASSES to supply with gas (a substance capable of indefinite expansion)

GASALIER _n_ pl. -S gaselier

GASBAG _n_ pl. -S a bag for holding gas

GASCON _n_ pl. -S a boaster

GASELIER _n_ pl. -S a gaslight chandelier

GASEOUS _adj_ pertaining to gas

GASH _v_ -ED, -ING, -ES to make a long deep cut in

GASH _adj_ GASHER, GASHEST knowing

GASHOUSE _n_ pl. -S a gasworks

GASIFIED past tense of gasify

GASIFIER _n_ pl. -S one that gasifies

GASIFORM _adj_ having the form of gas

GASIFY _v_ -IFIED, -IFYING, -IFIES to convert into gas

GASKET _n_ pl. -S packing for making something fluid-tight

GASKIN _n_ pl. -S a part of a horse's leg

GASKING _n_ pl. -S a gasket

GASLESS _adj_ having no gas

GASLIGHT _n_ pl. -S light made by burning gas

GASLIT _adj_ illuminated by gaslight

GASMAN _n_ pl. -MEN an employee of a gas company

GASOGENE _n_ pl. -S gazogene

GASOHOL _n_ pl. -S a fuel mixture of gasoline and ethyl alcohol

GASOLENE _n_ pl. -S gasoline

GASOLIER _n_ pl. -S gaselier

GASOLINE _n_ pl. -S a liquid fuel

GASP _v_ -ED, -ING, -S to breathe convulsively

GASPER _n_ pl. -S a cigarette

GASSED past tense of gas

GASSER _n_ pl. -S one that gasses

GASSES a present 3d person sing. of gas

GASSING _n_ pl. -S a poisoning by noxious gas

GASSY _adj_ -SIER, -SIEST containing gas **GASSILY** _adv_

GAST _v_ -ED, -ING, -S to scare

GASTER _n_ pl. -S the enlarged part of the abdomen in some insects

GASTIGHT _adj_ not allowing gas to escape or enter

GASTNESS _n_ pl. -ES fright

GASTRAEA _n_ pl. -S a type of metazoan

GASTRAL _adj_ pertaining to the stomach

GASTREA _n_ pl. -S gastraea

GASTRIC _adj_ pertaining to the stomach

GASTRIN _n_ pl. -S a hormone

GASTRULA _n_ pl. -LAS or -LAE a metazoan embryo

GASWORKS _n_ pl. GASWORKS a factory where gas is produced

GAT _n_ pl. -S a pistol

GATE _v_ GATED, GATING, GATES to supply with a gate (a movable barrier)

GATEAU _n_ pl. -TEAUX a rich layer cake

GATEFOLD _n_ pl. -S a folded insert in a book or magazine

GATELESS _adj_ lacking a gate

GATELIKE _adj_ resembling a gate

GATEMAN _n_ pl. -MEN a person in charge of a gate

GATEPOST _n_ pl. -S a post from which a gate is hung

GATEWAY _n_ pl. -WAYS a passage that may be closed by a gate

GATHER _v_ -ED, -ING, -S to bring together into one place or group

GATHERER _n_ pl. -S one that gathers

GATING present participle of gate

GATOR _n_ pl. -S an alligator

GAUCHE _adj_ GAUCHER, GAUCHEST lacking social grace **GAUCHELY** _adv_

GAUCHO _n_ pl. -CHOS a cowboy of the South American pampas

GAUD _n_ pl. -S a showy ornament

GAUDERY _n_ pl. -ERIES finery

GAUDY _adj_ GAUDIER, GAUDIEST tastelessly showy **GAUDILY** _adv_

GAUDY _n_ pl. -DIES a festival

GAUFFER	*v* -ED, -ING, -S to goffer
GAUGE	*v* GAUGED, GAUGING, GAUGES to measure precisely
GAUGER	*n* pl. -S one that gauges
GAULT	*n* pl. -S a heavy, thick clay soil
GAUM	*v* -ED, -ING, -S to smear
GAUN	present participle of gae
GAUNT	*adj* GAUNTER, GAUNTEST emaciated **GAUNTLY** *adv*
GAUNTLET	*v* -ED, -ING, -S to gantlet
GAUNTRY	*n* pl. -TRIES gantry
GAUR	*n* pl. -S a wild ox
GAUSS	*n* pl. -ES a unit of magnetic induction
GAUZE	*n* pl. -S a transparent fabric
GAUZY	*adj* GAUZIER, GAUZIEST resembling gauze **GAUZILY** *adv*
GAVAGE	*n* pl. -S introduction of material into the stomach by a tube
GAVE	past tense of give
GAVEL	*v* -ELED, -ELING, -ELS or -ELLED, -ELLING, -ELS to signal for attention or order by use of a gavel (a small mallet)
GAVELOCK	*n* pl. -S a crowbar
GAVIAL	*n* pl. -S a large reptile
GAVOT	*n* pl. -S a French dance
GAVOTTE	*v* -VOTTED, -VOTTING, -VOTTES to dance a gavot
GAWK	*v* -ED, -ING, -S to stare stupidly
GAWKER	*n* pl. -S one that gawks
GAWKIER	comparative of gawky
GAWKIES	pl. of gawky
GAWKISH	*adj* gawky
GAWKY	*adj* GAWKIER, GAWKIEST awkward **GAWKILY** *adv*
GAWKY	*n* pl. GAWKIES an awkward person
GAWP	*v* -ED, -ING, -S to stare stupidly
GAWPER	*n* pl. -S one that gawps
GAWSIE	*adj* well-fed and healthy looking
GAWSY	*adj* gawsie
GAY	*adj* GAYER, GAYEST merry
GAY	*n* pl. GAYS a homosexual
GAYAL	*n* pl. -S a domesticated ox
GAYETY	*n* pl. -ETIES gaiety
GAYLY	*adv* in a gay manner
GAYNESS	*n* pl. -ES gaiety
GAYWINGS	*n* pl. GAYWINGS a perennial herb
GAZABO	*n* pl. -BOS or -BOES a fellow
GAZANIA	*n* pl. -S a South African herb
GAZAR	*n* pl. -S silky sheer fabric
GAZE	*v* GAZED, GAZING, GAZES to look intently
GAZEBO	*n* pl. -BOS or -BOES a roofed structure open on the sides
GAZELLE	*n* pl. -S a small antelope
GAZER	*n* pl. -S one that gazes
GAZETTE	*v* -ZETTED, -ZETTING, -ZETTES to announce in an official journal
GAZING	present participle of gaze
GAZOGENE	*n* pl. -S an apparatus for carbonating liquids
GAZPACHO	*n* pl. -CHOS a cold, spicy soup
GAZUMP	*v* -ED, -ING, -S to cheat by raising the price originally agreed upon
GAZUMPER	*n* pl. -S one that gazumps
GEAR	*v* -ED, -ING, -S to provide with gears (toothed machine parts)
GEARBOX	*n* pl. -ES an automotive transmission
GEARCASE	*n* pl. -S a casing for gears
GEARING	*n* pl. -S a system of gears
GEARLESS	*adj* being without gears
GECK	*v* -ED, -ING, -S to mock
GECKO	*n* pl. GECKOS or GECKOES a small lizard
GED	*n* pl. -S a food fish
GEE	*v* GEED, GEEING, GEES to turn to the right
GEEGAW	*n* pl. -S gewgaw
GEEK	*n* pl. -S a carnival performer
GEEKY	*adj* GEEKIER, GEEKIEST socially awkward or unappealing
GEEPOUND	*n* pl. -S a unit of mass
GEESE	pl. of goose
GEEST	*n* pl. -S old alluvial matter
GEEZ	*interj* jeez
GEEZER	*n* pl. -S an eccentric man
GEISHA	*n* pl. -S a Japanese girl trained to entertain
GEL	*v* GELLED, GELLING, GELS to become like jelly **GELABLE** *adj*
GELADA	*n* pl. -S a baboon
GELANT	*n* pl. -S gellant

GELATE *v* -ATED, -ATING, -ATES to gel

GELATI a pl. of gelato

GELATIN *n* pl. -S a glutinous substance

GELATINE *n* pl. -S gelatin

GELATING present participle of gelate

GELATION *n* pl. -S the process of gelling

GELATO *n* pl. -TI or -TOS Italian ice cream

GELD *v* -ED, -ING, -S to castrate

GELDER *n* pl. -S one that gelds

GELDING *n* pl. -S a castrated animal

GELEE *n* pl. -S a cosmetic gel

GELID *adj* icy **GELIDLY** *adv*

GELIDITY *n* pl. -TIES iciness

GELLANT *n* pl. -S a substance used to produce gelling

GELLED past tense of gel

GELLING present participle of gel

GELSEMIA *n/pl* medicinal plant roots

GELT *n* pl. -S money

GEM *v* GEMMED, GEMMING, GEMS to adorn with gems (precious stones)

GEMINAL *adj* of or pertaining to two substituents on the same atom

GEMINATE *v* -NATED, -NATING, -NATES to arrange in pairs

GEMLIKE *adj* resembling a gem

GEMMA *n* pl. -MAE an asexual reproductive structure

GEMMATE *v* -MATED, -MATING, -MATES to produce gemmae

GEMMED past tense of gem

GEMMIER comparative of gemmy

GEMMIEST superlative of gemmy

GEMMILY *adv* in a manner suggesting a gem

GEMMING present participle of gem

GEMMULE *n* pl. -S a small gemma

GEMMY *adj* -MIER, -MIEST resembling a gem

GEMOLOGY *n* pl. -GIES the science of gems

GEMOT *n* pl. -S a public meeting in Anglo-Saxon England

GEMOTE *n* pl. -S gemot

GEMSBOK *n* pl. -S a large antelope

GEMSBUCK *n* pl. -S gemsbok

GEMSTONE *n* pl. -S a precious stone

GEN *n* pl. -S information obtained from study

GENDARME *n* pl. -S a policeman

GENDER *v* -ED, -ING, -S to engender

GENE *n* pl. -S a hereditary unit

GENERA a pl. of genus

GENERAL *n* pl. -S a military officer

GENERATE *v* -ATED, -ATING, -ATES to bring into existence

GENERIC *n* pl. -S a type of drug

GENEROUS *adj* willing to give

GENESIS *n* pl. GENESES an origin

GENET *n* pl. -S a carnivorous mammal

GENETIC *adj* pertaining to genetics

GENETICS *n/pl* the science of heredity

GENETTE *n* pl. -S genet

GENEVA *n* pl. -S a liquor

GENIAL *adj* having a pleasant or friendly manner **GENIALLY** *adv*

GENIC *adj* pertaining to genes

GENIE *n* pl. -S jinni

GENII a pl. of genius

GENIP *n* pl. -S a tropical tree

GENIPAP *n* pl. -S a tropical tree

GENITAL *adj* pertaining to reproduction

GENITALS *n/pl* the sexual organs

GENITIVE *n* pl. -S a grammatical case

GENITOR *n* pl. -S a male parent

GENITURE *n* pl. -S birth

GENIUS *n* pl. GENIUSES or GENII an exceptional natural aptitude

GENOA *n* pl. -S a triangular sail

GENOCIDE *n* pl. -S the deliberate extermination of a national or racial group

GENOISE *n* pl. -S a rich spongecake

GENOM *n* pl. -S genome

GENOME *n* pl. -S a haploid set of chromosomes **GENOMIC** *adj*

GENOTYPE *n* pl. -S the genetic constitution of an organism

GENRE *n* pl. -S a type or kind

GENRO *n* pl. -ROS a group of elder statesmen in Japan

GENS *n* pl. GENTES a type of clan

GENSENG *n* pl. -S ginseng

GENT *n* pl. -S a gentleman

GENTEEL	*adj* -TEELER, -TEELEST well-bred or refined
GENTES	pl. of gens
GENTIAN	*n* pl. -S a flowering plant
GENTIL	*adj* kind
GENTILE	*n* pl. -S a non-Jewish person
GENTLE	*adj* -TLER, -TLEST mild **GENTLY** *adv*
GENTLE	*v* -TLED, -TLING, -TLES to tame
GENTOO	*n* pl. -TOOS a gray-backed penguin
GENTRICE	*n* pl. -S good breeding
GENTRIFY	*v* -FIED, -FYING, -FIES to renew a decayed urban area so as to attract middle-class residents
GENTRY	*n* pl. -TRIES people of high social class
GENU	*n* pl. GENUA the knee
GENUINE	*adj* authentic
GENUS	*n* pl. GENERA or GENUSES a kind, sort, or class
GEODE	*n* pl. -S a type of rock
GEODESIC	*n* pl. -S a geometric line
GEODESY	*n* pl. -SIES geographical surveying
GEODETIC	*adj* pertaining to geodesy
GEODIC	*adj* of or pertaining to a geode
GEODUCK	*n* pl. -S a large, edible clam
GEOGNOSY	*n* pl. -SIES a branch of geology
GEOID	*n* pl. -S a hypothetical surface of the earth **GEOIDAL** *adj*
GEOLOGER	*n* pl. -S a specialist in geology
GEOLOGY	*n* pl. -GIES the science that deals with the origin and structure of the earth **GEOLOGIC** *adj*
GEOMANCY	*n* pl. -CIES a method of foretelling the future by geographical features
GEOMETER	*n* pl. -S a specialist in geometry
GEOMETRY	*n* pl. -TRIES a branch of mathematics
GEOPHAGY	*n* pl. -GIES the practice of eating earthy substances
GEOPHONE	*n* pl. -S a device that detects vibrations in the earth
GEOPHYTE	*n* pl. -S a plant having underground buds
GEOPONIC	*adj* pertaining to farming
GEOPROBE	*n* pl. -S a spacecraft for exploring space near the earth
GEORGIC	*n* pl. -S a poem about farming
GEOTAXIS	*n* pl. -TAXES the movement of an organism in response to gravity
GERAH	*n* pl. -S a Hebrew unit of weight
GERANIAL	*n* pl. -S citral
GERANIOL	*n* pl. -S an alcohol used in perfumes
GERANIUM	*n* pl. -S a flowering plant
GERARDIA	*n* pl. -S an herb
GERBERA	*n* pl. -S an herb
GERBIL	*n* pl. -S a burrowing rodent
GERBILLE	*n* pl. -S gerbil
GERENT	*n* pl. -S a ruler or manager
GERENUK	*n* pl. -S a long-necked antelope
GERM	*n* pl. -S a microorganism that causes disease
GERMAN	*n* pl. -S an elaborate dance
GERMANE	*adj* relevant
GERMANIC	*adj* containing germanium (a metallic element)
GERMEN	*n* pl. -MENS or -MINA something that serves as an origin
GERMFREE	*adj* free from germs
GERMIER	comparative of germy
GERMIEST	superlative of germy
GERMINA	a pl. of germen
GERMINAL	*adj* being in the earliest stage of development
GERMY	*adj* GERMIER, GERMIEST full of germs
GERONTIC	*adj* pertaining to old age
GERUND	*n* pl. -S a verbal noun
GESNERIA	*adj* designating a type of flowering plant
GESSO	*n* pl. -SOES a plaster mixture
GESSOED	*adj* having gesso as a coating
GEST	*n* pl. -S a feat
GESTALT	*n* pl. -STALTS or -STALTEN a unified whole
GESTAPO	*n* pl. -POS a secret-police organization
GESTATE	*v* -TATED, -TATING, -TATES to carry in the uterus during pregnancy
GESTE	*n* pl. -S gest
GESTIC	*adj* pertaining to bodily motion
GESTICAL	*adj* gestic

GESTURAL *adj* pertaining to or consisting of gestures (expressive bodily motions)

GESTURE *v* -TURED, -TURING, -TURES to express by bodily motion

GESTURER *n* pl. -S one that gestures

GET *v* GOT, GOTTEN, GETTING, GETS to obtain or acquire **GETABLE, GETTABLE** *adj*

GET *n* pl. GITTIN a divorce by Jewish law

GETA *n* pl. -S a Japanese wooden clog

GETAWAY *n* pl. -AWAYS an escape

GETTER *v* -ED, -ING, -S to purify with a chemically active substance

GETTING present participle of get

GETUP *n* pl. -S a costume

GEUM *n* pl. -S a perennial herb

GEWGAW *n* pl. -S a showy trinket

GEY *adv* very

GEYSER *n* pl. -S a spring that ejects jets of hot water and steam

GHARIAL *n* pl. -S a large reptile

GHARRI *n* pl. -S gharry

GHARRY *n* pl. -RIES a carriage used in India

GHAST *adj* ghastly

GHASTFUL *adj* frightful

GHASTLY *adj* -LIER, -LIEST terrifying

GHAT *n* pl. -S a passage to a river

GHAUT *n* pl. -S ghat

GHAZI *n* pl. -S or -ES a Muslim war hero

GHEE *n* pl. -S a kind of liquid butter

GHERAO *v* -ED, -ING, -ES to coerce by physical means

GHERKIN *n* pl. -S a small cucumber

GHETTO *v* -ED, -ING, -S or -ES to isolate in a slum

GHI *n* pl. -S ghee

GHIBLI *n* pl. -S a hot desert wind

GHILLIE *n* pl. -S a type of shoe

GHOST *v* -ED, -ING, -S to haunt

GHOSTING *n* pl. -S a false image on a television screen

GHOSTLY *adj* -LIER, -LIEST spectral

GHOSTY *adj* GHOSTIER, GHOSTIEST ghostly

GHOUL *n* pl. -S a demon **GHOULISH** *adj*

GHOULIE *n* pl. -S a ghoul

GHYLL *n* pl. -S a ravine

GIANT *n* pl. -S a person or thing of great size

GIANTESS *n* pl. -ES a female giant

GIANTISM *n* pl. -S the condition of being a giant

GIAOUR *n* pl. -S a non-Muslim

GIB *v* GIBBED, GIBBING, GIBS to fasten with a wedge of wood or metal

GIBBER *v* -ED, -ING, -S to jabber

GIBBET *v* -BETED, -BETING, -BETS or -BETTED, -BETTING, -BETS to execute by hanging

GIBBING present participle of gib

GIBBON *n* pl. -S an arboreal ape

GIBBOSE *adj* gibbous

GIBBOUS *adj* irregularly rounded

GIBBSITE *n* pl. -S a mineral

GIBE *v* GIBED, GIBING, GIBES to jeer **GIBINGLY** *adv*

GIBER *n* pl. -S one that gibes

GIBLET *n* pl. -S an edible part of a fowl

GIBSON *n* pl. -S a martini served with a tiny onion

GID *n* pl. -S a disease of sheep

GIDDAP *interj* — used as a command to a horse to go faster

GIDDY *adj* -DIER, -DIEST dizzy **GIDDILY** *adv*

GIDDY *v* -DIED, -DYING, -DIES to make giddy

GIDDYAP *interj* giddap

GIDDYUP *interj* giddap

GIE *v* GIED, GIEN, GIEING, GIES to give

GIFT *v* -ED, -ING, -S to present with a gift (something given without charge)

GIFTEDLY *adv* in a talented manner

GIFTLESS *adj* being without a gift

GIFTWARE *n* pl. -S wares suitable for gifts

GIG *v* GIGGED, GIGGING, GIGS to catch fish with a pronged spear

GIGA *n* pl. GIGHE a gigue

GIGABIT *n* pl. -S a unit of information

GIGABYTE *n* pl. -S 1,073,741,824 bytes

GIGANTIC *adj* huge

GIGAS *adj* pertaining to variations in plant development

GIGATON *n* pl. -S a unit of weight

GIGAWATT *n* pl. -S a unit of power

GIGGED past tense of gig

GIGGING present participle of gig

GIGGLE *v* -GLED, -GLING, -GLES to laugh in a silly manner

GIGGLER *n* pl. -S one that giggles

GIGGLY *adj* -GLIER, -GLIEST tending to giggle

GIGHE pl. of giga

GIGLET *n* pl. -S a playful girl

GIGLOT *n* pl. -S giglet

GIGOLO *n* pl. -LOS a man supported financially by a woman

GIGOT *n* pl. -S a leg of lamb

GIGUE *n* pl. -S a lively dance

GILBERT *n* pl. -S a unit of magnetomotive force

GILD *v* GILDED or GILT, GILDING, GILDS to cover with a thin layer of gold

GILDER *n* pl. -S one that gilds

GILDHALL *n* pl. -S a town hall

GILDING *n* pl. -S the application of gilt

GILL *v* -ED, -ING, -S to catch fish with a type of net

GILLER *n* pl. -S one that gills

GILLIE *n* pl. -S ghillie

GILLNET *v* -NETTED, -NETTING, -NETS to gill

GILLY *v* -LIED, -LYING, -LIES to transport on a type of wagon

GILT *n* pl. -S the gold with which something is gilded

GILTHEAD *n* pl. -S a marine fish

GIMBAL *v* -BALED, -BALING, -BALS or -BALLED, -BALLING, -BALS to support on a set of rings

GIMCRACK *n* pl. -S a gewgaw

GIMEL *n* pl. -S a Hebrew letter

GIMLET *v* -ED, -ING, -S to pierce with a boring tool

GIMMAL *n* pl. -S a pair of interlocked rings

GIMME *n* pl. -S something easily won

GIMMICK *v* -ED, -ING, -S to provide with a gimmick (a novel or tricky feature)

GIMMICKY *adj* having or being like a gimmick

GIMMIE *n* pl. -MIES an easy golf putt conceded to an opponent

GIMP *v* -ED, -ING, -S to limp

GIMPIER comparative of gimpy

GIMPIEST superlative of gimpy

GIMPY *adj* GIMPIER, GIMPIEST limping

GIN *v* GINNED, GINNING, GINS to remove seeds from cotton

GIN *v* GAN, GUNNEN, GINNING, GINS to begin

GINGAL *n* pl. -S jingal

GINGALL *n* pl. -S jingal

GINGELEY *n* pl. -LEYS gingelly

GINGELI *n* pl. -S gingelly

GINGELIES pl. of gingely

GINGELLI *n* pl. -S gingelly

GINGELLY *n* pl. -LIES the sesame seed or its oil

GINGELY *n* pl. -LIES gingelly

GINGER *v* -ED, -ING, -S to flavor with ginger (a pungent spice)

GINGERLY *adv* in a careful manner

GINGERY *adj* having the characteristics of ginger

GINGHAM *n* pl. -S a cotton fabric

GINGILI *n* pl. -LIS gingelly

GINGILLI *n* pl. -S gingelly

GINGIVA *n* pl. -VAE the fleshy tissue that surrounds the teeth **GINGIVAL** *adj*

GINGKO *n* pl. -KOES ginkgo

GINK *n* pl. -S a fellow

GINKGO *n* pl. -GOES or -GOS an ornamental tree

GINNED past tense of gin

GINNER *n* pl. -S one that gins cotton

GINNING *n* pl. -S cotton as it comes from a gin

GINNY *adj* GINNIER, GINNIEST affected with gin (a strong liquor)

GINSENG *n* pl. -S a perennial herb

GIP *v* GIPPED, GIPPING, GIPS to gyp

GIPON *n* pl. -S jupon

GIPPER *n* pl. -S one that gips

GIPPING present participle of gip

GIPSY	*v* -SIED, -SYING, -SIES to gypsy
GIRAFFE	*n* pl. -S a long-necked mammal
GIRASOL	*n* pl. -S a variety of opal
GIRASOLE	*n* pl. -S girasol
GIRD	*v* GIRDED or GIRT, GIRDING, GIRDS to surround
GIRDER	*n* pl. -S a horizontal support
GIRDLE	*v* -DLED, -DLING, -DLES to encircle with a belt
GIRDLER	*n* pl. -S one that girdles
GIRL	*n* pl. -S a female child
GIRLHOOD	*n* pl. -S the state of being a girl
GIRLIE	*adj* featuring scantily clothed women
GIRLISH	*adj* of, pertaining to, or having the characteristics of a girl
GIRLY	*adj* girlie
GIRN	*v* -ED, -ING, -S to snarl
GIRO	*n* pl. -ROS an autogiro
GIRON	*n* pl. -S gyron
GIROSOL	*n* pl. -S girasol
GIRSH	*n* pl. -ES qursh
GIRT	*v* -ED, -ING, -S to gird
GIRTH	*v* -ED, -ING, -S to encircle
GISARME	*n* pl. -S a medieval weapon
GISMO	*n* pl. -MOS a gadget
GIST	*n* pl. -S the main point
GIT	*n* pl. -S a foolish person
GITANO	*n* pl. -NOS a Spanish gypsy
GITTERN	*n* pl. -S a medieval guitar
GITTIN	pl. of get
GIVE	*v* GAVE, GIVEN, GIVING, GIVES to transfer freely to another's possession **GIVEABLE** *adj*
GIVEAWAY	*n* pl. -AWAYS something given away free of charge
GIVEBACK	*n* pl. -S a worker's benefit given back to management
GIVEN	*n* pl. -S something assigned as a basis for a calculation
GIVER	*n* pl. -S one that gives
GIVING	present participle of give
GIZMO	*n* pl. -MOS gismo
GIZZARD	*n* pl. -S a digestive organ
GJETOST	*n* pl. -S a hard brown cheese
GLABELLA	*n* pl. -BELLAE the smooth area between the eyebrows

GLABRATE	*adj* glabrous
GLABROUS	*adj* smooth
GLACE	*v* -CEED, -CEING, -CES to cover with icing
GLACIAL	*adj* of or pertaining to glaciers
GLACIATE	*v* -ATED, -ATING, -ATES to cover with glaciers
GLACIER	*n* pl. -S a huge mass of ice
GLACIS	*n* pl. -CISES a slope
GLAD	*adj* GLADDER, GLADDEST feeling pleasure
GLAD	*v* GLADDED, GLADDING, GLADS to gladden
GLADDEN	*v* -ED, -ING, -S to make glad
GLADDER	comparative of glad
GLADDEST	superlative of glad
GLADDING	present participle of glad
GLADE	*n* pl. -S an open space in a forest
GLADIATE	*adj* shaped like a sword
GLADIER	comparative of glady
GLADIEST	superlative of glady
GLADIOLA	*n* pl. -S a flowering plant
GLADIOLI	*n/pl* segments of the sternum
GLADLY	*adv* -LIER, -LIEST in a glad manner
GLADNESS	*n* pl. -ES the state of being glad
GLADSOME	*adj* -SOMER, -SOMEST glad
GLADY	*adj* GLADIER, GLADIEST having glades
GLAIKET	*adj* glaikit
GLAIKIT	*adj* foolish
GLAIR	*v* -ED, -ING, -S to coat with egg white
GLAIRE	*v* GLAIRED, GLAIRING, GLAIRES to glair
GLAIRY	*adj* GLAIRIER, GLAIRIEST resembling egg white
GLAIVE	*n* pl. -S a sword **GLAIVED** *adj*
GLAMOR	*n* pl. -S alluring attractiveness
GLAMOUR	*v* -ED, -ING, -S to bewitch
GLANCE	*v* GLANCED, GLANCING, GLANCES to look quickly
GLANCER	*n* pl. -S one that glances
GLAND	*n* pl. -S a secreting organ
GLANDERS	*n/pl* a disease of horses
GLANDULE	*n* pl. -S a small gland
GLANS	*n* pl. GLANDES the tip of the penis or clitoris

GLARE	*v* GLARED, GLARING, GLARES to shine with a harshly brilliant light
GLARY	*adj* GLARIER, GLARIEST glaring
GLASNOST	*n* pl. -S a Soviet policy of open political discussion
GLASS	*v* -ED, -ING, -ES to encase in glass (a transparent substance)
GLASSFUL	*n* pl. -FULS as much as a drinking glass will hold
GLASSIE	*n* pl. -S a type of playing marble
GLASSIER	comparative of glassy
GLASSIEST	superlative of glassy
GLASSILY	*adv* in a glassy manner
GLASSINE	*n* pl. -S a type of paper
GLASSMAN	*n* pl. -MEN a glazier
GLASSY	*adj* GLASSIER, GLASSIEST resembling glass
GLAUCOMA	*n* pl. -S a disease of the eye
GLAUCOUS	*adj* bluish green
GLAZE	*v* GLAZED, GLAZING, GLAZES to fit windows with glass panes
GLAZER	*n* pl. -S a glazier
GLAZIER	*n* pl. -S one that glazes
GLAZIERY	*n* pl. -ZIERIES the work of a glazier
GLAZING	*n* pl. -S glaziery
GLAZY	*adj* GLAZIER, GLAZIEST covered with a smooth, glossy coating
GLEAM	*v* -ED, -ING, -S to shine with a soft radiance
GLEAMER	*n* pl. -S one that gleams
GLEAMY	*adj* GLEAMIER, GLEAMIEST gleaming
GLEAN	*v* -ED, -ING, -S to gather little by little
GLEANER	*n* pl. -S one that gleans
GLEANING	*n* pl. -S something that is gleaned
GLEBA	*n* pl. -BAE a spore-bearing mass of some fungi
GLEBE	*n* pl. -S the soil or earth
GLED	*n* pl. -S glede
GLEDE	*n* pl. -S a bird of prey
GLEE	*n* pl. -S an unaccompanied song
GLEED	*n* pl. -S a glowing coal
GLEEFUL	*adj* merry
GLEEK	*v* -ED, -ING, -S to gibe
GLEEMAN	*n* pl. -MEN a minstrel
GLEESOME	*adj* gleeful
GLEET	*v* -ED, -ING, -S to discharge mucus from the urethra
GLEETY	*adj* GLEETIER, GLEETIEST resembling mucus
GLEG	*adj* alert **GLEGLY** *adv*
GLEGNESS	*n* pl. -ES alertness
GLEN	*n* pl. -S a small valley **GLENLIKE** *adj*
GLENOID	*adj* having the shallow or slightly cupped form of a bone socket
GLEY	*n* pl. GLEYS a clay soil layer **GLEYED** *adj*
GLEYING	*n* pl. -S development of gley
GLIA	*n* pl. -S supporting tissue that binds nerve tissue
GLIADIN	*n* pl. -S a simple protein
GLIADINE	*n* pl. -S gliadin
GLIAL	*adj* pertaining to the supporting tissue of the central nervous system
GLIB	*adj* GLIBBER, GLIBBEST fluent **GLIBLY** *adv*
GLIBNESS	*n* pl. -ES the quality of being glib
GLIDE	*v* GLIDED, GLIDING, GLIDES to move effortlessly
GLIDER	*n* pl. -S a type of aircraft
GLIFF	*n* pl. -S a brief moment
GLIM	*n* pl. -S a light or lamp
GLIME	*v* GLIMED, GLIMING, GLIMES to glance slyly
GLIMMER	*v* -ED, -ING, -S to shine faintly or unsteadily
GLIMPSE	*v* GLIMPSED, GLIMPSING, GLIMPSES to see for an instant
GLIMPSER	*n* pl. -S one that glimpses
GLINT	*v* -ED, -ING, -S to glitter
GLIOMA	*n* pl. -MAS or -MATA a type of tumor
GLISSADE	*v* -SADED, -SADING, -SADES to perform a gliding dance step
GLISTEN	*v* -ED, -ING, -S to shine by reflection
GLISTER	*v* -ED, -ING, -S to glisten
GLITCH	*n* pl. -ES a malfunction
GLITCHY	*adj* characterized by glitches
GLITTER	*v* -ED, -ING, -S to sparkle
GLITTERY	*adj* glittering

GLITZ *n* pl. -ES gaudy showiness

GLITZY *adj* GLITZIER, GLITZIEST showy

GLOAM *n* pl. -S twilight

GLOAMING *n* pl. -S twilight

GLOAT *v* -ED, -ING, -S to regard with great or excessive satisfaction

GLOATER *n* pl. -S one that gloats

GLOB *n* pl. -S a rounded mass

GLOBAL *adj* spherical **GLOBALLY** *adv*

GLOBATE *adj* spherical

GLOBATED *adj* spherical

GLOBBY *adj* -BIER, -BIEST full of globs

GLOBE *v* GLOBED, GLOBING, GLOBES to form into a perfectly round body

GLOBIN *n* pl. -S a simple protein

GLOBOID *n* pl. -S a spheroid

GLOBOSE *adj* spherical

GLOBOUS *adj* spherical

GLOBULAR *adj* spherical

GLOBULE *n* pl. -S a small spherical mass

GLOBULIN *n* pl. -S a simple protein

GLOCHID *n* pl. -S a barbed hair on some plants

GLOGG *n* pl. -S an alcoholic beverage

GLOM *v* GLOMMED, GLOMMING, GLOMS to steal

GLOMUS *n* pl. -MERA a type of vascular tuft

GLONOIN *n* pl. -S nitroglycerin

GLOOM *v* -ED, -ING, -S to become dark

GLOOMFUL *adj* gloomy

GLOOMING *n* pl. -S gloaming

GLOOMY *adj* GLOOMIER, GLOOMIEST dismally dark **GLOOMILY** *adv*

GLOP *v* GLOPPED, GLOPPING, GLOPS to cover with glop (a messy mass or mixture)

GLOPPY *adj* being or resembling glop

GLORIA *n* pl. -S a halo

GLORIED past tense of glory

GLORIES present 3d person sing. of glory

GLORIFY *v* -FIED, -FYING, -FIES to bestow honor or praise on

GLORIOLE *n* pl. -S a halo

GLORIOUS *adj* magnificent

GLORY *v* -RIED, -RYING, -RIES to rejoice proudly

GLOSS *v* -ED, -ING, -ES to make lustrous

GLOSSA *n* pl. -SAE or -SAS the tongue **GLOSSAL** *adj*

GLOSSARY *n* pl. -RIES a list of terms and their definitions

GLOSSEME *n* pl. -S the smallest linguistic unit that signals a meaning

GLOSSER *n* pl. -S one that glosses

GLOSSIER comparative of glossy

GLOSSIES pl. of glossy

GLOSSINA *n* pl. -S a tsetse fly

GLOSSY *adj* GLOSSIER, GLOSSIEST lustrous **GLOSSILY** *adv*

GLOSSY *n* pl. GLOSSIES a type of photograph

GLOST *n* pl. -S pottery that has been coated with a glassy surface

GLOTTIS *n* pl. -TISES or -TIDES the opening between the vocal cords **GLOTTAL, GLOTTIC** *adj*

GLOUT *v* -ED, -ING, -S to scowl

GLOVE *v* GLOVED, GLOVING, GLOVES to furnish with gloves (hand coverings)

GLOVER *n* pl. -S a maker or seller of gloves

GLOW *v* -ED, -ING, -S to emit light and heat

GLOWER *v* -ED, -ING, -S to scowl

GLOWFLY *n* pl. -FLIES a firefly

GLOWWORM *n* pl. -S a luminous insect

GLOXINIA *n* pl. -S a tropical plant

GLOZE *v* GLOZED, GLOZING, GLOZES to explain away

GLUCAGON *n* pl. -S a hormone

GLUCAN *n* pl. -S a polymer of glucose

GLUCINUM *n* pl. -S a metallic element **GLUCINIC** *adj*

GLUCOSE *n* pl. -S a sugar **GLUCOSIC** *adj*

GLUE *v* GLUED, GLUING or GLUEING, GLUES to fasten with glue (an adhesive substance)

GLUELIKE *adj* resembling glue

GLUEPOT *n* pl. -S a pot for melting glue

GLUER *n* pl. -S one that glues

GLUEY *adj* GLUIER, GLUIEST resembling glue **GLUILY** *adv*

GLUG *v* GLUGGED, GLUGGING, GLUGS to make a gurgling sound

GLUING	present participle of glue
GLUM	*adj* GLUMMER, GLUMMEST being in low spirits **GLUMLY** *adv*
GLUME	*n* pl. -S a bract on grassy plants
GLUMNESS	*n* pl. -ES the state of being glum
GLUMPY	*adj* GLUMPIER, GLUMPIEST glum **GLUMPILY** *adv*
GLUNCH	*v* -ED, -ING, -ES to frown
GLUON	*n* pl. -S a hypothetical massless particle binding quarks together
GLUT	*v* GLUTTED, GLUTTING, GLUTS to feed or fill to excess
GLUTEAL	*adj* of or pertaining to the buttock muscles
GLUTEI	pl. of gluteus
GLUTELIN	*n* pl. -S a plant protein
GLUTEN	*n* pl. -S a tough elastic plant protein substance
GLUTEUS	*n* pl. -TEI a buttock muscle
GLUTTED	past tense of glut
GLUTTING	present participle of glut
GLUTTON	*n* pl. -S a person who eats to excess
GLUTTONY	*n* pl. -TONIES excessive eating
GLYCAN	*n* pl. -S a carbohydrate
GLYCERIN	*n* pl. -S a glycerol **GLYCERIC** *adj*
GLYCEROL	*n* pl. -S a syrupy alcohol
GLYCERYL	*n* pl. -S a radical derived from glycerol
GLYCIN	*n* pl. -S a compound used in photography
GLYCINE	*n* pl. -S an amino acid
GLYCOGEN	*n* pl. -S a carbohydrate
GLYCOL	*n* pl. -S an alcohol **GLYCOLIC** *adj*
GLYCONIC	*n* pl. -S a type of verse line
GLYCOSYL	*n* pl. -S a radical derived from glucose
GLYCYL	*n* pl. -S a radical derived from glycine
GLYPH	*n* pl. -S an ornamental groove **GLYPHIC** *adj*
GLYPTIC	*n* pl. -S the art or process of engraving on gems
GNAR	*v* GNARRED, GNARRING, GNARS to snarl
GNARL	*v* -ED, -ING, -S to twist into a state of deformity
GNARLY	*adj* GNARLIER, GNARLIEST gnarled
GNARR	*v* -ED, -ING, -S to gnar
GNARRED	past tense of gnar
GNARRING	present participle of gnar
GNASH	*v* -ED, -ING, -ES to grind the teeth together
GNAT	*n* pl. -S a small winged insect
GNATHAL	*adj* gnathic
GNATHIC	*adj* of or pertaining to the jaw
GNATHION	*n* pl. -S the tip of the chin
GNATHITE	*n* pl. -S a jawlike appendage of an insect
GNATLIKE	*adj* resembling a gnat
GNATTY	*adj* -TIER, -TIEST infested with gnats
GNAW	*v* GNAWED, GNAWN, GNAWING, GNAWS to wear away by persistent biting **GNAWABLE** *adj*
GNAWER	*n* pl. -S one that gnaws
GNAWING	*n* pl. -S a persistent dull pain
GNAWN	a past participle of gnaw
GNEISS	*n* pl. -ES a type of rock **GNEISSIC** *adj*
GNOCCHI	*n/pl* dumplings made of pasta
GNOME	*n* pl. -S a dwarf
GNOMIC	*adj* resembling or containing aphorisms
GNOMICAL	*adj* gnomic
GNOMISH	*adj* resembling a gnome
GNOMIST	*n* pl. -S a writer of aphorisms
GNOMON	*n* pl. -S a part of a sundial **GNOMONIC** *adj*
GNOSIS	*n* pl. GNOSES mystical knowledge
GNOSTIC	*adj* possessing knowledge
GNU	*n* pl. -S a large antelope
GO	*v* WENT, GONE, GOING, GOES to move along
GOA	*n* pl. -S an Asian gazelle
GOAD	*v* -ED, -ING, -S to drive animals with a goad (a pointed stick)
GOADLIKE	*adj* resembling a goad
GOAL	*v* -ED, -ING, -S to score a goal (a point-scoring play in some games)
GOALIE	*n* pl. -S a player who defends against goals
GOALLESS	*adj* having no goal

GOALPOST *n* pl. -S a post that marks a boundary of the scoring area in some games

GOALWARD *adv* toward a goal (a point-scoring area)

GOANNA *n* pl. -S a large monitor lizard

GOAT *n* pl. -S a horned mammal

GOATEE *n* pl. -S a small pointed beard **GOATEED** *adj*

GOATFISH *n* pl. -ES a tropical fish

GOATHERD *n* pl. -S one who tends goats

GOATISH *adj* resembling a goat

GOATLIKE *adj* goatish

GOATSKIN *n* pl. -S the hide of a goat

GOB *v* GOBBED, GOBBING, GOBS to fill a mine pit with waste material

GOBAN *n* pl. -S gobang

GOBANG *n* pl. -S a Japanese game

GOBBED past tense of gob

GOBBET *n* pl. -S a piece of raw meat

GOBBING present participle of gob

GOBBLE *v* -BLED, -BLING, -BLES to eat hastily

GOBBLER *n* pl. -S a male turkey

GOBIES pl. of goby

GOBIOID *n* pl. -S a fish of the goby family

GOBLET *n* pl. -S a drinking vessel

GOBLIN *n* pl. -S an evil or mischievous creature

GOBO *n* pl. -BOS or -BOES a device used to shield a microphone from extraneous sounds

GOBONEE *adj* gobony

GOBONY *adj* compony

GOBY *n* pl. GOBIES a small fish

GOD *v* GODDED, GODDING, GODS to treat as a god (a supernatural being)

GODCHILD *n* pl. -CHILDREN one whom a person sponsors at baptism

GODDAM *v* -DAMMED, -DAMMING, -DAMS goddamn

GODDAMN *v* -ED, -ING, -S to damn

GODDED past tense of god

GODDESS *n* pl. -ES a female god

GODDING present participle of god

GODET *n* pl. -S insert of cloth in a seam

GODHEAD *n* pl. -S godhood

GODHOOD *n* pl. -S the state of being a god

GODLESS *adj* worshiping no god

GODLIER comparative of godly

GODLIEST superlative of godly

GODLIKE *adj* divine

GODLING *n* pl. -S a lesser god

GODLY *adj* -LIER, -LIEST pious **GODLILY** *adv*

GODOWN *n* pl. -S an oriental warehouse

GODROON *n* pl. -S gadroon

GODSEND *n* pl. -S an unexpected boon

GODSHIP *n* pl. -S the rank of a god

GODSON *n* pl. -S a male godchild

GODWIT *n* pl. -S a wading bird

GOER *n* pl. -S one that goes

GOETHITE *n* pl. -S an ore of iron

GOFER *n* pl. -S an employee who runs errands

GOFFER *v* -ED, -ING, -S to press ridges or pleats into

GOGGLE *v* -GLED, -GLING, -GLES to stare with wide eyes

GOGGLER *n* pl. -S one that goggles

GOGGLY *adj* -GLIER, -GLIEST wide-eyed

GOGLET *n* pl. -S a long-necked jar

GOGO *n* pl. -GOS a discotheque

GOING *n* pl. -S an advance toward an objective

GOITER *n* pl. -S an enlargement of the thyroid gland **GOITROUS** *adj*

GOITRE *n* pl. -S goiter

GOLCONDA *n* pl. -S a source of great wealth

GOLD *n* pl. -S a precious metallic element

GOLD *adj* GOLDER, GOLDEST golden

GOLDARN *n* pl. -S an expression of anger

GOLDBUG *n* pl. -S a gold beetle

GOLDEN *adj* -ENER, -ENEST of the color of gold **GOLDENLY** *adv*

GOLDEYE *n* pl. -S a freshwater fish

GOLDFISH *n* pl. -ES a freshwater fish

GOLDURN *n* pl. -S goldarn

GOLEM *n* pl. -S a legendary creature

GOLF *v* -ED, -ING, -S to play golf (a type of ball game)

GOLFER *n* pl. -S one that golfs

GOLFING *n* pl. -S the game of golf

GOLGOTHA	*n* pl. -S a place of burial
GOLIARD	*n* pl. -S a wandering student
GOLLIWOG	*n* pl. -S a grotesque doll
GOLLY	*interj* — used as a mild oath
GOLLYWOG	*n* pl. -S golliwog
GOLOSH	*n* pl. -ES galosh
GOLOSHE	*n* pl. -S galosh
GOMBO	*n* pl. -BOS gumbo
GOMBROON	*n* pl. -S a kind of Persian pottery
GOMERAL	*n* pl. -S a fool
GOMEREL	*n* pl. -S gomeral
GOMERIL	*n* pl. -S gomeral
GOMUTI	*n* pl. -S a palm tree
GONAD	*n* pl. -S a sex gland **GONADAL, GONADIAL, GONADIC** *adj*
GONDOLA	*n* pl. -S a long, narrow boat
GONE	*adj* departed
GONEF	*n* pl. -S ganef
GONENESS	*n* pl. -ES a state of exhaustion
GONER	*n* pl. -S one who is in a hopeless situation
GONFALON	*n* pl. -S a banner
GONFANON	*n* pl. -S gonfalon
GONG	*v* -ED, -ING, -S to make the sound of a gong (a disk-shaped percussion instrument)
GONGLIKE	*adj* resembling a gong
GONIA	pl. of gonion and of gonium
GONIDIUM	*n* pl. -IA an asexual reproductive cell **GONIDIAL, GONIDIC** *adj*
GONIF	*n* pl. -S ganef
GONIFF	*n* pl. -S ganef
GONION	*n* pl. -NIA a part of the lower jaw
GONIUM	*n* pl. -NIA an immature reproductive cell
GONOCYTE	*n* pl. -S a cell that produces gametes
GONOF	*n* pl. -S ganef
GONOPH	*n* pl. -S ganef
GONOPORE	*n* pl. -S a genital pore
GONZO	*adj* bizarre
GOO	*n* pl. GOOS a sticky or viscid substance
GOOBER	*n* pl. -S a peanut
GOOD	*adj* BETTER, BEST having positive or desirable qualities
GOOD	*n* pl. -S something that is good

GOODBY	*n* pl. -BYS goodbye
GOODBYE	*n* pl. -S a concluding remark or gesture at parting
GOODIE	*n* pl. -S goody
GOODIES	pl. of goody
GOODISH	*adj* somewhat good
GOODLY	*adj* -LIER, -LIEST of pleasing appearance
GOODMAN	*n* pl. -MEN the master of a household
GOODNESS	*n* pl. -ES the state of being good
GOODWIFE	*n* pl. -WIVES the mistress of a household
GOODWILL	*n* pl. -S an attitude of friendliness
GOODY	*n* pl. GOODIES a desirable food
GOOEY	*adj* GOOIER, GOOIEST sticky or viscid
GOOF	*v* -ED, -ING, -S to blunder
GOOFBALL	*n* pl. -S a sleeping pill
GOOFY	*adj* GOOFIER, GOOFIEST silly **GOOFILY** *adv*
GOOGLY	*n* pl. -GLIES a type of bowled ball in cricket
GOOGOL	*n* pl. -S an enormous number
GOOIER	comparative of gooey
GOOIEST	superlative of gooey
GOOK	*n* pl. -S goo **GOOKY** *adj*
GOOMBAH	*n* pl. -S an older man who is a friend
GOOMBAY	*n* pl. -BAYS calypso music of the Bahamas
GOON	*n* pl. -S a hired thug
GOONEY	*n* pl. -NEYS an albatross
GOONIE	*n* pl. -S gooney
GOONY	*n* pl. -NIES gooney
GOOP	*n* pl. -S goo, gunk
GOOPY	*adj* GOOPIER, GOOPIEST sticky, gooey
GOORAL	*n* pl. -S goral
GOOSE	*n* pl. GEESE a swimming bird
GOOSE	*v* GOOSED, GOOSING, GOOSES to poke between the buttocks
GOOSEY	*adj* GOOSIER, GOOSIEST goosy
GOOSY	*adj* GOOSIER, GOOSIEST resembling a goose
GOPHER	*n* pl. -S a burrowing rodent
GOR	*interj* — used as a mild oath

GORAL	*n* pl. -S a goat antelope
GORBELLY	*n* pl. -LIES a potbelly
GORBLIMY	*interj* blimey
GORCOCK	*n* pl. -S the male red grouse
GORE	*v* GORED, GORING, GORES to pierce with a horn or tusk
GORGE	*v* GORGED, GORGING, GORGES to stuff with food **GORGEDLY** *adv*
GORGEOUS	*adj* beautiful
GORGER	*n* pl. -S one that gorges
GORGERIN	*n* pl. -S a part of a column
GORGET	*n* pl. -S a piece of armor for the throat **GORGETED** *adj*
GORGING	present participle of gorge
GORGON	*n* pl. -S an ugly woman
GORHEN	*n* pl. -S the female red grouse
GORIER	comparative of gory
GORIEST	superlative of gory
GORILLA	*n* pl. -S a large ape
GORILY	*adv* in a gory manner
GORINESS	*n* pl. -ES the state of being gory
GORING	present participle of gore
GORMAND	*n* pl. -S gourmand
GORMLESS	*adj* stupid
GORP	*n* pl. -S a snack for quick energy
GORSE	*n* pl. -S furze
GORSY	*adj* GORSIER, GORSIEST abounding in gorse
GORY	*adj* GORIER, GORIEST bloody
GOSH	*interj* — used as an exclamation of surprise
GOSHAWK	*n* pl. -S a large hawk
GOSLING	*n* pl. -S a young goose
GOSPEL	*n* pl. -S the message concerning Christ, the kingdom of God, and salvation
GOSPELER	*n* pl. -S one that teaches the gospel
GOSPORT	*n* pl. -S a communication device in an airplane
GOSSAMER	*n* pl. -S a fine film of cobwebs
GOSSAN	*n* pl. -S a type of decomposed rock
GOSSIP	*v* -SIPED, -SIPING, -SIPS or -SIPPED, -SIPPING, -SIPS to talk idly about the affairs of others
GOSSIPER	*n* pl. -S one that gossips
GOSSIPRY	*n* pl. -RIES the practice of gossiping
GOSSIPY	*adj* inclined to gossip
GOSSOON	*n* pl. -S a boy
GOSSYPOL	*n* pl. -S a toxic pigment
GOT	past tense of get
GOTHIC	*n* pl. -S a style of printing
GOTHITE	*n* pl. -S goethite
GOTTEN	past participle of get
GOUACHE	*n* pl. -S a method of painting
GOUGE	*v* GOUGED, GOUGING, GOUGES to cut or scoop out
GOUGER	*n* pl. -S one that gouges
GOULASH	*n* pl. -ES a beef stew
GOURAMI	*n* pl. -S or -ES a food fish
GOURD	*n* pl. -S a hard-shelled fruit
GOURDE	*n* pl. -S a monetary unit of Haiti
GOURMAND	*n* pl. -S one who loves to eat
GOURMET	*n* pl. -S a connoisseur of fine food and drink
GOUT	*n* pl. -S a metabolic disease
GOUTY	*adj* GOUTIER, GOUTIEST affected with gout **GOUTILY** *adv*
GOVERN	*v* -ED, -ING, -S to rule or direct
GOVERNOR	*n* pl. -S one that governs
GOWAN	*n* pl. -S a daisy **GOWANED, GOWANY** *adj*
GOWD	*n* pl. -S gold
GOWK	*n* pl. -S a fool
GOWN	*v* -ED, -ING, -S to dress in a gown (a long, loose outer garment)
GOWNSMAN	*n* pl. -MEN a professional or academic person
GOX	*n* pl. -ES gaseous oxygen
GRAAL	*n* pl. -S grail
GRAB	*v* GRABBED, GRABBING, GRABS to grasp suddenly
GRABBER	*n* pl. -S one that grabs
GRABBIER	comparative of grabby
GRABBIEST	superlative of grabby
GRABBING	present participle of grab
GRABBLE	*v* -BLED, -BLING, -BLES to grope
GRABBLER	*n* pl. -S one that grabbles
GRABBY	*adj* -BIER, -BIEST tending to grab

GRABEN	*n* pl. -S a depression of the earth's crust
GRACE	*v* GRACED, GRACING, GRACES to give beauty to
GRACEFUL	*adj* -FULLER, -FULLEST having beauty of form or movement
GRACILE	*adj* gracefully slender
GRACILIS	*n* pl. -LES a thigh muscle
GRACING	present participle of grace
GRACIOSO	*n* pl. -SOS a clown in Spanish comedy
GRACIOUS	*adj* marked by kindness and courtesy
GRACKLE	*n* pl. -S a blackbird
GRAD	*n* pl. -S a graduate
GRADATE	*v* -DATED, -DATING, -DATES to change by degrees
GRADE	*v* GRADED, GRADING, GRADES to arrange in steps or degrees **GRADABLE** *adj*
GRADER	*n* pl. -S one that grades
GRADIENT	*n* pl. -S a rate of inclination
GRADIN	*n* pl. -S gradine
GRADINE	*n* pl. -S one of a series of steps
GRADING	present participle of grade
GRADUAL	*n* pl. -S a hymn sung in alternate parts
GRADUAND	*n* pl. -S one who is about to graduate
GRADUATE	*v* -ATED, -ATING, -ATES to receive an academic degree or diploma
GRADUS	*n* pl. -ES a dictionary of prosody
GRAECIZE	*v* -CIZED, -CIZING, -CIZES to grecize
GRAFFITO	*n* pl. -TI an inscription or drawing made on a rock or wall
GRAFT	*v* -ED, -ING, -S to unite with a growing plant by insertion
GRAFTAGE	*n* pl. -S the process of grafting
GRAFTER	*n* pl. -S one that grafts
GRAHAM	*n* pl. -S whole-wheat flour
GRAIL	*n* pl. -S the object of a long quest
GRAIN	*v* -ED, -ING, -S to form into small particles
GRAINER	*n* pl. -S one that grains
GRAINY	*adj* GRAINIER, GRAINIEST granular
GRAM	pl. -S a unit of mass and weight
GRAMA	*n* pl. -S a pasture grass
GRAMARY	*n* pl. -RIES gramarye
GRAMARYE	*n* pl. -S occult learning; magic
GRAMERCY	*n* pl. -CIES an expression of gratitude
GRAMMAR	*n* pl. -S the study of the formal features of a language
GRAMME	*n* pl. -S gram
GRAMP	*n* pl. -S grandfather
GRAMPUS	*n* pl. -ES a marine mammal
GRAN	*n* pl. -S a grandmother
GRANA	pl. of granum
GRANARY	*n* pl. -RIES a storehouse for grain
GRAND	*adj* GRANDER, GRANDEST large and impressive
GRAND	*n* pl. -S a type of piano
GRANDAD	*n* pl. -S granddad
GRANDAM	*n* pl. -S a grandmother
GRANDAME	*n* pl. -S grandam
GRANDDAD	*n* pl. -S a grandfather
GRANDDAM	*n* pl. -S the female parent of an animal with offspring
GRANDEE	*n* pl. -S man of high social position
GRANDEUR	*n* pl. -S the state of being grand
GRANDKID	*n* pl. -S the child of one's son or daughter
GRANDLY	*adv* in a grand manner
GRANDMA	*n* pl. -S a grandmother
GRANDPA	*n* pl. -S a grandfather
GRANDSIR	*n* pl. -S a grandfather
GRANDSON	*n* pl. -S a son of one's son or daughter
GRANGE	*n* pl. -S a farm
GRANGER	*n* pl. -S a farmer
GRANITA	*n* pl. -S an iced dessert
GRANITE	*n* pl. -S a type of rock **GRANITIC** *adj*
GRANNIE	*n* pl. -S granny
GRANNY	*n* pl. -NIES a grandmother
GRANOLA	*n* pl. -S a breakfast cereal
GRANT	*v* -ED, -ING, -S to bestow upon
GRANTEE	*n* pl. -S one to whom something is granted
GRANTER	*n* pl. -S one that grants
GRANTOR	*n* pl. -S granter
GRANULAR	*adj* composed of granules

GRANULE	*n* pl. -S a small particle
GRANUM	*n* pl. GRANA a part of a plant chloroplast
GRAPE	*n* pl. -S an edible berry
GRAPERY	*n* pl. -ERIES a vinery
GRAPEY	*adj* GRAPIER, GRAPIEST grapy
GRAPH	*v* -ED, -ING, -S to represent by means of a diagram
GRAPHEME	*n* pl. -S a unit of a writing system
GRAPHIC	*n* pl. -S a product of the art of representation
GRAPHITE	*n* pl. -S a variety of carbon
GRAPIER	comparative of grapy
GRAPIEST	superlative of grapy
GRAPLIN	*n* pl. -S a grapnel
GRAPLINE	*n* pl. -S graplin
GRAPNEL	*n* pl. -S a type of anchor
GRAPPA	*n* pl. -S an Italian brandy
GRAPPLE	*v* -PLED, -PLING, -PLES to struggle or contend
GRAPPLER	*n* pl. -S one that grapples
GRAPY	*adj* GRAPIER, GRAPIEST resembling grapes
GRASP	*v* -ED, -ING, -S to seize firmly with the hand
GRASPER	*n* pl. -S one that grasps
GRASS	*v* -ED, -ING, -ES to cover with grass (herbaceous plants)
GRASSY	*adj* GRASSIER, GRASSIEST of, resembling, or pertaining to grass **GRASSILY** *adv*
GRAT	past tense of greet (to weep)
GRATE	*v* GRATED, GRATING, GRATES to reduce to shreds by rubbing
GRATEFUL	*adj* -FULLER, -FULLEST deeply thankful
GRATER	*n* pl. -S one that grates
GRATIFY	*v* -FIED, -FYING, -FIES to satisfy
GRATIN	*n* pl. -S a type of food crust
GRATINE	*adj* covered with a crust
GRATINEE	*v* -NEED, -NEEING, -NEES to cook food that is covered with a crust
GRATING	*n* pl. -S a network of bars covering an opening
GRATIS	*adj* free of charge
GRATUITY	*n* pl. -ITIES a gift of money
GRAUPEL	*n* pl. -S granular snow pellets
GRAVAMEN	*n* pl. -MENS or -MINA the most serious part of an accusation
GRAVE	*adj* GRAVER, GRAVEST extremely serious
GRAVE	*v* GRAVED, GRAVEN, GRAVING, GRAVES to engrave
GRAVEL	*v* -ELED, -ELING, -ELS or -ELLED, -ELLING, -ELS to pave with gravel (a mixture of rock fragments)
GRAVELLY	*adj* containing gravel
GRAVELY	*adv* in a grave manner
GRAVEN	past participle of grave
GRAVER	*n* pl. -S an engraver
GRAVEST	superlative of grave
GRAVID	*adj* pregnant **GRAVIDLY** *adv*
GRAVIDA	*n* pl. -DAS or -DAE a pregnant woman
GRAVIES	pl. of gravy
GRAVING	present participle of grave
GRAVITAS	*n* pl. -ES reserved, dignified behavior
GRAVITON	*n* pl. -S a hypothetical particle
GRAVITY	*n* pl. -TIES the force of attraction toward the earth's center
GRAVLAKS	*n* pl. GRAVLAKS gravlax
GRAVLAX	*n* pl. GRAVLAX cured salmon
GRAVURE	*n* pl. -S a printing process
GRAVY	*n* pl. -VIES a sauce of the fat and juices from cooked meat
GRAY	*adj* GRAYER, GRAYEST of a color between white and black
GRAY	*v* -ED, -ING, -S to make gray
GRAYBACK	*n* pl. -S a gray bird
GRAYFISH	*n* pl. -ES a dogfish
GRAYISH	*adj* somewhat gray
GRAYLAG	*n* pl. -S a wild goose
GRAYLING	*n* pl. -S a food fish
GRAYLY	*adv* in a gray manner
GRAYMAIL	*n* pl. -S pressure on an official to reveal sensitive information
GRAYNESS	*n* pl. -ES the state of being gray
GRAYOUT	*n* pl. -S a temporary blurring of vision
GRAZE	*v* GRAZED, GRAZING, GRAZES to feed on growing grass **GRAZABLE** *adj*
GRAZER	*n* pl. -S one that grazes
GRAZIER	*n* pl. -S one that grazes cattle
GRAZING	*n* pl. -S land used for the feeding of animals

GRAZIOSO *adj* graceful in style

GREASE *v* GREASED, GREASING, GREASES to smear with grease (a lubricating substance)

GREASER *n* pl. -S one that greases

GREASY *adj* GREASIER, GREASIEST containing or resembling grease **GREASILY** *adv*

GREAT *adj* GREATER, GREATEST large

GREAT *n* pl. -S a distinguished or outstanding person

GREATEN *v* -ED, -ING, -S to make greater

GREATLY *adv* in a great manner

GREAVE *n* pl. -S a piece of armor for the leg **GREAVED** *adj*

GREBE *n* pl. -S a diving bird

GRECIZE *v* -CIZED, -CIZING, -CIZES to provide with a Greek style

GREE *v* GREED, GREEING, GREES to agree

GREED *n* pl. -S excessive desire for gain or wealth

GREEDY *adj* GREEDIER, GREEDIEST marked by greed **GREEDILY** *adv*

GREEGREE *n* pl. -S grigri

GREEK *n* pl. GREEK something unintelligible

GREEN *adj* GREENER, GREENEST of the color of growing foliage

GREEN *v* -ED, -ING, -S to become green

GREENBUG *n* pl. -S a green aphid

GREENERY *n* pl. -ERIES green vegetation

GREENFLY *n* pl. -FLIES a green aphid

GREENIE *n* pl. -S an amphetamine pill

GREENIER comparative of greeny

GREENIEST superlative of greeny

GREENING *n* pl. -S a variety of apple

GREENISH *adj* somewhat green

GREENLET *n* pl. -S a vireo

GREENLY *adv* in a green manner

GREENTH *n* pl. -S verdure

GREENWAY *n* pl. -WAYS piece of undeveloped land in a city

GREENY *adj* GREENIER, GREENIEST somewhat green

GREET *v* -ED, -ING, -S to address in a friendly and courteous way

GREET *v* GRAT, GRUTTEN, GREETING, GREETS to weep

GREETER *n* pl. -S one that greets

GREETING *n* pl. -S a salutation

GREGO *n* pl. -GOS a hooded coat

GREIGE *n* pl. -S fabric in a gray state

GREISEN *n* pl. -S a type of rock

GREMIAL *n* pl. -S a lap cloth used by a bishop during a service

GREMLIN *n* pl. -S a mischievous creature

GREMMIE *n* pl. -S an inexperienced surfer

GREMMY *n* pl. -MIES gremmie

GRENADE *n* pl. -S an explosive device

GREW past tense of grow

GREWSOME *adj* -SOMER, -SOMEST gruesome

GREY *adj* GREYER, GREYEST gray

GREY *v* -ED, -ING, -S to gray

GREYHEN *n* pl. -S the female black grouse

GREYISH *adj* grayish

GREYLAG *n* pl. -S graylag

GREYLY *adv* grayly

GREYNESS *n* pl. -ES grayness

GRIBBLE *n* pl. -S a marine isopod

GRID *n* pl. -S a grating

GRIDDER *n* pl. -S a football player

GRIDDLE *v* -DLED, -DLING, -DLES to cook on a flat pan

GRIDE *v* GRIDED, GRIDING, GRIDES to scrape harshly

GRIDIRON *n* pl. -S a grate for broiling food

GRIDLOCK *v* -ED, -ING, -S to bring to a standstill

GRIEF *n* pl. -S intense mental distress

GRIEVANT *n* pl. -S one that submits a complaint for arbitration

GRIEVE *v* GRIEVED, GRIEVING, GRIEVES to feel grief

GRIEVER *n* pl. -S one that grieves

GRIEVOUS *adj* causing grief

GRIFF *n* pl. -S griffe

GRIFFE *n* pl. -S the offspring of a black person and a mulatto

GRIFFIN *n* pl. -S a mythological creature

GRIFFON *n* pl. -S griffin

GRIFT *v* -ED, -ING, -S to swindle

GRIFTER *n* pl. -S a swindler

GRIG *n* pl. -S a lively person

GRIGRI *n* pl. -S a fetish or amulet

GRILL *v* -ED, -ING, -S to broil on a gridiron

GRILLADE *n* pl. -S a dish of grilled meat

GRILLAGE *n* pl. -S a framework of timber

GRILLE *n* pl. -S a grating

GRILLER *n* pl. -S one that grills

GRILSE *n* pl. -S a young salmon

GRIM *adj* GRIMMER, GRIMMEST stern and unrelenting

GRIMACE *v* -MACED, -MACING, -MACES to contort the facial features

GRIMACER *n* pl. -S one that grimaces

GRIME *v* GRIMED, GRIMING, GRIMES to make dirty

GRIMIER comparative of grimy

GRIMIEST superlative of grimy

GRIMILY *adv* in a grimy manner

GRIMING present participle of grime

GRIMLY *adv* in a grim manner

GRIMMER comparative of grim

GRIMMEST superlative of grim

GRIMNESS *n* pl. -ES the quality of being grim

GRIMY *adj* GRIMIER, GRIMIEST dirty

GRIN *v* GRINNED, GRINNING, GRINS to smile broadly

GRINCH *n* pl. -ES one who spoils the fun of others

GRIND *v* GROUND or GRINDED, GRINDING, GRINDS to wear, smooth, or sharpen by friction

GRINDER *n* pl. -S one that grinds

GRINDERY *n* pl. -ERIES a place where tools are ground

GRINNED past tense of grin

GRINNER *n* pl. -S one that grins

GRINNING present participle of grin

GRIOT *n* pl. -S a tribal entertainer in West Africa

GRIP *v* GRIPPED or GRIPT, GRIPPING, GRIPS to grasp

GRIPE *v* GRIPED, GRIPING, GRIPES to grasp

GRIPER *n* pl. -S one that gripes

GRIPEY *adj* GRIPIER, GRIPIEST gripy

GRIPIER comparative of gripy

GRIPIEST superlative of gripy

GRIPING present participle of gripe

GRIPMAN *n* pl. -MEN a cable car operator

GRIPPE *n* pl. -S a virus disease

GRIPPED a past tense of grip

GRIPPER *n* pl. -S one that grips

GRIPPIER comparative of grippy

GRIPPIEST superlative of grippy

GRIPPING present participle of grip

GRIPPLE *adj* greedy

GRIPPY *adj* GRIPPIER, GRIPPIEST affected with the grippe

GRIPSACK *n* pl. -S a valise

GRIPT a past tense of grip

GRIPY *adj* GRIPIER, GRIPIEST causing sharp pains in the bowels

GRISEOUS *adj* grayish

GRISETTE *n* pl. -S a young French working-class girl

GRISKIN *n* pl. -S the lean part of a loin of pork

GRISLY *adj* -LIER, -LIEST horrifying

GRISON *n* pl. -S a carnivorous mammal

GRIST *n* pl. -S grain for grinding

GRISTLE *n* pl. -S the tough part of meat

GRISTLY *adj* -TLIER, -TLIEST containing gristle

GRIT *v* GRITTED, GRITTING, GRITS to press the teeth together

GRITH *n* pl. -S sanctuary for a limited period of time

GRITTY *adj* -TIER, -TIEST plucky **GRITTILY** *adv*

GRIVET *n* pl. -S a small monkey

GRIZZLE *v* -ZLED, -ZLING, -ZLES to complain

GRIZZLER *n* pl. -S one that grizzles

GRIZZLY *adj* -ZLIER, -ZLIEST grayish

GRIZZLY *n* pl. -ZLIES a large bear

GROAN *v* -ED, -ING, -S to utter a low, mournful sound

GROANER *n* pl. -S one that groans

GROAT *n* pl. -S an old English coin

GROCER *n* pl. -S a dealer in foodstuffs and household supplies

GROCERY *n* pl. -CERIES a grocer's store

GROG *n* pl. -S a mixture of liquor and water

GROGGERY *n* pl. -GERIES a barroom

GROGGY *adj* -GIER, -GIEST dazed **GROGGILY** *adv*

GROGRAM   *n* pl. -S a coarse silk fabric

GROGSHOP   *n* pl. -S a groggery

GROIN   *v* -ED, -ING, -S to build with intersecting arches

GROMMET   *n* pl. -S a reinforcing ring of metal

GROMWELL   *n* pl. -S an herb

GROOM   *v* -ED, -ING, -S to clean and care for

GROOMER   *n* pl. -S one that grooms

GROOVE   *v* GROOVED, GROOVING, GROOVES to form a groove (a long, narrow depression)

GROOVER   *n* pl. -S one that grooves

GROOVY   *adj* GROOVIER, GROOVIEST marvelous

GROPE   *v* GROPED, GROPING, GROPES to feel about with the hands

GROPER   *n* pl. -S one that gropes

GROSBEAK   *n* pl. -S a finch

GROSCHEN   *n* pl. GROSCHEN an Austrian coin

GROSS   *adj* GROSSER, GROSSEST flagrant

GROSS   *v* -ED, -ING, -ES to earn exclusive of deductions

GROSSER   *n* pl. -S a product yielding a large volume of business

GROSSLY   *adv* in a gross manner

GROSZ   *n* pl. GROSZY a Polish coin

GROSZE   *n* pl. GROSZY grosz

GROT   *n* pl. -S a grotto

GROTTO   *n* pl. -TOES or -TOS a cave

GROTTY   *adj* -TIER, -TIEST wretched

GROUCH   *v* -ED, -ING, -ES to complain

GROUCHY   *adj* GROUCHIER, GROUCHIEST ill-tempered

GROUND   *v* -ED, -ING, -S to place on a foundation

GROUNDER   *n* pl. -S a type of batted baseball

GROUP   *v* -ED, -ING, -S to arrange in a group (an assemblage of persons or things)

GROUPER   *n* pl. -S a food fish

GROUPIE   *n* pl. -S a female follower of rock groups

GROUPING   *n* pl. -S a set of objects

GROUPOID   *n* pl. -S a type of mathematical set

GROUSE   *v* GROUSED, GROUSING, GROUSES to complain

GROUSER   *n* pl. -S one that grouses

GROUT   *v* -ED, -ING, -S to fill with a thin mortar

GROUTER   *n* pl. -S one that grouts

GROUTY   *adj* GROUTIER, GROUTIEST surly

GROVE   *n* pl. -S a small forested area **GROVED** *adj*

GROVEL   *v* -ELED, -ELING, -ELS or -ELLED, -ELLING, -ELS to crawl in an abject manner

GROVELER   *n* pl. -S one that grovels

GROW   *v* GREW, GROWN, GROWING, GROWS to cultivate **GROWABLE** *adj*

GROWER   *n* pl. -S one that grows

GROWL   *v* -ED, -ING, -S to utter a deep, harsh sound

GROWLER   *n* pl. -S one that growls

GROWLY   *adj* GROWLIER, GROWLIEST deep and harsh in speech

GROWN   *adj* mature

GROWNUP   *n* pl. -S a mature person

GROWTH   *n* pl. -S development

GROWTHY   *adj* GROWTHIER, GROWTHIEST fast-growing

GROYNE   *n* pl. -S a structure built to protect a shore from erosion

GRUB   *v* GRUBBED, GRUBBING, GRUBS to dig

GRUBBER   *n* pl. -S one that grubs

GRUBBY   *adj* -BIER, -BIEST dirty **GRUBBILY** *adv*

GRUBWORM   *n* pl. -S the larva of some insects

GRUDGE   *v* GRUDGED, GRUDGING, GRUDGES to be unwilling to give or admit

GRUDGER   *n* pl. -S one that grudges

GRUE   *n* pl. -S a shudder of fear

GRUEL   *v* -ELED, -ELING, -ELS or -ELLED, -ELLING, -ELS to disable by hard work

GRUELER   *n* pl. -S one that gruels

GRUELING   *n* pl. -S an exhausting experience

GRUELLED   a past tense of gruel

GRUELLER   *n* pl. -S grueler

GRUELLING   present participle of gruel

GRUESOME *adj* -SOMER, -SOMEST repugnant

GRUFF *adj* GRUFFER, GRUFFEST low and harsh in speech

GRUFF *v* -ED, -ING, -S to utter in a gruff voice

GRUFFIER comparative of gruffy

GRUFFIEST superlative of gruffy

GRUFFILY *adv* in a gruffy manner

GRUFFISH *adj* somewhat gruff

GRUFFLY *adv* in a gruff manner

GRUFFY *adj* GRUFFIER, GRUFFIEST gruff

GRUGRU *n* pl. -S a palm tree

GRUIFORM *adj* designating an order of birds

GRUM *adj* GRUMMER, GRUMMEST morose

GRUMBLE *v* -BLED, -BLING, -BLES to mutter in discontent **GRUMBLY** *adj*

GRUMBLER *n* pl. -S one that grumbles

GRUME *n* pl. -S a thick, viscid substance

GRUMMER comparative of grum

GRUMMEST superlative of grum

GRUMMET *n* pl. -S grommet

GRUMOSE *adj* grumous

GRUMOUS *adj* consisting of clustered grains

GRUMP *v* -ED, -ING, -S to complain

GRUMPHIE *n* pl. -S a pig

GRUMPHY *n* pl. GRUMPHIES grumphie

GRUMPISH *adj* grumpy

GRUMPY *adj* GRUMPIER, GRUMPIEST ill-tempered **GRUMPILY** *adv*

GRUNGE *n* pl. -S dirt

GRUNGY *adj* -GIER, -GIEST dirty

GRUNION *n* pl. -S a small food fish

GRUNT *v* -ED, -ING, -S to utter a deep, guttural sound

GRUNTER *n* pl. -S one that grunts

GRUNTLE *v* -TLED, -TLING, -TLES to put in a good humor

GRUSHIE *adj* thriving

GRUTCH *v* -ED, -ING, -ES to grudge

GRUTTEN past participle of greet (to weep)

GRUYERE *n* pl. -S a Swiss cheese

GRYPHON *n* pl. -S griffin

GUACHARO *n* pl. -ROS or -ROES a tropical bird

GUACO *n* pl. -COS a tropical plant

GUAIAC *n* pl. -S guaiacum

GUAIACOL *n* pl. -S a chemical compound

GUAIACUM *n* pl. -S a medicinal resin

GUAIOCUM *n* pl. -S guaiacum

GUAN *n* pl. -S a large bird

GUANACO *n* pl. -COS a South American mammal

GUANASE *n* pl. -S an enzyme

GUANAY *n* pl. -NAYS a Peruvian cormorant

GUANIDIN *n* pl. -S a chemical compound

GUANIN *n* pl. -S guanine

GUANINE *n* pl. -S a chemical compound

GUANO *n* pl. -NOS the accumulated excrement of sea birds

GUAR *n* pl. -S a drought-tolerant legume

GUARANI *n* pl. -NIS or -NIES a monetary unit of Paraguay

GUARANTY *v* -TIED, -TYING, -TIES to assume responsibility for the quality of

GUARD *v* -ED, -ING, -S to protect

GUARDANT *n* pl. -S a guardian

GUARDER *n* pl. -S one that guards

GUARDIAN *n* pl. -S one that guards

GUAVA *n* pl. -S a tropical shrub

GUAYULE *n* pl. -S a shrub that is a source of rubber

GUCK *n* pl. -S a messy substance

GUDE *n* pl. -S good

GUDGEON *v* -ED, -ING, -S to dupe

GUENON *n* pl. -S a long-tailed monkey

GUERDON *v* -ED, -ING, -S to reward

GUERIDON *n* pl. -S a small stand or table

GUERILLA *n* pl. -S a member of a small independent band of soldiers

GUERNSEY *n* pl. -SEYS a woolen shirt

GUESS *v* -ED, -ING, -ES to form an opinion from little or no evidence

GUESSER *n* pl. -S one that guesses

GUEST *v* -ED, -ING, -S to appear as a visitor

GUFF *n* pl. -S foolish talk

GUFFAW *v* -ED, -ING, -S to laugh loudly

GUGGLE *v* -GLED, -GLING, -GLES to gurgle

GUGLET   *n* pl. -S goglet

GUID   *n* pl. -S good

GUIDANCE   *n* pl. -S advice

GUIDE   *v* GUIDED, GUIDING, GUIDES to show the way to **GUIDABLE** *adj*

GUIDER   *n* pl. -S one that guides

GUIDEWAY   *n* pl. -WAYS a track for controlling the line of motion of something

GUIDON   *n* pl. -S a small flag

GUILD   *n* pl. -S an association of people of the same trade

GUILDER   *n* pl. -S a monetary unit of the Netherlands

GUILE   *v* GUILED, GUILING, GUILES to beguile

GUILEFUL   *adj* cunning

GUILT   *n* pl. -S the fact of having committed an offense

GUILTY   *adj* GUILTIER, GUILTIEST worthy of blame for an offense **GUILTILY** *adv*

GUIMPE   *n* pl. -S a short blouse

GUINEA   *n* pl. -S a former British coin

GUIPURE   *n* pl. -S a type of lace

GUIRO   *n* pl. -ROS a percussion instrument

GUISARD   *n* pl. -S a masker

GUISE   *v* GUISED, GUISING, GUISES to disguise

GUITAR   *n* pl. -S a stringed musical instrument

GUITGUIT   *n* pl. -S a tropical American bird

GUL   *n* pl. -S a design in oriental carpets

GULAG   *n* pl. -S a forced-labor camp

GULAR   *adj* of or pertaining to the throat

GULCH   *n* pl. -ES a deep, narrow ravine

GULDEN   *n* pl. -S a guilder

GULES   *n* pl. GULES the color red

GULF   *v* -ED, -ING, -S to swallow up

GULFIER   comparative of gulfy

GULFIEST   superlative of gulfy

GULFLIKE   *adj* resembling a deep chasm

GULFWEED   *n* pl. -S a brownish seaweed

GULFY   *adj* GULFIER, GULFIEST full of whirlpools

GULL   *v* -ED, -ING, -S to deceive

GULLABLE   *adj* gullible **GULLABLY** *adv*

GULLET   *n* pl. -S the throat

GULLEY   *n* pl. -LEYS a ravine

GULLIBLE   *adj* easily deceived **GULLIBLY** *adv*

GULLY   *v* -LIED, -LYING, -LIES to form ravines by the action of water

GULOSITY   *n* pl. -TIES gluttony

GULP   *v* -ED, -ING, -S to swallow rapidly

GULPER   *n* pl. -S one that gulps

GULPY   *adj* GULPIER, GULPIEST marked by gulping

GUM   *v* GUMMED, GUMMING, GUMS to smear, seal, or clog with gum (a sticky, viscid substance)

GUMBO   *n* pl. -BOS the okra plant

GUMBOIL   *n* pl. -S an abscess in the gum

GUMBOOT   *n* pl. -S a rubber boot

GUMBOTIL   *n* pl. -S a sticky clay

GUMDROP   *n* pl. -S a chewy candy

GUMLESS   *adj* having no gum

GUMLIKE   *adj* resembling gum

GUMMA   *n* pl. -MAS or -MATA a soft tumor

GUMMED   past tense of gum

GUMMER   *n* pl. -S one that gums

GUMMIER   comparative of gummy

GUMMIEST   superlative of gummy

GUMMING   present participle of gum

GUMMITE   *n* pl. -S a mixture of various minerals

GUMMOSE   *adj* gummy

GUMMOSIS   *n* pl. -MOSES a disease of plants

GUMMOUS   *adj* gummy

GUMMY   *adj* -MIER, -MIEST resembling gum

GUMPTION   *n* pl. -S shrewdness

GUMSHOE   *v* -SHOED, -SHOEING, -SHOES to investigate stealthily

GUMTREE   *n* pl. -S a tree that yields gum

GUMWEED   *n* pl. -S a plant covered with a gummy substance

GUMWOOD   *n* pl. -S the wood of a gumtree

GUN   *v* GUNNED, GUNNING, GUNS to shoot with a gun (a portable firearm)

GUNBOAT   *n* pl. -S an armed vessel

GUNDOG   *n* pl. -S a hunting dog

GUNFIGHT	*v* -FOUGHT, -FIGHTING, -FIGHTS to fight with guns	**GURNET**	*n* pl. -S a gurnard
GUNFIRE	*n* pl. -S the firing of guns	**GURNEY**	*n* pl. -NEYS a wheeled cot
GUNFLINT	*n* pl. -S the flint in a flintlock	**GURRY**	*n* pl. -RIES fish offal
GUNFOUGHT	past tense of gunfight	**GURSH**	*n* pl. -ES qursh
GUNITE	*n* pl. -S a mixture of cement, sand, and water	**GURU**	*n* pl. -S a Hindu spiritual teacher
		GURUSHIP	*n* pl. -S the office of a guru
GUNK	*n* pl. -S filthy, sticky, or greasy matter **GUNKY** *adj*	**GUSH**	*v* -ED, -ING, -ES to flow forth forcefully
GUNKHOLE	*v* -HOLED, -HOLING, -HOLES to make a series of short boat trips	**GUSHER**	*n* pl. -S a gushing oil well
GUNLESS	*adj* having no gun	**GUSHY**	*adj* GUSHIER, GUSHIEST overly sentimental **GUSHILY** *adv*
GUNLOCK	*n* pl. -S the mechanism which ignites the charge of a gun	**GUSSET**	*v* -ED, -ING, -S to furnish with a reinforcing piece of material
GUNMAN	*n* pl. -MEN one who is armed with a gun	**GUSSIE**	*v* -SIED, -SYING, -SIES gussy
GUNMETAL	*n* pl. -S a dark gray color	**GUSSY**	*v* -SIED, -SYING, -SIES to dress up in fine or showy clothes
GUNNED	past tense of gun	**GUST**	*v* -ED, -ING, -S to blow in gusts (sudden blasts of wind)
GUNNEL	*n* pl. -S a marine fish		
GUNNEN	past participle of gin	**GUSTABLE**	*n* pl. -S a savory food
GUNNER	*n* pl. -S one that operates a gun	**GUSTIER**	comparative of gusty
GUNNERY	*n* pl. -NERIES the use of guns	**GUSTIEST**	superlative of gusty
GUNNING	*n* pl. -S the sport of hunting with a gun	**GUSTILY**	*adv* in a gusty manner
		GUSTLESS	*adj* having no gusts
GUNNY	*n* pl. -NIES a coarse fabric	**GUSTO**	*n* pl. -TOES vigorous enjoyment
GUNNYBAG	*n* pl. -S a bag made of gunny	**GUSTY**	*adj* GUSTIER, GUSTIEST blowing in gusts
GUNPAPER	*n* pl. -S a type of explosive paper		
GUNPLAY	*n* pl. -PLAYS the shooting of guns	**GUT**	*v* GUTTED, GUTTING, GUTS to remove the guts (intestines) of
GUNPOINT	*n* pl. -S the point or aim of a gun	**GUTLESS**	*adj* lacking courage
GUNROOM	*n* pl. -S a room on a British warship	**GUTLIKE**	*adj* resembling guts
		GUTSILY	*adv* in a gutsy manner
GUNSEL	*n* pl. -S a gunman	**GUTSY**	*adj* GUTSIER, GUTSIEST brave
GUNSHIP	*n* pl. -S an armed helicopter	**GUTTA**	*n* pl. -TAE a drop of liquid
GUNSHOT	*n* pl. -S a projectile fired from a gun	**GUTTATE**	*adj* resembling a drop
		GUTTATED	*adj* guttate
GUNSMITH	*n* pl. -S one who makes or repairs firearms	**GUTTED**	past tense of gut
GUNSTOCK	*n* pl. -S the rear wooden part of a rifle	**GUTTER**	*v* -ED, -ING, -S to form channels for draining off water
GUNWALE	*n* pl. -S the upper edge of a ship's side	**GUTTERY**	*adj* marked by extreme vulgarity or indecency
GUPPY	*n* pl. -PIES a small, tropical fish	**GUTTIER**	comparative of gutty
GURGE	*v* GURGED, GURGING, GURGES to swirl	**GUTTIEST**	superlative of gutty
		GUTTING	present participle of gut
GURGLE	*v* -GLED, -GLING, -GLES to flow unevenly	**GUTTLE**	*v* -TLED, -TLING, -TLES to eat rapidly
GURGLET	*n* pl. -S goglet	**GUTTLER**	*n* pl. -S one that guttles
GURNARD	*n* pl. -S a marine fish	**GUTTURAL**	*n* pl. -S a throaty sound

GUTTY   *adj* -TIER, -TIEST marked by courage

GUV   *n* pl. -S a governor

GUY   *v* -ED, -ING, -S to ridicule

GUYLINE   *n* pl. -S a rope, chain, or wire used as a brace

GUYOT   *n* pl. -S a flat-topped seamount

GUZZLE   *v* -ZLED, -ZLING, -ZLES to drink rapidly

GUZZLER   *n* pl. -S one that guzzles

GWEDUC   *n* pl. -S geoduck

GWEDUCK   *n* pl. -S geoduck

GYBE   *v* GYBED, GYBING, GYBES to shift from side to side while sailing

GYM   *n* pl. -S a room for athletic activities

GYMKHANA   *n* pl. -S an athletic meet

GYMNASIA   *n/pl* gyms

GYMNAST   *n* pl. -S one who is skilled in physical exercises

GYNAECEA   *n/pl* gynecia

GYNAECIA   *n/pl* gynecia

GYNANDRY   *n* pl. -DRIES the condition of having both male and female sexual organs

GYNARCHY   *n* pl. -CHIES government by women

GYNECIC   *adj* pertaining to women

GYNECIUM   *n* pl. -CIA the pistil of a flower

GYNECOID   *adj* resembling a woman

GYNIATRY   *n* pl. -TRIES the treatment of women's diseases

GYNOECIA   *n/pl* gynecia

GYP   *v* GYPPED, GYPPING, GYPS to swindle

GYPLURE   *n* pl. -S a synthetic attractant to trap gypsy moths

GYPPER   *n* pl. -S one that gyps

GYPSEIAN   *adj* of or pertaining to gypsies

GYPSEOUS   *adj* containing gypsum

GYPSTER   *n* pl. -S one that gyps

GYPSUM   *n* pl. -S a mineral

GYPSY   *v* -SIED, -SYING, -SIES to live like a gypsy (a wanderer)

GYPSYDOM   *n* pl. -S the realm of gypsies

GYPSYISH   *adj* resembling a gypsy

GYPSYISM   *n* pl. -S the mode of life of gypsies

GYRAL   *adj* gyratory **GYRALLY** *adv*

GYRASE   *n* pl. -S an enzyme

GYRATE   *v* -RATED, -RATING, -RATES to revolve or rotate

GYRATION   *n* pl. -S the act of gyrating

GYRATOR   *n* pl. -S one that gyrates

GYRATORY   *adj* moving in a circle or spiral

GYRE   *v* GYRED, GYRING, GYRES to move in a circle or spiral

GYRENE   *n* pl. -S a marine

GYRI   pl. of gyrus

GYRING   present participle of gyre

GYRO   *n* pl. -ROS a gyroscope

GYROIDAL   *adj* spiral in arrangement

GYRON   *n* pl. -S a heraldic design

GYROSE   *adj* marked with wavy lines

GYROSTAT   *n* pl. -S a type of stabilizing device

GYRUS   *n* pl. -RI a ridge in the brain

GYVE   *v* GYVED, GYVING, GYVES to shackle

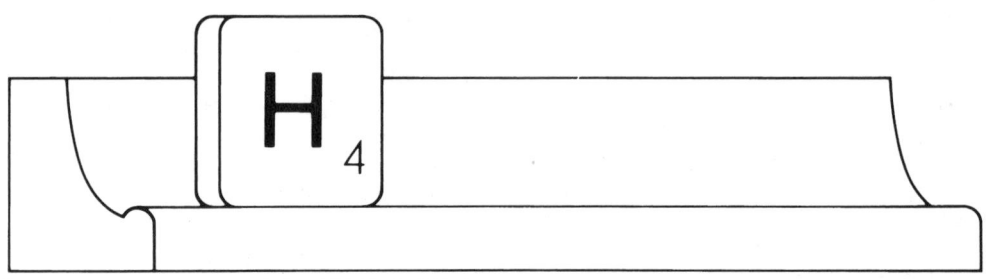

HA   *n* pl. -S a sound of surprise

HAAF   *n* pl. -S a deep-sea fishing ground

HAAR   *n* pl. -S a fog

HABANERA   *n* pl. -S a Cuban dance

HABDALAH   *n* pl. -S a Jewish ceremony

HABILE   *adj* skillful

HABIT   *v* -ED, -ING, -S to clothe or dress

HABITAN   *n* pl. -S a French settler

HABITANT   *n* pl. -S an inhabitant

HABITAT   *n* pl. -S the natural environment of an organism

HABITUAL   *adj* occurring frequently or constantly

HABITUDE   *n* pl. -S a usual course of action

HABITUE   *n* pl. -S a frequent customer

HABITUS   *n* pl. HABITUS bodily build and constitution

HABOOB   *n* pl. -S a violent sandstorm

HABU   *n* pl. -S a poisonous snake

HACEK   *n* pl. -S a mark placed over a letter to modify it

HACHURE   *v* -CHURED, -CHURING, -CHURES to make a hatching on a map

HACIENDA   *n* pl. -S an estate

HACK   *v* -ED, -ING, -S to cut or chop roughly

HACKBUT   *n* pl. -S a type of gun

HACKEE   *n* pl. -S a chipmunk

HACKER   *n* pl. -S one that hacks

HACKIE   *n* pl. -S a taxicab driver

HACKLE   *v* -LED, -LING, -LES to hack

HACKLER   *n* pl. -S one that hackles

HACKLY   *adj* -LIER, -LIEST jagged

HACKMAN   *n* pl. -MEN a hackie

HACKNEY   *v* -NEYED, -NEYING, -NEYS to make common

HACKSAW   *n* pl. -S a type of saw

HACKWORK   *n* pl. -S artistic work done according to formula

HAD   a past tense of have

HADAL   *adj* pertaining to deep parts of the ocean

HADARIM   a pl. of heder

HADDEST   a past 2d person sing. of have

HADDOCK   *n* pl. -S a food fish

HADE   *v* HADED, HADING, HADES to incline

HADITH   *n* pl. HADITH or HADITHS a record of the sayings of Muhammed

HADJ   *n* pl. -ES a pilgrimage to Mecca

HADJEE   *n* pl. -S hadji

HADJI   *n* pl. -S one who has made a hadj

HADRON   *n* pl. -S an elementary particle **HADRONIC** *adj*

HADST   a past 2d person sing. of have

HAE   *v* HAED, HAEN, HAEING, HAES to have

HAEM   *n* pl. -S heme

HAEMAL   *adj* hemal

HAEMATAL   *adj* hemal

HAEMATIC   *n* pl. -S hematic

HAEMATIN   *n* pl. -S hematin

HAEMIC   *adj* hemic

HAEMIN   *n* pl. -S hemin

HAEMOID   *adj* hemoid

HAEN   past participle of hae

HAERES   *n* pl. -REDES heres

HAET   *n* pl. -S a small amount

HAFFET   *n* pl. -S the cheekbone and temple

HAFFIT	*n* pl. -S haffet
HAFIZ	*n* pl. HAFIS a Muslim who knows the Koran by heart
HAFNIUM	*n* pl. -S a metallic element
HAFT	*v* -ED, -ING, -S to supply with a handle
HAFTARA	*n* pl. -RAS, -ROT or -ROTH haphtara
HAFTARAH	*n* pl. -RAHS, -ROT or -ROTH haphtara
HAFTER	*n* pl. -S one that hafts
HAFTORAH	*n* pl. -RAHS, -ROT or -ROTH haphtara
HAG	*v* HAGGED, HAGGING, HAGS to hack
HAGADIC	*adj* haggadic
HAGADIST	*n* pl. -S a haggadic scholar
HAGBERRY	*n* pl. -RIES a small cherry
HAGBORN	*adj* born of a witch
HAGBUSH	*n* pl. -ES a large tree
HAGBUT	*n* pl. -S hackbut
HAGDON	*n* pl. -S a seabird
HAGFISH	*n* pl. -ES an eellike fish
HAGGADA	*n* pl. -DAS, -DOT or -DOTH haggadah
HAGGADAH	*n* pl. -DAHS, -DOT or -DOTH a biblical narrative **HAGGADIC** *adj*
HAGGARD	*n* pl. -S an adult hawk
HAGGED	past tense of hag
HAGGING	present participle of hag
HAGGIS	*n* pl. -GISES a Scottish dish
HAGGISH	*adj* resembling a hag
HAGGLE	*v* -GLED, -GLING, -GLES to bargain
HAGGLER	*n* pl. -S one that haggles
HAGRIDE	*v* -RODE, -RIDDEN, -RIDING, -RIDES to harass
HAH	*n* pl. -S ha
HAHA	*n* pl. -S a fence set in a ditch
HAHNIUM	*n* pl. -S a radioactive element
HAIK	*n* pl. HAIKS or HAIKA an outer garment worn by Arabs
HAIKU	*n* pl. HAIKU a Japanese poem
HAIL	*v* -ED, -ING, -S to welcome
HAILER	*n* pl. -S one that hails
HAIR	*n* pl. -S a threadlike growth
HAIRBALL	*n* pl. -S a ball of hair
HAIRBAND	*n* pl. -S a headband
HAIRCAP	*n* pl. -S a hat
HAIRCUT	*n* pl. -S a cutting of the hair
HAIRDO	*n* pl. -DOS a style of wearing the hair
HAIRED	*adj* having hair
HAIRIER	comparative of hairy
HAIRIEST	superlative of hairy
HAIRLESS	*adj* having no hair
HAIRLIKE	*adj* resembling a hair
HAIRLINE	*n* pl. -S a very thin line
HAIRLOCK	*n* pl. -S a lock of hair
HAIRNET	*n* pl. -S a net worn to keep the hair in place
HAIRPIN	*n* pl. -S a hair fastener
HAIRWORK	*n* pl. -S the making of articles from hair
HAIRWORM	*n* pl. -S a parasitic worm
HAIRY	*adj* HAIRIER, HAIRIEST covered with hair
HAJ	*n* pl. -ES hadj
HAJI	*n* pl. -S hadji
HAJJ	*n* pl. -ES hadj
HAJJI	*n* pl. -S hadji
HAKE	*n* pl. -S a marine fish
HAKEEM	*n* pl. -S hakim
HAKIM	*n* pl. -S a Muslim physician
HALACHA	*n* pl. -CHAS or -CHOT halakah
HALAKAH	*n* pl. -KAHS or -KOTH the legal part of the Talmud
HALAKHA	*n* pl. -KHAS or -KHOT halakah
HALAKIC	*adj* pertaining to the halakah
HALAKIST	*n* pl. -S a halakic writer
HALAKOTH	a pl. of halakah
HALALA	*n* pl. -S a Saudi Arabian coin
HALALAH	*n* pl. -S halala
HALATION	*n* pl. -S a blurring of light in photographs
HALAVAH	*n* pl. -S halvah
HALAZONE	*n* pl. -S a disinfectant for drinking water
HALBERD	*n* pl. -S an axlike weapon of the 15th and 16th centuries
HALBERT	*n* pl. -S halberd
HALCYON	*n* pl. -S a mythical bird
HALE	*adj* HALER, HALEST healthy
HALE	*v* HALED, HALING, HALES to compel to go

HALENESS	*n* pl. -ES the state of being hale
HALER	*n* pl. -LERS or -LERU a coin of the Czech Republic
HALEST	superlative of hale
HALF	*n* pl. HALVES one of two equal parts
HALFBACK	*n* pl. -S a football player
HALFBEAK	*n* pl. -S a marine fish
HALFLIFE	*n* pl. -LIVES a measure of radioactive decay
HALFNESS	*n* pl. -ES the state of being half
HALFTIME	*n* pl. -S an intermission in a football game
HALFTONE	*n* pl. -S a shade between light and dark
HALFWAY	*adj* being in the middle
HALIBUT	*n* pl. -S a flatfish
HALID	*n* pl. -S halide
HALIDE	*n* pl. -S a chemical compound
HALIDOM	*n* pl. -S something holy
HALIDOME	*n* pl. -S halidom
HALING	present participle of hale
HALITE	*n* pl. -S a mineral
HALITUS	*n* pl. -ES an exhalation
HALL	*n* pl. -S a large room for assembly
HALLAH	*n* pl. -LAHS, -LOTH or -LOT challah
HALLEL	*n* pl. -S a chant of praise
HALLIARD	*n* pl. -S halyard
HALLMARK	*v* -ED, -ING, -S to mark with an official stamp
HALLO	*v* -ED, -ING, -S or -ES to shout
HALLOA	*v* -ED, -ING, -S to hallo
HALLOO	*v* -ED, -ING, -S to hallo
HALLOT	a pl. of hallah
HALLOTH	a pl. of hallah
HALLOW	*v* -ED, -ING, -S to make holy
HALLOWER	*n* pl. -S one that hallows
HALLUX	*n* pl. -LUCES the big toe
HALLWAY	*n* pl. -WAYS a hall
HALM	*n* pl. -S haulm
HALMA	*n* pl. -S a board game
HALO	*v* -ED, -ING, -ES or -S to form a halo (a ring of light)
HALOGEN	*n* pl. -S a nonmetallic element
HALOID	*n* pl. -S a chemical salt
HALOLIKE	*adj* resembling a halo
HALT	*v* -ED, -ING, -S to stop
HALTER	*v* -ED, -ING, -S to put restraint upon
HALTERE	*n* pl. -S a pair of wings of an insect
HALTLESS	*adj* not hesitant
HALUTZ	*n* pl. -LUTZIM an Israeli farmer
HALVA	*n* pl. -S halvah
HALVAH	*n* pl. -S a Turkish confection
HALVE	*v* HALVED, HALVING, HALVES to divide into two equal parts
HALVERS	*n* pl. HALVERS half shares
HALVES	pl. of half
HALVING	present participle of halve
HALYARD	*n* pl. -S a line used to hoist a sail
HAM	*v* HAMMED, HAMMING, HAMS to overact
HAMADA	*n* pl. -S hammada
HAMAL	*n* pl. -S a porter in eastern countries
HAMARTIA	*n* pl. -S a defect of character
HAMATE	*n* pl. -S a wrist bone
HAMAUL	*n* pl. -S hamal
HAMBONE	*v* -BONED, -BONING, -BONES to overact
HAMBURG	*n* pl. -S a patty of ground beef
HAME	*n* pl. -S a part of a horse collar
HAMLET	*n* pl. -S a small town
HAMMADA	*n* pl. -S a desert plateau of bedrock
HAMMAL	*n* pl. -S hamal
HAMMED	past tense of ham
HAMMER	*v* -ED, -ING, -S to strike repeatedly
HAMMERER	*n* pl. -S one that hammers
HAMMIER	comparative of hammy
HAMMIEST	superlative of hammy
HAMMILY	*adv* in a hammy manner
HAMMING	present participle of ham
HAMMOCK	*n* pl. -S a hanging cot
HAMMY	*adj* -MIER, -MIEST overly theatrical
HAMPER	*v* -ED, -ING, -S to hinder
HAMPERER	*n* pl. -S one that hampers
HAMSTER	*n* pl. -S a burrowing rodent

HAMULUS   *n* pl. -LI a small hook **HAMULAR, HAMULATE, HAMULOSE, HAMULOUS** *adj*

HAMZA   *n* pl. -S an Arabic diacritical mark

HAMZAH   *n* pl. -S hamza

HANAPER   *n* pl. -S a wicker receptacle

HANCE   *n* pl. -S a side of an arch

HAND   *v* -ED, -ING, -S to present with the hand (the end of the forearm)

HANDBAG   *n* pl. -S a small carrying bag

HANDBALL   *n* pl. -S a small rubber ball

HANDBELL   *n* pl. -S a small bell with a handle

HANDBILL   *n* pl. -S a circular

HANDBOOK   *n* pl. -S a manual

HANDCAR   *n* pl. -S a hand-operated railroad car

HANDCART   *n* pl. -S a cart pushed by hand

HANDCUFF   *v* -ED, -ING, -S to fetter with restraining cuffs

HANDFAST   *v* -ED, -ING, -S to grip securely

HANDFUL   *n* pl. HANDFULS or HANDSFUL as much as the hand can hold

HANDGRIP   *n* pl. -S a grip by the hand or hands

HANDGUN   *n* pl. -S a small firearm

HANDHELD   *n* pl. -S something held in the hand

HANDHOLD   *n* pl. -S a handgrip

HANDICAP   *v* -CAPPED, -CAPPING, -CAPS to hinder

HANDIER   comparative of handy

HANDIEST   superlative of handy

HANDILY   *adv* in a handy manner

HANDLE   *v* -DLED, -DLING, -DLES to touch with the hands

HANDLER   *n* pl. -S one that handles

HANDLESS   *adj* having no hands

HANDLIKE   *adj* resembling a hand

HANDLING   *n* pl. -S the manner in which something is handled

HANDLIST   *n* pl. -S a reference list

HANDLOOM   *n* pl. -S a manually operated loom

HANDMADE   *adj* made by hand

HANDMAID   *n* pl. -S a female servant

HANDOFF   *n* pl. -S a play in football

HANDOUT   *n* pl. -S something given out free

HANDOVER   *n* pl. -S an instance of giving up control

HANDPICK   *v* -ED, -ING, -S to choose carefully

HANDRAIL   *n* pl. -S a railing used for support

HANDSAW   *n* pl. -S a saw used manually

HANDSEL   *v* -SELED, -SELING, -SELS or -SELLED, -SELLING, -SELS to give a gift to

HANDSET   *n* pl. -S a type of telephone

HANDSEWN   *adj* sewn by hand

HANDSFUL   a pl. of handful

HANDSOME   *adj* -SOMER, -SOMEST attractive

HANDWORK   *n* pl. -S manual labor

HANDWRIT   *adj* written by hand

HANDY   *adj* HANDIER, HANDIEST convenient for handling

HANDYMAN   *n* pl. -MEN a man who does odd jobs

HANG   *v* HUNG or HANGED, HANGING, HANGS to attach from above only **HANGABLE** *adj*

HANGAR   *v* -ED, -ING, -S to place in an aircraft shelter

HANGBIRD   *n* pl. -S a type of bird

HANGDOG   *n* pl. -S a sneaky person

HANGER   *n* pl. -S one that hangs

HANGFIRE   *n* pl. -S a delay in detonation

HANGING   *n* pl. -S an execution by strangling with a suspended noose

HANGMAN   *n* pl. -MEN an executioner

HANGNAIL   *n* pl. -S an agnail

HANGNEST   *n* pl. -S a hangbird

HANGOUT   *n* pl. -S a place often visited

HANGOVER   *n* pl. -S the physical effects following a drinking binge

HANGTAG   *n* pl. -S a type of tag used commercially

HANGUL   *n* the Korean alphabetic script

HANGUP   *n* pl. -S an inhibition or obsession

HANIWA   *n/pl* Japanese clay sculptures

HANK   *v* -ED, -ING, -S to fasten a sail

HANKER   *v* -ED, -ING, -S to long for

HANKERER   *n* pl. -S one that hankers

HANKIE   *n* pl. -S hanky

HANKY   *n* pl. -KIES a handkerchief

HANSA   *n* pl. -S hanse

HANSE   *n* pl. -S a guild of merchants

HANSEL   *v* -SELED, -SELING, -SELS or -SELLED, -SELLING, -SELS to handsel

HANSOM   *n* pl. -S a light carriage

HANT   *v* -ED, -ING, -S to haunt

HANTLE   *n* pl. -S a large amount

HANUMAN   *n* pl. -S an East Indian monkey

HAO   *n* pl. HAO a monetary unit of Vietnam

HAP   *v* HAPPED, HAPPING, HAPS to happen

HAPAX   *n* pl. -ES a word that occurs only once

HAPHTARA   *n* pl. -RAS, -ROT or -ROTH a biblical selection

HAPLESS   *adj* luckless

HAPLITE   *n* pl. -S aplite

HAPLOID   *n* pl. -S a cell having only one set of chromosomes

HAPLOIDY   *n* pl. -DIES the state of being a haploid

HAPLONT   *n* pl. -S an organism having a particular chromosomal structure

HAPLOPIA   *n* pl. -S normal vision

HAPLOSIS   *n* pl. -LOSES the halving of the chromosome number

HAPLY   *adv* by chance

HAPPED   past tense of hap

HAPPEN   *v* -ED, -ING, -S to occur

HAPPING   present participle of hap

HAPPY   *adj* -PIER, -PIEST marked by joy **HAPPILY** *adv*

HAPTEN   *n* pl. -S a substance similar to an antigen **HAPTENIC** *adj*

HAPTENE   *n* pl. -S hapten

HAPTIC   *adj* pertaining to the sense of touch

HAPTICAL   *adj* haptic

HARANGUE   *v* -RANGUED, -RANGUING, -RANGUES to deliver a tirade to

HARASS   *v* -ED, -ING, -ES to bother persistently

HARASSER   *n* pl. -S one that harasses

HARBOR   *v* -ED, -ING, -S to shelter

HARBORER   *n* pl. -S one that harbors

HARBOUR   *v* -ED, -ING, -S to harbor

HARD   *adj* HARDER, HARDEST firm and unyielding

HARDBACK   *n* pl. -S a hardcover book

HARDBALL   *n* pl. -S baseball

HARDBOOT   *n* pl. -S a horseman

HARDCASE   *adj* tough

HARDCORE   *adj* unyielding

HARDEDGE   *n* pl. -S a geometric painting

HARDEN   *v* -ED, -ING, -S to make hard

HARDENER   *n* pl. -S one that hardens

HARDHACK   *n* pl. -S a woody plant

HARDHAT   *n* pl. -S a conservative

HARDHEAD   *n* pl. -S a practical person

HARDIER   comparative of hardy

HARDIES   pl. of hardy

HARDIEST   superlative of hardy

HARDILY   *adv* in a hardy manner

HARDLINE   *adj* unyielding

HARDLY   *adv* scarcely

HARDNESS   *n* pl. -ES the state of being hard

HARDNOSE   *n* pl. -S a stubborn person

HARDPAN   *n* pl. -S a layer of hard subsoil

HARDS   *n/pl* the coarse refuse of flax

HARDSET   *adj* rigid

HARDSHIP   *n* pl. -S a difficult, painful condition

HARDTACK   *n* pl. -S a hard biscuit

HARDTOP   *n* pl. -S a type of car

HARDWARE   *n* pl. -S metal goods

HARDWIRE   *v* -WIRED, -WIRING, -WIRES to permanently connect electronic components

HARDWOOD   *n* pl. -S the hard, compact wood of various trees

HARDY   *adj* -DIER, -DIEST very sturdy

HARDY   *n* pl. -DIES a blacksmith's chisel

HARE   *v* HARED, HARING, HARES to run

HAREBELL   *n* pl. -S a perennial herb

HAREEM   *n* pl. -S harem

HARELIKE   *adj* resembling a hare (a long-eared mammal)

HARELIP   *n* pl. -S a deformity of the upper lip

HAREM   *n* pl. -S the section of a Muslim household reserved for women

HARIANA   *n* pl. -S a breed of cattle

HARICOT   *n* pl. -S the seed of various string beans

HARIJAN   *n* pl. -S an outcaste in India

HARING	present participle of hare
HARK	v -ED, -ING, -S to listen to
HARKEN	v -ED, -ING, -S to hearken
HARKENER	n pl. -S one that harkens
HARL	n pl. -S a herl
HARLOT	n pl. -S a prostitute
HARLOTRY	n pl. -RIES prostitution
HARM	v -ED, -ING, -S to injure
HARMER	n pl. -S one that harms
HARMFUL	adj capable of harming
HARMIN	n pl. -S harmine
HARMINE	n pl. -S an alkaloid used as a stimulant
HARMLESS	adj not harmful
HARMONIC	n pl. -S an overtone
HARMONY	n pl. -NIES agreement
HARNESS	v -ED, -ING, -ES to put tackle on a draft animal
HARP	v -ED, -ING, -S to play on a harp (a type of stringed musical instrument)
HARPER	n pl. -S a harpist
HARPIES	pl. of harpy
HARPIN	n pl. -S harping
HARPING	n pl. -S a wooden plank used in shipbuilding
HARPIST	n pl. -S one that plays the harp
HARPOON	v -ED, -ING, -S to strike with a harpoon
HARPY	n pl. -PIES a shrewish person
HARRIDAN	n pl. -S a haggard woman
HARRIED	past tense of harry
HARRIER	n pl. -S a hunting dog
HARRIES	present 3d person sing. of harry
HARROW	v -ED, -ING, -S to break up and level soil
HARROWER	n pl. -S one that harrows
HARRUMPH	v -ED, -ING, -S to make a guttural sound
HARRY	v -RIED, -RYING, -RIES to pillage
HARSH	adj HARSHER, HARSHEST severe **HARSHLY** adv
HARSHEN	v -ED, -ING, -S to make harsh
HARSLET	n pl. -S haslet
HART	n pl. -S a male deer
HARTAL	n pl. -S a stoppage of work
HARUMPH	v -ED, -ING, -S harrumph
HARUSPEX	n pl. -PICES a soothsayer of ancient Rome
HARVEST	v -ED, -ING, -S to gather a crop
HAS	a present 3d person sing. of have
HASH	v -ED, -ING, -ES to mince
HASHEESH	n pl. -ES hashish
HASHHEAD	n pl. -S a hashish addict
HASHISH	n pl. -ES a mild narcotic
HASLET	n pl. -S the edible viscera of an animal
HASP	v -ED, -ING, -S to fasten with a clasp
HASSEL	n pl. -S an argument
HASSLE	v -SLED, -SLING, -SLES to argue
HASSOCK	n pl. -S a footstool
HAST	a present 2d person sing. of have
HASTATE	adj triangular
HASTE	v HASTED, HASTING, HASTES to hasten
HASTEFUL	adj hasty
HASTEN	v -ED, -ING, -S to hurry
HASTENER	n pl. -S one that hastens
HASTING	present participle of haste
HASTY	adj HASTIER, HASTIEST speedy **HASTILY** adv
HAT	v HATTED, HATTING, HATS to provide with a hat (a covering for the head)
HATABLE	adj hateable
HATBAND	n pl. -S a band worn on a hat
HATBOX	n pl. -ES a box for a hat
HATCH	v -ED, -ING, -ES to bring forth young from an egg
HATCHECK	adj pertaining to the checking of hats
HATCHEL	v -ELED, -ELING, -ELS or -ELLED, -ELLING, -ELS to separate flax fibers with a comb
HATCHER	n pl. -S one that hatches
HATCHERY	n pl. -ERIES a place for hatching eggs
HATCHET	n pl. -S a small ax
HATCHING	n pl. -S a series of lines used to show shading
HATCHWAY	n pl. -WAYS an opening in the deck of a ship

HATE	*v* HATED, HATING, HATES to despise
HATEABLE	*adj* meriting hatred
HATEFUL	*adj* detestable
HATER	*n* pl. -S one that hates
HATFUL	*n* pl. HATSFUL or HATFULS as much as a hat can hold
HATH	a present 3d person sing. of have
HATING	present participle of hate
HATLESS	*adj* lacking a hat
HATLIKE	*adj* resembling a hat
HATMAKER	*n* pl. -S one that makes hats
HATPIN	*n* pl. -S a pin for securing a hat
HATRACK	*n* pl. -S a rack for hats
HATRED	*n* pl. -S intense dislike or aversion
HATSFUL	a pl. of hatful
HATTED	past tense of hat
HATTER	*n* pl. -S a hatmaker
HATTERIA	*n* pl. -S a reptile
HATTING	present participle of hat
HAUBERK	*n* pl. -S a coat of armor
HAUGH	*n* pl. -S a low-lying meadow
HAUGHTY	*adj* -TIER, -TIEST arrogant
HAUL	*v* -ED, -ING, -S to pull with force
HAULAGE	*n* pl. -S the act of hauling
HAULER	*n* pl. -S one that hauls
HAULIER	*n* pl. -S hauler
HAULM	*n* pl. -S a plant stem
HAULMY	*adj* HAULMIER, HAULMIEST having haulms
HAULYARD	*n* pl. -S halyard
HAUNCH	*n* pl. -ES the hindquarter **HAUNCHED** *adj*
HAUNT	*v* -ED, -ING, -S to visit frequently
HAUNTER	*n* pl. -S one that haunts
HAUSEN	*n* pl. -S a Russian sturgeon
HAUSFRAU	*n* pl. -FRAUS or -FRAUEN a housewife
HAUT	*adj* haute
HAUTBOIS	*n* pl. HAUTBOIS hautboy
HAUTBOY	*n* pl. -BOYS an oboe
HAUTE	*adj* high-class
HAUTEUR	*n* pl. -S haughty manner or spirit
HAVARTI	*n* pl. -S a Danish cheese
HAVDALAH	*n* pl. -S habdalah
HAVE	*v* past 2d person sing. HAD, HADDEST or HADST, present participle HAVING, present 2d person sing. HAVE or HAST, 3d person sing. HAS or HATH to be in possession of
HAVE	*n* pl. -S a wealthy person
HAVELOCK	*n* pl. -S a covering for a cap
HAVEN	*v* -ED, -ING, -S to shelter
HAVER	*v* -ED, -ING, -S to hem and haw
HAVEREL	*n* pl. -S a fool
HAVING	present participle of have
HAVIOR	*n* pl. -S behavior
HAVIOUR	*n* pl. -S havior
HAVOC	*v* -OCKED, -OCKING, -OCS to destroy
HAVOCKER	*n* pl. -S one that havocs
HAW	*v* -ED, -ING, -S to turn left
HAWFINCH	*n* pl. -ES a Eurasian finch
HAWK	*v* -ED, -ING, -S to peddle
HAWKBILL	*n* pl. -S a sea turtle
HAWKER	*n* pl. -S one that hawks
HAWKEY	*n* pl. -EYS a hawkie
HAWKEYED	*adj* having keen sight
HAWKIE	*n* pl. -S a white-faced cow
HAWKING	*n* pl. -S falconry
HAWKISH	*adj* warlike
HAWKLIKE	*adj* resembling a hawk (a bird of prey)
HAWKMOTH	*n* pl. -S a large moth
HAWKNOSE	*n* pl. -S a large, curved nose
HAWKSHAW	*n* pl. -S a detective
HAWKWEED	*n* pl. -S a weedlike herb
HAWSE	*n* pl. -S a part of a ship's bow
HAWSER	*n* pl. -S a mooring rope
HAWTHORN	*n* pl. -S a thorny shrub
HAY	*v* -ED, -ING, -S to convert into hay (grass, cut and dried for fodder)
HAYCOCK	*n* pl. -S a pile of hay
HAYER	*n* pl. -S one that hays
HAYFIELD	*n* pl. -S a field where grasses for hay are grown
HAYFORK	*n* pl. -S a tool for pitching hay
HAYING	*n* pl. -S the season for harvesting hay
HAYLAGE	*n* pl. -S a type of hay
HAYLOFT	*n* pl. -S a loft for hay storage

HAYMAKER *n* pl. -S one that makes hay

HAYMOW *n* pl. -S a hayloft

HAYRACK *n* pl. -S a frame used in hauling hay

HAYRICK *n* pl. -S a haystack

HAYRIDE *n* pl. -S a wagon ride

HAYSEED *n* pl. -S a bumpkin

HAYSTACK *n* pl. -S a pile of hay

HAYWARD *n* pl. -S an officer who tends cattle

HAYWIRE *n* pl. -S wire used in baling hay

HAZAN *n* pl. -ZANIM or -ZANS a cantor

HAZARD *v* -ED, -ING, -S to venture

HAZE *v* HAZED, HAZING, HAZES to subject to a humiliating initiation

HAZEL *n* pl. -S a shrub

HAZELHEN *n* pl. -S a European grouse

HAZELLY *adj* yellowish brown

HAZELNUT *n* pl. -S an edible nut

HAZER *n* pl. -S one that hazes

HAZIER comparative of hazy

HAZIEST superlative of hazy

HAZILY *adv* in a hazy manner

HAZINESS *n* pl. -ES the state of being hazy

HAZING *n* pl. -S an attempt to embarrass or ridicule

HAZY *adj* HAZIER, HAZIEST unclear

HAZZAN *n* pl. HAZZANIM or HAZZANS hazan

HE *n* pl. -S a male person

HEAD *v* -ED, -ING, -S to be chief of

HEADACHE *n* pl. -S a pain inside the head

HEADACHY *adj* -ACHIER, -ACHIEST having a headache

HEADBAND *n* pl. -S a band worn on the head

HEADER *n* pl. -S a grain harvester

HEADFISH *n* pl. -ES a marine fish

HEADGATE *n* pl. -S a gate to control the flow of water

HEADGEAR *n* pl. -S a covering for the head

HEADHUNT *v* -ED, -ING, -S to seek out, decapitate, and preserve the heads of enemies

HEADIER comparative of heady

HEADIEST superlative of heady

HEADILY *adv* in a heady manner

HEADING *n* pl. -S a title

HEADLAMP *n* pl. -S a light on the front of a car

HEADLAND *n* pl. -S a cliff

HEADLESS *adj* lacking a head

HEADLINE *v* -LINED, -LINING, -LINES to provide with a title

HEADLOCK *n* pl. -S a wrestling hold

HEADLONG *adj* rash; impetuous

HEADMAN *n* pl. -MEN a foreman

HEADMOST *adj* foremost

HEADNOTE *n* pl. -S a prefixed note

HEADPIN *n* pl. -S a bowling pin

HEADRACE *n* pl. -S a water channel

HEADREST *n* pl. -S a support for the head

HEADROOM *n* pl. -S clear vertical space

HEADSAIL *n* pl. -S a type fo sail

HEADSET *n* pl. -S a pair of earphones

HEADSHIP *n* pl. -S the position of a leader

HEADSMAN *n* pl. -MEN an executioner

HEADSTAY *n* pl. -STAYS a support for a ship's foremast

HEADWAY *n* pl. -WAYS forward movement

HEADWIND *n* pl. -S an oncoming wind

HEADWORD *n* pl. -S a word put at the beginning

HEADWORK *n* pl. -S mental work

HEADY *adj* HEADIER, HEADIEST intoxicating

HEAL *v* -ED, -ING, -S to make sound or whole **HEALABLE** *adj*

HEALER *n* pl. -S one that heals

HEALTH *n* pl. -S the physical condition of an organism

HEALTHY *adj* HEALTHIER, HEALTHIEST having good health

HEAP *v* -ED, -ING, -S to pile up

HEAR *v* HEARD, HEARING, HEARS to perceive by the ear **HEARABLE** *adj*

HEARER *n* pl. -S one that hears

HEARING *n* pl. -S a preliminary examination

HEARKEN *v* -ED, -ING, -S to listen to

HEARSAY *n* pl. -SAYS secondhand information

HEARSE *v* HEARSED, HEARSING, HEARSES to transport in a hearse (a vehicle for conveying corpses)

HEART	v -ED, -ING, -S to hearten
HEARTEN	v -ED, -ING, -S to give courage to
HEARTH	n pl. -S the floor of a fireplace
HEARTY	adj HEARTIER, HEARTIEST very friendly **HEARTILY** adv
HEARTY	n pl. HEARTIES a comrade
HEAT	v HEATED or HET, HEATING, HEATS to make hot **HEATABLE** adj
HEATEDLY	adv in an inflamed or excited manner
HEATER	n pl. -S an apparatus for heating
HEATH	n pl. -S an evergreen shrub
HEATHEN	n pl. -S an uncivilized person
HEATHER	n pl. -S an evergreen shrub **HEATHERY** adj
HEATHY	adj HEATHIER, HEATHIEST abounding in heath
HEATLESS	adj having no warmth
HEAUME	n pl. -S a medieval helmet
HEAVE	v HEAVED or HOVE, HEAVING, HEAVES to lift forcefully
HEAVEN	n pl. -S the sky
HEAVENLY	adj -LIER, -LIEST full of beauty and peace
HEAVER	n pl. -S one that heaves
HEAVIER	comparative of heavy
HEAVIES	pl. of heavy
HEAVING	present participle of heave
HEAVY	adj HEAVIER, HEAVIEST having much weight **HEAVILY** adv
HEAVY	n pl. HEAVIES a villain
HEAVYSET	adj solidly built; stocky
HEBDOMAD	n pl. -S the number seven
HEBETATE	v -TATED, -TATING, -TATES to make dull
HEBETIC	adj pertaining to puberty
HEBETUDE	n pl. -S mental dullness
HEBRAIZE	v -IZED, -IZING, -IZES to make Hebrew
HECATOMB	n pl. -S a great sacrifice or slaughter
HECK	n pl. -S hell
HECKLE	v -LED, -LING, -LES to harass a speaker
HECKLER	n pl. -S one that heckles
HECTARE	n pl. -S a unit of area

HECTIC	adj filled with turmoil **HECTICLY** adv
HECTICAL	adj hectic
HECTOR	v -ED, -ING, -S to bully
HEDDLE	n pl. -S a part of a loom
HEDER	n pl. HEDERS or HADARIM a Jewish school
HEDGE	v HEDGED, HEDGING, HEDGES to surround with a hedge (a dense row of shrubs)
HEDGEHOG	n pl. -S a small mammal
HEDGEHOP	v -HOPPED, -HOPPING, -HOPS to fly near the ground
HEDGEPIG	n pl. -S a hedgehog
HEDGER	n pl. -S one that hedges
HEDGEROW	n pl. -S a row of bushes
HEDGING	present participle of hedge
HEDGY	adj HEDGIER, HEDGIEST abounding in hedges
HEDONIC	adj pertaining to pleasure
HEDONICS	n/pl a branch of psychology
HEDONISM	n pl. -S the pursuit of pleasure
HEDONIST	n pl. -S a follower of hedonism
HEED	v -ED, -ING, -S to pay attention to
HEEDER	n pl. -S one that heeds
HEEDFUL	adj paying close attention
HEEDLESS	adj paying little or no attention
HEEHAW	v -ED, -ING, -S to guffaw
HEEL	v -ED, -ING, -S to supply with a heel (the raised part of a shoe)
HEELBALL	n pl. -S a composition used for polishing
HEELER	n pl. -S one that puts heels on shoes
HEELING	n pl. -S the act of inclining laterally
HEELLESS	adj lacking heels
HEELPOST	n pl. -S a post fitted to the end of something
HEELTAP	n pl. -S material put on the heel of a shoe
HEEZE	v HEEZED, HEEZING, HEEZES to hoist
HEFT	v -ED, -ING, -S to lift up
HEFTER	n pl. -S one that hefts
HEFTY	adj HEFTIER, HEFTIEST heavy **HEFTILY** adv
HEGARI	n pl. -S a grain

HEGEMONY	n pl. -NIES great authority
HEGIRA	n pl. -S an exodus
HEGUMEN	n pl. -S the head of a monastery
HEGUMENE	n pl. -S the head of a nunnery
HEGUMENY	n pl. -NIES the office of a hegumen
HEH	n pl. -S a Hebrew letter
HEIFER	n pl. -S a young cow
HEIGH	interj — used to attract attention
HEIGHT	n pl. -S the highest point
HEIGHTEN	v -ED, -ING, -S to raise
HEIGHTH	n pl. -S height
HEIL	v -ED, -ING, -S to salute
HEIMISH	adj homelike
HEINIE	n pl. -S the buttocks
HEINOUS	adj very wicked
HEIR	v -ED, -ING, -S to inherit
HEIRDOM	n pl. -S heirship
HEIRESS	n pl. -ES a female inheritor
HEIRLESS	adj having no inheritors
HEIRLOOM	n pl. -S an inherited possession
HEIRSHIP	n pl. -S the right to inheritance
HEISHI	n/pl tiny beads made from shells
HEIST	v -ED, -ING, -S to steal
HEISTER	n pl. -S one that heists
HEJIRA	n pl. -S hegira
HEKTARE	n pl. -S hectare
HELD	past tense of hold
HELIAC	adj heliacal
HELIACAL	adj pertaining to the sun
HELIAST	n pl. -S an Athenian judge
HELICAL	adj shaped like a helix
HELICES	a pl. of helix
HELICITY	n pl. -TIES a component of a particle's spin
HELICOID	n pl. -S a type of geometrical surface
HELICON	n pl. -S a large bass tuba
HELICOPT	v -ED, -ING, -S to travel by helicopter
HELILIFT	v -ED, -ING, -S to transport by helicopter
HELIO	n pl. -LIOS a signaling mirror
HELIPAD	n pl. -S a heliport
HELIPORT	n pl. -S an airport for helicopters
HELISTOP	n pl. -S a heliport

HELIUM	n pl. -S a gaseous element
HELIX	n pl. -LIXES or -LICES something spiral in form
HELL	v -ED, -ING, -S to behave raucously
HELLBENT	adj stubbornly determined
HELLBOX	n pl. -ES a printer's receptacle
HELLCAT	n pl. -S a shrewish person
HELLER	n pl. -S a hellion
HELLERI	n pl. -ES a tropical fish
HELLERY	n pl. -LERIES rough play
HELLFIRE	n pl. -S the torment of hell
HELLHOLE	n pl. -S a horrible place
HELLION	n pl. -S a troublesome person
HELLISH	adj horrible
HELLKITE	n pl. -S a cruel person
HELLO	v -ED, -ING, -ES or -S to greet
HELLUVA	adj disagreeable
HELM	v -ED, -ING, -S to steer a ship
HELMET	v -ED, -ING, -S to supply with a helmet (a protective covering for the head)
HELMINTH	n pl. -S a worm
HELMLESS	adj lacking a helm (a steering system)
HELMSMAN	n pl. -MEN one that steers a ship
HELO	n pl. HELOS a helicopter
HELOT	n pl. -S a slave or serf
HELOTAGE	n pl. -S helotism
HELOTISM	n pl. -S slavery or or serfdom
HELOTRY	n pl. -RIES helotism
HELP	v HELPED or HOLP, HELPED or HOLPEN, HELPING, HELPS to give assistance to **HELPABLE** adj
HELPER	n pl. -S one that helps
HELPFUL	adj being of service or assistance
HELPING	n pl. -S a portion of food
HELPLESS	adj defenseless
HELPMATE	n pl. -S a helpful companion
HELPMEET	n pl. -S a helpmate
HELVE	v HELVED, HELVING, HELVES to provide with a handle
HEM	v HEMMED, HEMMING, HEMS to provide with an edge
HEMAGOG	n pl. -S an agent that promotes blood flow

HEMAL	*adj* pertaining to the blood
HEMATAL	*adj* hemal
HEMATEIN	*n* pl. -S a chemical compound
HEMATIC	*n* pl. -S a medicine for a blood disease
HEMATIN	*n* pl. -S heme
HEMATINE	*n* pl. -S hematin
HEMATITE	*n* pl. -S an ore of iron
HEMATOID	*adj* resembling blood
HEMATOMA	*n* pl. -MAS or -MATA a swelling filled with blood
HEME	*n* pl. -S a component of hemoglobin
HEMIC	*adj* hemal
HEMIN	*n* pl. -S a chloride of heme
HEMIOLA	*n* pl. -S a rhythmic alteration in music
HEMIOLIA	*n* pl. -S hemiola
HEMIPTER	*n* pl. -S an insect
HEMLINE	*n* pl. -S the bottom edge of a garment
HEMLOCK	*n* pl. -S a poisonous herb
HEMMED	past tense of hem
HEMMER	*n* pl. -S one that hems
HEMMING	present participle of hem
HEMOCOEL	*n* pl. -S a body cavity
HEMOCYTE	*n* pl. -S a blood cell
HEMOID	*adj* hemal
HEMOLYZE	*v* -LYZED, -LYZING, -LYZES to break down red blood cells
HEMOSTAT	*n* pl. -S an instrument for reducing bleeding
HEMP	*n* pl. -S a tall herb
HEMPEN	*adj* made of hemp
HEMPIE	*adj* HEMPIER, HEMPIEST hempy
HEMPIER	comparative of hempy
HEMPIEST	superlative of hempy
HEMPLIKE	*adj* resembling hemp
HEMPSEED	*n* pl. -S the seed of hemp
HEMPWEED	*n* pl. -S a climbing plant
HEMPY	*adj* HEMPIER, HEMPIEST mischievous
HEN	*n* pl. -S a female chicken
HENBANE	*n* pl. -S a poisonous herb
HENBIT	*n* pl. -S a perennial herb
HENCE	*adv* consequently
HENCHMAN	*n* pl. -MEN an unscrupulous supporter
HENCOOP	*n* pl. -S a cage for hens
HENEQUEN	*n* pl. -S a fiber used to make ropes
HENEQUIN	*n* pl. -S henequen
HENHOUSE	*n* pl. -S a shelter for poultry
HENIQUEN	*n* pl. -S henequen
HENLIKE	*adj* resembling a hen
HENNA	*v* -ED, -ING, -S to dye with a reddish coloring
HENNERY	*n* pl. -NERIES a poultry farm
HENPECK	*v* -ED, -ING, -S to dominate by nagging
HENRY	*n* pl. -RIES or -RYS a unit of inductance
HENT	*v* -ED, -ING, -S to grasp
HEP	*adj* hip
HEPARIN	*n* pl. -S a biochemical
HEPATIC	*n* pl. -S a drug acting on the liver
HEPATICA	*n* pl. -CAS or -CAE a perennial herb
HEPATIZE	*v* -TIZED, -TIZING, -TIZES to convert tissue into a firm mass
HEPATOMA	*n* pl. -MAS or -MATA a tumor of the liver
HEPCAT	*n* pl. -S a jazz enthusiast
HEPTAD	*n* pl. -S a group of seven
HEPTAGON	*n* pl. -S a seven-sided polygon
HEPTANE	*n* pl. -S a hydrocarbon used as a solvent
HEPTARCH	*n* pl. -S one of a group of seven rulers
HEPTOSE	*n* pl. -S a chemical compound
HER	*pron* the objective or possessive case of the pronoun she
HERALD	*v* -ED, -ING, -S to proclaim
HERALDIC	*adj* pertaining to heraldry
HERALDRY	*n* pl. -RIES the art or science of armorial bearings
HERB	*n* pl. -S a flowering plant with a nonwoody stem
HERBAGE	*n* pl. -S nonwoody plant life
HERBAL	*n* pl. -S a book about herbs and plants
HERBARIA	*n/pl* collections of dried plants
HERBED	*adj* flavored with herbs
HERBIER	comparative of herby
HERBIEST	superlative of herby

HERBLESS   *adj* lacking herbs

HERBLIKE   *adj* resembling an herb

HERBY   *adj* HERBIER, HERBIEST abounding in herbs

HERCULES   *n* pl. -LESES any man of great size and strength

HERD   *v* -ED, -ING, -S to bring together in a herd (a group of animals)

HERDER   *n* pl. -S one who tends a herd

HERDIC   *n* pl. -S a type of carriage

HERDLIKE   *adj* resembling a herd

HERDMAN   *n* pl. -MEN herdsman

HERDSMAN   *n* pl. -MEN a herder

HERE   *n* pl. -S this place

HEREAT   *adj* at this time

HEREAWAY   *adv* in this vicinity

HEREBY   *adv* by this means

HEREDES   pl. of heres

HEREDITY   *n* pl. -TIES the genetic transmission of chracteristics

HEREIN   *adv* in this

HEREINTO   *adv* into this place

HEREOF   *adv* of this

HEREON   *adv* on this

HERES   *n* pl. HEREDES an heir

HERESY   *n* pl. -SIES a belief contrary to a church doctrine

HERETIC   *n* pl. -S one that upholds heresy

HERETO   *adv* to this matter

HERETRIX   *n* pl. -TRIXES or -TRICES heritrix

HEREUNTO   *adv* hereto

HEREUPON   *adv* immediately following this

HEREWITH   *adv* along with this

HERIOT   *n* pl. -S a feudal tribute or payment

HERITAGE   *n* pl. -S something that is inherited

HERITOR   *n* pl. -S one that inherits

HERITRIX   *n* pl. -TRIXES or -TRICES a female heritor

HERL   *n* pl. -S a feathered fishing lure

HERM   *n* pl. -S a type of statue

HERMA   *n* pl. -MAE or -MAI a herm **HERMAEAN** *adj*

HERMETIC   *adj* airtight

HERMIT   *n* pl. -S a recluse **HERMITIC** *adj*

HERMITRY   *n* pl. -RIES the state of being a hermit

HERN   *n* pl. -S a heron

HERNIA   *n* pl. -NIAS or -NIAE the protrusion of an organ through its surrounding wall **HERNIAL** *adj*

HERNIATE   *v* -ATED, -ATING, -ATES to protrude through an abnormal bodily opening

HERO   *n* pl. -ROES or -ROS a hoagie

HEROIC   *n* pl. -S an epic verse

HEROICAL   *adj* courageous; noble

HEROIN   *n* pl. -S an addictive narcotic

HEROINE   *n* pl. -S a brave woman

HEROISM   *n* pl. -S heroic behavior

HEROIZE   *v* -IZED, -IZING, -IZES to make heroic

HERON   *n* pl. -S a wading bird

HERONRY   *n* pl. -RIES a place where herons breed

HERPES   *n* pl. HERPES a skin infection **HERPETIC** *adj*

HERRING   *n* pl. -S a food fish

HERRY   *v* -RIED, -RYING, -RIES to harry

HERS   *pron* the possessive case of the pronoun she

HERSELF   *pron* a form of the 3d person sing. feminine pronoun

HERSTORY   *n* pl. -RIES history with a feminist viewpoint

HERTZ   *n* pl. -ES a unit of frequency

HESITANT   *adj* tending to hesitate

HESITATE   *v* -TATED, -TATING, -TATES to hold back in uncertainty

HESSIAN   *n* pl. -S a coarse cloth

HESSITE   *n* pl. -S a mineral

HEST   *n* pl. -S a command

HET   *n* pl. -S heth

HETAERA   *n* pl. -RAE or -RAS a concubine **HETAERIC** *adj*

HETAIRA   *n* pl. -RAI or -RAS hetaera

HETERO   *n* pl. -EROS a heterosexual

HETH   *n* pl. -S a Hebrew letter

HETMAN   *n* pl. -S a cossack leader

HEUCH   *n* pl. -S heugh

HEUGH   *n* pl. -S a steep cliff

HEW   *v* HEWED, HEWN, HEWING, HEWS to cut with an ax **HEWABLE** *adj*

HEWER	*n* pl. -S one that hews
HEX	*v* -ED, -ING, -ES to cast an evil spell upon
HEXAD	*n* pl. -S a group of six **HEXADIC** *adj*
HEXADE	*n* pl. -S hexad
HEXAGON	*n* pl. -S a polygon having six sides
HEXAGRAM	*n* pl. -S a six-pointed star
HEXAMINE	*n* pl. -S a chemical compound
HEXANE	*n* pl. -S a volatile liquid
HEXAPLA	*n* pl. -S an edition in which six texts are set in parallel columns **HEXAPLAR** *adj*
HEXAPOD	*n* pl. -S a six-legged insect
HEXAPODY	*n* pl. -DIES a line of verse with six feet
HEXARCHY	*n* pl. -CHIES a group of six separate states
HEXER	*n* pl. -S one that hexes
HEXEREI	*n* pl. -S witchcraft
HEXONE	*n* pl. -S a hydrocarbon solvent
HEXOSAN	*n* pl. -S a carbohydrate
HEXOSE	*n* pl. -S a simple sugar
HEXYL	*n* pl. -S a hydrocarbon radical
HEY	*interj* — used to attract attention
HEYDAY	*n* pl. -DAYS the period of one's greatest success
HEYDEY	*n* pl. -DEYS heyday
HI	*interj* — used as a greeting
HIATUS	*n* pl. -ES a gap or missing section **HIATAL** *adj*
HIBACHI	*n* pl. -S a cooking device
HIBERNAL	*adj* pertaining to winter
HIBISCUS	*n* pl. -ES a tropical plant
HIC	*interj* — used to represent a hiccup
HICCOUGH	*v* -ED, -ING, -S to hiccup
HICCUP	*v* -CUPED, -CUPING, -CUPS or -CUPPED, -CUPPING, -CUPS to make a peculiar-sounding, spasmodic inhalation
HICK	*n* pl. -S a rural person **HICKISH** *adj*
HICKEY	*n* pl. HICKEYS or HICKIES a gadget
HICKORY	*n* pl. -RIES a hardwood tree
HID	a past tense of hide
HIDABLE	*adj* able to be hidden
HIDALGO	*n* pl. -GOS a minor Spanish nobleman
HIDDEN	*adj* concealed; obscure **HIDDENLY** *adv*
HIDE	*v* HID, HIDDEN, HIDING, HIDES to conceal
HIDE	*v* HIDED, HIDING, HIDES to flog
HIDEAWAY	*n* pl. -AWAYS a hideout
HIDELESS	*adj* lacking a skin
HIDEOUS	*adj* very ugly
HIDEOUT	*n* pl. -S a place of refuge
HIDER	*n* pl. -S one that hides
HIDING	*n* pl. -S a beating
HIDROSIS	*n* pl. -DROSES abnormal perspiration
HIDROTIC	*n* pl. -S a drug that induces perspiration
HIE	*v* HIED, HIEING or HYING, HIES to hurry
HIEMAL	*adj* pertaining to winter
HIERARCH	*n* pl. -S a religious leader
HIERATIC	*adj* pertaining to priests
HIGGLE	*v* -GLED, -GLING, -GLES to haggle
HIGGLER	*n* pl. -S one that higgles
HIGH	*adj* HIGHER, HIGHEST reaching far upward
HIGH	*n* pl. -S a high level
HIGHBALL	*v* -ED, -ING, -S to go at full speed
HIGHBORN	*adj* of noble birth
HIGHBOY	*n* pl. -BOYS a tall chest of drawers
HIGHBRED	*adj* highborn
HIGHBROW	*n* pl. -S a person who has superior tastes
HIGHBUSH	*adj* forming a tall bush
HIGHJACK	*v* -ED, -ING, -S to hijack
HIGHLAND	*n* pl. -S an elevated region
HIGHLIFE	*n* pl. -S the lifestyle of fashionable society
HIGHLY	*adv* to a high degree
HIGHNESS	*n* pl. -ES the state of being high
HIGHROAD	*n* pl. -S a highway
HIGHSPOT	*n* pl. -S an event of major importance
HIGHT	*v* -ED, -ING, -S to command
HIGHTAIL	*v* -ED, -ING, -S to retreat rapidly

HIGHTH	*n* pl. -S height
HIGHWAY	*n* pl. -WAYS a main road
HIJACK	*v* -ED, -ING, -S to seize a vehicle while in transit
HIJACKER	*n* pl. -S one that hijacks
HIJINKS	*n/pl* mischievous fun
HIKE	*v* HIKED, HIKING, HIKES to walk a long distance
HIKER	*n* pl. -S one that hikes
HILA	pl. of hilum
HILAR	*adj* pertaining to a hilum
HILARITY	*n* pl. -TIES noisy merriment
HILDING	*n* pl. -S a vile person
HILI	pl. of hilus
HILL	*v* -ED, -ING, -S to form into a hill (a rounded elevation)
HILLER	*n* pl. -S one that hills
HILLIER	comparative of hilly
HILLIEST	superlative of hilly
HILLO	*v* -ED, -ING, -S or -ES to hallo
HILLOA	*v* -ED, -ING, -S to hallo
HILLOCK	*n* pl. -S a small hill **HILLOCKY** *adj*
HILLSIDE	*n* pl. -S the side of a hill
HILLTOP	*n* pl. -S the top of a hill
HILLY	*adj* HILLIER, HILLIEST abounding in hills
HILT	*v* -ED, -ING, -S to provide with a hilt (a handle for a weapon)
HILTLESS	*adj* having no hilt
HILUM	*n* pl. HILA a small opening in a bodily organ
HILUS	*n* pl. HILI hilum
HIM	*pron* the objective case of the pronoun he
HIMATION	*n* pl. -MATIA or -MATIONS a loose outer garment
HIMSELF	*pron* a form of the 3d person sing. masculine pronoun
HIN	*n* pl. -S a Hebrew unit of liquid measure
HIND	*n* pl. -S a female red deer
HINDER	*v* -ED, -ING, -S to impede
HINDERER	*n/pl* -S one that hinders
HINDGUT	*n* pl. -S the rear part of the alimentary canal
HINDMOST	*adj* farthest to the rear
HINGE	*v* HINGED, HINGING, HINGES to attach a jointed device
HINGER	*n* pl. -S one that hinges
HINNY	*v* -NIED, -NYING, -NIES to whinny
HINT	*v* -ED, -ING, -S to suggest indirectly
HINTER	*n* pl. -S one that hints
HIP	*v* HIPPED, HIPPING, HIPS to build a type of roof
HIP	*adj* HIPPER, HIPPEST aware of the most current styles and trends
HIPBONE	*n* pl. -S a pelvic bone
HIPLESS	*adj* lacking a hip (the pelvic joint)
HIPLIKE	*adj* suggestive of a hip
HIPLINE	*n* pl. -S the distance around the hips
HIPNESS	*n* pl. -ES the state of being hip
HIPPARCH	*n* pl. -S a cavalry commander in ancient Greece
HIPPED	past tense of hip
HIPPER	comparative of hip
HIPPEST	superlative of hip
HIPPIE	*n* pl. -S a nonconformist
HIPPIER	comparative of hippy
HIPPIEST	superlative of hippy
HIPPING	present participle of hip
HIPPISH	*adj* depressed; sad
HIPPO	*n* pl. -POS a hippopotamus
HIPPY	*adj* -PIER, -PIEST having big hips
HIPSHOT	*adj* lame; awkward
HIPSTER	*n* pl. -S one that is hip
HIRABLE	*adj* available for hire
HIRAGANA	*n* pl. -S a Japanese cursive script
HIRCINE	*adj* pertaining to a goat
HIRE	*v* HIRED, HIRING, HIRES to engage the services of for payment **HIREABLE** *adj*
HIRELING	*n* pl. -S one that works for money only
HIRER	*n* pl. -S one that hires
HIRING	present participle of hire
HIRPLE	*v* -PLED, -PLING, -PLES to limp
HIRSEL	*v* -SELED, -SELING, -SELS or -SELLED, -SELLING, -SELS to herd sheep

HIRSLE	*v* -SLED, -SLING, -SLES to slide along
HIRSUTE	*adj* hairy
HIRUDIN	*n* pl. -S an anticoagulant
HIS	*pron* the possessive form of the pronoun he
HISN	*pron* his
HISPID	*adj* covered with stiff hairs
HISS	*v* -ED, -ING, -ES to make a sibilant sound
HISSELF	*pron* himself
HISSER	*n* pl. -S one that hisses
HISSING	*n* pl. -S an object of scorn
HISSY	*n* pl. HISSIES a tantrum
HIST	*v* -ED, -ING, -S to hoist
HISTAMIN	*n* pl. -S an amine released in allergic reactions
HISTIDIN	*n* pl. -S an amino acid
HISTOGEN	*n* pl. -S interior plant tissue
HISTOID	*adj* pertaining to connective tissue
HISTONE	*n* pl. -S a simple protein
HISTORIC	*adj* important in history
HISTORY	*n* pl. -RIES a chronological record of past events
HIT	*v* HIT, HITTING, HITS to strike forcibly
HITCH	*v* -ED, -ING, -ES to fasten with a knot or hook
HITCHER	*n* pl. -S one that hitches
HITHER	*adv* toward this place
HITHERTO	*adv* up to now
HITLESS	*adj* being without a hit
HITTER	*n* pl. -S one that hits
HITTING	present participle of hit
HIVE	*v* HIVED, HIVING, HIVES to cause to enter a hive (a bee's nest)
HIVELESS	*adj* lacking a hive
HIZZONER	*n* pl. -S — used as a title for a mayor
HM	*interj* hmm
HMM	*interj* — used to express thoughtful consideration
HO	*interj* — used to express surprise
HOACTZIN	*n* pl. -S or -ES hoatzin
HOAGIE	*n* pl. -S a long sandwich
HOAGY	*n* pl. -GIES hoagie
HOAR	*n* pl. -S a white coating
HOARD	*v* -ED, -ING, -S to gather and store away
HOARDER	*n* pl. -S one that hoards
HOARDING	*n* pl. -S something hoarded
HOARIER	comparative of hoary
HOARIEST	superlative of hoary
HOARILY	*adv* in a hoary manner
HOARSE	*adj* HOARSER, HOARSEST low and rough in sound **HOARSELY** *adv*
HOARSEN	*v* -ED, -ING, -S to make hoarse
HOARY	*adj* HOARIER, HOARIEST white with age
HOATZIN	*n* pl. -S or -ES a tropical bird
HOAX	*v* -ED, -ING, -ES to deceive
HOAXER	*n* pl. -S one that hoaxes
HOB	*v* HOBBED, HOBBING, HOBS to furnish with hobnails
HOBBIES	pl. of hobby
HOBBIT	*n* pl. -S a fictitious creature that lives underground
HOBBLE	*v* -BLED, -BLING, -BLES to limp
HOBBLER	*n* pl. -S one that hobbles
HOBBY	*n* pl. -BIES a recreational pastime
HOBBYIST	*n* pl. -S one that pursues a hobby
HOBLIKE	*adj* suggestive of an elf
HOBNAIL	*v* -ED, -ING, -S to put hobnails (short nails with a broad head) on a shoe sole
HOBNOB	*v* -NOBBED, -NOBBING, -NOBS to associate in a friendly way
HOBO	*v* -ED, -ING, -S or -ES to live like a hobo (a vagrant or tramp)
HOBOISM	*n* pl. -S the state of being a hobo
HOCK	*v* -ED, -ING, -S to pawn
HOCKER	*n* pl. -S one that hocks
HOCKEY	*n* pl. -EYS a game played on ice
HOCKSHOP	*n* pl. -S a pawnshop
HOCUS	*v* -CUSED, -CUSING, -CUSES or -CUSSED, -CUSSING, -CUSSES to deceive or cheat
HOD	*n* pl. -S a portable trough
HODAD	*n* pl. -S a nonsurfer
HODADDY	*n* pl. -DIES hodad
HODDEN	*n* pl. -S a coarse cloth
HODDIN	*n* pl. -S hodden

HOE   v HOED, HOEING, HOES to use a hoe (a gardening tool)

HOECAKE   n pl. -S a cornmeal cake

HOEDOWN   n pl. -S a square dance

HOELIKE   adj resembling a hoe

HOER   n pl. -S one that hoes

HOG   v HOGGED, HOGGING, HOGS to take more than one's share

HOGAN   n pl. -S a Navaho Indian dwelling

HOGBACK   n pl. -S a sharp ridge

HOGFISH   n pl. -ES a tropical fish

HOGG   n pl. -S a young sheep

HOGGED   past tense of hog

HOGGER   n pl. -S one that hogs

HOGGET   n pl. -S a young unshorn sheep

HOGGING   present participle of hog

HOGGISH   adj coarsely selfish

HOGLIKE   adj hoggish

HOGMANAY   n pl. -NAYS a Scottish celebration

HOGMANE   n pl. -S hogmanay

HOGMENAY   n pl. -NAYS hogmanay

HOGNOSE   n pl. -S a nonvenomous snake

HOGNUT   n pl. -S a hickory nut

HOGSHEAD   n pl. -S a large cask

HOGTIE   v -TIED, -TIEING or -TYING, -TIES to tie together the legs of

HOGWASH   n pl. -ES meaningless talk

HOGWEED   n pl. -S a coarse plant

HOICK   v -ED, -ING, -S to change directions abruptly

HOIDEN   v -ED, -ING, -S to hoyden

HOISE   v HOISED, HOISING, HOISES to hoist

HOIST   v -ED, -ING, -S to haul up by some mechanical means

HOISTER   n pl. -S one that hoists

HOKE   v HOKED, HOKING, HOKES to give false value to

HOKEY   adj HOKIER, HOKIEST false; contrived **HOKILY** adv

HOKINESS   n pl. -ES the state of being hokey

HOKKU   n pl. HOKKU haiku

HOKUM   n pl. -S nonsense

HOKYPOKY   n pl. -KIES trickery

HOLARD   n pl. -S the total quantity of water in the soil

HOLD   v HELD, HOLDEN, HOLDING, HOLDS to maintain possession of **HOLDABLE** adj

HOLDALL   n pl. -S a carrying case

HOLDBACK   n pl. -S a restraining device

HOLDEN   a past participle of hold

HOLDER   n pl. -S one that holds

HOLDFAST   n pl. -S a fastening device

HOLDING   n pl. -S something held

HOLDOUT   n pl. -S one who delays signing a contract

HOLDOVER   n pl. -S something left over

HOLDUP   n pl. -S a delay

HOLE   v HOLED, HOLING, HOLES to make a hole (a cavity in a solid)

HOLELESS   adj lacking a hole

HOLEY   adj full of holes

HOLIBUT   n pl. -S halibut

HOLIDAY   v -ED, -ING, -S to take a vacation

HOLIER   comparative of holy

HOLIES   pl. of holy

HOLIEST   superlative of holy

HOLILY   adv in a holy manner

HOLINESS   n pl. -ES the state of being holy

HOLING   present participle of hole

HOLISM   n pl. -S a philosophical theory

HOLIST   n pl. -S one who adheres to the theory of holism **HOLISTIC** adj

HOLK   v -ED, -ING, -S to howk

HOLLA   v -ED, -ING, -S to hallo

HOLLAND   n pl. -S a cotton fabric

HOLLER   v -ED, -ING, -S to yell

HOLLIES   pl. of holly

HOLLO   v -ED, -ING, -S or -ES to hallo

HOLLOA   v -ED, -ING, -S to hallo

HOLLOO   v -ED, -ING, -S to hallo

HOLLOW   adj -LOWER, -LOWEST not solid **HOLLOWLY** adv

HOLLOW   v -ED, -ING, -S to make hollow

HOLLY   n pl. -LIES a tree

HOLM   n pl. -S an island in a river

HOLMIUM   n pl. -S a metallic element **HOLMIC** adj

HOLOGAMY   n pl. -MIES the state of having gametes of the same size and form as other cells

HOLOGRAM *n* pl. -S a three-dimensional photograph

HOLOGYNY *n* pl. -NIES a trait transmitted solely in the female line

HOLOTYPE *n* pl. -S an animal or plant specimen

HOLOZOIC *adj* eating solid foods

HOLP a past tense of help

HOLPEN a past participle of help

HOLS *n/pl* a vacation

HOLSTEIN *n* pl. -S a breed of cattle

HOLSTER *n* pl. -S a case for a pistol

HOLT *n* pl. -S a grove

HOLY *adj* -LIER, -LIEST having a divine nature or origin

HOLY *n* pl. -LIES a holy place

HOLYDAY *n* pl. -DAYS a religious holiday

HOLYTIDE *n* pl. -S a time of religious observance

HOMAGE *v* -AGED, -AGING, -AGES to pay tribute to

HOMAGER *n* pl. -S a feudal vassal

HOMBRE *n* pl. -S a fellow

HOMBURG *n* pl. -S a felt hat

HOME *v* HOMED, HOMING, HOMES to return to one's home (place of residence)

HOMEBODY *n* pl. -BODIES one who likes to stay at home

HOMEBOY *n* pl. -BOYS a boy or man from one's neighborhood

HOMEBRED *n* pl. -S a native athlete

HOMED past tense of home

HOMELAND *n* pl. -S one's native land

HOMELESS *adj* lacking a home

HOMELIKE *adj* suggestive of a home

HOMELY *adj* -LIER, -LIEST unattractive

HOMEMADE *adj* made at home

HOMEOBOX *n* pl. -ES a short DNA sequence

HOMEOTIC *adj* being a gene producing a shift in development

HOMEPORT *v* -ED, -ING, -S to assign a ship to a port

HOMER *v* -ED, -ING, -S to hit a home run

HOMEROOM *n* pl. -S the classroom where pupils report before classes begin

HOMESICK *adj* longing for home

HOMESITE *n* pl. -S a location for a house

HOMESPUN *n* pl. -S a loosely woven fabric

HOMESTAY *n* pl. -STAYS a period during which a visitor in a foreign country lives with a local family

HOMETOWN *n* pl. -S the town of one's birth or residence

HOMEWARD *adv* toward home

HOMEWORK *n* pl. -S work done at home

HOMEY *adj* HOMIER, HOMIEST homelike

HOMICIDE *n* pl. -S the killing of one person by another

HOMIER comparative of homy

HOMIEST superlative of homy

HOMILIST *n* pl. -S one that delivers a homily

HOMILY *n* pl. -LIES a sermon

HOMINES a pl. of homo

HOMINESS *n* pl. -ES the quality of being homey

HOMING present participle of home

HOMINIAN *n* pl. -S a hominid

HOMINID *n* pl. -S a manlike creature

HOMINIES pl. of hominy

HOMININE *adj* characteristic of man

HOMINIZE *v* -NIZED, -NIZING, -NIZES to alter the environment to conform with evolving man

HOMINOID *n* pl. -S a manlike animal

HOMINY *n* pl. -NIES hulled, dried corn

HOMMOCK *n* pl. -S a ridge in an ice field

HOMMOS *n* pl. -ES hummus

HOMO *n* pl. HOMINES or HOMOS a member of the genus that includes modern man

HOMOGAMY *n* pl. -MIES the bearing of sexually similar flowers

HOMOGENY *n* pl. -NIES correspondence in form or structure

HOMOGONY *n* pl. -NIES the condition of having flowers with uniform stamens and pistils

HOMOLOG *n* pl. -S something that exhibits homology

HOMOLOGY *n* pl. -GIES similarity in structure

HOMONYM *n* pl. -S a namesake

HOMONYMY *n* pl. -MIES the condition of having the same name

HOMOSEX *n* pl. -ES homosexuality

HOMY *adj* HOMIER, HOMIEST homey

HON	*n* pl. -S a honeybun
HONAN	*n* pl. -S a fine silk
HONCHO	*v* -ED, -ING, -S to take charge of
HONDA	*n* pl. -S a part of a lariat
HONDLE	*v* -DLED, -DLING, -DLES to haggle
HONE	*v* HONED, HONING, HONES to sharpen
HONER	*n* pl. -S one that hones
HONEST	*adj* -ESTER, -ESTEST truthful **HONESTLY** *adv*
HONESTY	*n* pl. -TIES truthfulness
HONEWORT	*n* pl. -S a perennial herb
HONEY	*v* HONEYED or HONIED, HONEYING, HONEYS to sweeten with honey (a sweet, viscid fluid)
HONEYBEE	*n* pl. -S a type of bee
HONEYBUN	*n* pl. -S a sweetheart
HONEYDEW	*n* pl. -S a sweet fluid
HONEYFUL	*adj* containing much honey
HONG	*n* pl. -S a Chinese factory
HONIED	a past tense of honey
HONING	present participle of hone
HONK	*v* -ED, -ING, -S to emit a cry like that of a goose
HONKER	*n* pl. -S one that honks
HONOR	*v* -ED, -ING, -S to respect
HONORAND	*n* pl. -S an honoree
HONORARY	*n* pl. -ARIES an honor society
HONOREE	*n* pl. -S one that receives an honor
HONORER	*n* pl. -S one that honors
HONOUR	*v* -ED, -ING, -S to honor
HONOURER	*n* pl. -S honorer
HOOCH	*n* pl. -ES cheap whiskey
HOOD	*v* -ED, -ING, -S to furnish with a hood (a covering for the head)
HOODIE	*n* pl. -S a gray crow of Europe
HOODIER	comparative of hoody
HOODIEST	superlative of hoody
HOODLESS	*adj* lacking a hood
HOODLIKE	*adj* resembling a hood
HOODLUM	*n* pl. -S a thug
HOODOO	*v* -ED, -ING, -S to jinx
HOODWINK	*v* -ED, -ING, -S to trick
HOODY	*adj* HOODIER, HOODIEST resembling a hoodlum
HOOEY	*n* pl. -EYS nonsense

HOOF	*v* -ED, -ING, -S to dance
HOOF	*n* pl. HOOVES or HOOFS the hard covering on the feet of certain animals
HOOFBEAT	*n* pl. -S the sound of hooves striking the ground
HOOFER	*n* pl. -S a professional dancer
HOOFLESS	*adj* lacking hooves
HOOFLIKE	*adj* resembling a hoof
HOOK	*v* -ED, -ING, -S to catch with a hook (a bent piece of metal)
HOOKA	*n* pl. -S hookah
HOOKAH	*n* pl. -S a water pipe
HOOKER	*n* pl. -S a prostitute
HOOKEY	*n* pl. -EYS hooky
HOOKIER	comparative of hooky
HOOKIES	pl. of hooky
HOOKIEST	superlative of hooky
HOOKLESS	*adj* lacking a hook
HOOKLET	*n* pl. -S a small hook
HOOKLIKE	*adj* resembling a hook
HOOKNOSE	*n* pl. -S an aquiline nose
HOOKUP	*n* pl. -S an electrical assemblage
HOOKWORM	*n* pl. -S a parasitic worm
HOOKY	*n* pl. HOOKIES truancy
HOOKY	*adj* HOOKIER, HOOKIEST full of hooks
HOOLIE	*adj* easy; slow
HOOLIGAN	*n* pl. -S a hoodlum
HOOLY	*adj* hoolie
HOOP	*v* -ED, -ING, -S to fasten with a hoop (a circular band of metal)
HOOPER	*n* pl. -S one that hoops
HOOPLA	*n* pl. -S commotion
HOOPLESS	*adj* lacking a hoop
HOOPLIKE	*adj* suggestive of a hoop
HOOPOE	*n* pl. -S a European bird
HOOPOO	*n* pl. -POOS hoopoe
HOOPSTER	*n* pl. -S a basketball player
HOORAH	*v* -ED, -ING, -S to hurrah
HOORAY	*v* -ED, -ING, -S to hurrah
HOOSEGOW	*n* pl. -S a jail
HOOSGOW	*n* pl. -S hoosegow
HOOT	*v* -ED, -ING, -S to cry like an owl
HOOTCH	*n* pl. -ES hooch
HOOTER	*n* pl. -S one that hoots

HOOTY *adj* HOOTIER, HOOTIEST sounding like the cry of an owl

HOOVED *adj* having hooves

HOOVES a pl. of hoof

HOP *v* HOPPED, HOPPING, HOPS to move by jumping on one foot

HOPE *v* HOPED, HOPING, HOPES to have a desire or expectation

HOPEFUL *n* pl. -S one that aspires

HOPELESS *adj* despairing

HOPER *n* pl. -S one that hopes

HOPHEAD *n* pl. -S a drug addict

HOPING present participle of hope

HOPLITE *n* pl. -S a foot soldier of ancient Greece **HOPLITIC** *adj*

HOPPED past tense of hop

HOPPER *n* pl. -S one that hops

HOPPING *n* pl. -S a going from one place to another of the same kind

HOPPLE *v* -PLED, -PLING, -PLES to hobble

HOPPY *adj* -PIER, -PIEST having the taste of hops (catkins of a particular vine)

HOPSACK *n* pl. -S a coarse fabric

HOPTOAD *n* pl. -S a toad

HORA *n* pl. -S an Israeli dance

HORAH *n* pl. -S hora

HORAL *adj* hourly

HORARY *adj* hourly

HORDE *v* HORDED, HORDING, HORDES to gather in a large group

HORDEIN *n* pl. -S a simple protein

HORIZON *n* pl. -S the line where the sky seems to meet the earth

HORMONE *n* pl. -S a secretion of the endocrine organs **HORMONAL, HORMONIC** *adj*

HORN *v* -ED, -ING, -S to form a horn (a hard, bonelike projection of the head)

HORNBEAM *n* pl. -S a small tree

HORNBILL *n* pl. -S a large-billed bird

HORNBOOK *n* pl. -S a primer

HORNET *n* pl. -S a stinging insect

HORNFELS *n* pl. HORNFELS a silicate rock

HORNIER comparative of horny

HORNIEST superlative of horny

HORNILY *adv* in a horny manner

HORNIST *n* pl. -S a French horn player

HORNITO *n* pl. -TOS a mound of volcanic matter

HORNLESS *adj* lacking a horn

HORNLIKE *adj* resembling a horn

HORNPIPE *n* pl. -S a musical instrument

HORNPOUT *n* pl. -S a catfish

HORNTAIL *n* pl. -S a wasplike insect

HORNWORM *n* pl. -S the larva of a hawkmoth

HORNWORT *n* pl. -S an aquatic herb

HORNY *adj* HORNIER, HORNIEST hornlike in hardness

HOROLOGE *n* pl. -S a timepiece

HOROLOGY *n* pl. -GIES the science of measuring time

HORRENT *adj* bristling; standing erect

HORRIBLE *n* pl. -S something that causes horror

HORRIBLY *adv* dreadfully

HORRID *adj* repulsive **HORRIDLY** *adv*

HORRIFIC *adj* causing horror

HORRIFY *v* -FIED, -FYING, -FIES to cause to feel horror

HORROR *n* pl. -S a feeling of intense fear or repugnance

HORSE *v* HORSED, HORSING, HORSES to provide with a horse (a large, hoofed mammal)

HORSECAR *n* pl. -S a streetcar drawn by a horse

HORSEFLY *n* pl. -FLIES a large fly

HORSEMAN *n* pl. -MEN one who rides a horse

HORSEPOX *n* pl. -ES a skin disease of horses

HORSEY *adj* HORSIER, HORSIEST horsy

HORSIER comparative of horsy

HORSIEST superlative of horsy

HORSILY *adv* in a horsy manner

HORSING present participle of horse

HORST *n* pl. -S a portion of the earth's crust

HORSTE *n* pl. -S horst

HORSY *adj* HORSIER, HORSIEST resembling a horse

HOSANNA *v* -ED, -ING, -S to praise

HOSANNAH *interj* — used to express praise to God

HOSE   *v* HOSED, HOSING, HOSES to spray with water

HOSE   *n* pl. HOSEN stockings or socks

HOSEL   *n* pl. -S a part of a golf club

HOSEPIPE   *n* pl. -S a flexible tube for conveying fluids

HOSIER   *n* pl. -S one that makes hose

HOSIERY   *n* pl. -SIERIES hose

HOSING   present participle of hose

HOSPICE   *n* pl. -S a shelter

HOSPITAL   *n* pl. -S a medical institution

HOSPITIA   *n/pl* places of shelter

HOSPODAR   *n* pl. -S a governor of a region under Turkish rule

HOST   *v* -ED, -ING, -S to entertain socially

HOSTA   *n* pl. -S a plantain lily

HOSTAGE   *n* pl. -S a person held as security

HOSTEL   *v* -TELED, -TELING, -TELS or -TELLED, -TELLING, -TELS to stay at inns overnight while traveling

HOSTELER   *n* pl. -S an innkeeper

HOSTELRY   *n* pl. -RIES an inn

HOSTESS   *v* -ED, -ING, -ES to act as a hostess (a woman who entertains socially)

HOSTILE   *n* pl. -S an unfriendly person

HOSTLER   *n* pl. -S a person who tends horses or mules

HOSTLY   *adj* pertaining to one who hosts

HOT   *adj* HOTTER, HOTTEST having a high temperature

HOT   *v* HOTTED, HOTTING, HOTS to heat

HOTBED   *n* pl. -S a bed of rich soil

HOTBLOOD   *n* pl. -S a thoroughbred horse

HOTBOX   *n* pl. -ES an overheated bearing of a railroad car

HOTCAKE   *n* pl. -S a pancake

HOTCH   *v* -ED, -ING, -ES to wiggle

HOTCHPOT   *n* pl. -S the combining of properties in order to divide them equally among heirs

HOTDOG   *v* -DOGGED, -DOGGING, -DOGS to perform showily

HOTEL   *n* pl. -S a public lodging

HOTELDOM   *n* pl. -S hotels and hotel workers

HOTELIER   *n* pl. -S a hotel manager

HOTELMAN   *n* pl. -MEN a hotelier

HOTFOOT   *v* -FOOTED, -FOOTING, -FOOTS to hurry

HOTHEAD   *n* pl. -S a quick-tempered person

HOTHOUSE   *n* pl. -S a heated greenhouse

HOTLINE   *n* pl. -S a direct communications system for immediate contact

HOTLY   *adv* in a hot manner

HOTNESS   *n* pl. -ES the state of being hot

HOTPRESS   *v* -ED, -ING, -ES to subject to heat and pressure

HOTROD   *n* pl. -S a car modified for high speeds

HOTSHOT   *n* pl. -S a showily skillful person

HOTSPUR   *n* pl. -S a hothead

HOTTED   past tense of hot

HOTTER   comparative of hot

HOTTEST   superlative of hot

HOTTING   present participle of hot

HOTTISH   *adj* somewhat hot

HOUDAH   *n* pl. -S howdah

HOUND   *v* -ED, -ING, -S to pursue relentlessly

HOUNDER   *n* pl. -S one that hounds

HOUR   *n* pl. -S a period of sixty minutes

HOURI   *n* pl. -S a beautiful maiden in Muslim belief

HOURLY   *adj* occurring every hour

HOUSE   *v* HOUSED, HOUSING, HOUSES to lodge in a house (a building in which people live)

HOUSEBOY   *n* pl. -BOYS a male servant

HOUSEFLY   *n* pl. -FLIES a common fly

HOUSEFUL   *n* pl. -S as much as a house will hold

HOUSEL   *v* -SELED, -SELING, -SELS or -SELLED, -SELLING, -SELS to administer the Eucharist to

HOUSEMAN   *n* pl. -MEN a male servant

HOUSER   *n* pl. -S one who organizes housing projects

HOUSESIT   *v* -SAT, -SITTING, -SITS to occupy a dwelling while the tenants are away

HOUSETOP   *n* pl. -S the roof of a house

HOUSING   *n* pl. -S any dwelling place

HOVE   a past tense of heave

HOVEL   *v* -ELED, -ELING, -ELS or -ELLED, -ELLING, -ELS to live in a small, miserable dwelling

HOVER	*v* -ED, -ING, -S to hang suspended in the air
HOVERER	*n* pl. -S something that hovers
HOW	*n* pl. -S a method of doing something
HOWBEIT	*adv* nevertheless
HOWDAH	*n* pl. -S a seat on an elephant or camel for riders
HOWDIE	*n* pl. -S a midwife
HOWDY	*v* -DIED, -DYING, -DIES to greet with the words "how do you do"
HOWE	*n* pl. -S a valley
HOWEVER	*adv* nevertheless
HOWF	*n* pl. -S a place frequently visited
HOWFF	*n* pl. -S howf
HOWITZER	*n* pl. -S a short cannon
HOWK	*v* -ED, -ING, -S to dig
HOWL	*v* -ED, -ING, -S to cry like a dog
HOWLER	*n* pl. -S one that howls
HOWLET	*n* pl. -S an owl
HOY	*n* pl. HOYS a heavy barge or scow
HOYA	*n* pl. -S a flowering plant
HOYDEN	*v* -ED, -ING, -S to act like a tomboy
HOYLE	*n* pl. -S a rule book
HUARACHE	*n* pl. -S a flat-heeled sandal
HUARACHO	*n* pl. -CHOS huarache
HUB	*n* pl. -S the center of a wheel
HUBBLY	*adj* having an uneven surface
HUBBUB	*n* pl. -S an uproar
HUBBY	*n* pl. -BIES a husband
HUBCAP	*n* pl. -S a covering for the hub of a wheel
HUBRIS	*n* pl. -BRISES arrogance
HUCK	*n* pl. -S a durable fabric
HUCKLE	*n* pl. -S the hip
HUCKSTER	*v* -ED, -ING, -S to peddle
HUDDLE	*v* -DLED, -DLING, -DLES to crowd together
HUDDLER	*n* pl. -S one that huddles
HUE	*n* pl. -S color **HUED, HUELESS** *adj*
HUFF	*v* -ED, -ING, -S to breathe heavily
HUFFISH	*adj* sulky
HUFFY	*adj* HUFFIER, HUFFIEST easily offended **HUFFILY** *adv*
HUG	*v* HUGGED, HUGGING, HUGS to clasp tightly in the arms
HUGE	*adj* HUGER, HUGEST very large **HUGELY** *adv*
HUGENESS	*n* pl. -ES the quality of being huge
HUGEOUS	*adj* huge
HUGER	comparative of huge
HUGEST	superlative of huge
HUGGABLE	*adj* cuddlesome
HUGGED	past tense of hug
HUGGER	*n* pl. -S one that hugs
HUGGING	present participle of hug
HUH	*interj* — used to express surprise
HUIC	*interj* — used to encourage hunting hounds
HUIPIL	*n* pl. -S or -ES an embroidered blouse or dress of Mexico
HUISACHE	*n* pl. -S a flowering plant
HULA	*n* pl. -S a Hawaiian dance
HULK	*v* -ED, -ING, -S to appear impressively large
HULKY	*adj* HULKIER, HULKIEST massive
HULL	*v* -ED, -ING, -S to remove the shell from a seed
HULLER	*n* pl. -S one that hulls
HULLO	*v* -ED, -ING, -S or -ES to hallo
HULLOA	*v* -ED, -ING, -S to hallo
HUM	*v* HUMMED, HUMMING, HUMS to sing without opening the lips or saying words
HUMAN	*n* pl. -S a person
HUMANE	*adj* -MANER, -MANEST compassionate **HUMANELY** *adv*
HUMANISE	*v* -ISED, -ISING, -ISES to humanize
HUMANISM	*n* pl. -S the quality of being human
HUMANIST	*n* pl. -S one who studies human nature
HUMANITY	*n* pl. -TIES the human race
HUMANIZE	*v* -IZED, -IZING, -IZES to make human
HUMANLY	*adv* in a human manner
HUMANOID	*n* pl. -S something having human form
HUMATE	*n* pl. -S a chemical salt
HUMBLE	*adj* -BLER, -BLEST modest

HUMBLE   *v* -BLED, -BLING, -BLES to reduce the pride of

HUMBLER   *n* pl. -S one that humbles

HUMBLEST   superlative of humble

HUMBLING   present participle of humble

HUMBLY   *adv* in a humble manner

HUMBUG   *v* -BUGGED, -BUGGING, -BUGS to deceive

HUMDRUM   *n* pl. -S a dull, boring person

HUMERAL   *n* pl. -S a bone of the shoulder

HUMERUS   *n* pl. -MERI the large bone of the upper arm

HUMIC   *adj* derived from humus

HUMID   *adj* having much humidity

HUMIDIFY   *v* -FIED, -FYING, -FIES to make humid

HUMIDITY   *n* pl. -TIES moisture of the air

HUMIDLY   *adv* in a humid manner

HUMIDOR   *n* pl. -S a cigar case

HUMIFIED   *adj* converted into humus

HUMILITY   *n* pl. -TIES the quality of being humble

HUMMABLE   *adj* capable of being hummed

HUMMED   past tense of hum

HUMMER   *n* pl. -S one that hums

HUMMING   present participle of hum

HUMMOCK   *v* -ED, -ING, -S to form into hummocks (small rounded hills)

HUMMOCKY   *adj* abounding in hummocks

HUMMUS   *n* pl. -ES a paste of pureed chickpeas and tahini

HUMOR   *v* -ED, -ING, -S to indulge

HUMORAL   *adj* pertaining to bodily fluids

HUMORFUL   *adj* humorous

HUMORIST   *n* pl. -S a humorous writer or entertainer

HUMOROUS   *adj* funny; witty

HUMOUR   *v* -ED, -ING, -S to humor

HUMP   *v* -ED, -ING, -S to arch into a hump (a rounded protuberance)

HUMPBACK   *n* pl. -S a humped back

HUMPH   *v* -ED, -ING, -S to utter a grunt

HUMPLESS   *adj* lacking a hump

HUMPY   *adj* HUMPIER, HUMPIEST full of humps

HUMUS   *n* pl. -ES decomposed organic matter

HUMVEE   *n* pl. -S a type of motor vehicle

HUN   *n* pl. -S a barbarous, destructive person

HUNCH   *v* -ED, -ING, -ES to arch forward

HUNDRED   *n* pl. -S a number

HUNG   a past tense of hang

HUNGER   *v* -ED, -ING, -S to crave

HUNGOVER   *adj* suffering from a hangover

HUNGRY   *adj* -GRIER, -GRIEST wanting food **HUNGRILY** *adv*

HUNH   *interj* — used to ask for a repetition of an utterance

HUNK   *n* pl. -S a large piece

HUNKER   *v* -ED, -ING, -S to squat

HUNKY   *adj* HUNKIER, HUNKIEST muscular and attractive

HUNNISH   *adj* resembling a hun

HUNT   *v* -ED, -ING, -S to pursue for food or sport **HUNTABLE** *adj* **HUNTEDLY** *adv*

HUNTER   *n* pl. -S one that hunts

HUNTING   *n* pl. -S an instance of searching

HUNTRESS   *n* pl. -ES a female hunter

HUNTSMAN   *n* pl. -MEN a hunter

HUP   *interj* — used to mark a marching cadence

HURDIES   *n/pl* the buttocks

HURDLE   *v* -DLED, -DLING, -DLES to jump over

HURDLER   *n* pl. -S one that hurdles

HURDS   *n/pl* hards

HURL   *v* -ED, -ING, -S to throw with great force

HURLER   *n* pl. -S one that hurls

HURLEY   *n* pl. -LEYS hurling

HURLING   *n* pl. -S an Irish game

HURLY   *n* pl. -LIES commotion

HURRAH   *v* -ED, -ING, -S to cheer

HURRAY   *v* -ED, -ING, -S to hurrah

HURRIER   *n* pl. -S one that hurries

HURRY   *v* -RIED, -RYING, -RIES to move swiftly

HURST   *n* pl. -S a small hill

HURT   *v* HURT, HURTING, HURTS to injure

HURTER   *n* pl. -S one that hurts

HURTFUL   *adj* causing injury

HURTLE   *v* -TLED, -TLING, -TLES to rush violently

HURTLESS	*adj* harmless
HUSBAND	*v* -ED, -ING, -S to spend wisely
HUSH	*v* -ED, -ING, -ES to quiet **HUSHEDLY** *adv*
HUSHABY	*v* go to sleep — used imperatively to soothe a child
HUSHFUL	*adj* quiet
HUSK	*v* -ED, -ING, -S to remove the husk (the outer covering) from
HUSKER	*n* pl. -S one that husks
HUSKIER	comparative of husky
HUSKIES	pl. of husky
HUSKIEST	superlative of husky
HUSKILY	*adv* in a husky manner
HUSKING	*n* pl. -S a gathering of families to husk corn
HUSKLIKE	*adj* resembling a husk
HUSKY	*adj* -KIER, -KIEST hoarse
HUSKY	*n* pl. -KIES an Eskimo dog
HUSSAR	*n* pl. -S a cavalry soldier
HUSSY	*n* pl. -SIES a lewd woman
HUSTINGS	*n* pl. HUSTINGS a British court
HUSTLE	*v* -TLED, -TLING, -TLES to hurry
HUSTLER	*n* pl. -S one that hustles
HUSWIFE	*n* pl. -WIFES or -WIVES a sewing kit
HUT	*v* HUTTED, HUTTING, HUTS to live in a hut (a simple shelter)
HUTCH	*v* -ED, -ING, -ES to store away
HUTLIKE	*adj* resembling a hut
HUTMENT	*n* pl. -S a group of huts
HUTTED	past tense of hut
HUTTING	present participle of hut
HUTZPA	*n* pl. -S chutzpah
HUTZPAH	*n* pl. -S chutzpah
HUZZA	*v* -ED, -ING, -S to cheer
HUZZAH	*v* -ED, -ING, -S to huzza
HWAN	*n* pl. HWAN a monetary unit of South Korea
HYACINTH	*n* pl. -S a flowering plant
HYAENA	*n* pl. -S hyena **HYAENIC** *adj*
HYALIN	*n* pl. -S hyaline
HYALINE	*n* pl. -S a transparent substance
HYALITE	*n* pl. -S a colorless opal
HYALOGEN	*n* pl. -S a substance found in animal cells
HYALOID	*n* pl. -S a membrane of the eye
HYBRID	*n* pl. -S the offspring of genetically dissimilar parents
HYBRIS	*n* pl. -BRISES hubris
HYDATID	*n* pl. -S a cyst caused by a tapeworm
HYDRA	*n* pl. -DRAS or -DRAE a freshwater polyp
HYDRACID	*n* pl. -S an acid
HYDRAGOG	*n* pl. -S a purgative causing watery discharges
HYDRANT	*n* pl. -S an outlet from a water main
HYDRANTH	*n* pl. -S the oral opening of a hydra
HYDRASE	*n* pl. -S an enzyme
HYDRATE	*v* -DRATED, -DRATING, -DRATES to combine with water
HYDRATOR	*n* pl. -S one that hydrates
HYDRIA	*n* pl. -DRIAE a water jar
HYDRIC	*adj* pertaining to moisture
HYDRID	*n* pl. -S hydride
HYDRIDE	*n* pl. -S a chemical compound
HYDRO	*n* pl. -DROS electricity produced by waterpower
HYDROGEL	*n* pl. -S a colloid
HYDROGEN	*n* pl. -S a gaseous element
HYDROID	*n* pl. -S a polyp
HYDROMEL	*n* pl. -S a mixture of honey and water
HYDRONIC	*adj* pertaining to heating and cooling by water
HYDROPIC	*adj* affected with hydropsy
HYDROPS	*n* pl. -ES hydropsy
HYDROPSY	*n* pl. -SIES dropsy
HYDROSKI	*n* pl. -S a plate attached to a seaplane to facilitate takeoffs and landings
HYDROSOL	*n* pl. -S an aqueous solution of a colloid
HYDROUS	*adj* containing water
HYDROXY	*adj* containing hydroxyl
HYDROXYL	*n* pl. -S the radical or group containing oxygen and hydrogen
HYENA	*n* pl. -S a wolflike mammal **HYENIC, HYENINE, HYENOID** *adj*
HYETAL	*adj* pertaining to rain
HYGEIST	*n* pl. -S an expert in hygiene
HYGIEIST	*n* pl. -S hygeist

HYGIENE   *n* pl. -S the science of health **HYGIENIC** *adj*

HYING   present participle of hie

HYLA   *n* pl. -S a tree frog

HYLOZOIC   *adj* pertaining to the doctrine that life and matter are inseparable

HYMEN   *n* pl. -S a vaginal membrane **HYMENAL** *adj*

HYMENEAL   *n* pl. -S a wedding song or poem

HYMENIUM   *n* pl. -NIA or -NIUMS a layer in certain fungi **HYMENIAL** *adj*

HYMN   *v* -ED, -ING, -S to sing a hymn (a song of praise to God)

HYMNAL   *n* pl. -S a book of hymns

HYMNARY   *n* pl. -RIES a hymnal

HYMNBOOK   *n* pl. -S a hymnal

HYMNIST   *n* pl. -S one who composes hymns

HYMNLESS   *adj* lacking a hymn

HYMNLIKE   *adj* resembling a hymn

HYMNODY   *n* pl. -DIES the singing of hymns

HYOID   *n* pl. -S a bone of the tongue **HYOIDAL, HYOIDEAN** *adj*

HYOSCINE   *n* pl. -S a sedative

HYP   *n* pl. -S hypochondria

HYPE   *v* HYPED, HYPING, HYPES to promote extravagantly

HYPER   *adj* very excitable

HYPERGOL   *n* pl. -S a rocket fuel

HYPERON   *n* pl. -S an atomic particle

HYPEROPE   *n* pl. -S a farsighted person

HYPHA   *n* pl. -PHAE a threadlike element of a fungus **HYPHAL** *adj*

HYPHEMIA   *n* pl. -S deficiency of blood

HYPHEN   *v* -ED, -ING, -S to connect words or syllables with a hyphen (a mark of punctuation)

HYPING   present participle of hype

HYPNIC   *adj* pertaining to sleep

HYPNOID   *adj* pertaining to hypnosis or sleep

HYPNOSIS   *n* pl. -NOSES an artificially induced state resembling sleep

HYPNOTIC   *n* pl. -S a sleep-inducing drug

HYPO   *v* -ED, -ING, -S to inject with a hypodermic needle

HYPOACID   *adj* having a lower than normal degree of acidity

HYPODERM   *n* pl. -S a skin layer

HYPOGEA   pl. of hypogeum

HYPOGEAL   *adj* underground

HYPOGEAN   *adj* hypogeal

HYPOGENE   *adj* formed underground

HYPOGEUM   *n* pl. -GEA an underground chamber

HYPOGYNY   *n* pl. -NIES the condition of having flowers with organs situated below the ovary

HYPONEA   *n* pl. -S hyponoia

HYPONOIA   *n* pl. -S dulled mental activity

HYPOPNEA   *n* pl. -S abnormally shallow breathing

HYPOPYON   *n* pl. -S an accumulation of pus in the eye

HYPOTHEC   *n* pl. -S a type of mortgage

HYPOXIA   *n* pl. -S a deficiency of oxygen in body tissue **HYPOXIC** *adj*

HYRACOID   *n* pl. -S a hyrax

HYRAX   *n* pl. -RAXES or -RACES a small, harelike mammal

HYSON   *n* pl. -S a Chinese tea

HYSSOP   *n* pl. -S a medicinal herb

HYSTERIA   *n* pl. -S uncontrollable excitement or fear

HYSTERIC   *n* pl. -S one who is subject to fits of hysteria

HYTE   *adj* insane

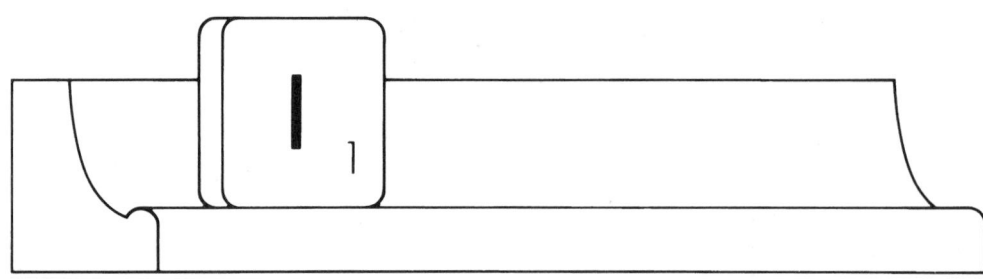

IAMB	*n* pl. -S a type of metrical foot	**ICICLE**	*n* pl. -S a hanging spike of ice **ICICLED** *adj*
IAMBIC	*n* pl. -S an iamb	**ICIER**	comparative of icy
IAMBUS	*n* pl. -BUSES or -BI an iamb	**ICIEST**	superlative of icy
IATRIC	*adj* pertaining to medicine	**ICILY**	*adv* in an icy manner
IATRICAL	*adj* iatric	**ICINESS**	*n* pl. -ES the state of being icy
IBEX	*n* pl. IBEXES or IBICES a wild goat	**ICING**	*n* pl. -S a sweet mixture for covering cakes
IBIDEM	*adv* in the same place	**ICK**	*interj* — used to express disgust
IBIS	*n* pl. IBISES a wading bird	**ICKER**	*n* pl. -S a head of grain
IBOGAINE	*n* pl. -S an alkaloid used as an antidepressant	**ICKINESS**	*n* pl. -ES the state of being icky
ICE	*v* ICED, ICING, ICES to cover with ice (frozen water)	**ICKY**	*adj* ICKIER, ICKIEST repulsive **ICKILY** *adv*
ICEBERG	*n* pl. -S a large floating body of ice	**ICON**	*n* pl. -S or -ES a representation **ICONIC, ICONICAL** *adj*
ICEBLINK	*n* pl. -S a glare over an ice field	**ICTERIC**	*n* pl. -S a remedy for icterus
ICEBOAT	*n* pl. -S a vehicle that sails on ice	**ICTERUS**	*n* pl. -ES a diseased condition of the liver
ICEBOUND	*adj* surrounded by ice	**ICTUS**	*n* pl. -ES a recurring stress or beat in a poetical form **ICTIC** *adj*
ICEBOX	*n* pl. -ES a cabinet for cooling food	**ICY**	*adj* ICIER, ICIEST covered with ice
ICECAP	*n* pl. -S a covering of ice and snow	**ID**	*n* pl. -S a part of the psyche
ICED	past tense of ice	**IDEA**	*n* pl. -S a conception existing in the mind **IDEALESS** *adj*
ICEFALL	*n* pl. -S a kind of frozen waterfall	**IDEAL**	*n* pl. -S a standard of perfection
ICEHOUSE	*n* pl. -S a building for storing ice	**IDEALISE**	*v* -ISED, -ISING, -ISES to idealize
ICEKHANA	*n* pl. -S an automotive event held on a frozen lake	**IDEALISM**	*n* pl. -S the pursuit of noble goals
ICELESS	*adj* having no ice	**IDEALIST**	*n* pl. -S an adherent of idealism
ICELIKE	*adj* resembling ice	**IDEALITY**	*n* pl. -TIES the state of being perfect; something idealized
ICEMAN	*n* pl. -MEN a man who supplies ice	**IDEALIZE**	*v* -IZED, -IZING, -IZES to regard as perfect
ICH	*n* pl. ICHS a disease of certain fishes	**IDEALLY**	*adv* perfectly
ICHNITE	*n* pl. -S a fossil footprint	**IDEALOGY**	*n* pl. -GIES ideology
ICHOR	*n* pl. -S a watery discharge from a wound **ICHOROUS** *adj*	**IDEATE**	*v* -ATED, -ATING, -ATES to form an idea
ICHTHYIC	*adj* pertaining to fishes		

IDEATION	*n* pl. -S the act of ideating
IDEATIVE	*adj* pertaining to ideation
IDEM	*adj* the same
IDENTIC	*adj* identical
IDENTIFY	*v* -FIED, -FYING, -FIES to establish the identity of
IDENTITY	*n* pl. -TIES the essential character of a person or thing
IDEOGRAM	*n* pl. -S a type of written symbol
IDEOLOGY	*n* pl. -GIES a systematic body of ideas
IDES	*n* pl. IDES a certain day in the ancient Roman calendar
IDIOCY	*n* pl. -CIES the condition of being an idiot
IDIOLECT	*n* pl. -S one's speech pattern
IDIOM	*n* pl. -S an expression peculiar to a language
IDIOT	*n* pl. -S a mentally deficient person **IDIOTIC** *adj*
IDIOTISM	*n* pl. -S idiocy
IDLE	*adj* IDLER, IDLEST inactive
IDLE	*v* IDLED, IDLING, IDLES to pass time idly
IDLENESS	*n* pl. -ES the state of being idle
IDLER	*n* pl. -S one that idles
IDLESSE	*n* pl. -S idleness
IDLEST	superlative of idle
IDLING	present participle of idle
IDLY	*adv* in an idle manner
IDOCRASE	*n* pl. -S a mineral
IDOL	*n* pl. -S an object of worship
IDOLATER	*n* pl. -S one that worships idols
IDOLATOR	*n* pl. -S idolater
IDOLATRY	*n* pl. -TRIES the worship of idols
IDOLISE	*v* -ISED, -ISING, -ISES to idolize
IDOLISER	*n* pl. -S one that idolises
IDOLISM	*n* pl. -S idolatry
IDOLIZE	*v* -IZED, -IZING, -IZES to worship
IDOLIZER	*n* pl. -S one that idolizes
IDONEITY	*n* pl. -TIES the state of being idoneous
IDONEOUS	*adj* suitable
IDYL	*n* pl. -S a poem or prose work depicting scenes of rural simplicity
IDYLIST	*n* pl. -S a writer of idyls
IDYLL	*n* pl. -S idyl **IDYLLIC** *adj*
IDYLLIST	*n* pl. -S idylist
IF	*n* pl. -S a possibility
IFF	*conj* if and only if
IFFINESS	*n* pl. -ES the state of being iffy
IFFY	*adj* IFFIER, IFFIEST full of uncertainty
IGLOO	*n* pl. -LOOS an Eskimo dwelling
IGLU	*n* pl. -S igloo
IGNATIA	*n* pl. -S a medicinal seed
IGNEOUS	*adj* pertaining to fire
IGNIFY	*v* -FIED, -FYING, -FIES to burn
IGNITE	*v* -NITED, -NITING, -NITES to set on fire
IGNITER	*n* pl. -S one that ignites
IGNITION	*n* pl. -S the act of igniting
IGNITOR	*n* pl. -S igniter
IGNITRON	*n* pl. -S a type of rectifier tube
IGNOBLE	*adj* of low character **IGNOBLY** *adv*
IGNOMINY	*n* pl. -NIES disgrace or dishonor
IGNORANT	*adj* having no knowledge
IGNORE	*v* -NORED, -NORING, -NORES to refuse to notice
IGNORER	*n* pl. -S one that ignores
IGUANA	*n* pl. -S a tropical lizard
IGUANIAN	*n* pl. -S a lizard related to the iguana
IHRAM	*n* pl. -S the garb worn by Muslim pilgrims
IKAT	*n* pl. -S a fabric of tie-dyed yarns
IKEBANA	*n* pl. -S the Japanese art of flower arranging
IKON	*n* pl. -S icon
ILEA	pl. of ileum
ILEAC	*adj* pertaining to the ileum
ILEAL	*adj* ileac
ILEITIS	*n* pl. ILEITIDES inflammation of the ileum
ILEUM	*n* pl. ILEA a part of the small intestine
ILEUS	*n* pl. -ES intestinal obstruction
ILEX	*n* pl. -ES a holly
ILIA	pl. of ilium
ILIAC	*adj* pertaining to the ilium
ILIAD	*n* pl. -S a long poem
ILIAL	*adj* iliac

ILIUM	*n* pl. ILIA a bone of the pelvis
ILK	*n* pl. -S a class or kind
ILKA	*adj* each
ILL	*n* pl. -S an evil
ILLATION	*n* pl. -S the act of inferring
ILLATIVE	*n* pl. -S a word or phrase introducing an inference
ILLEGAL	*n* pl. -S a person who enters a country without authorization
ILLICIT	*adj* not permitted
ILLINIUM	*n* pl. -S a radioactive element
ILLIQUID	*adj* not being cash
ILLITE	*n* pl. -S a group of minerals **ILLITIC** *adj*
ILLNESS	*n* pl. -ES sickness
ILLOGIC	*n* pl. -S absence of logic
ILLUME	*v* -LUMED, -LUMING, -LUMES to illuminate
ILLUMINE	*v* -MINED, -MINING, -MINES to illuminate
ILLUSION	*n* pl. -S a false perception
ILLUSIVE	*adj* illusory
ILLUSORY	*adj* based on illusion
ILLUVIUM	*n* pl. -VIA or -VIUMS a type of material accumulated in soil **ILLUVIAL** *adj*
ILLY	*adv* badly
ILMENITE	*n* pl. -S a mineral
IMAGE	*v* -AGED, -AGING, -AGES to imagine
IMAGER	*n* pl. -S one that images
IMAGERY	*n* pl. -ERIES mental pictures
IMAGINAL	*adj* pertaining to an imago
IMAGINE	*v* -INED, -INING, -INES to form a mental picture of
IMAGINER	*n* pl. -S one that imagines
IMAGING	*n* pl. -S the action of producing a visible representation
IMAGINING	present participle of imagine
IMAGISM	*n* pl. -S a movement in poetry
IMAGIST	*n* pl. -S an adherent of imagism
IMAGO	*n* pl. -GOES or -GOS an adult insect
IMAM	*n* pl. -S a Muslim priest
IMAMATE	*n* pl. -S the office of an imam
IMARET	*n* pl. -S a Turkish inn
IMAUM	*n* pl. -S imam
IMBALM	*v* -ED, -ING, -S to embalm

IMBALMER	*n* pl. -S embalmer
IMBARK	*v* -ED, -ING, -S to embark
IMBECILE	*n* pl. -S a mentally deficient person
IMBED	*v* -BEDDED, -BEDDING, -BEDS to embed
IMBIBE	*v* -BIBED, -BIBING, -BIBES to drink
IMBIBER	*n* pl. -S one that imbibes
IMBITTER	*v* -ED, -ING, -S to embitter
IMBLAZE	*v* -BLAZED, -BLAZING, -BLAZES to emblaze
IMBODY	*v* -BODIED, -BODYING, -BODIES to embody
IMBOLDEN	*v* -ED, -ING, -S to embolden
IMBOSOM	*v* -ED, -ING, -S to embosom
IMBOWER	*v* -ED, -ING, -S to embower
IMBROWN	*v* -ED, -ING, -S to embrown
IMBRUE	*v* -BRUED, -BRUING, -BRUES to stain
IMBRUTE	*v* -BRUTED, -BRUTING, -BRUTES to make brutal
IMBUE	*v* -BUED, -BUING, -BUES to make thoroughly wet
IMID	*n* pl. -S imide
IMIDE	*n* pl. -S a chemical compound **IMIDIC** *adj*
IMIDO	*adj* containing an imide
IMINE	*n* pl. -S a chemical compound
IMINO	*adj* containing an imine
IMITABLE	*adj* capable of being imitated
IMITATE	*v* -TATED, -TATING, -TATES to behave in the same way as
IMITATOR	*n* pl. -S one that imitates
IMMANE	*adj* great in size
IMMANENT	*adj* existing within
IMMATURE	*n* pl. -S an individual that is not fully grown or developed
IMMENSE	*adj* -MENSER, -MENSEST great in size
IMMERGE	*v* -MERGED, -MERGING, -MERGES to immerse
IMMERSE	*v* -MERSED, -MERSING, -MERSES to plunge into a liquid
IMMESH	*v* -ED, -ING, -ES to enmesh
IMMIES	pl. of immy
IMMINENT	*adj* ready to take place
IMMINGLE	*v* -GLED, -GLING, -GLES to blend

IMMIX	*v* -ED, -ING, -ES to mix in
IMMOBILE	*adj* incapable of being moved
IMMODEST	*adj* not modest
IMMOLATE	*v* -LATED, -LATING, -LATES to kill as a sacrifice
IMMORAL	*adj* contrary to established morality
IMMORTAL	*n* pl. -S one who is not subject to death
IMMOTILE	*adj* lacking mobility
IMMUNE	*n* pl. -S one who is protected from a disease
IMMUNISE	*v* -NISED, -NISING, -NISES to immunize
IMMUNITY	*n* pl. -TIES the state of being protected from a disease
IMMUNIZE	*v* -NIZED, -NIZING, -NIZES to protect from a disease
IMMURE	*v* -MURED, -MURING, -MURES to imprison
IMMY	*n* pl. -MIES a type of playing marble
IMP	*v* -ED, -ING, -S to graft feathers onto a bird's wing
IMPACT	*v* -ED, -ING, -S to pack firmly together
IMPACTER	*n* pl. -S one that impacts
IMPACTOR	*n* pl. -S impacter
IMPAINT	*v* -ED, -ING, -S to paint or depict
IMPAIR	*v* -ED, -ING, -S to make worse
IMPAIRER	*n* pl. -S one that impairs
IMPALA	*n* pl. -S an African antelope
IMPALE	*v* -PALED, -PALING, -PALES to pierce with a pointed object
IMPALER	*n* pl. -S one that impales
IMPANEL	*v* -ELED, -ELING, -ELS or -ELLED, -ELLING, -ELS to enter on a list for jury duty
IMPARITY	*n* pl. -TIES lack of equality
IMPARK	*v* -ED, -ING, -S to confine in a park
IMPART	*v* -ED, -ING, -S to make known
IMPARTER	*n* pl. -S one that imparts
IMPASSE	*n* pl. -S a road or passage having no exit
IMPASTE	*v* -PASTED, -PASTING, -PASTES to make into a paste
IMPASTO	*n* pl. -TOS a painting technique
IMPAVID	*adj* brave
IMPAWN	*v* -ED, -ING, -S to pawn
IMPEACH	*v* -ED, -ING, -ES to charge with misconduct in office
IMPEARL	*v* -ED, -ING, -S to make pearly
IMPEDE	*v* -PEDED, -PEDING, -PEDES to obstruct the progress of
IMPEDER	*n* pl. -S one that impedes
IMPEL	*v* -PELLED, -PELLING, -PELS to force into action
IMPELLER	*n* pl. -S one that impels
IMPELLOR	*n* pl. -S impeller
IMPEND	*v* -ED, -ING, -S to be imminent
IMPERIA	a pl. of imperium
IMPERIAL	*n* pl. -S an emperor or empress
IMPERIL	*v* -ILED, -ILING, -ILS or -ILLED, -ILLING, -ILS to place in jeopardy
IMPERIUM	*n* pl. -RIUMS or -RIA absolute power
IMPETIGO	*n* pl. -GOS a skin disease
IMPETUS	*n* pl. -ES an impelling force
IMPHEE	*n* pl. -S an African grass
IMPI	*n* pl. -S a body of warriors
IMPIETY	*n* pl. -TIES lack of piety
IMPING	*n* pl. -S the process of grafting
IMPINGE	*v* -PINGED, -PINGING, -PINGES to collide
IMPINGER	*n* pl. -S one that impinges
IMPIOUS	*adj* not pious
IMPISH	*adj* mischievous **IMPISHLY** *adv*
IMPLANT	*v* -ED, -ING, -S to set securely
IMPLEAD	*v* -ED, -ING, -S to sue in a court of law
IMPLEDGE	*v* -PLEDGED, -PLEDGING, -PLEDGES to pawn
IMPLICIT	*adj* implied
IMPLIED	past tense of imply
IMPLIES	present 3d person sing. of imply
IMPLODE	*v* -PLODED, -PLODING, -PLODES to collapse inward
IMPLORE	*v* -PLORED, -PLORING, -PLORES to beg for urgently
IMPLORER	*n* pl. -S one that implores
IMPLY	*v* -PLIED, -PLYING, -PLIES to indicate or suggest indirectly
IMPOLICY	*n* pl. -CIES an unwise course of action
IMPOLITE	*adj* not polite
IMPONE	*v* -PONED, -PONING, -PONES to wager

IMPOROUS	*adj* extremely dense	**INACTION**	*n* pl. -S lack of action
IMPORT	*v* -ED, -ING, -S to bring into a country from abroad	**INACTIVE**	*adj* not active
IMPORTER	*n* pl. -S one that imports	**INANE**	*adj* INANER, INANEST nonsensical **INANELY** *adv*
IMPOSE	*v* -POSED, -POSING, -POSES to establish as compulsory	**INANE**	*n* pl. -S empty space
IMPOSER	*n* pl. -S one that imposes	**INANITY**	*n* pl. -TIES something that is inane
IMPOST	*v* -ED, -ING, -S to determine customs duties	**INAPT**	*adj* not apt **INAPTLY** *adv*
IMPOSTER	*n* pl. -S impostor	**INARABLE**	*adj* not arable
IMPOSTOR	*n* pl. -S one that poses as another for deceptive purposes	**INARCH**	*v* -ED, -ING, -ES to graft with in a certain way
IMPOTENT	*n* pl. -S one that is powerless	**INARM**	*v* -ED, -ING, -S to encircle with the arms
IMPOUND	*v* -ED, -ING, -S to seize and retain in legal custody	**INBEING**	*n* pl. -S the state of being inherent
IMPOWER	*v* -ED, -ING, -S to empower	**INBOARD**	*n* pl. -S a type of boat motor
IMPREGN	*v* -ED, -ING, -S to make pregnant	**INBORN**	*adj* existing in one from birth
IMPRESA	*n* pl. -S a type of emblem	**INBOUND**	*v* -ED, -ING, -S to put a basketball in play from out of bounds
IMPRESE	*n* pl. -S impresa		
IMPRESS	*v* -ED, -ING, -ES to affect strongly	**INBOUNDS**	*adj* being within certain boundaries
IMPREST	*n* pl. -S a loan or advance of money	**INBRED**	*n* pl. -S a product of inbreeding
IMPRIMIS	*adv* in the first place	**INBREED**	*v* -BRED, -BREEDING, -BREEDS to breed closely related stock
IMPRINT	*v* -ED, -ING, -S to produce a mark by pressure		
IMPRISON	*v* -ED, -ING, -S to confine	**INBUILT**	*adj* forming an integral part of a structure
IMPROPER	*adj* not proper	**INBURST**	*n* pl. -S the act of bursting inward
IMPROV	*n* pl. -S improvisation	**INBY**	*adv* inward
IMPROVE	*v* -PROVED, -PROVING, -PROVES to make better	**INBYE**	*adv* inby
		INCAGE	*v* -CAGED, -CAGING, -CAGES to encage
IMPROVER	*n* pl. -S one that improves	**INCANT**	*v* -ED, -ING, -S to utter ritually
IMPUDENT	*adj* offensively bold or disrespectful	**INCASE**	*v* -CASED, -CASING, -CASES to encase
IMPUGN	*v* -ED, -ING, -S to make insinuations against	**INCENSE**	*v* -CENSED, -CENSING, -CENSES to make angry
IMPUGNER	*n* pl. -S one that impugns		
IMPULSE	*v* -PULSED, -PULSING, -PULSES to give impetus to	**INCENTER**	*n* pl. -S the point where the three lines bisecting the angles of a triangle meet
IMPUNITY	*n* pl. -TIES exemption from penalty	**INCEPT**	*v* -ED, -ING, -S to take in
IMPURE	*adj* not pure **IMPURELY** *adv*	**INCEPTOR**	*n* pl. -S one that incepts
IMPURITY	*n* pl. -TIES something that is impure	**INCEST**	*n* pl. -S sexual intercourse between closely related persons
IMPUTE	*v* -PUTED, -PUTING, -PUTES to credit to a person or a cause	**INCH**	*v* -ED, -ING, -ES to move very slowly
IMPUTER	*n* pl. -S one that imputes	**INCHMEAL**	*adv* little by little
IN	*v* INNED, INNING, INS to harvest	**INCHOATE**	*adj* being in an early stage
		INCHWORM	*n* pl. -S a type of worm

INCIDENT *n* pl. -S an event

INCIPIT *n* pl. -S the opening words of a text

INCISAL *adj* being the cutting edge of a tooth

INCISE *v* -CISED, -CISING, -CISES to cut into

INCISION *n* pl. -S the act of incising

INCISIVE *adj* penetrating

INCISOR *n* pl. -S a cutting tooth

INCISORY *adj* adapted for cutting

INCISURE *n* pl. -S a notch or cleft of a body part

INCITANT *n* pl. -S something that incites

INCITE *v* -CITED, -CITING, -CITES to arouse to action

INCITER *n* pl. -S one that incites

INCIVIL *adj* discourteous

INCLASP *v* -ED, -ING, -S to enclasp

INCLINE *v* -CLINED, -CLINING, -CLINES to slant

INCLINER *n* pl. -S one that inclines

INCLIP *v* -CLIPPED, -CLIPPING, -CLIPS to clasp

INCLOSE *v* -CLOSED, -CLOSING, -CLOSES to enclose

INCLOSER *n* pl. -S one that incloses

INCLUDE *v* -CLUDED, -CLUDING, -CLUDES to have as a part

INCOG *n* pl. -S a disguised person

INCOME *n* pl. -S a sum of money earned regularly

INCOMER *n* pl. -S one that comes in

INCOMING *n* pl. -S an arrival

INCONNU *n* pl. -S a large food fish

INCONY *adj* pretty

INCORPSE *v* -CORPSED, -CORPSING, -CORPSES to become combined with

INCREASE *v* -CREASED, -CREASING, -CREASES to make or become greater

INCREATE *adj* not created

INCROSS *v* -ED, -ING, -ES to inbreed

INCRUST *v* -ED, -ING, -S to encrust

INCUBATE *v* -BATED, -BATING, -BATES to warm eggs for hatching

INCUBUS *n* pl. -BI or -BUSES a demon

INCUDAL *adj* pertaining to the incus

INCUDATE *adj* incudal

INCUDES pl. of incus

INCULT *adj* uncultivated

INCUMBER *v* -ED, -ING, -S to encumber

INCUR *v* -CURRED, -CURRING, -CURS to bring upon oneself

INCURVE *v* -CURVED, -CURVING, -CURVES to curve inward

INCUS *n* pl. INCUDES a bone in the middle ear

INCUSE *v* -CUSED, -CUSING, -CUSES to mark by stamping

INDABA *n* pl. -S a meeting of South African tribes

INDAGATE *v* -GATED, -GATING, -GATES to investigate

INDAMIN *n* pl. -S indamine

INDAMINE *n* pl. -S a chemical compound

INDEBTED *adj* beholden

INDECENT *adj* -CENTER, -CENTEST not decent

INDEED *adv* in truth

INDENE *n* pl. -S a hydrocarbon

INDENT *v* -ED, -ING, -S to cut or tear irregularly

INDENTER *n* pl. -S one that indents

INDENTOR *n* pl. -S indenter

INDEVOUT *adj* not devout

INDEX *n* pl. INDEXES or INDICES a type of reference guide at the end of a book

INDEX *v* -ED, -ING, -ES to provide with an index

INDEXER *n* pl. -S one that indexes

INDEXING *n* pl. -S the linking of wages and prices to cost-of-living levels

INDICAN *n* pl. -S a chemical compound

INDICANT *n* pl. -S something that indicates

INDICATE *v* -CATED, -CATING, -CATES to point out

INDICES a pl. of index

INDICIA *n* pl. -S a distinctive mark

INDICIUM *n* pl. -S an indicia

INDICT *v* -ED, -ING, -S to charge with a crime

INDICTEE *n* pl. -S one that is indicted

INDICTER *n* pl. -S one that indicts

INDICTOR *n* pl. -S indicter

INDIE	*n* pl. -S a person who is independent
INDIGEN	*n* pl. -S indigene
INDIGENE	*n* pl. -S a native
INDIGENT	*n* pl. -S a needy person
INDIGN	*adj* disgraceful **INDIGNLY** *adv*
INDIGO	*n* pl. -GOS or -GOES a blue dye
INDIGOID	*n* pl. -S a blue dye
INDIRECT	*adj* not direct
INDITE	*v* -DITED, -DITING, -DITES to write or compose
INDITER	*n* pl. -S one that indites
INDIUM	*n* pl. -S a metallic element
INDOCILE	*adj* not docile
INDOL	*n* pl. -S indole
INDOLE	*n* pl. -S a chemical compound
INDOLENT	*adj* lazy
INDOOR	*adj* pertaining to the interior of a building
INDOORS	*adv* in or into a house
INDORSE	*v* -DORSED, -DORSING, -DORSES to endorse
INDORSEE	*n* pl. -S endorsee
INDORSER	*n* pl. -S endorser
INDORSING	present participle of indorse
INDORSOR	*n* pl. -S endorsor
INDOW	*v* -ED, -ING, -S to endow
INDOXYL	*n* pl. -S a chemical compound
INDRAFT	*n* pl. -S an inward flow or current
INDRAWN	*adj* drawn in
INDRI	*n* pl. -S a short-tailed lemur
INDUCE	*v* -DUCED, -DUCING, -DUCES to influence into doing something
INDUCER	*n* pl. -S one that induces
INDUCT	*v* -ED, -ING, -S to bring into military service
INDUCTEE	*n* pl. -S one that is inducted
INDUCTOR	*n* pl. -S one that inducts
INDUE	*v* -DUED, -DUING, -DUES to endue
INDULGE	*v* -DULGED, -DULGING, -DULGES to yield to the desire of
INDULGER	*n* pl. -S one that indulges
INDULIN	*n* pl. -S induline
INDULINE	*n* pl. -S a blue dye
INDULT	*n* pl. -S a privilege granted by the pope
INDURATE	*v* -RATED, -RATING, -RATES to make hard
INDUSIUM	*n* pl. -SIA an enclosing membrane **INDUSIAL** *adj*
INDUSTRY	*n* pl. -TRIES a group of productive enterprises
INDWELL	*v* -DWELT, -DWELLING, -DWELLS to live within
INEARTH	*v* -ED, -ING, -S to bury
INEDIBLE	*adj* not fit to be eaten
INEDITA	*n/pl* unpublished literary works
INEDITED	*adj* not published
INEPT	*adj* not suitable **INEPTLY** *adv*
INEQUITY	*n* pl. -TIES unfairness
INERRANT	*adj* free from error
INERT	*n* pl. -S something that lacks active properties
INERTIA	*n* pl. -TIAS or -TIAE the tendency of a body to resist acceleration **INERTIAL** *adj*
INERTLY	*adv* inactively
INEXACT	*adj* not exact
INEXPERT	*n* pl. -S a novice
INFALL	*n* pl. -S movement under the influence of gravity toward a celestial object
INFAMOUS	*adj* having a vile reputation
INFAMY	*n* pl. -MIES the state of being infamous
INFANCY	*n* pl. -CIES the state of being an infant
INFANT	*n* pl. -S a child in the earliest stages of life
INFANTA	*n* pl. -S a daughter of a Spanish or Portuguese monarch
INFANTE	*n* pl. -S a younger son of a Spanish or Portuguese monarch
INFANTRY	*n* pl. -TRIES a branch of the army composed of foot soldiers
INFARCT	*n* pl. -S an area of dead or dying tissue
INFARE	*n* pl. -S a reception for newlyweds
INFAUNA	*n* pl. -NAS or -NAE fauna living on a soft sea floor **INFAUNAL** *adj*
INFECT	*v* -ED, -ING, -S to contaminate with disease-producing germs
INFECTER	*n* pl. -S one that infects
INFECTOR	*n* pl. -S infecter
INFECUND	*adj* barren

INFEOFF   *v* -ED, -ING, -S to enfeoff

INFER   *v* -FERRED, -FERRING, -FERS to reach or derive by reasoning

INFERIOR   *n* pl. -S one of lesser rank

INFERNAL   *adj* pertaining to hell

INFERNO   *n* pl. -NOS a place that resembles or suggests hell

INFERRED   past tense of infer

INFERRER   *n* pl. -S one that infers

INFERRING   present participle of infer

INFEST   *v* -ED, -ING, -S to overrun in large numbers

INFESTER   *n* pl. -S one that infests

INFIDEL   *n* pl. -S one who has no religious faith

INFIELD   *n* pl. -S a part of a baseball field

INFIGHT   *v* -FOUGHT, -FIGHTING, -FIGHTS to contend with others within the same group

INFINITE   *n* pl. -S something that has no limits

INFINITY   *n* pl. -TIES the state of having no limits

INFIRM   *v* -ED, -ING, -S to weaken or destroy the validity of

INFIRMLY   *adv* in a feeble manner

INFIX   *v* -ED, -ING, -ES to implant

INFIXION   *n* pl. -S the act of infixing

INFLAME   *v* -FLAMED, -FLAMING, -FLAMES to set on fire

INFLAMER   *n* pl. -S one that inflames

INFLATE   *v* -FLATED, -FLATING, -FLATES to cause to expand by filling with gas or air

INFLATER   *n* pl. -S one that inflates

INFLATOR   *n* pl. -S inflater

INFLECT   *v* -ED, -ING, -S to bend

INFLEXED   *adj* bent inward

INFLICT   *v* -ED, -ING, -S to cause to be endured; impose

INFLIGHT   *adj* done during an air voyage

INFLOW   *n* pl. -S the act of flowing in

INFLUENT   *n* pl. -S a tributary

INFLUX   *n* pl. -ES a flowing in

INFO   *n* pl. -FOS information

INFOLD   *v* -ED, -ING, -S to fold inward

INFOLDER   *n* pl. -S one that infolds

INFORM   *v* -ED, -ING, -S to supply with information

INFORMAL   *adj* marked by the absence of formality or ceremony

INFORMER   *n* pl. -S one that informs

INFOUGHT   past tense of infight

INFRA   *adv* below

INFRACT   *v* -ED, -ING, -S to break a legal rule

INFRARED   *n* pl. -S a part of the invisible spectrum

INFRINGE   *v* -FRINGED, -FRINGING, -FRINGES to violate an oath or a law

INFRUGAL   *adj* not frugal

INFUSE   *v* -FUSED, -FUSING, -FUSES to permeate with something

INFUSER   *n* pl. -S one that infuses

INFUSION   *n* pl. -S the act of infusing

INFUSIVE   *adj* capable of infusing

INGATE   *n* pl. -S a channel by which molten metal enters a mold

INGATHER   *v* -ED, -ING, -S to gather in

INGENUE   *n* pl. -S a naive young woman

INGEST   *v* -ED, -ING, -S to take into the body

INGESTA   *n/pl* ingested material

INGLE   *n* pl. -S a fire

INGOING   *adj* entering

INGOT   *v* -ED, -ING, -S to shape into a convenient form for storage

INGRAFT   *v* -ED, -ING, -S to engraft

INGRAIN   *v* -ED, -ING, -S to impress firmly on the mind

INGRATE   *n* pl. -S an ungrateful person

INGRESS   *n* pl. -ES the act of entering

INGROUP   *n* pl. -S a group united by common interests

INGROWN   *adj* grown into the flesh

INGROWTH   *n* pl. -S growth inward

INGUINAL   *adj* pertaining to the groin

INGULF   *v* -ED, -ING, -S to engulf

INHABIT   *v* -ED, -ING, -S to live in

INHALANT   *n* pl. -S something that is inhaled

INHALE   *v* -HALED, -HALING, -HALES to take into the lungs

INHALER   *n* pl. -S one that inhales

INHAUL   *n* pl. -S a line for bringing in a sail

INHAULER   *n* pl. -S an inhaul

INHERE	*v* -HERED, -HERING, -HERES to be inherent
INHERENT	*adj* existing in something as an essential characteristic
INHERIT	*v* -ED, -ING, -S to receive by legal succession
INHESION	*n* pl. -S the state of inhering
INHIBIN	*n* pl. -S a human hormone
INHIBIT	*v* -ED, -ING, -S to restrain or hold back
INHUMAN	*adj* lacking desirable human qualities
INHUMANE	*adj* not humane
INHUME	*v* -HUMED, -HUMING, -HUMES to bury
INHUMER	*n* pl. -S one that inhumes
INIMICAL	*adj* unfriendly
INION	*n* pl. INIA a part of the skull
INIQUITY	*n* pl. -TIES a gross injustice
INITIAL	*v* -TIALED, -TIALING, -TIALS or -TIALLED, -TIALLING, -TIALS to mark with the first letters of one's name
INITIATE	*v* -ATED, -ATING, -ATES to originate
INJECT	*v* -ED, -ING, -S to force a fluid into
INJECTOR	*n* pl. -S one that injects
INJURE	*v* -JURED, -JURING, -JURES to do or cause injury to
INJURER	*n* pl. -S one that injures
INJURY	*n* pl. -RIES harm inflicted or suffered
INK	*v* -ED, -ING, -S to mark with ink (a colored fluid used for writing)
INKBERRY	*n* pl. -RIES a small shrub
INKBLOT	*n* pl. -S a blotted pattern of spilled ink
INKER	*n* pl. -S one that inks
INKHORN	*n* pl. -S a small container for ink
INKIER	comparative of inky
INKIEST	superlative of inky
INKINESS	*n* pl. -ES the state of being inky
INKJET	*adj* being a high-speed printing process using jets of ink
INKLE	*n* pl. -S a tape used for trimming
INKLESS	*adj* being without ink
INKLIKE	*adj* resembling ink
INKLING	*n* pl. -S a slight suggestion
INKPOT	*n* pl. -S an inkwell
INKSTAND	*n* pl. -S an inkwell
INKSTONE	*n* pl. -S a stone on which dry ink and water are mixed
INKWELL	*n* pl. -S a small container for ink
INKWOOD	*n* pl. -S an evergreen tree
INKY	*adj* INKIER, INKIEST resembling ink
INLACE	*v* -LACED, -LACING, -LACES to enlace
INLAID	past tense of inlay
INLAND	*n* pl. -S the interior of a region
INLANDER	*n* pl. -S one living in the interior of a region
INLAY	*v* -LAID, -LAYING, -LAYS to set into a surface
INLAYER	*n* pl. -S one that inlays
INLET	*v* -LET, -LETTING, -LETS to insert
INLIER	*n* pl. -S a type of rock formation
INLY	*adv* inwardly
INMATE	*n* pl. -S one who is confined to an institution
INMESH	*v* -ED, -ING, -ES to enmesh
INMOST	*adj* farthest within
INN	*v* -ED, -ING, -S to put up at an inn (a public lodging house)
INNARDS	*n/pl* the internal organs
INNATE	*adj* inborn **INNATELY** *adv*
INNED	past tense of in
INNER	*n* pl. -S something that is within
INNERLY	*adv* inwardly
INNERVE	*v* -NERVED, -NERVING, -NERVES to stimulate
INNING	*n* pl. -S a division of a baseball game
INNLESS	*adj* having no inns
INNOCENT	*adj* -CENTER, -CENTEST free from guilt or sin
INNOCENT	*n* pl. -S an innocent person
INNOVATE	*v* -VATED, -VATING, -VATES to introduce something new
INNUENDO	*v* -ED, -ING, -S or -ES to make a derogatory implication
INOCULUM	*n* pl. -LA or -LUMS the material used in an inoculation
INOSITE	*n* pl. -S inositol
INOSITOL	*n* pl. -S an alcohol found in plant and animal tissue

INPHASE *adj* having matching electrical phases

INPOUR *v* -ED, -ING, -S to pour in

INPUT *v* -PUTTED, -PUTTING, -PUTS to enter data into a computer

INQUEST *n* pl. -S a legal inquiry

INQUIET *v* -ED, -ING, -S to disturb

INQUIRE *v* -QUIRED, -QUIRING, -QUIRES to ask about

INQUIRER *n* pl. -S one that inquires

INQUIRY *n* pl. -RIES a question

INRO *n* pl. INRO a Japanese ornamental container

INROAD *n* pl. -S a hostile invasion

INRUSH *n* pl. -ES a rushing in

INSANE *adj* -SANER, -SANEST mentally unsound **INSANELY** *adv*

INSANITY *n* pl. -TIES the state of being insane; something utterly foolish

INSCAPE *n* pl. -S the inner essential quality of something

INSCRIBE *v* -SCRIBED, -SCRIBING, -SCRIBES to write or engrave as a lasting record

INSCROLL *v* -ED, -ING, -S to enscroll

INSCULP *v* -ED, -ING, -S to engrave

INSEAM *n* pl. -S an inner seam

INSECT *n* pl. -S any of a class of small invertebrate animals

INSECTAN *adj* pertaining to insects

INSECURE *adj* unsafe

INSERT *v* -ED, -ING, -S to put in

INSERTER *n* pl. -S one that inserts

INSET *v* -SETTED, -SETTING, -SETS to insert

INSETTER *n* pl. -S one that inserts

INSHEATH *v* -ED, -ING, -S to ensheath

INSHORE *adj* near the shore

INSHRINE *v* -SHRINED, -SHRINING, -SHRINES to enshrine

INSIDE *n* pl. -S something that lies within

INSIDER *n* pl. -S an accepted member of a clique

INSIGHT *n* pl. -S a perception of the inner nature of things

INSIGNE *n* pl. INSIGNIA an insignia

INSIGNIA *n* pl. -S an emblem of authority or honor

INSIPID *adj* dull and uninteresting

INSIST *v* -ED, -ING, -S to be resolute on some matter

INSISTER *n* pl. -S one that insists

INSNARE *v* -SNARED, -SNARING, -SNARES to ensnare

INSNARER *n* pl. -S ensnarer

INSOFAR *adv* to such an extent

INSOLATE *v* -LATED, -LATING, -LATES to expose to sunlight

INSOLE *n* pl. -S the inner sole of a boot or shoe

INSOLENT *n* pl. -S an extremely rude person

INSOMNIA *n* pl. -S chronic inability to sleep

INSOMUCH *adv* to such a degree

INSOUL *v* -ED, -ING, -S to ensoul

INSPAN *v* -SPANNED, -SPANNING, -SPANS to harness or yoke to a vehicle

INSPECT *v* -ED, -ING, -S to look carefully at or over

INSPHERE *v* -SPHERED, -SPHERING, -SPHERES to ensphere

INSPIRE *v* -SPIRED, -SPIRING, -SPIRES to animate the mind or emotions of

INSPIRER *n* pl. -S one that inspires

INSPIRIT *v* -ED, -ING, -S to fill with spirit or life

INSTABLE *adj* unstable

INSTAL *v* -STALLED, -STALLING, -STALS to install

INSTALL *v* -ED, -ING, -S to place in position for use

INSTANCE *v* -STANCED, -STANCING, -STANCES to cite as an example

INSTANCY *n* pl. -CIES urgency

INSTANT *n* pl. -S a very short time

INSTAR *v* -STARRED, -STARRING, -STARS to adorn with stars

INSTATE *v* -STATED, -STATING, -STATES to place in office

INSTEAD *adv* as a substitute or equivalent

INSTEP *n* pl. -S a part of the foot

INSTIL *v* -STILLED, -STILLING, -STILS to instill

INSTILL *v* -ED, -ING, -S to infuse slowly

INSTINCT *n* pl. -S an inborn behavioral pattern

INSTROKE *n* pl. -S an inward stroke

INSTRUCT   *v* -ED, -ING, -S to supply with knowledge

INSULANT   *n* pl. -S an insulating material

INSULAR   *n* pl. -S an islander

INSULATE   *v* -LATED, -LATING, -LATES to separate with nonconducting material

INSULIN   *n* pl. -S a hormone

INSULT   *v* -ED, -ING, -S to treat offensively

INSULTER   *n* pl. -S one that insults

INSURANT   *n* pl. -S one who is insured

INSURE   *v* -SURED, -SURING, -SURES to guarantee against loss

INSURED   *n* pl. -S one who is insured

INSURER   *n* pl. -S one that insures

INSURING   present participle of insure

INSWATHE   *v* -SWATHED, -SWATHING, -SWATHES to enswathe

INSWEPT   *adj* narrowed in front

INTACT   *adj* not damaged in any way

INTAGLIO   *n* pl. -GLIOS or -GLI an incised or sunken design

INTAGLIO   *v* -ED, -ING, -S to engrave in intaglio

INTAKE   *n* pl. -S the act of taking in

INTARSIA   *n* pl. -S a decorative technique

INTEGER   *n* pl. -S a whole number

INTEGRAL   *n* pl. -S a total unit

INTEND   *v* -ED, -ING, -S to have as a specific aim or purpose

INTENDED   *n* pl. -S one's spouse to-be

INTENDER   *n* pl. -S one that intends

INTENSE   *adj* -TENSER, -TENSEST existing in an extreme degree

INTENT   *n* pl. -S a purpose

INTENTLY   *adv* in an unwavering manner

INTER   *v* -TERRED, -TERRING, -TERS to bury

INTERACT   *v* -ED, -ING, -S to act on each other

INTERAGE   *adj* including persons of various ages

INTERBED   *v* -BEDDED, -BEDDING, -BEDS to insert between other layers

INTERCOM   *n* pl. -S a type of communication system

INTERCUT   *v* -CUT, -CUTTING, -CUTS to alternate camera shots

INTEREST   *v* -ED, -ING, -S to engage the attention of

INTERIM   *n* pl. -S an interval

INTERIOR   *n* pl. -S the inside

INTERLAP   *v* -LAPPED, -LAPPING, -LAPS to lap one over another

INTERLAY   *v* -LAID, -LAYING, -LAYS to place between

INTERMIT   *v* -MITTED, -MITTING, -MITS to stop temporarily

INTERMIX   *v* -ED, -ING, -ES to mix together

INTERN   *v* -ED, -ING, -S to confine during a war

INTERNAL   *n* pl. -S an inner attribute

INTERNE   *n* pl. -S a recent medical school graduate on a hospital staff

INTERNEE   *n* pl. -S one who has been interned

INTERRED   past tense of inter

INTERREX   *n* pl. -REGES a type of sovereign

INTERRING   present participle of inter

INTERROW   *adj* existing between rows

INTERSEX   *n* pl. -ES a person having characteristics of both sexes

INTERTIE   *n* pl. -S a type of electrical connection

INTERVAL   *n* pl. -S a space of time between periods or events

INTERWAR   *adj* happening between wars

INTHRAL   *v* -THRALLED, -THRALLING, -THRALS to enthrall

INTHRALL   *v* -ED, -ING, -S to enthrall

INTHRONE   *v* -THRONED, -THRONING, -THRONES to enthrone

INTI   *n* pl. -S a monetary unit of Peru

INTIMA   *n* pl. -MAE or -MAS the innermost layer of an organ **INTIMAL** *adj*

INTIMACY   *n* pl. -CIES the state of being closely associated

INTIMATE   *v* -MATED, -MATING, -MATES to make known indirectly

INTIME   *adj* cozy

INTIMIST   *n* pl. -S a writer or artist who deals with deep personal experiences

INTINE   *n* pl. -S the inner wall of a spore

INTITLE   *v* -TLED, -TLING, -TLES to entitle

INTITULE   *v* -ULED, -ULING, -ULES to entitle

INTO *prep* to the inside of

INTOMB *v* -ED, -ING, -S to entomb

INTONATE *v* -NATED, -NATING, -NATES to intone

INTONE *v* -TONED, -TONING, -TONES to speak in a singing voice

INTONER *n* pl. -S one that intones

INTORT *v* -ED, -ING, -S to twist inward

INTOWN *adj* located in the center of a city

INTRADAY *adj* occurring within a single day

INTRADOS *n* pl. -ES the inner curve of an arch

INTRANT *n* pl. -S an entrant

INTREAT *v* -ED, -ING, -S to entreat

INTRENCH *v* -ED, -ING, -ES to entrench

INTREPID *adj* fearless

INTRIGUE *v* -TRIGUED, -TRIGUING, -TRIGUES to arouse the curiosity of

INTRO *n* pl. -TROS an introduction

INTROFY *v* -FIED, -FYING, -FIES to increase the wetting properties of

INTROIT *n* pl. -S music sung at the beginning of a worship service

INTROMIT *v* -MITTED, -MITTING, -MITS to put in

INTRON *n* pl. -S an intervening sequence in the genetic code

INTRORSE *adj* facing inward

INTRUDE *v* -TRUDED, -TRUDING, -TRUDES to thrust or force oneself in

INTRUDER *n* pl. -S one that intrudes

INTRUST *v* -ED, -ING, -S to entrust

INTUBATE *v* -BATED, -BATING, -BATES to insert a tube into

INTUIT *v* -ED, -ING, -S to know without conscious reasoning

INTURN *n* pl. -S a turning inward **INTURNED** *adj*

INTWINE *v* -TWINED, -TWINING, -TWINES to entwine

INTWIST *v* -ED, -ING, -S to entwist

INULASE *n* pl. -S an enzyme

INULIN *n* pl. -S a chemical compound

INUNDANT *adj* inundating

INUNDATE *v* -DATED, -DATING, -DATES to overwhelm with water

INURBANE *adj* not urbane

INURE *v* -URED, -URING, -URES to accustom to accept something undesirable

INURN *v* -ED, -ING, -S to put in an urn

INUTILE *adj* useless

INVADE *v* -VADED, -VADING, -VADES to enter for conquest or plunder

INVADER *n* pl. -S one that invades

INVALID *v* -ED, -ING, -S to disable physically

INVAR *n* pl. -S an iron-nickel alloy

INVASION *n* pl. -S the act of invading **INVASIVE** *adj*

INVECTED *adj* edged by convex curves

INVEIGH *v* -ED, -ING, -S to protest angrily

INVEIGLE *v* -GLED, -GLING, -GLES to induce by guile or flattery

INVENT *v* -ED, -ING, -S to devise originally

INVENTER *n* pl. -S inventor

INVENTOR *n* pl. -S one that invents

INVERITY *n* pl. -TIES lack of truth

INVERSE *n* pl. -S something that is opposite

INVERT *v* -ED, -ING, -S to turn upside down

INVERTER *n* pl. -S one that inverts

INVERTOR *n* pl. -S a type of electrical device

INVEST *v* -ED, -ING, -S to commit something of value for future profit

INVESTOR *n* pl. -S one that invests

INVIABLE *adj* not viable **INVIABLY** *adv*

INVIRILE *adj* not virile

INVISCID *adj* not viscid

INVITAL *adj* not vital

INVITE *v* -VITED, -VITING, -VITES to request the presence of

INVITEE *n* pl. -S one that is invited

INVITER *n* pl. -S one that invites

INVITING present participle of invite

INVOCATE *v* -CATED, -CATING, -CATES to invoke

INVOICE *v* -VOICED, -VOICING, -VOICES to bill

INVOKE *v* -VOKED, -VOKING, -VOKES to appeal to for aid

INVOKER *n* pl. -S one that invokes

INVOLUTE *v* -LUTED, -LUTING, -LUTES to roll or curl up

INVOLVE *v* -VOLVED, -VOLVING, -VOLVES to contain or include as a part

INVOLVER *n* pl. -S one that involves

INWALL *v* -ED, -ING, -S to surround with a wall

INWARD *adv* toward the inside

INWARDLY *adv* on the inside

INWARDS *adv* inward

INWEAVE *v* -WOVE or -WEAVED, -WOVEN, -WEAVING, -WEAVES to weave together

INWIND *v* -WOUND, -WINDING, -WINDS to enwind

INWRAP *v* -WRAPPED, -WRAPPING, -WRAPS to enwrap

IODATE *v* -DATED, -DATING, -DATES to iodize

IODATION *n* pl. -S the act of iodating

IODIC *adj* pertaining to iodine

IODID *n* pl. -S iodide

IODIDE *n* pl. -S a compound of iodine

IODIN *n* pl. -S iodine

IODINATE *v* -ATED, -ATING, -ATES to iodize

IODINE *n* pl. -S a nonmetallic element

IODISE *v* -DISED, -DISING, -DISES iodize

IODISM *n* pl. -S iodine poisoning

IODIZE *v* -DIZED, -DIZING, -DIZES to treat with iodine

IODIZER *n* pl. -S one that iodizes

IODOFORM *n* pl. -S an iodine compound

IODOPHOR *n* pl. -S an iodine compound

IODOPSIN *n* pl. -S a pigment in the retina

IODOUS *adj* pertaining to iodine

IOLITE *n* pl. -S a mineral

ION *n* pl. -S an electrically charged atom

IONIC *n* pl. -S a style of type

IONICITY *n* pl. -TIES the state of existing as or like an ion

IONISE *v* -ISED, -ISING, -ISES to ionize

IONIUM *n* pl. -S an isotope of thorium

IONIZE *v* -IZED, -IZING, -IZES to convert into ions

IONIZER *n* pl. -S one that ionizes

IONOGEN *n* pl. -S a compound capable of forming ions

IONOMER *n* pl. -S a type of plastic

IONONE *n* pl. -S a chemical compound

IOTA *n* pl. -S a Greek letter

IOTACISM *n* pl. -S excessive use of the letter iota

IPECAC *n* pl. -S a medicinal plant

IPOMOEA *n* pl. -S a flowering plant

IRACUND *adj* easily angered

IRADE *n* pl. -S a decree of a Muslim ruler

IRATE *adj* IRATER, IRATEST angry **IRATELY** *adv*

IRE *v* IRED, IRING, IRES to anger

IREFUL *adj* angry **IREFULLY** *adv*

IRELESS *adj* not angry

IRENIC *adj* peaceful in purpose

IRENICAL *adj* irenic

IRENICS *n/pl* a branch of theology

IRID *n* pl. -S a plant of the iris family

IRIDES a pl. of iris

IRIDIC *adj* pertaining to iridium

IRIDIUM *n* pl. -S a metallic element

IRING present participle of ire

IRIS *n* pl. IRISES or IRIDES a part of the eye

IRIS *v* -ED, -ING, -ES to give the form of a rainbow to

IRITIS *n* pl. -TISES inflammation of the iris **IRITIC** *adj*

IRK *v* -ED, -ING, -S to annoy or weary

IRKSOME *adj* tending to irk

IROKO *n* pl. -KOS a large African tree

IRON *v* -ED, -ING, -S to furnish with iron (a metallic element)

IRONBARK *n* pl. -S a timber tree

IRONCLAD *n* pl. -S an armored warship

IRONE *n* pl. -S an aromatic oil

IRONER *n* pl. -S a machine for pressing clothes

IRONIC *adj* pertaining to irony

IRONICAL *adj* ironic

IRONIES pl. of irony

IRONING   *n* pl. -S clothes pressed or to be pressed

IRONIST   *n* pl. -S one who uses irony

IRONIZE   *v* -NIZED, -NIZING, -NIZES to mix with nutritional iron

IRONLIKE   *adj* resembling iron

IRONNESS   *n* pl. -ES the state of being iron

IRONSIDE   *n* pl. -S a man of great strength

IRONWARE   *n* pl. -S articles made of iron

IRONWEED   *n* pl. -S a shrub

IRONWOOD   *n* pl. -S a hardwood tree

IRONWORK   *n* pl. -S objects made of iron

IRONY   *n* pl. -NIES the use of words to express the opposite of what is literally said

IRREAL   *adj* not real

IRRIGATE   *v* -GATED, -GATING, -GATES to supply with water by artificial means

IRRITANT   *n* pl. -S something that irritates

IRRITATE   *v* -TATED, -TATING, -TATES to excite to impatience or anger

IRRUPT   *v* -ED, -ING, -S to rush in forcibly

IS   present 3d person sing. of be

ISAGOGE   *n* pl. -S a type of introduction to a branch of study

ISAGOGIC   *n* pl. -S a branch of theology

ISARITHM   *n* pl. -S an isopleth

ISATIN   *n* pl. -S a chemical compound **ISATINIC** *adj*

ISATINE   *n* pl. -S isatin

ISBA   *n* pl. -S a Russian log hut

ISCHEMIA   *n* pl. -S a type of anemia **ISCHEMIC** *adj*

ISCHIUM   *n* pl. -CHIA a pelvic bone **ISCHIAL** *adj*

ISLAND   *v* -ED, -ING, -S to make into an island (a land area entirely surrounded by water)

ISLANDER   *n* pl. -S one that lives on an island

ISLE   *v* ISLED, ISLING, ISLES to place on an isle (a small island)

ISLELESS   *adj* lacking an isle

ISLET   *n* pl. -S a small island

ISLING   present participle of isle

ISM   *n* pl. -S a distinctive theory or doctrine

ISOBAR   *n* pl. -S a type of atom **ISOBARIC** *adj*

ISOBARE   *n* pl. -S isobar

ISOBATH   *n* pl. -S a line on a map connecting points of equal water depth

ISOCHEIM   *n* pl. -S a type of isotherm

ISOCHIME   *n* pl. -S isocheim

ISOCHOR   *n* pl. -S isochore

ISOCHORE   *n* pl. -S a curve used to show a relationship between pressure and temperature

ISOCHRON   *n* pl. -S a line on a chart connecting points representing the same time

ISOCLINE   *n* pl. -S a type of rock formation

ISOCRACY   *n* pl. -CIES a form of government

ISODOSE   *adj* pertaining to zones that receive equal doses of radiation

ISOGAMY   *n* pl. -MIES the fusion of two similar gametes

ISOGENIC   *adj* genetically similar

ISOGENY   *n* pl. -NIES the state of being of similar origin

ISOGLOSS   *n* pl. -ES a line on a map between linguistically varied areas

ISOGON   *n* pl. -S a polygon having equal angles

ISOGONAL   *n* pl. -S isogone

ISOGONE   *n* pl. -S a line on a map used to show characteristics of the earth's magnetic field

ISOGONIC   *n* pl. -S isogone

ISOGONY   *n* pl. -NIES an equivalent relative growth of parts

ISOGRAFT   *v* -ED, -ING, -S to transplant from one individual to another of the same species

ISOGRAM   *n* pl. -S a line on a map connecting points of equal value

ISOGRAPH   *n* pl. -S a line on a map indicating areas that are linguistically similar

ISOGRIV   *n* pl. -S a line drawn on a map such that all points have equal grid variation

ISOHEL   *n* pl. -S a line on a map connecting points receiving equal sunshine

ISOHYET   *n* pl. -S a line on a map connecting points having equal rainfall

ISOLABLE	*adj* capable of being isolated	**ISSEI**	*n* pl. -S a Japanese immigrant to the United States
ISOLATE	*v* -LATED, -LATING, -LATES to set apart from others	**ISSUABLE**	*adj* authorized for issuing **ISSUABLY** *adv*
ISOLATOR	*n* pl. -S one that isolates	**ISSUANCE**	*n* pl. -S the act of issuing
ISOLEAD	*n* pl. -S a line on a ballistic graph	**ISSUANT**	*adj* coming forth
ISOLINE	*n* pl. -S an isogram	**ISSUE**	*v* -SUED, -SUING, -SUES to come forth
ISOLOG	*n* pl. -S isologue		
ISOLOGUE	*n* pl. -S a type of chemical compound	**ISSUER**	*n* pl. -S one that issues
		ISTHMI	a pl. of isthmus
ISOMER	*n* pl. -S a type of chemical compound **ISOMERIC** *adj*	**ISTHMIAN**	*n* pl. -S a native of an isthmus
		ISTHMIC	*adj* pertaining to an isthmus
ISOMETRY	*n* pl. -TRIES equality of measure	**ISTHMOID**	*adj* isthmic
ISOMORPH	*n* pl. -S something similar to something else in form	**ISTHMUS**	*n* pl. -MUSES or -MI a strip of land connecting two larger land masses
ISONOMY	*n* pl. -MIES equality of civil rights **ISONOMIC** *adj*		
		ISTLE	*n* pl. -S a strong fiber
ISOPACH	*n* pl. -S an isogram connecting points of equal thickness	**IT**	*pron* the 3d person sing. neuter pronoun
ISOPHOTE	*n* pl. -S a curve on a chart joining points of equal light intensity	**ITALIC**	*n* pl. -S a style of print
ISOPLETH	*n* pl. -S a type of isogram	**ITCH**	*v* -ED, -ING, -ES to have an uneasy or tingling skin sensation
ISOPOD	*n* pl. -S a kind of crustacean		
ISOPODAN	*n* pl. -S an isopod	**ITCHING**	*n* pl. -S an uneasy or tingling skin sensation
ISOPRENE	*n* pl. -S a volatile liquid		
ISOSPIN	*n* pl. -S a type of quantum number	**ITCHY**	*adj* ITCHIER, ITCHIEST causing an itching sensation **ITCHILY** *adv*
ISOSPORY	*n* pl. -RIES the condition of producing sexual or asexual spores of but one kind	**ITEM**	*v* -ED, -ING, -S to itemize
		ITEMISE	*v* -ISED, -ISING, -ISES itemize
ISOSTASY	*n* pl. -SIES the state of balance in the earth's crust	**ITEMIZE**	*v* -IZED, -IZING, -IZES to set down the particulars of
ISOTACH	*n* pl. -S a line on a map connecting points of equal wind velocity	**ITEMIZER**	*n* pl. -S one that itemizes
		ITERANCE	*n* pl. -S repetition
		ITERANT	*adj* repeating
ISOTHERE	*n* pl. -S a type of isotherm	**ITERATE**	*v* -ATED, -ATING, -ATES to repeat
ISOTHERM	*n* pl. -S a line on a map connecting points of equal mean temperature		
		ITERUM	*adv* again; once more
		ITHER	*adj* other
ISOTONE	*n* pl. -S a type of atom	**ITS**	*pron* the possessive form of the pronoun it
ISOTONIC	*adj* of equal tension		
ISOTOPE	*n* pl. -S a form of an element **ISOTOPIC** *adj*	**ITSELF**	*pron* a reflexive form of the pronoun it
ISOTOPY	*n* pl. -PIES the state of being an isotope	**IVIED**	*adj* covered with ivy
		IVORY	*n* pl. -RIES a hard white substance found in elephant tusks
ISOTROPY	*n* pl. -PIES the state of being identical in all directions		
ISOTYPE	*n* pl. -S a type of diagram **ISOTYPIC** *adj*	**IVY**	*n* pl. IVIES a climbing vine **IVYLIKE** *adj*
		IWIS	*adv* certainly
ISOZYME	*n* pl. -S a type of enzyme **ISOZYMIC** *adj*	**IXIA**	*n* pl. -S a flowering plant

IXODID   *n* pl. -S a bloodsucking insect
IXORA   *n* pl. -S a flowering plant
IXTLE   *n* pl. -S istle

IZAR   *n* pl. -S an outer garment worn by Muslim women
IZZARD   *n* pl. -S the letter Z

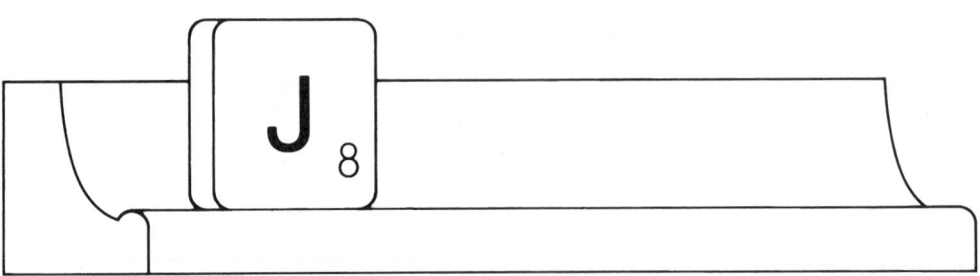

JAB *v* JABBED, JABBING, JABS to poke sharply

JABBER *v* -ED, -ING, -S to talk rapidly

JABBERER *n* pl. -S one that jabbers

JABBING present participle of jab

JABIRU *n* pl. -S a wading bird

JABOT *n* pl. -S a decoration on a shirt

JACAL *n* pl. -ES or -S a hut

JACAMAR *n* pl. -S a tropical bird

JACANA *n* pl. -S a wading bird

JACINTH *n* pl. -S a variety of zircon

JACINTHE *n* pl. -S an orange color

JACK *v* -ED, -ING, -S to raise with a type of lever

JACKAL *n* pl. -S a doglike mammal

JACKAROO *n* pl. -ROOS jackeroo

JACKASS *n* pl. -ES a male donkey

JACKBOOT *n* pl. -S a heavy boot

JACKDAW *n* pl. -S a crowlike bird

JACKER *n* pl. -S one that jacks

JACKEROO *n* pl. -ROOS an inexperienced ranch hand

JACKET *v* -ED, -ING, -S to provide with a jacket (a short coat)

JACKFISH *n* pl. -ES a food fish

JACKIES pl. of jacky

JACKLEG *n* pl. -S an unskilled worker

JACKPOT *n* pl. -S a top prize or reward

JACKROLL *v* -ED, -ING, -S to rob a drunken or sleeping person

JACKSTAY *n* pl. -STAYS a rope on a ship

JACKY *n* pl. JACKIES a sailor

JACOBIN *n* pl. -S a pigeon

JACOBUS *n* pl. -ES an old English coin

JACONET *n* pl. -S a cotton cloth

JACQUARD *n* pl. -S a fabric of intricate weave

JACULATE *v* -LATED, -LATING, -LATES to throw

JADE *v* JADED, JADING, JADES to weary **JADEDLY** *adv*

JADEITE *n* pl. -S a mineral **JADITIC** *adj*

JADISH *adj* worn-out **JADISHLY** *adv*

JAEGER *n* pl. -S a hunter

JAG *v* JAGGED, JAGGING, JAGS to cut unevenly

JAGER *n* pl. -S jaeger

JAGG *v* -ED, -ING, -S to jag

JAGGARY *n* pl. -RIES jaggery

JAGGED *adj* -GEDER, -GEDEST having a sharply uneven edge or surface **JAGGEDLY** *adv*

JAGGER *n* pl. -S one that jags

JAGGERY *n* pl. -GERIES a coarse, dark sugar

JAGGHERY *n* pl. -GHERIES jaggery

JAGGING present participle of jag

JAGGY *adj* -GIER, -GIEST jagged

JAGLESS *adj* smooth and even

JAGRA *n* pl. -S jaggery

JAGUAR *n* pl. -S a large feline animal

JAIL *v* -ED, -ING, -S to put in jail (a place of confinement)

JAILBAIT *n* pl. JAILBAIT a girl under the age of consent with whom sexual intercourse constitutes statutory rape

JAILBIRD *n* pl. -S a prisoner

JAILER *n* pl. -S a keeper of a jail

JAILOR *n* pl. -S jailer

JAKE *adj* all right; fine

JAKES *n/pl* an outhouse

JALAP	*n* pl. -S a Mexican plant **JALAPIC** *adj*
JALAPENO	*n* pl. -NOS a hot pepper
JALAPIN	*n* pl. -S a medicinal substance contained in jalap
JALOP	*n* pl. -S jalap
JALOPPY	*n* pl. -PIES jalopy
JALOPY	*n* pl. -LOPIES a decrepit car
JALOUSIE	*n* pl. -S a type of window
JAM	*v* JAMMED, JAMMING, JAMS to force together tightly
JAMB	*v* -ED, -ING, -S to jam
JAMBE	*n* pl. -S a jambeau
JAMBEAU	*n* pl. -BEAUX a piece of armor for the leg
JAMBOREE	*n* pl. -S a noisy celebration
JAMMED	past tense of jam
JAMMER	*n* pl. -S one that jams
JAMMIES	*n/pl* pajamas
JAMMING	present participle of jam
JAMMY	*adj* -MIER, -MIEST sticky with jam (boiled fruit and sugar)
JANE	*n* pl. -S a girl or woman
JANGLE	*v* -GLED, -GLING, -GLES to make a harsh, metallic sound
JANGLER	*n* pl. -S one that jangles
JANGLY	*adj* -GLIER, -GLIEST jangling
JANIFORM	*adj* hypocritical
JANISARY	*n* pl. -SARIES janizary
JANITOR	*n* pl. -S a maintenance man
JANIZARY	*n* pl. -ZARIES a Turkish soldier
JANTY	*adj* jaunty
JAPAN	*v* -PANNED, -PANNING, -PANS to coat with a glossy, black lacquer
JAPANIZE	*v* -NIZED, -NIZING, -NIZES to make Japanese
JAPANNER	*n* pl. -S one that japans
JAPANNING	present participle of japan
JAPE	*v* JAPED, JAPING, JAPES to mock
JAPER	*n* pl. -S one that japes
JAPERY	*n* pl. -ERIES mockery
JAPING	present participle of jape
JAPINGLY	*adv* in a japing manner
JAPONICA	*n* pl. -S an Asian shrub
JAR	*v* JARRED, JARRING, JARS to cause to shake
JARFUL	*n* pl. JARFULS or JARSFUL the quantity held by a jar (a cylindrical container)
JARGON	*v* -ED, -ING, -S to speak or write an obscure and often pretentious kind of language
JARGONEL	*n* pl. -S a variety of pear
JARGOON	*n* pl. -S a variety of zircon
JARHEAD	*n* pl. -S a marine soldier
JARINA	*n* pl. -S the hard seed of a palm tree
JARL	*n* pl. -S a Scandinavian nobleman
JARLDOM	*n* pl. -S the domain of a jarl
JAROSITE	*n* pl. -S a mineral
JAROVIZE	*v* -VIZED, -VIZING, -VIZES to hasten the flowering of a plant
JARRAH	*n* pl. -S an evergreen tree
JARRED	past tense of jar
JARRING	present participle of jar
JARSFUL	a pl. of jarful
JARVEY	*n* pl. -VEYS the driver of a carriage for hire
JASMIN	*n* pl. -S jasmine
JASMINE	*n* pl. -S a climbing shrub
JASPER	*n* pl. -S a variety of quartz **JASPERY** *adj*
JASSID	*n* pl. -S any of a family of plant pests
JATO	*n* pl. -TOS a takeoff aided by jet propulsion
JAUK	*v* -ED, -ING, -S to dawdle
JAUNCE	*v* JAUNCED, JAUNCING, JAUNCES to prance
JAUNDICE	*v* -DICED, -DICING, -DICES to prejudice unfavorably
JAUNT	*v* -ED, -ING, -S to make a pleasure trip
JAUNTY	*adj* -TIER, -TIEST having a lively and self-confident manner **JAUNTILY** *adv*
JAUP	*v* -ED, -ING, -S to splash
JAVA	*n* pl. -S coffee
JAVELIN	*v* -ED, -ING, -S to pierce with a javelin (a light spear)
JAVELINA	*n* pl. -S a peccary
JAW	*v* -ED, -ING, -S to jabber
JAWAN	*n* pl. -S a soldier of India
JAWBONE	*v* -BONED, -BONING, -BONES to attempt to convince

JAWBONER *n* pl. -S one that jawbones

JAWLIKE *adj* resembling the jaw (the framework of the mouth)

JAWLINE *n* pl. -S the outline of the lower jaw

JAY *n* pl. JAYS a corvine bird

JAYBIRD *n* pl. -S a jay

JAYGEE *n* pl. -S a military officer

JAYVEE *n* pl. -S a junior varsity player

JAYWALK *v* -ED, -ING, -S to cross a street recklessly

JAZZ *v* -ED, -ING, -ES to enliven

JAZZER *n* pl. -S one that jazzes

JAZZLIKE *adj* resembling a type of music

JAZZMAN *n* pl. -MEN a type of musician

JAZZY *adj* JAZZIER, JAZZIEST lively **JAZZILY** *adv*

JEALOUS *adj* resentful of another's advantages

JEALOUSY *n* pl. -SIES a jealous feeling

JEAN *n* pl. -S a durable cotton fabric

JEBEL *n* pl. -S a mountain

JEE *v* JEED, JEEING, JEES to gee

JEEP *v* -ED, -ING, -S to travel by a small type of motor vehicle

JEEPERS *interj* — used as a mild oath

JEEPNEY *n* pl. -NEYS a Philippine jitney

JEER *v* -ED, -ING, -S to mock

JEERER *n* pl. -S one that jeers

JEEZ *interj* — used as a mild oath

JEFE *n* pl. -S a chief

JEHAD *n* pl. -S jihad

JEHU *n* pl. -S a fast driver

JEJUNA pl. of jejunum

JEJUNAL *adj* pertaining to the jejunum

JEJUNE *adj* uninteresting; childish **JEJUNELY** *adv*

JEJUNITY *n* pl. -TIES something that is jejune

JEJUNUM *n* pl. -NA a part of the small intestine

JELL *v* -ED, -ING, -S to congeal

JELLABA *n* pl. -S djellaba

JELLIFY *v* -FIED, -FYING, -FIES to jelly

JELLY *v* -LIED, -LYING, -LIES to make into a jelly (a soft, semisolid substance)

JELUTONG *n* pl. -S a tropical tree

JEMADAR *n* pl. -S an officer in the army of India

JEMIDAR *n* pl. -S jemadar

JEMMY *v* -MIED, -MYING, -MIES to jimmy

JENNET *n* pl. -S a small horse

JENNY *n* pl. -NIES a female donkey

JEON *n* pl. JEON a monetary unit of South Korea

JEOPARD *v* -ED, -ING, -S to imperil

JEOPARDY *n* pl. -DIES risk of loss or injury

JERBOA *n* pl. -S a small rodent

JEREED *n* pl. -S a wooden javelin

JEREMIAD *n* pl. -S a tale of woe

JERID *n* pl. -S jereed

JERK *v* -ED, -ING, -S to move with a sharp, sudden motion

JERKER *n* pl. -S one that jerks

JERKIES pl. of jerky

JERKIN *n* pl. -S a sleeveless jacket

JERKY *adj* JERKIER, JERKIEST characterized by jerking movements **JERKILY** *adv*

JERKY *n* pl. -KIES dried meat

JEROBOAM *n* pl. -S a wine bottle

JERREED *n* pl. -S jereed

JERRICAN *n* pl. -S jerrycan

JERRID *n* pl. -S jereed

JERRY *n* pl. -RIES a German soldier

JERRYCAN *n* pl. -S a fuel container

JERSEY *n* pl. -SEYS a close-fitting knitted shirt **JERSEYED** *adj*

JESS *v* -ED, -ING, -ES to fasten straps around the legs of a hawk

JESSANT *adj* shooting forth

JESSE *v* JESSED, JESSING, JESSES to jess

JEST *v* -ED, -ING, -S to joke

JESTER *n* pl. -S one that jests

JESTFUL *adj* tending to jest

JESTING *n* pl. -S the act of one who jests

JET *v* JETTED, JETTING, JETS to spurt forth in a stream

JETBEAD *n* pl. -S an ornamental shrub

JETE *n* pl. -S a ballet leap

JETLIKE *adj* resembling a jet airplane

JETLINER *n* pl. -S a type of aircraft

JETON *n* pl. -S jetton

JETPORT *n* pl. -S a type of airport

JETSAM *n* pl. -S goods cast overboard

JETSOM *n* pl. -S jetsam

JETTED past tense of jet

JETTIED past tense of jetty

JETTIER comparative of jetty

JETTIES present 3d person sing. of jetty

JETTIEST superlative of jetty

JETTING present participle of jet

JETTISON *v* -ED, -ING, -S to cast overboard

JETTON *n* pl. -S a piece used in counting

JETTY *v* -TIED, -TYING, -TIES to jut

JETTY *adj* -TIER, -TIEST having the color jet black

JEU *n* pl. JEUX a game

JEWEL *v* -ELED, -ELING, -ELS or -ELLED, -ELLING, -ELS to adorn or equip with jewels (precious stones)

JEWELER *n* pl. -S a dealer or maker of jewelry

JEWELLER *n* pl. -S jeweler

JEWELLING a present participle of jewel

JEWELRY *n* pl. -RIES an article or articles for personal adornment

JEWFISH *n* pl. -ES a large marine fish

JEZAIL *n* pl. -S a type of firearm

JEZEBEL *n* pl. -S a scheming, wicked woman

JIAO *n* pl. JIAO chiao

JIB *v* JIBBED, JIBBING, JIBS to refuse to proceed further

JIBB *v* -ED, -ING, -S to shift from side to side while sailing

JIBBER *n* pl. -S a horse that jibs

JIBBING present participle of jib

JIBBOOM *n* pl. -S a ship's spar

JIBE *v* JIBED, JIBING, JIBES to gibe **JIBINGLY** *adv*

JIBER *n* pl. -S one that jibes

JICAMA *n* pl. -S a tropical plant with edible roots

JIFF *n* pl. -S jiffy

JIFFY *n* pl. -FIES a short time

JIG *v* JIGGED, JIGGING, JIGS to bob

JIGGER *v* -ED, -ING, -S to jerk up and down

JIGGERED *adj* damned

JIGGING present participle of jig

JIGGLE *v* -GLED, -GLING, -GLES to shake lightly

JIGGLY *adj* -GLIER, -GLIEST unsteady

JIGSAW *v* -SAWED, -SAWN, -SAWING, -SAWS to cut with a type of saw

JIHAD *n* pl. -S a Muslim holy war

JILL *n* pl. -S a unit of liquid measure

JILLION *n* pl. -S a very large number

JILT *v* -ED, -ING, -S to reject a lover

JILTER *n* pl. -S one that jilts

JIMINY *interj* — used to express surprise

JIMJAMS *n/pl* violent delirium

JIMMINY *interj* jiminy

JIMMY *v* -MIED, -MYING, -MIES to pry open with a crowbar

JIMP *adj* JIMPER, JIMPEST natty **JIMPLY** *adv*

JIMPY *adj* jimp

JIN *n* pl. -S jinn

JINGAL *n* pl. -S a heavy musket

JINGALL *n* pl. -S jingal

JINGKO *n* pl. -KOES ginkgo

JINGLE *v* -GLED, -GLING, -GLES to make a tinkling sound

JINGLER *n* pl. -S one that jingles

JINGLY *adj* -GLIER, -GLIEST jingling

JINGO *n* pl. -GOES a zealous patriot **JINGOISH** *adj*

JINGOISM *n* pl. -S the spirit or policy of jingoes

JINGOIST *n* pl. -S a jingo

JINK *v* -ED, -ING, -S to move quickly out of the way

JINKER *n* pl. -S one that jinks

JINN *n* pl. -S a supernatural being in Muslim mythology

JINNEE *n* pl. JINN jinn

JINNI *n* pl. JINN jinn

JINX *v* -ED, -ING, -ES to bring bad luck to

JIPIJAPA *n* pl. -S a tropical plant

JITNEY *n* pl. -NEYS a small bus

JITTER *v* -ED, -ING, -S to fidget

JITTERY *adj* -TERIER, -TERIEST extremely nervous

JIUJITSU *n* pl. -S jujitsu

JIUJUTSU *n* pl. -S jujitsu

JIVE *v* JIVED, JIVING, JIVES to play jazz or swing music

JIVEASS *adj* insincere, phony

JIVER *n* pl. -S one that jives

JIVEY *adj* JIVIER, JIVIEST jazzy, lively

JNANA *n* pl. -S knowledge acquired through meditation

JO *n* pl. JOES a sweetheart

JOANNES *n* pl. JOANNES johannes

JOB *v* JOBBED, JOBBING, JOBS to work by the piece

JOBBER *n* pl. -S a pieceworker

JOBBERY *n* pl. -BERIES corruption in public office

JOBBING present participle of job

JOBLESS *adj* having no job

JOBNAME *n* pl. -S a computer code for a job instruction

JOCK *n* pl. -S an athletic supporter

JOCKETTE *n* pl. -S a woman who rides horses in races

JOCKEY *v* -EYED, -EYING, -EYS to maneuver for an advantage

JOCKO *n* pl. JOCKOS a monkey

JOCOSE *adj* humorous **JOCOSELY** *adv*

JOCOSITY *n* pl. -TIES the state of being jocose

JOCULAR *adj* given to joking

JOCUND *adj* cheerful **JOCUNDLY** *adv*

JODHPUR *n* pl. -S a type of boot

JOE *n* pl. -S a fellow

JOEY *n* pl. -EYS a young kangaroo

JOG *v* JOGGED, JOGGING, JOGS to run at a slow, steady pace

JOGGER *n* pl. -S one that jogs

JOGGING *n* pl. -S the practice of running at a slow, steady pace

JOGGLE *v* -GLED, -GLING, -GLES to shake slightly

JOGGLER *n* pl. -S one that joggles

JOHANNES *n* pl. JOHANNES a Portuguese coin

JOHN *n* pl. -S a toilet

JOHNBOAT *n* pl. -S a narrow square-ended boat

JOHNNY *n* pl. -NIES a sleeveless hospital gown

JOIN *v* -ED, -ING, -S to unite **JOINABLE** *adj*

JOINDER *n* pl. -S a joining of parties in a lawsuit

JOINER *n* pl. -S a carpenter

JOINERY *n* pl. -ERIES the trade of a joiner

JOINING *n* pl. -S a juncture

JOINT *v* -ED, -ING, -S to fit together by means of a junction

JOINTER *n* pl. -S one that joints

JOINTLY *adv* together

JOINTURE *v* -TURED, -TURING, -TURES to set aside property as an inheritance

JOIST *v* -ED, -ING, -S to support with horizontal beams

JOJOBA *n* pl. -S a small tree

JOKE *v* JOKED, JOKING, JOKES to say something amusing

JOKER *n* pl. -S one that jokes

JOKESTER *n* pl. -S a practical joker

JOKEY *adj* JOKIER, JOKIEST amusing **JOKILY** *adv*

JOKIER comparative of jokey

JOKIEST superlative of jokey

JOKINESS *n* pl. -ES the state of being jokey

JOKING present participle of joke

JOKINGLY *adv* in a joking manner

JOKY *adj* JOKIER, JOKIEST jokey

JOLE *n* pl. -S jowl

JOLLIED past tense of jolly

JOLLIER comparative of jolly

JOLLIES present 3d person sing. of jolly

JOLLIEST superlative of jolly

JOLLIFY *v* -FIED, -FYING, -FIES to make jolly

JOLLITY *n* pl. -TIES mirth

JOLLY *adj* -LIER, -LIEST cheerful **JOLLILY** *adv*

JOLLY *v* -LIED, -LYING, -LIES to put in a good humor for one's own purposes

JOLT *v* -ED, -ING, -S to jar or shake roughly

JOLTER *n* pl. -S one that jolts

JOLTY *adj* JOLTIER, JOLTIEST marked by a jolting motion **JOLTILY** *adv*

JONES	*n* pl. JONESES a drug addiction
JONGLEUR	*n* pl. -S a minstrel
JONQUIL	*n* pl. -S a perennial herb
JORAM	*n* pl. -S jorum
JORDAN	*n* pl. -S a type of container
JORUM	*n* pl. -S a large drinking bowl
JOSEPH	*n* pl. -S a woman's long cloak
JOSH	*v* -ED, -ING, -ES to tease
JOSHER	*n* pl. -S one that joshes
JOSS	*n* pl. -ES a Chinese idol
JOSTLE	*v* -TLED, -TLING, -TLES to bump or push roughly
JOSTLER	*n* pl. -S one that jostles
JOT	*v* JOTTED, JOTTING, JOTS to write down quickly
JOTA	*n* pl. -S a Spanish dance
JOTTER	*n* pl. -S one that jots
JOTTING	*n* pl. -S a brief note
JOTTY	*adj* written down quickly
JOUAL	*n* pl. -S a dialect of Canadian French
JOUK	*v* -ED, -ING, -S to dodge
JOULE	*n* pl. -S a unit of energy
JOUNCE	*v* JOUNCED, JOUNCING, JOUNCES to move roughly up and down
JOUNCY	*adj* JOUNCIER, JOUNCIEST marked by a jouncing motion
JOURNAL	*n* pl. -S a record of daily events
JOURNEY	*v* -ED, -ING, -S to travel
JOUST	*v* -ED, -ING, -S to engage in personal combat
JOUSTER	*n* pl. -S one that jousts
JOVIAL	*adj* good-humored **JOVIALLY** *adv*
JOVIALTY	*n* pl. -TIES the quality or state of being jovial
JOW	*v* -ED, -ING, -S to toll
JOWAR	*n* pl. -S a durra grown in India
JOWL	*n* pl. -S the fleshy part under the lower jaw **JOWLED** *adj*
JOWLY	*adj* JOWLIER, JOWLIEST having prominent jowls
JOY	*v* -ED, -ING, -S to rejoice
JOYANCE	*n* pl. -S gladness
JOYFUL	*adj* -FULLER, -FULLEST happy **JOYFULLY** *adv*
JOYLESS	*adj* being without gladness
JOYOUS	*adj* joyful **JOYOUSLY** *adv*
JOYPOP	*v* -POPPED, -POPPING, -POPS to use habit-forming drugs occasionally
JOYRIDE	*v* -RODE, -RIDDEN, -RIDING, -RIDES to take an automobile ride for pleasure
JOYRIDER	*n* pl. -S one that joyrides
JOYSTICK	*n* pl. -S the control stick in an airplane
JUBA	*n* pl. -S a lively dance
JUBBAH	*n* pl. -S a loose outer garment
JUBE	*n* pl. -S a platform in a church
JUBHAH	*n* pl. -S jubbah
JUBILANT	*adj* exultant
JUBILATE	*v* -LATED, -LATING, -LATES to exult
JUBILE	*n* pl. -S jubilee
JUBILEE	*n* pl. -S a celebration
JUDAS	*n* pl. -ES a peephole
JUDDER	*v* -ED, -ING, -S to vibrate
JUDGE	*v* JUDGED, JUDGING, JUDGES to decide on critically
JUDGER	*n* pl. -S one that judges
JUDGMENT	*n* pl. -S an authoritative opinion
JUDICIAL	*adj* pertaining to courts of law
JUDO	*n* pl. -DOS a form of jujitsu
JUDOIST	*n* pl. -S one skilled in judo
JUDOKA	*n* pl. -S a judoist
JUG	*v* JUGGED, JUGGING, JUGS to put into a jug (a large, deep container with a narrow mouth and a handle)
JUGA	a pl. of jugum
JUGAL	*adj* pertaining to the cheek or cheekbone
JUGATE	*adj* occurring in pairs
JUGFUL	*n* pl. JUGFULS or JUGSFUL as much as a jug will hold
JUGGED	past tense of jug
JUGGING	present participle of jug
JUGGLE	*v* -GLED, -GLING, -GLES to perform feats of manual dexterity
JUGGLER	*n* pl. -S one that juggles
JUGGLERY	*n* pl. -GLERIES the art of a juggler
JUGGLING	*n* pl. -S jugglery
JUGHEAD	*n* pl. -S a dolt
JUGSFUL	a pl. of jugful

JUGULA pl. of jugulum

JUGULAR *n* pl. -S a vein of the neck

JUGULATE *v* -LATED, -LATING, -LATES to suppress a disease by extreme measures

JUGULUM *n* pl. -LA a part of a bird's neck

JUGUM *n* pl. -GA or -GUMS a pair of the opposite leaflets of a pinnate leaf

JUICE *v* JUICED, JUICING, JUICES to extract the juice (the liquid part of a fruit or vegetable) from

JUICER *n* pl. -S a juice extractor

JUICY *adj* JUICIER, JUICIEST full of juice **JUICILY** *adv*

JUJITSU *n* pl. -S a Japanese art of self-defense

JUJU *n* pl. -S an object regarded as having magical power

JUJUBE *n* pl. -S a fruit-flavored candy

JUJUISM *n* pl. -S the system of beliefs connected with jujus

JUJUIST *n* pl. -S a follower of jujuism

JUJUTSU *n* pl. -S jujitsu

JUKE *v* JUKED, JUKING, JUKES to fake out of position

JUKEBOX *n* pl. -ES a coin-operated phonograph

JULEP *n* pl. -S a sweet drink

JULIENNE *v* -ENNED, -ENNING, -ENNES to cut food into long thin strips

JUMBAL *n* pl. -S a ring-shaped cookie

JUMBLE *v* -BLED, -BLING, -BLES to mix in a disordered manner

JUMBLER *n* pl. -S one that jumbles

JUMBO *n* pl. -BOS a very large specimen of its kind

JUMBUCK *n* pl. -S a sheep

JUMP *v* -ED, -ING, -S to spring off the ground

JUMPER *n* pl. -S one that jumps

JUMPOFF *n* pl. -S a starting point

JUMPSUIT *n* pl. -S a one-piece garment

JUMPY *adj* JUMPIER, JUMPIEST nervous **JUMPILY** *adv*

JUN *n* pl. JUN a coin of North Korea

JUNCO *n* pl. -COS or -COES a small finch

JUNCTION *n* pl. -S a place where things join

JUNCTURE *n* pl. -S the act of joining

JUNGLE *n* pl. -S land covered with dense tropical vegetation **JUNGLED** *adj*

JUNGLY *adj* -GLIER, -GLIEST resembling a jungle

JUNIOR *n* pl. -S a person who is younger than another

JUNIPER *n* pl. -S an evergreen tree

JUNK *v* -ED, -ING, -S to discard as trash

JUNKER *n* pl. -S something ready for junking

JUNKET *v* -ED, -ING, -S to banquet

JUNKETER *n* pl. -S one that junkets

JUNKIE *n* pl. -S a drug addict

JUNKMAN *n* pl. -MEN one who buys and sells junk

JUNKY *adj* JUNKIER, JUNKIEST worthless

JUNKYARD *n* pl. -S a place where junk is stored

JUNTA *n* pl. -S a political or governmental council

JUNTO *n* pl. -TOS a political faction

JUPE *n* pl. -S a woman's jacket

JUPON *n* pl. -S a tunic

JURA pl. of jus

JURAL *adj* pertaining to law **JURALLY** *adv*

JURANT *n* pl. -S one that takes an oath

JURAT *n* pl. -S a statement on an affidavit

JURATORY *adj* pertaining to an oath

JUREL *n* pl. -S a food fish

JURIDIC *adj* pertaining to the law

JURIST *n* pl. -S one versed in the law **JURISTIC** *adj*

JUROR *n* pl. -S a member of a jury

JURY *v* -RIED, -RYING, -RIES to select material for exhibition

JURYMAN *n* pl. -MEN a juror

JUS *n* pl. JURA a legal right

JUSSIVE *n* pl. -S a word used to express command

JUST *v* -ED, -ING, -S to joust

JUST *adj* JUSTER, JUSTEST acting in conformity with what is morally good

JUSTER *n* pl. -S jouster

JUSTICE *n* pl. -S a judge

JUSTIFY   *v* -FIED, -FYING, -FIES to show to be just, right, or valid

JUSTLE   *v* -TLED, -TLING, -TLES to jostle

JUSTLY   *adv* in a just manner

JUSTNESS   *n* pl. -ES the quality of being just

JUT   *v* JUTTED, JUTTING, JUTS to protrude

JUTE   *n* pl. -S a strong, coarse fiber

JUTTY   *v* -TIED, -TYING, -TIES to jut

JUVENAL   *n* pl. -S a young bird's plumage

JUVENILE   *n* pl. -S a young person

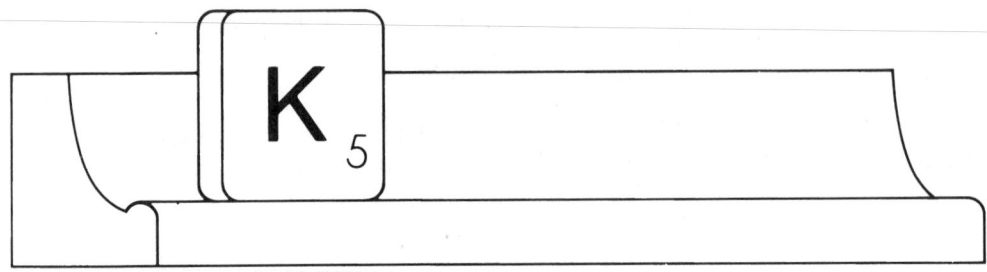

KA	*n* pl. -S the spiritual self of a human being in Egyptian religion
KAAS	*n* pl. KAAS kas
KAB	*n* pl. -S an ancient Hebrew unit of measure
KABAB	*n* pl. -S kabob
KABAKA	*n* pl. -S a Ugandan emperor
KABALA	*n* pl. -S cabala
KABAR	*n* pl. -S caber
KABAYA	*n* pl. -S a cotton jacket
KABBALA	*n* pl. -S cabala
KABBALAH	*n* pl. -S cabala
KABELJOU	*n* pl. -S a large food fish
KABIKI	*n* pl. -S a tropical tree
KABOB	*n* pl. -S cubes of meat cooked on a skewer
KABUKI	*n* pl. -S a form of Japanese theater
KACHINA	*n* pl. -S an ancestral spirit
KADDISH	*n* pl. -DISHIM a Jewish prayer
KADI	*n* pl. -S cadi
KAE	*n* pl. -S a bird resembling a crow
KAF	*n* pl. -S kaph
KAFFIR	*n* pl. -S kafir
KAFFIYEH	*n* pl. -S a large, square kerchief
KAFIR	*n* pl. -S a cereal grass
KAFTAN	*n* pl. -S caftan
KAGU	*n* pl. -S a flightless bird
KAHUNA	*n* pl. -S a medicine man
KAIAK	*n* pl. -S kayak
KAIF	*n* pl. -S kef
KAIL	*n* pl. -S kale
KAILYARD	*n* pl. -S kaleyard
KAIN	*n* pl. -S a tax paid in produce or livestock
KAINIT	*n* pl. -S kainite
KAINITE	*n* pl. -S a mineral salt
KAISER	*n* pl. -S an emperor
KAISERIN	*n* pl. -S a kaiser's wife
KAJEPUT	*n* pl. -S cajuput
KAKA	*n* pl. -S a parrot
KAKAPO	*n* pl. -POS a flightless parrot
KAKEMONO	*n* pl. -NOS a Japanese scroll
KAKI	*n* pl. -S a Japanese tree
KAKIEMON	*n* pl. -S a Japanese porcelain
KALAM	*n* pl. -S a type of Muslim theology
KALE	*n* pl. -S a variety of cabbage
KALENDS	*n* pl. KALENDS calends
KALEWIFE	*n* pl. -WIVES a female vegetable vendor
KALEYARD	*n* pl. -S a kitchen garden
KALIAN	*n* pl. -S a hookah
KALIF	*n* pl. -S caliph
KALIFATE	*n* pl. -S califate
KALIMBA	*n* pl. -S an African musical instrument
KALIPH	*n* pl. -S caliph
KALIUM	*n* pl. -S potassium
KALLIDIN	*n* pl. -S a hormone
KALMIA	*n* pl. -S an evergreen shrub
KALONG	*n* pl. -S a fruit-eating bat
KALPA	*n* pl. -S a period of time in Hindu religion
KALPAK	*n* pl. -S calpac
KALYPTRA	*n* pl. -S a thin veil
KAMAAINA	*n* pl. -S a longtime resident of Hawaii
KAMACITE	*n* pl. -S an alloy of nickel and iron
KAMALA	*n* pl. -S an Asian tree
KAME	*n* pl. -S a mound of detrital material

KAMI	*n* pl. KAMI a sacred power or force
KAMIK	*n* pl. -S a type of boot
KAMIKAZE	*n* pl. -S a plane to be flown in a suicide crash on a target
KAMPONG	*n* pl. -S a small village
KAMSEEN	*n* pl. -S khamsin
KAMSIN	*n* pl. -S khamsin
KANA	*n* pl. -S the Japanese syllabic script
KANBAN	*n* pl. -S a manufacturing strategy wherein parts are delivered only as needed
KANE	*n* pl. -S kain
KANGAROO	*n* pl. -ROOS an Australian mammal
KANJI	*n* pl. -S a system of Japanese writing
KANTAR	*n* pl. -S a unit of weight
KANTELE	*n* pl. -S a type of harp
KAOLIANG	*n* pl. -S an Asian sorghum
KAOLIN	*n* pl. -S a fine white clay **KAOLINIC** *adj*
KAOLINE	*n* pl. -S kaolin
KAON	*n* pl. -S a type of meson
KAPA	*n* pl. -S a coarse cloth
KAPH	*n* pl. -S a Hebrew letter
KAPOK	*n* pl. -S a mass of silky fibers
KAPPA	*n* pl. -S a Greek letter
KAPUT	*adj* ruined
KAPUTT	*adj* kaput
KARAKUL	*n* pl. -S an Asian sheep
KARAOKE	*n* pl. -S a musical device to which a user sings along
KARAT	*n* pl. -S a unit of quality for gold
KARATE	*n* pl. -S a Japanese art of self-defense
KARMA	*n* pl. -S the force generated by a person's actions **KARMIC** *adj*
KARN	*n* pl. -S cairn
KAROO	*n* pl. -ROOS karroo
KAROSS	*n* pl. -ES an African garment
KARROO	*n* pl. -ROOS a dry plateau
KARST	*n* pl. -S a limestone region **KARSTIC** *adj*
KART	*n* pl. -S a small motor vehicle
KARTING	*n* pl. -S the sport of racing karts

KARYOTIN	*n* pl. -S the nuclear material of a cell
KAS	*n* pl. KAS a large cupboard
KASBAH	*n* pl. -S casbah
KASHA	*n* pl. -S a cooked cereal
KASHER	*v* -ED, -ING, -S to kosher
KASHMIR	*n* pl. -S cashmere
KASHRUT	*n* pl. -S kashruth
KASHRUTH	*n* pl. -S the Jewish dietary laws
KAT	*n* pl. -S an evergreen shrub
KATA	*n* pl. -S an exercise of set movements
KATAKANA	*n* pl. -S a Japanese syllabic symbol
KATCHINA	*n* pl. -S kachina
KATCINA	*n* pl. -S kachina
KATHODE	*n* pl. -S cathode **KATHODAL, KATHODIC** *adj*
KATION	*n* pl. -S cation
KATYDID	*n* pl. -S a grasshopper
KAURI	*n* pl. -S a timber tree
KAURY	*n* pl. -RIES kauri
KAVA	*n* pl. -S a tropical shrub
KAVAKAVA	*n* pl. -S kava
KAVASS	*n* pl. -ES a Turkish policeman
KAY	*n* pl. KAYS the letter K
KAYAK	*v* -ED, -ING, -S to travel in a kayak (an Eskimo canoe)
KAYAKER	*n* pl. -S one that rides in a kayak
KAYAKING	*n* pl. -S the act or skill of managing a kayak
KAYLES	*n/pl* a British game
KAYO	*v* -ED, -ING, -S or -ES to knock out
KAZACHOK	*n* pl. -ZACHKI a Russian folk dance
KAZATSKI	*n* pl. -ES kazachok
KAZATSKY	*n* pl. -SKIES kazachok
KAZOO	*n* pl. -ZOOS a toy musical instrument
KBAR	*n* pl. -S a kilobar
KEA	*n* pl. -S a parrot
KEBAB	*n* pl. -S kabob
KEBAR	*n* pl. -S caber
KEBBIE	*n* pl. -S a rough walking stick
KEBBOCK	*n* pl. -S kebbuck
KEBBUCK	*n* pl. -S a whole cheese

KEBLAH	*n* pl. -S kiblah
KEBOB	*n* pl. -S kabob
KECK	*v* -ED, -ING, -S to retch
KECKLE	*v* -LED, -LING, -LES to wind with rope to prevent chafing
KEDDAH	*n* pl. -S an enclosure for elephants
KEDGE	*v* KEDGED, KEDGING, KEDGES to move a vessel with the use of an anchor
KEDGEREE	*n* pl. -S a food in India
KEEF	*n* pl. -S kef
KEEK	*v* -ED, -ING, -S to peep
KEEL	*v* -ED, -ING, -S to capsize
KEELAGE	*n* pl. -S the amount paid to keep a boat in a harbor
KEELBOAT	*n* pl. -S a freight boat
KEELHALE	*v* -HALED, -HALING, -HALES to keelhaul
KEELHAUL	*v* -ED, -ING, -S to rebuke severely
KEELLESS	*adj* having no keel (the main structural part of a ship)
KEELSON	*n* pl. -S a beam in a ship
KEEN	*adj* KEENER, KEENEST enthusiastic
KEEN	*v* -ED, -ING, -S to wail loudly over the dead
KEENER	*n* pl. -S one that keens
KEENLY	*adv* in a keen manner
KEENNESS	*n* pl. -ES sharpness
KEEP	*v* KEPT, KEEPING, KEEPS to continue to possess **KEEPABLE** *adj*
KEEPER	*n* pl. -S one that keeps
KEEPING	*n* pl. -S custody
KEEPSAKE	*n* pl. -S a memento
KEESHOND	*n* pl. -HONDS or -HONDEN a small, heavy-coated dog
KEESTER	*n* pl. -S keister
KEET	*n* pl. -S a young guinea fowl
KEEVE	*n* pl. -S a tub or vat
KEF	*n* pl. -S hemp smoked to produce euphoria
KEFFIYEH	*n* pl. -S kaffiyeh
KEFIR	*n* pl. -S a fermented beverage made from cow's milk
KEG	*n* pl. -S a small barrel
KEGELER	*n* pl. -S kegler
KEGLER	*n* pl. -S a bowler
KEGLING	*n* pl. -S bowling
KEIR	*n* pl. -S kier
KEISTER	*n* pl. -S the buttocks
KEITLOA	*n* pl. -S a rhinoceros
KELEP	*n* pl. -S a stinging ant
KELIM	*n* pl. -S kilim
KELLY	*n* pl. -LIES a bright green color
KELOID	*n* pl. -S a scar caused by excessive growth of fibrous tissue **KELOIDAL** *adj*
KELP	*v* -ED, -ING, -S to burn a type of seaweed
KELPIE	*n* pl. -S a water sprite
KELPY	*n* pl. -PIES kelpie
KELSON	*n* pl. -S keelson
KELTER	*n* pl. -S kilter
KELVIN	*n* pl. -S a unit of temperature
KEMP	*n* pl. -S a champion
KEMPT	*adj* neatly kept
KEN	*v* KENNED or KENT, KENNING, KENS to know
KENAF	*n* pl. -S an East Indian plant
KENCH	*n* pl. -ES a bin for salting fish
KENDO	*n* pl. -DOS a Japanese sport
KENNED	a past tense of ken
KENNEL	*v* -NELED, -NELING, -NELS or -NELLED, -NELLING, -NELS to keep in a shelter for dogs
KENNING	*n* pl. -S a metaphorical compound word or phrase
KENO	*n* pl. -NOS a game of chance
KENOSIS	*n* pl. -SISES the incarnation of Christ **KENOTIC** *adj*
KENOTRON	*n* pl. -S a type of diode
KENT	a past tense of ken
KEP	*v* KEPPED, KEPPEN or KIPPEN, KEPPING, KEPS to catch
KEPHALIN	*n* pl. -S cephalin
KEPI	*n* pl. -S a type of cap
KEPPED	past tense of kep
KEPPEN	a past participle of kep
KEPPING	present participle of kep
KEPT	past tense of keep
KERAMIC	*n* pl. -S ceramic
KERATIN	*n* pl. -S a fibrous protein
KERATOID	*adj* horny

KERATOMA	*n* pl. -MAS or -MATA a skin disease	**KEVIL**	*n* pl. -S kevel
KERATOSE	*adj* of or resembling horny tissue	**KEX**	*n* pl. -ES a dry, hollow stalk
KERB	*v* -ED, -ING, -S to provide with curbing	**KEY**	*v* -ED, -ING, -S to provide with a key (a device used to turn the bolt in a lock)
KERCHIEF	*n* pl. -CHIEFS or -CHIEVES a cloth worn as a head covering	**KEYBOARD**	*v* -ED, -ING, -S to operate a machine by means of a keyset
KERCHOO	*interj* ahchoo	**KEYCARD**	*n* pl. -S a coded card for operating a device
KERF	*v* -ED, -ING, -S to make an incision with a cutting tool	**KEYHOLE**	*n* pl. -S a hole for a key
KERMES	*n* pl. KERMES a red dye	**KEYLESS**	*adj* being without a key
KERMESS	*n* pl. -ES kermis	**KEYNOTE**	*v* -NOTED, -NOTING, -NOTES to deliver the main speech at a function
KERMESSE	*n* pl. -S kermis		
KERMIS	*n* pl. -MISES a local outdoor festival	**KEYNOTER**	*n* pl. -S one that keynotes
KERN	*v* -ED, -ING, -S to be formed with a projecting typeface	**KEYPAD**	*n* pl. -S a small keyboard
KERNE	*n* pl. -S a medieval foot soldier	**KEYPUNCH**	*v* -ED, -ING, -ES to perforate with a machine
KERNEL	*v* -NELED, -NELING, -NELS or -NELLED, -NELLING, -NELS to envelop as a kernel (the inner part of a nut)	**KEYSET**	*n* pl. -S a system of finger levers
		KEYSTER	*n* pl. -S keister
		KEYSTONE	*n* pl. -S the central stone of an arch
KERNITE	*n* pl. -S a mineral	**KEYWAY**	*n* pl. -WAYS a slot for a key
KEROGEN	*n* pl. -S a substance found in shale	**KEYWORD**	*n* pl. -S a significant word
KEROSENE	*n* pl. -S a fuel oil	**KHADDAR**	*n* pl. -S a cotton cloth
KEROSINE	*n* pl. -S kerosene	**KHADI**	*n* pl. -S khaddar
KERPLUNK	*v* -ED, -ING, -S to fall or drop with a heavy sound	**KHAF**	*n* pl. -S kaph
		KHAKI	*n* pl. -S a durable cloth
KERRIA	*n* pl. -S a Chinese shrub	**KHALIF**	*n* pl. -S caliph
KERRY	*n* pl. -RIES one of an Irish breed of cattle	**KHALIFA**	*n* pl. -S caliph
KERSEY	*n* pl. -SEYS a woolen cloth	**KHAMSEEN**	*n* pl. -S khamsin
KERYGMA	*n* pl. -MATA the preaching of the gospel	**KHAMSIN**	*n* pl. -S a hot, dry wind
		KHAN	*n* pl. -S an Asian ruler
KESTREL	*n* pl. -S a small falcon	**KHANATE**	*n* pl. -S the domain of a khan
KETCH	*n* pl. -ES a sailing vessel	**KHAPH**	*n* pl. -S kaph
KETCHUP	*n* pl. -S a spicy tomato sauce	**KHAT**	*n* pl. -S kat
KETENE	*n* pl. -S a toxic gas	**KHAZEN**	*n* pl. -ZENS or -ZENIM hazzan
KETO	*adj* of or pertaining to ketone	**KHEDA**	*n* pl. -S keddah
KETOL	*n* pl. -S a chemical compound	**KHEDAH**	*n* pl. -S keddah
KETONE	*n* pl. -S a type of chemical compound **KETONIC** *adj*	**KHEDIVE**	*n* pl. -S a Turkish viceroy **KHEDIVAL** *adj*
KETOSE	*n* pl. -S a simple sugar	**KHET**	*n* pl. -S heth
KETOSIS	*n* pl. -TOSES a buildup of ketones in the body **KETOTIC** *adj*	**KHETH**	*n* pl. -S heth
		KHI	*n* pl. -S chi
KETTLE	*n* pl. -S a vessel for boiling liquids	**KHIRKAH**	*n* pl. -S a patchwork garment
KEVEL	*n* pl. -S a belaying cleat or peg	**KHOUM**	*n* pl. -S a monetary unit of Mauritania

KIANG	*n* pl. -S a wild ass
KIAUGH	*n* pl. -S trouble; worry
KIBBE	*n* pl. -S a Near Eastern dish of ground lamb and bulgur
KIBBEH	*n* pl. -S kibbe
KIBBI	*n* pl. -S kibbe
KIBBITZ	*v* -ED, -ING, -ES kibitz
KIBBLE	*v* -BLED, -BLING, -BLES to grind coarsely
KIBBUTZ	*n* pl. -BUTZIM a collective farm in Israel
KIBE	*n* pl. -S a sore caused by exposure to cold
KIBEI	*n* pl. -S one born in America of immigrant Japanese parents and educated in Japan
KIBITZ	*v* -ED, -ING, -ES to meddle
KIBITZER	*n* pl. -S one that kibitzes
KIBLA	*n* pl. -S kiblah
KIBLAH	*n* pl. -S the direction toward which Muslims face while praying
KIBOSH	*v* -ED, -ING, -ES to stop
KICK	*v* -ED, -ING, -S to strike out with the foot or feet **KICKABLE** *adj*
KICKBACK	*n* pl. -S a strong reaction
KICKBALL	*n* pl. -S baseball using an inflated ball that is kicked
KICKER	*n* pl. -S one that kicks
KICKIER	comparative of kicky
KICKIEST	superlative of kicky
KICKOFF	*n* pl. -S the kick that begins play in football
KICKSHAW	*n* pl. -S a trifle or trinket
KICKUP	*n* pl. -S a noisy argument
KICKY	*adj* KICKIER, KICKIEST exciting
KID	*v* KIDDED, KIDDING, KIDS to tease
KIDDER	*n* pl. -S one that kids
KIDDIE	*n* pl. -S a small child
KIDDIES	pl. of kiddy
KIDDING	present participle of kid
KIDDISH	*adj* childish
KIDDO	*n* pl. -DOS or -DOES — used as a form of familiar address
KIDDUSH	*n* pl. -ES a Jewish prayer
KIDDY	*n* pl. -DIES kiddie
KIDLIKE	*adj* resembling a child

KIDNAP	*v* -NAPED, -NAPING, -NAPS or -NAPPED, -NAPPING, -NAPS to take a person by force and often for ransom
KIDNAPEE	*n* pl. -S one that is kidnaped
KIDNAPER	*n* pl. -S one that kidnaps
KIDNAPPER	*n* pl. -S kidnaper
KIDNAPPING	present participle of kidnap
KIDNEY	*n* pl. -NEYS a bodily organ
KIDSKIN	*n* pl. -S a type of leather
KIDVID	*n* pl. -S television programs for children
KIEF	*n* pl. -S kef
KIELBASA	*n* pl. -BASAS, -BASI, or -BASY a smoked sausage
KIER	*n* pl. -S a vat for boiling and dyeing fabrics
KIESTER	*n* pl. -S keister
KIF	*n* pl. -S kef
KILIM	*n* pl. -S an oriental tapestry
KILL	*v* -ED, -ING, -S to cause to die
KILLDEE	*n* pl. -S killdeer
KILLDEER	*n* pl. -S a wading bird
KILLER	*n* pl. -S one that kills
KILLICK	*n* pl. -S a small anchor
KILLIE	*n* pl. -S a freshwater fish
KILLING	*n* pl. -S a sudden notable success
KILLJOY	*n* pl. -JOYS one who spoils the fun of others
KILLOCK	*n* pl. -S killick
KILN	*v* -ED, -ING, -S to bake in a type of oven
KILO	*n* pl. KILOS a kilogram or kilometer
KILOBAR	*n* pl. -S a unit of atmospheric pressure
KILOBASE	*n* pl. -S unit of measure of a nucleic-acid chain
KILOBAUD	*n* pl. -S a unit of data transmission speed
KILOBIT	*n* pl. -S a unit of computer information
KILOBYTE	*n* pl. -S 1,024 bytes
KILOGRAM	*n* pl. -S a unit of mass and weight
KILOMOLE	*n* pl. -S one thousand moles
KILORAD	*n* pl. -S a unit of nuclear radiation
KILOTON	*n* pl. -S a unit of weight

KILOVOLT   *n* pl. -S a unit of electromotive force

KILOWATT   *n* pl. -S a unit of power

KILT   *v* -ED, -ING, -S to make creases or pleats in

KILTER   *n* pl. -S good condition

KILTIE   *n* pl. -S one who wears a kilt (a type of skirt)

KILTING   *n* pl. -S an arrangement of kilt pleats

KILTY   *n* pl. KILTIES kiltie

KIMCHEE   *n* pl. -S kimchi

KIMCHI   *n* pl. -S a spicy Korean dish of pickled cabbage

KIMONO   *n* pl. -NOS a loose robe
KIMONOED *adj*

KIN   *n* pl. -S a group of persons of common ancestry

KINA   *n* pl. -S a monetary unit of Papua New Guinea

KINASE   *n* pl. -S an enzyme

KIND   *adj* KINDER, KINDEST having a gentle, giving nature

KIND   *n* pl. -S a class of similar or related objects or individuals

KINDLE   *v* -DLED, -DLING, -DLES to cause to burn

KINDLER   *n* pl. -S one that kindles

KINDLESS   *adj* lacking kindness

KINDLING   *n* pl. -S material that is easily ignited

KINDLY   *adj* -LIER, -LIEST kind

KINDNESS   *n* pl. -ES the quality of being kind

KINDRED   *n* pl. -S a natural grouping

KINE   *n* pl. -S a type of television tube

KINEMA   *n* pl. -S cinema

KINESIC   *adj* pertaining to kinesics

KINESICS   *n/pl* the study of body motion in relation to communication

KINESIS   *n* pl. -NESES a type of movement

KINETIC   *adj* pertaining to motion

KINETICS   *n/pl* a branch of science dealing with motion

KINETIN   *n* pl. -S a substance that increases plant growth

KINFOLK   *n/pl* relatives

KINFOLKS   *n/pl* kinfolk

KING   *v* -ED, -ING, -S to reign as king (a male monarch)

KINGBIRD   *n* pl. -S an American bird

KINGBOLT   *n* pl. -S a kingpin

KINGCUP   *n* pl. -S a marsh plant

KINGDOM   *n* pl. -S the area ruled by a king

KINGFISH   *n* pl. -ES a marine food fish

KINGHOOD   *n* pl. -S the office of a king

KINGLESS   *adj* having no king

KINGLET   *n* pl. -S a king who rules over a small area

KINGLIKE   *adj* resembling a king

KINGLY   *adj* -LIER, -LIEST of or befitting a king

KINGPIN   *n* pl. -S a central bolt connecting an axle to a vehicle

KINGPOST   *n* pl. -S a supporting structure of a roof

KINGSHIP   *n* pl. -S the power or position of a king

KINGSIDE   *n* pl. -S a part of a chessboard

KINGWOOD   *n* pl. -S a hardwood tree

KININ   *n* pl. -S a hormone

KINK   *v* -ED, -ING, -S to form a tight curl or bend in

KINKAJOU   *n* pl. -S an arboreal mammal

KINKY   *adj* KINKIER, KINKIEST tightly curled **KINKILY** *adv*

KINO   *n* pl. -NOS a gum resin

KINSFOLK   *n/pl* kinfolk

KINSHIP   *n* pl. -S relationship

KINSMAN   *n* pl. -MEN a male relative

KIOSK   *n* pl. -S an open booth

KIP   *v* KIPPED, KIPPING, KIPS to sleep

KIPPEN   a past participle of kep

KIPPER   *v* -ED, -ING, -S to cure fish by salting and smoking

KIPPERER   *n* pl. -S one that kippers

KIPPING   present participle of kip

KIPSKIN   *n* pl. -S an animal hide that has not been tanned

KIR   *n* pl. -S an alcoholic beverage

KIRIGAMI   *n* pl. -S the Japanese art of folding paper

KIRK   *n* pl. -S a church

KIRKMAN   *n* pl. -MEN a member of a church

KIRMESS   *n* pl. -ES kermis

KIRN   *v* -ED, -ING, -S to churn

KIRSCH   *n* pl. -ES a kind of brandy

KIRTLE	*n* pl. -S a man's tunic or coat **KIRTLED** *adj*
KISHKA	*n* pl. -S kishke
KISHKE	*n* pl. -S a sausage
KISMAT	*n* pl. -S kismet
KISMET	*n* pl. -S destiny **KISMETIC** *adj*
KISS	*v* -ED, -ING, -ES to touch with the lips as a sign of affection **KISSABLE** *adj* **KISSABLY** *adv*
KISSER	*n* pl. -S one that kisses
KISSY	*adj* inclined to kiss
KIST	*n* pl. -S a chest, box, or coffin
KISTFUL	*n* pl. -S as much as a kist can hold
KIT	*v* KITTED, KITTING, KITS to equip
KITCHEN	*n* pl. -S a room where food is cooked
KITE	*v* KITED, KITING, KITES to obtain money or credit fraudulently
KITELIKE	*adj* resembling a kite (a light, covered frame flown in the wind)
KITER	*n* pl. -S one that kites
KITH	*n* pl. -S one's friends and neighbors
KITHARA	*n* pl. -S cithara
KITHE	*v* KITHED, KITHING, KITHES to make known
KITING	present participle of kite
KITLING	*n* pl. -S a young animal
KITSCH	*n* pl. -ES faddish art or literature **KITSCHY** *adj*
KITTED	past tense of kit
KITTEL	*n* pl. KITTEL a Jewish ceremonial robe
KITTEN	*v* -ED, -ING, -ES to bear kittens (young cats)
KITTIES	pl. of kitty
KITTING	present participle of kit
KITTLE	*v* -TLED, -TLING, -TLES to tickle
KITTLE	*adj* -TLER, -TLEST ticklish
KITTY	*n* pl. -TIES a kitten or cat
KIVA	*n* pl. -S an underground ceremonial chamber
KIWI	*n* pl. -S a flightless bird
KLATCH	*n* pl. -ES a social gathering
KLATSCH	*n* pl. -ES klatch

KLAVERN	*n* pl. -S a local branch of the Ku Klux Klan
KLAXON	*n* pl. -S a low-pitched horn
KLEAGLE	*n* pl. -S an official in the Ku Klux Klan
KLEPHT	*n* pl. -S a Greek guerrilla **KLEPHTIC** *adj*
KLEZMER	*n* pl. -MORIM a Jewish folk musician
KLISTER	*n* pl. -S a wax for skis
KLONG	*n* pl. -S a canal
KLOOF	*n* pl. -S a ravine
KLUDGE	*n* pl. -S a system composed of ill-fitting components
KLUGE	*n* pl. -S kludge
KLUTZ	*n* pl. -ES a clumsy person
KLUTZY	*adj* KLUTZIER, KLUTZIEST clumsy
KLYSTRON	*n* pl. -S a type of electron tube
KNACK	*v* -ED, -ING, -S to strike sharply
KNACKER	*n* pl. -S one that buys old livestock
KNACKERY	*n* pl. -ERIES the place of business of a knacker
KNAP	*v* KNAPPED, KNAPPING, KNAPS to strike sharply
KNAPPER	*n* pl. -S one that knaps
KNAPSACK	*n* pl. -S a bag carried on the back
KNAPWEED	*n* pl. -S a meadow plant
KNAR	*n* pl. -S a bump on a tree **KNARRED, KNARRY** *adj*
KNAUR	*n* pl. -S knar
KNAVE	*n* pl. -S a dishonest person **KNAVISH** *adj*
KNAVERY	*n* pl. -ERIES trickery
KNAWEL	*n* pl. -S a Eurasian plant
KNEAD	*v* -ED, -ING, -S to work into a uniform mixture with the hands
KNEADER	*n* pl. -S one that kneads
KNEE	*v* KNEED, KNEEING, KNEES to strike with the knee (a joint of the leg)
KNEECAP	*v* -CAPPED, -CAPPING, -CAPS to maim by shooting in the kneecap (a bone at the front of the knee)
KNEEHOLE	*n* pl. -S a space for the knees
KNEEL	*v* KNELT or KNEELED, KNEELING, KNEELS to rest on the knees
KNEELER	*n* pl. -S one that kneels

KNEEPAD — *n* pl. -S a covering for a knee

KNEEPAN — *n* pl. -S the kneecap

KNEESOCK — *n* pl. -S a sock reaching up to the knee

KNELL — *v* -ED, -ING, -S to sound a bell

KNELT — a past tense of kneel

KNESSET — *n* pl. -S the Israeli parliament

KNEW — past tense of know

KNICKERS — *n/pl* loose-fitting pants gathered at the knee

KNIFE — *n* pl. KNIVES a sharp-edged instrument used for cutting

KNIFE — *v* KNIFED, KNIFING, KNIFES to cut with a knife

KNIFER — *n* pl. -S one that knifes

KNIGHT — *v* -ED, -ING, -S to make a knight (a medieval gentleman-soldier) of

KNIGHTLY — *adj* of or befitting a knight

KNISH — *n* pl. -ES dough stuffed with filling and fried

KNIT — *v* KNITTED, KNITTING, KNITS to make a fabric or garment by joining loops of yarn

KNITTER — *n* pl. -S one that knits

KNITTING — *n* pl. -S work done by a knitter

KNITWEAR — *n* pl. KNITWEAR knitted clothing

KNIVES — pl. of knife

KNOB — *n* pl. -S a rounded protuberance **KNOBBED, KNOBLIKE** *adj*

KNOBBLY — *adj* -BLIER, -BLIEST having very small knobs

KNOBBY — *adj* -BIER, -BIEST full of knobs

KNOCK — *v* -ED, -ING, -S to strike sharply

KNOCKER — *n* pl. -S one that knocks

KNOCKOFF — *n* pl. -S a copy that sells for less than the original

KNOCKOUT — *n* pl. -S a blow that induces unconsciousness

KNOLL — *v* -ED, -ING, -S to knell

KNOLLER — *n* pl. -S one that knolls

KNOLLY — *adj* hilly

KNOP — *n* pl. -S a knob **KNOPPED** *adj*

KNOSP — *n* pl. -S a knob

KNOT — *v* KNOTTED, KNOTTING, KNOTS to tie in a knot (a closed loop)

KNOTHOLE — *n* pl. -S a hole in a plank

KNOTLESS — *adj* having no knots

KNOTLIKE — *adj* resembling a knot

KNOTTED — past tense of knot

KNOTTER — *n* pl. -S one that knots

KNOTTING — *n* pl. -S a fringe made of knotted threads

KNOTTY — *adj* -TIER, -TIEST full of knots **KNOTTILY** *adv*

KNOTWEED — *n* pl. -S a common weed

KNOUT — *v* -ED, -ING, -S to flog with a leather whip

KNOW — *v* KNEW, KNOWN, KNOWING, KNOWS to have a true understanding of **KNOWABLE** *adj*

KNOWER — *n* pl. -S one that knows

KNOWING — *adj* -INGER, -INGEST astute

KNOWING — *n* pl. -S knowledge

KNOWN — *n* pl. -S a mathematical quantity whose value is given

KNUBBY — *adj* -BIER, -BIEST nubby

KNUCKLE — *v* -LED, -LING, -LES to hit with the knuckles (the joints of the fingers)

KNUCKLER — *n* pl. -S a type of baseball pitch

KNUCKLY — *adj* -LIER, -LIEST having prominent knuckles

KNUR — *n* pl. -S a bump on a tree

KNURL — *v* -ED, -ING, -S to make grooves or ridges in

KNURLY — *adj* KNURLIER, KNURLIEST gnarly

KOA — *n* pl. -S a timber tree

KOALA — *n* pl. -S an Australian mammal

KOAN — *n* pl. -S a paradox meditated on by Buddhist monks

KOB — *n* pl. -S a reddish brown antelope

KOBO — *n* pl. KOBO a monetary unit of Nigeria

KOBOLD — *n* pl. -S an elf

KOEL — *n* pl. -S an Australian bird

KOHL — *n* pl. -S a type of eye makeup

KOHLRABI — *n* pl. -ES a variety of cabbage

KOI — *n* pl. KOI a large and colorful fish

KOINE — *n* pl. -S a type of dialect

KOKANEE — *n* pl. -S a food fish

KOLA — *n* pl. -S cola

KOLACKY — *n* pl. KOLACKY a kind of pastry

KOLBASI — *n* pl. -S kielbasa

KOLBASSI — *n* pl. -S kielbasa

KOLHOZ — *n* pl. -HOZY or -HOZES kolkhoz

KOLINSKI	*n* pl. -ES kolinsky
KOLINSKY	*n* pl. -SKIES an Asian mink
KOLKHOS	*n* pl. -KHOSY or -KHOSES kolkhoz
KOLKHOZ	*n* pl. -KHOZY or -KHOZES a collective farm in Russia
KOLKOZ	*n* pl. -KOZY or -KOZES kolkhoz
KOLO	*n* pl. -LOS a European folk dance
KOMATIK	*n* pl. -S an Eskimo sledge
KOMONDOR	*n* pl. -DORS, -DOROK, or -DOROCK a large, shaggy-coated dog
KONK	*v* -ED, -ING, -S conk
KOODOO	*n* pl. -DOOS kudu
KOOK	*n* pl. -S an eccentric person
KOOKIE	*adj* KOOKIER, KOOKIEST kooky
KOOKY	*adj* KOOKIER, KOOKIEST eccentric
KOP	*n* pl. -S a hill
KOPECK	*n* pl. -S a Russian coin
KOPEK	*n* pl. -S kopeck
KOPH	*n* pl. -S a Hebrew letter
KOPJE	*n* pl. -S a small hill
KOPPA	*n* pl. -S a Greek letter
KOPPIE	*n* pl. -S kopje
KOR	*n* pl. -S a Hebrew unit of measure
KORAT	*n* pl. -S a cat having a silver-blue coat
KORE	*n* pl. -RAI an ancient Greek statue of a young woman
KORUNA	*n* pl. KORUNAS, KORUNY, or KORUN a monetary unit of the Czech Republic
KOS	*n* pl. KOS a land measure in India
KOSHER	*v* -ED, -ING, -S to make fit to be eaten according to Jewish dietary laws
KOSS	*n* pl. KOSS kos
KOTO	*n* pl. -TOS a musical instrument
KOTOW	*v* -ED, -ING, -S to kowtow
KOTOWER	*n* pl. -S one that kotows
KOUMIS	*n* pl. -MISES koumiss
KOUMISS	*n* pl. -ES a beverage made from camel's milk
KOUMYS	*n* pl. -ES koumiss
KOUMYSS	*n* pl. -ES koumiss
KOUPREY	*n* pl. -PREYS a short-haired ox
KOUROS	*n* pl. -ROI an ancient Greek statue of a young man
KOUSSO	*n* pl. -SOS cusso
KOWTOW	*v* -ED, -ING, -S to behave in a servile manner
KOWTOWER	*n* pl. -S one that kowtows
KRAAL	*v* -ED, -ING, -S to pen in a type of enclosure
KRAFT	*n* pl. -S a strong paper
KRAIT	*n* pl. -S a venomous snake
KRAKEN	*n* pl. -S a legendary sea monster
KRATER	*n* pl. -S a type of vase
KRAUT	*n* pl. -S sauerkraut
KREEP	*n* pl. -S a basaltic lunar rock
KREMLIN	*n* pl. -S a Russian citadel
KREPLACH	*n* pl. KREPLACH dumplings filled with ground meat or cheese
KREUTZER	*n* pl. -S a former monetary unit of Austria
KREUZER	*n* pl. -S kreutzer
KRILL	*n* pl. -S an aggregate of small marine crustaceans
KRIMMER	*n* pl. -S a kind of fur
KRIS	*n* pl. -ES a short sword
KRONA	*n* pl. KRONUR a monetary unit of Iceland
KRONA	*n* pl. KRONOR a monetary unit of Sweden
KRONE	*n* pl. KRONER a monetary unit of Denmark
KRONE	*n* pl. KRONEN a former monetary unit of Austria
KRONOR	pl. of krona
KRONUR	pl. of krona
KROON	*n* pl. KROONS or KROONI a former monetary unit of Estonia
KRUBI	*n* pl. -S a tropical plant
KRUBUT	*n* pl. -S krubi
KRULLER	*n* pl. -S cruller
KRUMHORN	*n* pl. -S crumhorn
KRYOLITE	*n* pl. -S cryolite
KRYOLITH	*n* pl. -S cryolite
KRYPTON	*n* pl. -S a gaseous element
KUCHEN	*n* pl. KUCHEN a coffee cake
KUDO	*n* pl. -DOS award; honor
KUDU	*n* pl. -S a large antelope
KUDZU	*n* pl. -S an Asian vine
KUE	*n* pl. -S the letter Q

KUGEL   *n* pl. -S a baked pudding of potatoes or noodles

KUKRI   *n* pl. -S a long, curved knife of Nepal

KULAK   *n* pl. -LAKS or -LAKI a rich Russian peasant

KULTUR   *n* pl. -S culture; civilization

KUMISS   *n* pl. -ES koumiss

KUMMEL   *n* pl. -S a type of liqueur

KUMQUAT   *n* pl. -S a citrus fruit

KUMYS   *n* pl. -ES koumiss

KUNZITE   *n* pl. -S a mineral

KURBASH   *v* -ED, -ING, -ES to flog with a leather whip

KURGAN   *n* pl. -S a mound of earth over a grave

KURTA   *n* pl. -S a shirt worn in India

KURTOSIS   *n* pl. -SISES the relative degree of curvature in a statistical curve

KURU   *n* pl. -S a disease of the nervous system

KUSSO   *n* pl. -SOS cusso

KUVASZ   *n* pl. -VASZOK a large dog having a white coat

KVAS   *n* pl. -ES kvass

KVASS   *n* pl. -ES a Russian beer

KVETCH   *v* -ED, -ING, -ES to complain

KVETCHY   *adj* KVETCHIER, KVETCHIEST habitually complaining

KWACHA   *n* pl. KWACHA a monetary unit of Zambia

KWANZA   *n* pl. -S a monetary unit of Angola

KYACK   *n* pl. -S a packsack

KYAK   *n* pl. -S a kayak (an Eskimo canoe)

KYANISE   *v* -ISED, -ISING, -ISES to kyanize

KYANITE   *n* pl. -S cyanite

KYANIZE   *v* -IZED, -IZING, -IZES to treat wood with a type of preservative

KYAR   *n* pl. -S coir

KYAT   *n* pl. -S a monetary unit of Myanmar

KYBOSH   *v* -ED, -ING, -ES to kibosh

KYLIX   *n* pl. -LIKES a drinking vessel

KYMOGRAM   *n* pl. -S a record of fluid pressure

KYPHOSIS   *n* pl. -PHOSES abnormal curvature of the spine **KYPHOTIC** *adj*

KYRIE   *n* pl. -S a religious petition for mercy

KYTE   *n* pl. -S the stomach

KYTHE   *v* KYTHED, KYTHING, KYTHES to kithe

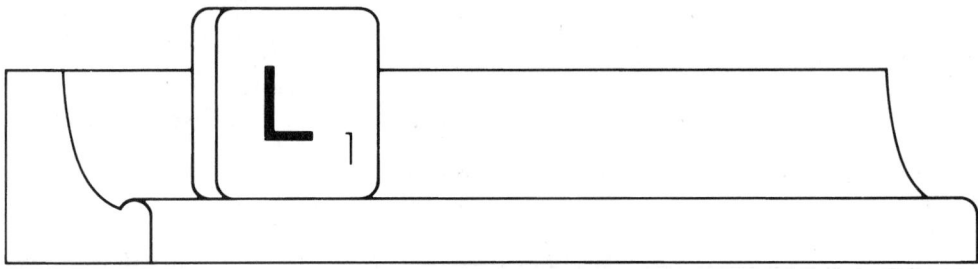

LA *n* pl. -S the sixth tone of the diatonic musical scale

LAAGER *v* -ED, -ING, -S to form a defensive encampment

LAARI *n* pl. LAARI a monetary unit of the Maldives

LAB *n* pl. -S a laboratory

LABARUM *n* pl. -RA or -RUMS an ecclesiastical banner

LABDANUM *n* pl. -S a fragrant resin

LABEL *v* -BELED, -BELING, -BELS or -BELLED, -BELLING, -BELS to describe or designate

LABELER *n* pl. -S one that labels

LABELLA pl. of labellum

LABELLED a past tense of label

LABELLER *n* pl. -S labeler

LABELLING a present participle of label

LABELLUM *n* pl. -LA the lower petal of an orchid

LABIA pl. of labium

LABIAL *n* pl. -S a labially produced sound

LABIALLY *adv* by means of the lips

LABIATE *n* pl. -S a labiated plant

LABIATED *adj* having corollas that are divided into two liplike parts

LABILE *adj* likely to change

LABILITY *n* pl. -TIES the state of being labile

LABIUM *n* pl. -BIA a fold of the vulva

LABOR *v* -ED, -ING, -S to work

LABORER *n* pl. -S one that labors

LABORITE *n* pl. -S a supporter of labor interests

LABOUR *v* -ED, -ING, -S to labor

LABOURER *n* pl. -S laborer

LABRA a pl. of labrum

LABRADOR *n* pl. -S a hunting dog

LABRET *n* pl. -S an ornament worn in a perforation of the lip

LABROID *n* pl. -S a marine fish

LABRUM *n* pl. -BRA or -BRUMS a lip or liplike structure

LABRUSCA *adj* designating a fox grape

LABURNUM *n* pl. -S an ornamental tree

LAC *n* pl. -S a resinous substance secreted by certain insects

LACE *v* LACED, LACING, LACES to fasten by means of a lace (a cord for drawing together two edges)

LACELESS *adj* lacking lace

LACELIKE *adj* resembling lace

LACER *n* pl. -S one that laces

LACERATE *v* -ATED, -ATING, -ATES to tear roughly

LACERTID *n* pl. -S a type of lizard

LACEWING *n* pl. -S a winged insect

LACEWOOD *n* pl. -S an Australian tree

LACEWORK *n* pl. -S a delicate openwork fabric

LACEY *adj* LACIER, LACIEST lacy

LACHES *n* pl. LACHES undue delay in asserting a legal right

LACIER comparative of lacy

LACIEST superlative of lacy

LACILY *adv* in a lacy manner

LACINESS *n* pl. -ES the quality of being lacy

LACING *n* pl. -S a contrasting marginal band of color

LACK *v* -ED, -ING, -S to be without

LACKADAY *interj* — used to express regret

LACKER *v* -ED, -ING, -S to lacquer

LACKEY *v* -ED, -ING, -S to act in a servile manner

LACONIC *adj* using a minimum of words

LACONISM	*n* pl. -S brevity of expression
LACQUER	*v* -ED, -ING, -S to coat with a glossy substance
LACQUEY	*v* -ED, -ING, -S to lackey
LACRIMAL	*n* pl. -S a type of vase
LACROSSE	*n* pl. -S a type of ball game
LACTAM	*n* pl. -S a chemical compound
LACTARY	*adj* pertaining to milk
LACTASE	*n* pl. -S an enzyme
LACTATE	*v* -TATED, -TATING, -TATES to secrete milk
LACTEAL	*n* pl. -S a lymphatic vessel
LACTEAN	*adj* lacteous
LACTEOUS	*adj* resembling milk
LACTIC	*adj* derived from milk
LACTONE	*n* pl. -S any of a group of esters **LACTONIC** *adj*
LACTOSE	*n* pl. -S a lactic sugar
LACUNA	*n* pl. -NAE or -NAS an empty space or missing part **LACUNAL, LACUNARY, LACUNATE** *adj*
LACUNAR	*n* pl. -NARS or -NARIA a ceiling with recessed panels
LACUNE	*n* pl. -S lacuna
LACUNOSE	*adj* marked by shallow depressions
LACY	*adj* LACIER, LACIEST resembling lacework
LAD	*n* pl. -S a boy or youth
LADANUM	*n* pl. -S labdanum
LADDER	*v* -ED, -ING, -S to cause a run in a stocking
LADDIE	*n* pl. -S a lad
LADE	*v* LADED, LADEN, LADING, LADES to load with a cargo
LADEN	*v* -ED, -ING, -S to lade
LADER	*n* pl. -S one that lades
LADIES	pl. of lady
LADING	*n* pl. -S cargo; freight
LADINO	*n* pl. -NOS a fast-growing clover
LADLE	*v* -DLED, -DLING, -DLES to lift out with a ladle (a type of spoon)
LADLEFUL	*n* pl. -S as much as a ladle will hold
LADLER	*n* pl. -S one that ladles
LADLING	present participle of ladle
LADRON	*n* pl. -S ladrone
LADRONE	*n* pl. -S a thief
LADY	*n* pl. -DIES a woman of refinement and gentle manners
LADYBIRD	*n* pl. -S a ladybug
LADYBUG	*n* pl. -S a small beetle
LADYFISH	*n* pl. -ES a bonefish
LADYHOOD	*n* pl. -S the state of being a lady
LADYISH	*adj* somewhat ladylike
LADYKIN	*n* pl. -S a small lady
LADYLIKE	*adj* resembling or suitable to a lady
LADYLOVE	*n* pl. -S a sweetheart
LADYPALM	*n* pl. -S a palm tree
LADYSHIP	*n* pl. -S the condition of being a lady
LAETRILE	*n* pl. -S a drug derived from apricot pits
LAEVO	*adj* levo
LAG	*v* LAGGED, LAGGING, LAGS to stay or fall behind
LAGAN	*n* pl. -S goods thrown into the sea with a buoy attached to enable recovery
LAGEND	*n* pl. -S lagan
LAGER	*v* -ED, -ING, -S to laager
LAGGARD	*n* pl. -S one that lags
LAGGED	past tense of lag
LAGGER	*n* pl. -S a laggard
LAGGING	*n* pl. -S an insulating material
LAGNAPPE	*n* pl. -S a small gift given to a customer with his purchase
LAGOON	*n* pl. -S a shallow body of water **LAGOONAL** *adj*
LAGUNA	*n* pl. -S lagoon
LAGUNE	*n* pl. -S lagoon
LAHAR	*n* pl. -S a flowing mass of volcanic debris
LAIC	*n* pl. -S a layman **LAICAL** *adj* **LAICALLY** *adv*
LAICH	*n* pl. -S laigh
LAICISE	*v* -ICISED, -ICISING, -ICISES to laicize
LAICISM	*n* pl. -S a political system free from clerical control
LAICIZE	*v* -ICIZED, -ICIZING, -ICIZES to free from clerical control
LAID	a past tense of lay
LAIGH	*n* pl. -S a lowland
LAIN	past participle of lie

LAIR   *v* -ED, -ING, -S to live in a lair (a wild animal's resting or dwelling place)

LAIRD   *n* pl. -S the owner of a landed estate **LAIRDLY** *adj*

LAITANCE   *n* pl. -S a milky deposit on the surface of fresh concrete

LAITH   *adj* loath **LAITHLY** *adv*

LAITY   *n* pl. -ITIES the nonclerical membership of a religious faith

LAKE   *n* pl. -S a sizable inland body of water **LAKELIKE** *adj*

LAKED   *adj* subjected to the process of laking

LAKEPORT   *n* pl. -S a city located on the shore of a lake

LAKER   *n* pl. -S a lake fish

LAKESIDE   *n* pl. -S the land along the edge of a lake

LAKH   *n* pl. -S the sum of one hundred thousand

LAKING   *n* pl. -S the reddening of blood plasma by the release of hemoglobin from the red corpuscles

LAKY   *adj* LAKIER, LAKIEST of the color of blood

LALL   *v* -ED, -ING, -S to articulate the letter *r* as *l*

LALLAN   *n* pl. -S a lowland

LALLAND   *n* pl. -S a lowland

LALLYGAG   *v* -GAGGED, -GAGGING, -GAGS to dawdle

LAM   *v* LAMMED, LAMMING, LAMS to flee hastily

LAMA   *n* pl. -S a Buddhist monk

LAMASERY   *n* pl. -SERIES a monastery of lamas

LAMB   *v* -ED, -ING, -S to give birth to a lamb (a young sheep)

LAMBAST   *v* -ED, -ING, -S to lambaste

LAMBASTE   *v* -BASTED, -BASTING, -BASTES to beat severely

LAMBDA   *n* pl. -S a Greek letter **LAMBDOID** *adj*

LAMBENCY   *n* pl. -CIES the quality or an instance of being lambent

LAMBENT   *adj* flickering lightly and gently over a surface

LAMBER   *n* pl. -S a ewe that is lambing

LAMBERT   *n* pl. -S a unit of brightness

LAMBIE   *n* pl. -S a lambkin

LAMBIER   comparative of lamby

LAMBIEST   superlative of lamby

LAMBKILL   *n* pl. -S an evergreen shrub

LAMBKIN   *n* pl. -S a small lamb

LAMBLIKE   *adj* resembling a lamb

LAMBSKIN   *n* pl. -S the skin of a lamb

LAMBY   *adj* LAMBIER, LAMBIEST resembling a lamb

LAME   *adj* LAMER, LAMEST physically disabled

LAME   *v* LAMED, LAMING, LAMES to make lame

LAMED   *n* pl. -S a Hebrew letter

LAMEDH   *n* pl. -S lamed

LAMELLA   *n* pl. -LAE or -LAS a thin plate, scale, or membrane **LAMELLAR** *adj*

LAMELY   *adv* in a lame manner

LAMENESS   *n* pl. -ES the state of being lame

LAMENT   *v* -ED, -ING, -S to express sorrow or regret for

LAMENTER   *n* pl. -S one that laments

LAMER   comparative of lame

LAMEST   superlative of lame

LAMIA   *n* pl. -MIAS or -MIAE a female demon

LAMINA   *n* pl. -NAE or -NAS a thin plate, scale, or layer **LAMINAL, LAMINAR, LAMINARY** *adj*

LAMINATE   *v* -NATED, -NATING, -NATES to compress into a thin plate

LAMING   present participle of lame

LAMINOSE   *adj* composed of laminae

LAMINOUS   *adj* laminose

LAMISTER   *n* pl. -S lamster

LAMMED   past tense of lam

LAMMING   present participle of lam

LAMP   *v* -ED, -ING, -S to look at

LAMPAD   *n* pl. -S a candlestick

LAMPAS   *n* pl. -ES inflammation of the roof of a horse's mouth

LAMPERS   *n* pl. -ES lampas

LAMPION   *n* pl. -S a type of light-generating device

LAMPOON   *v* -ED, -ING, -S to ridicule in a satirical composition

LAMPPOST   *n* pl. -S a post supporting a streetlight

LAMPREY   *n* pl. -PREYS an eellike fish

LAMPYRID *n* pl. -S any of a family of beetles

LAMSTER *n* pl. -S a fugitive

LANAI *n* pl. -S a veranda

LANATE *adj* covered with wool

LANATED *adj* lanate

LANCE *v* LANCED, LANCING, LANCES to pierce with a lance (a spearlike weapon)

LANCELET *n* pl. -S a small marine organism

LANCER *n* pl. -S a cavalryman armed with a lance

LANCET *n* pl. -S a narrow, pointed arch **LANCETED** *adj*

LANCIERS *n* pl. LANCIERS a French dance

LANCING present participle of lance

LAND *v* -ED, -ING, -S to set down upon land (solid ground)

LANDAU *n* pl. -S a type of carriage

LANDER *n* pl. -S one that lands

LANDFALL *n* pl. -S a sighting or approach to land

LANDFILL *n* pl. -S a system of waste disposal

LANDFORM *n* pl. -S a natural feature of the earth's surface

LANDGRAB *n* pl. -S a swift and often fraudulent seizure of land

LANDING *n* pl. -S a place for discharging or taking on passengers or cargo

LANDLADY *n* pl. -DIES a female landlord

LANDLER *n* pl. -S a slow Austrian dance

LANDLESS *adj* owning no land

LANDLINE *n* pl. -S a line of communication on land

LANDLORD *n* pl. -S one who owns and rents out real estate

LANDMAN *n* pl. -MEN one who lives and works on land

LANDMARK *n* pl. -S an object that marks a boundary line

LANDMASS *n* pl. -ES a large area of land

LANDMEN pl. of landman

LANDSIDE *n* pl. -S a part of a plow

LANDSKIP *n* pl. -S landscape

LANDSLEIT pl. of landsman

LANDSLID past tense of landslide (to win an election by an overwhelming majority)

LANDSLIP *n* pl. -S the fall of a mass of earth

LANDSMAN *n* pl. LANDSLEIT a fellow Jew coming from one's own section of Eastern Europe

LANDSMAN *n* pl. -MEN landman

LANDWARD *adv* toward the land

LANE *n* pl. -S a narrow passageway

LANELY *adj* lonely

LANEWAY *n* pl. -WAYS a lane

LANG *adj* long

LANGLAUF *n* pl. -S a cross-country ski run

LANGLEY *n* pl. -LEYS a unit of illumination

LANGRAGE *n* pl. -S a shot formerly used in naval warfare

LANGREL *n* pl. -S langrage

LANGSHAN *n* pl. -S any of a breed of large domestic fowl

LANGSYNE *n* pl. -S time long past

LANGUAGE *n* pl. -S a body of words and systems serving as a means of communication

LANGUE *n* pl. -S a type of language

LANGUET *n* pl. -S a tonguelike part

LANGUID *adj* lacking in vigor or vitality

LANGUISH *v* -ED, -ING, -ES to lose vigor or vitality

LANGUOR *n* pl. -S the state of being languid

LANGUR *n* pl. -S an Asian monkey

LANIARD *n* pl. -S lanyard

LANIARY *n* pl. -ARIES a cuspid

LANITAL *n* pl. -S a woollike fiber

LANK *adj* LANKER, LANKEST long and slender **LANKLY** *adv*

LANKNESS *n* pl. -ES the state of being lank

LANKY *adj* LANKIER, LANKIEST ungracefully tall and thin **LANKILY** *adv*

LANNER *n* pl. -S a falcon of Europe and Asia

LANNERET *n* pl. -S a male lanner

LANOLIN *n* pl. -S a fatty substance obtained from wool

LANOLINE *n* pl. -S lanolin

LANOSE *adj* lanate

LANOSITY *n* pl. -TIES the state of being lanose

LANTANA *n* pl. -S a tropical shrub

LANTERN *n* pl. -S a protective case for a light

LANTHORN *n* pl. -S a lantern

LANUGO	*n* pl. -GOS fine, soft hair
LANYARD	*n* pl. -S a fastening rope on a ship
LAP	*v* LAPPED, LAPPING, LAPS to fold over or around something
LAPBOARD	*n* pl. -S a flat board used as a table or desk
LAPDOG	*n* pl. -S a small dog
LAPEL	*n* pl. -S an extension of the collar of a garment **LAPELED, LAPELLED** *adj*
LAPFUL	*n* pl. -S as much as the lap can hold
LAPIDARY	*n* pl. -DARIES one who works with precious stones
LAPIDATE	*v* -DATED, -DATING, -DATES to hurl stones at
LAPIDES	pl. of lapis
LAPIDIFY	*v* -FIED, -FYING, -FIES to turn to stone
LAPIDIST	*n* pl. -S a lapidary
LAPILLUS	*n* pl. -LI a small fragment of lava
LAPIN	*n* pl. -S a rabbit
LAPIS	*n* pl. LAPIDES a stone
LAPIS	*n* pl. -PISES a mineral
LAPPED	past tense of lap
LAPPER	*v* -ED, -ING, -S to lopper
LAPPET	*n* pl. -S a decorative flap on a garment **LAPPETED** *adj*
LAPPING	present participle of lap
LAPSE	*v* LAPSED, LAPSING, LAPSES to fall from a previous standard **LAPSABLE, LAPSIBLE** *adj*
LAPSER	*n* pl. -S one that lapses
LAPSUS	*n* pl. LAPSUS a mistake
LAPTOP	*n* pl. -S a small computer for use on one's lap
LAPWING	*n* pl. -S a shore bird
LAR	*n* pl. -ES or -S a tutelary god or spirit of an ancient Roman household
LARBOARD	*n* pl. -S the left-hand side of a ship
LARCENER	*n* pl. -S one that commits larceny
LARCENY	*n* pl. -NIES the felonious taking and removal of another's personal goods
LARCH	*n* pl. -ES a coniferous tree
LARD	*v* -ED, -ING, -S to coat with lard (the melted fat of hogs)
LARDER	*n* pl. -S a place where food is stored
LARDIER	comparative of lardy
LARDIEST	superlative of lardy
LARDLIKE	*adj* resembling lard
LARDON	*n* pl. -S a thin slice of bacon or pork
LARDOON	*n* pl. -S lardon
LARDY	*adj* LARDIER, LARDIEST resembling lard
LAREE	*n* pl. -S lari
LARES	a pl. of lar
LARGANDO	*adj* becoming gradually slower — used as a musical direction
LARGE	*adj* LARGER, LARGEST of considerable size or quantity **LARGELY** *adv*
LARGE	*n* pl. -S generosity
LARGESS	*n* pl. -ES generosity
LARGESSE	*n* pl. -S largess
LARGEST	superlative of large
LARGISH	*adj* somewhat large
LARGO	*n* pl. -GOS a slow musical movement
LARI	*n* pl. -S a monetary unit of Maldives
LARIAT	*v* -ED, -ING, -S to lasso
LARINE	*adj* resembling a gull
LARK	*v* -ED, -ING, -S to behave playfully
LARKER	*n* pl. -S one that larks
LARKIER	comparative of larky
LARKIEST	superlative of larky
LARKISH	*adj* playful
LARKSOME	*adj* playful
LARKSPUR	*n* pl. -S a flowering plant
LARKY	*adj* LARKIER, LARKIEST playful
LARRIGAN	*n* pl. -S a type of moccasin
LARRIKIN	*n* pl. -S a rowdy
LARRUP	*v* -ED, -ING, -S to beat or thrash
LARRUPER	*n* pl. -S one that larrups
LARUM	*n* pl. -S an alarm
LARVA	*n* pl. -VAE or -VAS the immature form of various insects and animals when newly hatched **LARVAL** *adj*
LARYNX	*n* pl. LARYNGES or LARYNXES an organ of the respiratory tract **LARYNGAL** *adj*

LASAGNA *n* pl. -S an Italian baked dish

LASAGNE *n* pl. -S lasagna

LASCAR *n* pl. -S an East Indian sailor

LASE *v* LASED, LASING, LASES to function as a laser

LASER *n* pl. -S a device that amplifies light waves

LASH *v* -ED, -ING, -ES to strike with a whip

LASHER *n* pl. -S one that lashes

LASHING *n* pl. -S a flogging

LASHINS *n/pl* an abundance

LASHKAR *n* pl. -S lascar

LASING present participle of lase

LASS *n* pl. -ES a young woman

LASSIE *n* pl. -S a lass

LASSO *v* -ED, -ING, -S or -ES to catch with a lasso (a long rope with a running noose)

LASSOER *n* pl. -S one that lassos

LAST *v* -ED, -ING, -S to continue in existence

LASTER *n* pl. -S one that lasts

LASTING *n* pl. -S a durable fabric

LASTLY *adv* in conclusion

LAT *n* pl. LATS or LATI a former monetary unit of Latvia

LATAKIA *n* pl. -S a variety of Turkish tobacco

LATCH *v* -ED, -ING, -ES to close with a type of fastening device

LATCHET *n* pl. -S a thong used to fasten a shoe

LATCHKEY *n* pl. -KEYS a key for opening a latched door

LATE *adj* LATER, LATEST coming or occurring after the expected time

LATED *adj* belated

LATEEN *n* pl. -S a sailing vessel

LATEENER *n* pl. -S a lateen

LATELY *adv* not long ago

LATEN *v* -ED, -ING, -S to become late

LATENCY *n* pl. -CIES the state of being present but not manifest

LATENESS *n* pl. -ES the state of being late

LATENT *n* pl. -S a barely visible fingerprint that can be developed for study

LATENTLY *adv* dormantly

LATER comparative of late

LATERAD *adv* toward the side

LATERAL *v* -ED, -ING, -S to throw a sideward pass in football

LATERITE *n* pl. -S a type of soil

LATERIZE *v* -IZED, -IZING, -IZES to convert to laterite

LATEST *n* pl. -S the most recent development

LATEWOOD *n* pl. -S a part of an annual ring of wood

LATEX *n* pl. LATICES or LATEXES a milky liquid of certain plants

LATH *v* -ED, -ING, -S to cover with laths (thin strips of wood)

LATHE *v* LATHED, LATHING, LATHES to cut or shape on a type of machine

LATHER *v* -ED, -ING, -S to cover with lather (a light foam)

LATHERER *n* pl. -S one that lathers

LATHERY *adj* covered with lather

LATHI *n* pl. -S a heavy stick of bamboo and iron in India

LATHIER comparative of lathy

LATHIEST superlative of lathy

LATHING *n* pl. -S work made of or using laths

LATHWORK *n* pl. -S lathing

LATHY *adj* LATHIER, LATHIEST long and slender

LATI a pl. of lat

LATICES a pl. of latex

LATIGO *n* pl. -GOS or -GOES a strap used to fasten a saddle

LATINITY *n* pl. -TIES a manner of writing or speaking Latin

LATINIZE *v* -IZED, -IZING, -IZES to translate into Latin

LATINO *n* pl. -NOS a Latin American

LATISH *adj* somewhat late

LATITUDE *n* pl. -S freedom from narrow restrictions

LATKE *n* pl. -S a potato pancake

LATOSOL *n* pl. -S a tropical soil

LATRIA *n* pl. -S the supreme worship given to God only, in Roman Catholicism

LATRINE *n* pl. -S a type of toilet

LATTEN *n* pl. -S a brass-like alloy

LATTER	*adj* being the second mentioned of two
LATTERLY	*adv* lately
LATTICE	*v* -TICED, -TICING, -TICES to form a structure consisting of interlaced strips of material
LATTIN	*n* pl. -S latten
LAUAN	*n* pl. -S a Philippine timber
LAUD	*v* -ED, -ING, -S to praise
LAUDABLE	*adj* worthy of praise **LAUDABLY** *adv*
LAUDANUM	*n* pl. -S a type of opium preparation
LAUDATOR	*n* pl. -S a lauder
LAUDER	*n* pl. -S one that lauds
LAUGH	*v* -ED, -ING, -S to express emotion, typically mirth, by a series of inarticulate sounds
LAUGHER	*n* pl. -S one that laughs
LAUGHING	*n* pl. -S laughter
LAUGHTER	*n* pl. -S the act or sound of one that laughs
LAUNCE	*n* pl. -S a marine fish
LAUNCH	*v* -ED, -ING, -ES to set in motion
LAUNCHER	*n* pl. -S a launching device
LAUNDER	*v* -ED, -ING, -S to wash clothes
LAUNDRY	*n* pl. -DRIES a collection of clothes to be washed
LAURA	*n* pl. -RAS or -RAE a type of monastery
LAUREATE	*v* -ATED, -ATING, -ATES to laurel
LAUREL	*v* -RELED, -RELING, -RELS or -RELLED, -RELLING, -RELS to crown with a wreath of evergreen leaves
LAUWINE	*n* pl. -S an avalanche
LAV	*n* pl. -S a lavatory
LAVA	*n* pl. -S molten rock that issues from a volcano
LAVABO	*n* pl. -BOES or -BOS a ceremonial washing in certain Christian churches
LAVAGE	*n* pl. -S a washing
LAVALAVA	*n* pl. -S a Polynesian garment
LAVALIER	*n* pl. -S a pendant worn on a chain around the neck
LAVALIKE	*adj* resembling lava
LAVATION	*n* pl. -S the acting of washing
LAVATORY	*n* pl. -RIES a room equipped with washing and toilet facilities
LAVE	*v* LAVED, LAVING, LAVES to wash
LAVEER	*v* -ED, -ING, -S to sail against the wind
LAVENDER	*v* -ED, -ING, -S to sprinkle with a type of perfume
LAVER	*n* pl. -S a vessel used for ancient Hebrew ceremonial washings
LAVEROCK	*n* pl. -S a songbird
LAVING	present participle of lave
LAVISH	*adj* -ISHER, -ISHEST expending or giving in great amounts **LAVISHLY** *adv*
LAVISH	*v* -ED, -ING, -ES to expend or give in great amounts
LAVISHER	*n* pl. -S one that lavishes
LAVROCK	*n* pl. -S laverock
LAW	*v* -ED, -ING, -S to take a complaint to court for settlement
LAWBOOK	*n* pl. -S a book containing or dealing with laws
LAWFUL	*adj* allowed by law (the body of rules governing the affairs of a community) **LAWFULLY** *adv*
LAWGIVER	*n* pl. -S one who institutes a legal system
LAWINE	*n* pl. -S lauwine
LAWING	*n* pl. -S a bill for food or drink in a tavern
LAWLESS	*adj* having no system of laws
LAWLIKE	*adj* being like the law
LAWMAKER	*n* pl. -S a legislator
LAWMAN	*n* pl. -MEN a law-enforcement officer
LAWN	*n* pl. -S an area of grass-covered land **LAWNY** *adj*
LAWSUIT	*n* pl. -S a legal action
LAWYER	*v* -ED, -ING, -S to work as a member of the legal profession
LAWYERLY	*adj* befitting a member of the legal profession
LAX	*adj* LAXER, LAXEST not strict or stringent
LAXATION	*n* pl. -S the act of relaxing
LAXATIVE	*n* pl. -S a drug that stimulates evacuation of the bowels
LAXITY	*n* pl. -ITIES the state of being lax
LAXLY	*adv* in a lax manner
LAXNESS	*n* pl. -ES laxity

LAY   *v* LAID or LAYED, LAYING, LAYS to deposit as a wager

LAYABOUT   *n* pl. -S a lazy person

LAYAWAY   *n* pl. -AWAYS an item that has been reserved with a down payment

LAYER   *v* -ED, -ING, -S to form a layer (a single thickness, coating, or covering)

LAYERAGE   *n* pl. -S a method of plant propagation

LAYERING   *n* pl. -S layerage

LAYETTE   *n* pl. -S an outfit of clothing and equipment for a newborn child

LAYMAN   *n* pl. -MEN a member of the laity

LAYOFF   *n* pl. -S the suspension or dismissal of employees

LAYOUT   *n* pl. -S an arrangement or plan

LAYOVER   *n* pl. -S a stopover

LAYUP   *n* pl. -S a shot in basketball

LAYWOMAN   *n* pl. -WOMEN a female member of the laity

LAZAR   *n* pl. -S a beggar afflicted with a loathsome disease

LAZARET   *n* pl. -S a hospital treating contagious diseases

LAZE   *v* LAZED, LAZING, LAZES to pass time lazily

LAZIED   past tense of lazy

LAZIER   comparative of lazy

LAZIES   present 3d person sing. of lazy

LAZIEST   superlative of lazy

LAZILY   *adv* in a lazy manner

LAZINESS   *n* pl. -ES the state of being lazy

LAZING   present participle of laze

LAZULI   *n* pl. -S a mineral

LAZULITE   *n* pl. -S a mineral

LAZURITE   *n* pl. -S a mineral

LAZY   *adj* LAZIER, LAZIEST disinclined toward work or exertion

LAZY   *v* LAZIED, LAZING, LAZIES to move or lie lazily

LAZYISH   *adj* somewhat lazy

LEA   *n* pl. -S a meadow

LEACH   *v* -ED, -ING, -ES to subject to the filtering action of a liquid

LEACHATE   *n* pl. -S a solution obtained by leaching

LEACHER   *n* pl. -S one that leaches

LEACHY   *adj* LEACHIER, LEACHIEST porous

LEAD   *v* LED, LEADING, LEADS to show the way to by going in advance

LEAD   *v* -ED, -ING, -S to cover with lead (a heavy metallic element)

LEADEN   *adj* oppressively heavy **LEADENLY** *adv*

LEADER   *n* pl. -S one that leads or guides

LEADIER   comparative of leady

LEADIEST   superlative of leady

LEADING   *n* pl. -S a covering or border of lead

LEADLESS   *adj* having no lead

LEADMAN   *n* pl. -MEN a worker in charge of other workers

LEADOFF   *n* pl. -S an opening play or move

LEADSMAN   *n* pl. -MEN a seaman who measures the depth of water

LEADWORK   *n* pl. -S something made of lead

LEADWORT   *n* pl. -S a tropical plant

LEADY   *adj* LEADIER, LEADIEST resembling lead

LEAF   *n* pl. LEAVES a usually green, flattened organ of vascular plants

LEAF   *v* -ED, -ING, -S to turn pages rapidly

LEAFAGE   *n* pl. -S foliage

LEAFIER   comparative of leafy

LEAFIEST   superlative of leafy

LEAFLESS   *adj* having no leaves

LEAFLET   *v* -LETED, -LETING, -LETS or -LETTED, -LETTING, -LETS to distribute printed sheets of paper

LEAFLIKE   *adj* resembling a leaf

LEAFWORM   *n* pl. -S a moth larva that feeds on leaves

LEAFY   *adj* LEAFIER, LEAFIEST covered with leaves

LEAGUE   *v* LEAGUED, LEAGUING, LEAGUES to come together for a common purpose

LEAGUER   *v* -ED, -ING, -S to besiege

LEAK   *v* -ED, -ING, -S to permit the escape of something through a breach or flaw

LEAKAGE   *n* pl. -S the act or an instance of leaking

LEAKER   *n* pl. -S one that leaks

LEAKLESS   *adj* designed not to leak

LEAKY	*adj* LEAKIER, LEAKIEST tending to leak **LEAKILY** *adv*	**LEAVER**	*n* pl. -S one that leaves
LEAL	*adj* loyal **LEALLY** *adv*	**LEAVES**	pl. of leaf
LEALTY	*n* pl. -TIES loyalty	**LEAVING**	*n* pl. -S a leftover
LEAN	*v* LEANED or LEANT, LEANING, LEANS to deviate from a vertical position	**LEAVY**	*adj* LEAVIER, LEAVIEST leafy
LEAN	*adj* LEANER, LEANEST having little fat **LEANLY** *adv*	**LEBEN**	*n* pl. -S a type of liquid food
LEANER	*n* pl. -S one that leans	**LECH**	*v* -ED, -ING, -ES to engage in lechery
LEANING	*n* pl. -S a tendency	**LECHAYIM**	*n* pl. -S lehayim
LEANNESS	*n* pl. -ES the state of being lean	**LECHER**	*v* -ED, -ING, -S to engage in lechery
LEANT	a past tense of lean	**LECHERY**	*n* pl. -ERIES excessive sexual indulgence
LEAP	*v* LEAPED or LEAPT or LEPT, LEAPING, LEAPS to spring off the ground	**LECHWE**	*n* pl. -S an African antelope
LEAPER	*n* pl. -S one that leaps	**LECITHIN**	*n* pl. -S any of a group of fatty substances found in plant and animal tissues
LEAPFROG	*v* -FROGGED, -FROGGING, -FROGS to jump over with the legs wide apart	**LECTERN**	*n* pl. -S a reading desk
LEAPT	a past tense of leap	**LECTIN**	*n* pl. -S a protein that binds to a sugar molecule
LEAR	*n* pl. -S learning	**LECTION**	*n* pl. -S a portion of sacred writing read in a church service
LEARIER	comparative of leary	**LECTOR**	*n* pl. -S a reader of the lessons in a church service
LEARIEST	superlative of leary	**LECTURE**	*v* -TURED, -TURING, -TURES to expound on a specific subject
LEARN	*v* LEARNED or LEARNT, LEARNING, LEARNS to gain knowledge by experience, instruction, or study	**LECTURER**	*n* pl. -S one that lectures
LEARNER	*n* pl. -S one that learns	**LECYTHIS**	*adj* designating a family of tropical shrubs
LEARNING	*n* pl. -S acquired knowledge	**LECYTHUS**	*n* pl. -THI lekythos
LEARNT	a past tense of learn	**LED**	past tense of lead
LEARY	*adj* LEARIER, LEARIEST leery	**LEDGE**	*n* pl. -S a narrow, shelflike projection
LEASE	*v* LEASED, LEASING, LEASES to grant temporary use of in exchange for rent **LEASABLE** *adj*	**LEDGER**	*n* pl. -S an account book of final entry
LEASER	*n* pl. -S one that leases	**LEDGY**	*adj* LEDGIER, LEDGIEST abounding in ledges
LEASH	*v* -ED, -ING, -ES to restrain an animal with a line or thong	**LEE**	*n* pl. -S shelter from the wind
LEASING	*n* pl. -S a falsehood	**LEEBOARD**	*n* pl. -S a board attached to a sailing vessel to prevent leeway
LEAST	*n* pl. -S something that is smallest in size or degree	**LEECH**	*v* -ED, -ING, -ES to cling to and feed upon or drain
LEATHER	*v* -ED, -ING, -S to cover with leather (the dressed or tanned hide of an animal)	**LEEK**	*n* pl. -S an herb used in cookery
LEATHERN	*adj* made of leather	**LEER**	*v* -ED, -ING, -S to look with a sideways glance
LEATHERY	*adj* resembling leather	**LEERY**	*adj* LEERIER, LEERIEST suspicious **LEERILY** *adv*
LEAVE	*v* LEFT, LEAVING, LEAVES to go away from	**LEET**	*n* pl. -S a former English court for petty offenses
LEAVED	*adj* having a leaf or leaves	**LEEWARD**	*n* pl. -S the direction toward which the wind is blowing
LEAVEN	*v* -ED, -ING, -S to produce fermentation in		

LEEWAY   *n* pl. -WAYS the lateral drift of a ship

LEFT   *adj* LEFTER, LEFTEST pertaining to the side of the body to the north when one faces east

LEFT   *n* pl. -S the left side or hand

LEFTIES   pl. of lefty

LEFTISH   *adj* inclined to be a leftist

LEFTISM   *n* pl. -S a liberal political philosophy

LEFTIST   *n* pl. -S an advocate of leftism

LEFTOVER   *n* pl. -S an unused or unconsumed portion

LEFTWARD   *adv* toward the left

LEFTWING   *adj* favoring leftism

LEFTY   *n* pl. LEFTIES a left-handed person

LEG   *v* LEGGED, LEGGING, LEGS to move with the legs (appendages that serve as a means of support and locomotion)

LEGACY   *n* pl. -CIES something bequeathed

LEGAL   *n* pl. -S an authorized investment that may be made by investors such as savings banks

LEGALESE   *n* pl. -S the specialized language of lawyers

LEGALISE   *v* -ISED, -ISING, -ISES to legalize

LEGALISM   *n* pl. -S strict conformity to the law

LEGALIST   *n* pl. -S an adherent of legalism

LEGALITY   *n* pl. -TIES the condition of being lawful

LEGALIZE   *v* -IZED, -IZING, -IZES to make lawful

LEGALLY   *adv* in a lawful manner

LEGATE   *v* -GATED, -GATING, -GATES to bequeath

LEGATEE   *n* pl. -S the inheritor of a legacy

LEGATINE   *adj* pertaining to an official envoy

LEGATING   present participle of legate

LEGATION   *n* pl. -S the sending of an official envoy

LEGATO   *n* pl. -TOS a smooth and flowing musical style

LEGATOR   *n* pl. -S one that legates

LEGEND   *n* pl. -S an unverified story from earlier times

LEGENDRY   *n* pl. -RIES a collection of legends

LEGER   *n* pl. -S fishing bait made to lie on the bottom

LEGERITY   *n* pl. -TIES quickness of the mind or body

LEGES   pl. of lex

LEGGED   past tense of leg

LEGGIER   comparative of leggy

LEGGIERO   *adv* in a light or graceful manner — used as a musical direction

LEGGIEST   superlative of leggy

LEGGIN   *n* pl. -S legging

LEGGING   *n* pl. -S a covering for the leg

LEGGY   *adj* -GIER, -GIEST having long legs

LEGHORN   *n* pl. -S a smooth, plaited straw

LEGIBLE   *adj* capable of being read **LEGIBLY** *adv*

LEGION   *n* pl. -S a large military force

LEGIST   *n* pl. -S one learned or skilled in the law

LEGIT   *n* pl. -S legitimate drama

LEGLESS   *adj* having no legs

LEGLIKE   *adj* resembling a leg

LEGMAN   *n* pl. -MEN a newspaperman assigned to gather information

LEGONG   *n* pl. -S a Balinese dance

LEGROOM   *n* pl. -S space in which to extend the legs

LEGUME   *n* pl. -S a type of plant

LEGUMIN   *n* pl. -S a plant protein

LEGWORK   *n* pl. -S work that involves extensive walking

LEHAYIM   *n* pl. -S a traditional Jewish toast

LEHR   *n* pl. -S a type of oven

LEHUA   *n* pl. -S a tropical tree

LEI   *n* pl. -S a wreath of flowers

LEISTER   *v* -ED, -ING, -S to spear with a three-pronged fishing implement

LEISURE   *n* pl. -S freedom from the demands of work or duty **LEISURED** *adj*

LEK   *n* pl. LEKS or LEKE or LEKU a monetary unit of Albania

LEKVAR   *n* pl. -S a prune butter

LEKYTHOS   *n* pl. -THOI an oil jar used in ancient Greece

LEKYTHUS   *n* pl. -THI lekythos

LEMAN   *n* pl. -S a lover

LEMMA   *n* pl. -MAS or -MATA a type of proposition in logic

LEMMING   *n* pl. -S a mouselike rodent

LEMNISCI   *n/pl* bands of nerve fibers

LEMON   *n* pl. -S a citrus fruit **LEMONISH, LEMONY** *adj*

LEMONADE   *n* pl. -S a beverage

LEMPIRA   *n* pl. -S a monetary unit of Honduras

LEMUR   *n* pl. -S an arboreal mammal related to the monkeys

LEMURES   *n/pl* the ghosts of the dead in ancient Roman religion

LEMURINE   *adj* pertaining to a lemur

LEMUROID   *n* pl. -S a lemur

LEND   *v* LENT, LENDING, LENDS to give the temporary use of **LENDABLE** *adj*

LENDER   *n* pl. -S one that lends

LENES   pl. of lenis

LENGTH   *n* pl. -S the longer or longest dimension of an object

LENGTHEN   *v* -ED, -ING, -S to make or become longer

LENGTHY   *adj* LENGTHIER, LENGTHIEST very long

LENIENCE   *n* pl. -S leniency

LENIENCY   *n* pl. -CIES the quality of being lenient

LENIENT   *adj* gently tolerant

LENIS   *n* pl. LENES a speech sound pronounced with little or no aspiration

LENITION   *n* pl. -S a change in articulation

LENITIVE   *n* pl. -S a soothing medicine

LENITY   *n* pl. -TIES leniency

LENO   *n* pl. -NOS a style of weaving

LENS   *n* pl. -ES a piece of transparent material used in changing the convergence of light rays **LENSLESS** *adj*

LENS   *v* -ED, -ING, -ES to make a film of

LENSE   *n* pl. -S lens

LENSMAN   *n* pl. -MEN a photographer

LENT   past tense of lend

LENTANDO   *adv* becoming slower — used as a musical direction

LENTEN   *adj* meager

LENTIC   *adj* pertaining to still water

LENTICEL   *n* pl. -S a mass of cells on a plant stem

LENTIGO   *n* pl. -TIGINES a freckle

LENTIL   *n* pl. -S a Eurasian annual plant

LENTISK   *n* pl. -S an evergreen tree

LENTO   *n* pl. -TOS a slow musical movement

LENTOID   *adj* lens-shaped

LEONE   *n* pl. -S a monetary unit of Sierra Leone

LEONINE   *adj* pertaining to a lion

LEOPARD   *n* pl. -S a large, carnivorous feline mammal

LEOTARD   *n* pl. -S a close-fitting garment

LEPER   *n* pl. -S one affected with leprosy

LEPIDOTE   *n* pl. -S a flowering shrub

LEPORID   *n* pl. -RIDS or -RIDAE a gnawing mammal

LEPORINE   *adj* resembling a rabbit or hare

LEPROSE   *adj* leprous

LEPROSY   *n* pl. -SIES a chronic disease characterized by skin lesions and deformities

LEPROTIC   *adj* leprous

LEPROUS   *adj* affected with leprosy

LEPT   a past tense of leap

LEPTON   *n* pl. -TA a monetary unit of Greece

LEPTON   *n* pl. -S a subatomic particle **LEPTONIC** *adj*

LESBIAN   *n* pl. -S a female homosexual

LESION   *n* pl. -S an abnormal change in the structure of an organ or tissue **LESIONED** *adj*

LESS   *adj* LESSER, LEAST not as great in quantity or degree

LESSEE   *n* pl. -S one to whom a lease is granted

LESSEN   *v* -ED, -ING, -S to make or become less

LESSER   *adj* not as large or important

LESSON   *v* -ED, -ING, -S to instruct

LESSOR   *n* pl. -S one that grants a lease

LEST   *conj* for fear that

LET   *v* LETTED, LETTING, LETS to hinder

LETCH   *v* -ED, -ING, -ES lech

LETDOWN   *n* pl. -S a decrease

LETHAL   *n* pl. -S a death-causing genetic defect

LETHALLY   *adv* in a deadly manner

LETHARGY   *n* pl. -GIES drowsiness; sluggishness

LETHE   *n* pl. -S forgetfulness **LETHEAN** *adj*

LETTED   past tense of let

LETTER   *v* -ED, -ING, -S to mark with letters (written symbols representing speech sounds)

LETTERER   *n* pl. -S one that letters

LETTING   present participle of let

LETTUCE   *n* pl. -S an herb cultivated as a salad plant

LETUP   *n* pl. -S a lessening or relaxation

LEU   *n* pl. LEI a monetary unit of Romania

LEUCEMIA   *n* pl. -S leukemia **LEUCEMIC** *adj*

LEUCIN   *n* pl. -S leucine

LEUCINE   *n* pl. -S an amino acid

LEUCITE   *n* pl. -S a mineral **LEUCITIC** *adj*

LEUCOMA   *n* pl. -S leukoma

LEUD   *n* pl. -S or -ES a feudal vassal

LEUKEMIA   *n* pl. -S a disease of the blood-forming organs

LEUKEMIC   *n* pl. -S one affected with leukemia

LEUKOMA   *n* pl. -S an opacity of the cornea

LEUKON   *n* pl. -S a bodily organ consisting of the white blood cells

LEUKOSIS   *n* pl. -KOSES leukemia **LEUKOTIC** *adj*

LEV   *n* pl. LEVA a monetary unit of Bulgaria

LEVANT   *v* -ED, -ING, -S to avoid a debt

LEVANTER   *n* pl. -S an easterly Mediterranean wind

LEVATOR   *n* pl. -ES or -S a muscle that raises an organ or part

LEVEE   *v* LEVEED, LEVEEING, LEVEES to provide with an embankment

LEVEL   *v* -ELED, -ELING, -ELS or -ELLED, -ELLING, -ELS to make even

LEVELER   *n* pl. -S one that levels

LEVELLER   *n* pl. -S leveler

LEVELLING   a present participle of level

LEVELLY   *adv* in an even manner

LEVER   *v* -ED, -ING, -S to move with a lever (a rigid body used to lift weight)

LEVERAGE   *v* -AGED, -AGING, -AGES to provide with a type of economic advantage

LEVERET   *n* pl. -S a young hare

LEVIABLE   *adj* liable to be levied

LEVIED   past tense of levy

LEVIER   *n* pl. -S one that levies

LEVIES   present 3d person sing. of levy

LEVIGATE   *v* -GATED, -GATING, -GATES to reduce to a fine powder

LEVIN   *n* pl. -S lightning

LEVIRATE   *n* pl. -S the custom of marrying the widow of one's brother

LEVITATE   *v* -TATED, -TATING, -TATES to rise and float in the air

LEVITY   *n* pl. -TIES conduct characterized by a lack of seriousness

LEVO   *adj* turning toward the left

LEVODOPA   *n* pl. -S a form of dopa

LEVOGYRE   *adj* turning toward the left

LEVULIN   *n* pl. -S a chemical compound

LEVULOSE   *n* pl. -S a very sweet sugar

LEVY   *v* LEVIED, LEVYING, LEVIES to impose or collect by legal authority

LEWD   *adj* LEWDER, LEWDEST obscene **LEWDLY** *adv*

LEWDNESS   *n* pl. -ES the state of being lewd

LEWIS   *n* pl. -ISES a hoisting device

LEWISITE   *n* pl. -S a vesicant liquid

LEWISSON   *n* pl. -S lewis

LEX   *n* pl. LEGES law

LEXEME   *n* pl. -S a linguistic unit **LEXEMIC** *adj*

LEXICAL   *adj* pertaining to the words of a language

LEXICON   *n* pl. -CA or -CONS a dictionary

LEXIS   *n* pl. LEXES the vocabulary of a language, a group, or a subject field

LEY   *n* pl. LEYS lea

LI   *n* pl. -S a Chinese unit of distance

LIABLE   *adj* subject or susceptible to something possible or likely

LIAISE   *v* LIAISED, LIAISING, LIAISES to establish liaison

LIAISON *n* pl. -S a means for maintaining communication

LIANA *n* pl. -S a tropical vine

LIANE *n* pl. -S liana

LIANG *n* pl. -S a Chinese unit of weight

LIANOID *adj* pertaining to a liana

LIAR *n* pl. -S one that speaks falsely

LIARD *n* pl. -S a former silver coin of France

LIB *n* pl. -S liberation

LIBATION *n* pl. -S a ceremonial pouring of a liquid

LIBECCIO *n* pl. -CIOS a southwest wind

LIBEL *v* -BELED, -BELING, -BELS or -BELLED, -BELLING, -BELS to make or publish a defamatory statement about

LIBELANT *n* pl. -S a plaintiff in a type of lawsuit

LIBELEE *n* pl. -S a defendant in a type of lawsuit

LIBELER *n* pl. -S one that libels

LIBELIST *n* pl. -S a libeler

LIBELLED a past tense of libel

LIBELLEE *n* pl. -S libelee

LIBELLER *n* pl. -S libeler

LIBELLING a present participle of libel

LIBELOUS *adj* defamatory

LIBER *n* pl. LIBRI or LIBERS a book of public records

LIBERAL *n* pl. -S a person favorable to progress or reform

LIBERATE *v* -ATED, -ATING, -ATES to set free

LIBERTY *n* pl. -TIES the state of being free

LIBIDO *n* pl. -DOS the energy derived from instinctual biological drives

LIBLAB *n* pl. -S a person supporting a coalition of liberal and labor groups

LIBRA *n* pl. -BRAE an ancient Roman unit of weight

LIBRA *n* pl. -S a former gold coin of Peru

LIBRARY *n* pl. -BRARIES a place where literary materials are kept for reading and reference

LIBRATE *v* -BRATED, -BRATING, -BRATES to move from side to side

LIBRETTO *n* pl. -TOS or -TI the text of an opera

LIBRI a pl. of liber

LICE pl. of louse

LICENCE *v* -CENCED, -CENCING, -CENCES to license

LICENCEE *n* pl. -S licensee

LICENCER *n* pl. -S licenser

LICENSE *v* -CENSED, -CENSING, -CENSES to issue or grant authoritative permission to

LICENSEE *n* pl. -S one that is licensed

LICENSER *n* pl. -S one that licenses

LICENSOR *n* pl. -S licenser

LICENTE a pl. of sente

LICH *n* pl. -ES a corpse

LICHEE *n* pl. -S litchi

LICHEN *v* -ED, -ING, -S to cover with lichens (flowerless plants)

LICHENIN *n* pl. -S a chemical compound

LICHI *n* pl. -S litchi

LICHT *v* -ED, -ING, -S to light

LICHTLY *adv* lightly

LICIT *adj* lawful **LICITLY** *adv*

LICK *v* -ED, -ING, -S to pass the tongue over the surface of

LICKER *n* pl. -S one that licks

LICKING *n* pl. -S a thrashing or beating

LICKSPIT *n* pl. -S a fawning person

LICORICE *n* pl. -S a perennial herb

LICTOR *n* pl. -S a magistrate's attendant in ancient Rome

LID *v* LIDDED, LIDDING, LIDS to provide with a lid (a movable cover)

LIDAR *n* pl. -S an electronic locating device

LIDLESS *adj* having no lid

LIDO *n* pl. -DOS a fashionable beach resort

LIE *v* LIED, LYING, LIES to speak falsely

LIE *v* LAY, LAIN, LYING, LIES to be in or get into a horizontal position

LIED *n* pl. LIEDER a German song

LIEF *adj* LIEFER, LIEFEST willing **LIEFLY** *adv*

LIEGE *n* pl. -S a feudal lord

LIEGEMAN *n* pl. -MEN a feudal vassal

LIEN	*n* pl. -S a legal right to hold or sell a debtor's property	**LIGHT**	*adj* LIGHTER, LIGHTEST having little weight
LIENABLE	*adj* capable of being subjected to a lien	**LIGHT**	*v* LIGHTED or LIT, LIGHTING, LIGHTS to illuminate
LIENAL	*adj* pertaining to the spleen	**LIGHTEN**	*v* -ED, -ING, -S to reduce the weight of
LIENTERY	*n* pl. -TERIES a form of diarrhea	**LIGHTER**	*v* -ED, -ING, -S to convey in a type of barge
LIER	*n* pl. -S one that lies or reclines	**LIGHTFUL**	*adj* brightly illuminated
LIERNE	*n* pl. -S a connecting part in Gothic vaulting	**LIGHTING**	*n* pl. -S illumination
LIEU	*n* pl. -S place; stead	**LIGHTISH**	*adj* somewhat light
LIEVE	*adv* LIEVER, LIEVEST gladly	**LIGHTLY**	*adv* to a moderate degree
LIFE	*n* pl. LIVES the quality that distinguishes animals and plants from inanimate matter	**LIGNEOUS**	*adj* of or resembling wood
		LIGNIFY	*v* -FIED, -FYING, -FIES to convert into wood
LIFEBOAT	*n* pl. -S a small rescue boat	**LIGNIN**	*n* pl. -S an essential part of woody tissue
LIFEFUL	*adj* full of life		
LIFELESS	*adj* having no life	**LIGNITE**	*n* pl. -S a type of coal **LIGNITIC** *adj*
LIFELIKE	*adj* resembling a living thing		
LIFELINE	*n* pl. -S a rope used to aid a person in distress	**LIGROIN**	*n* pl. -S a flammable liquid
		LIGROINE	*n* pl. -S ligroin
LIFELONG	*adj* lasting for a lifetime	**LIGULA**	*n* pl. -LAE or -LAS a strap-shaped organ or part **LIGULAR, LIGULATE, LIGULOID** *adj*
LIFER	*n* pl. -S a prisoner serving a life sentence		
LIFETIME	*n* pl. -S the period of living existence	**LIGULE**	*n* pl. -S a strap-shaped plant part
		LIGURE	*n* pl. -S a precious stone
LIFEWAY	*n* pl. -WAYS a way of living	**LIKABLE**	*adj* pleasant
LIFEWORK	*n* pl. -S the major work of one's lifetime	**LIKE**	*v* LIKED, LIKING, LIKES to find pleasant
LIFT	*v* -ED, -ING, -S to move to a higher position **LIFTABLE** *adj*	**LIKE**	*adj* LIKER, LIKEST possessing the same or almost the same characteristics
LIFTER	*n* pl. -S one that lifts		
LIFTGATE	*n* pl. -S a rear panel on a station wagon that opens upward	**LIKEABLE**	*adj* likable
		LIKED	past tense of like
LIFTMAN	*n* pl. -MEN an elevator operator	**LIKELY**	*adj* -LIER, -LIEST probable
LIFTOFF	*n* pl. -S the vertical takeoff of a rocket	**LIKEN**	*v* -ED, -ING, -S to represent as similar
LIGAMENT	*n* pl. -S a band of firm, fibrous tissue	**LIKENESS**	*n* pl. -ES a pictorial representation
LIGAN	*n* pl. -S lagan	**LIKER**	*n* pl. -S one that likes
LIGAND	*n* pl. -S a type of ion or molecule	**LIKEST**	superlative of like
LIGASE	*n* pl. -S an enzyme	**LIKEWISE**	*adv* in a similar manner
LIGATE	*v* -GATED, -GATING, -GATES to bind	**LIKING**	*n* pl. -S a feeling of attraction or affection
LIGATION	*n* pl. -S the act of ligating **LIGATIVE** *adj*	**LIKUTA**	*n* pl. MAKUTA a monetary unit of Zaire
LIGATURE	*v* -TURED, -TURING, -TURES to ligate	**LILAC**	*n* pl. -S a flowering shrub
		LILIED	*adj* covered with lilies
LIGER	*n* pl. -S the offspring of a male lion and a female tiger	**LILIES**	pl. of lily

LILLIPUT   *n* pl. -S a very small person

LILT   *v* -ED, -ING, -S to sing or speak rhythmically

LILY   *n* pl. LILIES a flowering plant **LILYLIKE** *adj*

LIMA   *n* pl. -S the edible seed of a tropical American plant

LIMACINE   *adj* resembling a type of mollusk

LIMACON   *n* pl. -S a type of geometric curve

LIMAN   *n* pl. -S a lagoon

LIMB   *v* -ED, -ING, -S to cut off the arms or legs of

LIMBA   *n* pl. -S an African tree

LIMBATE   *adj* having an edge of a different color

LIMBECK   *n* pl. -S alembic

LIMBER   *adj* -BERER, -BEREST flexible **LIMBERLY** *adv*

LIMBER   *v* -ED, -ING, -S to make flexible

LIMBI   a pl. of limbus

LIMBIC   *adj* pertaining to a system of the brain

LIMBIER   comparative of limby

LIMBIEST   superlative of limby

LIMBLESS   *adj* having no arms or legs

LIMBO   *n* pl. -BOS a condition of oblivion or neglect

LIMBUS   *n* pl. -BUSES or -BI a distinctive border

LIMBY   *adj* LIMBIER, LIMBIEST having many large branches

LIME   *v* LIMED, LIMING, LIMES to treat with lime (a calcium compound)

LIMEADE   *n* pl. -S a beverage

LIMEKILN   *n* pl. -S a furnace in which shells are burned to produce lime

LIMELESS   *adj* having no lime

LIMEN   *n* pl. -MENS or -MINA a sensory threshold

LIMERICK   *n* pl. -S a humorous verse

LIMES   *n* pl. LIMITES a fortified boundary

LIMEY   *n* pl. -EYS a British sailor

LIMIER   comparative of limy

LIMIEST   superlative of limy

LIMINA   a pl. of limen

LIMINAL   *adj* pertaining to the limen

LIMINESS   *n* pl. -ES the state of being limy

LIMING   present participle of lime

LIMIT   *v* -ED, -ING, -S to restrict

LIMITARY   *adj* limiting

LIMITED   *n* pl. -S a train or bus making few stops

LIMITER   *n* pl. -S one that limits

LIMITES   pl. of limes

LIMMER   *n* pl. -S a scoundrel

LIMN   *v* -ED, -ING, -S to depict by painting or drawing

LIMNER   *n* pl. -S one that limns

LIMNETIC   *adj* pertaining to the open water of a lake or pond

LIMNIC   *adj* limnetic

LIMO   *n* pl. LIMOS a limousine

LIMONENE   *n* pl. -S a chemical compound

LIMONITE   *n* pl. -S a major ore of iron

LIMP   *v* -ED, -ING, -S to walk lamely

LIMP   *adj* LIMPER, LIMPEST lacking rigidity

LIMPA   *n* pl. -S rye bread made with molasses

LIMPER   *n* pl. -S one that limps

LIMPET   *n* pl. -S a type of mollusk

LIMPID   *adj* transparent **LIMPIDLY** *adv*

LIMPKIN   *n* pl. -S a wading bird

LIMPLY   *adv* in a limp manner

LIMPNESS   *n* pl. -ES the state of being limp

LIMPSEY   *adj* -SIER, -SIEST limpsy

LIMPSY   *adj* -SIER, -SIEST lacking strength or vigor

LIMULOID   *n* pl. -S a horseshoe crab

LIMULUS   *n* pl. -LI a horseshoe crab

LIMY   *adj* LIMIER, LIMIEST resembling or containing lime

LIN   *n* pl. -S linn

LINABLE   *adj* lineable

LINAC   *n* pl. -S a device for imparting high velocities to charged particles

LINAGE   *n* pl. -S the number of lines of printed material

LINALOL   *n* pl. -S linalool

LINALOOL   *n* pl. -S a fragrant alcohol

LINCHPIN   *n* pl. -S a locking pin inserted in the end of a shaft

LINDANE   *n* pl. -S an insecticide

LINDEN   *n* pl. -S a tall forest tree

LINDY   *n* pl. -DIES a lively dance

LINE   *v* LINED, LINING, LINES to mark with lines (slender, continuous marks)

LINEABLE   *adj* lying in a straight line

LINEAGE   *n* pl. -S direct descent from an ancestor

LINEAL   *adj* being directly descended from an ancestor **LINEALLY** *adv*

LINEAR   *adj* of or resembling a straight line **LINEARLY** *adv*

LINEATE   *adj* marked with lines

LINEATED   *adj* lineate

LINEBRED   *adj* produced by interbreeding within a particular line of descent

LINECUT   *n* pl. -S a type of printing plate

LINED   past tense of line

LINELESS   *adj* having no lines

LINELIKE   *adj* resembling a line

LINEMAN   *n* pl. -MEN one who installs or repairs telephone wires

LINEN   *n* pl. -S a fabric woven from the fibers of flax **LINENY** *adj*

LINER   *n* pl. -S a commercial ship or airplane

LINESMAN   *n* pl. -MEN a football official

LINEUP   *n* pl. -S a row of persons

LINEY   *adj* LINIER, LINIEST liny

LING   *n* pl. -S a heath plant

LINGA   *n* pl. -S lingam

LINGAM   *n* pl. -S a Hindu phallic symbol

LINGCOD   *n* pl. -S a marine food fish

LINGER   *v* -ED, -ING, -S to delay leaving

LINGERER   *n* pl. -S one that lingers

LINGERIE   *n* pl. -S women's underwear

LINGIER   comparative of lingy

LINGIEST   superlative of lingy

LINGO   *n* pl. -GOES strange or incomprehensible language

LINGUA   *n* pl. -GUAE the tongue or a tonguelike part

LINGUAL   *n* pl. -S a sound articulated with the tongue

LINGUINE   *n* pl. -S linguini

LINGUINI   *n* pl. -S a type of pasta

LINGUIST   *n* pl. -S a person skilled in several languages

LINGY   *adj* LINGIER, LINGIEST covered with heaths

LINIER   comparative of liney and liny

LINIEST   superlative of liney and liny

LINIMENT   *n* pl. -S a medicinal liquid

LININ   *n* pl. -S a substance in the nucleus of a cell

LINING   *n* pl. -S an inner layer

LINK   *v* -ED, -ING, -S to connect **LINKABLE** *adj*

LINKAGE   *n* pl. -S the act of linking

LINKBOY   *n* pl. -BOYS a man or boy hired to carry a torch to light the way along dark streets

LINKER   *n* pl. -S one that links

LINKMAN   *n* pl. -MEN a linkboy

LINKSMAN   *n* pl. -MEN a golfer

LINKUP   *n* pl. -S something that serves as a linking device

LINKWORK   *n* pl. -S something composed of interlocking rings

LINKY   *adj* full of interlocking rings

LINN   *n* pl. -S a waterfall

LINNET   *n* pl. -S a European songbird

LINO   *n* pl. -NOS linoleum

LINOCUT   *n* pl. -S a print made from a design cut into linoleum

LINOLEUM   *n* pl. -S a durable material used as a floor covering

LINSANG   *n* pl. -S a carnivorous mammal

LINSEED   *n* pl. -S flaxseed

LINSEY   *n* pl. -SEYS a coarse fabric

LINSTOCK   *n* pl. -S a stick having one end divided to hold a match

LINT   *n* pl. -S an accumulation of bits of fiber

LINTEL   *n* pl. -S a horizontal supporting beam

LINTER   *n* pl. -S a machine for removing fibers from cotton seeds

LINTIER   comparative of linty

LINTIEST   superlative of linty

LINTLESS   *adj* free from lint

LINTOL   *n* pl. -S lintel

LINTY   *adj* LINTIER, LINTIEST covered with lint

LINUM   *n* pl. -S a plant of the flax family

LINURON   *n* pl. -S a herbicide

LINY   *adj* LINIER, LINIEST resembling a line

LION   *n* pl. -S a large, carnivorous feline mammal

LIONESS	*n* pl. -ES a female lion
LIONFISH	*n* pl. -ES a tropical fish
LIONISE	*v* -ISED, -ISING, -ISES to lionize
LIONISER	*n* pl. -S one that lionises
LIONIZE	*v* -IZED, -IZING, -IZES to treat or regard as a celebrity
LIONIZER	*n* pl. -S one that lionizes
LIONLIKE	*adj* resembling a lion
LIP	*v* LIPPED, LIPPING, LIPS to touch with the lips (the folds of flesh around the mouth)
LIPASE	*n* pl. -S an enzyme
LIPID	*n* pl. -S any of a class of fatty substances **LIPIDIC** *adj*
LIPIDE	*n* pl. -S lipid
LIPIN	*n* pl. -S a lipid
LIPLESS	*adj* having no lips
LIPLIKE	*adj* resembling a lip
LIPOCYTE	*n* pl. -S a fat-producing cell
LIPOID	*n* pl. -S a lipid **LIPOIDAL** *adj*
LIPOMA	*n* pl. -MAS or -MATA a tumor of fatty tissue
LIPOSOME	*n* pl. -S a microscopic globule composed of lipids
LIPPED	past tense of lip
LIPPEN	*v* -ED, -ING, -S to trust
LIPPER	*v* -ED, -ING, -S to ripple
LIPPING	*n* pl. -S a liplike outgrowth of bone
LIPPY	*adj* -PIER, -PIEST impudent
LIPSTICK	*n* pl. -S a cosmetic used to color the lips
LIQUATE	*v* -QUATED, -QUATING, -QUATES to purify metal by heating
LIQUEFY	*v* -FIED, -FYING, -FIES to make or become liquid
LIQUEUR	*n* pl. -S a sweetened alcoholic beverage
LIQUID	*n* pl. -S a substance that flows freely
LIQUIDLY	*adv* in a free-flowing manner
LIQUIFY	*v* -FIED, -FYING, -FIES to liquefy
LIQUOR	*v* -ED, -ING, -S to intoxicate with liquor (an alcoholic beverage)
LIRA	*n* pl. LIRI a monetary unit of Malta
LIRA	*n* pl. LIRE or LIRAS a monetary unit of Italy
LIRA	*n* pl. LIROTH or LIROT a former monetary unit of Israel
LIRIPIPE	*n* pl. -S a long scarf
LISENTE	a pl. of sente
LISLE	*n* pl. -S a fine, tightly twisted cotton thread
LISP	*v* -ED, -ING, -S to pronounce the letters *s* and *z* imperfectly
LISPER	*n* pl. -S one that lisps
LISSOM	*adj* lissome **LISSOMLY** *adv*
LISSOME	*adj* lithe
LIST	*v* -ED, -ING, -S to write down in a particular order **LISTABLE** *adj*
LISTEE	*n* pl. -S one that is on a list
LISTEL	*n* pl. -S a narrow molding
LISTEN	*v* -ED, -ING, -S to make conscious use of the sense of hearing
LISTENER	*n* pl. -S one that listens
LISTER	*n* pl. -S a type of plow
LISTING	*n* pl. -S something that is listed
LISTLESS	*adj* languid
LIT	*n* pl. -S the litas
LITANY	*n* pl. -NIES a ceremonial form of prayer
LITAS	*n* pl. LITAI or LITU a former monetary unit of Lithuania
LITCHI	*n* pl. -S the edible fruit of a Chinese tree
LITE	*adj* lower in calories or having less of some ingredient
LITER	*n* pl. -S a unit of capacity
LITERACY	*n* pl. -CIES the ability to read and write
LITERAL	*n* pl. -S a small error in printing or writing
LITERARY	*adj* of, pertaining to, or having the characteristics of books and writings
LITERATE	*n* pl. -S one who can read and write
LITERATI	*n/pl* scholars collectively
LITHARGE	*n* pl. -S a monoxide of lead
LITHE	*adj* LITHER, LITHEST bending easily **LITHELY** *adv*
LITHEMIA	*n* pl. -S an excess of uric acid in the blood **LITHEMIC** *adj*
LITHIA	*n* pl. -S an oxide of lithium
LITHIC	*adj* pertaining to lithium
LITHIFY	*v* -FIED, -FYING, -FIES to petrify

LITHIUM	*n* pl. -S a metallic element	**LIVETRAP**	*v* -TRAPPED, -TRAPPING, -TRAPS to capture in a type of animal trap
LITHO	*v* -ED, -ING, -S to make prints by lithography	**LIVID**	*adj* having the skin abnormally discolored **LIVIDLY** *adv*
LITHOID	*adj* resembling stone	**LIVIDITY**	*n* pl. -TIES the state of being livid
LITHOSOL	*n* pl. -S a type of soil	**LIVIER**	*n* pl. -S livyer
LITIGANT	*n* pl. -S one who is engaged in a lawsuit	**LIVING**	*n* pl. -S a means of subsistence
LITIGATE	*v* -GATED, -GATING, -GATES to subject to legal proceedings	**LIVINGLY**	*adv* realistically
LITMUS	*n* pl. -ES a blue coloring matter	**LIVRE**	*n* pl. -S a former monetary unit of France
LITORAL	*adj* pertaining to a coastal region	**LIVYER**	*n* pl. -S a permanent resident of Newfoundland
LITOTES	*n* pl. LITOTES a figure of speech in which an assertion is made by the negation of its opposite **LITOTIC** *adj*	**LIXIVIUM**	*n* pl. -IA or -IUMS a solution obtained by leaching **LIXIVIAL** *adj*
LITRE	*n* pl. -S liter	**LIZARD**	*n* pl. -S any of a suborder of reptiles
LITTEN	*adj* lighted	**LLAMA**	*n* pl. -S a ruminant mammal
LITTER	*v* -ED, -ING, -S to scatter rubbish about	**LLANO**	*n* pl. -NOS an open, grassy plain
LITTERER	*n* pl. -S one that litters	**LO**	*interj* — used to attract attention or to express surprise
LITTERY	*adj* covered with rubbish	**LOACH**	*n* pl. -ES a freshwater fish
LITTLE	*adj* -TLER, -TLEST small	**LOAD**	*v* -ED, -ING, -S to place in or on a means of conveyance
LITTLE	*n* pl. -S a small amount	**LOADER**	*n* pl. -S one that loads
LITTLISH	*adj* somewhat little	**LOADING**	*n* pl. -S a burden
LITTORAL	*n* pl. -S a coastal region	**LOADSTAR**	*n* pl. -S lodestar
LITU	a pl. of litas	**LOAF**	*n* pl. LOAVES a shaped mass of bread
LITURGY	*n* pl. -GIES a prescribed system of public worship **LITURGIC** *adj*	**LOAF**	*v* -ED, -ING, -S to pass time idly
LIVABLE	*adj* suitable for living in	**LOAFER**	*n* pl. -S one that loafs
LIVE	*v* LIVED, LIVING, LIVES to function as an animal or plant	**LOAM**	*v* -ED, -ING, -S to cover with loam (a type of soil)
LIVE	*adj* LIVER, LIVEST having life	**LOAMLESS**	*adj* having no loam
LIVEABLE	*adj* livable	**LOAMY**	*adj* LOAMIER, LOAMIEST resembling loam
LIVELONG	*adj* long in passing	**LOAN**	*v* -ED, -ING, -S to lend **LOANABLE** *adj*
LIVELY	*adj* -LIER, -LIEST full of energy **LIVELILY** *adv*	**LOANER**	*n* pl. -S one that loans
LIVEN	*v* -ED, -ING, -S to make lively	**LOANING**	*n* pl. -S a lane
LIVENER	*n* pl. -S one that livens	**LOANWORD**	*n* pl. -S a word taken from another language
LIVENESS	*n* pl. -ES the state of being live	**LOATH**	*adj* unwilling
LIVER	*n* pl. -S a secreting organ	**LOATHE**	*v* LOATHED, LOATHING, LOATHES to detest greatly
LIVERIED	*adj* wearing a livery	**LOATHER**	*n* pl. -S one that loathes
LIVERISH	*adj* having a liver disorder	**LOATHFUL**	*adj* repulsive
LIVERY	*n* pl. -ERIES a uniform worn by servants	**LOATHING**	*n* pl. -S extreme dislike
LIVES	pl. of life		
LIVEST	superlative of live		

LOATHLY *adj* repulsive

LOAVES pl. of loaf

LOB *v* LOBBED, LOBBING, LOBS to throw or hit in a high arc

LOBAR *adj* pertaining to a lobe

LOBATE *adj* having lobes **LOBATELY** *adv*

LOBATED *adj* lobate

LOBATION *n* pl. -S the formation of lobes

LOBBED past tense of lob

LOBBER *n* pl. -S one that lobs

LOBBING present participle of lob

LOBBY *v* -BIED, -BYING, -BIES to attempt to influence legislators

LOBBYER *n* pl. -S a lobbyist

LOBBYGOW *n* pl. -S an errand boy

LOBBYISM *n* pl. -S the practice of lobbying

LOBBYIST *n* pl. -S one who lobbies

LOBE *n* pl. -S a rounded, projecting anatomical part **LOBED** *adj*

LOBEFIN *n* pl. -S a bony fish

LOBELIA *n* pl. -S a flowering plant

LOBELINE *n* pl. -S a poisonous alkaloid

LOBLOLLY *n* pl. -LIES a pine tree

LOBO *n* pl. -BOS the timber wolf

LOBOTOMY *n* pl. -MIES a type of surgical operation

LOBSTER *v* -ED, -ING, -S to fish for lobsters (marine crustaceans)

LOBSTICK *n* pl. -S a tree with its lower branches trimmed

LOBULE *n* pl. -S a small lobe **LOBULAR, LOBULATE, LOBULOSE** *adj*

LOBWORM *n* pl. -S a lugworm

LOCA a pl. of locus

LOCAL *n* pl. -S a train or bus making all stops

LOCALE *n* pl. -S a locality

LOCALISE *v* -ISED, -ISING, -ISES to localize

LOCALISM *n* pl. -S a custom or mannerism peculiar to a locality

LOCALIST *n* pl. -S one who is strongly concerned with the matters of a locality

LOCALITE *n* pl. -S a resident of a locality

LOCALITY *n* pl. -TIES an area or neighborhood

LOCALIZE *v* -IZED, -IZING, -IZES to confine to a particular area

LOCALLY *adv* in a particular area

LOCATE *v* -CATED, -CATING, -CATES to determine the position of

LOCATER *n* pl. -S one that locates

LOCATION *n* pl. -S the place where something is at a given moment

LOCATIVE *n* pl. -S a type of grammatical case

LOCATOR *n* pl. -S locater

LOCH *n* pl. -S a lake

LOCHAN *n* pl. -S a small lake

LOCHIA *n* pl. LOCHIA a vaginal discharge following childbirth **LOCHIAL** *adj*

LOCI a pl. of locus

LOCK *v* -ED, -ING, -S to secure by means of a mechanical fastening device **LOCKABLE** *adj*

LOCKAGE *n* pl. -S a toll on a ship passing through a canal

LOCKBOX *n* pl. -ES a box that locks

LOCKDOWN *n* pl. -S the confinement of prisoners to their cells

LOCKER *n* pl. -S an enclosure that may be locked

LOCKET *n* pl. -S a small ornamental case

LOCKJAW *n* pl. -S a form of tetanus

LOCKNUT *n* pl. -S a nut which keeps another from loosening

LOCKOUT *n* pl. -S a closing of a business to coerce employees to agree to terms

LOCKRAM *n* pl. -S a coarse, linen fabric

LOCKSTEP *n* pl. -S a mode of marching in close file

LOCKUP *n* pl. -S a jail

LOCO *n* pl. -COS or -COES locoweed

LOCO *v* -ED, -ING, -S to poison with locoweed

LOCOFOCO *n* pl. -COS a type of friction match

LOCOISM *n* pl. -S a disease of livestock

LOCOMOTE *v* -MOTED, -MOTING, -MOTES to move about

LOCOWEED *n* pl. -S a plant that causes poisoning when eaten by livestock

LOCULAR *adj* having or divided into loculi

LOCULATE *adj* locular

LOCULE *n* pl. -S loculus **LOCULED** *adj*

LOCULUS *n* pl. -LI a small, cell-like chamber

LOCUM *n* pl. -S a temporary substitute

LOCUS *n* pl. LOCI or LOCA a place

LOCUST *n* pl. -S a migratory grasshopper

LOCUSTA *n* pl. -TAE a spikelet **LOCUSTAL** *adj*

LOCUTION *n* pl. -S a particular form of expression

LOCUTORY *n* pl. -RIES a room in a monastery

LODE *n* pl. -S a deposit of ore

LODEN *n* pl. -S a thick, woolen fabric

LODESTAR *n* pl. -S a star used as a point of reference

LODGE *v* LODGED, LODGING, LODGES to furnish with temporary quarters

LODGER *n* pl. -S one that resides in rented quarters

LODGING *n* pl. -S a temporary place to live

LODGMENT *n* pl. -S a lodging

LODICULE *n* pl. -S a scale at the base of the ovary of a grass

LOESS *n* pl. -ES a soil deposit **LOESSAL, LOESSIAL** *adj*

LOFT *v* -ED, -ING, -S to store in a loft (an upper room)

LOFTER *n* pl. -S a type of golf club

LOFTIER comparative of lofty

LOFTIEST superlative of lofty

LOFTILY *adv* in a lofty manner

LOFTLESS *adj* having no loft

LOFTLIKE *adj* resembling a loft

LOFTY *adj* LOFTIER, LOFTIEST extending high in the air

LOG *v* LOGGED, LOGGING, LOGS to cut down trees for timber

LOGAN *n* pl. -S a stone balanced to permit easy movement

LOGANIA *adj* designating a family of flowering plants

LOGBOOK *n* pl. -S a record book of a ship or aircraft

LOGE *n* pl. -S a small compartment

LOGGATS *n/pl* loggets

LOGGED past tense of log

LOGGER *n* pl. -S one that logs

LOGGETS *n/pl* an old English throwing game

LOGGIA *n* pl. -GIAS or -GIE an open gallery

LOGGING *n* pl. -S the business of cutting down trees for timber

LOGGY *adj* -GIER, -GIEST logy

LOGIA a pl. of logion

LOGIC *n* pl. -S the science of reasoning

LOGICAL *adj* pertaining to logic

LOGICIAN *n* pl. -S one who is skilled in logic

LOGICISE *v* -CISED, -CISING, -CISES to logicize

LOGICIZE *v* -CIZED, -CIZING, -CIZES to reason

LOGIER comparative of logy

LOGIEST superlative of logy

LOGILY *adv* in a logy manner

LOGINESS *n* pl. -ES the state of being logy

LOGION *n* pl. -GIA or -GIONS a saying attributed to Jesus

LOGISTIC *n* pl. -S symbolic logic

LOGJAM *n* pl. -S a tangled mass of logs

LOGO *n* pl. LOGOS an identifying symbol

LOGOGRAM *n* pl. -S a symbol used to represent an entire word

LOGOMACH *n* pl. -S one given to arguing about words

LOGOS *n* pl. LOGOI the rational principle that governs the universe in ancient Greek philosophy

LOGOTYPE *n* pl. -S a piece of type bearing a syllable, word, or words

LOGOTYPY *n* pl. -TYPIES the use of logotypes

LOGROLL *v* -ED, -ING, -S to obtain passage of by exchanging political favors

LOGWAY *n* pl. -WAYS a ramp used in logging

LOGWOOD *n* pl. -S a tropical tree

LOGY *adj* -GIER, -GIEST sluggish

LOIN *n* pl. -S a part of the side and back between the ribs and the hipbone

LOITER *v* -ED, -ING, -S to stand idly about

LOITERER *n* pl. -S one that loiters

LOLL *v* -ED, -ING, -S to lounge

LOLLER *n* pl. -S one that lolls

LOLLIES pl. of lolly

LOLLIPOP   *n* pl. -S a piece of candy on the end of a stick

LOLLOP   *v* -ED, -ING, -S to loll

LOLLY   *n* pl. -LIES a lollipop

LOLLYGAG   *v* -GAGGED, -GAGGING, -GAGS to lallygag

LOLLYPOP   *n* pl. -S lollipop

LOMEIN   *n* pl. -S a Chinese dish of noodles, meat, and vegetables

LOMENT   *n* pl. -S a type of plant pod

LOMENTUM   *n* pl. -TA or -TUMS loment

LONE   *adj* having no companions

LONELY   *adj* -LIER, -LIEST sad from lack of companionship **LONELILY** *adv*

LONENESS   *n* pl. -ES the state of being lone

LONER   *n* pl. -S one that avoids others

LONESOME   *n* pl. -S self

LONG   *adj* LONGER, LONGEST extending for a considerable distance

LONG   *v* -ED, -ING, -S to desire strongly

LONGAN   *n* pl. -S the edible fruit of a Chinese tree

LONGBOAT   *n* pl. -S the largest boat carried by a sailing vessel

LONGBOW   *n* pl. -S a type of archery bow

LONGE   *v* LONGED, LONGEING, LONGES to guide a horse by means of a long rope

LONGER   *n* pl. -S one that longs

LONGERON   *n* pl. -S a longitudinal support of an airplane

LONGHAIR   *n* pl. -S an intellectual

LONGHAND   *n* pl. -S ordinary handwriting

LONGHEAD   *n* pl. -S a person having a long skull

LONGHORN   *n* pl. -S one of a breed of long-horned cattle

LONGIES   *n/pl* long underwear

LONGING   *n* pl. -S a strong desire

LONGISH   *adj* somewhat long

LONGLEAF   *n* pl. -LEAVES an evergreen tree

LONGLINE   *n* pl. -S a type of fishing line

LONGLY   *adv* for a considerable distance

LONGNESS   *n* pl. -ES the state of being long

LONGSHIP   *n* pl. -S a medieval ship

LONGSOME   *adj* tediously long

LONGSPUR   *n* pl. -S a long-clawed finch

LONGTIME   *adj* of long duration

LONGUEUR   *n* pl. -S a dull and tedious section

LONGWAYS   *adv* longwise

LONGWISE   *adv* lengthwise

LOO   *v* -ED, -ING, -S to subject to a forfeit at loo (a card game)

LOOBY   *n* pl. -BIES a large, awkward person

LOOEY   *n* pl. -EYS looie

LOOF   *n* pl. -S the palm of the hand

LOOFA   *n* pl. -S loofah

LOOFAH   *n* pl. -S a tropical vine

LOOIE   *n* pl. -S a lieutenant of the armed forces

LOOK   *v* -ED, -ING, -S to use one's eyes in seeing

LOOKDOWN   *n* pl. -S a marine fish

LOOKER   *n* pl. -S one that looks

LOOKOUT   *n* pl. -S one engaged in keeping watch

LOOKUP   *n* pl. -S the process of looking something up

LOOM   *v* -ED, -ING, -S to appear in an enlarged and indistinct form

LOON   *n* pl. -S a diving waterfowl

LOONEY   *adj* -NIER, -NIEST loony

LOONEY   *n* pl. -EYS loony

LOONY   *adj* -NIER, -NIEST crazy

LOONY   *n* pl. -NIES a loony person

LOOP   *v* -ED, -ING, -S to form loops (circular or oval openings)

LOOPER   *n* pl. -S one that loops

LOOPHOLE   *v* -HOLED, -HOLING, -HOLES to make small openings in

LOOPY   *adj* LOOPIER, LOOPIEST full of loops

LOOSE   *adj* LOOSER, LOOSEST not firm, taut, or rigid **LOOSELY** *adv*

LOOSE   *v* LOOSED, LOOSING, LOOSES to set free

LOOSEN   *v* -ED, -ING, -S to make looser

LOOSENER   *n* pl. -S one that loosens

LOOSER   comparative of loose

LOOSEST   superlative of loose

LOOSING   present participle of loose

LOOT   *v* -ED, -ING, -S to plunder

LOOTER   *n* pl. -S one that loots

LOP	*v* LOPPED, LOPPING, LOPS to cut off branches or twigs from
LOPE	*v* LOPED, LOPING, LOPES to run with a steady, easy gait
LOPER	*n* pl. -S one that lopes
LOPPED	past tense of lop
LOPPER	*v* -ED, -ING, -S to curdle
LOPPING	present participle of lop
LOPPY	*adj* -PIER, -PIEST hanging limply
LOPSIDED	*adj* leaning to one side
LOPSTICK	*n* pl. -S lobstick
LOQUAT	*n* pl. -S a small yellow fruit
LORAL	*adj* pertaining to the space between the eye and bill of a bird
LORAN	*n* pl. -S a type of navigational system
LORD	*v* -ED, -ING, -S to invest with the power of a lord (a person having dominion over others)
LORDING	*n* pl. -S a lordling
LORDLESS	*adj* having no lord
LORDLIER	comparative of lordly
LORDLIEST	superlative of lordly
LORDLIKE	*adj* lordly
LORDLING	*n* pl. -S a young or unimportant lord
LORDLY	*adj* -LIER, -LIEST of or befitting a lord
LORDOMA	*n* pl. -S lordosis
LORDOSIS	*n* pl. -DOSES a curvature of the spinal column **LORDOTIC** *adj*
LORDSHIP	*n* pl. -S the power of a lord
LORE	*n* pl. -S traditional knowledge or belief
LOREAL	*adj* loral
LORGNON	*n* pl. -S a pair of eyeglasses with a handle
LORICA	*n* pl. -CAE a protective covering or shell
LORICATE	*n* pl. -S an animal having a lorica
LORIES	pl. of lory
LORIKEET	*n* pl. -S a small parrot
LORIMER	*n* pl. -S a maker of implements for harnesses and saddles
LORINER	*n* pl. -S lorimer
LORIS	*n* pl. -RISES an Asian lemur
LORN	*adj* abandoned
LORNNESS	*n* pl. -ES the state of being lorn

LORRY	*n* pl. -RIES a type of wagon or truck
LORY	*n* pl. -RIES a small parrot
LOSE	*v* LOST, LOSING, LOSES to come to be without and be unable to find **LOSABLE** *adj*
LOSEL	*n* pl. -S a worthless person
LOSER	*n* pl. -S one that loses
LOSING	*n* pl. -S a loss
LOSINGLY	*adv* in a manner characterized by defeat
LOSS	*n* pl. -ES the act of one that loses
LOSSY	*adj* causing dissipation of electrical energy
LOST	*adj* not to be found or recovered
LOSTNESS	*n* pl. -ES the state of being lost
LOT	*v* LOTTED, LOTTING, LOTS to distribute proportionately
LOTA	*n* pl. -S lotah
LOTAH	*n* pl. -S a small water vessel used in India
LOTH	*adj* loath
LOTHARIO	*n* pl. -IOS a seducer of women
LOTHSOME	*adj* repulsive
LOTI	*n* pl. MALOTI a monetary unit of Lesotho
LOTIC	*adj* pertaining to moving water
LOTION	*n* pl. -S a liquid preparation for external application
LOTOS	*n* pl. -ES lotus
LOTTE	*n* pl. -S a monkfish
LOTTED	past tense of lot
LOTTERY	*n* pl. -TERIES a type of gambling game
LOTTING	present participle of lot
LOTTO	*n* pl. -TOS a game of chance
LOTUS	*n* pl. -ES an aquatic plant
LOUCHE	*adj* not reputable
LOUD	*adj* LOUDER, LOUDEST strongly audible
LOUDEN	*v* -ED, -ING, -S to make or become louder
LOUDISH	*adj* somewhat loud
LOUDLY	*adv* -LIER, -LIEST in a loud manner
LOUDNESS	*n* pl. -ES the quality of being loud
LOUGH	*n* pl. -S a lake
LOUIE	*n* pl. -S looie

LOUIS	*n* pl. LOUIS a former gold coin of France	**LOVEVINE**	*n* pl. -S a twining herb
		LOVING	*adj* affectionate
LOUNGE	*v* LOUNGED, LOUNGING, LOUNGES to recline or lean in a relaxed, lazy manner	**LOVINGLY**	*adv* in a loving manner
		LOW	*adj* LOWER, LOWEST having relatively little upward extension
LOUNGER	*n* pl. -S one that lounges		
LOUNGY	*adj* suitable for lounging	**LOW**	*v* -ED, -ING, -S to utter the sound characteristic of cattle
LOUP	*v* LOUPED, LOUPEN, LOUPING, LOUPS to leap	**LOWBALL**	*v* -ED, -ING, -S to give a customer a deceptively low price
LOUPE	*n* pl. -S a small magnifying glass	**LOWBORN**	*adj* of humble birth
LOUR	*v* -ED, -ING, -S to lower	**LOWBOY**	*n* pl. -BOYS a low chest of drawers
LOURY	*adj* lowery		
LOUSE	*n* pl. LICE a parasitic insect	**LOWBRED**	*adj* lowborn
LOUSE	*v* LOUSED, LOUSING, LOUSES to spoil or bungle	**LOWBROW**	*n* pl. -S an uncultivated person
		LOWDOWN	*n* pl. -S the whole truth
LOUSY	*adj* LOUSIER, LOUSIEST mean or contemptible **LOUSILY** *adv*	**LOWE**	*v* LOWED, LOWING, LOWES to blaze
LOUT	*v* -ED, -ING, -S to bow in respect	**LOWER**	*v* -ED, -ING, -S to appear dark and threatening
LOUTISH	*adj* clumsy		
LOUVER	*n* pl. -S a type of window **LOUVERED** *adj*	**LOWERY**	*adj* dark and threatening
		LOWING	*n* pl. -S the sound characteristic of cattle
LOUVRE	*n* pl. -S louver		
LOVABLE	*adj* having qualities that attract love **LOVABLY** *adv*	**LOWISH**	*adj* somewhat low
		LOWLAND	*n* pl. -S an area of land lying lower than the adjacent country
LOVAGE	*n* pl. -S a perennial herb		
LOVAT	*n* pl. -S a chiefly green color mixture in fabrics	**LOWLIFE**	*n* pl. -LIFES or -LIVES a despicable person
LOVE	*v* LOVED, LOVING, LOVES to feel great affection for	**LOWLIFER**	*n* pl. -S a lowlife
		LOWLIGHT	*n* pl. -S an unpleasant event, detail, or part
LOVEABLE	*adj* lovable **LOVEABLY** *adv*		
LOVEBIRD	*n* pl. -S a small parrot	**LOWLY**	*adj* -LIER, -LIEST low in position or rank
LOVEBUG	*n* pl. -S a small black fly that swarms along highways	**LOWN**	*adj* peaceful
LOVED	past tense of love	**LOWNESS**	*n* pl. -ES the state of being low
LOVELESS	*adj* feeling no love	**LOWRIDER**	*n* pl. -S a car having a lowered suspension
LOVELIER	comparative of lovely		
LOVELIES	pl. of lovely	**LOWSE**	*adj* loose
LOVELIEST	superlative of lovely	**LOX**	*v* -ED, -ING, -ES to supply with lox (liquid oxygen)
LOVELILY	*adv* in a lovely manner		
LOVELOCK	*n* pl. -S a lock of hair hanging separately	**LOYAL**	*adj* -ALER, -ALEST faithful to one's allegiance
		LOYALISM	*n* pl. -S loyalty
LOVELORN	*adj* not loved	**LOYALIST**	*n* pl. -S one who is loyal
LOVELY	*adj* -LIER, -LIEST beautiful	**LOYALLY**	*adv* in a loyal manner
LOVELY	*n* pl. -LIES a beautiful woman	**LOYALTY**	*n* pl. -TIES the state of being loyal
LOVER	*n* pl. -S one that loves another **LOVERLY** *adj*		
		LOZENGE	*n* pl. -S a small, often medicated candy
LOVESICK	*adj* languishing with love		
LOVESOME	*adj* lovely	**LUAU**	*n* pl. -S a Hawaiian feast

LUBBER   *n* pl. -S a clumsy person **LUBBERLY** *adj*

LUBE   *n* pl. -S a lubricant

LUBRIC   *adj* slippery

LUBRICAL   *adj* lubric

LUCARNE   *n* pl. -S a type of window

LUCE   *n* pl. -S a freshwater fish

LUCENCE   *n* pl. -S lucency

LUCENCY   *n* pl. -CIES the quality of being lucent

LUCENT   *adj* giving off light **LUCENTLY** *adv*

LUCERN   *n* pl. -S lucerne

LUCERNE   *n* pl. -S alfalfa

LUCES   a pl. of lux

LUCID   *adj* easily understood **LUCIDLY** *adv*

LUCIDITY   *n* pl. -TIES the quality of being lucid

LUCIFER   *n* pl. -S a friction match

LUCK   *v* -ED, -ING, -S to succeed by chance or good fortune

LUCKIE   *n* pl. -S an old woman

LUCKLESS   *adj* unlucky

LUCKY   *adj* LUCKIER, LUCKIEST having good fortune **LUCKILY** *adv*

LUCRE   *n* pl. -S monetary gain

LUCULENT   *adj* lucid

LUDE   *n* pl. -S a methaqualone pill

LUDIC   *adj* aimlessly playful

LUES   *n* pl. LUES syphilis

LUETIC   *n* pl. -S one infected with syphilis

LUFF   *v* -ED, -ING, -S to steer a sailing vessel nearer into the wind

LUFFA   *n* pl. -S loofah

LUG   *v* LUGGED, LUGGING, LUGS to carry or pull with effort

LUGE   *v* LUGED, LUGEING, LUGES to race on a luge (a small sled)

LUGER   *n* pl. -S one that luges

LUGGAGE   *n* pl. -S articles containing a traveler's belongings

LUGGED   past tense of lug

LUGGER   *n* pl. -S a small sailing vessel

LUGGIE   *n* pl. -S a small wooden dish or pail

LUGGING   present participle of lug

LUGSAIL   *n* pl. -S a type of sail

LUGWORM   *n* pl. -S a burrowing marine worm

LUKEWARM   *adj* moderately warm

LULL   *v* -ED, -ING, -S to cause to sleep or rest

LULLABY   *v* -BIED, -BYING, -BIES to lull with a soothing song

LULU   *n* pl. -S something remarkable

LUM   *n* pl. -S a chimney

LUMBAGO   *n* pl. -GOS pain in the lower back

LUMBAR   *n* pl. -S an anatomical part situated near the loins

LUMBER   *v* -ED, -ING, -S to cut down and prepare timber for market

LUMBERER   *n* pl. -S one that lumbers

LUMEN   *n* pl. -MENS or -MINA the inner passage of a tubular organ **LUMENAL, LUMINAL** *adj*

LUMINARY   *n* pl. -NARIES a body that gives light

LUMINISM   *n* pl. -S a style of painting

LUMINIST   *n* pl. -S a painter who uses the effects of light

LUMINOUS   *adj* giving off light

LUMMOX   *n* pl. -ES a clumsy person

LUMP   *v* -ED, -ING, -S to make into lumps (shapeless masses)

LUMPEN   *n* pl. -S an uprooted individual

LUMPER   *n* pl. -S a laborer employed to load and unload ships

LUMPFISH   *n* pl. -ES a marine fish

LUMPISH   *adj* stupid

LUMPY   *adj* LUMPIER, LUMPIEST full of lumps **LUMPILY** *adv*

LUNA   *n* pl. -S an alchemical designation for silver

LUNACY   *n* pl. -CIES insanity

LUNAR   *n* pl. -S an observation of the moon taken for navigational purposes

LUNARIAN   *n* pl. -S a supposed inhabitant of the moon

LUNATE   *adj* crescent-shaped **LUNATELY** *adv*

LUNATED   *adj* lunate

LUNATIC   *n* pl. -S an insane person

LUNATION   *n* pl. -S the interval between two successive new moons

LUNCH   *v* -ED, -ING, -ES to eat a noonday meal

LUNCHEON   *n* pl. -S a noonday meal

LUNCHER	*n* pl. -S one that lunches
LUNE	*n* pl. -S a crescent-shaped figure
LUNET	*n* pl. -S lunette
LUNETTE	*n* pl. -S a crescent-shaped object
LUNG	*n* pl. -S a respiratory organ
LUNGAN	*n* pl. -S longan
LUNGE	*v* LUNGED, LUNGING, LUNGES to make a forceful forward movement
LUNGEE	*n* pl. -S lungi
LUNGER	*n* pl. -S one that lunges
LUNGFISH	*n* pl. -ES a type of fish
LUNGFUL	*n* pl. -S as much as the lungs can hold
LUNGI	*n* pl. -S a loincloth worn by men in India
LUNGING	present participle of lunge
LUNGWORM	*n* pl. -S a parasitic worm
LUNGWORT	*n* pl. -S a European herb
LUNGYI	*n* pl. -S lungi
LUNIER	comparative of luny
LUNIES	pl. of luny
LUNIEST	superlative of luny
LUNK	*n* pl. -S a lunkhead
LUNKER	*n* pl. -S a large game fish
LUNKHEAD	*n* pl. -S a stupid person
LUNT	*v* -ED, -ING, -S to emit smoke
LUNULA	*n* pl. -LAE a small crescent-shaped structure **LUNULAR, LUNULATE** *adj*
LUNULE	*n* pl. -S lunula
LUNY	*adj* -NIER, -NIEST loony
LUNY	*n* pl. -NIES a loony
LUPANAR	*n* pl. -S a brothel
LUPIN	*n* pl. -S lupine
LUPINE	*n* pl. -S a flowering plant
LUPOUS	*adj* pertaining to lupus
LUPULIN	*n* pl. -S a medicinal powder obtained from the hop plant
LUPUS	*n* pl. -ES a skin disease
LURCH	*v* -ED, -ING, -ES to sway abruptly
LURCHER	*n* pl. -S one that lurks or prowls
LURDAN	*n* pl. -S a lazy or stupid person
LURDANE	*n* pl. -S lurdan
LURE	*v* LURED, LURING, LURES to attract with something desirable
LURER	*n* pl. -S one that lures
LURID	*adj* causing shock or horror **LURIDLY** *adv*
LURING	present participle of lure
LURK	*v* -ED, -ING, -S to wait in concealment
LURKER	*n* pl. -S one that lurks
LUSCIOUS	*adj* having a very pleasing taste or smell
LUSH	*adj* LUSHER, LUSHEST abounding in vegetation **LUSHLY** *adv*
LUSH	*v* -ED, -ING, -ES to drink to excess
LUSHNESS	*n* pl. -ES the state of being lush
LUST	*v* -ED, -ING, -S to have an intense desire
LUSTER	*v* -ED, -ING, -S to make or become lustrous
LUSTFUL	*adj* marked by excessive sexual desire
LUSTIER	comparative of lusty
LUSTIEST	superlative of lusty
LUSTILY	*adv* in a lusty manner
LUSTRA	a pl. of lustrum
LUSTRAL	*adj* pertaining to a lustrum
LUSTRATE	*v* -TRATED, -TRATING, -TRATES to purify ceremonially
LUSTRE	*v* -TRED, -TRING, -TRES to luster
LUSTRING	*n* pl. -S a glossy silk fabric
LUSTROUS	*adj* reflecting light evenly and efficiently
LUSTRUM	*n* pl. -TRUMS or -TRA a ceremonial purification of the population in ancient Rome
LUSTY	*adj* LUSTIER, LUSTIEST full of vigor
LUSUS	*n* pl. -ES an abnormality
LUTANIST	*n* pl. -S one who plays the lute
LUTE	*v* LUTED, LUTING, LUTES to play a lute (a stringed musical instrument)
LUTEA	pl. of luteum
LUTEAL	*adj* pertaining to the luteum
LUTECIUM	*n* pl. -S lutetium
LUTED	past tense of lute
LUTEFISK	*n* pl. -S dried codfish
LUTEIN	*n* pl. -S a yellow pigment
LUTENIST	*n* pl. -S lutanist

LUTEOLIN   *n* pl. -S a yellow pigment

LUTEOUS   *adj* light to moderate greenish yellow in color

LUTETIUM   *n* pl. -S a metallic element

LUTEUM   *n* pl. -TEA a hormone-secreting body

LUTHERN   *n* pl. -S a type of window

LUTHIER   *n* pl. -S one who makes stringed instruments

LUTING   *n* pl. -S a substance used as a sealant

LUTIST   *n* pl. -S a lutanist

LUTZ   *n* pl. -ES a jump in figure skating

LUV   *n* pl. -S a sweetheart

LUX   *n* pl. LUXES or LUCES a unit of illumination

LUXATE   *v* -ATED, -ATING, -ATES to put out of joint

LUXATION   *n* pl. -S the act of luxating

LUXE   *n* pl. -S luxury

LUXURY   *n* pl. -RIES free indulgence in that which affords pleasure or comfort

LWEI   *n* pl. -S a monetary unit of Angola

LYARD   *adj* streaked with gray

LYART   *adj* lyard

LYASE   *n* pl. -S an enzyme

LYCEE   *n* pl. -S a French secondary school

LYCEUM   *n* pl. -CEUMS or -CEA a hall for public lectures or discussions

LYCHEE   *n* pl. -S litchi

LYCHNIS   *n* pl. -NISES a flowering plant

LYCOPENE   *n* pl. -S a red pigment

LYCOPOD   *n* pl. -S an evergreen plant

LYDDITE   *n* pl. -S an explosive

LYE   *n* pl. -S a solution used in making soap

LYING   *n* pl. -S the act of telling lies

LYINGLY   *adv* falsely

LYMPH   *n* pl. -S a body fluid containing white blood cells **LYMPHOID** *adj*

LYMPHOMA   *n* pl. -MAS or -MATA a type of tumor

LYNCEAN   *adj* of or resembling a lynx

LYNCH   *v* -ED, -ING, -ES to put to death without legal sanction

LYNCHER   *n* pl. -S one that lynches

LYNCHING   *n* pl. -S the act of one who lynches

LYNCHPIN   *n* pl. -S linchpin

LYNX   *n* pl. -ES a short-tailed wildcat

LYOPHILE   *adj* pertaining to a type of colloid

LYRATE   *adj* having the shape of a lyre **LYRATELY** *adv*

LYRATED   *adj* lyrate

LYRE   *n* pl. -S an ancient harp-like instrument

LYREBIRD   *n* pl. -S an Australian bird

LYRIC   *n* pl. -S a lyrical poem

LYRICAL   *adj* having the form of a song

LYRICISE   *v* -CISED, -CISING, -CISES to lyricize

LYRICISM   *n* pl. -S the quality of being lyrics

LYRICIST   *n* pl. -S one who writes the words for songs

LYRICIZE   *v* -CIZED, -CIZING, -CIZES to write lyrics

LYRIFORM   *adj* lyrate

LYRISM   *n* pl. -S lyricism

LYRIST   *n* pl. -S one who plays the lyre

LYSATE   *n* pl. -S a product of lysis

LYSE   *v* LYSED, LYSING, LYSES to cause to undergo lysis

LYSIN   *n* pl. -S a substance capable of disintegrating blood cells or bacteria

LYSINE   *n* pl. -S an amino acid

LYSING   present participle of lyse

LYSIS   *n* pl. LYSES the disintegration of cells by lysins

LYSOGEN   *n* pl. -S a type of antigen

LYSOGENY   *n* pl. -NIES the state of being like a lysogen

LYSOSOME   *n* pl. -S a saclike part of a cell

LYSOZYME   *n* pl. -S an enzyme

LYSSA   *n* pl. -S rabies

LYTIC   *adj* pertaining to lysis

LYTTA   *n* pl. -TAE or -TAS a fibrous band in the tongue of certain carnivorous mammals

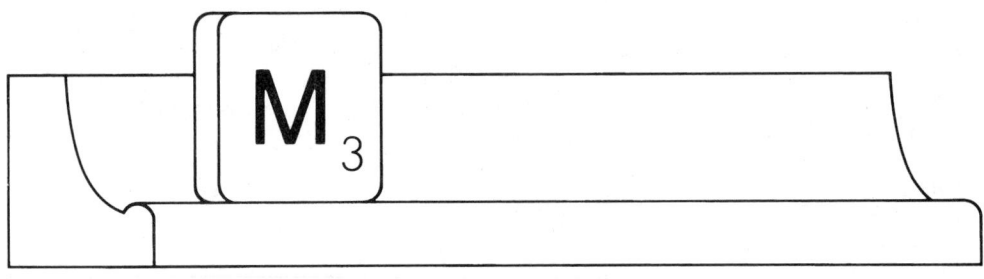

MA	*n* pl. -S mother	**MACK**	*n* pl. -S mac
MAAR	*n* pl. -S a volcanic crater	**MACKEREL**	*n* pl. -S a marine food fish
MABE	*n* pl. -S a cultured pearl	**MACKINAW**	*n* pl. -S a woolen fabric
MAC	*n* pl. -S a raincoat	**MACKLE**	*v* -LED, -LING, -LES to blur in printing
MACABER	*adj* macabre	**MACLE**	*n* pl. -S a spot or discoloration in a mineral **MACLED** *adj*
MACABRE	*adj* gruesome		
MACACO	*n* pl. -COS a lemur	**MACON**	*n* pl. -S a red or white French wine
MACADAM	*n* pl. -S a type of pavement		
MACAQUE	*n* pl. -S a short-tailed monkey	**MACRAME**	*n* pl. -S a trimming of knotted thread or cord
MACARONI	*n* pl. -NIS or -NIES a tubular pasta	**MACRO**	*n* pl. -ROS a type of computer instruction
MACAROON	*n* pl. -S a type of cookie	**MACRON**	*n* pl. -S a symbol placed over a vowel to show that it has a long sound
MACAW	*n* pl. -S a large parrot		
MACCABAW	*n* pl. -S maccaboy		
MACCABOY	*n* pl. -BOYS a type of snuff	**MACRURAL**	*adj* pertaining to macruran
MACCHIA	*n* pl. -CHIE a dense growth of small trees and shrubs	**MACRURAN**	*n* pl. -S any of a suborder of crustaceans
MACCOBOY	*n* pl. -BOYS maccaboy	**MACULA**	*n* pl. -LAE or -LAS a spot **MACULAR** *adj*
MACE	*v* MACED, MACING, MACES to attack with a clublike weapon	**MACULATE**	*v* -LATED, -LATING, -LATES to mark with spots
MACER	*n* pl. -S an official who carries a ceremonial staff	**MACULE**	*v* -ULED, -ULING, -ULES to mackle
MACERATE	*v* -ATED, -ATING, -ATES to soften by soaking in liquid	**MACUMBA**	*n* pl. -S a religion practiced in Brazil
MACH	*n* pl. -S a number indicating the ratio of the speed of a body to the speed of sound	**MAD**	*adj* MADDER, MADDEST insane
		MAD	*v* MADDED, MADDING, MADS to madden
MACHE	*n* pl. -S a European herb		
MACHETE	*n* pl. -S a large, heavy knife	**MADAM**	*n* pl. -S a woman who manages a brothel
MACHINE	*v* -CHINED, -CHINING, -CHINES to process by machine (a mechanical device)	**MADAME**	*n* pl. -S madam
		MADAME	*n* pl. MESDAMES the French title of respect for a married woman
MACHISMO	*n* pl. -MOS strong masculinity	**MADCAP**	*n* pl. -S an impulsive person
MACHO	*n* pl. -CHOS a person who exhibits machismo	**MADDED**	past tense of mad
MACHREE	*n* pl. -S dear	**MADDEN**	*v* -ED, -ING, -S to make or become mad
MACHZOR	*n* pl. -ZORIM or -ZORS mahzor		
MACING	present participle of mace	**MADDER**	*n* pl. -S a perennial herb

MADDEST	superlative of mad
MADDING	present participle of mad
MADDISH	*adj* somewhat mad
MADE	past tense of make
MADEIRA	*n* pl. -S a white wine
MADHOUSE	*n* pl. -S an insane asylum
MADLY	*adv* in a mad manner
MADMAN	*n* pl. -MEN a man who is insane
MADNESS	*n* pl. -ES the state of being mad
MADONNA	*n* pl. -S a former Italian title of respect for a woman
MADRAS	*n* pl. -ES a cotton fabric
MADRE	*n* pl. -S mother
MADRIGAL	*n* pl. -S a short lyric poem
MADRONA	*n* pl. -S an evergreen tree
MADRONE	*n* pl. -S madrona
MADRONO	*n* pl. -NOS madrona
MADURO	*n* pl. -ROS a dark-colored, relatively strong cigar
MADWOMAN	*n* pl. -WOMEN a woman who is insane
MADWORT	*n* pl. -S a flowering plant
MADZOON	*n* pl. -S matzoon
MAE	*n* pl. -S more
MAENAD	*n* pl. -S or -ES a female participant in ancient Greek orgies **MAENADIC** *adj*
MAESTOSO	*n* pl. -SOS a stately musical passage
MAESTRO	*n* pl. -STROS or -STRI a master of an art
MAFFIA	*n* pl. -S mafia
MAFFICK	*v* -ED, -ING, -S to celebrate boisterously
MAFIA	*n* pl. -S a secret criminal organization
MAFIC	*adj* pertaining to minerals rich in magnesium and iron
MAFIOSO	*n* pl. -SI a member of the mafia
MAFTIR	*n* pl. -S the concluding section of a parashah
MAG	*n* pl. -S a magazine
MAGAZINE	*n* pl. -S a type of periodical publication
MAGDALEN	*n* pl. -S a reformed prostitute
MAGE	*n* pl. -S a magician
MAGENTA	*n* pl. -S a purplish red dye
MAGGOT	*n* pl. -S the legless larva of certain insects **MAGGOTY** *adj*
MAGI	pl. of magus
MAGIAN	*n* pl. -S a magus
MAGIC	*v* -ICKED, -ICKING, -ICS to affect by magic (sorcery)
MAGICAL	*adj* resembling magic
MAGICIAN	*n* pl. -S one skilled in magic
MAGICKED	past tense of magic
MAGICKING	present participle of magic
MAGILP	*n* pl. -S megilp
MAGISTER	*n* pl. -S a master or teacher
MAGLEV	*adj* pertaining to a railroad system using magnets to move a train above the tracks
MAGMA	*n* pl. -MAS or -MATA the molten matter from which igneous rock is formed **MAGMATIC** *adj*
MAGNATE	*n* pl. -S a powerful or influential person
MAGNESIA	*n* pl. -S a medicinal compound **MAGNESIC** *adj*
MAGNET	*n* pl. -S a body that possesses the property of attracting iron
MAGNETIC	*n* pl. -S a magnet
MAGNETO	*n* pl. -TOS a type of electric generator
MAGNETON	*n* pl. -S a unit of magnetic moment
MAGNIFIC	*adj* magnificent
MAGNIFY	*v* -FIED, -FYING, -FIES to increase the perceived size of
MAGNOLIA	*n* pl. -S a flowering shrub or tree
MAGNUM	*n* pl. -S a large wine bottle
MAGOT	*n* pl. -S a tailless ape
MAGPIE	*n* pl. -S a corvine bird
MAGUEY	*n* pl. -GUEYS a tropical plant
MAGUS	*n* pl. -GI a magician
MAHARAJA	*n* pl. -S a king or prince in India
MAHARANI	*n* pl. -S the wife of a maharaja
MAHATMA	*n* pl. -S a Hindu sage
MAHIMAHI	*n* pl. MAHIMAHI a food fish in Hawaii
MAHJONG	*n* pl. -S a game of Chinese origin
MAHJONGG	*n* pl. -S mahjong
MAHOE	*n* pl. -S a tropical tree
MAHOGANY	*n* pl. -NIES a tropical tree
MAHONIA	*n* pl. -S a flowering shrub

MAHOUT *n* pl. -S the keeper and driver of an elephant

MAHUANG *n* pl. -S an Asian plant

MAHZOR *n* pl. -ZORIM or -ZORS a Jewish prayer book

MAID *n* pl. -S a maiden **MAIDISH** *adj*

MAIDEN *n* pl. -S a young unmarried woman **MAIDENLY** *adj*

MAIDHOOD *n* pl. -S the state of being a maiden

MAIEUTIC *adj* pertaining to a method of eliciting knowledge

MAIGRE *adj* containing neither flesh nor its juices

MAIHEM *n* pl. -S mayhem

MAIL *v* -ED, -ING, -S to send by a governmental postal system. **MAILABLE** *adj*

MAILBAG *n* pl. -S a bag for carrying mail (postal material)

MAILBOX *n* pl. -ES a box for depositing mail

MAILE *n* pl. -S a Pacific island vine

MAILER *n* pl. -S one that mails

MAILING *n* pl. -S a rented farm

MAILL *n* pl. -S a payment

MAILLESS *adj* having no armor

MAILLOT *n* pl. -S a woman's one-piece bathing suit

MAILMAN *n* pl. -MEN a man who carries and delivers mail

MAIM *v* -ED, -ING, -S to injure so as to cause lasting damage

MAIMER *n* pl. -S one that maims

MAIN *n* pl. -S the principal part

MAINLAND *n* pl. -S a principal land mass

MAINLINE *v* -LINED, -LINING, -LINES to inject a narcotic into a major vein

MAINLY *adv* for the most part

MAINMAST *n* pl. -S the principal mast of a vessel

MAINSAIL *n* pl. -S the principal sail of a vessel

MAINSTAY *n* pl. -STAYS a principal support

MAINTAIN *v* -ED, -ING, -S to keep in proper condition

MAINTOP *n* pl. -S a platform at the head of a mainmast

MAIOLICA *n* pl. -S majolica

MAIR *n* pl. -S more

MAIST *n* pl. -S most

MAIZE *n* pl. -S an American cereal grass

MAJAGUA *n* pl. -S a tropical tree

MAJESTIC *adj* having majesty

MAJESTY *n* pl. -TIES regal dignity

MAJOLICA *n* pl. -S a type of pottery

MAJOR *v* -ED, -ING, -S to pursue a specific principal course of study

MAJORITY *n* pl. -TIES the greater number or part

MAJORLY *adv* mainly

MAKAR *n* pl. -S a poet

MAKE *v* MADE, MAKING, MAKES to cause to exist **MAKABLE, MAKEABLE** *adj*

MAKEBATE *n* pl. -S one that encourages quarrels

MAKEFAST *n* pl. -S an object to which a boat is tied

MAKEOVER *n* pl. -S a changing of appearance

MAKER *n* pl. -S one that makes

MAKEUP *n* pl. -S the way in which the parts or ingredients of something are put together

MAKIMONO *n* pl. -NOS a Japanese ornamental scroll

MAKING *n* pl. -S material from which something can be developed

MAKO *n* pl. -KOS a large shark

MAKUTA pl. of likuta

MALACCA *n* pl. -S the cane of an Asian rattan palm

MALADY *n* pl. -DIES an illness

MALAISE *n* pl. -S a feeling of vague discomfort

MALAMUTE *n* pl. -S an Alaskan sled dog

MALANGA *n* pl. -S a yautia

MALAPERT *n* pl. -S an impudent person

MALAPROP *n* pl. -S a humorous misuse of a word

MALAR *n* pl. -S the cheekbone

MALARIA *n* pl. -S an infectious disease **MALARIAL, MALARIAN** *adj*

MALARKEY *n* pl. -KEYS nonsense

MALARKY *n* pl. -KIES malarkey

MALAROMA *n* pl. -S a malodor

MALATE *n* pl. -S a chemical salt

MALE	*n* pl. -S an individual that begets young by fertilizing the female
MALEATE	*n* pl. -S a chemical salt
MALEDICT	*v* -ED, -ING, -S to curse
MALEFIC	*adj* producing or causing evil
MALEMIUT	*n* pl. -S malamute
MALEMUTE	*n* pl. -S malamute
MALENESS	*n* pl. -ES the quality of being a male
MALFED	*adj* badly fed
MALGRE	*prep* in spite of
MALIC	*adj* pertaining to apples
MALICE	*n* pl. -S a desire to injure another
MALIGN	*v* -ED, -ING, -S to speak evil of
MALIGNER	*n* pl. -S one that maligns
MALIGNLY	*adv* in an evil manner
MALIHINI	*n* pl. -S a newcomer to Hawaii
MALINE	*n* pl. -S a delicate net used for veils
MALINGER	*v* -ED, -ING, -S to feign illness in order to avoid duty or work
MALISON	*n* pl. -S a curse
MALKIN	*n* pl. -S an untidy woman
MALL	*v* -ED, -ING, -S to maul
MALLARD	*n* pl. -S a wild duck
MALLEE	*n* pl. -S an evergreen tree
MALLEI	pl. of malleus
MALLEOLI	*n/pl* bony protuberances of the ankle
MALLET	*n* pl. -S a type of hammer
MALLEUS	*n* pl. -LEI a bone of the middle ear
MALLOW	*n* pl. -S a flowering plant
MALM	*n* pl. -S a soft, friable limestone
MALMSEY	*n* pl. -SEYS a white wine
MALMY	*adj* MALMIER, MALMIEST resembling malm
MALODOR	*n* pl. -S an offensive odor
MALOTI	pl. of loti
MALPOSED	*adj* being in the wrong position
MALT	*v* -ED, -ING, -S to treat or combine with malt (germinated grain)
MALTASE	*n* pl. -S an enzyme
MALTED	*n* pl. -S a sweet beverage
MALTHA	*n* pl. -S a natural tar
MALTIER	comparative of malty

MALTIEST	superlative of malty
MALTOL	*n* pl. -S a chemical compound
MALTOSE	*n* pl. -S a type of sugar
MALTREAT	*v* -ED, -ING, -S to treat badly
MALTSTER	*n* pl. -S one that makes malt
MALTY	*adj* MALTIER, MALTIEST resembling malt
MALVASIA	*n* pl. -S malmsey
MAMA	*n* pl. -S mother
MAMALIGA	*n* pl. -S a cornmeal porridge
MAMBA	*n* pl. -S a venomous snake
MAMBO	*v* -ED, -ING, -ES or -S to perform a ballroom dance
MAMELUKE	*n* pl. -S a slave in Muslim countries
MAMEY	*n* pl. -MEYS or -MEYES a tropical tree
MAMIE	*n* pl. -S mamey
MAMLUK	*n* pl. -S mameluke
MAMMA	*n* pl. -S mama
MAMMA	*n* pl. -MAE a milk-secreting organ
MAMMAL	*n* pl. -S any of a class of warm-blooded vertebrates
MAMMARY	*adj* pertaining to the mammae
MAMMATE	*adj* having mammae
MAMMATUS	*n* pl. -TI a type of cloud
MAMMEE	*n* pl. -S mamey
MAMMER	*v* -ED, -ING, -S to hesitate
MAMMET	*n* pl. -S maumet
MAMMEY	*n* pl. -MEYS mamey
MAMMIE	*n* pl. -S mammy
MAMMIES	pl. of mammy
MAMMILLA	*n* pl. -LAE a nipple
MAMMITIS	*n* pl. -MITIDES mastitis
MAMMOCK	*v* -ED, -ING, -S to shred
MAMMON	*n* pl. -S material wealth
MAMMOTH	*n* pl. -S an extinct elephant
MAMMY	*n* pl. -MIES mother
MAN	*n* pl. MEN an adult human male
MAN	*v* MANNED, MANNING, MANS to supply with men
MANA	*n* pl. -S a supernatural force in certain Pacific island religions
MANACLE	*v* -CLED, -CLING, -CLES to handcuff
MANAGE	*v* -AGED, -AGING, -AGES to control or direct

MANAGER *n* pl. -S one that manages

MANAKIN *n* pl. -S a tropical bird

MANANA *n* pl. -S tomorrow

MANATEE *n* pl. -S an aquatic mammal **MANATOID** *adj*

MANCHE *n* pl. -S a heraldic design

MANCHET *n* pl. -S a small loaf of fine white bread

MANCIPLE *n* pl. -S an officer authorized to purchase provisions

MANDALA *n* pl. -S a Hindu or Buddhist graphic symbol of the universe **MANDALIC** *adj*

MANDAMUS *v* -ED, -ING, -ES to command by means of writ issued by a superior court

MANDARIN *n* pl. -S a citrus fruit

MANDATE *v* -DATED, -DATING, -DATES to authorize or decree

MANDATOR *n* pl. -S one that mandates

MANDIBLE *n* pl. -S the bone of the lower jaw

MANDIOCA *n* pl. -S manioc

MANDOLA *n* pl. -S an ancient lute

MANDOLIN *n* pl. -S a stringed musical instrument

MANDRAKE *n* pl. -S a European herb

MANDREL *n* pl. -S a shaft on which a tool is mounted

MANDRIL *n* pl. -S mandrel

MANDRILL *n* pl. -S a large baboon

MANE *n* pl. -S the long hair growing on and about the neck of some animals **MANED, MANELESS** *adj*

MANEGE *n* pl. -S the art of training and riding horses

MANEUVER *v* -ED, -ING, -S to change the position of for a specific purpose

MANFUL *adj* courageous **MANFULLY** *adv*

MANGABEY *n* pl. -BEYS a long-tailed monkey

MANGABY *n* pl. -BIES mangabey

MANGANIC *adj* containing manganese (a metallic element)

MANGE *n* pl. -S a skin disease of domestic animals

MANGEL *n* pl. -S a variety of beet

MANGER *n* pl. -S a trough or box from which horses or cattle eat

MANGEY *adj* MANGIER, MANGIEST mangy

MANGIER comparative of mangy

MANGIEST superlative of mangy

MANGILY *adv* in a mangy manner

MANGLE *v* -GLED, -GLING, -GLES to cut, slash, or crush so as to disfigure

MANGLER *n* pl. -S one that mangles

MANGO *n* pl. -GOES or -GOS an edible tropical fruit

MANGOLD *n* pl. -S mangel

MANGONEL *n* pl. -S a medieval military device for hurling stones

MANGROVE *n* pl. -S a tropical tree or shrub

MANGY *adj* MANGIER, MANGIEST affected with mange

MANHOLE *n* pl. -S a hole providing entrance to an underground or enclosed structure

MANHOOD *n* pl. -S the state of being a man

MANHUNT *n* pl. -S an intensive search for a person

MANIA *n* pl. -S an excessive interest or enthusiasm

MANIAC *n* pl. -S an insane person **MANIACAL** *adj*

MANIC *n* pl. -S one that is affected with mania

MANICURE *v* -CURED, -CURING, -CURES to trim and polish the fingernails of

MANIFEST *v* -ED, -ING, -S to show clearly

MANIFOLD *v* -ED, -ING, -S to make several copies of

MANIHOT *n* pl. -S a tropical plant

MANIKIN *n* pl. -S an anatomical model of the human body

MANILA *n* pl. -S a strong paper

MANILLA *n* pl. -S manila

MANILLE *n* pl. -S the second highest trump in certain card games

MANIOC *n* pl. -S a tropical plant

MANIOCA *n* pl. -S manioc

MANIPLE *n* pl. -S a silk band worn on the left arm as a vestment

MANITO *n* pl. -TOS manitou

MANITOU *n* pl. -S an Algonquian Indian deity

MANITU *n* pl. -S manitou

MANKIND *n* pl. MANKIND the human race

MANLESS *adj* destitute of men

MANLIKE *adj* resembling a man

MANLY	*adj* -LIER, -LIEST having the qualities of a man **MANLILY** *adv*	**MANTRA**	*n* pl. -S a mystical formula of prayer or incantation in Hinduism **MANTRIC** *adj*
MANMADE	*adj* made by man		
MANNA	*n* pl. -S divinely supplied food	**MANTRAP**	*n* pl. -S a trap for catching men
MANNAN	*n* pl. -S a type of sugar	**MANTUA**	*n* pl. -S a woman's gown
MANNED	past tense of man	**MANUAL**	*n* pl. -S a small reference book
MANNER	*n* pl. -S a way of acting **MANNERED** *adj*	**MANUALLY**	*adv* by means of the hands
		MANUARY	*adj* involving the hands
MANNERLY	*adj* polite	**MANUBRIA**	*n/pl* handle-shaped anatomical parts
MANNIKIN	*n* pl. -S manikin		
MANNING	present participle of man	**MANUMIT**	*v* -MITTED, -MITTING, -MITS to free from slavery
MANNISH	*adj* resembling or characteristic of a man	**MANURE**	*v* -NURED, -NURING, -NURES to fertilize with manure (animal excrement)
MANNITE	*n* pl. -S mannitol **MANNITIC** *adj*		
MANNITOL	*n* pl. -S an alcohol	**MANURER**	*n* pl. -S one that manures
MANNOSE	*n* pl. -S a type of sugar	**MANURIAL**	*adj* of or pertaining to manure
MANO	*n* pl. -NOS a stone used for grinding foods	**MANURING**	present participle of manure
		MANUS	*n* pl. MANUS the end of the forelimb in vertebrates
MANOR	*n* pl. -S a landed estate or territorial unit **MANORIAL** *adj*		
		MANWARD	*adv* toward man
MANPACK	*adj* designed to be carried by one person	**MANWARDS**	*adv* manward
		MANWISE	*adv* in a manner characteristic of man
MANPOWER	*n* pl. -S the number of men available for service		
		MANY	*adj* MORE, MOST consisting of or amounting to a large number
MANQUE	*adj* frustrated in the fulfillment of one's aspirations		
		MANYFOLD	*adv* by many times
MANROPE	*n* pl. -S a rope used as a handrail	**MAP**	*v* MAPPED, MAPPING, MAPS to delineate on a map (a representation of a region)
MANSARD	*n* pl. -S a type of roof		
MANSE	*n* pl. -S a clergyman's house		
MANSION	*n* pl. -S a large, impressive house	**MAPLE**	*n* pl. -S a hardwood tree
		MAPLIKE	*adj* resembling a map
MANTA	*n* pl. -S a cotton fabric	**MAPMAKER**	*n* pl. -S one that makes maps
MANTEAU	*n* pl. -TEAUS or -TEAUX a loose cloak	**MAPPABLE**	*adj* capable of being mapped
		MAPPED	past tense of map
MANTEL	*n* pl. -S a shelf above a fireplace	**MAPPER**	*n* pl. -S one that maps
MANTELET	*n* pl. -S a mobile screen used to protect soldiers	**MAPPING**	*n* pl. -S a mathematical correspondence
MANTES	a pl. of mantis	**MAQUETTE**	*n* pl. -S a small preliminary model
MANTIC	*adj* having powers of prophecy		
MANTID	*n* pl. -S mantis	**MAQUI**	*n* pl. -S maquis
MANTILLA	*n* pl. -S a woman's scarf	**MAQUIS**	*n* pl. MAQUIS a thick underbrush
MANTIS	*n* pl. -TISES or -TES a predatory insect	**MAR**	*v* MARRED, MARRING, MARS to detract from the perfection or wholeness of
MANTISSA	*n* pl. -S the decimal part of a logarithm		
MANTLE	*v* -TLED, -TLING, -TLES to cloak	**MARABOU**	*n* pl. -S an African stork
MANTLET	*n* pl. -S mantelet	**MARABOUT**	*n* pl. -S a marabou
MANTLING	*n* pl. -S an ornamental cloth	**MARACA**	*n* pl. -S a percussion instrument
		MARANTA	*n* pl. -S a tropical plant

MARASCA *n* pl. -S a wild cherry

MARASMUS *n* pl. -ES a wasting away of the body **MARASMIC** *adj*

MARATHON *n* pl. -S a long-distance race

MARAUD *v* -ED, -ING, -S to rove in search of booty

MARAUDER *n* pl. -S one that marauds

MARAVEDI *n* pl. -S a former coin of Spain

MARBLE *v* -BLED, -BLING, -BLES to give a mottled appearance to

MARBLER *n* pl. -S one that marbles

MARBLING *n* pl. -S an intermixture of fat and lean in meat

MARBLY *adj* -BLIER, -BLIEST mottled

MARC *n* pl. -S the residue remaining after a fruit has been pressed

MARCATO *adv* with strong accentuation — used as a musical direction

MARCEL *v* -CELLED, -CELLING, -CELS to make a deep, soft wave in the hair

MARCH *v* -ED, -ING, -ES to walk in a formal military manner

MARCHEN *n* pl. MARCHEN a folktale

MARCHER *n* pl. -S one that marches

MARCHESA *n* pl. -CHESE the wife or widow of a marchese

MARCHESE *n* pl. -CHESI an Italian nobleman

MARE *n* pl. -S a mature female horse

MARE *n* pl. -RIA a dark area on the surface of the moon or Mars

MAREMMA *n* pl. -REMME a marshy coastal region

MARENGO *adj* served with a sauce of mushrooms, tomatoes, oil, and wine

MARGARIC *adj* pearly

MARGARIN *n* pl. -S a butter substitute

MARGAY *n* pl. -GAYS a small American wildcat

MARGE *n* pl. -S a margin

MARGENT *v* -ED, -ING, -S to margin

MARGIN *v* -ED, -ING, -S to provide with a margin (a border)

MARGINAL *adj* of or pertaining to a margin

MARGRAVE *n* pl. -S the military governor of a medieval German border province

MARIA pl. of mare

MARIACHI *n* pl. -S a Mexican musical band

MARIGOLD *n* pl. -S a flowering plant

MARIMBA *n* pl. -S a percussion instrument

MARINA *n* pl. -S a docking area for small boats

MARINADE *v* -NADED, -NADING, -NADES to marinate

MARINARA *n* pl. -S a seasoned tomato sauce

MARINATE *v* -NATED, -NATING, -NATES to soak in a seasoned liquid before cooking

MARINE *n* pl. -S a soldier trained for service at sea and on land

MARINER *n* pl. -S a sailor

MARIPOSA *n* pl. -S a flowering plant

MARISH *n* pl. -ES a marsh

MARITAL *adj* pertaining to marriage

MARITIME *adj* pertaining to navigation or commerce on the sea

MARJORAM *n* pl. -S fragrant herb

MARK *v* -ED, -ING, -S to make a visible impression on

MARKDOWN *n* pl. -S a reduction in price

MARKEDLY *adv* in an evident manner

MARKER *n* pl. -S one that marks

MARKET *v* -ED, -ING, -S to offer for sale

MARKETER *n* pl. -S one that markets

MARKHOOR *n* pl. -S markhor

MARKHOR *n* pl. -S a wild goat

MARKING *n* pl. -S a pattern of marks

MARKKA *n* pl. -KAA or -KAS a monetary unit of Finland

MARKSMAN *n* pl. -MEN a person skillful at hitting a target

MARKUP *n* pl. -S an increase in price

MARL *v* -ED, -ING, -S to fertilize with marl (an earthy deposit containing lime, clay, and sand)

MARLIER comparative of marly

MARLIEST superlative of marly

MARLIN *n* pl. -S a marine game fish

MARLINE *n* pl. -S a rope used on a ship

MARLING *n* pl. -S marline

MARLITE *n* pl. -S a type of marl **MARLITIC** *adj*

MARLY *adj* MARLIER, MARLIEST abounding with marl

MARMITE *n* pl. -S a large soup kettle

MARMOSET *n* pl. -S a small monkey

MARMOT *n* pl. -S a burrowing rodent

MAROCAIN *n* pl. -S a light crinkled fabric

MAROON *v* -ED, -ING, -S to abandon in an isolated place

MARPLOT *n* pl. -S one that ruins a plan by meddling

MARQUE *n* pl. -S reprisal

MARQUEE *n* pl. -S a rooflike structure projecting over an entrance

MARQUESS *n* pl. -ES marquis

MARQUIS *n* pl. -ES a European nobleman

MARQUISE *n* pl. -S the wife or widow of a marquis

MARRAM *n* pl. -S a beach grass

MARRANO *n* pl. -NOS a Jew in Spain who professed Christianity to avoid persecution

MARRED past tense of mar

MARRER *n* pl. -S one that mars

MARRIAGE *n* pl. -S the legal union of a man and woman

MARRIED *n* pl. -S one who has entered into marriage

MARRIER *n* pl. -S one that marries

MARRIES present 3d person sing. of marry

MARRING present participle of mar

MARRON *n* pl. -S a variety of chestnut

MARROW *v* -ED, -ING, -S to marry

MARROWY *adj* pithy

MARRY *v* -RIED, -RYING, -RIES to enter into marriage

MARSALA *n* pl. -S a Sicilian wine

MARSE *n* pl. -S master

MARSH *n* pl. -ES a tract of low, wet land

MARSHAL *v* -ED, -ING, -S to put in proper order

MARSHALL *v* -ED, -ING, -S to marshal

MARSHY *adj* MARSHIER, MARSHIEST resembling a marsh

MARSUPIA *n/pl* abdominal pouches of certain mammals

MART *v* -ED, -ING, -S to market

MARTAGON *n* pl. -S a flowering plant

MARTELLO *n* pl. -LOS a circular fort

MARTEN *n* pl. -S a carnivorous mammal

MARTIAL *adj* pertaining to war

MARTIAN *n* pl. -S a supposed inhabitant of the planet Mars

MARTIN *n* pl. -S a small bird

MARTINET *n* pl. -S one who demands rigid adherence to rules

MARTINI *n* pl. -S an alcoholic beverage

MARTLET *n* pl. -S a martin

MARTYR *v* -ED, -ING, -S to put to death for adhering to a belief

MARTYRLY *adj* resembling a martyr

MARTYRY *n* pl. -TYRIES a shrine erected in honor of a martyred person

MARVEL *v* -VELED, -VELING, -VELS or -VELLED, -VELLING, -VELS to be filled with wonder or astonishment

MARVY *adj* marvelous

MARYJANE *n* pl. -S marijuana

MARZIPAN *n* pl. -S an almond candy

MASCARA *v* -ED, -ING, -S to color the eyelashes or eyebrows with a cosmetic

MASCON *n* pl. -S a concentration of dense mass beneath the moon's surface

MASCOT *n* pl. -S a person, animal, or object believed to bring good luck

MASER *n* pl. -S a device for amplifying electrical impulses

MASH *v* -ED, -ING, -ES to reduce to a pulpy mass

MASHER *n* pl. -S one that mashes

MASHIE *n* pl. -S a golf club

MASHY *n* pl. MASHIES mashie

MASJID *n* pl. -S a mosque

MASK *v* -ED, -ING, -S to cover with a mask (a covering used to disguise the face) **MASKABLE** *adj*

MASKEG *n* pl. -S muskeg

MASKER *n* pl. -S one that wears a mask

MASKING *n* pl. -S a piece of scenery used to conceal parts of a stage from the audience

MASKLIKE *adj* suggestive of a mask

MASON *v* -ED, -ING, -S to build with stone or brick

MASONIC *adj* pertaining to masonry

MASONRY *n* pl. -RIES a structure built of stone or brick

MASQUE *n* pl. -S a dramatic entertainment formerly popular in England

MASQUER *n* pl. -S masker

MASS — *v* -ED, -ING, -ES to assemble in a mass (a body of coherent matter)

MASSA — *n* pl. -S master

MASSACRE — *v* -CRED, -CRING, -CRES to kill indiscriminately

MASSAGE — *v* -SAGED, -SAGING, -SAGES to manipulate parts of the body for remedial or hygienic purposes

MASSAGER — *n* pl. -S one that massages

MASSCULT — *n* pl. -S culture as popularized by the mass media

MASSE — *n* pl. -S a type of shot in billiards

MASSEDLY — *adv* in a massed manner

MASSETER — *n* pl. -S a muscle that raises the lower jaw

MASSEUR — *n* pl. -S a man who massages

MASSEUSE — *n* pl. -S a woman who massages

MASSICOT — *n* pl. -S a yellow pigment

MASSIER — comparative of massy

MASSIEST — superlative of massy

MASSIF — *n* pl. -S a principal mountain mass

MASSIVE — *adj* of considerable size

MASSLESS — *adj* having no mass

MASSY — *adj* MASSIER, MASSIEST massive

MAST — *v* -ED, -ING, -S to provide with a mast (a long pole on a ship that supports the sails and rigging)

MASTABA — *n* pl. -S an ancient Egyptian tomb

MASTABAH — *n* pl. -S mastaba

MASTER — *v* -ED, -ING, -S to become skilled in

MASTERLY — *adj* very skillful

MASTERY — *n* pl. -TERIES superior knowledge or skill

MASTHEAD — *v* -ED, -ING, -S to raise to the top of a mast

MASTIC — *n* pl. -S an aromatic resin

MASTICHE — *n* pl. -S mastic

MASTIFF — *n* pl. -S a large, short-haired dog

MASTITIS — *n* pl. -TITIDES inflammation of the breast **MASTITIC** *adj*

MASTIX — *n* pl. -ES mastic

MASTLESS — *adj* having no mast

MASTLIKE — *adj* resembling a mast

MASTODON — *n* pl. -S an extinct elephant-like mammal

MASTOID — *n* pl. -S the rear portion of the temporal bone

MASURIUM — *n* pl. -S a metallic element

MAT — *v* MATTED, MATTING, MATS to pack down into a dense mass

MATADOR — *n* pl. -S the bullfighter who kills the bull in a bullfight

MATAMBALA — a pl. of tambala

MATCH — *v* -ED, -ING, -ES to set in competition or opposition

MATCHBOX — *n* pl. -ES a small box

MATCHER — *n* pl. -S one that matches

MATCHUP — *n* pl. -S a setting of two players against each other

MATE — *v* MATED, MATING, MATES to join as mates (partners in a union)

MATELESS — *adj* having no mate

MATELOT — *n* pl. -S a sailor

MATELOTE — *n* pl. -S a fish stew

MATER — *n* pl. -TERS or -TRES mother

MATERIAL — *n* pl. -S the substance of which anything is or may be composed

MATERIEL — *n* pl. -S the aggregate of equipment and supplies used by an organization

MATERNAL — *adj* pertaining to a mother

MATESHIP — *n* pl. -S the state of being a mate

MATEY — *n* pl. -EYS a friend

MATH — *n* pl. -S mathematics

MATILDA — *n* pl. -S a hobo's bundle

MATIN — *n* pl. -S a morning song, as of birds

MATINAL — *adj* pertaining to the morning

MATINEE — *n* pl. -S a daytime performance

MATINESS — *n* pl. -ES friendliness

MATING — *n* pl. -S the period during which a seasonal-breeding animal can mate

MATLESS — *adj* having no mats (small floor coverings)

MATRASS — *n* pl. -ES a long-necked glass vessel

MATRES — a pl. of mater

MATRIX — *n* pl. -TRICES or -TRIXES something within which something else originates or develops

MATRON — *n* pl. -S a married woman of established social position **MATRONAL, MATRONLY** *adj*

MATSAH *n* pl. -S matzo

MATT *v* -ED, -ING, -S to matte

MATTE *v* MATTED, MATTING, MATTES to produce a dull finish on

MATTED past tense of mat, matt, and matte

MATTEDLY *adv* in a tangled manner

MATTER *v* -ED, -ING, -S to be of importance

MATTERY *adj* producing pus

MATTIN *n* pl. -S matin

MATTING *n* pl. -S a woven fabric used as a floor covering

MATTOCK *n* pl. -S a digging tool

MATTOID *n* pl. -S a mentally unbalanced person

MATTRASS *n* pl. -ES matrass

MATTRESS *n* pl. -ES a large pad filled with resilient material used on or as a bed

MATURATE *v* -RATED, -RATING, -RATES to mature

MATURE *adj* -TURER, -TUREST fully developed **MATURELY** *adv*

MATURE *v* -TURED, -TURING, -TURES to make or become mature

MATURITY *n* pl. -TIES the state of being mature

MATZA *n* pl. -S matzo

MATZAH *n* pl. -S matzo

MATZO *n* pl. -ZOS, -ZOT, or -ZOTH an unleavened bread

MATZOH *n* pl. -S matzo

MATZOON *n* pl. -S a food made from milk

MATZOT a pl. of matzo

MATZOTH a pl. of matzo

MAUD *n* pl. -S a Scottish gray and black plaid

MAUDLIN *adj* excessively emotional

MAUGER *prep* maugre

MAUGRE *prep* in spite of

MAUL *v* -ED, -ING, -S to injure by beating

MAULER *n* pl. -S one that mauls

MAUMET *n* pl. -S an idol

MAUMETRY *n* pl. -RIES idolatry

MAUN *v* must — MAUN is the only form of this verb; it cannot be conjugated

MAUND *n* pl. -S an Asian unit of weight

MAUNDER *v* -ED, -ING, -S to talk incoherently

MAUNDY *n* pl. -DIES the religious ceremony of washing the feet of the poor

MAUSOLEA *n/pl* large, stately tombs

MAUT *n* pl. -S malt

MAUVE *n* pl. -S a purple color

MAVEN *n* pl. -S mavin

MAVERICK *n* pl. -S an unbranded range animal

MAVIE *n* pl. -S mavis

MAVIN *n* pl. -S an expert

MAVIS *n* pl. -VISES a songbird

MAW *v* MAWED, MAWN, MAWING, MAWS to mow

MAWKISH *adj* offensively sentimental

MAX *n* pl. -ES maximum

MAXI *n* pl. -S a long skirt or coat

MAXICOAT *n* pl. -S a long coat

MAXILLA *n* pl. -LAE or -LAS the upper jaw or jawbone

MAXIM *n* pl. -S a brief statement of a general truth or principle

MAXIMA a pl. of maximum

MAXIMAL *n* pl. -S an element of a mathematical set that is followed by no other

MAXIMIN *n* pl. -S the maximum of a set of minima

MAXIMISE *v* -MISED, -MISING, -MISES to maximize

MAXIMITE *n* pl. -S a powerful explosive

MAXIMIZE *v* -MIZED, -MIZING, -MIZES to make as great as possible

MAXIMUM *n* pl. -MUMS or -MA the greatest possible amount, quantity, or degree

MAXIXE *n* pl. -S a Brazilian dance

MAXWELL *n* pl. -S a unit of magnetic flux

MAY *v* present 2d person sing. MAY, MAYEST, or MAYST, past tense MIGHT — used as an auxiliary to express permission

MAY *v* -ED, -ING, -S to gather flowers in the spring

MAYA *n* pl. -S the power to produce illusions, in Hindu philosophy **MAYAN** *adj*

MAYAPPLE *n* pl. -S a perennial herb

MAYBE	*n* pl. -S an uncertainty
MAYBUSH	*n* pl. -ES a flowering shrub
MAYDAY	*n* pl. -DAYS a radio distress call
MAYEST	a present 2d person sing. of may
MAYFLY	*n* pl. -FLIES a winged insect
MAYHAP	*adv* maybe
MAYHEM	*n* pl. -S the offense of willfully maiming a person
MAYING	*n* pl. -S the gathering of spring flowers
MAYO	*n* pl. -YOS mayonnaise
MAYOR	*n* pl. -S the chief executive official of a city or borough **MAYORAL** *adj*
MAYORESS	*n* pl. -ES a female mayor
MAYPOLE	*n* pl. -S a decorated pole used in a spring celebration
MAYPOP	*n* pl. -S a flowering vine
MAYST	a present 2d person sing. of may
MAYVIN	*n* pl. -S mavin
MAYWEED	*n* pl. -S a malodorous weed
MAZAEDIA	*n/pl* spore-producing organs of certain lichens
MAZARD	*n* pl. -S the head or face
MAZE	*v* MAZED, MAZING, MAZES to bewilder **MAZEDLY** *adv*
MAZELIKE	*adj* mazy
MAZER	*n* pl. -S a large drinking bowl
MAZIER	comparative of mazy
MAZIEST	superlative of mazy
MAZILY	*adv* in a mazy manner
MAZINESS	*n* pl. -ES the quality of being mazy
MAZING	present participle of maze
MAZOURKA	*n* pl. -S mazurka
MAZUMA	*n* pl. -S money
MAZURKA	*n* pl. -S a Polish dance
MAZY	*adj* MAZIER, MAZIEST full of confusing turns and passages
MAZZARD	*n* pl. -S a wild cherry
MBIRA	*n* pl. -S an African musical instrument
ME	*pron* the objective case of the pronoun I
MEAD	*n* pl. -S an alcoholic beverage
MEADOW	*n* pl. -S a tract of grassland **MEADOWY** *adj*

MEAGER	*adj* deficient in quantity or quality **MEAGERLY** *adv*
MEAGRE	*adj* meager **MEAGRELY** *adv*
MEAL	*n* pl. -S the food served and eaten in one sitting
MEALIE	*n* pl. -S an ear of corn
MEALIER	comparative of mealy
MEALIEST	superlative of mealy
MEALLESS	*adj* lacking a meal
MEALTIME	*n* pl. -S the usual time for a meal
MEALWORM	*n* pl. -S the destructive larva of certain beetles
MEALY	*adj* MEALIER, MEALIEST soft, dry, and friable
MEALYBUG	*n* pl. -S a destructive insect
MEAN	*v* MEANT, MEANING, MEANS to intend
MEAN	*adj* MEANER, MEANEST inferior in grade, quality, or character
MEANDER	*v* -ED, -ING, -S to wander
MEANER	*n* pl. -S one that means
MEANIE	*n* pl. -S a nasty person
MEANIES	pl. of meany
MEANING	*n* pl. -S something that one intends to convey by language
MEANLY	*adv* in a mean manner
MEANNESS	*n* pl. -ES the state of being mean
MEANT	past tense of mean
MEANTIME	*n* pl. -S the intervening time
MEANY	*n* pl. MEANIES meanie
MEASLE	*n* pl. -S a tapeworm larva **MEASLED** *adj*
MEASLY	*adj* -SLIER, -SLIEST meager
MEASURE	*v* -SURED, -SURING, -SURES to ascertain the dimensions, quantity, or capacity of
MEASURER	*n* pl. -S one that measures
MEAT	*n* pl. -S animal flesh used as food **MEATED** *adj*
MEATAL	*adj* pertaining to a meatus
MEATBALL	*n* pl. -S a small ball of chopped meat
MEATHEAD	*n* pl. -S a dolt
MEATIER	comparative of meaty
MEATIEST	superlative of meaty
MEATILY	*adv* in a meaty manner
MEATLESS	*adj* having no meat

MEATLOAF   *n* pl. -LOAVES a baked loaf of ground meat

MEATMAN   *n* pl. -MEN a vendor of meat

MEATUS   *n* pl. -ES a natural body passage

MEATY   *adj* MEATIER, MEATIEST full of meat

MECCA   *n* pl. -S a place visited by many people

MECHANIC   *n* pl. -S a person who works with machines

MECONIUM   *n* pl. -S the first fecal excretion of a newborn child

MED   *adj* medical

MEDAKA   *n* pl. -S a Japanese fish

MEDAL   *v* -ALED, -ALING, -ALS or -ALLED, -ALLING, -ALS to honor with a medal (a commemorative piece of metal)

MEDALIST   *n* pl. -S a person to whom a medal has been awarded

MEDALLIC   *adj* of or pertaining to a medal

MEDALLING   a present participle of medal

MEDDLE   *v* -DLED, -DLING, -DLES to interest oneself in what is not one's concern

MEDDLER   *n* pl. -S one that meddles

MEDEVAC   *v* -VACKED, -VACKING, -VACS to evacuate the wounded from a battlefield by helicopter

MEDFLY   *n* pl. -FLIES a Mediterranean fruit fly

MEDIA   *n* pl. -DIAE the middle layer of a blood or lymph vessel

MEDIA   *n* pl. -S a channel of communication

MEDIACY   *n* pl. -CIES the act of mediating

MEDIAD   *adv* toward the middle of a body or part

MEDIAE   pl. of media

MEDIAL   *n* pl. -S a sound, syllable, or letter in the middle of a word

MEDIALLY   *adv* in a central manner

MEDIAN   *n* pl. -S a central part

MEDIANLY   *adv* medially

MEDIANT   *n* pl. -S a type of musical tone

MEDIATE   *v* -ATED, -ATING, -ATES to act between disputing parties in order to bring about a settlement

MEDIATOR   *n* pl. -S one that mediates

MEDIC   *n* pl. -S one engaged in medical work

MEDICAID   *n* pl. -S a type of governmental health program

MEDICAL   *n* pl. -S a physical examination

MEDICARE   *n* pl. -S a type of governmental health program

MEDICATE   *v* -CATED, -CATING, -CATES to treat with medicine

MEDICINE   *v* -CINED, -CINING, -CINES to administer medicine (a substance used in the treatment of disease) to

MEDICK   *n* pl. -S a flowering plant

MEDICO   *n* pl. -COS a doctor or medical student

MEDIEVAL   *n* pl. -S a person belonging to the Middle Ages

MEDII   pl. of medius

MEDINA   *n* pl. -S the native quarter of a North African city

MEDIOCRE   *adj* neither good nor bad

MEDITATE   *v* -TATED, -TATING, -TATES to ponder

MEDIUM   *n* pl. -DIA or -DIUMS a surrounding environment in which something functions and thrives

MEDIUS   *n* pl. -DII the middle finger

MEDLAR   *n* pl. -S a Eurasian tree

MEDLEY   *n* pl. -LEYS a mixture

MEDULLA   *n* pl. -LAS or -LAE the central tissue in the stems of certain plants **MEDULLAR** *adj*

MEDUSA   *n* pl. -SAE or -SAS a jellyfish **MEDUSAL** *adj*

MEDUSAN   *n* pl. -S medusa

MEDUSOID   *n* pl. -S medusa

MEED   *n* pl. -S a deserved reward

MEEK   *adj* MEEKER, MEEKEST lacking in spirit and courage **MEEKLY** *adv*

MEEKNESS   *n* pl. -ES the quality of being meek

MEERKAT   *n* pl. -S an African mongoose

MEET   *v* MET, MEETING, MEETS to come into the company or presence of

MEETER   *n* pl. -S one that meets

MEETING   *n* pl. -S an assembly for a common purpose

MEETLY   *adv* suitably

MEETNESS   *n* pl. -ES suitability

MEGABAR   *n* pl. -S a unit of pressure

MEGABIT *n* pl. -S a unit of computer information

MEGABUCK *n* pl. -S one million dollars

MEGABYTE *n* pl. -S 1,048,576 bytes

MEGACITY *n* pl. -CITIES a very large city

MEGADEAL *n* pl. -S a business deal involving a lot of money

MEGADOSE *n* pl. -S an abnormally large dose

MEGADYNE *n* pl. -S a unit of force

MEGAHIT *n* pl. -S something extremely successful

MEGALITH *n* pl. -S a huge stone used in prehistoric monuments

MEGALOPS *n* pl. -LOPSES a larval stage of most crabs

MEGAPOD *n* pl. -S megapode

MEGAPODE *n* pl. -S a large-footed bird

MEGASS *n* pl. -ES a bagasse

MEGASSE *n* pl. -S megass

MEGASTAR *n* pl. -S an extremely successful performer

MEGATON *n* pl. -S a unit of explosive force

MEGAVOLT *n* pl. -S a unit of electromotive force

MEGAWATT *n* pl. -S a unit of power

MEGILLAH *n* pl. -S a long, involved story

MEGILP *n* pl. -S a substance with which pigments are mixed in painting

MEGILPH *n* pl. -S megilp

MEGOHM *n* pl. -S a unit of electrical resistance

MEGRIM *n* pl. -S a migraine

MEIKLE *adj* large

MEINIE *n* pl. -S meiny

MEINY *n* pl. -NIES a retinue

MEIOSIS *n* pl. -OSES a type of cell division **MEIOTIC** *adj*

MEL *n* pl. -S honey

MELAMED *n* pl. -LAMDIM a teacher in a Jewish school

MELAMINE *n* pl. -S a chemical compound

MELANGE *n* pl. -S a mixture

MELANIAN *adj* pertaining to dark pigmentation

MELANIC *n* pl. -S one who is affected with melanism

MELANIN *n* pl. -S a dark pigment

MELANISM *n* pl. -S abnormally dark pigmentation of the skin

MELANIST *n* pl. -S a melanic

MELANITE *n* pl. -S a black variety of garnet

MELANIZE *v* -NIZED, -NIZING, -NIZES to make dark

MELANOID *n* pl. -S a dark pigment

MELANOMA *n* pl. -MAS or -MATA a darkly pigmented tumor

MELANOUS *adj* having dark skin and hair

MELD *v* -ED, -ING, -S to blend

MELDER *n* pl. -S the amount of grain ground at one time

MELEE *n* pl. -S a confused struggle

MELIC *adj* pertaining to song

MELILITE *n* pl. -S a mineral group

MELILOT *n* pl. -S a flowering plant

MELINITE *n* pl. -S a powerful explosive

MELISMA *n* pl. -MAS or -MATA melodic embellishment

MELL *v* -ED, -ING, -S to mix

MELLIFIC *adj* producing honey

MELLOW *adj* -LOWER, -LOWEST soft and full-flavored from ripeness **MELLOWLY** *adv*

MELLOW *v* -ED, -ING, -S to make or become mellow

MELODEON *n* pl. -S a musical instrument

MELODIA *n* pl. -S a type of organ stop

MELODIC *adj* pertaining to melody

MELODICA *n* pl. -S a harmonica with a small keyboard at one end

MELODIES pl. of melody

MELODISE *v* -DISED, -DISING, -DISES to melodize

MELODIST *n* pl. -S a composer of melodies

MELODIZE *v* -DIZED, -DIZING, -DIZES to compose a melody

MELODY *n* pl. -DIES an agreeable succession of musical sounds

MELOID *n* pl. -S a type of beetle

MELON *n* pl. -S any of various gourds

MELT *v* -ED, -ING, -S to change from a solid to a liquid state by heat **MELTABLE** *adj*

MELTAGE *n* pl. -S the process of melting

MELTDOWN *n* pl. -S the melting of the core of a nuclear reactor

MELTER *n* pl. -S one that melts

MELTON *n* pl. -S a heavy woolen fabric

MEM *n* pl. -S a Hebrew letter

MEMBER   *n* pl. -S a distinct part of a whole **MEMBERED** *adj*

MEMBRANE   *n* pl. -S a thin, pliable layer of tissue

MEMENTO   *n* pl. -TOS or -TOES something that serves as a reminder of the past

MEMO   *n* pl. MEMOS a note designating something to be remembered

MEMOIR   *n* pl. -S a biography

MEMORIAL   *n* pl. -S something that serves as a remembrance of a person or event

MEMORISE   *v* -ISED, -ISING, -ISES memorize

MEMORIZE   *v* -RIZED, -RIZING, -RIZES to commit to memory

MEMORY   *n* pl. -RIES the mental faculty of retaining and recalling past experience

MEMSAHIB   *n* pl. -S a European woman living in colonial India

MEN   pl. of man

MENACE   *v* -ACED, -ACING, -ACES to theaten

MENACER   *n* pl. -S one that menaces

MENAD   *n* pl. -S maenad

MENAGE   *n* pl. -S a household

MENARCHE   *n* pl. -S the first occurrence of menstruation

MENAZON   *n* pl. -S an insecticide

MEND   *v* -ED, -ING, -S to repair **MENDABLE** *adj*

MENDER   *n* pl. -S one that mends

MENDIGO   *n* pl. -GOS a freshwater fish

MENDING   *n* pl. -S an accumulation of articles to be mended

MENFOLK   *n/pl* the men of a family or community

MENFOLKS   *n/pl* menfolk

MENHADEN   *n* pl. -S a marine fish

MENHIR   *n* pl. -S a prehistoric monument

MENIAL   *n* pl. -S a domestic servant

MENIALLY   *adv* in a servile manner

MENINX   *n* pl. -NINGES any of the membranes enclosing the brain and spinal cord

MENISCUS   *n* pl. -CI or -CUSES a crescent-shaped body **MENISCAL** *adj*

MENO   *adv* less — used as a musical direction

MENOLOGY   *n* pl. -GIES an ecclesiastical calendar

MENORAH   *n* pl. -S a candleholder used in Jewish worship

MENSA   *n* pl. -SAS or -SAE the grinding surface of a tooth

MENSAL   *adj* pertaining to or used at the table

MENSCH   *n* pl. MENSCHES or MENSCHEN an admirable person

MENSE   *v* MENSED, MENSING, MENSES to do honor to

MENSEFUL   *adj* proper

MENSTRUA   *n/pl* solvents

MENSURAL   *adj* pertaining to measure

MENSWEAR   *n* pl. MENSWEAR clothing for men

MENTA   pl. of mentum

MENTAL   *adj* pertaining to the mind **MENTALLY** *adv*

MENTHENE   *n* pl. -S a liquid hydrocarbon

MENTHOL   *n* pl. -S an alcohol

MENTION   *v* -ED, -ING, -S to refer to in a casual manner

MENTOR   *v* -ED, -ING, -S to serve as a friend and teacher to

MENTUM   *n* pl. -TA the chin

MENU   *n* pl. -S a list of the dishes available in a restaurant

MEOU   *v* -ED, -ING, -S meow

MEOW   *v* -ED, -ING, -S to make the crying sound of a cat

MEPHITIS   *n* pl. -TISES an offensive odor **MEPHITIC** *adj*

MERCAPTO   *adj* containing a particular chemical group

MERCER   *n* pl. -S a dealer in textiles

MERCERY   *n* pl. -CERIES a mercer's shop

MERCHANT   *v* -ED, -ING, -S to buy and sell goods for profit

MERCIES   pl. of mercy

MERCIFUL   *adj* full of mercy

MERCURY   *n* pl. -RIES a metallic element **MERCURIC** *adj*

MERCY   *n* pl. -CIES compassion shown to an offender or enemy

MERE   *n* pl. -S a pond or lake

MERE   *adj* MERER, MEREST being nothing more than **MERELY** *adv*

MERENGUE   *n* pl. -S a ballroom dance

MERGE	*v* MERGED, MERGING, MERGES to combine
MERGENCE	*n* pl. -S the act of merging
MERGER	*n* pl. -S the union of two or more businesses into a single enterprise
MERGING	present participle of merge
MERIDIAN	*n* pl. -S a circle around the earth passing through both poles
MERINGUE	*n* pl. -S a topping for pastries
MERINO	*n* pl. -NOS a fine wool
MERISIS	*n* pl. MERISES growth
MERISTEM	*n* pl. -S formative plant tissue
MERISTIC	*adj* made up of segments
MERIT	*v* -ED, -ING, -S to earn
MERK	*n* pl. -S a former coin of Scotland
MERL	*n* pl. -S merle
MERLE	*n* pl. -S a blackbird
MERLIN	*n* pl. -S a European falcon
MERLON	*n* pl. -S the solid part of an indented parapet
MERLOT	*n* pl. -S a dry red wine
MERMAID	*n* pl. -S a legendary marine creature
MERMAN	*n* pl. -MEN a legendary marine creature
MEROPIA	*n* pl. -S partial blindness **MEROPIC** *adj*
MERRY	*adj* -RIER, -RIEST cheerful **MERRILY** *adv*
MESA	*n* pl. -S a land formation having a flat top and steep sides
MESALLY	*adv* medially
MESARCH	*adj* originating in a mesic habitat
MESCAL	*n* pl. -S a cactus
MESDAMES	pl. of madame
MESEEMS	*v* past tense MESEEMED present 3d person sing. MESEEMETH it seems to me — MESEEMS is an impersonal verb and is used only in the 3d person sing.
MESH	*v* -ED, -ING, -ES to entangle
MESHIER	comparative of meshy
MESHIEST	superlative of meshy
MESHUGA	*adj* crazy
MESHUGAH	*adj* meshuga
MESHUGGA	*adj* meshuga
MESHUGGE	*adj* meshuga

MESHWORK	*n* pl. -S a network
MESHY	*adj* MESHIER, MESHIEST netty
MESIAL	*adj* situated in the middle **MESIALLY** *adv*
MESIAN	*adj* mesial
MESIC	*adj* characterized by a medium supply of moisture
MESMERIC	*adj* pertaining to hypnotism
MESNALTY	*n* pl. -TIES a type of feudal estate
MESNE	*n* pl. -S a feudal lord holding land from a superior
MESOCARP	*n* pl. -S the middle layer of a pericarp
MESODERM	*n* pl. -S the middle germ layer of an embryo
MESOGLEA	*n* pl. -S a gelatinous material in sponges
MESOMERE	*n* pl. -S an embryonic segment
MESON	*n* pl. -S a subatomic particle **MESONIC** *adj*
MESOPHYL	*n* pl. -S the soft tissue of a leaf
MESOSOME	*n* pl. -S a specialized cellular part
MESOTRON	*n* pl. -S a meson
MESQUIT	*n* pl. -S mesquite
MESQUITE	*n* pl. -S a spiny tree or shrub
MESS	*v* -ED, -ING, -ES to make dirty or untidy
MESSAGE	*v* -SAGED, -SAGING, -SAGES to send as a message (an oral, written, or signaled communication)
MESSAN	*n* pl. -S a lapdog
MESSIAH	*n* pl. -S an expected liberator
MESSIER	comparative of messy
MESSIEST	superlative of messy
MESSIEURS	pl. of monsieur
MESSILY	*adv* in a messy manner
MESSMAN	*n* pl. -MEN a serviceman who works in a dining facility
MESSMATE	*n* pl. -S a person with whom one eats regularly
MESSUAGE	*n* pl. -S a dwelling house with its adjacent buildings and land
MESSY	*adj* MESSIER, MESSIEST dirty or untidy
MESTEE	*n* pl. -S mustee
MESTESO	*n* pl. -SOS or -SOES mestizo
MESTINO	*n* pl. -NOS or -NOES mestizo

MESTIZA	*n* pl. -S a female mestizo
MESTIZO	*n* pl. -ZOS or -ZOES a person of mixed ancestry
MET	past tense of meet
META	*adj* pertaining to positions in a benzene ring separated by one carbon atom
METAGE	*n* pl. -S an official measurement of weight or contents
METAL	*v* -ALED, -ALING, -ALS or -ALLED, -ALLING, -ALS to cover with metal (any of various ductile, fusible, and lustrous substances)
METALISE	*v* -ISED, -ISING, -ISES to metalize
METALIST	*n* pl. -S one who works with metals
METALIZE	*v* -IZED, -IZING, -IZES to treat with metal
METALLED	a past tense of metal
METALLIC	*n* pl. -S a fabric or yarn made of or coated with metal
METALLING	a present participle of metal
METAMER	*n* pl. -S a type of chemical compound
METAMERE	*n* pl. -S a somite
METAPHOR	*n* pl. -S a type of figure of speech
METATE	*n* pl. -S a stone used for grinding grains
METAZOAN	*n* pl. -S any of a major division of multicellular animals **METAZOAL, METAZOIC** *adj*
METAZOON	*n* pl. -ZOA a metazoan
METE	*v* METED, METING, METES to distribute by measure
METEOR	*n* pl. -S a small celestial body that enters the earth's atmosphere **METEORIC** *adj*
METEPA	*n* pl. -S a chemical compound
METER	*v* -ED, -ING, -S to measure by mechanical means
METERAGE	*n* pl. -S the process of metering
METH	*n* pl. -S a stimulant drug
METHADON	*n* pl. -S a narcotic drug
METHANE	*n* pl. -S a flammable gas
METHANOL	*n* pl. -S a toxic alcohol
METHINKS	*v* past tense METHOUGHT it seems to me — METHINKS is an impersonal verb and is used only in the 3d person sing.
METHOD	*n* pl. -S a means of procedure

METHODIC	*adj* systematic
METHOUGHT	past tense of methinks
METHOXY	*adj* containing a certain chemical group
METHOXYL	*adj* methoxy
METHYL	*n* pl. -S a univalent radical **METHYLIC** *adj*
METHYLAL	*n* pl. -S a flammable liquid
METICAL	*n* pl. -CAIS or -CALS a monetary unit of Mozambique
METIER	*n* pl. -S a vocation
METING	present participle of mete
METIS	*n* pl. METIS a person of mixed ancestry
METISSE	*n* pl. -S a female metis
METONYM	*n* pl. -S a word used in metonymy
METONYMY	*n* pl. -MIES a type of figure of speech
METOPE	*n* pl. -PES or -PAE a space between two triglyphs
METOPIC	*adj* pertaining to the forehead
METOPON	*n* pl. -S a narcotic drug
METRE	*v* -TRED, -TRING, -TRES to meter
METRIC	*n* pl. -S a standard of measurement
METRICAL	*adj* pertaining to or composed in a system of arranged and measured rhythm
METRIFY	*v* -FIED, -FYING, -FIES to compose in metrical form
METRING	present participle of metre
METRIST	*n* pl. -S one who metrifies
METRITIS	*n* pl. -TISES inflammation of the uterus
METRO	*n* pl. -ROS a subway
METTLE	*n* pl. -S quality of character **METTLED** *adj*
METUMP	*n* pl. -S a tumpline
MEUNIERE	*adj* cooked in browned butter
MEW	*v* -ED, -ING, -S to confine
MEWL	*v* -ED, -ING, -S to whimper
MEWLER	*n* pl. -S one that mewls
MEZCAL	*n* pl. -S mescal
MEZE	*n* pl. -S a Greek or Middle Eastern appetizer
MEZEREON	*n* pl. -S a flowering shrub
MEZEREUM	*n* pl. -S mezereon

MEZQUIT	*n* pl. -S mesquite
MEZQUITE	*n* pl. -S mesquite
MEZUZA	*n* pl. -S mezuzah
MEZUZAH	*n* pl. -ZAHS, -ZOT, or -ZOTH a Judaic scroll
MEZZO	*n* pl. -ZOS a female voice of a full, deep quality
MHO	*n* pl. MHOS a unit of electrical conductance
MI	*n* pl. -S the third tone of the diatonic musical scale
MIAOU	*v* -ED, -ING, -S to meow
MIAOW	*v* -ED, -ING, -S to meow
MIASM	*n* pl. -S miasma
MIASMA	*n* pl. -MAS or -MATA a noxious vapor **MIASMAL, MIASMIC** *adj*
MIAUL	*v* -ED, -ING, -S to meow
MIB	*n* pl. -S a type of playing marble
MICA	*n* pl. -S a mineral
MICAWBER	*n* pl. -S a person who remains hopeful despite adversity
MICE	pl. of mouse
MICELL	*n* pl. -S micelle
MICELLA	*n* pl. -LAE micelle
MICELLE	*n* pl. -S a coherent strand or structure in a fiber **MICELLAR** *adj*
MICHE	*v* MICHED, MICHING, MICHES to skulk
MICKEY	*n* pl. -EYS a drugged drink
MICKLE	*adj* -LER, -LEST large
MICKLE	*n* pl. -S a large amount
MICRA	a pl. of micron
MICRIFY	*v* -FIED, -FYING, -FIES to make small
MICRO	*n* pl. -CROS a very small computer
MICROBAR	*n* pl. -S a unit of atmospheric pressure
MICROBE	*n* pl. -S a minute life form **MICROBIC** *adj*
MICROBUS	*n* pl. -BUSES or -BUSSES a small bus
MICRODOT	*n* pl. -S a copy of printed matter reduced to the size of a dot
MICROHM	*n* pl. -S a unit of electrical resistance
MICROLUX	*n* pl. -LUXES or -LUCES a unit of illumination
MICROMHO	*n* pl. -S a unit of electrical conductance

MICRON	*n* pl. -CRONS or -CRA a unit of length
MICRURGY	*n* pl. -GIES the use of minute tools under high magnification
MID	*n* pl. -S the middle
MIDAIR	*n* pl. -S a region in the middle of the air
MIDBRAIN	*n* pl. -S the middle region of the brain
MIDCULT	*n* pl. -S middle-class culture
MIDDAY	*n* pl. -DAYS the middle of the day
MIDDEN	*n* pl. -S a dunghill
MIDDIES	pl. of middy
MIDDLE	*v* -DLED, -DLING, -DLES to place in the middle (the area or point equidistant from extremes or limits)
MIDDLER	*n* pl. -S a student in an intermediate grade
MIDDLING	*n* pl. -S a cut of pork
MIDDY	*n* pl. -DIES a loosely fitting blouse
MIDFIELD	*n* pl. -S the middle portion of a playing field
MIDGE	*n* pl. -S a small winged insect
MIDGET	*n* pl. -S a very small person
MIDGUT	*n* pl. -S the middle part of the embryonic digestive tract
MIDI	*n* pl. -S a skirt or coat that extends to the middle of the calf
MIDIRON	*n* pl. -S a golf club
MIDLAND	*n* pl. -S the middle part of a country
MIDLEG	*n* pl. -S the middle of the leg
MIDLIFE	*n* pl. -LIVES middle age
MIDLINE	*n* pl. -S a median line
MIDMONTH	*n* pl. -S the middle of the month
MIDMOST	*n* pl. -S a part exactly in the middle
MIDNIGHT	*n* pl. -S the middle of the night
MIDNOON	*n* pl. -S midday
MIDPOINT	*n* pl. -S a point at the middle
MIDRANGE	*n* pl. -S the middle of a range
MIDRASH	*n* pl. -RASHIM or -RASHOTH an early Jewish interpretation of a biblical text
MIDRIB	*n* pl. -S the central vein of a leaf
MIDRIFF	*n* pl. -S the middle part of the body

MIDSHIP *adj* pertaining to the middle of a ship

MIDSHIPS *adv* toward the middle of a ship

MIDSIZE *adj* of intermediate size

MIDSIZED *adj* midsize

MIDSOLE *n* pl. -S a middle layer of the sole of a shoe

MIDSPACE *n* pl. -S the middle of a space

MIDST *n* pl. -S the middle

MIDSTORY *n* pl. -RIES the middle of a story

MIDTERM *n* pl. -S an examination given in the middle of an academic semester

MIDTOWN *n* pl. -S the central part of a city

MIDWATCH *n* pl. -ES a watch on a ship between midnight and 4 A.M.

MIDWAY *n* pl. -WAYS an avenue at a fair or carnival for concessions and amusements

MIDWEEK *n* pl. -S the middle of the week

MIDWIFE *v* -WIFED, -WIFING, -WIFES or -WIVED, -WIVING, -WIVES to assist a woman in childbirth

MIDYEAR *n* pl. -S the middle of the year

MIEN *n* pl. -S demeanor

MIFF *v* -ED, -ING, -S to annoy

MIFFY *adj* MIFFIER, MIFFIEST easily annoyed

MIG *n* pl. -S a type of playing marble

MIGG *n* pl. -S mig

MIGGLE *n* pl. -S a mig

MIGHT *n* pl. -S strength

MIGHTY *adj* MIGHTIER, MIGHTIEST strong **MIGHTILY** *adv*

MIGNON *n* pl. -S a cut of beef

MIGNONNE *adj* daintily small

MIGRAINE *n* pl. -S a severe headache

MIGRANT *n* pl. -S one that migrates

MIGRATE *v* -GRATED, -GRATING, -GRATES to move from one region to another

MIGRATOR *n* pl. -S a migrant

MIHRAB *n* pl. -S a niche in a mosque

MIJNHEER *n* pl. -S mynheer

MIKADO *n* pl. -DOS an emperor of Japan

MIKE *v* MIKED, MIKING, MIKES to amplify or record by use of a microphone

MIKRON *n* pl. -KRONS or -KRA micron

MIKVAH *n* pl. -VAHS or -VOTH a place for ritual bathing by Orthodox Jews

MIKVEH *n* pl. -S mikvah

MIL *n* pl. -S a unit of length

MILADI *n* pl. -S milady

MILADY *n* pl. -DIES an English gentlewoman

MILAGE *n* pl. -S mileage

MILCH *adj* giving milk

MILCHIG *adj* made of or derived from milk

MILD *adj* MILDER, MILDEST not harsh or rough

MILDEN *v* -ED, -ING, -S to make or become mild

MILDEW *v* -ED, -ING, -S to affect with mildew (a whitish growth produced by fungi)

MILDEWY *adj* affected with or resembling mildew

MILDLY *adj* in a mild manner

MILDNESS *n* pl. -ES the quality of being mild

MILE *n* pl. -S a unit of distance

MILEAGE *n* pl. -S total distance expressed in miles

MILEPOST *n* pl. -S a post indicating distance in miles

MILER *n* pl. -S one that runs a mile race

MILESIMO *n* pl. -MOS a former monetary unit of Chile

MILFOIL *n* pl. -S a perennial herb

MILIA pl. of milium

MILIARIA *n* pl. -S a skin disease

MILIARY *adj* made up of many small projections

MILIEU *n* pl. -LIEUS or -LIEUX environment

MILITANT *n* pl. -S a person who is aggressively engaged in a cause

MILITARY *n* pl. -TARIES armed forces

MILITATE *v* -TATED, -TATING, -TATES to have influence or effect

MILITIA *n* pl. -S a citizen army

MILIUM *n* pl. -IA a small, whitish lump in the skin

MILK *v* -ED, -ING, -S to draw milk (a whitish, nutritious liquid) from the udder of

MILKER *n* pl. -S one that milks

MILKFISH *n* pl. -ES a marine food fish

MILKIER comparative of milky

MILKIEST	superlative of milky
MILKILY	*adv* in a milky manner
MILKMAID	*n* pl. -S a woman who milks cows
MILKMAN	*n* pl. -MEN a man who sells or delivers milk
MILKSHED	*n* pl. -S a region supplying milk to a particular community
MILKSOP	*n* pl. -S an effeminate man
MILKWEED	*n* pl. -S a plant that secretes a milky juice
MILKWOOD	*n* pl. -S a tropical tree
MILKWORT	*n* pl. -S a flowering plant
MILKY	*adj* MILKIER, MILKIEST resembling or suggestive of milk
MILL	*v* -ED, -ING, -S to grind by mechanical means **MILLABLE** *adj*
MILLAGE	*n* pl. -S a type of monetary rate
MILLCAKE	*n* pl. -S a residue from pressed linseed
MILLDAM	*n* pl. -S a dam built to form a millpond
MILLE	*n* pl. -S a thousand
MILLEPED	*n* pl. -S milliped
MILLER	*n* pl. -S one that mills
MILLET	*n* pl. -S a cereal grass
MILLIARD	*n* pl. -S a billion
MILLIARE	*n* pl. -S a unit of area
MILLIARY	*n* pl. -ARIES an ancient Roman milestone
MILLIBAR	*n* pl. -S a unit of atmospheric pressure
MILLIEME	*n* pl. -S unit of value of Egypt and Sudan
MILLIER	*n* pl. -S a unit of weight
MILLIGAL	*n* pl. -S a unit of acceleration
MILLILUX	*n* pl. -LUXES or -LUCES a unit of illumination
MILLIME	*n* pl. -S a coin of Tunisia
MILLIMHO	*n* pl. -MHOS a unit of electrical conductance
MILLINE	*n* pl. -S a unit of advertising space
MILLINER	*n* pl. -S one who makes or sells women's hats
MILLING	*n* pl. -S a corrugated edge on a coin
MILLIOHM	*n* pl. -S a unit of electrical resistance
MILLION	*n* pl. -S a number
MILLIPED	*n* pl. -S a multi-legged arthropod
MILLIREM	*n* pl. -S a quantity of ionizing radiation
MILLPOND	*n* pl. -S a pond for supplying water to run a mill wheel (a type of waterwheel)
MILLRACE	*n* pl. -S the current of water that drives a mill wheel
MILLRUN	*n* pl. -S a millrace
MILLWORK	*n* pl. -S woodwork produced by milling
MILNEB	*n* pl. -S a fungicide
MILO	*n* pl. -LOS a cereal grass
MILORD	*n* pl. -S an English gentleman
MILPA	*n* pl. -S a field that is cleared from a jungle for farming purposes
MILREIS	*n* pl. MILREIS a former monetary unit of Portugal
MILT	*v* -ED, -ING, -S to impregnate with milt (fish sperm)
MILTER	*n* pl. -S a male fish at breeding time
MILTY	*adj* MILTIER, MILTIEST full of milt
MIM	*adj* primly demure
MIMBAR	*n* pl. -S a pulpit in a mosque
MIME	*v* MIMED, MIMING, MIMES to mimic
MIMEO	*v* -ED, -ING, -S to make copies of by use of a mimeograph
MIMER	*n* pl. -S one that mimes
MIMESIS	*n* pl. -SISES mimicry **MIMETIC** *adj*
MIMETITE	*n* pl. -S an ore of lead
MIMIC	*v* -ICKED, -ICKING, -ICS to imitate closely
MIMICAL	*adj* of the nature of mimicry
MIMICKER	*n* pl. -S one that mimics
MIMICKING	present participle of mimic
MIMICRY	*n* pl. -RIES an instance of mimicking
MIMING	present participle of mime
MIMOSA	*n* pl. -S a tropical plant
MINA	*n* pl. -NAS or -NAE an ancient unit of weight and value
MINABLE	*adj* capable of being mined
MINACITY	*n* pl. -TIES the state of being threatening
MINAE	a pl. of mina

MINARET	*n* pl. -S a slender tower attached to a mosque
MINATORY	*adj* threatening
MINCE	*v* MINCED, MINCING, MINCES to cut into very small pieces
MINCER	*n* pl. -S one that minces
MINCY	*adj* MINCIER, MINCIEST affectedly dainty
MIND	*v* -ED, -ING, -S to heed
MINDER	*n* pl. -S one that minds
MINDFUL	*adj* heedful
MINDLESS	*adj* lacking intelligence
MINDSET	*n* pl. -S a fixed mental attitude
MINE	*v* MINED, MINING, MINES to dig into for valuable materials
MINEABLE	*adj* minable
MINER	*n* pl. -S one that mines
MINERAL	*n* pl. -S a naturally occurring inorganic substance having a characteristic set of physical properties
MINGIER	comparative of mingy
MINGIEST	superlative of mingy
MINGLE	*v* -GLED, -GLING, -GLES to mix together
MINGLER	*n* pl. -S one that mingles
MINGY	*adj* -GIER, -GIEST mean and stingy
MINI	*n* pl. -S something distinctively smaller than others of its kind
MINIBIKE	*n* pl. -S a small motorcycle
MINIBUS	*n* pl. -BUSES or -BUSSES a small bus
MINICAB	*n* pl. -S a small taxicab
MINICAMP	*n* pl. -S a short training camp for football players
MINICAR	*n* pl. -S a small automobile
MINIFY	*v* -FIED, -FYING, -FIES to make small or smaller
MINIKIN	*n* pl. -S a small or dainty creature
MINILAB	*n* pl. -S a retail outlet offering rapid on-site film development
MINIM	*n* pl. -S a unit of liquid measure
MINIMA	a pl. of minimum
MINIMAL	*n* pl. -S an element of a mathematical set that precedes all others
MINIMAX	*n* pl. -ES the minimum of a set of maxima
MINIMILL	*n* pl. -S a small-scale steel mill
MINIMISE	*v* -MISED, -MISING, -MISES to minimize
MINIMIZE	*v* -MIZED, -MIZING, -MIZES to make as small as possible
MINIMUM	*n* pl. -MUMS or -MA the least possible amount, quantity, or degree
MINING	*n* pl. -S the process or business of working mines (excavations in the earth)
MINION	*n* pl. -S a servile follower
MINIPARK	*n* pl. -S a small city park
MINISH	*v* -ED, -ING, -ES to diminish
MINISKI	*n* pl. -S a short ski
MINISTER	*v* -ED, -ING, -S to give aid or service
MINISTRY	*n* pl. -TRIES the act of ministering
MINIUM	*n* pl. -S a red pigment
MINIVAN	*n* pl. -S a small van
MINIVER	*n* pl. -S a white fur
MINK	*n* pl. -S a carnivorous mammal
MINKE	*n* pl. -S a small whale
MINNOW	*n* pl. -S a small fish
MINNY	*n* pl. -NIES minnow
MINOR	*v* -ED, -ING, -S to pursue a specific subordinate course of study
MINORCA	*n* pl. -S any of a breed of large domestic fowls
MINORITY	*n* pl. -TIES the smaller number or part
MINSTER	*n* pl. -S a large or important church
MINSTREL	*n* pl. -S a medieval musician
MINT	*v* -ED, -ING, -S to produce by stamping metal, as coins
MINTAGE	*n* pl. -S the act of minting
MINTER	*n* pl. -S one that mints
MINTY	*adj* MINTIER, MINTIEST having the flavor mint (an aromatic herb)
MINUEND	*n* pl. -S a number from which another is to be subtracted
MINUET	*n* pl. -S a slow, stately dance
MINUS	*n* pl. -ES a negative quantity
MINUTE	*v* -UTED, -UTING, -UTES to make a brief note of
MINUTE	*adj* -NUTER, -NUTEST very small **MINUTELY** *adv*

MINUTIA   *n* pl. -TIAE a small detail
MINUTIAL *adj*

MINUTING   present participle of minute

MINX   *n* pl. -ES a pert girl **MINXISH** *adj*

MINYAN   *n* pl. -YANS or -YANIM the minimum number required to be present for the conduct of a Jewish service

MIOSIS   *n* pl. -OSES excessive contraction of the pupil of the eye

MIOTIC   *n* pl. -S an agent that causes miosis

MIQUELET   *n* pl. -S a former Spanish or French soldier

MIR   *n* pl. MIRS or MIRI a Russian peasant commune

MIRACLE   *n* pl. -S an event ascribed to supernatural or divine origin

MIRADOR   *n* pl. -S an architectural feature designed to afford an extensive view

MIRAGE   *n* pl. -S a type of optical illusion

MIRE   *v* MIRED, MIRING, MIRES to cause to stick in swampy ground

MIREX   *n* pl. -ES an insecticide

MIRI   a pl. of mir

MIRIER   comparative of miry

MIRIEST   superlative of miry

MIRINESS   *n* pl. -ES the state of being miry

MIRING   present participle of mire

MIRK   *adj* MIRKER, MIRKEST murk

MIRK   *n* pl. -S murk

MIRKY   *adj* MIRKIER, MIRKIEST murky
MIRKILY *adv*

MIRLITON   *n* pl. -S a chayote

MIRROR   *v* -ED, -ING, -S to reflect an image of

MIRTH   *n* pl. -S spirited gaiety
MIRTHFUL *adj*

MIRY   *adj* MIRIER, MIRIEST swampy

MIRZA   *n* pl. -S a Persian title of honor

MISACT   *v* -ED, -ING, -S to act badly

MISADAPT   *v* -ED, -ING, -S to adapt wrongly

MISADD   *v* -ED, -ING, -S to add incorrectly

MISAGENT   *n* pl. -S a bad agent

MISAIM   *v* -ED, -ING, -S to aim badly

MISALIGN   *v* -ED, -ING, -S to align improperly

MISALLY   *v* -LIED, -LYING, -LIES to ally badly

MISALTER   *v* -ED, -ING, -S to alter wrongly

MISANDRY   *n* pl. -DRIES hatred of men

MISAPPLY   *v* -PLIED, -PLYING, -PLIES to apply wrongly

MISASSAY   *v* -ED, -ING, -S to attempt unsuccessfully

MISATE   past tense of miseat

MISATONE   *v* -ATONED, -ATONING, -ATONES to atone wrongly

MISAVER   *v* -AVERRED, -AVERRING, -AVERS to speak erroneously

MISAWARD   *v* -ED, -ING, -S to award wrongly

MISBEGIN   *v* -GAN, -GUN, -GINNING, -GINS to begin wrongly

MISBEGOT   *adj* born out of wedlock

MISBIAS   *v* -ASED, -ASING, -ASES or -ASSED, -ASSING, -ASSES to bias wrongly

MISBILL   *v* -ED, -ING, -S to bill wrongly

MISBIND   *v* -BOUND, -BINDING, -BINDS to bind imperfectly

MISBRAND   *v* -ED, -ING, -S to brand incorrectly

MISBUILD   *v* -BUILT, -BUILDING, -BUILDS to build imperfectly

MISCALL   *v* -ED, -ING, -S to call by a wrong name

MISCARRY   *v* -RIED, -RYING, -RIES to be unsuccessful

MISCAST   *v* -CAST, -CASTING, -CASTS to cast in an unsuitable role

MISCHIEF   *n* pl. -S action that causes irritation, harm, or trouble

MISCIBLE   *adj* capable of being mixed

MISCITE   *v* -CITED, -CITING, -CITES to misquote

MISCLAIM   *v* -ED, -ING, -S to claim wrongfully

MISCLASS   *v* -ED, -ING, -ES to put in the wrong class

MISCODE   *v* -CODED, -CODING, -CODES to code wrongly

MISCOIN   *v* -ED, -ING, -S to coin improperly

MISCOLOR   *v* -ED, -ING, -S to color incorrectly

MISCOOK   *v* -ED, -ING, -S to cook badly

MISCOPY   *v* -COPIED, -COPYING, -COPIES to copy incorrectly

MISCOUNT   *v* -ED, -ING, -S to count incorrectly

MISCUE   v -CUED, -CUING, -CUES to make a faulty stroke in billiards

MISCUT   v -CUT, -CUTTING, -CUTS to cut incorrectly

MISDATE   v -DATED, -DATING, -DATES to date incorrectly

MISDEAL   v -DEALT, -DEALING, -DEALS to deal cards incorrectly

MISDEED   n pl. -S an evil act

MISDEEM   v -ED, -ING, -S to judge unfavorably

MISDIAL   v -DIALED, -DIALING, -DIALS or -DIALLED, -DIALLING, -DIALS to dial wrongly

MISDO   v -DID, -DONE, -DOING, -DOES to do wrongly

MISDOER   n pl. -S one that misdoes

MISDOING   n pl. -S an instance of doing wrong

MISDONE   past participle of misdo

MISDOUBT   v -ED, -ING, -S to doubt

MISDRAW   v -DREW, -DRAWN, -DRAWING, -DRAWS to draw incorrectly

MISDRIVE   v -DROVE, -DRIVEN, -DRIVING, -DRIVES to drive wrongly or improperly

MISE   n pl. -S an agreement or settlement

MISEASE   n pl. -S discomfort

MISEAT   v -ATE, -EATEN, -EATING, -EATS to eat improperly

MISEDIT   v -ED, -ING, -S to edit incorrectly

MISENROL   v -ROLLED, -ROLLING, -ROLS to misenroll

MISENROLL   v -ED, -ING, -S to enroll improperly

MISENTER   v -ED, -ING, -S to enter erroneously

MISENTRY   n pl. -TRIES an erroneous entry

MISER   n pl. -S one who hoards money greedily

MISERERE   n pl. -S a part of a church seat

MISERLY   adj characteristic of a miser

MISERY   n pl. -ERIES a state of great suffering

MISEVENT   n pl. -S a mishap

MISFAITH   n pl. -S lack of faith; disbelief

MISFIELD   v -ED, -ING, -S to field badly

MISFILE   v -FILED, -FILING, -FILES to file in the wrong place

MISFIRE   v -FIRED, -FIRING, -FIRES to fail to fire

MISFIT   v -FITTED, -FITTING, -FITS to fit badly

MISFOCUS   v -CUSED, -CUSING, -CUSES or -CUSSED, -CUSSING, -CUSSES to focus badly

MISFORM   v -ED, -ING, -S to misshape

MISFRAME   v -FRAMED, -FRAMING, -FRAMES to frame badly

MISGAUGE   v -GAUGED, -GAUGING, -GAUGES to gauge wrongly or inaccurately

MISGIVE   v -GAVE, -GIVEN, -GIVING, -GIVES to make doubtful or fearful

MISGRADE   v -GRADED, -GRADING, -GRADES to grade incorrectly

MISGRAFT   v -ED, -ING, -S to graft wrongly

MISGROW   v -GREW, -GROWN, -GROWING, -GROWS to grow abnormally

MISGUESS   v -ED, -ING, -ES to guess wrongly

MISGUIDE   v -GUIDED, -GUIDING, -GUIDES to guide wrongly

MISHAP   n pl. -S an unfortunate accident

MISHEAR   v -HEARD, -HEARING, -HEARS to hear incorrectly

MISHIT   v -HIT, -HITTING, -HITS to hit poorly

MISHMASH   n pl. -ES a confused mixture

MISHMOSH   n pl. -ES mishmash

MISINFER   v -FERRED, -FERRING, -FERS to infer wrongly

MISINTER   v -TERRED, -TERRING, -TERS to inter improperly

MISJOIN   v -ED, -ING, -S to join improperly

MISJUDGE   v -JUDGED, -JUDGING, -JUDGES to judge wrongly

MISKAL   n pl. -S an Oriental unit of weight

MISKEEP   v -KEPT, -KEEPING, -KEEPS to keep wrongly

MISKICK   v -ED, -ING, -S to kick badly

MISKNOW   v -KNEW, -KNOWN, -KNOWING, -KNOWS to fail to understand or recognize

MISLABEL   v -BELED, -BELING, -BELS or -BELLED, -BELLING, -BELS to label incorrectly or falsely

MISLABOR   v -ED, -ING, -S to labor badly

MISLAIN   past participle of mislie

MISLAY *v* -LAID, -LAYING, -LAYS to put in a forgotten place

MISLAYER *n* pl. -S one that mislays

MISLEAD *v* -LED, -LEADING, -LEADS to lead astray

MISLEARN *v* -LEARNED or -LEARNT, -LEARNING, -LEARNS to learn wrongly

MISLIE *v* -LAY, -LAIN, -LYING, -LIES to lie in a wrong position

MISLIGHT *v* -LIGHTED or -LIT, -LIGHTING, -LIGHTS to lead astray by its light

MISLIKE *v* -LIKED, -LIKING, -LIKES to dislike

MISLIKER *n* pl. -S one that mislikes

MISLIT a past tense of mislight

MISLIVE *v* -LIVED, -LIVING, -LIVES to live a bad life

MISLODGE *v* -LODGED, -LODGING, -LODGES to lodge in a wrong place

MISLYING present participle of mislie

MISMAKE *v* -MADE, -MAKING, -MAKES to make incorrectly

MISMARK *v* -ED, -ING, -S to mark wrongly

MISMATCH *v* -ED, -ING, -ES to match badly

MISMATE *v* -MATED, -MATING, -MATES to mate unsuitably

MISMEET *v* -MET, -MEETING, -MEETS to meet under unfortunate circumstances

MISMOVE *v* -MOVED, -MOVING, -MOVES to move wrongly

MISNAME *v* -NAMED, -NAMING, -NAMES to call by a wrong name

MISNOMER *n* pl. -S a name wrongly used

MISO *n* pl. -SOS a type of food paste

MISOGAMY *n* pl. -MIES a hatred of marriage

MISOGYNY *n* pl. -NIES a hatred of women

MISOLOGY *n* pl. -GIES a hatred of debate or reasoning

MISORDER *v* -ED, -ING, -S to order incorrectly

MISPAGE *v* -PAGED, -PAGING, -PAGES to page incorrectly

MISPAINT *v* -ED, -ING, -S to paint wrongly

MISPARSE *v* -PARSED, -PARSING, -PARSES to parse incorrectly

MISPART *v* -ED, -ING, -S to part badly

MISPATCH *v* -ED, -ING, -ES to patch badly

MISPEN *v* -PENNED, -PENNING, -PENS to write incorrectly

MISPLACE *v* -PLACED, -PLACING, -PLACES to put in a wrong place

MISPLAN *v* -PLANNED, -PLANNING, -PLANS to plan badly

MISPLANT *v* -ED, -ING, -S to plant wrongly

MISPLAY *v* -ED, -ING, -S to make a bad play in a game

MISPLEAD *v* -PLEADED or -PLED, -PLEADING, -PLEADS to plead wrongly or falsely

MISPOINT *v* -ED, -ING, -S to point improperly

MISPOISE *v* -POISED, -POISING, -POISES to poise incorrectly

MISPRICE *v* -PRICED, -PRICING, -PRICES to price incorrectly

MISPRINT *v* -ED, -ING, -S to print incorrectly

MISPRIZE *v* -PRIZED, -PRIZING, -PRIZES to despise

MISQUOTE *v* -QUOTED, -QUOTING, -QUOTES to quote incorrectly

MISRAISE *v* -RAISED, -RAISING, -RAISES to raise wrongly

MISRATE *v* -RATED, -RATING, -RATES to rate incorrectly

MISREAD *v* -READ, -READING, -READS to read incorrectly

MISREFER *v* -FERRED, -FERRING, -FERS to refer incorrectly

MISRELY *v* -LIED, -LYING, -LIES to rely wrongly

MISROUTE *v* -ROUTED, -ROUTING, -ROUTES to route incorrectly

MISRULE *v* -RULED, -RULING, -RULES to rule unwisely or unjustly

MISS *v* -ED, -ING, -ES to fail to make contact with

MISSABLE *adj* able to be missed

MISSAL *n* pl. -S a prayer book

MISSAY *v* -SAID, -SAYING, -SAYS to say incorrectly

MISSEAT *v* -ED, -ING, -S to seat wrongly

MISSEL *n* pl. -S a European thrush

MISSEND *v* -SENT, -SENDING, -SENDS to send incorrectly

MISSENSE *n* pl. -S a form of genetic mutation

MISSET *v* -SET, -SETTING, -SETS to set incorrectly

MISSHAPE	*v* -SHAPED, -SHAPEN, -SHAPING, -SHAPES to shape badly
MISSHOD	*adj* improperly shod
MISSIES	pl. of missy
MISSILE	*n* pl. -S an object or weapon that is thrown or projected
MISSILRY	*n* pl. -RIES the science of designing and operating guided missiles
MISSION	*v* -ED, -ING, -S to send to perform a specific task
MISSIS	*n* pl. -SISES a wife
MISSIVE	*n* pl. -S a written communication
MISSORT	*v* -ED, -ING, -S to sort badly or improperly
MISSOUND	*v* -ED, -ING, -S to sound wrongly
MISSOUT	*n* pl. -S a losing throw of dice
MISSPACE	*v* -SPACED, -SPACING, -SPACES to space incorrectly
MISSPEAK	*v* -SPOKE, -SPOKEN, -SPEAKING, -SPEAKS to speak incorrectly
MISSPELL	*v* -SPELLED or -SPELT, -SPELLING, -SPELLS to spell incorrectly
MISSPEND	*v* -SPENT, -SPENDING, -SPENDS to spend wrongly
MISSPOKE	past tense of misspeak
MISSPOKEN	past participle of misspeak
MISSTART	*v* -ED, -ING, -S to start off badly
MISSTATE	*v* -STATED, -STATING, -STATES to state wrongly
MISSTEER	*v* -ED, -ING, -S to steer wrongly
MISSTEP	*n* pl. -S a false step
MISSTOP	*v* -STOPPED, -STOPPING, -STOPS to stop wrongly
MISSTYLE	*v* -STYLED, -STYLING, -STYLES to style or call wrongly
MISSUIT	*v* -ED, -ING, -S to suit badly
MISSUS	*n* pl. -ES missis
MISSY	*n* pl. MISSIES a young girl
MIST	*v* -ED, -ING, -S to become blurry
MISTAKE	*v* -TOOK or -TEUK, -TAKEN, -TAKING, -TAKES to interpret wrongly
MISTAKER	*n* pl. -S one that mistakes
MISTBOW	*n* pl. -S a fogbow
MISTEACH	*v* -TAUGHT, -TEACHING, -TEACHES to teach wrongly or badly

MISTEND	*v* -ED, -ING, -S to tend to improperly
MISTER	*n* pl. -S sir
MISTERM	*v* -ED, -ING, -S to call by a wrong name
MISTEUK	a past tense of mistake
MISTHINK	*v* -THOUGHT, -THINKING, -THINKS to think wrongly
MISTHROW	*v* -THREW, -THROWN, -THROWING, -THROWS to throw errantly
MISTIER	comparative of misty
MISTIEST	superlative of misty
MISTILY	*adv* in a misty manner
MISTIME	*v* -TIMED, -TIMING, -TIMES to time wrongly
MISTITLE	*v* -TLED, -TLING, -TLES to call by a wrong title
MISTOOK	a past tense of mistake
MISTOUCH	*v* -ED, -ING, -ES to touch improperly
MISTRACE	*v* -TRACED, -TRACING, -TRACES to trace wrongly
MISTRAIN	*v* -ED, -ING, -S to train improperly
MISTRAL	*n* pl. -S a cold, dry wind
MISTREAT	*v* -ED, -ING, -S to treat badly
MISTRESS	*n* pl. -ES a woman in a position of authority
MISTRIAL	*n* pl. -S a trial made invalid because of some error in procedure
MISTRUST	*v* -ED, -ING, -S to distrust
MISTRUTH	*n* pl. -S a lie
MISTRYST	*v* -ED, -ING, -S to fail to keep an appointment with
MISTUNE	*v* -TUNED, -TUNING, -TUNES to tune incorrectly
MISTUTOR	*v* -ED, -ING, -S to instruct or bring up badly
MISTY	*adj* MISTIER, MISTIEST blurry
MISTYPE	*v* -TYPED, -TYPING, -TYPES to type incorrectly
MISUNION	*n* pl. -S a bad union
MISUSAGE	*n* pl. -S incorrect use
MISUSE	*v* -USED, -USING, -USES to use incorrectly
MISUSER	*n* pl. -S one that misuses
MISVALUE	*v* -UED, -UING, -UES to value incorrectly

MISWORD *v* -ED, -ING, -S to word wrongly

MISWRITE *v* -WROTE or -WRIT, -WRITTEN, -WRITING, -WRITES to write incorrectly

MISYOKE *v* -YOKED, -YOKING, -YOKES to yoke improperly

MITE *n* pl. -S a small arachnid

MITER *v* -ED, -ING, -S to raise to the rank of a bishop

MITERER *n* pl. -S one that miters

MITHER *n* pl. -S mother

MITICIDE *n* pl. -S a substance used to kill mites

MITIER comparative of mity

MITIEST superlative of mity

MITIGATE *v* -GATED, -GATING, -GATES to make less severe

MITIS *n* pl. -TISES a type of wrought iron

MITOGEN *n* pl. -S a substance that induces mitosis

MITOSIS *n* pl. -TOSES a type of cell division **MITOTIC** *adj*

MITRAL *adj* pertaining to a valve of the heart

MITRE *v* -TRED, -TRING, -TRES to miter

MITSVAH *n* pl. -VAHS or -VOTH mitzvah

MITT *n* pl. -S a type of baseball glove

MITTEN *n* pl. -S a type of covering for the hand

MITTIMUS *n* pl. -ES a warrant committing a person to prison

MITY *adj* MITIER, MITIEST infested with mites

MITZVAH *n* pl. -VAHS or -VOTH a commandment of Jewish law

MIX *v* MIXED or MIXT, MIXING, MIXES to put together into one mass **MIXABLE, MIXIBLE** *adj*

MIXER *n* pl. -S one that mixes

MIXOLOGY *n* pl. -GIES the art of making mixed drinks

MIXT a past tense of mix

MIXTURE *n* pl. -S something produced by mixing

MIXUP *n* pl. -S a state of confusion

MIZEN *n* pl. -S mizzen

MIZZEN *n* pl. -S a type of sail

MIZZLE *v* -ZLED, -ZLING, -ZLES to rain in fine droplets

MIZZLY *adj* characterized by a fine rain

MM *interj* — used to express assent or satisfaction

MNEMONIC *n* pl. -S a device to assist the memory

MO *n* pl. MOS a moment

MOA *n* pl. -S an extinct flightless bird

MOAN *v* -ED, -ING, -S to utter a low, mournful sound

MOANER *n* pl. -S one that moans

MOANFUL *adj* moaning

MOAT *v* -ED, -ING, -S to surround with a moat (a water-filled trench)

MOATLIKE *adj* suggestive of a moat

MOB *v* MOBBED, MOBBING, MOBS to crowd about

MOBBER *n* pl. -S one that mobs

MOBBISH *adj* characteristic of a mob (a disorderly crowd of people)

MOBCAP *n* pl. -S a woman's cap

MOBILE *n* pl. -S a form of sculpture

MOBILISE *v* -LISED, -LISING, -LISES to mobilize

MOBILITY *n* pl. -TIES the ability to move

MOBILIZE *v* -LIZED, -LIZING, -LIZES to put into movement

MOBLED *adj* wrapped in or as if in a hood

MOBOCRAT *n* pl. -S a supporter of mob rule

MOBSTER *n* pl. -S a gangster

MOC *n* pl. -S a moccasin

MOCCASIN *n* pl. -S a type of shoe

MOCHA *n* pl. -S a choice, pungent coffee

MOCHILA *n* pl. -S a leather covering for a saddle

MOCK *v* -ED, -ING, -S to ridicule **MOCKABLE** *adj*

MOCKER *n* pl. -S one that mocks

MOCKERY *n* pl. -ERIES the act of mocking

MOCKUP *n* pl. -S a full-sized model

MOD *n* pl. -S one who wears boldly stylish clothes

MODAL *adj* pertaining to a mode **MODALLY** *adv*

MODALITY *n* pl. -TIES the state of being modal

MODE *n* pl. -S a method of doing or acting

MODEL	v -ELED, -ELING, -ELS or -ELLED, -ELLING, -ELS to plan or form after a pattern	**MOG**	v MOGGED, MOGGING, MOGS to move away
MODELER	n pl. -S one that models	**MOGGIE**	n pl. -S moggy
MODELING	n pl. -S the treatment of volume in sculpture	**MOGGY**	n pl. -GIES a cat
MODELIST	n pl. -S one who makes models	**MOGUL**	n pl. -S an important person
MODELLED	a past tense of model	**MOHAIR**	n pl. -S the long, silky hair of the Angora goat
MODELLER	n pl. -S modeler	**MOHEL**	n pl. -HALIM, -HELIM or -HELS a person who performs Jewish ritual circumcisions
MODELLING	a present participle of model		
MODEM	n pl. -S a device for converting signals from one form to another	**MOHUR**	n pl. -S a former gold coin of India
MODERATE	v -ATED, -ATING, -ATES to make less extreme	**MOIDORE**	n pl. -S a former gold coin of Portugal
MODERATO	n pl. -TOS a musical passage played at a medium tempo	**MOIETY**	n pl. -ETIES a half
		MOIL	v -ED, -ING, -S to work hard
MODERN	adj -ERNER, -ERNEST pertaining to present or recent time **MODERNLY** adv	**MOILER**	n pl. -S one that moils
		MOIRA	n pl. -RAI fate or destiny, in ancient Greek religion
MODERN	n pl. -S a person of modern times or views	**MOIRE**	n pl. -S a fabric having a wavy pattern
MODERNE	adj pretentiously modern	**MOIST**	adj MOISTER, MOISTEST slightly wet
MODEST	adj -ESTER, -ESTEST having a moderate regard for oneself **MODESTLY** adv	**MOISTEN**	v -ED, -ING, -S to make or become moist
		MOISTFUL	adj moist
MODESTY	n pl. -TIES the quality of being modest	**MOISTLY**	adv in a moist manner
MODI	pl. of modus	**MOISTURE**	n pl. -S condensed or diffused liquid
MODICUM	n pl. -CA or -CUMS a small amount	**MOJARRA**	n pl. -S a marine fish
MODIFIER	n pl. -S one that modifies	**MOJO**	n pl. -JOS or -JOES a magic charm
MODIFY	v -FIED, -FYING, -FIES to change in form or character	**MOKE**	n pl. -S a donkey
MODIOLUS	n pl. -LI a bony shaft of the inner ear	**MOL**	n pl. -S mole
		MOLA	n pl. -S a marine fish
MODISH	adj stylish **MODISHLY** adv	**MOLAL**	adj pertaining to a mole
MODISTE	n pl. -S a dealer in stylish women's clothing	**MOLALITY**	n pl. -TIES the number of moles of solute per liter of solvent
MODULAR	adj pertaining to a module	**MOLAR**	n pl. -S a grinding tooth
MODULATE	v -LATED, -LATING, -LATES to adjust to a certain proportion	**MOLARITY**	n pl. -TIES the number of moles of solute per liter of solution
MODULE	n pl. -S a standard of measurement	**MOLASSES**	n pl. -LASSESES a thick syrup
MODULO	adv with respect to a modulus	**MOLD**	v -ED, -ING, -S to work into a particular shape **MOLDABLE** adj
MODULUS	n pl. -LI a number that produces the same remainder when divided into each of two numbers	**MOLDER**	v -ED, -ING, -S to turn to dust by natural decay
MODUS	n pl. -DI a mode	**MOLDIER**	comparative of moldy
MOFETTE	n pl. -S a noxious emanation from a fissure in the earth	**MOLDIEST**	superlative of moldy
		MOLDING	n pl. -S a long, narrow strip used to decorate a surface
MOFFETTE	n pl. -S mofette		

MOLDWARP	*n* pl. -S a burrowing mammal
MOLDY	*adj* MOLDIER, MOLDIEST musty
MOLE	*n* pl. -S the quantity of a compound that has a weight equal to the compound's molecular weight
MOLECULE	*n* pl. -S the smallest physical unit of an element
MOLEHILL	*n* pl. -S a small mound of earth
MOLESKIN	*n* pl. -S a cotton fabric
MOLEST	*v* -ED, -ING, -S to disturb or annoy
MOLESTER	*n* pl. -S one that molests
MOLIES	pl. of moly
MOLINE	*adj* having arms forked and curved at the ends — used of a heraldic cross
MOLL	*n* pl. -S a gangster's girlfriend
MOLLAH	*n* pl. -S mullah
MOLLIE	*n* pl. -S a tropical fish
MOLLIES	pl. of molly
MOLLIFY	*v* -FIED, -FYING, -FIES to soothe
MOLLUSC	*n* pl. -S mollusk
MOLLUSK	*n* pl. -S any of a phylum of soft-bodied invertebrates
MOLLY	*n* pl. -LIES mollie
MOLOCH	*n* pl. -S a spiny lizard
MOLT	*v* -ED, -ING, -S to cast off an outer covering
MOLTEN	*adj* made liquid by heat **MOLTENLY** *adv*
MOLTER	*n* pl. -S one that molts
MOLTO	*adv* very — used in musical directions
MOLY	*n* pl. -LIES a wild garlic
MOLYBDIC	*adj* pertaining to a certain metallic element
MOM	*n* pl. -S mother
MOME	*n* pl. -S a fool
MOMENT	*n* pl. -S a brief period of time
MOMENTA	a pl. of momentum
MOMENTLY	*adv* from moment to moment
MOMENTO	*n* pl. -TOS or -TOES memento
MOMENTUM	*n* pl. -TA or -TUMS force of movement
MOMI	a pl. of momus
MOMISM	*n* pl. -S an excessive dependence on mothers
MOMMA	*n* pl. -S mother
MOMMY	*n* pl. -MIES mother
MOMSER	*n* pl. -S a bastard
MOMUS	*n* pl. -MUSES or -MI a carping person
MOMZER	*n* pl. -S momser
MON	*n* pl. MEN man
MONACHAL	*adj* pertaining to monks
MONACID	*n* pl. -S monoacid
MONAD	*n* pl. -S a single-celled organism **MONADAL, MONADIC** *adj*
MONADES	pl. of monas
MONADISM	*n* pl. -S a philosophical doctrine
MONANDRY	*n* pl. -DRIES the condition of having one husband at a time
MONARCH	*n* pl. -S an absolute ruler
MONARCHY	*n* pl. -CHIES rule by a monarch
MONARDA	*n* pl. -S an aromatic herb
MONAS	*n* pl. MONADES a monad
MONASTIC	*n* pl. -S a monk
MONAURAL	*adj* pertaining to sound transmission, recording, or reproduction involving a single transmission path
MONAXIAL	*adj* having one axis
MONAXON	*n* pl. -S a straight spicule in sponges
MONAZITE	*n* pl. -S a mineral
MONDE	*n* pl. -S the world
MONDO	*n* pl. -DOS a rapid question and answer technique employed in Zen Buddhism
MONECIAN	*adj* having both male and female sex organs in the same individual
MONELLIN	*n* pl. -S a protein extracted from a West African red berry
MONERAN	*n* pl. -S a cellular organism that does not have a distinct nucleus
MONETARY	*adj* pertaining to money
MONETISE	*v* -TISED, -TISING, -TISES to monetize
MONETIZE	*v* -TIZED, -TIZING, -TIZES to coin into money
MONEY	*n* pl. MONEYS or MONIES an official medium of exchange and measure of value
MONEYBAG	*n* pl. -S a bag for holding money
MONEYED	*adj* having much money
MONEYER	*n* pl. -S one that coins money

MONEYMAN *n* pl. -MEN a person who invests large sums of money

MONGEESE a pl. of mongoose

MONGER *v* -ED, -ING, -S to peddle

MONGO *n* pl. -GOS mungo

MONGOE *n* pl. -S mungo

MONGOL *n* pl. -S a person affected with a form of mental deficiency

MONGOOSE *n* pl. -GOOSES or -GEESE a carnivorous mammal

MONGREL *n* pl. -S an animal or plant of mixed breed

MONGST *prep* amongst

MONICKER *n* pl. -S moniker

MONIE *adj* many

MONIED *adj* moneyed

MONIES a pl. of money

MONIKER *n* pl. -S a name

MONISH *v* -ED, -ING, -ES to warn

MONISM *n* pl. -S a philosophical theory

MONIST *n* pl. -S an adherent of monism **MONISTIC** *adj*

MONITION *n* pl. -S a warning

MONITIVE *adj* giving warning

MONITOR *v* -ED, -ING, -S to keep track of

MONITORY *n* pl. -RIES a letter of warning

MONK *n* pl. -S a man who is a member of a secluded religious order

MONKERY *n* pl. -ERIES the mode of life of monks

MONKEY *v* -ED, -ING, -S to mimic

MONKFISH *n* pl. -ES a marine fish

MONKHOOD *n* pl. -S the state of being a monk

MONKISH *adj* pertaining to monks

MONO *n* pl. MONOS an infectious disease

MONOACID *n* pl. -S a type of acid

MONOCARP *n* pl. -S a plant that yields fruit only once before dying

MONOCLE *n* pl. -S an eyeglass for one eye **MONOCLED** *adj*

MONOCOT *n* pl. -S a type of seed plant

MONOCRAT *n* pl. -S an autocrat

MONOCYTE *n* pl. -S a type of white blood cell

MONODIST *n* pl. -S one who writes monodies

MONODY *n* pl. -DIES an elegy performed by one person **MONODIC** *adj*

MONOECY *n* pl. -CIES the condition of being monecian

MONOFIL *n* pl. -S a single filament of synthetic fiber

MONOFUEL *n* pl. -S a type of rocket propellant

MONOGAMY *n* pl. -MIES marriage with one person at a time

MONOGENY *n* pl. -NIES asexual reproduction

MONOGERM *adj* being a fruit that produces a single plant

MONOGLOT *n* pl. -S a person speaking or writing only one language

MONOGRAM *v* -GRAMED, -GRAMING, -GRAMS or -GRAMMED, -GRAMMING, -GRAMS to mark with a design of one's initials

MONOGYNY *n* pl. -NIES the condition of having one wife at a time

MONOHULL *n* pl. -S a vessel with a single hull

MONOLITH *n* pl. -S a large block of stone

MONOLOG *n* pl. -S a lengthy speech by one person

MONOLOGY *n* pl. -GIES the act of uttering a monolog

MONOMER *n* pl. -S a type of chemical compound

MONOMIAL *n* pl. -S an algebraic expression consisting of a single term

MONOPODE *n* pl. -S a creature having one foot

MONOPODY *n* pl. -DIES a measure consisting of a single metrical foot

MONOPOLE *n* pl. -S a type of radio antenna

MONOPOLY *n* pl. -LIES exclusive control of a commodity or service in a particular market

MONORAIL *n* pl. -S a single rail serving as a track for a wheeled vehicle

MONOSOME *n* pl. -S an unpaired chromosome

MONOSOMY *n* pl. -MIES a condition of having one unpaired chromosome

MONOTINT *n* pl. -S a painting done in different shades of one color

MONOTONE *n* pl. -S a vocal utterance in one unvaried tone

MONOTONY *n* pl. -NIES tedious sameness

MONOTYPE *n* pl. -S the only representative of its group

MONOXIDE *n* pl. -S a type of oxide

MONS *n* pl. MONTES a protuberance of the body

MONSIEUR *n* pl. MESSIEURS a French title of courtesy for a man

MONSOON *n* pl. -S a seasonal wind

MONSTER *n* pl. -S a strange or terrifying creature

MONSTERA *n* pl. -S a tropical American plant

MONTAGE *v* -TAGED, -TAGING, -TAGES to combine into a composite picture

MONTANE *n* pl. -S the lower vegetation belt of a mountain

MONTE *n* pl. -S a card game

MONTEITH *n* pl. -S a large punch bowl

MONTERO *n* pl. -ROS a type of cap

MONTES pl. of mons

MONTH *n* pl. -S a period of approximately 30 days

MONTHLY *n* pl. -LIES a publication issued once a month

MONUMENT *n* pl. -S a structure built as a memorial

MONURON *n* pl. -S an herbicide

MONY *adj* many

MOO *v* -ED, -ING, -S to make the deep, moaning sound of a cow

MOOCH *v* -ED, -ING, -ES to obtain without paying

MOOCHER *n* pl. -S one that mooches

MOOD *n* pl. -S a person's emotional state at a particular moment

MOODY *adj* MOODIER, MOODIEST given to changing moods **MOODILY** *adv*

MOOL *n* pl. -S soft soil

MOOLA *n* pl. -S moolah

MOOLAH *n* pl. -S money

MOOLEY *n* pl. -EYS muley

MOON *v* -ED, -ING, -S to spend time idly

MOONBEAM *n* pl. -S a ray of light from the moon (the earth's natural satellite)

MOONBOW *n* pl. -S a rainbow formed by light from the moon

MOONCALF *n* pl. -CALVES a foolish person

MOONDUST *n* pl. -S dust on the moon

MOONEYE *n* pl. -S a freshwater fish

MOONFISH *n* pl. -ES a marine fish

MOONIER comparative of moony

MOONIEST superlative of moony

MOONILY *adv* in a moony manner

MOONISH *adj* fickle

MOONLESS *adj* lacking the light of the moon

MOONLET *n* pl. -S a small satellite

MOONLIKE *adj* resembling the moon

MOONLIT *adj* lighted by the moon

MOONPORT *n* pl. -S a facility for launching spacecraft to the moon

MOONRISE *n* pl. -S the rising of the moon above the horizon

MOONSAIL *n* pl. -S a light, square sail

MOONSEED *n* pl. -S a climbing plant

MOONSET *n* pl. -S the setting of the moon below the horizon

MOONSHOT *n* pl. -S the launching of a spacecraft to the moon

MOONWALK *n* pl. -S an instance of walking on the moon

MOONWARD *adv* toward the moon

MOONWORT *n* pl. -S a flowering plant

MOONY *adj* MOONIER, MOONIEST resembling the moon

MOOR *v* -ED, -ING, -S to secure a vessel by means of cables

MOORAGE *n* pl. -S the act of mooring

MOORCOCK *n* pl. -S the male moorfowl

MOORFOWL *n* pl. -S a game bird

MOORHEN *n* pl. -S the female moorfowl

MOORIER comparative of moory

MOORIEST superlative of moory

MOORING *n* pl. -S a place where a vessel may be moored

MOORISH *adj* marshy

MOORLAND *n* pl. -S a tract of marshy land

MOORWORT *n* pl. -S a marsh plant

MOORY *adj* MOORIER, MOORIEST marshy

MOOSE *n* pl. MOOSE a ruminant mammal

MOOT *v* -ED, -ING, -S to bring up for discussion

MOOTER *n* pl. -S one that moots

MOP *v* MOPPED, MOPPING, MOPS to wipe with a mop (an implement for cleaning floors)

MOPBOARD *n* pl. -S a board at the base of a wall

MOPE   v MOPED, MOPING, MOPES to act in a dejected or gloomy manner

MOPED   n pl. -S a type of motorbike

MOPER   n pl. -S one that mopes

MOPERY   n pl. -PERIES an act of dawdling

MOPEY   adj MOPIER, MOPIEST dejected

MOPIER   comparative of mopy

MOPIEST   superlative of mopy

MOPING   present participle of mope

MOPINGLY   adv in a moping manner

MOPISH   adj given to moping **MOPISHLY** adv

MOPOKE   n pl. -S an Australian bird

MOPPED   past tense of mop

MOPPER   n pl. -S one that mops

MOPPET   n pl. -S a child

MOPPING   present participle of mop

MOPY   adj MOPIER, MOPIEST mopey

MOQUETTE   n pl. -S a woolen fabric

MOR   n pl. -S a forest humus

MORA   n pl. -RAE or -RAS a unit of metrical time in prosody

MORAINE   n pl. -S an accumulation of debris deposited by a glacier **MORAINAL, MORAINIC** adj

MORAL   adj pertaining to principles of right and wrong **MORALLY** adv

MORALE   n pl. -S the state of the spirits of an individual or group

MORALISE   v -ISED, -ISING, -ISES to moralize

MORALISM   n pl. -S the practice of moralizing

MORALIST   n pl. -S a teacher of morality

MORALITY   n pl. -TIES conformity to the rules of right conduct

MORALIZE   v -IZED, -IZING, -IZES to explain in a moral sense

MORALS   n/pl rules of conduct with respect to right and wrong

MORASS   n pl. -ES a marsh **MORASSY** adj

MORATORY   adj authorizing delay of payment

MORAY   n pl. -RAYS a tropical eel

MORBID   adj gruesome **MORBIDLY** adv

MORBIFIC   adj causing disease

MORBILLI   n/pl a virus disease

MORCEAU   n pl. -CEAUX a short literary or musical composition

MORDANCY   n pl. -CIES a sarcastic quality

MORDANT   v -ED, -ING, -S to treat with a caustic substance

MORDENT   n pl. -S a melodic embellishment

MORE   n pl. -S a greater amount

MOREEN   n pl. -S a heavy fabric

MOREL   n pl. -S an edible mushroom

MORELLE   n pl. -S a flowering plant

MORELLO   n pl. -LOS a variety of sour cherry

MOREOVER   adv in addition

MORESQUE   n pl. -S an ancient decorative style

MORGAN   n pl. -S a unit of distance between genes

MORGEN   n pl. -S a Dutch unit of land area

MORGUE   n pl. -S a place where dead bodies are kept for identification

MORIBUND   adj being about to die

MORION   n pl. -S a type of helmet

MORN   n pl. -S morning

MORNING   n pl. -S the early part of the day

MOROCCO   n pl. -COS a soft leather

MORON   n pl. -S a mentally deficient person **MORONIC** adj

MORONISM   n pl. -S the condition of being a moron

MORONITY   n pl. -TIES moronism

MOROSE   adj sullen **MOROSELY** adv

MOROSITY   n pl. -TIES the state of being morose

MORPH   n pl. -S a type of phoneme

MORPHEME   n pl. -S a linguistic unit

MORPHIA   n pl. -S morphine

MORPHIC   adj pertaining to form

MORPHIN   n pl. -S morphine

MORPHINE   n pl. -S a narcotic alkaloid

MORPHO   n pl. -PHOS a tropical butterfly

MORRION   n pl. -S morion

MORRIS   n pl. -RISES an English folk dance

MORRO   n pl. -ROS a rounded elevation

MORROW   n pl. -S the next day

MORSE   adj designating a code used in telegraphy

MORSEL   v -SELED, -SELING, -SELS or -SELLED, -SELLING, -SELS to divide into small pieces

MORT   *n* pl. -S a note sounded on a hunting horn to announce the killing of an animal

MORTAL   *n* pl. -S a human being

MORTALLY   *adv* fatally

MORTAR   *v* -ED, -ING, -S to secure with mortar (a type of cement)

MORTARY   *adj* containing or resembling mortar

MORTGAGE   *v* -GAGED, -GAGING, -GAGES to pledge to a creditor as security

MORTICE   *v* -TICED, -TICING, -TICES to mortise

MORTIFY   *v* -FIED, -FYING, -FIES to humiliate

MORTISE   *v* -TISED, -TISING, -TISES to join or fasten securely

MORTISER   *n* pl. -S one that mortises

MORTMAIN   *n* pl. -S perpetual ownership of land

MORTUARY   *n* pl. -ARIES a place where dead bodies are kept until burial

MORULA   *n* pl. -LAE or -LAS an embryonic mass of cells **MORULAR** *adj*

MOSAIC   *v* -ICKED, -ICKING, -ICS to form into a mosaic (a type of inlaid surface decoration)

MOSASAUR   *n* pl. -S an extinct lizard

MOSCHATE   *adj* musky

MOSEY   *v* -ED, -ING, -S to saunter

MOSHAV   *n* pl. -SHAVIM a cooperative settlement of small farms in Israel

MOSK   *n* pl. -S mosque

MOSQUE   *n* pl. -S a Muslim house of worship

MOSQUITO   *n* pl. -TOES or -TOS a winged insect

MOSS   *v* -ED, -ING, -ES to cover with moss (a growth of small, leafy-stemmed plants)

MOSSBACK   *n* pl. -S a large, old fish

MOSSER   *n* pl. -S one that gathers or works with moss

MOSSIER   comparative of mossy

MOSSIEST   superlative of mossy

MOSSLIKE   *adj* resembling moss

MOSSO   *adv* rapidly — used as a musical direction

MOSSY   *adj* MOSSIER, MOSSIEST covered with moss

MOST   *n* pl. -S the greatest amount

MOSTE   past tense of mote

MOSTEST   *n* pl. -S most

MOSTLY   *adv* mainly

MOT   *n* pl. -S a witty saying

MOTE   *v* past tense MOSTE may

MOTE   *n* pl. -S a small particle

MOTEL   *n* pl. -S a roadside hotel

MOTET   *n* pl. -S a type of choral composition

MOTEY   *adj* full of motes

MOTH   *n* pl. -S a winged insect

MOTHBALL   *v* -ED, -ING, -S to put into storage

MOTHER   *v* -ED, -ING, -S to give birth to

MOTHERLY   *adj* maternal

MOTHERY   *adj* slimy

MOTHLIKE   *adj* resembling a moth

MOTHY   *adj* MOTHIER, MOTHIEST full of moths

MOTIF   *n* pl. -S a recurring thematic element in an artistic work **MOTIFIC** *adj*

MOTILE   *n* pl. -S one whose mental imagery consists chiefly of inner feelings of action

MOTILITY   *n* pl. -TIES the ability to move

MOTION   *v* -ED, -ING, -S to signal by a bodily movement

MOTIONAL   *adj* pertaining to movement

MOTIONER   *n* pl. -S one that motions

MOTIVATE   *v* -VATED, -VATING, -VATES to provide with an incentive

MOTIVE   *v* -TIVED, -TIVING, -TIVES to motivate

MOTIVIC   *adj* pertaining to a musical motif

MOTIVITY   *n* pl. -TIES the ability to move

MOTLEY   *adj* -LEYER, -LEYEST or -LIER, -LIEST composed of diverse elements

MOTLEY   *n* pl. -LEYS a garment of various colors

MOTMOT   *n* pl. -S a tropical bird

MOTOR   *v* -ED, -ING, -S to travel by automobile

MOTORBUS   *n* pl. -BUSES or -BUSSES a bus

MOTORCAR   *n* pl. -S an automobile

MOTORDOM   *n* pl. -S the motor vehicle industry

MOTORIC *adj* pertaining to muscular movement

MOTORING *n* pl. -S the recreation of traveling by automobile

MOTORISE *v* -ISED, -ISING, -ISES to motorize

MOTORIST *n* pl. -S one who travels by automobile

MOTORIZE *v* -IZED, -IZING, -IZES to equip with motor vehicles

MOTORMAN *n* pl. -MEN one who operates an electric streetcar or subway train

MOTORWAY *n* pl. -WAYS a type of highway

MOTT *n* pl. -S motte

MOTTE *n* pl. -S a small growth of trees on a prairie

MOTTLE *v* -TLED, -TLING, -TLES to mark with spots or streaks of different colors

MOTTLER *n* pl. -S one that mottles

MOTTO *n* pl. -TOES or -TOS a short expression of a guiding principle

MOUCH *v* -ED, -ING, -ES to mooch

MOUCHOIR *n* pl. -S a small handkerchief

MOUE *n* pl. -S a pouting grimace

MOUFFLON *n* pl. -S mouflon

MOUFLON *n* pl. -S a wild sheep

MOUILLE *adj* pronounced with the front of the tongue against the palate

MOUJIK *n* pl. -S muzhik

MOULAGE *n* pl. -S the making of a cast or mold of a mark for use in a criminal investigation

MOULD *v* -ED, -ING, -S to mold

MOULDER *v* -ED, -ING, -S to molder

MOULDING *n* pl. -S molding

MOULDY *adj* MOULDIER, MOULDIEST moldy

MOULIN *n* pl. -S a vertical cavity in a glacier

MOULT *v* -ED, -ING, -S to molt

MOULTER *n* pl. -S molter

MOUND *v* -ED, -ING, -S to pile

MOUNT *v* -ED, -ING, -S to get up on

MOUNTAIN *n* pl. -S a large, natural elevation of the earth's surface

MOUNTER *n* pl. -S one that mounts

MOUNTING *n* pl. -S something that provides a backing or appropriate setting for something else

MOURN *v* -ED, -ING, -S to feel or express grief or sorrow

MOURNER *n* pl. -S one that mourns

MOURNFUL *adj* -FULLER, -FULLEST expressing grief or sorrow

MOURNING *n* pl. -S an outward sign of grief

MOUSE *n* pl. MICE a small rodent

MOUSE *v* MOUSED, MOUSING, MOUSES to catch mice

MOUSER *n* pl. -S an animal that catches mice

MOUSEY *adj* MOUSIER, MOUSIEST mousy

MOUSIER comparative of mousy

MOUSIEST superlative of mousy

MOUSILY *adv* in a mousy manner

MOUSING *n* pl. -S a wrapping around the shank end of a hook

MOUSSAKA *n* pl. -S a Middle Eastern dish of meat and eggplant

MOUSSE *v* MOUSSED, MOUSSING, MOUSSES to style with mousse (foamy preparation used in styling hair)

MOUSY *adj* MOUSIER, MOUSIEST resembling a mouse

MOUTH *v* -ED, -ING, -S to put into the mouth

MOUTHER *n* pl. -S a speaker

MOUTHFUL *n* pl. -S as much as the mouth can hold

MOUTHY *adj* MOUTHIER, MOUTHIEST very talkative **MOUTHILY** *adv*

MOUTON *n* pl. -S sheepskin processed to resemble seal or beaver

MOVABLE *n* pl. -S something that can be moved

MOVABLY *adv* so as to be capable of being moved

MOVE *v* MOVED, MOVING, MOVES to change from one position to another

MOVEABLE *n* pl. -S movable

MOVEABLY *adv* movably

MOVED past tense of move

MOVELESS *adj* incapable of movement

MOVEMENT *n* pl. -S the act of moving

MOVER *n* pl. -S one that moves

MOVIE *n* pl. -S a motion picture

MOVIEDOM *n* pl. -S filmdom

MOVIEOLA *n* pl. -S a device for viewing and editing film

MOVING present participle of move

MOVINGLY *adv* so as to affect the emotions

MOVIOLA *n* pl. -S movieola

MOW *v* MOWED, MOWN, MOWING, MOWS to cut down standing herbage

MOWER *n* pl. -S one that mows

MOWING *n* pl. -S the act of cutting down standing herbage

MOXA *n* pl. -S a Chinese plant

MOXIE *n* pl. -S spirit or courage

MOZETTA *n* pl. -TAS or -TE mozzetta

MOZO *n* pl. -ZOS a manual laborer

MOZZETTA *n* pl. -TAS or -TE a hooded cape worn by bishops

MRIDANGA *n* pl. -S a drum of India

MU *n* pl. -S a Greek letter

MUCH *n* pl. -ES a great amount

MUCHACHO *n* pl. -CHOS a young man

MUCHLY *adv* very much

MUCHNESS *n* pl. -ES the quality of being great

MUCID *adj* musty

MUCIDITY *n* pl. -TIES the state of being mucid

MUCILAGE *n* pl. -S an adhesive substance

MUCIN *n* pl. -S a protein secreted by the mucous membranes **MUCINOID, MUCINOUS** *adj*

MUCK *v* -ED, -ING, -S to fertilize with manure

MUCKER *n* pl. -S a vulgar person

MUCKIER comparative of mucky

MUCKIEST superlative of mucky

MUCKILY *adv* in a mucky manner

MUCKLE *n* pl. -S a large amount

MUCKLUCK *n* pl. -S mukluk

MUCKRAKE *v* -RAKED, -RAKING, -RAKES to search for and expose corruption

MUCKWORM *n* pl. -S a worm found in manure

MUCKY *adj* MUCKIER, MUCKIEST filthy

MUCLUC *n* pl. -S mukluk

MUCOID *n* pl. -S a complex protein **MUCOIDAL** *adj*

MUCOR *n* pl. -S a type of fungus

MUCOSA *n* pl. -SAE or -SAS a mucous membrane **MUCOSAL** *adj*

MUCOSE *adj* mucous

MUCOSITY *n* pl. -TIES the state of being mucous

MUCOUS *adj* secreting or containing mucus

MUCRO *n* pl. -CRONES a sharp point at the end of certain plant and animal organs

MUCUS *n* pl. -ES a viscid bodily fluid

MUD *v* MUDDED, MUDDING, MUDS to cover with mud (soft, wet earth)

MUDCAP *v* -CAPPED, -CAPPING, -CAPS to cover an explosive with mud before detonating

MUDCAT *n* pl. -S a type of catfish

MUDDER *n* pl. -S a racehorse that runs well on a muddy track

MUDDIED past tense of muddy

MUDDIER comparative of muddy

MUDDIES present 3d person sing. of muddy

MUDDIEST superlative of muddy

MUDDILY *adv* in a muddy manner

MUDDING present participle of mud

MUDDLE *v* -DLED, -DLING, -DLES to mix in a disordered manner

MUDDLER *n* pl. -S one that muddles

MUDDLY *adj* disordered

MUDDY *adj* -DIER, -DIEST covered or filled with mud

MUDDY *v* -DIED, -DYING, -DIES to make or become muddy

MUDFISH *n* pl. -ES a fish found in mud or muddy water

MUDFLAT *n* pl. -S a level tract alternately covered and left bare by the tide

MUDFLOW *n* pl. -S a moving mass of mud

MUDGUARD *n* pl. -S a fender

MUDHOLE *n* pl. -S a hole or hollow place full of mud

MUDLARK *n* pl. -S a street urchin

MUDPACK *n* pl. -S cosmetic paste for the face

MUDPUPPY *n* pl. -PIES a large salamander

MUDRA *n* pl. -S a hand gesture in East Indian classical dancing

MUDROCK *n* pl. -S pelite

MUDROOM *n* pl. -S a room for shedding muddy clothing or footwear

MUDSILL *n* pl. -S the lowest supporting timber of a structure

MUDSLIDE *n* pl. -S a mudflow down a slope

MUDSTONE *n* pl. -S a type of rock

MUEDDIN *n* pl. -S muezzin

MUENSTER *n* pl. -S a mild cheese

MUESLI *n* pl. -S a breakfast cereal

MUEZZIN *n* pl. -S a Muslim crier who calls the faithful to prayer

MUFF *v* -ED, -ING, -S to bungle

MUFFIN *n* pl. -S a small, round bread

MUFFLE *v* -FLED, -FLING, -FLES to wrap with something to deaden sound

MUFFLER *n* pl. -S a device for deadening sound

MUFTI *n* pl. -S a judge who interprets Muslim religious law

MUG *v* MUGGED, MUGGING, MUGS to assault with intent to rob

MUGFUL *n* pl. -S as much as a mug can hold

MUGG *v* -ED, -ING, -S to make funny faces

MUGGAR *n* pl. -S mugger

MUGGED past tense of mug

MUGGEE *n* pl. -S one who is mugged

MUGGER *n* pl. -S a large Asian crocodile

MUGGIER comparative of muggy

MUGGIEST superlative of muggy

MUGGILY *adv* in a muggy manner

MUGGING *n* pl. -S a street assault or beating

MUGGINS *n* pl. MUGGINS a card game

MUGGUR *n* pl. -S mugger

MUGGY *adj* -GIER, -GIEST warm and humid

MUGWORT *n* pl. -S a flowering plant

MUGWUMP *n* pl. -S a political independent

MUHLY *n* pl. MUHLIES a perennial grass

MUJIK *n* pl. -S muzhik

MUKLUK *n* pl. -S a soft boot worn by Eskimos

MUKTUK *n* pl. -S whale skin used for food

MULATTO *n* pl. -TOES or -TOS the offspring of one white and one black parent

MULBERRY *n* pl. -RIES a tree bearing an edible, berrylike fruit

MULCH *v* -ED, -ING, -ES to provide with a protective covering for the soil

MULCT *v* -ED, -ING, -S to defraud

MULE *v* MULED, MULING, MULES to strike from dies belonging to two different issues, as a coin

MULETA *n* pl. -S a red cloth used by a matador

MULETEER *n* pl. -S one who drives mules (hoofed work animals)

MULEY *n* pl. -LEYS a hornless cow

MULING present participle of mule

MULISH *adj* stubborn **MULISHLY** *adv*

MULL *v* -ED, -ING, -S to ponder

MULLA *n* pl. -S mullah

MULLAH *n* pl. -S a Muslim religious leader or teacher

MULLEIN *n* pl. -S a Eurasian herb

MULLEN *n* pl. -S mullein

MULLER *n* pl. -S a grinding implement

MULLET *n* pl. -S an edible fish

MULLEY *n* pl. -LEYS muley

MULLIGAN *n* pl. -S a stew of various meats and vegetables

MULLION *v* -ED, -ING, -S to provide with vertical dividing strips

MULLITE *n* pl. -S a mineral

MULLOCK *n* pl. -S waste earth or rock from a mine **MULLOCKY** *adj*

MULTIAGE *adj* including people of various ages

MULTICAR *adj* owning or involving several cars

MULTIFID *adj* divided into many parts

MULTIJET *adj* having more than two jets

MULTIPED *n* pl. -S an animal having many feet

MULTIPLE *n* pl. -S the product of a quantity by an integer

MULTIPLY *v* -PLIED, -PLYING, -PLIES to increase in number

MULTITON *adj* weighing many tons

MULTIUSE *adj* having many uses

MULTURE *n* pl. -S a fee paid to a miller for grinding grain

MUM *v* MUMMED, MUMMING, MUMS to act in a disguise

MUMBLE *v* -BLED, -BLING, -BLES to speak unclearly

MUMBLER *n* pl. -S one that mumbles

MUMBLY *adj* given to mumbling

MUMM *v* -ED, -ING, -S to mum

MUMMED past tense of mum and mumm

MUMMER *n* pl. -S one that mums

MUMMERY *n* pl. -MERIES a performance by mummers

MUMMIED past tense of mummy

MUMMIES present 3d person sing. of mummy

MUMMIFY *v* -FIED, -FYING, -FIES to preserve by embalming

MUMMING present participle of mum

MUMMY *v* -MIED, -MYING, -MIES to mummify

MUMP *v* -ED, -ING, -S to beg

MUMPER *n* pl. -S one that mumps

MUMU *n* pl. -S muumuu

MUN *n* pl. -S man; fellow

MUNCH *v* -ED, -ING, -ES to chew with a crackling sound

MUNCHER *n* pl. -S one that munches

MUNCHIES *n/pl* hunger pangs

MUNCHKIN *n* pl. -S a small friendly person

MUNDANE *adj* ordinary

MUNDUNGO *n* pl. -GOS a foul-smelling tobacco

MUNGO *n* pl. -GOS a low-quality wool

MUNGOOSE *n* pl. -S mongoose

MUNI *n* pl. -S a security issued by a state or local government

MUNIMENT *n* pl. -S a means of defense

MUNITION *v* -ED, -ING, -S to furnish with war materiel

MUNNION *n* pl. -S a muntin

MUNSTER *n* pl. -S muenster

MUNTIN *n* pl. -S a dividing strip for window panes

MUNTING *n* pl. -S muntin

MUNTJAC *n* pl. -S a small Asian deer

MUNTJAK *n* pl. -S muntjac

MUON *n* pl. -S a subatomic particle **MUONIC** *adj*

MUONIUM *n* pl. -S an electron and a positive muon bound together

MURA *n* pl. -S a Japanese village

MURAENID *n* pl. -S a moray

MURAL *n* pl. -S a painting applied directly to a wall or ceiling

MURALIST *n* pl. -S a painter of murals

MURDER *v* -ED, -ING, -S to kill unlawfully with premediated malice

MURDEREE *n* pl. -S one that is murdered

MURDERER *n* pl. -S one that murders

MURE *v* MURED, MURING, MURES to immure

MUREIN *n* pl. -S a type of polymer

MUREX *n* pl. -RICES or -REXES a marine mollusk

MURIATE *n* pl. -S chloride

MURIATED *adj* pickled

MURICATE *adj* covered with short, sharp points

MURICES a pl. of murex

MURID *n* pl. -S a murine

MURINE *n* pl. -S any of a family of small rodents

MURING present participle of mure

MURK *adj* MURKER, MURKEST dark **MURKLY** *adv*

MURK *n* pl. -S darkness

MURKY *adj* MURKIER, MURKIEST dark **MURKILY** *adv*

MURMUR *v* -ED, -ING, -S to speak unclearly

MURMURER *n* pl. -S one that murmurs

MURPHY *n* pl. -PHIES a potato

MURR *n* pl. -S murre

MURRA *n* pl. -S a substance used to make fine vases and cups in ancient Rome

MURRAIN *n* pl. -S a disease of cattle

MURRE *n* pl. -S a diving bird

MURRELET *n* pl. -S a small diving bird

MURREY *n* pl. -REYS a dark purple color

MURRHA *n* pl. -S murra **MURRHINE** *adj*

MURRINE *adj* pertaining to murra

MURRY *n* pl. -RIES a moray

MURTHER *v* -ED, -ING, -S to murder

MUSCA *n* pl. -CAE any of a genus of flies

MUSCADEL *n* pl. -S muscatel

MUSCADET *n* pl. -S a dry white French wine

MUSCAT *n* pl. -S a sweet, white grape

MUSCATEL *n* pl. -S a wine made from muscat grapes

MUSCID *n* pl. -S musca

MUSCLE *v* -CLED, -CLING, -CLES to proceed by force

MUSCLY *adj* composed of muscle (tissue that produces bodily movement)

MUSCULAR *adj* pertaining to muscle

MUSE *v* MUSED, MUSING, MUSES to ponder

MUSEFUL *adj* pensive

MUSER *n* pl. -S one that muses

MUSETTE *n* pl. -S a small bagpipe

MUSEUM *n* pl. -S a place where objects of lasting interest or value are cared for and exhibited

MUSH *v* -ED, -ING, -ES to travel over snow with a dog sled

MUSHER *n* pl. -S one that mushes

MUSHROOM *v* -ED, -ING, -S to grow or spread rapidly

MUSHY *adj* MUSHIER, MUSHIEST pulpy **MUSHILY** *adv*

MUSIC *n* pl. -S vocal or instrumental sounds organized to produce a unified composition

MUSICAL *n* pl. -S a play in which dialogue is interspersed with songs and dances

MUSICALE *n* pl. -S a program of music performed at a social gathering

MUSICIAN *n* pl. -S one who performs or composes music

MUSING *n* pl. -S contemplation

MUSINGLY *adv* in a pensive manner

MUSJID *n* pl. -S a mosque

MUSK *n* pl. -S a strongly odorous substance secreted by certain animals

MUSKEG *n* pl. -S a marsh

MUSKET *n* pl. -S a type of firearm

MUSKETRY *n* pl. -RIES the technique of firing small arms

MUSKIE *n* pl. -S a freshwater fish

MUSKIER comparative of musky

MUSKIEST superlative of musky

MUSKILY *adv* in a musky manner

MUSKIT *n* pl. -S mesquite

MUSKRAT *n* pl. -S an aquatic rodent

MUSKY *adj* MUSKIER, MUSKIEST resembling musk

MUSLIN *n* pl. -S a cotton fabric

MUSPIKE *n* pl. -S a freshwater fish

MUSQUASH *n* pl. -ES the muskrat

MUSS *v* -ED, -ING, -ES to mess

MUSSEL *n* pl. -S a bivalve mollusk

MUSSY *adj* MUSSIER, MUSSIEST messy **MUSSILY** *adv*

MUST *v* -ED, -ING, -S to become musty

MUSTACHE *n* pl. -S a growth of hair on the upper lip

MUSTANG *n* pl. -S a wild horse

MUSTARD *n* pl. -S a pungent seasoning

MUSTARDY *adj* resembling mustard

MUSTEE *n* pl. -S an octoroon

MUSTER *v* -ED, -ING, -S to summon or assemble

MUSTH *n* pl. -S a state of frenzy occurring in male elephants

MUSTY *adj* MUSTIER, MUSTIEST having a stale odor **MUSTILY** *adv*

MUT *n* pl. -S mutt

MUTABLE *adj* capable of change **MUTABLY** *adv*

MUTAGEN *n* pl. -S a substance that causes biological mutation

MUTANT *n* pl. -S something that undergoes mutation

MUTASE *n* pl. -S an enzyme

MUTATE *v* -TATED, -TATING, -TATES to undergo mutation

MUTATION *n* pl. -S the act of changing **MUTATIVE** *adj*

MUTCH *n* pl. -ES a close-fitting cap

MUTCHKIN *n* pl. -S a Scottish unit of liquid measure

MUTE *adj* MUTER, MUTEST characterized by an absence of speech **MUTELY** *adv*

MUTE *v* MUTED, MUTING, MUTES to deaden the sound of **MUTEDLY** *adv*

MUTENESS *n* pl. -ES the state of being mute

MUTER comparative of mute

MUTEST superlative of mute

MUTICOUS *adj* lacking a point

MUTILATE *v* -LATED, -LATING, -LATES to deprive of a limb or other essential part

MUTINE   v -TINED, -TINING, -TINES to mutiny

MUTINEER   v -ED, -ING, -S to mutiny

MUTING   present participle of mute

MUTINIED   past tense of mutiny

MUTINIES   present 3d person sing. of mutiny

MUTINING   present participle of mutine

MUTINOUS   adj disposed to mutiny

MUTINY   v -NIED, -NYING, -NIES to revolt against constituted authority

MUTISM   n pl. -S muteness

MUTON   n pl. -S a unit of nucleic acid

MUTT   n pl. -S a mongrel dog

MUTTER   v -ED, -ING, -S to speak unclearly

MUTTERER   n pl. -S one that mutters

MUTTON   n pl. -S the flesh of sheep used as food **MUTTONY** adj

MUTUAL   adj shared in common **MUTUALLY** adv

MUTUEL   n pl. -S a system of betting on races

MUTULE   n pl. -S an ornamental block used in classical Greek architecture **MUTULAR** adj

MUUMUU   n pl. -S a long, loose dress

MUZHIK   n pl. -S a Russian peasant

MUZJIK   n pl. -S muzhik

MUZZIER   comparative of muzzy

MUZZIEST   superlative of muzzy

MUZZILY   adv in a muzzy manner

MUZZLE   v -ZLED, -ZLING, -ZLES to put a covering over the mouth of to prevent biting or eating

MUZZLER   n pl. -S one that muzzles

MUZZY   adj -ZIER, -ZIEST confused

MY   pron the possessive form of the pronoun I

MYALGIA   n pl. -S muscular pain **MYALGIC** adj

MYASIS   n pl. MYASES myiasis

MYCELE   n pl. -S mycelium

MYCELIUM   n pl. -LIA the vegetative portion of a fungus **MYCELIAL, MYCELIAN, MYCELOID** adj

MYCETOMA   n pl. -MAS or -MATA a fungous infection

MYCOLOGY   n pl. -GIES the branch of botany dealing with fungi

MYCOSIS   n pl. -COSES a disease caused by a fungus **MYCOTIC** adj

MYELIN   n pl. -S a fatty substance that encases certain nerve fibers **MYELINIC** adj

MYELINE   n pl. -S myelin

MYELITIS   n pl. -LITIDES inflammation of the bone marrow

MYELOID   adj pertaining to bone marrow

MYELOMA   n pl. -MAS or -MATA a tumor of the bone marrow

MYIASIS   n pl. MYIASES infestation of human tissue by fly maggots

MYLONITE   n pl. -S a type of rock

MYNA   n pl. -S an Asian bird

MYNAH   n pl. -S myna

MYNHEER   n pl. -S a Dutch title of courtesy for a man

MYOBLAST   n pl. -S a cell capable of giving rise to muscle cells

MYOGENIC   adj originating in muscle tissue

MYOGRAPH   n pl. -S an instrument for recording muscular contractions

MYOID   adj resembling muscle

MYOLOGY   n pl. -GIES the study of muscles **MYOLOGIC** adj

MYOMA   n pl. -MAS or -MATA a tumor composed of muscle tissue

MYOPATHY   n pl. -THIES a disorder of muscle tissue

MYOPE   n pl. -S one who is affected with myopia

MYOPIA   n pl. -S a visual defect **MYOPIC** adj

MYOPY   n pl. -PIES myopia

MYOSCOPE   n pl. -S an instrument for observing muscular contractions

MYOSIN   n pl. -S a protein found in muscle tissue

MYOSIS   n pl. MYOSES miosis

MYOSITIS   n pl. -TISES muscular pain from infection

MYOSOTE   n pl. -S myosotis

MYOSOTIS   n pl. -TISES a flowering plant

MYOTIC   n pl. -S miotic

MYOTOME   n pl. -S a portion of an embryonic somite

MYOTONIA   n pl. -S temporary muscular rigidity **MYOTONIC** adj

MYRIAD   n pl. -S a very large number

MYRIAPOD   *n* pl. -S a multi-legged arthropod

MYRICA   *n* pl. -S a medicinal tree bark

MYRIOPOD   *n* pl. -S myriapod

MYRMIDON   *n* pl. -S a loyal follower

MYRRH   *n* pl. -S an aromatic gum resin
MYRRHIC *adj*

MYRTLE   *n* pl. -S an evergreen shrub

MYSELF   *pron* a form of the 1st person sing. pronoun

MYSID   *n* pl. -S a small crustacean

MYSOST   *n* pl. -S a mild cheese

MYSTAGOG   *n* pl. -S a teacher of religious mysteries

MYSTERY   *n* pl. -TERIES something that is not or cannot be known, understood, or explained

MYSTIC   *n* pl. -S one who professes to have had mystical experiences

MYSTICAL   *adj* spiritually significant or symbolic

MYSTICLY   *adv* in a mystical manner

MYSTIFY   *v* -FIED, -FYING, -FIES to perplex

MYSTIQUE   *n* pl. -S an aura of mystery or mystical power surrounding a particular person or thing

MYTH   *n* pl. -S a type of traditional story

MYTHIC   *adj* mythical

MYTHICAL   *adj* based on or described in a myth

MYTHOS   *n* pl. -THOI a myth

MYTHY   *adj* MYTHIER, MYTHIEST resembling myth

MYXEDEMA   *n* pl. -S a disease caused by decreased activity of the thyroid gland

MYXOCYTE   *n* pl. -S a large cell found in mucous tissue

MYXOID   *adj* containing mucus

MYXOMA   *n* pl. -MAS or -MATA a tumor composed of mucous tissue

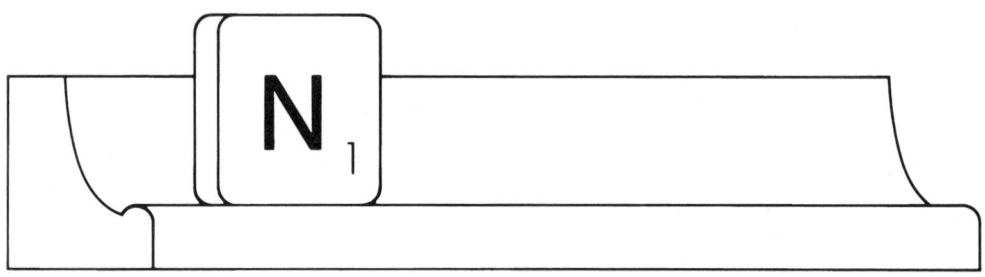

NA	*adv* no; not	**NAH**	*adv* no
NAAN	*n* pl. -S nan	**NAIAD**	*n* pl. -S or -ES a water nymph
NAB	*v* NABBED, NABBING, NABS to capture or arrest	**NAIF**	*n* pl. -S a naive person
NABBER	*n* pl. -S one that nabs	**NAIL**	*v* -ED, -ING, -S to fasten with a nail (a slender piece of metal)
NABE	*n* pl. -S a neighborhood movie theater	**NAILER**	*n* pl. -S one that nails
NABIS	*n* pl. NABIS a group of French artists	**NAILFOLD**	*n* pl. -S a fold of skin around the fingernail
NABOB	*n* pl. -S one who becomes rich and prominent **NABOBISH** *adj*	**NAILHEAD**	*n* pl. -S the top of a nail
NABOBERY	*n* pl. -ERIES the state of being a nabob	**NAILSET**	*n* pl. -S a steel rod for driving a nail into something
NABOBESS	*n* pl. -ES a female nabob	**NAINSOOK**	*n* pl. -S a cotton fabric
NABOBISM	*n* pl. -S great wealth and luxury	**NAIRA**	*n* pl. NAIRA a monetary unit of Nigeria
NACELLE	*n* pl. -S a shelter on an aircraft	**NAIVE**	*adj* NAIVER, NAIVEST lacking sophistication **NAIVELY** *adv*
NACHAS	*n* pl. NACHAS pride in another's accomplishments	**NAIVE**	*n* pl. -S a naive person
NACHES	*n* pl. NACHES nachas	**NAIVETE**	*n* pl. -S the quality of being naive
NACHO	*n* pl. -CHOS a tortilla chip topped with cheese and a savory mixture and broiled	**NAIVETY**	*n* pl. -TIES naivete
NACRE	*n* pl. -S the pearly internal layer of certain shells **NACRED, NACREOUS** *adj*	**NAKED**	*adj* -KEDER, -KEDEST being without clothing or covering **NAKEDLY** *adv*
NADA	*n* pl. -S nothing	**NALED**	*n* pl. -S an insecticide
NADIR	*n* pl. -S a point on the celestial sphere **NADIRAL** *adj*	**NALOXONE**	*n* pl. -S a chemical compound
NAE	*adv* no; not	**NAM**	a past tense of nim
NAETHING	*n* pl. -S nothing	**NAME**	*v* NAMED, NAMING, NAMES to give a title to **NAMABLE, NAMEABLE** *adj*
NAEVUS	*n* pl. -VI nevus **NAEVOID** *adj*	**NAMELESS**	*adj* lacking distinction or fame
NAG	*v* NAGGED, NAGGING, NAGS to find fault incessantly	**NAMELY**	*adv* that is to say
NAGANA	*n* pl. -S a disease of horses in Africa	**NAMER**	*n* pl. -S one that names
NAGGER	*n* pl. -S one that nags	**NAMESAKE**	*n* pl. -S one who is named after another
NAGGING	present participle of nag	**NAMETAG**	*n* pl. -S a tag bearing one's name worn for identification
NAGGY	*adj* -GIER, -GIEST given to nagging	**NAMING**	present participle of name
		NAN	*n* pl. -S a round flat bread
		NANA	*n* pl. -S a grandmother

NANDIN	*n* pl. -S an evergreen shrub
NANDINA	*n* pl. -S an Asian shrub
NANISM	*n* pl. -S abnormal smallness
NANKEEN	*n* pl. -S a cotton fabric
NANKIN	*n* pl. -S nankeen
NANNIE	*n* pl. -S nanny
NANNY	*n* pl. -NIES a children's nurse
NANOGRAM	*n* pl. -S a unit of mass and weight
NANOWATT	*n* pl. -S a unit of power
NAOS	*n* pl. NAOI an ancient temple
NAP	*v* NAPPED, NAPPING, NAPS to sleep briefly
NAPALM	*v* -ED, -ING, -S to assault with a type of incendiary bomb
NAPE	*n* pl. -S the back of the neck
NAPERY	*n* pl. -PERIES table linen
NAPHTHA	*n* pl. -S a volatile liquid
NAPHTHOL	*n* pl. -S a chemical compound
NAPHTHYL	*n* pl. -S a radical derived from naphthalene
NAPHTOL	*n* pl. -S naphthol
NAPIFORM	*adj* shaped like a turnip
NAPKIN	*n* pl. -S a piece of material used to wipe the hands and mouth
NAPLESS	*adj* threadbare
NAPOLEON	*n* pl. -S a type of pastry
NAPPE	*n* pl. -S a type of rock formation
NAPPED	past tense of nap
NAPPER	*n* pl. -S one that naps
NAPPIE	*n* pl. -S a diaper
NAPPING	present participle of nap
NAPPY	*adj* -PIER, -PIEST kinky
NARC	*n* pl. -S an undercover drug agent
NARCEIN	*n* pl. -S narceine
NARCEINE	*n* pl. -S an opium derivative
NARCISM	*n* pl. -S excessive love of oneself
NARCISSI	*n/pl* bulbous flowering plants
NARCIST	*n* pl. -S one given to narcism
NARCO	*n* pl. -COS narc
NARCOSE	*adj* characterized by stupor
NARCOSIS	*n* pl. -COSES a drug-induced stupor
NARCOTIC	*n* pl. -S a drug that dulls the senses

NARD	*n* pl. -S a fragrant ointment **NARDINE** *adj*
NARES	pl. of naris
NARGHILE	*n* pl. -S a hookah
NARGILE	*n* pl. -S narghile
NARGILEH	*n* pl. -S narghile
NARIS	*n* pl. NARES a nostril **NARIAL, NARIC, NARINE** *adj*
NARK	*v* -ED, -ING, -S to spy or inform
NARKY	*adj* irritable
NARRATE	*v* -RATED, -RATING, -RATES to tell a story
NARRATER	*n* pl. -S narrator
NARRATOR	*n* pl. -S one that narrates
NARROW	*adj* -ROWER, -ROWEST of little width **NARROWLY** *adv*
NARROW	*v* -ED, -ING, -S to make narrow
NARTHEX	*n* pl. -ES a vestibule in a church
NARWAL	*n* pl. -S narwhal
NARWHAL	*n* pl. -S an arctic aquatic mammal
NARWHALE	*n* pl. -S narwhal
NARY	*adj* not one
NASAL	*n* pl. -S a sound uttered through the nose
NASALISE	*v* -ISED, -ISING, -ISES to nasalize
NASALITY	*n* pl. -TIES the quality or an instance of being produced nasally
NASALIZE	*v* -IZED, -IZING, -IZES to produce sounds through the nose
NASALLY	*adv* through the nose
NASCENCE	*n* pl. -S nascency
NASCENCY	*n* pl. -CIES birth; origin
NASCENT	*adj* coming into existence
NASION	*n* pl. -S a point in the skull **NASIAL** *adj*
NASTIC	*adj* pertaining to an automatic response of plants
NASTY	*adj* -TIER, -TIEST offensive to the senses **NASTILY** *adv*
NASTY	*n* pl. -TIES something that is nasty
NATAL	*adj* pertaining to one's birth
NATALITY	*n* pl. -TIES birth rate
NATANT	*adj* floating or swimming **NATANTLY** *adv*

NATATION *n* pl. -S the act of swimming

NATATORY *adj* pertaining to swimming

NATCH *adv* naturally

NATES *n/pl* the buttocks

NATHLESS *adv* nevertheless

NATION *n* pl. -S a politically organized people who share a territory, customs, and history

NATIONAL *n* pl. -S a citizen of a nation

NATIVE *n* pl. -S an original inhabitant of an area

NATIVELY *adv* in an inborn manner

NATIVISM *n* pl. -S a policy of favoring the interests of native inhabitants

NATIVIST *n* pl. -S an advocate of nativism

NATIVITY *n* pl. -TIES the process of being born

NATRIUM *n* pl. -S sodium

NATRON *n* pl. -S a chemical compound

NATTER *v* -ED, -ING, -S to chatter

NATTY *adj* -TIER, -TIEST neatly dressed **NATTILY** *adv*

NATURAL *n* pl. -S a type of musical note

NATURE *n* pl. -S the essential qualities of a person or thing **NATURED** *adj*

NATURISM *n* pl. -S nudism

NATURIST *n* pl. -S a nudist

NAUGHT *n* pl. -S a zero

NAUGHTY *adj* -TIER, -TIEST disobedient

NAUMACHY *n* pl. -CHIES a mock sea battle

NAUPLIUS *n* pl. -PLII a form of certain crustaceans **NAUPLIAL** *adj*

NAUSEA *n* pl. -S a stomach disturbance

NAUSEANT *n* pl. -S an agent that induces nausea

NAUSEATE *v* -ATED, -ATING, -ATES to affect with nausea

NAUSEOUS *adj* affected with nausea

NAUTCH *n* pl. -ES a dancing exhibition in India

NAUTICAL *adj* pertaining to ships

NAUTILUS *n* pl. -LUSES or -LI a spiral-shelled mollusk

NAVAID *n* pl. -S a navigational device

NAVAL *adj* pertaining to ships **NAVALLY** *adv*

NAVAR *n* pl. -S a system of air navigation

NAVE *n* pl. -S the main part of a church

NAVEL *n* pl. -S a depression in the abdomen

NAVETTE *n* pl. -S a gem cut in a pointed oval form

NAVICERT *n* pl. -S a document permitting a vessel passage through a naval blockade

NAVIES pl. of navy

NAVIGATE *v* -GATED, -GATING, -GATES to plan and control the course of

NAVVY *n* pl. -VIES a manual laborer

NAVY *n* pl. -VIES a nation's warships

NAW *adv* no

NAWAB *n* pl. -S a nabob

NAY *n* pl. NAYS a negative vote

NAYSAYER *n* pl. -S one that denies or opposes something

NAZI *n* pl. -S a type of fascist

NAZIFY *v* -FIED, -FYING, -FIES to cause to be like a nazi

NE *adj* born with the name of

NEAP *n* pl. -S a tide of lowest range

NEAR *adj* NEARER, NEAREST situated within a short distance

NEAR *v* -ED, -ING, -S to approach

NEARBY *adj* near

NEARLY *adv* -LIER, -LIEST with close approximation

NEARNESS *n* pl. -ES the state of being near

NEARSIDE *n* pl. -S the left side

NEAT *adj* NEATER, NEATEST being in a state of cleanliness and order

NEAT *n* pl. -S a bovine

NEATEN *v* -ED, -ING, -S to make neat

NEATH *prep* beneath

NEATHERD *n* pl. -S a cowherd

NEATLY *adv* in a neat manner

NEATNESS *n* pl. -ES the state of being neat

NEB *n* pl. -S the beak of a bird

NEBBISH *n* pl. -ES a meek person **NEBBISHY** *adj*

NEBULA *n* pl. -LAS or -LAE a cloud-like interstellar mass **NEBULAR** *adj*

NEBULE *adj* composed of successive short curves

NEBULISE *v* -LISED, -LISING, -LISES to nebulize

NEBULIZE   *v* -LIZED, -LIZING, -LIZES to reduce to a fine spray

NEBULOSE   *adj* nebulous

NEBULOUS   *adj* unclear

NEBULY   *adj* nebule

NECK   *v* -ED, -ING, -S to kiss and caress in lovemaking

NECKBAND   *n* pl. -S a band worn around the neck (the part of the body joining the head to the trunk)

NECKER   *n* pl. -S one that necks

NECKING   *n* pl. -S a small molding near the top of a column

NECKLACE   *n* pl. -S an ornament worn around the neck

NECKLESS   *adj* having no neck

NECKLIKE   *adj* resembling the neck

NECKLINE   *n* pl. -S the line formed by the neck opening of a garment

NECKTIE   *n* pl. -S a strip of fabric worn around the neck

NECKWEAR   *n* pl. NECKWEAR something that is worn around the neck

NECROPSY   *v* -SIED, -SYING, -SIES to perform an autopsy on

NECROSE   *v* -CROSED, -CROSING, -CROSES to affect with necrosis

NECROSIS   *n* pl. -CROSES the death of living tissue **NECROTIC** *adj*

NECTAR   *n* pl. -S a delicious drink

NECTARY   *n* pl. -TARIES a plant gland

NEE   *adj* born with the name of

NEED   *v* -ED, -ING, -S to have an urgent or essential use for

NEEDER   *n* pl. -S one that needs

NEEDFUL   *n* pl. -S something that is needed

NEEDIER   comparative of needy

NEEDIEST   superlative of needy

NEEDILY   *adv* in a needy manner

NEEDLE   *v* -DLED, -DLING, -DLES to sew with a slender, pointed instrument

NEEDLER   *n* pl. -S one that needles

NEEDLESS   *adj* not necessary

NEEDLING   *n* pl. -S the act of one who needles

NEEDY   *adj* NEEDIER, NEEDIEST in a state of poverty

NEEM   *n* pl. -S an East Indian tree

NEEP   *n* pl. -S a turnip

NEGATE   *v* -GATED, -GATING, -GATES to nullify

NEGATER   *n* pl. -S one that negates

NEGATION   *n* pl. -S the act of negating

NEGATIVE   *v* -TIVED, -TIVING, -TIVES to veto

NEGATON   *n* pl. -S negatron

NEGATOR   *n* pl. -S negater

NEGATRON   *n* pl. -S an electron

NEGLECT   *v* -ED, -ING, -S to fail to pay attention to

NEGLIGE   *n* pl. -S negligee

NEGLIGEE   *n* pl. -S a woman's dressing gown

NEGROID   *n* pl. -S member of the black race

NEGRONI   *n* pl. -S an alcoholic beverage

NEGUS   *n* pl. -ES an alcoholic beverage

NEIF   *n* pl. -S nieve

NEIGH   *v* -ED, -ING, -S to utter the cry of a horse

NEIGHBOR   *v* -ED, -ING, -S to live close to

NEIST   *adj* next

NEITHER   *adj* not one or the other

NEKTON   *n* pl. -S free-swimming marine animals **NEKTONIC** *adj*

NELLIE   *n* pl. -S an effeminate male

NELLY   *n* pl. -LIES nellie

NELSON   *n* pl. -S a wrestling hold

NELUMBO   *n* pl. -BOS an aquatic herb

NEMA   *n* pl. -S a nematode

NEMATIC   *adj* pertaining to a phase of a liquid crystal

NEMATODE   *n* pl. -S a kind of worm

NEMESIS   *n* pl. NEMESES an unbeatable opponent

NENE   *n* pl. NENE a Hawaiian goose

NEOLITH   *n* pl. -S an ancient stone implement

NEOLOGY   *n* pl. -GIES a new word or phrase **NEOLOGIC** *adj*

NEOMORPH   *n* pl. -S a type of biological structure

NEOMYCIN   *n* pl. -S an antibiotic drug

NEON   *n* pl. -S a gaseous element **NEONED** *adj*

NEONATE   *n* pl. -S a newborn child **NEONATAL** *adj*

NEOPHYTE   *n* pl. -S a novice

NEOPLASM *n* pl. -S a tumor

NEOPRENE *n* pl. -S a synthetic rubber

NEOTENY *n* pl. -NIES attainment of sexual maturity in the larval stage **NEOTENIC** *adj*

NEOTERIC *n* pl. -S a modern author

NEOTYPE *n* pl. -S a specimen of a species

NEPENTHE *n* pl. -S a drug that induces forgetfulness

NEPHEW *n* pl. -S a son of one's brother or sister

NEPHRIC *adj* renal

NEPHRISM *n* pl. -S ill health caused by a kidney disease

NEPHRITE *n* pl. -S a mineral

NEPHRON *n* pl. -S an excretory unit of a kidney

NEPOTISM *n* pl. -S favoritism shown to a relative **NEPOTIC** *adj*

NEPOTIST *n* pl. -S one who practices nepotism

NERD *n* pl. -S a socially inept person **NERDISH** *adj*

NERDY *adj* NERDIER, NERDIEST socially inept

NEREID *n* pl. -S a sea nymph

NEREIS *n* pl. -REIDES a marine worm

NERITIC *adj* pertaining to shallow water

NEROL *n* pl. -S a fragrant alcohol

NEROLI *n* pl. -S a fragrant oil

NERTS *interj* — used to express defiance

NERTZ *interj* nerts

NERVATE *adj* having veins

NERVE *v* NERVED, NERVING, NERVES to give courage to

NERVIER comparative of nervy

NERVIEST superlative of nervy

NERVILY *adv* in a nervy manner

NERVINE *n* pl. -S a soothing medicine

NERVING *n* pl. -S a type of veterinary operation

NERVOUS *adj* easily excited

NERVULE *n* pl. -S nervure

NERVURE *n* pl. -S a vascular ridge on a leaf

NERVY *adj* NERVIER, NERVIEST impudent

NESCIENT *n* pl. -S one who is ignorant

NESS *n* pl. -ES a headland

NEST *v* -ED, -ING, -S to build a nest (a structure for holding bird eggs)

NESTABLE *adj* capable of being fitted closely within another container

NESTER *n* pl. -S one that nests

NESTLE *v* -TLED, -TLING, -TLES to lie snugly

NESTLER *n* pl. -S one that nestles

NESTLIKE *adj* resembling a nest

NESTLING *n* pl. -S a young bird

NESTOR *n* pl. -S a wise old man

NET *v* NETTED, NETTING, NETS to catch in a net (a type of openwork fabric)

NETHER *adj* situated below

NETLESS *adj* having no net

NETLIKE *adj* resembling a net

NETOP *n* pl. -S friend; companion

NETSUKE *n* pl. -S a button-like fixture on Japanese clothing

NETT *v* -ED, -ING, -S to net

NETTABLE *adj* capable of being netted

NETTED past tense of net, nett

NETTER *n* pl. -S one that nets

NETTIER comparative of netty

NETTIEST superlative of netty

NETTING *n* pl. -S a net

NETTLE *v* -TLED, -TLING, -TLES to make angry

NETTLER *n* pl. -S one that nettles

NETTLY *adj* -TLIER, -TLIEST prickly

NETTY *adj* -TIER, -TIEST resembling a net

NETWORK *v* -ED, -ING, -S to cover with or as if with crossing lines

NEUK *n* pl. -S nook

NEUM *n* pl. -S neume

NEUME *n* pl. -S a sign used in musical notation **NEUMATIC, NEUMIC** *adj*

NEURAL *adj* pertaining to the nervous system **NEURALLY** *adv*

NEURAXON *n* pl. -S a part of a neuron

NEURINE *n* pl. -S a ptomaine poison

NEURITIC *n* pl. -S one affected with neuritis

NEURITIS *n* pl. -RITIDES or -RITISES inflammation of a nerve

NEUROID *adj* resembling a nerve

NEUROMA *n* pl. -MAS or -MATA a type of tumor

NEURON *n* pl. -S the basic cellular unit of the nervous system **NEURONAL, NEURONIC** *adj*

NEURONE *n* pl. -S neuron

NEUROSIS *n* pl. -ROSES a type of emotional disturbance **NEUROSAL** *adj*

NEUROTIC *n* pl. -S one affected with a neurosis

NEURULA *n* pl. -LAE or -LAS a vertebrate embryo

NEUSTON *n* pl. -S an aggregate of small aquatic organisms

NEUTER *v* -ED, -ING, -S to castrate

NEUTRAL *n* pl. -S one that is impartial

NEUTRINO *n* pl. -NOS a subatomic particle

NEUTRON *n* pl. -S a subatomic particle

NEVE *n* pl. -S a granular snow

NEVER *adv* at no time

NEVUS *n* pl. -VI a birthmark **NEVOID** *adj*

NEW *adj* NEWER, NEWEST existing only a short time

NEW *n* pl. -S something that is new

NEWBORN *n* pl. -S a recently born infant

NEWCOMER *n* pl. -S one that has recently arrived

NEWEL *n* pl. -S a staircase support

NEWFOUND *adj* newly found

NEWIE *n* pl. -S something new

NEWISH *adj* somewhat new

NEWLY *adv* recently

NEWLYWED *n* pl. -S a person recently married

NEWMOWN *adj* recently mown

NEWNESS *n* pl. -ES the state of being new

NEWS *n/pl* a report of recent events

NEWSBOY *n* pl. -BOYS a boy who delivers or sells newspapers

NEWSCAST *n* pl. -S a news broadcast

NEWSHAWK *n* pl. -S a newspaper reporter

NEWSIE *n* pl. -S newsy

NEWSIER comparative of newsy

NEWSIES pl. of newsy

NEWSIEST superlative of newsy

NEWSLESS *adj* having no news

NEWSMAN *n* pl. -MEN a news reporter

NEWSPEAK *n* pl. -S a deliberately ambiguous language

NEWSREEL *n* pl. -S a short movie presenting current events

NEWSROOM *n* pl. -S a room where the news is gathered

NEWSY *adj* NEWSIER, NEWSIEST full of news

NEWSY *n* pl. NEWSIES a newsboy

NEWT *n* pl. -S a small salamander

NEWTON *n* pl. -S a unit of force

NEXT *adj* coming immediately after; adjoining

NEXTDOOR *adj* located in the next building or room

NEXUS *n* pl. -ES a connection or link

NGULTRUM *n* pl. -S a monetary unit of Bhutan

NGWEE *n* pl. NGWEE a monetary unit of Zambia

NIACIN *n* pl. -S a B vitamin

NIB *v* NIBBED, NIBBING, NIBS to provide with a penpoint

NIBBLE *v* -BLED, -BLING, -BLES to eat with small bites

NIBBLER *n* pl. -S one that nibbles

NIBLICK *n* pl. -S a golf club

NIBLIKE *adj* resembling a penpoint

NICAD *n* pl. -S nickel cadmium

NICE *adj* NICER, NICEST pleasing to the senses **NICELY** *adv*

NICENESS *n* pl. -ES the quality of being nice

NICETY *n* pl. -TIES a fine point or distinction

NICHE *v* NICHED, NICHING, NICHES to place in a receding space or hollow

NICK *v* -ED, -ING, -S to make a shallow cut in

NICKEL *v* -ELED, -ELING, -ELS or -ELLED, -ELLING, -ELS to plate with nickel (a metallic element)

NICKELIC *adj* pertaining to or containing nickel

NICKER *v* -ED, -ING, -S to neigh

NICKLE *v* -LED, -LING, -LES nickel

NICKNACK *n* pl. -S a trinket

NICKNAME *v* -NAMED, -NAMING, -NAMES to give an alternate name to

NICOL *n* pl. -S a type of prism

NICOTIN *n* pl. -S nicotine

NICOTINE *n* pl. -S a poisonous alkaloid in tobacco

NICTATE *n* -TATED, -TATING, -TATES to wink

NIDAL *adj* pertaining to a nidus

NIDE *n* NIDED, NIDING, NIDES to nest

NIDERING *n* pl. -S a coward

NIDGET *n* pl. -S an idiot

NIDI a pl. of nidus

NIDIFY *v* -FIED, -FYING, -FIES to nest

NIDING present participle of nide

NIDUS *n* pl. NIDI or NIDUSES a nest or breeding place

NIECE *n* pl. -S a daughter of one's brother or sister

NIELLIST *n* pl. -S one that niellos

NIELLO *n* pl. -LI or -LOS a black metallic substance

NIELLO *v* -ED, -ING, -S to decorate with niello

NIEVE *n* pl. -S the fist or hand

NIFFER *v* -ED, -ING, -S to barter

NIFTY *adj* -TIER, -TIEST stylish; pleasing **NIFTILY** *adv*

NIFTY *n* pl. -TIES something that is nifty

NIGGARD *v* -ED, -ING, -S to act stingily

NIGGLE *v* -GLED, -GLING, -GLES to worry over petty details

NIGGLER *n* pl. -S one that niggles

NIGGLING *n* pl. -S petty or meticulous work

NIGH *adj* NIGHER, NIGHEST near

NIGH *v* -ED, -ING, -S to approach

NIGHNESS *n* pl. -ES the state of being nigh

NIGHT *n* pl. -S the period from sunset to sunrise

NIGHTCAP *n* pl. -S a cap worn to bed

NIGHTIE *n* pl. -S a nightgown

NIGHTIES pl. of nighty

NIGHTJAR *n* pl. -S a nocturnal bird

NIGHTLY *adv* every night; at night

NIGHTY *n* pl. NIGHTIES nightie

NIGRIFY *v* -FIED, -FYING, -FIES to make black

NIGROSIN *n* pl. -S a type of dye

NIHIL *n* pl. -S nothing

NIHILISM *n* pl. -S a doctrine that denies traditional values

NIHILIST *n* pl. -S an adherent of nihilism

NIHILITY *n* pl. -TIES the state of being nothing

NIL *n* pl. -S nothing

NILGAI *n* pl. -S a large antelope

NILGAU *n* pl. -S nilgai

NILGHAI *n* pl. -S nilgai

NILGHAU *n* pl. -S nilgai

NILL *v* -ED, -ING, -S to be unwilling

NIM *v* NAM or NIMMED, NIMMING, NIMS to steal

NIMBLE *adj* -BLER, -BLEST agile **NIMBLY** *adv*

NIMBUS *n* pl. -BI or -BUSES a luminous cloud **NIMBUSED** *adj*

NIMIETY *n* pl. -ETIES excess **NIMIOUS** *adj*

NIMMED past tense of nim

NIMMING present participle of nim

NIMROD *n* pl. -S a hunter

NINE *n* pl. -S a number

NINEBARK *n* pl. -S a flowering shrub

NINEFOLD *adj* nine times as great

NINEPIN *n* pl. -S a wooden pin used in a bowling game

NINETEEN *n* pl. -S a number

NINETY *n* pl. -TIES a number

NINJA *n* pl. -S a feudal Japanese warrior

NINNY *n* pl. -NIES a fool **NINNYISH** *adj*

NINON *n* pl. -S a sheer fabric

NINTH *n* pl. -S one of nine equal parts

NINTHLY *adv* in the ninth place

NIOBATE *n* pl. -S a chemical salt

NIOBIUM *n* pl. -S a metallic element **NIOBIC, NIOBOUS** *adj*

NIP *v* NIPPED, NIPPING, NIPS to pinch

NIPA *n* pl. -S a palm tree

NIPPER *n* pl. -S one that nips

NIPPIER comparative of nippy

NIPPIEST superlative of nippy

NIPPILY *adv* in a nippy manner

NIPPING present participle of nip

NIPPLE *n* pl. -S a protuberance on the breast **NIPPLED** *adj*

NIPPY	*adj* -PIER, -PIEST sharp or biting
NIRVANA	*n* pl. -S a blessed state in Buddhism **NIRVANIC** *adj*
NISEI	*n* pl. -S one born in America of immigrant Japanese parents
NISI	*adj* not yet final
NISUS	*n* pl. NISUS an effort
NIT	*n* pl. -S the egg of a parasitic insect
NITE	*n* pl. -S night
NITER	*n* pl. -S a chemical salt
NITERIE	*n* pl. -S nitery
NITERY	*n* pl. -ERIES a nightclub
NITID	*adj* bright
NITINOL	*n* pl. -S an alloy of nickel and titanium
NITON	*n* pl. -S radon
NITPICK	*v* -ED, -ING, -S to fuss over petty details
NITPICKY	*adj* -PICKIER, -PICKIEST tending to nitpick
NITRATE	*v* -TRATED, -TRATING, -TRATES to treat with nitric acid
NITRATOR	*n* pl. -S one that nitrates
NITRE	*n* pl. -S niter
NITRIC	*adj* containing nitrogen
NITRID	*n* pl. -S nitride
NITRIDE	*v* -TRIDED, -TRIDING, -TRIDES to convert into a nitride (a compound of nitrogen)
NITRIFY	*v* -FIED, -FYING, -FIES to combine with nitrogen
NITRIL	*n* pl. -S nitrile
NITRILE	*n* pl. -S a chemical compound
NITRITE	*n* pl. -S a salt of nitrous acid
NITRO	*n* pl. -TROS a nitrated product
NITROGEN	*n* pl. -S a gaseous element
NITROLIC	*adj* pertaining to a class of acids
NITROSO	*adj* containing nitrosyl
NITROSYL	*n* pl. -S a univalent radical
NITROUS	*adj* containing nitrogen
NITTY	*adj* -TIER, -TIEST full of nits
NITWIT	*n* pl. -S a stupid person
NIVAL	*adj* pertaining to snow
NIVEOUS	*adj* resembling snow
NIX	*v* -ED, -ING, -ES to veto
NIX	*n* pl. NIXES or NIXE a water sprite
NIXIE	*n* pl. -S a female water sprite
NIXY	*n* pl. NIXIES an undeliverable piece of mail
NIZAM	*n* pl. -S a former sovereign of India
NIZAMATE	*n* pl. -S the territory of a nizam
NO	*n* pl. NOS or NOES a negative reply
NOB	*n* pl. -S a wealthy person
NOBBIER	comparative of nobby
NOBBIEST	superlative of nobby
NOBBILY	*adv* in a nobby manner
NOBBLE	*v* -BLED, -BLING, -BLES to disable a racehorse
NOBBLER	*n* pl. -S one that nobbles
NOBBY	*adj* -BIER, -BIEST elegant
NOBELIUM	*n* pl. -S a radioactive element
NOBILITY	*n* pl. -TIES the social class composed of nobles
NOBLE	*adj* -BLER, -BLEST possessing qualities of excellence
NOBLE	*n* pl. -S a person of high birth, rank, or title
NOBLEMAN	*n* pl. -MEN a noble
NOBLER	comparative of noble
NOBLESSE	*n* pl. -S the nobility
NOBLEST	superlative of noble
NOBLY	*adv* in a noble manner
NOBODY	*n* pl. -BODIES an unimportant person
NOCENT	*adj* harmful
NOCK	*v* -ED, -ING, -S to notch a bow or arrow
NOCTUID	*n* pl. -S a night-flying moth **NOCTUOID** *adj*
NOCTULE	*n* pl. -S a large bat
NOCTURN	*n* pl. -S a religious service
NOCTURNE	*n* pl. -S a musical composition
NOCUOUS	*adj* harmful
NOD	*v* NODDED, NODDING, NODS to briefly lower the head forward
NODAL	*adj* of the nature of a node **NODALLY** *adv*
NODALITY	*n* pl. -TIES the state of being nodal
NODDED	past tense of nod
NODDER	*n* pl. -S one that nods
NODDIES	pl. of noddy

NODDING	present participle of nod
NODDLE	*v* -DLED, -DLING, -DLES to nod frequently
NODDY	*n* pl. -DIES a fool
NODE	*n* pl. -S a swollen enlargement
NODI	pl. of nodus
NODICAL	*adj* pertaining to an astronomical point
NODOSE	*adj* having nodes
NODOSITY	*n* pl. -TIES the state of being nodose
NODOUS	*adj* nodose
NODULE	*n* pl. -S a small node **NODULAR, NODULOSE, NODULOUS** *adj*
NODUS	*n* pl. -DI a difficulty
NOEL	*n* pl. -S a Christmas carol
NOES	a pl. of no
NOESIS	*n* pl. -SISES the process of reason
NOETIC	*adj* pertaining to reason
NOG	*v* NOGGED, NOGGING, NOGS to fill in a space in a wall with bricks
NOGG	*n* pl. -S a strong ale
NOGGIN	*n* pl. -S a small cup
NOGGING	*n* pl. -S a type of masonry
NOH	*n* pl. NOH the classical drama of Japan
NOHOW	*adv* in no manner
NOIL	*n* pl. -S a kind of short fiber **NOILY** *adj*
NOIR	*n* pl. -S a bleak type of crime fiction **NOIRISH** *adj*
NOISE	*v* NOISED, NOISING, NOISES to spread as a rumor or report
NOISETTE	*n* pl. -S a small round piece of meat
NOISOME	*adj* disgusting; harmful
NOISY	*adj* NOISIER, NOISIEST making loud sounds **NOISILY** *adv*
NOLO	*n* pl. -LOS a type of legal plea
NOM	*n* pl. -S a name
NOMA	*n* pl. -S a severe inflammation of the mouth
NOMAD	*n* pl. -S a wanderer **NOMADIC** *adj*
NOMADISM	*n* pl. -S the mode of life of a nomad
NOMARCH	*n* pl. -S the head of a nome
NOMARCHY	*n* pl. -ARCHIES a nome
NOMBLES	*n/pl* numbles
NOMBRIL	*n* pl. -S a point on a heraldic shield
NOME	*n* pl. -S a province of modern Greece
NOMEN	*n* pl. -MINA the second name of an ancient Roman
NOMINAL	*n* pl. -S a word used as a noun
NOMINATE	*v* -NATED, -NATING, -NATES to name as a candidate
NOMINEE	*n* pl. -S one that is nominated
NOMISM	*n* pl. -S strict adherence to moral law **NOMISTIC** *adj*
NOMOGRAM	*n* pl. -S a type of graph
NOMOLOGY	*n* pl. -GIES the science of law
NOMOS	*n* pl. NOMOI law
NONA	*n* pl. -S a virus disease
NONACID	*n* pl. -S a substance that is not an acid
NONACTOR	*n* pl. -S a person who is not an actor
NONADULT	*n* pl. -S a person who is not an adult
NONAGE	*n* pl. -S a period of immaturity
NONAGON	*n* pl. -S a nine-sided polygon
NONART	*n* pl. -S something that is not art
NONBANK	*n* pl. -S a business that is not a bank
NONBASIC	*adj* not basic
NONBEING	*n* pl. -S lack of being
NONBLACK	*n* pl. -S one that is not black
NONBODY	*n* pl. -BODIES a person's nonphysical nature
NONBOOK	*n* pl. -S a book of little literary merit
NONBRAND	*adj* lacking a brand name
NONCASH	*adj* other than cash
NONCE	*n* pl. -S the present occasion
NONCLASS	*n* pl. -ES a lack of class
NONCLING	*adj* not clinging
NONCOLA	*adj* being a drink that is not a cola
NONCOLOR	*n* pl. -S a lack of color
NONCOM	*n* pl. -S a noncommissioned officer
NONCRIME	*n* pl. -S something that is not a crime
NONDAIRY	*adj* having no milk products
NONDANCE	*n* pl. -S an unrhythmic dance

NONDRUG *adj* not involving drugs

NONE *n* pl. -S one of seven canonical daily periods for prayer and devotion

NONEGO *n* pl. -GOS all that is not part of the ego

NONELECT *adj* not chosen

NONELITE *adj* not belonging to an elite group

NONEMPTY *adj* not empty

NONENTRY *n* pl. -TRIES the fact of not entering

NONEQUAL *n* pl. -S one that is not equal

NONESUCH *n* pl. -ES a person or thing without an equal

NONET *n* pl. -S a composition for nine instruments or voices

NONEVENT *n* pl. -S an expected event that does not occur

NONFACT *n* pl. -S a statement not based on fact

NONFAN *n* pl. -S a person who is not a fan (an enthusiast)

NONFARM *adj* not pertaining to the farm

NONFAT *adj* having no fat solids

NONFATAL *adj* not fatal

NONFATTY *adj* not fatty

NONFINAL *adj* not being the last

NONFLUID *n* pl. -S a substance that is not a fluid

NONFOCAL *adj* not focal

NONFOOD *adj* pertaining to something other than food

NONFUEL *adj* not used as a fuel

NONGAME *adj* not hunted for food, sport, or fur

NONGAY *n* pl. -S a person who is not a homosexual

NONGLARE *adj* that does not glare

NONGREEN *adj* not green

NONGUEST *n* pl. -S one who is not a guest

NONGUILT *n* pl. -S the absence of guilt

NONHARDY *adj* not hardy

NONHEME *adj* not containing iron that is bound like that of heme

NONHERO *n* pl. -ROES an antihero

NONHOME *adj* not taking place in the home

NONHUMAN *adj* not human

NONIDEAL *adj* not ideal

NONIMAGE *adj* not having an image

NONIONIC *adj* not ionic

NONIRON *adj* not needing to be ironed

NONISSUE *n* pl. -S a topic that is not controversial

NONJUROR *n* pl. -S one who refuses to take a required oath

NONJURY *adj* not involving a jury

NONLABOR *adj* not pertaining to labor

NONLEAFY *adj* not having leaves

NONLEGAL *adj* not legal

NONLIFE *n* pl. -LIVES the absence of life

NONLOCAL *n* pl. -S one that is not local

NONMAJOR *n* pl. -S a student who is not majoring in a specified subject

NONMAN *n* pl. -MEN a being that is not a man

NONMEAT *adj* not containing meat

NONMETAL *n* pl. -S an element that lacks metallic properties

NONMETRO *adj* not metropolitan

NONMODAL *adj* not modal

NONMONEY *adj* not involving money

NONMORAL *adj* not pertaining to morals

NONMUSIC *n* pl. -S inferior music

NONNAVAL *adj* not naval

NONNEWS *adj* not being news

NONNOVEL *n* pl. -S a literary work that is not a novel

NONOBESE *adj* not obese

NONOHMIC *adj* not measured in ohms

NONOILY *adj* not oily

NONOWNER *n* pl. -S one who is not the owner

NONPAGAN *n* pl. -S one who is not a pagan

NONPAID *adj* not paid

NONPAPAL *adj* not papal

NONPAR *adj* being a stock that has no face value

NONPARTY *adj* not affiliated with any political party

NONPAST *n* pl. -S a verb form that lacks an inflection for a past tense

NONPEAK *adj* being a time when something is not at its highest level

NONPLAY *n* pl. -PLAYS a theatrical work that is not a play

NONPLUS *v* -PLUSED, -PLUSING, -PLUSES or -PLUSSED, -PLUSSING, -PLUSSES to baffle

NONPOINT *adj* not occurring at a definite single site

NONPOLAR *adj* not polar

NONPOOR *adj* not being poor

NONPRINT *adj* not involving printed material

NONPROS *v* -PROSSED, -PROSSING, -PROSSES to enter a judgment against a plaintiff who fails to prosecute

NONQUOTA *adj* not included in or subject to a quota

NONRATED *adj* not rated

NONRIGID *adj* not rigid

NONRIVAL *n* pl. -S an unimportant rival

NONROYAL *adj* not royal

NONRURAL *adj* not rural

NONSELF *n* pl. -SELVES foreign material in a body

NONSENSE *n* pl. -S behavior or language that is meaningless or absurd

NONSKED *n* pl. -S an airline without scheduled flying times

NONSKID *adj* designed to inhibit skidding

NONSKIER *n* pl. -S one that does not ski

NONSLIP *adj* designed to prevent slipping

NONSOLAR *adj* not solar

NONSOLID *n* pl. -S a substance that is not a solid

NONSTICK *adj* allowing of easy removal of cooked food particles

NONSTOP *adj* making no stops

NONSTORY *n* pl. -RIES an insignificant news story

NONSTYLE *n* pl. -S a style that is not identifiable

NONSUCH *n* pl. -ES nonesuch

NONSUGAR *n* pl. -S a substance that is not a sugar

NONSUIT *v* -ED, -ING, -S to dismiss the lawsuit of

NONTAX *n* pl. -ES a tax of little consequence

NONTIDAL *adj* not tidal

NONTITLE *adj* pertaining to an athletic contest in which a title is not at stake

NONTONAL *adj* lacking tonality

NONTOXIC *adj* not toxic

NONTRUMP *adj* not having a trump

NONTRUTH *n* pl. -S something that is not true

NONUNION *n* pl. -S failure of a broken bone to heal

NONUPLE *n* pl. -S a number nine times as great as another

NONURBAN *adj* not urban

NONUSE *n* pl. -S failure to use

NONUSER *n* pl. -S one that is not a user

NONUSING *adj* not using

NONVALID *adj* not valid

NONVIRAL *adj* not viral

NONVOCAL *adj* not vocal

NONVOTER *n* pl. -S one that does not vote

NONWAR *n* pl. -S a war that is not officially declared

NONWHITE *n* pl. -S a person who is not of the white race

NONWOODY *adj* not woody

NONWORD *n* pl. -S a word that has no meaning

NONWORK *adj* not involving work

NONWOVEN *n* pl. -S a fabric not made by weaving

NONYL *n* pl. -S an alkyl radical

NONZERO *adj* having a value other than zero

NOO *adv* now

NOODGE *v* NOODGED, NOODGING, NOODGES to nag

NOODLE *v* -DLED, -DLING, -DLES to play idly on a musical instrument

NOOK *n* pl. -S a corner, as in a room **NOOKLIKE** *adj*

NOON *n* pl. -S midday

NOONDAY *n* pl. -DAYS noon

NOONING *n* pl. -S a meal eaten at noon

NOONTIDE *n* pl. -S noon

NOONTIME *n* pl. -S noon

NOOSE *v* NOOSED, NOOSING, NOOSES to secure with a type of loop

NOOSER *n* pl. -S one that nooses

NOPAL *n* pl. -S a cactus

NOPE *adv* no

NOR *conj* and not

NORDIC *adj* pertaining to cross-country ski racing and ski jumping

NORI *n* pl. -S dried seaweed pressed into sheets

NORIA *n* pl. -S a type of waterwheel

NORITE *n* pl. -S a granular rock **NORITIC** *adj*

NORLAND *n* pl. -S a region in the north

NORM *n* pl. -S a standard regarded as typical for a specific group

NORMAL *n* pl. -S the usual or expected state or form

NORMALCY *n* pl. -CIES conformity with the norm

NORMALLY *adv* as a rule; usually

NORMANDE *adj* prepared with foods associated with Normandy

NORMED *adj* having a norm

NORMLESS *adj* having no norm

NORTH *n* pl. -S a point of the compass

NORTHER *n* pl. -S a wind or storm from the north

NORTHERN *n* pl. -S a person living in the north

NORTHING *n* pl. -S movement toward the north

NOSE *v* NOSED, NOSING, NOSES to sniff with the nose (the organ of smell)

NOSEBAG *n* pl. -S a feedbag

NOSEBAND *n* pl. -S a part of a horse's bridle

NOSED past tense of nose

NOSEDIVE *n* pl. -S a steep downward plunge

NOSEGAY *n* pl. -GAYS a bouquet

NOSELESS *adj* having no nose

NOSELIKE *adj* resembling a nose

NOSEY *adj* NOSIER, NOSIEST nosy

NOSH *v* -ED, -ING, -ES to eat snacks between meals

NOSHER *n* pl. -S one that noshes

NOSIER comparative of nosy, nosey

NOSIEST superlative of nosy, nosey

NOSILY *adv* in a nosy manner

NOSINESS *n* pl. -ES the quality of being nosy

NOSING *n* pl. -S a projecting edge

NOSOLOGY *n* pl. -GIES a classification of diseases

NOSTOC *n* pl. -S a freshwater alga

NOSTRIL *n* pl. -S an external opening of the nose

NOSTRUM *n* pl. -S a medicine of one's own invention

NOSY *adj* NOSIER, NOSIEST unduly curious

NOT *adv* in no way

NOTA pl. of notum

NOTABLE *n* pl. -S a person of distinction

NOTABLY *adv* in a distinguished manner

NOTAL *adj* pertaining to a notum

NOTARIAL *adj* pertaining to a notary

NOTARIZE *v* -RIZED, -RIZING, -RIZES to certify through a notary

NOTARY *n* pl. -RIES a public officer who certifies documents

NOTATE *v* -TATED, -TATING, -TATES to put into notation

NOTATION *n* pl. -S a system of symbols

NOTCH *v* -ED, -ING, -ES to make an angular cut in

NOTCHER *n* pl. -S one that notches

NOTE *v* NOTED, NOTING, NOTES to write down

NOTEBOOK *n* pl. -S a book in which to write

NOTECASE *n* pl. -S a billfold

NOTED past tense of note

NOTEDLY *adv* in a famous manner

NOTELESS *adj* undistinguished

NOTEPAD *n* pl. -S a number of sheets of paper glued together at one end

NOTER *n* pl. -S one that notes

NOTHER *adj* different

NOTHING *n* pl. -S the absence of all quantity or magnitude

NOTICE *v* -TICED, -TICING, -TICES to become aware of

NOTICER *n* pl. -S one that notices

NOTIFIER *n* pl. -S one that notifies

NOTIFY *v* -FIED, -FYING, -FIES to inform

NOTING present participle of note

NOTION *n* pl. -S a general idea **NOTIONAL** *adj*

NOTORNIS *n* pl. NOTORNIS a flightless bird

NOTTURNO *n* pl. -NI a nocturne

NOTUM *n* pl. -TA a part of the thorax of an insect

NOUGAT   *n* pl. -S a chewy candy

NOUGHT   *n* pl. -S naught

NOUMENON   *n* pl. -MENA an object of intellectual intuition **NOUMENAL** *adj*

NOUN   *n* pl. -S a word used to denote the name of something **NOUNAL, NOUNLESS** *adj* **NOUNALLY** *adv*

NOURISH   *v* -ED, -ING, -ES to sustain with food

NOUS   *n* pl. -ES mind, reason, or intellect

NOUVEAU   *adj* newly arrived or developed

NOUVELLE   *adj* pertaining to a form of French cooking

NOVA   *n* pl. -VAS or -VAE a type of star **NOVALIKE** *adj*

NOVATION   *n* pl. -S the substitution of a new legal obligation for an old one

NOVEL   *n* pl. -S a fictional prose narrative

NOVELISE   *v* -ISED, -ISING, -ISES to novelize

NOVELIST   *n* pl. -S a writer of novels

NOVELIZE   *v* -IZED, -IZING, -IZES to put into the form of a novel

NOVELLA   *n* pl. -LAS or -LE a short novel

NOVELLY   *adv* in a new or unusual manner

NOVELTY   *n* pl. -TIES something new or unusual

NOVENA   *n* pl. -NAS or -NAE a religious devotion lasting nine days

NOVERCAL   *adj* pertaining to a stepmother

NOVICE   *n* pl. -S a person new to any field or activity

NOW   *n* pl. -S the present time

NOWADAYS   *adv* in these times

NOWAY   *adv* in no way

NOWAYS   *adv* noway

NOWHERE   *n* pl. -S a nonexistent place

NOWISE   *adv* not at all

NOWNESS   *n* pl. -ES the state of existing at the present time

NOWT   *n* pl. -S naught

NOXIOUS   *adj* harmful to health

NOYADE   *n* pl. -S an execution by drowning

NOZZLE   *n* pl. -S a projecting spout

NTH   *adj* pertaining to an indefinitely large ordinal number

NU   *n* pl. -S a Greek letter

NUANCE   *n* pl. -S a slight variation **NUANCED** *adj*

NUB   *n* pl. -S a protuberance or knob

NUBBIER   comparative of nubby

NUBBIEST   superlative of nubby

NUBBIN   *n* pl. -S an undeveloped fruit

NUBBLE   *n* pl. -S a small nub

NUBBLY   *adj* -BLIER, -BLIEST having nubbles

NUBBY   *adj* -BIER, -BIEST having nubs

NUBIA   *n* pl. -S a woman's scarf

NUBILE   *adj* suitable for marriage

NUBILITY   *n* pl. -TIES the quality of being nubile

NUBILOSE   *adj* nubilous

NUBILOUS   *adj* cloudy

NUCELLUS   *n* pl. -LI the essential part of a plant ovule **NUCELLAR** *adj*

NUCHA   *n* pl. -CHAE the nape of the neck

NUCHAL   *n* pl. -S an anatomical part lying in the region of the nape

NUCLEAL   *adj* nuclear

NUCLEAR   *adj* pertaining to a nucleus

NUCLEASE   *n* pl. -S an enzyme

NUCLEATE   *v* -ATED, -ATING, -ATES to form into a nucleus

NUCLEI   a pl. of nucleus

NUCLEIN   *n* pl. -S a protein found in nuclei

NUCLEOID   *n* pl. -S the DNA-containing area of certain cells

NUCLEOLE   *n* pl. -S a part of a nucleus

NUCLEOLI   *n/pl* nucleoles

NUCLEON   *n* pl. -S a subatomic particle

NUCLEUS   *n* pl. -CLEI or -CLEUSES an essential part of a cell

NUCLIDE   *n* pl. -S a species of atom **NUCLIDIC** *adj*

NUDE   *adj* NUDER, NUDEST being without clothing or covering **NUDELY** *adv*

NUDE   *n* pl. -S a nude figure

NUDENESS   *n* pl. -ES nudity

NUDER   comparative of nude

NUDEST   superlative of nude

NUDGE   *v* NUDGED, NUDGING, NUDGES to push gently

NUDGER   *n* pl. -S one that nudges

NUDICAUL   *adj* having leafless stems

NUDIE *n* pl. -S a movie featuring nude performers

NUDISM *n* pl. -S the practice of going nude

NUDIST *n* pl. -S an advocate of nudism

NUDITY *n* pl. -TIES the state of being nude

NUDNICK *n* pl. -S nudnik

NUDNIK *n* pl. -S an annoying person

NUDZH *v* -ED, -ING, -ES to noodge

NUGATORY *adj* having no power

NUGGET *n* pl. -S a mass of solid matter **NUGGETY** *adj*

NUISANCE *n* pl. -S a source of annoyance

NUKE *v* NUKED, NUKING, NUKES to attack with nuclear weapons

NULL *v* -ED, -ING, -S to reduce to nothing

NULLAH *n* pl. -S a ravine

NULLIFY *v* -FIED, -FYING, -FIES to make useless or ineffective

NULLITY *n* pl. -TIES something of no legal force

NUMB *adj* NUMBER, NUMBEST lacking sensation

NUMB *v* -ED, -ING, -S to make numb

NUMBAT *n* pl. -S a small Australian mammal

NUMBER *v* -ED, -ING, -S to count

NUMBERER *n* pl. -S one that numbers

NUMBFISH *n* pl. -ES a fish capable of emitting electric shocks

NUMBLES *n/pl* animal entrails

NUMBLY *adv* in a numb manner

NUMBNESS *n* pl. -ES the state of being numb

NUMEN *n* pl. -MINA a deity

NUMERACY *n* pl. -CIES the ability to understand basic mathematics

NUMERAL *n* pl. -S a symbol that expresses a number

NUMERARY *adj* pertaining to numbers

NUMERATE *v* -ATED, -ATING, -ATES to count

NUMERIC *n* pl. -S a numeral

NUMEROUS *adj* many

NUMINA pl. of numen

NUMINOUS *n* pl. -ES the presence or revelation of the numen

NUMMARY *adj* pertaining to coins

NUMMULAR *adj* shaped like a coin

NUMSKULL *n* pl. -S a dunce

NUN *n* pl. -S a woman belonging to a religious order

NUNATAK *n* pl. -S a mountain peak completely surrounded by glacial ice

NUNCHAKU *n* pl. -S a Japanese weapon

NUNCIO *n* pl. -CIOS an ambassador from the pope

NUNCLE *n* pl. -S an uncle

NUNLIKE *adj* resembling a nun

NUNNERY *n* pl. -NERIES a religious house for nuns

NUNNISH *adj* of, pertaining to, or characteristic of a nun

NUPTIAL *n* pl. -S a wedding

NURD *n* pl. -S nerd

NURL *n* -ED, -ING, -S to knurl

NURSE *v* NURSED, NURSING, NURSES to care for the sick or infirm

NURSER *n* pl. -S a baby's bottle

NURSERY *n* pl. -ERIES a room for young children

NURSING *n* pl. -S the profession of one who nurses

NURSLING *n* pl. -S an infant

NURTURAL *adj* pertaining to the process of nurturing

NURTURE *v* -TURED, -TURING, -TURES to nourish

NURTURER *n* pl. -S one that nurtures

NUT *v* NUTTED, NUTTING, NUTS to gather nuts (hard-shelled dry fruits)

NUTANT *adj* drooping

NUTATE *v* -TATED, -TATING, -TATES to exhibit nutation

NUTATION *n* pl. -S an oscillatory movement of the axis of a rotating body

NUTBROWN *adj* of a dark brown

NUTCASE *n* pl. -S a crazy person

NUTGALL *n* pl. -S a gallnut

NUTGRASS *n* pl. -ES a perennial herb

NUTHATCH *n* pl. -ES a small bird

NUTHOUSE *n* pl. -S an insane asylum

NUTLET *n* pl. -S a small nut

NUTLIKE *adj* resembling a nut

NUTMEAT *n* pl. -S the edible kernel of a nut

NUTMEG   *n* pl. -S an aromatic seed used as a spice

NUTPICK   *n* pl. -S a device for extracting the kernels from nuts

NUTRIA   *n* pl. -S the coypu

NUTRIENT   *n* pl. -S a nourishing substance

NUTSEDGE   *n* pl. -S nutgrass

NUTSHELL   *n* pl. -S the shell of a nut

NUTSY   *adj* NUTSIER, NUTSIEST crazy

NUTTED   past tense of nut

NUTTER   *n* pl. -S one that gathers nuts

NUTTING   *n* pl. -S the act of gathering nuts

NUTTY   *adj* -TIER, -TIEST silly; crazy
NUTTILY *adv*

NUTWOOD   *n* pl. -S a nut-bearing tree

NUZZLE   *v* -ZLED, -ZLING, -ZLES to push with the nose

NUZZLER   *n* pl. -S one that nuzzles

NYALA   *n* pl. -S an antelope

NYLGHAI   *n* pl. -S nilgai

NYLGHAU   *n* pl. -S nilgai

NYLON   *n* pl. -S a synthetic material

NYMPH   *n* pl. -S a female spirit
NYMPHAL, NYMPHEAN *adj*

NYMPHA   *n* pl. -PHAE a fold of the vulva

NYMPHET   *n* pl. -S a young nymph

NYMPHO   *n* pl. -PHOS a woman obsessed by sexual desire

NYSTATIN   *n* pl. -S an antibiotic

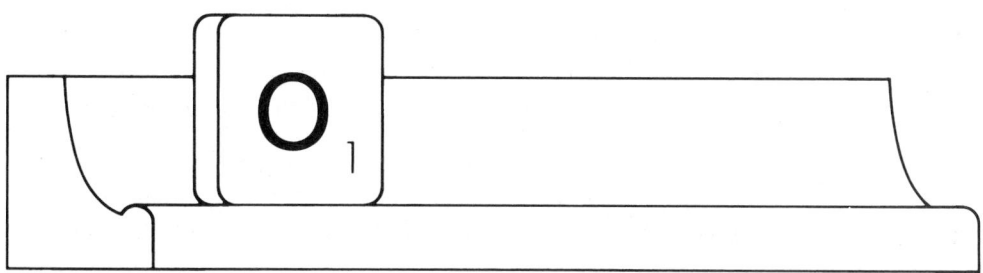

OAF	*n* pl. OAFS or OAVES a clumsy, stupid person **OAFISH** *adj* **OAFISHLY** *adv*	**OBEDIENT**	*adj* obeying or willing to obey
OAK	*n* pl. -S a hardwood tree or shrub **OAKEN, OAKLIKE** *adj*	**OBEISANT**	*adj* showing reverence or respect
		OBELI	pl. of obelus
OAKMOSS	*n* pl. -ES a lichen that grows on oak trees	**OBELIA**	*n* pl. -S a marine hydroid
OAKUM	*n* pl. -S loosely twisted hemp fiber	**OBELISE**	*v* -LISED, -LISING, -LISES to obelize
OAR	*v* -ED, -ING, -S to propel with oars (long, broad-bladed poles)	**OBELISK**	*n* pl. -S a four-sided shaft of stone with a pyramidal top
OARFISH	*n* pl. -ES a marine fish	**OBELISM**	*n* pl. -S the act of obelizing
OARLESS	*adj* having no oars	**OBELIZE**	*v* -LIZED, -LIZING, -LIZES to mark with an obelus
OARLIKE	*adj* resembling an oar	**OBELUS**	*n* pl. -LI a symbol used in ancient manuscripts to indicate a doubtful passage
OARLOCK	*n* pl. -S a device for holding an oar in place		
OARSMAN	*n* pl. -MEN a person who rows a boat	**OBESE**	*adj* very fat **OBESELY** *adv*
		OBESITY	*n* pl. -TIES the state or condition of being obese
OASIS	*n* pl. OASES a green area in a desert region	**OBEY**	*v* -ED, -ING, -S to follow the commands or guidance of **OBEYABLE** *adj*
OAST	*n* pl. -S a type of kiln		
OAT	*n* pl. -S a cereal grass	**OBEYER**	*n* pl. -S one that obeys
OATCAKE	*n* pl. -S a cake made of oatmeal	**OBI**	*n* pl. -S obeah
OATEN	*adj* pertaining to oats	**OBIA**	*n* pl. -S obeah
OATER	*n* pl. -S a cowboy movie	**OBIISM**	*n* pl. -S obeahism
OATH	*n* pl. -S a formal declaration or promise to fulfill a pledge	**OBIT**	*n* pl. -S an obituary
		OBITUARY	*n* pl. -ARIES a published notice of a death
OATLIKE	*adj* resembling oats		
OATMEAL	*n* pl. -S meal made from oats	**OBJECT**	*v* -ED, -ING, -S to argue in opposition
OAVES	a pl. of oaf	**OBJECTOR**	*n* pl. -S one that objects
OBCONIC	*adj* conical with the apex below	**OBJET**	*n* pl. -S an article of artistic value
OBDURACY	*n* pl. -CIES the quality or an instance of being obdurate	**OBLAST**	*n* pl. -LASTS or -LASTI an administrative division of Russia
OBDURATE	*adj* stubborn		
OBE	*n* pl. -S obeah	**OBLATE**	*n* pl. -S a layman residing in a monastery
OBEAH	*n* pl. -S a form of sorcery of African origin	**OBLATELY**	*adv* elliptically
		OBLATION	*n* pl. -S the act of making a religious offering **OBLATORY** *adj*
OBEAHISM	*n* pl. -S the use of obeah		

OBLIGATE   *v* -GATED, -GATING, -GATES to oblige

OBLIGATO   *n* pl. -TI or -TOS an important musical part

OBLIGE   *v* OBLIGED, OBLIGING, OBLIGES to put in one's debt by a favor or service

OBLIGEE   *n* pl. -S one that is obliged

OBLIGER   *n* pl. -S one that obliges

OBLIGING   present participle of oblige

OBLIGOR   *n* pl. -S one who places himself under a legal obligation

OBLIQUE   *v* OBLIQUED, OBLIQUING, OBLIQUES to slant

OBLIVION   *n* pl. -S the state of being forgotten; the act of forgetting

OBLONG   *n* pl. -S something that is oblong (elongated)

OBLONGLY   *adv* in an oblong manner

OBLOQUY   *n* pl. -QUIES abusive language

OBOE   *n* pl. -S a woodwind instrument

OBOIST   *n* pl. -S one who plays the oboe

OBOL   *n* pl. -S a coin of ancient Greece

OBOLE   *n* pl. -S a coin of medieval France

OBOLUS   *n* pl. -LI an obol

OBOVATE   *adj* ovate with the narrow end at the base

OBOVOID   *adj* ovoid with the narrow end at the base

OBSCENE   *adj* -SCENER, -SCENEST indecent

OBSCURE   *adj* -SCURER, -SCUREST dark or indistinct

OBSCURE   *v* -SCURED, -SCURING, -SCURES to make obscure

OBSEQUY   *n* pl. -QUIES a funeral rite

OBSERVE   *v* -SERVED, -SERVING, -SERVES to look attentively

OBSERVER   *n* pl. -S one that observes

OBSESS   *v* -ED, -ING, -ES to dominate the thoughts of

OBSESSOR   *n* pl. -S something that obsesses

OBSIDIAN   *n* pl. -S a volcanic glass

OBSOLETE   *v* -LETED, -LETING, -LETES to make out-of-date

OBSTACLE   *n* pl. -S something that obstructs

OBSTRUCT   *v* -ED, -ING, -S to get in the way of

OBTAIN   *v* -ED, -ING, -S to gain possession of

OBTAINER   *n* pl. -S one that obtains

OBTECT   *adj* covered by a hardened secretion

OBTECTED   *adj* obtect

OBTEST   *v* -ED, -ING, -S to beseech

OBTRUDE   *v* -TRUDED, -TRUDING, -TRUDES to thrust forward

OBTRUDER   *n* pl. -S one that obtrudes

OBTUND   *v* -ED, -ING, -S to deaden

OBTURATE   *v* -RATED, -RATING, -RATES to close or stop up

OBTUSE   *adj* -TUSER, -TUSEST dull **OBTUSELY** *adv*

OBTUSITY   *n* pl. -TIES the state of being obtuse

OBVERSE   *n* pl. -S the side of a coin bearing the main design

OBVERT   *v* -ED, -ING, -S to turn so as to show a different surface

OBVIATE   *v* -ATED, -ATING, -ATES to prevent or eliminate by effective measures **OBVIABLE** *adj*

OBVIATOR   *n* pl. -S one that obviates

OBVIOUS   *adj* easily perceived or understood

OBVOLUTE   *adj* rolled or tuned in

OCA   *n* pl. -S a South American herb

OCARINA   *n* pl. -S a wind instrument

OCCASION   *v* -ED, -ING, -S to cause

OCCIDENT   *n* pl. -S the west

OCCIPUT   *n* pl. -PITA or -PUTS the back part of the skull

OCCLUDE   *v* -CLUDED, -CLUDING, -CLUDES to close or stop up

OCCLUSAL   *adj* pertaining to the biting surface of a tooth

OCCULT   *v* -ED, -ING, -S to conceal

OCCULTER   *n* pl. -S one that occults

OCCULTLY   *adv* secretly

OCCUPANT   *n* pl. -S a resident

OCCUPIER   *n* pl. -S one that occupies

OCCUPY   *v* -PIED, -PYING, -PIES to engage the attention or energies of

OCCUR   *v* -CURRED, -CURRING, -CURS to take place

OCEAN *n* pl. -S the vast body of salt water that covers most of the earth's surface **OCEANIC** *adj*

OCEANAUT *n* pl. -S an aquanaut

OCELLAR *adj* pertaining to an ocellus

OCELLATE *adj* having ocelli

OCELLUS *n* pl. -LI a minute simple eye

OCELOT *n* pl. -S an American wildcat **OCELOID** *adj*

OCHER *v* -ED, -ING, -S to color with ocher (a red or yellow iron ore used as a pigment)

OCHEROUS *adj* containing or resembling ocher

OCHERY *adj* ocherous

OCHONE *interj* — used to express grief

OCHRE *v* OCHRED, OCHRING, OCHRES to ocher

OCHREA *n* pl. -REAE ocrea

OCHREOUS *adj* ocherous

OCHRING present participle of ochre

OCHROID *adj* ocherous

OCHROUS *adj* ocherous

OCHRY *adj* ochery

OCKER *n* pl. -S a boorish person

OCOTILLO *n* pl. -LOS a Mexican shrub

OCREA *n* pl. -REAE a sheathing plant part

OCREATE *adj* having ocreae

OCTAD *n* pl. -S a group of eight **OCTADIC** *adj*

OCTAGON *n* pl. -S an eight-sided polygon

OCTAL *adj* pertaining to a number system with a base of eight

OCTAN *n* pl. -S a fever recurring every eighth day

OCTANE *n* pl. -S a liquid hydrocarbon

OCTANGLE *n* pl. -S an octagon

OCTANOL *n* pl. -S an alcohol

OCTANT *n* pl. -S an eighth of a circle **OCTANTAL** *adj*

OCTARCHY *n* pl. -TARCHIES a government by eight persons

OCTAVE *n* pl. -S a type of musical interval **OCTAVAL** *adj*

OCTAVO *n* pl. -VOS a page size

OCTET *n* pl. -S a group of eight

OCTETTE *n* pl. -S octet

OCTONARY *n* pl. -NARIES a stanza of eight lines

OCTOPOD *n* pl. -S any of an order of eight-armed mollusks

OCTOPUS *n* pl. -PUSES, -PI, or -PODES a nocturnal octopod

OCTOROON *n* pl. -S a person of one-eighth black ancestry

OCTROI *n* pl. -S a tax on certain articles brought into a city

OCTUPLE *v* -PLED, -PLING, -PLES to multiply by eight

OCTUPLET *n* pl. -S a group of eight related items

OCTUPLEX *adj* being eight times as great

OCTUPLING present participle of octuple

OCTUPLY *adv* to eight times the degree

OCTYL *n* pl. -S a univalent radical

OCULAR *n* pl. -S an eyepiece

OCULARLY *adv* by means of the eyes or sight

OCULIST *n* pl. -S a physician who treats diseases of the eye

OCULUS *n* pl. -LI a circular window

OD *n* pl. -S a hypothetical force of natural power

ODALISK *n* pl. -S a female slave in a harem

ODD *adj* ODDER, ODDEST unusual

ODD *n* pl. -S one that is odd

ODDBALL *n* pl. -S an eccentric person

ODDISH *adj* somewhat odd

ODDITY *n* pl. -TIES one that is odd

ODDLY *adv* in an odd manner

ODDMENT *n* pl. -S a remnant

ODDNESS *n* pl. -ES the state of being odd

ODE *n* pl. -S a lyric poem

ODEON *n* pl. -S odeum

ODEUM *n* pl. ODEA or ODEUMS a theater or concert hall

ODIC *adj* pertaining to an ode

ODIOUS *adj* deserving or causing hatred **ODIOUSLY** *adv*

ODIST *n* pl. -S one who writes odes

ODIUM *n* pl. -S hatred

ODOGRAPH *n* pl. -S an odometer

ODOMETER *n* pl. -S a device for measuring distance traveled

ODOMETRY *n* pl. -TRIES the process of using an odometer

ODONATE *n* pl. -S any of an order of predacious insects

ODONTOID *n* pl. -S a toothlike vertebral projection

ODOR *n* pl. -S the property of a substance that affects the sense of smell **ODORED, ODORFUL** *adj*

ODORANT *n* pl. -S an odorous substance

ODORIZE *v* -IZED, -IZING, -IZES to make odorous

ODORLESS *adj* having no odor

ODOROUS *adj* having an odor

ODOUR *n* pl. -S odor **ODOURFUL** *adj*

ODYL *n* pl. -S an od

ODYLE *n* pl. -S odyl

ODYSSEY *n* pl. -SEYS a long, wandering journey

OE *n* pl. -S a whirlwind off the Faeroe islands

OECOLOGY *n* pl. -GIES ecology

OEDEMA *n* pl. -MAS or -MATA edema

OEDIPAL *adj* pertaining to the libidinal feelings in a child toward the parent of the opposite sex

OEDIPEAN *adj* oedipal

OEILLADE *n* pl. -S an amorous look

OENOLOGY *n* pl. -GIES the study of wines

OENOMEL *n* pl. -S an ancient Greek beverage of wine and honey

OERSTED *n* pl. -S a unit of magnetic intensity

OESTRIN *n* pl. -S estrin

OESTRIOL *n* pl. -S estriol

OESTRONE *n* pl. -S estrone

OESTROUS *adj* estrous

OESTRUM *n* pl. -S estrum

OESTRUS *n* pl. -ES estrus

OEUVRE *n* pl. -S a work of art

OF *prep* coming from

OFF *v* -ED, -ING, -S to go away

OFFAL *n* pl. -S waste material

OFFBEAT *n* pl. -S an unaccented beat in a musical measure

OFFCAST *n* pl. -S a castoff

OFFCUT *n* pl. -S something that is cut off

OFFENCE *n* pl. -S offense

OFFEND *v* -ED, -ING, -S to commit an offense

OFFENDER *n* pl. -S one that offends

OFFENSE *n* pl. -S a violation of a moral or social code

OFFER *v* -ED, -ING, -S to present for acceptance or rejection

OFFERER *n* pl. -S one that offers

OFFERING *n* pl. -S a contribution

OFFEROR *n* pl. -S offerer

OFFHAND *adv* without preparation

OFFICE *n* pl. -S a position of authority

OFFICER *v* -ED, -ING, -S to furnish with officers (persons holding positions of authority)

OFFICIAL *n* pl. -S one that holds a position of authority

OFFING *n* pl. -S the near future

OFFISH *adj* aloof **OFFISHLY** *adv*

OFFKEY *adj* pitched higher or lower than the correct musical tone

OFFLOAD *v* -ED, -ING, -S to unload

OFFPRINT *v* -ED, -ING, -S to reprint an excerpt

OFFRAMP *n* pl. -S a road leading off an expressway

OFFSET *v* -SET, -SETTING, -SETS to compensate for

OFFSHOOT *n* pl. -S a lateral shoot from a main stem

OFFSHORE *adv* away from the shore

OFFSIDE *n* pl. -S an improper football play

OFFSTAGE *n* pl. -S a part of a stage not visible to the audience

OFFTRACK *adj* away from a racetrack

OFT *adv* OFTER, OFTEST often

OFTEN *adv* -ENER, -ENEST frequently

OFTTIMES *adv* often

OGAM *n* pl. -S ogham

OGDOAD *n* pl. -S a group of eight

OGEE *n* pl. -S an S-shaped molding

OGHAM *n* pl. -S an Old Irish alphabet **OGHAMIC** *adj*

OGHAMIST *n* pl. -S one who writes in ogham

OGIVE *n* pl. -S a pointed arch **OGIVAL** *adj*

OGLE *v* OGLED, OGLING, OGLES to stare at

OGLER *n* pl. -S one that ogles

OGRE	*n* pl. -S a monster
OGREISH	*adj* resembling an ogre
OGREISM	*n* pl. -S the state of being ogreish
OGRESS	*n* pl. -ES a female ogre
OGRISH	*adj* ogreish **OGRISHLY** *adv*
OGRISM	*n* pl. -S ogreism
OH	*v* -ED, -ING, -S to exclaim in surprise, pain, or desire
OHIA	*n* pl. -S lehua
OHM	*n* pl. -S a unit of electrical resistance **OHMIC** *adj*
OHMAGE	*n* pl. -S electrical resistance expressed in ohms
OHMMETER	*n* pl. -S an instrument for measuring ohmage
OHO	*interj* — used to express surprise or exultation
OIDIUM	*n* pl. OIDIA a type of fungus
OIL	*v* -ED, -ING, -S to supply with oil (a greasy liquid used for lubrication, fuel, or illumination)
OILBIRD	*n* pl. -S a tropical bird
OILCAMP	*n* pl. -S a living area for workers at an oil well
OILCAN	*n* pl. -S a can for applying lubricating oil
OILCLOTH	*n* pl. -S a waterproof fabric
OILCUP	*n* pl. -S a closed cup for supplying lubricant
OILER	*n* pl. -S one that oils
OILHOLE	*n* pl. -S a hole through which lubricating oil is injected
OILIER	comparative of oily
OILIEST	superlative of oily
OILILY	*adv* in an oily manner
OILINESS	*n* pl. -ES the state of being oily
OILMAN	*n* pl. -MEN one who owns or operates oil wells
OILPAPER	*n* pl. -S a water-resistant paper
OILPROOF	*adj* impervious to oil
OILSEED	*n* pl. -S a seed from which oil is pressed out
OILSKIN	*n* pl. -S a waterproof fabric
OILSTONE	*n* pl. -S a stone for sharpening tools
OILTIGHT	*adj* being so tight as to prevent the passage of oil
OILWAY	*n* pl. -WAYS a channel for the passage of oil
OILY	*adj* OILIER, OILIEST covered or soaked with oil
OINK	*v* -ED, -ING, -S to utter the natural grunt of a hog
OINOLOGY	*n* pl. -GIES oenology
OINOMEL	*n* pl. -S oenomel
OINTMENT	*n* pl. -S a viscous preparation applied to the skin as a medicine or cosmetic
OITICICA	*n* pl. -S a South American tree
OKA	*n* pl. -S a Turkish unit of weight
OKAPI	*n* pl. -S an African ruminant mammal
OKAY	*v* -ED, -ING, -S to approve
OKE	*n* pl. -S oka
OKEH	*n* pl. -S approval
OKEYDOKE	*adj* perfectly all right
OKRA	*n* pl. -S a tall annual herb
OLD	*adj* OLDER, OLDEST or ELDER, ELDEST living or existing for a relatively long time
OLD	*n* pl. -S an individual of a specified age
OLDEN	*adj* pertaining to a bygone era
OLDIE	*n* pl. -S a popular song of an earlier day
OLDISH	*adj* somewhat old
OLDNESS	*n* pl. -ES the state of being old
OLDSQUAW	*n* pl. -S a sea duck
OLDSTER	*n* pl. -S an old person
OLDSTYLE	*n* pl. -S a style of printing type
OLDWIFE	*n* pl. -WIVES a marine fish
OLDY	*n* pl. OLDIES oldie
OLE	*n* pl. -S a shout of approval
OLEA	pl. of oleum
OLEANDER	*n* pl. -S a flowering shrub
OLEASTER	*n* pl. -S a flowering shrub
OLEATE	*n* pl. -S a chemical salt
OLEFIN	*n* pl. -S an alkene **OLEFINIC** *adj*
OLEFINE	*n* pl. -S olefin
OLEIC	*adj* pertaining to oil
OLEIN	*n* pl. -S the liquid portion of a fat
OLEINE	*n* pl. -S olein
OLEO	*n* pl. OLEOS margarine
OLEUM	*n* pl. OLEA oil
OLEUM	*n* pl. -S a corrosive liquid
OLIBANUM	*n* pl. -S a fragrant resin

OLIGARCH *n* pl. -S a ruler in a government by the few

OLIGOMER *n* pl. -S a type of polymer

OLIGURIA *n* pl. -S reduced excretion of urine

OLIO *n* pl. OLIOS a miscellaneous collection

OLIVARY *adj* shaped like an olive

OLIVE *n* pl. -S the small oval fruit of a Mediterranean tree

OLIVINE *n* pl. -S a mineral **OLIVINIC** *adj*

OLLA *n* pl. -S a wide-mouthed pot or jar

OLOGIST *n* pl. -S an expert in a particular ology

OLOGY *n* pl. -GIES a branch of knowledge

OLOROSO *n* pl. -SOS a dark sherry

OLYMPIAD *n* pl. -S a celebration of the Olympic Games

OM *n* pl. -S a mantra used in contemplation of ultimate reality

OMASUM *n* pl. -SA the third stomach of a ruminant

OMBER *n* pl. -S ombre

OMBRE *n* pl. -S a card game

OMEGA *n* pl. -S a Greek letter

OMELET *n* pl. -S a dish of beaten eggs cooked and folded around a filling

OMELETTE *n* pl. -S omelet

OMEN *v* -ED, -ING, -S to be an omen (a prophetic sign) of

OMENTUM *n* pl. -TA or -TUMS a fold in an abdominal membrane **OMENTAL** *adj*

OMER *n* pl. -S a Hebrew unit of dry measure

OMICRON *n* pl. -S a Greek letter

OMIKRON *n* pl. -S omicron

OMINOUS *adj* portending evil

OMISSION *n* pl. -S something left undone

OMISSIVE *adj* marked by omission

OMIT *v* OMITTED, OMITTING, OMITS to leave out

OMITTER *n* pl. -S one that omits

OMNIARCH *n* pl. -S an almighty ruler

OMNIBUS *n* pl. -ES a bus

OMNIFIC *adj* unlimited in creative power

OMNIFORM *adj* of all forms

OMNIMODE *adj* of all modes

OMNIVORA *n/pl* omnivores

OMNIVORE *n* pl. -S an animal that eats all kinds of food

OMOPHAGY *n* pl. -GIES the eating of raw flesh

OMPHALOS *n* pl. -LI a central point

ON *n* pl. -S the side of the wicket where a batsman stands in cricket

ONAGER *n* pl. -GERS or -GRI a wild ass of central Asia

ONANISM *n* pl. -S coitus deliberately interrupted to prevent insemination

ONANIST *n* pl. -S one who practices onanism

ONBOARD *adj* carried aboard a vehicle

ONCE *n* one single time

ONCIDIUM *n* pl. -S a tropical orchid

ONCOGENE *n* pl. -S a gene that causes a cell to become cancerous

ONCOLOGY *n* pl. -GIES the science of tumors

ONCOMING *n* pl. -S an approach

ONDOGRAM *n* pl. -S a graph of electric wave forms

ONE *n* pl. -S a number

ONEFOLD *adj* constituting a single, undivided whole

ONEIRIC *adj* pertaining to dreams

ONENESS *n* pl. -ES unity

ONEROUS *adj* burdensome or oppressive

ONERY *adj* -ERIER, -ERIEST ornery

ONESELF *pron* a person's self

ONETIME *adj* former

ONGOING *adj* continuing without interruption

ONION *n* pl. -S the edible bulb of a cultivated herb **ONIONY** *adj*

ONIUM *adj* characterized by a complex cation

ONLOOKER *n* pl. -S a spectator

ONLY *adv* with nothing or no one else

ONRUSH *n* pl. -ES a forward rush or flow

ONSET *n* pl. -S a beginning

ONSHORE *adv* toward the shore

ONSIDE *adj* not offside

ONSTAGE *adj* being on a part of the stage visible to the audience

ONSTREAM *adv* in or into production

ONTIC *adj* having real being or existence

ONTO *prep* to a position upon

ONTOGENY *n* pl. -NIES the development of an individual organism

ONTOLOGY *n* pl. -GIES the branch of philosophy that deals with being

ONUS *n* pl. -ES a burden or responsibility

ONWARD *adv* toward a point ahead or in front

ONWARDS *adv* onward

ONYX *n* pl. -ES a variety of quartz

OOCYST *n* pl. -S a zygote

OOCYTE *n* pl. -S an egg before maturation

OODLES *n* pl. OODLES a large amount

OODLINS *n* pl. OODLINS oodles

OOGAMETE *n* pl. -S a female gamete of certain protozoa

OOGAMOUS *adj* having structurally dissimilar gametes

OOGAMY *n* pl. -MIES the state of being oogamous

OOGENY *n* pl. -NIES the development of ova

OOGONIUM *n* pl. -NIA or -NIUMS a female sexual organ in certain algae and fungi **OOGONIAL** *adj*

OOH *v* -ED, -ING, -S to exclaim in amazement, joy, or surprise

OOLACHAN *n* pl. -S eulachon

OOLITE *n* pl. -S a variety of limestone **OOLITIC** *adj*

OOLITH *n* pl. -S oolite

OOLOGIST *n* pl. -S an expert in oology

OOLOGY *n* pl. -GIES the study of birds' eggs **OOLOGIC** *adj*

OOLONG *n* pl. -S a dark Chinese tea

OOMIAC *n* pl. -S umiak

OOMIACK *n* pl. -S umiak

OOMIAK *n* pl. -S umiak

OOMPAH *v* -ED, -ING, -S to play a repeated rhythmic bass accompaniment

OOMPH *n* pl. -S spirited vigor

OOPHYTE *n* pl. -S a stage of development in certain plants **OOPHYTIC** *adj*

OOPS *interj* — used to express mild apology, surprise, or dismay

OORALI *n* pl. -S curare

OORIE *adj* ourie

OOSPERM *n* pl. -S a fertilized egg

OOSPHERE *n* pl. -S an unfertilized egg within an oogonium

OOSPORE *n* pl. -S a fertilized egg within an oogonium **OOSPORIC** *adj*

OOT *n* pl. -S out

OOTHECA *n* pl. -CAE an egg case of certain insects **OOTHECAL** *adj*

OOTID *n* pl. -S one of the four sections into which a mature ovum divides

OOZE *v* OOZED, OOZING, OOZES to flow or leak out slowly

OOZINESS *n* pl. -ES the state of being oozy

OOZY *adj* OOZIER, OOZIEST containing or resembling soft mud or slime **OOZILY** *adv*

OP *n* pl. -S a style of abstract art

OPACIFY *v* -FIED, -FYING, -FIES to make opaque

OPACITY *n* pl. -TIES something that is opaque

OPAH *n* pl. -S a marine fish

OPAL *n* pl. -S a mineral

OPALESCE *v* -ESCED, -ESCING, -ESCES to emit an iridescent shimmer of colors

OPALINE *n* pl. -S an opaque white glass

OPAQUE *adj* OPAQUER, OPAQUEST impervious to light **OPAQUELY** *adv*

OPAQUE *v* OPAQUED, OPAQUING, OPAQUES to make opaque

OPE *v* OPED, OPING, OPES to open

OPEN *adj* OPENER, OPENEST affording unobstructed access, passage, or view

OPEN *v* -ED, -ING, -S to cause to become open **OPENABLE** *adj*

OPENCAST *adj* worked from a surface open to the air

OPENER *n* pl. -S one that opens

OPENING *n* pl. -S a vacant or unobstructed space

OPENLY *adv* in an open manner

OPENNESS *n* pl. -ES the state of being open

OPENWORK *n* pl. -S ornamental or structural work containing numerous openings

OPERA *n* pl. -S a form of musical drama

OPERABLE *adj* capable of being used **OPERABLY** *adv*

OPERAND *n* pl. -S a quantity on which a mathematical operation is performed

OPERANT *n* pl. -S one that operates

OPERATE *v* -ATED, -ATING, -ATES to perform a function

OPERATIC *n* pl. -S the technique of staging operas

OPERATOR *n* pl. -S a symbol that represents a mathematical function

OPERCELE *n* pl. -S opercule

OPERCULA *n/pl* opercules

OPERCULE *n* pl. -S an anatomical part that serves as a lid or cover

OPERETTA *n* pl. -S a light musical drama with spoken dialogue

OPERON *n* pl. -S a type of gene cluster

OPEROSE *adj* involving great labor

OPHIDIAN *n* pl. -S a snake

OPHITE *n* pl. -S a green mottled igneous rock **OPHITIC** *adj*

OPIATE *v* -ATED, -ATING, -ATES to treat with opium

OPINE *v* OPINED, OPINING, OPINES to hold or state as an opinion

OPING present participle of ope

OPINION *n* pl. -S a conclusion or judgment one holds to be true

OPIOID *n* pl. -S a peptide that acts like opium

OPIUM *n* pl. -S an addictive narcotic

OPIUMISM *n* pl. -S opium addiction

OPPIDAN *n* pl. -S a townsman

OPPILATE *v* -LATED, -LATING, -LATES to obstruct **OPPILANT** *adj*

OPPONENT *n* pl. -S one that opposes another

OPPOSE *v* -POSED, -POSING, -POSES to be in contention or conflict with

OPPOSER *n* pl. -S one that opposes

OPPOSITE *n* pl. -S one that is radically different from another in some related way

OPPRESS *v* -ED, -ING, -ES to burden by abuse of power or authority

OPPUGN *v* -ED, -ING, -S to assail with argument

OPPUGNER *n* pl. -S one that oppugns

OPSIN *n* pl. -S a type of protein

OPSONIC *adj* pertaining to opsonin

OPSONIFY *v* -FIED, -FYING, -FIES to opsonize

OPSONIN *n* pl. -S an antibody of blood serum

OPSONIZE *v* -NIZED, -NIZING, -NIZES to form opsonins in

OPT *v* -ED, -ING, -S to choose

OPTATIVE *n* pl. -S a mood of verbs that expresses a wish or desire

OPTIC *n* pl. -S an eye

OPTICAL *adj* pertaining to sight

OPTICIAN *n* pl. -S one who makes or deals in optical goods

OPTICIST *n* pl. -S one engaged in the study of light and vision

OPTIMA a pl. of optimum

OPTIMAL *adj* most desirable

OPTIME *n* pl. -S an honor student in mathematics at Cambridge University

OPTIMISE *v* -MISED, -MISING, -MISES to optimize

OPTIMISM *n* pl. -S a disposition to look on the favorable side of things

OPTIMIST *n* pl. -S one who exhibits optimism

OPTIMIZE *v* -MIZED, -MIZING, -MIZES to make as perfect, useful, or effective as possible

OPTIMUM *n* pl. -MA or -MUMS the most favorable condition for obtaining a given result

OPTION *v* -ED, -ING, -S to grant an option (a right to buy or sell something at a specified price within a specified time) on

OPTIONAL *n* pl. -S an elective course of study

OPTIONEE *n* pl. -S one who holds a legal option

OPULENCE *n* pl. -S wealth

OPULENCY *n* pl. -CIES opulence

OPULENT *adj* wealthy

OPUNTIA *n* pl. -S an American cactus

OPUS *n* pl. OPERA or OPUSES a literary of musical work

OPUSCULA *n/pl* opuscules

OPUSCULE *n* pl. -S a minor work

OQUASSA *n* pl. -S a small lake trout

OR *n* pl. -S the heraldic color gold

ORA pl. of os

ORACH *n* pl. -ES a cultivated plant

ORACHE *n* pl. -S orach

ORACLE *n* pl. -S a person through whom a deity is believed to speak **ORACULAR** *adj*

ORAD *adv* toward the mouth

ORAL *n* pl. -S an examination requiring spoken answers

ORALISM *n* pl. -S the use of oral methods of teaching the deaf

ORALIST *n* pl. -S an advocate of oralism

ORALITY *n* pl. -TIES the state of being produced orally

ORALLY *adv* through the mouth

ORANG *n* pl. -S a large ape

ORANGE *n* pl. -S a citrus fruit

ORANGERY *n* pl. -RIES a place where orange trees are cultivated

ORANGEY *adj* -ANGIER, -ANGIEST orangy

ORANGISH *adj* of a somewhat orange color

ORANGY *adj* -ANGIER, -ANGIEST resembling or suggestive of an orange

ORATE *v* ORATED, ORATING, ORATES to speak formally

ORATION *n* pl. -S a formal speech

ORATOR *n* pl. -S one that orates

ORATORIO *n* pl. -RIOS a type of musical composition

ORATORY *n* pl. -RIES the art of public speaking

ORATRESS *n* pl. -ES oratrix

ORATRIX *n* pl. -TRICES a female orator

ORB *v* -ED, -ING, -S to form into a circle or sphere

ORBIER comparative of orby

ORBIEST superlative of orby

ORBIT *v* -ED, -ING, -S to move or revolve around

ORBITAL *n* pl. -S a subdivision of a nuclear shell

ORBITER *n* pl. -S one that orbits

ORBY *adj* ORBIER, ORBIEST resembling a circle or sphere

ORC *n* pl. -S a marine mammal

ORCA *n* pl. -S orc

ORCEIN *n* pl. -S a reddish brown dye

ORCHARD *n* pl. -S an area for the cultivation of fruit trees

ORCHID *n* pl. -S a flowering plant

ORCHIL *n* pl. -S a purple dye

ORCHIS *n* pl. -CHISES an orchid

ORCHITIS *n* pl. -TISES inflammation of the testicle **ORCHITIC** *adj*

ORCIN *n* pl. -S orcinol

ORCINOL *n* pl. -S a chemical compound

ORDAIN *v* -ED, -ING, -S to invest with holy authority

ORDAINER *n* pl. -S one that ordains

ORDEAL *n* pl. -S a severely difficult or painful experience

ORDER *v* -ED, -ING, -S to give a command or instruction to

ORDERER *n* pl. -S one that orders

ORDERLY *n* pl. -LIES a male attendant

ORDINAL *n* pl. -S a number designating position in a series

ORDINAND *n* pl. -S a person about to be ordained

ORDINARY *adj* -NARIER, -NARIEST of a kind to be expected in the normal order of events

ORDINARY *n* pl. -NARIES something that is ordinary

ORDINATE *n* pl. -S a particular geometric coordinate

ORDINES a pl. of ordo

ORDNANCE *n* pl. -S artillery; a cannon

ORDO *n* pl. -DINES or -DOS a calendar of religious directions

ORDURE *n* pl. -S manure

ORE *n* pl. -S a mineral or rock containing a valuable metal

OREAD *n* pl. -S a mountain nymph in Greek mythology

ORECTIC *adj* pertaining to appetites or desires

ORECTIVE *adj* orectic

OREGANO *n* pl. -NOS an aromatic herb used as a seasoning

OREIDE *n* pl. -S oroide

ORFRAY *n* pl. -FRAYS orphrey

ORGAN *n* pl. -S a differentiated part of an organism performing a specific function

ORGANA a pl. of organon and organum

ORGANDIE	*n* pl. -S organdy
ORGANDY	*n* pl. -DIES a cotton fabric
ORGANIC	*n* pl. -S a substance of animal or vegetable origin
ORGANISE	*v* -NISED, -NISING, -NISES to organize
ORGANISM	*n* pl. -S any form of animal or plant life
ORGANIST	*n* pl. -S one who plays the organ (a keyboard musical instrument)
ORGANIZE	*v* -NIZED, -NIZING, -NIZES to form into an orderly whole
ORGANON	*n* pl. -GANA or -GANONS a system of rules for scientific investigation
ORGANUM	*n* pl. -GANA or -GANUMS organon
ORGANZA	*n* pl. -S a sheer fabric
ORGASM	*n* pl. -S the climax of sexual excitement **ORGASMIC, ORGASTIC** *adj*
ORGEAT	*n* pl. -S an almond-flavored syrup
ORGIAC	*adj* of the nature of an orgy
ORGIC	*adj* orgiac
ORGONE	*n* pl. -S a postulated energy pervading the universe
ORGULOUS	*adj* proud
ORGY	*n* pl. -GIES a party marked by unrestrained sexual indulgence
ORIBATID	*n* pl. -S any of a family of eyeless mites
ORIBI	*n* pl. -S an African antelope
ORIEL	*n* pl. -S a type of projecting window
ORIENT	*v* -ED, -ING, -S to adjust in relation to something else
ORIENTAL	*n* pl. -S an inhabitant of an eastern country
ORIFICE	*n* pl. -S a mouth or mouthlike opening
ORIGAMI	*n* pl. -S the Japanese art of paper folding
ORIGAN	*n* pl. -S marjoram
ORIGANUM	*n* pl. -S an aromatic herb
ORIGIN	*n* pl. -S a coming into being
ORIGINAL	*n* pl. -S the first form of something
ORINASAL	*n* pl. -S a sound pronounced through both the mouth and nose
ORIOLE	*n* pl. -S an American songbird
ORISON	*n* pl. -S a prayer

ORLE	*n* pl. -S a heraldic border
ORLOP	*n* pl. -S the lowest deck of a ship
ORMER	*n* pl. -S an abalone
ORMOLU	*n* pl. -S an alloy used to imitate gold
ORNAMENT	*v* -ED, -ING, -S to decorate
ORNATE	*adj* elaborately or excessively ornamented **ORNATELY** *adv*
ORNERY	*adj* -NERIER, -NERIEST stubborn and mean-spirited
ORNIS	*n* pl. ORNITHES avifauna
ORNITHIC	*adj* pertaining to birds
OROGENY	*n* pl. -NIES the process of mountain formation **OROGENIC** *adj*
OROIDE	*n* pl. -S an alloy used to imitate gold
OROLOGY	*n* pl. -GIES the study of mountains
OROMETER	*n* pl. -S a type of barometer
OROTUND	*adj* full and clear in sound
ORPHAN	*v* -ED, -ING, -S to deprive of both parents
ORPHIC	*adj* mystical
ORPHICAL	*adj* orphic
ORPHREY	*n* pl. -PHREYS an ornamental band or border
ORPIMENT	*n* pl. -S a yellow dye
ORPIN	*n* pl. -S orpine
ORPINE	*n* pl. -S a perennial herb
ORRA	*adj* occasional
ORRERY	*n* pl. -RERIES a mechanical model of the solar system
ORRICE	*n* pl. -S orris
ORRIS	*n* pl. -RISES a flowering plant
ORT	*n* pl. -S a scrap of food
ORTHICON	*n* pl. -S a type of television camera tube
ORTHO	*adj* pertaining to reproduction in a photograph of the full range of colors in nature
ORTHODOX	*n* pl. -ES one holding traditional beliefs
ORTHOEPY	*n* pl. -EPIES the study of correct pronunciation
ORTHOSIS	*n* pl. -THOSES an orthotic
ORTHOTIC	*n* pl. -S a brace for weak joints or muscles
ORTOLAN	*n* pl. -S a European bird

ORYX	*n* pl. -ES an African antelope
ORZO	*n* pl. -ZOS rice-shaped pasta
OS	*n* pl. ORA an orifice
OS	*n* pl. OSSA a bone
OS	*n* pl. OSAR an esker
OSCINE	*n* pl. -S any of a family of songbirds **OSCININE** *adj*
OSCITANT	*adj* yawning
OSCULA	pl. of osculum
OSCULANT	*adj* adhering closely
OSCULAR	*adj* pertaining to the mouth
OSCULATE	*v* -LATED, -LATING, -LATES to kiss
OSCULE	*n* pl. -S osculum
OSCULUM	*n* pl. -LA an opening in a sponge
OSE	*n* pl. -S an esker
OSIER	*n* pl. -S a European tree
OSMATIC	*adj* depending mainly on the sense of smell
OSMICS	*n/pl* the study of the sense of smell
OSMIUM	*n* pl. -S a metallic element **OSMIC, OSMIOUS** *adj*
OSMOL	*n* pl. -S a unit of osmotic pressure **OSMOLAL** *adj*
OSMOLAR	*adj* osmotic
OSMOLE	*n* pl. -S osmol
OSMOSE	*v* -MOSED, -MOSING, -MOSES to undergo osmosis
OSMOSIS	*n* pl. -MOSES a form of diffusion of a fluid through a membrane
OSMOTIC	*adj* pertaining to osmosis
OSMOUS	*adj* containing osmium
OSMUND	*n* pl. -S any of a genus of large ferns
OSMUNDA	*n* pl. -S osmund
OSNABURG	*n* pl. -S a cotton fabric
OSPREY	*n* pl. -PREYS an American hawk
OSSA	pl. of os
OSSEIN	*n* pl. -S a protein substance in bone
OSSEOUS	*adj* resembling bone
OSSIA	*conj* or else — used as a musical direction
OSSICLE	*n* pl. -S a small bone
OSSIFIC	*adj* pertaining to the formation of bone
OSSIFIER	*n* pl. -S one that ossifies
OSSIFY	*v* -FIED, -FYING, -FIES to convert into bone
OSSUARY	*n* pl. -ARIES a receptacle for the bones of the dead
OSTEAL	*adj* osseous
OSTEITIS	*n* pl. -ITIDES inflammation of bone **OSTEITIC** *adj*
OSTEOID	*n* pl. -S uncalcified bone matrix
OSTEOMA	*n* pl. -MAS or -MATA a tumor of bone tissue
OSTEOSIS	*n* pl. -OSES or -OSISES the formation of bone
OSTIA	pl. of ostium
OSTIARY	*n* pl. -ARIES a doorkeeper at a church
OSTINATO	*n* pl. -TOS a constantly recurring musical phrase
OSTIOLE	*n* pl. -S a small bodily opening **OSTIOLAR** *adj*
OSTIUM	*n* pl. OSTIA an opening in a bodily organ
OSTLER	*n* pl. -S hostler
OSTMARK	*n* pl. -S a former East German monetary unit
OSTOMY	*n* pl. -MIES a type of surgical operation
OSTOSIS	*n* pl. -TOSES or -TOSISES the formation of bone
OSTRACOD	*n* pl. -S a minute freshwater crustacean
OSTRACON	*n* pl. -CA a fragment containing an inscription
OSTRICH	*n* pl. -ES a large, flightless bird
OTALGIA	*n* pl. -S pain in the ear **OTALGIC** *adj*
OTALGY	*n* pl. -GIES otalgia
OTHER	*n* pl. -S one that remains of two or more
OTIC	*adj* pertaining to the ear
OTIOSE	*adj* lazy **OTIOSELY** *adv*
OTIOSITY	*n* pl. -TIES the state of being otiose
OTITIS	*n* pl. OTITIDES inflammation of the ear **OTITIC** *adj*
OTOCYST	*n* pl. -S an organ of balance in many invertebrates
OTOLITH	*n* pl. -S a hard mass that forms in the inner ear
OTOLOGY	*n* pl. -GIES the science of the ear
OTOSCOPE	*n* pl. -S an instrument for examining the ear

OTOSCOPY *n* pl. -PIES the use of an otoscope

OTOTOXIC *adj* adversely affecting hearing or balance

OTTAR *n* pl. -S attar

OTTAVA *n* pl. -S an octave

OTTER *n* pl. -S a carnivorous mammal

OTTO *n* pl. -TOS attar

OTTOMAN *n* pl. -S a type of sofa

OUABAIN *n* pl. -S a cardiac stimulant

OUCH *v* -ED, -ING, -ES to ornament with ouches (settings for precious stones)

OUD *n* pl. -S a stringed instrument of northern Africa

OUGHT *v* -ED, -ING, -S to owe

OUGUIYA *n* pl. OUGUIYA a monetary unit of Mauritania

OUISTITI *n* pl. -S a South American monkey

OUNCE *n* pl. -S a unit of weight

OUPH *n* pl. -S ouphe

OUPHE *n* pl. -S an elf

OUR *pron* a possessive form of the pronoun we

OURANG *n* pl. -S orang

OURARI *n* pl. -S curare

OUREBI *n* pl. -S oribi

OURIE *adj* shivering with cold

OURS *pron* a possessive form of the pronoun we

OURSELF *pron* myself — used in formal or regal contexts

OUSEL *n* pl. -S ouzel

OUST *v* -ED, -ING, -S to expel or remove from a position or place

OUSTER *n* pl. -S the act of ousting

OUT *v* -ED, -ING, -S to be revealed

OUTACT *v* -ED, -ING, -S to surpass in acting

OUTADD *v* -ED, -ING, -S to surpass in adding

OUTAGE *n* pl. -S a failure or interruption in use or functioning

OUTARGUE *v* -GUED, -GUING, -GUES to get the better of by arguing

OUTASK *v* -ED, -ING, -S to surpass in asking

OUTATE past tense of outeat

OUTBACK *n* pl. -S isolated rural country

OUTBAKE *v* -BAKED, -BAKING, -BAKES to surpass in baking

OUTBARK *v* -ED, -ING, -S to surpass in barking

OUTBAWL *v* -ED, -ING, -S to surpass in bawling

OUTBEAM *v* -ED, -ING, -S to surpass in beaming

OUTBEG *v* -BEGGED, -BEGGING, -BEGS to surpass in begging

OUTBID *v* -BID, -BIDDEN, -BIDDING, -BIDS to bid higher than

OUTBITCH *v* -ED, -ING, -ES to surpass in bitching

OUTBLAZE *v* -BLAZED, -BLAZING, -BLAZES to surpass in brilliance of light

OUTBLEAT *v* -ED, -ING, -S to surpass in bleating

OUTBLESS *v* -ED, -ING, -ES to surpass in blessing

OUTBLOOM *v* -ED, -ING, -S to surpass in blooming

OUTBLUFF *v* -ED, -ING, -S to surpass in bluffing

OUTBLUSH *v* -ED, -ING, -ES to surpass in blushing

OUTBOARD *n* pl. -S a type of motor

OUTBOAST *v* -ED, -ING, -S to surpass in boasting

OUTBOUGHT past tense of outbuy

OUTBOUND *adj* outward bound

OUTBOX *v* -ED, -ING, -ES to surpass in boxing

OUTBRAG *v* -BRAGGED, -BRAGGING, -BRAGS to surpass in bragging

OUTBRAVE *v* -BRAVED, -BRAVING, -BRAVES to surpass in courage

OUTBRAWL *v* -ED, -ING, -S to surpass in brawling

OUTBREAK *n* pl. -S a sudden eruption

OUTBREED *v* -BRED, -BREEDING, -BREEDS to interbreed relatively unrelated stocks

OUTBRIBE *v* -BRIBED, -BRIBING, -BRIBES to surpass in bribing

OUTBUILD *v* -BUILT, -BUILDING, -BUILDS to surpass in building

OUTBULK *v* -ED, -ING, -S to surpass in bulking

OUTBULLY *v* -LIED, -LYING, -LIES to surpass in bullying

OUTBURN	*v* -BURNED or -BURNT, -BURNING, -BURNS to burn longer than	**OUTCURSE**	*v* -CURSED, -CURSING, -CURSES to surpass in cursing
OUTBURST	*n* pl. -S a sudden and violent outpouring	**OUTCURVE**	*n* pl. -S a type of pitch in baseball
OUTBUY	*v* -BOUGHT, -BUYING, -BUYS to surpass in buying	**OUTDANCE**	*v* -DANCED, -DANCING, -DANCES to surpass in dancing
OUTBY	*adv* outdoors	**OUTDARE**	*v* -DARED, -DARING, -DARES to surpass in daring
OUTBYE	*adv* outby	**OUTDATE**	*v* -DATED, -DATING, -DATES to make out-of-date
OUTCAPER	*v* -ED, -ING, -S to surpass in capering	**OUTDO**	*v* -DID, -DONE, -DOING, -DOES to exceed in performance
OUTCAST	*n* pl. -S one that is cast out	**OUTDODGE**	*v* -DODGED, -DODGING, -DODGES to surpass in dodging
OUTCASTE	*n* pl. -S a Hindu who has been expelled from his caste	**OUTDOER**	*n* pl. -S one that outdoes
OUTCATCH	*v* -CAUGHT, -CATCHING, -CATCHES to surpass in catching	**OUTDONE**	past participle of outdo
OUTCAVIL	*v* -ILED, -ILING, -ILS or -ILLED, -ILLING, -ILS to surpass in caviling	**OUTDOOR**	*adj* pertaining to the open air
		OUTDOORS	*adv* in the open air
OUTCHARM	*v* -ED, -ING, -S to surpass in charming	**OUTDRAG**	*v* -DRAGGED, -DRAGGING, -DRAGS to surpass in drag racing
OUTCHEAT	*v* -ED, -ING, -S to surpass in cheating	**OUTDRANK**	past tense of outdrink
OUTCHIDE	*v* -CHIDED or -CHID, -CHIDDEN, -CHIDING, -CHIDES to surpass in chiding	**OUTDRAW**	*v* -DREW, -DRAWN, -DRAWING, -DRAWS to attract a larger audience than
OUTCLASS	*v* -ED, -ING, -ES to surpass so decisively as to appear of a higher class	**OUTDREAM**	*v* -DREAMED or -DREAMT, -DREAMING, -DREAMS to surpass in dreaming
OUTCLIMB	*v* -CLIMBED or -CLOMB, -CLIMBING, -CLIMBS to surpass in climbing	**OUTDRESS**	*v* -ED, -ING, -ES to surpass in dressing
		OUTDREW	past tense of outdraw
OUTCOACH	*v* -ED, -ING, -ES to surpass in coaching	**OUTDRINK**	*v* -DRANK, -DRUNK, -DRINKING, -DRINKS to surpass in drinking
OUTCOME	*n* pl. -S a result	**OUTDRIVE**	*v* -DROVE, -DRIVEN, -DRIVING, -DRIVES to drive a golf ball farther than
OUTCOOK	*v* -ED, -ING, -S to surpass in cooking	
OUTCOUNT	*v* -ED, -ING, -S to surpass in counting	**OUTDROP**	*v* -DROPPED, -DROPPING, -DROPS to surpass in dropping
OUTCRAWL	*v* -ED, -ING, -S to surpass in crawling	**OUTDRUNK**	past participle of outdrink
OUTCRIED	past tense of outcry	**OUTDUEL**	*v* -DUELED, -DUELING, -DUELS or -DUELLED, -DUELLING, -DUELS to surpass in dueling
OUTCRIES	present 3d person sing. of outcry	
OUTCROP	*v* -CROPPED, -CROPPING, -CROPS to protrude above the soil	**OUTEARN**	*v* -ED, -ING, -S to surpass in earning
		OUTEAT	*v* -ATE, -EATEN, -EATING, -EATS to surpass in eating
OUTCROSS	*v* -ED, -ING, -ES to cross with a relatively unrelated individual	**OUTECHO**	*v* -ED, -ING, -ES to surpass in echoing
OUTCROW	*v* -ED, -ING, -S to surpass in crowing	**OUTER**	*n* pl. -S a part of a target
OUTCRY	*v* -CRIED, -CRYING, -CRIES to cry louder than	**OUTFABLE**	*v* -BLED, -BLING, -BLES to surpass in fabling

OUTFACE *v* -FACED, -FACING, -FACES to confront unflinchingly

OUTFALL *n* pl. -S the outlet of a body of water

OUTFAST *v* -ED, -ING, -S to surpass in fasting

OUTFAWN *v* -ED, -ING, -S to surpass in fawning

OUTFEAST *v* -ED, -ING, -S to surpass in feasting

OUTFEEL *v* -FELT, -FEELING, -FEELS to surpass in feeling

OUTFIELD *n* pl. -S a part of a baseball field

OUTFIGHT *v* -FOUGHT, -FIGHTING, -FIGHTS to defeat

OUTFIND *v* -FOUND, -FINDING, -FINDS to surpass in finding

OUTFIRE *v* -FIRED, -FIRING, -FIRES to surpass in firing

OUTFISH *v* -ED, -ING, -ES to surpass in fishing

OUTFIT *v* -FITTED, -FITTING, -FITS to equip

OUTFLANK *v* -ED, -ING, -S to gain a tactical advantage over

OUTFLOW *v* -ED, -ING, -S to flow out

OUTFLY *v* -FLEW, -FLOWN, -FLYING, -FLIES to surpass in speed of flight

OUTFOOL *v* -ED, -ING, -S to surpass in fooling

OUTFOOT *v* -ED, -ING, -S to surpass in speed

OUTFOUGHT past tense of outfight

OUTFOUND past tense of outfind

OUTFOX *v* -ED, -ING, -ES to outwit

OUTFROWN *v* -ED, -ING, -S to frown more than

OUTGAIN *v* -ED, -ING, -S to gain more than

OUTGAS *v* -GASSED, -GASSING, -GASSES to remove gas from

OUTGIVE *v* -GAVE, -GIVEN, -GIVING, -GIVES to give more than

OUTGLARE *v* -GLARED, -GLARING, -GLARES to surpass in glaring

OUTGLOW *v* -ED, -ING, -S to surpass in glowing

OUTGNAW *v* -GNAWED, -GNAWN, -GNAWING, -GNAWS to surpass in gnawing

OUTGO *v* -WENT, -GONE, -GOING, -GOES to go beyond

OUTGOING *n* pl. -S a departure

OUTGREW past tense of outgrow

OUTGRIN *v* -GRINNED, -GRINNING, -GRINS to surpass in grinning

OUTGROSS *v* -ED, -ING, -ES to surpass in gross earnings

OUTGROUP *n* pl. -S a group of people outside one's own group

OUTGROW *v* -GREW, -GROWN, -GROWING, -GROWS to grow too large for

OUTGUESS *v* -ED, -ING, -ES to anticipate the actions of

OUTGUIDE *v* -GUIDED, -GUIDING, -GUIDES to surpass in guiding

OUTGUN *v* -GUNNED, -GUNNING, -GUNS to surpass in firepower

OUTGUSH *n* pl. -ES a gushing out

OUTHAUL *n* pl. -S a rope for extending a sail along a spar

OUTHEAR *v* -HEARD, -HEARING, -HEARS to surpass in hearing

OUTHIT *v* -HIT, -HITTING, -HITS to get more hits than

OUTHOMER *v* -ED, -ING, -S to surpass in hitting home runs

OUTHOUSE *n* pl. -S a toilet housed in a small structure

OUTHOWL *v* -ED, -ING, -S to surpass in howling

OUTHUMOR *v* -ED, -ING, -S to surpass in humoring

OUTHUNT *v* -ED, -ING, -S to surpass in hunting

OUTING *n* pl. -S a short pleasure trip

OUTJINX *v* -ED, -ING, -ES to surpass in jinxing

OUTJUMP *v* -ED, -ING, -S to surpass in jumping

OUTJUT *v* -JUTTED, -JUTTING, -JUTS to stick out

OUTKEEP *v* -KEPT, -KEEPING, -KEEPS to surpass in keeping

OUTKICK *v* -ED, -ING, -S to surpass in kicking

OUTKILL *v* -ED, -ING, -S to surpass in killing

OUTKISS *v* -ED, -ING, -ES to surpass in kissing

OUTLAID past tense of outlay

OUTLAIN past participle of outlie

OUTLAND *n* pl. -S a foreign land

OUTLAST v -ED, -ING, -S to last longer than

OUTLAUGH v -ED, -ING, -S to surpass in laughing

OUTLAW v -ED, -ING, -S to prohibit

OUTLAWRY n pl. -RIES habitual defiance of the law

OUTLAY v -LAID, -LAYING, -LAYS to pay out

OUTLEAP v -LEAPED or -LEAPT, -LEAPING, -LEAPS to surpass in leaping

OUTLEARN v -LEARNED or -LEARNT, -LEARNING, -LEARNS to surpass in learning

OUTLET n pl. -S a passage for escape or discharge

OUTLIE v -LAY, -LAIN, -LYING, -LIES to lie beyond

OUTLIER n pl. -S an outlying area or portion

OUTLINE v -LINED, -LINING, -LINES to indicate the main features or different parts of

OUTLINER n pl. -S one that outlines

OUTLIVE v -LIVED, -LIVING, -LIVES to live longer than

OUTLIVER n pl. -S one that outlives

OUTLOOK n pl. -S a point of view

OUTLOVE v -LOVED, -LOVING, -LOVES to surpass in loving

OUTLYING present participle of outlie

OUTMAN v -MANNED, -MANNING, -MANS to surpass in manpower

OUTMARCH v -ED, -ING, -ES to surpass in marching

OUTMATCH v -ED, -ING, -ES to outdo

OUTMODE v -MODED, -MODING, -MODES to outdate

OUTMOST adj farthest out

OUTMOVE v -MOVED, -MOVING, -MOVES to move faster or farther than

OUTPACE v -PACED, -PACING, -PACES to surpass in speed

OUTPAINT v -ED, -ING, -S to surpass in painting

OUTPASS v -ED, -ING, -ES to excel in passing a football

OUTPITCH v -ED, -ING, -ES to surpass in pitching

OUTPITY v -PITIED, -PITYING, -PITIES to surpass in pitying

OUTPLAN v -PLANNED, -PLANNING, -PLANS to surpass in planning

OUTPLAY v -ED, -ING, -S to excel or defeat in a game

OUTPLOD v -PLODDED, -PLODDING, -PLODS to surpass in plodding

OUTPLOT v -PLOTTED, -PLOTTING, -PLOTS to surpass in plotting

OUTPOINT v -ED, -ING, -S to score more points than

OUTPOLL v -ED, -ING, -S to get more votes than

OUTPORT n pl. -S a port of export or departure

OUTPOST n pl. -S a body of troops stationed at a distance from the main body

OUTPOUR v -ED, -ING, -S to pour out

OUTPOWER v -ED, -ING, -S to surpass in power

OUTPRAY v -ED, -ING, -S to surpass in praying

OUTPREEN v -ED, -ING, -S to surpass in preening

OUTPRESS v -ED, -ING, -ES to surpass in pressing

OUTPRICE v -PRICED, -PRICING, -PRICES to surpass in pricing

OUTPULL v -ED, -ING, -S to attract a larger audience or following than

OUTPUNCH v -ED, -ING, -ES to surpass in punching

OUTPUSH v -ED, -ING, -ES to surpass in pushing

OUTPUT v -PUTTED, -PUTTING, -PUTS to produce

OUTQUOTE v -QUOTED, -QUOTING, -QUOTES to surpass in quoting

OUTRACE v -RACED, -RACING, -RACES to run faster or farther than

OUTRAGE v -RAGED, -RAGING, -RAGES to arouse anger or resentment in

OUTRAISE v -RAISED, -RAISING, -RAISES to surpass in raising

OUTRAN past tense of outrun

OUTRANCE n pl. -S the last extremity

OUTRANG past tense of outring

OUTRANGE v -RANGED, -RANGING, -RANGES to surpass in range

OUTRANK v -ED, -ING, -S to rank higher than

OUTRATE *v* -RATED, -RATING, -RATES to surpass in a rating

OUTRAVE *v* -RAVED, -RAVING, -RAVES to surpass in raving

OUTRE *adj* deviating from what is usual or proper

OUTREACH *v* -ED, -ING, -ES to reach beyond

OUTREAD *v* -READ, -READING, -READS to surpass in reading

OUTRIDE *v* -RODE, -RIDDEN, -RIDING, -RIDES to ride faster or better than

OUTRIDER *n* pl. -S a mounted attendant who rides before or beside a carriage

OUTRIGHT *adj* being without limit or reservation

OUTRING *v* -RANG, -RUNG, -RINGING, -RINGS to ring louder than

OUTRIVAL *v* -VALED, -VALING, -VALS or -VALLED, -VALLING, -VALS to outdo in a competition or rivalry

OUTROAR *v* -ED, -ING, -S to roar louder than

OUTROCK *v* -ED, -ING, -S to surpass in rocking

OUTRODE past tense of outride

OUTROLL *v* -ED, -ING, -S to roll out

OUTROOT *v* -ED, -ING, -S to pull up by the roots

OUTROW *v* -ED, -ING, -S to surpass in rowing

OUTRUN *v* -RAN, -RUNNING, -RUNS to run faster than

OUTRUNG past participle of outring

OUTRUSH *v* -ED, -ING, -ES to surpass in rushing

OUTSAIL *v* -ED, -ING, -S to sail faster than

OUTSANG past tense of outsing

OUTSAT past tense of outsit

OUTSAVOR *v* -ED, -ING, -S to surpass in a distinctive taste or smell

OUTSAW past tense of outsee

OUTSCOLD *v* -ED, -ING, -S to surpass in scolding

OUTSCOOP *v* -ED, -ING, -S to surpass in scooping

OUTSCORE *v* -SCORED, -SCORING, -SCORES to score more points than

OUTSCORN *v* -ED, -ING, -S to surpass in scorning

OUTSEE *v* -SAW, -SEEN, -SEEING, -SEES to see beyond

OUTSELL *v* -SOLD, -SELLING, -SELLS to sell more than

OUTSERT *n* pl. -S a folded sheet placed around a folded section of printed matter

OUTSERVE *v* -SERVED, -SERVING, -SERVES to surpass in serving

OUTSET *n* pl. -S a beginning

OUTSHAME *v* -SHAMED, -SHAMING, -SHAMES to surpass in shaming

OUTSHINE *v* -SHONE or -SHINED, -SHINING, -SHINES to shine brighter than

OUTSHOOT *v* -SHOT, -SHOOTING, -SHOOTS to shoot better than

OUTSHOUT *v* -ED, -ING, -S to shout louder than

OUTSIDE *n* pl. -S the outer side, surface, or part

OUTSIDER *n* pl. -S one that does not belong to a particular group

OUTSIGHT *n* pl. -S the power of perceiving external things

OUTSIN *v* -SINNED, -SINNING, -SINS to surpass in sinning

OUTSING *v* -SANG, -SUNG, -SINGING, -SINGS to surpass in singing

OUTSIT *v* -SAT, -SITTING, -SITS to remain sitting or in session longer than

OUTSIZE *n* pl. -S an unusual size **OUTSIZED** *adj*

OUTSKATE *v* -SKATED, -SKATING, -SKATES to surpass in skating

OUTSKIRT *n* pl. -S an outlying area

OUTSLEEP *v* -SLEPT, -SLEEPING, -SLEEPS to sleep later than

OUTSLICK *v* -ED, -ING, -S to get the better of by trickery or cunning

OUTSMART *v* -ED, -ING, -S to outwit

OUTSMILE *v* -SMILED, -SMILING, -SMILES to surpass in smiling

OUTSMOKE *v* -SMOKED, -SMOKING, -SMOKES to surpass in smoking

OUTSNORE *v* -SNORED, -SNORING, -SNORES to surpass in snoring

OUTSOAR *v* -ED, -ING, -S to soar beyond

OUTSOLD past tense of outsell

OUTSOLE *n* pl. -S the outer sole of a boot or shoe

OUTSPAN *v* -SPANNED, -SPANNING, -SPANS to unharness a draft animal

OUTSPEAK *v* -SPOKE, -SPOKEN, -SPEAKING, -SPEAKS to outdo in speaking

OUTSPEED *v* -SPED or -SPEEDED, -SPEEDING, -SPEEDS to go faster than

OUTSPELL *v* -SPELLED or -SPELT, -SPELLING, -SPELLS to surpass in spelling

OUTSPEND *v* -SPENT, -SPENDING, -SPENDS to exceed the limits of in spending

OUTSPOKE past tense of outspeak

OUTSPOKEN past participle of outspeak

OUTSTAND *v* -STOOD, -STANDING, -STANDS to endure beyond

OUTSTARE *v* -STARED, -STARING, -STARES to outface

OUTSTART *v* -ED, -ING, -S to get ahead of at the start

OUTSTATE *v* -STATED, -STATING, -STATES to surpass in stating

OUTSTAY *v* -ED, -ING, -S to surpass in staying power

OUTSTEER *v* -ED, -ING, -S to surpass in steering

OUTSTOOD past tense of outstand

OUTSTRIP *v* -STRIPPED, -STRIPPING, -STRIPS to go faster or farther than

OUTSTUDY *v* -STUDIED, -STUDYING, -STUDIES to surpass in studying

OUTSTUNT *v* -ED, -ING, -S to surpass in stunting

OUTSULK *v* -ED, -ING, -S to surpass in sulking

OUTSUNG past participle of outsing

OUTSWEAR *v* -SWORE or -SWARE, -SWORN, -SWEARING, -SWEARS to surpass in swearing

OUTSWIM *v* -SWAM, -SWUM, -SWIMMING, -SWIMS to swim faster or farther than

OUTTAKE *n* pl. -S a passage outwards

OUTTALK *v* -ED, -ING, -S to surpass in talking

OUTTASK *v* -ED, -ING, -S to surpass in tasking

OUTTELL *v* -TOLD, -TELLING, -TELLS to say openly

OUTTHANK *v* -ED, -ING, -S to surpass in thanking

OUTTHINK *v* -THOUGHT, -THINKING, -THINKS to get the better of by thinking

OUTTHROB *v* -THROBBED, -THROBBING, -THROBS to surpass in throbbing

OUTTHROW *v* -THREW, -THROWN, -THROWING, -THROWS to throw farther or more accurately than

OUTTOLD past tense of outtell

OUTTOWER *v* -ED, -ING, -S to tower above

OUTTRADE *v* -TRADED, -TRADING, -TRADES to get the better of in a trade

OUTTRICK *v* -ED, -ING, -S to get the better of by trickery

OUTTROT *v* -TROTTED, -TROTTING, -TROTS to surpass in trotting

OUTTRUMP *v* -ED, -ING, -S to outplay

OUTTURN *n* pl. -S a quantity produced

OUTVALUE *v* -UED, -UING, -UES to be worth more than

OUTVAUNT *v* -ED, -ING, -S to surpass in vaunting

OUTVIE *v* -VIED, -VYING, -VIES to surpass in a competition

OUTVOICE *v* -VOICED, -VOICING, -VOICES to surpass in loudness of voice

OUTVOTE *v* -VOTED, -VOTING, -VOTES to defeat by a majority of votes

OUTVYING present participle of outvie

OUTWAIT *v* -ED, -ING, -S to exceed in patience

OUTWALK *v* -ED, -ING, -S to surpass in walking

OUTWAR *v* -WARRED, -WARRING, -WARS to surpass in warring

OUTWARD *adv* toward the outside

OUTWARDS *adv* outward

OUTWARRED past tense of outwar

OUTWARRING present participle of outwar

OUTWASH *n* pl. -ES detritus washed from a glacier

OUTWASTE *v* -WASTED, -WASTING, -WASTES to surpass in wasting

OUTWATCH *v* -ED, -ING, -ES to watch longer than

OUTWEAR *v* -WORE, -WORN, -WEARING, -WEARS to last longer than

OUTWEARY *v* -RIED, -RYING, -RIES to surpass in wearying

OUTWEEP *v* -WEPT, -WEEPING, -WEEPS to weep more than

OUTWEIGH *v* -ED, -ING, -S to weigh more than

OUTWENT past tense of outgo

OUTWEPT past tense of outweep

OUTWHIRL *v* -ED, -ING, -S to surpass in whirling

OUTWILE *v* -WILED, -WILING, -WILES to surpass in wiling

OUTWILL *v* -ED, -ING, -S to surpass in willpower

OUTWIND *v* -ED, -ING, -S to cause to be out of breath

OUTWISH *v* -ED, -ING, -ES to surpass in wishing

OUTWIT *v* -WITTED, -WITTING, -WITS to get the better of by superior cleverness

OUTWORE past tense of outwear

OUTWORK *v* -WORKED or -WROUGHT, -WORKING, -WORKS to work faster or better than

OUTWORN past participle of outwear

OUTWRITE *v* -WROTE or -WRIT, -WRITTEN, -WRITING, -WRITES to write better than

OUT-WROUGHT a past tense of outwork

OUTYELL *v* -ED, -ING, -S to yell louder than

OUTYELP *v* -ED, -ING, -S to surpass in yelping

OUTYIELD *v* -ED, -ING, -S to surpass in yield

OUZEL *n* pl. -S a European bird

OUZO *n* pl. -ZOS a Greek liqueur

OVA pl. of ovum

OVAL *n* pl. -S an oval (egg-shaped) figure or object

OVALITY *n* pl. -TIES ovalness

OVALLY *adv* in the shape of an oval

OVALNESS *n* pl. -ES the state of being oval

OVARIAL *adj* ovarian

OVARIAN *adj* pertaining to an ovary

OVARIES pl. of ovary

OVARIOLE *n* pl. -S one of the tubes of which the ovaries of most insects are composed

OVARITIS *n* pl. -RITIDES inflammation of an ovary

OVARY *n* pl. -RIES a female reproductive gland

OVATE *adj* egg-shaped **OVATELY** *adv*

OVATION *n* pl. -S an expression or demonstration of popular acclaim

OVEN *n* pl. -S an enclosed compartment in which substances are heated **OVENLIKE** *adj*

OVENBIRD *n* pl. -S an American songbird

OVENWARE *n* pl. -S heat-resistant dishes for baking and serving food

OVER *v* -ED, -ING, -S to leap above and to the other side of

OVERABLE *adj* excessively able

OVERACT *v* -ED, -ING, -S to act with exaggeration

OVERAGE *n* pl. -S an amount in excess

OVERAGED *adj* too old to be useful

OVERALL *n* pl. -S a loose outer garment

OVERAPT *adj* excessively apt

OVERARCH *v* -ED, -ING, -ES to form an arch over

OVERARM *adj* done with the arm above the shoulder

OVERATE past tense of overeat

OVERAWE *v* -AWED, -AWING, -AWES to subdue by inspiring awe

OVERBAKE *v* -BAKED, -BAKING, -BAKES to bake too long

OVERBEAR *v* -BORE, -BORNE or -BORN, -BEARING, -BEARS to bring down by superior weight or force

OVERBEAT *v* -BEAT, -BEATEN, -BEATING, -BEATS to beat too much

OVERBED *adj* spanning a bed

OVERBET *v* -BET or -BETTED, -BETTING, -BETS to bet too much

OVERBID *v* -BID, -BID or -BIDDEN, -BIDDING, -BIDS to bid higher than

OVERBIG *adj* too big

OVERBILL *v* -ED, -ING, -S to bill too much

OVERBITE *n* pl. -S a faulty closure of the teeth

OVERBLOW *v* -BLEW, -BLOWN, -BLOWING, -BLOWS to give excessive importance to

OVERBOIL *v* -ED, -ING, -S to boil too long

OVERBOLD *adj* excessively bold or forward

OVERBOOK *v* -ED, -ING, -S to issue reservations in excess of the space available

OVERBORE past tense of overbear

OVERBORN a past participle of overbear

OVERBORNE a past participle of overbear

OVER-BOUGHT past tense of overbuy

OVERBRED *adj* bred too finely or to excess

OVERBURN *v* -BURNED or -BURNT, -BURNING, -BURNS to burn too long

OVERBUSY *adj* too busy

OVERBUY *v* -BOUGHT, -BUYING, -BUYS to buy in quantities exceeding need or demand

OVERCALL *v* -ED, -ING, -S to overbid

OVERCAME past tense of overcome

OVERCAST *v* -CAST or -CASTED, -CASTING, -CASTS to become cloudy or dark

OVERCOAT *n* pl. -S a warm coat worn over indoor clothing

OVERCOLD *adj* too cold

OVERCOME *v* -CAME, -COMING, -COMES to get the better of

OVERCOOK *v* -ED, -ING, -S to cook too long

OVERCOOL *v* -ED, -ING, -S to make too cool

OVERCOY *adj* too coy

OVERCRAM *v* -CRAMMED, -CRAMMING, -CRAMS to stuff or cram to excess

OVERCROP *v* -CROPPED, -CROPPING, -CROPS to exhaust the fertility of by cultivating to excess

OVERCURE *v* -CURED, -CURING, -CURES to cure too long

OVERCUT *v* -CUT, -CUTTING, -CUTS to cut too much

OVERDARE *v* -DARED, -DARING, -DARES to become too daring

OVERDEAR *adj* too dear; too costly

OVERDECK *v* -ED, -ING, -S to adorn extravagantly

OVERDO *v* -DID, -DONE, -DOING, -DOES to do to excess

OVERDOER *n* pl. -S one that overdoes

OVERDOG *n* pl. -S one that is dominant or victorious

OVERDOSE *v* -DOSED, -DOSING, -DOSES to give an excessive dose to

OVERDRAW *v* -DREW, -DRAWN, -DRAWING, -DRAWS to draw checks on in excess of the balance

OVERDRY *v* -DRIED, -DRYING, -DRIES to dry too much

OVERDUB *v* -DUBBED, -DUBBING, -DUBS to add sound to an existing recording

OVERDUE *adj* not paid when due

OVERDYE *v* -DYED, -DYEING, -DYES to dye with too much color

OVEREASY *adj* too easy

OVEREAT *v* -ATE, -EATEN, -EATING, -EATS to eat to excess

OVEREDIT *v* -ED, -ING, -S to edit more than necessary

OVERFAR *adj* too great in distance, extent, or degree

OVERFAST *adj* too fast

OVERFAT *adj* too fat

OVERFEAR *v* -ED, -ING, -S to fear too much

OVERFEED *v* -FED, -FEEDING, -FEEDS to feed too much

OVERFILL *v* -ED, -ING, -S to fill to overflowing

OVERFISH *v* -ED, -ING, -ES to deplete the supply of fish in an area by fishing to excess

OVERFLOW *v* -FLOWED, -FLOWN, -FLOWING, -FLOWS to flow over the top of

OVERFLY *v* -FLEW, -FLOWN, -FLYING, -FLIES to fly over

OVERFOND *adj* too fond or affectionate

OVERFOUL *adj* too foul

OVERFREE *adj* too free

OVERFULL *adj* too full

OVERFUND *v* -ED, -ING, -S to fund more than required

OVERGILD *v* -GILDED or -GILT, -GILDING, -GILDS to gild over

OVERGIRD *v* -GIRDED or -GIRT, -GIRDING, -GIRDS to gird to excess

OVERGLAD *adj* too glad

OVERGOAD *v* -ED, -ING, -S to goad too much

OVERGROW *v* -GREW, -GROWN, -GROWING, -GROWS to grow over

OVERHAND *v* -ED, -ING, -S to sew with short, vertical stitches

OVERHANG *v* -HUNG, -HANGING, -HANGS to hang or project over

OVERHARD *adj* too hard

OVERHATE *v* -HATED, -HATING, -HATES to hate to excess

OVERHAUL *v* -ED, -ING, -S to examine carefully for needed repairs

OVERHEAD *n* pl. -S the general cost of running a business

OVERHEAP *v* -ED, -ING, -S to heap up or accumulate to excess

OVERHEAR *v* -HEARD, -HEARING, -HEARS to hear without the speaker's knowledge or intention

OVERHEAT *v* -ED, -ING, -S to heat to excess

OVERHIGH *adj* too high

OVERHOLD *v* -HELD, -HOLDING, -HOLDS to rate too highly

OVERHOLY *adj* too holy

OVERHOPE *v* -HOPED, -HOPING, -HOPES to hope exceedingly

OVERHOT *adj* too hot

OVERHUNG past tense of overhang

OVERHUNT *v* -ED, -ING, -S to deplete the supply of game in an area by hunting to excess

OVERHYPE *v* -HYPED, -HYPING, -HYPES to hype to excess

OVERIDLE *adj* too idle

OVERJOY *v* -ED, -ING, -S to fill with great joy

OVERJUST *adj* too just

OVERKEEN *adj* too keen

OVERKILL *v* -ED, -ING, -S to destroy with more nuclear force than required

OVERKIND *adj* too kind

OVERLADE *v* -LADED, -LADEN, -LADING, -LADES to load with too great a burden

OVERLAID past tense of overlay

OVERLAIN past participle of overlie

OVERLAND *n* pl. -S a train or stagecoach that travels over land

OVERLAP *v* -LAPPED, -LAPPING, -LAPS to extend over and cover a part of

OVERLATE *adj* too late

OVERLAX *adj* too lax

OVERLAY *v* -LAID, -LAYING, -LAYS to lay over

OVERLEAF *adv* on the other side of the page

OVERLEAP *v* -LEAPED or -LEAPT, -LEAPING, -LEAPS to leap over

OVERLEND *v* -LENT, -LENDING, -LENDS to lend too much

OVERLET *v* -LET, -LETTING, -LETS to let to excess

OVERLEWD *adj* too lewd

OVERLIE *v* -LAY, -LAIN, -LYING, -LIES to lie over

OVERLIT a past tense of overlight

OVERLIVE *v* -LIVED, -LIVING, -LIVES to outlive

OVERLOAD *v* -ED, -ING, -S to load to excess

OVERLONG *adj* too long

OVERLOOK *v* -ED, -ING, -S to fail to notice

OVERLORD *v* -ED, -ING, -S to rule tyrannically

OVERLOUD *adj* too loud

OVERLOVE *v* -LOVED, -LOVING, -LOVES to love to excess

OVERLUSH *adj* excessively lush

OVERLY *adv* to an excessive degree

OVERLYING present participle of overlie

OVERMAN *n* pl. -MEN a foreman

OVERMAN *v* -MANNED, -MANNING, -MANS to provide with more men than are needed

OVERMANY *adj* too many

OVERMEEK *adj* excessively meek

OVERMELT *v* -ED, -ING, -S to melt too much

OVERMEN pl. of overman

OVERMILD *adj* too mild

OVERMILK *v* -ED, -ING, -S to milk to excess

OVERMINE *v* -MINED, -MINING, -MINES to mine to excess

OVERMIX *v* -ED, -ING, -ES to mix too much

OVERMUCH *n* pl. -ES an excess

OVERNEAR *adj* too near

OVERNEAT *adj* too neat

OVERNEW *adj* too new

OVERNICE *adj* excessively nice

OVERPASS *v* -PASSED or -PAST, -PASSING, -PASSES to pass over

OVERPAY *v* -PAID, -PAYING, -PAYS to pay too much

OVERPERT *adj* too pert

OVERPLAN *v* -PLANNED, -PLANNING, -PLANS to plan to excess

OVERPLAY *v* -ED, -ING, -S to exaggerate

OVERPLOT v -PLOTTED, -PLOTTING, -PLOTS to devise an overly complex plot for

OVERPLUS n pl. -ES a surplus

OVERPLY v -PLIED, -PLYING, -PLIES to ply to excess; overwork

OVERPUMP v -ED, -ING, -S to pump to excess

OVERRAN past tense of overrun

OVERRANK adj too luxuriant in growth

OVERRASH adj too rash

OVERRATE v -RATED, -RATING, -RATES to rate too highly

OVERRICH adj too rich

OVERRIDE v -RODE, -RIDDEN, -RIDING, -RIDES to ride over

OVERRIFE adj too rife

OVERRIPE adj too ripe

OVERRODE past tense of override

OVERRUDE adj excessively rude

OVERRUFF v -ED, -ING, -S to trump with a higher trump card than has already been played

OVERRULE v -RULED, -RULING, -RULES to disallow the arguments of

OVERRUN v -RAN, -RUNNING, -RUNS to spread or swarm over

OVERSAD adj excessively sad

OVERSALE n pl. -S the act of overselling

OVERSALT v -ED, -ING, -S to salt to excess

OVERSAVE v -SAVED, -SAVING, -SAVES to save too much

OVERSAW past tense of oversee

OVERSEA adv overseas

OVERSEAS adv beyond or across the sea

OVERSEE v -SAW, -SEEN, -SEEING, -SEES to watch over and direct

OVERSEED v -ED, -ING, -S to seed to excess

OVERSEER n pl. -S one that oversees

OVERSELL v -SOLD, -SELLING, -SELLS to sell more of than can be delivered

OVERSET v -SET, -SETTING, -SETS to turn or tip over

OVERSEW v -SEWED, -SEWN, -SEWING, -SEWS to overhand

OVERSHOE n pl. -S a protective outer shoe

OVERSHOT n pl. -S a type of fabric weave

OVERSICK adj too sick

OVERSIDE n pl. -S the other side of a phonograph record

OVERSIZE n pl. -S an unusually large size

OVERSLIP v -SLIPPED or -SLIPT, -SLIPPING, -SLIPS to leave out

OVERSLOW adj too slow

OVERSOAK v -ED, -ING, -S to soak too much

OVERSOFT adj too soft

OVERSOLD past tense of oversell

OVERSOON adv too soon

OVERSOUL n pl. -S a supreme reality or mind in transcendentalism

OVERSPIN n pl. -S a forward spin imparted to a ball

OVERSTAY v -ED, -ING, -S to stay beyond the limits or duration of

OVERSTEP v -STEPPED, -STEPPING, -STEPS to go beyond

OVERSTIR v -STIRRED, -STIRRING, -STIRS to stir too much

OVERSUDS v -ED, -ING, -ES to form an excessive amount of suds

OVERSUP v -SUPPED, -SUPPING, -SUPS to sup to excess

OVERSURE adj too sure

OVERT adj open to view

OVERTAKE v -TOOK, -TAKEN, -TAKING, -TAKES to catch up with

OVERTALK v -ED, -ING, -S to talk to excess

OVERTAME adj too tame

OVERTART adj too tart

OVERTASK v -ED, -ING, -S to task too severely

OVERTAX v -ED, -ING, -ES to tax too heavily

OVERTHIN adj too thin

OVERTIME v -TIMED, -TIMING, -TIMES to exceed the desired timing for

OVERTIP v -TIPPED, -TIPPING, -TIPS to tip more than what is customary

OVERTIRE v -TIRED, -TIRING, -TIRES to tire excessively

OVERTLY adj in an overt manner

OVERTOIL v -ED, -ING, -S to wear out or exhaust by excessive toil

OVERTONE n pl. -S a higher partial tone

OVERTOOK past tense of overtake

OVERTOP v -TOPPED, -TOPPING, -TOPS to rise above the top of

OVERTRIM *v* -TRIMMED, -TRIMMING, -TRIMS to trim too much

OVERTURE *v* -TURED, -TURING, -TURES to propose

OVERTURN *v* -ED, -ING, -S to turn over

OVERURGE *v* -URGED, -URGING, -URGES to urge too much

OVERUSE *v* -USED, -USING, -USES to use too much

OVERVIEW *n* pl. -S a summary

OVERVOTE *v* -VOTED, -VOTING, -VOTES to defeat by a majority of votes

OVERWARM *v* -ED, -ING, -S to warm too much

OVERWARY *adj* too wary

OVERWEAK *adj* too weak

OVERWEAR *v* -WORE, -WORN, -WEARING, -WEARS to wear out

OVERWEEN *v* -ED, -ING, -S to be arrogant

OVERWET *v* -WETTED, -WETTING, -WETS to wet too much

OVERWIDE *adj* too wide

OVERWILY *adj* too wily

OVERWIND *v* -WOUND, -WINDING, -WINDS to wind too much, as a watch

OVERWISE *adj* too wise

OVERWORD *n* pl. -S a word or phrase repeated at intervals in a song

OVERWORE past tense of overwear

OVERWORK *v* -WORKED or -WROUGHT, -WORKING, -WORKS to cause to work too hard

OVERWORN past participle of overwear

OVER-WOUND past tense of overwind

OVER-WROUGHT a past tense of overwork

OVERZEAL *n* pl. -S excess of zeal

OVIBOS *n* pl. OVIBOS a wild ox

OVICIDE *n* pl. -S an agent that kills eggs **OVICIDAL** *adj*

OVIDUCT *n* pl. -S a tube through which ova travel from an ovary **OVIDUCAL** *adj*

OVIFORM *adj* shaped like an egg

OVINE *n* pl. -S a sheep or a closely related animal

OVIPARA *n/pl* egg-laying animals

OVIPOSIT *v* -ED, -ING, -S to lay eggs

OVISAC *n* pl. -S a sac containing an ovum or ova

OVOID *n* pl. -S an egg-shaped body **OVOIDAL** *adj*

OVOLO *n* pl. -LI or -LOS a convex molding

OVONIC *n* pl. -S an electronic device

OVULATE *v* -LATED, -LATING, -LATES to produce ova

OVULE *n* pl. -S a rudimentary seed **OVULAR, OVULARY** *adj*

OVUM *n* pl. OVA the female reproductive cell of animals

OW *interj* — used to express sudden pain

OWE *v* OWED, OWING, OWES to be under obligation to pay or repay

OWL *n* pl. -S a nocturnal bird

OWLET *n* pl. -S a young owl

OWLISH *adj* resembling an owl **OWLISHLY** *adv*

OWLLIKE *adj* owlish

OWN *v* -ED, -ING, -S to have as a belonging **OWNABLE** *adj*

OWNER *n* pl. -S one that owns

OWSE *n* pl. OWSEN ox

OX *n* pl. OXEN a hoofed mammal

OX *n* pl. -ES a clumsy person

OXALATE *v* -LATED, -LATING, -LATES to treat with an oxalate (a chemical salt)

OXALIS *n* pl. -ALISES a flowering plant **OXALIC** *adj*

OXAZEPAM *n* pl. -S a tranquilizing drug

OXAZINE *n* pl. -S a chemical compound

OXBLOOD *n* pl. -S a deep red color

OXBOW *n* pl. -S a U-shaped piece of wood in an ox yoke

OXCART *n* pl. -S an ox-drawn cart

OXEN pl. of ox

OXEYE *n* pl. -S a flowering plant

OXFORD *n* pl. -S a type of shoe

OXHEART *n* pl. -S a variety of sweet cherry

OXID *n* pl. -S oxide

OXIDABLE *adj* capable of being oxidized

OXIDANT *n* pl. -S an oxidizing agent

OXIDASE *n* pl. -S an oxidizing enzyme **OXIDASIC** *adj*

OXIDATE	*v* -DATED, -DATING, -DATES to oxidize
OXIDE	*n* pl. -S a binary compound of oxygen with another element or radical **OXIDIC** *adj*
OXIDISE	*v* -DISED, -DISING, -DISES to oxidize
OXIDISER	*n* pl. -S oxidizer
OXIDIZE	*v* -DIZED, -DIZING, -DIZES to combine with oxygen
OXIDIZER	*n* pl. -S an oxidant
OXIM	*n* pl. -S oxime
OXIME	*n* pl. -S a chemical compound
OXLIP	*n* pl. -S a flowering plant
OXO	*adj* containing oxygen
OXPECKER	*n* pl. -S an African bird
OXTAIL	*n* pl. -S the tail of an ox
OXTER	*n* pl. -S the armpit
OXTONGUE	*n* pl. -S a European herb
OXY	*adj* containing oxygen
OXYACID	*n* pl. -S an acid that contains oxygen
OXYGEN	*n* pl. -S a gaseous element **OXYGENIC** *adj*
OXYMORON	*n* pl. -MORA a combination of contradictory or incongruous words
OXYPHIL	*n* pl. -S oxyphile
OXYPHILE	*n* pl. -S an organism that thrives in a relatively acid environment
OXYSALT	*n* pl. -S a salt of an oxyacid
OXYSOME	*n* pl. -S a structural unit of cellular cristae
OXYTOCIC	*n* pl. -S a drug that hastens the process of childbirth
OXYTOCIN	*n* pl. -S a pituitary hormone
OXYTONE	*n* pl. -S a word having heavy stress on the last syllable
OY	*interj* — used to express dismay or pain
OYER	*n* pl. -S a type of legal writ
OYES	*n* pl. OYESSES oyez
OYEZ	*n* pl. OYESSES a cry used to introduce the opening of a court of law
OYSTER	*v* -ED, -ING, -S to gather oysters (edible mollusks)
OYSTERER	*n* pl. -S one that gathers or sells oysters
OZONATE	*v* -ATED, -ATING, -ATES to treat or combine with ozone
OZONE	*n* pl. -S a form of oxygen **OZONIC** *adj*
OZONIDE	*n* pl. -S a compound of ozone
OZONISE	*v* -ISED, -ISING, -ISES to ozonize
OZONIZE	*v* -IZED, -IZING, -IZES to convert into ozone
OZONIZER	*n* pl. -S a device for converting oxygen into ozone
OZONOUS	*adj* pertaining to ozone

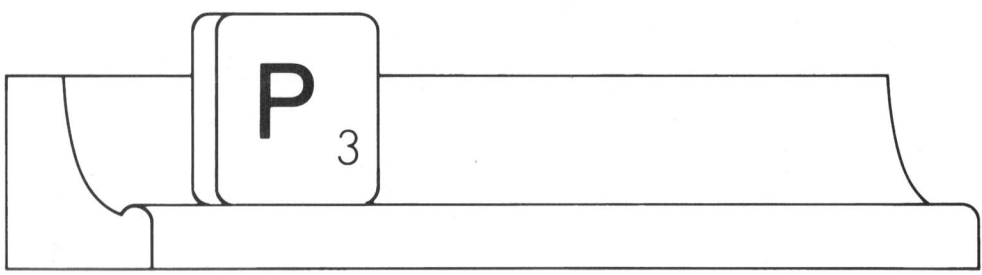

PA	*n* pl. -S a father	**PACKING**	*n* pl. -S material used to pack
PABLUM	*n* pl. -S insipid writing or speech	**PACKLY**	*adv* intimately
PABULUM	*n* pl. -S food **PABULAR** *adj*	**PACKMAN**	*n* pl. -MEN a peddler
PAC	*n* pl. -S a shoe like a moccasin	**PACKNESS**	*n* pl. -ES intimacy
PACA	*n* pl. -S a large rodent	**PACKSACK**	*n* pl. -S a carrying bag to be worn on the back
PACE	*v* PACED, PACING, PACES to walk with a regular step	**PACKWAX**	*n* pl. -ES paxwax
PACER	*n* pl. -S a horse whose gait is a pace	**PACT**	*n* pl. -S an agreement
		PACTION	*n* pl. -S a pact
PACHA	*n* pl. -S pasha	**PAD**	*v* PADDED, PADDING, PADS to line or stuff with soft material
PACHADOM	*n* pl. -S pashadom		
PACHALIC	*n* pl. -S pashalik	**PADAUK**	*n* pl. -S a tropical tree
PACHINKO	*n* pl. -KOS a Japanese pinball game	**PADDER**	*n* pl. -S one that pads
		PADDIES	pl. of paddy
PACHISI	*n* pl. -S a board game of India	**PADDING**	*n* pl. -S material with which to pad
PACHOULI	*n* pl. -S an East Indian herb		
PACHUCO	*n* pl. -COS a flashy Mexican-American youth	**PADDLE**	*v* -DLED, -DLING, -DLES to propel with a broad-bladed implement
PACIFIC	*adj* peaceful	**PADDLER**	*n* pl. -S one that paddles
PACIFIED	past tense of pacify	**PADDLING**	*n* pl. -S the act of one who paddles
PACIFIER	*n* pl. -S one that pacifies		
PACIFIES	present 3d person sing. of pacify	**PADDOCK**	*v* -ED, -ING, -S to confine in an enclosure for horses
PACIFISM	*n* pl. -S opposition to war or violence		
		PADDY	*n* pl. -DIES a rice field
PACIFIST	*n* pl. -S an advocate of pacifism	**PADI**	*n* pl. -S paddy
PACIFY	*v* -FIED, -FYING, -FIES to make peaceful	**PADISHAH**	*n* pl. -S a sovereign
		PADLE	*n* pl. -S a hoe
PACING	present participle of pace	**PADLOCK**	*v* -ED, -ING, -S to secure with a type of lock
PACK	*v* -ED, -ING, -S to put into a receptacle for transportation or storage **PACKABLE** *adj*		
		PADNAG	*n* pl. -S a horse that moves along at an easy pace
PACKAGE	*v* -AGED, -AGING, -AGES to make into a package (a wrapped or boxed object)	**PADOUK**	*n* pl. -S padauk
		PADRE	*n* pl. PADRES or PADRI a Christian clergyman
PACKAGER	*n* pl. -S one that packages		
PACKER	*n* pl. -S one that packs	**PADRONE**	*n* pl. -NES or -NI a master
PACKET	*v* -ED, -ING, -S to make into a small package	**PADSHAH**	*n* pl. -S padishah
		PADUASOY	*n* pl. -SOYS a strong silk fabric

PAEAN *n* pl. -S a song of joy

PAEANISM *n* pl. -S the chanting of a paean

PAELLA *n* pl. -S a saffron-flavored stew

PAEON *n* pl. -S a metrical foot of four syllables

PAESAN *n* pl. -S paesano

PAESANO *n* pl. -NI or -NOS a fellow countryman

PAGAN *n* pl. -S an irreligious person

PAGANDOM *n* pl. -S the realm of pagans

PAGANISE *v* -ISED, -ISING, -ISES to paganize

PAGANISH *adj* resembling a pagan

PAGANISM *n* pl. -S an irreligious attitude

PAGANIST *n* pl. -S a pagan

PAGANIZE *v* -IZED, -IZING, -IZES to make irreligious

PAGE *v* PAGED, PAGING, PAGES to summon by calling out the name of

PAGEANT *n* pl. -S an elaborate public spectacle

PAGEBOY *n* pl. -BOYS a woman's hairstyle

PAGED past tense of page

PAGER *n* pl. -S a beeper

PAGINAL *adj* pertaining to the pages of a book

PAGINATE *v* -NATED, -NATING, -NATES to number the pages of

PAGING *n* pl. -S a transfer of computer pages

PAGOD *n* pl. -S pagoda

PAGODA *n* pl. -S a Far Eastern temple

PAGURIAN *n* pl. -S a hermit crab

PAGURID *n* pl. -S pagurian

PAH *interj* — used as an exclamation of disgust

PAHLAVI *n* pl. -S a former coin of Iran

PAHOEHOE *n* pl. -S smooth solidified lava

PAID a past tense of pay

PAIK *v* -ED, -ING, -S to beat or strike

PAIL *n* pl. -S a watertight cylindrical container

PAILFUL *n* pl. PAILFULS or PAILSFUL as much as a pail can hold

PAILLARD *n* pl. -S a slice of meat pounded thin and grilled

PAIN *v* -ED, -ING, -S to cause pain (suffering or distress)

PAINCH *n* pl. -ES paunch

PAINFUL *adj* -FULLER, -FULLEST causing pain

PAINLESS *adj* not causing pain

PAINT *v* -ED, -ING, -S to make a representation of with paints (coloring substances)

PAINTER *n* pl. -S one that paints

PAINTING *n* pl. -S a picture made with paints

PAINTY *adj* PAINTIER, PAINTIEST covered with paint

PAIR *v* -ED, -ING, -S to arrange in sets of two

PAIRING *n* pl. -S a matching of two opponents in a tournament

PAISA *n* pl. PAISE or PAISAS a coin of Pakistan

PAISAN *n* pl. -S paisano

PAISANA *n* pl. -S a female compatriot

PAISANO *n* pl. -NOS a fellow countryman

PAISE a pl. of paisa

PAISLEY *n* pl. -LEYS a patterned wool fabric

PAJAMA *n* pl. -S a garment for sleeping or lounging

PAJAMAED *adj* wearing pajamas

PAKEHA *n* pl. -S a person who is not of Maori descent

PAL *v* PALLED, PALLING, PALS to associate as friends

PALABRA *n* pl. -S a word

PALACE *n* pl. -S a royal residence **PALACED** *adj*

PALADIN *n* pl. -S a knightly champion

PALAIS *n* pl. PALAIS a palace

PALATAL *n* pl. -S a bone of the palate

PALATE *n* pl. -S the roof of the mouth

PALATIAL *adj* resembling a palace

PALATINE *n* pl. -S a high officer of an empire

PALAVER *v* -ED, -ING, -S to chatter

PALAZZO *n* pl. -ZI an impressive building

PALAZZOS *n/pl* wide-legged pants for women

PALE *adj* PALER, PALEST lacking intensity of color

PALE *v* PALED, PALING, PALES to make or become pale

PALEA   *n* pl. -LEAE a small bract
PALEAL *adj*

PALEFACE   *n* pl. -S a white person

PALELY   *adv* in a pale manner

PALENESS   *n* pl. -ES the quality of being pale

PALEOSOL   *n* pl. -S a layer of ancient soil

PALER   comparative of pale

PALEST   superlative of pale

PALESTRA   *n* pl. -TRAS or -TRAE a school for athletics in ancient Greece

PALET   *n* pl. -S a palea

PALETOT   *n* pl. -S a loose overcoat

PALETTE   *n* pl. -S a board on which an artist mixes colors

PALEWAYS   *adv* palewise

PALEWISE   *adv* vertically

PALFREY   *n* pl. -FREYS a riding horse

PALIER   comparative of paly

PALIEST   superlative of paly

PALIKAR   *n* pl. -S a Greek soldier

PALIMONY   *n* pl. -NIES an allowance paid to one member of an unmarried couple who have separated

PALING   *n* pl. -S a picket fence

PALINODE   *n* pl. -S a formal retraction

PALISADE   *v* -SADED, -SADING, -SADES to fortify with a heavy fence

PALISH   *adj* somewhat pale

PALL   *v* -ED, -ING, -S to become insipid

PALLADIA   *n/pl* safeguards

PALLADIC   *adj* pertaining to the metallic element palladium

PALLED   past tense of pal

PALLET   *n* pl. -S a bed or mattress of straw

PALLETTE   *n* pl. -S a piece of armor protecting the armpit

PALLIA   a pl. of pallium

PALLIAL   *adj* pertaining to a part of the brain

PALLIATE   *v* -ATED, -ATING, -ATES to conceal the seriousness of

PALLID   *adj* pale **PALLIDLY** *adv*

PALLIER   comparative of pally

PALLIEST   superlative of pally

PALLING   present participle of pal

PALLIUM   *n* pl. -LIA or -LIUMS a cloak worn in ancient Rome

PALLOR   *n* pl. -S paleness

PALLY   *adj* -LIER, -LIEST marked by close friendship

PALM   *v* -ED, -ING, -S to touch with the palm (inner surface) of the hand

PALMAR   *adj* pertaining to the palm

PALMARY   *adj* worthy of praise

PALMATE   *adj* resembling an open hand

PALMATED   *adj* palmate

PALMER   *n* pl. -S a religious pilgrim

PALMETTE   *n* pl. -S a type of ornament

PALMETTO   *n* pl. -TOS or -TOES a tropical tree

PALMIER   comparative of palmy

PALMIEST   superlative of palmy

PALMIST   *n* pl. -S a fortune-teller

PALMITIN   *n* pl. -S a chemical compound

PALMLIKE   *adj* resembling a palm tree

PALMY   *adj* PALMIER, PALMIEST marked by prosperity

PALMYRA   *n* pl. -S a tropical tree

PALOMINO   *n* pl. -NOS a slender-legged horse

PALOOKA   *n* pl. -S an inferior boxer

PALP   *n* pl. -S a palpus

PALPABLE   *adj* capable of being felt **PALPABLY** *adv*

PALPAL   *adj* pertaining to a palpus

PALPATE   *v* -PATED, -PATING, -PATES to examine by touch

PALPATOR   *n* pl. -S one that palpates

PALPEBRA   *n* pl. -BRAE an eyelid

PALPUS   *n* pl. -PI a sensory organ of an arthropod

PALSHIP   *n* pl. -S the relation existing between close friends

PALSY   *v* -SIED, -SYING, -SIES to paralyze

PALTER   *v* -ED, -ING, -S to talk or act insincerely

PALTERER   *n* pl. -S one that palters

PALTRY   *adj* -TRIER, -TRIEST petty **PALTRILY** *adv*

PALUDAL   *adj* pertaining to a marsh

PALUDISM   *n* pl. -S malaria

PALY   *adj* PALIER, PALIEST somewhat pale

PAM   *n* pl. -S the jack of clubs in certain card games

PAMPA   *n* pl. -S a grassland of South America

PAMPEAN   *n* pl. -S a native of the pampas

PAMPER   *v* -ED, -ING, -S to treat with extreme or excessive indulgence

PAMPERER   *n* pl. -S one that pampers

PAMPERO   *n* pl. -ROS a cold, dry wind

PAMPHLET   *n* pl. -S a printed work with a paper cover

PAN   *v* PANNED, PANNING, PANS to criticize harshly

PANACEA   *n* pl. -S a remedy for all diseases or ills **PANACEAN** *adj*

PANACHE   *n* pl. -S an ornamental tuft of feathers

PANADA   *n* pl. -S a thick sauce

PANAMA   *n* pl. -S a lightweight hat

PANATELA   *n* pl. -S a long, slender cigar

PANBROIL   *v* -ED, -ING, -S to fry in a pan with little or no fat

PANCAKE   *v* -CAKED, -CAKING, -CAKES to land an airplane in a certain manner

PANCETTA   *n* pl. -S unsmoked Italian bacon

PANCHAX   *n* pl. -ES a tropical fish

PANCREAS   *n* pl. -ES a large gland

PANDA   *n* pl. -S an herbivorous mammal

PANDANUS   *n* pl. -NI or -NUSES a tropical plant

PANDECT   *n* pl. -S a complete body of laws

PANDEMIC   *n* pl. -S a widespread disease

PANDER   *v* -ED, -ING, -S to provide gratification for others' desires

PANDERER   *n* pl. -S one that panders

PANDIED   past tense of pandy

PANDIES   present 3d person sing. of pandy

PANDIT   *n* pl. -S a wise or learned man in India

PANDOOR   *n* pl. -S pandour

PANDORA   *n* pl. -S bandore

PANDORE   *n* pl. -S bandore

PANDOUR   *n* pl. -S a marauding soldier

PANDOWDY   *n* pl. -DIES an apple dessert

PANDURA   *n* pl. -S bandore

PANDY   *v* -DIED, -DYING, -DIES to punish by striking the hand

PANE   *n* pl. -S a sheet of glass for a window **PANED** *adj*

PANEL   *v* -ELED, -ELING, -ELS or -ELLED, -ELLING, -ELS to decorate with thin sheets of material

PANELING   *n* pl. -S material with which to panel

PANELIST   *n* pl. -S a member of a discussion or advisory group

PANELLED   a past tense of panel

PANELLING   a present participle of panel

PANETELA   *n* pl. -S panatela

PANFISH   *n* pl. -ES any small fish that can be fried whole

PANFRY   *v* -FRIED, -FRYING, -FRIES to fry in a frying pan

PANFUL   *n* pl. -S as much as a pan will hold

PANG   *v* -ED, -ING, -S to cause to have spasms of pain

PANGA   *n* pl. -S a large knife

PANGEN   *n* pl. -S a hypothetical heredity-controlling particle of protoplasm

PANGENE   *n* pl. -S pangen

PANGOLIN   *n* pl. -S a toothless mammal

PANHUMAN   *adj* pertaining to all humanity

PANIC   *v* -ICKED, -ICKING, -ICS to be overwhelmed by fear

PANICKY   *adj* -ICKIER, -ICKIEST tending to panic

PANICLE   *n* pl. -S a loosely branched flower cluster **PANICLED** *adj*

PANICUM   *n* pl. -S a grass

PANIER   *n* pl. -S pannier

PANMIXIA   *n* pl. -S random mating within a breeding population

PANMIXIS   *n* pl. -MIXES panmixia

PANNE   *n* pl. -S a lustrous velvet

PANNED   past tense of pan

PANNIER   *n* pl. -S a large basket

PANNIKIN   *n* pl. -S a small saucepan

PANNING   present participle of pan

PANOCHA   *n* pl. -S a coarse Mexican sugar

PANOCHE   *n* pl. -S panocha

PANOPLY   *n* pl. -PLIES a suit of armor

PANOPTIC   *adj* including everything visible in one view

PANORAMA   *n* pl. -S a complete view

PANPIPE   *n* pl. -S a musical instrument

PANSOPHY   *n* pl. -PHIES universal knowledge

PANSY   *n* pl. -SIES a flowering plant

PANT   *v* -ED, -ING, -S to breathe quickly and with difficulty

PANTHEON   *n* pl. -S a temple dedicated to all the gods

PANTHER   *n* pl. -S a leopard

PANTIE   *n* pl. -S a woman's or child's undergarment

PANTIES   pl. of panty

PANTILE   *n* pl. -S a roofing tile **PANTILED** *adj*

PANTO   *n* pl. -TOS a pantomime

PANTOFLE   *n* pl. -S a slipper

PANTOUM   *n* pl. -S a verse form

PANTRY   *n* pl. -TRIES a closet or room for storing kitchen utensils

PANTSUIT   *n* pl. -S a type of woman's suit

PANTY   *n* pl. PANTIES pantie

PANZER   *n* pl. -S an armored combat vehicle

PAP   *n* pl. -S a soft food for infants

PAPA   *n* pl. -S a father

PAPACY   *n* pl. -CIES the office of the pope

PAPAIN   *n* pl. -S an enzyme

PAPAL   *adj* pertaining to the pope **PAPALLY** *adv*

PAPAW   *n* pl. -S a fleshy fruit

PAPAYA   *n* pl. -S a melon-like fruit **PAPAYAN** *adj*

PAPER   *v* -ED, -ING, -S to cover or wrap with paper (a thin sheet material made of cellulose pulp)

PAPERBOY   *n* pl. -BOYS a newsboy

PAPERER   *n* pl. -S one that papers

PAPERY   *adj* resembling paper

PAPHIAN   *n* pl. -S a prostitute

PAPILLA   *n* pl. -LAE a nipple-like projection **PAPILLAR** *adj*

PAPILLON   *n* pl. -S a small dog having large ears

PAPOOSE   *n* pl. -S an American Indian baby

PAPPI   a pl. of pappus

PAPPIER   comparative of pappy

PAPPIES   pl. of pappy

PAPPIEST   superlative of pappy

PAPPOOSE   *n* pl. -S papoose

PAPPUS   *n* pl. -PI a tuft of bristles on the achene of certain plants **PAPPOSE, PAPPOUS** *adj*

PAPPY   *adj* -PIER, -PIEST resembling pap

PAPPY   *n* pl. -PIES a father

PAPRICA   *n* pl. -S paprika

PAPRIKA   *n* pl. -S a seasoning made from red peppers

PAPULA   *n* pl. -LAE papule

PAPULE   *n* pl. -S a pimple **PAPULAR, PAPULOSE** *adj*

PAPYRUS   *n* pl. -RUSES or -RI a tall aquatic plant **PAPYRAL, PAPYRIAN, PAPYRINE** *adj*

PAR   *v* PARRED, PARRING, PARS to shoot in a standard number of strokes in golf

PARA   *n* pl. -S a monetary unit of Yugoslavia

PARABLE   *n* pl. -S a simple story conveying a moral or religious lesson

PARABOLA   *n* pl. -S a conic section

PARACHOR   *n* pl. -S a mathematical constant that relates molecular volume to surface tension

PARADE   *v* -RADED, -RADING, -RADES to march in a public procession

PARADER   *n* pl. -S one that parades

PARADIGM   *n* pl. -S a pattern or example

PARADING   present participle of parade

PARADISE   *n* pl. -S a place of extreme beauty or delight

PARADOR   *n* pl. -S a government-owned hotel in Spain

PARADOS   *n* pl. -ES a protective embankment

PARADOX   *n* pl. -ES a statement seemingly contradictory or absurd yet perhaps true

PARADROP   *v* -DROPPED, -DROPPING, -DROPS to deliver by parachute

PARAFFIN   *v* -ED, -ING, -S to coat with a waxy substance

PARAFORM   *n* pl. -S a substance used as an antiseptic

PARAGOGE   *n* pl. -S the addition of a sound or sounds at the end of a word

PARAGON   *v* -ED, -ING, -S to compare with

PARAKEET   *n* pl. -S a small parrot

PARAKITE   *n* pl. -S a parachute kite for towing a person through the air by a motorboat

PARALLAX   *n* pl. -ES an apparent optical displacement of an object

PARALLEL   *v* -LELED, -LELING, -LELS or -LELLED, -LELLING, -LELS to be similar or analogous to

PARALYSE   *v* -LYSED, -LYSING, -LYSES to paralyze

PARALYZE   *v* -LYZED, -LYZING, -LYZES to render incapable of movement

PARAMENT   *n* pl. -MENTS or -MENTA an ornamental vestment

PARAMO   *n* pl. -MOS a plateau region of South America

PARAMOUR   *n* pl. -S an illicit lover

PARANG   *n* pl. -S a heavy knife

PARANOEA   *n* pl. -S paranoia

PARANOIA   *n* pl. -S a mental disorder

PARANOIC   *n* pl. -S a paranoid

PARANOID   *n* pl. -S one affected with paranoia

PARAPET   *n* pl. -S a protective wall

PARAPH   *n* pl. -S a flourish at the end of a signature

PARAQUAT   *n* pl. -S a weed killer

PARAQUET   *n* pl. -S parakeet

PARASANG   *n* pl. -S a Persian unit of distance

PARASHAH   *n* pl. -SHOTH or -SHIOTH a passage in Jewish scripture

PARASITE   *n* pl. -S an organism that lives and feeds on or in another organism

PARASOL   *n* pl. -S a small, light umbrella

PARAVANE   *n* pl. -S an underwater device used to cut cables

PARAWING   *n* pl. -S a winglike parachute

PARAZOAN   *n* pl. -S any of a major division of multicellular animals

PARBOIL   *v* -ED, -ING, -S to cook partially by boiling for a short time

PARCEL   *v* -CELED, -CELING, -CELS or -CELLED, -CELLING, -CELS to divide into parts or shares

PARCENER   *n* pl. -S a joint heir

PARCH   *v* -ED, -ING, -ES to make very dry

PARCHESI   *n* pl. -S pachisi

PARCHISI   *n* pl. -S pachisi

PARD   *n* pl. -S a leopard

PARDAH   *n* pl. -S purdah

PARDEE   *interj* pardi

PARDI   *interj* — used as a mild oath

PARDIE   *interj* pardi

PARDINE   *adj* pertaining to a leopard

PARDNER   *n* pl. -S chum; friend

PARDON   *v* -ED, -ING, -S to release from liability for an offense

PARDONER   *n* pl. -S one that pardons

PARDY   *interj* pardi

PARE   *v* PARED, PARING, PARES to cut off the outer covering of

PARECISM   *n* pl. -S the state of having the male and female sexual organs beside or near each other

PAREIRA   *n* pl. -S a medicinal plant root

PARENT   *v* -ED, -ING, -S to exercise the functions of a parent (a father or mother)

PARENTAL   *adj* pertaining to a parent

PAREO   *n* pl. -REOS pareu

PARER   *n* pl. -S one that pares

PARERGON   *n* pl. -GA a composition derived from a larger work

PARESIS   *n* pl. -RESES partial loss of the ability to move

PARETIC   *n* pl. -S one affected with paresis

PAREU   *n* pl. -S a Polynesian garment

PAREVE   *adj* parve

PARFAIT   *n* pl. -S a frozen dessert

PARFLESH   *n* pl. -ES a rawhide soaked in lye to remove the hair and dried

PARFOCAL   *adj* having lenses with the corresponding focal points in the same plane

PARGE   *v* PARGED, PARGING, PARGES to parget

PARGET   *v* -GETED, -GETING, -GETS or -GETTED, -GETTING, -GETS to cover with plaster

PARGING   *n* pl. -S a thin coat of mortar or plaster for sealing masonry

PARGO   *n* pl. -GOS a food fish

PARHELIA   *n/pl* bright circular spots appearing on a solar halo

PARHELIC   *adj* pertaining to parhelia

PARIAH   *n* pl. -S a social outcast

PARIAN   *n* pl. -S a hard, white porcelain

PARIES   *n* pl. PARIETES the wall of an organ

PARIETAL   *n* pl. -S a bone of the skull

PARING   *n* pl. -S something pared off

PARIS   *n* pl. -ISES a European herb

PARISH   *n* pl. -ES an ecclesiastical district

PARITY   *n* pl. -TIES equality

PARK   *v* -ED, -ING, -S to leave a vehicle in a location for a time

PARKA   *n* pl. -S a hooded garment

PARKER   *n* pl. -S one that parks

PARKING   *n* pl. -S an area in which vehicles may be left

PARKLAND   *n* pl. -S a grassland region with isolated or grouped trees

PARKLIKE   *adj* resembling an outdoor recreational area

PARKWAY   *n* pl. -WAYS a wide highway

PARLANCE   *n* pl. -S a manner of speaking

PARLANDO   *adj* sung in a manner suggestive of speech

PARLANTE   *adj* parlando

PARLAY   *v* -ED, -ING, -S to bet an original wager and its winnings on a subsequent event

PARLE   *v* PARLED, PARLING, PARLES to parley

PARLEY   *v* -LEYED, -LEYING, -LEYS to discuss terms with an enemy

PARLEYER   *n* pl. -S one that parleys

PARLING   present participle of parle

PARLOR   *n* pl. -S a room for the entertainment of visitors

PARLOUR   *n* pl. -S parlor

PARLOUS   *adj* dangerous

PARODIC   *adj* comically imitative

PARODIED   past tense of parody

PARODIES   present 3d person sing. of parody

PARODIST   *n* pl. -S one who parodies

PARODOS   *n* pl. -DOI an ode sung in ancient Greek drama

PARODY   *v* -DIED, -DYING, -DIES to imitate a serious literary work for comic effect

PAROL   *n* pl. -S an utterance

PAROLE   *v* -ROLED, -ROLING, -ROLES to release from prison before completion of the imposed sentence

PAROLEE   *n* pl. -S one who is paroled

PARONYM   *n* pl. -S a word having the same root as another

PAROQUET   *n* pl. -S parakeet

PAROTIC   *adj* situated near the ear

PAROTID   *n* pl. -S a salivary gland

PAROTOID   *n* pl. -S a gland of certain toads and frogs

PAROUS   *adj* having produced offspring

PAROXYSM   *n* pl. -S a sudden fit or attack

PARQUET   *v* -ED, -ING, -S to furnish with a floor of inlaid design

PARR   *n* pl. -S a young salmon

PARRAL   *n* pl. -S parrel

PARRED   past tense of par

PARREL   *n* pl. -S a sliding loop of rope or chain used on a ship

PARRIDGE   *n* pl. -S porridge

PARRIED   past tense of parry

PARRIES   present 3d person sing. of parry

PARRING   present participle of par

PARRITCH   *n* pl. -ES porridge

PARROKET   *n* pl. -S parakeet

PARROT   *v* -ED, -ING, -S to repeat or imitate without thought or understanding

PARROTER   *n* pl. -S one that parrots

PARROTY   *adj* resembling a parrot (a hook-billed tropical bird)

PARRY   *v* -RIED, -RYING, -RIES to ward off a blow

PARSE   *v* PARSED, PARSING, PARSES to describe and analyze grammatically **PARSABLE** *adj*

PARSEC   *n* pl. -S a unit of astronomical distance

PARSER   *n* pl. -S one that parses

PARSING   present participle of parse

PARSLEY   *n* pl. -LEYS a cultivated herb **PARSLEYED, PARSLIED** *adj*

PARSNIP   *n* pl. -S a European herb

PARSON   *n* pl. -S a clergyman **PARSONIC** *adj*

PART   *v* -ED, -ING, -S to divide or break into separate pieces

PARTAKE   *v* -TOOK, -TAKEN, -TAKING, -TAKES to participate

PARTAKER   *n* pl. -S one that partakes

PARTAN   *n* pl. -S an edible crab

PARTERRE   *n* pl. -S a section of a theater

PARTIAL   *n* pl. -S a simple component of a complex tone

PARTIBLE	*adj* divisible
PARTICLE	*n* pl. -S a very small piece or part
PARTIED	past tense of party
PARTIER	*n* pl. -S partyer
PARTIES	present 3d person sing. of party
PARTING	*n* pl. -S a division or separation
PARTISAN	*n* pl. -S a firm supporter of a person, party, or cause
PARTITA	*n* pl. -S a set of related instrumental pieces
PARTITE	*adj* divided into parts
PARTIZAN	*n* pl. -S partisan
PARTLET	*n* pl. -S a woman's garment
PARTLY	*adv* in some measure or degree
PARTNER	*v* -ED, -ING, -S to associate with in some activity of common interest
PARTON	*n* pl. -S a hypothetical atomic particle
PARTOOK	past tense of partake
PARTWAY	*adv* to some extent
PARTY	*v* -TIED, -TYING, -TIES to attend a social gathering
PARTYER	*n* pl. -S one that parties
PARURA	*n* pl. -S parure
PARURE	*n* pl. -S a set of matched jewelry
PARVE	*adj* made without milk or meat
PARVENU	*n* pl. -S one who has suddenly risen above his class
PARVENUE	*adj* characteristic of a parvenu
PARVIS	*n* pl. -VISES an enclosed area in front of a church
PARVISE	*n* pl. -S parvis
PARVO	*n* pl. -VOS a contagious disease of dogs
PARVOLIN	*n* pl. -S an oily liquid obtained from fish
PAS	*n* pl. PAS a dance step
PASCAL	*n* pl. -S a unit of pressure
PASCHAL	*n* pl. -S a candle used in certain religious ceremonies
PASE	*n* pl. -S a movement of a matador's cape
PASEO	*n* pl. -SEOS a leisurely stroll
PASH	*v* -ED, -ING, -ES to strike violently
PASHA	*n* pl. -S a former Turkish high official
PASHADOM	*n* pl. -S the rank of a pasha
PASHALIC	*n* pl. -S pashalik
PASHALIK	*n* pl. -S the territory of a pasha
PASQUIL	*n* pl. -S a satire or lampoon
PASS	*v* -ED, -ING, -ES to go by
PASSABLE	*adj* fairly good or acceptable **PASSABLY** *adv*
PASSADE	*n* pl. -S a turn of a horse backward or forward on the same ground
PASSADO	*n* pl. -DOS or -DOES a forward thrust in fencing
PASSAGE	*v* -SAGED, -SAGING, -SAGES to make a voyage
PASSANT	*adj* walking with the farther forepaw raised — used of a heraldic animal
PASSBAND	*n* pl. -S a frequency band that permits transmission with maximum efficiency
PASSBOOK	*n* pl. -S a bankbook
PASSE	*adj* outmoded
PASSEE	*adj* passe
PASSEL	*n* pl. -S a large quantity or number
PASSER	*n* pl. -S one that passes
PASSERBY	*n* pl. PASSERSBY one who passes by
PASSIBLE	*adj* capable of feeling or suffering
PASSIM	*adv* here and there
PASSING	*n* pl. -S a death
PASSION	*n* pl. -S an intense emotion
PASSIVE	*n* pl. -S a verb form
PASSKEY	*n* pl. -KEYS a key that opens several different locks
PASSLESS	*adj* incapable of being traveled over or through
PASSOVER	*n* pl. -S the lamb eaten at the feast of a Jewish holiday
PASSPORT	*n* pl. -S a document allowing travel from one country to another
PASSUS	*n* pl. -ES a section of a story or poem
PASSWORD	*n* pl. -S a secret word that must be spoken to gain admission
PAST	*n* pl. -S time gone by
PASTA	*n* pl. -S a food made of dough
PASTE	*v* PASTED, PASTING, PASTES to fasten with a sticky mixture
PASTEL	*n* pl. -S a soft, delicate hue
PASTER	*n* pl. -S one that pastes

PASTERN *n* pl. -S a part of a horse's foot

PASTEUP *n* pl. -S a finished copy to be photographed for making a printing plate

PASTICCI *n/pl* pastiches

PASTICHE *n* pl. -S an artistic work made of fragments from various sources

PASTIE *n* pl. -S pasty

PASTIER comparative of pasty

PASTIES pl. of pasty

PASTIEST superlative of pasty

PASTIL *n* pl. -S pastille

PASTILLE *n* pl. -S a lozenge

PASTIME *n* pl. -S a recreational activity

PASTINA *n* pl. -S a type of macaroni

PASTING present participle of paste

PASTIS *n* pl. -TISES a French liqueur

PASTLESS *adj* having no past

PASTNESS *n* pl. -ES the state of being past or gone by

PASTOR *v* -ED, -ING, -S to serve as the spiritual overseer of

PASTORAL *n* pl. -S a literary or artistic work that depicts country life

PASTRAMI *n* pl. -S a highly seasoned smoked beef

PASTROMI *n* pl. -S pastrami

PASTRY *n* pl. -TRIES a sweet baked food

PASTURAL *adj* pertaining to a pasture

PASTURE *v* -TURED, -TURING, -TURES to put in a pasture (a grazing area)

PASTURER *n* pl. -S one that pastures livestock

PASTY *adj* PASTIER, PASTIEST pale and unhealthy in appearance

PASTY *n* pl. PASTIES a meat pie

PAT *v* PATTED, PATTING, PATS to touch lightly

PATACA *n* pl. -S a monetary unit of Macao

PATAGIAL *adj* pertaining to a patagium

PATAGIUM *n* pl. -GIA a wing membrane of a bat

PATAMAR *n* pl. -S a sailing vessel

PATCH *v* -ED, -ING, -ES to mend or cover a hole or weak spot in

PATCHER *n* pl. -S one that patches

PATCHY *adj* PATCHIER, PATCHIEST uneven in quality **PATCHILY** *adv*

PATE *n* pl. -S the top of the head **PATED** *adj*

PATELLA *n* pl. -LAE or -LAS the flat movable bone at the front of the knee **PATELLAR** *adj*

PATEN *n* pl. -S a plate

PATENCY *n* pl. -CIES the state of being obvious

PATENT *v* -ED, -ING, -S to obtain a patent (a government grant protecting the rights of an inventor) on

PATENTEE *n* pl. -S one that holds a patent

PATENTLY *adv* obviously

PATENTOR *n* pl. -S one that grants a patent

PATER *n* pl. -S a father

PATERNAL *adj* pertaining to a father

PATH *n* pl. -S a trodden way or track

PATHETIC *adj* arousing pity

PATHLESS *adj* having no path

PATHOGEN *n* pl. -S any disease-producing organism

PATHOS *n* pl. -ES a quality that arouses feelings of pity or compassion

PATHWAY *n* pl. -WAYS a path

PATIENCE *n* pl. -S the quality of being patient

PATIENT *adj* -TIENTER, -TIENTEST able to endure disagreeable circumstances without complaint

PATIENT *n* pl. -S one who is under medical treatment

PATIN *n* pl. -S paten

PATINA *n* pl. -NAE or -NAS a green film that forms on bronze

PATINATE *v* -NATED, -NATING, -NATES to give a patina to

PATINE *v* -TINED, -TINING, -TINES to cover with a patina

PATINIZE *v* -NIZED, -NIZING, -NIZES to patinate

PATIO *n* pl. -TIOS an outdoor paved area adjoining a house

PATLY *adv* suitably

PATNESS *n* pl. -ES suitability

PATOIS *n* pl. PATOIS a dialect

PATRIOT *n* pl. -S one who loves his country

PATROL *v* -TROLLED, -TROLLING, -TROLS to pass through an area for the purposes of observation or security

PATRON   *n* pl. -S a regular customer **PATRONAL, PATRONLY** *adj*

PATROON   *n* pl. -S a landowner granted manorial rights under old Dutch law

PATSY   *n* pl. -SIES a person who is easily fooled

PATTAMAR   *n* pl. -S patamar

PATTED   past tense of pat

PATTEE   *adj* paty

PATTEN   *n* pl. -S a shoe having a thick wooden sole

PATTER   *v* -ED, -ING, -S to talk glibly or rapidly

PATTERER   *n* pl. -S one that patters

PATTERN   *v* -ED, -ING, -S to make according to a prescribed design

PATTIE   *n* pl. -S patty

PATTING   present participle of pat

PATTY   *n* pl. -TIES a small, flat cake of chopped food

PATTYPAN   *n* pl. -S a pan in which patties are baked

PATULENT   *adj* patulous

PATULOUS   *adj* spreading; open

PATY   *adj* formee

PATZER   *n* pl. -S an inept chess player

PAUCITY   *n* pl. -TIES smallness of number or quantity

PAUGHTY   *adj* arrogant

PAULDRON   *n* pl. -S a piece of armor for the shoulder

PAULIN   *n* pl. -S a sheet of waterproof material

PAUNCH   *n* pl. -ES the belly or abdomen **PAUNCHED** *adj*

PAUNCHY   *adj* PAUNCHIER, PAUNCHIEST having a protruding belly

PAUPER   *v* -ED, -ING, -S to reduce to poverty

PAUSAL   *adj* pertaining to a break or rest in speaking or writing

PAUSE   *v* PAUSED, PAUSING, PAUSES to stop temporarily

PAUSER   *n* pl. -S one that pauses

PAVAN   *n* pl. -S a slow, stately dance

PAVANE   *n* pl. -S pavan

PAVE   *v* PAVED, PAVING, PAVES to cover with material that forms a firm, level surface

PAVEED   *adj* set close together to conceal a metal base

PAVEMENT   *n* pl. -S a paved surface

PAVER   *n* pl. -S one that paves

PAVID   *adj* timid

PAVILION   *v* -ED, -ING, -S to cover with a large tent

PAVILLON   *n* pl. -S the bell of a wind instrument

PAVIN   *n* pl. -S pavan

PAVING   *n* pl. -S pavement

PAVIOR   *n* pl. -S a paver

PAVIOUR   *n* pl. -S a paver

PAVIS   *n* pl. -ISES a large medieval shield

PAVISE   *n* pl. -S pavis

PAVISER   *n* pl. -S a soldier carrying a pavis

PAVLOVA   *n* pl. -S a meringue dessert

PAVONINE   *adj* resembling a peacock

PAW   *v* -ED, -ING, -S to strike or scrape with a beating motion

PAWER   *n* pl. -S one that paws

PAWKY   *adj* PAWKIER, PAWKIEST sly **PAWKILY** *adv*

PAWL   *n* pl. -S a hinged mechanical part

PAWN   *v* -ED, -ING, -S to give as security for something borrowed **PAWNABLE** *adj*

PAWNAGE   *n* pl. -S an act of pawning

PAWNEE   *n* pl. -S one to whom something is pawned

PAWNER   *n* pl. -S one that pawns something

PAWNOR   *n* pl. -S pawner

PAWNSHOP   *n* pl. -S a place where things are pawned

PAWPAW   *n* pl. -S papaw

PAX   *n* pl. -ES a ceremonial embrace given to signify Christian love and unity

PAXWAX   *n* pl. -ES the nuchal ligament of a quadruped

PAY   *v* PAID or PAYED, PAYING, PAYS to give money or something of value in exchange for goods or services

PAYABLE   *adj* profitable **PAYABLY** *adv*

PAYABLES   *n/pl* accounts payable

PAYBACK *n* pl. -S a return on an investment equal to the original capital outlay

PAYCHECK *n* pl. -S a check in payment of wages or salary

PAYDAY *n* pl. -DAYS the day on which wages are paid

PAYEE *n* pl. -S one to whom money is paid

PAYER *n* pl. -S one that pays

PAYGRADE *n* pl. -S the grade of military personnel according to a base pay scale

PAYLOAD *n* pl. -S the part of a cargo producing income

PAYMENT *n* pl. -S something that is paid

PAYNIM *n* pl. -S a pagan

PAYOFF *n* pl. -S the act of distributing gains

PAYOLA *n* pl. -S a secret payment for favors

PAYOR *n* pl. -S payer

PAYOUT *n* pl. -S money that is paid out

PAYROLL *n* pl. -S a list of employees entitled to payment

PAZAZZ *n* pl. -ES pizazz

PE *n* pl. -S a Hebrew letter

PEA *n* pl. -S the edible seed of an annual herb

PEACE *v* PEACED, PEACING, PEACES to be or become silent

PEACEFUL *adj* -FULLER, -FULLEST undisturbed; calm

PEACENIK *n* pl. -S one who demonstrates against a war

PEACH *v* -ED, -ING, -ES to inform against someone

PEACHER *n* pl. -S one that peaches

PEACHY *adj* PEACHIER, PEACHIEST dandy

PEACING present participle of peace

PEACOAT *n* pl. -S a heavy woolen jacket

PEACOCK *v* -ED, -ING, -S to strut vainly

PEACOCKY *adj* -COCKIER, -COCKIEST flamboyant, showy

PEAFOWL *n* pl. -S a large pheasant

PEAG *n* pl. -S wampum

PEAGE *n* pl. -S peag

PEAHEN *n* pl. -S a female peafowl

PEAK *v* -ED, -ING, -S to reach a maximum

PEAKIER comparative of peaky

PEAKIEST superlative of peaky

PEAKISH *adj* somewhat sickly

PEAKLESS *adj* having no peak (a pointed top)

PEAKLIKE *adj* resembling a peak

PEAKY *adj* PEAKIER, PEAKIEST sickly

PEAL *v* -ED, -ING, -S to ring out

PEALIKE *adj* resembling a pea

PEAN *n* pl. -S paean

PEANUT *n* pl. -S the nutlike seed or pod of an annual vine

PEAR *n* pl. -S a fleshy fruit

PEARL *v* -ED, -ING, -S to adorn with pearls (smooth, rounded masses formed in certain mollusks)

PEARLASH *n* pl. -ES an alkaline compound

PEARLER *n* pl. -S one that dives for pearls

PEARLITE *n* pl. -S a cast-iron alloy

PEARLY *adj* PEARLIER, PEARLIEST resembling a pearl

PEARMAIN *n* pl. -S a variety of apple

PEART *adj* PEARTER, PEARTEST lively **PEARTLY** *adv*

PEASANT *n* pl. -S a person of inferior social rank

PEASCOD *n* pl. -S peasecod

PEASE *n* pl. PEASEN or PEASES a pea

PEASECOD *n* pl. -S a pea pod

PEAT *n* pl. -S a substance composed of partially decayed vegetable matter

PEATY *adj* PEATIER, PEATIEST resembling or containing peat

PEAVEY *n* pl. -VEYS a lever used to move logs

PEAVY *n* pl. -VIES peavey

PEBBLE *v* -BLED, -BLING, -BLES to cover with pebbles (small, rounded stones)

PEBBLY *adj* -BLIER, -BLIEST resembling pebbles

PEC *n* pl. -S a chest muscle

PECAN *n* pl. -S a nut-bearing tree

PECCABLE *adj* liable to sin

PECCANCY *n* pl. -CIES the state of being peccant

PECCANT	*adj* sinful
PECCARY	*n* pl. -RIES a piglike hoofed mammal
PECCAVI	*n* pl. -S a confession of sin
PECH	*v* -ED, -ING, -S to pant
PECHAN	*n* pl. -S the stomach
PECK	*v* -ED, -ING, -S to strike with the beak or something pointed
PECKER	*n* pl. -S one that pecks
PECKISH	*adj* irritable
PECKY	*adj* PECKIER, PECKIEST marked by decay caused by fungi
PECORINO	*n* pl. -NOS or -NI a hard cheese made from sheep's milk
PECTASE	*n* pl. -S an enzyme
PECTATE	*n* pl. -S a chemical salt
PECTEN	*n* pl. -TENS or -TINES a comblike anatomical part
PECTIN	*n* pl. -S a carbohydrate derivative **PECTIC** *adj*
PECTIZE	*v* -TIZED, -TIZING, -TIZES to change into a jelly
PECTORAL	*n* pl. -S something worn on the breast
PECULATE	*v* -LATED, -LATING, -LATES to embezzle
PECULIAR	*n* pl. -S something belonging exclusively to a person
PECULIUM	*n* pl. -LIA private property
PED	*n* pl. -S a natural soil aggregate
PEDAGOG	*n* pl. -S a teacher
PEDAGOGY	*n* pl. -GIES the work of a teacher
PEDAL	*v* -ALED, -ALING, -ALS or -ALLED, -ALLING, -ALS to operate by means of foot levers
PEDALFER	*n* pl. -S a type of soil
PEDALIER	*n* pl. -S the pedal keyboard of an organ
PEDALLED	a past tense of pedal
PEDALLING	a present participle of pedal
PEDALO	*n* pl. -LOS a paddleboat powered by pedals
PEDANT	*n* pl. -S one who flaunts his knowledge **PEDANTIC** *adj*
PEDANTRY	*n* pl. -RIES ostentatious display of knowledge
PEDATE	*adj* resembling a foot **PEDATELY** *adv*
PEDDLE	*v* -DLED, -DLING, -DLES to travel about selling wares

PEDDLER	*n* pl. -S one that peddles
PEDDLERY	*n* pl. -RIES the trade of a peddler
PEDDLING	present tense of peddle
PEDERAST	*n* pl. -S a man who engages in sexual activities with boys
PEDES	pl. of pes
PEDESTAL	*v* -TALED, -TALING, -TALS or -TALLED, -TALLING, -TALS to provide with an architectural support or base
PEDICAB	*n* pl. -S a passenger vehicle that is pedaled
PEDICEL	*n* pl. -S a slender basal part of an organism
PEDICLE	*n* pl. -S pedicel **PEDICLED** *adj*
PEDICURE	*v* -CURED, -CURING, -CURES to administer a cosmetic treatment to the feet and toenails
PEDIFORM	*adj* shaped like a foot
PEDIGREE	*n* pl. -S a line of ancestors
PEDIMENT	*n* pl. -S a triangular architectural part
PEDIPALP	*n* pl. -S an appendage of an arachnid
PEDLAR	*n* pl. -S peddler
PEDLARY	*n* pl. -LARIES peddlery
PEDLER	*n* pl. -S peddler
PEDLERY	*n* pl. -LERIES peddlery
PEDOCAL	*n* pl. -S a type of soil
PEDOLOGY	*n* pl. -GIES the scientific study of the behavior and development of children
PEDRO	*n* pl. -DROS a card game
PEDUNCLE	*n* pl. -S a flower stalk
PEE	*n* pl. -S the letter P
PEEBEEN	*n* pl. -S a large hardwood evergreen tree
PEEK	*v* -ED, -ING, -S to look furtively or quickly
PEEKABOO	*n* pl. -BOOS a children's game
PEEL	*v* -ED, -ING, -S to strip off an outer covering of **PEELABLE** *adj*
PEELER	*n* pl. -S one that peels
PEELING	*n* pl. -S a piece or strip that has been peeled off
PEEN	*v* -ED, -ING, -S to beat with the non-flat end of a hammerhead
PEEP	*v* -ED, -ING, -S to utter a short, shrill cry
PEEPER	*n* pl. -S one that peeps

PEEPHOLE *n* pl. -S a small opening through which one may look

PEEPSHOW *n* pl. -S an exhibition viewed through a small opening

PEEPUL *n* pl. -S pipal

PEER *v* -ED, -ING, -S to look narrowly or searchingly

PEERAGE *n* pl. -S the rank of a nobleman

PEERESS *n* pl. -ES a noblewoman

PEERIE *n* pl. -S peery

PEERLESS *adj* having no equal

PEERY *n* pl. PEERIES a child's toy

PEESWEEP *n* pl. -S a lapwing

PEETWEET *n* pl. -S a wading bird

PEEVE *v* PEEVED, PEEVING, PEEVES to annoy

PEEVISH *adj* irritable

PEEWEE *n* pl. -S an unusually small person or thing

PEEWIT *n* pl. -S pewit

PEG *v* PEGGED, PEGGING, PEGS to fasten with a peg (a wooden pin)

PEGBOARD *n* pl. -S a board with holes for pegs

PEGBOX *n* pl. -ES a part of a stringed instrument

PEGGED past tense of peg

PEGGING present participle of peg

PEGLESS *adj* lacking a peg

PEGLIKE *adj* resembling a peg

PEH *n* pl. -S pe

PEIGNOIR *n* pl. -S a woman's gown

PEIN *v* -ED, -ING, -S to peen

PEISE *v* PEISED, PEISING, PEISES to weigh

PEKAN *n* pl. -S a carnivorous mammal

PEKE *n* pl. -S a small, long-haired dog

PEKIN *n* pl. -S a silk fabric

PEKOE *n* pl. -S a black tea

PELAGE *n* pl. -S the coat or covering of a mammal **PELAGIAL** *adj*

PELAGIC *adj* oceanic

PELE *n* pl. -S a medieval fortified tower

PELERINE *n* pl. -S a woman's cape

PELF *n* pl. -S money or wealth

PELICAN *n* pl. -S a large, web-footed bird

PELISSE *n* pl. -S a long outer garment

PELITE *n* pl. -S a rock composed of fine fragments **PELITIC** *adj*

PELLAGRA *n* pl. -S a niacin-deficiency disease

PELLET *v* -ED, -ING, -S to strike with pellets (small rounded masses)

PELLETAL *adj* resembling a pellet

PELLICLE *n* pl. -S a thin skin or film

PELLMELL *n* pl. -S a jumbled mass

PELLUCID *adj* transparent

PELMET *n* pl. -S a decorative cornice

PELON *adj* hairless

PELORIA *n* pl. -S abnormal regularity of a flower form **PELORIAN, PELORIC** *adj*

PELORUS *n* pl. -ES a navigational instrument

PELOTA *n* pl. -S a court game of Spanish origin

PELT *v* -ED, -ING, -S to strike repeatedly with blows or missiles

PELTAST *n* pl. -S a soldier of ancient Greece

PELTATE *adj* shaped like a shield

PELTER *v* -ED, -ING, -S to pelt

PELTRY *n* pl. -RIES an animal skin

PELVIC *n* pl. -S a bone of the pelvis

PELVIS *n* pl. -VES or -VISES a part of the skeleton

PEMBINA *n* pl. -S a variety of cranberry

PEMICAN *n* pl. -S pemmican

PEMMICAN *n* pl. -S a food prepared by North American Indians

PEMOLINE *n* pl. -S a drug used as a stimulant

PEMPHIX *n* pl. -ES a skin disease

PEN *v* PENNED, PENNING, PENS to write with a pen (an instrument for writing with fluid ink)

PENAL *adj* pertaining to punishment

PENALISE *v* -ISED, -ISING, -ISES to penalize

PENALITY *n* pl. -TIES liability to punishment

PENALIZE *v* -IZED, -IZING, -IZES to subject to a penalty

PENALLY *adv* in a penal manner

PENALTY *n* pl. -TIES a punishment imposed for violation of a law, rule, or agreement

PENANCE	*v* -ANCED, -ANCING, -ANCES to impose a type of punishment upon	**PENNINE**	*n* pl. -S a mineral
		PENNING	present participle of pen
PENANG	*n* pl. -S a cotton fabric	**PENNON**	*n* pl. -S a pennant **PENNONED** *adj*
PENATES	*n/pl* the Roman gods of the household	**PENNY**	*n* pl. PENNIES or PENCE a coin of the United Kingdom
PENCE	a pl. of penny		
PENCEL	*n* pl. -S a small flag	**PENOCHE**	*n* pl. -S penuche
PENCHANT	*n* pl. -S a strong liking for something	**PENOLOGY**	*n* pl. -GIES the science of the punishment of crime
PENCIL	*v* -CILED, -CILING, -CILS or -CILLED, -CILLING, -CILS to produce by using a pencil (a writing and drawing implement)	**PENONCEL**	*n* pl. -S a small pennon
		PENPOINT	*n* pl. -S the point of a pen
		PENSEE	*n* pl. -S a thought
		PENSIL	*n* pl. -S pencel
PENCILER	*n* pl. -S one that pencils	**PENSILE**	*adj* hanging loosely
PEND	*v* -ED, -ING, -S to remain undecided or unsettled	**PENSION**	*v* -ED, -ING, -S to grant a retirement allowance to
PENDANT	*n* pl. -S a hanging ornament	**PENSIONE**	*n* pl. -S a boarding house
PENDENCY	*n* pl. -CIES a pending state	**PENSIVE**	*adj* engaged in deep thought
PENDENT	*n* pl. -S pendant	**PENSTER**	*n* pl. -S a writer
PENDULUM	*n* pl. -S a type of free swinging body **PENDULAR** *adj*	**PENSTOCK**	*n* pl. -S a conduit for conveying water to a waterwheel
PENES	a pl. of penis	**PENT**	*adj* confined
PENGO	*n* pl. -GOS a former monetary unit of Hungary	**PENTACLE**	*n* pl. -S a five-pointed star
		PENTAD	*n* pl. -S a group of five
PENGUIN	*n* pl. -S a flightless, aquatic bird	**PENTAGON**	*n* pl. -S a five-sided polygon
PENICIL	*n* pl. -S a small tuft of hairs	**PENTANE**	*n* pl. -S a volatile liquid
PENIS	*n* pl. -NES or -NISES the male organ of copulation **PENIAL, PENILE** *adj*	**PENTANOL**	*n* pl. -S an alcohol
		PENTARCH	*n* pl. -S one of five joint rulers
		PENTENE	*n* pl. -S a liquid hydrocarbon
PENITENT	*n* pl. -S a person who repents his sins	**PENTODE**	*n* pl. -S a type of electron tube
		PENTOMIC	*adj* made up of five battle groups
PENKNIFE	*n* pl. -KNIVES a small pocketknife	**PENTOSAN**	*n* pl. -S a complex carbohydrate
PENLIGHT	*n* pl. -S a small flashlight	**PENTOSE**	*n* pl. -S a sugar having five carbon atoms per molecule
PENLITE	*n* pl. -S penlight		
PENMAN	*n* pl. -MEN an author	**PENTYL**	*n* pl. -S amyl
PENNA	*n* pl. -NAE any of the feathers that determine a bird's shape	**PENUCHE**	*n* pl. -S a fudge-like candy
		PENUCHI	*n* pl. -S penuche
PENNAME	*n* pl. -S a name used by an author instead of his real name	**PENUCHLE**	*n* pl. -S pinochle
		PENUCKLE	*n* pl. -S pinochle
PENNANT	*n* pl. -S a long, narrow flag	**PENULT**	*n* pl. -S the next to last syllable in a word
PENNATE	*adj* having wings or feathers		
PENNATED	*adj* pennate	**PENUMBRA**	*n* pl. -BRAE or -BRAS a partial shadow
PENNE	*n* pl. PENNE short tubular pasta		
PENNED	past tense of pen	**PENURY**	*n* pl. -RIES extreme poverty
PENNER	*n* pl. -S one that pens	**PEON**	*n* pl. -S or -ES an unskilled laborer
PENNI	*n* pl. -NIA or -NIS a Finnish coin		
PENNIES	a pl. of penny		

PEONAGE *n* pl. -S the condition of being a peon

PEONISM *n* pl. -S peonage

PEONY *n* pl. -NIES a flowering plant

PEOPLE *v* -PLED, -PLING, -PLES to furnish with inhabitants

PEOPLER *n* pl. -S one that peoples

PEP *v* PEPPED, PEPPING, PEPS to fill with energy

PEPERONI *n* pl. -S a highly seasoned sausage

PEPLOS *n* pl. -ES a garment worn by women in ancient Greece

PEPLUM *n* pl. -LUMS or -LA a short section attached to the waistline of a garment **PEPLUMED** *adj*

PEPLUS *n* pl. -ES peplos

PEPO *n* pl. -POS a fruit having a fleshy interior and a hard rind

PEPONIDA *n* pl. -S pepo

PEPONIUM *n* pl. -S pepo

PEPPED past tense of pep

PEPPER *v* -ED, -ING, -S to season with pepper (a pungent condiment)

PEPPERER *n* pl. -S one that peppers

PEPPERY *adj* resembling pepper

PEPPING present participle of pep

PEPPY *adj* -PIER, -PIEST full of energy **PEPPILY** *adv*

PEPSIN *n* pl. -S a digestive enzyme of the stomach

PEPSINE *n* pl. -S pepsin

PEPTIC *n* pl. -S a substance that promotes digestion

PEPTID *n* pl. -S peptide

PEPTIDE *n* pl. -S a combination of amino acids **PEPTIDIC** *adj*

PEPTIZE *v* -TIZED, -TIZING, -TIZES to increase the colloidal dispersion of

PEPTIZER *n* pl. -S one that peptizes

PEPTONE *n* pl. -S a protein compound **PEPTONIC** *adj*

PER *prep* for each

PERACID *n* pl. -S a type of acid

PERCALE *n* pl. -S a cotton fabric

PERCEIVE *v* -CEIVED, -CEIVING, -CEIVES to become aware of through the senses

PERCENT *n* pl. -S one part in a hundred

PERCEPT *n* pl. -S something perceived

PERCH *v* -ED, -ING, -ES to sit or rest on an elevated place

PERCHER *n* pl. -S one that perches

PERCOID *n* pl. -S a spiny-finned fish

PERCUSS *v* -ED, -ING, -ES to strike with force

PERDIE *interj* pardi

PERDU *n* pl. -S a soldier sent on a dangerous mission

PERDUE *n* pl. -S perdu

PERDURE *v* -DURED, -DURING, -DURES to continue to exist

PERDY *interj* pardi

PEREGRIN *n* pl. -S a swift falcon much used in falconry

PEREION *n* pl. -REIA the thorax of some crustaceans

PEREON *n* pl. -REA pereion

PEREOPOD *n* pl. -S an appendage of the pereion

PERFECT *adj* -FECTER, -FECTEST lacking fault or defect; of an extreme kind

PERFECT *v* -ED, -ING, -S to make perfect

PERFECTA *n* pl. -S a system of betting

PERFECTO *n* pl. -TOS a medium-sized cigar

PERFIDY *n* pl. -DIES deliberate breach of faith or trust

PERFORCE *adv* of necessity

PERFORM *v* -ED, -ING, -S to begin and carry through to completion

PERFUME *v* -FUMED, -FUMING, -FUMES to fill with a fragrant odor

PERFUMER *n* pl. -S one that perfumes

PERFUSE *v* -FUSED, -FUSING, -FUSES to spread over or through something

PERGOLA *n* pl. -S a shaded shelter or passageway

PERHAPS *n* pl. -ES something open to doubt or conjecture

PERI *n* pl. -S a supernatural being of Persian mythology

PERIANTH *n* pl. -S an outer covering of a flower

PERIAPT *n* pl. -S an amulet

PERIBLEM *n* pl. -S a region of plant tissue

PERICARP *n* pl. -S the wall of a ripened plant ovary or fruit

PERICOPE *n* pl. -PES or -PAE a selection from a book

PERIDERM *n* pl. -S an outer layer of plant tissue

PERIDIUM *n* pl. -IA the covering of the spore-bearing organ in many fungi **PERIDIAL** *adj*

PERIDOT *n* pl. -S a mineral

PERIGEE *n* pl. -S the point in the orbit of a celestial body which is nearest to the earth **PERIGEAL, PERIGEAN** *adj*

PERIGON *n* pl. -S an angle equal to 360 degrees

PERIGYNY *n* pl. -NIES the state of being situated on a cuplike organ surrounding the pistil

PERIL *v* -ILED, -ILING, -ILS or -ILLED, -ILLING, -ILS to imperil

PERILLA *n* pl. -S an Asian herb

PERILOUS *adj* dangerous

PERILUNE *n* pl. -S the point in the orbit of a celestial body which is nearest to the moon

PERINEUM *n* pl. -NEA a region of the body at the lower end of the trunk **PERINEAL** *adj*

PERIOD *n* pl. -S a portion of time

PERIODIC *adj* recurring at regular intervals

PERIODID *n* pl. -S an iodide

PERIOTIC *adj* surrounding the ear

PERIPETY *n* pl. -TIES a sudden change in a course of events

PERIPTER *n* pl. -S a structure with a row of columns around all sides

PERIQUE *n* pl. -S a dark tobacco

PERISARC *n* pl. -S a protective covering of certain hydrozoans

PERISH *v* -ED, -ING, -ES to die

PERIWIG *n* pl. -S a wig

PERJURE *v* -JURED, -JURING, -JURES to make a perjurer of

PERJURER *n* pl. -S one guilty of perjury

PERJURY *n* pl. -RIES the willful giving of false testimony under oath in a judicial proceeding

PERK *v* -ED, -ING, -S to carry oneself jauntily

PERKISH *adj* somewhat perky

PERKY *adj* PERKIER, PERKIEST jaunty **PERKILY** *adv*

PERLITE *n* pl. -S a volcanic glass **PERLITIC** *adj*

PERM *v* -ED, -ING, -S to give hair a permanent wave

PERMEANT *adj* that permeates

PERMEASE *n* pl. -S a catalyzing agent

PERMEATE *v* -ATED, -ATING, -ATES to spread through

PERMIT *v* -MITTED, -MITTING, -MITS to allow

PERMUTE *v* -MUTED, -MUTING, -MUTES to change the order of

PERONEAL *adj* pertaining to the fibula

PERORAL *adj* occurring through the mouth

PERORATE *v* -RATED, -RATING, -RATES to make a lengthy speech

PEROXID *n* pl. -S peroxide

PEROXIDE *v* -IDED, -IDING, -IDES to treat with peroxide (a bleaching agent)

PEROXY *adj* containing the bivalent group O_2

PERPEND *v* -ED, -ING, -S to ponder

PERPENT *n* pl. -S a large building stone

PERPLEX *v* -ED, -ING, -ES to make mentally uncertain

PERRON *n* pl. -S an outdoor stairway

PERRY *n* pl. -RIES a beverage of pear juice often fermented

PERSALT *n* pl. -S a chemical salt

PERSE *n* pl. -S a blue color

PERSIST *v* -ED, -ING, -S to continue resolutely in some activity

PERSON *n* pl. -S a human being

PERSONA *n* pl. -NAE a character in a literary work

PERSONA *n* pl. -S the public role that a person assumes

PERSONAL *n* pl. -S a brief, private notice in a newspaper

PERSPIRE *v* -SPIRED, -SPIRING, -SPIRES to give off moisture through the pores of the skin **PERSPIRY** *adj*

PERSUADE *v* -SUADED, -SUADING, -SUADES to cause to do something by means of argument, reasoning, or entreaty

PERT *adj* PERTER, PERTEST impudent **PERTLY** *adv*

PERTAIN *v* -ED, -ING, -S to have reference or relation

PERTNESS *n* pl. -ES the quality of being pert

PERTURB *v* -ED, -ING, -S to disturb greatly

PERUKE *n* pl. -S a wig **PERUKED** *adj*

PERUSAL	n pl. -S the act of perusing	**PETCOCK**	n pl. -S a small valve or faucet
PERUSE	v -RUSED, -RUSING, -RUSES to read	**PETECHIA**	n pl. -CHIAE a small hemorrhagic spot on a body surface
PERUSER	n pl. -S one that peruses	**PETER**	v -ED, -ING, -S to diminish gradually
PERVADE	v -VADED, -VADING, -VADES to spread through every part of		
PERVADER	n pl. -S one that pervades	**PETIOLAR**	adj pertaining to a petiole
PERVERSE	adj willfully deviating from desired or expected conduct	**PETIOLE**	n pl. -S the stalk of a leaf **PETIOLED** adj
PERVERT	v -ED, -ING, -S to turn away from the right course of action	**PETIT**	adj small; minor
		PETITE	n pl. -S a clothing size for short women
PERVIOUS	adj capable of being penetrated	**PETITION**	v -ED, -ING, -S to make a formal request
PES	n pl. PEDES a foot or footlike part		
PESADE	n pl. -S the position of a horse when rearing	**PETNAP**	v -NAPPED, -NAPPING, -NAPS to steal a pet for profit
PESETA	n pl. -S a monetary unit of Spain	**PETRALE**	n pl. -S a food fish
PESEWA	n pl. -S a monetary unit of Ghana	**PETREL**	n pl. -S a small seabird
PESKY	adj -KIER, -KIEST annoying **PESKILY** adv	**PETRIFY**	v -FIED, -FYING, -FIES to convert into stone
		PETROL	n pl. -S gasoline
PESO	n pl. -SOS a monetary unit of various Spanish-speaking countries	**PETROLIC**	adj derived from petroleum
		PETRONEL	n pl. -S a portable firearm
PESSARY	n pl. -RIES a contraceptive device worn in the vagina	**PETROSAL**	adj petrous
		PETROUS	adj resembling stone in hardness
PEST	n pl. -S an annoying person or thing	**PETSAI**	n pl. -S Chinese cabbage
PESTER	v -ED, -ING, -S to bother	**PETTED**	past tense of pet
PESTERER	n pl. -S one that pesters	**PETTEDLY**	adv peevishly
PESTHOLE	n pl. -S a place liable to epidemic disease	**PETTER**	n pl. -S one that pets
		PETTI	pl. of petto
PESTLE	v -TLED, -TLING, -TLES to crush with a club-shaped hand tool	**PETTIER**	comparative of petty
		PETTIEST	superlative of petty
PESTO	n pl. -TOS a sauce of basil, garlic, and olive oil	**PETTIFOG**	v -FOGGED, -FOGGING, -FOGS to quibble
PESTY	adj PESTIER, PESTIEST annoying	**PETTILY**	adv in a petty manner
		PETTING	n pl. -S amorous caressing and kissing
PET	v PETTED, PETTING, PETS to caress with the hand		
		PETTISH	adj peevish
PETAL	n pl. -S a leaflike part of a corolla **PETALED, PETALLED** adj	**PETTLE**	v -TLED, -TLING, -TLES to caress
PETALINE	adj resembling a petal	**PETTO**	n pl. -TI the breast
PETALODY	n pl. -DIES the metamorphosis of various floral organs into petals	**PETTY**	adj -TIER, -TIEST insignificant
		PETULANT	adj peevish
PETALOID	adj resembling a petal	**PETUNIA**	n pl. -S a tropical herb
PETALOUS	adj having petals	**PETUNTSE**	n pl. -S a mineral
PETARD	n pl. -S an explosive device	**PETUNTZE**	n pl. -S petuntse
PETASOS	n pl. -ES petasus	**PEW**	n pl. -S a bench in church
PETASUS	n pl. -ES a broad-brimmed hat worn in ancient Greece	**PEWEE**	n pl. -S a small bird

PEWIT	*n* pl. -S the lapwing	**PHASEOUT**	*n* pl. -S a gradual stopping of operations
PEWTER	*n* pl. -S a tin alloy	**PHASIS**	*n* pl. PHASES a phase
PEWTERER	*n* pl. -S one that makes articles of pewter	**PHASMID**	*n* pl. -S a tropical insect
PEYOTE	*n* pl. -S a cactus	**PHAT**	*adj* susceptible of easy and rapid typesetting
PEYOTL	*n* pl. -S peyote	**PHATIC**	*adj* sharing feelings rather than ideas
PEYTRAL	*n* pl. -S a piece of armor for the breast of a horse	**PHEASANT**	*n* pl. -S a large, long-tailed bird
PEYTREL	*n* pl. -S peytral	**PHELLEM**	*n* pl. -S a layer of plant cells
PFENNIG	*n* pl. -NIGS or -NIGE a bronze coin of Germany	**PHELONIA**	*n/pl* liturgical vestments
PFFT	*interj* — used to express a sudden ending	**PHENATE**	*n* pl. -S a salt of carbolic acid
PFUI	*interj* phooey	**PHENAZIN**	*n* pl. -S a chemical compound
PHAETON	*n* pl. -S a light carriage	**PHENETIC**	*adj* pertaining to a type of classificatory system
PHAGE	*n* pl. -S an organism that destroys bacteria	**PHENETOL**	*n* pl. -S a volatile liquid
		PHENIX	*n* pl. -ES phoenix
PHALANGE	*n* pl. -S any bone of a finger or toe	**PHENOL**	*n* pl. -S a caustic compound
PHALANX	*n* pl. -ES a formation of infantry in ancient Greece	**PHENOLIC**	*n* pl. -S a synthetic resin
PHALLI	a pl. of phallus	**PHENOM**	*n* pl. -S a person of extraordinary ability or promise
PHALLIC	*adj* pertaining to a phallus	**PHENOXY**	*adj* containing a radical derived from phenol
PHALLISM	*n* pl. -S worship of the phallus as symbolic of nature's creative power	**PHENYL**	*n* pl. -S a univalent chemical radical **PHENYLIC** *adj*
PHALLIST	*n* pl. -S one who practices phallism	**PHEW**	*interj* — used to express relief, fatigue, or disgust
PHALLUS	*n* pl. -LI or -LUSES the penis	**PHI**	*n* pl. -S a Greek letter
PHANTASIED past tense of phantasy		**PHIAL**	*n* pl. -S a vial
PHANTASIES present 3d person sing. of phantasy		**PHILABEG**	*n* pl. -S filibeg
		PHILIBEG	*n* pl. -S filibeg
PHANTASM	*n* pl. -S a creation of the imagination	**PHILOMEL**	*n* pl. -S a songbird
PHANTAST	*n* pl. -S fantast	**PHILTER**	*v* -ED, -ING, -S to put under the spell of a love potion
PHANTASY	*v* -SIED, -SYING, -SIES to fantasy	**PHILTRE**	*v* -TRED, -TRING, -TRES to philter
PHANTOM	*n* pl. -S something existing in appearance only	**PHILTRUM**	*n* pl. -TRA the indentation between the upper lip and the nose
PHARAOH	*n* pl. -S a ruler of ancient Egypt	**PHIMOSIS**	*n* pl. -MOSES the abnormal constriction of the opening of the prepuce **PHIMOTIC** *adj*
PHARISEE	*n* pl. -S a hypocritically self-righteous person		
PHARMACY	*n* pl. -CIES a drugstore	**PHIZ**	*n* pl. -ES a face or facial expression
PHAROS	*n* pl. -ES a lighthouse or beacon to guide seamen	**PHLEGM**	*n* pl. -S a thick mucus secreted in the air passages
PHARYNX	*n* pl. -YNGES or -YNXES a section of the digestive tract	**PHLEGMY**	*adj* PHLEGMIER, PHLEGMIEST resembling phlegm
PHASE	*v* PHASED, PHASING, PHASES to plan or carry out by phases (distinct stages of development) **PHASEAL, PHASIC** *adj*	**PHLOEM**	*n* pl. -S a complex plant tissue
		PHLOX	*n* pl. -ES a flowering plant

PHOBIA — *n* pl. -S an obsessive or irrational fear

PHOBIC — *n* pl. -S one affected with a phobia

PHOCINE — *adj* pertaining to seals

PHOEBE — *n* pl. -S a small bird

PHOEBUS — *n* pl. -ES the sun

PHOENIX — *n* pl. -ES a mythical bird

PHON — *n* pl. -S a unit of loudness

PHONAL — *adj* pertaining to speech sounds

PHONATE — *v* -NATED, -NATING, -NATES to produce speech sounds

PHONE — *v* PHONED, PHONING, PHONES to telephone

PHONEME — *n* pl. -S a unit of speech **PHONEMIC** *adj*

PHONETIC — *adj* pertaining to speech sounds

PHONEY — *v* -ED, -ING, -S to phony

PHONEY — *adj* -NIER, -NIEST phony

PHONIC — *adj* pertaining to the nature of sound

PHONICS — *n/pl* the science of sound

PHONIED — past tense of phony

PHONIER — comparative of phoney and phony

PHONIES — present 3d person sing. of phony

PHONIEST — superlative of phoney and phony

PHONILY — *adv* in a phony manner

PHONING — present participle of phone

PHONO — *n* pl. -NOS a record player

PHONON — *n* pl. -S a quantum of vibrational energy

PHONY — *adj* -NIER, -NIEST not genuine or real

PHONY — *v* -NIED, -NYING, -NIES to alter so as to make appear genuine

PHOOEY — *interj* — used as an exclamation of disgust or contempt

PHORATE — *n* pl. -S an insecticide

PHORONID — *n* pl. -S a wormlike marine animal

PHOSGENE — *n* pl. -S a poisonous gas

PHOSPHID — *n* pl. -S a chemical compound

PHOSPHIN — *n* pl. -S a poisonous gas

PHOSPHOR — *n* pl. -S a substance that will emit light when exposed to radiation

PHOT — *n* pl. -S a unit of illumination

PHOTIC — *adj* pertaining to light

PHOTICS — *n/pl* the science of light

PHOTO — *v* -ED, -ING, -S to photograph

PHOTOG — *n* pl. -S one who takes photographs

PHOTOMAP — *v* -MAPPED, -MAPPING, -MAPS to map by means of aerial photography

PHOTON — *n* pl. -S an elementary particle **PHOTONIC** *adj*

PHOTOPIA — *n* pl. -S vision in bright light **PHOTOPIC** *adj*

PHOTOSET — *v* -SET, -SETTING, -SETS to prepare for printing by photographic means

PHPHT — *interj* pht

PHRASAL — *adj* pertaining to a group of two or more associated words

PHRASE — *v* PHRASED, PHRASING, PHRASES to express in words

PHRASING — *n* pl. -S manner or style of verbal expression

PHRATRY — *n* pl. -TRIES a tribal unit among primitive peoples **PHRATRAL, PHRATRIC** *adj*

PHREATIC — *adj* pertaining to underground waters

PHRENIC — *adj* pertaining to the mind

PHRENSY — *v* -SIED, -SYING, -SIES to frenzy

PHT — *interj* — used as an expression of mild anger or annoyance

PHTHALIC — *adj* pertaining to a certain acid

PHTHALIN — *n* pl. -S a chemical compound

PHTHISIC — *n* pl. -S phthisis

PHTHISIS — *n* pl. PHTHISES a disease of the lungs

PHUT — *n* pl. -S a dull, abrupt sound

PHYLA — pl. of phylon and phylum

PHYLAE — pl. of phyle

PHYLAR — *adj* pertaining to a phylum

PHYLAXIS — *n* pl. -AXISES an inhibiting of infection by the body

PHYLE — *n* pl. -LAE a political subdivision in ancient Greece **PHYLIC** *adj*

PHYLESIS — *n* pl. -LESES or -LESISES the course of evolutionary development **PHYLETIC** *adj*

PHYLLARY — *n* pl. -RIES a bract of certain plants

PHYLLITE — *n* pl. -S a foliated rock

PHYLLO — *n* pl. -LOS very thin pastry dough

PHYLLODE — *n* pl. -S a flattened petiole that serves as a leaf

PHYLLOID — *n* pl. -S a leaflike plant part

PHYLLOME *n* pl. -S a leaf of a plant

PHYLON *n* pl. -LA a genetically related group

PHYLUM *n* pl. -LA a taxonomic division

PHYSED *n* pl. -S physical education

PHYSES pl. of physis

PHYSIC *v* -ICKED, -ICKING, -ICS to treat with medicine

PHYSICAL *n* pl. -S a medical examination of the body

PHYSIQUE *n* pl. -S the form or structure of the body

PHYSIS *n* pl. PHYSES the principle of growth or change in nature

PHYTANE *n* pl. -S a chemical compound

PHYTOID *adj* resembling a plant

PHYTOL *n* pl. -S an alcohol

PHYTON *n* pl. -S a structural unit of a plant **PHYTONIC** *adj*

PI *n* pl. -S a Greek letter

PI *v* PIED, PIEING or PIING, PIES to jumble or disorder

PIA *n* pl. -S a membrane of the brain

PIACULAR *adj* atoning

PIAFFE *v* PIAFFED, PIAFFING, PIAFFES to perform a piaffer

PIAFFER *n* pl. -S a movement in horsemanship

PIAL *adj* pertaining to a pia

PIAN *n* pl. -S a tropical disease **PIANIC** *adj*

PIANISM *n* pl. -S performance on the piano

PIANIST *n* pl. -S one who plays the piano

PIANO *n* pl. -NOS a musical instrument

PIASABA *n* pl. -S piassava

PIASAVA *n* pl. -S piassava

PIASSABA *n* pl. -S piassava

PIASSAVA *n* pl. -S a coarse, stiff fiber

PIASTER *n* pl. -S a monetary unit of several Arab countries

PIASTRE *n* pl. -S piaster

PIAZZA *n* pl. -ZAS or -ZE a public square in an Italian town

PIBAL *n* pl. -S a small balloon for determining the direction and speed of the wind

PIBROCH *n* pl. -S a musical piece played on the bagpipe

PIC *n* pl. -S a photograph

PICA *n* pl. -S a craving for unnatural food

PICACHO *n* pl. -CHOS an isolated peak of a hill

PICADOR *n* pl. -ES or -S a horseman in a bullfight

PICAL *adj* resembling a pica

PICARA *n* pl. -S a female picaro

PICARO *n* pl. -ROS a vagabond

PICAROON *v* -ED, -ING, -S to act as a pirate

PICAYUNE *n* pl. -S a former Spanish-American coin

PICCOLO *n* pl. -LOS a small flute

PICE *n* pl. PICE a former coin of India and Pakistan

PICEOUS *adj* glossy-black in color

PICIFORM *adj* pertaining to an order of birds

PICK *v* -ED, -ING, -S to select

PICKADIL *n* pl. -S a type of collar

PICKAX *v* -ED, -ING, -ES to use a pickax (a tool for breaking hard surfaces)

PICKAXE *v* -AXED, -AXING, -AXES to pickax

PICKEER *v* -ED, -ING, -S to skirmish in advance of an army

PICKER *n* pl. -S one that picks

PICKEREL *n* pl. -S a freshwater fish

PICKET *v* -ED, -ING, -S to stand outside of some location, as a business, to publicize one's grievances against it

PICKETER *n* pl. -S one who pickets

PICKIER comparative of picky

PICKIEST superlative of picky

PICKING *n* pl. -S the act of one that picks

PICKLE *v* -LED, -LING, -LES to preserve or flavor in a solution of brine or vinegar

PICKLOCK *n* pl. -S a tool for opening locks

PICKOFF *n* pl. -S a play in baseball

PICKUP *n* pl. -S a small truck

PICKWICK *n* pl. -S a device for raising wicks in oil lamps

PICKY *adj* PICKIER, PICKIEST fussy

PICLORAM *n* pl. -S an herbicide

PICNIC *v* -NICKED, -NICKING, -NICS to go on a picnic (an outdoor excursion with food)

PICNICKY	adj pertaining to a picnic
PICOGRAM	n pl. -S one trillionth of a gram
PICOLIN	n pl. -S picoline
PICOLINE	n pl. -S a chemical compound
PICOMOLE	n pl. -S one trillionth of a mole
PICOT	v -ED, -ING, -S to edge with ornamental loops
PICOTEE	n pl. -S a variety of carnation
PICQUET	n pl. -S piquet
PICRATE	n pl. -S a chemical salt **PICRATED** adj
PICRIC	adj having a very bitter taste
PICRITE	n pl. -S an igneous rock **PICRITIC** adj
PICTURE	v -TURED, -TURING, -TURES to make a visual representation of
PICUL	n pl. -S an Asian unit of weight
PIDDLE	v -DLED, -DLING, -DLES to waste time
PIDDLER	n pl. -S one that piddles
PIDDLY	adj insignificant
PIDDOCK	n pl. -S a bivalve mollusk
PIDGIN	n pl. -S a mixed language
PIE	v PIED, PIEING, PIES to pi
PIEBALD	n pl. -S a spotted animal
PIECE	v PIECED, PIECING, PIECES to join into a whole
PIECER	n pl. -S one that pieces
PIECING	n pl. -S material to be sewn together
PIECRUST	n pl. -S the crust of a pie
PIED	past tense of pie
PIEDFORT	n pl. -S piefort
PIEDMONT	n pl. -S an area lying at the foot of a mountain
PIEFORT	n pl. -S an unusually thick coin
PIEING	a present participle of pi
PIEPLANT	n pl. -S a rhubarb
PIER	n pl. -S a structure extending from land out over water
PIERCE	v PIERCED, PIERCING, PIERCES to cut or pass into or through
PIERCER	n pl. -S one that pierces
PIEROGI	n pl. -ES a small dumpling with a filling
PIERROT	n pl. -S a clown

PIETA	n pl. -S a representation of the Virgin Mary mourning over the body of Christ
PIETIES	pl. of piety
PIETISM	n pl. -S piety
PIETIST	n pl. -S a pious person
PIETY	n pl. -TIES the quality or state of being pious
PIFFLE	v -FLED, -FLING, -FLES to babble
PIG	v PIGGED, PIGGING, PIGS to bear pigs (cloven-hoofed mammals)
PIGBOAT	n pl. -S a submarine
PIGEON	n pl. -S a short-legged bird
PIGFISH	n pl. -ES a marine fish
PIGGED	past tense of pig
PIGGERY	n pl. -GERIES a pigpen
PIGGIE	n pl. -S piggy
PIGGIER	comparative of piggy
PIGGIES	pl. of piggy
PIGGIEST	superlative of piggy
PIGGIN	n pl. -S a small wooden pail
PIGGING	present participle of pig
PIGGISH	adj greedy or dirty
PIGGY	n pl. -GIES a small pig
PIGGY	adj -GIER, -GIEST piggish
PIGLET	n pl. -S a small pig
PIGLIKE	adj resembling a pig
PIGMENT	v -ED, -ING, -S to add a coloring matter to
PIGMY	n pl. -MIES pygmy
PIGNOLI	n pl. -S pignolia
PIGNOLIA	n pl. -S the edible seed of nut pines
PIGNUS	n pl. -NORA property held as security for a debt
PIGNUT	n pl. -S a hickory nut
PIGOUT	n pl. -S an instance of eating to excess
PIGPEN	n pl. -S a place where pigs are kept
PIGSKIN	n pl. -S the skin of a pig
PIGSNEY	n pl. -NEYS a darling
PIGSTICK	v -ED, -ING, -S to hunt for wild boar
PIGSTY	n pl. -STIES a pigpen
PIGTAIL	n pl. -S a tight braid of hair

PIGWEED	*n* pl. -S a weedy plant	**PILLAGER**	*n* pl. -S one that pillages
PIING	a present participle of pi	**PILLAR**	*v* -ED, -ING, -S to provide with vertical building supports
PIKA	*n* pl. -S a small mammal	**PILLBOX**	*n* pl. -ES a small box for pills
PIKAKE	*n* pl. -S an East Indian vine	**PILLION**	*n* pl. -S a pad or cushion for an extra rider on a horse or motorcycle
PIKE	*v* PIKED, PIKING, PIKES to pierce with a pike (a long spear)		
PIKEMAN	*n* pl. -MEN a soldier armed with a pike	**PILLORY**	*v* -RIED, -RYING, -RIES to expose to public ridicule or abuse
PIKER	*n* pl. -S a stingy person	**PILLOW**	*v* -ED, -ING, -S to rest on a pillow (a cushion for the head)
PIKI	*n* pl. -S thin blue cornmeal bread		
PIKING	present participle of pike	**PILLOWY**	*adj* resembling a pillow
PILAF	*n* pl. -S a dish made of seasoned rice and often meat	**PILOSE**	*adj* covered with hair
		PILOSITY	*n* pl. -TIES the state of being pilose
PILAFF	*n* pl. -S pilaf		
PILAR	*adj* pertaining to hair	**PILOT**	*v* -ED, -ING, -S to control the course of
PILASTER	*n* pl. -S a rectangular column		
PILAU	*n* pl. -S pilaf	**PILOTAGE**	*n* pl. -S the act of piloting
PILAW	*n* pl. -S pilaf	**PILOTING**	*n* pl. -S a branch of navigation
PILCHARD	*n* pl. -S a small marine fish	**PILOUS**	*adj* pilose
PILE	*v* PILED, PILING, PILES to lay one upon the other	**PILSENER**	*n* pl. -S pilsner
		PILSNER	*n* pl. -S a light beer
PILEA	pl. of pileum	**PILULE**	*n* pl. -S a small pill **PILULAR** *adj*
PILEATE	*adj* having a pileus	**PILUS**	*n* pl. -LI a hair or hairlike structure
PILEATED	*adj* pileate		
PILED	past tense of pile	**PILY**	*adj* divided into a number of wedge-shaped heraldic designs
PILEI	pl. of pileus		
PILELESS	*adj* not having a raised surface of yarn	**PIMA**	*n* pl. -S a strong, high-grade cotton
PILEOUS	*adj* pilose	**PIMENTO**	*n* pl. -TOS pimiento
PILEUM	*n* pl. -LEA the top of a bird's head	**PIMIENTO**	*n* pl. -TOS a sweet pepper
		PIMP	*v* -ED, -ING, -S to solicit clients for a prostitute
PILEUP	*n* pl. -S a collision involving several motor vehicles		
		PIMPLE	*n* pl. -S an inflamed swelling of the skin **PIMPLED** *adj*
PILEUS	*n* pl. -LEI the umbrella-shaped portion of a mushroom		
		PIMPLY	*adj* -PLIER, -PLIEST covered with pimples
PILEWORT	*n* pl. -S a medicinal plant		
PILFER	*v* -ED, -ING, -S to steal	**PIN**	*v* PINNED, PINNING, PINS to fasten with a pin (a slender, pointed piece of metal)
PILFERER	*n* pl. -S one that pilfers		
PILGRIM	*n* pl. -S a traveler or wanderer	**PINA**	*n* pl. -S a pineapple
PILI	*n* pl. -S a Philippine tree	**PINAFORE**	*n* pl. -S a child's apron
PILIFORM	*adj* resembling a hair	**PINANG**	*n* pl. -S a palm tree
PILING	*n* pl. -S a structure of building supports	**PINASTER**	*n* pl. -S a pine tree
		PINATA	*n* pl. -S a pottery jar used in a Mexican game
PILL	*v* -ED, -ING, -S to dose with pills (small, rounded masses of medicine)		
		PINBALL	*n* pl. -S an electric game
		PINBONE	*n* pl. -S the hipbone
PILLAGE	*v* -LAGED, -LAGING, -LAGES to plunder	**PINCER**	*n* pl. -S one of the two pivoted parts of a grasping tool

PINCH _v_ -ED, -ING, -ES to squeeze between two edges or surfaces

PINCHBUG _n_ pl. -S a large beetle

PINCHECK _n_ pl. -S a fabric design

PINCHER _n_ pl. -S one that pinches

PINDER _n_ pl. -S an official who formerly impounded stray animals

PINDLING _adj_ puny or sickly

PINE _v_ PINED, PINING, PINES to yearn intensely

PINEAL _n_ pl. -S a gland in the brain

PINECONE _n_ pl. -S a cone-shaped fruit of a pine tree

PINED past tense of pine

PINELAND _n_ pl. -S land forested with pine

PINELIKE _adj_ resembling a pine (an evergreen tree)

PINENE _n_ pl. -S the main constituent of turpentine

PINERY _n_ pl. -ERIES an area where pineapples are grown

PINESAP _n_ pl. -S a fragrant herb

PINETUM _n_ pl. -TA a plantation of pine trees

PINEWOOD _n_ pl. -S the wood of a pine tree

PINEY _adj_ PINIER, PINIEST piny

PINFISH _n_ pl. -ES a small marine fish

PINFOLD _v_ -ED, -ING, -S to confine in an enclosure for stray animals

PING _v_ -ED, -ING, -S to produce a brief, high-pitched sound

PINGER _n_ pl. -S a device for producing pulses of sound

PINGO _n_ pl. -GOS a hill forced up by the effects of frost

PINGRASS _n_ pl. -ES a European weed

PINGUID _adj_ greasy

PINHEAD _n_ pl. -S the head of a pin

PINHOLE _n_ pl. -S a small hole made by a pin

PINIER comparative of piney and piny

PINIEST superlative of piney and piny

PINING present participle of pine

PINION _v_ -ED, -ING, -S to remove or bind the wing feathers of to prevent flight

PINITE _n_ pl. -S a mineral

PINITOL _n_ pl. -S an alcohol

PINK _adj_ PINKER, PINKEST of a pale reddish hue

PINK _v_ -ED, -ING, -S to cut a saw-toothed edge on cloth

PINKEN _v_ -ED, -ING, -S to become pink

PINKER _n_ pl. -S one that pinks

PINKEY _n_ pl. -EYS a ship with a narrow overhanging stern

PINKEYE _n_ pl. -S an inflammation of the eye

PINKIE _n_ pl. -S the little finger

PINKIES pl. of pinky

PINKING _n_ pl. -S a method of cutting or decorating

PINKISH _adj_ somewhat pink

PINKLY _adv_ with a pink hue

PINKNESS _n_ pl. -ES the state of being pink

PINKO _n_ pl. PINKOS or PINKOES a person who holds somewhat radical political views

PINKROOT _n_ pl. -S a medicinal plant root

PINKY _n_ pl. PINKIES pinkie

PINNA _n_ pl. -NAE or -NAS a feather, wing, or winglike part

PINNACE _n_ pl. -S a small sailing ship

PINNACLE _v_ -CLED, -CLING, -CLES to place on a summit

PINNAE a pl. of pinna

PINNAL _adj_ pertaining to a pinna

PINNATE _adj_ resembling a feather

PINNATED _adj_ pinnate

PINNED past tense of pin

PINNER _n_ pl. -S one that pins

PINNIES pl. of pinny

PINNING present participle of pin

PINNIPED _n_ pl. -S a mammal with limbs modified into flippers

PINNULA _n_ pl. -LAE pinnule **PINNULAR** _adj_

PINNULE _n_ pl. -S a pinnate part or organ

PINNY _n_ pl. -NIES a pinafore

PINOCHLE _n_ pl. -S a card game

PINOCLE _n_ pl. -S pinochle

PINOLE _n_ pl. -S a finely ground flour

PINON _n_ pl. -S or -ES a pine tree

PINOT _n_ pl. -S a red or white grape

PINPOINT _v_ -ED, -ING, -S to locate precisely

PINPRICK   *v* -ED, -ING, -S to puncture with a pin

PINSCHER   *n* pl. -S a large, short-haired dog

PINT   *n* pl. -S a liquid and dry measure of capacity

PINTA   *n* pl. -S a skin disease

PINTADA   *n* pl. -S pintado

PINTADO   *n* pl. -DOS or -DOES a large food fish

PINTAIL   *n* pl. -S a river duck

PINTANO   *n* pl. -NOS a tropical fish

PINTLE   *n* pl. -S a pin on which something turns

PINTO   *n* pl. -TOS or -TOES a spotted horse

PINTSIZE   *adj* small

PINUP   *n* pl. -S a picture that may be pinned up on a wall

PINWALE   *n* pl. -S a type of fabric

PINWEED   *n* pl. -S a perennial herb

PINWHEEL   *v* -ED, -ING, -S to revolve at the end of a stick

PINWORK   *n* pl. -S a type of embroidery

PINWORM   *n* pl. -S a parasitic worm

PINY   *adj* PINIER, PINIEST suggestive of or covered with pine trees

PINYIN   *n* a system for transliterating Chinese ideograms into the Latin alphabet

PINYON   *n* pl. -S pinon

PIOLET   *n* pl. -S an ice ax

PION   *n* pl. -S a subatomic particle **PIONIC** *adj*

PIONEER   *v* -ED, -ING, -S to take part in the beginnings of

PIOSITY   *n* pl. -TIES an excessive show of piety

PIOUS   *adj* marked by religious reverence **PIOUSLY** *adv*

PIP   *v* PIPPED, PIPPING, PIPS to break through the shell of an egg

PIPAGE   *n* pl. -S a system of pipes

PIPAL   *n* pl. -S a fig tree of India

PIPE   *v* PIPED, PIPING, PIPES to convey by means of a pipe (a hollow cylinder)

PIPEAGE   *n* pl. -S pipage

PIPEFISH   *n* pl. -ES a slender fish

PIPEFUL   *n* pl. -S a quantity sufficient to fill a tobacco pipe

PIPELESS   *adj* having no pipe

PIPELIKE   *adj* resembling a pipe

PIPELINE   *v* -LINED, -LINING, -LINES to convey by a line of pipe

PIPER   *n* pl. -S one that plays on a tubular musical instrument

PIPERINE   *n* pl. -S a chemical compound

PIPESTEM   *n* pl. -S the stem of a tobacco pipe

PIPET   *v* -PETTED, -PETTING, -PETS to pipette

PIPETTE   *v* -PETTED, -PETTING, -PETTES to measure liquid with a calibrated tube

PIPIER   comparative of pipy

PIPIEST   superlative of pipy

PIPINESS   *n* pl. -ES the quality of being pipy

PIPING   *n* pl. -S a system of pipes

PIPINGLY   *adv* shrilly

PIPIT   *n* pl. -S a songbird

PIPKIN   *n* pl. -S a small pot

PIPPED   past tense of pip

PIPPIN   *n* pl. -S any of several varieties of apple

PIPPING   present participle of pip

PIPY   *adj* PIPIER, PIPIEST shrill

PIQUANCE   *n* pl. -S piquancy

PIQUANCY   *n* pl. -CIES the quality of being piquant

PIQUANT   *adj* agreeably sharp in taste

PIQUE   *v* PIQUED, PIQUING, PIQUES to arouse anger or resentment in

PIQUET   *n* pl. -S a card game

PIRACY   *n* pl. -CIES robbery on the high seas

PIRAGUA   *n* pl. -S a dugout canoe

PIRANA   *n* pl. -S piranha

PIRANHA   *n* pl. -S a voracious fish

PIRARUCU   *n* pl. -S a large food fish

PIRATE   *v* -RATED, -RATING, -RATES to commit piracy

PIRATIC   *adj* pertaining to piracy

PIRAYA   *n* pl. -S piranha

PIRIFORM   *adj* pyriform

PIRN   *n* pl. -S a spinning-wheel bobbin

PIROG   *n* pl. -ROGEN, -ROGHI or -ROGI a large Russian pastry

PIROGI   *n* pl. -ES pierogi

PIROGUE *n* pl. -S piragua

PIROQUE *n* pl. -S piragua

PIROZHOK *n* pl. -ROZHKI, -ROSHKI or -ROJKI a small Russian pastry

PISCARY *n* pl. -RIES a place for fishing

PISCATOR *n* pl. -S a fisherman

PISCINA *n* pl. -NAE or -NAS a basin used in certain church ceremonies **PISCINAL** *adj*

PISCINE *adj* pertaining to fish

PISCO *n* pl. -COS a Peruvian brandy

PISH *v* -ED, -ING, -ES to express contempt

PISHOGE *n* pl. -S pishogue

PISHOGUE *n* pl. -S an evil spell

PISIFORM *n* pl. -S a small bone of the wrist

PISMIRE *n* pl. -S an ant

PISO *n* pl. -SOS the Philippine peso

PISOLITE *n* pl. -S a limestone

PISSOIR *n* pl. -S a public urinal

PISTACHE *n* pl. -S a shade of green

PISTE *n* pl. -S a downhill ski trail

PISTIL *n* pl. -S the seed-bearing organ of flowering plants

PISTOL *v* -TOLED, -TOLING, -TOLS or -TOLLED, -TOLLING, -TOLS to shoot with a small firearm

PISTOLE *n* pl. -S a former European gold coin

PISTON *n* pl. -S a part of an engine

PIT *v* PITTED, PITTING, PITS to mark with cavities or depressions

PITA *n* pl. -S a strong fiber

PITAPAT *v* -PATTED, -PATTING, -PATS to make a repeated tapping sound

PITCH *v* -ED, -ING, -ES to throw

PITCHER *n* pl. -S a container for holding and pouring liquids

PITCHIER comparative of pitchy

PITCHIEST superlative of pitchy

PITCHILY *adv* in a very dark manner

PITCHMAN *n* pl. -MEN a salesman of small wares

PITCHOUT *n* pl. -S a type of pitch in baseball

PITCHY *adj* PITCHIER, PITCHIEST tarry

PITEOUS *adj* pitiful

PITFALL *n* pl. -S a hidden danger or difficulty

PITH *v* -ED, -ING, -S to sever the spinal cord of

PITHEAD *n* pl. -S a mine entrance

PITHLESS *adj* lacking force

PITHY *adj* PITHIER, PITHIEST concise **PITHILY** *adv*

PITIABLE *adj* pitiful **PITIABLY** *adv*

PITIED past tense of pity

PITIER *n* pl. -S one that pities

PITIES present 3d person sing. of pity

PITIFUL *adj* -FULLER, -FULLEST arousing pity

PITILESS *adj* having no pity

PITMAN *n* pl. -MEN a mine worker

PITMAN *n* pl. -S a connecting rod

PITON *n* pl. -S a metal spike used in mountain climbing

PITSAW *n* pl. -S a large saw for cutting logs

PITTANCE *n* pl. -S a small allowance of money

PITTED past tense of pit

PITTING *n* pl. -S an arrangement of cavities or depressions

PITY *v* PITIED, PITYING, PITIES to feel pity (sorrow aroused by another's misfortune)

PIU *adv* more — used as a musical direction

PIVOT *v* -ED, -ING, -S to turn on a shaft or rod

PIVOTAL *adj* critically important

PIVOTMAN *n* pl. -MEN a center on a basketball team

PIX *n* pl. -ES pyx

PIXEL *n* pl. -S a basic unit of a video image

PIXIE *n* pl. -S pixy **PIXIEISH** *adj*

PIXINESS *n* pl. -ES the state of being playfully mischievous

PIXY *n* pl. PIXIES a playfully mischievous fairy or elf **PIXYISH** *adj*

PIZAZZ *n* pl. -ES the quality of being exciting or attractive

PIZAZZY *adj* having pizazz

PIZZA *n* pl. -S an Italian open pie

PIZZERIA *n* pl. -S a place where pizzas are made and sold

PIZZLE *n* pl. -S the penis of an animal

PLACABLE	*adj* capable of being placated **PLACABLY** *adv*	**PLAITING**	*n* pl. -S something that is plaited
PLACARD	*v* -ED, -ING, -S to publicize by means of posters	**PLAN**	*v* PLANNED, PLANNING, PLANS to formulate a plan (a method for achieving an end)
PLACATE	*v* -CATED, -CATING, -CATES to soothe or mollify	**PLANAR**	*adj* flat
		PLANARIA	*n* pl. -S an aquatic flatworm
PLACATER	*n* pl. -S one that placates	**PLANATE**	*adj* having a flat surface
PLACE	*v* PLACED, PLACING, PLACES to set in a particular position	**PLANCH**	*n* pl. -ES a plank
		PLANCHE	*n* pl. -S planch
PLACEBO	*n* pl. -BOS or -BOES a substance containing no medication that is given for its psychological effect	**PLANCHET**	*n* pl. -S a flat piece of metal for stamping into a coin
		PLANE	*v* PLANED, PLANING, PLANES to make smooth or even
PLACEMAN	*n* pl. -MEN a political appointee to a public office	**PLANER**	*n* pl. -S one that planes
		PLANET	*n* pl. -S a celestial body
PLACENTA	*n* pl. -TAS or -TAE a vascular organ in most mammals	**PLANFORM**	*n* pl. -S the contour of an object as viewed from above
PLACER	*n* pl. -S one that places	**PLANGENT**	*adj* resounding loudly
PLACET	*n* pl. -S a vote of assent	**PLANING**	present participle of plane
PLACID	*adj* calm or peaceful **PLACIDLY** *adv*	**PLANISH**	*v* -ED, -ING, -ES to toughen and smooth by hammering lightly
PLACING	present participle of place	**PLANK**	*v* -ED, -ING, -S to cover with planks (long, flat pieces of lumber)
PLACK	*n* pl. -S a former coin of Scotland		
PLACKET	*n* pl. -S a slit in a garment		
PLACOID	*n* pl. -S a fish having platelike scales	**PLANKING**	*n* pl. -S covering made of planks
		PLANKTER	*n* pl. -S any organism that is an element of plankton
PLAFOND	*n* pl. -S an elaborately decorated ceiling	**PLANKTON**	*n* pl. -S the minute animal and plant life of a body of water
PLAGAL	*adj* designating a medieval musical mode	**PLANLESS**	*adj* having no plan
PLAGE	*n* pl. -S a bright region on the sun	**PLANNED**	past tense of plan
		PLANNER	*n* pl. -S one that plans
PLAGIARY	*n* pl. -RIES the act of passing off another's work as one's own	**PLANNING**	*n* pl. -S the establishment of goals or policies
PLAGUE	*v* PLAGUED, PLAGUING, PLAGUES to harass or torment	**PLANOSOL**	*n* pl. -S a type of soil
		PLANT	*v* -ED, -ING, -S to place in the ground for growing
PLAGUER	*n* pl. -S one that plagues		
PLAGUEY	*adj* plaguy	**PLANTAIN**	*n* pl. -S a short-stemmed herb
PLAGUING	present participle of plague	**PLANTAR**	*adj* pertaining to the sole of the foot
PLAGUY	*adj* troublesome **PLAGUILY** *adv*		
PLAICE	*n* pl. -S a European flatfish	**PLANTER**	*n* pl. -S one that plants
PLAID	*n* pl. -S a woolen scarf of a checkered pattern **PLAIDED** *adj*	**PLANTING**	*n* pl. -S an area where plants are grown
PLAIN	*adj* PLAINER, PLAINEST evident **PLAINLY** *adv*	**PLANTLET**	*n* pl. -S a small plant
		PLANULA	*n* pl. -LAE the free-swimming larva of certain organisms **PLANULAR** *adj*
PLAIN	*v* -ED, -ING, -S to complain		
PLAINT	*n* pl. -S a complaint		
PLAISTER	*v* -ED, -ING, -S to plaster	**PLAQUE**	*n* pl. -S an ornamental plate or disk
PLAIT	*v* -ED, -ING, -S to braid		
PLAITER	*n* pl. -S one that plaits		

PLASH	*v* -ED, -ING, -ES to weave together
PLASHER	*n* pl. -S one that plashes
PLASHY	*adj* PLASHIER, PLASHIEST marshy
PLASM	*n* pl. -S plasma
PLASMA	*n* pl. -S the liquid part of blood **PLASMIC** *adj*
PLASMID	*n* pl. -S a hereditary structure of a cell
PLASMIN	*n* pl. -S an enzyme
PLASMOID	*n* pl. -S a type of high energy particle
PLASMON	*n* pl. -S a determinant of inheritance believed to exist in cells
PLASTER	*v* -ED, -ING, -S to cover with plaster (a mixture of lime, sand, and water)
PLASTERY	*adj* resembling plaster
PLASTIC	*n* pl. -S any of a group of synthetic or natural moldable materials
PLASTID	*n* pl. -S a structure in plant cells
PLASTRON	*n* pl. -S a part of the shell of a turtle **PLASTRAL** *adj*
PLASTRUM	*n* pl. -S plastron
PLAT	*v* PLATTED, PLATTING, PLATS to plait
PLATAN	*n* pl. -S a large tree
PLATANE	*n* pl. -S platan
PLATE	*v* PLATED, PLATING, PLATES to coat with a thin layer of metal
PLATEAU	*n* pl. -TEAUS or -TEAUX a level stretch of elevated land
PLATEAU	*v* -ED, -ING, -S to reach a period or condition of stability
PLATED	past tense of plate
PLATEFUL	*n* pl. PLATEFULS or PLATESFUL the quantity that fills a plate (a shallow dish)
PLATELET	*n* pl. -S a small, flattened body
PLATEN	*n* pl. -S the roller of a typewriter
PLATER	*n* pl. -S one that plates
PLATESFUL	a pl. of plateful
PLATFORM	*n* pl. -S a raised floor or flat surface
PLATIER	comparative of platy
PLATIES	a pl. of platy
PLATIEST	superlative of platy

PLATINA	*n* pl. -S platinum
PLATING	*n* pl. -S a thin layer of metal
PLATINIC	*adj* pertaining to platinum
PLATINUM	*n* pl. -S a metallic element
PLATONIC	*adj* purely spiritual and free from sensual desire
PLATOON	*v* -ED, -ING, -S to alternate with another player at the same position
PLATTED	past tense of plat
PLATTER	*n* pl. -S a large, shallow dish
PLATTING	present participle of plat
PLATY	*adj* PLATIER, PLATIEST split into thin, flat pieces
PLATY	*n* pl. PLATYS or PLATIES a small tropical fish
PLATYPUS	*n* pl. -PUSES or -PI an aquatic mammal
PLAUDIT	*n* pl. -S an expression of praise
PLAUSIVE	*adj* expressing praise
PLAY	*v* -ED, -ING, -S to engage in amusement or sport **PLAYABLE** *adj*
PLAYA	*n* pl. -S the bottom of a desert basin
PLAYACT	*v* -ED, -ING, -S to take part in a theatrical performance
PLAYBACK	*n* pl. -S the act of replaying a newly made recording
PLAYBILL	*n* pl. -S a program for a theatrical performance
PLAYBOOK	*n* pl. -S a book containing one or more literary works for the stage
PLAYBOY	*n* pl. -BOYS a man devoted to pleasurable activities
PLAYDATE	*n* pl. -S the scheduled date for showing a theatrical production
PLAYDAY	*n* pl. -DAYS a holiday
PLAYDOWN	*n* pl. -S a playoff
PLAYER	*n* pl. -S one that plays
PLAYFUL	*adj* frolicsome
PLAYGIRL	*n* pl. -S a woman devoted to pleasurable activities
PLAYGOER	*n* pl. -S one who attends the theater
PLAYLAND	*n* pl. -S a recreational area
PLAYLESS	*adj* lacking playfulness
PLAYLET	*n* pl. -S a short theatrical performance

PLAYLIKE *adj* resembling a theatrical performance

PLAYLIST *n* pl. -S a list of recordings to be played on the air

PLAYMATE *n* pl. -S a companion in play

PLAYOFF *n* pl. -S a series of games played to determine a championship

PLAYPEN *n* pl. -S an enclosure in which a young child may play

PLAYROOM *n* pl. -S a recreation room

PLAYSUIT *n* pl. -S a sports outfit for women and children

PLAYTIME *n* pl. -S a time for play or amusement

PLAYWEAR *n* pl. PLAYWEAR clothing worn for leisure activities

PLAZA *n* pl. -S a public square

PLEA *n* pl. -S an entreaty

PLEACH *v* -ED, -ING, -ES to weave together

PLEAD *v* PLEADED or PLED, PLEADING, PLEADS to ask for earnestly

PLEADER *n* pl. -S one that pleads

PLEADING *n* pl. -S an allegation in a legal action

PLEASANT *adj* -ANTER, -ANTEST pleasing

PLEASE *v* PLEASED, PLEASING, PLEASES to give enjoyment or satisfaction to

PLEASER *n* pl. -S one that pleases

PLEASURE *v* -SURED, -SURING, -SURES to please

PLEAT *v* -ED, -ING, -S to fold in an even manner

PLEATER *n* pl. -S one that pleats

PLEB *n* pl. -S a commoner

PLEBE *n* pl. -S a freshman at a military or naval academy

PLEBEIAN *n* pl. -S a commoner

PLECTRON *n* pl. -TRONS or -TRA plectrum

PLECTRUM *n* pl. -TRUMS or -TRA an implement used to pluck the strings of a stringed instrument

PLED a past tense of plead

PLEDGE *v* PLEDGED, PLEDGING, PLEDGES to give as security for something borrowed

PLEDGEE *n* pl. -S one to whom something is pledged

PLEDGEOR *n* pl. -S pledger

PLEDGER *n* pl. -S one that pledges something

PLEDGET *n* pl. -S a pad of absorbent cotton

PLEDGING present participle of pledge

PLEDGOR *n* pl. -S pledger

PLEIAD *n* pl. -S or -ES a group of seven illustrious persons

PLENA a pl. of plenum

PLENARY *adj* complete in every respect

PLENCH *n* pl. -ES a tool serving as pliers and a wrench

PLENISH *v* -ED, -ING, -ES to fill up

PLENISM *n* pl. -S the doctrine that space is fully occupied by matter

PLENIST *n* pl. -S an advocate of plenism

PLENTY *n* pl. -TIES a sufficient or abundant amount

PLENUM *n* pl. -NUMS or -NA space considered as fully occupied by matter

PLEONASM *n* pl. -S the use of needless words

PLEOPOD *n* pl. -S an appendage of crustaceans

PLESSOR *n* pl. -S plexor

PLETHORA *n* pl. -S an excess

PLEURA *n* pl. -RAE or -RAS a membrane that envelops the lungs **PLEURAL** *adj*

PLEURISY *n* pl. -SIES inflammation of the pleura

PLEURON *n* pl. -RA a part of a thoracic segment of an insect

PLEUSTON *n* pl. -S aquatic vegetation

PLEW *n* pl. -S a beaver skin

PLEXAL *adj* pertaining to a plexus

PLEXOR *n* pl. -S a small, hammer-like medical instrument

PLEXUS *n* pl. -ES an interlacing of parts

PLIABLE *adj* easily bent **PLIABLY** *adv*

PLIANCY *n* pl. -CIES the quality of being pliant

PLIANT *adj* easily bent **PLIANTLY** *adv*

PLICA *n* pl. -CAE a fold of skin **PLICAL** *adj*

PLICATE *adj* pleated

PLICATED *adj* plicate

PLIE *n* pl. -S a movement in ballet

PLIED past tense of ply

PLIER *n* pl. -S one that plies

PLIES present 3d person sing. of ply

PLIGHT *v* -ED, -ING, -S to promise or bind by a solemn pledge

PLIGHTER *n* pl. -S one that plights

PLIMSOL *n* pl. -S plimsoll

PLIMSOLE *n* pl. -S plimsoll

PLIMSOLL *n* pl. -S a rubber-soled cloth shoe

PLINK *v* -ED, -ING, -S to shoot at random targets

PLINKER *n* pl. -S one that plinks

PLINTH *n* pl. -S a stone or slab upon which a column or pedestal rests

PLIOTRON *n* pl. -S a type of vacuum tube

PLISKIE *n* pl. -S a practical joke

PLISKY *n* pl. -KIES pliskie

PLISSE *n* pl. -S a puckered texture of cloth

PLOD *v* PLODDED, PLODDING, PLODS to walk heavily

PLODDER *n* pl. -S one that plods

PLOIDY *n* pl. -DIES the extent of repetition of the basic number of chromosomes

PLONK *v* -ED, -ING, -S to plunk

PLOP *v* PLOPPED, PLOPPING, PLOPS to drop or fall heavily

PLOSION *n* pl. -S a release of breath after the articulation of certain consonants

PLOSIVE *n* pl. -S a sound produced by plosion

PLOT *v* PLOTTED, PLOTTING, PLOTS to plan secretly

PLOTLESS *adj* planless

PLOTLINE *n* pl. -S the main story of a book

PLOTTAGE *n* pl. -S an area of land

PLOTTED past tense of plot

PLOTTER *n* pl. -S one that plots

PLOTTIER comparative of plotty

PLOTTIES pl. of plotty

PLOTTING present participle of plot

PLOTTY *adj* -TIER, -TIEST full of intrigue, as a novel

PLOTTY *n* pl. -TIES a hot, spiced beverage

PLOTZ *v* -ED, -ING, -ES to be overwhelmed by an emotion

PLOUGH *v* -ED, -ING, -S to plow

PLOUGHER *n* pl. -S one that ploughs

PLOVER *n* pl. -S a shore bird

PLOW *v* -ED, -ING, -S to turn up land with a plow (a farm implement) **PLOWABLE** *adj*

PLOWBACK *n* pl. -S a reinvestment of profits in a business

PLOWBOY *n* pl. -BOYS a boy who leads a plow team

PLOWER *n* pl. -S one that plows

PLOWHEAD *n* pl. -S the clevis of a plow

PLOWLAND *n* pl. -S land suitable for cultivation

PLOWMAN *n* pl. -MEN a man who plows

PLOY *v* -ED, -ING, -S to move from a line into column

PLUCK *v* -ED, -ING, -S to pull out or off

PLUCKER *n* pl. -S one that plucks

PLUCKY *adj* PLUCKIER, PLUCKIEST brave and spirited **PLUCKILY** *adv*

PLUG *v* PLUGGED, PLUGGING, PLUGS to seal or close with a plug (a piece of material used to fill a hole)

PLUGGER *n* pl. -S one that plugs

PLUGLESS *adj* having no plug

PLUGOLA *n* pl. -S free incidental advertising on radio or television

PLUGUGLY *n* pl. -LIES a hoodlum

PLUM *n* pl. -S a fleshy fruit

PLUMAGE *n* pl. -S the feathers of a bird **PLUMAGED** *adj*

PLUMATE *adj* resembling a feather

PLUMB *v* -ED, -ING, -S to determine the depth of

PLUMBAGO *n* pl. -GOS graphite

PLUMBER *n* pl. -S one who installs and repairs plumbing

PLUMBERY *n* pl. -ERIES the work of a plumber

PLUMBIC *adj* containing lead

PLUMBING *n* pl. -S the pipe system of a building

PLUMBISM *n* pl. -S lead poisoning

PLUMBOUS *adj* containing lead

PLUMBUM *n* pl. -S lead

PLUME *v* PLUMED, PLUMING, PLUMES to cover with feathers

PLUMELET *n* pl. -S a small feather

PLUMERIA *n* pl. -S a flowering shrub

PLUMIER comparative of plumy

PLUMIEST superlative of plumy

PLUMING present participle of plume

PLUMIPED *n* pl. -S a bird having feathered feet

PLUMLIKE *adj* resembling a plum

PLUMMET *v* -ED, -ING, -S to drop straight down

PLUMMY *adj* -MIER, -MIEST full of plums

PLUMOSE *adj* having feathers

PLUMP *adj* PLUMPER, PLUMPEST well-rounded and full in form

PLUMP *v* -ED, -ING, -S to make plump

PLUMPEN *v* -ED, -ING, -S to plump

PLUMPER *n* pl. -S a heavy fall

PLUMPISH *adj* somewhat plump

PLUMPLY *adv* in a plump way

PLUMULE *n* pl. -S the primary bud of a plant embryo **PLUMULAR** *adj*

PLUMY *adj* PLUMIER, PLUMIEST covered with feathers

PLUNDER *v* -ED, -ING, -S to rob of goods by force

PLUNGE *v* PLUNGED, PLUNGING, PLUNGES to throw or thrust suddenly or forcibly into something

PLUNGER *n* pl. -S one that plunges

PLUNK *v* -ED, -ING, -S to fall or drop heavily

PLUNKER *n* pl. -S one that plunks

PLURAL *n* pl. -S a word that expresses more than one

PLURALLY *adv* in a manner or form that expresses more than one

PLUS *n* pl. PLUSES or PLUSSES an additional quantity

PLUSH *adj* PLUSHER, PLUSHEST luxurious **PLUSHLY** *adv*

PLUSH *n* pl. -ES a fabric with a long pile

PLUSHY *adj* PLUSHIER, PLUSHIEST luxurious **PLUSHILY** *adv*

PLUSSAGE *n* pl. -S an amount over and above another

PLUSSES a pl. of plus

PLUTEUS *n* pl. -TEI the larva of a sea urchin

PLUTON *n* pl. -S a formation of igneous rock **PLUTONIC** *adj*

PLUVIAL *n* pl. -S a prolonged period of wet climate

PLUVIAN *adj* characterized by much rain

PLUVIOSE *adj* pluvious

PLUVIOUS *adj* pertaining to rain

PLY *v* PLIED, PLYING, PLIES to supply with or offer repeatedly **PLYINGLY** *adv*

PLYER *n* pl. -S plier

PLYWOOD *n* pl. -S a building material

PNEUMA *n* pl. -S the soul or spirit

POACEOUS *adj* pertaining to plants of the grass family

POACH *v* -ED, -ING, -ES to trespass for the purpose of taking game or fish

POACHER *n* pl. -S one that poaches

POACHY *adj* POACHIER, POACHIEST swampy

POCHARD *n* pl. -S a sea duck

POCK *v* -ED, -ING, -S to mark with pocks (pustules caused by an eruptive disease)

POCKET *v* -ED, -ING, -S to place in a pouch sewed into a garment

POCKETER *n* pl. -S one that pockets

POCKMARK *v* -ED, -ING, -S to mark with scars caused by an eruptive disease

POCKY *adj* POCKIER, POCKIEST covered with pocks **POCKILY** *adv*

POCO *adv* a little — used as a musical direction

POCOSIN *n* pl. -S an upland swamp

POD *v* PODDED, PODDING, PODS to produce seed vessels

PODAGRA *n* pl. -S gout in the foot **PODAGRAL, PODAGRIC** *adj*

PODESTA *n* pl. -S an Italian magistrate

PODGY *adj* PODGIER, PODGIEST pudgy **PODGILY** *adv*

PODIA a pl. of podium

PODIATRY *n* pl. -TRIES the study and treatment of the human foot

PODITE *n* pl. -S a limb segment of an arthropod **PODITIC** *adj*

PODIUM *n* pl. -DIUMS or -DIA a small platform

PODLIKE *adj* resembling a pod (a seed vessel)

PODOCARP   *adj* designating a family of evergreen trees

PODOMERE   *n* pl. -S a podite

PODSOL   *n* pl. -S podzol **PODSOLIC** *adj*

PODZOL   *n* pl. -S an infertile soil **PODZOLIC** *adj*

POECHORE   *n* pl. -S a semiarid region

POEM   *n* pl. -S a composition in verse

POESY   *n* pl. -ESIES poetry

POET   *n* pl. -S one who writes poems

POETESS   *n* pl. -ES a female poet

POETIC   *adj* pertaining to poetry

POETICAL   *adj* poetic

POETICS   *n/pl* poetic theory or practice

POETISE   *v* -ISED, -ISING, -ISES to poetize

POETISER   *n* pl. -S poetizer

POETIZE   *v* -IZED, -IZING, -IZES to write poetry

POETIZER   *n* pl. -S one that poetizes

POETLESS   *adj* lacking a poet

POETLIKE   *adj* resembling a poet

POETRY   *n* pl. -RIES literary work in metrical form

POGEY   *n* pl. -GEYS any form of government relief

POGIES   pl. of pogy

POGONIA   *n* pl. -S a small orchid

POGONIP   *n* pl. -S a dense fog of suspended ice particles

POGROM   *v* -ED, -ING, -S to massacre systematically

POGY   *n* pl. -GIES a marine fish

POH   *interj* — used to express disgust

POI   *n* pl. -S a Hawaiian food

POIGNANT   *adj* emotionally distressing

POILU   *n* pl. -S a French soldier

POIND   *v* -ED, -ING, -S to seize and sell the property of to satisfy a debt

POINT   *v* -ED, -ING, -S to indicate direction with the finger

POINTE   *n* pl. -S a ballet position

POINTER   *n* pl. -S one that points

POINTMAN   *n* pl. -MEN a certain player in hockey

POINTY   *adj* POINTIER, POINTIEST coming to a sharp, tapering end

POISE   *v* POISED, POISING, POISES to hold in a state of equilibrium

POISER   *n* pl. -S one that poises

POISHA   *n* pl. POISHA the paisa of Bangladesh

POISON   *v* -ED, -ING, -S to administer a harmful substance to

POISONER   *n* pl. -S one that poisons

POITREL   *n* pl. -S peytral

POKE   *v* POKED, POKING, POKES to push or prod

POKER   *n* pl. -S one that pokes

POKEROOT   *n* pl. -S pokeweed

POKEWEED   *n* pl. -S a perennial herb

POKEY   *n* pl. -KEYS poky

POKIER   comparative of poky

POKIES   pl. of poky

POKIEST   superlative of poky

POKILY   *adv* in a poky manner

POKINESS   *n* pl. -ES the state of being poky

POKING   present participle of poke

POKY   *n* pl. POKIES a jail

POKY   *adj* POKIER, POKIEST slow

POL   *n* pl. -S a politician

POLAR   *n* pl. -S a straight line related to a point

POLARISE   *v* -ISED, -ISING, -ISES to polarize

POLARITY   *n* pl. -TIES the possession of two opposite qualities

POLARIZE   *v* -IZED, -IZING, -IZES to give polarity to

POLARON   *n* pl. -S a type of electron

POLDER   *n* pl. -S a tract of low land reclaimed from a body of water

POLE   *v* POLED, POLING, POLES to propel with a pole (a long, thin piece of wood or metal)

POLEAX   *v* -ED, -ING, -ES to strike with an axlike weapon

POLEAXE   *v* -AXED, -AXING, -AXES to poleax

POLECAT   *n* pl. -S a carnivorous mammal

POLED   past tense of pole

POLEIS   pl. of polis

POLELESS   *adj* having no pole

POLEMIC   *n* pl. -S a controversial argument

POLEMIST   *n* pl. -S one who engages in polemics

POLEMIZE   *v* -MIZED, -MIZING, -MIZES to engage in polemics

POLENTA   *n* pl. -S a thick mush of cornmeal

POLER   *n* pl. -S one that poles

POLESTAR   *n* pl. -S a guiding principle

POLEWARD   *adv* in the direction of either extremity of the earth's axis

POLEYN   *n* pl. -S a protective piece of leather for the knee

POLICE   *v* -LICED, -LICING, -LICES to make clean or orderly

POLICY   *n* pl. -CIES an action or a procedure considered with reference to prudence or expediency

POLING   present participle of pole

POLIO   *n* pl. -LIOS an infectious virus disease

POLIS   *n* pl. -LEIS an ancient Greek city-state

POLISH   *v* -ED, -ING, -ES to make smooth and lustrous by rubbing

POLISHER   *n* pl. -S one that polishes

POLITE   *adj* -LITER, -LITEST showing consideration for others **POLITELY** *adv*

POLITIC   *adj* shrewd

POLITICK   *v* -ED, -ING, -S to engage in politics

POLITICO   *n* pl. -COS or -COES one who politicks

POLITICS   *n/pl* the art or science of government

POLITY   *n* pl. -TIES a form or system of government

POLKA   *v* -ED, -ING, -S to perform a lively dance

POLL   *v* -ED, -ING, -S to question for the purpose of surveying public opinion

POLLACK   *n* pl. -S a marine food fish

POLLARD   *v* -ED, -ING, -S to cut the top branches of a tree back to the trunk

POLLEE   *n* pl. -S one who is polled

POLLEN   *v* -ED, -ING, -S to convey pollen (the fertilizing element in a seed plant) to

POLLER   *n* pl. -S one that polls

POLLEX   *n* pl. -LICES the innermost digit of the forelimb **POLLICAL** *adj*

POLLINIA   *n/pl* masses of pollen grains

POLLINIC   *adj* pertaining to pollen

POLLIST   *n* pl. -S a poller

POLLIWOG   *n* pl. -S a tadpole

POLLOCK   *n* pl. -S pollack

POLLSTER   *n* pl. -S a poller

POLLUTE   *v* -LUTED, -LUTING, -LUTES to make unclean or impure

POLLUTER   *n* pl. -S one that pollutes

POLLYWOG   *n* pl. -S polliwog

POLO   *n* pl. -LOS a game played on horseback

POLOIST   *n* pl. -S a polo player

POLONIUM   *n* pl. -S a radioactive element

POLTROON   *n* pl. -S a base coward

POLY   *n* pl. POLYS a type of white blood cell

POLYBRID   *n* pl. -S a type of hybrid plant

POLYCOT   *n* pl. -S a type of plant

POLYENE   *n* pl. -S a chemical compound **POLYENIC** *adj*

POLYGALA   *n* pl. -S a flowering plant

POLYGAMY   *n* pl. -MIES the condition of having more than one spouse at the same time

POLYGENE   *n* pl. -S a type of gene

POLYGLOT   *n* pl. -S one that speaks or writes several languages

POLYGON   *n* pl. -S a closed plane figure bounded by straight lines

POLYGONY   *n* pl. -NIES an herb

POLYGYNY   *n* pl. -NIES the condition of having more than one wife at the same time

POLYMATH   *n* pl. -S a person of great and varied learning

POLYMER   *n* pl. -S a complex chemical compound

POLYNYA   *n* pl. -YAS or -YI an area of open water surrounded by sea ice

POLYOMA   *n* pl. -S a type of virus

POLYP   *n* pl. -S an invertebrate

POLYPARY   *n* pl. -ARIES the common supporting structure of a polyp colony

POLYPI   a pl. of polypus

POLYPIDE   *n* pl. -S a polyp

POLYPNEA   *n* pl. -S rapid breathing

POLYPOD   *n* pl. -S a many-footed organism

POLYPODY   *n* pl. -DIES a fern

POLYPOID	*adj* resembling a polyp
POLYPORE	*n* pl. -S a type of fungus
POLYPOUS	*adj* pertaining to a polyp
POLYPUS	*n* pl. -PI or -PUSES a growth protruding from the mucous lining of an organ
POLYSEMY	*n* pl. -MIES diversity of meanings
POLYSOME	*n* pl. -S a cluster of protein particles
POLYTENE	*adj* having chromosomes of a certain type
POLYTENY	*n* pl. -NIES the state of being polytene
POLYTYPE	*n* pl. -S a crystal structure
POLYURIA	*n* pl. -S excessive urination **POLYURIC** *adj*
POLYZOAN	*n* pl. -S a bryozoan
POLYZOIC	*adj* composed of many zooids
POMACE	*n* pl. -S the pulpy residue of crushed fruits
POMADE	*v* -MADED, -MADING, -MADES to apply a perfumed hair dressing to
POMANDER	*n* pl. -S a mixture of aromatic substances
POMATUM	*n* pl. -S a perfumed hair dressing
POME	*n* pl. -S a fleshy fruit with a core
POMELO	*n* pl. -LOS a grapefruit
POMFRET	*n* pl. -S a marine fish
POMMEE	*adj* having arms with knoblike ends — used of a heraldic cross
POMMEL	*v* -MELED, -MELING, -MELS or -MELLED, -MELLING, -MELS to strike with the fists
POMOLOGY	*n* pl. -GIES the study of fruits
POMP	*n* pl. -S stately or splendid display
POMPANO	*n* pl. -NOS a marine food fish
POMPOM	*n* pl. -S an antiaircraft cannon
POMPON	*n* pl. -S an ornamental tuft or ball
POMPOUS	*adj* marked by exaggerated self-importance
PONCE	*v* PONCED, PONCING, PONCES to pimp
PONCHO	*n* pl. -CHOS a type of cloak
POND	*v* -ED, -ING, -S to collect into a pond (a small body of water)
PONDER	*v* -ED, -ING, -S to consider something deeply and thoroughly
PONDERER	*n* pl. -S one that ponders
PONDWEED	*n* pl. -S an aquatic plant
PONE	*n* pl. -S a corn bread
PONENT	*adj* affirmative
PONG	*v* -ED, -ING, -S to stink
PONGEE	*n* pl. -S a type of silk
PONGID	*n* pl. -S an anthropoid ape
PONIARD	*v* -ED, -ING, -S to stab with a dagger
PONIED	past tense of pony
PONIES	present 3d person sing. of pony
PONS	*n* pl. PONTES a band of nerve fibers in the brain
PONTIFEX	*n* pl. -FICES an ancient Roman priest
PONTIFF	*n* pl. -S a pope or bishop
PONTIFIC	*adj* pertaining to a pope or bishop
PONTIFICES	pl. of pontifex
PONTIL	*n* pl. -S a punty
PONTINE	*adj* pertaining to bridges
PONTON	*n* pl. -S pontoon
PONTOON	*n* pl. -S a flat-bottomed boat
PONY	*v* -NIED, -NYING, -NIES to prepare lessons with the aid of a literal translation
PONYTAIL	*n* pl. -S a hairstyle
POOCH	*v* -ED, -ING, -ES to bulge
POOD	*n* pl. -S a Russian unit of weight
POODLE	*n* pl. -S a heavy-coated dog
POOF	*interj* — used to indicate an instantaneous occurrence
POOH	*v* -ED, -ING, -S to express contempt for
POOL	*v* -ED, -ING, -S to combine in a common fund
POOLHALL	*n* pl. -S a poolroom
POOLROOM	*n* pl. -S an establishment for the playing of billiards
POOLSIDE	*n* pl. -S the area surrounding a swimming pool
POON	*n* pl. -S an East Indian tree
POOP	*v* -ED, -ING, -S to tire out
POOR	*adj* POORER, POOREST lacking the means of support
POORI	*n* pl. -S a light, flat wheat cake
POORISH	*adj* somewhat poor
POORLY	*adv* in a poor manner
POORNESS	*n* pl. -ES the state of being poor

POORTITH	*n* pl. -S poverty
POP	*v* POPPED, POPPING, POPS to make a sharp, explosive sound
POPCORN	*n* pl. -S a variety of corn
POPE	*n* pl. -S the head of the Roman Catholic Church **POPELESS, POPELIKE** *adj*
POPEDOM	*n* pl. -S the office of a pope
POPEYED	*adj* having bulging eyes
POPGUN	*n* pl. -S a toy gun
POPINJAY	*n* pl. -JAYS a vain person
POPLAR	*n* pl. -S a fast-growing tree
POPLIN	*n* pl. -S a durable fabric
POPLITIC	*adj* pertaining to the part of the leg behind the knee
POPOVER	*n* pl. -S a very light egg muffin
POPPA	*n* pl. -S papa
POPPED	past tense of pop
POPPER	*n* pl. -S one that pops
POPPET	*n* pl. -S a mechanical valve
POPPIED	*adj* covered with poppies
POPPIES	pl. of poppy
POPPING	present participle of pop
POPPLE	*v* -PLED, -PLING, -PLES to move in a bubbling or rippling manner
POPPY	*n* pl. -PIES a flowering plant
POPSIE	*n* pl. -S popsy
POPSY	*n* pl. -SIES a girlfriend
POPULACE	*n* pl. -S the common people
POPULAR	*adj* liked by many people
POPULATE	*v* -LATED, -LATING, -LATES to inhabit
POPULISM	*n* pl. -S populists' doctrines
POPULIST	*n* pl. -S a member of a party which represents the common people
POPULOUS	*adj* containing many inhabitants
PORCH	*n* pl. -ES a covered structure at the entrance to a building
PORCINE	*adj* pertaining to swine
PORCINO	*n* pl. -NI an edible mushroom
PORE	*v* PORED, PORING, PORES to gaze intently
PORGY	*n* pl. -GIES a marine food fish
PORISM	*n* pl. -S a type of mathematical proposition

PORK	*n* pl. -S the flesh of swine used as food
PORKER	*n* pl. -S a pig
PORKIER	comparative of porky
PORKIES	pl. of porky
PORKIEST	superlative of porky
PORKPIE	*n* pl. -S a man's hat
PORKWOOD	*n* pl. -S a tropical tree
PORKY	*adj* PORKIER, PORKIEST resembling pork
PORKY	*n* pl. -KIES a porcupine
PORN	*n* pl. -S pornography
PORNO	*n* pl. -NOS pornography
PORNY	*adj* PORNIER, PORNIEST pornographic
POROSE	*adj* porous
POROSITY	*n* pl. -TIES the state of being porous
POROUS	*adj* having minute openings **POROUSLY** *adv*
PORPHYRY	*n* pl. -RIES an igneous rock
PORPOISE	*n* pl. -S an aquatic mammal
PORRECT	*adj* extended forward
PORRIDGE	*n* pl. -S a soft food **PORRIDGY** *adj*
PORT	*v* -ED, -ING, -S to shift to the left side
PORTABLE	*n* pl. -S something that can be carried
PORTABLY	*adv* so as to be capable of being carried
PORTAGE	*v* -TAGED, -TAGING, -TAGES to transport from one navigable waterway to another
PORTAL	*n* pl. -S a door, gate, or entrance **PORTALED** *adj*
PORTANCE	*n* pl. -S demeanor
PORTAPAK	*n* pl. -S a portable combined video recorder and camera
PORTEND	*v* -ED, -ING, -S to serve as an omen of
PORTENT	*n* pl. -S an omen
PORTER	*v* -ED, -ING, -S to carry luggage for pay
PORTHOLE	*n* pl. -S a small window in a ship's side
PORTICO	*n* pl. -COS or -COES a type of porch
PORTIERE	*n* pl. -S a curtain for a doorway

PORTION *v* -ED, -ING, -S to divide into shares for distribution

PORTLESS *adj* having no place for ships to load or unload

PORTLY *adj* -LIER, -LIEST rather heavy or fat

PORTRAIT *n* pl. -S a likeness of a person

PORTRAY *v* -ED, -ING, -S to represent pictorially

PORTRESS *n* pl. -ES a female doorkeeper

POSADA *n* pl. -S an inn

POSE *v* POSED, POSING, POSES to assume a fixed position

POSER *n* pl. -S one that poses

POSEUR *n* pl. -S an affected or insincere person

POSH *adj* POSHER, POSHEST stylish or elegant **POSHLY** *adv*

POSHNESS *n* pl. -ES the quality of being posh

POSIES pl. of posy

POSING present participle of pose

POSINGLY *adv* in a posing manner

POSIT *v* -ED, -ING, -S to place

POSITION *v* -ED, -ING, -S to put in a particular location

POSITIVE *adj* -TIVER, -TIVEST certain

POSITIVE *n* pl. -S a quantity greater than zero

POSITRON *n* pl. -S a subatomic particle

POSOLOGY *n* pl. -GIES a branch of medicine that deals with drug dosages

POSSE *n* pl. -S a body of men summoned to aid a peace officer

POSSESS *v* -ED, -ING, -ES to have as property

POSSET *n* pl. -S a hot, spiced drink

POSSIBLE *adj* -BLER, -BLEST capable of happening or proving true **POSSIBLY** *adv*

POSSUM *n* pl. -S opossum

POST *v* -ED, -ING, -S to affix in a public place

POSTAGE *n* pl. -S the charge for mailing an item

POSTAL *n* pl. -S a postcard

POSTALLY *adv* in a manner pertaining to the mails

POSTANAL *adj* situated behind the anus

POSTBAG *n* pl. -S a mailbag

POSTBASE *adj* following a base word

POSTBOX *n* pl. -ES a mailbox

POSTBOY *n* pl. -BOYS a boy who carries mail

POSTBURN *adj* following a burn

POSTCARD *n* pl. -S a card for use in the mail

POSTCAVA *n* pl. -VAE a vein in higher vertebrates

POSTCODE *n* pl. -S a code of numbers and letters used in a mailing address

POSTCOUP *adj* following a coup

POSTDATE *v* -DATED, -DATING, -DATES to give a date later than the actual date to

POSTDIVE *adj* following a dive

POSTDOC *n* pl. -S one engaged in postdoctoral study

POSTDRUG *adj* following the taking of a drug

POSTEEN *n* pl. -S an Afghan outer garment

POSTER *n* pl. -S a printed or written notice for posting

POSTERN *n* pl. -S a rear door or gate

POSTFACE *n* pl. -S a brief note placed at the end of a publication

POSTFIRE *adj* following a fire

POSTFIX *v* -ED, -ING, -ES to affix at the end of something

POSTFORM *v* -ED, -ING, -S to shape subsequently

POSTGAME *adj* following a game

POSTHEAT *n* pl. -S heat applied to a metal after welding

POSTHOLE *n* pl. -S a hole for a fence post

POSTICHE *n* pl. -S an imitation

POSTIN *n* pl. -S posteen

POSTING *n* pl. -S the act of transferring to a ledger

POSTIQUE *n* pl. -S postiche

POSTLUDE *n* pl. -S a closing musical piece

POSTMAN *n* pl. -MEN a mailman

POSTMARK *v* -ED, -ING, -S to stamp mail with an official mark

POSTORAL *adj* situated behind the mouth

POSTPAID *adv* with the postage prepaid

POSTPONE *v* -PONED, -PONING, -PONES to put off to a future time

POSTRACE *adj* following a race

POSTRIOT *adj* following a riot

POSTSHOW *adj* following a show

POSTSYNC *v* -ED, -ING, -S to add sound to a film after a scene has been photographed

POSTTAX *adj* remaining after taxes

POSTTEEN *adj* occurring after one's teenage years

POSTTEST *n* pl. -S a test given after an instructional program

POSTURAL *adj* pertaining to the position of the body

POSTURE *v* -TURED, -TURING, -TURES to assume a particular position

POSTURER *n* pl. -S one that postures

POSTWAR *adj* occurring or existing after a war

POSY *n* pl. -SIES a flower or bouquet

POT *v* POTTED, POTTING, POTS to put in a pot (a round, fairly deep container)

POTABLE *n* pl. -S a liquid suitable for drinking

POTAGE *n* pl. -S a thick soup

POTAMIC *adj* pertaining to rivers

POTASH *n* pl. -ES an alkaline compound

POTASSIC *adj* pertaining to potassium (a metallic element)

POTATION *n* pl. -S the act of drinking

POTATO *n* pl. -TOES the edible tuber of a cultivated plant

POTATORY *adj* pertaining to drinking

POTBELLY *n* pl. -LIES a protruding abdominal region

POTBOIL *v* -ED, -ING, -S to produce inferior literary or artistic work

POTBOY *n* pl. -BOYS a boy who serves customers in a tavern

POTEEN *n* pl. -S Irish whiskey that is distilled unlawfully

POTENCE *n* pl. -S potency

POTENCY *n* pl. -CIES the quality of being potent

POTENT *adj* powerful **POTENTLY** *adv*

POTFUL *n* pl. -S as much as a pot can hold

POTHEAD *n* pl. -S one who smokes marijuana

POTHEEN *n* pl. -S poteen

POTHER *v* -ED, -ING, -S to trouble

POTHERB *n* pl. -S any herb used as a food or seasoning

POTHOLE *n* pl. -S a deep hole in a road **POTHOLED** *adj*

POTHOOK *n* pl. -S a hook for lifting or hanging pots

POTHOUSE *n* pl. -S a tavern

POTICHE *n* pl. -S a type of vase

POTION *n* pl. -S a magical or medicinal drink

POTLACH *n* pl. -ES a ceremonial feast

POTLACHE *n* pl. -S potlach

POTLATCH *v* -ED, -ING, -ES to hold a ceremonial feast for

POTLIKE *adj* resembling a pot

POTLINE *n* pl. -S a row of electrolytic cells

POTLUCK *n* pl. -S food which is incidentally available

POTMAN *n* pl. -MEN a man who serves customers in a tavern

POTPIE *n* pl. -S a deep-dish pie containing meat and vegetables

POTSHARD *n* pl. -S potsherd

POTSHERD *n* pl. -S a fragment of broken pottery

POTSHOT *v* -SHOT, -SHOTTING, -SHOTS to shoot randomly at

POTSIE *n* pl. -S potsy

POTSTONE *n* pl. -S a variety of steatite

POTSY *n* pl. -SIES a children's game

POTTAGE *n* pl. -S a thick soup

POTTED past tense of pot

POTTEEN *n* pl. -S poteen

POTTER *v* -ED, -ING, -S to putter

POTTERER *n* pl. -S one that potters

POTTERY *n* pl. -TERIES ware molded from clay and hardened by heat

POTTIER comparative of potty

POTTIES pl. of potty

POTTIEST superlative of potty

POTTING present participle of pot

POTTLE *n* pl. -S a drinking vessel

POTTO *n* pl. -TOS a lemur of tropical Africa

POTTY *adj* -TIER, -TIEST of little importance

POTTY *n* pl. -TIES a small toilet seat

POTZER *n* pl. -S patzer

POUCH *v* -ED, -ING, -ES to put in a pouch (a small, flexible receptacle)

POUCHY	*adj* POUCHIER, POUCHIEST resembling a pouch
POUF	*n* pl. -S a loose roll of hair **POUFED** *adj*
POUFF	*n* pl. -S pouf **POUFFED** *adj*
POUFFE	*n* pl. -S pouf
POULARD	*n* pl. -S a spayed hen
POULARDE	*n* pl. -S poulard
POULT	*n* pl. -S a young domestic fowl
POULTER	*n* pl. -S one that deals in poultry
POULTICE	*v* -TICED, -TICING, -TICES to apply a healing substance to
POULTRY	*n* pl. -TRIES domestic fowls kept for eggs or meat
POUNCE	*v* POUNCED, POUNCING, POUNCES to make a sudden assault or approach
POUNCER	*n* pl. -S one that pounces
POUND	*v* -ED, -ING, -S to strike heavily and repeatedly
POUNDAGE	*n* pl. -S the act of impounding
POUNDAL	*n* pl. -S a unit of force
POUNDER	*n* pl. -S one that pounds
POUR	*v* -ED, -ING, -S to cause to flow **POURABLE** *adj*
POURER	*n* pl. -S one that pours
POUSSIE	*n* pl. -S pussy
POUT	*v* -ED, -ING, -S to protrude the lips in ill humor
POUTER	*n* pl. -S one that pouts
POUTFUL	*adj* pouty
POUTY	*adj* POUTIER, POUTIEST tending to pout
POVERTY	*n* pl. -TIES the state of being poor
POW	*n* pl. -S an explosive sound
POWDER	*v* -ED, -ING, -S to reduce to powder (matter in a finely divided state)
POWDERER	*n* pl. -S one that powders
POWDERY	*adj* resembling powder
POWER	*v* -ED, -ING, -S to provide with means of propulsion
POWERFUL	*adj* possessing great force
POWTER	*n* pl. -S a domestic pigeon
POWWOW	*v* -ED, -ING, -S to hold a conference
POX	*v* -ED, -ING, -ES to infect with syphilis
POXVIRUS	*n* pl. -ES a type of virus
POYOU	*n* pl. -S an armadillo of Argentina
POZZOLAN	*n* pl. -S a finely divided material used to make cement
PRAAM	*n* pl. -S pram
PRACTIC	*adj* practical
PRACTICE	*v* -TICED, -TICING, -TICES to perform often so as to acquire skill
PRACTISE	*v* -TISED, -TISING, -TISES to practice
PRAECIPE	*n* pl. -S a legal writ
PRAEDIAL	*adj* pertaining to land
PRAEFECT	*n* pl. -S prefect
PRAELECT	*v* -ED, -ING, -S to prelect
PRAETOR	*n* pl. -S an ancient Roman magistrate
PRAHU	*n* pl. -S prau
PRAIRIE	*n* pl. -S a tract of grassland
PRAISE	*v* PRAISED, PRAISING, PRAISES to express approval or admiration of
PRAISER	*n* pl. -S one that praises
PRALINE	*n* pl. -S a confection made of nuts cooked in sugar
PRAM	*n* pl. -S a flat-bottomed boat
PRANCE	*v* PRANCED, PRANCING, PRANCES to spring forward on the hind legs
PRANCER	*n* pl. -S one that prances
PRANDIAL	*adj* pertaining to a meal
PRANG	*v* -ED, -ING, -S to cause to crash
PRANK	*v* -ED, -ING, -S to adorn gaudily
PRANKISH	*adj* mischievous
PRAO	*n* pl. PRAOS prau
PRASE	*n* pl. -S a mineral
PRAT	*n* pl. -S the buttocks
PRATE	*v* PRATED, PRATING, PRATES to chatter
PRATER	*n* pl. -S one that prates
PRATFALL	*n* pl. -S a fall on the buttocks
PRATING	present participle of prate
PRATIQUE	*n* pl. -S clearance given a ship by the health authority of a port
PRATTLE	*v* -TLED, -TLING, -TLES to babble
PRATTLER	*n* pl. -S one that prattles
PRAU	*n* pl. -S a swift Malaysian sailing vessel

PRAWN   *v* -ED, -ING, -S to fish for prawns (edible shellfish)

PRAWNER   *n* pl. -S one that prawns

PRAXIS   *n* pl. PRAXISES or PRAXES practical use of a theory

PRAY   *v* -ED, -ING, -S to address prayers to

PRAYER   *n* pl. -S a devout petition to a deity

PREACH   *v* -ED, -ING, -ES to advocate or recommend urgently

PREACHER   *n* pl. -S one that preaches

PREACHY   *adj* PREACHIER, PREACHIEST tending to preach

PREACT   *v* -ED, -ING, -S to act beforehand

PREADAPT   *v* -ED, -ING, -S to adapt beforehand

PREADMIT   *v* -MITTED, -MITTING, -MITS to admit beforehand

PREADOPT   *v* -ED, -ING, -S to adopt beforehand

PREADULT   *adj* preceding adulthood

PREAGED   *adj* previously aged

PREALLOT   *v* -LOTTED, -LOTTING, -LOTS to allot beforehand

PREAMBLE   *n* pl. -S an introductory statement

PREAMP   *n* pl. -S an amplifier

PREANAL   *adj* situated in front of the anus

PREARM   *v* -ED, -ING, -S to arm beforehand

PREAUDIT   *n* pl. -S an audit made prior to a final settlement of a transaction

PREAVER   *v* -VERRED, -VERRING, -VERS to aver or assert beforehand

PREAXIAL   *adj* situated in front of an axis

PREBAKE   *v* -BAKED, -BAKING, -BAKES to bake beforehand

PREBASAL   *adj* situated in front of a base

PREBEND   *n* pl. -S a clergyman's stipend

PREBILL   *v* -ED, -ING, -S to bill beforehand

PREBIND   *v* -BOUND, -BINDING, -BINDS to bind beforehand

PREBLESS   *v* -ED, -ING, -ES to bless beforehand

PREBOIL   *v* -ED, -ING, -S to boil beforehand

PREBOOK   *v* -ED, -ING, -S to book beforehand

PREBOOM   *adj* preceding a sudden expansion of business

PREBOUND   past tense of prebind

PRECAST   *v* -CAST, -CASTING, -CASTS to cast before placing into position

PRECAVA   *n* pl. -VAE a vein in higher vertebrates **PRECAVAL** *adj*

PRECEDE   *v* -CEDED, -CEDING, -CEDES to go before

PRECENT   *v* -ED, -ING, -S to lead a church choir in singing

PRECEPT   *n* pl. -S a rule of conduct

PRECESS   *v* -ED, -ING, -ES to rotate with a complex motion

PRECHECK   *v* -ED, -ING, -S to check beforehand

PRECHILL   *v* -ED, -ING, -S to chill beforehand

PRECIEUX   *adj* excessively refined

PRECINCT   *n* pl. -S a subdivision of a city or town

PRECIOUS   *n* pl. -ES a darling

PRECIPE   *n* pl. -S praecipe

PRECIS   *v* -ED, -ING, -ES to make a concise summary of

PRECISE   *adj* -CISER, -CISEST sharply and clearly defined or stated

PRECITED   *adj* previously cited

PRECLEAN   *v* -ED, -ING, -S to clean beforehand

PRECLEAR   *v* -ED, -ING, -S to clear beforehand

PRECLUDE   *v* -CLUDED, -CLUDING, -CLUDES to make impossible by previous action

PRECODE   *v* -CODED, -CODING, -CODES to code beforehand

PRECOOK   *v* -ED, -ING, -S to cook beforehand

PRECOOL   *v* -ED, -ING, -S to cool beforehand

PRECOUP   *adj* preceding a coup

PRECRASH   *adj* preceding a crash

PRECURE   *v* -CURED, -CURING, -CURES to cure beforehand

PRECUT   *v* -CUT, -CUTTING, -CUTS to cut beforehand

PREDATE   *v* -DATED, -DATING, -DATES to date before the actual or a specified time

PREDATOR   *n* pl. -S one that plunders

PREDAWN   *n* pl. -S the time just before dawn

PREDIAL   *adj* praedial

PREDICT *v* -ED, -ING, -S to tell of or about in advance

PREDIVE *adj* preceding a dive

PREDRILL *v* -ED, -ING, -S to drill beforehand

PREDUSK *n* pl. -S the time just before dusk

PREE *v* PREED, PREEING, PREES to test by tasting

PREEDIT *v* -ED, -ING, -S to edit beforehand

PREELECT *v* -ED, -ING, -S to elect or choose beforehand

PREEMIE *n* pl. -S an infant born prematurely

PREEMPT *v* -ED, -ING, -S to acquire by prior right

PREEN *v* -ED, -ING, -S to smooth or clean with the beak or tongue

PREENACT *v* -ED, -ING, -S to enact beforehand

PREENER *n* pl. -S one that preens

PREERECT *v* -ED, -ING, -S to erect beforehand

PREEXIST *v* -ED, -ING, -S to exist before

PREFAB *v* -FABBED, -FABBING, -FABS to construct beforehand

PREFACE *v* -ACED, -ACING, -ACES to provide with an introductory statement

PREFACER *n* pl. -S one that prefaces

PREFADE *v* -FADED, -FADING, -FADES to fade beforehand

PREFECT *n* pl. -S an ancient Roman official

PREFER *v* -FERRED, -FERRING, -FERS to hold in higher regard or esteem

PREFIGHT *adj* preceding a fight

PREFILE *v* -FILED, -FILING, -FILES to file beforehand

PREFIRE *v* -FIRED, -FIRING, -FIRES to fire beforehand

PREFIX *v* -ED, -ING, -ES to add as a prefix (a form affixed to the beginning of a root word)

PREFIXAL *adj* pertaining to or being a prefix

PREFLAME *adj* preceding a flame

PREFOCUS *v* -CUSED, -CUSING, -CUSES or -CUSSED, -CUSSING, -CUSSES to focus beforehand

PREFORM *v* -ED, -ING, -S to form beforehand

PREFRANK *v* -ED, -ING, -S to frank beforehand

PREFREEZE *v* -FROZE, -FROZEN, -FREEZING, -FREEZES to freeze beforehand

PREGAME *adj* preceding a game

PREGGERS *adj* pregnant

PREGNANT *adj* carrying a developing fetus in the uterus

PREHEAT *v* -ED, -ING, -S to heat beforehand

PREHUMAN *n* pl. -S a prototype of man

PREJUDGE *v* -JUDGED, -JUDGING, -JUDGES to judge beforehand

PRELACY *n* pl. -CIES the office of a prelate

PRELATE *n* pl. -S a high-ranking clergyman **PRELATIC** *adj*

PRELECT *v* -ED, -ING, -S to lecture

PRELEGAL *adj* occurring before the commencement of studies in law

PRELIFE *n* pl. -LIVES a life conceived as lived before one's earthly life

PRELIM *n* pl. -S a preliminary match

PRELIMIT *v* -ED, -ING, -S to limit beforehand

PRELUDE *v* -LUDED, -LUDING, -LUDES to play a musical introduction

PRELUDER *n* pl. -S one that preludes

PRELUNCH *adj* preceding lunch

PREMADE *adj* made beforehand

PREMAN *n* pl. -MEN a hypothetical ancestor of man

PREMEAL *adj* preceding a meal

PREMED *n* pl. -S a student preparing for the study of medicine

PREMEDIC *n* pl. -S a premed

PREMEET *adj* preceding a meet

PREMEN pl. of preman

PREMIE *n* pl. -S preemie

PREMIER *n* pl. -S a prime minister

PREMIERE *v* -MIERED, -MIERING, -MIERES to present publicly for the first time

PREMISE *v* -MISED, -MISING, -MISES to state in advance

PREMISS *n* pl. -ES a proposition in logic

PREMIUM *n* pl. -S an additional payment

PREMIX *v* -MIXED or -MIXT, -MIXING, -MIXES to mix before use

PREMOLAR *n* pl. -S a tooth

PREMOLD *v* -ED, -ING, -S to mold beforehand

PREMOLT *adj* preceding a molt

PREMORAL *adj* preceding the development of a moral code

PREMORSE *adj* ending abruptly, as if bitten off

PREMUNE *adj* resistant to a disease

PRENAME *n* pl. -S a forename

PRENATAL *adj* prior to birth

PRENOMEN *n* pl. -MENS or -MINA the first name of an ancient Roman

PRENOON *adj* preceding noon

PRENTICE *v* -TICED, -TICING, -TICES to place with an employer for instruction in a trade

PREORDER *v* -ED, -ING, -S to order beforehand

PREP *v* PREPPED, PREPPING, PREPS to attend a preparatory school

PREPACK *v* -ED, -ING, -S to package before retail distribution

PREPAID past tense of prepay

PREPARE *v* -PARED, -PARING, -PARES to put in proper condition or readiness

PREPARER *n* pl. -S one that prepares

PREPASTE *v* -PASTED, -PASTING, -PASTES to paste beforehand

PREPAY *v* -PAID, -PAYING, -PAYS to pay in advance

PREPENSE *adj* planned in advance

PREPILL *adj* preceding the development of a contraceptive pill

PREPLACE *v* -PLACED, -PLACING, -PLACES to place beforehand

PREPLAN *v* -PLANNED, -PLANNING, -PLANS to plan in advance

PREPLANT *adj* occurring before planting

PREPPED past tense of prep

PREPPIE *n* pl. -S one who preps

PREPPING present participle of prep

PREPPY *adj* -PIER, -PIEST associated with the style and behavior of preparatory school students **PREPPILY** *adv*

PREPREG *n* pl. -S reinforcing material already impregnated with a synthetic resin

PREPRICE *v* -PRICED, -PRICING, -PRICES to price beforehand

PREPRINT *v* -ED, -ING, -S to print in advance

PREPUCE *n* pl. -S a fold of skin covering the penis

PREPUNCH *v* -ED, -ING, -ES to punch in advance

PREPUPAL *adj* preceding the pupal stage

PREQUEL *n* pl. -S a book whose story precedes that of an earlier work

PRERACE *adj* preceding a race

PRERENAL *adj* situated in front of the kidney

PRERINSE *n* pl. -S a rinsing beforehand

PRERIOT *adj* preceding a riot

PREROCK *adj* preceding the development of rock music

PRESA *n* pl. -SE a musical symbol

PRESAGE *v* -SAGED, -SAGING, -SAGES to foretell

PRESAGER *n* pl. -S one that presages

PRESALE *adj* preceding a sale

PRESCIND *v* -ED, -ING, -S to consider separately

PRESCORE *v* -SCORED, -SCORING, -SCORES to record the sound of before filming

PRESE pl. of presa

PRESELL *v* -SOLD, -SELLING, -SELLS to promote a product not yet being sold to the public

PRESENCE *n* pl. -S close proximity

PRESENT *v* -ED, -ING, -S to bring into the presence of someone

PRESERVE *v* -SERVED, -SERVING, -SERVES to keep free from harm or danger

PRESET *v* -SET, -SETTING, -SETS to set beforehand

PRESHAPE *v* -SHAPED, -SHAPING, -SHAPES to shape beforehand

PRESHOW *v* -SHOWED, -SHOWN, -SHOWING, -SHOWS to show beforehand

PRESIDE *v* -SIDED, -SIDING, -SIDES to occupy the position of authority

PRESIDER *n* pl. -S one that presides

PRESIDIA *n/pl* Soviet executive committees

PRESIDIO *n* pl. -DIOS a Spanish fort

PRESIFT *v* -ED, -ING, -S to sift beforehand

PRESLEEP *adj* preceding sleep

PRESLICE *v* -SLICED, -SLICING, -SLICES to slice beforehand

PRESOAK *v* -ED, -ING, -S to soak beforehand

PRESOLD	past tense of presell
PRESONG	*adj* preceding a song
PRESORT	*v* -ED, -ING, -S to sort beforehand
PRESPLIT	*adj* preceding a split
PRESS	*v* -ED, -ING, -ES to act upon with steady force
PRESSER	*n* pl. -S one that presses
PRESSING	*n* pl. -S an instance of stamping with a press
PRESSMAN	*n* pl. -MEN a printing press operator
PRESSOR	*n* pl. -S a substance that raises blood pressure
PRESSRUN	*n* pl. -S a continuous operation of a printing press
PRESSURE	*v* -SURED, -SURING, -SURES to apply force to
PREST	*n* pl. -S a loan
PRESTAMP	*v* -ED, -ING, -S to stamp beforehand
PRESTER	*n* pl. -S a priest
PRESTIGE	*n* pl. -S distinction or reputation in the eyes of people
PRESTO	*n* pl. -TOS a musical passage played in rapid tempo
PRESUME	*v* -SUMED, -SUMING, -SUMES to take for granted
PRESUMER	*n* pl. -S one that presumes
PRETAPE	*v* -TAPED, -TAPING, -TAPES to tape beforehand
PRETASTE	*v* -TASTED, -TASTING, -TASTES to taste beforehand
PRETAX	*adj* existing before provision for taxes
PRETEEN	*n* pl. -S a child under the age of thirteen
PRETENCE	*n* pl. -S pretense
PRETEND	*v* -ED, -ING, -S to assume or display a false appearance of
PRETENSE	*n* pl. -S the act of pretending
PRETERIT	*n* pl. -S a past tense in grammar
PRETERM	*adj* pertaining to premature birth
PRETEST	*v* -ED, -ING, -S to give a preliminary test to
PRETEXT	*v* -ED, -ING, -S to allege as an excuse
PRETOR	*n* pl. -S praetor
PRETRAIN	*v* -ED, -ING, -S to train beforehand
PRETREAT	*v* -ED, -ING, -S to treat beforehand
PRETRIAL	*n* pl. -S a proceeding that precedes a trial
PRETRIM	*v* -TRIMMED, -TRIMMING, -TRIMS to trim beforehand
PRETTIED	past tense of pretty
PRETTIER	comparative of pretty
PRETTIES	present 3d person sing. of pretty
PRETTIEST	superlative of pretty
PRETTIFY	*v* -FIED, -FYING, -FIES to make pretty
PRETTY	*v* -TIED, -TYING, -TIES to make pretty
PRETTY	*adj* -TIER, -TIEST pleasing to the eye **PRETTILY** *adv*
PRETYPE	*v* -TYPED, -TYPING, -TYPES to type beforehand
PRETZEL	*n* pl. -S a glazed, salted cracker
PREUNION	*n* pl. -S a union beforehand
PREUNITE	*v* -UNITED, -UNITING, -UNITES to unite beforehand
PREVAIL	*v* -ED, -ING, -S to triumph
PREVENT	*v* -ED, -ING, -S to keep from happening
PREVIEW	*v* -ED, -ING, -S to view or exhibit in advance
PREVIOUS	*adj* coming or occurring before in time or order
PREVISE	*v* -VISED, -VISING, -VISES to foresee
PREVISOR	*n* pl. -S one that previses
PREVUE	*v* -VUED, -VUING, -VUES to preview
PREWAR	*adj* occurring or existing before a war
PREWARM	*v* -ED, -ING, -S to warm beforehand
PREWARN	*v* -ED, -ING, -S to warn in advance
PREWASH	*v* -ED, -ING, -ES to wash beforehand
PREWORK	*adj* preceding work
PREWRAP	*v* -WRAPPED, -WRAPPING, -WRAPS to wrap beforehand
PREX	*n* pl. -ES prexy
PREXY	*n* pl. PREXIES a president
PREY	*v* -ED, -ING, -S to seize and devour animals for food
PREYER	*n* pl. -S one that preys

PREZ   *n* pl. -ES a president

PRIAPEAN   *adj* priapic

PRIAPI   a pl. of priapus

PRIAPIC   *adj* phallic

PRIAPISM   *n* pl. -S a persistent erection of the penis

PRIAPUS   *n* pl. -PUSES or -PI a representation of the phallus

PRICE   *v* PRICED, PRICING, PRICES to set a value on

PRICER   *n* pl. -S one that prices

PRICEY   *adj* PRICIER, PRICIEST expensive

PRICIER   comparative of pricey and pricy

PRICIEST   superlative of pricey and pricy

PRICING   present participle of price

PRICK   *v* -ED, -ING, -S to puncture slightly

PRICKER   *n* pl. -S one that pricks

PRICKET   *n* pl. -S a spike for holding a candle upright

PRICKIER   comparative of pricky

PRICKIEST   superlative of pricky

PRICKING   *n* pl. -S a prickly feeling

PRICKLE   *v* -LED, -LING, -LES to prick

PRICKLY   *adj* -LIER, -LIEST having many sharp points

PRICKY   *adj* PRICKIER, PRICKIEST prickly

PRICY   *adj* PRICIER, PRICIEST pricey

PRIDE   *v* PRIDED, PRIDING, PRIDES to feel pride (a feeling of self-esteem)

PRIDEFUL   *adj* full of pride

PRIED   past tense of pry

PRIEDIEU   *n* pl. -DIEUS or -DIEUX a piece of furniture for kneeling on during prayer

PRIER   *n* pl. -S one that pries

PRIES   present 3d person sing. of pry

PRIEST   *v* -ED, -ING, -S to ordain as a priest (one authorized to perform religious rites)

PRIESTLY   *adj* -LIER, -LIEST characteristic of or befitting a priest

PRIG   *v* PRIGGED, PRIGGING, PRIGS to steal

PRIGGERY   *n* pl. -GERIES priggism

PRIGGISH   *adj* marked by priggism

PRIGGISM   *n* pl. -S prim adherence to convention

PRILL   *v* -ED, -ING, -S to convert into pellets

PRIM   *adj* PRIMMER, PRIMMEST formally precise or proper

PRIM   *v* PRIMMED, PRIMMING, PRIMS to give a prim expression to

PRIMA   *n* pl. -S primo

PRIMACY   *n* pl. -CIES the state of being first

PRIMAGE   *n* pl. -S an amount paid as an addition to freight charges

PRIMAL   *adj* being at the beginning or foundation

PRIMARY   *n* pl. -RIES a preliminary election

PRIMATAL   *n* pl. -S a primate

PRIMATE   *n* pl. -S any of an advanced order of mammals

PRIME   *v* PRIMED, PRIMING, PRIMES to make ready

PRIMELY   *adv* excellently

PRIMER   *n* pl. -S a book that covers the basics of a subject

PRIMERO   *n* pl. -ROS a card game

PRIMEVAL   *adj* pertaining to the earliest ages

PRIMI   a pl. of primo

PRIMINE   *n* pl. -S the outer covering of an ovule

PRIMING   *n* pl. -S the act of one that primes

PRIMLY   *adv* in a prim manner

PRIMMED   past tense of prim

PRIMMER   comparative of prim

PRIMMEST   superlative of prim

PRIMMING   present participle of prim

PRIMNESS   *n* pl. -ES the state of being prim

PRIMO   *n* pl. -MOS or -MI the main part in a musical piece

PRIMP   *v* -ED, -ING, -S to dress or adorn carefully

PRIMROSE   *n* pl. -S a perennial herb

PRIMSIE   *adj* prim

PRIMULA   *n* pl. -S primrose

PRIMUS   *n* pl. -ES the head bishop of Scotland

PRINCE   *n* pl. -S a non-reigning male member of a royal family

PRINCELY   *adj* -LIER, -LIEST of or befitting a prince

PRINCESS	*n* pl. -ES a non-reigning female member of a royal family	**PRIVATE**	*adj* -VATER, -VATEST not for public use or knowledge
PRINCIPE	*n* pl. -PI a prince	**PRIVATE**	*n* pl. -S a soldier of lower rank
PRINCOCK	*n* pl. -S a coxcomb	**PRIVET**	*n* pl. -S an ornamental shrub
PRINCOX	*n* pl. -ES princock	**PRIVIER**	comparative of privy
PRINK	*v* -ED, -ING, -S to dress or adorn in a showy manner	**PRIVIES**	pl. of privy
		PRIVITY	*n* pl. -TIES private knowledge
PRINKER	*n* pl. -S one that prinks	**PRIVY**	*adj* PRIVIER, PRIVIEST private **PRIVILY** *adv*
PRINT	*v* -ED, -ING, -S to produce by pressed type on a surface	**PRIVY**	*n* pl. PRIVIES an outhouse
PRINTER	*n* pl. -S one that prints	**PRIZE**	*v* PRIZED, PRIZING, PRIZES to value highly
PRINTERY	*n* pl. -ERIES a place where printing is done	**PRIZER**	*n* pl. -S one who vies for a reward
PRINTING	*n* pl. -S a reproduction from a printing surface		
PRINTOUT	*n* pl. -S the printed output of a computer	**PRO**	*n* pl. PROS an argument or vote in favor of something
		PROA	*n* pl. -S prau
PRION	*n* pl. -S a protein particle	**PROBABLE**	*n* pl. -S something likely to occur or prove true
PRIOR	*n* pl. -S an officer in a monastery		
PRIORATE	*n* pl. -S the office of a prior	**PROBABLY**	*adv* without much doubt
PRIORESS	*n* pl. -ES a nun corresponding in rank to a prior	**PROBAND**	*n* pl. -S one whose reactions or responses are studied
PRIORIES	pl. of priory	**PROBANG**	*n* pl. -S a surgical rod
PRIORITY	*n* pl. -TIES precedence established by importance	**PROBATE**	*v* -BATED, -BATING, -BATES to establish the validity of
PRIORLY	*adv* previously	**PROBE**	*v* PROBED, PROBING, PROBES to investigate or examine thoroughly
PRIORY	*n* pl. -RIES a religious house		
PRISE	*v* PRISED, PRISING, PRISES to raise or force with a lever	**PROBER**	*n* pl. -S one that probes
		PROBIT	*n* pl. -S a unit of statistical probability
PRISERE	*n* pl. -S a succession of vegetational stages	**PROBITY**	*n* pl. -TIES complete and confirmed integrity
PRISM	*n* pl. -S a solid which disperses light into a spectrum	**PROBLEM**	*n* pl. -S a perplexing question or situation
PRISMOID	*n* pl. -S a geometric solid		
PRISON	*v* -ED, -ING, -S to imprison	**PROCAINE**	*n* pl. -S a compound used as a local anesthetic
PRISONER	*n* pl. -S one that is imprisoned	**PROCARP**	*n* pl. -S a female sexual organ in certain algae
PRISS	*v* -ED, -ING, -ES to act in a prissy manner	**PROCEED**	*v* -ED, -ING, -S to go forward or onward
PRISSY	*adj* -SIER, -SIEST excessively or affectedly proper **PRISSILY** *adv*	**PROCESS**	*v* -ED, -ING, -ES to treat or prepare by a special method
PRISSY	*n* pl. -SIES one who is prissy	**PROCHAIN**	*adj* prochein
PRISTANE	*n* pl. -S a chemical compound	**PROCHEIN**	*adj* nearest in time, relation, or degree
PRISTINE	*adj* pertaining to the earliest time or state		
		PROCLAIM	*v* -ED, -ING, -S to make known publicly or officially
PRITHEE	*interj* — used to express a wish or request	**PROCTOR**	*v* -ED, -ING, -S to supervise
PRIVACY	*n* pl. -CIES the state of being private	**PROCURAL**	*n* pl. -S the act of procuring

PROCURE v -CURED, -CURING, -CURES to obtain by effort

PROCURER n pl. -S one that procures

PROD v PRODDED, PRODDING, PRODS to jab with something pointed

PRODDER n pl. -S one that prods

PRODIGAL n pl. -S one who spends lavishly and foolishly

PRODIGY n pl. -GIES a child having exceptional talent or ability

PRODROME n pl. -DROMES or -DROMATA a sign of impending disease

PRODUCE v -DUCED, -DUCING, -DUCES to bring into existence

PRODUCER n pl. -S one that produces

PRODUCT n pl. -S something produced by labor or effort

PROEM n pl. -S an introductory statement **PROEMIAL** adj

PROETTE n pl. -S a female professional athlete

PROF n pl. -S a professor

PROFANE v -FANED, -FANING, -FANES to treat with irreverence or abuse

PROFANER n pl. -S one that profanes

PROFESS v -ED, -ING, -ES to affirm openly

PROFFER v -ED, -ING, -S to present for acceptance

PROFILE v -FILED, -FILING, -FILES to draw an outline of

PROFILER n pl. -S one that profiles

PROFIT v -ED, -ING, -S to gain an advantage or benefit

PROFITER n pl. -S one that profits

PROFOUND adj -FOUNDER, -FOUNDEST intellectually deep and penetrating

PROFOUND n pl. -S something that is very deep

PROFUSE adj pouring forth generously

PROG v PROGGED, PROGGING, PROGS to prowl about for food or plunder

PROGENY n pl. -NIES a descendant or offspring

PROGERIA n pl. -S premature aging

PROGGER n pl. -S one that progs

PROGGING present participle of prog

PROGNOSE v -NOSED, -NOSING, -NOSES to forecast the probable course of a disease

PROGRADE adj pertaining to the orbital motion of a body

PROGRAM v -GRAMED, -GRAMING, -GRAMS or -GRAMMED, -GRAMMING, -GRAMS to arrange in a plan of proceedings

PROGRESS v -ED, -ING, -ES to move forward or onward

PROHIBIT v -ED, -ING, -S to forbid by authority

PROJECT v -ED, -ING, -S to extend outward

PROJET n pl. -S a plan or outline

PROLABOR adj favoring organized labor

PROLAMIN n pl. -S a simple protein

PROLAN n pl. -S a sex hormone

PROLAPSE v -LAPSED, -LAPSING, -LAPSES to fall or slip out of place

PROLATE adj extended lengthwise

PROLE n pl. -S a member of the working class

PROLEG n pl. -S an abdominal leg of certain insect larvae

PROLIFIC adj producing abundantly

PROLINE n pl. -S an amino acid

PROLIX adj tediously long and wordy **PROLIXLY** adv

PROLOG v -ED, -ING, -S to prologue

PROLOGUE v -LOGUED, -LOGUING, -LOGUES to preface

PROLONG v -ED, -ING, -S to lengthen in duration

PROLONGE n pl. -S a rope used for pulling a gun carriage

PROM n pl. -S a formal dance

PROMINE n pl. -S a substance that promotes growth

PROMISE v -ISED, -ISING, -ISES to make a declaration of assurance

PROMISEE n pl. -S one who is promised something

PROMISER n pl. -S promisor

PROMISING present participle of promise

PROMISOR n pl. -S one that promises

PROMO n pl. -MOS a promotional presentation

PROMOTE *v* -MOTED, -MOTING, -MOTES to contribute to the progress of

PROMOTER *n* pl. -S one that promotes

PROMPT *adj* PROMPTER, PROMPTEST quick to act or respond

PROMPT *v* -ED, -ING, -S to induce to action

PROMPTER *n* pl. -S one that prompts

PROMPTLY *adv* in a prompt manner

PROMULGE *v* -MULGED, -MULGING, -MULGES to proclaim

PRONATE *v* -NATED, -NATING, -NATES to turn the palm downward or backward

PRONATOR *n* pl. -S or -ES a forearm or forelimb muscle

PRONE *adj* lying with the front or face downward **PRONELY** *adv*

PRONG *v* -ED, -ING, -S to pierce with a pointed projection

PRONOTUM *n* pl. -NOTA a hard outer plate of an insect

PRONOUN *n* pl. -S a word that may be used in place of a noun

PRONTO *adv* quickly

PROOF *v* -ED, -ING, -S to examine for errors

PROOFER *n* pl. -S one that proofs

PROP *v* PROPPED, PROPPING, PROPS to keep from falling

PROPANE *n* pl. -S a flammable gas

PROPEL *v* -PELLED, -PELLING, -PELS to cause to move forward or onward

PROPEND *v* -ED, -ING, -S to have a tendency toward

PROPENE *n* pl. -S a flammable gas

PROPENOL *n* pl. -S a flammable liquid

PROPENSE *adj* tending toward

PROPENYL *adj* pertaining to a certain chemical group

PROPER *adj* -ERER, -EREST suitable **PROPERLY** *adv*

PROPER *n* pl. -S a portion of the Mass

PROPERTY *n* pl. -TIES something owned

PROPHAGE *n* pl. -S a form of virus

PROPHASE *n* pl. -S the first stage in mitosis

PROPHECY *n* pl. -CIES a prediction

PROPHESY *v* -SIED, -SYING, -SIES to predict

PROPHET *n* pl. -S one who predicts

PROPINE *v* -PINED, -PINING, -PINES to offer as a gift

PROPJET *n* pl. -S a type of airplane

PROPMAN *n* pl. -MEN a man in charge of stage properties

PROPOLIS *n* pl. -LISES a resinous substance used as a cement by bees

PROPONE *v* -PONED, -PONING, -PONES to propose

PROPOSAL *n* pl. -S something that is proposed

PROPOSE *v* -POSED, -POSING, -POSES to put forward for consideration or acceptance

PROPOSER *n* pl. -S one that proposes

PROPOUND *v* -ED, -ING, -S to propose

PROPPED past tense of prop

PROPPING present participle of prop

PROPYL *n* pl. -S a univalent radical **PROPYLIC** *adj*

PROPYLON *n* pl. -LA an entrance to a temple

PRORATE *v* -RATED, -RATING, -RATES to divide proportionately

PROROGUE *v* -ROGUED, -ROGUING, -ROGUES to discontinue a session of

PROSAIC *adj* pertaining to prose

PROSAISM *n* pl. -S a prosaic style

PROSAIST *n* pl. -S a writer of prose

PROSE *v* PROSED, PROSING, PROSES to write prose (writing without metrical structure)

PROSECT *v* -ED, -ING, -S to dissect

PROSER *n* pl. -S a prosaist

PROSIER comparative of prosy

PROSIEST superlative of prosy

PROSILY *adv* in a prosy manner

PROSING present participle of prose

PROSIT *interj* — used as a drinking toast

PROSO *n* pl. -SOS millet

PROSODY *n* pl. -DIES the study of poetical forms **PROSODIC** *adj*

PROSOMA *n* pl. -S the front region of the body of an invertebrate **PROSOMAL** *adj*

PROSPECT *v* -ED, -ING, -S to explore for mineral deposits

PROSPER *v* -ED, -ING, -S to be successful or fortunate

PROSS	*n* pl. -ES a prostitute	**PROTRACT**	*v* -ED, -ING, -S to prolong
PROSSIE	*n* pl. -S a prostitute	**PROTRUDE**	*v* -TRUDED, -TRUDING, -TRUDES to extend beyond the main portion
PROST	*interj* prosit		
PROSTATE	*n* pl. -S a gland in male mammals	**PROTYL**	*n* pl. -S protyle
PROSTIE	*n* pl. -S a prostitute	**PROTYLE**	*n* pl. -S a hypothetical substance from which all the elements are supposedly derived
PROSTYLE	*n* pl. -S a building having a row of columns across the front only		
PROSY	*adj* PROSIER, PROSIEST prosaic	**PROUD**	*adj* PROUDER, PROUDEST having or displaying pride **PROUDLY** *adv*
PROTAMIN	*n* pl. -S a simple protein	**PROUDFUL**	*adj* prideful
PROTASIS	*n* pl. -ASES the introductory part of a classical drama **PROTATIC** *adj*	**PROUNION**	*adj* favoring labor unions
		PROVE	*v* PROVED, PROVEN, PROVING, PROVES to establish the truth or validity of **PROVABLE** *adj* **PROVABLY** *adv*
PROTEA	*n* pl. -S an evergreen shrub		
PROTEAN	*n* pl. -S a type of protein		
PROTEASE	*n* pl. -S an enzyme	**PROVENLY**	*adv* without doubt
PROTECT	*v* -ED, -ING, -S to keep from harm, attack, or injury	**PROVER**	*n* pl. -S one that proves
		PROVERB	*v* -ED, -ING, -S to make a byword of
PROTEGE	*n* pl. -S one whose career is promoted by an influential person	**PROVIDE**	*v* -VIDED, -VIDING, -VIDES to supply
PROTEGEE	*n* pl. -S a female protege	**PROVIDER**	*n* pl. -S one that provides
PROTEI	pl. of proteus	**PROVINCE**	*n* pl. -S an administrative division of a country
PROTEID	*n* pl. -S protein		
PROTEIDE	*n* pl. -S proteid	**PROVING**	present participle of prove
PROTEIN	*n* pl. -S a nitrogenous organic compound	**PROVIRUS**	*n* pl. -ES a form of virus **PROVIRAL** *adj*
PROTEND	*v* -ED, -ING, -S to extend	**PROVISO**	*n* pl. -SOS or -SOES a clause in a document introducing a condition or restriction
PROTEOSE	*n* pl. -S a water-soluble protein		
PROTEST	*v* -ED, -ING, -S to express strong objection		
		PROVOKE	*v* -VOKED, -VOKING, -VOKES to incite to anger or resentment
PROTEUS	*n* pl. -TEI any of a genus of aerobic bacteria		
		PROVOKER	*n* pl. -S one that provokes
PROTEUS	*n* pl. -ES one that readily changes his appearance or principles	**PROVOST**	*n* pl. -S a high-ranking university official
		PROW	*n* pl. -S the forward part of a ship
PROTIST	*n* pl. -S any of a group of unicellular organisms	**PROW**	*adj* PROWER, PROWEST brave
PROTIUM	*n* pl. -S an isotope of hydrogen	**PROWAR**	*adj* favoring war
		PROWESS	*n* pl. -ES exceptional ability
PROTOCOL	*v* -COLED, -COLING, -COLS or -COLLED, -COLLING, -COLS to form a preliminary draft of an official document	**PROWL**	*v* -ED, -ING, -S to move about stealthily
		PROWLER	*n* pl. -S one that prowls
PROTON	*n* pl. -S a subatomic particle **PROTONIC** *adj*	**PROXEMIC**	*adj* pertaining to a branch of environmental study
PROTOPOD	*n* pl. -S a part of a crustacean appendage	**PROXIES**	pl. of proxy
		PROXIMAL	*adj* located near the point of origin
PROTOXID	*n* pl. -S an oxide		
PROTOZOA	*n/pl* unicellular microscopic organisms	**PROXIMO**	*adj* of or occurring in the following month

PROXY   *n* pl. PROXIES a person authorized to act for another

PRUDE   *n* pl. -S a prudish person

PRUDENCE   *n* pl. -S the quality of being prudent

PRUDENT   *adj* having, showing, or exercising good judgment

PRUDERY   *n* pl. -ERIES excessive regard for propriety, modesty, or morality

PRUDISH   *adj* marked by prudery

PRUINOSE   *adj* having a powdery covering

PRUNE   *v* PRUNED, PRUNING, PRUNES to cut off branches or parts from **PRUNABLE** *adj*

PRUNELLA   *n* pl. -S a strong woolen fabric

PRUNELLE   *n* pl. -S a plum-flavored liqueur

PRUNELLO   *n* pl. -LOS prunella

PRUNER   *n* pl. -S one that prunes

PRUNING   present participle of prune

PRUNUS   *n* pl. -ES a flowering tree

PRURIENT   *adj* having lustful thoughts or desires

PRURIGO   *n* pl. -GOS a skin disease

PRURITUS   *n* pl. -ES intense itching **PRURITIC** *adj*

PRUSSIC   *adj* pertaining to a type of acid

PRUTA   *n* pl. PRUTOT prutah

PRUTAH   *n* pl. PRUTOTH a monetary unit of Israel

PRY   *v* PRIED, PRYING, PRIES to inquire impertinently into private matters **PRYINGLY** *adv*

PRYER   *n* pl. -S prier

PRYTHEE   *interj* prithee

PSALM   *v* -ED, -ING, -S to praise in psalms (sacred songs)

PSALMIC   *adj* of or pertaining to a psalm

PSALMIST   *n* pl. -S a writer of psalms

PSALMODY   *n* pl. -DIES the use of psalms in worship

PSALTER   *n* pl. -S a book of psalms

PSALTERY   *n* pl. -TERIES an ancient stringed musical instrument

PSALTRY   *n* pl. -TRIES psaltery

PSAMMITE   *n* pl. -S a fine-grained rock

PSAMMON   *n* pl. -S a group of microorganisms living in waterlogged sands

PSCHENT   *n* pl. -S a crown worn by ancient Egyptian kings

PSEPHITE   *n* pl. -S a rock composed of small pebbles

PSEUD   *n* pl. -S a person pretending to be an intellectual

PSEUDO   *n* pl. PSEUDOS a pseud

PSHAW   *v* -ED, -ING, -S to utter an expression of disapproval

PSI   *n* pl. -S a Greek letter

PSILOCIN   *n* pl. -S a hallucinogenic drug

PSILOSIS   *n* pl. -LOSES a tropical disease **PSILOTIC** *adj*

PSOAS   *n* pl. PSOAI or PSOAE a muscle of the loin **PSOATIC** *adj*

PSOCID   *n* pl. -S a minute winged insect

PSORALEA   *n* pl. -S a plant of the bean family

PSORALEN   *n* pl. -S a drug used to treat psoriasis

PSST   *interj* — used to attract someone's attention

PSYCH   *v* -ED, -ING, -S to put into the proper frame of mind

PSYCHE   *n* pl. -S the mental structure of a person

PSYCHIC   *n* pl. -S one sensitive to extrasensory phenomena

PSYCHO   *n* pl. -CHOS a mentally unstable person

PSYLLA   *n* pl. -S any of various plant lice

PSYLLID   *n* pl. -S psylla

PSYLLIUM   *n* pl. -S the seed of a fleawort

PSYWAR   *n* pl. -S psychological warfare

PTERIN   *n* pl. -S a chemical compound

PTEROPOD   *n* pl. -S a type of mollusk

PTERYGIA   *n/pl* fleshy growths over the cornea

PTERYLA   *n* pl. -LAE a feathered area on the skin of a bird

PTISAN   *n* pl. -S a tea of herbs or barley

PTOMAIN   *n* pl. -S ptomaine

PTOMAINE   *n* pl. -S a compound produced by the decomposition of protein

PTOSIS   *n* pl. PTOSES a drooping of the upper eyelid **PTOTIC** *adj*

PTYALIN   *n* pl. -S a salivary enzyme

PTYALISM   *n* pl. -S an excessive flow of saliva

PUB   *n* pl. -S a tavern

PUBERTY   *n* pl. -TIES a period of sexual maturation **PUBERAL, PUBERTAL** *adj*

PUBES	*n* pl. PUBES the lower part of the abdomen
PUBIC	*adj* pertaining to the pubes or pubis
PUBIS	*n* pl. PUBES the forward portion of either of the hipbones
PUBLIC	*n* pl. -S the community or the people as a whole
PUBLICAN	*n* pl. -S one who owns or manages a pub
PUBLICLY	*adv* by the public
PUBLISH	*v* -ED, -ING, -ES to print and issue to the public
PUCCOON	*n* pl. -S an herb that yields a red dye
PUCE	*n* pl. -S a dark red color
PUCK	*n* pl. -S a rubber disk used in ice hockey
PUCKA	*adj* pukka
PUCKER	*v* -ED, -ING, -S to gather into small wrinkles or folds
PUCKERER	*n* pl. -S one that puckers
PUCKERY	*adj* -ERIER, -ERIEST having a tendency to pucker
PUCKISH	*adj* impish
PUD	*n* pl. -S pudding
PUDDING	*n* pl. -S a thick, soft dessert
PUDDLE	*v* -DLED, -DLING, -DLES to strew with puddles (small pools of water)
PUDDLER	*n* pl. -S one who subjects iron to puddling
PUDDLING	*n* pl. -S the process of converting pig iron to wrought iron
PUDDLY	*adj* -DLIER, -DLIEST full of puddles
PUDENCY	*n* pl. -CIES modesty
PUDENDUM	*n* pl. -DA the external genital organs of a woman **PUDENDAL** *adj*
PUDGY	*adj* PUDGIER, PUDGIEST short and fat **PUDGILY** *adv*
PUDIBUND	*adj* prudish
PUDIC	*adj* to the pudendum
PUEBLO	*n* pl. -LOS a communal dwelling of certain Indian tribes
PUERILE	*adj* childish
PUFF	*v* -ED, -ING, -S to blow in short gusts
PUFFBALL	*n* pl. -S any of various globular fungi

PUFFER	*n* pl. -S one that puffs
PUFFERY	*n* pl. -ERIES excessive public praise
PUFFIN	*n* pl. -S a sea bird
PUFFY	*adj* -FIER, -FIEST swollen **PUFFILY** *adv*
PUG	*v* PUGGED, PUGGING, PUGS to fill in with clay or mortar
PUGAREE	*n* pl. -S pugree
PUGGAREE	*n* pl. -S pugree
PUGGED	past tense of pug
PUGGIER	comparative of puggy
PUGGIEST	superlative of puggy
PUGGING	present participle of pug
PUGGISH	*adj* somewhat stubby
PUGGREE	*n* pl. -S pugree
PUGGRY	*n* pl. -GRIES pugree
PUGGY	*adj* -GIER, -GIEST puggish
PUGH	*interj* — used to express disgust
PUGILISM	*n* pl. -S the art or practice of fighting with the fists
PUGILIST	*n* pl. -S one who fights with his fists
PUGMARK	*n* pl. -S a footprint
PUGREE	*n* pl. -S a cloth band wrapped around a hat
PUISNE	*n* pl. -S one of lesser rank
PUISSANT	*adj* powerful
PUJA	*n* pl. -S a Hindu prayer ritual
PUJAH	*n* pl. -S puja
PUKE	*v* PUKED, PUKING, PUKES to vomit
PUKKA	*adj* genuine
PUL	*n* pl. PULS or PULI a coin of Afghanistan
PULA	*n* pl. PULA a monetary unit of Botswana
PULE	*v* PULED, PULING, PULES to whine
PULER	*n* pl. -S one that pules
PULI	*n* pl. -LIK or -LIS a long-haired sheepdog
PULICENE	*adj* pertaining to fleas
PULICIDE	*n* pl. -S an agent used for destroying fleas
PULIK	a pl. of puli
PULING	*n* pl. -S a plaintive cry
PULINGLY	*adv* in a whining manner

PULL — *v* -ED, -ING, -S to exert force in order to cause motion toward the force

PULLBACK — *n* pl. -S a restraint or drawback

PULLER — *n* pl. -S one that pulls

PULLET — *n* pl. -S a young hen

PULLEY — *n* pl. -LEYS a device used for lifting weight

PULLMAN — *n* pl. -S a railroad sleeping car

PULLOUT — *n* pl. -S a withdrawal

PULLOVER — *n* pl. -S a garment that is put on by being drawn over the head

PULLUP — *n* pl. -S the act of raising oneself while hanging by the hands

PULMONIC — *adj* pertaining to the lungs

PULMOTOR — *n* pl. -S a respiratory device

PULP — *v* -ED, -ING, -S to reduce to pulp (a soft, moist mass of matter)

PULPAL — *adj* pertaining to pulp **PULPALLY** *adv*

PULPER — *n* pl. -S one that pulps

PULPIER — comparative of pulpy

PULPIEST — superlative of pulpy

PULPILY — *adv* in a pulpy manner

PULPIT — *n* pl. -S a platform in a church **PULPITAL** *adj*

PULPLESS — *adj* having no pulp

PULPOUS — *adj* pulpy

PULPWOOD — *n* pl. -S soft wood used in making paper

PULPY — *adj* PULPIER, PULPIEST resembling pulp

PULQUE — *n* pl. -S a fermented Mexican beverage

PULSANT — *adj* pulsating

PULSAR — *n* pl. -S a celestial source of radio waves

PULSATE — *v* -SATED, -SATING, -SATES to expand and contract rhythmically

PULSATOR — *n* pl. -S something that pulsates

PULSE — *v* PULSED, PULSING, PULSES to pulsate

PULSEJET — *n* pl. -S a type of engine

PULSER — *n* pl. -S a device that causes pulsations

PULSING — present participle of pulse

PULSION — *n* pl. -S propulsion

PULSOJET — *n* pl. -S pulsejet

PULVILLI — *n/pl* pads between the claws of an insect's foot

PULVINUS — *n* pl. -NI a swelling at the base of a leaf **PULVINAR** *adj*

PUMA — *n* pl. -S a cougar

PUMELO — *n* pl. -LOS pomelo

PUMICE — *v* -ICED, -ICING, -ICES to polish with a porous volcanic rock

PUMICER — *n* pl. -S one that pumices

PUMICITE — *n* pl. -S a porous volcanic rock

PUMMEL — *v* -MELED, -MELING, -MELS or -MELLED, -MELLING, -MELS to pommel

PUMMELO — *n* pl. -LOS a shaddock

PUMP — *v* -ED, -ING, -S to cause to flow by means of a pump (a device for moving fluids)

PUMPER — *n* pl. -S one that pumps

PUMPKIN — *n* pl. -S a large, edible fruit

PUMPLESS — *adj* lacking a pump

PUMPLIKE — *adj* resembling a pump

PUN — *v* PUNNED, PUNNING, PUNS to make a pun (a play on words)

PUNA — *n* pl. -S a cold, arid plateau

PUNCH — *v* -ED, -ING, -ES to perforate with a type of tool

PUNCHEON — *n* pl. -S a vertical supporting timber

PUNCHER — *n* pl. -S one that punches

PUNCHY — *adj* PUNCHIER, PUNCHIEST dazed **PUNCHILY** *adv*

PUNCTATE — *adj* covered with dots

PUNCTUAL — *adj* being on time

PUNCTURE — *v* -TURED, -TURING, -TURES to pierce with a pointed object

PUNDIT — *n* pl. -S a Hindu scholar **PUNDITIC** *adj*

PUNDITRY — *n* pl. -RIES the learning of pundits

PUNG — *n* pl. -S a box-shaped sleigh

PUNGENCY — *n* pl. -CIES the state of being pungent

PUNGENT — *adj* sharply affecting the organs of taste or smell

PUNGLE — *v* -GLED, -GLING, -GLES to contribute

PUNIER — comparative of puny

PUNIEST — superlative of puny

PUNILY — *adv* in a puny manner

PUNINESS — *n* pl. -ES the state of being puny

PUNISH *v* -ED, -ING, -ES to impose a penalty on in requital for wrongdoing

PUNISHER *n* pl. -S one that punishes

PUNITION *n* pl. -S the act of punishing; punishment

PUNITIVE *adj* inflicting punishment

PUNITORY *adj* punitive

PUNK *n* pl. -S dry, decayed wood used as tinder

PUNK *adj* PUNKER, PUNKEST of inferior quality

PUNKA *n* pl. -S a ceiling fan used in India

PUNKAH *n* pl. -S punka

PUNKER *n* pl. -S a punk rock musician

PUNKEY *n* pl. -KEYS punkie

PUNKIE *n* pl. -S a biting gnat

PUNKIN *n* pl. -S pumpkin

PUNKISH *adj* pertaining to a style inspired by punk rock

PUNKY *adj* PUNKIER, PUNKIEST resembling punk

PUNNED past tense of pun

PUNNER *n* pl. -S a punster

PUNNET *n* pl. -S a small basket

PUNNING present participle of pun

PUNNY *adj* -NIER, -NIEST being or involving a pun

PUNSTER *n* pl. -S one who is given to punning

PUNT *v* -ED, -ING, -S to propel through water with a pole

PUNTER *n* pl. -S one that punts

PUNTO *n* pl. -TOS a hit or thrust in fencing

PUNTY *n* pl. -TIES an iron rod used in glassmaking

PUNY *adj* PUNIER, PUNIEST of inferior size, strength, or significance

PUP *v* PUPPED, PUPPING, PUPS to give birth to puppies

PUPA *n* pl. -PAS or -PAE an intermediate stage of a metamorphic insect **PUPAL** *adj*

PUPARIUM *n* pl. -IA a pupal shell **PUPARIAL** *adj*

PUPATE *v* -PATED, -PATING, -PATES to pass through the pupal stage

PUPATION *n* pl. -S the act of pupating

PUPFISH *n* pl. -ES a small, freshwater fish

PUPIL *n* pl. -S a student under the close supervision of a teacher

PUPILAGE *n* pl. -S the state of being a pupil

PUPILAR *adj* pertaining to a part of the eye

PUPILARY *adj* pupilar

PUPPED past tense of pup

PUPPET *n* pl. -S a small figure, as of a person or animal, manipulated by the hand

PUPPETRY *n* pl. -RIES the art of making or manipulating puppets

PUPPING present participle of pup

PUPPY *n* pl. -PIES a young dog **PUPPYISH** *adj*

PUPPYDOM *n* pl. -S the world of puppies

PUR *v* PURRED, PURRING, PURS to purr

PURANA *n* pl. -S a Hindu scripture **PURANIC** *adj*

PURBLIND *adj* partially blind

PURCHASE *v* -CHASED, -CHASING, -CHASES to acquire by the payment of money

PURDA *n* pl. -S purdah

PURDAH *n* pl. -S a curtain used in India to seclude women

PURE *adj* PURER, PUREST free from anything different, inferior, or contaminating

PUREBRED *n* pl. -S an animal of unmixed stock

PUREE *v* -REED, -REEING, -REES to reduce to a thick pulp by cooking and sieving

PURELY *adv* in a pure manner

PURENESS *n* pl. -ES the quality of being pure

PURER comparative of pure

PUREST superlative of pure

PURFLE *v* -FLED, -FLING, -FLES to decorate the border of

PURFLING *n* pl. -S an ornamental border

PURGE *v* PURGED, PURGING, PURGES to purify

PURGER *n* pl. -S one that purges

PURGING *n* pl. -S the act of purifying

PURI *n* pl. -S poori

PURIFIER *n* pl. -S one that purifies

PURIFY *v* -FIED, -FYING, -FIES to free from impurities

PURIN	*n* pl. -S purine
PURINE	*n* pl. -S a chemical compound
PURISM	*n* pl. -S strict adherence to traditional correctness
PURIST	*n* pl. -S one who practices purism **PURISTIC** *adj*
PURITAN	*n* pl. -S a rigorously moral or religious person
PURITY	*n* pl. -TIES the quality of being pure
PURL	*v* -ED, -ING, -S to knit with a particular stitch
PURLIEU	*n* pl. -S an outlying or neighboring area
PURLIN	*n* pl. -S a horizontal supporting timber
PURLINE	*n* pl. -S purlin
PURLOIN	*v* -ED, -ING, -S to steal
PURPLE	*adj* -PLER, -PLEST of a color intermediate between red and blue
PURPLE	*v* -PLED, -PLING, -PLES to make purple
PURPLISH	*adj* somewhat purple
PURPLY	*adj* purplish
PURPORT	*v* -ED, -ING, -S to profess or claim
PURPOSE	*v* -POSED, -POSING, -POSES to resolve to perform or accomplish
PURPURA	*n* pl. -S a disease characterized by purple spots on the skin
PURPURE	*n* pl. -S the heraldic color purple
PURPURIC	*adj* pertaining to purpura
PURPURIN	*n* pl. -S a reddish dye
PURR	*v* -ED, -ING, -S to utter a low, vibrant sound
PURRED	past tense of pur and purr
PURRING	present participle of pur and purr
PURSE	*v* PURSED, PURSING, PURSES to pucker
PURSER	*n* pl. -S an officer in charge of a ship's accounts
PURSIER	comparative of pursy
PURSIEST	superlative of pursy
PURSILY	*adv* in a pursy manner
PURSING	present participle of purse
PURSLANE	*n* pl. -S a common garden herb
PURSUANT	*adv* in accordance
PURSUE	*v* -SUED, -SUING, -SUES to follow in order to overtake or capture
PURSUER	*n* pl. -S one that pursues
PURSUIT	*n* pl. -S the act of pursuing
PURSY	*adj* PURSIER, PURSIEST short of breath
PURULENT	*adj* secreting pus
PURVEY	*v* -ED, -ING, -S to supply
PURVEYOR	*n* pl. -S one that purveys
PURVIEW	*n* pl. -S the extent of operation, authority, or concern
PUS	*n* pl. -ES a viscous fluid formed in infected tissue
PUSH	*v* -ED, -ING, -ES to exert force in order to cause motion away from the force
PUSHBALL	*n* pl. -S a type of ball game
PUSHCART	*n* pl. -S a light cart pushed by hand
PUSHDOWN	*n* pl. -S a store of computer data
PUSHER	*n* pl. -S one that pushes
PUSHFUL	*adj* pushy
PUSHIER	comparative of pushy
PUSHIEST	superlative of pushy
PUSHILY	*adv* in a pushy manner
PUSHOVER	*n* pl. -S an easily defeated person or team
PUSHPIN	*n* pl. -S a large-headed pin
PUSHROD	*n* pl. -S a rod for operating the valves in an engine
PUSHUP	*n* pl. -S a type of exercise
PUSHY	*adj* PUSHIER, PUSHIEST offensively aggressive
PUSLEY	*n* pl. -LEYS pussley
PUSLIKE	*adj* resembling pus
PUSS	*n* pl. -ES a cat
PUSSIER	comparative of pussy
PUSSIES	pl. of pussy
PUSSIEST	superlative of pussy
PUSSLEY	*n* pl. -LEYS purslane
PUSSLIKE	*adj* catlike
PUSSLY	*n* pl. -LIES pussley
PUSSY	*n* pl. PUSSIES a cat
PUSSY	*adj* -SIER, -SIEST full of pus
PUSSYCAT	*n* pl. -S a cat

PUSTULE   *n* pl. -S a small elevation of the skin containing pus **PUSTULAR, PUSTULED** *adj*

PUT   *v* PUT, PUTTING, PUTS to place in a particular position

PUTAMEN   *n* pl. -MINA the hard covering of the kernel of certain fruits

PUTATIVE   *adj* generally regarded as such

PUTLOG   *n* pl. -S a horizontal supporting timber

PUTOFF   *n* pl. -S an excuse

PUTON   *n* pl. -S a hoax or deception

PUTOUT   *n* pl. -S an act of causing an out in baseball

PUTREFY   *v* -FIED, -FYING, -FIES to make or become putrid

PUTRID   *adj* being in a decomposed, foul-smelling state **PUTRIDLY** *adv*

PUTSCH   *n* pl. -ES a suddenly executed attempt to overthrow a government

PUTT   *v* -ED, -ING, -S to hit with a light stroke in golf

PUTTEE   *n* pl. -S a strip of cloth wound around the leg

PUTTER   *v* -ED, -ING, -S to occupy oneself in a leisurely or ineffective manner

PUTTERER   *n* pl. -S one that putters

PUTTI   pl. of putto

PUTTIED   past tense of putty

PUTTIER   *n* pl. -S one that putties

PUTTING   present participle of put

PUTTO   *n* pl. -TI an infant boy in art

PUTTY   *v* -TIED, -TYING, -TIES to fill with a type of cement

PUTZ   *v* -ED, -ING, -ES to waste time

PUZZLE   *v* -ZLED, -ZLING, -ZLES to cause uncertainty and indecision in

PUZZLER   *n* pl. -S something that puzzles

PYA   *n* pl. -S a copper coin of Burma

PYAEMIA   *n* pl. -S pyemia **PYAEMIC** *adj*

PYCNIDIA   *n/pl* spore-bearing organs of certain fungi

PYCNOSIS   *n* pl. -NOSES pyknosis

PYCNOTIC   *adj* pyknotic

PYE   *n* pl. -S a book of ecclesiastical rules in the pre-Reformation English church

PYELITIS   *n* pl. -TISES inflammation of the pelvis or the kidney **PYELITIC** *adj*

PYEMIA   *n* pl. -S the presence of pus in the blood **PYEMIC** *adj*

PYGIDIUM   *n* pl. -IA the posterior region of certain invertebrates **PYGIDIAL** *adj*

PYGMY   *n* pl. -MIES a small person **PYGMAEAN, PYGMEAN, PYGMOID, PYGMYISH** *adj*

PYGMYISM   *n* pl. -S a stunted or dwarfish condition

PYIC   *adj* pertaining to pus

PYIN   *n* pl. -S a protein compound contained in pus

PYJAMAS   *n* pl. PYJAMAS pajamas

PYKNIC   *n* pl. -S a person having a broad, stocky build

PYKNOSIS   *n* pl. -NOSES a shrinking and thickening of a cell nucleus

PYKNOTIC   *adj* exhibiting pyknosis

PYLON   *n* pl. -S a tall structure marking an entrance or approach

PYLORUS   *n* pl. -RI or -RUSES the opening between the stomach and the duodenum **PYLORIC** *adj*

PYODERMA   *n* pl. -S a pus-causing skin disease

PYOGENIC   *adj* producing pus

PYOID   *adj* puslike

PYORRHEA   *n* pl. -S a discharge of pus

PYOSIS   *n* pl. -OSES the formation of pus

PYRALID   *n* pl. -S a long-legged moth

PYRAMID   *v* -ED, -ING, -S to raise or increase by adding amounts gradually

PYRAN   *n* pl. -S a chemical compound **PYRANOID** *adj*

PYRANOSE   *n* pl. -S a simple sugar

PYRE   *n* pl. -S a pile of combustible material

PYRENE   *n* pl. -S a putamen

PYRENOID   *n* pl. -S a protein body of certain lower organisms

PYRETIC   *adj* pertaining to fever

PYREXIA   *n* pl. -S fever **PYREXIAL, PYREXIC** *adj*

PYRIC   *adj* pertaining to burning

PYRIDINE   *n* pl. -S a flammable liquid **PYRIDIC** *adj*

PYRIFORM   *adj* pear-shaped

PYRITE   *n* pl. -S a metallic sulfide **PYRITIC, PYRITOUS** *adj*

PYROGEN   *n* pl. -S a substance that produces fever

PYROLA   *n* pl. -S a perennial herb

PYROLOGY   *n* pl. -GIES the scientific examination of materials by heat

PYROLYZE   *v* -LYZED, -LYZING, -LYZES to affect compounds by the application of heat

PYRONE   *n* pl. -S a chemical compound

PYRONINE   *n* pl. -S a dye

PYROPE   *n* pl. -S a variety of garnet

PYROSIS   *n* pl. -SISES heartburn

PYROSTAT   *n* pl. -S a thermostat

PYROXENE   *n* pl. -S any of a group of minerals common in igneous rocks

PYRRHIC   *n* pl. -S a type of metrical foot

PYRROL   *n* pl. -S pyrrole

PYRROLE   *n* pl. -S a chemical compound **PYRROLIC** *adj*

PYRUVATE   *n* pl. -S a chemical salt

PYTHON   *n* pl. -S a large snake **PYTHONIC** *adj*

PYURIA   *n* pl. -S the presence of pus in the urine

PYX   *n* pl. -ES a container in which the eucharistic bread is kept

PYXIDES   pl. of pyxis

PYXIDIUM   *n* pl. -IA a type of seed vessel

PYXIE   *n* pl. -S an evergreen shrub

PYXIS   *n* pl. PYXIDES a pyxidium

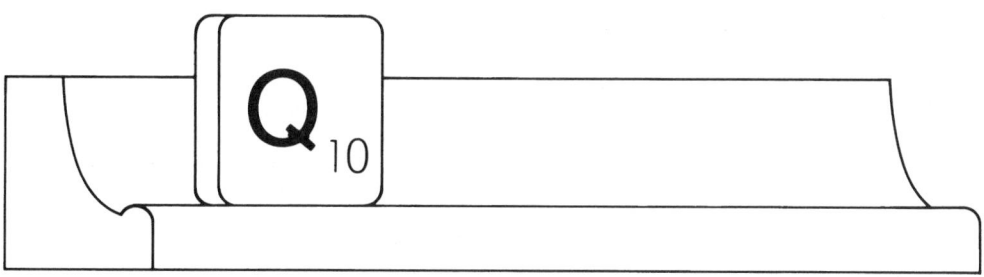

QAID	*n* pl. -S caid	**QUAFF**	*v* -ED, -ING, -S to drink deeply
QANAT	*n* pl. -S a system of underground tunnels and wells in the Middle East	**QUAFFER**	*n* pl. -S one that quaffs
		QUAG	*n* pl. -S a quagmire
QAT	*n* pl. -S kat	**QUAGGA**	*n* pl. -S an extinct zebralike mammal
QINDAR	*n* pl. -DARS or -DARKA qintar	**QUAGGY**	*adj* -GIER, -GIEST marshy
QINTAR	*n* pl. -S a monetary unit of Albania	**QUAGMIRE**	*n* pl. -S an area of marshy ground
QIVIUT	*n* pl. -S the wool of a musk-ox	**QUAGMIRY**	*adj* -MIRIER, -MIRIEST marshy
QOPH	*n* pl. -S koph	**QUAHAUG**	*n* pl. -S quahog
QUA	*adv* in the capacity of	**QUAHOG**	*n* pl. -S an edible clam
QUAALUDE	*n* pl. -S a sedative drug	**QUAI**	*n* pl. -S quay
QUACK	*v* -ED, -ING, -S to utter the characteristic cry of a duck	**QUAICH**	*n* pl. -ES or -S a small drinking vessel
QUACKERY	*n* pl. -ERIES fraudulent practice	**QUAIGH**	*n* pl. -S quaich
QUACKISH	*adj* fraudulent	**QUAIL**	*v* -ED, -ING, -S to cower
QUACKISM	*n* pl. -S quackery	**QUAINT**	*adj* QUAINTER, QUAINTEST pleasingly old-fashioned or unfamiliar **QUAINTLY** *adv*
QUAD	*v* QUADDED, QUADDING, QUADS to space out by means of quadrats		
		QUAKE	*v* QUAKED, QUAKING, QUAKES to shake or vibrate
QUADPLEX	*n* pl. -ES a building having four units	**QUAKER**	*n* pl. -S one that quakes
QUADRANS	*n* pl. -RANTES an ancient Roman coin	**QUAKY**	*adj* QUAKIER, QUAKIEST tending to quake **QUAKILY** *adv*
QUADRANT	*n* pl. -S a quarter section of a circle	**QUALE**	*n* pl. -LIA a property considered apart from things having the property
QUADRAT	*n* pl. -S a piece of type metal used for filling spaces		
		QUALIFY	*v* -FIED, -FYING, -FIES to make suitable or capable
QUADRATE	*v* -RATED, -RATING, -RATES to correspond or agree	**QUALITY**	*n* pl. -TIES a characteristic or attribute
QUADRIC	*n* pl. -S a type of geometric surface	**QUALM**	*n* pl. -S a feeling of doubt or misgiving
QUADRIGA	*n* pl. -GAE a chariot drawn by four horses	**QUALMISH**	*adj* having qualms
QUADROON	*n* pl. -S a person of one-quarter black ancestry	**QUALMY**	*adj* QUALMIER, QUALMIEST qualmish
		QUAMASH	*n* pl. -ES camass
QUAERE	*n* pl. -S a question	**QUANDANG**	*n* pl. -S quandong
QUAESTOR	*n* pl. -S an ancient Roman magistrate	**QUANDARY**	*n* pl. -RIES a dilemma

QUANDONG *n* pl. -S an Australian tree

QUANGO *n* pl. -GOS a public administrative board

QUANT *v* -ED, -ING, -S to propel through water with a pole

QUANTA pl. of quantum

QUANTAL *adj* pertaining to a quantum

QUANTIC *n* pl. -S a type of mathematical function

QUANTIFY *v* -FIED, -FYING, -FIES to determine the quantity of

QUANTILE *n* pl. -S any of the values of a random variable that divides a frequency distribution

QUANTITY *n* pl. -TIES a specified or indefinite amount or number

QUANTIZE *v* -TIZED, -TIZING, -TIZES to limit the possible values of to a discrete set

QUANTONG *n* pl. -S quandong

QUANTUM *n* pl. -TA a fundamental unit of energy

QUARE *adj* queer

QUARK *n* pl. -S a hypothetical atomic particle

QUARREL *v* -RELED, -RELING, -RELS or -RELLED, -RELLING, -RELS to engage in an angry dispute

QUARRIER *n* pl. -S one that quarries

QUARRY *v* -RIED, -RYING, -RIES to dig stone from an excavation

QUART *n* pl. -S a liquid measure of capacity

QUARTAN *n* pl. -S a recurrent malarial fever

QUARTE *n* pl. -S a fencing thrust

QUARTER *v* -ED, -ING, -S to divide into four equal parts

QUARTERN *n* pl. -S one-fourth of something

QUARTET *n* pl. -S a group of four

QUARTIC *n* pl. -S a type of mathematical function

QUARTILE *n* pl. -S a portion of a frequency distribution

QUARTO *n* pl. -TOS the size of a piece of paper cut four from a sheet

QUARTZ *n* pl. -ES a mineral

QUASAR *n* pl. -S a distant celestial object emitting strong radio waves

QUASH *v* -ED, -ING, -ES to suppress completely

QUASHER *n* pl. -S one that quashes

QUASI *adj* similar but not exactly the same

QUASS *n* pl. -ES kvass

QUASSIA *n* pl. -S a tropical tree

QUASSIN *n* pl. -S a medicinal compound obtained from the wood of a quassia

QUATE *adj* quiet

QUATORZE *n* pl. -S a set of four cards of the same denomination scoring fourteen points

QUATRAIN *n* pl. -S a stanza of four lines

QUATRE *n* pl. -S the four at cards or dice

QUAVER *v* -ED, -ING, -S to quiver

QUAVERER *n* pl. -S one that quavers

QUAVERY *adj* quivery

QUAY *n* pl. QUAYS a wharf **QUAYLIKE** *adj*

QUAYAGE *n* pl. -S a charge for the use of a quay

QUAYSIDE *n* pl. -S the area adjacent to a quay

QUEAN *n* pl. -S a harlot

QUEASY *adj* -SIER, -SIEST easily nauseated **QUEASILY** *adv*

QUEAZY *adj* -ZIER, -ZIEST queasy

QUEEN *v* -ED, -ING, -S to make a queen (a female monarch) of

QUEENDOM *n* pl. -S the area ruled by a queen

QUEENLY *adj* -LIER, -LIEST of or befitting a queen

QUEER *adj* QUEERER, QUEEREST deviating from the expected or normal

QUEER *v* -ED, -ING, -S to spoil the effect or success of

QUEERISH *adj* somewhat queer

QUEERLY *adv* in a queer manner

QUELL *v* -ED, -ING, -S to suppress

QUELLER *n* pl. -S one that quells

QUENCH *v* -ED, -ING, -ES to put out or extinguish

QUENCHER *n* pl. -S one that quenches

QUENELLE *n* pl. -S a type of dumpling

QUERCINE *adj* pertaining to oaks

QUERIDA *n* pl. -S a female sweetheart

QUERIED past tense of query

QUERIER *n* pl. -S a querist

QUERIES	present 3d person sing. of query
QUERIST	*n* pl. -S one who queries
QUERN	*n* pl. -S a hand-turned grain mill
QUERY	*v* -RIED, -RYING, -RIES to question
QUEST	*v* -ED, -ING, -S to make a search
QUESTER	*n* pl. -S one that quests
QUESTION	*v* -ED, -ING, -S to put a question (an inquiry) to
QUESTOR	*n* pl. -S quaestor
QUETZAL	*n* pl. -S or -ES a tropical bird
QUEUE	*v* QUEUED, QUEUING or QUEUEING, QUEUES to line up
QUEUER	*n* pl. -S one that queues
QUEY	*n* pl. QUEYS a young cow
QUEZAL	*n* pl. -S or -ES quetzal
QUIBBLE	*v* -BLED, -BLING, -BLES to argue over trivialities
QUIBBLER	*n* pl. -S one that quibbles
QUICHE	*n* pl. -S a custard-filled pastry
QUICK	*adj* QUICKER, QUICKEST acting or capable of acting with speed
QUICK	*n* pl. -S a sensitive area of flesh
QUICKEN	*v* -ED, -ING, -S to speed up
QUICKIE	*n* pl. -S something done quickly
QUICKLY	*adv* in a quick manner
QUICKSET	*n* pl. -S a plant suitable for hedges
QUID	*n* pl. -S a portion of something to be chewed
QUIDDITY	*n* pl. -TIES the true nature of a thing
QUIDNUNC	*n* pl. -S a nosy person
QUIET	*adj* -ETER, -ETEST making little or no noise
QUIET	*v* -ED, -ING, -S to cause to be quiet
QUIETEN	*v* -ED, -ING, -S to quiet
QUIETER	*n* pl. -S one that quiets
QUIETISM	*n* pl. -S a form of religious mysticism
QUIETIST	*n* pl. -S an advocate of quietism
QUIETLY	*adv* in a quiet manner
QUIETUDE	*n* pl. -S a state of tranquillity
QUIETUS	*n* pl. -ES a final settlement
QUIFF	*n* pl. -S a forelock
QUILL	*v* -ED, -ING, -S to press small ridges in
QUILLAI	*n* pl. -S an evergreen tree
QUILLAIA	*n* pl. -S a quillai
QUILLAJA	*n* pl. -S a quillai
QUILLET	*n* pl. -S a trivial distinction
QUILLING	*n* pl. -S material that is quilled
QUILT	*v* -ED, -ING, -S to stitch together with padding in between
QUILTER	*n* pl. -S one that quilts
QUILTING	*n* pl. -S material that is used for making quilts
QUIN	*n* pl. -S a quintuplet
QUINARY	*n* pl. -RIES a group of five
QUINATE	*adj* arranged in groups of five
QUINCE	*n* pl. -S an apple-like fruit
QUINCUNX	*n* pl. -ES an arrangement of five objects
QUINELA	*n* pl. -S quinella
QUINELLA	*n* pl. -S a type of bet in horse racing
QUINIC	*adj* pertaining to quinine
QUINIELA	*n* pl. -S quinella
QUININ	*n* pl. -S quinine
QUININA	*n* pl. -S quinine
QUININE	*n* pl. -S a medicinal alkaloid
QUINNAT	*n* pl. -S a food fish
QUINOA	*n* pl. -S a weedy plant
QUINOID	*n* pl. -S a chemical compound
QUINOL	*n* pl. -S a chemical compound
QUINOLIN	*n* pl. -S a chemical compound
QUINONE	*n* pl. -S a chemical compound
QUINSY	*n* pl. -SIES an inflammation of the tonsils
QUINT	*n* pl. -S a group of five
QUINTA	*n* pl. -S a country estate in Portugal or Latin America
QUINTAIN	*n* pl. -S an object used as a target in a medieval sport
QUINTAL	*n* pl. -S a unit of weight
QUINTAN	*n* pl. -S a recurrent fever
QUINTAR	*n* pl. -S qintar
QUINTE	*n* pl. -S a position in fencing
QUINTET	*n* pl. -S a group of five
QUINTIC	*n* pl. -S a type of mathematical function
QUINTILE	*n* pl. -S a portion of a frequency distribution
QUINTIN	*n* pl. -S a fine linen

QUIP	*v* QUIPPED, QUIPPING, QUIPS to make witty remarks
QUIPPER	*n* pl. -S one that quips
QUIPPISH	*adj* witty
QUIPPU	*n* pl. -S quipu
QUIPSTER	*n* pl. -S one that quips
QUIPU	*n* pl. -S an ancient calculating device
QUIRE	*v* QUIRED, QUIRING, QUIRES to arrange sheets of paper in sets of twenty-four
QUIRK	*v* -ED, -ING, -S to twist
QUIRKISH	*adj* quirky
QUIRKY	*adj* QUIRKIER, QUIRKIEST peculiar **QUIRKILY** *adv*
QUIRT	*v* -ED, -ING, -S to strike with a riding whip
QUISLING	*n* pl. -S a traitor who aids the invaders of his country
QUIT	*v* QUITTED, QUITTING, QUITS to end one's engagement in or occupation with
QUITCH	*n* pl. -ES a perennial grass
QUITE	*adv* to the fullest extent
QUITRENT	*n* pl. -S a fixed rent due from a socage tenant
QUITTED	past tense of quit
QUITTER	*n* pl. -S one that quits
QUITTING	present participle of quit
QUITTOR	*n* pl. -S an inflammation of an animal's hoof
QUIVER	*v* -ED, -ING, -S to shake with a slight but rapid motion
QUIVERER	*n* pl. -S one that quivers
QUIVERY	*adj* marked by quivering
QUIXOTE	*n* pl. -S a quixotic person
QUIXOTIC	*adj* extremely idealistic
QUIXOTRY	*n* pl. -TRIES quixotic action or thought
QUIZ	*v* QUIZZED, QUIZZING, QUIZZES to test the knowledge of by asking questions
QUIZZER	*n* pl. -S one that quizzes
QUOD	*n* pl. -S a prison
QUOHOG	*n* pl. -S quahog
QUOIN	*v* -ED, -ING, -S to secure with a type of wedge
QUOIT	*v* -ED, -ING, -S to play a throwing game similar to ringtoss
QUOKKA	*n* pl. -S a short-tailed wallaby
QUOMODO	*n* pl. -DOS a means or manner
QUONDAM	*adj* that once was
QUORUM	*n* pl. -S a particularly chosen group
QUOTA	*n* pl. -S a proportional part or share
QUOTE	*v* QUOTED, QUOTING, QUOTES to repeat the words of **QUOTABLE** *adj* **QUOTABLY** *adv*
QUOTER	*n* pl. -S one that quotes
QUOTH	*v* said — QUOTH is the only accepted form of this verb; it cannot be conjugated
QUOTHA	*interj* — used to express surprise or sarcasm
QUOTIENT	*n* pl. -S the number resulting from the division of one number by another
QUOTING	present participle of quote
QURSH	*n* pl. -ES a monetary unit of Saudi Arabia
QURUSH	*n* pl. -ES qursh
QWERTY	*n* pl. -TYS a standard keyboard

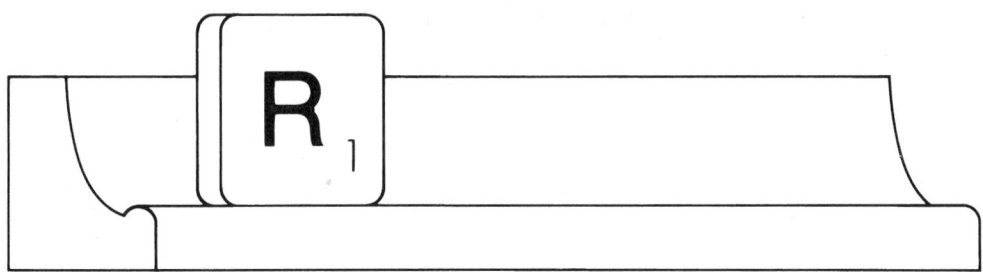

RABAT   *n* pl. -S a dickey attached to a clerical collar

RABATO   *n* pl. -TOS a wide, lace-edged collar

RABBET   *v* -ED, -ING, -S to cut a groove in

RABBI   *n* pl. -S or -ES a Jewish spiritual leader

RABBIN   *n* pl. -S rabbi

RABBINIC   *adj* pertaining to rabbis

RABBIT   *v* -ED, -ING, -S to hunt rabbits (rodent-like mammals)

RABBITER   *n* pl. -S one that rabbits

RABBITRY   *n* pl. -RIES a place where rabbits are kept

RABBITY   *adj* resembling a rabbit

RABBLE   *v* -BLED, -BLING, -BLES to mob

RABBLER   *n* pl. -S an iron bar used in puddling

RABBONI   *n* pl. -S master; teacher — used as a Jewish title of respect

RABIC   *adj* pertaining to rabies

RABID   *adj* affected with rabies **RABIDLY** *adv*

RABIDITY   *n* pl. -TIES the state of being rabid

RABIES   *n* pl. RABIES an infectious virus disease **RABIETIC** *adj*

RACCOON   *n* pl. -S a carnivorous mammal

RACE   *v* RACED, RACING, RACES to compete in a contest of speed

RACEMATE   *n* pl. -S a chemical salt

RACEME   *n* pl. -S a mode of arrangement of flowers along an axis **RACEMED** *adj*

RACEMIC   *adj* pertaining to a racemate

RACEMISM   *n* pl. -S the state of being racemic

RACEMIZE   *v* -MIZED, -MIZING, -MIZES to convert into a racemic compound

RACEMOID   *adj* pertaining to a raceme

RACEMOSE   *adj* having the form of a raceme

RACEMOUS   *adj* racemose

RACER   *n* pl. -S one that races

RACEWAY   *n* pl. -WAYS a channel for conducting water

RACHET   *n* pl. -S ratchet

RACHILLA   *n* pl. -LAE the central stalk of a grass spikelet

RACHIS   *n* pl. -CHISES or -CHIDES the spinal column **RACHIAL** *adj*

RACHITIS   *n* pl. -TIDES rickets **RACHITIC** *adj*

RACIAL   *adj* pertaining to an ethnic group **RACIALLY** *adv*

RACIER   comparative of racy

RACIEST   superlative of racy

RACILY   *adv* in a racy manner

RACINESS   *n* pl. -ES the quality of being racy

RACING   *n* pl. -S the sport of engaging in contests of speed

RACISM   *n* pl. -S a doctrine of racial superiority

RACIST   *n* pl. -S an advocate of racism

RACK   *v* -ED, -ING, -S to place in a type of framework

RACKER   *n* pl. -S one that racks

RACKET   *v* -ED, -ING, -S to make a loud noise

RACKETY   *adj* -ETIER, -ETIEST noisy

RACKFUL   *n* pl. -S as much as a rack can hold

RACKLE   *adj* impetuous; rash

RACKWORK   *n* pl. -S a type of mechanism

RACLETTE   *n* pl. -S a cheese dish

RACON   *n* pl. -S a type of radar transmitter

RACOON   *n* pl. -S raccoon

RACQUET *n* pl. -S a lightweight implement used in various ball games

RACY *adj* RACIER, RACIEST bordering on impropriety or indecency

RAD *v* RADDED, RADDING, RADS to fear

RADAR *n* pl. -S an electronic locating device

RADDLE *v* -DLED, -DLING, -DLES to weave together

RADIABLE *adj* capable of radiating

RADIAL *n* pl. -S a part diverging from a center

RADIALE *n* pl. -LIA a bone of the carpus

RADIALLY *adv* in a diverging manner

RADIAN *n* pl. -S a unit of angular measure

RADIANCE *n* pl. -S brightness

RADIANCY *n* pl. -CIES radiance

RADIANT *n* pl. -S a point from which rays are emitted

RADIATE *v* -ATED, -ATING, -ATES to emit rays

RADIATOR *n* pl. -S a heating device

RADICAL *n* pl. -S a group of atoms that acts as a unit in chemical compounds

RADICAND *n* pl. -S a quantity in mathematics

RADICATE *v* -CATED, -CATING, -CATES to cause to take root

RADICEL *n* pl. -S a rootlet

RADICES a pl. of radix

RADICLE *n* pl. -S a part of a plant embryo

RADII a pl. of radius

RADIO *v* -ED, -ING, -S to transmit by radio (an apparatus for wireless communication)

RADIOMAN *n* pl. -MEN a radio operator or technician

RADISH *n* pl. -ES a pungent, edible root

RADIUM *n* pl. -S a radioactive element

RADIUS *n* pl. -DII or -DIUSES a straight line from the center of a circle to the circumference

RADIX *n* pl. -DICES or -DIXES the root of a plant

RADOME *n* pl. -S a domelike device used to shelter a radar antenna

RADON *n* pl. -S a radioactive element

RADULA *n* pl. -LAE or -LAS a tonguelike organ of mollusks **RADULAR** *adj*

RADWASTE *n* pl. -S radioactive waste

RAFF *n* pl. -S riffraff

RAFFIA *n* pl. -S a palm tree

RAFFISH *adj* tawdry

RAFFLE *v* -FLED, -FLING, -FLES to dispose of by a form of lottery

RAFFLER *n* pl. -S one that raffles

RAFT *v* -ED, -ING, -S to transport on a raft (a type of buoyant structure)

RAFTER *n* pl. -S a supporting beam

RAFTERED *adj* furnished with rafters

RAFTSMAN *n* pl. -MEN one who manages a raft

RAG *v* RAGGED, RAGGING, RAGS to scold

RAGA *n* pl. -S a Hindu musical form

RAGBAG *n* pl. -S a bag for storing scraps of cloth

RAGE *v* RAGED, RAGING, RAGES to act or speak with violent anger

RAGEE *n* pl. -S ragi

RAGGED *adj* -GEDER, -GEDEST tattered **RAGGEDLY** *adv*

RAGGEDY *adj* somewhat ragged

RAGGEE *n* pl. -S ragi

RAGGIES pl. of raggy

RAGGING present participle of rag

RAGGLE *n* pl. -S a groove cut in masonry

RAGGY *n* pl. -GIES ragi

RAGI *n* pl. -S an East Indian cereal grass

RAGING present participle of rage

RAGINGLY *adv* in a furious manner

RAGLAN *n* pl. -S a type of overcoat

RAGMAN *n* pl. -MEN one who gathers and sells scraps of cloth

RAGOUT *v* -ED, -ING, -S to make into a highly seasoned stew

RAGTAG *n* pl. -S riffraff

RAGTIME *n* pl. -S a style of American dance music

RAGTOP *n* pl. -S a convertible automobile

RAGWEED *n* pl. -S a weedy herb

RAGWORT *n* pl. -S a flowering plant

RAH *interj* — used to cheer on a team or player

RAIA	*n* pl. -S rayah	**RAISONNE**	*adj* arranged systematically
RAID	*v* -ED, -ING, -S to make a sudden assault on	**RAJ**	*n* pl. -ES dominion; sovereignty
RAIDER	*n* pl. -S one that raids	**RAJA**	*n* pl. -S rajah
RAIL	*v* -ED, -ING, -S to scold in abusive or insolent language	**RAJAH**	*n* pl. -S a king or prince in India
RAILBIRD	*n* pl. -S a racing enthusiast	**RAKE**	*v* RAKED, RAKING, RAKES to gather with a toothed implement
RAILBUS	*n* pl. -BUSES or -BUSSES a passenger car equipped for operation on rails	**RAKEE**	*n* pl. -S raki
		RAKEHELL	*n* pl. -S a man lacking in moral restraint
RAILCAR	*n* pl. -S a railroad car	**RAKEOFF**	*n* pl. -S a share of profits
RAILER	*n* pl. -S one that rails	**RAKER**	*n* pl. -S one that rakes
RAILHEAD	*n* pl. -S the end of a railroad line	**RAKI**	*n* pl. -S a Turkish liqueur
RAILING	*n* pl. -S a fence-like barrier	**RAKING**	present participle of rake
RAILLERY	*n* pl. -LERIES good-natured teasing	**RAKISH**	*adj* dapper **RAKISHLY** *adv*
RAILROAD	*v* -ED, -ING, -S to transport by railroad (a type of road on which locomotives are run)	**RALE**	*n* pl. -S an abnormal respiratory sound
		RALLIED	past tense of rally
RAILWAY	*n* pl. -WAYS a railroad	**RALLIER**	*n* pl. -S one that rallies
RAIMENT	*n* pl. -S clothing	**RALLINE**	*adj* pertaining to a family of marsh birds
RAIN	*v* -ED, -ING, -S to fall like rain (drops of water condensed from atmospheric vapor)	**RALLY**	*v* -LIED, -LYING, -LIES to call together for a common purpose
RAINBAND	*n* pl. -S a dark band in the solar spectrum	**RALLYE**	*n* pl. -S a type of automobile race
		RALLYING	*n* pl. -S the sport of driving in rallyes
RAINBIRD	*n* pl. -S a type of bird	**RALLYIST**	*n* pl. -S a participant in a rallye
RAINBOW	*n* pl. -S an arc of spectral colors formed in the sky	**RALPH**	*v* -ED, -ING, -S to vomit
RAINCOAT	*n* pl. -S a waterproof coat	**RAM**	*v* RAMMED, RAMMING, RAMS to strike with great force
RAINDROP	*n* pl. -S a drop of rain	**RAMATE**	*adj* having branches
RAINFALL	*n* pl. -S a fall of rain	**RAMBLE**	*v* -BLED, -BLING, -BLES to wander
RAINIER	comparative of rainy		
RAINIEST	superlative of rainy	**RAMBLER**	*n* pl. -S one that rambles
RAINILY	*adv* in a rainy manner	**RAMBUTAN**	*n* pl. -S the edible fruit of a Malayan tree
RAINLESS	*adj* having no rain		
RAINOUT	*n* pl. -S atomic fallout occurring in precipitation	**RAMEE**	*n* pl. -S ramie
		RAMEKIN	*n* pl. -S a cheese dish
RAINWASH	*v* -ED, -ING, -ES to wash material downhill by rain	**RAMENTUM**	*n* pl. -TA a scale formed on the surface of leaves
RAINWEAR	*n* pl. -S waterproof clothing	**RAMEQUIN**	*n* pl. -S ramekin
RAINY	*adj* RAINIER, RAINIEST marked by rain	**RAMET**	*n* pl. -S an independent member of a clone
RAISE	*v* RAISED, RAISING, RAISES to move to a higher position **RAISABLE** *adj*	**RAMI**	pl. of ramus
		RAMIE	*n* pl. -S an Asian shrub
RAISER	*n* pl. -S one that raises	**RAMIFORM**	*adj* shaped like a branch
RAISIN	*n* pl. -S a dried grape **RAISINY** *adj*	**RAMIFY**	*v* -FIED, -FYING, -FIES to divide into branches
RAISING	*n* pl. -S an elevation	**RAMILIE**	*n* pl. -S ramillie

RAMILLIE	*n* pl. -S a type of wig
RAMJET	*n* pl. -S a type of engine
RAMMED	past tense of ram
RAMMER	*n* pl. -S one that rams
RAMMIER	comparative of rammy
RAMMIEST	superlative of rammy
RAMMING	present participle of ram
RAMMISH	*adj* resembling a ram (a male sheep)
RAMMY	*adj* -MIER, -MIEST rammish
RAMOSE	*adj* having many branches **RAMOSELY** *adv*
RAMOSITY	*n* pl. -TIES the state of being ramose
RAMOUS	*adj* ramose
RAMP	*v* -ED, -ING, -S to rise or stand on the hind legs
RAMPAGE	*v* -PAGED, -PAGING, -PAGES to move about wildly or violently
RAMPAGER	*n* pl. -S one that rampages
RAMPANCY	*n* pl. -CIES the state of being rampant
RAMPANT	*adj* unrestrained
RAMPART	*v* -ED, -ING, -S to furnish with a fortifying embankment
RAMPIKE	*n* pl. -S a standing dead tree
RAMPION	*n* pl. -S a European plant
RAMPOLE	*n* pl. -S rampike
RAMROD	*v* -RODDED, -RODDING, -RODS to supervise
RAMSHORN	*n* pl. -S a snail used as an aquarium scavenger
RAMSON	*n* pl. -S a broad-leaved garlic
RAMTIL	*n* pl. -S a tropical plant
RAMULOSE	*adj* having many small branches
RAMULOUS	*adj* ramulose
RAMUS	*n* pl. -MI a branch-like part of a structure
RAN	past tense of run and rin
RANCE	*n* pl. -S a variety of marble
RANCH	*v* -ED, -ING, -ES to work on a ranch (an establishment for raising livestock)
RANCHER	*n* pl. -S one that owns or works on a ranch
RANCHERO	*n* pl. -ROS a rancher
RANCHMAN	*n* pl. -MEN a rancher
RANCHO	*n* pl. -CHOS a ranch

RANCID	*adj* having an unpleasant odor or taste **RANCIDLY** *adv*
RANCOR	*n* pl. -S bitter and vindictive enmity **RANCORED** *adj*
RANCOUR	*n* pl. -S rancor
RAND	*n* pl. -S a strip of leather at the heel of a shoe
RANDAN	*n* pl. -S a boat rowed by three persons
RANDIER	comparative of randy
RANDIES	pl. of randy
RANDIEST	superlative of randy
RANDOM	*n* pl. -S a haphazard course
RANDOMLY	*adv* in a haphazard manner
RANDY	*adj* -DIER, -DIEST lustful
RANDY	*n* pl. RANDIES a rude person
RANEE	*n* pl. -S rani
RANG	past tense of ring
RANGE	*v* RANGED, RANGING, RANGES to place in a particular order
RANGER	*n* pl. -S an officer supervising the care of a forest
RANGY	*adj* RANGIER, RANGIEST tall and slender
RANI	*n* pl. -S the wife of a rajah
RANID	*n* pl. -S any of a large family of frogs
RANK	*v* -ED, -ING, -S to determine the relative position of
RANK	*adj* RANKER, RANKEST strong and disagreeable in odor or taste
RANKER	*n* pl. -S an enlisted soldier
RANKING	*n* pl. -S a listing of ranked individuals
RANKISH	*adj* somewhat rank
RANKLE	*v* -KLED, -KLING, -KLES to cause irritation or resentment in
RANKLY	*adv* in a rank manner
RANKNESS	*n* pl. -ES the state of being rank
RANPIKE	*n* pl. -S rampike
RANSACK	*v* -ED, -ING, -S to search thoroughly
RANSOM	*v* -ED, -ING, -S to obtain the release of by paying a demanded price
RANSOMER	*n* pl. -S one that ransoms
RANT	*v* -ED, -ING, -S to speak in a loud or vehement manner
RANTER	*n* pl. -S one that rants

RANULA	*n* pl. -S a cyst formed under the tongue
RAP	*v* RAPPED, RAPPING, RAPS to strike sharply
RAPACITY	*n* pl. -TIES the quality of being ravenous
RAPE	*v* RAPED, RAPING, RAPES to force to submit to sexual intercourse
RAPER	*n* pl. -S a rapist
RAPESEED	*n* pl. -S the seed of a European herb
RAPHE	*n* pl. RAPHAE or RAPHES a seamlike ridge between two halves of an organ or part
RAPHIA	*n* pl. -S raffia
RAPHIDE	*n* pl. -S a needle-shaped crystal occurring in plant cells
RAPHIS	*n* pl. -PHIDES raphide
RAPID	*adj* -IDER, -IDEST fast-moving **RAPIDLY** *adv*
RAPID	*n* pl. -S a fast-moving part of a river
RAPIDITY	*n* pl. -TIES swiftness
RAPIER	*n* pl. -S a long, slender sword **RAPIERED** *adj*
RAPINE	*n* pl. -S the taking of property by force
RAPING	present participle of rape
RAPINI	*n/pl* rappini
RAPIST	*n* pl. -S one who rapes
RAPPAREE	*n* pl. -S a plunderer
RAPPED	past tense of rap
RAPPEE	*n* pl. -S a strong snuff
RAPPEL	*v* -PELED, -PELING, -PELS or -PELLED, -PELLING, -PELS to descend from a steep height by means of a rope
RAPPEN	*n* pl. RAPPEN a monetary unit of Switzerland
RAPPER	*n* pl. -S one that raps
RAPPING	present participle of rap
RAPPINI	*n/pl* immature turnip plants
RAPPORT	*n* pl. -S a harmonious relationship
RAPT	*adj* deeply engrossed **RAPTLY** *adv*
RAPTNESS	*n* pl. -ES the state of being rapt
RAPTOR	*n* pl. -S a bird of prey
RAPTURE	*v* -TURED, -TURING, -TURES to fill with great joy
RARE	*adj* RARER, RAREST occurring infrequently
RARE	*v* RARED, RARING, RARES to be enthusiastic
RAREBIT	*n* pl. -S a cheese dish
RAREFIER	*n* pl. -S one that rarefies
RAREFY	*v* -EFIED, -EFYING, -EFIES to make less dense
RARELY	*adv* not often
RARENESS	*n* pl. -ES the quality of being rare
RARER	comparative of rare
RARERIPE	*n* pl. -S a fruit that ripens early
RAREST	superlative of rare
RARIFY	*v* -FIED, -FYING, -FIES to rarefy
RARING	*adj* full of enthusiasm
RARITY	*n* pl. -TIES rareness
RAS	*n* pl. -ES an Ethiopian prince
RASBORA	*n* pl. -S a tropical fish
RASCAL	*n* pl. -S an unscrupulous or dishonest person
RASCALLY	*adj* characteristic of a rascal
RASE	*v* RASED, RASING, RASES to raze
RASER	*n* pl. -S one that rases
RASH	*adj* RASHER, RASHEST acting without due caution or forethought
RASH	*n* pl. -ES a skin eruption **RASHLIKE** *adj*
RASHER	*n* pl. -S a thin slice of meat
RASHLY	*adv* in a rash manner
RASHNESS	*n* pl. -ES the state of being rash
RASING	present participle of rase
RASORIAL	*adj* habitually scratching the ground for food
RASP	*v* -ED, -ING, -S to rub with something rough
RASPER	*n* pl. -S one that rasps
RASPISH	*adj* irritable
RASPY	*adj* RASPIER, RASPIEST rough
RASSLE	*v* -SLED, -SLING, -SLES to wrestle
RASTER	*n* pl. -S the area reproducing images on the picture tube of a television set
RASURE	*n* pl. -S erasure
RAT	*v* RATTED, RATTING, RATS to hunt rats (long-tailed rodents)

RATABLE	*adj* capable of being rated **RATABLY** *adv*
RATAFEE	*n* pl. -S ratafia
RATAFIA	*n* pl. -S an almond-flavored liqueur
RATAL	*n* pl. -S an amount on which rates are assessed
RATAN	*n* pl. -S rattan
RATANY	*n* pl. -NIES rhatany
RATAPLAN	*v* -PLANNED, -PLANNING, -PLANS to make a rapidly repeating sound
RATATAT	*n* pl. -S a quick, sharp rapping sound
RATBAG	*n* pl. -S an eccentric or disagreeable person
RATCH	*n* pl. -ES a ratchet
RATCHET	*v* -ED, -ING, -S to increase or decrease by small amounts
RATE	*v* RATED, RATING, RATES to estimate the value of
RATEABLE	*adj* ratable **RATEABLY** *adv*
RATEL	*n* pl. -S a carnivorous mammal
RATER	*n* pl. -S one that rates
RATFINK	*n* pl. -S a contemptible person
RATFISH	*n* pl. -ES a marine fish
RATH	*adj* rathe
RATHE	*adj* appearing or ripening early
RATHER	*adv* preferably
RATHOLE	*n* pl. -S a hole made by a rat
RATICIDE	*n* pl. -S a substance for killing rats
RATIFIER	*n* pl. -S one that ratifies
RATIFY	*v* -FIED, -FYING, -FIES to approve and sanction formally
RATINE	*n* pl. -S a heavy fabric woven loosely
RATING	*n* pl. -S relative estimate or evaluation
RATIO	*n* pl. -TIOS a proportional relationship
RATION	*v* -ED, -ING, -S to distribute in fixed portions
RATIONAL	*n* pl. -S a number that can be expressed as a quotient of integers
RATITE	*n* pl. -S a flightless bird
RATLIKE	*adj* resembling a rat
RATLIN	*n* pl. -S ratline
RATLINE	*n* pl. -S one of the ropes forming the steps of a ship's rope ladder
RATO	*n* pl. -TOS a rocket-assisted airplane takeoff
RATOON	*v* -ED, -ING, -S to sprout from a root planted the previous year
RATOONER	*n* pl. -S a plant that ratoons
RATSBANE	*n* pl. -S rat poison
RATTAIL	*n* pl. -S a marine fish
RATTAN	*n* pl. -S a palm tree
RATTED	past tense of rat
RATTEEN	*n* pl. -S a coarse woolen fabric
RATTEN	*v* -ED, -ING, -S to harass
RATTENER	*n* pl. -S one that rattens
RATTER	*n* pl. -S an animal used for catching rats
RATTIER	comparative of ratty
RATTIEST	superlative of ratty
RATTING	present participle of rat
RATTISH	*adj* ratlike
RATTLE	*v* -TLED, -TLING, -TLES to make a quick succession of short, sharp sounds
RATTLER	*n* pl. -S one that rattles
RATTLING	*n* pl. -S ratline
RATTLY	*adj* tending to rattle
RATTON	*n* pl. -S a rat
RATTOON	*v* -ED, -ING, -S to ratoon
RATTRAP	*n* pl. -S a trap for catching rats
RATTY	*adj* -TIER, -TIEST infested with rats
RAUCITY	*n* pl. -TIES the state of being raucous
RAUCOUS	*adj* loud and unruly
RAUNCH	*n* pl. -ES vulgarity
RAUNCHY	*adj* -CHIER, -CHIEST slovenly
RAVAGE	*v* -AGED, -AGING, -AGES to destroy
RAVAGER	*n* pl. -S one that ravages
RAVE	*v* RAVED, RAVING, RAVES to speak irrationally or incoherently
RAVEL	*v* -ELED, -ELING, -ELS or -ELLED, -ELLING, -ELS to separate the threads of
RAVELER	*n* pl. -S one that ravels
RAVELIN	*n* pl. -S a type of fortification
RAVELING	*n* pl. -S a loose thread
RAVELLED	a past tense of ravel

RAVELLER	*n* pl. -S raveler	**RAZING**	present participle of raze
RAVELLING	*n* pl. -S raveling	**RAZOR**	*v* -ED, -ING, -S to shave or cut with a sharp-edged instrument
RAVELLY	*adj* tangled		
RAVEN	*v* -ED, -ING, -S to eat in a ravenous manner	**RAZZ**	*v* -ED, -ING, -ES to deride
		RE	*n* pl. -S the second tone of the diatonic musical scale
RAVENER	*n* pl. -S one that ravens		
RAVENING	*n* pl. -S rapacity		
RAVENOUS	*adj* extremely hungry		
RAVER	*n* pl. -S one that raves		
RAVIGOTE	*n* pl. -S a spiced vinegar sauce		

Following is a list of self-explanatory verbs containing the prefix RE- (again):

RAVIN	*v* -ED, -ING, -S to raven
RAVINE	*n* pl. -S a narrow, steep-sided valley
RAVING	*n* pl. -S irrational, incoherent speech
RAVINGLY	*adv* in a delirious manner
RAVIOLI	*n* pl. -S an Italian pasta dish
RAVISH	*v* -ED, -ING, -ES to seize and carry off by force
RAVISHER	*n* pl. -S one that ravishes
RAW	*adj* RAWER, RAWEST uncooked
RAW	*n* pl. -S a sore or irritated spot
RAWBONED	*adj* having little flesh
RAWHIDE	*v* -HIDED, -HIDING, -HIDES to beat with a type of whip
RAWIN	*n* pl. -S a wind measurement made by tracking a balloon with radar
RAWISH	*adj* somewhat raw
RAWLY	*adv* in a raw manner
RAWNESS	*n* pl. -ES the state of being raw
RAX	*v* -ED, -ING, -ES to stretch out
RAY	*v* -ED, -ING, -S to emit rays (narrow beams of light)
RAYA	*n* pl. -S rayah
RAYAH	*n* pl. -S a non-Muslim inhabitant of Turkey
RAYGRASS	*n* pl. -ES ryegrass
RAYLESS	*adj* having no rays
RAYLIKE	*adj* resembling a narrow beam of light
RAYON	*n* pl. -S a synthetic fiber
RAZE	*v* RAZED, RAZING, RAZES to tear down or demolish
RAZEE	*v* -ZEED, -ZEEING, -ZEES to make lower by removing the upper deck, as a ship
RAZER	*n* pl. -S one that razes

REABSORB	*v* -ED, -ING, -S
REACCEDE	*v* -CEDED, -CEDING, -CEDES
REACCENT	*v* -ED, -ING, -S
REACCEPT	*v* -ED, -ING, -S
REACCUSE	*v* -CUSED, -CUSING, -CUSES
READAPT	*v* -ED, -ING, -S
READD	*v* -ED, -ING, -S
READDICT	*v* -ED, -ING, -S
READJUST	*v* -ED, -ING, -S
READMIT	*v* -MITTED, -MITTING, -MITS
READOPT	*v* -ED, -ING, -S
READORN	*v* -ED, -ING, -S
REAFFIRM	*v* -ED, -ING, -S
REAFFIX	*v* -ED, -ING, -ES
REALIGN	*v* -ED, -ING, -S
REALLOT	*v* -LOTTED, -LOTTING, -LOTS
REALTER	*v* -ED, -ING, -S
REANNEX	*v* -ED, -ING, -ES
REANOINT	*v* -ED, -ING, -S
REAPPEAR	*v* -ED, -ING, -S
REAPPLY	*v* -PLIED, -PLYING, -PLIES
REARGUE	*v* -GUED, -GUING, -GUES
REARM	*v* -ED, -ING, -S
REAROUSE	*v* -AROUSED, -AROUSING, -AROUSES
REARREST	*v* -ED, -ING, -S
REASCEND	*v* -ED, -ING, -S
REASSAIL	*v* -ED, -ING, -S
REASSERT	*v* -ED, -ING, -S
REASSESS	*v* -ED, -ING, -ES
REASSIGN	*v* -ED, -ING, -S
REASSORT	*v* -ED, -ING, -S
REASSUME	*v* -SUMED, -SUMING, -SUMES
REASSURE	*v* -SURED, -SURING, -SURES
REATTACH	*v* -ED, -ING, -ES
REATTACK	*v* -ED, -ING, -S
REATTAIN	*v* -ED, -ING, -S
REAVAIL	*v* -ED, -ING, -S
REAVOW	*v* -ED, -ING, -S

REAWAKE	v -AWAKED or -AWOKE, -AWOKEN, -AWAKING, -AWAKES
REAWAKEN	v -ED, -ING, -S
REBAIT	v -ED, -ING, -S
REBEGIN	v -GAN, -GUN, -GINNING, -GINS
REBID	v -BID, -BIDDEN, -BIDDING, -BIDS
REBILL	v -ED, -ING, -S
REBIND	v -BOUND, -BINDING, -BINDS
REBLEND	v -ED, -ING, -S
REBLOOM	v -ED, -ING, -S
REBOARD	v -ED, -ING, -S
REBODY	v -BODIED, -BODYING, -BODIES
REBOIL	v -ED, -ING, -S
REBOOK	v -ED, -ING, -S
REBOOT	v -ED, -ING, -S
REBORE	v -BORED, -BORING, -BORES
REBOTTLE	v -TLED, -TLING, -TLES
REBOUGHT	past tense of rebuy
REBOUND	past tense of rebind
REBREED	v -BRED, -BREEDING, -BREEDS
REBUILD	v -BUILT or -BUILDED, -BUILDING, -BUILDS
REBURY	v -BURIED, -BURYING, -BURIES
REBUTTON	v -ED, -ING, -S
REBUY	v -BOUGHT, -BUYING, -BUYS
RECANE	v -CANED, -CANING, -CANES
RECARRY	v -RIED, -RYING, -RIES
RECAST	v -CAST, -CASTING, -CASTS
RECHANGE	v -CHANGED, -CHANGING, -CHANGES
RECHARGE	v -CHARGED, -CHARGING, -CHARGES
RECHART	v -ED, -ING, -S
RECHECK	v -ED, -ING, -S
RECHEW	v -ED, -ING, -S
RECHOOSE	v -CHOSE, -CHOSEN, -CHOOSING, -CHOOSES
RECIRCLE	v -CLED, -CLING, -CLES
RECLAD	a past tense of reclothe
RECLASP	v -ED, -ING, -S
RECLEAN	v -ED, -ING, -S
RECLOTHE	v -CLOTHED or -CLAD, -CLOTHING, -CLOTHES
RECOAL	v -ED, -ING, -S
RECOCK	v -ED, -ING, -S
RECODE	v -CODED, -CODING, -CODES
RECODIFY	v -FIED, -FYING, -FIES
RECOIN	v -ED, -ING, -S
RECOLOR	v -ED, -ING, -S
RECOMB	v -ED, -ING, -S
RECOMMIT	v -MITTED, -MITTING, -MITS
RECOOK	v -ED, -ING, -S
RECOPY	v -COPIED, -COPYING, -COPIES
RECORK	v -ED, -ING, -S

RECOUPLE	v -PLED, -PLING, -PLES
RECRATE	v -CRATED, -CRATING, -CRATES
RECROSS	v -ED, -ING, -ES
RECROWN	v -ED, -ING, -S
RECUT	v -CUT, -CUTTING, -CUTS
REDAMAGE	v -AGED, -AGING, -AGES
REDATE	v -DATED, -DATING, -DATES
REDECIDE	v -CIDED, -CIDING, -CIDES
REDEFEAT	v -ED, -ING, -S
REDEFECT	v -ED, -ING, -S
REDEFINE	v -FINED, -FINING, -FINES
REDEFY	v -FIED, -FYING, -FIES
REDEMAND	v -ED, -ING, -S
REDENY	v -NIED, -NYING, -NIES
REDEPLOY	v -ED, -ING, -S
REDESIGN	v -ED, -ING, -S
REDIAL	v -DIALED, -DIALING, -DIALS or -DIALLED, -DIALLING, -DIALS
REDID	past tense of redo
REDIGEST	v -ED, -ING, -S
REDIP	v -DIPPED or -DIPT, -DIPPING, -DIPS
REDIVIDE	v -VIDED, -VIDING, -VIDES
REDO	v -DID, -DONE, -DOING, -DOES
REDOCK	v -ED, -ING, -S
REDON	v -DONNED, -DONNING, -DONS
REDONE	past participle of redo
REDRAW	v -DREW, -DRAWN, -DRAWING, -DRAWS
REDREAM	v -DREAMED or -DREAMT, -DREAMING, -DREAMS
REDRIED	past tense of redry
REDRIES	present 3d person sing. of redry
REDRILL	v -ED, -ING, -S
REDRIVE	v -DROVE, -DRIVEN, -DRIVING, -DRIVES
REDRY	v -DRIED, -DRYING, -DRIES
REDUB	v -DUBBED, -DUBBING, -DUBS
REDYE	v -DYED, -DYEING, -DYES
REEARN	v -ED, -ING, -S
REECHO	v -ED, -ING, -ES
REEDIT	v -ED, -ING, -S
REEJECT	v -ED, -ING, -S
REELECT	v -ED, -ING, -S
REEMBARK	v -ED, -ING, -S
REEMBODY	v -BODIED, -BODYING, -BODIES
REEMERGE	v -EMERGED, -EMERGING, -EMERGES
REEMIT	v -EMITTED, -EMITTING, -EMITS
REEMPLOY	v -ED, -ING, -S
REENACT	v -ED, -ING, -S
REENDOW	v -ED, -ING, -S
REENGAGE	v -GAGED, -GAGING, -GAGES
REENJOY	v -ED, -ING, -S
REENLIST	v -ED, -ING, -S

REENROLL	v -ED, -ING, -S
REENTER	v -ED, -ING, -S
REEQUIP	v -EQUIPPED, -EQUIPPING, -EQUIPS
REERECT	v -ED, -ING, -S
REEVOKE	v -EVOKED, -EVOKING, -EVOKES
REEXPEL	v -PELLED, -PELLING, -PELS
REEXPORT	v -ED, -ING, -S
REEXPOSE	v -POSED, -POSING, -POSES
REFALL	v -FELL, -FALLEN, -FALLING, -FALLS
REFASTEN	v -ED, -ING, -S
REFEED	v -FED, -FEEDING, -FEEDS
REFEEL	v -FELT, -FEELING, -FEELS
REFELL	past tense of refall
REFENCE	v -FENCED, -FENCING, -FENCES
REFIGHT	v -FOUGHT, -FIGHTING, -FIGHTS
REFIGURE	v -URED, -URING, -URES
REFILE	v -FILED, -FILING, -FILES
REFILL	v -ED, -ING, -S
REFILM	v -ED, -ING, -S
REFILTER	v -ED, -ING, -S
REFIND	v -FOUND, -FINDING, -FINDS
REFIRE	v -FIRED, -FIRING, -FIRES
REFIX	v -ED, -ING, -ES
REFLEW	past tense of refly
REFLIES	present 3d person sing. of refly
REFLOAT	v -ED, -ING, -S
REFLOOD	v -ED, -ING, -S
REFLOW	v -ED, -ING, -S
REFLOWER	v -ED, -ING, -S
REFLY	v -FLEW, -FLOWN, -FLYING, -FLIES
REFOCUS	v -CUSED, -CUSING, -CUSES or -CUSSED, -CUSSING, -CUSSES
REFOLD	v -ED, -ING, -S
REFORGE	v -FORGED, -FORGING, -FORGES
REFORMAT	v -MATTED, -MATTING, -MATS
REFOUGHT	past tense of refight
REFOUND	v -ED, -ING, -S
REFRAME	v -FRAMED, -FRAMING, -FRAMES
REFREEZE	v -FROZE, -FROZEN, -FREEZING, -FREEZES
REFRONT	v -ED, -ING, -S
REFRY	v -FRIED, -FRYING, -FRIES
REFUEL	v -ELED, -ELING, -ELS or -ELLED, -ELLING, -ELS
REGAIN	v -ED, -ING, -S
REGATHER	v -ED, -ING, -S
REGAUGE	v -GAUGED, -GAUGING, -GAUGES
REGAVE	past tense of regive
REGEAR	v -ED, -ING, -S
REGILD	v -GILDED or -GILT, -GILDING, -GILDS
REGIVE	v -GAVE, -GIVEN, -GIVING, -GIVES
REGLAZE	v -GLAZED, -GLAZING, -GLAZES
REGLOSS	v -ED, -ING, -ES
REGLOW	v -ED, -ING, -S
REGLUE	v -GLUED, -GLUING, -GLUES
REGRADE	v -GRADED, -GRADING, -GRADES
REGRAFT	v -ED, -ING, -S
REGRANT	v -ED, -ING, -S
REGREEN	v -ED, -ING, -S
REGREW	past tense of regrow
REGRIND	v -GROUND, -GRINDING, -GRINDS
REGROOM	v -ED, -ING, -S
REGROOVE	v -GROOVED, -GROOVING, -GROOVES
REGROUND	past tense of regrind
REGROUP	v -ED, -ING, -S
REGROW	v -GREW, -GROWN, -GROWING, -GROWS
REHAMMER	v -ED, -ING, -S
REHANDLE	v -DLED, -DLING, -DLES
REHANG	v -HUNG or -HANGED, -HANGING, -HANGS
REHARDEN	v -ED, -ING, -S
REHASH	v -ED, -ING, -ES
REHEAR	v -HEARD, -HEARING, -HEARS
REHEAT	v -ED, -ING, -S
REHEEL	v -ED, -ING, -S
REHEM	v -HEMMED, -HEMMING, -HEMS
REHINGE	v -HINGED, -HINGING, -HINGES
REHIRE	v -HIRED, -HIRING, -HIRES
REHUNG	a past tense of rehang
REIGNITE	v -NITED, -NITING, -NITES
REIMAGE	v -AGED, -AGING, -AGES
REIMPORT	v -ED, -ING, -S
REIMPOSE	v -POSED, -POSING, -POSES
REINCITE	v -CITED, -CITING, -CITES
REINCUR	v -CURRED, -CURRING, -CURS
REINDEX	v -ED, -ING, -ES
REINDICT	v -ED, -ING, -S
REINDUCE	v -DUCED, -DUCING, -DUCES
REINDUCT	v -ED, -ING, -S
REINFECT	v -ED, -ING, -S
REINFORM	v -ED, -ING, -S
REINFUSE	v -FUSED, -FUSING, -FUSES
REINJECT	v -ED, -ING, -S
REINJURE	v -JURED, -JURING, -JURES
REINK	v -ED, -ING, -S
REINSERT	v -ED, -ING, -S
REINSURE	v -SURED, -SURING, -SURES
REINTER	v -TERRED, -TERRING, -TERS
REINVADE	v -VADED, -VADING, -VADES
REINVENT	v -ED, -ING, -S
REINVEST	v -ED, -ING, -S
REINVITE	v -VITED, -VITING, -VITES
REINVOKE	v -VOKED, -VOKING, -VOKES
REISSUE	v -SUED, -SUING, -SUES

REJACKET	v -ED, -ING, -S	**REOIL**	v -ED, -ING, -S
REJOIN	v -ED, -ING, -S	**REOPEN**	v -ED, -ING, -S
REJUDGE	v -JUDGED, -JUDGING, -JUDGES	**REOPPOSE**	v -POSED, -POSING, -POSES
REJUGGLE	v -GLED, -GLING, -GLES	**REORDAIN**	v -ED, -ING, -S
REKEY	v -ED, -ING, -S	**REORDER**	v -ED, -ING, -S
REKINDLE	v -DLED, -DLING, -DLES	**REORIENT**	v -ED, -ING, -S
REKNIT	v -KNITTED, -KNITTING, -KNITS	**REOUTFIT**	v -FITTED, -FITTING, -FITS
RELABEL	v -BELED, -BELING, -BELS or	**REPACIFY**	v -FIED, -FYING, -FIES
	-BELLED, -BELLING, -BELS	**REPACK**	v -ED, -ING, -S
RELACE	v -LACED, -LACING, -LACES	**REPAINT**	v -ED, -ING, -S
RELAUNCH	v -ED, -ING, -ES	**REPANEL**	v -ELED, -ELING, -ELS or -ELLED,
RELAY	v -LAID, -LAYING, -LAYS		-ELLING, -ELS
RELEARN	v -LEARNED or -LEARNT,	**REPAPER**	v -ED, -ING, -S
	-LEARNING, -LEARNS	**REPARK**	v -ED, -ING, -S
RELEND	v -LENT, -LENDING, -LENDS	**REPASS**	v -ED, -ING, -ES
RELET	v -LET, -LETTING, -LETS	**REPATCH**	v -ED, -ING, -ES
RELETTER	v -ED, -ING, -S	**REPAVE**	v -PAVED, -PAVING, -PAVES
RELIGHT	v -LIGHTED or -LIT, -LIGHTING,	**REPEG**	v -PEGGED, -PEGGING, -PEGS
	-LIGHTS	**REPEOPLE**	v -PLED, -PLING, -PLES
RELINE	v -LINED, -LINING, -LINES	**REPERK**	v -ED, -ING, -S
RELINK	v -ED, -ING, -S	**REPHRASE**	v -PHRASED, -PHRASING,
RELIST	v -ED, -ING, -S		-PHRASES
RELIT	a past tense of relight	**REPIN**	v -PINNED, -PINNING, -PINS
RELOAD	v -ED, -ING, -S	**REPLAN**	v -PLANNED, -PLANNING, -PLANS
RELOAN	v -ED, -ING, -S	**REPLANT**	v -ED, -ING, -S
RELOCK	v -ED, -ING, -S	**REPLATE**	v -PLATED, -PLATING, -PLATES
RELOOK	v -ED, -ING, -S	**REPLAY**	v -ED, -ING, -S
REMAIL	v -ED, -ING, -S	**REPLEAD**	v -PLEADED or -PLED, -PLEADING,
REMAKE	v -MADE, -MAKING, -MAKES		-PLEADS
REMAP	v -MAPPED, -MAPPING, -MAPS	**REPLEDGE**	v -PLEDGED, -PLEDGING,
REMARKET	v -ED, -ING, -S		-PLEDGES
REMARRY	v -RIED, -RYING, -RIES	**REPLOT**	v -PLOTTED, -PLOTTING, -PLOTS
REMASTER	v -ED, -ING, -S	**REPLUMB**	v -ED, -ING, -S
REMATCH	v -ED, -ING, -ES	**REPLUNGE**	v -PLUNGED, -PLUNGING,
REMATE	v -MATED, -MATING, -MATES		-PLUNGES
REMEET	v -MET, -MEETING, -MEETS	**REPOLISH**	v -ED, -ING, -ES
REMELT	v -ED, -ING, -S	**REPOLL**	v -ED, -ING, -S
REMEND	v -ED, -ING, -S	**REPOT**	v -POTTED, -POTTING, -POTS
REMERGE	v -MERGED, -MERGING, -MERGES	**REPOUR**	v -ED, -ING, -S
REMET	past tense of remeet	**REPOWER**	v -ED, -ING, -S
REMIX	v -MIXED or -MIXT, -MIXING, -MIXES	**REPRICE**	v -PRICED, -PRICING, -PRICES
REMODIFY	v -FIED, -FYING, -FIES	**REPRINT**	v -ED, -ING, -S
REMOLD	v -ED, -ING, -S	**REPROBE**	v -PROBED, -PROBING, -PROBES
REMOUNT	v -ED, -ING, -S	**REPUMP**	v -ED, -ING, -S
RENAIL	v -ED, -ING, -S	**REPURIFY**	v -FIED, -FYING, -FIES
RENAME	v -NAMED, -NAMING, -NAMES	**REPURSUE**	v -SUED, -SUING, -SUES
RENEST	v -ED, -ING, -S	**RERACK**	v -ED, -ING, -S
RENOTIFY	v -FIED, -FYING, -FIES	**RERAISE**	v -RAISED, -RAISING, -RAISES
RENUMBER	v -ED, -ING, -S	**REREAD**	v -READ, -READING, -READS
REOBJECT	v -ED, -ING, -S	**RERECORD**	v -ED, -ING, -S
REOBTAIN	v -ED, -ING, -S	**REREMIND**	v -ED, -ING, -S
REOCCUPY	v -PIED, -PYING, -PIES	**REREPEAT**	v -ED, -ING, -S
REOCCUR	v -CURRED, -CURRING, -CURS	**REREVIEW**	v -ED, -ING, -S
		RERIG	v -RIGGED, -RIGGING, -RIGS

RERISE	v -ROSE, -RISEN, -RISING, -RISES	**RESOLD**	past tense of resell
REROLL	v -ED, -ING, -S	**RESOLDER**	v -ED, -ING, -S
REROOF	v -ED, -ING, -S	**RESOLE**	v -SOLED, -SOLING, -SOLES
REROSE	past tense of rerise	**RESOUGHT**	past tense of reseek
REROUTE	v -ROUTED, -ROUTING, -ROUTES	**RESOW**	v -SOWED, -SOWN, -SOWING, -SOWS
RESADDLE	v -DLED, -DLING, -DLES		
RESAID	past tense of resay	**RESPACE**	v -SPACED, -SPACING, -SPACES
RESAIL	v -ED, -ING, -S	**RESPADE**	v -SPADED, -SPADING, -SPADES
RESALUTE	v -LUTED, -LUTING, -LUTES	**RESPEAK**	v -SPOKE, -SPOKEN, -SPEAKING, -SPEAKS
RESAMPLE	v -PLED, -PLING, -PLES		
RESAW	v -SAWED, -SAWN, -SAWING, -SAWS	**RESPELL**	v -SPELLED or -SPELT, -SPELLING, -SPELLS
RESAY	v -SAID, -SAYING, -SAYS	**RESPLICE**	v -SPLICED, -SPLICING, -SPLICES
RESCHOOL	v -ED, -ING, -S	**RESPLIT**	v -SPLIT, -SPLITTING, -SPLITS
RESCORE	v -SCORED, -SCORING, -SCORES	**RESPOKE**	past tense of respeak
RESCREEN	v -ED, -ING, -S	**RESPOKEN**	past participle of respeak
RESCULPT	v -ED, -ING, -S	**RESPOT**	v -SPOTTED, -SPOTTING, -SPOTS
RESEAL	v -ED, -ING, -S	**RESPRANG**	a past tense of respring
RESEASON	v -ED, -ING, -S	**RESPRAY**	v -ED, -ING, -S
RESEAT	v -ED, -ING, -S	**RESPREAD**	v -SPREAD, -SPREADING, -SPREADS
RESECURE	v -CURED, -CURING, -CURES	**RESPRING**	v -SPRANG or -SPRUNG, -SPRINGING, -SPRINGS
RESEE	v -SAW, -SEEN, -SEEING, -SEES		
RESEED	v -ED, -ING, -S	**RESPROUT**	v -ED, -ING, -S
RESEEK	v -SOUGHT, -SEEKING, -SEEKS	**RESTACK**	v -ED, -ING, -S
RESEEN	past participle of resee	**RESTAFF**	v -ED, -ING, -S
RESEIZE	v -SEIZED, -SEIZING, -SEIZES	**RESTAGE**	v -STAGED, -STAGING, -STAGES
RESELL	v -SOLD, -SELLING, -SELLS	**RESTAMP**	v -ED, -ING, -S
RESEND	v -SENT, -SENDING, -SENDS	**RESTART**	v -ED, -ING, -S
RESET	v -SET, -SETTING, -SETS	**RESTATE**	v -STATED, -STATING, -STATES
RESETTLE	v -TLED, -TLING, -TLES	**RESTITCH**	v -ED, -ING, -ES
RESEW	v -SEWED, -SEWN, -SEWING, -SEWS	**RESTOCK**	v -ED, -ING, -S
		RESTOKE	v -STOKED, -STOKING, -STOKES
RESHAPE	v -SHAPED, -SHAPING, -SHAPES	**RESTRESS**	v -ED, -ING, -ES
RESHAVE	v -SHAVED, -SHAVEN, -SHAVING, -SHAVES	**RESTRIKE**	v -STRUCK, -STRICKEN, -STRIKING, -STRIKES
RESHINE	v -SHONE or -SHINED, -SHINING, -SHINES	**RESTRING**	v -STRUNG, -STRINGING, -STRINGS
RESHIP	v -SHIPPED, -SHIPPING, -SHIPS	**RESTRIVE**	v -STROVE, -STRIVEN, -STRIVING, -STRIVES
RESHOE	v -SHOD, -SHOEING, -SHOES		
RESHONE	a past tense of reshine	**RESTRUCK**	past tense of restrike
RESHOOT	v -SHOT, -SHOOTING, -SHOOTS	**RESTRUNG**	past tense of restring
RESHOW	v -SHOWED, -SHOWN, -SHOWING, -SHOWS	**RESTUDY**	v -STUDIED, -STUDYING, -STUDIES
		RESTUFF	v -ED, -ING, -S
RESIFT	v -ED, -ING, -S	**RESTYLE**	v -STYLED, -STYLING, -STYLES
RESIGHT	v -ED, -ING, -S	**RESUBMIT**	v -MITTED, -MITTING, -MITS
RESILVER	v -ED, -ING, -S	**RESUMMON**	v -ED, -ING, -S
RESITE	v -SITED, -SITING, -SITES	**RESUPPLY**	v -PLIED, -PLYING, -PLIES
RESIZE	v -SIZED, -SIZING, -SIZES	**RESURVEY**	v -ED, -ING, -S
RESKETCH	v -ED, -ING, -ES	**RETACK**	v -ED, -ING, -S
RESLATE	v -SLATED, -SLATING, -SLATES	**RETACKLE**	v -LED, -LING, -LES
RESMELT	v -ED, -ING, -S	**RETAG**	v -TAGGED, -TAGGING, -TAGS
RESMOOTH	v -ED, -ING, -S	**RETAILOR**	v -ED, -ING, -S
RESOAK	v -ED, -ING, -S	**RETAPE**	v -TAPED, -TAPING, -TAPES
RESOD	v -SODDED, -SODDING, -SODS	**RETARGET**	v -ED, -ING, -S

RETASTE	v -TASTED, -TASTING, -TASTES
RETAX	v -ED, -ING, -ES
RETEACH	v -TAUGHT, -TEACHING, -TEACHES
RETEAM	v -ED, -ING, -S
RETEAR	v -TORE, -TORN, -TEARING, -TEARS
RETELL	v -TOLD, -TELLING, -TELLS
RETEMPER	v -ED, -ING, -S
RETEST	v -ED, -ING, -S
RETHINK	v -THOUGHT, -THINKING, -THINKS
RETHREAD	v -ED, -ING, -S
RETIE	v -TIED, -TYING, -TIES
RETILE	v -TILED, -TILING, -TILES
RETIME	v -TIMED, -TIMING, -TIMES
RETINT	v -ED, -ING, -S
RETITLE	v -TLED, -TLING, -TLES
RETOLD	past tense of retell
RETORE	past tense of retear
RETORN	past participle of retear
RETRACK	v -ED, -ING, -S
RETRAIN	v -ED, -ING, -S
RETRIM	v -TRIMMED, -TRIMMING, -TRIMS
RETRY	v -TRIED, -TRYING, -TRIES
RETUNE	v -TUNED, -TUNING, -TUNES
RETWIST	v -ED, -ING, -S
RETYING	present participle of retie
RETYPE	v -TYPED, -TYPING, -TYPES
REUNIFY	v -FIED, -FYING, -FIES
REUNITE	v -UNITED, -UNITING, -UNITES
REUSE	v -USED, -USING, -USES
REUTTER	v -ED, -ING, -S
REVALUE	v -UED, -UING, -UES
REVERIFY	v -FIED, -FYING, -FIES
REVEST	v -ED, -ING, -S
REVIEW	v -ED, -ING, -S
REVISIT	v -ED, -ING, -S
REVOICE	v -VOICED, -VOICING, -VOICES
REVOTE	v -VOTED, -VOTING, -VOTES
REWAKE	v -WAKED or -WOKE, -WOKEN, -WAKING, -WAKES
REWAKEN	v -ED, -ING, -S
REWAN	a past tense of rewin
REWARM	v -ED, -ING, -S
REWASH	v -ED, -ING, -ES
REWAX	v -ED, -ING, -ES
REWEAVE	v -WOVE or -WEAVED, -WOVEN, -WEAVING, -WEAVES
REWED	v -WEDDED, -WEDDING, -WEDS
REWEIGH	v -ED, -ING, -S
REWELD	v -ED, -ING, -S
REWET	v -WETTED, -WETTING, -WETS
REWIDEN	v -ED, -ING, -S
REWIN	v -WON or -WAN, -WINNING, -WINS

REWIND	v -WOUND or -WINDED, -WINDING, -WINDS
REWIRE	v -WIRED, -WIRING, -WIRES
REWOKE	a past tense of rewake
REWOKEN	past participle of rewake
REWON	a past tense of rewin
REWORK	v -WORKED or -WROUGHT, -WORKING, -WORKS
REWOUND	a past tense of rewind
REWOVE	a past tense of reweave
REWOVEN	past participle of reweave
REWRAP	v -WRAPPED, or -WRAPT, -WRAPPING, -WRAPS
REWRITE	v -WROTE, -WRITTEN, -WRITING, -WRITES
REWROUGHT	a past tense of rework
REZONE	v -ZONED, -ZONING, -ZONES
REACH	v -ED, -ING, -ES to stretch out or put forth
REACHER	n pl. -S one that reaches
REACT	v -ED, -ING, -S to respond to a stimulus
REACTANT	n pl. -S one that reacts
REACTION	n pl. -S the act of reacting
REACTIVE	adj tending to react
REACTOR	n pl. -S one that reacts
READ	v READ, READING, READS to look at so as to take in the meaning of, as something written or printed **READABLE** adj **READABLY** adv
READER	n pl. -S one that reads
READERLY	adj typical of a reader
READIED	past tense of ready
READIER	comparative of ready
READIES	present 3d person sing. of ready
READIEST	superlative of ready
READILY	adv in a ready manner
READING	n pl. -S material that is read
READOUT	n pl. -S a presentation of computer data
READY	adj READIER, READIEST prepared
READY	v READIED, READYING, READIES to make ready
REAGENT	n pl. -S a substance used in a chemical reaction to ascertain the nature or composition of another

REAGIN   *n* pl. -S a type of antibody
     REAGINIC *adj*

REAL   *adj* REALER, REALEST having actual existence

REAL   *n* pl. -S or -ES a former monetary unit of Spain

REAL   *n* pl. REIS a former monetary unit of Portugal and Brazil

REALGAR   *n* pl. -S a mineral

REALIA   *n/pl* objects used by a teacher to illustrate everyday living

REALISE   *v* -ISED, -ISING, -ISES to realize

REALISER   *n* pl. -S one that realises

REALISM   *n* pl. -S concern with fact or reality

REALIST   *n* pl. -S one who is concerned with fact or reality

REALITY   *n* pl. -TIES something that is real

REALIZE   *v* -IZED, -IZING, -IZES to understand completely

REALIZER   *n* pl. -S one that realizes

REALLY   *adv* actually

REALM   *n* pl. -S a kingdom

REALNESS   *n* pl. -ES the state of being real

REALTY   *n* pl. -TIES property in buildings and land

REAM   *v* -ED, -ING, -S to enlarge with a reamer

REAMER   *n* pl. -S a tool used to enlarge holes

REAP   *v* -ED, -ING, -S to cut for harvest
     REAPABLE *adj*

REAPER   *n* pl. -S one that reaps

REAPHOOK   *n* pl. -S an implement used in reaping

REAR   *v* -ED, -ING, -S to lift upright

REARER   *n* pl. -S one that rears

REARMICE   *n/pl* reremice

REARMOST   *adj* coming or situated last

REARWARD   *n* pl. -S the rearmost division of an army

REASCENT   *n* pl. -S a new or second ascent

REASON   *v* -ED, -ING, -S to derive inferences or conclusions from known or presumed facts

REASONER   *n* pl. -S one that reasons

REATA   *n* pl. -S riata

REAVE   *v* REAVED or REFT, REAVING, REAVES to plunder

REAVER   *n* pl. -S one that reaves

REB   *n* pl. -S a Confederate soldier

REBAR   *n* pl. -S a steel rod for use in reinforced concrete

REBATE   *v* -BATED, -BATING, -BATES to deduct or return from a payment or bill

REBATER   *n* pl. -S one that rebates

REBATO   *n* pl. -TOS rabato

REBBE   *n* pl. -S a rabbi

REBEC   *n* pl. -S an ancient stringed instrument

REBECK   *n* pl. -S rebec

REBEL   *v* -BELLED, -BELLING, -BELS to oppose the established government of one's land

REBELDOM   *n* pl. -S an area controlled by rebels

REBIRTH   *n* pl. -S a new or second birth

REBOANT   *adj* resounding loudly

REBOP   *n* pl. -S a type of music

REBORN   *adj* born again

REBOUND   *v* -ED, -ING, -S to spring back

REBOZO   *n* pl. -ZOS a long scarf

REBRANCH   *v* -ED, -ING, -ES to form secondary branches

REBUFF   *v* -ED, -ING, -S to reject or refuse curtly

REBUKE   *v* -BUKED, -BUKING, -BUKES to criticize sharply

REBUKER   *n* pl. -S one that rebukes

REBURIAL   *n* pl. -S a second burial

REBUS   *n* pl. -ES a type of puzzle

REBUT   *v* -BUTTED, -BUTTING, -BUTS to refute

REBUTTAL   *n* pl. -S argument or proof that rebuts

REBUTTER   *n* pl. -S one that rebuts

REBUTTING   present participle of rebut

REC   *n* pl. -S recreation

RECALL   *v* -ED, -ING, -S to call back

RECALLER   *n* pl. -S one that recalls

RECAMIER   *n* pl. -S a backless couch

RECANT   *v* -ED, -ING, -S to make a formal retraction or disavowal of

RECANTER   *n* pl. -S one that recants

RECAP   *v* -CAPPED, -CAPPING, -CAPS to review by a brief summary

RECCE   *n* pl. -S a recon

RECEDE   v -CEDED, -CEDING, -CEDES to move back or away

RECEIPT   v -ED, -ING, -S to mark as having been paid

RECEIVE   v -CEIVED, -CEIVING, -CEIVES to come into possession of

RECEIVER   n pl. -S one that receives

RECENCY   n pl. -CIES the state of being recent

RECENT   adj -CENTER, -CENTEST of or pertaining to a time not long past **RECENTLY** adv

RECEPT   n pl. -S a type of mental image

RECEPTOR   n pl. -S a nerve ending specialized to receive stimuli

RECESS   v -ED, -ING, -ES to place in a receding space or hollow

RECHEAT   n pl. -S a hunting call

RECIPE   n pl. -S a set of instructions for making something

RECISION   n pl. -S a cancellation

RECITAL   n pl. -S a detailed account

RECITE   v -CITED, -CITING, -CITES to declaim or say from memory

RECITER   n pl. -S one that recites

RECK   v -ED, -ING, -S to be concerned about

RECKLESS   adj foolishly heedless of danger

RECKON   v -ED, -ING, -S to count or compute

RECKONER   n pl. -S one that reckons

RECLAIM   v -ED, -ING, -S to make suitable for cultivation or habitation

RECLAME   n pl. -S publicity

RECLINE   v -CLINED, -CLINING, -CLINES to lean or lie back

RECLINER   n pl. -S one that reclines

RECLUSE   n pl. -S one who lives in solitude and seclusion

RECOIL   v -ED, -ING, -S to draw back in fear or disgust

RECOILER   n pl. -S one that recoils

RECON   n pl. -S a preliminary survey

RECONVEY   v -ED, -ING, -S to convey back to a previous position

RECORD   v -ED, -ING, -S to set down for preservation

RECORDER   n pl. -S one that records

RECOUNT   v -ED, -ING, -S to relate in detail

RECOUP   v -ED, -ING, -S to get back the equivalent of

RECOUPE   adj divided twice

RECOURSE   n pl. -S a turning or applying to someone or something for aid

RECOVER   v -ED, -ING, -S to obtain again after losing

RECOVERY   n pl. -ERIES an economic upturn

RECREANT   n pl. -S a coward

RECREATE   v -ATED, -ATING, -ATES to refresh mentally or physically

RECRUIT   v -ED, -ING, -S to engage for military service

RECTA   a pl. of rectum

RECTAL   adj pertaining to the rectum **RECTALLY** adv

RECTI   pl. of rectus

RECTIFY   v -FIED, -FYING, -FIES to correct

RECTO   n pl. -TOS a right-hand page of a book

RECTOR   n pl. -S a clergyman in charge of a parish

RECTORY   n pl. -RIES a rector's dwelling

RECTRIX   n pl. -TRICES a feather of a bird's tail

RECTUM   n pl. -TUMS or -TA the terminal portion of the large intestine

RECTUS   n pl. -TI a straight muscle

RECUR   v -CURRED, -CURRING, -CURS to happen again

RECURVE   v -CURVED, -CURVING, -CURVES to curve backward or downward

RECUSAL   n pl. -S the act of recusing

RECUSANT   n pl. -S one who refuses to accept established authority

RECUSE   v -CUSED, -CUSING, -CUSES to disqualify or challenge as judge in a particular case

RECYCLE   v -CLED, -CLING, -CLES to process in order to extract useful materials

RECYCLER   n pl. -S one that recycles

RED   adj REDDER, REDDEST of the color of blood

RED   v REDDED, REDDING, REDS to redd

REDACT   v -ED, -ING, -S to prepare for publication

REDACTOR   n pl. -S one that redacts

REDAN   *n* pl. -S a type of fortification

REDARGUE   *v* -GUED, -GUING, -GUES to disprove

REDBAIT   *v* -ED, -ING, -S to denounce as Communist

REDBAY   *n* pl. -BAYS a small tree

REDBIRD   *n* pl. -S a bird with red plummage

REDBONE   *n* pl. -S a hunting dog

REDBRICK   *n* pl. -S a modern British university

REDBUD   *n* pl. -S a small tree

REDBUG   *n* pl. -S a chigger

REDCAP   *n* pl. -S a porter

REDCOAT   *n* pl. -S a British soldier during the American Revolution

REDD   *v* -ED, -ING, -S to put in order

REDDED   past tense of red and redd

REDDEN   *v* -ED, -ING, -S to make or become red

REDDER   *n* pl. -S one that redds

REDDEST   superlative of red

REDDING   present participle of red and redd

REDDISH   *adj* somewhat red

REDDLE   *v* -DLED, -DLING, -DLES to ruddle

REDE   *v* REDED, REDING, REDES to advise

REDEAR   *n* pl. -S a common sunfish

REDEEM   *v* -ED, -ING, -S to buy back

REDEEMER   *n* pl. -S one that redeems

REDEYE   *n* pl. -S a railroad danger signal

REDFIN   *n* pl. -S a freshwater fish

REDFISH   *n* pl. -ES an edible rockfish

REDHEAD   *n* pl. -S a person with red hair

REDHORSE   *n* pl. -S a freshwater fish

REDIA   *n* pl. -DIAE or -DIAS the larva of certain flatworms **REDIAL** *adj*

REDING   present participle of rede

REDIRECT   *v* -ED, -ING, -S to change the course or direction of

REDLEG   *n* pl. -S a bird with red legs

REDLINE   *v* -LINED, -LINING, -LINES to withhold loans or insurance from certain neighborhoods

REDLY   *adv* with red color

REDNESS   *n* pl. -ES the state of being red

REDO   *n* pl. -DOS something that is done again

REDOLENT   *adj* fragrant

REDOUBLE   *v* -BLED, -BLING, -BLES to double

REDOUBT   *n* pl. -S an enclosed fortification

REDOUND   *v* -ED, -ING, -S to have an effect

REDOUT   *n* pl. -S a condition in which blood is driven to the head

REDOWA   *n* pl. -S a lively dance

REDOX   *n* pl. -ES a type of chemical reaction

REDPOLL   *n* pl. -S a small finch

REDRAFT   *v* -ED, -ING, -S to make a revised copy of

REDRAWER   *n* pl. -S one that redraws

REDRESS   *v* -ED, -ING, -ES to set right

REDROOT   *n* pl. -S a perennial herb

REDSHANK   *n* pl. -S a shore bird

REDSHIFT   *n* pl. -S a displacement of the spectrum of a celestial body toward the longer wavelengths

REDSHIRT   *v* -ED, -ING, -S to keep a college athlete out of varsity play in order to extend his eligibility

REDSTART   *n* pl. -S a small songbird

REDTAIL   *n* pl. -S a type of hawk

REDTOP   *n* pl. -S a type of grass

REDUCE   *v* -DUCED, -DUCING, -DUCES to diminish

REDUCER   *n* pl. -S one that reduces

REDUCTOR   *n* pl. -S an apparatus for the reduction of metallic ions in solution

REDUVIID   *n* pl. -S a bloodsucking insect

REDUX   *adj* brought back

REDWARE   *n* pl. -S an edible seaweed

REDWING   *n* pl. -S a European thrush

REDWOOD   *n* pl. -S a very tall evergreen tree

REE   *n* pl. -S the female Eurasian sandpiper

REECHY   *adj* REECHIER, REECHIEST foul, rancid

REED   *v* -ED, -ING, -S to fasten with reeds (the stalks of tall grasses)

REEDBIRD   *n* pl. -S the bobolink

REEDBUCK   *n* pl. -S an African antelope

REEDIER   comparative of reedy

REEDIEST   superlative of reedy

REEDIFY   *v* -FIED, -FYING, -FIES to rebuild

REEDILY *adv* with a thin, piping sound

REEDING *n* pl. -S a convex molding

REEDLIKE *adj* resembling a reed

REEDLING *n* pl. -S a marsh bird

REEDMAN *n* pl. -MEN one who plays a reed instrument

REEDY *adj* REEDIER, REEDIEST abounding in reeds

REEF *v* -ED, -ING, -S to reduce the area of a sail **REEFABLE** *adj*

REEFER *n* pl. -S one that reefs

REEFY *adj* REEFIER, REEFIEST abounding in ridges of rock

REEK *v* -ED, -ING, -S to give off a strong, unpleasant odor

REEKER *n* pl. -S one that reeks

REEKY *adj* REEKIER, REEKIEST reeking

REEL *v* -ED, -ING, -S to wind on a type of rotary device **REELABLE** *adj*

REELER *n* pl. -S one that reels

REENTRY *n* pl. -TRIES a new or second entry

REEST *v* -ED, -ING, -S to balk

REEVE *v* REEVED or ROVE, ROVEN, REEVING, REEVES to fasten by passing through or around something

REF *v* REFFED, REFFING, REFS to referee

REFACE *v* -FACED, -FACING, -FACES to repair the outer surface of

REFECT *v* -ED, -ING, -S to refresh with food and drink

REFEL *v* -FELLED, -FELLING, -FELS to reject

REFER *v* -FERRED, -FERRING, -FERS to direct to a source for help or information

REFEREE *v* -EED, -EEING, -EES to supervise the play in certain sports

REFERENT *n* pl. -S something referred to

REFERRAL *n* pl. -S one that is referred

REFERRED past tense of refer

REFERRER *n* pl. -S one that refers

REFERRING present participle of refer

REFFED past tense of ref

REFFING present participle of ref

REFINE *v* -FINED, -FINING, -FINES to free from impurities

REFINER *n* pl. -S one that refines

REFINERY *n* pl. -ERIES a place where crude material is refined

REFINING present participle of refine

REFINISH *v* -ED, -ING, -ES to give a new surface to

REFIT *v* -FITTED, -FITTING, -FITS to prepare and equip for additional use

REFLATE *v* -FLATED, -FLATING, -FLATES to inflate again

REFLECT *v* -ED, -ING, -S to turn or throw back from a surface

REFLET *n* pl. -S special brilliance of surface

REFLEX *v* -ED, -ING, -ES to bend back

REFLEXLY *adv* in a reflexed manner

REFLUENT *adj* flowing back

REFLUX *v* -ED, -ING, -ES to cause to flow back

REFOREST *v* -ED, -ING, -S to replant with trees

REFORM *v* -ED, -ING, -S to change to a better state

REFORMER *n* pl. -S one that reforms

REFRACT *v* -ED, -ING, -S to deflect in a particular manner, as a ray of light

REFRAIN *v* -ED, -ING, -S to keep oneself back

REFRESH *v* -ED, -ING, -ES to restore the well-being and vigor of

REFT a past tense of reave

REFUGE *v* -UGED, -UGING, -UGES to give or take shelter

REFUGEE *n* pl. -S one who flees for safety

REFUGIUM *n* pl. -GIA a stable area during a period of continental climactic change

REFUND *v* -ED, -ING, -S to give back

REFUNDER *n* pl. -S one that refunds

REFUSAL *n* pl. -S the act of refusing

REFUSE *v* -FUSED, -FUSING, -FUSES to express oneself as unwilling to accept, do, or comply with

REFUSER *n* pl. -S one that refuses

REFUSNIK *n* pl. -S a Soviet citizen who is refused permission to emigrate

REFUTAL *n* pl. -S the act of refuting

REFUTE *v* -FUTED, -FUTING, -FUTES to prove to be false or erroneous

REFUTER *n* pl. -S one that refutes

REG *n* pl. -S a regulation

REGAINER *n* pl. -S one that regains

REGAL *adj* of or befitting a king

REGALE *v* -GALED, -GALING, -GALES to delight

REGALER *n* pl. -S one that regales

REGALIA *n/pl* the rights and privileges of a king

REGALITY *n* pl. -TIES regal authority

REGALLY *adv* in a regal manner

REGARD *v* -ED, -ING, -S to look upon with a particular feeling

REGATTA *n* pl. -S a boat race

REGELATE *v* -LATED, -LATING, -LATES to refreeze ice by reducing the pressure

REGENCY *n* pl. -CIES the office of a regent

REGENT *n* pl. -S one who rules in the place of a sovereign **REGENTAL** *adj*

REGES pl. of rex

REGGAE *n* pl. -S a form of popular Jamaican music

REGICIDE *n* pl. -S the killing of a king

REGIME *n* pl. -S a system of government

REGIMEN *n* pl. -S a systematic plan

REGIMENT *v* -ED, -ING, -S to form into military units

REGINA *n* pl. -NAE or -NAS queen **REGINAL** *adj*

REGION *n* pl. -S an administrative area or division

REGIONAL *n* pl. -S something that serves as a region

REGISTER *v* -ED, -ING, -S to record officially

REGISTRY *n* pl. -TRIES the act of registering

REGIUS *adj* holding a professorship founded by the sovereign

REGLET *n* pl. -S a flat, narrow molding

REGMA *n* pl. -MATA a type of fruit

REGNA pl. of regnum

REGNAL *adj* pertaining to a king or his reign

REGNANCY *n* pl. -CIES the state of being regnant

REGNANT *adj* reigning

REGNUM *n* pl. -NA dominion

REGOLITH *n* pl. -S a layer of loose rock

REGORGE *v* -GORGED, -GORGING, -GORGES to vomit

REGOSOL *n* pl. -S a type of soil

REGRATE *v* -GRATED, -GRATING, -GRATES to buy up in order to sell for a higher price in the same area

REGREET *v* -ED, -ING, -S to greet in return

REGRESS *v* -ED, -ING, -ES to go back

REGRET *v* -GRETTED, -GRETTING, -GRETS to look back upon with sorrow or remorse

REGROWTH *n* pl. -S a new or second growth

REGULAR *n* pl. -S an habitual customer

REGULATE *v* -LATED, -LATING, -LATES to control according to rule

REGULUS *n* pl. -LI or -LUSES a mass that forms beneath the slag in a furnace **REGULINE** *adj*

REHAB *v* -HABBED, -HABBING, -HABS to restore to a good condition

REHABBER *n* pl. -S one that rehabs

REHEARSE *v* -HEARSED, -HEARSING, -HEARSES to practice in preparation for a public appearance

REHEATER *n* pl. -S one that reheats

REHOBOAM *n* pl. -S a wine bottle

REHOUSE *v* -HOUSED, -HOUSING, -HOUSES to establish in a new housing unit

REI *n* pl. -S an erroneous English form for a former Portuguese coin

REIF *n* pl. -S robbery

REIFIER *n* pl. -S one that reifies

REIFY *v* -IFIED, -IFYING, -IFIES to regard as real or concrete

REIGN *v* -ED, -ING, -S to exercise sovereign power

REIN *v* -ED, -ING, -S to restrain

REINDEER *n* pl. -S a large deer

REINJURY *n* pl. -RIES a second injury

REINLESS *adj* unrestrained

REINSMAN *n* pl. -MEN a skilled rider of horses

REIS pl. of real

REISSUER *n* pl. -S one that reissues

REITBOK *n* pl. -S the reedbuck

REIVE *v* REIVED, REIVING, REIVES to plunder

REIVER *n* pl. -S one that reives

REJECT *v* -ED, -ING, -S to refuse to accept, consider, or make use of

REJECTEE *n* pl. -S one that is rejected

REJECTER *n* pl. -S one that rejects

REJECTOR *n* pl. -S rejecter

REJIGGER *v* -ED, -ING, -S to alter

REJOICE *v* -JOICED, -JOICING, -JOICES to feel joyful

REJOICER *n* pl. -S one that rejoices

RELAPSE *v* -LAPSED, -LAPSING, -LAPSES to fall or slip back into a former state

RELAPSER *n* pl. -S one that relapses

RELATE *v* -LATED, -LATING, -LATES to give an account of

RELATER *n* pl. -S one that relates

RELATION *n* pl. -S a significant association between two or more things

RELATIVE *n* pl. -S one who is connected with another by blood or marriage

RELATOR *n* pl. -S relater

RELAX *v* -ED, -ING, -ES to make less tense or rigid

RELAXANT *n* pl. -S a drug that relieves muscular tension

RELAXER *n* pl. -S one that relaxes

RELAXIN *n* pl. -S a female hormone

RELAY *v* -ED, -ING, -S to send along by using fresh sets to replace tired ones

RELEASE *v* -LEASED, -LEASING, -LEASES to set free

RELEASER *n* pl. -S one that releases

RELEGATE *v* -GATED, -GATING, -GATES to assign

RELENT *v* -ED, -ING, -S to become less severe

RELEVANT *adj* pertaining to the matter at hand

RELEVE *n* pl. -S a raising onto the toe in ballet

RELIABLE *n* pl. -S one that can be relied on

RELIABLY *adv* in a manner that can be relied on

RELIANCE *n* pl. -S confident or trustful dependence

RELIANT *adj* showing reliance

RELIC *n* pl. -S a surviving memorial of something past

RELICT *n* pl. -S an organism surviving in a changed environment

RELIED past tense of rely

RELIEF *n* pl. -S aid in the form of money or necessities

RELIER *n* pl. -S one that relies

RELIES present 3d person sing. of rely

RELIEVE *v* -LIEVED, -LIEVING, -LIEVES to lessen or free from pain or discomfort

RELIEVER *n* pl. -S one that relieves

RELIEVO *n* pl. -VOS the projection of figures or forms from a flat background

RELIGION *n* pl. -S the worship of a god or the supernatural

RELIQUE *n* pl. -S relic

RELISH *v* -ED, -ING, -ES to enjoy

RELIVE *v* -LIVED, -LIVING, -LIVES to experience again

RELOADER *n* pl. -S one that reloads

RELOCATE *v* -CATED, -CATING, -CATES to establish in a new place

RELUCENT *adj* reflecting light

RELUCT *v* -ED, -ING, -S to show opposition

RELUME *v* -LUMED, -LUMING, -LUMES to light again

RELUMINE *v* -MINED, -MINING, -MINES to relume

RELY *v* -LIED, -LYING, -LIES to place trust or confidence

REM *n* pl. -S a quantity of ionizing radiation

REMAIN *v* -ED, -ING, -S to continue in the same state

REMAKER *n* pl. -S one that remakes

REMAN *v* -MANNED, -MANNING, -MANS to furnish with a fresh supply of men

REMAND *v* -ED, -ING, -S to send back

REMANENT *adj* remaining

REMANNED past tense of reman

REMANNING present participle of reman

REMARK *v* -ED, -ING, -S to say or write briefly or casually

REMARKER *n* pl. -S one that remarks

REMARQUE *n* pl. -S a mark made in the margin of an engraved plate

REMEDIAL *adj* intended to correct something

REMEDY *v* -DIED, -DYING, -DIES to relieve or cure

REMEMBER *v* -ED, -ING, -S to bring to mind again

REMEX *n* pl. REMIGES a flight feather of a bird's wing **REMIGIAL** *adj*

REMIND *v* -ED, -ING, -S to cause to remember

REMINDER *n* pl. -S one that reminds

REMINT *v* -ED, -ING, -S to melt down and make into new coin

REMISE *v* -MISED, -MISING, -MISES to give up a claim to

REMISS *adj* careless **REMISSLY** *adv*

REMIT *v* -MITTED, -MITTING, -MITS to send money in payment

REMITTAL *n* pl. -S the act of remitting

REMITTER *n* pl. -S one that remits

REMITTING present participle of remit

REMITTOR *n* pl. -S remitter

REMNANT *n* pl. -S something remaining

REMODEL *v* -ELED, -ELING, -ELS or -ELLED, -ELLING, -ELS to make over

REMOLADE *n* pl. -S a piquant sauce

REMORA *n* pl. -S a type of marine fish **REMORID** *adj*

REMORSE *n* pl. -S deep anguish caused by a sense of guilt

REMOTE *adj* -MOTER, -MOTEST situated far away **REMOTELY** *adv*

REMOTE *n* pl. -S a broadcast originating outside a studio

REMOTION *n* pl. -S the act of removing

REMOVAL *n* pl. -S the act of removing

REMOVE *v* -MOVED, -MOVING, -MOVES to take or move away

REMOVER *n* pl. -S one that removes

REMUDA *n* pl. -S a herd of horses

RENAL *adj* pertaining to the kidneys

RENATURE *v* -TURED, -TURING, -TURES to restore natural qualities

REND *v* RENT or RENDED, RENDING, RENDS to tear apart forcibly

RENDER *v* -ED, -ING, -S to cause to be or become

RENDERER *n* pl. -S one that renders

RENDIBLE *adj* capable of being rent

RENDZINA *n* pl. -S a type of soil

RENEGADE *v* -GADED, -GADING, -GADES to become a traitor

RENEGADO *n* pl. -DOS or -DOES a traitor

RENEGE *v* -NEGED, -NEGING, -NEGES to fail to carry out a promise or commitment

RENEGER *n* pl. -S one that reneges

RENEW *v* -ED, -ING, -S to make new or as if new again

RENEWAL *n* pl. -S the act of renewing

RENEWER *n* pl. -S one that renews

RENIFORM *adj* kidney-shaped

RENIG *v* -NIGGED, -NIGGING, -NIGS to renege

RENIN *n* pl. -S an enzyme

RENITENT *adj* resisting physical pressure

RENMINBI *n* pl. RENMINBI currency in the People's Republic of China

RENNASE *n* pl. -S rennin

RENNET *n* pl. -S a lining membrane in the stomach of certain young animals

RENNIN *n* pl. -S an enzyme

RENOGRAM *n* pl. -S a photographic depiction of the course of renal excretion

RENOUNCE *v* -NOUNCED, -NOUNCING, -NOUNCES to disown

RENOVATE *v* -VATED, -VATING, -VATES to make like new

RENOWN *v* -ED, -ING, -S to make famous

RENT *v* -ED, -ING, -S to obtain temporary use of in return for compensation **RENTABLE** *adj*

RENTAL *n* pl. -S an amount paid or collected as rent

RENTE *n* pl. -S annual income under French law

RENTER *n* pl. -S one that rents

RENTIER *n* pl. -S one that receives a fixed income

RENVOI *n* pl. -S the expulsion by a government of an alien

REOFFER *v* -ED, -ING, -S to offer for public sale

REOVIRUS *n* pl. -ES a type of virus

REP *n* pl. -S a cross-ribbed fabric

REPAID past tense of repay

REPAIR *v* -ED, -ING, -S to restore to good condition

REPAIRER *n* pl. -S one that repairs

REPAND *adj* having a wavy margin
REPANDLY *adv*

REPARTEE *n* pl. -S a quick, witty reply

REPAST *v* -ED, -ING, -S to eat or feast

REPAY *v* -PAID, -PAYING, -PAYS to pay back

REPEAL *v* -ED, -ING, -S to revoke

REPEALER *n* pl. -S one that repeals

REPEAT *v* -ED, -ING, -S to say or do again

REPEATER *n* pl. -S one that repeats

REPEL *v* -PELLED, -PELLING, -PELS to drive back

REPELLER *n* pl. -S one that repels

REPENT *v* -ED, -ING, -S to feel remorse or self-reproach for a past action

REPENTER *n* pl. -S one that repents

REPETEND *n* pl. -S a phrase or sound that is repeated

REPINE *v* -PINED, -PINING, -PINES to express discontent

REPINER *n* pl. -S one that repines

REPLACE *v* -PLACED, -PLACING, -PLACES to take the place of

REPLACER *n* pl. -S one that replaces

REPLETE *adj* abundantly supplied

REPLEVIN *v* -ED, -ING, -S to replevy

REPLEVY *v* -PLEVIED, -PLEVYING, -PLEVIES to regain possession of by legal action

REPLICA *n* pl. -S a close copy or reproduction

REPLICON *n* pl. -S a section of nucleic acid that replicates as a unit

REPLIER *n* pl. -S one that replies

REPLY *v* -PLIED, -PLYING, -PLIES to answer

REPO *n* pl. -POS something repossessed

REPORT *v* -ED, -ING, -S to give an account of

REPORTER *n* pl. -S one that reports

REPOSAL *n* pl. -S the act of reposing

REPOSE *v* -POSED, -POSING, -POSES to lie at rest

REPOSER *n* pl. -S one that reposes

REPOSIT *v* -ED, -ING, -S to put away

REPOUSSE *n* pl. -S a raised design hammered in metal

REPP *n* pl. -S rep

REPPED *adj* resembling rep

REPRESS *v* -ED, -ING, -ES to keep under control

REPRIEVE *v* -PRIEVED, -PRIEVING, -PRIEVES to postpone the punishment of

REPRISAL *n* pl. -S an act of retaliation

REPRISE *v* -PRISED, -PRISING, -PRISES to take back by force

REPRO *n* pl. -PROS a trial sheet of printed material suitable for photographic reproduction

REPROACH *v* -ED, -ING, -ES to find fault with

REPROOF *n* pl. -S criticism for a fault

REPROVAL *n* pl. -S reproof

REPROVE *v* -PROVED, -PROVING, -PROVES to rebuke

REPROVER *n* pl. -S one that reproves

REPTANT *adj* creeping or crawling

REPTILE *n* pl. -S any of a class of cold-blooded, air-breathing vertebrates

REPUBLIC *n* pl. -S a constitutional form of government

REPUGN *v* -ED, -ING, -S to oppose

REPULSE *v* -PULSED, -PULSING, -PULSES to drive back

REPULSER *n* pl. -S one that repulses

REPUTE *v* -PUTED, -PUTING, -PUTES to consider to be as specified

REQUEST *v* -ED, -ING, -S to express a desire for

REQUIEM *n* pl. -S a musical composition for the dead

REQUIN *n* pl. -S a voracious shark

REQUIRE *v* -QUIRED, -QUIRING, -QUIRES to have need of

REQUIRER *n* pl. -S one that requires

REQUITAL *n* pl. -S something given in return, compensation, or retaliation

REQUITE *v* -QUITED, -QUITING, -QUITES to make equivalent return for

REQUITER *n* pl. -S one that requites

RERAN past tense of rerun

REREDOS *n* pl. -ES an ornamental screen behind an altar

REREMICE *n/pl* bats (flying mammals)

REREWARD *n* pl. -S rearward

REROLLER *n* pl. -S one that rerolls

RERUN   v -RAN, -RUNNING, -RUNS to present a repetition of a recorded performance

RES   n pl. RES a particular thing or matter

RESALE   n pl. -S the act of selling again

RESCALE   v -SCALED, -SCALING, -SCALES to plan on a new scale

RESCIND   v -ED, -ING, -S to annul

RESCRIPT   n pl. -S something rewritten

RESCUE   v -CUED, -CUING, -CUES to free from danger

RESCUER   n pl. -S one that rescues

RESEARCH   v -ED, -ING, -ES to investigate thoroughly

RESEAU   n pl. -SEAUS or -SEAUX a filter screen for making color films

RESECT   v -ED, -ING, -S to excise part of an organ or structure surgically

RESEDA   n pl. -S a flowering plant

RESELLER   n pl. -S one that resells

RESEMBLE   v -BLED, -BLING, -BLES to be similar to

RESENT   v -ED, -ING, -S to feel or express annoyance or ill will at

RESERVE   v -SERVED, -SERVING, -SERVES to keep back for future use

RESERVER   n pl. -S one that reserves

RESETTER   n pl. -S one that resets

RESH   n pl. -ES a Hebrew letter

RESHAPER   n pl. -S one that reshapes something

RESID   n pl. -S a type of fuel oil

RESIDE   v -SIDED, -SIDING, -SIDES to dwell permanently or continuously

RESIDENT   n pl. -S one who resides

RESIDER   n pl. -S a resident

RESIDUA   a pl. of residuum

RESIDUAL   n pl. -S something left over

RESIDUE   n pl. -S something remaining after the removal of a part

RESIDUUM   n pl. -SIDUA or -SIDUUMS residue

RESIGN   v -ED, -ING, -S to give up one's office or position

RESIGNER   n pl. -S one that resigns

RESILE   v -SILED, -SILING, -SILES to spring back

RESIN   v -ED, -ING, -S to treat with resin (a viscous substance obtained from certain plants)

RESINATE   v -ATED, -ATING, -ATES to resin

RESINIFY   v -FIED, -FYING, -FIES to convert into resin

RESINOID   n pl. -S a resinous substance

RESINOUS   adj resembling resin

RESINY   adj resinous

RESIST   v -ED, -ING, -S to strive against

RESISTER   n pl. -S one that resists

RESISTOR   n pl. -S a device in an electric circuit

RESOJET   n pl. -S a pulsejet

RESOLUTE   adj -LUTER, -LUTEST characterized by firmness or determination

RESOLUTE   n pl. -S one who is resolute

RESOLVE   v -SOLVED, -SOLVING, -SOLVES to make a firm decision about

RESOLVER   n pl. -S one that resolves

RESONANT   n pl. -S a resounding sound

RESONATE   v -NATED, -NATING, -NATES to resound

RESORB   v -ED, -ING, -S to absorb again

RESORCIN   n pl. -S a chemical compound

RESORT   v -ED, -ING, -S to go frequently or habitually

RESORTER   n pl. -S one that resorts

RESOUND   v -ED, -ING, -S to make a loud, long, or echoing sound

RESOURCE   n pl. -S an available supply

RESPECT   v -ED, -ING, -S to have a high regard for

RESPIRE   v -SPIRED, -SPIRING, -SPIRES to breathe

RESPITE   v -SPITED, -SPITING, -SPITES to relieve temporarily

RESPOND   v -ED, -ING, -S to say or act in return

RESPONSA   n/pl written rabbinic decisions

RESPONSE   n pl. -S a reply or reaction

REST   v -ED, -ING, -S to refresh oneself by ceasing work or activity

RESTER   n pl. -S one that rests

RESTFUL   adj -FULLER, -FULLEST tranquil

RESTIVE   adj difficult to control

RESTLESS   adj unable or disinclined to remain at rest

RESTORAL *n* pl. -S the act of restoring

RESTORE *v* -STORED, -STORING, -STORES to bring back to a former or original condition

RESTORER *n* pl. -S one that restores

RESTRAIN *v* -ED, -ING, -S to hold back from action

RESTRICT *v* -ED, -ING, -S to keep within certain boundaries

RESTROOM *n* pl. -S a room furnished with toilets and sinks

RESULT *v* -ED, -ING, -S to occur as a consequence

RESUME *v* -SUMED, -SUMING, -SUMES to take up again after interruption

RESUMER *n* pl. -S one that resumes

RESUPINE *adj* lying on the back

RESURGE *v* -SURGED, -SURGING, -SURGES to rise again

RET *v* RETTED, RETTING, RETS to soak in order to loosen the fiber from the woody tissue

RETABLE *n* pl. -S a raised shelf above an altar

RETAIL *v* -ED, -ING, -S to sell in small quantities

RETAILER *n* pl. -S one that retails

RETAIN *v* -ED, -ING, -S to keep possession of

RETAINER *n* pl. -S one that retains

RETAKE *v* -TOOK, -TAKEN, -TAKING, -TAKES to take back

RETAKER *n* pl. -S one that retakes

RETARD *v* -ED, -ING, -S to slow the progress of

RETARDER *n* pl. -S one that retards

RETCH *v* -ED, -ING, -ES to make an effort to vomit

RETE *n* pl. -TIA an anatomical mesh or network

RETEM *n* pl. -S a desert shrub

RETENE *n* pl. -S a chemical compound

RETIA pl. of rete

RETIAL *adj* pertaining to a rete

RETIARII *n/pl* ancient Roman gladiators

RETIARY *adj* resembling a net

RETICENT *adj* tending to be silent

RETICLE *n* pl. -S a network of lines in the eyepiece of an optical instrument

RETICULA *n/pl* netlike structures

RETICULE *n* pl. -S a woman's handbag

RETIFORM *adj* arranged like a net

RETINA *n* pl. -NAS or -NAE a membrane of the eye

RETINAL *n* pl. -S retinene

RETINE *n* pl. -S a substance in cells that retards growth and cell division

RETINENE *n* pl. -S a pigment in the retina

RETINITE *n* pl. -S a fossil resin

RETINOID *n* pl. -S a compound analogous to vitamin A

RETINOL *n* pl. -S a liquid hydrocarbon

RETINUE *n* pl. -S a group of attendants **RETINUED** *adj*

RETINULA *n* pl. -LAE or -LAS a neural receptor of an arthropod's eye

RETIRANT *n* pl. -S a retiree

RETIRE *v* -TIRED, -TIRING, -TIRES to go away or withdraw

RETIREE *n* pl. -S one who has retired from his vocation

RETIRER *n* pl. -S one that retires

RETIRING *adj* shy

RETOOK past tense of retake

RETOOL *v* -ED, -ING, -S to reequip with tools

RETORT *v* -ED, -ING, -S to answer back sharply

RETORTER *n* pl. -S one that retorts

RETOUCH *v* -ED, -ING, -ES to add new details or touches to

RETRACE *v* -TRACED, -TRACING, -TRACES to go back over

RETRACT *v* -ED, -ING, -S to take back

RETRAL *adj* situated toward the back **RETRALLY** *adv*

RETREAD *v* -ED, -ING, -S to furnish with a new tread

RETREAT *v* -ED, -ING, -S to go back or backward

RETRENCH *v* -ED, -ING, -ES to curtail

RETRIAL *n* pl. -S a second trial

RETRIEVE *v* -TRIEVED, -TRIEVING, -TRIEVES to get back

RETRO *n* pl. -ROS a rocket on a spacecraft that produces thrust in a direction opposite to the line of flight

RETROACT *v* -ED, -ING, -S to act in return

RETROFIT	*v* -FITTED, -FITTING, -FITS to furnish with new parts not originally available
RETRORSE	*adj* bent backward
RETSINA	*n* pl. -S a resin-flavored Greek wine
RETTED	past tense of ret
RETTING	present participle of ret
RETURN	*v* -ED, -ING, -S to come or go back
RETURNEE	*n* pl. -S one that has returned
RETURNER	*n* pl. -S one that returns
RETUSE	*adj* having a rounded apex with a shallow notch — used of leaves
REUNION	*n* pl. -S a reuniting of persons after separation
REUNITER	*n* pl. -S one that reunites
REUSABLE	*adj* capable of being used again
REV	*v* REVVED, REVVING, REVS to increase the speed of
REVAMP	*v* -ED, -ING, -S to make over
REVAMPER	*n* pl. -S one that revamps
REVANCHE	*n* pl. -S a political policy designed to regain lost territory
REVEAL	*v* -ED, -ING, -S to make known
REVEALER	*n* pl. -S one that reveals
REVEHENT	*adj* carrying back
REVEILLE	*n* pl. -S a morning bugle call
REVEL	*v* -ELED, -ELING, -ELS or -ELLED, -ELLING, -ELS to engage in revelry
REVELER	*n* pl. -S one that revels
REVELLER	*n* pl. -S reveler
REVELLING	present participle of revel
REVELRY	*n* pl. -RIES noisy merrymaking
REVENANT	*n* pl. -S one that returns
REVENGE	*v* -VENGED, -VENGING, -VENGES to inflict injury in return for
REVENGER	*n* pl. -S one that revenges
REVENUE	*n* pl. -S the income of a government **REVENUAL**, **REVENUED** *adj*
REVENUER	*n* pl. -S a revenue officer
REVERB	*v* -ED, -ING, -S to continue in a series of echoes
REVERE	*v* -VERED, -VERING, -VERES to regard with great respect
REVEREND	*n* pl. -S a clergyman
REVERENT	*adj* deeply respectful
REVERER	*n* pl. -S one that reveres
REVERIE	*n* pl. -S a daydream
REVERIES	pl. of revery
REVERING	present participle of revere
REVERS	*n* pl. REVERS a part of a garment turned back to show the inside
REVERSAL	*n* pl. -S the act of reversing
REVERSE	*v* -VERSED, -VERSING, -VERSES to turn or move in the opposite direction
REVERSER	*n* pl. -S one that reverses
REVERSO	*n* pl. -VERSOS verso
REVERT	*v* -ED, -ING, -S to return to a former state
REVERTER	*n* pl. -S one that reverts
REVERY	*n* pl. -ERIES reverie
REVET	*v* -VETTED, -VETTING, -VETS to face with masonry
REVIEWAL	*n* pl. -S the act of reviewing
REVIEWER	*n* pl. -S one that reviews
REVILE	*v* -VILED, -VILING, -VILES to denounce with abusive language
REVILER	*n* pl. -S one that reviles
REVISAL	*n* pl. -S a revision
REVISE	*v* -VISED, -VISING, -VISES to make a new or improved version of
REVISER	*n* pl. -S one that revises
REVISION	*n* pl. -S a revised version
REVISOR	*n* pl. -S reviser
REVISORY	*adj* pertaining to revision
REVIVAL	*n* pl. -S renewed attention to or interest in something
REVIVE	*v* -VIVED, -VIVING, -VIVES to bring back to life or consciousness
REVIVER	*n* pl. -S one that revives
REVIVIFY	*v* -FIED, -FYING, -FIES to give new life to
REVIVING	present participle of revive
REVOKE	*v* -VOKED, -VOKING, -VOKES to annul by taking back
REVOKER	*n* pl. -S one that revokes
REVOLT	*v* -ED, -ING, -S to rise up against authority
REVOLTER	*n* pl. -S one that revolts
REVOLUTE	*adj* rolled backward or downward

REVOLVE	*v* -VOLVED, -VOLVING, -VOLVES to turn about an axis
REVOLVER	*n* pl. -S a type of handgun
REVUE	*n* pl. -S a type of musical show
REVUIST	*n* pl. -S a writer of revues
REVULSED	*adj* affected with revulsion
REVVED	past tense of rev
REVVING	present participle of rev
REWARD	*v* -ED, -ING, -S to give recompense to for worthy behavior
REWARDER	*n* pl. -S one that rewards
REWINDER	*n* pl. -S one that rewinds
REWORD	*v* -ED, -ING, -S to state again in other words
REWRITER	*n* pl. -S one that rewrites
REX	*n* pl. REGES king
REX	*n* pl. -ES an animal with a single wavy layer of hair
REYNARD	*n* pl. -S a fox
RHABDOM	*n* pl. -S a rodlike structure in the retinula
RHABDOME	*n* pl. -S rhabdom
RHACHIS	*n* pl. -CHISES or -CHIDES rachis
RHAMNOSE	*n* pl. -S a sugar found in plants
RHAMNUS	*n* pl. -ES a thorny tree or shrub
RHAPHE	*n* pl. -PHAE or -PHES raphe
RHAPSODE	*n* pl. -S a reciter of epic poetry in ancient Greece
RHAPSODY	*n* pl. -DIES an exalted expression of feeling
RHATANY	*n* pl. -NIES a South American shrub
RHEA	*n* pl. -S a flightless bird
RHEBOK	*n* pl. -S a large antelope
RHEMATIC	*adj* pertaining to a verb
RHENIUM	*n* pl. -S a metallic element
RHEOBASE	*n* pl. -S the smallest amount of electricity required to stimulate a nerve
RHEOLOGY	*n* pl. -GIES the study of matter in the fluid state
RHEOPHIL	*adj* living in flowing water
RHEOSTAT	*n* pl. -S a resistor used to control electric current
RHESUS	*n* pl. -ES an Asian monkey
RHETOR	*n* pl. -S a teacher of rhetoric
RHETORIC	*n* pl. -S the study of effective speech and writing
RHEUM	*n* pl. -S a watery discharge from the eyes or nose **RHEUMIC** *adj*
RHEUMY	*adj* RHEUMIER, RHEUMIEST marked by rheum
RHINAL	*adj* pertaining to the nose
RHINITIS	*n* pl. RHINITIDES inflammation of the mucous membranes of the nose
RHINO	*n* pl. -NOS a rhinoceros
RHIZOBIA	*n/pl* rod-shaped bacteria
RHIZOID	*n* pl. -S a rootlike structure
RHIZOMA	*n* pl. -MATA rhizome
RHIZOME	*n* pl. -S a rootlike, underground stem **RHIZOMIC** *adj*
RHIZOPOD	*n* pl. -S any of a class of protozoans
RHIZOPUS	*n* pl. -PI or -PUSES any of a genus of mold fungi
RHO	*n* pl. RHOS a Greek letter
RHODAMIN	*n* pl. -S a red dye
RHODIUM	*n* pl. -S a metallic element **RHODIC** *adj*
RHODORA	*n* pl. -S a flowering shrub
RHOMB	*n* pl. -S a rhombus
RHOMBI	a pl. of rhombus
RHOMBIC	*adj* having the shape of a rhombus
RHOMBOID	*n* pl. -S a type of geometric figure
RHOMBUS	*n* pl. -BUSES or -BI a type of geometric figure
RHONCHUS	*n* pl. -CHI a rattling respiratory sound **RHONCHAL** *adj*
RHUBARB	*n* pl. -S a perennial herb
RHUMB	*n* pl. -S a point of the mariner's compass
RHUMBA	*v* -ED, -ING, -S to rumba
RHUS	*n* pl. -ES any of a genus of shrubs and trees
RHYME	*v* RHYMED, RHYMING, RHYMES to compose verse with corresponding terminal sounds
RHYMER	*n* pl. -S one that rhymes
RHYOLITE	*n* pl. -S a volcanic rock
RHYTA	pl. of rhyton
RHYTHM	*n* pl. -S movement or procedure with uniform recurrence of strong and weak elements
RHYTHMIC	*n* pl. -S the science of rhythm
RHYTON	*n* pl. -TONS or -TA an ancient Greek drinking horn

RIA   *n* pl. -S a long, narrow inlet

RIAL   *n* pl. -S a monetary unit of Iran

RIALTO   *n* pl. -TOS a marketplace

RIANT   *adj* cheerful **RIANTLY** *adv*

RIATA   *n* pl. -S a lasso

RIB   *v* RIBBED, RIBBING, RIBS to poke fun at

RIBALD   *n* pl. -S one who uses crude language

RIBALDLY   *adv* crudely

RIBALDRY   *n* pl. -RIES crude language

RIBAND   *n* pl. -S a ribbon

RIBBAND   *n* pl. -S a long, narrow strip used in shipbuilding

RIBBED   past tense of rib

RIBBER   *n* pl. -S one that ribs

RIBBIER   comparative of ribby

RIBBIEST   superlative of ribby

RIBBING   *n* pl. -S the act of one that ribs

RIBBON   *v* -ED, -ING, -S to decorate with ribbons (narrow strips of fine fabric)

RIBBONY   *adj* resembling ribbon

RIBBY   *adj* -BIER, -BIEST marked by prominent ribs (curved bony rods in the body)

RIBES   *n* pl. RIBES a flowering shrub

RIBGRASS   *n* pl. -ES a weedy plant

RIBIER   *n* pl. -S a large, black grape

RIBLESS   *adj* having no ribs

RIBLET   *n* pl. -S the rib end in a breast of lamb or veal

RIBLIKE   *adj* resembling a rib

RIBOSE   *n* pl. -S a pentose sugar

RIBOSOME   *n* pl. -S a particle composed of protein and ribonucleic acid

RIBWORT   *n* pl. -S ribgrass

RICE   *v* RICED, RICING, RICES to press through a ricer

RICEBIRD   *n* pl. -S the bobolink

RICER   *n* pl. -S a kitchen utensil consisting of a container perforated with small holes

RICERCAR   *n* pl. -S an instrumental composition

RICH   *adj* RICHER, RICHEST having wealth

RICHEN   *v* -ED, -ING, -S to make rich

RICHES   *n/pl* wealth

RICHLY   *adv* in a rich manner

RICHNESS   *n* pl. -ES the state of being rich

RICHWEED   *n* pl. -S a flowering plant

RICIN   *n* pl. -S a poisonous protein

RICING   present participle of rice

RICINUS   *n* pl. -ES a large-leaved plant

RICK   *v* -ED, -ING, -S to pile hay in stacks

RICKETS   *n/pl* a disease resulting from vitamin D deficiency

RICKETY   *adj* -ETIER, -ETIEST likely to fall or collapse

RICKEY   *n* pl. -EYS an alcoholic beverage containing lime juice, sugar, and soda water

RICKRACK   *n* pl. -S a flat braid used as a trimming

RICKSHA   *n* pl. -S rickshaw

RICKSHAW   *n* pl. -S a small, two-wheeled passenger vehicle

RICOCHET   *v* -CHETED, -CHETING, -CHETS or -CHETTED, -CHETTING, -CHETS to rebound from a surface

RICOTTA   *n* pl. -S an Italian cheese

RICRAC   *n* pl. -S rickrack

RICTUS   *n* pl. -ES the expanse of the open mouth **RICTAL** *adj*

RID   *v* RID or RIDDED, RIDDING, RIDS to free from something objectionable

RIDABLE   *adj* capable of being ridden

RIDDANCE   *n* pl. -S deliverance

RIDDED   a past tense of rid

RIDDEN   past participle of ride

RIDDER   *n* pl. -S one that rids

RIDDING   present participle of rid

RIDDLE   *v* -DLED, -DLING, -DLES to pierce with many holes

RIDDLER   *n* pl. -S one that riddles

RIDE   *v* RODE, RIDDEN, RIDING, RIDES to sit on, control, and be conveyed by an animal or machine

RIDEABLE   *adj* ridable

RIDENT   *adj* laughing

RIDER   *n* pl. -S one that rides

RIDGE   *v* RIDGED, RIDGING, RIDGES to form into ridges (long, narrow elevations)

RIDGEL   *n* pl. -S a ridgling

RIDGIER   comparative of ridgy

RIDGIEST   superlative of ridgy

RIDGIL   *n* pl. -S a ridgling

RIDGING   present participle of ridge

RIDGLING   *n* pl. -S a male animal with undescended testicles

RIDGY   *adj* RIDGIER, RIDGIEST having ridges

RIDICULE   *v* -CULED, -CULING, -CULES to make fun of

RIDING   *n* pl. -S the act of one that rides

RIDLEY   *n* pl. -LEYS a sea turtle

RIDOTTO   *n* pl. -TOS a public musical entertainment in 18th century England

RIEL   *n* pl. -S a monetary unit of Cambodia

RIESLING   *n* pl. -S a white Rhine wine

RIEVER   *n* pl. -S reaver

RIF   *v* RIFFED, RIFFING, RIFS to dismiss from employment

RIFAMPIN   *n* pl. -S an antibiotic

RIFE   *adj* RIFER, RIFEST abundant **RIFELY** *adv*

RIFENESS   *n* pl. -ES the state of being rife

RIFF   *v* -ED, -ING, -S to riffle

RIFFED   past tense of rif

RIFFING   present participle of rif

RIFFLE   *v* -FLED, -FLING, -FLES to flip through hastily

RIFFLER   *n* pl. -S a filing and scraping tool

RIFFRAFF   *n* pl. -S the disreputable element of society

RIFLE   *v* -FLED, -FLING, -FLES to search through and rob

RIFLEMAN   *n* pl. -MEN a soldier armed with a rifle (a type of firearm)

RIFLER   *n* pl. -S one that rifles

RIFLERY   *n* pl. -RIES the practice of shooting at targets with a rifle

RIFLING   *n* pl. -S the system of grooves in a gun barrel

RIFT   *v* -ED, -ING, -S to form rifts (clefts)

RIFTLESS   *adj* having no rift

RIG   *v* RIGGED, RIGGING, RIGS to put in proper condition for use

RIGADOON   *n* pl. -S a lively dance

RIGATONI   *n* pl. -S a tubular pasta

RIGAUDON   *n* pl. -S rigadoon

RIGGED   past tense of rig

RIGGER   *n* pl. -S one that rigs

RIGGING   *n* pl. -S the system of lines, chains, and tackle used aboard a ship

RIGHT   *adj* RIGHTER, RIGHTEST being in accordance with what is good, proper, or just

RIGHT   *v* -ED, -ING, -S to put in proper order or condition

RIGHTER   *n* pl. -S one that rights

RIGHTFUL   *adj* just or proper

RIGHTIES   pl. of righty

RIGHTISM   *n* pl. -S a conservative political philosophy

RIGHTIST   *n* pl. -S an advocate of rightism

RIGHTLY   *adv* in a right manner

RIGHTO   *interj* — used to express cheerful consent

RIGHTY   *n* pl. RIGHTIES a right-handed person

RIGID   *adj* not flexible

RIGIDIFY   *v* -FIED, -FYING, -FIES to make rigid

RIGIDITY   *n* pl. -TIES the state of being rigid

RIGIDLY   *adv* in a rigid manner

RIGOR   *n* pl. -S strictness or severity

RIGORISM   *n* pl. -S strictness or severity in conduct or attitude

RIGORIST   *n* pl. -S one that professes rigorism

RIGOROUS   *adj* characterized by rigor

RIGOUR   *n* pl. -S rigor

RIKISHA   *n* pl. -S rickshaw

RIKSHAW   *n* pl. -S rickshaw

RILE   *v* RILED, RILING, RILES to anger

RILEY   *adj* angry

RILIEVO   *n* pl. -VI relievo

RILING   present participle of rile

RILL   *v* -ED, -ING, -S to flow like a rill (a small brook)

RILLE   *n* pl. -S a valley on the moon's surface

RILLET   *n* pl. -S a small rill

RIM	v RIMMED, RIMMING, RIMS to provide with a rim (an outer edge)	**RINGNECK**	n pl. -S a bird having a ring of color around the neck
RIME	v RIMED, RIMING, RIMES to rhyme	**RINGSIDE**	n pl. -S the area just outside a boxing or wrestling ring (a square enclosure)
RIMER	n pl. -S one that rimes		
RIMESTER	n pl. -S a rimer	**RINGTAIL**	n pl. -S an animal having a tail with ringlike markings
RIMFIRE	n pl. -S a cartridge having the primer set in the rim of the shell	**RINGTAW**	n pl. -S a game of marbles
RIMIER	comparative of rimy	**RINGTOSS**	n pl. -ES a game in which the object is to toss a ring onto an upright stick
RIMIEST	superlative of rimy		
RIMINESS	n pl. -ES the condition of being rimy	**RINGWORM**	n pl. -S a skin disease
		RINK	n pl. -S a surface of ice for skating
RIMING	present participle of rime		
RIMLAND	n pl. -S an outlying area	**RINNING**	present participle of rin
RIMLESS	adj having no rim	**RINSE**	v RINSED, RINSING, RINSES to cleanse with clear water **RINSABLE, RINSIBLE** adj
RIMMED	past tense of rim		
RIMMER	n pl. -S a reamer		
RIMMING	present participle of rim	**RINSER**	n pl. -S one that rinses
RIMOSE	adj marked by cracks **RIMOSELY** adv	**RINSING**	n pl. -S the act of one that rinses
		RIOJA	n pl. -S a dry red Spanish wine
RIMOSITY	n pl. -TIES the state of being rimose	**RIOT**	v -ED, -ING, -S to take part in a violent public disturbance
RIMOUS	adj rimose	**RIOTER**	n pl. -S one that riots
RIMPLE	v -PLED, -PLING, -PLES to wrinkle	**RIOTOUS**	adj characterized by rioting
		RIP	v RIPPED, RIPPING, RIPS to tear or cut apart roughly
RIMROCK	n pl. -S a type of rock formation		
RIMY	adj RIMIER, RIMIEST frosty	**RIPARIAN**	adj pertaining to the bank of a river
RIN	v RAN, RINNING, RINS to run or melt		
		RIPCORD	n pl. -S a cord pulled to release a parachute
RIND	n pl. -S a thick and firm outer covering **RINDED** adj	**RIPE**	adj RIPER, RIPEST fully developed **RIPELY** adv
RING	v -ED, -ING, -S to form a ring (a circular band) around	**RIPE**	v RIPED, RIPING, RIPES to cleanse
RING	v RANG, RUNG, RINGING, RINGS to give forth a clear, resonant sound	**RIPEN**	v -ED, -ING, -S to become ripe
		RIPENER	n pl. -S one that ripens
RINGBARK	v -ED, -ING, -S to make an encircling cut through the bark of	**RIPENESS**	n pl. -ES the state of being ripe
		RIPER	comparative of ripe
RINGBOLT	n pl. -S a type of eyebolt	**RIPEST**	superlative of ripe
RINGBONE	n pl. -S a bony growth on a horse's foot	**RIPIENO**	n pl. -NI or -NOS tutti
		RIPING	present participle of ripe
RINGDOVE	n pl. -S a European pigeon	**RIPOFF**	n pl. -S an instance of stealing
RINGENT	adj having open liplike parts	**RIPOST**	v -ED, -ING, -S to riposte
RINGER	n pl. -S one that rings	**RIPOSTE**	v -POSTED, -POSTING, -POSTES to make a return thrust in fencing
RINGGIT	n pl. -S a monetary unit of Malaysia		
RINGHALS	n pl. -ES a venomous snake	**RIPPABLE**	adj capable of being ripped
RINGLET	n pl. -S a small ring	**RIPPED**	past tense of rip
RINGLIKE	adj resembling a ring	**RIPPER**	n pl. -S one that rips

RIPPING   *adj* excellent

RIPPLE   *v* -PLED, -PLING, -PLES to form ripples (small waves)

RIPPLER   *n* pl. -S a toothed tool for cleaning flax fiber

RIPPLET   *n* pl. -S a small ripple

RIPPLING   present participle of ripple

RIPPLY   *adj* -PLIER, -PLIEST marked by ripples

RIPRAP   *v* -RAPPED, -RAPPING, -RAPS to strengthen with a foundation of broken stones

RIPSAW   *n* pl. -S a type of saw

RIPSTOP   *n* pl. -S a fabric woven so that small tears do not spread

RIPTIDE   *n* pl. -S a tide that opposes other tides

RISE   *v* ROSE, RISEN, RISING, RISES to move upward

RISER   *n* pl. -S one that rises

RISHI   *n* pl. -S a Hindu sage

RISIBLE   *adj* inclined to laugh **RISIBLY** *adv*

RISIBLES   *n/pl* a sense of the ridiculous

RISING   *n* pl. -S the act of one that rises

RISK   *v* -ED, -ING, -S to expose to a risk (a chance of injury or loss)

RISKER   *n* pl. -S one that risks

RISKLESS   *adj* free of risk

RISKY   *adj* RISKIER, RISKIEST dangerous **RISKILY** *adv*

RISOTTO   *n* pl. -TOS a rice dish

RISQUE   *adj* bordering on impropriety or indecency

RISSOLE   *n* pl. -S a small roll filled with meat or fish

RISUS   *n* pl. -ES a grin or laugh

RITARD   *n* pl. -S a musical passage with a gradual slackening in tempo

RITE   *n* pl. -S a ceremonial act or procedure

RITTER   *n* pl. -S a knight

RITUAL   *n* pl. -S a system of rites

RITUALLY   *adv* ceremonially

RITZ   *n* pl. -ES pretentious display

RITZY   *adj* RITZIER, RITZIEST elegant **RITZILY** *adv*

RIVAGE   *n* pl. -S a coast, shore, or bank

RIVAL   *v* -VALED, -VALING, -VALS or -VALLED, -VALLING, -VALS to strive to equal or surpass

RIVALRY   *n* pl. -RIES competition

RIVE   *v* RIVED, RIVEN, RIVING, RIVES to tear apart

RIVER   *n* pl. -S a large, natural stream of water

RIVERBED   *n* pl. -S the area covered or once covered by a river

RIVERINE   *adj* pertaining to a river

RIVET   *v* -ETED, -ETING, -ETS or -ETTED, -ETTING, -ETS to fasten with a type of metal bolt

RIVETER   *n* pl. -S one that rivets

RIVIERA   *n* pl. -S a coastal resort area

RIVIERE   *n* pl. -S a necklace of precious stones

RIVING   present participle of rive

RIVULET   *n* pl. -S a small stream

RIVULOSE   *adj* having narrow, winding lines

RIYAL   *n* pl. -S a monetary unit of Saudi Arabia

ROACH   *v* -ED, -ING, -ES to cause to arch

ROAD   *n* pl. -S an open way for public passage

ROADBED   *n* pl. -S the foundation for a railroad track

ROADEO   *n* pl. -EOS a competition for truck drivers

ROADIE   *n* pl. -S a person who works for traveling entertainers

ROADKILL   *n* pl. -S an animal that has been killed on a road

ROADLESS   *adj* having no roads

ROADSHOW   *n* pl. -S a theatrical show on tour

ROADSIDE   *n* pl. -S the area along the side of a road

ROADSTER   *n* pl. -S a light, open automobile

ROADWAY   *n* pl. -WAYS a road

ROADWORK   *n* pl. -S outdoor running as a form of physical conditioning

ROAM   *v* -ED, -ING, -S to move about without purpose or plan

ROAMER   *n* pl. -S one that roams

ROAN   *n* pl. -S an animal having a coat sprinkled with white or gray

ROAR   *v* -ED, -ING, -S to utter a loud, deep sound

ROARER   *n* pl. -S one that roars

ROARING *n* pl. -S a loud, deep sound

ROAST *v* -ED, -ING, -S to cook with dry heat

ROASTER *n* pl. -S one that roasts

ROB *v* ROBBED, ROBBING, ROBS to take property from illegally

ROBALO *n* pl. -LOS a marine food fish

ROBAND *n* pl. -S a piece of yarn used to fasten a sail

ROBBED past tense of rob

ROBBER *n* pl. -S one that robs

ROBBERY *n* pl. -BERIES the act of one who robs

ROBBIN *n* pl. -S a roband

ROBBING present participle of rob

ROBE *v* ROBED, ROBING, ROBES to cover with a robe (a long, loose outer garment)

ROBIN *n* pl. -S a songbird

ROBLE *n* pl. -S an oak tree

ROBORANT *n* pl. -S an invigorating drug

ROBOT *n* pl. -S a humanlike machine that performs various functions **ROBOTIC** *adj*

ROBOTICS *n/pl* a field of interest concerned with robots

ROBOTISM *n* pl. -S the state of being a robot

ROBOTIZE *v* -IZED, -IZING, -IZES to make automatic

ROBOTRY *n* pl. -RIES the science of robots

ROBUST *adj* -BUSTER, -BUSTEST strong and healthy **ROBUSTLY** *adv*

ROBUSTA *n* pl. -S a coffee grown in Africa

ROC *n* pl. -S a legendary bird of prey

ROCAILLE *n* pl. -S rococo

ROCHET *n* pl. -S a linen vestment

ROCK *v* -ED, -ING, -S to move back and forth

ROCKABY *n* pl. -BIES a song used to lull a child to sleep

ROCKABYE *n* pl. -S rockaby

ROCKAWAY *n* pl. -WAYS a light carriage

ROCKER *n* pl. -S a rocking chair

ROCKERY *n* pl. -ERIES a rock garden

ROCKET *v* -ED, -ING, -S to convey by means of a rocket (a device propelled by the reaction of escaping gases)

ROCKETER *n* pl. -S one that designs or launches rockets

ROCKETRY *n* pl. -RIES the science of rockets

ROCKFALL *n* pl. -S a mass of fallen rocks

ROCKFISH *n* pl. -ES a fish living around rocks

ROCKIER comparative of rocky

ROCKIEST superlative of rocky

ROCKLESS *adj* having no rocks

ROCKLIKE *adj* resembling a rock (a large mass of stone)

ROCKLING *n* pl. -S a marine fish

ROCKOON *n* pl. -S a small rocket

ROCKROSE *n* pl. -S a flowering plant

ROCKWEED *n* pl. -S a brown seaweed

ROCKWORK *n* pl. -S a natural mass of rocks

ROCKY *adj* ROCKIER, ROCKIEST unsteady

ROCOCO *n* pl. -COS a style of architecture and decoration

ROD *v* RODDED, RODDING, RODS to provide with a rod (a straight, slender piece of wood, metal, or other material)

RODE past tense of ride

RODENT *n* pl. -S a gnawing mammal

RODEO *v* -ED, -ING, -S to perform cowboy skills in a contest

RODLESS *adj* having no rod

RODLIKE *adj* resembling a rod

RODMAN *n* pl. -MEN a surveyor's assistant

RODSMAN *n* pl. -MEN rodman

ROE *n* pl. -S the mass of eggs within a female fish

ROEBUCK *n* pl. -S the male of a small Eurasian deer

ROENTGEN *n* pl. -S a unit of radiation dosage

ROGATION *n* pl. -S the proposal of a law in ancient Rome

ROGATORY *adj* requesting information

ROGER *n* pl. -S the pirate flag bearing the skull and crossbones

ROGUE *v* ROGUED, ROGUEING or ROGUING, ROGUES to defraud

ROGUERY *n* pl. -ERIES roguish conduct

ROGUISH *adj* dishonest

ROIL *v* -ED, -ING, -S to make muddy

ROILY *adj* ROILIER, ROILIEST muddy

ROISTER *v* -ED, -ING, -S to revel

ROLAMITE	*n* pl. -S a nearly frictionless mechanical device
ROLE	*n* pl. -S a part played by an actor
ROLF	*v* -ED, -ING, -S to practice a type of massage
ROLFER	*n* pl. -S one that rolfs
ROLL	*v* -ED, -ING, -S to move along by repeatedly turning over
ROLLAWAY	*adj* mounted on rollers
ROLLBACK	*n* pl. -S a return to a lower level of prices or wages
ROLLER	*n* pl. -S a rotating cylinder
ROLLICK	*v* -ED, -ING, -S to frolic
ROLLICKY	*adj* given to rollicking
ROLLING	*n* pl. -S the act of one that rolls
ROLLMOP	*n* pl. -S a fillet of herring
ROLLOUT	*n* pl. -S a type of play in football
ROLLOVER	*n* pl. -S a motor vehicle accident in which the vehicle overturns
ROLLTOP	*adj* having a flexible, sliding cover
ROLLWAY	*n* pl. -WAYS an incline for rolling logs
ROM	*n* pl. -S a Gypsy man or boy
ROMAINE	*n* pl. -S a variety of lettuce
ROMAN	*n* pl. -S a metrical narrative of medieval France
ROMANCE	*v* -MANCED, -MANCING, -MANCES to woo
ROMANCER	*n* pl. -S one that romances
ROMANISE	*v* -ISED, -ISING, -ISES to romanize
ROMANIZE	*v* -IZED, -IZING, -IZES to write in the Roman alphabet
ROMANO	*n* pl. -NOS an Italian cheese
ROMANTIC	*n* pl. -S a fanciful person
ROMAUNT	*n* pl. -S a long, medieval tale
ROMEO	*n* pl. -MEOS a male lover
ROMP	*v* -ED, -ING, -S to play boisterously
ROMPER	*n* pl. -S one that romps
ROMPISH	*adj* inclined to romp
RONDEAU	*n* pl. -DEAUX a short poem of fixed form
RONDEL	*n* pl. -S a rondeau of 14 lines
RONDELET	*n* pl. -S a rondeau of 5 or 7 lines
RONDELLE	*n* pl. -S rondel
RONDO	*n* pl. -DOS a type of musical composition
RONDURE	*n* pl. -S a circle or sphere
RONION	*n* pl. -S a mangy animal or person
RONNEL	*n* pl. -S an insecticide
RONTGEN	*n* pl. -S roentgen
RONYON	*n* pl. -S ronion
ROOD	*n* pl. -S a crucifix
ROOF	*v* -ED, -ING, -S to provide with a roof (the external upper covering of a building)
ROOFER	*n* pl. -S one that builds or repairs roofs
ROOFING	*n* pl. -S material for a roof
ROOFLESS	*adj* having no roof
ROOFLIKE	*adj* resembling a roof
ROOFLINE	*n* pl. -S the profile of a roof
ROOFTOP	*n* pl. -S a roof
ROOFTREE	*n* pl. -S a horizontal timber in a roof
ROOK	*v* -ED, -ING, -S to swindle
ROOKERY	*n* pl. -ERIES a colony of rooks (European crows)
ROOKIE	*n* pl. -S a novice
ROOKY	*adj* ROOKIER, ROOKIEST abounding in rooks
ROOM	*v* -ED, -ING, -S to occupy a room (a walled space within a building)
ROOMER	*n* pl. -S a lodger
ROOMETTE	*n* pl. -S a small room
ROOMFUL	*n* pl. -S as much as a room can hold
ROOMIE	*n* pl. -S a roommate
ROOMMATE	*n* pl. -S one with whom a room is shared
ROOMY	*adj* ROOMIER, ROOMIEST spacious **ROOMILY** *adv*
ROORBACH	*n* pl. -S roorback
ROORBACK	*n* pl. -S a false story used for political advantage
ROOSE	*v* ROOSED, ROOSING, ROOSES to praise
ROOSER	*n* pl. -S one that rooses
ROOST	*v* -ED, -ING, -S to settle down for rest or sleep
ROOSTER	*n* pl. -S a male chicken
ROOT	*v* -ED, -ING, -S to put forth a root (an underground portion of a plant)
ROOTAGE	*n* pl. -S a system of roots

ROOTER	*n* pl. -S one that gives encouragement or support
ROOTHOLD	*n* pl. -S the embedding of a plant to soil through the growing of roots
ROOTIER	comparative of rooty
ROOTIEST	superlative of rooty
ROOTLESS	*adj* having no roots
ROOTLET	*n* pl. -S a small root
ROOTLIKE	*adj* resembling a root
ROOTY	*adj* ROOTIER, ROOTIEST full of roots
ROPE	*v* ROPED, ROPING, ROPES to bind with a rope (a thick line of twisted fibers) **ROPABLE** *adj*
ROPELIKE	*adj* resembling a rope
ROPER	*n* pl. -S one that ropes
ROPERY	*n* pl. -ERIES a place where ropes are made
ROPEWALK	*n* pl. -S a long path where ropes are made
ROPEWAY	*n* pl. -WAYS an aerial cable used to transport freight
ROPEY	*adj* ROPIER, ROPIEST ropy
ROPIER	comparative of ropy
ROPIEST	superlative of ropy
ROPILY	*adv* in a ropy manner
ROPINESS	*n* pl. -ES the quality of being ropy
ROPING	present participle of rope
ROPY	*adj* ROPIER, ROPIEST resembling a rope or ropes
ROQUE	*n* pl. -S a form of croquet
ROQUET	*v* -ED, -ING, -S to cause one's own ball to hit another in croquet
RORQUAL	*n* pl. -S a large whale
ROSARIAN	*n* pl. -S a cultivator of roses
ROSARIUM	*n* pl. -IA or -IUMS a rose garden
ROSARY	*n* pl. -RIES a series of prayers in the Roman Catholic Church
ROSCOE	*n* pl. -S a pistol
ROSE	*v* ROSED, ROSING, ROSES to make the color of a rose (a reddish flower)
ROSEATE	*adj* rose-colored
ROSEBAY	*n* pl. -BAYS an evergreen shrub
ROSEBUD	*n* pl. -S the bud of a rose
ROSEBUSH	*n* pl. -ES a shrub that bears roses
ROSED	past tense of rose
ROSEFISH	*n* pl. -ES a marine food fish
ROSELIKE	*adj* resembling a rose
ROSELLE	*n* pl. -S a tropical plant
ROSEMARY	*n* pl. -MARIES an evergreen shrub
ROSEOLA	*n* pl. -S a rose-colored skin rash **ROSEOLAR** *adj*
ROSEROOT	*n* pl. -S a perennial herb
ROSERY	*n* pl. -ERIES a place where roses are grown
ROSESLUG	*n* pl. -S a larval sawfly that eats rose leaves
ROSET	*n* pl. -S resin
ROSETTE	*n* pl. -S an ornament resembling a rose
ROSEWOOD	*n* pl. -S a tropical tree
ROSIER	comparative of rosy
ROSIEST	superlative of rosy
ROSILY	*adv* in a rosy manner
ROSIN	*v* -ED, -ING, -S to treat with rosin (a brittle resin)
ROSINESS	*n* pl. -ES the state of being rosy
ROSING	present participle of rose
ROSINOL	*n* pl. -S rosin oil
ROSINOUS	*adj* resembling rosin
ROSINY	*adj* rosinous
ROSOLIO	*n* pl. -LIOS a liqueur made from raisins and brandy
ROSTELLA	*n/pl* small, beaklike structures
ROSTER	*n* pl. -S a list of names
ROSTRA	a pl. of rostrum
ROSTRAL	*adj* pertaining to a rostrum
ROSTRATE	*adj* having a rostrum
ROSTRUM	*n* pl. -TRA or -TRUMS a beaklike process or part
ROSULATE	*adj* arranged in the form of a rosette
ROSY	*adj* ROSIER, ROSIEST rose-colored
ROT	*v* ROTTED, ROTTING, ROTS to decompose
ROTA	*n* pl. -S a roster
ROTARY	*n* pl. -RIES a rotating part or device
ROTATE	*v* -TATED, -TATING, -TATES to turn about an axis
ROTATION	*n* pl. -S the act or an instance of rotating **ROTATIVE** *adj*
ROTATOR	*n* pl. -S one that rotates

ROTATOR	*n* pl. -ES a muscle serving to rotate a part of the body
ROTATORY	*adj* pertaining to rotation
ROTCH	*n* pl. -ES rotche
ROTCHE	*n* pl. -S a seabird
ROTE	*n* pl. -S mechanical routine
ROTENONE	*n* pl. -S an insecticide
ROTGUT	*n* pl. -S inferior liquor
ROTI	*n* pl. -S an unleavened bread
ROTIFER	*n* pl. -S a microscopic aquatic organism
ROTIFORM	*adj* shaped like a wheel
ROTL	*n* pl. ROTLS or ARTAL a unit of weight in Muslim countries
ROTO	*n* pl. -TOS a type of printing process
ROTOR	*n* pl. -S a rotating part of a machine
ROTOTILL	*v* -ED, -ING, -S to till soil with a type of farming implement
ROTTE	*n* pl. -S a medieval stringed instrument
ROTTED	past tense of rot
ROTTEN	*adj* -TENER, -TENEST being in a state of decay **ROTTENLY** *adv*
ROTTER	*n* pl. -S a scoundrel
ROTTING	present participle of rot
ROTUND	*adj* marked by roundness **ROTUNDLY** *adv*
ROTUNDA	*n* pl. -S a round building
ROTURIER	*n* pl. -S a commoner
ROUBLE	*n* pl. -S ruble
ROUCHE	*n* pl. -S ruche
ROUE	*n* pl. -S a lecherous man
ROUEN	*n* pl. -S any of a breed of domestic ducks
ROUGE	*v* ROUGED, ROUGING, ROUGES to color with a red cosmetic
ROUGH	*adj* ROUGHER, ROUGHEST having an uneven surface
ROUGH	*v* -ED, -ING, -S to make rough
ROUGHAGE	*n* pl. -S coarse, bulky food
ROUGHDRY	*v* -DRIED, -DRYING, -DRIES to dry without ironing, as washed clothes
ROUGHEN	*v* -ED, -ING, -S to make rough
ROUGHER	*n* pl. -S one that roughs
ROUGHHEW	*v* -HEWED, -HEWN, -HEWING, -HEWS to shape roughly
ROUGHISH	*adj* somewhat rough
ROUGHLEG	*n* pl. -S a large hawk
ROUGHLY	*adv* in a rough manner
ROUGING	present participle of rouge
ROUILLE	*n* pl. -S a peppery garlic sauce
ROULADE	*n* pl. -S a musical embellishment
ROULEAU	*n* pl. -LEAUX or -LEAUS a roll of coins wrapped in paper
ROULETTE	*v* -LETTED, -LETTING, -LETTES to make tiny slits in
ROUND	*adj* ROUNDER, ROUNDEST shaped like a sphere
ROUND	*v* -ED, -ING, -S to make round
ROUNDEL	*n* pl. -S a round figure or object
ROUNDER	*n* pl. -S a tool for rounding
ROUNDISH	*adj* somewhat round
ROUNDLET	*n* pl. -S a small circle
ROUNDLY	*adv* in a round manner
ROUNDUP	*n* pl. -S the driving together of cattle scattered over a range
ROUP	*v* -ED, -ING, -S to auction
ROUPET	*adj* roupy
ROUPY	*adj* ROUPIER, ROUPIEST hoarse **ROUPILY** *adv*
ROUSE	*v* ROUSED, ROUSING, ROUSES to bring out of a state of sleep or inactivity
ROUSER	*n* pl. -S one that rouses
ROUSSEAU	*n* pl. -S fried pemmican
ROUST	*v* -ED, -ING, -S to arouse and drive out
ROUSTER	*n* pl. -S a wharf laborer and deckhand
ROUT	*v* -ED, -ING, -S to defeat overwhelmingly
ROUTE	*v* ROUTED, ROUTING, ROUTES to send on a particular course
ROUTEMAN	*n* pl. -MEN one who conducts business on a customary course
ROUTER	*n* pl. -S a scooping tool
ROUTEWAY	*n* pl. -WAYS an established course of travel
ROUTH	*n* pl. -S an abundance
ROUTINE	*n* pl. -S a regular course of procedure
ROUTING	present participle of route

ROUX   *n* pl. ROUX a mixture of butter and flour

ROVE   *v* ROVED, ROVING, ROVES to roam

ROVEN   a past participle of reeve

ROVER   *n* pl. -S one that roves

ROVING   *n* pl. -S a roll of textile fibers

ROVINGLY   *adv* in a roving manner

ROW   *v* -ED, -ING, -S to propel by means of oars **ROWABLE** *adj*

ROWAN   *n* pl. -S a Eurasian tree

ROWBOAT   *n* pl. -S a small boat designed to be rowed

ROWDY   *adj* -DIER, -DIEST disorderly in behavior **ROWDILY** *adv*

ROWDY   *n* pl. -DIES a rowdy person

ROWDYISH   *adj* tending to be rowdy

ROWDYISM   *n* pl. -S disorderly behavior

ROWEL   *v* -ELED, -ELING, -ELS or -ELLED, -ELLING, -ELS to prick with a spiked wheel in order to urge forward

ROWEN   *n* pl. -S a second growth of grass

ROWER   *n* pl. -S one that rows

ROWING   *n* pl. -S the sport of racing in light, long, and narrow rowboats

ROWLOCK   *n* pl. -S an oarlock

ROWTH   *n* pl. -S routh

ROYAL   *n* pl. -S a size of printing paper

ROYALISM   *n* pl. -S support of a monarch or monarchy

ROYALIST   *n* pl. -S a supporter of a monarch or monarchy

ROYALLY   *adv* in a kingly manner

ROYALTY   *n* pl. -TIES the status or power of a monarch

ROYSTER   *v* -ED, -ING, -S to roister

ROZZER   *n* pl. -S a policeman

RUANA   *n* pl. -S a woolen poncho

RUB   *v* RUBBED, RUBBING, RUBS to move along the surface of a body with pressure

RUBABOO   *n* pl. -BOOS a type of soup

RUBACE   *n* pl. -S rubasse

RUBAIYAT   *n* pl. RUBAIYAT four-lined stanzas in Persian poetry

RUBASSE   *n* pl. -S a variety of quartz

RUBATO   *n* pl. -TOS a fluctuation of speed within a musical phrase

RUBBABOO   *n* pl. -BOOS rubaboo

RUBBED   past tense of rub

RUBBER   *v* -ED, -ING, -S to stretch one's neck in looking at something

RUBBERY   *adj* resembling rubber (an elastic substance)

RUBBING   *n* pl. -S an image produced by rubbing

RUBBISH   *n* pl. -ES worthless, unwanted matter **RUBBISHY** *adj*

RUBBLE   *v* -BLED, -BLING, -BLES to reduce to rubble (broken pieces)

RUBBLY   *adj* -BLIER, -BLIEST abounding in rubble

RUBDOWN   *n* pl. -S a brisk rubbing of the body

RUBE   *n* pl. -S a rustic

RUBELLA   *n* pl. -S a virus disease

RUBEOLA   *n* pl. -S a virus disease **RUBEOLAR** *adj*

RUBICUND   *adj* ruddy

RUBIDIUM   *n* pl. -S a metallic element **RUBIDIC** *adj*

RUBIED   past tense of ruby

RUBIER   comparative of ruby

RUBIES   present 3d person sing. of ruby

RUBIEST   superlative of ruby

RUBIGO   *n* pl. -GOS red iron oxide

RUBIOUS   *adj* ruby-colored

RUBLE   *n* pl. -S a monetary unit of the Soviet Union

RUBOFF   *n* pl. -S a deep impression made by close contact

RUBOUT   *n* pl. -S an instance of obliterating something

RUBRIC   *n* pl. -S a part of a manuscript or book that appears in red **RUBRICAL** *adj*

RUBUS   *n* pl. RUBUS a plant of the rose family

RUBY   *v* -BIED, -BYING, -BIES to tint with the color of a ruby (a deep-red precious stone)

RUBY   *adj* -BIER, -BIEST of a deep-red color

RUBYLIKE   *adj* resembling a ruby

RUCHE   *n* pl. -S a pleated strip of fine fabric

RUCHED   *adj* trimmed with a ruche

RUCHING   *n* pl. -S a ruche

RUCK	*v* -ED, -ING, -S to wrinkle or crease
RUCKLE	*v* -LED, -LING, -LES to ruck
RUCKSACK	*n* pl. -S a knapsack
RUCKUS	*n* pl. -ES a noisy disturbance
RUCTION	*n* pl. -S a ruckus
RUCTIOUS	*adj* quarrelsome
RUDD	*n* pl. -S a freshwater fish
RUDDER	*n* pl. -S a vertical blade used to direct the course of a vessel
RUDDIER	comparative of ruddy
RUDDIEST	superlative of ruddy
RUDDILY	*adv* in a ruddy manner
RUDDLE	*v* -DLED, -DLING, -DLES to color with a red dye
RUDDOCK	*n* pl. -S a European bird
RUDDY	*adj* -DIER, -DIEST having a healthy, reddish color
RUDE	*adj* RUDER, RUDEST discourteous or impolite **RUDELY** *adv*
RUDENESS	*n* pl. -ES the quality of being rude
RUDERAL	*n* pl. -S a plant growing in poor land
RUDESBY	*n* pl. -BIES a rude person
RUDEST	superlative of rude
RUDIMENT	*n* pl. -S a basic principle or element
RUE	*v* RUED, RUING, RUES to feel sorrow or remorse for
RUEFUL	*adj* feeling sorrow or remorse **RUEFULLY** *adv*
RUER	*n* pl. -S one that rues
RUFF	*v* -ED, -ING, -S to trump
RUFFE	*n* pl. -S a freshwater fish
RUFFIAN	*n* pl. -S a tough, lawless person
RUFFLE	*v* -FLED, -FLING, -FLES to destroy the smoothness of
RUFFLER	*n* pl. -S one that ruffles
RUFFLIER	comparative of ruffly
RUFFLIEST	superlative of ruffly
RUFFLIKE	*adj* resembling a ruff (a pleated collar)
RUFFLING	present participle of ruffle
RUFFLY	*adj* -FLIER, -FLIEST not smooth
RUFIYAA	*n* pl. RUFIYAA a monetary unit of the Maldives
RUFOUS	*adj* reddish
RUG	*v* RUGGED, RUGGING, RUGS to tear roughly
RUGA	*n* pl. -GAE an anatomical fold or wrinkle **RUGAL, RUGATE** *adj*
RUGBY	*n* pl. -BIES a form of football
RUGGED	*adj* -GEDER, -GEDEST having an uneven surface **RUGGEDLY** *adv*
RUGGER	*n* pl. -S rugby
RUGGING	present participle of rug
RUGLIKE	*adj* resembling a rug (a thick fabric used as a floor covering)
RUGOLA	*n* pl. -S arugula
RUGOSA	*n* pl. -S a flowering plant
RUGOSE	*adj* full of wrinkles **RUGOSELY** *adv*
RUGOSITY	*n* pl. -TIES the state of being rugose
RUGOUS	*adj* rugose
RUGULOSE	*adj* having small wrinkles
RUIN	*v* -ED, -ING, -S to destroy **RUINABLE** *adj*
RUINATE	*v* -ATED, -ATING, -ATES to ruin
RUINER	*n* pl. -S one that ruins
RUING	present participle of rue
RUINOUS	*adj* destructive
RULE	*v* RULED, RULING, RULES to exercise control over **RULABLE** *adj*
RULELESS	*adj* not restrained or regulated by law
RULER	*n* pl. -S one that rules
RULING	*n* pl. -S an authoritative decision
RULY	*adj* RULIER, RULIEST orderly
RUM	*n* pl. -S an alcoholic liquor
RUM	*adj* RUMMER, RUMMEST odd
RUMAKI	*n* pl. -S chicken liver wrapped together with water chestnuts in a bacon slice
RUMBA	*v* -ED, -ING, -S to perform a ballroom dance
RUMBLE	*v* -BLED, -BLING, -BLES to make a deep, thunderous sound
RUMBLER	*n* pl. -S one that rumbles
RUMBLING	*n* pl. -S a thunderous sound
RUMBLY	*adj* tending to rumble
RUMEN	*n* pl. -MINA or -MENS a part of the stomach of a ruminant **RUMINAL** *adj*

RUMINANT   *n* pl. -S a hoofed, even-toed mammal

RUMINATE   *v* -NATED, -NATING, -NATES to chew again

RUMMAGE   *v* -MAGED, -MAGING, -MAGES to search thoroughly through

RUMMAGER   *n* pl. -S one that rummages

RUMMER   *n* pl. -S a large drinking glass

RUMMEST   superlative of rum

RUMMY   *n* pl. -MIES a card game

RUMMY   *adj* -MIER, -MIEST odd

RUMOR   *v* -ED, -ING, -S to spread by hearsay

RUMOUR   *v* -ED, -ING, -S to rumor

RUMP   *n* pl. -S the lower and back part of the trunk **RUMPLESS** *adj*

RUMPLE   *v* -PLED, -PLING, -PLES to wrinkle

RUMPLY   *adj* -PLIER, -PLIEST rumpled

RUMPUS   *n* pl. -ES a noisy disturbance

RUN   *v* RAN, RUNNING, RUNS to move by rapid steps

RUNABOUT   *n* pl. -S a small, open auto

RUNAGATE   *n* pl. -S a deserter

RUNAWAY   *n* pl. -AWAYS one that runs away

RUNBACK   *n* pl. -S a type of run in football

RUNDLE   *n* pl. -S a rung

RUNDLET   *n* pl. -S a small barrel

RUNDOWN   *n* pl. -S a summary

RUNE   *n* pl. -S a letter of an ancient alphabet **RUNELIKE** *adj*

RUNG   *n* pl. -S a crosspiece forming a step of a ladder **RUNGLESS** *adj*

RUNIC   *adj* pertaining to a rune

RUNKLE   *v* -KLED, -KLING, -KLES to wrinkle

RUNLESS   *adj* scoring no runs in baseball

RUNLET   *n* pl. -S a small stream

RUNNEL   *n* pl. -S a small stream

RUNNER   *n* pl. -S one that runs

RUNNING   *n* pl. -S a race

RUNNY   *adj* -NIER, -NIEST tending to drip

RUNOFF   *n* pl. -S rainfall that is not absorbed by the soil

RUNOUT   *n* pl. -S the end of a film strip

RUNOVER   *n* pl. -S matter for publication that exceeds the allotted space

RUNROUND   *n* pl. -S evasive action

RUNT   *n* pl. -S a small person or animal **RUNTISH** *adj*

RUNTY   *adj* RUNTIER, RUNTIEST small

RUNWAY   *n* pl. -WAYS a landing and takeoff strip for aircraft

RUPEE   *n* pl. -S a monetary unit of India

RUPIAH   *n* pl. -S a monetary unit of Indonesia

RUPTURE   *v* -TURED, -TURING, -TURES to burst

RURAL   *adj* pertaining to the country

RURALISE   *v* -ISED, -ISING, -ISES to ruralize

RURALISM   *n* pl. -S the state of being rural

RURALIST   *n* pl. -S one who lives in the country

RURALITE   *n* pl. -S a ruralist

RURALITY   *n* pl. -TIES the state of being rural

RURALIZE   *v* -IZED, -IZING, -IZES to make rural

RURALLY   *adv* in a rural manner

RURBAN   *adj* partially rural and urban

RUSE   *n* pl. -S a deception

RUSH   *v* -ED, -ING, -ES to move swiftly

RUSHEE   *n* pl. -S a college student seeking admission to a fraternity or sorority

RUSHER   *n* pl. -S one that rushes

RUSHIER   comparative of rushy

RUSHIEST   superlative of rushy

RUSHING   *n* pl. -S yardage gained in football by running plays

RUSHLIKE   *adj* resembling a rush (a grasslike marsh plant)

RUSHY   *adj* RUSHIER, RUSHIEST abounding in rushes

RUSINE   *adj* pertaining to a genus of deer

RUSK   *n* pl. -S a sweetened biscuit

RUSSET   *n* pl. -S a reddish or yellowish brown color **RUSSETY** *adj*

RUSSIFY   *v* -FIED, -FYING, -FIES to make Russian

RUST   *v* -ED, -ING, -S to form rust (a reddish coating that forms on iron) **RUSTABLE** *adj*

RUSTIC   *n* pl. -S one who lives in the country

RUSTICAL   *n* pl. -S a rustic

RUSTICLY	*adv* in a rural manner
RUSTIER	comparative of rusty
RUSTIEST	superlative of rusty
RUSTILY	*adv* in a rusty manner
RUSTLE	*v* -TLED, -TLING, -TLES to make a succession of slight, soft sounds
RUSTLER	*n* pl. -S one that rustles
RUSTLESS	*adj* free from rust
RUSTLING	present participle of rustle
RUSTY	*adj* RUSTIER, RUSTIEST covered with rust
RUT	*v* RUTTED, RUTTING, RUTS to make ruts (grooves) in
RUTABAGA	*n* pl. -S a plant having a thick, edible root
RUTH	*n* pl. -S compassion
RUTHENIC	*adj* pertaining to a rare, metallic element
RUTHFUL	*adj* full of compassion
RUTHLESS	*adj* having no compassion
RUTILANT	*adj* having a reddish glow
RUTILE	*n* pl. -S a mineral
RUTIN	*n* pl. -S a chemical compound
RUTTED	past tense of rut
RUTTIER	comparative of rutty
RUTTIEST	superlative of rutty
RUTTILY	*adv* in a rutty manner
RUTTING	present participle of rut
RUTTISH	*adj* lustful
RUTTY	*adj* -TIER, -TIEST marked by ruts
RYA	*n* pl. -S a Scandinavian handwoven rug
RYE	*n* pl. -S a cereal grass
RYEGRASS	*n* pl. -ES a European grass
RYKE	*v* RYKED, RYKING, RYKES to reach
RYND	*n* pl. -S an iron support
RYOKAN	*n* pl. -S a Japanese inn
RYOT	*n* pl. -S a tenant farmer in India

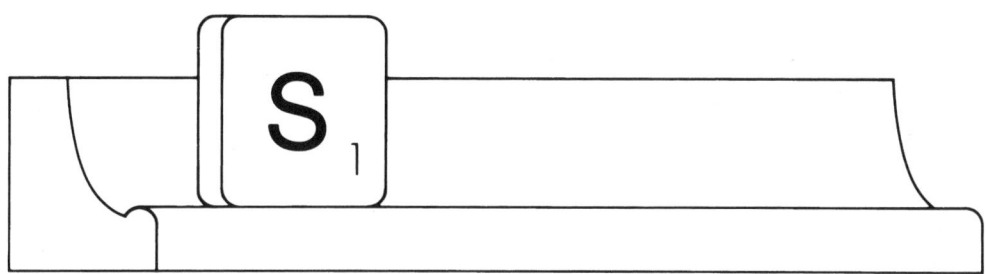

SAB   *v* SABBED, SABBING, SABS to sob

SABATON   *n* pl. -S a piece of armor for the foot

SABAYON   *n* pl. -S a sauce of whipped egg yolks, sugar, and wine

SABBAT   *n* pl. -S an assembly of demons and witches

SABBATH   *n* pl. -S sabbat

SABBATIC   *adj* bringing a period of rest

SABBED   past tense of sab

SABBING   present participle of sab

SABE   *v* SABED, SABEING, SABES to savvy

SABER   *v* -ED, -ING, -S to strike with a saber (a type of sword)

SABIN   *n* pl. -S a unit of sound absorption

SABINE   *n* pl. -S savin

SABIR   *n* pl. -S a French-based pidgin language

SABLE   *n* pl. -S a carnivorous mammal

SABOT   *n* pl. -S a wooden shoe

SABOTAGE   *v* -TAGED, -TAGING, -TAGES to destroy maliciously

SABOTEUR   *n* pl. -S one who sabotages

SABRA   *n* pl. -S a native Israeli

SABRE   *v* -BRED, -BRING, -BRES to saber

SABULOSE   *adj* sabulous

SABULOUS   *adj* sandy

SAC   *n* pl. -S a pouchlike structure in an animal or plant

SACATON   *n* pl. -S a perennial grass

SACBUT   *n* pl. -S sackbut

SACCADE   *n* pl. -S a rapid, jerky movement of the eye **SACCADIC** *adj*

SACCATE   *adj* having a sac

SACCULAR   *adj* resembling a sac

SACCULE   *n* pl. -S a small sac

SACCULUS   *n* pl. -LI saccule

SACHEM   *n* pl. -S a North American Indian chief **SACHEMIC** *adj*

SACHET   *n* pl. -S a small bag containing perfumed powder **SACHETED** *adj*

SACK   *v* -ED, -ING, -S to put into a sack (a large bag)

SACKBUT   *n* pl. -S a medieval trombone

SACKER   *n* pl. -S one that sacks

SACKFUL   *n* pl. SACKFULS or SACKSFUL as much as a sack can hold

SACKING   *n* pl. -S material for making sacks

SACKLIKE   *adj* resembling a sack

SACKSFUL   a pl. of sackful

SACLIKE   *adj* resembling a sac

SACQUE   *n* pl. -S a loose-fitting dress

SACRA   pl. of sacrum

SACRAL   *n* pl. -S a vertebra or nerve situated near the sacrum

SACRARIA   *n/pl* ancient Roman shrines

SACRED   *adj* dedicated to or set apart for the worship of a deity **SACREDLY** *adv*

SACRING   *n* pl. -S the consecration of bread and wine of the Eucharist

SACRIST   *n* pl. -S a person in charge of a sacristy

SACRISTY   *n* pl. -TIES a room in which sacred vessels and vestments are kept

SACRUM   *n* pl. -CRA or -CRUMS a bone of the pelvis

SAD   *adj* SADDER, SADDEST unhappy

SADDEN   *v* -ED, -ING, -S to make sad

SADDHU	*n* pl. -S sadhu
SADDLE	*v* -DLED, -DLING, -DLES to put a saddle (a leather seat for a rider) on
SADDLER	*n* pl. -S one that makes, repairs, or sells saddles
SADDLERY	*n* pl. -DLERIES the shop of a saddler
SADDLING	present participle of saddle
SADE	*n* pl. -S a Hebrew letter
SADHE	*n* pl. -S sade
SADHU	*n* pl. -S a Hindu holy man
SADI	*n* pl. -S sade
SADIRON	*n* pl. -S a heavy flatiron
SADISM	*n* pl. -S a tendency to take delight in inflicting pain
SADIST	*n* pl. -S one marked by sadism **SADISTIC** *adj*
SADLY	*adv* in a sad manner
SADNESS	*n* pl. -ES the state of being sad
SAE	*adv* so
SAFARI	*v* -ED, -ING, -S to go on a hunting expedition
SAFE	*adj* SAFER, SAFEST free from danger **SAFELY** *adv*
SAFE	*n* pl. -S a metal receptacle for storing valuables
SAFENESS	*n* pl. -ES the quality of being safe
SAFER	comparative of safe
SAFEST	superlative of safe
SAFETY	*v* -TIED, -TYING, -TIES to protect against failure, breakage, or accident
SAFFRON	*n* pl. -S a flowering plant
SAFRANIN	*n* pl. -S a red dye
SAFROL	*n* pl. -S safrole
SAFROLE	*n* pl. -S a poisonous liquid
SAG	*v* SAGGED, SAGGING, SAGS to bend or sink downward from weight or pressure
SAGA	*n* pl. -S a medieval Scandinavian narrative
SAGACITY	*n* pl. -TIES wisdom
SAGAMAN	*n* pl. -MEN a writer of sagas
SAGAMORE	*n* pl. -S an Algonquian Indian chief
SAGANASH	*n* pl. -ES a white man — an Algonquian Indian term
SAGBUT	*n* pl. -S sackbut

SAGE	*adj* SAGER, SAGEST wise **SAGELY** *adv*
SAGE	*n* pl. -S an aromatic herb used as seasoning
SAGENESS	*n* pl. -ES wisdom
SAGER	comparative of sage
SAGEST	superlative of sage
SAGGAR	*v* -ED, -ING, -S to bake in a saggar (a protective clay casing)
SAGGARD	*n* pl. -S a saggar
SAGGED	past tense of sag
SAGGER	*v* -ED, -ING, -S to saggar
SAGGING	present participle of sag
SAGGY	*adj* -GIER, -GIEST characterized by sagging
SAGIER	comparative of sagy
SAGIEST	superlative of sagy
SAGITTAL	*adj* resembling an arrow or arrowhead
SAGO	*n* pl. -GOS a tropical tree
SAGUARO	*n* pl. -ROS a tall cactus
SAGUM	*n* pl. -GA a cloak worn by ancient Roman soldiers
SAGY	*adj* SAGIER, SAGIEST flavored with sage
SAHIB	*n* pl. -S sir; master — used as a term of respect in colonial India
SAHIWAL	*n* pl. -S any of a breed of humped dairy cattle
SAHUARO	*n* pl. -ROS saguaro
SAICE	*n* pl. -S syce
SAID	*n* pl. -S sayyid
SAIGA	*n* pl. -S a small antelope
SAIL	*v* -ED, -ING, -S to move across the surface of water by the action of wind **SAILABLE** *adj*
SAILBOAT	*n* pl. -S a boat that sails
SAILER	*n* pl. -S a vessel that sails
SAILFISH	*n* pl. -ES a large marine fish
SAILING	*n* pl. -S the act of one that sails
SAILOR	*n* pl. -S a member of a ship's crew **SAILORLY** *adj*
SAIMIN	*n* pl. -S a Hawaiian noodle soup
SAIN	*v* -ED, -ING, -S to make the sign of the cross on
SAINFOIN	*n* pl. -S a perennial herb
SAINT	*v* -ED, -ING, -S to declare to be a saint (a person of exceptional holiness)

SAINTDOM *n* pl. -S the condition of being a saint

SAINTLY *adj* -LIER, -LIEST of or befitting a saint

SAITH a present 3d person sing. of say

SAITHE *n* pl. SAITHE a marine food fish

SAIYID *n* pl. -S sayyid

SAJOU *n* pl. -S a capuchin

SAKE *n* pl. -S benefit, interest, or advantage

SAKER *n* pl. -S a Eurasian falcon

SAKI *n* pl. -S a Japanese liquor

SAL *n* pl. -S salt

SALAAM *v* -ED, -ING, -S to greet with a low bow

SALABLE *adj* capable of being or fit to be sold **SALABLY** *adv*

SALACITY *n* pl. -TIES lewdness

SALAD *n* pl. -S a dish of green, raw vegetables

SALADANG *n* pl. -S a wild ox

SALAL *n* pl. -S a small shrub

SALAMI *n* pl. -S a seasoned sausage

SALARIAT *n* pl. -S the class of salaried persons

SALARY *v* -RIED, -RYING, -RIES to pay a periodic, fixed compensation to

SALCHOW *n* pl. -S a figure-skating jump

SALE *n* pl. -S the act or an instance of selling

SALEABLE *adj* salable **SALEABLY** *adv*

SALEP *n* pl. -S a starchy meal ground from the roots of certain orchids

SALEROOM *n* pl. -S a room in which goods are displayed for sale

SALESMAN *n* pl. -MEN a man who sells merchandise

SALIC *adj* pertaining to a group of igneous rocks

SALICIN *n* pl. -S a chemical compound

SALICINE *n* pl. -S salicin

SALIENCE *n* pl. -S a projecting feature or detail

SALIENCY *n* pl. -CIES salience

SALIENT *n* pl. -S the part of a fortification projecting closest to the enemy

SALIFY *v* -FIED, -FYING, -FIES to combine with a salt

SALINA *n* pl. -S a pond, marsh, or lake containing salt water

SALINE *n* pl. -S a salt solution

SALINITY *n* pl. -TIES a concentration of salt

SALINIZE *v* -NIZED, -NIZING, -NIZES to treat with salt

SALIVA *n* pl. -S a fluid secreted by the glands of the mouth **SALIVARY** *adj*

SALIVATE *v* -VATED, -VATING, -VATES to secrete saliva

SALL *v* shall — SALL is the only form of this verb; it cannot be conjugated

SALLET *n* pl. -S a light medieval helmet

SALLIED past tense of sally

SALLIER *n* pl. -S one that sallies

SALLIES present 3d person sing. of sally

SALLOW *adj* -LOWER, -LOWEST of a sickly yellowish color **SALLOWLY** *adv*

SALLOW *v* -ED, -ING, -S to make sallow

SALLOWY *adj* abounding in willow trees

SALLY *v* -LIED, -LYING, -LIES to rush out suddenly

SALMI *n* pl. -S a dish of roasted game birds

SALMON *n* pl. -S a food fish

SALMONID *n* pl. -S a fish of the salmon family

SALOL *n* pl. -S a chemical compound

SALON *n* pl. -S a large room in which guests are received

SALOON *n* pl. -S a tavern

SALOOP *n* pl. -S a hot drink made from an infusion of aromatic herbs

SALP *n* pl. -S salpa

SALPA *n* pl. -PAE or -PAS a free-swimming tunicate

SALPIAN *n* pl. -S salpa

SALPID *n* pl. -S salpa

SALPINX *n* pl. -PINGES an anatomical tube

SALSA *n* pl. -S a spicy sauce of tomatoes, onions, and peppers

SALSIFY *n* pl. -FIES a European herb

SALSILLA *n* pl. -S a tropical plant

SALT *v* -ED, -ING, -S to treat with salt (a crystalline compound used as a seasoning and preservative)

SALT *adj* SALTER, SALTEST salty

SALTANT	*adj* jumping or dancing
SALTBOX	*n* pl. -ES a type of house
SALTBUSH	*n* pl. -ES a salt-tolerant plant
SALTER	*n* pl. -S one that salts
SALTERN	*n* pl. -S a place where salt is produced
SALTIE	*n* pl. -S a deep-sea vessel sailing the Great Lakes
SALTIER	*n* pl. -S saltire
SALTIEST	superlative of salty
SALTILY	*adv* in a salty manner
SALTINE	*n* pl. -S a salted cracker
SALTING	*n* pl. -S land regularly flooded by tides
SALTIRE	*n* pl. -S a heraldic design
SALTISH	*adj* somewhat salty
SALTLESS	*adj* having no salt
SALTLIKE	*adj* resembling salt
SALTNESS	*n* pl. -ES the state of being salty
SALTPAN	*n* pl. -S a large pan for making salt by evaporation
SALTWORK	*n* pl. -S a saltern
SALTWORT	*n* pl. -S a seaside herb
SALTY	*adj* SALTIER, SALTIEST tasting of or containing salt
SALUKI	*n* pl. -S a tall, slender dog
SALUTARY	*adj* producing a beneficial effect
SALUTE	*v* -LUTED, -LUTING, -LUTES to greet with a sign of welcome or respect
SALUTER	*n* pl. -S one that salutes
SALVABLE	*adj* capable of being saved **SALVABLY** *adv*
SALVAGE	*v* -VAGED, -VAGING, -VAGES to save from loss or destruction
SALVAGEE	*n* pl. -S one in whose favor salvage has been effected
SALVAGER	*n* pl. -S one that salvages
SALVAGING	present participle of salvage
SALVE	*v* SALVED, SALVING, SALVES to soothe
SALVER	*n* pl. -S a tray or serving platter
SALVIA	*n* pl. -S a flowering plant
SALVIFIC	*adj* having the power to save
SALVING	present participle of salve
SALVO	*v* -ED, -ING, -S or -ES to discharge firearms simultaneously

SALVOR	*n* pl. -S a salvager
SAMARA	*n* pl. -S a dry, one-seeded fruit
SAMARIUM	*n* pl. -S a metallic element
SAMBA	*v* -ED, -ING, -S to perform a Brazilian dance
SAMBAR	*n* pl. -S a large Asian deer
SAMBHAR	*n* pl. -S sambar
SAMBHUR	*n* pl. -S sambar
SAMBO	*n* pl. -BOS a Latin American of mixed black and Indian ancestry
SAMBUCA	*n* pl. -S an ancient stringed instrument
SAMBUKE	*n* pl. -S sambuca
SAMBUR	*n* pl. -S sambar
SAME	*adj* resembling in every relevant respect
SAMECH	*n* pl. -S samek
SAMEK	*n* pl. -S a Hebrew letter
SAMEKH	*n* pl. -S samek
SAMENESS	*n* pl. -ES lack of change or variety
SAMIEL	*n* pl. -S the simoom
SAMISEN	*n* pl. -S a Japanese stringed instrument
SAMITE	*n* pl. -S a silk fabric
SAMIZDAT	*n* pl. -S a system in the Soviet Union for printing and distributing unauthorized literature
SAMLET	*n* pl. -S a young salmon
SAMOSA	*n* pl. -S a filled pastry turnover
SAMOVAR	*n* pl. -S a metal urn for heating water
SAMP	*n* pl. -S coarsely ground corn
SAMPAN	*n* pl. -S a flat-bottomed Chinese skiff
SAMPHIRE	*n* pl. -S a European herb
SAMPLE	*v* -PLED, -PLING, -PLES to test a representative portion of a whole
SAMPLER	*n* pl. -S one that samples
SAMPLING	*n* pl. -S a small part selected for analysis
SAMSARA	*n* pl. -S the cycle of birth, death, and rebirth in Buddhism
SAMSHU	*n* pl. -S a Chinese liquor
SAMURAI	*n* pl. -S a Japanese warrior
SANATIVE	*adj* having the power to cure or heal
SANCTA	a pl. of sanctum

SANCTIFY	*v* -FIED, -FYING, -FIES to make holy	**SANDY**	*adj* SANDIER, SANDIEST containing or covered with sand
SANCTION	*v* -ED, -ING, -S to authorize	**SANE**	*adj* SANER, SANEST mentally sound **SANELY** *adv*
SANCTITY	*n* pl. -TIES holiness		
SANCTUM	*n* pl. -TUMS or -TA a sacred place	**SANE**	*v* SANED, SANING, SANES to sain
SAND	*v* -ED, -ING, -S to cover with sand (a loose, granular rock material)	**SANENESS**	*n* pl. -ES sanity
		SANER	comparative of sane
		SANEST	superlative of sane
SANDAL	*v* -DALED, -DALING, -DALS or -DALLED, -DALLING, -DALS to provide with sandals (light, open shoes)	**SANG**	past tense of sing
		SANGA	*n* pl. -S sangar
		SANGAR	*n* pl. -S a temporary fortification for two or three men
SANDARAC	*n* pl. -S an aromatic resin		
SANDBAG	*v* -BAGGED, -BAGGING, -BAGS to surround with bags of sand	**SANGAREE**	*n* pl. -S an alcoholic beverage
		SANGER	*n* pl. -S sangar
SANDBANK	*n* pl. -S a large mass of sand	**SANGH**	*n* pl. -S an association promoting unity between the different groups in Hinduism
SANDBAR	*n* pl. -S a ridge of sand formed in a river or sea		
SANDBOX	*n* pl. -ES a box containing sand for children to play in	**SANGRIA**	*n* pl. -S an alcoholic beverage
		SANGUINE	*n* pl. -S a red color
SANDBUR	*n* pl. -S an annual herb	**SANICLE**	*n* pl. -S a medicinal herb
SANDBURR	*n* pl. -S sandbur	**SANIES**	*n* pl. SANIES a fluid discharged from wounds **SANIOUS** *adj*
SANDDAB	*n* pl. -S a small flatfish		
SANDER	*n* pl. -S one that sands	**SANING**	present participle of sane
SANDFISH	*n* pl. -ES a marine fish	**SANITARY**	*n* pl. -TARIES a public urinal
SANDFLY	*n* pl. -FLIES a biting fly	**SANITATE**	*v* -TATED, -TATING, -TATES to sanitize
SANDHI	*n* pl. -S a process of phonetic modification		
		SANITIES	pl. of sanity
SANDHOG	*n* pl. -S a worker who digs or works in sand	**SANITISE**	*v* -TISED, -TISING, -TISES to sanitize
SANDIER	comparative of sandy	**SANITIZE**	*v* -TIZED, -TIZING, -TIZES to guard against infection or disease by cleaning or sterilizing
SANDIEST	superlative of sandy		
SANDLIKE	*adj* resembling sand		
SANDLING	*n* pl. -S a marine fish	**SANITY**	*n* pl. -TIES the state of being sane
SANDLOT	*n* pl. -S a vacant lot	**SANJAK**	*n* pl. -S an administrative district of Turkey
SANDMAN	*n* pl. -MEN a mythical person who makes children sleepy by sprinkling sand in their eyes		
		SANK	past tense of sink
		SANNOP	*n* pl. -S sannup
SANDPEEP	*n* pl. -S a wading bird	**SANNUP**	*n* pl. -S a married male American Indian
SANDPILE	*n* pl. -S a pile of sand		
SANDPIT	*n* pl. -S a pit dug in sandy soil	**SANNYASI**	*n* pl. -S a Hindu monk
SANDSHOE	*n* pl. -S a lightweight sneaker	**SANS**	*prep* without
SANDSOAP	*n* pl. -S a type of soap	**SANSAR**	*n* pl. -S sarsar
SANDSPUR	*n* pl. -S a sandbur	**SANSEI**	*n* pl. -S a grandchild of Japanese immigrants to the United States
SANDWICH	*v* -ED, -ING, -ES to place between two layers or objects		
		SANSERIF	*n* pl. -S a typeface without serifs
SANDWORM	*n* pl. -S a sand-dwelling worm	**SANTALIC**	*adj* pertaining to sandalwood
SANDWORT	*n* pl. -S a flowering plant	**SANTALOL**	*n* pl. -S sandalwood oil

SANTIMS	*n* pl. -TIMI a former coin of Latvia
SANTIR	*n* pl. -S a Persian dulcimer
SANTO	*n* pl. -TOS a wooden image of a saint
SANTOL	*n* pl. -S a tropical tree
SANTONIN	*n* pl. -S a chemical compound
SANTOUR	*n* pl. -S santir
SANTUR	*n* pl. -S santir
SAP	*v* SAPPED, SAPPING, SAPS to deplete or weaken gradually
SAPAJOU	*n* pl. -S a capuchin
SAPHEAD	*n* pl. -S a foolish, stupid, or gullible person
SAPHENA	*n* pl. -NAE a vein of the leg
SAPID	*adj* pleasant to the taste
SAPIDITY	*n* pl. -TIES the state of being sapid
SAPIENCE	*n* pl. -S wisdom
SAPIENCY	*n* pl. -CIES sapience
SAPIENS	*adj* pertaining to recent man
SAPIENT	*adj* wise
SAPLESS	*adj* lacking vitality
SAPLING	*n* pl. -S a young tree
SAPONIFY	*v* -FIED, -FYING, -FIES to convert into soap
SAPONIN	*n* pl. -S a soapy substance obtained from plants
SAPONINE	*n* pl. -S saponin
SAPONITE	*n* pl. -S a mineral found in veins and cavities of rocks
SAPOR	*n* pl. -S flavor **SAPOROUS** *adj*
SAPOTA	*n* pl. -S an evergreen tree
SAPOTE	*n* pl. -S a tropical American tree
SAPOUR	*n* pl. -S sapor
SAPPED	past tense of sap
SAPPER	*n* pl. -S a military engineer
SAPPHIC	*n* pl. -S a type of verse form
SAPPHIRE	*n* pl. -S a blue gem
SAPPHISM	*n* pl. -S lesbianism
SAPPHIST	*n* pl. -S a lesbian
SAPPING	present participle of sap
SAPPY	*adj* -PIER, -PIEST silly **SAPPILY** *adv*
SAPREMIA	*n* pl. -S a form of blood poisoning **SAPREMIC** *adj*
SAPROBE	*n* pl. -S an organism that derives its nourishment from decaying organic matter **SAPROBIC** *adj*
SAPROPEL	*n* pl. -S mud consisting chiefly of decaying organic matter
SAPSAGO	*n* pl. -GOS a hard green cheese
SAPWOOD	*n* pl. -S the newly formed outer wood of a tree
SARABAND	*n* pl. -S a stately Spanish dance
SARAN	*n* pl. -S a thermoplastic resin
SARAPE	*n* pl. -S serape
SARCASM	*n* pl. -S a sharply mocking or contemptuous remark
SARCENET	*n* pl. -S a silk fabric
SARCOID	*n* pl. -S a disease of horses
SARCOMA	*n* pl. -MAS or -MATA a type of tumor
SARCOUS	*adj* composed of flesh or muscle
SARD	*n* pl. -S a variety of quartz
SARDANA	*n* pl. -S a Spanish folk dance
SARDAR	*n* pl. -S sirdar
SARDINE	*n* pl. -S a small food fish
SARDIUS	*n* pl. -ES sard
SARDONIC	*adj* mocking
SARDONYX	*n* pl. -ES a variety of quartz
SAREE	*n* pl. -S sari
SARGASSO	*n* pl. -GASSOS a brownish seaweed
SARGE	*n* pl. -S sergeant
SARI	*n* pl. -S an outer garment worn by Hindu women
SARIN	*n* pl. -S a toxic gas
SARK	*n* pl. -S a shirt
SARKY	*adj* SARKIER, SARKIEST sarcastic
SARMENT	*n* pl. -S a type of plant stem
SARMENTA	*n/pl* sarments
SAROD	*n* pl. -S a lute of northern India
SARODE	*n* pl. -S sarod
SARODIST	*n* pl. -S one who plays the sarod
SARONG	*n* pl. -S an outer garment worn in the Pacific islands
SAROS	*n* pl. -ES the eclipse cycle of the sun and moon
SARSAR	*n* pl. -S a cold, whistling wind
SARSEN	*n* pl. -S a large sandstone block
SARSENET	*n* pl. -S sarcenet
SARTOR	*n* pl. -S a tailor
SARTORII	*n/pl* flat, narrow thigh muscles

SASH   *v* -ED, -ING, -ES to furnish with a frame in which glass is set

SASHAY   *v* -ED, -ING, -S to flounce

SASHIMI   *n* pl. -S a Japanese dish of sliced raw fish

SASIN   *n* pl. -S an antelope of India

SASS   *v* -ED, -ING, -ES to talk impudently to

SASSABY   *n* pl. -BIES an African antelope

SASSIER   comparative of sassy

SASSIES   pl. of sassy

SASSIEST   superlative of sassy

SASSILY   *adv* in a sassy manner

SASSWOOD   *n* pl. -S an African tree

SASSY   *n* pl. -SIES sasswood

SASSY   *adj* SASSIER, SASSIEST impudent

SASTRUGA   *n* pl. -GI a ridge of snow formed by the wind in polar regions

SAT   past tense of sit

SATANG   *n* pl. -S a monetary unit of Thailand

SATANIC   *adj* extremely evil

SATANISM   *n* pl. -S worship of the powers of evil

SATANIST   *n* pl. -S one who practices satanism

SATARA   *n* pl. -S a woolen fabric

SATAY   *n* pl. -TAYS marinated meat that is skewered and broiled and dipped in peanut sauce

SATCHEL   *n* pl. -S a small carrying bag

SATE   *v* SATED, SATING, SATES to satiate

SATEEN   *n* pl. -S a cotton fabric

SATEM   *adj* pertaining to a group of Indo-European languages

SATI   *n* pl. -S suttee

SATIABLE   *adj* capable of being satiated **SATIABLY** *adv*

SATIATE   *v* -ATED, -ATING, -ATES to satisfy to or beyond capacity

SATIETY   *n* pl. -ETIES the state of being satiated

SATIN   *n* pl. -S a smooth fabric

SATINET   *n* pl. -S a thin satin

SATING   present participle of sate

SATINPOD   *n* pl. -S a flowering plant

SATINY   *adj* resembling satin

SATIRE   *n* pl. -S the use of derisive wit to attack folly or wickedness **SATIRIC** *adj*

SATIRISE   *v* -RISED, -RISING, -RISES to satirize

SATIRIST   *n* pl. -S one who satirizes

SATIRIZE   *v* -RIZED, -RIZING, -RIZES to subject to satire

SATISFY   *v* -FIED, -FYING, -FIES to provide fully with what is desired, expected, or needed

SATORI   *n* pl. -S the illumination of spirit sought by Zen Buddhists

SATRAP   *n* pl. -S a governor of a province in ancient Persia

SATRAPY   *n* pl. -PIES the territory of a satrap

SATSUMA   *n* pl. -S a variety of orange

SATURANT   *n* pl. -S a substance used to saturate

SATURATE   *v* -RATED, -RATING, -RATES to fill completely with something that permeates

SATYR   *n* pl. -S a woodland deity of Greek mythology **SATYRIC** *adj*

SATYRID   *n* pl. -S a brownish butterfly

SAU   *n* pl. SAU xu

SAUCE   *v* SAUCED, SAUCING, SAUCES to season with sauce (a flavorful liquid dressing)

SAUCEBOX   *n* pl. -ES a saucy person

SAUCEPAN   *n* pl. -S a cooking utensil

SAUCER   *n* pl. -S a small, shallow dish

SAUCH   *n* pl. -S saugh

SAUCING   present participle of sauce

SAUCY   *adj* SAUCIER, SAUCIEST impudent **SAUCILY** *adv*

SAUGER   *n* pl. -S a freshwater fish

SAUGH   *n* pl. -S a willow tree **SAUGHY** *adj*

SAUL   *n* pl. -S soul

SAULT   *n* pl. -S a waterfall

SAUNA   *n* pl. -S a Finnish steam bath

SAUNTER   *v* -ED, -ING, -S to walk in a leisurely manner

SAUREL   *n* pl. -S a marine fish

SAURIAN   *n* pl. -S any of a suborder of reptiles

SAUROPOD   *n* pl. -S any of a suborder of large dinosaurs

SAURY   *n* pl. -RIES a marine fish

SAUSAGE *n* pl. -S finely chopped and seasoned meat stuffed into a casing

SAUTE *v* -TEED or -TED, -TEING, -TES to fry in a small amount of fat

SAUTERNE *n* pl. -S a sweet white wine

SAUTOIR *n* pl. -S a saltire

SAUTOIRE *n* pl. -S sautoir

SAVABLE *adj* capable of being saved

SAVAGE *adj* -AGER, -AGEST fierce **SAVAGELY** *adv*

SAVAGE *v* -AGED, -AGING, -AGES to attack or treat brutally

SAVAGERY *n* pl. -RIES the quality of being savage

SAVAGEST superlative of savage

SAVAGING present participle of savage

SAVAGISM *n* pl. -S savagery

SAVANNA *n* pl. -S a flat, treeless grassland

SAVANNAH *n* pl. -S savanna

SAVANT *n* pl. -S a man of profound learning

SAVARIN *n* pl. -S a yeast cake baked in a ring mold

SAVATE *n* pl. -S a pugilistic sport

SAVE *v* SAVED, SAVING, SAVES to rescue from danger, injury, or loss **SAVEABLE** *adj*

SAVELOY *n* pl. -LOYS a highly seasoned sausage

SAVER *n* pl. -S one that saves

SAVIN *n* pl. -S an evergreen shrub

SAVINE *n* pl. -S savin

SAVING *n* pl. -S the act or an instance of saving

SAVINGLY *adv* in a thrifty manner

SAVIOR *n* pl. -S one that saves

SAVIOUR *n* pl. -S savior

SAVOR *v* -ED, -ING, -S to taste or smell with pleasure

SAVORER *n* pl. -S one that savors

SAVORIER comparative of savory

SAVORIES pl. of savory

SAVOROUS *adj* savory

SAVORY *adj* -VORIER, -VORIEST pleasant to the taste or smell **SAVORILY** *adv*

SAVORY *n* pl. -VORIES a savory dish served before or after a meal

SAVOUR *v* -ED, -ING, -S to savor

SAVOURER *n* pl. -S savorer

SAVOURY *adj* -VOURIER, -VOURIEST savory

SAVOURY *n* pl. -VOURIES a savory

SAVOY *n* pl. -VOYS a variety of cabbage

SAVVY *v* -VIED, -VYING, -VIES to understand

SAVVY *adj* -VIER, -VIEST shrewd

SAW *v* SAWED, SAWN, SAWING, SAWS to cut or divide with a saw (a type of cutting tool)

SAWBILL *n* pl. -S a tropical bird

SAWBONES *n* pl. -BONESES a surgeon

SAWBUCK *n* pl. -S a sawhorse

SAWDUST *n* pl. -S small particles of wood produced in sawing

SAWER *n* pl. -S one that saws

SAWFISH *n* pl. -ES a marine fish

SAWFLY *n* pl. -FLIES a winged insect

SAWHORSE *n* pl. -S a rack used to support a piece of wood being sawed

SAWLIKE *adj* resembling a saw

SAWLOG *n* pl. -S a log large enough to saw into boards

SAWMILL *n* pl. -S a place where logs are sawed

SAWN a past participle of saw

SAWNEY *n* pl. -NEYS a foolish person

SAWTOOTH *n* pl. -TEETH a cutting edge on a saw

SAWYER *n* pl. -S one that saws wood for a living

SAX *n* pl. -ES a saxophone

SAXATILE *adj* living or growing among rocks

SAXHORN *n* pl. -S a brass wind instrument

SAXONY *n* pl. -NIES a woolen fabric

SAXTUBA *n* pl. -S a bass saxhorn

SAY *v* SAID, SAYING, present sing. 2d person SAY, SAYEST, or SAYST, 3d person SAYS or SAITH to utter **SAYABLE** *adj*

SAYER *n* pl. -S one that says

SAYID *n* pl. -S sayyid

SAYING *n* pl. -S a maxim

SAYONARA *n* pl. -S goodby

SAYST a present 2d person sing. of say

SAYYID   *n* pl. -S lord; sir — used as a title of respect for a Muslim dignitary

SCAB   *v* SCABBED, SCABBING, SCABS to become covered with a scab (a crust that forms over a healing wound)

SCABBARD   *v* -ED, -ING, -S to put into a sheath, as a sword

SCABBLE   *v* -BLED, -BLING, -BLES to shape roughly

SCABBY   *adj* -BIER, -BIEST covered with scabs **SCABBILY** *adv*

SCABIES   *n* pl. SCABIES a skin disease

SCABIOSA   *n* pl. -S scabious

SCABIOUS   *n* pl. -ES a flowering plant

SCABLAND   *n* pl. -S rocky land with little soil cover

SCABLIKE   *adj* resembling a scab

SCABROUS   *adj* roughened with small projections

SCAD   *n* pl. -S a marine fish

SCAFFOLD   *v* -ED, -ING, -S to provide with a scaffold (a temporary platform for workmen)

SCAG   *n* pl. -S heroin

SCALABLE   *adj* capable of being scaled **SCALABLY** *adv*

SCALADE   *n* pl. -S an act of scaling the walls of a fortification

SCALADO   *n* pl. -DOS scalade

SCALAGE   *n* pl. -S a percentage deduction to compensate for shrinkage

SCALAR   *n* pl. -S a mathematical quantity possessing only magnitude

SCALARE   *n* pl. -S a tropical fish

SCALAWAG   *n* pl. -S a rascal

SCALD   *v* -ED, -ING, -S to burn with hot liquid or steam

SCALDIC   *adj* skaldic

SCALE   *v* SCALED, SCALING, SCALES to climb up or over

SCALENE   *adj* designating a triangle having no two sides equal

SCALENUS   *n* pl. -NI a muscle of the neck

SCALEPAN   *n* pl. -S a pan on a weighing scale

SCALER   *n* pl. -S one that scales

SCALEUP   *n* pl. -S an increase based on a fixed ratio

SCALIER   comparative of scaly

SCALIEST   superlative of scaly

SCALING   present participle of scale

SCALL   *n* pl. -S a scaly eruption of the skin

SCALLION   *n* pl. -S an onion-like plant

SCALLOP   *v* -ED, -ING, -S to bake in a sauce topped with bread crumbs

SCALP   *v* -ED, -ING, -S to remove an upper part from

SCALPEL   *n* pl. -S a small surgical knife

SCALPER   *n* pl. -S one that scalps

SCALY   *adj* SCALIER, SCALIEST peeling off in flakes

SCAM   *v* SCAMMED, SCAMMING, SCAMS to cheat or swindle

SCAMMONY   *n* pl. -NIES a climbing plant

SCAMP   *v* -ED, -ING, -S to perform in a hasty or careless manner

SCAMPER   *v* -ED, -ING, -S to run playfully about

SCAMPI   *n* pl. SCAMPI or SCAMPIES large shrimp used in Italian cooking

SCAMPISH   *adj* rascally

SCAN   *v* SCANNED, SCANNING, SCANS to examine closely

SCANDAL   *v* -DALED, -DALING, -DALS or -DALLED, -DALLING, -DALS to defame

SCANDENT   *adj* climbing, as a plant

SCANDIA   *n* pl. -S an oxide of scandium

SCANDIUM   *n* pl. -S a metallic element **SCANDIC** *adj*

SCANNED   past tense of scan

SCANNER   *n* pl. -S one that scans

SCANNING   *n* pl. -S close examination

SCANSION   *n* pl. -S the analysis of verse into metrical feet and rhythm patterns

SCANT   *adj* SCANTER, SCANTEST meager

SCANT   *v* -ED, -ING, -S to provide with a meager portion

SCANTIER   comparative of scanty

SCANTIES   *n/pl* brief panties for women

SCANTLY   *adv* in a scant manner

SCANTY   *adj* SCANTIER, SCANTIEST meager **SCANTILY** *adv*

SCAPE   *v* SCAPED, SCAPING, SCAPES to escape

SCAPHOID   *n* pl. -S a bone of the wrist

SCAPOSE   *adj* bearing a leafless stalk

SCAPULA *n* pl. -LAE or -LAS a bone of the shoulder

SCAPULAR *n* pl. -S a sleeveless outer garment worn by monks

SCAR *v* SCARRED, SCARRING, SCARS to form a scar (a mark left by the healing of injured tissue)

SCARAB *n* pl. -S a large, black beetle

SCARCE *adj* SCARCER, SCARCEST infrequently seen or found

SCARCELY *adv* by a narrow margin

SCARCITY *n* pl. -TIES the quality of being scarce

SCARE *v* SCARED, SCARING, SCARES to frighten

SCARER *n* pl. -S one that scares

SCAREY *adj* SCARIER, SCARIEST scary

SCARF *n* pl. SCARFS or SCARVES a piece of cloth worn for warmth or protection

SCARF *v* -ED, -ING, -S to cover with a scarf

SCARFPIN *n* pl. -S a tiepin

SCARIER comparative of scarey and scary

SCARIEST superlative of scarey and scary

SCARIFY *v* -FIED, -FYING, -FIES to make superficial cuts in

SCARILY *adv* in a scary manner

SCARING present participle of scare

SCARIOSE *adj* scarious

SCARIOUS *adj* thin, dry, and membranous

SCARLESS *adj* having no scars

SCARLET *n* pl. -S a red color

SCARP *v* -ED, -ING, -S to cut or make into a steep slope

SCARPER *v* -ED, -ING, -S to flee

SCARPH *v* -ED, -ING, -S to unite by means of a type of joint

SCARRED past tense of scar

SCARRING present participle of scar

SCARRY *adj* -RIER, -RIEST marked with scars

SCART *v* -ED, -ING, -S to scratch

SCARVES a pl. of scarf

SCARY *adj* SCARIER, SCARIEST frightening

SCAT *v* SCATTED, SCATTING, SCATS to leave hastily

SCATBACK *n* pl. -S a type of player in football

SCATHE *v* SCATHED, SCATHING, SCATHES to criticize severely

SCATT *n* pl. -S a tax

SCATTED past tense of scat

SCATTER *v* -ED, -ING, -S to go or send in various directions

SCATTING present participle of scat

SCATTY *adj* -TIER, -TIEST crazy

SCAUP *n* pl. -S a sea duck

SCAUPER *n* pl. -S an engraving tool

SCAUR *n* pl. -S a protruding, isolated rock

SCAVENGE *v* -ENGED, -ENGING, -ENGES to search through rubbish for usable items

SCENA *n* pl. -S an elaborate composition for a single voice

SCENARIO *n* pl. -IOS a summary of the plot of a dramatic work

SCEND *v* -ED, -ING, -S to rise upward, as a ship on a wave

SCENE *n* pl. -S the place where some action or event occurs

SCENERY *n* pl. -ERIES a picturesque landscape or view

SCENIC *adj* pertaining to scenery

SCENICAL *adj* scenic

SCENT *v* -ED, -ING, -S to fill with an odor

SCEPTER *v* -ED, -ING, -S to invest with royal authority

SCEPTIC *n* pl. -S skeptic

SCEPTRAL *adj* pertaining to royal authority

SCEPTRE *v* -TRED, -TRING, -TRES to scepter

SCHAPPE *n* pl. -S a silk fabric

SCHAV *n* pl. -S a chilled soup

SCHEDULE *v* -ULED, -ULING, -ULES to assign to a certain date or time

SCHEMA *n* pl. -MATA or -MAS a generalized diagram or plan

SCHEME *v* SCHEMED, SCHEMING, SCHEMES to plan or plot

SCHEMER *n* pl. -S one that schemes

SCHERZO *n* pl. -ZOS or -ZI a lively musical movement

SCHILLER *n* pl. -S a brownish luster occurring on certain minerals

SCHISM *n* pl. -S a division into opposing parties

SCHIST *n* pl. -S a rock that readily splits into parallel layers

SCHIZIER comparative of schizy

SCHIZIEST superlative of schizy

SCHIZO *n* pl. SCHIZOS a schizoid

SCHIZOID *n* pl. -S a person affected with a type of psychotic disorder

SCHIZONT *n* pl. -S an organism that reproduces by a form of asexual reproduction

SCHIZY *adj* SCHIZIER, SCHIZIEST affected with schizophrenia

SCHIZZY *adj* SCHIZZIER, SCHIZZIEST schizy

SCHLEP *v* SCHLEPPED, SCHLEPPING, SCHLEPS to lug or drag

SCHLEPP *v* -ED, -ING, -S to schlep

SCHLIERE *n* pl. -REN a small streak in an igneous rock

SCHLOCK *n* pl. -S inferior merchandise

SCHLOCKY *adj* of inferior quality

SCHLUMP *v* -ED, -ING, -S to go about lazily or sloppily dressed

SCHMALTZ *n* pl. -ES excessive sentimentality

SCHMALZ *n* pl. -ES schmaltz

SCHMALZY *adj* SCHMALZIER, SCHMALZIEST characterized by schmaltz

SCHMEAR *n* pl. -S an aggregate of related things

SCHMEER *v* -ED, -ING, -S to bribe

SCHMELZE *n* pl. -S a type of decorative glass

SCHMO *n* pl. SCHMOES or SCHMOS a stupid person

SCHMOE *n* pl. -S schmo

SCHMOOS *v* -ED, -ING, -ES to schmooze

SCHMOOSE *v* SCHMOOSED, SCHMOOSING, SCHMOOSES to schmooze

SCHMOOZE *v* SCHMOOZED, SCHMOOZING, SCHMOOZES to gossip

SCHMUCK *n* pl. -S a foolish or clumsy person

SCHNAPPS *n* pl. SCHNAPPS a strong liquor

SCHNAPS *n* pl. SCHNAPS schnapps

SCHNECKE *n* pl. -KEN a sweet roll

SCHNOOK *n* pl. -S an easily deceived person

SCHNOZ *n* pl. SCHNOZZES the nose

SCHNOZZ *n* pl. -ES schnoz

SCHOLAR *n* pl. -S a learned person

SCHOLIUM *n* pl. -LIA or -LIUMS an explanatory marginal note

SCHOOL *v* -ED, -ING, -S to educate in an institution of learning

SCHOONER *n* pl. -S a sailing vessel

SCHORL *n* pl. -S a mineral

SCHRIK *n* pl. -S sudden fright

SCHROD *n* pl. -S scrod

SCHTICK *n* pl. -S shtick

SCHTIK *n* pl. -S shtick

SCHUIT *n* pl. -S a Dutch sailing vessel

SCHUL *n* pl. SCHULN shul

SCHUSS *v* -ED, -ING, -ES to make a fast, straight run in skiing

SCHUSSER *n* pl. -S one that schusses

SCHWA *n* pl. -S a type of vowel sound

SCIAENID *n* pl. -S a carnivorous fish

SCIATIC *n* pl. -S a nerve, vein, or artery situated near the hip

SCIATICA *n* pl. -S a painful disorder of the hip and adjoining areas

SCIENCE *n* pl. -S a department of systematized knowledge

SCILICET *adv* namely

SCILLA *n* pl. -S a flowering plant

SCIMETAR *n* pl. -S scimitar

SCIMITAR *n* pl. -S a curved Oriental sword

SCIMITER *n* pl. -S scimitar

SCINCOID *n* pl. -S one of a family of smooth, short-limbed lizards

SCIOLISM *n* pl. -S superficial knowledge

SCIOLIST *n* pl. -S one whose knowledge is superficial

SCION *n* pl. -S a child or descendant

SCIROCCO *n* pl. -COS sirocco

SCIRRHUS *n* pl. -RHI or -RHUSES a hard tumor

SCISSILE *adj* capable of being cut or split easily

SCISSION *n* pl. -S the act of cutting or splitting

SCISSOR *v* -ED, -ING, -S to cut with a two-bladed cutting implement

SCISSURE *n* pl. -S a lengthwise cut

SCIURID *n* pl. -S a sciurine

SCIURINE *n* pl. -S a rodent of the squirrel family

SCIUROID *adj* resembling a squirrel

SCLAFF *v* -ED, -ING, -S to strike the ground with the club before hitting the ball in golf

SCLAFFER *n* pl. -S one that sclaffs

SCLERA *n* pl. -RAS or -RAE the white, fibrous outer coat of the eyeball **SCLERAL** *adj*

SCLEREID *n* pl. -S a type of plant cell

SCLERITE *n* pl. -S one of the hard plates forming the outer covering of an arthropod

SCLEROID *adj* sclerous

SCLEROMA *n* pl. -MATA a hardened patch of cellular tissue

SCLEROSE *v* -ROSED, -ROSING, -ROSES to become hard, as tissue

SCLEROUS *adj* hardened

SCOFF *v* -ED, -ING, -S to express rude doubt or derision

SCOFFER *n* pl. -S one that scoffs

SCOFFLAW *n* pl. -S an habitual law violator

SCOLD *v* -ED, -ING, -S to rebuke harshly

SCOLDER *n* pl. -S one that scolds

SCOLDING *n* pl. -S a harsh reproof

SCOLEX *n* pl. -LECES or -LICES the knoblike head of a tapeworm

SCOLIOMA *n* pl. -S abnormal curvature of the spine

SCOLLOP *v* -ED, -ING, -S to scallop

SCONCE *v* SCONCED, SCONCING, SCONCES to fine

SCONE *n* pl. -S a flat, round cake

SCOOP *v* -ED, -ING, -S to take up with a scoop (a spoonlike utensil)

SCOOPER *n* pl. -S one that scoops

SCOOPFUL *n* pl. SCOOPFULS or SCOOPSFUL as much as a scoop will hold

SCOOT *v* -ED, -ING, -S to go quickly

SCOOTER *n* pl. -S a two-wheeled vehicle

SCOP *n* pl. -S an Old English poet

SCOPE *v* SCOPED, SCOPING, SCOPES to look at in order to evaluate

SCOPULA *n* pl. -LAE or -LAS a dense tuft of hairs

SCORCH *v* -ED, -ING, -ES to burn slightly so as to alter the color or taste

SCORCHER *n* pl. -S one that scorches

SCORE *v* SCORED, SCORING, SCORES to make a point in a game or contest

SCOREPAD *n* pl. -S a pad on which scored points are recorded

SCORER *n* pl. -S one that scores

SCORIA *n* pl. -RIAE the refuse of a smelted metal or ore

SCORIFY *v* -FIED, -FYING, -FIES to reduce to scoria

SCORING present participle of score

SCORN *v* -ED, -ING, -S to treat or regard with contempt

SCORNER *n* pl. -S one that scorns

SCORNFUL *adj* feeling or expressing contempt

SCORPION *n* pl. -S a stinging arachnid

SCOT *n* pl. -S a tax

SCOTCH *v* -ED, -ING, -ES to put a definite end to

SCOTER *n* pl. -S a sea duck

SCOTIA *n* pl. -S a concave molding

SCOTOMA *n* pl. -MAS or -MATA a blind spot in the field of vision

SCOTOPIA *n* pl. -S vision in dim light **SCOTOPIC** *adj*

SCOTTIE *n* pl. -S a short-legged terrier

SCOUR *v* -ED, -ING, -S to cleanse or polish by hard rubbing

SCOURER *n* pl. -S one that scours

SCOURGE *v* SCOURGED, SCOURGING, SCOURGES to punish severely

SCOURGER *n* pl. -S one that scourges

SCOURING *n* pl. -S material removed by scouring

SCOUSE *n* pl. -S a type of meat stew

SCOUT *v* -ED, -ING, -S to observe for the purpose of obtaining information

SCOUTER *n* pl. -S one that scouts

SCOUTH *n* pl. -S plenty

SCOUTHER *v* -ED, -ING, -S to scorch

SCOUTING *n* pl. -S the act of one that scouts

SCOW *v* -ED, -ING, -S to transport by scow (a flat-bottomed boat)

SCOWDER *v* -ED, -ING, -S to scouther

SCOWL *v* -ED, -ING, -S to frown angrily

SCOWLER *n* pl. -S one that scowls

SCRABBLE *v* -BLED, -BLING, -BLES to claw or grope about frantically

SCRABBLY *adj* -BLIER, -BLIEST raspy

SCRAG *v* SCRAGGED, SCRAGGING, SCRAGS to wring the neck of

SCRAGGLY *adj* -GLIER, -GLIEST uneven

SCRAGGY *adj* -GIER, -GIEST scrawny

SCRAICH *v* -ED, -ING, -S to utter a shrill cry

SCRAIGH *v* -ED, -ING, -S to scraich

SCRAM *v* SCRAMMED, SCRAMMING, SCRAMS to leave quickly

SCRAMBLE *v* -BLED, -BLING, -BLES to move or climb hurriedly

SCRAMJET *n* pl. -S a type of aircraft engine

SCRANNEL *n* pl. -S a thin person

SCRAP *v* SCRAPPED, SCRAPPING, SCRAPS to discard

SCRAPE *v* SCRAPED, SCRAPING, SCRAPES to rub so as to remove an outer layer

SCRAPER *n* pl. -S one that scrapes

SCRAPIE *n* pl. -S a disease of sheep

SCRAPING *n* pl. -S something scraped off

SCRAPPED past tense of scrap

SCRAPPER *n* pl. -S a fighter

SCRAPPIER comparative of scrappy

SCRAPPIEST superlative of scrappy

SCRAPPING present participle of scrap

SCRAPPLE *n* pl. -S a seasoned mixture of ground meat and cornmeal

SCRAPPY *adj* -PIER, -PIEST marked by fighting spirit

SCRATCH *v* -ED, -ING, -ES to make a thin, shallow cut or mark on

SCRATCHY *adj* SCRATCHIER, SCRATCHIEST made by scratching

SCRAWL *v* -ED, -ING, -S to write hastily or illegibly

SCRAWLER *n* pl. -S one that scrawls

SCRAWLY *adj* SCRAWLIER, SCRAWLIEST written hastily or illegibly

SCRAWNY *adj* -NIER, -NIEST extremely thin

SCREAK *v* -ED, -ING, -S to screech

SCREAKY *adj* screechy

SCREAM *v* -ED, -ING, -S to utter a prolonged, piercing cry

SCREAMER *n* pl. -S one that screams

SCREE *n* pl. -S a mass of rocks at the foot of a slope

SCREECH *v* -ED, -ING, -ES to utter a harsh, shrill cry

SCREECHY *adj* SCREECHIER, SCREECHIEST screaching

SCREED *v* -ED, -ING, -S to shred

SCREEN *v* -ED, -ING, -S to provide with a screen (a device designed to divide, conceal, or protect)

SCREENER *n* pl. -S one that screens

SCREW *v* -ED, -ING, -S to attach with a screw (a type of metal fastener)

SCREWER *n* pl. -S one that screws

SCREWUP *n* pl. -S an instance of bungling

SCREWY *adj* SCREWIER, SCREWIEST crazy

SCRIBAL *adj* pertaining to a public clerk or secretary

SCRIBBLE *v* -BLED, -BLING, -BLES to write hastily or carelessly

SCRIBE *v* SCRIBED, SCRIBING, SCRIBES to mark with a scriber

SCRIBER *n* pl. -S a pointed instrument used for marking off material to be cut

SCRIED past tense of scry

SCRIES present 3d person sing. of scry

SCRIEVE *v* SCRIEVED, SCRIEVING, SCRIEVES to move along swiftly and smoothly

SCRIM *n* pl. -S a cotton fabric

SCRIMP *v* -ED, -ING, -S to be very or overly thrifty

SCRIMPER *n* pl. -S one that scrimps

SCRIMPIT *adj* meager

SCRIMPY *adj* SCRIMPIER, SCRIMPIEST meager

SCRIP *n* pl. -S a small piece of paper

SCRIPT *v* -ED, -ING, -S to prepare a written text for, as a play or motion picture

SCRIPTER *n* pl. -S one that scripts

SCRIVE *v* SCRIVED, SCRIVING, SCRIVES to engrave

SCROD *n* pl. -S a young cod

SCROFULA *n* pl. -S a disease of the lymph glands

SCROGGY *adj* -GIER, -GIEST of stunted growth

SCROLL   *v* -ED, -ING, -S to move text across a display screen

SCROOCH   *v* -ED, -ING, -ES to crouch

SCROOGE   *n* pl. -S a miserly person

SCROOP   *v* -ED, -ING, -S to make a harsh, grating sound

SCROOTCH   *v* -ED, -ING, -ES to scrooch

SCROTUM   *n* pl. -TA or -TUMS the pouch of skin that contains the testes **SCROTAL** *adj*

SCROUGE   *v* SCROUGED, SCROUGING, SCROUGES to crowd

SCROUNGE   *v* SCROUNGED, SCROUNGING, SCROUNGES to gather by foraging

SCROUNGY   *adj* SCROUNGIER, SCROUNGIEST dirty

SCRUB   *v* SCRUBBED, SCRUBBING, SCRUBS to rub hard in order to clean

SCRUBBER   *n* pl. -S one that scrubs

SCRUBBY   *adj* -BIER, -BIEST inferior in size or quality

SCRUFF   *n* pl. -S the back of the neck

SCRUFFY   *adj* -FIER, -FIEST shabby

SCRUM   *v* SCRUMMED, SCRUMMING, SCRUMS to engage in a scrummage (a formation around the ball in rugby)

SCRUNCH   *v* -ED, -ING, -ES to crush

SCRUPLE   *v* -PLED, -PLING, -PLES to hesitate because of ethical considerations

SCRUTINY   *n* pl. -NIES a close examination

SCRY   *v* SCRIED, SCRYING, SCRIES to engage in crystal gazing

SCUBA   *n* pl. -S an underwater breathing device

SCUD   *v* SCUDDED, SCUDDING, SCUDS to run or move swiftly

SCUDO   *n* pl. -DI a former Italian coin

SCUFF   *v* -ED, -ING, -S to walk without lifting the feet

SCUFFLE   *v* -FLED, -FLING, -FLES to struggle in a rough, confused manner

SCUFFLER   *n* pl. -S one that scuffles

SCULK   *v* -ED, -ING, -S to skulk

SCULKER   *n* pl. -S skulker

SCULL   *v* -ED, -ING, -S to propel with a type of oar

SCULLER   *n* pl. -S one that sculls

SCULLERY   *n* pl. -LERIES a room in which kitchen utensils are cleaned and stored

SCULLION   *n* pl. -S a kitchen servant who does menial work

SCULP   *v* -ED, -ING, -S to sculpt

SCULPIN   *n* pl. -S a freshwater fish

SCULPT   *v* -ED, -ING, -S to form an image or representation of from solid material

SCULPTOR   *n* pl. -S one that sculpts

SCUM   *v* SCUMMED, SCUMMING, SCUMS to remove the scum (impure or extraneous matter) from

SCUMBAG   *n* pl. -S a dirtbag

SCUMBLE   *v* -BLED, -BLING, -BLES to soften the outlines or colors of by rubbing lightly

SCUMLIKE   *adj* resembling scum

SCUMMED   past tense of scum

SCUMMER   *n* pl. -S one that scums

SCUMMING   present participle of scum

SCUMMY   *adj* -MIER, -MIEST covered with scum

SCUNNER   *v* -ED, -ING, -S to feel loathing or disgust

SCUP   *n* pl. -S a marine food fish

SCUPPAUG   *n* pl. -S scup

SCUPPER   *v* -ED, -ING, -S to ambush

SCURF   *n* pl. -S scaly or shredded dry skin

SCURFY   *adj* SCURFIER, SCURFIEST covered with scurf

SCURRIED   past tense of scurry

SCURRIES   present 3d person sing. of scurry

SCURRIL   *adj* scurrile

SCURRILE   *adj* expressed in coarse and abusive language

SCURRY   *v* -RIED, -RYING, -RIES to move hurriedly

SCURVY   *adj* -VIER, -VIEST base or contemptible **SCURVILY** *adv*

SCURVY   *n* pl. -VIES a disease resulting from vitamin C deficiency

SCUT   *n* pl. -S a short tail, as of a rabbit

SCUTA   pl. of scutum

SCUTAGE   *n* pl. -S a tax exacted by a feudal lord in lieu of military service

SCUTATE   *adj* shaped like a shield

SCUTCH	*v* -ED, -ING, -ES to separate the woody fiber from by beating
SCUTCHER	*n* pl. -S one that scutches
SCUTE	*n* pl. -S a horny plate or scale
SCUTELLA	*n/pl* small, scutate organs or parts
SCUTTER	*v* -ED, -ING, -S to scurry
SCUTTLE	*v* -TLED, -TLING, -TLES to scurry
SCUTUM	*n* pl. -TA scute
SCUZZY	*adj* -ZIER, -ZIEST dirty or shabby
SCYPHATE	*adj* shaped like a cup
SCYPHUS	*n* pl. -PHI a Greek cup with two handles
SCYTHE	*v* SCYTHED, SCYTHING, SCYTHES to cut with a scythe (a single-bladed cutting implement)
SEA	*n* pl. -S the ocean
SEABAG	*n* pl. -S a bag used by a sailor
SEABEACH	*n* pl. -ES a beach lying along the sea
SEABED	*n* pl. -S a seafloor
SEABIRD	*n* pl. -S a bird frequenting the ocean or seacoast
SEABOARD	*n* pl. -S the seacoast
SEABOOT	*n* pl. -S a waterproof boot
SEABORNE	*adj* carried on or over the sea
SEACOAST	*n* pl. -S land bordering on the sea
SEACOCK	*n* pl. -S a valve in a ship's hull
SEACRAFT	*n* pl. -S skill in sea navigation
SEADOG	*n* pl. -S a fogbow
SEADROME	*n* pl. -S an airport in the sea
SEAFARER	*n* pl. -S a sailor
SEAFLOOR	*n* pl. -S the bottom of a sea
SEAFOOD	*n* pl. -S edible fish or shellfish from the sea
SEAFOWL	*n* pl. -S a seabird
SEAFRONT	*n* pl. -S an area along the edge of the sea
SEAGIRT	*adj* surrounded by the sea
SEAGOING	*adj* designed for use on the sea
SEAGULL	*n* pl. -S a gull frequenting the sea
SEAL	*v* -ED, -ING, -S to close or make secure against access, leakage, or passage **SEALABLE** *adj*
SEALANT	*n* pl. -S a sealing agent
SEALER	*n* pl. -S one that seals
SEALERY	*n* pl. -ERIES the occupation of hunting seals
SEALLIKE	*adj* resembling a seal (an aquatic mammal)
SEALSKIN	*n* pl. -S the skin of a seal
SEAM	*v* -ED, -ING, -S to join with a seam (a line formed by sewing two pieces of fabric together)
SEAMAN	*n* pl. -MEN a sailor **SEAMANLY** *adj*
SEAMARK	*n* pl. -S a landmark serving as a navigational guide to mariners
SEAMER	*n* pl. -S one that seams
SEAMIER	comparative of seamy
SEAMIEST	superlative of seamy
SEAMLESS	*adj* having no seam
SEAMLIKE	*adj* resembling a seam
SEAMOUNT	*n* pl. -S an undersea mountain
SEAMSTER	*n* pl. -S a person whose occupation is sewing
SEAMY	*adj* SEAMIER, SEAMIEST unpleasant
SEANCE	*n* pl. -S a meeting of persons seeking spiritualistic messages
SEAPIECE	*n* pl. -S a seascape
SEAPLANE	*n* pl. -S an airplane designed to take off from or land on the water
SEAPORT	*n* pl. -S a harbor or town accessible to seagoing ships
SEAQUAKE	*n* pl. -S an undersea earthquake
SEAR	*adj* SEARER, SEAREST sere
SEAR	*v* -ED, -ING, -S to burn the surface of
SEARCH	*v* -ED, -ING, -ES to look through or over carefully in order to find something
SEARCHER	*n* pl. -S one that searches
SEAROBIN	*n* pl. -S a marine fish
SEASCAPE	*n* pl. -S a picture of the sea
SEASCOUT	*n* pl. -S a boy scout trained in water activities
SEASHELL	*n* pl. -S the shell of a marine mollusk
SEASHORE	*n* pl. -S land bordering on the sea
SEASICK	*adj* affected with nausea caused by the motion of a vessel at sea
SEASIDE	*n* pl. -S the seashore
SEASON	*v* -ED, -ING, -S to heighten or improve the flavor of by adding savory ingredients

SEASONAL   *adj* occurring at a certain time of the year

SEASONER   *n* pl. -S one that seasons

SEAT   *v* -ED, -ING, -S to place on a seat (something on which one sits)

SEATER   *n* pl. -S one that seats

SEATING   *n* pl. -S material for covering seats

SEATLESS   *adj* having no seat

SEATMATE   *n* pl. -S one with whom one shares a seat

SEATRAIN   *n* pl. -S a ship equipped to carry railroad cars

SEATWORK   *n* pl. -S work done at one's seat

SEAWALL   *n* pl. -S a wall to protect a shoreline from erosion

SEAWAN   *n* pl. -S wampum

SEAWANT   *n* pl. -S seawan

SEAWARD   *n* pl. -S the direction toward the open sea

SEAWARE   *n* pl. -S seaweed used as fertilizer

SEAWATER   *n* pl. -S water from the sea

SEAWAY   *n* pl. -WAYS the headway made by a ship

SEAWEED   *n* pl. -S a plant growing in the sea

SEBACIC   *adj* derived from a certain acid

SEBASIC   *adj* sebacic

SEBUM   *n* pl. -S a fatty matter secreted by certain glands of the skin

SEC   *n* pl. -S secant

SECALOSE   *n* pl. -S a complex carbohydrate

SECANT   *n* pl. -S a trigonometric function of an angle

SECANTLY   *adv* in an intersecting manner

SECATEUR   *n* pl. -S a pruning tool

SECCO   *n* pl. -COS the art of painting on dry plaster

SECEDE   *v* -CEDED, -CEDING, -CEDES to withdraw formally from an alliance or association

SECEDER   *n* pl. -S one that secedes

SECERN   *v* -ED, -ING, -S to discern as separate

SECLUDE   *v* -CLUDED, -CLUDING, -CLUDES to remove or set apart from others

SECOND   *v* -ED, -ING, -S to give support or encouragement to

SECONDE   *n* pl. -S a position in fencing

SECONDER   *n* pl. -S one that seconds

SECONDLY   *adv* in the next place after the first

SECONDO   *n* pl. -DI the lower part in a piano duet

SECPAR   *n* pl. -S a parsec

SECRECY   *n* pl. -CIES the condition of being secret

SECRET   *adj* -CRETER, -CRETEST kept from knowledge or view

SECRET   *n* pl. -S something kept from the knowledge of others

SECRETE   *v* -CRETED, -CRETING, -CRETES to generate and separate out from cells or bodily fluids

SECRETIN   *n* pl. -S a hormone

SECRETLY   *adv* in a secret manner

SECRETOR   *n* pl. -S one that secretes

SECT   *n* pl. -S a group of people united by common beliefs or interests

SECTARY   *n* pl. -RIES a member of a sect

SECTILE   *adj* capable of being cut smoothly

SECTION   *v* -ED, -ING, -S to divide into sections (distinct parts)

SECTOR   *v* -ED, -ING, -S to divide into sectors (sections)

SECTORAL   *adj* of or pertaining to a sector

SECULAR   *n* pl. -S a layman

SECUND   *adj* having the parts or organs arranged on one side only **SECUNDLY** *adv*

SECUNDUM   *adv* according to

SECURE   *adj* -CURER, -CUREST free from danger **SECURELY** *adv*

SECURE   *v* -CURED, -CURING, -CURES to make firm or tight

SECURER   *n* pl. -S one that secures

SECUREST   superlative of secure

SECURING   present participle of secure

SECURITY   *n* pl. -TIES the state of being secure

SEDAN   *n* pl. -S a type of automobile

SEDARIM   a pl. of seder

SEDATE   *adj* -DATER, -DATEST calm **SEDATELY** *adv*

SEDATE   *v* -DATED, -DATING, -DATES to administer a sedative to

SEDATION	*n* pl. -S the reduction of stress or excitement by the use of sedatives
SEDATIVE	*n* pl. -S a drug that induces a calm state
SEDER	*n* pl. -DARIM or -DERS a Jewish ceremonial dinner
SEDERUNT	*n* pl. -S a prolonged sitting
SEDGE	*n* pl. -S a marsh plant
SEDGY	*adj* SEDGIER, SEDGIEST abounding in sedge
SEDILE	*n* pl. -LIA one of the seats in a church for the use of the officiating clergy
SEDILIUM	*n* pl. -LIA sedile
SEDIMENT	*v* -ED, -ING, -S to settle to the bottom of a liquid
SEDITION	*n* pl. -S incitement of rebellion against a government
SEDUCE	*v* -DUCED, -DUCING, -DUCES to lead astray **SEDUCIVE** *adj*
SEDUCER	*n* pl. -S one that seduces
SEDULITY	*n* pl. -TIES the state of being sedulous
SEDULOUS	*adj* diligent
SEDUM	*n* pl. -S a flowering plant
SEE	*v* SAW, SEEN, SEEING, SEES to perceive with the eyes **SEEABLE** *adj*
SEECATCH	*n* pl. -CATCHIE an adult male fur seal
SEED	*v* -ED, -ING, -S to plant seeds (propagative plant structures) in
SEEDBED	*n* pl. -S land prepared for seeding
SEEDCAKE	*n* pl. -S a sweet cake containing aromatic seeds
SEEDCASE	*n* pl. -S a pericarp
SEEDER	*n* pl. -S one that seeds
SEEDIER	comparative of seedy
SEEDIEST	superlative of seedy
SEEDILY	*adv* in a seedy manner
SEEDLESS	*adj* having no seeds
SEEDLIKE	*adj* resembling a seed
SEEDLING	*n* pl. -S a young plant
SEEDMAN	*n* pl. -MEN seedsman
SEEDPOD	*n* pl. -S a type of seed vessel
SEEDSMAN	*n* pl. -MEN a dealer in seeds
SEEDTIME	*n* pl. -S the season for sowing seeds

SEEDY	*adj* SEEDIER, SEEDIEST containing seeds; inferior in condition or quality
SEEING	*n* pl. -S the act of one that sees
SEEK	*v* SOUGHT, SEEKING, SEEKS to go in search of
SEEKER	*n* pl. -S one that seeks
SEEL	*v* -ED, -ING, -S to stitch closed the eyes of, as a falcon during training
SEELY	*adj* frail
SEEM	*v* -ED, -ING, -S to give the impression of being
SEEMER	*n* pl. -S one that seems
SEEMING	*n* pl. -S outward appearance
SEEMLY	*adj* -LIER, -LIEST of pleasing appearance
SEEN	past participle of see
SEEP	*v* -ED, -ING, -S to pass slowly through small openings
SEEPAGE	*n* pl. -S the quantity of fluid that has seeped
SEEPY	*adj* SEEPIER, SEEPIEST soaked or oozing with water
SEER	*n* pl. -S a prophet
SEERESS	*n* pl. -ES a female seer
SEESAW	*v* -ED, -ING, -S to move up and down or back and forth
SEETHE	*v* SEETHED, SEETHING, SEETHES to surge or foam as if boiling
SEG	*n* pl. -S one who advocates racial segregation
SEGETAL	*adj* growing in fields of grain
SEGGAR	*n* pl. -S a saggar
SEGMENT	*v* -ED, -ING, -S to divide into sections
SEGNO	*n* pl. -GNI or -GNOS a musical sign
SEGO	*n* pl. -GOS a perennial herb
SEGUE	*v* -GUED, -GUEING, -GUES to proceed without pause from one musical theme to another
SEI	*n* pl. -S a rorqual
SEICENTO	*n* pl. -TOS the seventeenth century
SEICHE	*n* pl. -S an oscillation of the surface of a lake or landlocked sea
SEIDEL	*n* pl. -S a large beer glass
SEIF	*n* pl. -S a long, narrow sand dune

SEIGNEUR	*n* pl. -S seignior
SEIGNIOR	*n* pl. -S a feudal lord
SEIGNORY	*n* pl. -GNORIES the power of a seignior
SEINE	*v* SEINED, SEINING, SEINES to catch fish with a large, vertically hanging net
SEINER	*n* pl. -S one that seines
SEISE	*v* SEISED, SEISING, SEISES to seize **SEISABLE** *adj*
SEISER	*n* pl. -S seizer
SEISIN	*n* pl. -S seizin
SEISING	*n* pl. -S seizing
SEISM	*n* pl. -S an earthquake **SEISMAL, SEISMIC** *adj*
SEISMISM	*n* pl. -S the natural activity involved in earthquakes
SEISOR	*n* pl. -S seizor
SEISURE	*n* pl. -S seizure
SEIZE	*v* SEIZED, SEIZING, SEIZES to take hold of suddenly and forcibly **SEIZABLE** *adj*
SEIZER	*n* pl. -S one that seizes
SEIZIN	*n* pl. -S legal possession of land
SEIZING	*n* pl. -S the act of one that seizes
SEIZOR	*n* pl. -S one that takes seizin
SEIZURE	*n* pl. -S the act of seizing
SEJANT	*adj* represented in a sitting position — used of a heraldic animal
SEJEANT	*adj* sejant
SEL	*n* pl. -S self
SELADANG	*n* pl. -S saladang
SELAH	*n* pl. -S a word of unknown meaning often marking the end of a verse in the Psalms
SELAMLIK	*n* pl. -S the portion of a Turkish house reserved for men
SELCOUTH	*adj* unusual
SELDOM	*adj* infrequent **SELDOMLY** *adv*
SELECT	*v* -ED, -ING, -S to choose
SELECTEE	*n* pl. -S one that is selected
SELECTLY	*adv* by selection
SELECTOR	*n* pl. -S one that selects
SELENATE	*n* pl. -S a chemical salt
SELENIC	*adj* pertaining to selenium
SELENIDE	*n* pl. -S a compound of selenium
SELENITE	*n* pl. -S a variety of gypsum

SELENIUM	*n* pl. -S a nonmetallic element **SELENOUS** *adj*
SELF	*n* pl. SELVES the total, essential, or particular being of one person
SELF	*v* -ED, -ING, -S to inbreed
SELFDOM	*n* pl. -S selfhood
SELFHEAL	*n* pl. -S a perennial herb
SELFHOOD	*n* pl. -S the state of being an individual person
SELFISH	*adj* concerned chiefly or only with oneself
SELFLESS	*adj* unselfish
SELFNESS	*n* pl. -ES selfhood
SELFSAME	*adj* identical
SELFWARD	*adv* toward oneself
SELL	*v* SOLD, SELLING, SELLS to give up to another for money or other valuable consideration **SELLABLE** *adj*
SELLE	*n* pl. -S a saddle
SELLER	*n* pl. -S one that sells
SELLOUT	*n* pl. -S a performance for which all seats have been sold
SELSYN	*n* pl. -S a type of remote-control device
SELTZER	*n* pl. -S carbonated mineral water
SELVA	*n* pl. -S a tropical rain forest
SELVAGE	*n* pl. -S the edge of a woven fabric finished to prevent raveling **SELVAGED** *adj*
SELVEDGE	*n* pl. -S selvage
SELVES	pl. of self
SEMANTIC	*adj* pertaining to meaning
SEMATIC	*adj* serving as a warning
SEME	*n* pl. -S a type of ornamental pattern
SEMEME	*n* pl. -S the meaning of a morpheme **SEMEMIC** *adj*
SEMEN	*n* pl. -MINA or -MENS a fluid produced in the male reproductive organs
SEMESTER	*n* pl. -S a period constituting half of an academic year
SEMI	*n* pl. -S a freight trailer
SEMIARID	*adj* characterized by light rainfall
SEMIBALD	*adj* partly bald
SEMICOMA	*n* pl. -S a coma from which a person can be aroused
SEMIDEAF	*adj* partly deaf
SEMIDOME	*n* pl. -S a half dome

SEMIDRY *adj* moderately dry

SEMIFIT *adj* conforming somewhat to the lines of the body

SEMIGALA *adj* somewhat gala

SEMIHARD *adj* moderately hard

SEMIHIGH *adj* moderately high

SEMIHOBO *n* pl. -BOS or -BOES a person having some of the characteristics of a hobo

SEMILOG *adj* having one scale logarithmic and the other arithmetic

SEMIMAT *adj* having a slight luster

SEMIMATT *adj* semimat

SEMIMUTE *adj* having partially lost the faculty of speech

SEMINA a pl. of semen

SEMINAL *adj* pertaining to semen

SEMINAR *n* pl. -S an advanced study group at a college or university

SEMINARY *n* pl. -NARIES a school for the training of priests, ministers, or rabbis

SEMINUDE *adj* partly nude

SEMIOSIS *n* pl. -OSES a process in which something functions as a sign to an organism

SEMIOTIC *n* pl. -S a general theory of signs and symbolism

SEMIPRO *n* pl. -PROS one who is engaged in some field or sport for pay on a part-time basis

SEMIRAW *adj* somewhat raw

SEMIS *n* pl. -MISES a coin of ancient Rome

SEMISOFT *adj* moderately soft

SEMITIST *n* pl. -S one who favors Jewish interests

SEMITONE *n* pl. -S a type of musical tone

SEMIWILD *adj* somewhat wild

SEMOLINA *n* pl. -S a granular product of wheat used for pasta

SEMPLE *adj* of humble birth

SEMPLICE *adj* simple — used as a musical direction

SEMPRE *adv* in the same manner throughout — used as a musical direction

SEN *n* pl. SEN a monetary unit of Japan

SENARIUS *n* pl. -NARII a Greek or Latin verse consisting of six metrical feet

SENARY *adj* pertaining to the number six

SENATE *n* pl. -S an assembly having high deliberative and legislative functions

SENATOR *n* pl. -S a member of a senate

SEND *v* SENT, SENDING, SENDS to cause to go **SENDABLE** *adj*

SEND *v* -ED, -ING, -S to scend

SENDAL *n* pl. -S a silk fabric

SENDER *n* pl. -S one that sends

SENDOFF *n* pl. -S a farewell celebration

SENDUP *n* pl. -S a parody

SENE *n* pl. SENE a monetary unit of Western Samoa

SENECA *n* pl. -S senega

SENECIO *n* pl. -CIOS a flowering plant

SENEGA *n* pl. -S a medicinal plant root

SENGI *n* pl. SENGI a monetary unit of Zaire

SENHOR *n* pl. -S or -ES a Portuguese or Brazilian gentleman

SENHORA *n* pl. -S a married Portuguese or Brazilian woman

SENILE *n* pl. -S one who exhibits senility

SENILELY *adv* in a senile manner

SENILITY *n* pl. -TIES mental and physical infirmity due to old age

SENIOR *n* pl. -S a person who is older than another

SENITI *n* pl. SENITI a monetary unit of Tonga

SENNA *n* pl. -S a medicinal plant

SENNET *n* pl. -S a call sounded on a trumpet signaling the entrance or exit of actors

SENNIGHT *n* pl. -S a week

SENNIT *n* pl. -S braided straw used in making hats

SENOPIA *n* pl. -S an improvement of near vision

SENOR *n* pl. -S or -ES a Spanish gentleman

SENORA *n* pl. -S a married Spanish woman

SENORITA *n* pl. -S an unmarried Spanish girl or woman

SENRYU *n* pl. SENRYU a Japanese poem

SENSA	pl. of sensum
SENSATE	v -SATED, -SATING, -SATES to sense
SENSE	v SENSED, SENSING, SENSES to perceive by the senses (any of certain agencies through which an individual receives impressions of the external world)
SENSEFUL	adj sensible
SENSIBLE	adj -BLER, -BLEST having or showing good judgment **SENSIBLY** adv
SENSIBLE	n pl. -S something that can be sensed
SENSILLA	n pl. -LAE a simple sense organ
SENSING	present participle of sense
SENSOR	n pl. -S a device that receives and responds to a stimulus
SENSORIA	n/pl the parts of the brain concerned with the reception and interpretation of sensory stimuli
SENSORY	adj pertaining to the senses or sensation
SENSUAL	adj pertaining to the physical senses
SENSUM	n pl. -SA an object of perception or sensation
SENSUOUS	adj pertaining to or derived from the senses
SENT	past tense of send (to cause to go)
SENTE	n pl. LICENTE or LISENTE a monetary unit of Lesotho
SENTENCE	v -TENCED, -TENCING, -TENCES to declare judicially the extent of punishment to be imposed
SENTI	n pl. SENTI a former monetary unit of Tanzania
SENTIENT	n pl. -S a person or thing capable of sensation
SENTIMO	n pl. -MOS a monetary unit of the Philippines
SENTINEL	v -NELED, -NELING, -NELS or -NELLED, -NELLING, -NELS to stand guard
SENTRY	n pl. -TRIES one who stands guard
SEPAL	n pl. -S one of the individual leaves of a calyx **SEPALED, SEPALINE, SEPALLED, SEPALOID, SEPALOUS** adj
SEPARATE	v -RATED, -RATING, -RATES to set or keep apart
SEPIA	n pl. -S a brown pigment **SEPIC** adj
SEPOY	n pl. -POYS a native of India serving in the British army
SEPPUKU	n pl. -S a Japanese form of suicide
SEPSIS	n pl. SEPSES bacterial invasion of the body
SEPT	n pl. -S a clan
SEPTA	pl. of septum
SEPTAL	adj pertaining to a septum
SEPTARIA	n/pl limestone nodules
SEPTATE	adj having a septum
SEPTET	n pl. -S a group of seven
SEPTETTE	n pl. -S septet
SEPTIC	n pl. -S an agent producing sepsis **SEPTICAL** adj
SEPTIME	n pl. -S a position in fencing
SEPTUM	n pl. -TA or -TUMS a dividing membrane or partition
SEPTUPLE	v -PLED, -PLING, -PLES to make seven times as great
SEQUEL	n pl. -S something that follows and serves as a continuation
SEQUELA	n pl. -QUELAE an abnormal condition resulting from a preceding disease
SEQUENCE	v -QUENCED, -QUENCING, -QUENCES to arrange in consecutive order
SEQUENCY	n pl. -CIES the following of one thing after another
SEQUENT	n pl. -S something that follows
SEQUIN	n pl. -S a shiny ornamental disk **SEQUINED** adj
SEQUITUR	n pl. -S the conclusion of an inference
SEQUOIA	n pl. -S a large evergreen tree
SER	n pl. -S a unit of weight of India
SERA	a pl. of serum
SERAC	n pl. -S a large mass of ice broken off of a glacier
SERAGLIO	n pl. -GLIOS a harem
SERAI	n pl. -S a Turkish palace
SERAIL	n pl. -S a seraglio
SERAL	adj pertaining to a series of ecological changes
SERAPE	n pl. -S a colorful woolen shawl

SERAPH *n* pl. -APHS, -APHIM, or -APHIN a winged celestial being **SERAPHIC** *adj*

SERAPHIM *n* pl. -S seraph

SERDAB *n* pl. -S a chamber within an ancient Egyptian tomb

SERE *adj* SERER, SEREST withered; dry

SERE *v* SERED, SERING, SERES to sear

SEREIN *n* pl. -S a fine rain falling from an apparently clear sky

SERENADE *v* -NADED, -NADING, -NADES to perform an honorific evening song for

SERENATA *n* pl. -TAS or -TE a dramatic cantata

SERENE *adj* SERENER, SERENEST calm; tranquil **SERENELY** *adv*

SERENE *n* pl. -S a serene condition or expanse

SERENITY *n* pl. -TIES the state of being serene

SERER comparative of sere

SEREST superlative of sere

SERF *n* pl. -S a feudal slave

SERFAGE *n* pl. -S serfdom

SERFDOM *n* pl. -S the state of being a serf

SERFHOOD *n* pl. -S serfdom

SERFISH *adj* characteristic of a serf

SERFLIKE *adj* serfish

SERGE *n* pl. -S a twilled fabric

SERGEANT *n* pl. -S a noncommissioned military officer

SERGING *n* pl. -S a process of finishing the raw edges of a fabric

SERIAL *n* pl. -S a literary or dramatic work presented in successive installments

SERIALLY *adv* in the manner or form of a serial

SERIATE *v* -ATED, -ATING, -ATES to put into a series

SERIATIM *adv* serially

SERICIN *n* pl. -S a kind of protein

SERIEMA *n* pl. -S a Brazilian bird

SERIES *n* pl. SERIES an arrangement of one after another

SERIF *n* pl. -S a fine line used to finish off the main stroke of a letter **SERIFED, SERIFFED** *adj*

SERIN *n* pl. -S a European finch

SERINE *n* pl. -S an amino acid

SERING present participle of sere

SERINGA *n* pl. -S a Brazilian tree

SERIOUS *adj* thoughtful or subdued in appearance or manner

SERJEANT *n* pl. -S sergeant

SERMON *n* pl. -S a religious discourse **SERMONIC** *adj*

SEROLOGY *n* pl. -GIES the science of serums

SEROSA *n* pl. -SAS or -SAE a thin membrane lining certain bodily cavities **SEROSAL** *adj*

SEROSITY *n* pl. -TIES the quality or state of being serous

SEROTINE *n* pl. -S a European bat

SEROTYPE *n* pl. -S a group of closely related organisms distinguished by a common set of antigens

SEROUS *adj* of or resembling serum

SEROW *n* pl. -S an Asian antelope

SERPENT *n* pl. -S a snake

SERPIGO *n* pl. -GOES or -GINES a spreading skin eruption

SERRANID *n* pl. -S a marine fish

SERRANO *n* pl. -NOS a small hot pepper

SERRATE *v* -RATED, -RATING, -RATES to furnish with toothlike projections

SERRY *v* -RIED, -RYING, -RIES to crowd together

SERUM *n* pl. -RUMS or -RA the watery portion of whole blood **SERUMAL** *adj*

SERVABLE *adj* capable of serving or being served

SERVAL *n* pl. -S an African wildcat

SERVANT *n* pl. -S one that serves others

SERVE *v* SERVED, SERVING, SERVES to work for

SERVER *n* pl. -S one that serves another

SERVICE *v* -VICED, -VICING, -VICES to repair

SERVICER *n* pl. -S one that services

SERVILE *adj* slavishly submissive

SERVING *n* pl. -S a portion of food

SERVITOR *n* pl. -S a male servant

SERVO *n* pl. -VOS an automatic device used to control another mechanism

SESAME	*n* pl. -S an East Indian plant
SESAMOID	*n* pl. -S a nodular mass of bone or cartilage
SESSILE	*adj* permanently attached
SESSION	*n* pl. -S a meeting of a legislative or judicial body for the transaction of business
SESSPOOL	*n* pl. -S cesspool
SESTERCE	*n* pl. -S a coin of ancient Rome
SESTET	*n* pl. -S a stanza of six lines
SESTINA	*n* pl. -S a type of verse form
SESTINE	*n* pl. -S sestina
SET	*v* SET, SETTING, SETS to put in a particular position
SETA	*n* pl. -TAE a coarse, stiff hair **SETAL** *adj*
SETBACK	*n* pl. -S a defeat
SETENANT	*n* pl. -S a postage stamp that differs in design from others in the same sheet
SETIFORM	*adj* having the form of a seta
SETLINE	*n* pl. -S a strong fishing line
SETOFF	*n* pl. -S something that offsets something else
SETON	*n* pl. -S a type of surgical thread
SETOSE	*adj* covered with setae
SETOUS	*adj* setose
SETOUT	*n* pl. -S a display
SETSCREW	*n* pl. -S a type of screw
SETT	*n* pl. -S the burrow of a badger
SETTEE	*n* pl. -S a long seat with a high back
SETTER	*n* pl. -S one that sets
SETTING	*n* pl. -S the scenery used in a dramatic production
SETTLE	*v* -TLED, -TLING, -TLES to place in a desired state or order
SETTLER	*n* pl. -S one that settles
SETTLING	*n* pl. -S sediment
SETTLOR	*n* pl. -S one that makes a legal settlement
SETULOSE	*adj* covered with seta
SETULOUS	*adj* setulose
SETUP	*n* pl. -S the way something is arranged
SEVEN	*n* pl. -S a number
SEVENTH	*n* pl. -S one of seven equal parts
SEVENTY	*n* pl. -TIES a number
SEVER	*v* -ED, -ING, -S to divide or cut into parts
SEVERAL	*n* pl. -S a few persons or things
SEVERE	*adj* -VERER, -VEREST unsparing in the treatment of others **SEVERELY** *adv*
SEVERITY	*n* pl. -TIES the quality or state of being severe
SEVICHE	*n* pl. -S a dish of raw fish
SEW	*v* SEWED, SEWN, SEWING, SEWS to mend or fasten with a needle and thread **SEWABLE** *adj*
SEWAGE	*n* pl. -S the waste matter carried off by sewers
SEWAN	*n* pl. -S seawan
SEWAR	*n* pl. -S a medieval servant
SEWER	*v* -ED, -ING, -S to clean or maintain sewers (underground conduits for waste)
SEWERAGE	*n* pl. -S sewage
SEWING	*n* pl. -S material that has been or is to be sewed
SEWN	a past participle of sew
SEX	*v* -ED, -ING, -ES to determine the sex (the property by which organisms are classified according to reproductive functions) of
SEXIER	comparative of sexy
SEXIEST	superlative of sexy
SEXILY	*adv* in a sexy manner
SEXINESS	*n* pl. -ES the quality or state of being sexy
SEXISM	*n* pl. -S prejudice or discrimination against women
SEXIST	*n* pl. -S one that practices sexism
SEXLESS	*adj* lacking sexual characteristics
SEXOLOGY	*n* pl. -GIES the study of human sexual behavior
SEXPOT	*n* pl. -S a sexually attractive woman
SEXT	*n* pl. -S one of seven canonical daily periods for prayer and devotion
SEXTAIN	*n* pl. -S a stanza of six lines
SEXTAN	*n* pl. -S a recurrent malarial fever
SEXTANT	*n* pl. -S an instrument for measuring angular distances
SEXTARII	*n/pl* ancient Roman units of liquid measure
SEXTET	*n* pl. -S a group of six

SEXTETTE   *n* pl. -S sextet

SEXTILE   *n* pl. -S the position of two celestial bodies when they are sixty degrees apart

SEXTO   *n* pl. -TOS sixmo

SEXTON   *n* pl. -S a maintenance worker of a church

SEXTUPLE   *v* -PLED, -PLING, -PLES to make six times as great

SEXTUPLY   *adv* to six times as much or as many

SEXUAL   *adj* pertaining to sex **SEXUALLY** *adv*

SEXY   *adj* SEXIER, SEXIEST arousing sexual desire

SFERICS   *n/pl* an electronic detector of storms

SFORZATO   *n* pl. -TOS the playing of a tone or chord with sudden force

SFUMATO   *n* pl. -TOS a technique used in painting

SH   *interj* — used to urge silence

SHA   *interj* — used to urge silence

SHABBY   *adj* -BIER, -BIEST ragged **SHABBILY** *adv*

SHACK   *n* pl. -S a shanty

SHACKLE   *v* -LED, -LING, -LES to confine with metal fastenings placed around the wrists or ankles

SHACKLER   *n* pl. -S one that shackles

SHACKO   *n* pl. -KOS or -KOES shako

SHAD   *n* pl. -S a food fish

SHADBLOW   *n* pl. -S a shadbush

SHADBUSH   *n* pl. -ES a flowering tree or shrub

SHADCHAN   *n* pl. -CHANIM or -CHANS a Jewish marriage broker

SHADDOCK   *n* pl. -S a citrus fruit

SHADE   *v* SHADED, SHADING, SHADES to screen from light or heat

SHADER   *n* pl. -S one that shades

SHADFLY   *n* pl. -FLIES a winged insect

SHADIER   comparative of shady

SHADIEST   superlative of shady

SHADILY   *adv* in a shady manner

SHADING   *n* pl. -S protection against light or heat

SHADOOF   *n* pl. -S a device used in Egypt for raising water for irrigation

SHADOW   *v* -ED, -ING, -S to make dark or gloomy

SHADOWER   *n* pl. -S one that shadows

SHADOWY   *adj* -OWIER, -OWIEST dark

SHADRACH   *n* pl. -S a mass of unfused material in the hearth of a blast furnace

SHADUF   *n* pl. -S shadoof

SHADY   *adj* SHADIER, SHADIEST shaded

SHAFT   *v* -ED, -ING, -S to push or propel with a pole

SHAFTING   *n* pl. -S a system of rods for transmitting motion or power

SHAG   *v* SHAGGED, SHAGGING, SHAGS to make shaggy

SHAGBARK   *n* pl. -S a hardwood tree

SHAGGY   *adj* -GIER, -GIEST covered with long, coarse hair **SHAGGILY** *adv*

SHAGREEN   *n* pl. -S the rough skin of certain sharks

SHAH   *n* pl. -S an Iranian ruler

SHAHDOM   *n* pl. -S the territory ruled by a shah

SHAIRD   *n* pl. -S shard

SHAIRN   *n* pl. -S sharn

SHAITAN   *n* pl. -S an evil spirit

SHAKE   *v* SHOOK, SHAKEN, SHAKING, SHAKES to move to and fro with short, rapid movements **SHAKABLE** *adj*

SHAKEOUT   *n* pl. -S a minor economic recession

SHAKER   *n* pl. -S one that shakes

SHAKEUP   *n* pl. -S a total reorganization

SHAKIER   comparative of shaky

SHAKIEST   superlative of shaky

SHAKILY   *adv* in a shaky manner

SHAKING   present participle of shake

SHAKO   *n* pl. -KOS or -KOES a type of military hat

SHAKY   *adj* SHAKIER, SHAKIEST shaking

SHALE   *n* pl. -S a fissile rock

SHALED   *adj* having a shell or husk

SHALEY   *adj* SHALIER, SHALIEST shaly

SHALIER   comparative of shaly

SHALIEST   superlative of shaly

SHALL *v* present sing. 2d person SHALL or SHALT, past sing. 2d person SHOULD, SHOULDST, or SHOULDEST — used as an auxiliary to express futurity, inevitability, or command

SHALLOON *n* pl. -S a woolen fabric

SHALLOP *n* pl. -S a small, open boat

SHALLOT *n* pl. -S a plant resembling an onion

SHALLOW *adj* -LOWER, -LOWEST having little depth

SHALLOW *v* -ED, -ING, -S to make shallow

SHALOM *n* pl. -S a word used as a Jewish greeting or farewell

SHALT a present 2d person sing. of shall

SHALY *adj* SHALIER, SHALIEST resembling shale

SHAM *v* SHAMMED, SHAMMING, SHAMS to feign

SHAMABLE *adj* capable of being shamed

SHAMAN *n* pl. -S a medicine man among certain North American Indians **SHAMANIC** *adj*

SHAMAS *n* pl. -MOSIM shammes

SHAMBLE *v* -BLED, -BLING, -BLES to walk awkwardly

SHAME *v* SHAMED, SHAMING, SHAMES to cause to feel a painful sense of guilt or degradation

SHAMEFUL *adj* disgraceful

SHAMES *n* pl. -MOSIM shammes

SHAMING present participle of shame

SHAMMAS *n* pl. -MASIM shammes

SHAMMASH *n* pl. -MASHIM shammes

SHAMMED past tense of sham

SHAMMER *n* pl. -S one that shams

SHAMMES *n* pl. -MOSIM a minor official of a synagogue

SHAMMIED past tense of shammy

SHAMMIES present 3d person sing. of shammy

SHAMMING present participle of sham

SHAMMOS *n* pl. -MOSIM shammes

SHAMMOSIM pl. of shammes

SHAMMY *v* -MIED, -MYING, -MIES to chamois

SHAMOIS *n* pl. SHAMOIS chamois

SHAMOS *n* pl. -MOSIM shammes

SHAMOSIM pl. of shames

SHAMOY *v* -ED, -ING, -S to chamois

SHAMPOO *v* -ED, -ING, -S to cleanse with a special preparation

SHAMROCK *n* pl. -S a three-leaved plant

SHAMUS *n* pl. -ES a private detective

SHANDY *n* pl. -DIES an alcoholic drink

SHANGHAI *v* -ED, -ING, -S to kidnap for service aboard a ship

SHANK *v* -ED, -ING, -S to hit sharply to the right, as a golf ball

SHANNY *n* pl. -NIES a marine fish

SHANTEY *n* pl. -TEYS chantey

SHANTI *n* pl. -S peace

SHANTIES pl. of shanty

SHANTIH *n* pl. -S shanti

SHANTUNG *n* pl. -S a silk fabric

SHANTY *n* pl. -TIES a small, crudely built dwelling

SHAPE *v* SHAPED, SHAPEN, SHAPING, SHAPES to give shape (outward form) to **SHAPABLE** *adj*

SHAPELY *adj* -LIER, -LIEST having a pleasing shape

SHAPER *n* pl. -S one that shapes

SHAPEUP *n* pl. -S a system of hiring a work crew

SHAPING present participle of shape

SHARD *n* pl. -S a fragment of broken pottery

SHARE *v* SHARED, SHARING, SHARES to have, get, or use in common with another or others **SHARABLE** *adj*

SHARER *n* pl. -S one that shares

SHARIF *n* pl. -S sherif

SHARING present participle of share

SHARK *v* -ED, -ING, -S to live by trickery

SHARKER *n* pl. -S one that sharks

SHARN *n* pl. -S cow dung **SHARNY** *adj*

SHARP *adj* SHARPER, SHARPEST suitable for or capable of cutting or piercing

SHARP *v* -ED, -ING, -S to raise in pitch, as a musical tone

SHARPEN *v* -ED, -ING, -S to make sharp

SHARPER *n* pl. -S a swindler

SHARPIE *n* pl. -S a very alert person

SHARPLY *adv* in a sharp manner

SHARPY *n* pl. SHARPIES sharpie

SHASHLIK *n* pl. -S kabob

SHASLIK *n* pl. -S shashlik

SHATTER *v* -ED, -ING, -S to break into pieces

SHAUGH *n* pl. -S a thicket

SHAUL *v* -ED, -ING, -S to shoal

SHAVE *v* SHAVED, SHAVEN, SHAVING, SHAVES to sever the hair close to the roots **SHAVABLE** *adj*

SHAVER *n* pl. -S one that shaves

SHAVIE *n* pl. -S a trick or prank

SHAVING *n* pl. -S something shaved off

SHAW *v* SHAWED, SHAWN, SHAWING, SHAWS to show

SHAWL *v* -ED, -ING, -S to wrap in a shawl (a piece of cloth worn as a covering)

SHAWM *n* pl. -S an early woodwind instrument

SHAWN past participle of shaw

SHAY *n* pl. SHAYS a chaise

SHE *n* pl. -S a female person

SHEA *n* pl. -S an African tree

SHEAF *v* -ED, -ING, -S to sheave

SHEAL *n* pl. -S shealing

SHEALING *n* pl. -S a shepherd's hut

SHEAR *v* SHEARED or SHORE, SHORN, SHEARING, SHEARS to cut the hair or wool from

SHEARER *n* pl. -S one that shears

SHEARING *n* pl. -S an instance of cutting hair or wool

SHEATH *v* -ED, -ING, -S to sheathe

SHEATHE *v* SHEATHED, SHEATHING, SHEATHES to put into a protective case

SHEATHER *n* pl. -S one that sheathes

SHEAVE *v* SHEAVED, SHEAVING, SHEAVES to gather into a bundle

SHEBANG *n* pl. -S a situation, organization, or matter

SHEBEAN *n* pl. -S shebeen

SHEBEEN *n* pl. -S a place where liquor is sold illegally

SHED *v* SHEDDED, SHEDDING, SHEDS to house in a shed (a small, low structure)

SHEDABLE *adj* capable of being cast off

SHEDDER *n* pl. -S one that casts off something

SHEDDING present participle of shed

SHEDLIKE *adj* resembling a shed

SHEEN *v* -ED, -ING, -S to shine

SHEENFUL *adj* shining

SHEENY *adj* SHEENIER, SHEENIEST shining

SHEEP *n* pl. SHEEP a ruminant mammal

SHEEPCOT *n* pl. -S an enclosure for sheep

SHEEPDOG *n* pl. -S a dog trained to guard and herd sheep

SHEEPISH *adj* embarrassed

SHEEPMAN *n* pl. -MEN a person who raises sheep

SHEER *v* -ED, -ING, -S to swerve

SHEER *adj* SHEERER, SHEEREST of very thin texture **SHEERLY** *adv*

SHEET *v* -ED, -ING, -S to cover with a sheet (a thin, rectangular piece of material)

SHEETER *n* pl. -S one that sheets

SHEETFED *adj* pertaining to a type of printing press

SHEETING *n* pl. -S material in the form of sheets

SHEEVE *n* pl. -S a grooved pulley wheel

SHEIK *n* pl. -S an Arab chief

SHEIKDOM *n* pl. -S the area ruled by a sheik

SHEIKH *n* pl. -S sheik

SHEILA *n* pl. -S a young woman

SHEITAN *n* pl. -S shaitan

SHEKEL *n* pl. -S an ancient unit of weight and money

SHELDUCK *n* pl. -S a European duck

SHELF *n* pl. SHELVES a flat rigid structure used to support articles

SHELFFUL *n* pl. -S as much as a shelf can hold

SHELL *v* -ED, -ING, -S to divest of a shell (a hard outer covering)

SHELLAC *v* -LACKED, -LACKING, -LACS to cover with a thin varnish

SHELLACK *v* -ED, -ING, -S to shellac

SHELLER *n* pl. -S one that shells

SHELLY *adj* SHELLIER, SHELLIEST abounding in seashells

SHELTA *n* pl. -S an esoteric jargon of Gaelic

SHELTER   *v* -ED, -ING, -S to provide cover or protection for

SHELTIE   *n* pl. -S a small, shaggy pony

SHELTY   *n* pl. -TIES sheltie

SHELVE   *v* SHELVED, SHELVING, SHELVES to place on a shelf

SHELVER   *n* pl. -S one that shelves

SHELVES   pl. of shelf

SHELVING   *n* pl. -S material for shelves

SHELVY   *adj* SHELVIER, SHELVIEST inclining gradually

SHEND   *v* SHENT, SHENDING, SHENDS to disgrace

SHEOL   *n* pl. -S hell

SHEPHERD   *v* -ED, -ING, -S to watch over carefully

SHEQEL   *n* pl. SHEQALIM shekel

SHERBERT   *n* pl. -S sherbet

SHERBET   *n* pl. -S a frozen fruit-flavored mixture

SHERD   *n* pl. -S shard

SHEREEF   *n* pl. -S sherif

SHERIF   *n* pl. -S an Arab ruler

SHERIFF   *n* pl. -S a law-enforcement officer of a county

SHERLOCK   *n* pl. -S a detective

SHEROOT   *n* pl. -S cheroot

SHERPA   *n* pl. -S a soft fabric for linings

SHERRIS   *n* pl. -RISES sherry

SHERRY   *n* pl. -RIES a fortified wine with a nutty flavor

SHETLAND   *n* pl. -S a wool yarn

SHEUCH   *n* pl. -S sheugh

SHEUGH   *n* pl. -S a ditch

SHEW   *v* SHEWED, SHEWN, SHEWING, SHEWS to show

SHEWER   *n* pl. -S one that shews

SHH   *interj* sh

SHIATSU   *n* pl. -S a massage using finger pressure

SHIATZU   *n* pl. -S shiatsu

SHIBAH   *n* pl. -S shiva

SHICKER   *n* pl. -S a drunkard

SHIED   past tense of shy

SHIEL   *n* pl. -S shieling

SHIELD   *v* -ED, -ING, -S to provide with a protective cover or shelter

SHIELDER   *n* pl. -S one that shields

SHIELING   *n* pl. -S shealing

SHIER   *n* pl. -S a horse having a tendency to shy

SHIES   present 3d person sing. of shy

SHIEST   a superlative of shy

SHIFT   *v* -ED, -ING, -S to move from one position to another

SHIFTER   *n* pl. -S one that shifts

SHIFTY   *adj* SHIFTIER, SHIFTIEST tricky **SHIFTILY** *adv*

SHIGELLA   *n* pl. -LAE or -LAS any of a genus of aerobic bacteria

SHIITAKE   *n* pl. -S a dark Oriental mushroom

SHIKAR   *v* -KARRED, -KARRING, -KARS to hunt

SHIKAREE   *n* pl. -S a big game hunter

SHIKARI   *n* pl. -S shikaree

SHIKARRED   past tense of shikar

SHIKARRING   present participle of shikar

SHIKKER   *n* pl. -S shicker

SHILINGI   *n* pl. SHILINGI a monetary unit of Tanzania

SHILL   *v* -ED, -ING, -S to act as a decoy

SHILLALA   *n* pl. -S a short, thick club

SHILLING   *n* pl. -S a former monetary unit of Great Britain

SHILPIT   *adj* sickly

SHILY   *adv* in a shy manner

SHIM   *v* SHIMMED, SHIMMING, SHIMS to fill out or level by inserting a thin wedge

SHIMMER   *v* -ED, -ING, -S to glimmer

SHIMMERY   *adj* shimmering

SHIMMING   present participle of shim

SHIMMY   *v* -MIED, -MYING, -MIES to vibrate or wobble

SHIN   *v* SHINNED, SHINNING, SHINS to climb by gripping and pulling alternately with the hands and legs

SHINBONE   *n* pl. -S the tibia

SHINDIG   *n* pl. -S an elaborate dance or party

SHINDY   *n* pl. -DYS or -DIES a shindig

SHINE   *v* SHONE or SHINED, SHINING, SHINES to emit light

SHINER   *n* pl. -S one that shines

SHINGLE	v -GLED, -GLING, -GLES to cover with shingles (thin, oblong pieces of building material)
SHINGLER	n pl. -S one that shingles
SHINGLY	adj covered with small, loose stones
SHINIER	comparative of shiny
SHINIEST	superlative of shiny
SHINILY	adv in a shiny manner
SHINING	adj emitting or reflecting light
SHINLEAF	n pl. -LEAFS or -LEAVES a perennial herb
SHINNED	past of shin
SHINNERY	n pl. -NERIES a dense growth of small trees
SHINNEY	v -ED, -ING, -S to play a form of hockey
SHINNING	present participle of shin
SHINNY	v -NIED, -NYING, -NIES to shin
SHINY	adj SHINIER, SHINIEST filled with light
SHIP	v SHIPPED, SHIPPING, SHIPS to transport by ship (a vessel suitable for navigation in deep water)
SHIPLAP	n pl. -S an overlapping joint used in carpentry
SHIPLOAD	n pl. -S as much as a ship can carry
SHIPMAN	n pl. -MEN a sailor
SHIPMATE	n pl. -S a fellow sailor
SHIPMENT	n pl. -S something that is shipped
SHIPPED	past tense of ship
SHIPPEN	n pl. -S a cowshed
SHIPPER	n pl. -S one that ships
SHIPPING	n pl. -S the business of one that ships
SHIPPON	n pl. -S shippen
SHIPSIDE	n pl. -S the area alongside a ship
SHIPWAY	n pl. -WAYS a canal deep enough to serve ships
SHIPWORM	n pl. -S a wormlike mollusk
SHIPYARD	n pl. -S a place where ships are built or repaired
SHIRE	n pl. -S a territorial division of Great Britain
SHIRK	v -ED, -ING, -S to avoid work or duty
SHIRKER	n pl. -S one that shirks
SHIRR	v -ED, -ING, -S to draw into three or more parallel rows, as cloth
SHIRRING	n pl. -S a shirred arrangement of cloth
SHIRT	n pl. -S a garment for the upper part of the body
SHIRTING	n pl. -S fabric used for making shirts
SHIRTY	adj SHIRTIER, SHIRTIEST angry
SHIST	n pl. -S schist
SHITAKE	n pl. -S shiitake
SHITTAH	n pl. -S a hardwood tree
SHITTIM	n pl. -S the wood of the shittah
SHIV	n pl. -S a knife
SHIVA	n pl. -S a period of mourning
SHIVAH	n pl. -S shiva
SHIVAREE	v -REED, -REEING, -REES to chivaree
SHIVE	n pl. -S a thin fragment
SHIVER	v -ED, -ING, -S to tremble with fear or cold
SHIVERER	n pl. -S one that shivers
SHIVERY	adj shivering
SHLEMIEL	n pl. -S an unlucky bungler
SHLEP	v SHLEPPED, SHLEPPING, SHLEPS to schlep
SHLEPP	v -ED, -ING, -S to schlep
SHLOCK	n pl. -S schlock
SHLUMP	v -ED, -ING, -S to schlump
SHLUMPY	adj slovenly
SHMALTZ	n pl. -ES schmaltz
SHMALTZY	adj SHMALTZIER, SHMALTZIEST schmalzy
SHMEAR	n pl. -S schmear
SHMO	n pl. SHMOES schmo
SHMOOZE	v SHMOOZED, SHMOOZING, SHMOOZES to schmooze
SHMUCK	n pl. -S schmuck
SHNAPS	n pl. SHNAPS schnapps
SHNOOK	n pl. -S schnook
SHOAL	adj SHOALER, SHOALEST shallow
SHOAL	v -ED, -ING, -S to become shallow
SHOALY	adj SHOALIER, SHOALIEST full of shallow areas
SHOAT	n pl. -S a young hog

SHOCK   *v* -ED, -ING, -S to strike with great surprise, horror, or disgust

SHOCKER   *n* pl. -S one that shocks

SHOD   a past tense of shoe

SHODDEN   a past participle of shoe

SHODDY   *adj* -DIER, -DIEST of inferior quality **SHODDILY** *adv*

SHODDY   *n* pl. -DIES a low-quality wool

SHOE   *n* pl. SHOES or SHOON a covering for the foot

SHOE   *v* SHOD or SHOED, SHODDEN, SHOEING, SHOES to provide with shoes

SHOEBILL   *n* pl. -S a wading bird

SHOEHORN   *v* -ED, -ING, -S to force into a small space

SHOELACE   *n* pl. -S a lace for fastening a shoe

SHOELESS   *adj* having no shoe

SHOEPAC   *n* pl. -S a waterproof boot

SHOEPACK   *n* pl. -S shoepac

SHOER   *n* pl. -S one that shoes horses

SHOETREE   *n* pl. -S a device shaped like a foot that is inserted into a shoe to preserve its shape

SHOFAR   *n* pl. SHOFARS or SHOFROTH a ram's-horn trumpet blown in certain Jewish rituals

SHOG   *v* SHOGGED, SHOGGING, SHOGS to move along

SHOGUN   *n* pl. -S a former military leader of Japan **SHOGUNAL** *adj*

SHOJI   *n* pl. -S a paper screen used as a partition or door in a Japanese house

SHOLOM   *n* pl. -S shalom

SHONE   a past tense of shine

SHOO   *v* -ED, -ING, -S to drive away

SHOOFLY   *n* pl. -FLIES a child's rocker

SHOOK   *n* pl. -S a set of parts for assembling a barrel or packing

SHOOL   *v* -ED, -ING, -S to shovel

SHOON   a pl. of shoe

SHOOT   *v* SHOT, SHOOTING, SHOOTS to hit, wound, or kill with a missile discharged from a weapon

SHOOTER   *n* pl. -S one that shoots

SHOOTING   *n* pl. -S the act of one that shoots

SHOOTOUT   *n* pl. -S a battle fought with handguns or rifles

SHOP   *v* SHOPPED, SHOPPING, SHOPS to examine goods with intent to buy

SHOPBOY   *n* pl. -BOYS a salesclerk

SHOPGIRL   *n* pl. -S a salesgirl

SHOPHAR   *n* pl. -PHARS or -PHROTH shofar

SHOPLIFT   *v* -ED, -ING, -S to steal goods from a store

SHOPMAN   *n* pl. -MEN one who owns or operates a small store

SHOPPE   *n* pl. -S a small store

SHOPPED   past tense of shop

SHOPPER   *n* pl. -S one that shops

SHOPPING   *n* pl. -S the act of one that shops

SHOPTALK   *n* pl. -S conversation concerning one's business or occupation

SHOPWORN   *adj* worn out from being on display in a store

SHORAN   *n* pl. -S a type of navigational system

SHORE   *v* SHORED, SHORING, SHORES to prop with a supporting timber

SHORING   *n* pl. -S a system of supporting timbers

SHORL   *n* pl. -S schorl

SHORN   a past participle of shear

SHORT   *adj* SHORTER, SHORTEST having little length

SHORT   *v* -ED, -ING, -S to cause a type of electrical malfunction in

SHORTAGE   *n* pl. -S an insufficient supply or amount

SHORTCUT   *v* -CUT, -CUTTING, -CUTS to take a shorter or quicker way

SHORTEN   *v* -ED, -ING, -S to make or become shorter

SHORTIA   *n* pl. -S a perennial herb

SHORTIE   *n* pl. -S shorty

SHORTIES   pl. of shorty

SHORTISH   *adj* somewhat short

SHORTLY   *adv* in a short time

SHORTY   *n* pl. SHORTIES one that is short

SHOT   *v* SHOTTED, SHOTTING, SHOTS to load with shot (small lead or steel pellets)

SHOTE   *n* pl. -S shoat

SHOTGUN   *v* -GUNNED, -GUNNING, -GUNS to shoot with a type of gun

SHOTT	*n* pl. -S chott	**SHOWROOM**	*n* pl. -S a room used for the display of merchandise
SHOTTED	past tense of shot		
SHOTTEN	*adj* having spawned — used of a fish	**SHOWY**	*adj* SHOWIER, SHOWIEST making a great or brilliant display
SHOTTING	present participle of shot	**SHOYU**	*n* pl. -S soy sauce
SHOULD	past tense of shall	**SHRANK**	past tense of shrink
SHOULDER	*v* -ED, -ING, -S to assume the burden or responsibility of	**SHRAPNEL**	*n* pl. SHRAPNEL fragments from an exploding bomb, mine, or shell
SHOULDEST	a 2d person sing. past tense of shall	**SHRED**	*v* SHREDDED, SHREDDING, SHREDS to tear into small strips
SHOULDST	a 2d person sing. past tense of shall	**SHREDDER**	*n* pl. -S one that shreds
		SHREW	*v* -ED, -ING, -S to curse
SHOUT	*v* -ED, -ING, -S to utter loudly	**SHREWD**	*adj* SHREWDER, SHREWDEST having keen insight **SHREWDLY** *adv*
SHOUTER	*n* pl. -S one that shouts		
SHOVE	*v* SHOVED, SHOVING, SHOVES to push roughly	**SHREWDIE**	*n* pl. -S a shrewd person
		SHREWISH	*adj* ill-tempered
SHOVEL	*v* -ELED, -ELING, -ELS or -ELLED, -ELLING, -ELS to take up with a shovel (a digging implement)	**SHRI**	*n* pl. -S sri
		SHRIEK	*v* -ED, -ING, -S to utter a shrill cry
SHOVELER	*n* pl. -S one that shovels	**SHRIEKER**	*n* pl. -S one that shrieks
SHOVER	*n* pl. -S one that shoves	**SHRIEKY**	*adj* SHRIEKIER, SHRIEKIEST shrill
SHOVING	present participle of shove		
SHOW	*v* SHOWED, SHOWN, SHOWING, SHOWS to cause or permit to be seen **SHOWABLE** *adj*	**SHRIEVAL**	*adj* pertaining to a sheriff
		SHRIEVE	*v* SHRIEVED, SHRIEVING, SHRIEVES to shrive
SHOWBIZ	*n* pl. -BIZZES show business	**SHRIFT**	*n* pl. -S the act of shriving
SHOWBOAT	*v* -ED, -ING, -S to show off	**SHRIKE**	*n* pl. -S a predatory bird
SHOWCASE	*v* -CASED, -CASING, -CASES to exhibit	**SHRILL**	*adj* SHRILLER, SHRILLEST having a high-pitched and piercing quality **SHRILLY** *adv*
SHOWDOWN	*n* pl. -S an event that forces the conclusion of an issue		
SHOWER	*v* -ED, -ING, -S to bathe in a spray of water	**SHRILL**	*v* -ED, -ING, -S to utter a shrill sound
SHOWERER	*n* pl. -S one that showers	**SHRIMP**	*v* -ED, -ING, -S to catch shrimps (small marine decapods)
SHOWERY	*adj* abounding with brief periods of rain	**SHRIMPER**	*n* pl. -S a shrimp fisher
		SHRIMPY	*adj* SHRIMPIER, SHRIMPIEST abounding in shrimp
SHOWGIRL	*n* pl. -S a chorus girl		
SHOWIER	comparative of showy	**SHRINE**	*v* SHRINED, SHRINING, SHRINES to place in a shrine (a receptacle for sacred relics)
SHOWIEST	superlative of showy		
SHOWILY	*adv* in a showy manner		
SHOWING	*n* pl. -S an exhibition or display	**SHRINK**	*v* SHRANK, SHRUNK or SHRUNKEN, SHRINKING, SHRINKS to contract or draw back
SHOWMAN	*n* pl. -MEN a theatrical producer		
SHOWN	past participle of show	**SHRINKER**	*n* pl. -S one that shrinks
SHOWOFF	*n* pl. -S one given to pretentious display	**SHRIVE**	*v* SHROVE or SHRIVED, SHRIVEN, SHRIVING, SHRIVES to hear the confession of and grant absolution to
SHOWRING	*n* pl. -S a ring where animals are displayed		

SHRIVEL   *v* -ELED, -ELING, -ELS or -ELLED, -ELLING, -ELS to contract into wrinkles

SHRIVER   *n* pl. -S one that shrives

SHRIVING   present participle of shrive

SHROFF   *v* -ED, -ING, -S to test the genuineness of, as a coin

SHROUD   *v* -ED, -ING, -S to wrap in burial clothing

SHROVE   a past tense of shrive

SHRUB   *n* pl. -S a low, woody plant

SHRUBBY   *adj* -BIER, -BIEST covered with shrubs

SHRUG   *v* SHRUGGED, SHRUGGING, SHRUGS to raise and contract the shoulders

SHRUNK   a past tense of shrink

SHRUNKEN   a past participle of shrink

SHTETEL   *n* pl. SHTETLACH or SHTETELS a Jewish village

SHTETL   *n* pl. SHTETLACH or SHTETLS shtetel

SHTICK   *n* pl. -S an entertainment routine

SHTIK   *n* pl. -S shtick

SHUCK   *v* -ED, -ING, -S to remove the husk or shell from

SHUCKER   *n* pl. -S one that shucks

SHUCKING   *n* pl. -S the act of one that shucks

SHUDDER   *v* -ED, -ING, -S to tremble

SHUDDERY   *adj* shuddering

SHUFFLE   *v* -FLED, -FLING, -FLES to walk without lifting the feet

SHUFFLER   *n* pl. -S one that shuffles

SHUL   *n* pl. SHULN or SHULS a synagogue

SHUN   *v* SHUNNED, SHUNNING, SHUNS to avoid

SHUNNER   *n* pl. -S one that shuns

SHUNPIKE   *v* -PIKED, -PIKING, -PIKES to travel on side roads to avoid expressways

SHUNT   *v* -ED, -ING, -S to turn aside

SHUNTER   *n* pl. -S one that shunts

SHUSH   *v* -ED, -ING, -ES to silence

SHUT   *v* SHUT, SHUTTING, SHUTS to close

SHUTDOWN   *n* pl. -S a temporary closing of an industrial plant

SHUTE   *v* SHUTED, SHUTING, SHUTES to chute

SHUTEYE   *n* pl. -S sleep

SHUTOFF   *n* pl. -S a device that shuts something off

SHUTOUT   *n* pl. -S a game in which one team fails to score

SHUTTER   *v* -ED, -ING, -S to provide with shutters (hinged window covers)

SHUTTING   present participle of shut

SHUTTLE   *v* -TLED, -TLING, -TLES to move or travel back and forth

SHWANPAN   *n* pl. -S swanpan

SHY   *adj* SHIER, SHIEST or SHYER, SHYEST timid

SHY   *v* SHIED, SHYING, SHIES to move suddenly back or aside, as in fear

SHYER   *n* pl. -S shier

SHYLOCK   *v* -ED, -ING, -S to lend money at high interest rates

SHYLY   *adv* in a shy manner

SHYNESS   *n* pl. -ES the state of being shy

SHYSTER   *n* pl. -S an unscrupulous lawyer or politician

SI   *n* pl. -S ti

SIAL   *n* pl. -S a type of rock formation **SIALIC** *adj*

SIALID   *n* pl. -S an alderfly

SIALIDAN   *n* pl. -S sialid

SIALOID   *adj* resembling saliva

SIAMANG   *n* pl. -S a large, black gibbon

SIAMESE   *n* pl. -S a water pipe with a connection for two hoses

SIB   *n* pl. -S a sibling

SIBB   *n* pl. -S sib

SIBILANT   *n* pl. -S a speech sound produced by the fricative passage of breath through a narrow orifice

SIBILATE   *v* -LATED, -LATING, -LATES to hiss

SIBLING   *n* pl. -S one having the same parents as another

SIBYL   *n* pl. -S a female prophet **SIBYLIC, SIBYLLIC** *adj*

SIC   *v* SICCED, SICCING, SICS to urge to attack

SICCAN   *adj* such

SICE   *n* pl. -S syce

SICK   *adj* SICKER, SICKEST affected with disease or ill health

SICK   *v* -ED, -ING, -S to sic

SICKBAY   *n* pl. -BAYS a ship's hospital

SICKBED   *n* pl. -S a sick person's bed

SICKEE   *n* pl. -S sickie

SICKEN   *v* -ED, -ING, -S to make sick

SICKENER   *n* pl. -S one that sickens

SICKERLY   *adv* securely

SICKIE   *n* pl. -S an emotionally sick person

SICKISH   *adj* somewhat sick

SICKLE   *v* -LED, -LING, -LES to cut with an agricultural implement having a single blade

SICKLY   *adj* -LIER, -LIEST appearing as if sick **SICKLILY** *adv*

SICKLY   *v* -LIED, -LYING, -LIES to make sickly

SICKNESS   *n* pl. -ES the state of being sick

SICKO   *n* pl. SICKOS sickie

SICKOUT   *n* pl. -S an organized absence of workers claiming to be sick

SICKROOM   *n* pl. -S a room occupied by a sick person

SIDDUR   *n* pl. -DURIM or -DURS a Jewish prayer book

SIDE   *v* SIDED, SIDING, SIDES to agree with or support

SIDEARM   *adj* thrown with a sideways sweep of the arm

SIDEBAND   *n* pl. -S a band of radio frequencies

SIDEBAR   *n* pl. -S a short news story accompanying a major story

SIDECAR   *n* pl. -S a passenger car attached to a motorcycle

SIDED   past tense of side

SIDEHILL   *n* pl. -S a hillside

SIDEKICK   *n* pl. -S a close friend
SIDELINE   *v* -LINED, -LINING, -LINES to put out of action

SIDELING   *adj* sloping

SIDELONG   *adj* directed to one side

SIDEMAN   *n* pl. -MEN a member of a jazz band

SIDEREAL   *adj* pertaining to the stars

SIDERITE   *n* pl. -S a mineral

SIDESHOW   *n* pl. -S a small show offered in addition to a main attraction

SIDESLIP   *v* -SLIPPED, -SLIPPING, -SLIPS to slip to one side

SIDESPIN   *n* pl. -S a type of spin imparted to a ball

SIDESTEP   *v* -STEPPED, -STEPPING, -STEPS to step to one side

SIDEWALK   *n* pl. -S a paved walk for pedestrians

SIDEWALL   *n* pl. -S a side surface of a tire

SIDEWARD   *adv* toward one side

SIDEWAY   *adv* sideways

SIDEWAYS   *adv* toward or from one side

SIDEWISE   *adv* sideways

SIDING   *n* pl. -S material used for surfacing a frame building

SIDLE   *v* -DLED, -DLING, -DLES to move sideways

SIDLER   *n* pl. -S one that sidles

SIEGE   *v* SIEGED, SIEGING, SIEGES to attempt to capture or gain

SIEMENS   *n* pl. SIEMENS a unit of electrical conductance

SIENITE   *n* pl. -S syenite

SIENNA   *n* pl. -S a brown pigment

SIEROZEM   *n* pl. -S a type of soil

SIERRA   *n* pl. -S a mountain range **SIERRAN** *adj*

SIESTA   *n* pl. -S an afternoon nap or rest

SIEUR   *n* pl. -S an old French title of respect for a man

SIEVE   *v* SIEVED, SIEVING, SIEVES to pass through a sieve (a utensil for separating the coarse parts from the fine parts of loose matter)

SIFAKA   *n* pl. -S a lemur of Madagascar

SIFFLEUR   *n* pl. -S an animal that makes a whistling noise

SIFT   *v* -ED, -ING, -S to sieve

SIFTER   *n* pl. -S one that sifts

SIFTING   *n* pl. -S the work of a sifter

SIGANID   *n* pl. -S any of a family of fishes

SIGH   *v* -ED, -ING, -S to let out a sigh (a deep, audible breath)

SIGHER   *n* pl. -S one that sighs

SIGHLESS   *adj* uttering no sigh

SIGHLIKE   *adj* resembling a sigh

SIGHT   *v* -ED, -ING, -S to observe or notice

SIGHTER   *n* pl. -S one that sights

SIGHTING	*n* pl. -S an observation	**SILENT**	*adj* -LENTER, -LENTEST making no sound or noise **SILENTLY** *adv*
SIGHTLY	*adj* -LIER, -LIEST pleasing to look at	**SILENTS**	*n/pl* silent movies
SIGHTSEE	*v* -SAW, -SEEN, -SEEING, -SEES to visit and view places of interest	**SILENUS**	*n* pl. -NI a woodland deity of Greek mythology
		SILESIA	*n* pl. -S a cotton fabric
SIGIL	*n* pl. -S an official seal	**SILEX**	*n* pl. -ES silica
SIGLOS	*n* pl. -LOI an ancient Persian coin	**SILICA**	*n* pl. -S a form of silicon
		SILICATE	*n* pl. -S a chemical salt
SIGMA	*n* pl. -S a Greek letter **SIGMATE** *adj*	**SILICIC**	*adj* pertaining to silicon
SIGMOID	*n* pl. -S an S-shaped curve in a bodily part	**SILICIDE**	*n* pl. -S a silicon compound
		SILICIFY	*v* -FIED, -FYING, -FIES to convert into silica
SIGN	*v* -ED, -ING, -S to write one's name on	**SILICIUM**	*n* pl. -S silicon
SIGNAGE	*n* pl. -S a system of signs in a community	**SILICLE**	*n* pl. -S a short, flat silique
		SILICON	*n* pl. -S a nonmetallic element
SIGNAL	*v* -NALED, -NALING, -NALS or -NALLED, -NALLING, -NALS to notify by a means of communication	**SILICONE**	*n* pl. -S a silicon compound
		SILICULA	*n* pl. -LAE a silicle
		SILIQUA	*n* pl. -QUAE silique
SIGNALER	*n* pl. -S one that signals	**SILIQUE**	*n* pl. -LIQUES a type of seed capsule
SIGNALLY	*adv* notably		
SIGNEE	*n* pl. -S a signer of a document	**SILK**	*v* -ED, -ING, -S to cover with silk (a soft, lustrous fabric)
SIGNER	*n* pl. -S one that signs	**SILKEN**	*adj* made of silk
SIGNET	*v* -ED, -ING, -S to mark with an official seal	**SILKIER**	comparative of silky
		SILKIES	pl. of silky
SIGNIFY	*v* -FIED, -FYING, -FIES to make known	**SILKIEST**	superlative of silky
SIGNIOR	*n* pl. -GNIORI or -GNIORS signor	**SILKILY**	*adv* in a silky manner
SIGNIORY	*n* pl. -GNIORIES signory	**SILKLIKE**	*adj* resembling silk
SIGNOR	*n* pl. -GNORI or -GNORS an Italian title of courtesy for a man	**SILKWEED**	*n* pl. -S milkweed
		SILKWORM	*n* pl. -S a caterpillar that spins a cocoon of silk fibers
SIGNORA	*n* pl. -GNORE or -GNORAS an Italian title of courtesy for a married woman	**SILKY**	*adj* SILKIER, SILKIEST resembling silk
		SILKY	*n* pl. SILKIES a glossy-coated terrier
SIGNORE	*n* pl. -GNORI signor		
SIGNORY	*n* pl. -GNORIES seignory	**SILL**	*n* pl. -S the horizontal piece at the base of a window
SIGNPOST	*v* -ED, -ING, -S to provide with signposts (posts bearing signs)	**SILLABUB**	*n* pl. -S an alcoholic dessert
SIKE	*n* pl. -S syke	**SILLER**	*n* pl. -S silver
SIKER	*adj* secure	**SILLIBUB**	*n* pl. -S sillabub
SILAGE	*n* pl. -S fodder that has been preserved in a silo	**SILLY**	*adj* -LIER, -LIEST showing a lack of good sense **SILLILY** *adv*
SILANE	*n* pl. -S a chemical compound	**SILLY**	*n* pl. -LIES a silly person
SILD	*n* pl. -S a young herring	**SILO**	*v* -ED, -ING, -S to store in a silo (a tall, cylindrical structure)
SILENCE	*v* -LENCED, -LENCING, -LENCES to make silent		
		SILOXANE	*n* pl. -S a chemical compound
SILENCER	*n* pl. -S one that silences	**SILT**	*v* -ED, -ING, -S to fill with silt (a sedimentary material)
SILENI	pl. of silenus		

SILTY	*adj* SILTIER, SILTIEST full of silt	**SIMPLE**	*adj* SIMPLER, SIMPLEST not complex or complicated
SILURID	*n* pl. -S any of a family of catfishes	**SIMPLE**	*n* pl. -S something that is simple
SILUROID	*n* pl. -S a silurid	**SIMPLEX**	*n* pl. -PLEXES, -PLICES, or -PLICIA a simple word
SILVA	*n* pl. -VAS or -VAE sylva	**SIMPLIFY**	*v* -FIED, -FYING, -FIES to make simple
SILVAN	*n* pl. -S sylvan	**SIMPLISM**	*n* pl. -S the tendency to oversimplify an issue or problem
SILVER	*v* -ED, -ING, -S to cover with silver (a metallic element)		
SILVERER	*n* pl. -S one that silvers	**SIMPLIST**	*n* pl. -S a person given to simplism
SILVERLY	*adv* with a silvery appearance	**SIMPLY**	*adv* in a simple manner
SILVERN	*adj* silvery	**SIMULANT**	*n* pl. -S one that simulates
SILVERY	*adj* resembling silver	**SIMULAR**	*n* pl. -S a simulant
SILVEX	*n* pl. -ES an herbicide	**SIMULATE**	*v* -LATED, -LATING, -LATES to take on the appearance of
SILVICAL	*adj* pertaining to silvics		
SILVICS	*n/pl* the study of forest trees	**SIN**	*v* SINNED, SINNING, SINS to commit a sin (an offense against religious or moral law)
SIM	*n* pl. -S simulation		
SIMA	*n* pl. -S an igneous rock		
SIMAR	*n* pl. -S a woman's light jacket or robe	**SINAPISM**	*n* pl. -S a pasty mixture applied to an irritated part of the body
SIMARUBA	*n* pl. -S a tropical tree	**SINCE**	*adv* from then until now
SIMAZINE	*n* pl. -S an herbicide	**SINCERE**	*adj* -CERER, -CEREST free from hypocrisy or falseness
SIMIAN	*n* pl. -S an ape or monkey		
SIMILAR	*adj* being like but not completely identical to	**SINCIPUT**	*n* pl. -CIPUTS or -CIPITA the forehead
SIMILE	*n* pl. -S a figure of speech	**SINE**	*n* pl. -S a trigonometric function of an angle
SIMIOID	*adj* simious	**SINECURE**	*n* pl. -S an office or position requiring little or no work
SIMIOUS	*adj* pertaining to simians		
SIMITAR	*n* pl. -S scimitar	**SINEW**	*v* -ED, -ING, -S to strengthen
SIMLIN	*n* pl. -S cymling	**SINEWY**	*adj* lean and muscular
SIMMER	*v* -ED, -ING, -S to cook below or just at the boiling point	**SINFONIA**	*n* pl. -NIE a symphony
		SINFUL	*adj* marked by sin **SINFULLY** *adv*
SIMNEL	*n* pl. -S a crisp bread		
SIMOLEON	*n* pl. -S a dollar	**SING**	*v* SANG, SUNG, SINGING, SINGS to utter with musical inflections of the voice **SINGABLE** *adj*
SIMONIAC	*n* pl. -S one who practices simony		
SIMONIES	pl. of simony	**SINGE**	*v* SINGED, SINGEING, SINGES to burn slightly
SIMONIST	*n* pl. -S a simoniac		
SIMONIZE	*v* -NIZED, -NIZING, -NIZES to polish with wax	**SINGER**	*n* pl. -S one that sings
		SINGLE	*v* -GLED, -GLING, -GLES to select from a group
SIMONY	*n* pl. -NIES the buying or selling of a church office	**SINGLET**	*n* pl. -S a man's undershirt or jersey
SIMOOM	*n* pl. -S a hot, dry desert wind		
SIMOON	*n* pl. -S simoom	**SINGLY**	*adv* without the company of others
SIMP	*n* pl. -S a foolish person		
SIMPER	*v* -ED, -ING, -S to smile in a silly manner	**SINGSONG**	*n* pl. -S monotonous cadence in speaking or reading
SIMPERER	*n* pl. -S one who simpers	**SINGULAR**	*n* pl. -S a word form that denotes one person or thing

SINH	*n* pl. -S a hyperbolic function of an angle
SINICIZE	*v* -CIZED, -CIZING, -CIZES to modify by Chinese influence
SINISTER	*adj* threatening or portending evil
SINK	*v* SANK, SUNK or SUNKEN, SINKING, SINKS to move to a lower level **SINKABLE** *adj*
SINKAGE	*n* pl. -S the act, process, or degree of sinking
SINKER	*n* pl. -S one that sinks
SINKHOLE	*n* pl. -S a natural depression in a land surface
SINLESS	*adj* free from sin
SINNED	past tense of sin
SINNER	*n* pl. -S one that sins
SINNING	present participle of sin
SINOLOGY	*n* pl. -GIES the study of the Chinese
SINOPIA	*n* pl. -PIAS or -PIE a red pigment
SINSYNE	*adv* since
SINTER	*v* -ED, -ING, -S to make cohesive by the combined action of heat and pressure
SINUATE	*v* -ATED, -ATING, -ATES to curve in and out
SINUOUS	*adj* characterized by curves, bends, or turns
SINUS	*n* pl. -ES a cranial cavity
SINUSOID	*n* pl. -S a mathematical curve
SIP	*v* SIPPED, SIPPING, SIPS to drink in small quantities
SIPE	*v* SIPED, SIPING, SIPES to seep
SIPHON	*v* -ED, -ING, -S to draw off through a siphon (a type of tube)
SIPHONAL	*adj* of or pertaining to a siphon
SIPHONIC	*adj* siphonal
SIPING	present participle of sipe
SIPPED	past tense of sip
SIPPER	*n* pl. -S one that sips
SIPPET	*n* pl. -S a small piece of bread soaked in gravy
SIPPING	present participle of sip
SIR	*n* pl. -S a respectful form of address used to a man
SIRDAR	*n* pl. -S a person of rank in India
SIRE	*v* SIRED, SIRING, SIRES to beget
SIREE	*n* pl. -S sirree
SIREN	*n* pl. -S a device that produces a penetrating warning sound
SIRENIAN	*n* pl. -S any of an order of aquatic mammals
SIRING	present participle of sire
SIRLOIN	*n* pl. -S a cut of beef
SIROCCO	*n* pl. -COS a hot, dry wind
SIRRA	*n* pl. -S sirrah
SIRRAH	*n* pl. -S a form of address used to inferiors
SIRREE	*n* pl. -S sir
SIRUP	*n* pl. -S syrup **SIRUPY** *adj*
SIRVENTE	*n* pl. -S a satirical medieval song or poem
SIS	*n* pl. SISES sister
SISAL	*n* pl. -S a strong fiber used for rope
SISKIN	*n* pl. -S a Eurasian finch
SISSY	*n* pl. -SIES an effeminate man or boy
SISSY	*adj* SISSIER, SISSIEST sissyish
SISSYISH	*adj* resembling a sissy
SISTER	*v* -ED, -ING, -S to treat like a sister (a female sibling)
SISTERLY	*adj* of or resembling a sister
SISTROID	*adj* included between the convex sides of two intersecting curves
SISTRUM	*n* pl. -TRUMS or -TRA an ancient Egyptian percussion instrument
SIT	*v* SAT, SAT or SITTEN, SITTING, SITS to rest on the buttocks
SITAR	*n* pl. -S a lute of India
SITARIST	*n* pl. -S one who plays the sitar
SITCOM	*n* pl. -S a television comedy series with continuing characters
SITE	*v* SITED, SITING, SITES to place in position for operation
SITH	*adv* since
SITHENCE	*adv* since
SITHENS	*adv* since
SITING	present participle of site
SITOLOGY	*n* pl. -GIES the science of nutrition and diet
SITTEN	a past participle of sit
SITTER	*n* pl. -S one that sits
SITTING	*n* pl. -S a meeting or session
SITUATE	*v* -ATED, -ATING, -ATES to place in a certain position

SITUP *n* pl. -S an exercise in which one moves from a lying to a sitting position

SITUS *n* pl. -TUSES a position or location

SITZMARK *n* pl. -S a mark left in the snow by a skier who has fallen backward

SIVER *n* pl. -S a sewer

SIX *n* pl. -ES a number

SIXFOLD *adj* being six times as great as

SIXMO *n* pl. -MOS a paper size

SIXPENCE *n* pl. -S a British coin worth six pennies

SIXPENNY *adj* worth sixpence

SIXTE *n* pl. -S a fencing parry

SIXTEEN *n* pl. -S a number

SIXTH *n* pl. -S one of six equal parts

SIXTHLY *adv* in the sixth place

SIXTIETH *n* pl. -S one of sixty equal parts

SIXTY *n* pl. -TIES a number

SIXTYISH *adj* being about sixty years old

SIZABLE *adj* of considerable size **SIZABLY** *adv*

SIZAR *n* pl. -S a British student who receives financial assistance frcm his college

SIZE *v* SIZED, SIZING, SIZES to arrange according to size (physical proportions)

SIZEABLE *adj* sizable **SIZEABLY** *adv*

SIZER *n* pl. -S sizar

SIZIER comparative of sizy

SIZIEST superlative of sizy

SIZINESS *n* pl. -ES the quality or state of being sizy

SIZING *n* pl. -S a substance used as a glaze or filler for porous materials

SIZY *adj* SIZIER, SIZIEST viscid

SIZZLE *v* -ZLED, -ZLING, -ZLES to burn or fry with a hissing sound

SIZZLER *n* pl. -S a very hot day

SJAMBOK *v* -ED, -ING, -S to strike with a whip used in South Africa

SKA *n* pl. -S a popular music of Jamaica

SKAG *n* pl. -S heroin

SKALD *n* pl. -S an ancient Scandinavian poet **SKALDIC** *adj*

SKAT *n* pl. -S a card game

SKATE *v* SKATED, SKATING, SKATES to glide over ice or the ground on skates (shoes fitted with runners or wheels)

SKATER *n* pl. -S one that skates

SKATING *n* pl. -S the sport of gliding on skates

SKATOL *n* pl. -S skatole

SKATOLE *n* pl. -S a chemical compound

SKEAN *n* pl. -S a type of dagger

SKEANE *n* pl. -S a length of yarn wound in a loose coil

SKEE *v* SKEED, SKEEING, SKEES to ski

SKEEN *n* pl. -S skean

SKEET *n* pl. -S the sport of shooting at clay pigeons hurled in the air by spring traps

SKEETER *n* pl. -S a skeet shooter

SKEG *n* pl. -S a timber that connects the keel and sternpost of a ship

SKEIGH *adj* proud

SKEIN *v* -ED, -ING, -S to wind into long, loose coils

SKELETON *n* pl. -S the supporting or protective framework of a human or animal body **SKELETAL** *adj*

SKELLUM *n* pl. -S a rascal

SKELM *n* pl. -S skellum

SKELP *v* SKELPED or SKELPIT, SKELPING, SKELPS to slap

SKELTER *v* -ED, -ING, -S to scurry

SKENE *n* pl. -S skean

SKEP *n* pl. -S a beehive

SKEPSIS *n* pl. -SISES the attitude or outlook of a skeptic

SKEPTIC *n* pl. -S a person who doubts generally accepted ideas

SKERRY *n* pl. -RIES a small, rocky island

SKETCH *v* -ED, -ING, -ES to make a rough, hasty drawing of

SKETCHER *n* pl. -S one that sketches

SKETCHY *adj* SKETCHIER, SKETCHIEST lacking in completeness or clearness

SKEW *v* -ED, -ING, -S to turn aside

SKEWBACK *n* pl. -S a sloping surface against which the end of an arch rests

SKEWBALD *n* pl. -S a horse having patches of brown and white

SKEWER *v* -ED, -ING, -S to pierce with a long pin, as meat

SKEWNESS *n* pl. -ES lack of symmetry

SKI *v* -ED, -ING, -S to travel on skis (long, narrow strips of wood or metal)

SKIABLE *adj* capable of being skied over

SKIAGRAM *n* pl. -S a picture made up of shadows or outlines

SKIBOB *n* pl. -S a vehicle used for traveling over snow

SKID *v* SKIDDED, SKIDDING, SKIDS to slide sideways as a result of a loss of traction

SKIDDER *n* pl. -S one that skids

SKIDDOO *v* -ED, -ING, -S to go away

SKIDDY *adj* -DIER, -DIEST likely to cause skidding

SKIDOO *v* -ED, -ING, -S to skiddoo

SKIDWAY *n* pl. -WAYS a platform on which logs are piled for loading or sawing

SKIED past tense of ski and sky

SKIER *n* pl. -S one that skis

SKIES present 3d person sing. of sky

SKIEY *adj* skyey

SKIFF *n* pl. -S a small, open boat

SKIFFLE *v* -FLED, -FLING, -FLES to play a particular style of music

SKIING *n* pl. -S the sport of traveling on skis

SKIJORER *n* pl. -S a skier who is drawn over snow by a horse or vehicle

SKILFUL *adj* skillful

SKILL *n* pl. -S the ability to do something well **SKILLED** *adj*

SKILLESS *adj* having no skill

SKILLET *n* pl. -S a frying pan

SKILLFUL *adj* having skill

SKILLING *n* pl. -S a former coin of Scandinavian countries

SKIM *v* SKIMMED, SKIMMING, SKIMS to remove floating matter from the surface of

SKIMMER *n* pl. -S one that skims

SKIMMING *n* pl. -S something that is skimmed from a liquid

SKIMP *v* -ED, -ING, -S to scrimp

SKIMPY *adj* SKIMPIER, SKIMPIEST scanty **SKIMPILY** *adv*

SKIN *v* SKINNED, SKINNING, SKINS to strip or deprive of skin (the membranous tissue covering the body of an animal)

SKINFUL *n* pl. -S as much as a skin container can hold

SKINHEAD *n* pl. -S one whose hair is cut very short

SKINK *v* -ED, -ING, -S to pour out or serve, as liquor

SKINKER *n* pl. -S one that skinks

SKINLESS *adj* having no skin

SKINLIKE *adj* resembling skin

SKINNED past tense of skin

SKINNER *n* pl. -S one that skins

SKINNING present participle of skin

SKINNY *adj* -NIER, -NIEST very thin

SKINT *adj* having no money

SKIORING *n* pl. -S a form of skiing

SKIP *v* SKIPPED, SKIPPING, SKIPS to move with light springing steps

SKIPJACK *n* pl. -S a marine fish

SKIPLANE *n* pl. -S an airplane designed to take off from or land on snow

SKIPPED past tense of skip

SKIPPER *v* -ED, -ING, -S to act as master or captain of

SKIPPET *n* pl. -S a small box for protecting an official seal

SKIPPING present participle of skip

SKIRL *v* -ED, -ING, -S to produce a shrill sound

SKIRMISH *v* -ED, -ING, -ES to engage in a minor battle

SKIRR *v* -ED, -ING, -S to move rapidly

SKIRRET *n* pl. -S an Asian herb

SKIRT *v* -ED, -ING, -S to go or pass around

SKIRTER *n* pl. -S one that skirts

SKIRTING *n* pl. -S a board at the base of a wall

SKIT *n* pl. -S a short dramatic scene

SKITE *v* SKITED, SKITING, SKITES to move away quickly

SKITTER *v* -ED, -ING, -S to move lightly or rapidly along a surface

SKITTERY *adj* -TERIER, -TERIEST skittish

SKITTISH *adj* easily frightened

SKITTLE *n* pl. -S a wooden pin used in a bowling game

SKIVE   *v* SKIVED, SKIVING, SKIVES to pare

SKIVER   *n* pl. -S one that skives

SKIVVY   *v* -VIED, -VYING, -VIES to work as a female servant

SKIWEAR   *n* pl. SKIWEAR clothing suitable for wear while skiing

SKLENT   *v* -ED, -ING, -S to slant

SKOAL   *v* -ED, -ING, -S to drink to the health of

SKOOKUM   *adj* excellent

SKOSH   *n* pl. -ES a small amount

SKREEGH   *v* -ED, -ING, -S to screech

SKREIGH   *v* -ED, -ING, -S to screech

SKUA   *n* pl. -S a predatory seabird

SKULK   *v* -ED, -ING, -S to move about stealthily

SKULKER   *n* pl. -S one that skulks

SKULL   *n* pl. -S the framework of the head **SKULLED** *adj*

SKULLCAP   *n* pl. -S a close-fitting cap

SKUNK   *v* -ED, -ING, -S to defeat overwhelmingly

SKY   *v* SKIED or SKYED, SKYING, SKIES to hit or throw toward the sky (the upper atmosphere)

SKYBORNE   *adj* airborne

SKYBOX   *n* pl. -ES an enclosure of seats situated high in a stadium

SKYCAP   *n* pl. -S a porter at an airport

SKYDIVE   *v* -DIVED or -DOVE, -DIVING, -DIVES to parachute from an airplane for sport

SKYDIVER   *n* pl. -S one that skydives

SKYEY   *adj* resembling the sky

SKYHOOK   *n* pl. -S a hook conceived as being suspended from the sky

SKYJACK   *v* -ED, -ING, -S to hijack an airplane

SKYLARK   *v* -ED, -ING, -S to frolic

SKYLIGHT   *n* pl. -S a window in a roof or ceiling

SKYLINE   *n* pl. -S the horizon

SKYLIT   *adj* having a skylight

SKYMAN   *n* pl. -MEN an aviator

SKYPHOS   *n* pl. -PHOI a drinking vessel used in ancient Greece

SKYSAIL   *n* pl. -S a type of sail

SKYWALK   *n* pl. -S an elevated walkway between two buildings

SKYWARD   *adv* toward the sky

SKYWARDS   *adv* skyward

SKYWAY   *n* pl. -WAYS an elevated highway

SKYWRITE   *v* -WROTE, -WRITTEN, -WRITING, -WRITES to write in the sky by releasing a visible vapor from an airplane

SLAB   *v* SLABBED, SLABBING, SLABS to cover with slabs (broad, flat pieces of solid material)

SLABBER   *v* -ED, -ING, -S to slobber

SLABBERY   *adj* slobbery

SLABBING   present participle of slab

SLABLIKE   *adj* resembling a slab

SLACK   *adj* SLACKER, SLACKEST not tight or taut

SLACK   *v* -ED, -ING, -S to slacken

SLACKEN   *v* -ED, -ING, -S to make less tight or taut

SLACKER   *n* pl. -S a shirker

SLACKLY   *adv* in a slack manner

SLAG   *v* SLAGGED, SLAGGING, SLAGS to convert into slag (the fused residue of a smelted ore)

SLAGGY   *adj* -GIER, -GIEST resembling slag

SLAIN   past participle of slay

SLAINTE   *interj* — used to toast one's health

SLAKE   *v* SLAKED, SLAKING, SLAKES to quench **SLAKABLE** *adj*

SLAKER   *n* pl. -S one that slakes

SLALOM   *v* -ED, -ING, -S to ski in a zigzag course

SLAM   *v* SLAMMED, SLAMMING, SLAMS to shut forcibly and noisily

SLAMMER   *n* pl. -S a jail

SLANDER   *v* -ED, -ING, -S to defame

SLANG   *v* -ED, -ING, -S to use slang (extremely informal or vulgar language)

SLANGY   *adj* SLANGIER, SLANGIEST being or containing slang **SLANGILY** *adv*

SLANK   a past tense of slink

SLANT   *v* -ED, -ING, -S to deviate from the horizontal or vertical

SLANTY   *adj* deviating from the horizontal or vertical

SLAP	*v* SLAPPED, SLAPPING, SLAPS to strike with the open hand
SLAPDASH	*n* pl. -ES careless work
SLAPJACK	*n* pl. -S a pancake
SLAPPED	past tense of slap
SLAPPER	*n* pl. -S one that slaps
SLAPPING	present participle of slap
SLASH	*v* -ED, -ING, -ES to cut with violent sweeping strokes
SLASHER	*n* pl. -S one that slashes
SLASHING	*n* pl. -S the act of one that slashes
SLAT	*v* SLATTED, SLATTING, SLATS to provide with slats (narrow strips of wood or metal)
SLATCH	*n* pl. -ES a calm between breaking waves
SLATE	*v* SLATED, SLATING, SLATES to cover with slate (a roofing material)
SLATER	*n* pl. -S one that slates
SLATEY	*adj* SLATIER, SLATIEST slaty
SLATHER	*v* -ED, -ING, -S to spread thickly
SLATIER	comparative of slaty
SLATIEST	superlative of slaty
SLATING	*n* pl. -S the act of one that slates
SLATTED	past tense of slat
SLATTERN	*n* pl. -S a slovenly woman
SLATTING	*n* pl. -S material for making slats
SLATY	*adj* SLATIER, SLATIEST resembling slate
SLAVE	*v* SLAVED, SLAVING, SLAVES to work like a slave (one who is owned by another)
SLAVER	*v* -ED, -ING, -S to drool
SLAVERER	*n* pl. -S one that slavers
SLAVERY	*n* pl. -ERIES ownership of one person by another
SLAVEY	*n* pl. -EYS a female servant
SLAVING	present participle of slave
SLAVISH	*adj* pertaining to or characteristic of a slave
SLAW	*n* pl. -S coleslaw
SLAY	*v* SLEW, SLAIN, SLAYING, SLAYS to kill violently
SLAY	*v* SLAYED, SLAIN, SLAYING, SLAYS to amuse overwhelmingly
SLAYER	*n* pl. -S one that slays
SLEAVE	*v* SLEAVED, SLEAVING, SLEAVES to separate into filaments
SLEAZE	*n* pl. -S a sleazy quality
SLEAZO	*adj* sleazy
SLEAZY	*adj* SLEAZIER, SLEAZIEST shoddy **SLEAZILY** *adv*
SLED	*v* SLEDDED, SLEDDING, SLEDS to convey on a sled (a vehicle for carrying people or loads over snow or ice)
SLEDDER	*n* pl. -S one that sleds
SLEDDING	*n* pl. -S the act of one that sleds
SLEDGE	*v* SLEDGED, SLEDGING, SLEDGES to convey on a type of sled
SLEEK	*adj* SLEEKER, SLEEKEST smooth and glossy
SLEEK	*v* -ED, -ING, -S to make sleek
SLEEKEN	*v* -ED, -ING, -S to sleek
SLEEKIER	comparative of sleeky
SLEEKIEST	superlative of sleeky
SLEEKIT	*adj* sleek
SLEEKLY	*adv* in a sleek manner
SLEEKY	*adj* SLEEKIER, SLEEKIEST sleek
SLEEP	*v* SLEPT, SLEEPING, SLEEPS to be in a natural, periodic state of rest
SLEEPER	*n* pl. -S one that sleeps
SLEEPING	*n* pl. -S the act of one that sleeps
SLEEPY	*adj* SLEEPIER, SLEEPIEST ready or inclined to sleep **SLEEPILY** *adv*
SLEET	*v* -ED, -ING, -S to shower sleet (frozen rain)
SLEETY	*adj* SLEETIER, SLEETIEST resembling sleet
SLEEVE	*v* SLEEVED, SLEEVING, SLEEVES to furnish with a sleeve (the part of a garment covering the arm)
SLEIGH	*v* -ED, -ING, -S to ride in a sled
SLEIGHER	*n* pl. -S one that sleighs
SLEIGHT	*n* pl. -S deftness
SLENDER	*adj* -DERER, -DEREST thin
SLEPT	past tense of sleep
SLEUTH	*v* -ED, -ING, -S to act as a detective
SLEW	*v* -ED, -ING, -S to slue

SLICE	v SLICED, SLICING, SLICES to cut into thin, flat pieces	**SLINKY**	adj SLINKIER, SLINKIEST stealthy **SLINKILY** adv
SLICER	n pl. -S one that slices	**SLIP**	v SLIPPED or SLIPT, SLIPPING, SLIPS to slide suddenly and accidentally
SLICK	adj SLICKER, SLICKEST smooth and slippery		
SLICK	v -ED, -ING, -S to make slick	**SLIPCASE**	n pl. -S a protective box for a book
SLICKER	n pl. -S an oilskin raincoat		
SLICKLY	adv in a slick manner	**SLIPE**	v SLIPED, SLIPING, SLIPES to peel
SLIDE	v SLID, SLIDDEN, SLIDING, SLIDES to move smoothly along a surface **SLIDABLE** adj	**SLIPFORM**	v -ED, -ING, -S to construct with the use of a mold in which concrete is placed to set
SLIDER	n pl. -S one that slides	**SLIPKNOT**	n pl. -S a type of knot
SLIDEWAY	n pl. -WAYS a route along which something slides	**SLIPLESS**	adj free from errors
SLIDING	present participle of slide	**SLIPOUT**	n pl. -S an insert in a newspaper
SLIER	a comparative of sly	**SLIPOVER**	n pl. -S a pullover
SLIEST	a superlative of sly	**SLIPPAGE**	n pl. -S a falling off from a standard or level
SLIGHT	adj SLIGHTER, SLIGHTEST small in size or amount **SLIGHTLY** adv	**SLIPPED**	a past tense of slip
		SLIPPER	n pl. -S a light, low shoe
SLIGHT	v -ED, -ING, -S to treat with disregard	**SLIPPERY**	adj -PERIER, -PERIEST causing or tending to cause slipping
SLILY	adv in a sly manner	**SLIPPING**	present participle of slip
SLIM	adj SLIMMER, SLIMMEST slender	**SLIPPY**	adj -PIER, -PIEST slippery
		SLIPSHOD	adj carelessly done or made
SLIM	v SLIMMED, SLIMMING, SLIMS to make slim	**SLIPSLOP**	n pl. -S watery food
SLIME	v SLIMED, SLIMING, SLIMES to cover with slime (viscous mud)	**SLIPSOLE**	n pl. -S a thin insole
		SLIPT	a past tense of slip
SLIMIER	comparative of slimy	**SLIPUP**	n pl. -S a mistake
SLIMIEST	superlative of slimy	**SLIPWARE**	n pl. -S a type of pottery
SLIMILY	adv in a slimy manner	**SLIPWAY**	n pl. -WAYS an area sloping toward the water in a shipyard
SLIMING	present participle of slime		
SLIMLY	adv in a slim manner	**SLIT**	v SLITTED, SLITTING, SLITS to make a slit (a long, narrow cut) in
SLIMMED	past tense of slim		
SLIMMER	n pl. -S a dieter	**SLITHER**	v -ED, -ING, -S to slide from side to side
SLIMMEST	superlative of slim	**SLITHERY**	adj slippery
SLIMMING	present participle of slim	**SLITLESS**	adj having no slits
SLIMNESS	n pl. -ES the state of being slim	**SLITTED**	past tense of slit
SLIMPSY	adj -SIER, -SIEST slimsy	**SLITTER**	n pl. -S one that slits
SLIMSY	adj -SIER, -SIEST flimsy	**SLITTING**	present participle of slit
SLIMY	adj SLIMIER, SLIMIEST resembling slime	**SLIVER**	v -ED, -ING, -S to cut into long, thin pieces
SLING	v SLUNG, SLINGING, SLINGS to throw with a sudden motion	**SLIVERER**	n pl. -S one that slivers
		SLIVOVIC	n pl. -ES a plum brandy
SLINGER	n pl. -S one that slings	**SLOB**	n pl. -S a slovenly or boorish person
SLINK	v SLUNK or SLANK or SLINKED, SLINKING, SLINKS to move stealthily	**SLOBBER**	v -ED, -ING, -S to drool
		SLOBBERY	adj slobbering

SLOBBISH	*adj* resembling a slob
SLOBBY	*adj* SLOBBIER, SLOBBIEST characteristic of a slob
SLOE	*n* pl. -S a plumlike fruit
SLOG	*v* SLOGGED, SLOGGING, SLOGS to plod
SLOGAN	*n* pl. -S a motto adopted by a group
SLOGGER	*n* pl. -S one that slogs
SLOGGING	present participle of slog
SLOID	*n* pl. -S sloyd
SLOJD	*n* pl. -S sloyd
SLOOP	*n* pl. -S a type of sailing vessel
SLOP	*v* SLOPPED, SLOPPING, SLOPS to spill or splash
SLOPE	*v* SLOPED, SLOPING, SLOPES to slant
SLOPER	*n* pl. -S one that slopes
SLOPPED	past tense of slop
SLOPPING	present participle of slop
SLOPPY	*adj* -PIER, -PIEST messy **SLOPPILY** *adv*
SLOPWORK	*n* pl. -S the manufacture of cheap clothing
SLOSH	*v* -ED, -ING, -ES to move with a splashing motion
SLOSHY	*adj* SLOSHIER, SLOSHIEST slushy
SLOT	*v* SLOTTED, SLOTTING, SLOTS to cut a long, narrow opening in
SLOTBACK	*n* pl. -S a type of football player
SLOTH	*n* pl. -S a slow-moving arboreal mammal
SLOTHFUL	*adj* sluggish
SLOTTED	past tense of slot
SLOTTING	present participle of slot
SLOUCH	*v* -ED, -ING, -ES to sit, stand, or move with a drooping posture
SLOUCHER	*n* pl. -S one that slouches
SLOUCHY	*adj* SLOUCHIER, SLOUCHIEST slouching
SLOUGH	*v* -ED, -ING, -S to cast off
SLOUGHY	*adj* SLOUGHIER, SLOUGHIEST miry
SLOVEN	*n* pl. -S a slovenly person
SLOVENLY	*adj* -LIER, -LIEST habitually untidy or unclean
SLOW	*adj* SLOWER, SLOWEST moving with little speed
SLOW	*v* -ED, -ING, -S to lessen the speed of
SLOWDOWN	*n* pl. -S a lessening of pace
SLOWISH	*adj* somewhat slow
SLOWLY	*adv* in a slow manner
SLOWNESS	*n* pl. -ES the state of being slow
SLOWPOKE	*n* pl. -S a slow individual
SLOWWORM	*n* pl. -S a European lizard having no legs
SLOYD	*n* pl. -S a Swedish system of manual training
SLUB	*v* SLUBBED, SLUBBING, SLUBS to draw out and twist slightly
SLUBBER	*v* -ED, -ING, -S to stain or dirty
SLUBBING	*n* pl. -S a slightly twisted roll of textile fibers
SLUDGE	*n* pl. -S a muddy deposit
SLUDGY	*adj* SLUDGIER, SLUDGIEST covered with sludge
SLUE	*v* SLUED, SLUING, SLUES to cause to move sideways
SLUFF	*v* -ED, -ING, -S to discard a card or cards
SLUG	*v* SLUGGED, SLUGGING, SLUGS to strike heavily
SLUGABED	*n* pl. -S one inclined to stay in bed out of laziness
SLUGFEST	*n* pl. -S a vigorous fight
SLUGGARD	*n* pl. -S an habitually lazy person
SLUGGED	past tense of slug
SLUGGER	*n* pl. -S one that slugs
SLUGGING	present participle of slug
SLUGGISH	*adj* displaying little movement or activity
SLUICE	*v* SLUICED, SLUICING, SLUICES to wash with a sudden flow of water
SLUICY	*adj* falling in streams
SLUING	present participle of slue
SLUM	*v* SLUMMED, SLUMMING, SLUMS to visit slums (squalid urban areas)
SLUMBER	*v* -ED, -ING, -S to sleep
SLUMBERY	*adj* sleepy
SLUMGUM	*n* pl. -S the residue remaining after honey is extracted from a honeycomb
SLUMISM	*n* pl. -S the prevalence of slums
SLUMLORD	*n* pl. -S a landlord of slum property

SLUMMED	past tense of slum
SLUMMER	*n* pl. -S one that slums
SLUMMING	present participle of slum
SLUMMY	*adj* -MIER, -MIEST resembling a slum
SLUMP	*v* -ED, -ING, -S to fall or sink suddenly
SLUNG	past tense of sling
SLUNK	a past tense of slink
SLUR	*v* SLURRED, SLURRING, SLURS to pass over lightly or carelessly
SLURB	*n* pl. -S a poorly planned suburban area **SLURBAN** *adj*
SLURP	*v* -ED, -ING, -S to eat or drink noisily
SLURRED	past tense of slur
SLURRING	present participle of slur
SLURRY	*v* -RIED, -RYING, -RIES to convert into a type of watery mixture
SLUSH	*v* -ED, -ING, -ES to splash with slush (partly melted snow)
SLUSHY	*adj* SLUSHIER, SLUSHIEST resembling slush **SLUSHILY** *adv*
SLUT	*n* pl. -S a slovenly woman **SLUTTISH** *adj*
SLUTTY	*adj* SLUTTIER, SLUTTIEST characteristic of a slut
SLY	*adj* SLIER, SLIEST or SLYER, SLYEST crafty **SLYLY** *adv*
SLYBOOTS	*n* pl. SLYBOOTS a sly person
SLYNESS	*n* pl. -ES the quality or state of being sly
SLYPE	*n* pl. -S a narrow passage in an English cathedral
SMACK	*v* -ED, -ING, -S to strike sharply
SMACKER	*n* pl. -S one that smacks
SMALL	*adj* SMALLER, SMALLEST of limited size or quantity
SMALL	*n* pl. -S a small part
SMALLAGE	*n* pl. -S a wild celery
SMALLISH	*adj* somewhat small
SMALLPOX	*n* pl. -ES a virus disease
SMALT	*n* pl. -S a blue pigment
SMALTI	a pl. of smalto
SMALTINE	*n* pl. -S smaltite
SMALTITE	*n* pl. -S a mineral
SMALTO	*n* pl. -TOS or -TI colored glass used in mosaics
SMARAGD	*n* pl. -S an emerald
SMARAGDE	*n* pl. -S smaragd
SMARM	*n* pl. -S trite sentimentality
SMARMY	*adj* SMARMIER, SMARMIEST marked by excessive flattery **SMARMILY** *adv*
SMART	*v* -ED, -ING, -S to cause a sharp, stinging pain
SMART	*adj* SMARTER, SMARTEST characterized by mental acuity
SMARTASS	*n* pl. -ES a smarty
SMARTEN	*v* -ED, -ING, -S to improve in appearance
SMARTIE	*n* pl. -S smarty
SMARTLY	*adv* in a smart manner
SMARTY	*n* pl. SMARTIES an obnoxiously conceited person
SMASH	*v* -ED, -ING, -ES to shatter violently
SMASHER	*n* pl. -S one that smashes
SMASHUP	*n* pl. -S a collision of motor vehicles
SMATTER	*v* -ED, -ING, -S to speak with little knowledge
SMAZE	*n* pl. -S an atmospheric mixture of smoke and haze
SMEAR	*v* -ED, -ING, -S to spread with a sticky, greasy, or dirty substance
SMEARER	*n* pl. -S one that smears
SMEARY	*adj* SMEARIER, SMEARIEST smeared
SMECTIC	*adj* pertaining to a phase of a liquid crystal
SMECTITE	*n* pl. -S a clayey mineral
SMEDDUM	*n* pl. -S ground malt powder
SMEEK	*v* -ED, -ING, -S to smoke
SMEGMA	*n* pl. -S sebum
SMELL	*v* SMELLED or SMELT, SMELLING, SMELLS to perceive by means of the olfactory nerves
SMELLER	*n* pl. -S one that smells
SMELLY	*adj* SMELLIER, SMELLIEST having an unpleasant odor
SMELT	*v* -ED, -ING, -S to melt or fuse, as ores
SMELTER	*n* pl. -S one that smelts
SMELTERY	*n* pl. -ERIES a place for smelting
SMERK	*v* -ED, -ING, -S to smirk
SMEW	*n* pl. -S a Eurasian duck
SMIDGE	*n* pl. -S a smidgen

SMIDGEN *n* pl. -S a very small amount

SMIDGEON *n* pl. -S smidgen

SMIDGIN *n* pl. -S smidgen

SMILAX *n* pl. -ES a twining plant

SMILE *v* SMILED, SMILING, SMILES to upturn the corners of the mouth in pleasure

SMILER *n* pl. -S one that smiles

SMILEY *adj* exhibiting a smile (a facial expression)

SMIRCH *v* -ED, -ING, -ES to soil

SMIRK *v* -ED, -ING, -S to smile in an affected or smug manner

SMIRKER *n* pl. -S one that smirks

SMIRKY *adj* SMIRKIER, SMIRKIEST smirking

SMITE *v* SMOTE, SMIT or SMITTEN, SMITING, SMITES to strike heavily

SMITER *n* pl. -S one that smites

SMITH *n* pl. -S a worker in metals

SMITHERS *n/pl* small fragments

SMITHERY *n* pl. -ERIES the trade of a smith

SMITHY *n* pl. SMITHIES the workshop of a smith

SMITING present participle of smite

SMITTEN a past participle of smite

SMOCK *v* -ED, -ING, -S to furnish with a smock (a loose outer garment)

SMOCKING *n* pl. -S a type of embroidery

SMOG *n* pl. -S an atmospheric mixture of smoke and fog **SMOGLESS** *adj*

SMOGGY *adj* -GIER, -GIEST filled with smog

SMOKE *v* SMOKED, SMOKING, SMOKES to emit smoke (the gaseous product of burning materials) **SMOKABLE** *adj*

SMOKEPOT *n* pl. -S a container for giving off smoke

SMOKER *n* pl. -S one that smokes

SMOKEY *adj* SMOKIER, SMOKIEST smoky

SMOKING present participle of smoke

SMOKY *adj* SMOKIER, SMOKIEST filled with smoke **SMOKILY** *adv*

SMOLDER *v* -ED, -ING, -S to burn with no flame

SMOLT *n* pl. -S a young salmon

SMOOCH *v* -ED, -ING, -ES to kiss

SMOOCHY *adj* smudgy

SMOOTH *adj* SMOOTHER, SMOOTHEST having a surface that is free from irregularities

SMOOTH *v* -ED, -ING, -S or -ES to make smooth

SMOOTHEN *v* -ED, -ING, -S to smooth

SMOOTHER *n* pl. -S one that smooths

SMOOTHIE *n* pl. -S a person with polished manners

SMOOTHLY *adv* in a smooth manner

SMOOTHY *n* pl. SMOOTHIES smoothie

SMOTE past tense of smite

SMOTHER *v* -ED, -ING, -S to prevent from breathing

SMOTHERY *adj* tending to smother

SMOULDER *v* -ED, -ING, -S to smolder

SMUDGE *v* SMUDGED, SMUDGING, SMUDGES to smear or dirty

SMUDGY *adj* SMUDGIER, SMUDGIEST smudged **SMUDGILY** *adv*

SMUG *adj* SMUGGER, SMUGGEST highly self-satisfied

SMUGGLE *v* -GLED, -GLING, -GLES to import or export illicitly

SMUGGLER *n* pl. -S one that smuggles

SMUGLY *adv* in a smug manner

SMUGNESS *n* pl. -ES the quality or state of being smug

SMUT *v* SMUTTED, SMUTTING, SMUTS to soil

SMUTCH *v* -ED, -ING, -ES to smudge

SMUTCHY *adj* SMUTCHIER, SMUTCHIEST smudgy

SMUTTED past tense of smut

SMUTTING present participle of smut

SMUTTY *adj* -TIER, -TIEST obscene **SMUTTILY** *adv*

SNACK *v* -ED, -ING, -S to eat a light meal

SNAFFLE *v* -FLED, -FLING, -FLES to obtain by devious means

SNAFU *v* -ED, -ING, -S to bring into a state of confusion

SNAG *v* SNAGGED, SNAGGING, SNAGS to catch on a snag (a jagged protuberance)

SNAGGY *adj* -GIER, -GIEST full of snags

SNAGLIKE *adj* resembling a snag

SNAIL   *v* -ED, -ING, -S to move slowly

SNAKE   *v* SNAKED, SNAKING, SNAKES to move like a snake (a limbless reptile)

SNAKEBIT   *adj* unlucky

SNAKEY   *adj* SNAKIER, SNAKIEST snaky

SNAKY   *adj* SNAKIER, SNAKIEST resembling a snake **SNAKILY** *adv*

SNAP   *v* SNAPPED, SNAPPING, SNAPS to make a sharp cracking sound

SNAPBACK   *n* pl. -S a sudden rebound or recovery

SNAPLESS   *adj* lacking a snap (a type of fastening device)

SNAPPED   past tense of snap

SNAPPER   *n* pl. -S one that snaps

SNAPPIER   comparative of snappy

SNAPPIEST   superlative of snappy

SNAPPILY   *adv* in a snappy manner

SNAPPING   present participle of snap

SNAPPISH   *adj* tending to speak in an impatient or irritable manner

SNAPPY   *adj* -PIER, -PIEST snappish

SNAPSHOT   *v* -SHOTTED, -SHOTTING, -SHOTS to photograph informally and quickly

SNAPWEED   *n* pl. -S a flowering plant

SNARE   *v* SNARED, SNARING, SNARES to trap

SNARER   *n* pl. -S one that snares

SNARK   *n* pl. -S an imaginary animal

SNARKY   *adj* SNARKIER, SNARKIEST snappish

SNARL   *v* -ED, -ING, -S to growl viciously

SNARLER   *n* pl. -S one that snarls

SNARLY   *adj* SNARLIER, SNARLIEST tangled

SNASH   *n* pl. -ES abusive language

SNATCH   *v* -ED, -ING, -ES to seize suddenly

SNATCHER   *n* pl. -S one that snatches

SNATCHY   *adj* SNATCHIER, SNATCHIEST occurring irregularly

SNATH   *n* pl. -S the handle of a scythe

SNATHE   *n* pl. -S snath

SNAW   *v* -ED, -ING, -S to snow

SNAZZY   *adj* -ZIER, -ZIEST very stylish

SNEAK   *v* SNEAKED or SNUCK, SNEAKING, SNEAKS to move stealthily

SNEAKER   *n* pl. -S one that sneaks

SNEAKY   *adj* SNEAKIER, SNEAKIEST deceitful **SNEAKILY** *adv*

SNEAP   *v* -ED, -ING, -S to chide

SNECK   *n* pl. -S a latch

SNED   *v* SNEDDED, SNEDDING, SNEDS to prune

SNEER   *v* -ED, -ING, -S to curl the lip in contempt

SNEERER   *n* pl. -S one that sneers

SNEERFUL   *adj* given to sneering

SNEESH   *n* pl. -ES snuff

SNEEZE   *v* SNEEZED, SNEEZING, SNEEZES to make a sudden, involuntary expiration of breath

SNEEZER   *n* pl. -S one that sneezes

SNEEZY   *adj* SNEEZIER, SNEEZIEST tending to sneeze

SNELL   *v* -ED, -ING, -S to attach a short line to a fishhook

SNELL   *adj* SNELLER, SNELLEST keen

SNIB   *v* SNIBBED, SNIBBING, SNIBS to latch

SNICK   *v* -ED, -ING, -S to nick

SNICKER   *v* -ED, -ING, -S to utter a partly stifled laugh

SNICKERY   *adj* tending to snicker

SNIDE   *adj* SNIDER, SNIDEST maliciously derogatory **SNIDELY** *adv*

SNIFF   *v* -ED, -ING, -S to inhale audibly through the nose

SNIFFER   *n* pl. -S one that sniffs

SNIFFIER   comparative of sniffy

SNIFFIEST   superlative of sniffy

SNIFFILY   *adv* in a sniffy manner

SNIFFISH   *adj* haughty

SNIFFLE   *v* -FLED, -FLING, -FLES to sniff repeatedly

SNIFFLER   *n* pl. -S one that sniffles

SNIFFY   *adj* -FIER, -FIEST sniffish

SNIFTER   *n* pl. -S a pear-shaped liquor glass

SNIGGER   *v* -ED, -ING, -S to snicker

SNIGGLE   *v* -GLED, -GLING, -GLES to fish for eels

SNIGGLER   *n* pl. -S one that sniggles

SNIP   *v* SNIPPED, SNIPPING, SNIPS to cut with a short, quick stroke

SNIPE   *v* SNIPED, SNIPING, SNIPES to shoot at individuals from a concealed place

SNIPER   *n* pl. -S one that snipes

SNIPPED   past tense of snip

SNIPPER   *n* pl. -S one that snips

SNIPPET   *n* pl. -S a small piece snipped off

SNIPPETY   *adj* -PETIER, -PETIEST snippy

SNIPPING   present participle of snip

SNIPPY   *adj* -PIER, -PIEST snappish **SNIPPILY** *adv*

SNIT   *n* pl. -S a state of agitation

SNITCH   *v* -ED, -ING, -ES to tattle

SNITCHER   *n* pl. -S one who snitches

SNIVEL   *v* -ELED, -ELING, -ELS or -ELLED, -ELLING, -ELS to cry or whine with sniffling

SNIVELER   *n* pl. -S one that snivels

SNOB   *n* pl. -S one who tends to avoid or rebuff those regarded as inferior

SNOBBERY   *n* pl. -BERIES snobbish behavior

SNOBBIER   comparative of snobby

SNOBBIEST   superlative of snobby

SNOBBILY   *adv* in a snobby manner

SNOBBISH   *adj* characteristic of a snob

SNOBBISM   *n* pl. -S snobbery

SNOBBY   *adj* -BIER, -BIEST snobbish

SNOG   *v* SNOGGED, SNOGGING, SNOGS to kiss

SNOOD   *v* -ED, -ING, -S to secure with a snood (a net or fabric cap for the hair)

SNOOK   *v* -ED, -ING, -S to sniff

SNOOKER   *v* -ED, -ING, -S to trick

SNOOL   *v* -ED, -ING, -S to yield meekly

SNOOP   *v* -ED, -ING, -S to pry about

SNOOPER   *n* pl. -S one that snoops

SNOOPY   *adj* SNOOPIER, SNOOPIEST given to snooping **SNOOPILY** *adv*

SNOOT   *v* -ED, -ING, -S to treat with disdain

SNOOTY   *adj* SNOOTIER, SNOOTIEST snobbish **SNOOTILY** *adv*

SNOOZE   *v* SNOOZED, SNOOZING, SNOOZES to sleep lightly

SNOOZER   *n* pl. -S one that snoozes

SNOOZLE   *v* -ZLED, -ZLING, -ZLES to nuzzle

SNOOZY   *adj* SNOOZIER, SNOOZIEST drowsy

SNORE   *v* SNORED, SNORING, SNORES to breathe loudly while sleeping

SNORER   *n* pl. -S one that snores

SNORKEL   *v* -ED, -ING, -S to swim underwater with a type of breathing device

SNORT   *v* -ED, -ING, -S to exhale noisily through the nostrils

SNORTER   *n* pl. -S one that snorts

SNOT   *n* pl. -S nasal mucus

SNOTTY   *adj* -TIER, -TIEST arrogant **SNOTTILY** *adv*

SNOUT   *v* -ED, -ING, -S to provide with a nozzle

SNOUTISH   *adj* snouty

SNOUTY   *adj* SNOUTIER, SNOUTIEST resembling a long, projecting nose

SNOW   *v* -ED, -ING, -S to fall as snow (precipitation in the form of ice crystals)

SNOWBALL   *v* -ED, -ING, -S to increase at a rapidly accelerating rate

SNOWBANK   *n* pl. -S a mound of snow

SNOWBELL   *n* pl. -S a flowering shrub

SNOWBELT   *n* pl. -S a region that receives an appreciable amount of snow each year

SNOWBIRD   *n* pl. -S a small bird

SNOWBUSH   *n* pl. -ES a flowering shrub

SNOWCAP   *n* pl. -S a covering of snow

SNOWDROP   *n* pl. -S a European herb

SNOWFALL   *n* pl. -S a fall of snow

SNOWIER   comparative of snowy

SNOWIEST   superlative of snowy

SNOWILY   *adv* in a snowy manner

SNOWLAND   *n* pl. -S an area marked by a great amount of snow

SNOWLESS   *adj* having no snow

SNOWLIKE   *adj* resembling snow

SNOWMAN   *n* pl. -MEN a figure of a person that is made of snow

SNOWMELT   *n* pl. -S water produced by the melting of snow

SNOWMOLD n pl. -S a fungus disease of grasses near the edge of melting snow

SNOWPACK n pl. -S an accumulation of packed snow

SNOWPLOW v -ED, -ING, -S to execute a type of skiing maneuver

SNOWSHED n pl. -S a structure built to provide protection against snow

SNOWSHOE v -SHOED, -SHOEING, -SHOES to walk on snowshoes (oval frames that allow a person to walk on deep snow)

SNOWSUIT n pl. -S a child's garment for winter wear

SNOWY adj SNOWIER, SNOWIEST abounding in snow

SNUB v SNUBBED, SNUBBING, SNUBS to treat with contempt or neglect

SNUBBER n pl. -S one that snubs

SNUBBY adj -BIER, -BIEST blunt

SNUBNESS n pl. -ES bluntness

SNUCK a past tense of sneak

SNUFF v -ED, -ING, -S to use or inhale snuff (powdered tobacco)

SNUFFBOX n pl. -ES a box for holding snuff

SNUFFER n pl. -S one that snuffs

SNUFFIER comparative of snuffy

SNUFFIEST superlative of snuffy

SNUFFILY adv in a snuffy manner

SNUFFLE v -FLED, -FLING, -FLES to sniffle

SNUFFLER n pl. -S one that snuffles

SNUFFLY adj -FLIER, -FLIEST tending to snuffle

SNUFFY adj SNUFFIER, SNUFFIEST dingy

SNUG adj SNUGGER, SNUGGEST warmly comfortable

SNUG v SNUGGED, SNUGGING, SNUGS to make snug

SNUGGERY n pl. -GERIES a snug place

SNUGGEST superlative of snug

SNUGGIES n/pl women's long underwear

SNUGGING present participle of snug

SNUGGLE v -GLED, -GLING, -GLES to lie or press closely

SNUGLY adv in a snug manner

SNUGNESS n pl. -ES the quality or state of being snug

SNYE n pl. -S a side channel in a river or creek

SO n pl. SOS sol

SOAK v -ED, -ING, -S to saturate thoroughly in liquid

SOAKAGE n pl. -S the act of soaking

SOAKER n pl. -S one that soaks

SOAP v -ED, -ING, -S to treat with soap (a cleansing agent)

SOAPBARK n pl. -S a tropical tree

SOAPBOX n pl. -ES a box for soap

SOAPER n pl. -S a serial melodrama on radio or television

SOAPIER comparative of soapy

SOAPIEST superlative of soapy

SOAPILY adv in a soapy manner

SOAPLESS adj having no soap

SOAPLIKE adj resembling soap

SOAPSUDS n/pl suds (soapy water)

SOAPWORT n pl. -S a perennial herb

SOAPY adj SOAPIER, SOAPIEST containing or resembling soap

SOAR v -ED, -ING, -S to fly at a great height

SOARER n pl. -S one that soars

SOARING n pl. -S the sport of flying in a heavier-than-air craft without power

SOAVE n pl. -S an Italian wine

SOB v SOBBED, SOBBING, SOBS to cry with a convulsive catching of the breath

SOBBER n pl. -S one that sobs

SOBEIT conj provided that

SOBER adj SOBERER, SOBEREST having control of one's faculties

SOBER v -ED, -ING, -S to make sober

SOBERIZE v -IZED, -IZING, -IZES to sober

SOBERLY adv in a sober manner

SOBFUL adj given to sobbing

SOBRIETY n pl. -ETIES the quality or state of being sober

SOCAGE n pl. -S a form of feudal land tenure

SOCAGER n pl. -S a tenant by socage

SOCCAGE n pl. -S socage

SOCCER n pl. -S a type of ball game

SOCIABLE n pl. -S a social

SOCIABLY *adv* in a friendly manner

SOCIAL *n* pl. -S a friendly gathering

SOCIALLY *adv* with respect to society

SOCIETY *n* pl. -ETIES an organized group of persons **SOCIETAL** *adj*

SOCK *n* pl. SOCKS or SOX a knitted or woven covering for the foot

SOCK *v* -ED, -ING, -S to strike forcefully

SOCKET *v* -ED, -ING, -S to furnish with a socket (an opening for receiving something)

SOCKEYE *n* pl. -S a food fish

SOCKLESS *adj* having no socks

SOCKMAN *n* pl. -MEN socman

SOCKO *adj* strikingly impressive

SOCLE *n* pl. -S a block used as a base for a column or pedestal

SOCMAN *n* pl. -MEN a socager

SOD *v* SODDED, SODDING, SODS to cover with sod (turf)

SODA *n* pl. -S a type of chemical compound **SODALESS** *adj*

SODALIST *n* pl. -S a member of a sodality

SODALITE *n* pl. -S a mineral

SODALITY *n* pl. -TIES a society

SODAMIDE *n* pl. -S a chemical compound

SODDED past tense of sod

SODDEN *v* -ED, -ING, -S to make soggy

SODDENLY *adv* in a soggy manner

SODDING present participle of sod

SODDY *n* pl. -DIES a house built of sod

SODIUM *n* pl. -S a metallic element **SODIC** *adj*

SODOM *n* pl. -S a place notorious for vice and corruption

SODOMIST *n* pl. -S a sodomite

SODOMITE *n* pl. -S one who practices sodomy

SODOMIZE *v* -IZED, -IZING, -IZES to engage in sodomy with

SODOMY *n* pl. -OMIES unnatural copulation

SOEVER *adv* at all

SOFA *n* pl. -S a long, upholstered seat

SOFAR *n* pl. -S a system for locating underwater explosions

SOFFIT *n* pl. -S the underside of an architectural structure

SOFT *adj* SOFTER, SOFTEST yielding readily to pressure

SOFT *n* pl. -S a soft object or part

SOFTA *n* pl. -S a Muslim theological student

SOFTBACK *n* pl. -S a book bound in a flexible paper cover

SOFTBALL *n* pl. -S a type of ball

SOFTEN *v* -ED, -ING, -S to make soft

SOFTENER *n* pl. -S one that softens

SOFTHEAD *n* pl. -S a foolish person

SOFTIE *n* pl. -S softy

SOFTIES pl. of softy

SOFTISH *adj* somewhat soft

SOFTLY *adv* in a soft manner

SOFTNESS *n* pl. -ES the quality or state of being soft

SOFTWARE *n* pl. -S written or printed data used in computer operations

SOFTWOOD *n* pl. -S the soft wood of various trees

SOFTY *n* pl. SOFTIES a sentimental person

SOGGED *adj* soggy

SOGGY *adj* -GIER, -GIEST heavy with moisture **SOGGILY** *adv*

SOIGNE *adj* carefully done

SOIGNEE *adj* soigne

SOIL *v* -ED, -ING, -S to make dirty

SOILAGE *n* pl. -S green crops for feeding animals

SOILLESS *adj* carried on without soil (finely divided rock mixed with organic matter)

SOILURE *n* pl. -S a stain or smudge

SOIREE *n* pl. -S an evening party

SOJA *n* pl. -S the soybean

SOJOURN *v* -ED, -ING, -S to stay temporarily

SOKE *n* pl. -S a feudal right to administer justice within a certain territory

SOKEMAN *n* pl. -MEN socman

SOKOL *n* pl. -S an international group promoting physical fitness

SOL *n* pl. -S the fifth tone of the diatonic musical scale

SOLA a pl. of solum

SOLACE *v* -LACED, -LACING, -LACES to console

SOLACER *n* pl. -S one that solaces

SOLAN *n* pl. -S a gannet

SOLAND *n* pl. -S solan

SOLANDER *n* pl. -S a protective box for library materials

SOLANIN *n* pl. -S solanine

SOLANINE *n* pl. -S a poisonous alkaloid

SOLANO *n* pl. -NOS a strong, hot wind

SOLANUM *n* pl. -S any of a genus of herbs and shrubs

SOLAR *adj* pertaining to the sun

SOLARIA a pl. of solarium

SOLARISE *v* -ISED, -ISING, -ISES to solarize

SOLARISM *n* pl. -S an interpretation of folk tales as concepts of the nature of the sun

SOLARIUM *n* pl. -IA or -IUMS a room exposed to the sun

SOLARIZE *v* -IZED, -IZING, -IZES to expose to sunlight

SOLATE *v* -ATED, -ATING, -ATES to change to a fluid colloidal system

SOLATION *n* pl. -S the act of solating

SOLATIUM *n* pl. -TIA a compensation given for damage to the feelings

SOLD past tense of sell

SOLDAN *n* pl. -S a Muslim ruler

SOLDER *v* -ED, -ING, -S to join closely together

SOLDERER *n* pl. -S one that solders

SOLDI pl. of soldo

SOLDIER *v* -ED, -ING, -S to perform military service

SOLDIERY *n* pl. -DIERIES the military profession

SOLDO *n* pl. -DI a former coin of Italy

SOLE *v* SOLED, SOLING, SOLES to furnish with a sole (the bottom surface of a shoe or boot)

SOLECISE *v* -CISED, -CISING, -CISES to solecize

SOLECISM *n* pl. -S an ungrammatical combination of words in a sentence

SOLECIST *n* pl. -S one who solecizes

SOLECIZE *v* -CIZED, -CIZING, -CIZES to use solecisms

SOLED past tense of sole

SOLEI pl. of soleus

SOLELESS *adj* having no sole

SOLELY *adv* singly

SOLEMN *adj* -EMNER, -EMNEST serious **SOLEMNLY** *adv*

SOLENESS *n* pl. -ES the state of being the only one

SOLENOID *n* pl. -S a type of electric coil

SOLERET *n* pl. -S solleret

SOLEUS *n* pl. -LEI a leg muscle

SOLFEGE *n* pl. -S a type of singing exercise

SOLFEGGI *n/pl* solfeges

SOLGEL *adj* involving some changes in the state of a colloidal system

SOLI a pl. of solo

SOLICIT *v* -ED, -ING, -S to ask for earnestly

SOLID *adj* -IDER, -IDEST having definite shape and volume

SOLID *n* pl. -S a solid substance

SOLIDAGO *n* pl. -GOS a flowering plant

SOLIDARY *adj* united

SOLIDI pl. of solidus

SOLIDIFY *v* -FIED, -FYING, -FIES to make solid

SOLIDITY *n* pl. -TIES the quality or state of being solid

SOLIDLY *adv* in a solid manner

SOLIDUS *n* pl. -DI a coin of ancient Rome

SOLING present participle of sole

SOLION *n* pl. -S an electronic detecting and amplifying device

SOLIQUID *n* pl. -S a fluid colloidal system

SOLITARY *n* pl. -TARIES one who lives alone

SOLITON *n* pl. -S a solitary wave in physics

SOLITUDE *n* pl. -S the state of being alone

SOLLERET *n* pl. -S a sabaton

SOLO *n* pl. -LOS or -LI a musical composition for a single voice or instrument

SOLO *v* -ED, -ING, -S to perform alone

SOLOIST *n* pl. -S one that performs a solo

SOLON *n* pl. -S a wise lawgiver

SOLONETS *n* pl. -ES solonetz

SOLONETZ *n* pl. -ES a type of soil

SOLSTICE *n* pl. -S the time of the year when the sun is at its greatest distance from the celestial equator

SOLUBLE   *n* pl. -S something that is soluble (capable of being dissolved)

SOLUBLY   *adv* in a soluble manner

SOLUM   *n* pl. -LA or -LUMS a soil layer

SOLUS   *adj* alone

SOLUTE   *n* pl. -S a dissolved substance

SOLUTION   *n* pl. -S a homogeneous liquid mixture

SOLVABLE   *adj* capable of being solved

SOLVATE   *v* -VATED, -VATING, -VATES to convert into a type of ion

SOLVE   *v* SOLVED, SOLVING, SOLVES to find the answer or explanation for

SOLVENCY   *n* pl. -CIES the ability to pay all debts

SOLVENT   *n* pl. -S a substance capable of dissolving others

SOLVER   *n* pl. -S one that solves

SOLVING   present participle of solve

SOMA   *n* pl. -MATA or -MAS the body of an organism **SOMATIC** *adj*

SOMBER   *adj* gloomy **SOMBERLY** *adv*

SOMBRE   *adj* somber **SOMBRELY** *adv*

SOMBRERO   *n* pl. -ROS a broad-brimmed hat

SOMBROUS   *adj* somber

SOME   *adj* being an unspecified number or part

SOMEBODY   *n* pl. -BODIES an important person

SOMEDAY   *adv* at some future time

SOMEDEAL   *adv* to some degree

SOMEHOW   *adv* by some means

SOMEONE   *n* pl. -S a somebody

SOMERSET   *v* -SETED, -SETING, -SETS or -SETTED, -SETTING, -SETS to roll the body in a complete circle, head over heels

SOMETIME   *adv* at some future time

SOMEWAY   *adv* somehow

SOMEWAYS   *adv* someway

SOMEWHAT   *n* pl. -S an unspecified number or part

SOMEWHEN   *adv* sometime

SOMEWISE   *adv* somehow

SOMITE   *n* pl. -S a longitudinal segment of the body of some animals **SOMITAL, SOMITIC** *adj*

SON   *n* pl. -S a male child

SONANCE   *n* pl. -S sound

SONANT   *n* pl. -S a sound uttered with vibration of the vocal cords **SONANTAL, SONANTIC** *adj*

SONAR   *n* pl. -S an underwater locating device

SONARMAN   *n* pl. -MEN a person who operates sonar equipment

SONATA   *n* pl. -S a type of musical composition

SONATINA   *n* pl. -TINAS or -TINE a short sonata

SONDE   *n* pl. -S a device for observing atmospheric phenomena

SONDER   *n* pl. -S a class of small yachts

SONE   *n* pl. -S a unit of loudness

SONG   *n* pl. -S a musical composition written or adapted for singing

SONGBIRD   *n* pl. -S a bird that utters a musical call

SONGBOOK   *n* pl. -S a book of songs

SONGFEST   *n* pl. -S an informal gathering for group singing

SONGFUL   *adj* melodious

SONGLESS   *adj* incapable of singing

SONGLIKE   *adj* resembling a song

SONGSTER   *n* pl. -S a singer

SONHOOD   *n* pl. -S the state of being a son

SONIC   *adj* pertaining to sound

SONICATE   *v* -CATED, -CATING, -CATES to disrupt with sound waves

SONICS   *n/pl* the science dealing with the practical applications of sound

SONLESS   *adj* having no son

SONLIKE   *adj* resembling a son

SONLY   *adj* pertaining to a son

SONNET   *v* -NETED, -NETING, -NETS or -NETTED, -NETTING, -NETS to compose a sonnet (a type of poem)

SONNY   *n* pl. -NIES a small boy

SONOBUOY   *n* pl. -BUOYS a buoy that detects and transmits underwater sounds

SONOGRAM   *n* pl. -S an image produced by ultrasound

SONORANT   *n* pl. -S a type of voiced sound

SONORITY   *n* pl. -TIES the quality or state of being sonorous

SONOROUS   *adj* characterized by a full and loud sound

SONOVOX   *n* pl. -ES a sound effects device

SONSHIP   *n* pl. -S the state of being a son

SONSIE   *adj* -SIER, -SIEST sonsy

SONSY   *adj* -SIER, -SIEST comely

SOOCHONG   *n* pl. -S souchong

SOOEY   *interj* — used in calling pigs

SOOK   *n* pl. -S souk

SOON   *adv* SOONER, SOONEST in the near future

SOONER   *n* pl. -S one who settles on government land before it is officially opened for settlement

SOOT   *v* -ED, -ING, -S to cover with soot (a black substance produced by combustion)

SOOTH   *adj* SOOTHER, SOOTHEST true

SOOTH   *n* pl. -S truth

SOOTHE   *v* SOOTHED, SOOTHING, SOOTHES to restore to a quiet or normal state

SOOTHER   *n* pl. -S one that soothes

SOOTHLY   *adv* in truth

SOOTHSAY   *v* -SAID, -SAYING, -SAYS to predict

SOOTY   *adj* SOOTIER, SOOTIEST covered with soot **SOOTILY** *adv*

SOP   *v* SOPPED, SOPPING, SOPS to dip or soak in a liquid

SOPH   *n* pl. -S a sophomore

SOPHIES   pl. of sophy

SOPHISM   *n* pl. -S a plausible but fallacious argument

SOPHIST   *n* pl. -S one that uses sophisms

SOPHY   *n* pl. -PHIES a ruler of Persia

SOPITE   *v* -PITED, -PITING, -PITES to put to sleep

SOPOR   *n* pl. -S an abnormally deep sleep

SOPPED   past tense of sop

SOPPING   *adj* very wet

SOPPY   *adj* -PIER, -PIEST very wet

SOPRANO   *n* pl. -NOS or -NI the highest singing voice

SORA   *n* pl. -S a marsh bird

SORB   *v* -ED, -ING, -S to take up and hold by absorption or adsorption **SORBABLE** *adj*

SORBATE   *n* pl. -S a sorbed substance

SORBENT   *n* pl. -S a substance that sorbs

SORBET   *n* pl. -S sherbet

SORBIC   *adj* pertaining to a type of fruit

SORBITOL   *n* pl. -S a chemical compound

SORBOSE   *n* pl. -S a type of sugar

SORCERER   *n* pl. -S one who practices sorcery

SORCERY   *n* pl. -CERIES alleged use of supernatural powers

SORD   *n* pl. -S a flight of mallards

SORDID   *adj* filthy **SORDIDLY** *adv*

SORDINE   *n* pl. -S a device used to muffle the tone of a musical instrument

SORDINO   *n* pl. -NI sordine

SORDOR   *n* pl. -S a sordid state

SORE   *adj* SORER, SOREST painfully sensitive to the touch

SORE   *n* pl. -S a sore area on the body

SOREHEAD   *n* pl. -S a person who is easily angered or offended

SOREL   *n* pl. -S sorrel

SORELY   *adv* in a sore manner

SORENESS   *n* pl. -ES the quality or state of being sore

SORER   comparative of sore

SOREST   superlative of sore

SORGHO   *n* pl. -GHOS sorgo

SORGHUM   *n* pl. -S a cereal grass

SORGO   *n* pl. -GOS a variety of sorghum

SORI   pl. of sorus

SORICINE   *adj* belonging to the shrew family of mammals

SORING   *n* pl. -S the practice of making a horse's front feet sore to force high stepping

SORITES   *n* pl. SORITES a type of argument used in logic **SORITIC** *adj*

SORN   *v* -ED, -ING, -S to force oneself on others for food and lodging

SORNER   *n* pl. -S one that sorns

SOROCHE   *n* pl. -S mountain sickness

SORORAL   *adj* sisterly

SORORATE   *n* pl. -S the marriage of a man usually with his deceased wife's sister

SORORITY   *n* pl. -TIES a social club for women

SOROSIS   *n* pl. -ROSES or -ROSISES a women's club or society

SORPTION *n* pl. -S the act or process of sorbing **SORPTIVE** *adj*

SORREL *n* pl. -S a reddish brown color

SORRIER comparative of sorry

SORRIEST superlative of sorry

SORRILY *adv* in a sorry manner

SORROW *v* -ED, -ING, -S to grieve

SORROWER *n* pl. -S one that sorrows

SORRY *adj* -RIER, -RIEST feeling grief or penitence

SORT *v* -ED, -ING, -S to arrange according to kind, class, or size **SORTABLE** *adj* **SORTABLY** *adv*

SORTER *n* pl. -S one that sorts

SORTIE *v* -TIED, -TIEING, -TIES to attack suddenly from a defensive position

SORUS *n* pl. -RI a cluster of plant reproductive bodies

SOT *n* pl. -S an habitual drunkard

SOTH *n* pl. -S sooth

SOTOL *n* pl. -S a flowering plant

SOTTED *adj* besotted

SOTTISH *adj* resembling a sot

SOU *n* pl. -S a former French coin

SOUARI *n* pl. -S a tropical tree

SOUBISE *n* pl. -S a sauce of onions and butter

SOUCAR *n* pl. -S a Hindu banker

SOUCHONG *n* pl. -S a Chinese tea

SOUDAN *n* pl. -S soldan

SOUFFLE *n* pl. -S a light, baked dish

SOUFFLED *adj* made puffy by beating and baking

SOUGH *v* -ED, -ING, -S to make a moaning or sighing sound

SOUGHT past tense of seek

SOUK *n* pl. -S a marketplace in northern Africa and the Middle East

SOUL *n* pl. -S the spiritual aspect of human beings **SOULED, SOULLESS, SOULLIKE** *adj*

SOULFUL *adj* full of emotion

SOUND *adj* SOUNDER, SOUNDEST being in good health or condition

SOUND *v* -ED, -ING, -S to make a sound (something that stimulates the auditory receptors)

SOUNDBOX *n* pl. -ES a resonant cavity in a musical instrument

SOUNDER *n* pl. -S one that sounds

SOUNDING *n* pl. -S a sampling of opinions

SOUNDLY *adv* in a sound manner

SOUNDMAN *n* pl. -MEN a person who controls the quality of sound being recorded

SOUP *v* -ED, -ING, -S to increase the power or efficiency of

SOUPCON *n* pl. -S a minute amount

SOUPY *adj* SOUPIER, SOUPIEST foggy

SOUR *adj* SOURER, SOUREST sharp or biting to the taste

SOUR *v* -ED, -ING, -S to make or become sour

SOURBALL *n* pl. -S a sour candy

SOURCE *v* SOURCED, SOURCING, SOURCES to obtain from a point of origin

SOURDINE *n* pl. -S sordine

SOURISH *adj* somewhat sour

SOURLY *adv* in a sour manner

SOURNESS *n* pl. -ES the quality or state of being sour

SOURPUSS *n* pl. -ES a grouchy person

SOURSOP *n* pl. -S a tropical tree

SOURWOOD *n* pl. -S a flowering tree

SOUSE *v* SOUSED, SOUSING, SOUSES to immerse

SOUTACHE *n* pl. -S a flat, narrow braid

SOUTANE *n* pl. -S a cassock

SOUTER *n* pl. -S a shoemaker

SOUTH *v* -ED, -ING, -S to move toward the south (a cardinal point of the compass)

SOUTHER *n* pl. -S a wind or storm from the south

SOUTHERN *n* pl. -S a person living in the south

SOUTHING *n* pl. -S movement toward the south

SOUTHPAW *n* pl. -S a left-handed person

SOUTHRON *n* pl. -S a southern

SOUVENIR *n* pl. -S a memento

SOUVLAKI *n* pl. -S a Greek shish kebab

SOVIET *n* pl. -S a legislative body in a Communist country

SOVKHOZ *n* pl. -KHOZES or -KHOZY a state-owned farm in the Soviet Union

SOVRAN	*n* pl. -S a monarch
SOVRANLY	*adv* supremely
SOVRANTY	*n* pl. -TIES a monarchy
SOW	*v* SOWED, SOWN, SOWING, SOWS to scatter over land for growth, as seed **SOWABLE** *adj*
SOWANS	*n* pl. SOWANS sowens
SOWAR	*n* pl. -S a mounted native soldier in India
SOWBELLY	*n* pl. -LIES pork cured in salt
SOWBREAD	*n* pl. -S a flowering plant
SOWCAR	*n* pl. -S soucar
SOWENS	*n* pl. SOWENS porridge made from oat husks
SOWER	*n* pl. -S one that sows
SOWN	past participle of sow
SOX	a pl. of sock
SOY	*n* pl. SOYS the soybean
SOYA	*n* pl. -S soy
SOYBEAN	*n* pl. -S the seed of a cultivated Asian herb
SOYMILK	*n* pl. -S a milk substitute made from soybeans
SOYUZ	*n* pl. -ES a Soviet manned spacecraft
SOZIN	*n* pl. -S a type of protein
SOZINE	*n* pl. -S sozin
SOZZLED	*adj* drunk
SPA	*n* pl. -S a mineral spring
SPACE	*v* SPACED, SPACING, SPACES to set some distance apart
SPACEMAN	*n* pl. -MEN an astronaut
SPACER	*n* pl. -S one that spaces
SPACEY	*adj* SPACIER, SPACIEST weird in behavior
SPACIAL	*adj* spatial
SPACING	*n* pl. -S the distance between any two objects
SPACIOUS	*adj* vast or ample in extent
SPACKLE	*v* -LED, -LING, -LES to fill cracks or holes in a surface with paste
SPACY	*adj* SPACIER, SPACIEST spacey
SPADE	*v* SPADED, SPADING, SPADES to take up with a spade (a digging implement)
SPADEFUL	*n* pl. -S as much as a spade can hold
SPADER	*n* pl. -S one that spades
SPADICES	pl. of spadix
SPADILLE	*n* pl. -S the highest trump in certain card games
SPADING	present participle of spade
SPADIX	*n* pl. -DICES or -DIXES a flower cluster
SPADO	*n* pl. -DONES a castrated man or animal
SPAE	*v* SPAED, SPAEING, SPAES to foretell
SPAEING	*n* pl. -S the act of foretelling
SPAETZLE	*n/pl* tiny dumplings
SPAGYRIC	*n* pl. -S a person skilled in alchemy
SPAHEE	*n* pl. -S spahi
SPAHI	*n* pl. -S a Turkish cavalryman
SPAIL	*n* pl. -S spale
SPAIT	*n* pl. -S spate
SPAKE	a past tense of speak
SPALE	*n* pl. -S a splinter or chip
SPALL	*v* -ED, -ING, -S to break up into fragments
SPALLER	*n* pl. -S one that spalls
SPALPEEN	*n* pl. -S a rascal
SPAN	*v* SPANNED, SPANNING, SPANS to extend over or across
SPANCEL	*v* -CELED, -CELING, -CELS or -CELLED, -CELLING, -CELS to bind or fetter with a rope
SPANDEX	*n* pl. -ES a synthetic elastic fiber
SPANDREL	*n* pl. -S a space between two adjoining arches
SPANDRIL	*n* pl. -S spandrel
SPANG	*adv* directly
SPANGLE	*v* -GLED, -GLING, -GLES to adorn with spangles (bits of sparkling metal)
SPANGLY	*adj* -GLIER, -GLIEST covered with spangles
SPANIEL	*n* pl. -S a dog with silky hair
SPANK	*v* -ED, -ING, -S to slap on the buttocks
SPANKER	*n* pl. -S one that spanks
SPANKING	*n* pl. -S the act of one that spanks
SPANLESS	*adj* having no extent
SPANNED	past tense of span
SPANNER	*n* pl. -S one that spans
SPANNING	present participle of span

SPANWORM *n* pl. -S an inchworm

SPAR *v* SPARRED, SPARRING, SPARS to provide with spars (stout poles used to support rigging)

SPARABLE *n* pl. -S a type of nail

SPARE *v* SPARED, SPARING, SPARES to refrain from punishing, harming, or destroying

SPARE *adj* SPARER, SPAREST meager **SPARELY** *adv*

SPARER *n* pl. -S one that spares

SPARERIB *n* pl. -S a cut of pork

SPAREST *adj* superlative of spare

SPARGE *v* SPARGED, SPARGING, SPARGES to sprinkle

SPARGER *n* pl. -S one that sparges

SPARID *n* pl. -S any of a family of marine fishes

SPARING present participle of spare

SPARK *v* -ED, -ING, -S to give off sparks (small fiery particles)

SPARKER *n* pl. -S something that sparks

SPARKIER comparative of sparky

SPARKIEST superlative of sparky

SPARKILY *adv* in a lively manner

SPARKISH *adj* jaunty

SPARKLE *v* -KLED, -KLING, -KLES to give off or reflect flashes of light

SPARKLER *n* pl. -S something that sparkles

SPARKLY *adj* -KLIER, -KLIEST tending to sparkle

SPARKY *adj* SPARKIER, SPARKIEST lively

SPARLIKE *adj* resembling a spar

SPARLING *n* pl. -S a young herring

SPAROID *n* pl. -S a sparid

SPARRED past tense of spar

SPARRIER comparative of sparry

SPARRIEST superlative of sparry

SPARRING present participle of spar

SPARROW *n* pl. -S a small bird

SPARRY *adj* -RIER, -RIEST resembling spar (a lustrous mineral)

SPARSE *adj* SPARSER, SPARSEST thinly distributed **SPARSELY** *adv*

SPARSITY *n* pl. -TIES the quality or state of being sparse

SPARTAN *adj* avoiding luxury and comfort

SPASM *n* pl. -S an abnormal, involuntary muscular contraction

SPASTIC *n* pl. -S one suffering from a paralysis with muscle spasms

SPAT *v* SPATTED, SPATTING, SPATS to strike lightly

SPATE *n* pl. -S a freshet

SPATHE *n* pl. -S a leaflike organ of certain plants **SPATHAL, SPATHED, SPATHOSE** *adj*

SPATHIC *adj* sparry

SPATIAL *adj* of or pertaining to space

SPATTED past tense of spat

SPATTER *v* -ED, -ING, -S to scatter in drops

SPATTING present participle of spat

SPATULA *n* pl. -S a mixing implement **SPATULAR** *adj*

SPATZLE *n/pl* spaetzle

SPAVIE *n* pl. -S spavin **SPAVIET** *adj*

SPAVIN *n* pl. -S a disease of horses **SPAVINED** *adj*

SPAWN *v* -ED, -ING, -S to deposit eggs

SPAWNER *n* pl. -S one that spawns

SPAY *v* -ED, -ING, -S to remove the ovaries of

SPAZ *n* pl. SPAZZES a clumsy, foolish, or incompetent person

SPEAK *v* SPOKE or SPAKE, SPOKEN, SPEAKING, SPEAKS to utter words

SPEAKER *n* pl. -S one that speaks

SPEAKING *n* pl. -S a speech or discourse

SPEAN *v* -ED, -ING, -S to wean

SPEAR *v* -ED, -ING, -S to pierce with a spear (a long, pointed weapon)

SPEARER *n* pl. -S one that spears

SPEARGUN *n* pl. -S a gun that shoots a spear

SPEARMAN *n* pl. -MEN a person armed with a spear

SPEC *v* SPECCED, SPECCING, SPECS to write specifications for

SPECIAL *adj* -CIALER, -CIALEST of a distinct kind or character

SPECIAL *n* pl. -S a special person or thing

SPECIATE *v* -ATED, -ATING, -ATES to undergo a type of evolutionary process

SPECIE *n* pl. -S coined money

SPECIFIC	*n* pl. -S a remedy intended for a particular disease	**SPEISS**	*n* pl. -ES a metallic mixture obtained in smelting certain ores
SPECIFY	*v* -FIED, -FYING, -FIES to state in detail	**SPELAEAN**	*adj* spelean
SPECIMEN	*n* pl. -S a part or individual representative of a group or whole	**SPELEAN**	*adj* living in caves
		SPELL	*v* SPELLED or SPELT, SPELLING, SPELLS to name or write the letters of in order
SPECIOUS	*adj* having a false look of truth or authenticity	**SPELLER**	*n* pl. -S one that spells words
SPECK	*v* -ED, -ING, -S to mark with small spots	**SPELLING**	*n* pl. -S a sequence of letters composing a word
SPECKLE	*v* -LED, -LING, -LES to speck	**SPELT**	*n* pl. -S a variety of wheat
SPECS	*n/pl* eyeglasses	**SPELTER**	*n* pl. -S zinc in the form of ingots
SPECTATE	*v* -TATED, -TATING, -TATES to attend and view	**SPELTZ**	*n* pl. -ES spelt
		SPELUNK	*v* -ED, -ING, -S to explore caves
SPECTER	*n* pl. -S a visible disembodied spirit	**SPENCE**	*n* pl. -S a pantry
		SPENCER	*n* pl. -S a trysail
SPECTRA	a pl. of spectrum	**SPEND**	*v* SPENT, SPENDING, SPENDS to pay out
SPECTRAL	*adj* resembling a specter		
SPECTRE	*n* pl. -S specter	**SPENDER**	*n* pl. -S one that spends
SPECTRUM	*n* pl. -TRA or -TRUMS an array of the components of a light wave	**SPENSE**	*n* pl. -S spence
		SPENT	past tense of spend
SPECULUM	*n* pl. -LA or -LUMS a medical instrument **SPECULAR** *adj*	**SPERM**	*n* pl. -S a male gamete **SPERMIC** *adj*
SPEECH	*n* pl. -ES the faculty or act of speaking	**SPERMARY**	*n* pl. -RIES an organ in which sperms are formed
SPEED	*v* SPED or SPEEDED, SPEEDING, SPEEDS to move swiftly	**SPERMINE**	*n* pl. -S a chemical compound
		SPERMOUS	*adj* resembling or made up of sperms
SPEEDER	*n* pl. -S one that speeds	**SPEW**	*v* -ED, -ING, -S to vomit
SPEEDIER	comparative of speedy	**SPEWER**	*n* pl. -S one that spews
SPEEDIEST	superlative of speedy	**SPHAGNUM**	*n* pl. -S a grayish moss
SPEEDILY	*adv* in a speedy manner	**SPHENE**	*n* pl. -S a mineral
SPEEDING	*n* pl. -S the act of driving faster than the law allows	**SPHENIC**	*adj* shaped like a wedge
SPEEDO	*n* pl. SPEEDOS a speedometer	**SPHENOID**	*n* pl. -S a bone of the skull
SPEEDUP	*n* pl. -S an acceleration of production without an increase in pay	**SPHERAL**	*adj* of, pertaining to, or having the form of a sphere
		SPHERE	*v* SPHERED, SPHERING, SPHERES to form into a sphere (a type of geometric solid)
SPEEDWAY	*n* pl. -WAYS a road designed for rapid travel		
SPEEDY	*adj* SPEEDIER, SPEEDIEST swift	**SPHERIC**	*adj* spheral
		SPHERICS	*n/pl* the geometry of figures on the surface of a sphere
SPEEL	*v* -ED, -ING, -S to climb		
SPEER	*v* -ED, -ING, -S to inquire	**SPHERIER**	comparative of sphery
SPEERING	*n* pl. -S inquiry	**SPHERIEST**	superlative of sphery
SPEIL	*v* -ED, -ING, -S to speel	**SPHERING**	present participle of sphere
SPEIR	*v* -ED, -ING, -S to speer	**SPHEROID**	*n* pl. -S a type of geometric solid
SPEISE	*n* pl. -S speiss	**SPHERULE**	*n* pl. -S a small sphere

SPHERY *adj* SPHERIER, SPHERIEST resembling a sphere

SPHINGES a pl. of sphinx

SPHINGID *n* pl. -S the hawkmoth

SPHINX *n* pl. SPHINXES or SPHINGES a monster in Egyptian mythology

SPHYGMUS *n* pl. -ES the pulse **SPHYGMIC** *adj*

SPICA *n* pl. -CAE or -CAS an ear of grain **SPICATE, SPICATED** *adj*

SPICCATO *n* pl. -TOS a method of playing a stringed instrument

SPICE *v* SPICED, SPICING, SPICES to season with a spice (an aromatic vegetable substance)

SPICER *n* pl. -S one that spices

SPICERY *n* pl. -ERIES a spicy quality

SPICEY *adj* SPICIER, SPICIEST spicy

SPICIER comparative of spicy

SPICIEST superlative of spicy

SPICILY *adv* in a spicy manner

SPICING present participle of spice

SPICULA *n* pl. -LAE spicule **SPICULAR** *adj*

SPICULE *n* pl. -S a needlelike structure

SPICULUM *n* pl. -LA spicule

SPICY *adj* SPICIER, SPICIEST containing spices

SPIDER *n* pl. -S a type of arachnid

SPIDERY *adj* -DERIER, -DERIEST resembling a spider

SPIED past tense of spy

SPIEGEL *n* pl. -S a type of cast iron

SPIEL *v* -ED, -ING, -S to talk at length

SPIELER *n* pl. -S one that spiels

SPIER *v* -ED, -ING, -S to speer

SPIES present 3d person sing. of spy

SPIFF *v* -ED, -ING, -S to make spiffy

SPIFFING *adj* spiffy

SPIFFY *adj* -FIER, -FIEST stylish **SPIFFILY** *adv*

SPIGOT *n* pl. -S a faucet

SPIKE *v* SPIKED, SPIKING, SPIKES to fasten with a spike (a long, thick nail)

SPIKELET *n* pl. -S a type of flower cluster

SPIKER *n* pl. -S one that spikes

SPIKEY *adj* SPIKIER, SPIKIEST spiky

SPIKING present participle of spike

SPIKY *adj* SPIKIER, SPIKIEST resembling a spike **SPIKILY** *adv*

SPILE *v* SPILED, SPILING, SPILES to stop up with a wooden plug

SPILIKIN *n* pl. -S a strip of wood used in a game

SPILING *n* pl. -S a piling

SPILL *v* SPILLED or SPILT, SPILLING, SPILLS to cause to run out of a container

SPILLAGE *n* pl. -S something that is spilled

SPILLER *n* pl. -S one that spills

SPILLWAY *n* pl. -WAYS a channel for surplus water in a reservoir

SPILT a past tense of spill

SPILTH *n* pl. -S spillage

SPIN *v* SPUN, SPINNING, SPINS to draw out and twist into threads

SPINACH *n* pl. -ES a cultivated herb **SPINACHY** *adj*

SPINAGE *n* pl. -S spinach

SPINAL *n* pl. -S an injection of an anesthetic into the spinal cord

SPINALLY *adv* with respect to the spine

SPINATE *adj* bearing thorns

SPINDLE *v* -DLED, -DLING, -DLES to impale on a slender rod

SPINDLER *n* pl. -S one that spindles

SPINDLY *adj* -DLIER, -DLIEST long and slender

SPINE *n* pl. -S the vertebral column **SPINED** *adj*

SPINEL *n* pl. -S a mineral

SPINELLE *n* pl. -S spinel

SPINET *n* pl. -S a small piano

SPINIER comparative of spiny

SPINIEST superlative of spiny

SPINIFEX *n* pl. -ES an Australian grass

SPINLESS *adj* having no rotation

SPINNER *n* pl. -S one that spins

SPINNERY *n* pl. -NERIES a spinning mill

SPINNEY *n* pl. -NEYS a thicket

SPINNING *n* pl. -S the act of one that spins

SPINNY *n* pl. -NIES spinney

SPINOFF *n* pl. -S a new application or incidental result

SPINOR *n* pl. -S a type of mathematical vector

SPINOSE *adj* spiny

SPINOUS	*adj* spiny
SPINOUT	*n* pl. -S a rotational skid by an automobile
SPINSTER	*n* pl. -S an unmarried woman who is past the usual age for marrying
SPINTO	*n* pl. -TOS a singing voice that is lyric and dramatic
SPINULA	*n* pl. -LAE spinule
SPINULE	*n* pl. -S a small thorn
SPINY	*adj* SPINIER, SPINIEST bearing or covered with thorns
SPIRACLE	*n* pl. -S an orifice through which breathing occurs
SPIRAEA	*n* pl. -S spirea
SPIRAL	*v* -RALED, -RALING, -RALS or -RALLED, -RALLING, -RALS to move like a spiral (a type of plane curve)
SPIRALLY	*adv* in a spiral manner
SPIRANT	*n* pl. -S a speech sound produced by the forcing of breath through a narrow passage
SPIRE	*v* SPIRED, SPIRING, SPIRES to rise in a tapering manner
SPIREA	*n* pl. -S a flowering shrub
SPIREM	*n* pl. -S spireme
SPIREME	*n* pl. -S a filament forming part of a cell nucleus during mitosis
SPIRIER	comparative of spiry
SPIRIEST	superlative of spiry
SPIRILLA	*n/pl* spirally twisted, aerobic bacteria
SPIRING	present participle of spire
SPIRIT	*v* -ED, -ING, -S to carry off secretly
SPIROID	*adj* resembling a spiral
SPIRT	*v* -ED, -ING, -S to spurt
SPIRULA	*n* pl. -LAE or -LAS a spiral-shelled mollusk
SPIRY	*adj* SPIRIER, SPIRIEST tall, slender, and tapering
SPIT	*v* SPITTED, SPITTING, SPITS to impale on a spit (a pointed rod on which meat is turned)
SPITAL	*n* pl. -S a hospital
SPITBALL	*n* pl. -S a type of pitch in baseball
SPITE	*v* SPITED, SPITING, SPITES to treat with malice
SPITEFUL	*adj* -FULLER, -FULLEST malicious

SPITFIRE	*n* pl. -S a quick-tempered person
SPITING	present participle of spite
SPITTED	past tense of spit
SPITTER	*n* pl. -S a spitball
SPITTING	present participle of spit
SPITTLE	*n* pl. -S saliva
SPITTOON	*n* pl. -S a receptacle for saliva
SPITZ	*n* pl. -ES a dog having a heavy coat
SPIV	*n* pl. -S a petty criminal
SPLAKE	*n* pl. -S a freshwater fish
SPLASH	*v* -ED, -ING, -ES to scatter a liquid about
SPLASHER	*n* pl. -S one that splashes
SPLASHY	*adj* SPLASHIER, SPLASHIEST showy
SPLAT	*v* SPLATTED, SPLATTING, SPLATS to flatten on impact
SPLATTER	*v* -ED, -ING, -S to spatter
SPLAY	*v* -ED, -ING, -S to spread out
SPLEEN	*n* pl. -S a ductless organ of the body
SPLEENY	*adj* SPLEENIER, SPLEENIEST peevish
SPLENDID	*adj* -DIDER, -DIDEST magnificent
SPLENDOR	*n* pl. -S magnificence
SPLENIA	pl. of splenium
SPLENIAL	*adj* pertaining to the splenius
SPLENIC	*adj* pertaining to the spleen
SPLENIUM	*n* pl. -NIA a surgical bandage
SPLENIUS	*n* pl. -NII a muscle of the neck
SPLENT	*n* pl. -S a splint
SPLICE	*v* SPLICED, SPLICING, SPLICES to join at the ends
SPLICER	*n* pl. -S one that splices
SPLIFF	*n* pl. -S a marijuana cigarette
SPLINE	*v* SPLINED, SPLINING, SPLINES to provide with a spline (a key that connects two rotating mechanical parts)
SPLINT	*v* -ED, -ING, -S to brace with a splint (a thin piece of wood)
SPLINTER	*v* -ED, -ING, -S to split into sharp, slender pieces
SPLIT	*v* SPLIT, SPLITTING, SPLITS to separate lengthwise
SPLITTER	*n* pl. -S one that splits

SPLODGE	v SPLODGED, SPLODGING, SPLODGES to splotch
SPLORE	n pl. -S a carousal
SPLOSH	v -ED, -ING, -ES to splash
SPLOTCH	v -ED, -ING, -ES to mark with large, irregular spots
SPLOTCHY	adj SPLOTCHIER, SPLOTCHIEST splotched
SPLURGE	v SPLURGED, SPLURGING, SPLURGES to spend money lavishly
SPLURGER	n pl. -S one that splurges
SPLURGY	adj SPLURGIER, SPLURGIEST tending to splurge
SPLUTTER	v -ED, -ING, -S to speak rapidly and confusedly
SPODE	n pl. -S a fine china
SPOIL	v SPOILED or SPOILT, SPOILING, SPOILS to impair the value or quality of
SPOILAGE	n pl. -S something that is spoiled or wasted
SPOILER	n pl. -S one that spoils
SPOILT	a past tense of spoil
SPOKE	v SPOKED, SPOKING, SPOKES to provide with spokes (rods that support the rim of a wheel)
SPOKEN	past participle of speak
SPOLIATE	v -ATED, -ATING, -ATES to plunder
SPONDAIC	n pl. -S a spondee
SPONDEE	n pl. -S a type of metrical foot
SPONGE	v SPONGED, SPONGING, SPONGES to wipe with a sponge (a mass of absorbent material)
SPONGER	n pl. -S one that sponges
SPONGIER	comparative of spongy
SPONGIEST	superlative of spongy
SPONGILY	adv in a spongy manner
SPONGIN	n pl. -S a fibrous material
SPONGING	present participle of sponge
SPONGY	adj SPONGIER, SPONGIEST resembling a sponge
SPONSAL	adj pertaining to marriage
SPONSION	n pl. -S the act of sponsoring
SPONSON	n pl. -S a projection from the side of a ship
SPONSOR	v -ED, -ING, -S to make oneself responsible for
SPONTOON	n pl. -S a spear-like weapon
SPOOF	v -ED, -ING, -S to ridicule in fun
SPOOFER	n pl. -S one that spoofs
SPOOFERY	n pl. -ERIES good-natured ridicule
SPOOFY	adj humorously satiric
SPOOK	v -ED, -ING, -S to scare
SPOOKERY	n pl. -ERIES something spooky
SPOOKISH	adj spooky
SPOOKY	adj SPOOKIER, SPOOKIEST scary **SPOOKILY** adv
SPOOL	v -ED, -ING, -S to wind on a small cylinder
SPOOLING	n pl. -S the temporary storage of data for later output
SPOON	v -ED, -ING, -S to take up with a spoon (a type of eating utensil)
SPOONEY	adj SPOONIER, SPOONIEST spoony
SPOONEY	n pl. -EYS a spoony
SPOONFUL	n pl. SPOONFULS or SPOONSFUL as much as a spoon can hold
SPOONIER	comparative of spooney
SPOONIES	pl. of spoony
SPOONIEST	superlative of spooney
SPOONSFUL	a pl. of spoonful
SPOONY	adj SPOONIER, SPOONIEST overly sentimental **SPOONILY** adv
SPOONY	n pl. SPOONIES a spoony person
SPOOR	v -ED, -ING, -S to track
SPORADIC	adj occurring at irregular intervals
SPORAL	adj of, pertaining to, or resembling a spore
SPORE	v SPORED, SPORING, SPORES to produce spores (asexual, usually single-celled reproductive bodies)
SPOROID	adj resembling a spore
SPOROZOA	n/pl parasitic one-celled animals
SPORRAN	n pl. -S a large purse worn by Scottish Highlanders
SPORT	v -ED, -ING, -S to frolic
SPORTER	n pl. -S one that sports
SPORTFUL	adj sportive
SPORTIF	adj sporty
SPORTIVE	adj playful

SPORTY   *adj* SPORTIER, SPORTIEST showy **SPORTILY** *adv*

SPORULE   *n* pl. -S a small spore **SPORULAR** *adj*

SPOT   *v* SPOTTED, SPOTTING, SPOTS to mark with spots (small, roundish discolorations)

SPOTLESS   *adj* perfectly clean

SPOTLIT   a past tense of spotlight

SPOTTER   *n* pl. -S one that spots

SPOTTING   present participle of spot

SPOTTY   *adj* -TIER, -TIEST marked with spots **SPOTTILY** *adv*

SPOUSAL   *n* pl. -S marriage

SPOUSE   *v* SPOUSED, SPOUSING, SPOUSES to marry

SPOUT   *v* -ED, -ING, -S to eject in a rapid stream

SPOUTER   *n* pl. -S one that spouts

SPRADDLE   *v* -DLED, -DLING, -DLES to straddle

SPRAG   *n* pl. -S a device used to prevent a vehicle from rolling backward

SPRAIN   *v* -ED, -ING, -S to weaken by a sudden and violent twisting or wrenching

SPRANG   *n* pl. -S a weaving technique to form an openwork mesh

SPRAT   *n* pl. -S a small herring

SPRATTLE   *v* -TLED, -TLING, -TLES to struggle

SPRAWL   *v* -ED, -ING, -S to stretch out ungracefully

SPRAWLER   *n* pl. -S one that sprawls

SPRAWLY   *adj* SPRAWLIER, SPRAWLIEST tending to sprawl

SPRAY   *v* -ED, -ING, -S to disperse in fine particles

SPRAYER   *n* pl. -S one that sprays

SPREAD   *v* SPREAD, SPREADING, SPREADS to open or expand over a larger area

SPREADER   *n* pl. -S one that spreads

SPREE   *n* pl. -S an unrestrained indulgence in an activity

SPRENT   *adj* sprinkled over

SPRIER   a comparative of spry

SPRIEST   a superlative of spry

SPRIG   *v* SPRIGGED, SPRIGGING, SPRIGS to fasten with small, thin nails

SPRIGGER   *n* pl. -S one that sprigs

SPRIGGY   *adj* -GIER, -GIEST having small branches

SPRIGHT   *n* pl. -S sprite

SPRING   *v* SPRANG or SPRUNG, SPRINGING, SPRINGS to move upward suddenly and swiftly

SPRINGAL   *n* pl. -S a young man

SPRINGE   *v* SPRINGED, SPRINGEING, SPRINGES to catch with a type of snare

SPRINGER   *n* pl. -S one that springs

SPRINGY   *adj* SPRINGIER, SPRINGIEST resilient

SPRINKLE   *v* -KLED, -KLING, -KLES to scatter drops or particles on

SPRINT   *v* -ED, -ING, -S to run at top speed

SPRINTER   *n* pl. -S one that sprints

SPRIT   *n* pl. -S a ship's spar

SPRITE   *n* pl. -S an elf or fairy

SPRITZ   *v* -ED, -ING, -ES to spray

SPRITZER   *n* pl. -S a beverage of white wine and soda water

SPROCKET   *n* pl. -S a toothlike projection that engages with the links of a chain

SPROUT   *v* -ED, -ING, -S to begin to grow

SPRUCE   *adj* SPRUCER, SPRUCEST neat and trim in appearance **SPRUCELY** *adv*

SPRUCE   *v* SPRUCED, SPRUCING, SPRUCES to make spruce

SPRUCY   *adj* SPRUCIER, SPRUCIEST spruce

SPRUE   *n* pl. -S a tropical disease

SPRUG   *n* pl. -S a sparrow

SPRUNG   a past tense of spring

SPRY   *adj* SPRYER, SPRYEST or SPRIER, SPRIEST nimble **SPRYLY** *adv*

SPRYNESS   *n* pl. -ES the quality or state of being spry

SPUD   *v* SPUDDED, SPUDDING, SPUDS to remove with a spade-like tool

SPUDDER   *n* pl. -S a tool for removing bark from trees

SPUE   *v* SPUED, SPUING, SPUES to spew

SPUME   *v* SPUMED, SPUMING, SPUMES to foam

SPUMIER comparative of spumy

SPUMIEST superlative of spumy

SPUMING present participle of spume

SPUMONE n pl. -S an Italian ice cream

SPUMONI n pl. -S spumone

SPUMOUS adj spumy

SPUMY adj SPUMIER, SPUMIEST foamy

SPUN past tense of spin

SPUNK v -ED, -ING, -S to begin to burn

SPUNKIE n pl. -S a light caused by the combustion of marsh gas

SPUNKY adj SPUNKIER, SPUNKIEST plucky **SPUNKILY** adv

SPUR v SPURRED, SPURRING, SPURS to urge on with a spur (a horseman's goad)

SPURGALL v -ED, -ING, -S to injure with a spur

SPURGE n pl. -S a tropical plant

SPURIOUS adj not genuine

SPURN v -ED, -ING, -S to reject with contempt

SPURNER n pl. -S one that spurns

SPURRED past tense of spur

SPURRER n pl. -S one that spurs

SPURREY n pl. -REYS spurry

SPURRIER n pl. -S one that makes spurs

SPURRING present participle of spur

SPURRY n pl. -RIES a European weed

SPURT v -ED, -ING, -S to gush forth

SPURTLE n pl. -S a stick for stirring porridge

SPUTA pl. of sputum

SPUTNIK n pl. -S a Soviet artificial earth satellite

SPUTTER v -ED, -ING, -S to eject particles in short bursts

SPUTUM n pl. -TA saliva

SPY v SPIED, SPYING, SPIES to watch secretly

SPYGLASS n pl. -ES a small telescope

SQUAB n pl. -S a young pigeon

SQUABBLE v -BLED, -BLING, -BLES to quarrel

SQUABBY adj -BIER, -BIEST short and fat

SQUAD v SQUADDED, SQUADDING, SQUADS to form into squads (small organized groups)

SQUADRON v -ED, -ING, -S to arrange in squadrons (units of military organization)

SQUALENE n pl. -S a chemical compound

SQUALID adj -IDER, -IDEST marked by filthiness caused by neglect or poverty

SQUALL v -ED, -ING, -S to cry or scream loudly

SQUALLER n pl. -S one that squalls

SQUALLY adj SQUALLIER, SQUALLIEST gusty

SQUALOR n pl. -S the quality or state of being squalid

SQUAMA n pl. -MAE a scale **SQUAMATE, SQUAMOSE, SQUAMOUS** adj

SQUANDER v -ED, -ING, -S to spend wastefully

SQUARE adj SQUARER, SQUAREST having four equal sides and four right angles; rigidly conventional

SQUARE v SQUARED, SQUARING, SQUARES to make square

SQUARELY adv in a straightforward or honest manner

SQUARER n pl. -S one that squares

SQUAREST superlative of square

SQUARING present participle of square

SQUARISH adj somewhat square

SQUASH v -ED, -ING, -ES to press into a pulp or flat mass

SQUASHER n pl. -S one that squashes

SQUASHY adj SQUASHIER, SQUASHIEST soft and moist

SQUAT v SQUATTED, SQUATTING, SQUATS to bend one's knees and sit on one's heels

SQUAT adj SQUATTER, SQUATTEST short and thick **SQUATLY** adv

SQUATTER v -ED, -ING, -S to move through water

SQUATTING present participle of squat

SQUATTY adj -TIER, -TIEST squat

SQUAWK v -ED, -ING, -S to utter a loud, harsh cry

SQUAWKER n pl. -S one that squawks

SQUEAK v -ED, -ING, -S to make a sharp, high-pitched sound

SQUEAKER n pl. -S one that squeaks

SQUEAKY adj SQUEAKIER, SQUEAKIEST tending to squeak

SQUEAL	*v* -ED, -ING, -S to utter a sharp, shrill cry
SQUEALER	*n* pl. -S one that squeals
SQUEEGEE	*v* -GEED, -GEEING, -GEES to wipe with a squeegee (an implement for removing water from a surface)
SQUEEZE	*v* SQUEEZED, SQUEEZING, SQUEEZES to press hard upon
SQUEEZER	*n* pl. -S one that squeezes
SQUEG	*v* SQUEGGED, SQUEGGING, SQUEGS to oscillate in an irregular manner
SQUELCH	*v* -ED, -ING, -ES to squash
SQUELCHY	*adj* SQUELCHIER, SQUELCHIEST squashy
SQUIB	*v* SQUIBBED, SQUIBBING, SQUIBS to lampoon
SQUID	*v* SQUIDDED, SQUIDDING, SQUIDS to fish for squid (ten-armed marine mollusks)
SQUIFFED	*adj* drunk
SQUIFFY	*adj* -FIER, -FIEST squiffed
SQUIGGLE	*v* -GLED, -GLING, -GLES to wriggle
SQUIGGLY	*adj* -GLIER, -GLIEST wriggly
SQUILGEE	*v* -GEED, -GEEING, -GEES to squeegee
SQUILL	*n* pl. -S a Eurasian herb
SQUILLA	*n* pl. -LAS or -LAE a burrowing crustacean
SQUINCH	*v* -ED, -ING, -ES to squint
SQUINNY	*v* -NIED, -NYING, -NIES to squint
SQUINNY	*adj* -NIER, -NIEST squinty
SQUINT	*adj* SQUINTER, SQUINTEST cross-eyed
SQUINT	*v* -ED, -ING, -S to look with the eyes partly closed
SQUINTER	*n* pl. -S one that squints
SQUINTY	*adj* SQUINTIER, SQUINTIEST marked by squinting
SQUIRE	*v* SQUIRED, SQUIRING, SQUIRES to serve as a squire (an escort)
SQUIREEN	*n* pl. -S an owner of a small estate
SQUIRISH	*adj* of, resembling, or befitting a squire
SQUIRM	*v* -ED, -ING, -S to wriggle
SQUIRMER	*n* pl. -S one that squirms
SQUIRMY	*adj* SQUIRMIER, SQUIRMIEST wriggly
SQUIRREL	*v* -RELED, -RELING, -RELS or -RELLED, -RELLING, -RELS to store up for future use
SQUIRT	*v* -ED, -ING, -S to eject in a thin, swift stream
SQUIRTER	*n* pl. -S one that squirts
SQUISH	*v* -ED, -ING, -ES to squash
SQUISHY	*adj* SQUISHIER, SQUISHIEST squashy
SQUOOSH	*v* -ED, -ING, -ES to squash
SQUOOSHY	*adj* SQUOOSHIER, SQUOOSHIEST squashy
SQUUSH	*v* -ED, -ING, -ES to squash
SRADDHA	*n* pl. -S sradha
SRADHA	*n* pl. -S a Hindu ceremonial offering
SRI	*n* pl. -S mister; sir — used as a Hindu title of respect
STAB	*v* STABBED, STABBING, STABS to pierce with a pointed weapon
STABBER	*n* pl. -S one that stabs
STABILE	*n* pl. -S a stationary abstract sculpture
STABLE	*adj* -BLER, -BLEST resistant to sudden change or position or condition
STABLE	*v* -BLED, -BLING, -BLES to put in a stable (a shelter for domestic animals)
STABLER	*n* pl. -S one that keeps a stable
STABLEST	superlative of stable
STABLING	*n* pl. -S accommodation for animals in a stable
STABLISH	*v* -ED, -ING, -ES to establish
STABLY	*adv* in a stable manner
STACCATO	*n* pl. -TOS or -TI a musical passage marked by the short, clear-cut playing of tones
STACK	*v* -ED, -ING, -S to pile
STACKER	*n* pl. -S one that stacks
STACKUP	*n* pl. -S an arrangement of circling airplanes over an airport waiting to land
STACTE	*n* pl. -S a spice used by the ancient Jews in making incense
STADDLE	*n* pl. -S a platform on which hay is stacked
STADE	*n* pl. -S an ancient Greek unit of length

STADIA	n pl. -S a method of surveying distances	**STAKE**	v STAKED, STAKING, STAKES to fasten with a stake (a pointed piece of wood or metal)
STADIUM	n pl. -S a structure in which athletic events are held	**STAKEOUT**	n pl. -S a surveillance of an area especially by the police
STAFF	v -ED, -ING, -S to provide with a staff (a body of assistants)	**STALAG**	n pl. -S a German prisoner-of-war camp
STAFFER	n pl. -S a member of a staff	**STALE**	adj STALER, STALEST not fresh **STALELY** adv
STAG	v STAGGED, STAGGING, STAGS to attend a social function without a female companion	**STALE**	v STALED, STALING, STALES to become stale
STAGE	v STAGED, STAGING, STAGES to produce for public view	**STALK**	v -ED, -ING, -S to pursue stealthily
STAGEFUL	n pl. -S as much or as many as a stage can hold	**STALKER**	n pl. -S one that stalks
STAGER	n pl. -S an experienced person	**STALKY**	adj STALKIER, STALKIEST long and slender **STALKILY** adv
STAGEY	adj STAGIER, STAGIEST stagy	**STALL**	v -ED, -ING, -S to stop the progress of
STAGGARD	n pl. -S a full-grown male red deer	**STALLION**	n pl. -S an uncastrated male horse
STAGGART	n pl. -S staggard	**STALWART**	n pl. -S an unwavering partisan
STAGGED	past tense of stag	**STAMEN**	n pl. -S the pollen-bearing organ of flowering plants
STAGGER	v -ED, -ING, -S to walk or stand unsteadily	**STAMINA**	n pl. -S endurance **STAMINAL** adj
STAGGERY	adj unsteady	**STAMMEL**	n pl. -S a red color
STAGGIE	n pl. -S a colt	**STAMMER**	v -ED, -ING, -S to speak with involuntary breaks and pauses
STAGGING	present participle of stag		
STAGGY	adj -GIER, -GIEST having the appearance of a mature male	**STAMP**	v -ED, -ING, -S to bring the foot down heavily
STAGIER	comparative of stagey and stagy	**STAMPEDE**	v -PEDED, -PEDING, -PEDES to cause to run away in headlong panic
STAGIEST	superlative of stagey and stagy		
STAGILY	adv in a stagy manner	**STAMPER**	n pl. -S one that stamps
STAGING	n pl. -S a temporary platform	**STANCE**	n pl. -S a manner of standing
STAGNANT	adj not moving or flowing	**STANCH**	adj STANCHER, STANCHEST staunch
STAGNATE	v -NATED, -NATING, -NATES to become stagnant	**STANCH**	v -ED, -ING, -ES to stop the flow of blood from
STAGY	adj STAGIER, STAGIEST having a theatrical quality	**STANCHER**	n pl. -S one that stanches
STAID	adj STAIDER, STAIDEST sober and sedate **STAIDLY** adv	**STANCHLY**	adv in a stanch manner
STAIG	n pl. -S a colt	**STAND**	v STOOD, STANDING, STANDS to assume or maintain an upright position
STAIN	v -ED, -ING, -S to discolor or dirty		
STAINER	n pl. -S one that stains	**STANDARD**	n pl. -S an established measure of comparison
STAIR	n pl. -S a rest for the foot used in going from one level to another	**STANDBY**	n pl. -BYS one that can be relied on
STAIRWAY	n pl. -WAYS a flight of stairs		
STAITHE	n pl. -S a wharf equipped for transferring coal from railroad cars into ships	**STANDEE**	n pl. -S one who stands because of the lack of seats
		STANDER	n pl. -S one that stands

STANDING *n* pl. -S a position or condition in society

STANDISH *n* pl. -ES a receptacle for pens and ink

STANDOFF *n* pl. -S a tie or draw, as in a game

STANDOUT *n* pl. -S one that shows marked superiority

STANDPAT *adj* resisting or opposing change

STANDUP *adj* having an upright position

STANE *v* STANED, STANING, STANES to stone

STANG *v* -ED, -ING, -S to sting

STANHOPE *n* pl. -S a light, open carriage

STANINE *n* pl. -S one of the nine classes into which a set of scores are divided

STANING present participle of stane

STANK *n* pl. -S a pond

STANNARY *n* pl. -RIES a tin-mining region

STANNIC *adj* pertaining to tin

STANNITE *n* pl. -S an ore of tin

STANNOUS *adj* pertaining to tin

STANNUM *n* pl. -S tin

STANZA *n* pl. -S a division of a poem **STANZAED, STANZAIC** *adj*

STAPEDES pl. of stapes

STAPELIA *n* pl. -S an African plant

STAPES *n* pl. -PEDES a bone of the middle ear

STAPH *n* pl. -S any of various spherical bacteria

STAPLE *v* -PLED, -PLING, -PLES to fasten by means of a U-shaped metal loop

STAPLER *n* pl. -S a stapling device

STAR *v* STARRED, STARRING, STARS to shine as a star (a natural luminous body visible in the sky)

STARCH *v* -ED, -ING, -ES to treat with starch (a solid carbohydrate)

STARCHY *adj* STARCHIER, STARCHIEST containing starch

STARDOM *n* pl. -S the status of a preeminent performer

STARDUST *n* pl. -S a romantic quality

STARE *v* STARED, STARING, STARES to gaze fixedly

STARER *n* pl. -S one that stares

STARETS *n* pl. STARTSY a spiritual adviser in the Eastern Orthodox Church

STARFISH *n* pl. -ES a star-shaped marine animal

STARGAZE *v* -GAZED, -GAZING, -GAZES to gaze at the stars

STARING present participle of stare

STARK *adj* STARKER, STARKEST harsh in appearance **STARKLY** *adv*

STARKERS *adj* naked

STARLESS *adj* having no stars

STARLET *n* pl. -S a small star

STARLIKE *adj* resembling a star

STARLING *n* pl. -S a European bird

STARLIT *adj* lighted by the stars

STARNOSE *n* pl. -S a burrowing mammal

STARRED past tense of star

STARRING present participle of star

STARRY *adj* -RIER, -RIEST abounding with stars

STARSHIP *n* pl. -S a spaceship for interstellar travel

START *v* -ED, -ING, -S to set out

STARTER *n* pl. -S one that starts

STARTLE *v* -TLED, -TLING, -TLES to frighten or surprise suddenly

STARTLER *n* pl. -S one that startles

STARTSY pl. of starets

STARTUP *n* pl. -S the act of starting something

STARVE *v* STARVED, STARVING, STARVES to die from lack of food

STARVER *n* pl. -S one that starves

STARWORT *n* pl. -S a flowering plant

STASES pl. of stasis

STASH *v* -ED, -ING, -ES to store in a secret place

STASIMON *n* pl. -MA a choral ode in ancient Greek drama

STASIS *n* pl. STASES a stoppage of the normal flow of bodily fluids

STAT *n* pl. -S a statistic

STATABLE *adj* capable of being stated

STATAL *adj* pertaining to a national government

STATANT *adj* standing with all feet on the ground — used of a heraldic animal

STATE	*v* STATED, STATING, STATES to set forth in words
STATEDLY	*adv* regularly
STATELY	*adj* -LIER, -LIEST dignified
STATER	*n* pl. -S one that states
STATIC	*n* pl. -S random noise produced in a radio or television receiver **STATICAL** *adj*
STATICE	*n* pl. -S a flowering plant
STATICKY	*adj* marked by static
STATING	present participle of state
STATION	*v* -ED, -ING, -S to assign to a position
STATISM	*n* pl. -S a theory of government
STATIST	*n* pl. -S an adherent of statism
STATIVE	*n* pl. -S a verb that expresses a condition
STATOR	*n* pl. -S the part of a machine about which the rotor revolves
STATUARY	*n* pl. -ARIES a group of statues
STATUE	*n* pl. -S a three-dimensional work of art **STATUED** *adj*
STATURE	*n* pl. -S the natural height of a human or animal body
STATUS	*n* pl. -ES relative position
STATUSY	*adj* conferring prestige
STATUTE	*n* pl. -S a law enacted by the legislative branch of a government
STAUMREL	*n* pl. -S a dolt
STAUNCH	*adj* STAUNCHER, STAUNCHEST firm and dependable
STAUNCH	*v* -ED, -ING, -ES to stanch
STAVE	*v* STAVED or STOVE, STAVING, STAVES to drive or thrust away
STAW	a past tense of steal
STAY	*v* STAYED or STAID, STAYING, STAYS to continue in a place or condition
STAYER	*n* pl. -S one that stays
STAYSAIL	*n* pl. -S a type of sail
STEAD	*v* -ED, -ING, -S to be of advantage to
STEADIED	past tense of steady
STEADIER	*n* pl. -S one that steadies
STEADIES	present 3d person sing. of steady
STEADING	*n* pl. -S a small farm
STEADY	*adj* STEADIER, STEADIEST firm in position **STEADILY** *adv*

STEADY	*v* STEADIED, STEADYING, STEADIES to make steady
STEAK	*n* pl. -S a slice of meat
STEAL	*v* STOLE or STAW, STOLEN, STEALING, STEALS to take without right or permission
STEALAGE	*n* pl. -S theft
STEALER	*n* pl. -S one that steals
STEALING	*n* pl. -S the act of one that steals
STEALTH	*n* pl. -S stealthy procedure
STEALTHY	*adj* STEALTHIER, STEALTHIEST intended to escape observation
STEAM	*v* -ED, -ING, -S to expose to steam (water in the form of vapor)
STEAMER	*v* -ED, -ING, -S to travel by steamship
STEAMY	*adj* STEAMIER, STEAMIEST marked by steam **STEAMILY** *adv*
STEAPSIN	*n* pl. -S an enzyme
STEARATE	*n* pl. -S a chemical salt
STEARIN	*n* pl. -S the solid portion of a fat **STEARIC** *adj*
STEARINE	*n* pl. -S stearin
STEATITE	*n* pl. -S a variety of talc
STEDFAST	*adj* staunch
STEED	*n* pl. -S a horse
STEEK	*v* -ED, -ING, -S to shut
STEEL	*v* -ED, -ING, -S to cover with steel (a tough iron alloy)
STEELIE	*n* pl. -S a steel playing marble
STEELY	*adj* STEELIER, STEELIEST resembling steel
STEENBOK	*n* pl. -S an African antelope
STEEP	*adj* STEEPER, STEEPEST inclined sharply
STEEP	*v* -ED, -ING, -S to soak in a liquid
STEEPEN	*v* -ED, -ING, -S to make steep
STEEPER	*n* pl. -S one that steeps
STEEPISH	*adj* somewhat steep
STEEPLE	*n* pl. -S a tapering structure on a church tower **STEEPLED** *adj*
STEEPLY	*adv* in a steep manner
STEER	*v* -ED, -ING, -S to direct the course of
STEERAGE	*n* pl. -S the act of steering
STEERER	*n* pl. -S one that steers

STEEVE   *v* STEEVED, STEEVING, STEEVES to stow in the hold of a ship

STEEVING   *n* pl. -S the angular elevation of a bowsprit from a ship's keel

STEGODON   *n* pl. -S an extinct elephant-like mammal

STEIN   *n* pl. -S a beer mug

STEINBOK   *n* pl. -S steenbok

STELA   *n* pl. -LAE or -LAI an inscribed slab used as a monument **STELAR, STELENE** *adj*

STELE   *n* pl. -S the central portion of vascular tissue in a plant stem **STELIC** *adj*

STELLA   *n* pl. -S a former coin of the United States

STELLAR   *adj* pertaining to the stars

STELLATE   *adj* shaped like a star

STELLIFY   *v* -FIED, -FYING, -FIES to convert into a star

STEM   *v* STEMMED, STEMMING, STEMS to remove stems (ascending axes of a plant) from

STEMLESS   *adj* having no stem

STEMLIKE   *adj* resembling a stem

STEMMA   *n* pl. -MAS or -MATA a scroll recording the genealogy of a family in ancient Rome

STEMMED   past tense of stem

STEMMER   *n* pl. -S one that removes stems

STEMMERY   *n* pl. -MERIES a place where tobacco leaves are stripped

STEMMING   present participle of stem

STEMMY   *adj* -MIER, -MIEST abounding in stems

STEMSON   *n* pl. -S a supporting timber of a ship

STEMWARE   *n* pl. -S a type of glassware

STENCH   *n* pl. -ES a foul odor

STENCHY   *adj* STENCHIER, STENCHIEST having a stench

STENCIL   *v* -CILED, -CILING, -CILS or -CILLED, -CILLING, -CILS to mark by means of a perforated sheet of material

STENGAH   *n* pl. -S a mixed drink

STENO   *n* pl. STENOS a stenographer

STENOKY   *n* pl. -KIES the ability of an organism to live only under a narrow range of conditions

STENOSED   *adj* affected with stenosis

STENOSIS   *n* pl. -NOSES a narrowing of a bodily passage **STENOTIC** *adj*

STENTOR   *n* pl. -S a person having a very loud voice

STEP   *v* STEPPED, STEPPING, STEPS to move by lifting the foot and setting it down in another place

STEPDAME   *n* pl. -S a stepmother

STEPLIKE   *adj* resembling a stair

STEPPE   *n* pl. -S a vast treeless plain

STEPPED   past tense of step

STEPPER   *n* pl. -S one that steps

STEPPING   present participle of step

STEPSON   *n* pl. -S a son of one's spouse by a former marriage

STEPWISE   *adj* marked by a gradual progression

STERE   *n* pl. -S a unit of volume

STEREO   *v* -ED, -ING, -S to make a type of printing plate

STERIC   *adj* pertaining to the spatial relationships of atoms in a molecule

STERICAL   *adj* steric

STERIGMA   *n* pl. -MAS or -MATA a spore-bearing stalk of certain fungi

STERILE   *adj* incapable of producing offspring

STERLET   *n* pl. -S a small sturgeon

STERLING   *n* pl. -S British money

STERN   *adj* STERNER, STERNEST unyielding

STERN   *n* pl. -S the rear part of a ship

STERNA   a pl. of sternum

STERNAL   *adj* pertaining to the sternum

STERNITE   *n* pl. -S a somitic sclerite

STERNLY   *adv* in a stern manner

STERNSON   *n* pl. -S a reinforcing post of a ship

STERNUM   *n* pl. -NA or -NUMS a long, flat supporting bone of most vertebrates

STERNWAY   *n* pl. -WAYS the backward movement of a vessel

STEROID   *n* pl. -S a type of chemical compound

STEROL   *n* pl. -S a type of solid alcohol

STERTOR   *n* pl. -S a deep snoring sound

STET	*v* STETTED, STETTING, STETS to cancel a previously made printing correction
STEW	*v* -ED, -ING, -S to cook by boiling slowly
STEWARD	*v* -ED, -ING, -S to manage
STEWBUM	*n* pl. -S a drunken bum
STEWPAN	*n* pl. -S a pan used for stewing
STEY	*adj* steep
STHENIA	*n* pl. -S excessive energy **STHENIC** *adj*
STIBIAL	*adj* pertaining to stibium
STIBINE	*n* pl. -S a poisonous gas
STIBIUM	*n* pl. -S antimony
STIBNITE	*n* pl. -S an ore of antimony
STICH	*n* pl. -S a line of poetry **STICHIC** *adj*
STICK	*v* -ED, -ING, -S to support with slender pieces of wood
STICK	*v* STUCK, STICKING, STICKS to pierce with a pointed object
STICKER	*n* pl. -S an adhesive label
STICKFUL	*n* pl. -S an amount of set type
STICKIER	comparative of sticky
STICKIEST	superlative of sticky
STICKILY	*adv* in a sticky manner
STICKIT	*adj* unsuccessful
STICKLE	*v* -LED, -LING, -LES to argue stubbornly
STICKLER	*n* pl. -S one that stickles
STICKMAN	*n* pl. -MEN one who supervises the play at a dice table
STICKOUT	*n* pl. -S one that is conspicuous
STICKPIN	*n* pl. -S a decorative tiepin
STICKUM	*n* pl. -S a substance that causes adhesion
STICKUP	*n* pl. -S a robbery at gunpoint
STICKY	*adj* STICKIER, STICKIEST tending to adhere
STICTION	*n* pl. -S the force required to begin to move a body that is in contact with another body
STIED	a past tense of sty
STIES	present 3d person sing. of sty
STIFF	*adj* STIFFER, STIFFEST difficult to bend or stretch
STIFF	*v* -ED, -ING, -S to cheat someone by not paying
STIFFEN	*v* -ED, -ING, -S to make stiff
STIFFISH	*adj* somewhat stiff
STIFFLY	*adv* in a stiff manner
STIFLE	*v* -FLED, -FLING, -FLES to smother
STIFLER	*n* pl. -S one that stifles
STIGMA	*n* pl. -MAS or -MATA a mark of disgrace **STIGMAL** *adj*
STILBENE	*n* pl. -S a chemical compound
STILBITE	*n* pl. -S a mineral
STILE	*n* pl. -S a series of steps for passing over a fence or wall
STILETTO	*v* -ED, -ING, -S or -ES to stab with a stiletto (a short dagger)
STILL	*adj* STILLER, STILLEST free from sound or motion
STILL	*v* -ED, -ING, -S to make still
STILLMAN	*n* pl. -MEN one who operates a distillery
STILLY	*adj* STILLIER, STILLIEST still
STILT	*v* -ED, -ING, -S to raise on stilts (long, slender poles)
STIME	*n* pl. -S a glimpse
STIMULUS	*n* pl. -LI something that causes a response
STIMY	*v* -MIED, -MYING, -MIES to stymie
STING	*v* STUNG, STINGING, STINGS to prick painfully
STINGER	*n* pl. -S one that stings
STINGIER	comparative of stingy
STINGIEST	superlative of stingy
STINGILY	*adv* in a stingy manner
STINGO	*n* pl. -GOS a strong ale or beer
STINGRAY	*n* pl. -RAYS a flat-bodied marine fish
STINGY	*adj* -GIER, -GIEST unwilling to spend or give
STINK	*v* STANK or STUNK, STINKING, STINKS to emit a foul odor
STINKARD	*n* pl. -S a despicable person
STINKBUG	*n* pl. -S an insect that emits a foul odor
STINKER	*n* pl. -S one that stinks
STINKIER	comparative of stinky
STINKIEST	superlative of stinky
STINKO	*adj* drunk
STINKPOT	*n* pl. -S a jar containing foul-smelling combustibles formerly used in warfare

STINKY	*adj* STINKIER, STINKIEST emitting a foul odor
STINT	*v* -ED, -ING, -S to limit
STINTER	*n* pl. -S one that stints
STIPE	*n* pl. -S a slender supporting part of a plant **STIPED** *adj*
STIPEL	*n* pl. -S a small stipule
STIPEND	*n* pl. -S a fixed sum of money paid periodically
STIPES	*n* pl. STIPITES a stipe
STIPPLE	*v* -PLED, -PLING, -PLES to draw, paint, or engrave by means of dots or short touches
STIPPLER	*n* pl. -S one that stipples
STIPULE	*n* pl. -S an appendage at the base of a leaf in certain plants **STIPULAR, STIPULED** *adj*
STIR	*v* STIRRED, STIRRING, STIRS to pass an implement through in circular motions
STIRK	*n* pl. -S a young cow
STIRP	*n* pl. -S lineage
STIRPS	*n* pl. STIRPES a family or branch of a family
STIRRED	past tense of stir
STIRRER	*n* pl. -S one that stirs
STIRRING	present participle of stir
STIRRUP	*n* pl. -S a support for the foot of a horseman
STITCH	*v* -ED, -ING, -ES to join by making in-and-out movements with a threaded needle
STITCHER	*n* pl. -S one that stitches
STITHY	*v* STITHIED, STITHYING, STITHIES to forge on an anvil
STIVER	*n* pl. -S a former Dutch coin
STOA	*n* pl. STOAE, STOAI, or STOAS an ancient Greek covered walkway
STOAT	*n* pl. -S a weasel with a black-tipped tail
STOB	*v* STOBBED, STOBBING, STOBS to stab
STOCCADO	*n* pl. -DOS a thrust with a rapier
STOCCATA	*n* pl. -S stoccado
STOCK	*v* -ED, -ING, -S to keep for future sale or use
STOCKADE	*v* -ADED, -ADING, -ADES to build a type of protective fence around
STOCKCAR	*n* pl. -S a boxcar for carrying livestock
STOCKER	*n* pl. -S a young animal suitable for being fattened for market
STOCKIER	comparative of stocky
STOCKIEST	superlative of stocky
STOCKILY	*adv* in a stocky manner
STOCKING	*n* pl. -S a knitted or woven covering for the foot and leg
STOCKISH	*adj* stupid
STOCKIST	*n* pl. -S one who stocks goods
STOCKMAN	*n* pl. -MEN one who owns or raises livestock
STOCKPOT	*n* pl. -S a pot in which broth is prepared
STOCKY	*adj* STOCKIER, STOCKIEST having a short, thick body
STODGE	*v* STODGED, STODGING, STODGES to stuff full with food
STODGY	*adj* STODGIER, STODGIEST boring **STODGILY** *adv*
STOGEY	*n* pl. -GEYS stogy
STOGIE	*n* pl. -S stogy
STOGY	*n* pl. -GIES a long, slender cigar
STOIC	*n* pl. -S one who is indifferent to pleasure or pain **STOICAL** *adj*
STOICISM	*n* pl. -S indifference to pleasure or pain
STOKE	*v* STOKED, STOKING, STOKES to supply a furnace with fuel
STOKER	*n* pl. -S one that stokes
STOKESIA	*n* pl. -S a perennial herb
STOKING	present participle of stoke
STOLE	*n* pl. -S a long-wide scarf **STOLED** *adj*
STOLEN	past participle of steal
STOLID	*adj* -IDER, -IDEST showing little or no emotion **STOLIDLY** *adv*
STOLLEN	*n* pl. -S a sweet bread
STOLON	*n* pl. -S a type of plant stem **STOLONIC** *adj*
STOLPORT	*n* pl. -S an airport for aircraft needing comparatively short runways
STOMA	*n* pl. -MAS or -MATA a minute opening in the epidermis of a plant organ
STOMACH	*v* -ED, -ING, -S to tolerate
STOMACHY	*adj* paunchy
STOMAL	*adj* stomatal

STOMATA	a pl. of stoma	**STOPPED**	a past tense of stop
STOMATAL	*adj* pertaining to a stoma	**STOPPER**	*v* -ED, -ING, -S to plug
STOMATE	*n* pl. -S a stoma	**STOPPING**	present participle of stop
STOMATIC	*adj* pertaining to the mouth	**STOPPLE**	*v* -PLED, -PLING, -PLES to stopper
STOMODEA	*n/pl* embryonic oral cavities	**STOPT**	a past tense of stop
STOMP	*v* -ED, -ING, -S to tread heavily	**STORABLE**	*n* pl. -S something that can be stored
STOMPER	*n* pl. -S one that stomps	**STORAGE**	*n* pl. -S a place for storing
STONE	*v* STONED, STONING, STONES to pelt with stones (pieces of concreted earthy or mineral matter) **STONABLE** *adj*	**STORAX**	*n* pl. -ES a fragrant resin
		STORE	*v* STORED, STORING, STORES to put away for future use
STONEFLY	*n* pl. -FLIES a winged insect	**STOREY**	*n* pl. -REYS a horizontal division of a building **STOREYED** *adj*
STONER	*n* pl. -S one that stones		
STONEY	*adj* STONIER, STONIEST stony	**STORIED**	past tense of story
STONIER	comparative of stony	**STORIES**	present 3d person sing. of story
STONIEST	superlative of stony	**STORING**	present participle of store
STONILY	*adv* in a stony manner	**STORK**	*n* pl. -S a wading bird
STONING	present participle of stone	**STORM**	*v* -ED, -ING, -S to blow violently
STONISH	*v* -ED, -ING, -ES to astonish	**STORMY**	*adj* STORMIER, STORMIEST storming **STORMILY** *adv*
STONY	*adj* STONIER, STONIEST abounding in stones		
		STORY	*v* -RIED, -RYING, -RIES to relate as a story (an account of an event or series of events)
STOOD	past tense of stand		
STOOGE	*v* STOOGED, STOOGING, STOOGES to act as a comedian's straight man	**STOSS**	*adj* facing the direction from which a glacier moves
		STOTINKA	*n* pl. -KI a monetary unit of Bulgaria
STOOK	*v* -ED, -ING, -S to stack upright in a field for drying, as bundles of grain		
		STOUND	*v* -ED, -ING, -S to ache
		STOUP	*n* pl. -S a basin for holy water
STOOKER	*n* pl. -S one that stooks	**STOUR**	*n* pl. -S dust
STOOL	*v* -ED, -ING, -S to defecate	**STOURE**	*n* pl. -S stour
STOOLIE	*n* pl. -S an informer	**STOURIE**	*adj* stoury
STOOP	*v* -ED, -ING, -S to bend the body forward and down	**STOURY**	*adj* dusty
		STOUT	*adj* STOUTER, STOUTEST fat
STOOPER	*n* pl. -S one that stoops	**STOUT**	*n* pl. -S a strong, dark ale
STOP	*v* STOPPED or STOPT, STOPPING, STOPS to discontinue the progress or motion of	**STOUTEN**	*v* -ED, -ING, -S to make stout
		STOUTISH	*adj* somewhat stout
		STOUTLY	*adv* in a stout manner
STOPBANK	*n* pl. -S an embankment along a river	**STOVE**	*n* pl. -S a heating apparatus
		STOVER	*n* pl. -S coarse food for cattle
STOPCOCK	*n* pl. -S a type of faucet	**STOW**	*v* -ED, -ING, -S to pack **STOWABLE** *adj*
STOPE	*v* STOPED, STOPING, STOPES to excavate in layers, as ore		
		STOWAGE	*n* pl. -S goods in storage
STOPER	*n* pl. -S one that stopes	**STOWAWAY**	*n* pl. -AWAYS one who hides aboard a conveyance to obtain free passage
STOPGAP	*n* pl. -S a temporary substitute		
STOPING	present participle of stope		
STOPOVER	*n* pl. -S a brief stop in the course of a journey		
		STOWP	*n* pl. -S stoup
STOPPAGE	*n* pl. -S the act of stopping		

STRADDLE	*v* -DLED, -DLING, -DLES to sit, stand, or walk with the legs wide apart	**STRATI**	pl. of stratus
STRAFE	*v* STRAFED, STRAFING, STRAFES to attack with machine-gun fire from an airplane	**STRATIFY**	*v* -FIED, -FYING, -FIES to form or arrange in layers
		STRATOUS	*adj* stratal
STRAFER	*n* pl. -S one that strafes	**STRATUM**	*n* pl. -TA or -TUMS a layer of material
STRAGGLE	*v* -GLED, -GLING, -GLES to stray	**STRATUS**	*n* pl. -TI a type of cloud
STRAGGLY	*adj* -GLIER, -GLIEST irregularly spread out	**STRAVAGE**	*v* -VAGED, -VAGING, -VAGES to stroll
STRAIGHT	*adj* STRAIGHTER, STRAIGHTEST extending uniformly in one direction without bends or irregularities	**STRAVAIG**	*v* -ED, -ING, -S to stravage
		STRAW	*v* -ED, -ING, -S to cover with straw (stalks of threshed grain)
STRAIGHT	*v* -ED, -ING, -S to make straight	**STRAWHAT**	*adj* pertaining to a summer theater situated in a resort area
STRAIN	*v* -ED, -ING, -S to exert to the utmost	**STRAWY**	*adj* STRAWIER, STRAWIEST resembling straw
STRAINER	*n* pl. -S a utensil used to separate liquids from solids	**STRAY**	*v* -ED, -ING, -S to wander from the proper area or course
STRAIT	*n* pl. -S a narrow waterway connecting two larger bodies of water	**STRAYER**	*n* pl. -S one that strays
		STREAK	*v* -ED, -ING, -S to cover with streaks (long, narrow marks)
STRAIT	*adj* STRAITER, STRAITEST narrow **STRAITLY** *adv*	**STREAKER**	*n* pl. -S one that streaks
STRAITEN	*v* -ED, -ING, -S to make strait	**STREAKY**	*adj* STREAKIER, STREAKIEST covered with streaks
STRAKE	*n* pl. -S a line of planking extending along a ship's hull **STRAKED** *adj*	**STREAM**	*v* -ED, -ING, -S to flow in a steady current
STRAMASH	*n* pl. -ES an uproar	**STREAMER**	*n* pl. -S a long, narrow flag
STRAMONY	*n* pl. -NIES a poisonous weed	**STREAMY**	*adj* STREAMIER, STREAMIEST streaming
STRAND	*v* -ED, -ING, -S to leave in an unfavorable situation	**STREEK**	*v* -ED, -ING, -S to stretch
		STREEKER	*n* pl. -S one that streeks
STRANDER	*n* pl. -S a machine that twists fibers into rope	**STREEL**	*v* -ED, -ING, -S to saunter
STRANG	*adj* strong	**STREET**	*n* pl. -S a public thoroughfare
STRANGE	*adj* STRANGER, STRANGEST unusual or unfamiliar	**STRENGTH**	*n* pl. -S capacity for exertion or endurance
STRANGER	*v* -ED, -ING, -S to estrange	**STREP**	*n* pl. -S any of various spherical or oval bacteria
STRANGLE	*v* -GLED, -GLING, -GLES to choke to death	**STRESS**	*v* -ED, -ING, -ES to place emphasis on
STRAP	*v* STRAPPED, STRAPPING, STRAPS to fasten with a strap (a narrow strip of flexible material)	**STRESSOR**	*n* pl. -S a type of stimulus
		STRETCH	*v* -ED, -ING, -ES to draw out or open to full length
STRAPPER	*n* pl. -S one that straps	**STRETCHY**	*adj* STRETCHIER, STRETCHIEST having a tendency to stretch
STRASS	*n* pl. -ES a brilliant glass used in making imitation gems		
STRATA	*n* pl. -S a stratum	**STRETTA**	*n* pl. -TE or -TAS stretto
STRATAL	*adj* pertaining to a stratum	**STRETTO**	*n* pl. -TI or -TOS a concluding musical passage played at a faster tempo
STRATEGY	*n* pl. -GIES a plan for obtaining a specific goal		
STRATH	*n* pl. -S a wide river valley	**STREUSEL**	*n* pl. -S a topping for coffee cakes

STREW	*v* STREWED, STREWN, STREWING, STREWS to scatter about
STREWER	*n* pl. -S one that strews
STRIA	*n* pl. STRIAE a thin groove, stripe, or streak
STRIATE	*v* -ATED, -ATING, -ATES to mark with striae
STRICK	*n* pl. -S a bunch of flax fibers
STRICKEN	*adj* strongly affected or afflicted
STRICKLE	*v* -LED, -LING, -LES to shape or smooth with a strickle (an instrument for leveling off grain)
STRICT	*adj* STRICTER, STRICTEST kept within narrow and specific limits **STRICTLY** *adv*
STRIDE	*v* STRODE, STRIDDEN, STRIDING, STRIDES to walk with long steps
STRIDENT	*adj* shrill
STRIDER	*n* pl. -S one that strides
STRIDING	present participle of stride
STRIDOR	*n* pl. -S a strident sound
STRIFE	*n* pl. -S bitter conflict or dissension
STRIGIL	*n* pl. -S a scraping instrument
STRIGOSE	*adj* covered with short, stiff hairs
STRIKE	*v* STRUCK or STROOK, STRICKEN or STRUCKEN, STRIKING, STRIKES to come or cause to come into contact with
STRIKER	*n* pl. -S one that strikes
STRING	*v* STRUNG or STRINGED, STRINGING, STRINGS to provide with strings (slender cords)
STRINGER	*n* pl. -S one that strings
STRINGY	*adj* STRINGIER, STRINGIEST resembling a string or strings
STRIP	*v* STRIPPED or STRIPT, STRIPPING, STRIPS to remove the outer covering from
STRIPE	*v* STRIPED, STRIPING, STRIPES to mark with stripes (long, distinct bands)
STRIPER	*n* pl. -S a food and game fish
STRIPIER	comparative of stripy
STRIPIEST	superlative of stripy
STRIPING	*n* pl. -S the stripes marked or painted on something
STRIPPED	a past tense of strip
STRIPPER	*n* pl. -S one that strips
STRIPPING	present participle of strip
STRIPT	a past tense of strip
STRIPY	*adj* STRIPIER, STRIPIEST marked with stripes
STRIVE	*v* STROVE or STRIVED, STRIVEN, STRIVING, STRIVES to exert much effort or energy
STRIVER	*n* pl. -S one that strives
STROBE	*n* pl. -S a device that produces brief, high-intensity flashes of light
STROBIC	*adj* spinning
STROBIL	*n* pl. -S strobile
STROBILA	*n* pl. -LAE the entire body of a tapeworm
STROBILE	*n* pl. -S the conical, multiple fruit of certain trees
STROBILI	*n/pl* strobiles
STRODE	a past tense of stride
STROKE	*v* STROKED, STROKING, STROKES to rub gently
STROKER	*n* pl. -S one that strokes
STROLL	*v* -ED, -ING, -S to walk in a leisurely manner
STROLLER	*n* pl. -S one that strolls
STROMA	*n* pl. -MATA the substance that forms the framework of an organ or cell **STROMAL** *adj*
STRONG	*adj* STRONGER, STRONGEST having great strength **STRONGLY** *adv*
STRONGYL	*n* pl. -S a parasitic worm
STRONTIA	*n* pl. -S a chemical compound **STRONTIC** *adj*
STROOK	a past tense of strike
STROP	*v* STROPPED, STROPPING, STROPS to sharpen on a strip of leather
STROPHE	*n* pl. -S a part of an ancient Greek choral ode **STROPHIC** *adj*
STROPPER	*n* pl. -S one that strops
STROPPY	*adj* -PIER, -PIEST unruly
STROUD	*n* pl. -S a coarse woolen blanket
STROVE	a past tense of strive
STROW	*v* STROWED, STROWN, STROWING, STROWS to strew
STROY	*v* -ED, -ING, -S to destroy
STROYER	*n* pl. -S one that stroys
STRUCK	a past tense of strike
STRUCKEN	a past participle of strike

STRUDEL	*n* pl. -S a type of pastry
STRUGGLE	*v* -GLED, -GLING, -GLES to make strenuous efforts against opposition
STRUM	*v* STRUMMED, STRUMMING, STRUMS to play a stringed instrument by running the fingers lightly across the strings
STRUMA	*n* pl. -MAE or -MAS scrofula
STRUMMER	*n* pl. -S one that strums
STRUMMING	present participle of strum
STRUMOSE	*adj* having a struma
STRUMOUS	*adj* having or pertaining to a struma
STRUMPET	*n* pl. -S a prostitute
STRUNG	a past tense of string
STRUNT	*v* -ED, -ING, -S to strut
STRUT	*v* STRUTTED, STRUTTING, STRUTS to walk with a pompous air
STRUTTER	*n* pl. -S one that struts
STUB	*v* STUBBED, STUBBING, STUBS to strike accidentally against a projecting object
STUBBIER	comparative of stubby
STUBBIEST	superlative of stubby
STUBBILY	*adv* in a stubby manner
STUBBING	present participle of stub
STUBBLE	*n* pl. -S a short, rough growth of beard **STUBBLED** *adj*
STUBBLY	*adj* -BLIER, -BLIEST covered with stubble
STUBBORN	*adj* unyielding
STUBBY	*adj* -BIER, -BIEST short and thick
STUCCO	*v* -ED, -ING, -ES or -S to coat with a type of plaster
STUCCOER	*n* pl. -S one that stuccoes
STUCK	past tense of stick
STUD	*v* STUDDED, STUDDING, STUDS to set thickly with small projections
STUDBOOK	*n* pl. -S a record of the pedigree of purebred animals
STUDDIE	*n* pl. -S an anvil
STUDDING	*n* pl. -S the framework of a wall
STUDENT	*n* pl. -S a person formally engaged in learning
STUDFISH	*n* pl. -ES a freshwater fish
STUDIED	past tense of study

STUDIER	*n* pl. -S one that studies
STUDIES	present 3d person sing. of study
STUDIO	*n* pl. -DIOS an artist's workroom
STUDIOUS	*adj* given to study
STUDLY	*adj* -LIER, -LIEST muscular and attractive
STUDWORK	*n* pl. -S studding
STUDY	*v* STUDIED, STUDYING, STUDIES to apply the mind to the acquisition of knowledge
STUFF	*v* -ED, -ING, -S to fill or pack tightly
STUFFER	*n* pl. -S one that stuffs
STUFFING	*n* pl. -S material with which something is stuffed
STUFFY	*adj* STUFFIER, STUFFIEST poorly ventilated **STUFFILY** *adv*
STUIVER	*n* pl. -S stiver
STULL	*n* pl. -S a supporting timber in a mine
STULTIFY	*v* -FIED, -FYING, -FIES to cause to appear absurd
STUM	*v* STUMMED, STUMMING, STUMS to increase the fermentation of by adding grape juice
STUMBLE	*v* -BLED, -BLING, -BLES to miss one's step in walking or running
STUMBLER	*n* pl. -S one that stumbles
STUMMED	past tense of stum
STUMMING	present participle of stum
STUMP	*v* -ED, -ING, -S to baffle
STUMPAGE	*n* pl. -S uncut marketable timber
STUMPER	*n* pl. -S a baffling question
STUMPY	*adj* STUMPIER, STUMPIEST short and thick
STUN	*v* STUNNED, STUNNING, STUNS to render senseless or incapable of action
STUNG	past tense of sting
STUNK	a past tense of stink
STUNNED	past tense of stun
STUNNER	*n* pl. -S one that stuns
STUNNING	*adj* strikingly beautiful or attractive
STUNSAIL	*n* pl. -S a type of sail
STUNT	*v* -ED, -ING, -S to hinder the normal growth of

STUNTMAN	*n* pl. -MEN a person who substitutes for an actor in scenes involving dangerous activities
STUPA	*n* pl. -S a Buddhist shrine
STUPE	*n* pl. -S a medicated cloth to be applied to a wound
STUPEFY	*v* -FIED, -FYING, -FIES to dull the senses of
STUPID	*adj* -PIDER, -PIDEST mentally slow **STUPIDLY** *adv*
STUPID	*n* pl. -S a stupid person
STUPOR	*n* pl. -S a state of reduced sensibility
STURDY	*adj* -DIER, -DIEST strong and durable **STURDILY** *adv*
STURDY	*n* pl. -DIES a disease of sheep **STURDIED** *adj*
STURGEON	*n* pl. -S an edible fish
STURT	*n* pl. -S contention
STUTTER	*v* -ED, -ING, -S to speak with spasmodic repetition
STY	*v* STIED or STYED, STYING, STIES to keep in a pigpen
STYE	*n* pl. -S an inflamed swelling of the eyelid
STYGIAN	*adj* gloomy
STYLAR	*adj* pertaining to a stylus
STYLATE	*adj* bearing a stylet
STYLE	*v* STYLED, STYLING, STYLES to name
STYLER	*n* pl. -S one that styles
STYLET	*n* pl. -S a small, stiff organ or appendage of certain animals
STYLI	a pl. of stylus
STYLING	*n* pl. -S the way in which something is styled
STYLISE	*v* -ISED, -ISING, -ISES to stylize
STYLISER	*n* pl. -S one that stylises
STYLISH	*adj* fashionable
STYLISING	present participle of stylise
STYLIST	*n* pl. -S one who is a master of a literary or rhetorical style
STYLITE	*n* pl. -S an early Christian ascetic **STYLITIC** *adj*
STYLIZE	*v* -IZED, -IZING, -IZES to make conventional
STYLIZER	*n* pl. -S one that stylizes
STYLOID	*adj* slender and pointed
STYLUS	*n* pl. -LI or -LUSES a pointed instrument for writing, marking, or engraving
STYMIE	*v* -MIED, -MIEING, -MIES to thwart
STYMY	*v* -MIED, -MYING, -MIES to stymie
STYPSIS	*n* pl. -SISES the use of a styptic
STYPTIC	*n* pl. -S a substance used to check bleeding
STYRAX	*n* pl. -ES storax
STYRENE	*n* pl. -S a liquid hydrocarbon
SUABLE	*adj* capable of being sued **SUABLY** *adv*
SUASION	*n* pl. -S persuasion **SUASIVE, SUASORY** *adj*
SUAVE	*adj* SUAVER, SUAVEST smoothly affable and polite **SUAVELY** *adv*
SUAVITY	*n* pl. -TIES the state of being suave
SUB	*v* SUBBED, SUBBING, SUBS to act as a substitute
SUBA	*n* pl. -S subah
SUBABBOT	*n* pl. -S a subordinate abbot
SUBACID	*adj* slightly sour
SUBACRID	*adj* somewhat acrid
SUBACUTE	*adj* somewhat acute
SUBADAR	*n* pl. -S subahdar
SUBADULT	*n* pl. -S an individual approaching adulthood
SUBAGENT	*n* pl. -S a subordinate agent
SUBAH	*n* pl. -S a province of India
SUBAHDAR	*n* pl. -S a governor of a subah
SUBALAR	*adj* somewhat alar
SUBAREA	*n* pl. -S a subdivision of an area
SUBARID	*adj* somewhat arid
SUBATOM	*n* pl. -S a component of an atom
SUBAXIAL	*adj* somewhat axial
SUBBASE	*n* pl. -S the lowest part of a base
SUBBASIN	*n* pl. -S a section of an area drained by a river
SUBBASS	*n* pl. -ES a pedal stop producing the lowest tones of an organ
SUBBED	past tense of sub
SUBBING	*n* pl. -S a thin coating on the support of a photographic film
SUBBLOCK	*n* pl. -S a subdivision of a block

SUBBREED *n* pl. -S a distinguishable strain within a breed

SUBCASTE *n* pl. -S a subdivision of a caste

SUBCAUSE *n* pl. -S a subordinate cause

SUBCELL *n* pl. -S a subdivision of a cell

SUBCHIEF *n* pl. -S a subordinate chief

SUBCLAN *n* pl. -S a subdivision of a clan

SUBCLASS *v* -ED, -ING, -ES to place in a subdivision of a class

SUBCLERK *n* pl. -S a subordinate clerk

SUBCODE *n* pl. -S a subdivision of a code

SUBCOOL *v* -ED, -ING, -S to cool below the freezing point without solidification

SUBCULT *n* pl. -S a subdivision of a cult

SUBCUTIS *n* pl. -CUTES or -CUTISES the deeper part of the dermis

SUBDEAN *n* pl. -S a subordinate dean

SUBDEB *n* pl. -S a girl the year before she becomes a debutante

SUBDEPOT *n* pl. -S a military depot that operates under the jurisdiction of another depot

SUBDUAL *n* pl. -S the act of subduing

SUBDUCE *v* -DUCED, -DUCING, -DUCES to take away

SUBDUCT *v* -ED, -ING, -S to subduce

SUBDUE *v* -DUED, -DUING, -DUES to bring under control

SUBDUER *n* pl. -S one that subdues

SUBDURAL *adj* situated under the dura mater

SUBECHO *n* pl. -ECHOES an inferior echo

SUBEDIT *v* -ED, -ING, -S to act as the assistant editor of

SUBENTRY *n* pl. -TRIES an entry made under a more general entry

SUBEPOCH *n* pl. -S a subdivision of an epoch

SUBER *n* pl. -S phellem

SUBERECT *adj* nearly erect

SUBERIC *adj* pertaining to cork

SUBERIN *n* pl. -S a substance found in cork cells

SUBERISE *v* -ISED, -ISING, -ISES to suberize

SUBERIZE *v* -IZED, -IZING, -IZES to convert into cork tissue

SUBEROSE *adj* corky

SUBEROUS *adj* suberose

SUBFIELD *n* pl. -S a subset of a mathematical field that is itself a field

SUBFILE *n* pl. -S a subdivision of a file

SUBFIX *n* pl. -ES a distinguishing symbol or letter written below another character

SUBFLOOR *n* pl. -S a rough floor laid as a base for a finished floor

SUBFLUID *adj* somewhat fluid

SUBFRAME *n* pl. -S a frame for the attachment of a finish frame

SUBFUSC *adj* dark in color

SUBGENRE *n* pl. -S a subdivision of a genre

SUBGENUS *n* pl. -GENERA or -GENUSES a subdivision of a genus

SUBGOAL *n* pl. -S a subordinate goal

SUBGRADE *n* pl. -S a surface on which a pavement is placed

SUBGRAPH *n* pl. -S a graph contained within a larger graph

SUBGROUP *n* pl. -S a distinct group within a group

SUBGUM *n* pl. -S a Chinese dish of mixed vegetables

SUBHEAD *n* pl. -S the heading of a subdivision

SUBHUMAN *n* pl. -S one that is less than human

SUBHUMID *adj* somewhat humid

SUBIDEA *n* pl. -S an inferior idea

SUBINDEX *n* pl. -DEXES or -DICES a subfix

SUBITEM *n* pl. -S an item that forms a subdivision of a larger topic

SUBITO *adv* quickly — used as a musical direction

SUBJECT *v* -ED, -ING, -S to cause to experience

SUBJOIN *v* -ED, -ING, -S to add at the end

SUBLATE *v* -LATED, -LATING, -LATES to cancel

SUBLEASE *v* -LEASED, -LEASING, -LEASES to sublet

SUBLET *v* -LET, -LETTING, -LETS to rent leased property to another

SUBLEVEL *n* pl. -S a lower level

SUBLIME *adj* -LIMER, -LIMEST of elevated or noble quality

SUBLIME *v* -LIMED, -LIMING, -LIMES to make sublime

SUBLIMER *n* pl. -S one that sublimes

SUBLIMEST	superlative of sublime
SUBLIMING	present participle of sublime
SUBLINE	*n* pl. -S an inbred line within a strain
SUBLOT	*n* pl. -S a subdivision of a lot
SUBLUNAR	*adj* pertaining to the earth
SUBMENU	*n* pl. -S a secondary list of options for a computer
SUBMERGE	*v* -MERGED, -MERGING, -MERGES to place below the surface of a liquid
SUBMERSE	*v* -MERSED, -MERSING, -MERSES to submerge
SUBMISS	*adj* inclined to submit
SUBMIT	*v* -MITTED, -MITTING, -MITS to yield to the power of another
SUBNASAL	*adj* situated under the nose
SUBNET	*n* pl. -S a system of interconnections within a communications system
SUBNICHE	*n* pl. -S a subdivision of a habitat
SUBNODAL	*adj* situated under a node
SUBOPTIC	*adj* situated under the eyes
SUBORAL	*adj* situated under the mouth
SUBORDER	*n* pl. -S a category of related families within an order
SUBORN	*v* -ED, -ING, -S to induce to commit perjury
SUBORNER	*n* pl. -S one that suborns
SUBOVAL	*adj* nearly oval
SUBOVATE	*adj* nearly ovate
SUBOXIDE	*n* pl. -S an oxide containing relatively little oxygen
SUBPANEL	*n* pl. -S a subdivision of a panel
SUBPAR	*adj* below par
SUBPART	*n* pl. -S a subdivision of a part
SUBPENA	*v* -ED, -ING, -S to subpoena
SUBPHASE	*n* pl. -S a subdivision of a phase
SUBPHYLA	*n/pl* divisions within a phylum
SUBPLOT	*n* pl. -S a secondary literary plot
SUBPOENA	*v* -ED, -ING, -S to summon with a type of judicial writ
SUBPOLAR	*adj* situated just outside the polar circles
SUBPUBIC	*adj* situated under the pubis
SUBRACE	*n* pl. -S a subdivision of a race
SUBRENT	*n* pl. -S rent from a subtenant
SUBRING	*n* pl. -S a subset of a mathematical ring that is itself a ring
SUBRULE	*n* pl. -S a subordinate rule
SUBSALE	*n* pl. -S a resale of purchased goods
SUBSCALE	*n* pl. -S a subdivision of a scale
SUBSEA	*adj* situated below the surface of the sea
SUBSECT	*n* pl. -S a sect directly derived from another
SUBSENSE	*n* pl. -S a subdivision of a sense
SUBSERE	*n* pl. -S a type of ecological succession
SUBSERVE	*v* -SERVED, -SERVING, -SERVES to serve to promote
SUBSET	*n* pl. -S a mathematical set contained within a larger set
SUBSHAFT	*n* pl. -S a shaft that is beneath another shaft
SUBSHELL	*n* pl. -S one of the orbitals making up an electron shell of an atom
SUBSHRUB	*n* pl. -S a low shrub
SUBSIDE	*v* -SIDED, -SIDING, -SIDES to sink to a lower or normal level
SUBSIDER	*n* pl. -S one that subsides
SUBSIDY	*n* pl. -DIES a grant or contribution of money
SUBSIST	*v* -ED, -ING, -S to continue to exist
SUBSITE	*n* pl. -S a subdivision of a site
SUBSKILL	*n* pl. -S a subordinate skill
SUBSOIL	*v* -ED, -ING, -S to plow so as to turn up the subsoil (the layer of earth beneath the surface soil)
SUBSOLAR	*adj* situated directly beneath the sun
SUBSONIC	*adj* moving at a speed less than that of sound
SUBSPACE	*n* pl. -S a subset of a mathematical space
SUBSTAGE	*n* pl. -S a part of a microscope for supporting accessories
SUBSTATE	*n* pl. -S a subdivision of a state
SUBSUME	*v* -SUMED, -SUMING, -SUMES to include within a larger group
SUBTASK	*n* pl. -S a subordinate task
SUBTAXON	*n* pl. -TAXA or -TAXONS a subdivision of a taxon
SUBTEEN	*n* pl. -S a person approaching the teenage years

SUBTEND	*v* -ED, -ING, -S to extend under or opposite to
SUBTEST	*n* pl. -S a subdivision of a test
SUBTEXT	*n* pl. -S written or printed matter under a more general text
SUBTHEME	*n* pl. -S a subordinate theme
SUBTILE	*adj* -TILER, -TILEST subtle
SUBTILIN	*n* pl. -S an antibiotic
SUBTILTY	*n* pl. -TIES subtlety
SUBTITLE	*v* -TLED, -TLING, -TLES to give a secondary title to
SUBTLE	*adj* -TLER, -TLEST so slight as to be difficult to detect **SUBTLY** *adv*
SUBTLETY	*n* pl. -TIES the state of being subtle
SUBTONE	*n* pl. -S a low or subdued tone
SUBTONIC	*n* pl. -S a type of musical tone
SUBTOPIA	*n* pl. -S the suburbs of a city
SUBTOPIC	*n* pl. -S a secondary topic
SUBTOTAL	*v* -TALED, -TALING, -TALS or -TALLED, -TALLING, -TALS to total a portion of
SUBTRACT	*v* -ED, -ING, -S to take away
SUBTREND	*n* pl. -S a subordinate trend
SUBTRIBE	*n* pl. -S a subdivision of a tribe
SUBTUNIC	*n* pl. -S a tunic worn under another tunic
SUBTYPE	*n* pl. -S a type that is subordinate to or included in another type
SUBULATE	*adj* slender and tapering to a point
SUBUNIT	*n* pl. -S a unit that is a part of a larger unit
SUBURB	*n* pl. -S a residential area adjacent to a city **SUBURBED** *adj*
SUBURBAN	*n* pl. -S one who lives in a suburb
SUBURBIA	*n* pl. -S the suburbs of a city
SUBVENE	*v* -VENED, -VENING, -VENES to arrive or occur as a support or relief
SUBVERT	*v* -ED, -ING, -S to destroy completely
SUBVICAR	*n* pl. -S a subordinate vicar
SUBVIRAL	*adj* pertaining to a part of a virus
SUBVOCAL	*adj* mentally formulated as words
SUBWAY	*v* -ED, -ING, -S to travel by an underground railroad
SUBWORLD	*n* pl. -S a subdivision of a sphere of interest or activity
SUBZERO	*adj* registering less than zero
SUBZONE	*n* pl. -S a subdivision of a zone
SUCCAH	*n* pl. -CAHS or -COTH sukkah
SUCCEED	*v* -ED, -ING, -S to accomplish something desired or intended
SUCCESS	*n* pl. -ES the attainment of something desired or intended
SUCCINCT	*adj* -CINCTER, -CINCTEST clearly expressed in few words
SUCCINIC	*adj* pertaining to amber
SUCCINYL	*n* pl. -S a univalent radical
SUCCOR	*v* -ED, -ING, -S to go to the aid of
SUCCORER	*n* pl. -S one that succors
SUCCORY	*n* pl. -RIES chicory
SUCCOTH	a pl. of succah
SUCCOUR	*v* -ED, -ING, -S to succor
SUCCUBA	*n* pl. -BAE a succubus
SUCCUBUS	*n* pl. -BI or -BUSES a female demon
SUCCUMB	*v* -ED, -ING, -S to yield to superior force
SUCCUSS	*v* -ED, -ING, -ES to shake violently
SUCH	*adj* of that kind
SUCHLIKE	*adj* of a similar kind
SUCHNESS	*n* pl. -ES essential or characteristic quality
SUCK	*v* -ED, -ING, -S to draw in by establishing a partial vacuum
SUCKER	*v* -ED, -ING, -S to strip of lower shoots or branches
SUCKFISH	*n* pl. -ES a remora
SUCKLE	*v* -LED, -LING, -LES to give milk to from the breast
SUCKLER	*n* pl. -S one that suckles
SUCKLESS	*adj* having no juice
SUCKLING	*n* pl. -S an unweaned mammal
SUCRASE	*n* pl. -S an enzyme
SUCRE	*n* pl. -S a monetary unit of Ecuador
SUCROSE	*n* pl. -S a type of sugar
SUCTION	*v* -ED, -ING, -S to remove by the process of sucking
SUDARIUM	*n* pl. -IA a cloth for wiping the face
SUDARY	*n* pl. -RIES sudarium
SUDATION	*n* pl. -S excessive sweating
SUDATORY	*n* pl. -RIES a hot-air bath for inducing sweating

SUDD   *n* pl. -S a floating mass of vegetation

SUDDEN   *adj* happening quickly and without warning **SUDDENLY** *adv*

SUDDEN   *n* pl. -S a sudden occurrence

SUDOR   *n* pl. -S sweat **SUDORAL** *adj*

SUDS   *v* -ED, -ING, -ES to wash in soapy water

SUDSER   *n* pl. -S one that sudses

SUDSLESS   *adj* having no suds

SUDSY   *adj* SUDSIER, SUDSIEST foamy

SUE   *v* SUED, SUING, SUES to institute legal proceedings against

SUEDE   *v* SUEDED, SUEDING, SUEDES to finish leather with a soft, napped surface

SUER   *n* pl. -S one that sues

SUET   *n* pl. -S the hard, fatty tissue around the kidneys of cattle and sheep **SUETY** *adj*

SUFFARI   *n* pl. -S a safari

SUFFER   *v* -ED, -ING, -S to feel pain or distress

SUFFERER   *n* pl. -S one that suffers

SUFFICE   *v* -FICED, -FICING, -FICES to be adequate

SUFFICER   *n* pl. -S one that suffices

SUFFIX   *v* -ED, -ING, -ES to add as a suffix (a form affixed to the end of a root word)

SUFFIXAL   *adj* pertaining to or being a suffix

SUFFLATE   *v* -FLATED, -FLATING, -FLATES to inflate

SUFFRAGE   *n* pl. -S the right to vote

SUFFUSE   *v* -FUSED, -FUSING, -FUSES to spread through or over

SUGAR   *v* -ED, -ING, -S to cover with sugar (a sweet carbohydrate)

SUGARY   *adj* -ARIER, -ARIEST containing or resembling sugar

SUGGEST   *v* -ED, -ING, -S to bring or put forward for consideration

SUGH   *v* -ED, -ING, -S to sough

SUICIDAL   *adj* self-destructive

SUICIDE   *v* -CIDED, -CIDING, -CIDES to kill oneself intentionally

SUING   present participle of sue

SUINT   *n* pl. -S a natural grease found in the wool of sheep

SUIT   *v* -ED, -ING, -S to be appropriate to

SUITABLE   *adj* appropriate **SUITABLY** *adv*

SUITCASE   *n* pl. -S a flat, rectangular piece of luggage

SUITE   *n* pl. -S a series of things forming a unit

SUITER   *n* pl. -S a suitcase holding a specified number of suits (sets of garments)

SUITING   *n* pl. -S fabric for making suits

SUITLIKE   *adj* resembling a suit (a set of garments)

SUITOR   *n* pl. -S one that is courting a woman

SUKIYAKI   *n* pl. -S a Japanese dish

SUKKAH   *n* pl. -KAHS or -KOTH or -KOT a temporary shelter in which meals are eaten during a Jewish festival

SULCATE   *adj* having long, narrow furrows

SULCATED   *adj* sulcate

SULCUS   *n* pl. -CI a narrow furrow **SULCAL** *adj*

SULDAN   *n* pl. -S soldan

SULFA   *n* pl. -S a bacteria-inhibiting drug

SULFATE   *v* -FATED, -FATING, -FATES to treat with sulfuric acid

SULFID   *n* pl. -S sulfide

SULFIDE   *n* pl. -S a sulfur compound

SULFINYL   *n* pl. -S a bivalent radical

SULFITE   *n* pl. -S a chemical salt **SULFITIC** *adj*

SULFO   *adj* sulfonic

SULFONE   *n* pl. -S a sulfur compound

SULFONIC   *adj* containing a certain univalent radical

SULFONYL   *n* pl. -S a bivalent radical

SULFUR   *v* -ED, -ING, -S to treat with sulfur (a nonmetallic element)

SULFURET   *v* -RETED, -RETING, -RETS or -RETTED, -RETTING, -RETS to treat with sulfur

SULFURIC   *adj* pertaining to sulfur

SULFURY   *adj* resembling sulfur

SULFURYL   *n* pl. -S sulfonyl

SULK   *v* -ED, -ING, -S to be sulky

SULKER   *n* pl. -S one that sulks

SULKY   *adj* SULKIER, SULKIEST sullenly aloof or withdrawn **SULKILY** *adv*

SULKY   *n* pl. SULKIES a light horse-drawn vehicle

SULLAGE   *n* pl. -S sewage

SULLEN   *adj* -LENER, -LENEST showing a brooding ill humor or resentment **SULLENLY** *adv*

SULLY   *v* -LIED, -LYING, -LIES to soil

SULPHA   *n* pl. -S sulfa

SULPHATE   *v* -PHATED, -PHATING, -PHATES to sulfate

SULPHID   *n* pl. -S sulfide

SULPHIDE   *n* pl. -S sulfide

SULPHITE   *n* pl. -S sulfite

SULPHONE   *n* pl. -S sulfone

SULPHUR   *v* -ED, -ING, -S to sulfur

SULPHURY   *adj* sulfury

SULTAN   *n* pl. -S the ruler of a Muslim country **SULTANIC** *adj*

SULTANA   *n* pl. -S a sultan's wife

SULTRY   *adj* -TRIER, -TRIEST very hot and humid **SULTRILY** *adv*

SULU   *n* pl. -S a Melanesian skirt

SUM   *v* SUMMED, SUMMING, SUMS to add into one total

SUMAC   *n* pl. -S a flowering tree or shrub

SUMACH   *n* pl. -S sumac

SUMLESS   *adj* too large for calculation

SUMMA   *n* pl. -MAE or -MAS a comprehensive work on a topic

SUMMABLE   *adj* capable of being summed

SUMMAND   *n* pl. -S an addend

SUMMARY   *n* pl. -RIES a short restatement

SUMMATE   *v* -MATED, -MATING, -MATES to sum

SUMMED   past tense of sum

SUMMER   *v* -ED, -ING, -S to pass the summer (the warmest season of the year)

SUMMERLY   *adj* summery

SUMMERY   *adj* -MERIER, -MERIEST characteristic of summer

SUMMING   present participle of sum

SUMMIT   *v* -ED, -ING, -S to participate in a highest-level conference

SUMMITAL   *adj* pertaining to the highest point

SUMMITRY   *n* pl. -RIES the use of conferences between chiefs of state for international negotiation

SUMMON   *v* -ED, -ING, -S to order to appear

SUMMONER   *n* pl. -S one that summons

SUMMONS   *v* -ED, -ING, -ES to summon with a court order

SUMO   *n* pl. -MOS a Japanese form of wrestling

SUMP   *n* pl. -S a low area serving as a drain or receptacle for liquids

SUMPTER   *n* pl. -S a pack animal

SUMPWEED   *n* pl. -S a marsh plant

SUN   *v* SUNNED, SUNNING, SUNS to expose to the sun (the star around which the earth revolves)

SUNBACK   *adj* cut low to expose the back to sunlight

SUNBAKED   *adj* baked by the sun

SUNBATH   *n* pl. -S an exposure to sunlight

SUNBATHE   *v* -BATHED, -BATHING, -BATHES to take a sunbath

SUNBEAM   *n* pl. -S a beam of sunlight **SUNBEAMY** *adj*

SUNBELT   *n* pl. -S the southern and southwestern states of the U.S.

SUNBIRD   *n* pl. -S a tropical bird

SUNBLOCK   *n* pl. -S a preparation to protect the skin from the sun's rays

SUNBOW   *n* pl. -S an arc of spectral colors formed by the sun shining through a mist

SUNBURN   *v* -BURNED or -BURNT, -BURNING, -BURNS to burn or discolor from exposure to the sun

SUNBURST   *n* pl. -S a burst of sunlight

SUNCHOKE   *n* pl. -S a type of sunflower

SUNDAE   *n* pl. -S a dish of ice cream served with a topping

SUNDECK   *n* pl. -S a deck that is exposed to the sun

SUNDER   *v* -ED, -ING, -S to break apart

SUNDERER   *n* pl. -S one that sunders

SUNDEW   *n* pl. -S a marsh plant

SUNDIAL   *n* pl. -S a type of time-telling device

SUNDOG   *n* pl. -S a small rainbow

SUNDOWN   *n* pl. -S sunset

SUNDRESS   *n* pl. -ES a dress with an abbreviated bodice

SUNDRIES   *n/pl* miscellaneous items

SUNDROPS   *n* pl. SUNDROPS a flowering plant

SUNDRY   *adj* miscellaneous

SUNFAST   *adj* resistant to fading by the sun

SUNFISH   *n* pl. -ES a marine fish

SUNG   past participle of sing

SUNGLASS   *n* pl. -ES a lens for concentrating the sun's rays in order to produce heat

SUNGLOW   *n* pl. -S a glow in the sky caused by the sun

SUNK   a past participle of sink

SUNKEN   a past participle of sink

SUNKET   *n* pl. -S a tidbit

SUNLAMP   *n* pl. -S a lamp that radiates ultraviolet rays

SUNLAND   *n* pl. -S an area marked by a great amount of sunshine

SUNLESS   *adj* having no sunlight

SUNLIGHT   *n* pl. -S the light of the sun

SUNLIKE   *adj* resembling the sun

SUNLIT   *adj* lighted by the sun

SUNN   *n* pl. -S an East Indian shrub

SUNNA   *n* pl. -S the body of traditional Muslim law

SUNNAH   *n* pl. -S sunna

SUNNED   past tense of sun

SUNNING   present participle of sun

SUNNY   *adj* -NIER, -NIEST filled with sunlight **SUNNILY** *adv*

SUNPORCH   *n* pl. -ES a porch that admits much sunlight

SUNPROOF   *adj* resistant to damage by sunlight

SUNRISE   *n* pl. -S the ascent of the sun above the horizon in the morning

SUNROOF   *n* pl. -S an automobile roof having an openable panel

SUNROOM   *n* pl. -S a room built to admit a great amount of sunlight

SUNSCALD   *n* pl. -S an injury of woody plants caused by the sun

SUNSET   *n* pl. -S the descent of the sun below the horizon in the evening

SUNSHADE   *n* pl. -S something used as a protection from the sun

SUNSHINE   *n* pl. -S the light of the sun **SUNSHINY** *adj*

SUNSPOT   *n* pl. -S a dark spot on the surface of the sun

SUNSTONE   *n* pl. -S a variety of quartz

SUNSUIT   *n* pl. -S a type of playsuit

SUNTAN   *n* pl. -S a brown color on the skin produced by exposure to the sun

SUNUP   *n* pl. -S sunrise

SUNWARD   *adv* toward the sun

SUNWARDS   *adv* sunward

SUNWISE   *adv* from left to right

SUP   *v* SUPPED, SUPPING, SUPS to eat supper

SUPE   *n* pl. -S an actor without a speaking part

SUPER   *v* -ED, -ING, -S to reinforce with a thin cotton mesh, as a book

SUPERADD   *v* -ED, -ING, -S to add further

SUPERB   *adj* -PERBER, -PERBEST of excellent quality **SUPERBLY** *adv*

SUPERBAD   *adj* exceedingly bad

SUPERCAR   *n* pl. -S a superior car

SUPERCOP   *n* pl. -S a superior police officer

SUPEREGO   *n* pl. -EGOS a part of the psyche

SUPERFAN   *n* pl. -S an exceedingly devoted enthusiast

SUPERFIX   *n* pl. -ES a recurrent pattern of stress in speech

SUPERHIT   *n* pl. -S something exceedingly successful

SUPERHOT   *adj* exceedingly hot

SUPERIOR   *n* pl. -S one of higher rank, quality, or authority than another

SUPERJET   *n* pl. -S a type of jet airplane

SUPERLIE   *v* -LAY, -LAIN, -LYING, -LIES to lie above

SUPERMAN   *n* pl. -MEN a hypothetical superior man

SUPERMOM   *n* pl. -S a superior mom

SUPERNAL   *adj* pertaining to the sky

SUPERPRO   *n* pl. -PROS a superior professional

SUPERSEX   *n* pl. -ES a type of sterile organism

SUPERSPY   *n* pl. -SPIES a superior spy

SUPERTAX   *n* pl. -ES an additional tax

SUPINATE   *v* -NATED, -NATING, -NATES to turn so that the palm is facing upward

SUPINE   *n* pl. -S a Latin verbal noun

SUPINELY   *adv* in an inactive manner

SUPPED   past tense of sup

SUPPER   *n* pl. -S an evening meal

SUPPING	present participle of sup
SUPPLANT	v -ED, -ING, -S to take the place of
SUPPLE	adj -PLER, -PLEST pliant **SUPPLELY** adv
SUPPLE	v -PLED, -PLING, -PLES to make supple
SUPPLIER	n pl. -S one that supplies
SUPPLY	v -PLIED, -PLYING, -PLIES to furnish with what is needed
SUPPORT	v -ED, -ING, -S to hold up or add strength to
SUPPOSAL	n pl. -S something supposed
SUPPOSE	v -POSED, -POSING, -POSES to assume to be true
SUPPOSER	n pl. -S one that supposes
SUPPRESS	v -ED, -ING, -ES to put an end to forcibly
SUPRA	adv above
SUPREME	adj -PREMER, -PREMEST highest in power or authority
SUPREMO	n pl. -MOS one who is highest in authority
SUQ	n pl. -S souk
SURA	n pl. -S a chapter of the Koran
SURAH	n pl. -S a silk fabric
SURAL	adj pertaining to the calf of the leg
SURBASE	n pl. -S a molding or border above the base of a structure **SURBASED** adj
SURCEASE	v -CEASED, -CEASING, -CEASES to cease
SURCOAT	n pl. -S an outer coat or cloak
SURD	n pl. -S a voiceless speech sound
SURE	adj SURER, SUREST free from doubt
SUREFIRE	adj sure to meet expectations
SURELY	adv certainly
SURENESS	n pl. -ES the state of being sure
SURER	comparative of sure
SUREST	superlative of sure
SURETY	n pl. -TIES sureness
SURF	v -ED, -ING, -S to ride breaking waves on a long, narrow board **SURFABLE** adj
SURFACE	v -FACED, -FACING, -FACES to apply an outer layer to
SURFACER	n pl. -S one that surfaces
SURFBIRD	n pl. -S a shore bird
SURFBOAT	n pl. -S a strong rowboat
SURFEIT	v -ED, -ING, -S to supply to excess
SURFER	n pl. -S one that surfs
SURFFISH	n pl. -ES a marine fish
SURFIER	comparative of surfy
SURFIEST	superlative of surfy
SURFING	n pl. -S the act or sport of riding the surf (breaking waves)
SURFLIKE	adj resembling breaking waves
SURFY	adj SURFIER, SURFIEST abounding in breaking waves
SURGE	v SURGED, SURGING, SURGES to move in a swelling manner
SURGEON	n pl. -S one who practices surgery
SURGER	n pl. -S one that surges
SURGERY	n pl. -GERIES the treatment of medical problems by operation
SURGICAL	adj pertaining to surgery
SURGING	present participle of surge
SURGY	adj surging
SURICATE	n pl. -S a burrowing mammal
SURIMI	n pl. SURIMI an inexpensive fish product
SURLY	adj -LIER, -LIEST sullenly rude **SURLILY** adv
SURMISE	v -MISED, -MISING, -MISES to infer with little evidence
SURMISER	n pl. -S one that surmises
SURMOUNT	v -ED, -ING, -S to get over or across
SURNAME	v -NAMED, -NAMING, -NAMES to give a family name to
SURNAMER	n pl. -S one that surnames
SURPASS	v -ED, -ING, -ES to go beyond
SURPLICE	n pl. -S a loose-fitting vestment
SURPLUS	n pl. -ES an excess
SURPRINT	v -ED, -ING, -S to print over something already printed
SURPRISE	v -PRISED, -PRISING, -PRISES to come upon unexpectedly
SURPRIZE	v -PRIZED, -PRIZING, -PRIZES to surprise
SURRA	n pl. -S a disease of domestic animals
SURREAL	adj having dreamlike qualities

SURREY	*n* pl. -REYS a light carriage
SURROUND	*v* -ED, -ING, -S to extend completely around
SURROYAL	*n* pl. -S the topmost prong of a stag's antler
SURTAX	*v* -ED, -ING, -ES to assess with an extra tax
SURTOUT	*n* pl. -S a close-fitting overcoat
SURVEIL	*v* -VEILLED, -VEILLING, -VEILS to watch closely
SURVEY	*v* -ED, -ING, -S to determine the boundaries, area, or elevations of by measuring angles and distances
SURVEYOR	*n* pl. -S one that surveys land
SURVIVAL	*n* pl. -S a living or continuing longer than another person or thing
SURVIVE	*v* -VIVED, -VIVING, -VIVES to remain in existence
SURVIVER	*n* pl. -S survivor
SURVIVOR	*n* pl. -S one that survives
SUSHI	*n* pl. -S a dish of cold rice cakes topped with strips of raw fish
SUSLIK	*n* pl. -S a Eurasian rodent
SUSPECT	*v* -ED, -ING, -S to think guilty on slight evidence
SUSPEND	*v* -ED, -ING, -S to cause to stop for a period
SUSPENSE	*n* pl. -S a state of mental uncertainty or excitement
SUSPIRE	*v* -PIRED, -PIRING, -PIRES to sigh
SUSS	*v* -ED, -ING, -ES to figure out
SUSTAIN	*v* -ED, -ING, -S to maintain by providing with food and drink
SUSURRUS	*n* pl. -ES a soft rustling sound
SUTLER	*n* pl. -S one that peddles goods to soldiers
SUTRA	*n* pl. -S a Hindu aphorism
SUTTA	*n* pl. -S sutra
SUTTEE	*n* pl. -S a Hindu widow cremated on her husband's funeral pile to show her devotion to him
SUTURAL	*adj* pertaining to the line of junction between two bones
SUTURE	*v* -TURED, -TURING, -TURES to unite by sewing
SUZERAIN	*n* pl. -S a feudal lord
SVARAJ	*n* pl. -ES swaraj
SVEDBERG	*n* pl. -S a unit of time
SVELTE	*adj* SVELTER, SVELTEST gracefully slender **SVELTELY** *adv*
SWAB	*v* SWABBED, SWABBING, SWABS to clean with a large mop
SWABBER	*n* pl. -S one that swabs
SWABBIE	*n* pl. -S a sailor
SWABBING	present participle of swab
SWABBY	*n* pl. -BIES swabbie
SWACKED	*adj* drunk
SWADDLE	*v* -DLED, -DLING, -DLES to wrap in bandages
SWAG	*v* SWAGGED, SWAGGING, SWAGS to sway
SWAGE	*v* SWAGED, SWAGING, SWAGES to shape with a hammering tool
SWAGER	*n* pl. -S one that swages
SWAGGED	past tense of swag
SWAGGER	*v* -ED, -ING, -S to walk with a pompous air
SWAGGIE	*n* pl. -S a swagman
SWAGGING	present participle of swag
SWAGING	present participle of swage
SWAGMAN	*n* pl. -MEN a hobo
SWAIL	*n* pl. -S swale
SWAIN	*n* pl. -S a country boy **SWAINISH** *adj*
SWALE	*n* pl. -S a tract of low, marshy ground
SWALLOW	*v* -ED, -ING, -S to take through the mouth and esophagus into the stomach
SWAM	past tense of swim
SWAMI	*n* pl. -S a Hindu religious teacher
SWAMIES	pl. of swamy
SWAMP	*v* -ED, -ING, -S to inundate
SWAMPER	*n* pl. -S one that lives in a swampy area
SWAMPISH	*adj* swampy
SWAMPY	*adj* SWAMPIER, SWAMPIEST marshy
SWAMY	*n* pl. -MIES swami
SWAN	*v* SWANNED, SWANNING, SWANS to swear
SWANG	a past tense of swing
SWANHERD	*n* pl. -S one who tends swans (large aquatic birds)
SWANK	*adj* SWANKER, SWANKEST imposingly elegant

SWANK	*v* -ED, -ING, -S to swagger
SWANKY	*adj* SWANKIER, SWANKIEST swank **SWANKILY** *adv*
SWANLIKE	*adj* resembling a swan
SWANNED	past tense of swan
SWANNERY	*n* pl. -NERIES a place where swans are raised
SWANNING	present participle of swan
SWANPAN	*n* pl. -S a Chinese abacus
SWANSKIN	*n* pl. -S the skin of a swan
SWAP	*v* SWAPPED, SWAPPING, SWAPS to trade
SWAPPER	*n* pl. -S one that swaps
SWARAJ	*n* pl. -ES self-government in British India
SWARD	*v* -ED, -ING, -S to cover with turf
SWARE	a past tense of swear
SWARF	*n* pl. -S material removed by a cutting tool
SWARM	*v* -ED, -ING, -S to move in a large group
SWARMER	*n* pl. -S one that swarms
SWART	*adj* swarthy
SWARTH	*n* pl. -S turf
SWARTHY	*adj* -THIER, -THIEST having a dark complexion
SWARTY	*adj* swarthy
SWASH	*v* -ED, -ING, -ES to swagger
SWASHER	*n* pl. -S one that swashes
SWASTICA	*n* pl. -S swastika
SWASTIKA	*n* pl. -S a geometrical figure used as a symbol or ornament
SWAT	*v* SWATTED, SWATTING, SWATS to hit sharply
SWATCH	*n* pl. -ES a sample piece of cloth
SWATH	*n* pl. -S a row of cut grass or grain
SWATHE	*v* SWATHED, SWATHING, SWATHES to wrap in bandages
SWATHER	*n* pl. -S one that swathes
SWATTED	past tense of swat
SWATTER	*n* pl. -S one that swats
SWATTING	present participle of swat
SWAY	*v* -ED, -ING, -S to move slowly back and forth **SWAYABLE** *adj*
SWAYBACK	*n* pl. -S an abnormal sagging of the back
SWAYER	*n* pl. -S one that sways
SWAYFUL	*adj* capable of influencing
SWEAR	*v* SWORE or SWARE, SWORN, SWEARING, SWEARS to utter a solemn oath
SWEARER	*n* pl. -S one that swears
SWEAT	*v* -ED, -ING, -S to perspire
SWEATBOX	*n* pl. -ES a small enclosure in which one is made to sweat
SWEATER	*n* pl. -S a knitted outer garment
SWEATY	*adj* SWEATIER, SWEATIEST covered with perspiration **SWEATILY** *adv*
SWEDE	*n* pl. -S a rutabaga
SWEENY	*n* pl. -NIES atrophy of the shoulder muscles in horses
SWEEP	*v* SWEPT, SWEEPING, SWEEPS to clear or clean with a brush or broom
SWEEPER	*n* pl. -S one that sweeps
SWEEPING	*n* pl. -S the act of one that sweeps
SWEEPY	*adj* SWEEPIER, SWEEPIEST of wide range or scope
SWEER	*adj* lazy
SWEET	*adj* SWEETER, SWEETEST pleasing to the taste
SWEET	*n* pl. -S something that is sweet
SWEETEN	*v* -ED, -ING, -S to make sweet
SWEETIE	*n* pl. -S darling
SWEETING	*n* pl. -S a sweet apple
SWEETISH	*adj* somewhat sweet
SWEETLY	*adv* in a sweet manner
SWEETSOP	*n* pl. -S a tropical tree
SWELL	*v* SWELLED, SWOLLEN, SWELLING, SWELLS to increase in size or volume
SWELL	*adj* SWELLER, SWELLEST stylish
SWELLING	*n* pl. -S something that is swollen
SWELTER	*v* -ED, -ING, -S to suffer from oppressive heat
SWELTRY	*adj* -TRIER, -TRIEST oppressively hot
SWEPT	past tense of sweep
SWERVE	*v* SWERVED, SWERVING, SWERVES to turn aside suddenly from a straight course
SWERVER	*n* pl. -S one that swerves
SWEVEN	*n* pl. -S a dream or vision

SWIDDEN   *n* pl. -S an agricultural plot produced by burning off the vegetative cover

SWIFT   *adj* SWIFTER, SWIFTEST moving with a great rate of motion

SWIFT   *n* pl. -S a fast-flying bird

SWIFTER   *n* pl. -S a rope on a ship

SWIFTLET   *n* pl. -S a cave-dwelling swift

SWIFTLY   *adv* in a swift manner

SWIG   *v* SWIGGED, SWIGGING, SWIGS to drink deeply or rapidly

SWIGGER   *n* pl. -S one that swigs

SWILL   *v* -ED, -ING, -S to swig

SWILLER   *n* pl. -S one that swills

SWIM   *v* SWAM, SWUM, SWIMMING, SWIMS to propel oneself in water by natural means

SWIMMER   *n* pl. -S one that swims

SWIMMING   *n* pl. -S the act of one that swims

SWIMMY   *adj* -MIER, -MIEST dizzy **SWIMMILY** *adv*

SWIMSUIT   *n* pl. -S a bathing suit

SWIMWEAR   *n* pl. SWIMWEAR clothing suitable for swimming

SWINDLE   *v* -DLED, -DLING, -DLES to take money or property from by fraudulent means

SWINDLER   *n* pl. -S one that swindles

SWINE   *n* pl. SWINE a domestic pig

SWINEPOX   *n* pl. -ES a disease of swine

SWING   *v* SWUNG or SWANG, SWINGING, SWINGS to move freely back and forth

SWINGBY   *n* pl. -BYS a mission in which a spacecraft uses a planet's gravitational pull for making course changes

SWINGE   *v* SWINGED, SWINGEING, SWINGES to flog

SWINGER   *n* pl. -S one that swings

SWINGIER   comparative of swingy

SWINGIEST   superlative of swingy

SWINGING   *adj* -INGEST lively and hip

SWINGING   *n* pl. -S the practice of swapping sex partners

SWINGLE   *v* -GLED, -GLING, -GLES to scutch

SWINGMAN   *n* pl. -MEN a basketball player who can play guard or forward

SWINGY   *adj* SWINGIER, SWINGIEST marked by swinging

SWINISH   *adj* resembling or befitting swine

SWINK   *v* -ED, -ING, -S to toil

SWINNEY   *n* pl. -NEYS sweeny

SWIPE   *v* SWIPED, SWIPING, SWIPES to strike with a sweeping blow

SWIPLE   *n* pl. -S a part of a threshing device

SWIPPLE   *n* pl. -S swiple

SWIRL   *v* -ED, -ING, -S to move with a whirling motion

SWIRLY   *adj* SWIRLIER, SWIRLIEST swirling

SWISH   *v* -ED, -ING, -ES to move with a prolonged hissing sound

SWISHER   *n* pl. -S one that swishes

SWISHY   *adj* SWISHIER, SWISHIEST swishing

SWISS   *n* pl. -ES a cotton fabric

SWITCH   *v* -ED, -ING, -ES to beat with a flexible rod

SWITCHER   *n* pl. -S one that switches

SWITH   *adv* quickly

SWITHE   *adv* swith

SWITHER   *v* -ED, -ING, -S to doubt

SWITHLY   *adv* swith

SWIVE   *v* SWIVED, SWIVING, SWIVES to copulate with

SWIVEL   *v* -ELED, -ELING, -ELS or -ELLED, -ELLING, -ELS to turn on a pivoted support

SWIVET   *n* pl. -S a state of nervous excitement

SWIVING   present participle of swive

SWIZZLE   *v* -ZLED, -ZLING, -ZLES to drink excessively

SWIZZLER   *n* pl. -S one that swizzles

SWOB   *v* SWOBBED, SWOBBING, SWOBS to swab

SWOBBER   *n* pl. -S swabber

SWOLLEN   past participle of swell

SWOON   *v* -ED, -ING, -S to faint

SWOONER   *n* pl. -S one that swoons

SWOOP   *v* -ED, -ING, -S to make a sudden descent

SWOOPER   *n* pl. -S one that swoops

SWOOSH   *v* -ED, -ING, -ES to move with a rustling sound

SWOP   *v* SWOPPED, SWOPPING, SWOPS to swap

SWORD   *n* pl. -S a weapon having a long blade for cutting or thrusting

SWORDMAN   *n* pl. -MEN one skilled in the use of a sword

SWORE   a past tense of swear

SWORN   past participle of swear

SWOT   *v* SWOTTED, SWOTTING, SWOTS to swat

SWOTTER   *n* pl. -S one that swots

SWOUN   *v* -ED, -ING, -S to swoon

SWOUND   *v* -ED, -ING, -S to swoon

SWUM   past participle of swim

SWUNG   a past tense of swing

SYBARITE   *n* pl. -S a person devoted to pleasure and luxury

SYBO   *n* pl. -BOES the cibol

SYCAMINE   *n* pl. -S the mulberry tree

SYCAMORE   *n* pl. -S a North American tree

SYCE   *n* pl. -S a male servant in India

SYCEE   *n* pl. -S fine uncoined silver formerly used in China as money

SYCOMORE   *n* pl. -S sycamore

SYCONIUM   *n* pl. -NIA a fleshy multiple fruit

SYCOSIS   *n* pl. -COSES an inflammatory disease of the hair follicles

SYENITE   *n* pl. -S an igneous rock **SYENITIC** *adj*

SYKE   *n* pl. -S a small stream

SYLI   *n* pl. -S a former monetary unit of Guinea

SYLLABI   a pl. of syllabus

SYLLABIC   *n* pl. -S a speech sound of high sonority

SYLLABLE   *v* -BLED, -BLING, -BLES to pronounce syllables (units of spoken language)

SYLLABUB   *n* pl. -S sillabub

SYLLABUS   *n* pl. -BI or -BUSES an outline of a course of study

SYLPH   *n* pl. -S a slender, graceful girl or woman **SYLPHIC, SYLPHISH, SYLPHY** *adj*

SYLPHID   *n* pl. -S a young sylph

SYLVA   *n* pl. -VAS or -VAE the forest trees of an area

SYLVAN   *n* pl. -S one that lives in a forest

SYLVATIC   *adj* pertaining to a forest

SYLVIN   *n* pl. -S sylvite

SYLVINE   *n* pl. -S sylvite

SYLVITE   *n* pl. -S an ore of potassium

SYMBION   *n* pl. -S symbiont

SYMBIONT   *n* pl. -S an organism living in close association with another

SYMBIOT   *n* pl. -S symbiont

SYMBIOTE   *n* pl. -S symbiont

SYMBOL   *v* -BOLED, -BOLING, -BOLS or -BOLLED, -BOLLING, -BOLS to serve as a symbol (a representation) of

SYMBOLIC   *adj* pertaining to a symbol

SYMMETRY   *n* pl. -TRIES an exact correspondence between the opposite halves of a figure

SYMPATHY   *n* pl. -THIES a feeling of compassion for another's suffering

SYMPATRY   *n* pl. -RIES the state of occupying the same area without loss of identity from interbreeding

SYMPHONY   *n* pl. -NIES an orchestral composition

SYMPODIA   *n/pl* plant stems made up of a series of superposed branches

SYMPOSIA   *n/pl* conferences for the purpose of discussion

SYMPTOM   *n* pl. -S an indication of something

SYN   *adv* syne

SYNAGOG   *n* pl. -S a building for Jewish worship

SYNANON   *n* pl. -S a method of group therapy for drug addicts

SYNAPSE   *v* -APSED, -APSING, -APSES to come together in synapsis

SYNAPSID   *n* pl. -S one of a group of extinct reptiles

SYNAPSIS   *n* pl. -APSES the point at which a nervous impulse passes from one neuron to another **SYNAPTIC** *adj*

SYNC   *v* -ED, -ING, -S to cause to operate in unison

SYNCARP   *n* pl. -S a fleshy multiple fruit

SYNCARPY   *n* pl. -PIES the state of being a syncarp

SYNCH   *v* -ED, -ING, -S to sync

SYNCHRO   *n* pl. -CHROS a selsyn

SYNCLINE   *n* pl. -S a type of rock formation

SYNCOM   *n* pl. -S a type of communications satellite

SYNCOPE *n* pl. -S the contraction of a word by omitting one or more sounds from the middle **SYNCOPAL, SYNCOPIC** *adj*

SYNCYTIA *n/pl* masses of protoplasm resulting from cell fusion

SYNDESIS *n* pl. -DESES or -DESISES synapsis

SYNDET *n* pl. -S a synthetic detergent

SYNDETIC *adj* serving to connect

SYNDIC *n* pl. -S a business agent **SYNDICAL** *adj*

SYNDROME *n* pl. -S a group of symptoms that characterize a particular disorder

SYNE *adv* since

SYNECTIC *adj* pertaining to a system of problem solving

SYNERGIA *n* pl. -S synergy

SYNERGID *n* pl. -S a cell found in the embryo sac of a seed plant

SYNERGY *n* pl. -GIES combined action **SYNERGIC** *adj*

SYNESIS *n* pl. -SISES a type of grammatical construction

SYNFUEL *n* pl. -S a fuel derived from fossil fuels

SYNGAMY *n* pl. -MIES the union of two gametes **SYNGAMIC** *adj*

SYNGAS *n* pl. -GASES or -GASSES a mixture of carbon monoxide and hydrogen used in chemical synthesis

SYNOD *n* pl. -S a church council **SYNODAL, SYNODIC** *adj*

SYNONYM *n* pl. -S a word having the same meaning as another

SYNONYME *n* pl. -S synonym

SYNONYMY *n* pl. -MIES equivalence of meaning

SYNOPSIS *n* pl. -OPSES a summary **SYNOPTIC** *adj*

SYNOVIA *n* pl. -S a lubricating fluid secreted by certain membranes **SYNOVIAL** *adj*

SYNTAGMA *n* pl. -MAS or -MATA a syntactic element

SYNTAX *n* pl. -ES the way in which words are put together to form phrases and sentences

SYNTH *n* pl. -S a synthesizer

SYNTONY *n* pl. -NIES the tuning of transmitters and receivers with each other **SYNTONIC** *adj*

SYNURA *n* pl. -RAE any of a genus of protozoa

SYPH *n* pl. -S syphilis

SYPHER *v* -ED, -ING, -S to overlap so as to make an even surface, as beveled plank edges

SYPHILIS *n* pl. -LISES a venereal disease

SYPHON *v* -ED, -ING, -S to siphon

SYREN *n* pl. -S siren

SYRINGA *n* pl. -S an ornamental shrub

SYRINGE *v* -RINGED, -RINGING, -RINGES to cleanse or treat with injected fluid

SYRINX *n* pl. -INGES or -INXES the vocal organ of a bird

SYRPHIAN *n* pl. -S syrphid

SYRPHID *n* pl. -S a winged insect

SYRUP *n* pl. -S a thick, sweet liquid **SYRUPY** *adj*

SYSOP *n* pl. -S the administrator of a computer bulletin board

SYSTEM *n* pl. -S a group of interacting elements forming a unified whole

SYSTEMIC *n* pl. -S a type of pesticide

SYSTOLE *n* pl. -S the normal rhythmic contraction of the heart **SYSTOLIC** *adj*

SYZYGY *n* pl. -GIES the configuration of the earth, moon, and sun lying in a straight line **SYZYGAL, SYZYGIAL** *adj*

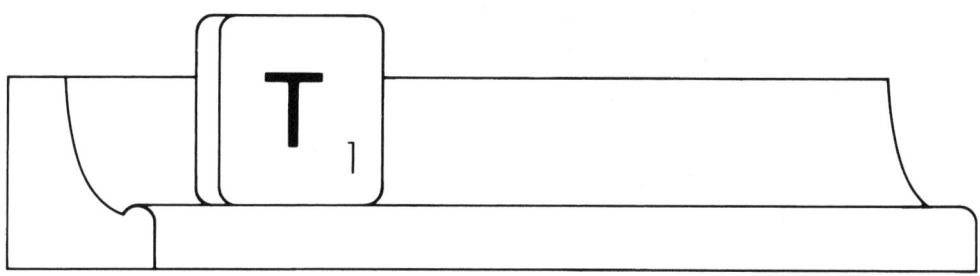

TA   *n* pl. -S an expression of gratitude

TAB   *v* TABBED, TABBING, TABS to name or designate

TABANID   *n* pl. -S a bloodsucking insect

TABARD   *n* pl. -S a sleeveless outer garment **TABARDED** *adj*

TABARET   *n* pl. -S a silk fabric

TABBED   past tense of tab

TABBIED   past tense of tabby

TABBIES   present 3d person sing. of tabby

TABBING   present participle of tab

TABBIS   *n* pl. -BISES a silk fabric

TABBY   *v* -BIED, -BYING, -BIES to give a wavy appearance to

TABER   *v* -ED, -ING, -S to tabor

TABES   *n* pl. TABES a syphilitic disease

TABETIC   *n* pl. -S one affected with tabes

TABID   *adj* affected with tabes

TABLA   *n* pl. -S a small drum

TABLE   *v* -BLED, -BLING, -BLES to place on a table (a piece of furniture having a flat upper surface)

TABLEAU   *n* pl. -LEAUX or -LEAUS a picture

TABLEFUL   *n* pl. TABLEFULS or TABLESFUL as much as a table can hold

TABLET   *v* -LETED, -LETING, -LETS or -LETTED, -LETTING, -LETS to inscribe on a small, flat surface

TABLETOP   *n* pl. -S the top of a table

TABLING   present participle of table

TABLOID   *n* pl. -S a small newspaper

TABOO   *v* -ED, -ING, -S to exclude from use, approach, or mention

TABOOLEY   *n* pl. -LEYS tabouli

TABOR   *v* -ED, -ING, -S to beat on a small drum

TABORER   *n* pl. -S one that tabors

TABORET   *n* pl. -S a small drum

TABORIN   *n* pl. -S taborine

TABORINE   *n* pl. -S a taboret

TABOULI   *n* pl. -S a Lebanese salad containing bulgur wheat, tomatoes, parsley, onions, and mint

TABOUR   *v* -ED, -ING, -S to tabor

TABOURER   *n* pl. -S taborer

TABOURET   *n* pl. -S taboret

TABU   *v* -ED, -ING, -S to taboo

TABULAR   *adj* of or pertaining to a list

TABULATE   *v* -LATED, -LATING, -LATES to arrange in a list

TABULI   *n* pl. -S tabouli

TABUN   *n* pl. -S a chemical compound

TACE   *n* pl. -S tasse

TACET   *interj* be silent — used as a musical direction

TACH   *n* pl. -S a device for indicating speed of rotation

TACHE   *n* pl. -S a clasp or buckle

TACHINID   *n* pl. -S a grayish fly

TACHISM   *n* pl. -S action painting

TACHISME   *n* pl. -S tachism

TACHIST   *n* pl. -S an action painter

TACHISTE   *n* pl. -S tachist

TACHYON   *n* pl. -S a theoretical subatomic particle

TACIT   *adj* unspoken **TACITLY** *adv*

TACITURN   *adj* habitually silent

TACK   *v* -ED, -ING, -S to fasten with tacks (short, sharp-pointed nails)

TACKER   *n* pl. -S one that tacks

TACKET *n* pl. -S a hobnail

TACKEY *adj* TACKIER, TACKIEST tacky

TACKIER comparative of tacky

TACKIEST superlative of tacky

TACKIFY *v* -FIED, -FYING, -FIES to make tacky

TACKILY *adv* in a tacky manner

TACKLE *v* -LED, -LING, -LES to seize and throw to the ground

TACKLER *n* pl. -S one that tackles

TACKLESS *adj* having no tacks

TACKLING *n* pl. -S equipment

TACKY *adj* TACKIER, TACKIEST adhesive

TACNODE *n* pl. -S a point of contact between two curves

TACO *n* pl. -COS a tortilla folded around a filling

TACONITE *n* pl. -S a low-grade iron ore

TACT *n* pl. -S skill in dealing with delicate situations

TACTFUL *adj* having tact

TACTIC *n* pl. -S a maneuver for gaining an objective **TACTICAL** *adj*

TACTILE *adj* pertaining to the sense of touch

TACTION *n* pl. -S the act of touching

TACTLESS *adj* lacking tact

TACTUAL *adj* tactile

TAD *n* pl. -S a small boy

TADPOLE *n* pl. -S the aquatic larva of an amphibian

TAE *prep* to

TAEL *n* pl. -S a Chinese unit of weight

TAENIA *n* pl. -NIAE or -NIAS a headband worn in ancient Greece

TAFFAREL *n* pl. -S taffrail

TAFFEREL *n* pl. -S taffrail

TAFFETA *n* pl. -S a lustrous fabric

TAFFIA *n* pl. -S tafia

TAFFRAIL *n* pl. -S a rail around the stern of a ship

TAFFY *n* pl. -FIES a chewy candy

TAFIA *n* pl. -S an inferior rum

TAG *v* TAGGED, TAGGING, TAGS to provide with a tag (an identifying marker)

TAGALONG *n* pl. -S one that follows another

TAGBOARD *n* pl. -S a material for making shipping tags

TAGGED past tense of tag

TAGGER *n* pl. -S one that tags

TAGGING present participle of tag

TAGLIKE *adj* resembling a tag

TAGMEME *n* pl. -S the smallest unit of meaningful grammatical relation

TAGMEMIC *adj* pertaining to a grammar in which a tagmeme is the basic unit

TAGRAG *n* pl. -S riffraff

TAHINI *n* pl. -S a paste of sesame seeds

TAHR *n* pl. -S a goatlike mammal

TAHSIL *n* pl. -S a district in India

TAIGA *n* pl. -S a subarctic evergreen forest

TAIGLACH *n* pl. TAIGLACH teiglach

TAIL *v* -ED, -ING, -S to provide with a tail (a hindmost part)

TAILBACK *n* pl. -S a member of the backfield in some football formations

TAILBONE *n* pl. -S the coccyx

TAILCOAT *n* pl. -S a man's coat

TAILER *n* pl. -S one that secretly follows another

TAILFAN *n* pl. -S a fanlike swimming organ at the rear of some crustaceans

TAILGATE *v* -GATED, -GATING, -GATES to drive dangerously close behind another vehicle

TAILING *n* pl. -S the part of a projecting stone or brick that is inserted into a wall

TAILLAMP *n* pl. -S a light at the rear of a vehicle

TAILLE *n* pl. -S a former French tax

TAILLESS *adj* having no tail

TAILLEUR *n* pl. -S a woman's tailored suit

TAILLIKE *adj* resembling a tail

TAILOR *v* -ED, -ING, -S to fit with clothes

TAILPIPE *n* pl. -S an exhaust pipe

TAILRACE *n* pl. -S a part of a millrace

TAILSKID *n* pl. -S a support on which the tail of an airplane rests

TAILSPIN *n* pl. -S the spiral descent of a stalled airplane

TAILWIND *n* pl. -S a wind coming from behind a moving vehicle

TAIN *n* pl. -S a thin plate

TAINT *v* -ED, -ING, -S to touch or affect slightly with something bad

TAIPAN *n* pl. -S a venomous snake

TAJ *n* pl. -ES a tall, conical cap worn in Muslim countries

TAKA *n* pl. TAKA a monetary unit of Bangladesh

TAKAHE *n* pl. -S a flightless bird

TAKE *v* TOOK, TAKEN, TAKING, TAKES to get possession of **TAKABLE, TAKEABLE** *adj*

TAKEAWAY *adj* designating prepared food that is sold for consumption elsewhere

TAKEDOWN *n* pl. -S an article that can be taken apart easily

TAKEOFF *n* pl. -S the act of rising in flight

TAKEOUT *n* pl. -S the act of removing

TAKEOVER *n* pl. -S the act of assuming control

TAKER *n* pl. -S one that takes

TAKEUP *n* pl. -S the act of taking something up

TAKIN *n* pl. -S a goatlike mammal

TAKING *n* pl. -S a seizure

TAKINGLY *adv* in an attractive manner

TALA *n* pl. -S a traditional rhythmic pattern of music in India

TALAPOIN *n* pl. -S a small African monkey

TALAR *n* pl. -S a long cloak

TALARIA *n/pl* winged sandals worn by various figures of classical mythology

TALC *v* TALCKED, TALCKING, TALCS or TALCED, TALCING, TALCS to treat with talc (a soft mineral with a soapy texture) **TALCKY, TALCOSE, TALCOUS** *adj*

TALCUM *n* pl. -S a powder made from talc

TALE *n* pl. -S a story

TALENT *n* pl. -S a special natural ability **TALENTED** *adj*

TALER *n* pl. -S a former German coin

TALESMAN *n* pl. -MEN a person summoned to fill a vacancy on a jury

TALEYSIM a pl. of tallith

TALI pl. of talus

TALION *n* pl. -S a retaliation for a crime

TALIPED *n* pl. -S a person afflicted with clubfoot

TALIPES *n* pl. TALIPES clubfoot

TALIPOT *n* pl. -S a tall palm tree

TALISMAN *n* pl. -S an object believed to possess magical powers

TALK *v* -ED, -ING, -S to communicate by speaking

TALKABLE *adj* able to be talked about

TALKER *n* pl. -S one that talks

TALKIE *n* pl. -S a moving picture with synchronized sound

TALKING *n* pl. -S conversation

TALKY *adj* TALKIER, TALKIEST tending to talk a great deal

TALL *adj* TALLER, TALLEST having great height

TALLAGE *v* -LAGED, -LAGING, -LAGES to tax

TALLAISIM a pl. of tallith

TALLBOY *n* pl. -BOYS a highboy

TALLIED past tense of tally

TALLIER *n* pl. -S one that tallies

TALLIES present 3d person sing. of tally

TALLIS *n* pl. -LISIM tallith

TALLISH *adj* somewhat tall

TALLIT *n* pl. -LITIM tallith

TALLITH *n* pl. TALLITHES, TALLITHIM, TALLITOTH, TALEYSIM, or TALLAISIM a Jewish prayer shawl

TALLNESS *n* pl. -ES the state of being tall

TALLOL *n* pl. -S a resinous liquid

TALLOW *v* -ED, -ING, -S to smear with tallow (a mixture of animal fats)

TALLOWY *adj* resembling tallow

TALLY *v* -LIED, -LYING, -LIES to count

TALLYHO *v* -ED, -ING, -S to make an encouraging shout to hunting hounds

TALLYMAN *n* pl. -MEN a person who tallies

TALMUDIC *adj* pertaining to the body of Jewish civil and religious law

TALON *n* pl. -S a claw of a bird of prey **TALONED** *adj*

TALOOKA *n* pl. -S taluk

TALUK *n* pl. -S an estate in India

TALUKA *n* pl. -S taluk

TALUS *n* pl. -LI a bone of the foot

TALUS *n* pl. -ES a slope formed by an accumulation of rock debris

TAM *n* pl. -S a tight-fitting Scottish cap

TAMABLE	*adj* capable of being tamed	**TAMPER**	*v* -ED, -ING, -S to interfere in a harmful manner
TAMAL	*n* pl. -S tamale	**TAMPERER**	*n* pl. -S one that tampers
TAMALE	*n* pl. -S a Mexican dish	**TAMPION**	*n* pl. -S a plug for the muzzle of a cannon
TAMANDU	*n* pl. -S tamandua		
TAMANDUA	*n* pl. -S an arboreal anteater	**TAMPON**	*v* -ED, -ING, -S to plug with a cotton pad
TAMARACK	*n* pl. -S a timber tree		
TAMARAO	*n* pl. -RAOS tamarau	**TAN**	*v* TANNED, TANNING, TANS to convert hide into leather by soaking in chemicals
TAMARAU	*n* pl. -S a small buffalo of the Philippines		
TAMARI	*n* pl. -S a Japanese soy sauce	**TAN**	*adj* TANNER, TANNEST brown from the sun's rays
TAMARIN	*n* pl. -S a South American monkey	**TANAGER**	*n* pl. -S a brightly colored bird
TAMARIND	*n* pl. -S a tropical tree	**TANBARK**	*n* pl. -S a tree bark used as a source of tannin
TAMARISK	*n* pl. -S an evergreen shrub	**TANDEM**	*n* pl. -S a bicycle built for two
TAMASHA	*n* pl. -S a public entertainment in India	**TANDOOR**	*n* pl. -DOORI a clay oven
TAMBAC	*n* pl. -S tombac	**TANG**	*v* -ED, -ING, -S to provide with a pungent flavor
TAMBAK	*n* pl. -S tombac	**TANGELO**	*n* pl. -LOS a citrus fruit
TAMBALA	*n* pl. -S or MATAMBALA a monetary unit of Malawi	**TANGENCE**	*n* pl. -S tangency
		TANGENCY	*n* pl. -CIES the state of being in immediate physical contact
TAMBOUR	*v* -ED, -ING, -S to embroider on a round wooden frame	**TANGENT**	*n* pl. -S a straight line in contact with a curve at one point
TAMBOURA	*n* pl. -S tambura	**TANGIBLE**	*n* pl. -S something palpable
TAMBUR	*n* pl. -S tambura	**TANGIBLY**	*adv* palpably
TAMBURA	*n* pl. -S a stringed instrument	**TANGIER**	comparative of tangy
TAME	*adj* TAMER, TAMEST gentle or docile	**TANGIEST**	superlative of tangy
TAME	*v* TAMED, TAMING, TAMES to make tame	**TANGLE**	*v* -GLED, -GLING, -GLES to bring together in intricate confusion
TAMEABLE	*adj* tamable	**TANGLER**	*n* pl. -S one that tangles
TAMEIN	*n* pl. -S a garment worn by Burmese women	**TANGLY**	*adj* -GLIER, -GLIEST tangled
TAMELESS	*adj* not capable of being tamed	**TANGO**	*v* -ED, -ING, -S to perform a Latin-American dance
TAMELY	*adv* in a tame manner		
TAMENESS	*n* pl. -ES the state of being tame	**TANGRAM**	*n* pl. -S a Chinese puzzle
TAMER	*n* pl. -S one that tames	**TANGY**	*adj* TANGIER, TANGIEST pungent
TAMEST	superlative of tame		
TAMING	present participle of tame	**TANIST**	*n* pl. -S the heir apparent to a Celtic chief
TAMIS	*n* pl. -ISES a strainer made of cloth mesh	**TANISTRY**	*n* pl. -RIES the system of electing a tanist
TAMMIE	*n* pl. -S tammy	**TANK**	*v* -ED, -ING, -S to store in a tank (a container usually for liquids)
TAMMY	*n* pl. -MIES a fabric of mixed fibers		
		TANKA	*n* pl. -S a Japanese verse form
TAMP	*v* -ED, -ING, -S to pack down by tapping	**TANKAGE**	*n* pl. -S the capacity of a tank
		TANKARD	*n* pl. -S a tall drinking vessel
TAMPALA	*n* pl. -S an annual herb	**TANKER**	*n* pl. -S a ship designed to transport liquids
TAMPAN	*n* pl. -S a biting insect		

TANKFUL *n* pl. -S the amount a tank can hold

TANKLIKE *adj* resembling a tank

TANKSHIP *n* pl. -S a tanker

TANNABLE *adj* capable of being tanned

TANNAGE *n* pl. -S the process of tanning

TANNATE *n* pl. -S a chemical salt

TANNED past tense of tan

TANNER *n* pl. -S one that tans

TANNERY *n* pl. -NERIES a place where hides are tanned

TANNEST superlative of tan

TANNIC *adj* pertaining to tannin

TANNIN *n* pl. -S a chemical compound used in tanning

TANNING *n* pl. -S the process of converting hides into leather

TANNISH *adj* somewhat tan

TANREC *n* pl. -S tenrec

TANSY *n* pl. -SIES a perennial herb

TANTALUM *n* pl. -S a metallic element **TANTALIC** *adj*

TANTALUS *n* pl. -ES a case for wine bottles

TANTARA *n* pl. -S the sound of a trumpet or horn

TANTIVY *n* pl. -TIVIES a hunting cry

TANTO *adv* so much — used as a musical direction

TANTRA *n* pl. -S one of a class of Hindu religious writings **TANTRIC** *adj*

TANTRUM *n* pl. -S a fit of rage

TANUKI *n* pl. -S a raccoon dog

TANYARD *n* pl. -S the section of a tannery containing the vats

TAO *n* pl. -S the path of virtuous conduct according to a Chinese philosophy

TAP *v* TAPPED, TAPPING, TAPS to strike gently

TAPA *n* pl. -S a cloth made from tree bark

TAPADERA *n* pl. -S a part of a saddle

TAPADERO *n* pl. -ROS tapadera

TAPALO *n* pl. -LOS a scarf worn in Latin-American countries

TAPE *v* TAPED, TAPING, TAPES to fasten with tape (a long, narrow strip or band)

TAPELESS *adj* being without tape

TAPELIKE *adj* resembling tape

TAPELINE *n* pl. -S a tape for measuring distances

TAPER *v* -ED, -ING, -S to become gradually narrower toward one end

TAPERER *n* pl. -S one that carries a candle in a religious procession

TAPESTRY *v* -TRIED, -TRYING, -TRIES to decorate with woven wall hangings

TAPETUM *n* pl. -TA a layer of cells in some plants **TAPETAL** *adj*

TAPEWORM *n* pl. -S a parasitic worm

TAPHOLE *n* pl. -S a hole in a blast furnace

TAPHOUSE *n* pl. -S a tavern

TAPING present participle of tape

TAPIOCA *n* pl. -S a starchy food

TAPIR *n* pl. -S a hoofed mammal

TAPIS *n* pl. -PISES material used for wall hangings and floor coverings

TAPPED past tense of tap

TAPPER *n* pl. -S one that taps

TAPPET *n* pl. -S a sliding rod that causes another part of a mechanism to move

TAPPING *n* pl. -S the process or means by which something is tapped

TAPROOM *n* pl. -S a barroom

TAPROOT *n* pl. -S the main root of a plant

TAPSTER *n* pl. -S one that dispenses liquor in a barroom

TAR *v* TARRED, TARRING, TARS to cover with tar (a black viscous liquid)

TARAMA *n* pl. -S a Greek paste of fish roe, garlic, lemon juice, and olive oil

TARANTAS *n* pl. -ES a Russian carriage

TARBOOSH *n* pl. -ES a cap worn by Muslim men

TARBUSH *n* pl. -ES tarboosh

TARDIER comparative of tardy

TARDIES pl. of tardy

TARDO *adj* slow — used as a musical direction

TARDY *adj* TARDIER, TARDIEST late **TARDILY** *adv*

TARDY *n* pl. -DIES an instance of being late

TARDYON	*n* pl. -S a subatomic particle that travels slower than the speed of light
TARE	*v* TARED, TARING, TARES to determine the weight of a container holding goods
TARGE	*n* pl. -S a small, round shield
TARGET	*v* -ED, -ING, -S to make a goal of
TARIFF	*v* -ED, -ING, -S to tax imported or exported goods
TARING	present participle of tare
TARLATAN	*n* pl. -S a cotton fabric
TARLETAN	*n* pl. -S tarlatan
TARMAC	*n* pl. -S an asphalt road
TARN	*n* pl. -S a small mountain lake
TARNAL	*adj* damned **TARNALLY** *adv*
TARNISH	*v* -ED, -ING, -ES to dull the luster of
TARO	*n* pl. -ROS a tropical plant
TAROC	*n* pl. -S tarok
TAROK	*n* pl. -S a card game
TAROT	*n* pl. -S any of a set of playing cards used for fortune-telling
TARP	*n* pl. -S a protective canvas covering
TARPAN	*n* pl. -S an Asian wild horse
TARPAPER	*n* pl. -S a heavy paper coated with tar
TARPON	*n* pl. -S a marine game fish
TARRAGON	*n* pl. -S a perennial herb
TARRE	*v* TARRED, TARRING, TARRES to urge to action
TARRED	past tense of tar
TARRIED	past tense of tarry
TARRIER	*n* pl. -S one that tarries
TARRIES	present 3d person sing. of tarry
TARRIEST	superlative of tarry
TARRING	present participle of tar and tarre
TARRY	*v* -RIED, -RYING, -RIES to delay or be slow in acting or doing
TARRY	*adj* -RIER, -RIEST resembling tar
TARSAL	*n* pl. -S a bone of the foot
TARSI	pl. of tarsus
TARSIA	*n* pl. -S intarsia
TARSIER	*n* pl. -S a nocturnal primate
TARSUS	*n* pl. TARSI a part of the foot
TART	*adj* TARTER, TARTEST having a sharp, sour taste
TART	*v* -ED, -ING, -S to dress up
TARTAN	*n* pl. -S a patterned woolen fabric
TARTANA	*n* pl. -S a Mediterranean sailing vessel
TARTAR	*n* pl. -S a crust on the teeth **TARTARIC** *adj*
TARTISH	*adj* somewhat tart
TARTLET	*n* pl. -S a small pie
TARTLY	*adv* in a tart manner
TARTNESS	*n* pl. -ES the state of being tart
TARTRATE	*n* pl. -S a chemical salt
TARTUFE	*n* pl. -S tartuffe
TARTUFFE	*n* pl. -S a hypocrite
TARTY	*adj* resembling a prostitute
TARWEED	*n* pl. -S a flowering plant
TARZAN	*n* pl. -S a person of superior strength and agility
TASK	*v* -ED, -ING, -S to assign a job to
TASKWORK	*n* pl. -S hard work
TASS	*n* pl. -ES a drinking cup
TASSE	*n* pl. -S tasset
TASSEL	*v* -SELED, -SELING, -SELS or -SELLED, -SELLING, -SELS to adorn with dangling ornaments
TASSET	*n* pl. -S a piece of plate armor for the upper thigh
TASSIE	*n* pl. -S tass
TASTE	*v* TASTED, TASTING, TASTES to perceive the flavor of by taking into the mouth **TASTABLE** *adj*
TASTEFUL	*adj* tasty
TASTER	*n* pl. -S one that tastes
TASTING	present participle of taste
TASTY	*adj* TASTIER, TASTIEST pleasant to the taste **TASTILY** *adv*
TAT	*v* TATTED, TATTING, TATS to make tatting
TATAMI	*n* pl. -S straw matting used as a floor covering
TATAR	*n* pl. -S a ferocious person
TATE	*n* pl. -S a tuft of hair
TATER	*n* pl. -S a potato
TATOUAY	*n* pl. -AYS a South American armadillo
TATTED	past tense of tat
TATTER	*v* -ED, -ING, -S to become torn and worn
TATTIE	*n* pl. -S a potato

TATTIER   comparative of tatty

TATTIEST   superlative of tatty

TATTILY   *adv* in a tatty manner

TATTING   *n* pl. -S delicate handmade lace

TATTLE   *v* -TLED, -TLING, -TLES to reveal the activities of another

TATTLER   *n* pl. -S one that tattles

TATTOO   *v* -ED, -ING, -S to mark the skin with indelible pigments

TATTOOER   *n* pl. -S one that tattoos

TATTY   *adj* -TIER, -TIEST shabby

TAU   *n* pl. -S a Greek letter

TAUGHT   past tense of teach

TAUNT   *v* -ED, -ING, -S to challenge or reproach sarcastically

TAUNTER   *n* pl. -S one that taunts

TAUPE   *n* pl. -S a dark gray color

TAURINE   *n* pl. -S a chemical compound

TAUT   *adj* TAUTER, TAUTEST fully stretched, so as not to be slack

TAUT   *v* -ED, -ING, -S to tangle

TAUTAUG   *n* pl. -S tautog

TAUTEN   *v* -ED, -ING, -S to make taut

TAUTLY   *adv* in a taut manner

TAUTNESS   *n* pl. -ES the state of being taut

TAUTOG   *n* pl. -S a marine fish

TAUTOMER   *n* pl. -S a type of chemical compound

TAUTONYM   *n* pl. -S a type of taxonomic designation

TAV   *n* pl. -S a Hebrew letter

TAVERN   *n* pl. -S a place where liquor is sold to be drunk on the premises

TAVERNA   *n* pl. -S a cafe in Greece

TAVERNER   *n* pl. -S one that runs a tavern

TAW   *v* -ED, -ING, -S to convert into white leather by the application of minerals

TAWDRY   *adj* -DRIER, -DRIEST gaudy **TAWDRILY** *adv*

TAWDRY   *n* pl. -DRIES gaudy finery

TAWER   *n* pl. -S one that taws

TAWIE   *adj* docile

TAWNEY   *n* pl. -NEYS tawny

TAWNY   *adj* -NIER, -NIEST light brown **TAWNILY** *adv*

TAWNY   *n* pl. -NIES a light brown color

TAWPIE   *n* pl. -S a foolish young person

TAWSE   *v* TAWSED, TAWSING, TAWSES to flog

TAX   *v* -ED, -ING, -ES to place a tax (a charge imposed by authority for public purposes) on

TAXA   a pl. of taxon

TAXABLE   *adj* subject to tax **TAXABLY** *adv*

TAXABLE   *n* pl. -S a taxable item

TAXATION   *n* pl. -S the process of taxing

TAXEME   *n* pl. -S a minimum grammatical feature of selection **TAXEMIC** *adj*

TAXER   *n* pl. -S one that taxes

TAXI   *v* TAXIED, TAXIING or TAXYING, TAXIS or TAXIES to travel in a taxicab

TAXICAB   *n* pl. -S an automobile for hire

TAXIMAN   *n* pl. -MEN the operator of a taxicab

TAXINGLY   *adv* in an onerous manner

TAXITE   *n* pl. -S a volcanic rock **TAXITIC** *adj*

TAXIWAY   *n* pl. -WAYS a paved strip at an airport

TAXLESS   *adj* free from taxation

TAXMAN   *n* pl. -MEN one who collects taxes

TAXON   *n* pl. TAXA or TAXONS a unit of scientific classification

TAXONOMY   *n* pl. -MIES the study of scientific classification

TAXPAID   *adj* paid for by taxes

TAXPAYER   *n* pl. -S one that pays taxes

TAXUS   *n* pl. TAXUS an evergreen tree or shrub

TAXWISE   *adj* pertaining to taxes

TAXYING   a present participle of taxi

TAZZA   *n* pl. -ZAS or -ZE an ornamental bowl

TEA   *n* pl. -S a beverage made by infusing dried leaves in boiling water

TEABERRY   *n* pl. -RIES a North American shrub

TEABOARD   *n* pl. -S a tray for serving tea

TEABOWL   *n* pl. -S a teacup having no handle

TEABOX   *n* pl. -ES a box for tea leaves

TEACAKE   *n* pl. -S a small cake served with tea

TEACART	*n* pl. -S a wheeled table used in serving tea
TEACH	*v* TAUGHT, TEACHING, TEACHES to impart knowledge or skill to
TEACHER	*n* pl. -S one that teaches
TEACHING	*n* pl. -S a doctrine
TEACUP	*n* pl. -S a cup in which tea is served
TEAHOUSE	*n* pl. -S a public establishment serving tea
TEAK	*n* pl. -S an East Indian tree
TEAKWOOD	*n* pl. -S the wood of the teak
TEAL	*n* pl. -S a river duck
TEALIKE	*adj* resembling tea
TEAM	*v* -ED, -ING, -S to form a team (a group of persons associated in a joint action)
TEAMAKER	*n* pl. -S one that makes tea
TEAMMATE	*n* pl. -S a member of the same team
TEAMSTER	*n* pl. -S a truck driver
TEAMWORK	*n* pl. -S cooperative effort to achieve a common goal
TEAPOT	*n* pl. -S a vessel used in making and serving tea
TEAPOY	*n* pl. -POYS a small table used in serving tea
TEAR	*v* -ED, -ING, -S to emit tears (drops of saline liquid secreted by a gland of the eye)
TEAR	*v* TORE, TORN, TEARING, TEARS to pull apart or into pieces **TEARABLE** *adj*
TEARAWAY	*n* pl. -AWAYS a rebellious person
TEARDOWN	*n* pl. -S the process of disassembling
TEARDROP	*n* pl. -S a tear
TEARER	*n* pl. -S one that tears or rips
TEARFUL	*adj* full of tears
TEARGAS	*v* -GASSED, -GASSING, -GASES or -GASSES to subject to a gas that irritates the eyes
TEARIER	comparative of teary
TEARIEST	superlative of teary
TEARILY	*adv* in a teary manner
TEARLESS	*adj* being without tears
TEAROOM	*n* pl. -S a restaurant serving tea
TEARY	*adj* TEARIER, TEARIEST tearful
TEASE	*v* TEASED, TEASING, TEASES to make fun of
TEASEL	*v* -SELED, -SELING, -SELS or -SELLED, -SELLING, -SELS to raise a soft surface on fabric with a bristly flower head
TEASELER	*n* pl. -S one that teasels
TEASER	*n* pl. -S one that teases
TEASHOP	*n* pl. -S a tearoom
TEASING	present participle of tease
TEASPOON	*n* pl. -S a small spoon
TEAT	*n* pl. -S a mammary gland **TEATED** *adj*
TEATIME	*n* pl. -S the customary time for tea
TEAWARE	*n* pl. -S a tea service
TEAZEL	*v* -ZELED, -ZELING, -ZELS or -ZELLED, -ZELLING, -ZELS to teasel
TEAZLE	*v* -ZLED, -ZLING, -ZLES to teasel
TECHED	*adj* crazy
TECHIE	*n* pl. -S a technician
TECHNIC	*n* pl. -S technique
TECHY	*adj* TECHIER, TECHIEST tetchy **TECHILY** *adv*
TECTA	pl. of tectum
TECTAL	*adj* pertaining to a tectum
TECTITE	*n* pl. -S tektite
TECTONIC	*adj* pertaining to construction
TECTRIX	*n* pl. -TRICES a small feather of a bird's wing
TECTUM	*n* pl. -TA a bodily structure resembling or serving as a roof
TED	*v* TEDDED, TEDDING, TEDS to spread for drying
TEDDER	*n* pl. -S one that teds
TEDDY	*n* pl. -DIES a woman's undergarment
TEDIOUS	*adj* causing weariness
TEDIUM	*n* pl. -S the state of being tedious
TEE	*v* TEED, TEEING, TEES to place a golf ball on a small peg
TEEL	*n* pl. -S sesame
TEEM	*v* -ED, -ING, -S to be full to overflowing
TEEMER	*n* pl. -S one that teems
TEEN	*n* pl. -S a teenager
TEENAGE	*adj* pertaining to teenagers

TEENAGED   *adj* teenage

TEENAGER   *n* pl. -S a person between the ages of thirteen and nineteen

TEENER   *n* pl. -S a teenager

TEENFUL   *adj* filled with grief

TEENIER   comparative of teeny

TEENIEST   superlative of teeny

TEENSY   *adj* -SIER, -SIEST tiny

TEENTSY   *adj* -SIER, -SIEST tiny

TEENY   *adj* -NIER, -NIEST tiny

TEENYBOP   *adj* pertaining to a young teenager

TEEPEE   *n* pl. -S tepee

TEETER   *v* -ED, -ING, -S to move unsteadily

TEETH   pl. of tooth

TEETHE   *v* TEETHED, TEETHING, TEETHES to cut teeth

TEETHER   *n* pl. -S an object for a baby to bite on during teething

TEETHING   *n* pl. -S the first growth of teeth

TEETOTAL   *v* -TALED, -TALING, -TALS or -TALLED, -TALLING, -TALS to abstain completely from alcoholic beverages

TEETOTUM   *n* pl. -S a spinning toy

TEFF   *n* pl. -S a cereal grass

TEFILLIN   *n/pl* the phylacteries worn by Jews

TEG   *n* pl. -S a yearling sheep

TEGMEN   *n* pl. -MINA a covering

TEGMENTA   *n/pl* anatomical coverings

TEGMINAL   *adj* pertaining to a tegmen

TEGUA   *n* pl. -S a type of moccasin

TEGULAR   *adj* resembling a tile

TEGUMEN   *n* pl. -MINA tegmen

TEGUMENT   *n* pl. -S a covering

TEIGLACH   *n* pl. TEIGLACH a confection consisting of balls of dough boiled in honey

TEIID   *n* pl. -S a tropical American lizard

TEIND   *n* pl. -S a tithe

TEKTITE   *n* pl. -S a glassy body believed to be of meteoritic origin **TEKTITIC** *adj*

TEL   *n* pl. -S an ancient mound in the Middle East

TELA   *n* pl. -LAE an anatomical tissue

TELAMON   *n* pl. -ES a male figure used as a supporting column

TELE   *n* pl. -S a television set

TELECAST   *v* -ED, -ING, -S to broadcast by television

TELEDU   *n* pl. -S a carnivorous mammal

TELEFILM   *n* pl. -S a motion picture made for television

TELEGA   *n* pl. -S a Russian wagon

TELEGONY   *n* pl. -NIES the supposed influence of a previous sire on the offspring of later matings of the mother with other males

TELEGRAM   *v* -GRAMMED, -GRAMMING, -GRAMS to send a message by telegraph

TELEMAN   *n* pl. -MEN a naval officer

TELEMARK   *n* pl. -S a type of turn in skiing

TELEOST   *n* pl. -S a bony fish

TELEPATH   *n* pl. -S one who can communicate with another by some means other than the senses

TELEPLAY   *n* pl. -PLAYS a play written for television

TELEPORT   *v* -ED, -ING, -S to transport by a process that involves no physical means

TELERAN   *n* pl. -S a system of air navigation

TELESIS   *n* pl. TELESES planned progress

TELESTIC   *n* pl. -S a type of acrostic

TELETEXT   *n* pl. -S a communications system in which printed matter is telecast to subscribers

TELETHON   *n* pl. -S a fund-raising television program

TELEVIEW   *v* -ED, -ING, -S to observe by means of television

TELEVISE   *v* -VISED, -VISING, -VISES to broadcast by television (an electronic system of transmitting images and sound)

TELEX   *v* -ED, -ING, -ES to send a message by a type of telegraphic system

TELFER   *v* -ED, -ING, -S to telpher

TELFORD   *n* pl. -S a road made of stones

TELIA   pl. of telium

TELIAL   *adj* pertaining to a telium

TELIC   *adj* directed toward a goal

TELIUM   *n* pl. -LIA a sorus on the host plant of a rust fungus

TELL   *v* TOLD, TELLING, TELLS to give a detailed account of **TELLABLE** *adj*

TELLER   *n* pl. -S one that tells

TELLIES   a pl. of telly

TELLTALE   *n* pl. -S a tattler

TELLURIC   *adj* pertaining to the earth

TELLY   *n* pl. -LIES or -LYS a television set

TELOME   *n* pl. -S a structural unit of a vascular plant **TELOMIC** *adj*

TELOMERE   *n* pl. -S the natural end of a chromosome

TELOS   *n* pl. TELOI an ultimate end

TELPHER   *v* -ED, -ING, -S to transport by a system of aerial cable cars

TELSON   *n* pl. -S the terminal segment of an arthropod **TELSONIC** *adj*

TEMBLOR   *n* pl. -S or -ES an earthquake

TEMERITY   *n* pl. -TIES foolish boldness

TEMP   *v* -ED, -ING, -S to work as a temporary employee

TEMPEH   *n* pl. -S an Asian food

TEMPER   *v* -ED, -ING, -S to moderate by adding a counterbalancing agent

TEMPERA   *n* pl. -S a technique of painting

TEMPERER   *n* pl. -S one that tempers

TEMPEST   *v* -ED, -ING, -S to agitate violently

TEMPI   a pl. of tempo

TEMPLAR   *n* pl. -S a lawyer or student of law in London

TEMPLATE   *n* pl. -S a pattern used as a guide in making something

TEMPLE   *n* pl. -S a house of worship **TEMPLED** *adj*

TEMPLET   *n* pl. -S template

TEMPO   *n* pl. -PI or -POS the rate of speed of a musical piece

TEMPORAL   *n* pl. -S a bone of the skull

TEMPT   *v* -ED, -ING, -S to entice to commit an unwise or immoral act

TEMPTER   *n* pl. -S one that tempts

TEMPURA   *n* pl. -S a Japanese dish

TEN   *n* pl. -S a number

TENABLE   *adj* capable of being held **TENABLY** *adv*

TENACE   *n* pl. -S a combination of two high cards in some card games

TENACITY   *n* pl. -TIES perseverance or persistence

TENACULA   *n/pl* hooked surgical instruments

TENAIL   *n* pl. -S tenaille

TENAILLE   *n* pl. -S an outer defense

TENANCY   *n* pl. -CIES the temporary occupancy of something that belongs to another

TENANT   *v* -ED, -ING, -S to inhabit

TENANTRY   *n* pl. -RIES tenancy

TENCH   *n* pl. -ES a freshwater fish

TEND   *v* -ED, -ING, -S to be disposed or inclined

TENDANCE   *n* pl. -S watchful care

TENDENCE   *n* pl. -S tendance

TENDENCY   *n* pl. -CIES an inclination to act or think in a particular way

TENDER   *adj* -DERER, -DEREST soft or delicate

TENDER   *v* -ED, -ING, -S to present for acceptance

TENDERER   *n* pl. -S one that tenders

TENDERLY   *adv* in a tender manner

TENDON   *n* pl. -S a band of tough, fibrous tissue

TENDRIL   *n* pl. -S a leafless organ of climbing plants

TENEBRAE   *n/pl* a religious service

TENEMENT   *n* pl. -S an apartment house

TENESMUS   *n* pl. -ES an urgent but ineffectual effort to defecate or urinate **TENESMIC** *adj*

TENET   *n* pl. -S a principle, belief, or doctrine held to be true

TENFOLD   *n* pl. -S an amount ten times as great as a given unit

TENIA   *n* pl. -NIAE or -NIAS a tapeworm

TENIASIS   *n* pl. -SISES infestation with tapeworms

TENNER   *n* pl. -S a ten-dollar bill

TENNIES   *n/pl* low-cut sneakers

TENNIS   *n* pl. -NISES an outdoor ball game

TENNIST   *n* pl. -S a tennis player

TENON   *v* -ED, -ING, -S to unite by means of a tenon (a projection on the end of a piece of wood)

TENONER   *n* pl. -S one that tenons

TENOR	*n* pl. -S a high male singing voice	**TENURE**	*n* pl. -S the holding of something **TENURED, TENURIAL** *adj*
TENORIST	*n* pl. -S one who sings tenor or plays a tenor instrument	**TENUTO**	*n* pl. -TI or -TOS a musical note or chord held longer than its normal duration
TENORITE	*n* pl. -S a mineral		
TENOTOMY	*n* pl. -MIES the surgical division of a tendon	**TEOCALLI**	*n* pl. -S an Aztec temple
		TEOPAN	*n* pl. -S a teocalli
TENOUR	*n* pl. -S tenor	**TEOSINTE**	*n* pl. -S an annual grass
TENPENCE	*n* pl. -S the sum of ten pennies	**TEPA**	*n* pl. -S a chemical compound
TENPENNY	*adj* worth tenpence	**TEPAL**	*n* pl. -S a division of a perianth
TENPIN	*n* pl. -S a bowling pin	**TEPEE**	*n* pl. -S a conical tent of some North American Indians
TENREC	*n* pl. -S a mammal that feeds on insects		
TENSE	*adj* TENSER, TENSEST taut **TENSELY** *adv*	**TEPEFY**	*v* -FIED, -FYING, -FIES to make tepid
		TEPHRA	*n* pl. -S solid material ejected from a volcano
TENSE	*v* TENSED, TENSING, TENSES to make tense	**TEPHRITE**	*n* pl. -S a volcanic rock
TENSIBLE	*adj* capable of being stretched **TENSIBLY** *adv*	**TEPID**	*adj* moderately warm **TEPIDLY** *adv*
TENSILE	*adj* tensible	**TEPIDITY**	*n* pl. -TIES the state of being tepid
TENSING	present participle of tense		
TENSION	*v* -ED, -ING, -S to make tense	**TEPOY**	*n* pl. -POYS teapoy
TENSITY	*n* pl. -TIES the state of being tense	**TEQUILA**	*n* pl. -S a Mexican liquor
		TERAI	*n* pl. -S a sun hat with a wide brim
TENSIVE	*adj* causing tensity		
TENSOR	*n* pl. -S a muscle that stretches a body part	**TERAOHM**	*n* pl. -S one trillion ohms
		TERAPH	*n* pl. -APHIM an image of a Semitic household god
TENT	*v* -ED, -ING, -S to live in a tent (a type of portable shelter)		
TENTACLE	*n* pl. -S an elongated, flexible appendage of some animals	**TERATISM**	*n* pl. -S a malformed fetus **TERATOID** *adj*
		TERATOMA	*n* pl. -MAS or -MATA a type of tumor
TENTAGE	*n* pl. -S a supply of tents		
TENTER	*v* -ED, -ING, -S to stretch on a type of frame	**TERAWATT**	*n* pl. -S one trillion watts
		TERBIA	*n* pl. -S an oxide of terbium
TENTH	*n* pl. -S one of ten equal parts	**TERBIUM**	*n* pl. -S a metallic element **TERBIC** *adj*
TENTHLY	*adv* in the tenth place		
TENTIE	*adj* TENTIER, TENTIEST tenty	**TERCE**	*n* pl. -S tierce
TENTIER	comparative of tenty	**TERCEL**	*n* pl. -S a male falcon
TENTIEST	superlative of tenty	**TERCELET**	*n* pl. -S tercel
TENTLESS	*adj* having no tent	**TERCET**	*n* pl. -S a group of three lines of verse
TENTLIKE	*adj* resembling a tent		
TENTY	*adj* TENTIER, TENTIEST watchful	**TEREBENE**	*n* pl. -S a mixture of terpenes
		TEREBIC	*adj* pertaining to an acid derived from oil of turpentine
TENUIS	*n* pl. -UES a voiceless phonetic stop	**TEREDO**	*n* pl. -DOS or -DINES a bivalve mollusk
TENUITY	*n* pl. -ITIES lack of substance or strength		
		TEREFAH	*adj* tref
TENUOUS	*adj* having little substance or strength	**TERETE**	*adj* cylindrical and slightly tapering
		TERGA	pl. of tergum

TERGAL	*adj* pertaining to a tergum
TERGITE	*n* pl. -S a tergum
TERGUM	*n* pl. -GA a back part of a segment of an arthropod
TERIYAKI	*n* pl. -S a Japanese food
TERM	*v* -ED, -ING, -S to give a name to
TERMER	*n* pl. -S a prisoner serving a specified sentence
TERMINAL	*n* pl. -S an end or extremity
TERMINUS	*n* pl. -NI or -NUSES a terminal
TERMITE	*n* pl. -S an insect resembling an ant **TERMITIC** *adj*
TERMLESS	*adj* having no limits
TERMLY	*adv* periodically
TERMOR	*n* pl. -S one that holds land for a certain number of years
TERMTIME	*n* pl. -S the time when a school or court is in session
TERN	*n* pl. -S a seabird
TERNARY	*n* pl. -RIES a group of three
TERNATE	*adj* arranged in groups of three
TERNE	*n* pl. -S an alloy of lead and tin
TERNION	*n* pl. -S a group of three
TERPENE	*n* pl. -S a chemical compound **TERPENIC** *adj*
TERPINOL	*n* pl. -S a fragrant liquid
TERRA	*n* pl. -RAE earth; land
TERRACE	*v* -RACED, -RACING, -RACES to provide with a terrace (a raised embankment)
TERRAIN	*n* pl. -S a tract of land
TERRANE	*n* pl. -S a rock formation
TERRAPIN	*n* pl. -S a North American tortoise
TERRARIA	*n/pl* glass enclosures for plants or small animals
TERRAS	*n* pl. -ES trass
TERRAZZO	*n* pl. -ZOS a mosaic flooring
TERREEN	*n* pl. -S terrine
TERRELLA	*n* pl. -S a spherical magnet
TERRENE	*n* pl. -S a land area
TERRET	*n* pl. -S a metal ring on a harness
TERRIBLE	*adj* very bad **TERRIBLY** *adv*
TERRIER	*n* pl. -S a small, active dog
TERRIES	pl. of terry
TERRIFIC	*adj* very good; fine
TERRIFY	*v* -FIED, -FYING, -FIES to fill with terror

TERRINE	*n* pl. -S an earthenware jar
TERRIT	*n* pl. -S terret
TERROR	*n* pl. -S intense fear
TERRY	*n* pl. -RIES an absorbent fabric
TERSE	*adj* TERSER, TERSEST succinct **TERSELY** *adv*
TERTIAL	*n* pl. -S a flight feather of a bird's wing
TERTIAN	*n* pl. -S a recurrent fever
TERTIARY	*n* pl. -ARIES a tertial
TESLA	*n* pl. -S a unit of magnetic induction
TESSERA	*n* pl. -SERAE a small square used in mosaic work
TEST	*v* -ED, -ING, -S to subject to an examination **TESTABLE** *adj*
TESTA	*n* pl. -TAE the hard outer coating of a seed
TESTACY	*n* pl. -CIES the state of being testate
TESTATE	*n* pl. -S a testator
TESTATOR	*n* pl. -S one that makes a will
TESTEE	*n* pl. -S one that is tested
TESTER	*n* pl. -S one that tests
TESTES	pl. of testis
TESTICLE	*n* pl. -S a testis
TESTIER	comparative of testy
TESTIEST	superlative of testy
TESTIFY	*v* -FIED, -FYING, -FIES to make a declaration of truth under oath
TESTILY	*adv* in a testy manner
TESTIS	*n* pl. TESTES a male reproductive gland
TESTON	*n* pl. -S a former French coin
TESTOON	*n* pl. -S teston
TESTUDO	*n* pl. -DINES or -DOS a portable screen used as a shield by the ancient Romans
TESTY	*adj* TESTIER, TESTIEST irritable
TET	*n* pl. -S teth
TETANAL	*adj* pertaining to tetanus
TETANIC	*n* pl. -S a drug capable of causing convulsions
TETANIES	pl. of tetany
TETANISE	*v* -NISED, -NISING, -NISES to tetanize
TETANIZE	*v* -NIZED, -NIZING, -NIZES to affect with convulsions

TETANUS	*n* pl. -ES an infectious disease **TETANOID** *adj*
TETANY	*n* pl. -NIES a condition marked by painful muscular spasms
TETCHED	*adj* crazy
TETCHY	*adj* TETCHIER, TETCHIEST irritable **TETCHILY** *adv*
TETH	*n* pl. -S a Hebrew letter
TETHER	*v* -ED, -ING, -S to fasten to a fixed object with a rope
TETOTUM	*n* pl. -S teetotum
TETRA	*n* pl. -S a tropical fish
TETRACID	*n* pl. -S a type of acid
TETRAD	*n* pl. -S a group of four **TETRADIC** *adj*
TETRAGON	*n* pl. -S a four-sided polygon
TETRAMER	*n* pl. -S a type of polymer
TETRAPOD	*n* pl. -S a four-footed animal
TETRARCH	*n* pl. -S one of four joint rulers
TETRODE	*n* pl. -S a type of electron tube
TETROXID	*n* pl. -S a type of oxide
TETRYL	*n* pl. -S a chemical compound
TETTER	*n* pl. -S a skin disease
TEUCH	*adj* teugh
TEUGH	*adj* tough **TEUGHLY** *adv*
TEW	*v* -ED, -ING, -S to work hard
TEXAS	*n* pl. -ES the uppermost structure on a steamboat
TEXT	*n* pl. -S the main body of a written or printed work
TEXTBOOK	*n* pl. -S a book used in the study of a subject
TEXTILE	*n* pl. -S a woven fabric
TEXTLESS	*adj* having no text
TEXTUAL	*adj* pertaining to a text
TEXTUARY	*n* pl. -ARIES a specialist in the study of the Scriptures
TEXTURAL	*adj* pertaining to the surface characteristics of something
TEXTURE	*v* -TURED, -TURING, -TURES to make by weaving
THACK	*v* -ED, -ING, -S to thatch
THAE	*adj* these; those
THAIRM	*n* pl. -S tharm
THALAMUS	*n* pl. -MI a part of the brain **THALAMIC** *adj*
THALER	*n* pl. -S taler
THALLIUM	*n* pl. -S a metallic element **THALLIC, THALLOUS** *adj*
THALLUS	*n* pl. -LI or -LUSES a plant body without true root, stem, or leaf **THALLOID** *adj*
THAN	*conj* — used to introduce the second element of a comparison
THANAGE	*n* pl. -S the land held by a thane
THANATOS	*n* pl. -ES an instinctual desire for death
THANE	*n* pl. -S a man holding land by military service in Anglo-Saxon England
THANK	*v* -ED, -ING, -S to express gratitude to
THANKER	*n* pl. -S one that thanks
THANKFUL	*adj* -FULLER, -FULLEST feeling gratitude
THARM	*n* pl. -S the belly
THAT	*pron* pl. THOSE the one indicated
THATAWAY	*adv* in that direction
THATCH	*v* -ED, -ING, -ES to cover with thatch (plant stalks or foliage)
THATCHER	*n* pl. -S one that thatches
THATCHY	*adj* THATCHIER, THATCHIEST resembling thatch
THAW	*v* -ED, -ING, -S to melt
THAWER	*n* pl. -S one that thaws
THAWLESS	*adj* never thawing
THE	*definite article* — used to specify or make particular
THEARCHY	*n* pl. -CHIES rule by a god
THEATER	*n* pl. -S a building for dramatic presentations **THEATRIC** *adj*
THEATRE	*n* pl. -S theater
THEBAINE	*n* pl. -S a poisonous alkaloid
THEBE	*n* pl. THEBE a monetary unit of Botswana
THECA	*n* pl. -CAE a protective anatomical covering **THECAL, THECATE** *adj*
THEE	*pron* the objective case of the pronoun thou
THEELIN	*n* pl. -S estrone
THEELOL	*n* pl. -S estriol
THEFT	*n* pl. -S the act of stealing
THEGN	*n* pl. -S thane **THEGNLY** *adj*
THEIN	*n* pl. -S theine
THEINE	*n* pl. -S caffeine

THEIR	*pron* a possessive form of the pronoun they
THEIRS	*pron* a possessive form of the pronoun they
THEISM	*n* pl. -S belief in the existence of a god
THEIST	*n* pl. -S one who believes in the existence of a god **THEISTIC** *adj*
THELITIS	*n* pl. -TISES inflammation of the nipple
THEM	*pron* the objective case of the pronoun they
THEMATIC	*n* pl. -S a stamp collected according to its subject
THEME	*v* THEMED, THEMING, THEMES to plan something according to a central subject
THEN	*n* pl. -S that time
THENAGE	*n* pl. -S thanage
THENAL	*adj* pertaining to the palm of the hand
THENAR	*n* pl. -S the palm of the hand
THENCE	*adv* from that place
THEOCRAT	*n* pl. -S a person who rules as a representative of a god
THEODICY	*n* pl. -CIES a defense of God's goodness in respect to the existence of evil
THEOGONY	*n* pl. -NIES an account of the origin of the gods
THEOLOG	*n* pl. -S a student of theology
THEOLOGY	*n* pl. -GIES the study of religion
THEONOMY	*n* pl. -MIES rule by a god
THEORBO	*n* pl. -BOS a stringed musical instrument
THEOREM	*n* pl. -S a proposition that is demonstrably true or is assumed to be so
THEORIES	pl. of theory
THEORISE	*v* -RISED, -RISING, -RISES to theorize
THEORIST	*n* pl. -S one that theorizes
THEORIZE	*v* -RIZED, -RIZING, -RIZES to form theories
THEORY	*n* pl. -RIES a group of propositions used to explain a class of phenomena
THERAPY	*n* pl. -PIES the treatment of illness or disability
THERE	*n* pl. -S that place
THEREAT	*adv* at that place or time
THEREBY	*adv* by that means
THEREFOR	*adv* for that
THEREIN	*adv* in that place
THEREMIN	*n* pl. -S a musical instrument
THEREOF	*adv* of that
THEREON	*adv* on that
THERETO	*adv* to that
THERIAC	*n* pl. -S molasses
THERIACA	*n* pl. -S theriac
THERM	*n* pl. -S a unit of quantity of heat
THERMAE	*n/pl* hot springs
THERMAL	*n* pl. -S a rising mass of warm air
THERME	*n* pl. -S therm
THERMEL	*n* pl. -S a device for temperature measurement
THERMIC	*adj* pertaining to heat
THERMION	*n* pl. -S an ion emitted by a heated body
THERMITE	*n* pl. -S a metallic mixture that produces intense heat when ignited
THERMOS	*n* pl. -ES a container used to keep liquids either hot or cold
THEROID	*adj* resembling a beast
THEROPOD	*n* pl. -S a carnivorous dinosaur
THESAURI	*n/pl* dictionaries of synonyms and antonyms
THESE	pl. of this
THESIS	*n* pl. THESES a proposition put forward for discussion
THESPIAN	*n* pl. -S an actor or actress
THETA	*n* pl. -S a Greek letter
THETIC	*adj* arbitrary
THETICAL	*adj* thetic
THEURGY	*n* pl. -GIES divine intervention in human affairs **THEURGIC** *adj*
THEW	*n* pl. -S a well-developed muscle
THEWLESS	*adj* weak
THEWY	*adj* THEWIER, THEWIEST brawny
THEY	*pron* the 3d person pl. pronoun in the nominative case
THIAMIN	*n* pl. -S thiamine
THIAMINE	*n* pl. -S a B vitamin
THIAZIDE	*n* pl. -S a drug used to treat high blood pressure
THIAZIN	*n* pl. -S thiazine
THIAZINE	*n* pl. -S a chemical compound

THIAZOL	*n* pl. -S thiazole	**THINNISH**	*adj* somewhat thin
THIAZOLE	*n* pl. -S a chemical compound	**THIO**	*adj* containing sulfur
THICK	*adj* THICKER, THICKEST having relatively great extent from one surface to its opposite	**THIOL**	*n* pl. -S a sulfur compound **THIOLIC** *adj*
THICK	*n* pl. -S the thickest part	**THIONATE**	*n* pl. -S a chemical salt
THICKEN	*v* -ED, -ING, -S to make thick	**THIONIC**	*adj* pertaining to sulfur
THICKET	*n* pl. -S a dense growth of shrubs or small trees **THICKETY** *adj*	**THIONIN**	*n* pl. -S a violet dye
THICKISH	*adj* somewhat thick	**THIONINE**	*n* pl. -S thionin
THICKLY	*adv* in a thick manner	**THIONYL**	*n* pl. -S sulfinyl
THICKSET	*n* pl. -S a thicket	**THIOPHEN**	*n* pl. -S a chemical compound
THIEF	*n* pl. THIEVES one that steals	**THIOTEPA**	*n* pl. -S a chemical compound
THIEVE	*v* THIEVED, THIEVING, THIEVES to steal	**THIOUREA**	*n* pl. -S a chemical compound
		THIR	*pron* these
THIEVERY	*n* pl. -ERIES the act or practice of stealing	**THIRAM**	*n* pl. -S a chemical compound
THIEVES	pl. of thief	**THIRD**	*n* pl. -S one of three equal parts
THIEVING	present participle of thieve	**THIRDLY**	*adv* in the third place
THIEVISH	*adj* given to stealing	**THIRL**	*v* -ED, -ING, -S to thrill
THIGH	*n* pl. -S a part of the leg **THIGHED** *adj*	**THIRLAGE**	*n* pl. -S an obligation requiring feudal tenants to grind grain at a certain mill
THILL	*n* pl. -S a shaft of a vehicle	**THIRST**	*v* -ED, -ING, -S to feel a desire or need to drink
THIMBLE	*n* pl. -S a cap used to protect the fingertip during sewing	**THIRSTER**	*n* pl. -S one that thirsts
THIN	*adj* THINNER, THINNEST having relatively little density or thickness	**THIRSTY**	*adj* THIRSTIER, THIRSTIEST feeling a desire or need to drink
THIN	*v* THINNED, THINNING, THINS to make thin	**THIRTEEN**	*n* pl. -S a number
		THIRTY	*n* pl. -TIES a number
THINCLAD	*n* pl. -S a runner on a track team	**THIS**	*pron* pl. THESE the person or thing just mentioned
THINDOWN	*n* pl. -S a lessening in the number of atomic particles and cosmic rays passing through the earth's atmosphere	**THISTLE**	*n* pl. -S a prickly plant
		THISTLY	*adj* -TLIER, -TLIEST prickly
		THITHER	*adv* in that direction
		THO	*conj* though
THINE	*pron* a possessive form of the pronoun thou	**THOLE**	*v* THOLED, THOLING, THOLES to endure
THING	*n* pl. -S an inanimate object	**THOLEPIN**	*n* pl. -S a pin that serves as an oarlock
THINK	*v* THOUGHT, THINKING, THINKS to formulate in the mind	**THOLOS**	*n* pl. -LOI a circular, underground tomb
THINKER	*n* pl. -S one that thinks		
THINKING	*n* pl. -S an opinion or judgment	**THONG**	*n* pl. -S a narrow strip of leather used for binding **THONGED** *adj*
THINLY	*adv* in a thin manner	**THORAX**	*n* pl. -RACES or -RAXES the part of the body between the neck and the abdomen **THORACAL, THORACIC** *adj*
THINNED	past tense of thin		
THINNER	*n* pl. -S one that thins		
THINNESS	*n* pl. -ES the quality or state of being thin	**THORIA**	*n* pl. -S an oxide of thorium
THINNEST	superlative of thin	**THORIC**	*adj* pertaining to thorium
THINNING	present participle of thin	**THORITE**	*n* pl. -S a thorium ore

THORIUM	*n* pl. -S a metallic element	**THREW**	past tense of throw
THORN	*v* -ED, -ING, -S to prick with a thorn (a sharp, rigid projection on a plant)	**THRICE**	*adv* three times
		THRIFT	*n* pl. -S care and wisdom in the management of one's resources
THORNY	*adj* THORNIER, THORNIEST full of thorns **THORNILY** *adv*	**THRIFTY**	*adj* THRIFTIER, THRIFTIEST displaying thrift
THORO	*adj* thorough	**THRILL**	*v* -ED, -ING, -S to excite greatly
THORON	*n* pl. -S a radioactive isotope of radon	**THRILLER**	*n* pl. -S one that thrills
		THRIP	*n* pl. -S a British coin
THOROUGH	*adj* THOROUGHER, THOROUGHEST complete in all respects	**THRIVE**	*v* THROVE or THRIVED, THRIVEN, THRIVING, THRIVES to grow vigorously
THORP	*n* pl. -S a small village	**THRIVER**	*n* pl. -S one that thrives
THORPE	*n* pl. -S thorp	**THRO**	*prep* through
THOSE	pl. of that	**THROAT**	*v* -ED, -ING, -S to utter in a hoarse voice
THOU	*v* -ED, -ING, -S to address as "thou" (the 2d person sing. pronoun in the nominative case)	**THROATY**	*adj* THROATIER, THROATIEST hoarse
THOUGH	*conj* despite the fact that	**THROB**	*v* THROBBED, THROBBING, THROBS to pulsate
THOUGHT	*n* pl. -S a product of thinking		
THOUSAND	*n* pl. -S a number	**THROBBER**	*n* pl. -S one that throbs
THOWLESS	*adj* listless	**THROE**	*n* pl. -S a violent spasm of pain
THRALDOM	*n* pl. -S servitude	**THROMBIN**	*n* pl. -S an enzyme
THRALL	*v* -ED, -ING, -S to enslave	**THROMBUS**	*n* pl. -BI a clot occluding a blood vessel
THRASH	*v* -ED, -ING, -ES to beat		
THRASHER	*n* pl. -S one that thrashes	**THRONE**	*v* THRONED, THRONING, THRONES to place on a throne (a royal chair)
THRAVE	*n* pl. -S a unit of measure for grain		
THRAW	*v* -ED, -ING, -S to twist	**THRONG**	*v* -ED, -ING, -S to crowd into
THRAWART	*adj* stubborn	**THROSTLE**	*n* pl. -S a songbird
THRAWN	*adj* twisted **THRAWNLY** *adv*	**THROTTLE**	*v* -TLED, -TLING, -TLES to strangle
THREAD	*v* -ED, -ING, -S to pass a thread (a very slender cord) through	**THROUGH**	*prep* by way of
		THROVE	a past tense of thrive
THREADER	*n* pl. -S one that threads	**THROW**	*v* THREW, THROWN, THROWING, THROWS to propel through the air with a movement of the arm
THREADY	*adj* THREADIER, THREADIEST resembling a thread		
THREAP	*v* -ED, -ING, -S to dispute		
THREAPER	*n* pl. -S one that threaps	**THROWER**	*n* pl. -S one that throws
THREAT	*v* -ED, -ING, -S to threaten	**THRU**	*prep* through
THREATEN	*v* -ED, -ING, -S to be a source of danger to	**THRUM**	*v* THRUMMED, THRUMMING, THRUMS to play a stringed instrument idly or monotonously
THREE	*n* pl. -S a number		
THREEP	*v* -ED, -ING, -S to threap	**THRUMMER**	*n* pl. -S one that thrums
THRENODE	*n* pl. -S a threnody	**THRUMMY**	*adj* -MIER, -MIEST shaggy
THRENODY	*n* pl. -DIES a song of lamentation	**THRUPUT**	*n* pl. -S the amount of raw material processed within a given time
THRESH	*v* -ED, -ING, -ES to separate the grain or seeds from a plant mechanically		
		THRUSH	*n* pl. -ES a songbird
THRESHER	*n* pl. -S one that threshes	**THRUST**	*v* -ED, -ING, -S to push forcibly

THRUSTER	*n* pl. -S one that thrusts
THRUSTOR	*n* pl. -S thruster
THRUWAY	*n* pl. -WAYS an express highway
THUD	*v* THUDDED, THUDDING, THUDS to make a dull, heavy sound
THUG	*n* pl. -S a brutal ruffian or assassin
THUGGEE	*n* pl. -S thuggery in India
THUGGERY	*n* pl. -GERIES thuggish behavior
THUGGISH	*adj* characteristic of a thug
THUJA	*n* pl. -S an evergreen tree or shrub
THULIA	*n* pl. -S an oxide of thulium
THULIUM	*n* pl. -S a metallic element
THUMB	*v* -ED, -ING, -S to leaf through with the thumb (the short, thick digit of the human hand)
THUMBKIN	*n* pl. -S a screw that is turned by the thumb and fingers
THUMBNUT	*n* pl. -S a nut that is turned by the thumb and fingers
THUMP	*v* -ED, -ING, -S to strike so as to make a dull, heavy sound
THUMPER	*n* pl. -S one that thumps
THUNDER	*v* -ED, -ING, -S to produce a loud, resounding sound
THUNDERY	*adj* accompanied with thunder
THUNK	*v* -ED, -ING, -S to make a sudden, muffled sound
THURIBLE	*n* pl. -S a censer
THURIFER	*n* pl. -S one who carries a thurible in a religious ceremony
THURL	*n* pl. -S the hip joint in cattle
THUS	*adv* in this manner
THUSLY	*adv* thus
THUYA	*n* pl. -S thuja
THWACK	*v* -ED, -ING, -S to strike with something flat
THWACKER	*n* pl. -S one that thwacks
THWART	*v* -ED, -ING, -S to prevent the accomplishment of
THWARTER	*n* pl. -S one that thwarts
THWARTLY	*adv* athwart
THY	*pron* a possessive form of the pronoun thou
THYME	*n* pl. -S an aromatic herb
THYMEY	*adj* THYMIER, THYMIEST thymy
THYMI	a pl. of thymus
THYMIC	*adj* pertaining to thyme
THYMIER	comparative of thymey and thymy
THYMIEST	superlative of thymey and thymy
THYMINE	*n* pl. -S a chemical compound
THYMOL	*n* pl. -S a chemical compound
THYMOSIN	*n* pl. -S a hormone secreted by the thymus
THYMUS	*n* pl. -MI or -MUSES a glandular structure in the body
THYMY	*adj* THYMIER, THYMIEST abounding in thyme
THYREOID	*adj* pertaining to the thyroid
THYROID	*n* pl. -S an endocrine gland
THYROXIN	*n* pl. -S an amino acid
THYRSE	*n* pl. -S thyrsus
THYRSUS	*n* pl. -SI a type of flower cluster **THYRSOID** *adj*
THYSELF	*pron* yourself
TI	*n* pl. -S the seventh tone of the diatonic musical scale
TIARA	*n* pl. -S a jeweled headpiece worn by women **TIARAED** *adj*
TIBIA	*n* pl. -IAE or -IAS a bone of the leg **TIBIAL** *adj*
TIC	*n* pl. -S an involuntary muscular contraction
TICAL	*n* pl. -S a former Thai unit of weight
TICK	*v* -ED, -ING, -S to make a recurrent clicking sound
TICKER	*n* pl. -S one that ticks
TICKET	*v* -ED, -ING, -S to attach a tag to
TICKING	*n* pl. -S a strong cotton fabric
TICKLE	*v* -LED, -LING, -LES to touch lightly so as to produce a tingling sensation
TICKLER	*n* pl. -S one that tickles
TICKLISH	*adj* sensitive to tickling
TICKSEED	*n* pl. -S a flowering plant
TICKTACK	*v* -ED, -ING, -S to ticktock
TICKTOCK	*v* -ED, -ING, -S to make the ticking sound of a clock
TICTAC	*v* -TACKED, -TACKING, -TACS to ticktack
TICTOC	*v* -TOCKED, -TOCKING, -TOCS to ticktock
TIDAL	*adj* pertaining to the tides **TIDALLY** *adv*
TIDBIT	*n* pl. -S a choice bit of food

TIDDLER   *n* pl. -S a small fish

TIDDLY   *adj* slightly drunk

TIDE   *v* TIDED, TIDING, TIDES to flow like the tide (the rise and fall of the ocean's waters)

TIDELAND   *n* pl. -S land alternately covered and uncovered by the tide

TIDELESS   *adj* lacking a tide

TIDELIKE   *adj* resembling a tide

TIDEMARK   *n* pl. -S a mark showing the highest or lowest point of a tide

TIDERIP   *n* pl. -S a riptide

TIDEWAY   *n* pl. -WAYS a tidal channel

TIDIED   past tense of tidy

TIDIER   *n* pl. -S one that tidies

TIDIES   present 3d person sing. of tidy

TIDIEST   superlative of tidy

TIDILY   *adv* in a tidy manner

TIDINESS   *n* pl. -ES the state of being tidy

TIDING   *n* pl. -S a piece of news

TIDY   *adj* -DIER, -DIEST neat and orderly

TIDY   *v* -DIED, -DYING, -DIES to make tidy

TIDYTIPS   *n* pl. TIDYTIPS an annual herb

TIE   *v* TIED, TYING or TIEING, TIES to fasten with a cord or rope

TIEBACK   *n* pl. -S a loop for holding a curtain back to one side

TIECLASP   *n* pl. -S a clasp for securing a necktie

TIED   past tense of tie

TIELESS   *adj* having no necktie

TIEPIN   *n* pl. -S a pin for securing a necktie

TIER   *v* -ED, -ING, -S to arrange in tiers (rows placed one above another)

TIERCE   *n* pl. -S one of seven canonical daily periods for prayer and devotion

TIERCED   *adj* divided into three equal parts

TIERCEL   *n* pl. -S tercel

TIFF   *v* -ED, -ING, -S to have a petty quarrel

TIFFANY   *n* pl. -NIES a thin, mesh fabric

TIFFIN   *v* -ED, -ING, -S to lunch

TIGER   *n* pl. -S a large feline mammal

TIGEREYE   *n* pl. -S a gemstone

TIGERISH   *adj* resembling a tiger

TIGHT   *adj* TIGHTER, TIGHTEST firmly or closely fixed in place **TIGHTLY** *adv*

TIGHTEN   *v* -ED, -ING, -S to make tight

TIGHTS   *n/pl* a close-fitting garment

TIGHTWAD   *n* pl. -S a miser

TIGLON   *n* pl. -S the offspring of a male tiger and a female lion

TIGON   *n* pl. -S tiglon

TIGRESS   *n* pl. -ES a female tiger

TIGRISH   *adj* tigerish

TIKE   *n* pl. -S tyke

TIKI   *n* pl. -S a wood or stone image of a Polynesian god

TIL   *n* pl. -S the sesame plant

TILAK   *n* pl. -S a mark worn on the forehead by Hindus

TILAPIA   *n* pl. -S an African fish

TILBURY   *n* pl. -BURIES a carriage having two wheels

TILDE   *n* pl. -S a mark placed over a letter to indicate its sound

TILE   *v* TILED, TILING, TILES to cover with tiles (thin slabs of baked clay)

TILEFISH   *n* pl. -ES a marine food fish

TILELIKE   *adj* resembling a tile

TILER   *n* pl. -S one that tiles

TILING   *n* pl. -S a surface of tiles

TILL   *v* -ED, -ING, -S to prepare land for crops by plowing **TILLABLE** *adj*

TILLAGE   *n* pl. -S cultivated land

TILLER   *v* -ED, -ING, -S to put forth stems from a root

TILLITE   *n* pl. -S rock made up of consolidated clay, sand, gravel, and boulders

TILT   *v* -ED, -ING, -S to cause to slant **TILTABLE** *adj*

TILTER   *n* pl. -S one that tilts

TILTH   *n* pl. -S tillage

TILTYARD   *n* pl. -S an area for jousting contests

TIMARAU   *n* pl. -S tamarau

TIMBAL   *n* pl. -S a large drum

TIMBALE   *n* pl. -S a pastry shell shaped like a drum

TIMBER   *v* -ED, -ING, -S to furnish with timber (wood used as a building material)

TIMBRE   *n* pl. -S the quality given to a sound by its overtones **TIMBRAL** *adj*

TIMBREL   *n* pl. -S a percussion instrument

TIME   *v* TIMED, TIMING, TIMES to determine the speed or duration of

TIMECARD   *n* pl. -S a card for recording an employee's times of arrival and departure

TIMELESS   *adj* having no beginning or end

TIMELINE   *n* pl. -S a schedule of events

TIMELY   *adj* -LIER, -LIEST occurring at the right moment

TIMEOUS   *adj* timely

TIMEOUT   *n* pl. -S a brief suspension of activity

TIMER   *n* pl. -S one that times

TIMEWORK   *n* pl. -S work paid for by the hour or by the day

TIMEWORN   *adj* showing the effects of long use or wear

TIMID   *adj* -IDER, -IDEST lacking courage or self-confidence **TIMIDLY** *adv*

TIMIDITY   *n* pl. -TIES the quality of being timid

TIMING   *n* pl. -S the selection of the proper moment for doing something

TIMOLOL   *n* pl. -S a drug used to treat glaucoma

TIMOROUS   *adj* fearful

TIMOTHY   *n* pl. -THIES a European grass

TIMPANO   *n* pl. -NI a kettledrum

TIMPANUM   *n* pl. -NA or -NUMS tympanum

TIN   *v* TINNED, TINNING, TINS to coat with tin (a metallic element)

TINAMOU   *n* pl. -S a South American game bird

TINCAL   *n* pl. -S crude borax

TINCT   *v* -ED, -ING, -S to tinge

TINCTURE   *v* -TURED, -TURING, -TURES to tinge

TINDER   *n* pl. -S readily combustible material **TINDERY** *adj*

TINE   *v* TINED, TINING, TINES to lose

TINEA   *n* pl. -S a fungous skin disease **TINEAL** *adj*

TINEID   *n* pl. -S one of a family of moths

TINFOIL   *n* pl. -S a thin metal sheeting

TINFUL   *n* pl. -S as much as a tin container can hold

TING   *v* -ED, -ING, -S to emit a high-pitched metallic sound

TINGE   *v* TINGED, TINGEING or TINGING, TINGES to apply a trace of color to

TINGLE   *v* -GLED, -GLING, -GLES to cause a prickly, stinging sensation

TINGLER   *n* pl. -S one that tingles

TINGLY   *adj* -GLIER, -GLIEST tingling

TINHORN   *n* pl. -S a showily pretentious person

TINIER   comparative of tiny

TINIEST   superlative of tiny

TINILY   *adv* in a tiny manner

TININESS   *n* pl. -ES the quality of being tiny

TINING   present participle of tine

TINKER   *v* -ED, -ING, -S to repair in an unskilled or experimental manner

TINKERER   *n* pl. -S one that tinkers

TINKLE   *v* -KLED, -KLING, -KLES to make slight, sharp, metallic sounds

TINKLER   *n* pl. -S one that tinkles

TINKLING   *n* pl. -S the sound made by something that tinkles

TINKLY   *adj* -KLIER, -KLIEST producing a tinkling sound

TINLIKE   *adj* resembling tin

TINMAN   *n* pl. -MEN a tinsmith

TINNED   past tense of tin

TINNER   *n* pl. -S a tin miner

TINNIER   comparative of tinny

TINNIEST   superlative of tinny

TINNILY   *adv* in a tinny manner

TINNING   present participle of tin

TINNITUS   *n* pl. -ES a ringing sound in the ears

TINNY   *adj* -NIER, -NIEST of or resembling tin

TINPLATE   *n* pl. -S thin sheet iron coated with tin

TINSEL   *v* -SELED, -SELING, -SELS or -SELLED, -SELLING, -SELS to give a showy or gaudy appearance to

TINSELLY	*adj* cheaply gaudy
TINSMITH	*n* pl. -S one who works with tin
TINSTONE	*n* pl. -S a tin ore
TINT	*v* -ED, -ING, -S to color slightly or delicately
TINTER	*n* pl. -S one that tints
TINTING	*n* pl. -S the process of one that tints
TINTLESS	*adj* lacking color
TINTYPE	*n* pl. -S a kind of photograph
TINWARE	*n* pl. -S articles made of tinplate
TINWORK	*n* pl. -S something made of tin
TINY	*adj* TINIER, TINIEST very small
TIP	*v* TIPPED, TIPPING, TIPS to tilt
TIPCART	*n* pl. -S a type of cart
TIPCAT	*n* pl. -S a game resembling baseball
TIPI	*n* pl. -S tepee
TIPLESS	*adj* having no point or extremity
TIPOFF	*n* pl. -S a hint or warning
TIPPABLE	*adj* capable of being tipped
TIPPED	past tense of tip
TIPPER	*n* pl. -S one that tips
TIPPET	*n* pl. -S a covering for the shoulders
TIPPIER	comparative of tippy
TIPPIEST	superlative of tippy
TIPPING	present participle of tip
TIPPLE	*v* -PLED, -PLING, -PLES to drink alcoholic beverages
TIPPLER	*n* pl. -S one that tipples
TIPPY	*adj* -PIER, -PIEST unsteady
TIPPYTOE	*v* -TOED, -TOEING, -TOES to tiptoe
TIPSIER	comparative of tipsy
TIPSIEST	superlative of tipsy
TIPSILY	*adv* in a tipsy manner
TIPSTAFF	*n* pl. -STAFFS or -STAVES an attendant in a court of law
TIPSTER	*n* pl. -S one that sells information to gamblers
TIPSTOCK	*n* pl. -S a part of a gun
TIPSY	*adj* -SIER, -SIEST slightly drunk
TIPTOE	*v* -TOED, -TOEING, -TOES to walk on the tips of one's toes
TIPTOP	*n* pl. -S the highest point
TIRADE	*n* pl. -S a long, vehement speech
TIRAMISU	*n* pl. -S a dessert made with ladyfingers, mascarpone, chocolate, and espresso
TIRE	*v* TIRED, TIRING, TIRES to grow tired
TIRED	*adj* TIREDER, TIREDEST sapped of strength **TIREDLY** *adv*
TIRELESS	*adj* seemingly incapable of tiring
TIRESOME	*adj* tedious
TIRING	present participle of tire
TIRL	*v* -ED, -ING, -S to make a vibrating sound
TIRO	*n* pl. -ROS tyro
TIRRIVEE	*n* pl. -S a tantrum
TISANE	*n* pl. -S a ptisan
TISSUAL	*adj* pertaining to tissue
TISSUE	*v* -SUED, -SUING, -SUES to weave into tissue (a fine sheer fabric)
TISSUEY	*adj* resembling tissue
TISSULAR	*adj* affecting an organism's tissue (structural material)
TIT	*n* pl. -S a small bird
TITAN	*n* pl. -S a person of great size
TITANATE	*n* pl. -S a chemical salt
TITANESS	*n* pl. -ES a female titan
TITANIA	*n* pl. -S a mineral
TITANIC	*adj* of great size
TITANISM	*n* pl. -S revolt against social conventions
TITANITE	*n* pl. -S a mineral
TITANIUM	*n* pl. -S a metallic element
TITANOUS	*adj* pertaining to titanium
TITBIT	*n* pl. -S tidbit
TITER	*n* pl. -S the strength of a chemical solution
TITFER	*n* pl. -S a hat
TITHABLE	*adj* subject to the payment of tithes
TITHE	*v* TITHED, TITHING, TITHES to pay a tithe (a small tax)
TITHER	*n* pl. -S one that tithes
TITHING	*n* pl. -S the act of levying tithes
TITHONIA	*n* pl. -S a tall herb
TITI	*n* pl. -S an evergreen shrub or tree
TITIAN	*n* pl. -S a reddish brown color
TITIVATE	*v* -VATED, -VATING, -VATES to dress smartly

TITLARK	*n* pl. -S a songbird
TITLE	*v* -TLED, -TLING, -TLES to furnish with a title (a distinctive appellation)
TITLIST	*n* pl. -S a sports champion
TITMAN	*n* pl. -MEN the smallest of a litter of pigs
TITMOUSE	*n* pl. -MICE a small bird
TITRABLE	*adj* capable of being titrated
TITRANT	*n* pl. -S the reagent used in titration
TITRATE	*v* -TRATED, -TRATING, -TRATES to determine the strength of a solution by adding a reagent until a desired reaction occurs
TITRATOR	*n* pl. -S one that titrates
TITRE	*n* pl. -S titer
TITTER	*v* -ED, -ING, -S to utter a restrained, nervous laugh
TITTERER	*n* pl. -S one that titters
TITTIE	*n* pl. -S a sister
TITTIES	pl. of titty
TITTLE	*n* pl. -S a very small mark in writing or printing
TITTUP	*v* -TUPED, -TUPING, -TUPS or -TUPPED, -TUPPING, -TUPS to move in a lively manner
TITTUPPY	*adj* shaky; unsteady
TITTY	*n* pl. -TIES a teat
TITULAR	*n* pl. -S one who holds a title
TITULARY	*n* pl. -LARIES a titular
TIVY	*adv* with great speed
TIZZY	*n* pl. -ZIES a state of nervous confusion
TMESIS	*n* pl. TMESES the separation of the parts of a compound word by an intervening word or words
TO	*prep* in the direction of
TOAD	*n* pl. -S a tailless, jumping amphibian
TOADFISH	*n* pl. -ES a marine fish
TOADFLAX	*n* pl. -ES a perennial herb
TOADIED	past tense of toady
TOADIES	present 3d person sing. of toady
TOADISH	*adj* resembling a toad
TOADLESS	*adj* having no toads
TOADLIKE	*adj* resembling a toad
TOADY	*v* TOADIED, TOADYING, TOADIES to engage in servile flattering
TOADYISH	*adj* characteristic of one that toadies
TOADYISM	*n* pl. -S toadyish behavior
TOAST	*v* -ED, -ING, -S to brown by exposure to heat
TOASTER	*n* pl. -S a device for toasting
TOASTY	*adj* TOASTIER, TOASTIEST comfortably warm
TOBACCO	*n* pl. -COS or -COES an annual herb cultivated for its leaves
TOBOGGAN	*v* -ED, -ING, -S to ride on a long, narrow sled
TOBY	*n* pl. -BIES a type of drinking mug
TOCCATA	*n* pl. -TAS or -TE a musical composition usually for an organ
TOCHER	*v* -ED, -ING, -S to give a dowry to
TOCOLOGY	*n* pl. -GIES the branch of medicine dealing with childbirth
TOCSIN	*n* pl. -S an alarm sounded on a bell
TOD	*n* pl. -S a British unit of weight
TODAY	*n* pl. -DAYS the present day
TODDIES	pl. of toddy
TODDLE	*v* -DLED, -DLING, -DLES to walk unsteadily
TODDLER	*n* pl. -S one that toddles
TODDY	*n* pl. -DIES an alcoholic beverage
TODY	*n* pl. -DIES a West Indian bird
TOE	*v* TOED, TOEING, TOES to touch with the toe (one of the terminal members of the foot)
TOEA	*n* pl. TOEA a monetary unit of Papua New Guinea
TOECAP	*n* pl. -S a covering for the tip of a shoe or boot
TOEHOLD	*n* pl. -S a space that supports the toes in climbing
TOELESS	*adj* having no toes
TOELIKE	*adj* resembling a toe
TOENAIL	*v* -ED, -ING, -S to fasten with obliquely driven nails
TOEPIECE	*n* pl. -S a piece of a shoe designed to cover the toes
TOEPLATE	*n* pl. -S a metal tab attached to the tip of a shoe

TOESHOE *n* pl. -S a dance slipper without a heel

TOFF *n* pl. -S a dandy

TOFFEE *n* pl. -S a chewy candy

TOFFY *n* pl. -FIES toffee

TOFT *n* pl. -S a hillock

TOFU *n* pl. -S a soft Oriental cheese made from soybean milk

TOG *v* TOGGED, TOGGING, TOGS to clothe

TOGA *n* pl. -GAS or -GAE an outer garment worn in ancient Rome **TOGAED** *adj*

TOGATE *adj* pertaining to ancient Rome

TOGATED *adj* wearing a toga

TOGETHER *adv* into a union or relationship

TOGGED past tense of tog

TOGGERY *n* pl. -GERIES clothing

TOGGING present participle of tog

TOGGLE *v* -GLED, -GLING, -GLES to fasten with a type of pin or short rod

TOGGLER *n* pl. -S one that toggles

TOGUE *n* pl. -S a freshwater fish

TOIL *v* -ED, -ING, -S to work strenuously

TOILE *n* pl. -S a sheer linen fabric

TOILER *n* pl. -S one that toils

TOILET *v* -ED, -ING, -S to dress and groom oneself

TOILETRY *n* pl. -TRIES an article used in dressing and grooming oneself

TOILETTE *n* pl. -S the act of dressing and grooming oneself

TOILFUL *adj* toilsome

TOILSOME *adj* demanding much exertion

TOILWORN *adj* worn by toil

TOIT *v* -ED, -ING, -S to saunter

TOKAMAK *n* pl. -S a doughnut-shaped nuclear reactor

TOKAY *n* pl. -KAYS a Malaysian gecko

TOKE *v* TOKED, TOKING, TOKES to take a puff on a marijuana cigarette

TOKEN *v* -ED, -ING, -S to serve as a sign of

TOKENISM *n* pl. -S the policy of making only a superficial effort

TOKER *n* pl. -S one that tokes

TOKING present participle of toke

TOKOLOGY *n* pl. -GIES tocology

TOKOMAK *n* pl. -S tokamak

TOKONOMA *n* pl. -S a small alcove in a Japanese house

TOLA *n* pl. -S a unit of weight used in India

TOLAN *n* pl. -S a chemical compound

TOLANE *n* pl. -S tolan

TOLBOOTH *n* pl. -S a prison

TOLD past tense of tell

TOLE *v* TOLED, TOLING, TOLES to allure

TOLEDO *n* pl. -DOS a finely tempered sword

TOLERANT *adj* inclined to tolerate

TOLERATE *v* -ATED, -ATING, -ATES to allow without active opposition

TOLIDIN *n* pl. -S tolidine

TOLIDINE *n* pl. -S a chemical compound

TOLING present participle of tole

TOLL *v* -ED, -ING, -S to collect or impose a toll (a fixed charge for a service or privilege)

TOLLAGE *n* pl. -S a toll

TOLLBAR *n* pl. -S a tollgate

TOLLER *n* pl. -S a collector of tolls

TOLLGATE *n* pl. -S a gate where a toll is collected

TOLLMAN *n* pl. -MEN a toller

TOLLWAY *n* pl. -WAYS a road on which tolls are collected

TOLU *n* pl. -S a fragrant resin

TOLUATE *n* pl. -S a chemical salt

TOLUENE *n* pl. -S a flammable liquid

TOLUIC *adj* pertaining to any of four isomeric acids derived from toluene

TOLUID *n* pl. -S toluide

TOLUIDE *n* pl. -S an amide

TOLUIDIN *n* pl. -S an amine

TOLUOL *n* pl. -S toluene

TOLUOLE *n* pl. -S toluol

TOLUYL *n* pl. -S a univalent chemical radical

TOLYL *n* pl. -S a univalent chemical radical

TOM *n* pl. -S the male of various animals

TOMAHAWK *v* -ED, -ING, -S to strike with a light ax

TOMALLEY *n* pl. -LEYS the liver of a lobster

TOMAN *n* pl. -S a coin of Iran

TOMATO *n* pl. -TOES the fleshy, edible fruit of a perennial plant **TOMATOEY** *adj*

TOMB *v* -ED, -ING, -S to place in a tomb (a burial vault or chamber)

TOMBAC *n* pl. -S an alloy of copper and zinc

TOMBACK *n* pl. -S tombac

TOMBAK *n* pl. -S tombac

TOMBAL *adj* pertaining to a tomb

TOMBLESS *adj* having no tomb

TOMBLIKE *adj* resembling a tomb

TOMBOLA *n* pl. -S a gambling game that is a type of lottery

TOMBOLO *n* pl. -LOS a sandbar connecting an island to the mainland

TOMBOY *n* pl. -BOYS a girl who prefers boyish activities

TOMCAT *v* -CATTED, -CATTING, -CATS to engage in sexually promiscuous behavior — used of a male

TOMCOD *n* pl. -S a marine fish

TOME *n* pl. -S a large book

TOMENTUM *n* pl. -TA a network of small blood vessels

TOMFOOL *n* pl. -S a foolish person

TOMMY *n* pl. -MIES a loaf of bread

TOMMYROT *n* pl. -S nonsense

TOMOGRAM *n* pl. -S a photograph made with X rays

TOMORROW *n* pl. -S the day following today

TOMPION *n* pl. -S tampion

TOMTIT *n* pl. -S any of various small active birds

TON *n* pl. -S a unit of weight

TONAL *adj* pertaining to tone **TONALLY** *adv*

TONALITY *n* pl. -TIES a system of tones

TONDO *n* pl. -DI or -DOS a circular painting

TONE *v* TONED, TONING, TONES to give a particular tone (a sound of definite pitch and vibration) to

TONEARM *n* pl. -S the pivoted part of a record player that holds the needle

TONELESS *adj* lacking in tone

TONEME *n* pl. -S a tonal unit of speech **TONEMIC** *adj*

TONER *n* pl. -S one that tones

TONETICS *n/pl* the phonetic study of tone in language **TONETIC** *adj*

TONETTE *n* pl. -S a simple flute

TONEY *adj* TONIER, TONIEST tony

TONG *v* -ED, -ING, -S to lift with a type of grasping device

TONGA *n* pl. -S a light cart used in India

TONGER *n* pl. -S one that tongs

TONGMAN *n* pl. -MEN a member of a Chinese secret society

TONGUE *v* TONGUED, TONGUING, TONGUES to touch with the tongue (an organ of the mouth)

TONGUING *n* pl. -S the use of the tongue in articulating notes on a wind instrument

TONIC *n* pl. -S something that invigorates or refreshes

TONICITY *n* pl. -TIES normal, healthy bodily condition

TONIER comparative of tony

TONIEST superlative of tony

TONIGHT *n* pl. -S the present night

TONING present participle of tone

TONISH *adj* stylish **TONISHLY** *adv*

TONLET *n* pl. -S a skirt of plate armor

TONNAGE *n* pl. -S total weight in tons

TONNE *n* pl. -S a unit of weight

TONNEAU *n* pl. -NEAUS or -NEAUX the rear seating compartment of an automobile

TONNER *n* pl. -S an object having a specified tonnage

TONNISH *adj* tonish

TONSIL *n* pl. -S a lymphoid organ **TONSILAR** *adj*

TONSURE *v* -SURED, -SURING, -SURES to shave the head of

TONTINE *n* pl. -S a form of collective life insurance

TONUS *n* pl. -ES a normal state of tension in muscle tissue

TONY *adj* TONIER, TONIEST stylish

TOO   *adv* in addition

TOOK   past tense of take

TOOL   *v* -ED, -ING, -S to form or finish with a tool (an implement used in manual work)

TOOLBOX   *n* pl. -ES a box for tools

TOOLER   *n* pl. -S one that tools

TOOLHEAD   *n* pl. -S a part of a machine

TOOLING   *n* pl. -S ornamentation done with tools

TOOLLESS   *adj* having no tools

TOOLROOM   *n* pl. -S a room where tools are stored

TOOLSHED   *n* pl. -S a building where tools are stored

TOOM   *adj* empty

TOON   *n* pl. -S an East Indian tree

TOOT   *v* -ED, -ING, -S to sound a horn or whistle in short blasts

TOOTER   *n* pl. -S one that toots

TOOTH   *n* pl. TEETH one of the hard structures attached in a row to each jaw

TOOTH   *v* -ED, -ING, -S to furnish with toothlike projections

TOOTHY   *adj* TOOTHIER, TOOTHIEST having or showing prominent teeth **TOOTHILY** *adv*

TOOTLE   *v* -TLED, -TLING, -TLES to toot softly or repeatedly

TOOTLER   *n* pl. -S one that tootles

TOOTS   *n* pl. -ES a woman or girl — usually used as a form of address

TOOTSIE   *n* pl. -S tootsy

TOOTSY   *n* pl. -SIES a foot

TOP   *v* TOPPED, TOPPING, TOPS to cut off the top (the highest part, point, or surface) of

TOPAZ   *n* pl. -ES a mineral **TOPAZINE** *adj*

TOPCOAT   *n* pl. -S a lightweight overcoat

TOPCROSS   *n* pl. -ES a cross between a purebred male and inferior female stock

TOPE   *v* TOPED, TOPING, TOPES to drink liquor to excess

TOPEE   *n* pl. -S topi

TOPER   *n* pl. -S one that topes

TOPFUL   *adj* topfull

TOPFULL   *adj* full to the top

TOPH   *n* pl. -S tufa

TOPHE   *n* pl. -S tufa

TOPHUS   *n* pl. -PHI a deposit of urates in the tissue around a joint

TOPI   *n* pl. -S a sun helmet

TOPIARY   *n* pl. -ARIES the art of trimming shrubs into shapes

TOPIC   *n* pl. -S a subject of discourse **TOPICAL** *adj*

TOPING   present participle of tope

TOPKICK   *n* pl. -S a first sergeant

TOPKNOT   *n* pl. -S an ornament for the hair

TOPLESS   *adj* having no top

TOPLINE   *n* pl. -S the outline of the top of an animal's body

TOPLOFTY   *adj* -LOFTIER, -LOFTIEST haughty

TOPMAST   *n* pl. -S a mast of a ship

TOPMOST   *adj* highest

TOPNOTCH   *adj* excellent

TOPOI   pl. of topos

TOPOLOGY   *n* pl. -GIES a branch of mathematics

TOPONYM   *n* pl. -S the name of a place

TOPONYMY   *n* pl. -MIES the study of toponyms

TOPOS   *n* pl. -POI a stock rhetorical theme

TOPOTYPE   *n* pl. -S a specimen selected from a locality typical of a species

TOPPED   past tense of top

TOPPER   *n* pl. -S one that tops

TOPPING   *n* pl. -S something that forms a top

TOPPLE   *v* -PLED, -PLING, -PLES to fall forward

TOPSAIL   *n* pl. -S a sail of a ship

TOPSIDE   *n* pl. -S the upper portion of a ship

TOPSIDER   *n* pl. -S one who is at the highest level of authority

TOPSOIL   *v* -ED, -ING, -S to remove the surface layer of soil from

TOPSPIN   *n* pl. -S a forward spin imparted to a ball

TOPSTONE   *n* pl. -S the stone at the top of a structure

TOPWORK   *v* -ED, -ING, -S to graft scions of another variety of plant on the main branches of

TOQUE   *n* pl. -S a close-fitting woman's hat

TOQUET   *n* pl. -S toque

TOR   *n* pl. -S a high, craggy hill

TORA   *n* pl. -S torah

TORAH   *n* pl. -RAHS, -ROTH, or -ROT a law or precept

TORC   *n* pl. -S a metal collar or necklace

TORCH   *v* -ED, -ING, -ES to set on fire

TORCHERE   *n* pl. -S a type of electric lamp

TORCHIER   *n* pl. -S torchere

TORCHON   *n* pl. -S a coarse lace

TORCHY   *adj* TORCHIER, TORCHIEST characteristic of a torch song

TORE   *n* pl. -S a torus

TOREADOR   *n* pl. -S a bullfighter

TORERO   *n* pl. -ROS a bullfighter

TOREUTIC   *adj* pertaining to a type of metalwork

TORI   pl. of torus

TORIC   *adj* pertaining to a torus

TORIES   pl. of tory

TORII   *n* pl. TORII the gateway of a Japanese temple

TORMENT   *v* -ED, -ING, -S to inflict with great bodily or mental suffering

TORN   past participle of tear

TORNADO   *n* pl. -DOES or -DOS a violent windstorm **TORNADIC** *adj*

TORNILLO   *n* pl. -LOS a flowering shrub

TORO   *n* pl. -ROS a bull

TOROID   *n* pl. -S a type of geometric surface **TOROIDAL** *adj*

TOROSE   *adj* cylindrical and swollen at intervals

TOROSITY   *n* pl. -TIES the quality or state of being torose

TOROT   a pl. of torah

TOROTH   a pl. of torah

TOROUS   *adj* torose

TORPEDO   *v* -ED, -ING, -ES or -S to damage or sink with an underwater missile

TORPID   *n* pl. -S a racing boat

TORPIDLY   *adv* in a sluggish manner

TORPOR   *n* pl. -S mental or physical inactivity

TORQUATE   *adj* having a torques

TORQUE   *v* TORQUED, TORQUING, TORQUES to cause to twist

TORQUER   *n* pl. -S one that torques

TORQUES   *n* pl. -QUESES a band of feathers, hair, or coloration around the neck

TORQUING   present participle of torque

TORR   *n* pl. TORR a unit of pressure

TORREFY   *v* -FIED, -FYING, -FIES to subject to intense heat

TORRENT   *n* pl. -S a rapid stream of water

TORRID   *adj* -RIDER, -RIDEST extremely hot **TORRIDLY** *adv*

TORRIFY   *v* -FIED, -FYING, -FIES to torrefy

TORSADE   *n* pl. -S a twisted cord

TORSE   *n* pl. -S a wreath of twisted silks

TORSI   a pl. of torso

TORSION   *n* pl. -S the act of twisting

TORSK   *n* pl. -S a marine food fish

TORSO   *n* pl. -SI or -SOS the trunk of the human body

TORT   *n* pl. -S a civil wrong

TORTE   *n* pl. TORTEN or TORTES a rich cake

TORTILE   *adj* twisted; coiled

TORTILLA   *n* pl. -S a round, flat cake of unleavened cornmeal

TORTIOUS   *adj* of the nature of a tort

TORTOISE   *n* pl. -S any of an order of reptiles having the body enclosed in a bony shell

TORTONI   *n* pl. -S a type of ice cream

TORTRIX   *n* pl. -ES a small moth

TORTUOUS   *adj* marked by repeated turns or bends

TORTURE   *v* -TURED, -TURING, -TURES to subject to severe physical pain

TORTURER   *n* pl. -S one that tortures

TORULA   *n* pl. -LAE or -LAS a type of fungus

TORUS   *n* pl. -RI a large convex molding

TORY   *n* pl. -RIES a political conservative

TOSH   *n* pl. -ES nonsense

TOSS   *v* TOSSED or TOST, TOSSING, TOSSES to throw lightly

TOSSER   *n* pl. -S one that tosses

TOSSPOT   *n* pl. -S a drunkard

TOSSUP *n* pl. -S an even choice or chance

TOST a past tense of toss

TOSTADA *n* pl. -S a tortilla fried in deep fat

TOSTADO *n* pl. -DOS tostada

TOT *v* TOTTED, TOTTING, TOTS to total

TOTABLE *adj* capable of being toted

TOTAL *v* -TALED, -TALING, -TALS or -TALLED, -TALLING, -TALS to ascertain the entire amount of

TOTALISE *v* -ISED, -ISING, -ISES to totalize

TOTALISM *n* pl. -S centralized control by an autocratic authority

TOTALIST *n* pl. -S one who tends to regard things as a unified whole

TOTALITY *n* pl. -TIES the quality or state of being complete

TOTALIZE *v* -IZED, -IZING, -IZES to make complete

TOTALLED a past tense of total

TOTALLING a present participle of total

TOTALLY *adv* completely

TOTE *v* TOTED, TOTING, TOTES to carry by hand

TOTEM *n* pl. -S a natural object serving as the emblem of a family or clan **TOTEMIC** *adj*

TOTEMISM *n* pl. -S a system of tribal division according to totems

TOTEMIST *n* pl. -S a specialist in totemism

TOTEMITE *n* pl. -S a totemist

TOTER *n* pl. -S one that totes

TOTHER *pron* the other

TOTING present participle of tote

TOTTED past tense of tot

TOTTER *v* -ED, -ING, -S to walk unsteadily

TOTTERER *n* pl. -S one that totters

TOTTERY *adj* shaky

TOTTING present participle of tot

TOUCAN *n* pl. -S a tropical bird

TOUCH *v* -ED, -ING, -ES to be in or come into contact with

TOUCHE *interj* — used to acknowledge a hit in fencing

TOUCHER *n* pl. -S one that touches

TOUCHUP *n* pl. -S an act of finishing by adding minor improvements

TOUCHY *adj* TOUCHIER, TOUCHIEST overly sensitive **TOUCHILY** *adv*

TOUGH *adj* TOUGHER, TOUGHEST strong and resilient

TOUGH *v* -ED, -ING, -S to endure hardship

TOUGHEN *v* -ED, -ING, -S to make tough

TOUGHIE *n* pl. -S a tough

TOUGHIES pl. of toughy

TOUGHISH *adj* somewhat tough

TOUGHLY *adv* in a tough manner

TOUGHY *n* pl. TOUGHIES toughie

TOUPEE *n* pl. -S a wig worn to cover a bald spot

TOUR *v* -ED, -ING, -S to travel from place to place

TOURACO *n* pl. -COS an African bird

TOURER *n* pl. -S a large, open automobile

TOURING *n* pl. -S cross-country skiing for pleasure

TOURISM *n* pl. -S the practice of touring for pleasure

TOURIST *n* pl. -S one who tours for pleasure **TOURISTY** *adj*

TOURNEY *v* -ED, -ING, -S to compete in a tournament

TOUSE *v* TOUSED, TOUSING, TOUSES to tousle

TOUSLE *v* -SLED, -SLING, -SLES to dishevel

TOUT *v* -ED, -ING, -S to solicit brazenly

TOUTER *n* pl. -S one that touts

TOUZLE *v* -ZLED, -ZLING, -ZLES to tousle

TOVARICH *n* pl. -ES comrade

TOVARISH *n* pl. -ES tovarich

TOW *v* -ED, -ING, -S to pull by means of a rope or chain

TOWAGE *n* pl. -S the price paid for towing

TOWARD *prep* in the direction of

TOWARDLY *adj* favorable

TOWARDS *prep* toward

TOWAWAY *n* pl. -AWAYS the act of towing away a vehicle

TOWBOAT *n* pl. -S a tugboat

TOWEL *v* -ELED, -ELING, -ELS or -ELLED, -ELLING, -ELS to wipe with a towel (an absorbent cloth)

TOWELING *n* pl. -S material used for towels

TOWER   *v* -ED, -ING, -S to rise to a great height

TOWERY   *adj* -ERIER, -ERIEST very tall

TOWHEAD   *n* pl. -S a head of light blond hair

TOWHEE   *n* pl. -S a common finch

TOWIE   *n* pl. -S a form of contract bridge for three players

TOWLINE   *n* pl. -S a line used in towing

TOWMOND   *n* pl. -S a year

TOWMONT   *n* pl. -S towmond

TOWN   *n* pl. -S a center of population smaller than a city

TOWNEE   *n* pl. -S a townsman

TOWNFOLK   *n/pl* the inhabitants of a town

TOWNHOME   *n* pl. -S one of a series of contiguous houses of two or three stories

TOWNIE   *n* pl. -S a nonstudent who lives in a college town

TOWNIES   pl. of towny

TOWNISH   *adj* characteristic of a town

TOWNLESS   *adj* having no towns

TOWNLET   *n* pl. -S a small town

TOWNSHIP   *n* pl. -S an administrative division of a county

TOWNSMAN   *n* pl. -MEN a resident of a town

TOWNWEAR   *n* pl. -S apparel that is suitable for wear in the city

TOWNY   *n* pl. TOWNIES townie

TOWPATH   *n* pl. -S a path along a river that is used by animals towing boats

TOWROPE   *n* pl. -S a rope used in towing

TOWY   *adj* resembling coarse hemp or flax fiber

TOXAEMIA   *n* pl. -S toxemia **TOXAEMIC** *adj*

TOXEMIA   *n* pl. -S the condition of having toxins in the blood **TOXEMIC** *adj*

TOXIC   *n* pl. -S a poisonous substance

TOXICAL   *adj* toxic

TOXICANT   *n* pl. -S a poisonous substance

TOXICITY   *n* pl. -TIES the quality of being poisonous

TOXIN   *n* pl. -S a poisonous substance

TOXINE   *n* pl. -S toxin

TOXOID   *n* pl. -S a type of toxin

TOY   *v* -ED, -ING, -S to amuse oneself as if with a toy (a child's plaything)

TOYER   *n* pl. -S one that toys

TOYISH   *adj* frivolous

TOYLESS   *adj* having no toy

TOYLIKE   *adj* resembling a toy

TOYO   *n* pl. -YOS a smooth straw used in making hats

TOYON   *n* pl. -S an ornamental evergreen shrub

TOYSHOP   *n* pl. -S a shop where toys are sold

TRABEATE   *adj* constructed with horizontal beams

TRACE   *v* TRACED, TRACING, TRACES to follow the course of

TRACER   *n* pl. -S one that traces

TRACERY   *n* pl. -ERIES ornamental work of interlaced lines

TRACHEA   *n* pl. -CHEAE or -CHEAS the passage for conveying air to the lungs **TRACHEAL** *adj*

TRACHEID   *n* pl. -S a long, tubular plant cell

TRACHLE   *v* -LED, -LING, -LES to draggle

TRACHOMA   *n* pl. -S a disease of the eye

TRACHYTE   *n* pl. -S a light-colored igneous rock

TRACING   *n* pl. -S something that is traced

TRACK   *v* -ED, -ING, -S to follow the marks left by an animal, a person, or a vehicle

TRACKAGE   *n* pl. -S the track system of a railroad

TRACKER   *n* pl. -S one that tracks

TRACKING   *n* pl. -S the placement of students within a curriculum

TRACKMAN   *n* pl. -MEN a railroad worker

TRACKWAY   *n* pl. -WAYS a trodden path

TRACT   *n* pl. -S an expanse of land

TRACTATE   *n* pl. -S a treatise

TRACTILE   *adj* capable of being drawn out in length

TRACTION   *n* pl. -S the act of pulling or drawing over a surface **TRACTIVE** *adj*

TRACTOR   *n* pl. -S a motor vehicle used in farming

TRAD   *adj* traditional

TRADE   *v* TRADED, TRADING, TRADES to give in exchange for another commodity **TRADABLE** *adj*

TRADEOFF   *n* pl. -S a giving up of one thing in return for another

TRADER   *n* pl. -S one that trades

TRADITOR   *n* pl. -ES a traitor among the early Christians

TRADUCE   *v* -DUCED, -DUCING, -DUCES to defame

TRADUCER   *n* pl. -S one that traduces

TRAFFIC   *v* -FICKED, -FICKING, -FICS to engage in buying and selling

TRAGEDY   *n* pl. -DIES a disastrous event

TRAGI   pl. of tragus

TRAGIC   *n* pl. -S the element of a drama that produces tragedy

TRAGICAL   *adj* of the nature of a tragedy

TRAGOPAN   *n* pl. -S an Asian pheasant

TRAGUS   *n* pl. -GI a part of the external opening of the ear

TRAIK   *v* -ED, -ING, -S to trudge

TRAIL   *v* -ED, -ING, -S to drag along a surface

TRAILER   *v* -ED, -ING, -S to transport by means of a trailer (a vehicle drawn by another)

TRAIN   *v* -ED, -ING, -S to instruct systematically

TRAINEE   *n* pl. -S a person receiving training

TRAINER   *n* pl. -S one that trains

TRAINFUL   *n* pl. -S as much as a railroad train can hold

TRAINING   *n* pl. -S systematic instruction

TRAINMAN   *n* pl. -MEN a railroad employee

TRAINWAY   *n* pl. -WAYS a railway

TRAIPSE   *v* TRAIPSED, TRAIPSING, TRAIPSES to walk about in an idle or aimless manner

TRAIT   *n* pl. -S a distinguishing characteristic

TRAITOR   *n* pl. -S one who betrays another

TRAJECT   *v* -ED, -ING, -S to transmit

TRAM   *v* TRAMMED, TRAMMING, TRAMS to convey in a tramcar

TRAMCAR   *n* pl. -S a streetcar

TRAMEL   *v* -ELED, -ELING, -ELS or -ELLED, -ELLING, -ELS to trammel

TRAMELL   *v* -ED, -ING, -S to trammel

TRAMLESS   *adj* having no tramcar

TRAMLINE   *n* pl. -S a streetcar line

TRAMMED   past tense of tram

TRAMMEL   *v* -MELED, -MELING, -MELS or -MELLED, -MELLING, -MELS to hinder

TRAMMING   present participle of tram

TRAMP   *v* -ED, -ING, -S to walk with a firm, heavy step

TRAMPER   *n* pl. -S one that tramps

TRAMPISH   *adj* resembling a vagabond

TRAMPLE   *v* -PLED, -PLING, -PLES to tread on heavily

TRAMPLER   *n* pl. -S one that tramples

TRAMROAD   *n* pl. -S a railway in a mine

TRAMWAY   *n* pl. -WAYS a tramline

TRANCE   *v* TRANCED, TRANCING, TRANCES to put into a trance (a semiconscious state)

TRANCHE   *n* pl. -S a portion

TRANGAM   *n* pl. -S a gewgaw

TRANK   *n* pl. -S a drug that tranquilizes

TRANQ   *n* pl. -S trank

TRANQUIL   *adj* -QUILER, -QUILEST or -QUILLER, -QUILLEST free from disturbance

TRANS   *adj* characterized by the arrangement of different atoms on opposite sides of the molecule

TRANSACT   *v* -ED, -ING, -S to carry out

TRANSECT   *v* -ED, -ING, -S to cut across

TRANSEPT   *n* pl. -S a major transverse part of the body of a church

TRANSFER   *v* -FERRED, -FERRING, -FERS to convey from one source to another

TRANSFIX   *v* -FIXED or -FIXT, -FIXING, -FIXES to impale

TRANSHIP   *v* -SHIPPED, -SHIPPING, -SHIPS to transfer from one conveyance to another

TRANSIT   *v* -ED, -ING, -S to pass across or through

TRANSMIT   *v* -MITTED, -MITTING, -MITS to send from one place or person to another

TRANSOM   *n* pl. -S a small window above a door or another window

TRANSUDE   *v* -SUDED, -SUDING, -SUDES to pass through a membrane

TRAP   *v* TRAPPED or TRAPT, TRAPPING, TRAPS to catch in a trap (a device for capturing and holding animals)

TRAPAN   *v* -PANNED, -PANNING, -PANS to trepan

TRAPBALL *n* pl. -S a type of ball game

TRAPDOOR *n* pl. -S a lifting or sliding door covering an opening

TRAPES *v* -ED, -ING, -ES to traipse

TRAPEZE *n* pl. -S a gymnastic apparatus

TRAPEZIA *n/pl* four-sided polygons having no parallel sides

TRAPLIKE *adj* resembling a trap

TRAPLINE *n* pl. -S a series of traps

TRAPNEST *v* -ED, -ING, -S to determine the productivity of hens with a type of nest

TRAPPEAN *adj* pertaining to traprock

TRAPPED a past tense of trap

TRAPPER *n* pl. -S one that traps

TRAPPING *n* pl. -S a covering for a horse

TRAPPOSE *adj* trappean

TRAPPOUS *adj* trappean

TRAPROCK *n* pl. -S an igneous rock

TRAPT a past tense of trap

TRAPUNTO *n* pl. -TOS a decorative quilted design

TRASH *v* -ED, -ING, -ES to free from trash (worthless or waste matter)

TRASHMAN *n* pl. -MEN a person who removes trash

TRASHY *adj* TRASHIER, TRASHIEST resembling trash **TRASHILY** *adv*

TRASS *n* pl. -ES a volcanic rock

TRAUCHLE *v* -LED, -LING, -LES to trachle

TRAUMA *n* pl. -MAS or -MATA a severe emotional shock

TRAVAIL *v* -ED, -ING, -S to toil

TRAVE *n* pl. -S a frame for confining a horse

TRAVEL *v* -ELED, -ELING, -ELS or -ELLED, -ELLING, -ELS to go from one place to another

TRAVELER *n* pl. -S one that travels

TRAVELOG *n* pl. -S a lecture or film on traveling

TRAVERSE *v* -VERSED, -VERSING, -VERSES to pass across or through

TRAVESTY *v* -TIED, -TYING, -TIES to parody

TRAVOIS *n* pl. -ES a type of sled

TRAVOISE *n* pl. -S travois

TRAWL *v* -ED, -ING, -S to fish by dragging a net along the sea bottom

TRAWLER *n* pl. -S a boat used for trawling

TRAWLEY *n* pl. -LEYS a small truck or car for conveying material

TRAWLNET *n* pl. -S the large net used in trawling

TRAY *n* pl. TRAYS a flat, shallow receptacle

TRAYFUL *n* pl. -S as much as a tray will hold

TREACLE *n* pl. -S molasses **TREACLY** *adj*

TREAD *v* TROD, TRODE, or TREADED, TRODDEN, TREADING, TREADS to walk on, over, or along

TREADER *n* pl. -S one that treads

TREADLE *v* -LED, -LING, -LES to work a foot lever

TREADLER *n* pl. -S one that treadles

TREASON *n* pl. -S violation of allegiance toward one's country

TREASURE *v* -URED, -URING, -URES to value highly

TREASURY *n* pl. -URIES a place where funds are received, kept, and disbursed

TREAT *v* -ED, -ING, -S to behave in a particular way toward

TREATER *n* pl. -S one that treats

TREATISE *n* pl. -S a formal and systematic written account of a subject

TREATY *n* pl. -TIES a formal agreement between two or more nations

TREBLE *v* -BLED, -BLING, -BLES to triple

TREBLY *adv* triply

TRECENTO *n* pl. -TOS the fourteenth century

TREDDLE *v* -DLED, -DLING, -DLES to treadle

TREE *v* TREED, TREEING, TREES to drive up a tree (a tall, woody plant)

TREELAWN *n* pl. -S the strip of lawn between the street and the sidewalk

TREELESS *adj* having no tree

TREELIKE *adj* resembling a tree

TREEN *n* pl. -S an article made from wood

TREENAIL *n* pl. -S a wooden peg used for fastening timbers

TREETOP *n* pl. -S the top of a tree

TREF *adj* unfit for use according to Jewish law

TREFAH *adj* tref

TREFOIL *n* pl. -S a plant having ternate leaves

TREHALA *n* pl. -S a sweet, edible substance forming the pupal case of certain weevils

TREK *v* TREKKED, TREKKING, TREKS to make a slow or arduous journey

TREKKER *n* pl. -S one that treks

TRELLIS *v* -ED, -ING, -ES to provide with a trellis (a frame used as a support for climbing plants)

TREMBLE *v* -BLED, -BLING, -BLES to shake involuntarily

TREMBLER *n* pl. -S one that trembles

TREMBLY *adj* -BLIER, -BLIEST marked by trembling

TREMOLO *n* pl. -LOS a vibrating musical effect

TREMOR *n* pl. -S a shaking movement

TRENAIL *n* pl. -S treenail

TRENCH *v* -ED, -ING, -ES to dig a long, narrow excavation in the ground

TRENCHER *n* pl. -S a wooden platter for serving food

TREND *v* -ED, -ING, -S to take a particular course

TRENDY *adj* TRENDIER, TRENDIEST very fashionable **TRENDILY** *adv*

TRENDY *n* pl. TRENDIES a trendy person

TREPAN *v* -PANNED, -PANNING, -PANS to trephine

TREPANG *n* pl. -S a marine animal

TREPHINE *v* -PHINED, -PHINING, -PHINES to operate on with a surgical saw

TREPID *adj* timorous

TRESPASS *v* -ED, -ING, -ES to enter upon the land of another unlawfully

TRESS *n* pl. -ES a long lock of hair **TRESSED** *adj*

TRESSEL *n* pl. -S trestle

TRESSIER comparative of tressy

TRESSIEST superlative of tressy

TRESSOUR *n* pl. -S tressure

TRESSURE *n* pl. -S a type of heraldic design

TRESSY *adj* TRESSIER, TRESSIEST abounding in tresses

TRESTLE *n* pl. -S a framework for supporting a bridge

TRET *n* pl. -S an allowance formerly paid to purchasers for waste incurred in transit

TREVET *n* pl. -S trivet

TREWS *n/pl* close-fitting tartan trousers

TREY *n* pl. TREYS a three in cards, dice, or dominoes

TRIABLE *adj* subject to judicial examination

TRIAC *n* pl. -S an electronic device used to control power

TRIACID *n* pl. -S a type of acid

TRIAD *n* pl. -S a group of three

TRIADIC *n* pl. -S a member of a triad

TRIADISM *n* pl. -S the quality or state of being a triad

TRIAGE *v* -AGED, -AGING, -AGES to practice a system of treating disaster victims

TRIAL *n* pl. -S a judicial examination

TRIANGLE *n* pl. -S a polygon having three sides

TRIARCHY *n* pl. -CHIES government by three persons

TRIAXIAL *adj* having three axes

TRIAZIN *n* pl. -S triazine

TRIAZINE *n* pl. -S a chemical compound

TRIAZOLE *n* pl. -S a chemical compound

TRIBADE *n* pl. -S a lesbian **TRIBADIC** *adj*

TRIBAL *adj* pertaining to a tribe **TRIBALLY** *adv*

TRIBASIC *adj* having three replaceable hydrogen atoms

TRIBE *n* pl. -S a group of people sharing a common ancestry and culture

TRIBRACH *n* pl. -S a type of metrical foot

TRIBUNAL *n* pl. -S a court of justice

TRIBUNE *n* pl. -S a defender of the rights of the people

TRIBUTE *n* pl. -S something given to show respect, gratitude, or admiration

TRICE *v* TRICED, TRICING, TRICES to haul up with a rope

TRICEPS *n* pl. -ES an arm muscle

TRICHINA *n* pl. -NAE or -NAS a parasitic worm

TRICHITE *n* pl. -S a minute mineral body found in volcanic rocks

TRICHOID	*adj* hairlike	**TRIFOLD**	*adj* having three parts
TRICHOME	*n* pl. -S a hairlike outgrowth	**TRIFORIA**	*n/pl* galleries in a church
TRICING	present participle of trice	**TRIFORM**	*adj* having three forms
TRICK	*v* -ED, -ING, -S to deceive	**TRIG**	*adj* TRIGGER, TRIGGEST neat
TRICKER	*n* pl. -S one that tricks	**TRIG**	*v* TRIGGED, TRIGGING, TRIGS to make trig
TRICKERY	*n* pl. -ERIES deception	**TRIGGER**	*v* -ED, -ING, -S to actuate
TRICKIE	*adj* TRICKIER, TRICKIEST tricky	**TRIGGEST**	superlative of trig
TRICKIER	comparative of tricky	**TRIGGING**	present participle of trig
TRICKIEST	superlative of tricky	**TRIGLY**	*adv* in a trig manner
TRICKILY	*adv* in a tricky manner	**TRIGLYPH**	*n* pl. -S an architectural ornament
TRICKISH	*adj* tricky		
TRICKLE	*v* -LED, -LING, -LES to flow or fall in drops	**TRIGNESS**	*n* pl. -ES the quality or state of being trig
TRICKLY	*adj* -LIER, -LIEST marked by trickling	**TRIGO**	*n* pl. -GOS wheat
TRICKSY	*adj* -SIER, -SIEST mischievous	**TRIGON**	*n* pl. -S an ancient stringed instrument
TRICKY	*adj* TRICKIER, TRICKIEST characterized by deception	**TRIGONAL**	*adj* shaped like a triangle
TRICLAD	*n* pl. -S an aquatic flatworm	**TRIGRAM**	*n* pl. -S a cluster of three successive letters
TRICOLOR	*n* pl. -S a flag having three colors	**TRIGRAPH**	*n* pl. -S a group of three letters representing one sound
TRICORN	*n* pl. -S a hat with the brim turned up on three sides	**TRIHEDRA**	*n/pl* figures having three plane surfaces meeting at a point
TRICORNE	*n* pl. -S tricorn	**TRIJET**	*n* pl. -S an airplane powered by three jet engines
TRICOT	*n* pl. -S a knitted fabric		
TRICTRAC	*n* pl. -S a form of backgammon	**TRIKE**	*n* pl. -S a tricycle
TRICYCLE	*n* pl. -S a vehicle having three wheels	**TRILBY**	*n* pl. -BIES a soft felt hat
TRIDENT	*n* pl. -S a spear having three prongs	**TRILL**	*v* -ED, -ING, -S to sing or play with a vibrating effect
TRIDUUM	*n* pl. -S a period of three days of prayer	**TRILLER**	*n* pl. -S one that trills
TRIED	past tense of try	**TRILLION**	*n* pl. -S a number
TRIENE	*n* pl. -S a type of chemical compound	**TRILLIUM**	*n* pl. -S a flowering plant
		TRILOBAL	*adj* trilobed
TRIENNIA	*n/pl* periods of three years	**TRILOBED**	*adj* having three lobes
TRIENS	*n* pl. -ENTES a coin of ancient Rome	**TRILOGY**	*n* pl. -GIES a group of three related literary works
TRIER	*n* pl. -S one that tries	**TRIM**	*adj* TRIMMER, TRIMMEST neat and orderly
TRIES	present 3d person sing. of try	**TRIM**	*v* TRIMMED, TRIMMING, TRIMS to make trim by cutting
TRIETHYL	*adj* containing three ethyl groups		
TRIFECTA	*n* pl. -S a system of betting	**TRIMARAN**	*n* pl. -S a sailing vessel
TRIFID	*adj* divided into three parts	**TRIMER**	*n* pl. -S a type of chemical compound **TRIMERIC** *adj*
TRIFLE	*v* -FLED, -FLING, -FLES to waste time	**TRIMETER**	*n* pl. -S a verse of three metrical feet
TRIFLER	*n* pl. -S one that trifles	**TRIMLY**	*adv* in a trim manner
TRIFLING	*n* pl. -S a waste of time	**TRIMMED**	past tense of trim
TRIFOCAL	*n* pl. -S a type of lens	**TRIMMER**	*n* pl. -S one that trims

TRIMMEST superlative of trim

TRIMMING *n* pl. -S something added as a decoration

TRIMNESS *n* pl. -ES the state of being trim

TRIMORPH *n* pl. -S a substance existing in three forms

TRIMOTOR *n* pl. -S an airplane powered by three engines

TRINAL *adj* having three parts

TRINARY *adj* consisting of three parts

TRINDLE *v* -DLED, -DLING, -DLES to trundle

TRINE *v* TRINED, TRINING, TRINES to place in a particular astrological position

TRINITY *n* pl. -TIES a group of three

TRINKET *v* -ED, -ING, -S to deal secretly

TRINKUMS *n/pl* small ornaments

TRINODAL *adj* having three nodes

TRIO *n* pl. TRIOS a group of three

TRIODE *n* pl. -S a type of electron tube

TRIOL *n* pl. -S a type of chemical compound

TRIOLET *n* pl. -S a short poem of fixed form

TRIOSE *n* pl. -S a simple sugar

TRIOXID *n* pl. -S trioxide

TRIOXIDE *n* pl. -S a type of oxide

TRIP *v* TRIPPED, TRIPPING, TRIPS to stumble

TRIPACK *n* pl. -S a type of film pack

TRIPART *adj* divided into three parts

TRIPE *n* pl. -S a part of the stomach of a ruminant that is used as food

TRIPEDAL *adj* having three feet

TRIPHASE *adj* having three phases

TRIPLANE *n* pl. -S a type of airplane

TRIPLE *v* -PLED, -PLING, -PLES to make three times as great

TRIPLET *n* pl. -S a group of three of one kind

TRIPLEX *n* pl. -ES an apartment having three floors

TRIPLING present participle of triple

TRIPLITE *n* pl. -S a mineral

TRIPLOID *n* pl. -S a cell having a chromosome number that is three times the basic number

TRIPLY *adv* in a triple degree, manner, or number

TRIPOD *n* pl. -S a stand having three legs **TRIPODAL, TRIPODIC** *adj*

TRIPODY *n* pl. -DIES a verse of three metrical feet

TRIPOLI *n* pl. -S a soft, friable rock

TRIPOS *n* pl. -ES a tripod

TRIPPED past tense of trip

TRIPPER *n* pl. -S one that trips

TRIPPET *n* pl. -S a part of a mechanism designed to strike another part

TRIPPING *n* pl. -S the act of one that trips

TRIPPY *adj* -PIER, -PIEST suggesting a trip on psychedelic drugs

TRIPTANE *n* pl. -S a chemical compound

TRIPTYCA *n* pl. -S a triptych

TRIPTYCH *n* pl. -S an ancient writing tablet

TRIPWIRE *n* pl. -S a low-placed hidden wire that sets off an alarm or a trap

TRIREME *n* pl. -S an ancient Greek or Roman warship

TRISCELE *n* pl. -S triskele

TRISECT *v* -ED, -ING, -S to divide into three equal parts

TRISEME *n* pl. -S a type of metrical foot **TRISEMIC** *adj*

TRISHAW *n* pl. -S a pedicab

TRISKELE *n* pl. -S a figure consisting of three branches radiating from a center

TRISMUS *n* pl. -ES lockjaw **TRISMIC** *adj*

TRISOME *n* pl. -S an organism having one chromosome in addition to the usual diploid number

TRISOMIC *n* pl. -S a trisome

TRISOMY *n* pl. -MIES the condition of being a trisome

TRISTATE *adj* pertaining to an area made up of three adjoining states

TRISTE *adj* sad

TRISTEZA *n* pl. -S a disease of citrus trees

TRISTFUL *adj* sad

TRISTICH *n* pl. -S a stanza of three lines

TRITE *adj* TRITER, TRITEST used so often as to be made commonplace **TRITELY** *adv*

TRITHING *n* pl. -S an administrative division in England

TRITICUM *n* pl. -S a cereal grass

TRITIUM	*n* pl. -S an isotope of hydrogen	
TRITOMA	*n* pl. -S an African herb	
TRITON	*n* pl. -S a marine mollusk	
TRITONE	*n* pl. -S a musical interval of three whole tones	
TRIUMPH	*v* -ED, -ING, -S to be victorious	
TRIUMVIR	*n* pl. -VIRS or -VIRI one of a ruling body of three in ancient Rome.	
TRIUNE	*n* pl. -S a trinity	
TRIUNITY	*n* pl. -TIES a trinity	
TRIVALVE	*n* pl. -S a type of shell	
TRIVET	*n* pl. -S a small stand having three legs	
TRIVIA	*n/pl* insignificant matters	
TRIVIAL	*adj* insignificant	
TRIVIUM	*n* pl. -IA a group of studies in medieval schools	
TROAK	*v* -ED, -ING, -S to troke	
TROCAR	*n* pl. -S a surgical instrument	
TROCHAIC	*n* pl. -S a trochee	
TROCHAL	*adj* shaped like a wheel	
TROCHAR	*n* pl. -S trocar	
TROCHE	*n* pl. -S a medicated lozenge	
TROCHEE	*n* pl. -S a type of metrical foot	
TROCHIL	*n* pl. -S an African bird	
TROCHILI	*n/pl* trochils	
TROCHLEA	*n* pl. -LEAE or -LEAS an anatomical structure resembling a pulley	
TROCHOID	*n* pl. -S a type of geometric curve	
TROCK	*v* -ED, -ING, -S to troke	
TROD	a past tense of tread	
TRODDEN	past participle of tread	
TRODE	a past tense of tread	
TROFFER	*n* pl. -S a fixture for fluorescent lighting	
TROGON	*n* pl. -S a tropical bird	
TROIKA	*n* pl. -S a Russian carriage	
TROILISM	*n* pl. -S sexual relations involving three persons	
TROILITE	*n* pl. -S a mineral	
TROILUS	*n* pl. -ES a large butterfly	
TROIS	*n* pl. TROIS the number three	
TROKE	*v* TROKED, TROKING, TROKES to exchange	
TROLAND	*n* pl. -S a unit of measurement of retinal response to light	
TROLL	*v* -ED, -ING, -S to fish with a slowly trailing line	
TROLLER	*n* pl. -S one that trolls	
TROLLEY	*v* -ED, -ING, -S to convey by streetcar	
TROLLIED	past tense of trolly	
TROLLIES	present 3d person sing. of trolly	
TROLLING	*n* pl. -S the act of one that trolls	
TROLLOP	*n* pl. -S a prostitute **TROLLOPY** *adj*	
TROLLY	*v* -LIED, -LYING, -LIES to trolley	
TROMBONE	*n* pl. -S a brass wind instrument	
TROMMEL	*n* pl. -S a screen used for sifting rock, ore, or coal	
TROMP	*v* -ED, -ING, -S to tramp	
TROMPE	*n* pl. -S a device used for supplying air to a furnace	
TRONA	*n* pl. -S a mineral	
TRONE	*n* pl. -S a weighing device	
TROOP	*v* -ED, -ING, -S to move or gather in crowds	
TROOPER	*n* pl. -S a cavalryman	
TROOPIAL	*n* pl. -S troupial	
TROOZ	*n/pl* trews	
TROP	*adv* too much	
TROPE	*n* pl. -S the figurative use of a word	
TROPHIC	*adj* pertaining to nutrition	
TROPHY	*v* -PHIED, -PHYING, -PHIES to honor with a trophy (a symbol of victory)	
TROPIC	*n* pl. -S either of two circles of the celestial sphere on each side of the equator **TROPICAL** *adj*	
TROPIN	*n* pl. -S tropine	
TROPINE	*n* pl. -S a poisonous alkaloid	
TROPISM	*n* pl. -S the involuntary response of an organism to an external stimulus	
TROPONIN	*n* pl. -S a protein of muscle	
TROT	*v* TROTTED, TROTTING, TROTS to go at a gait between a walk and a run	
TROTH	*v* -ED, -ING, -S to betroth	
TROTLINE	*n* pl. -S a strong fishing line	
TROTTED	past tense of trot	
TROTTER	*n* pl. -S a horse that trots	
TROTTING	present participle of trot	
TROTYL	*n* pl. -S an explosive	

TROUBLE   *v* -BLED, -BLING, -BLES to distress

TROUBLER   *n* pl. -S one that troubles

TROUGH   *n* pl. -S a long, narrow receptacle

TROUNCE   *v* TROUNCED, TROUNCING, TROUNCES to beat severely

TROUNCER   *n* pl. -S one that trounces

TROUPE   *v* TROUPED, TROUPING, TROUPES to tour with a theatrical company

TROUPER   *n* pl. -S a member of a theatrical company

TROUPIAL   *n* pl. -S a tropical bird

TROUPING   present participle of troupe

TROUSER   *adj* pertaining to trousers

TROUSERS   *n/pl* a garment for the lower part of the body

TROUT   *n* pl. -S a freshwater fish

TROUTY   *adj* TROUTIER, TROUTIEST abounding in trout

TROUVERE   *n* pl. -S a medieval poet

TROUVEUR   *n* pl. -S trouvere

TROVE   *n* pl. -S a valuable discovery

TROVER   *n* pl. -S a type of legal action

TROW   *v* -ED, -ING, -S to suppose

TROWEL   *v* -ELED, -ELING, -ELS or -ELLED, -ELLING, -ELS to smooth with a trowel (a hand tool having a flat blade)

TROWELER   *n* pl. -S one that trowels

TROWSERS   *n/pl* trousers

TROWTH   *n* pl. -S truth

TROY   *n* pl. TROYS a system of weights

TRUANCY   *n* pl. -CIES an act of truanting

TRUANT   *v* -ED, -ING, -S to stay out of school without permission

TRUANTRY   *n* pl. -RIES truancy

TRUCE   *v* TRUCED, TRUCING, TRUCES to suspend hostilities by mutual agreement

TRUCK   *v* -ED, -ING, -S to transport by truck (an automotive vehicle designed to carry loads)

TRUCKAGE   *n* pl. -S transportation of goods by trucks

TRUCKER   *n* pl. -S a truck driver

TRUCKFUL   *n* pl. -S as much as a truck can hold

TRUCKING   *n* pl. -S truckage

TRUCKLE   *v* -LED, -LING, -LES to yield weakly

TRUCKLER   *n* pl. -S one that truckles

TRUCKMAN   *n* pl. -MEN a trucker

TRUDGE   *v* TRUDGED, TRUDGING, TRUDGES to walk tiredly

TRUDGEN   *n* pl. -S a swimming stroke

TRUDGEON   *n* pl. -S trudgen

TRUDGER   *n* pl. -S one that trudges

TRUDGING   present participle of trudge

TRUE   *adj* TRUER, TRUEST consistent with fact or reality

TRUE   *v* TRUED, TRUING or TRUEING, TRUES to bring to conformity with a standard or requirement

TRUEBLUE   *n* pl. -S a person of unwavering loyalty

TRUEBORN   *adj* genuinely such by birth

TRUEBRED   *adj* designating an animal of unmixed stock

TRUED   past tense of true

TRUELOVE   *n* pl. -S a sweetheart

TRUENESS   *n* pl. -ES the quality or state of being true

TRUER   comparative of true

TRUEST   superlative of true

TRUFFE   *n* pl. -S truffle

TRUFFLE   *n* pl. -S an edible fungus **TRUFFLED** *adj*

TRUG   *n* pl. -S a gardener's basket

TRUING   a present participle of true

TRUISM   *n* pl. -S an obvious truth **TRUISTIC** *adj*

TRULL   *n* pl. -S a prostitute

TRULY   *adv* in conformity with fact or reality

TRUMEAU   *n* pl. -MEAUX a column supporting part of a doorway

TRUMP   *v* -ED, -ING, -S to outdo

TRUMPERY   *n* pl. -ERIES worthless finery

TRUMPET   *v* -ED, -ING, -S to sound on a trumpet (a brass wind instrument)

TRUNCATE   *v* -CATED, -CATING, -CATES to shorten by cutting off a part

TRUNDLE   *v* -DLED, -DLING, -DLES to propel by causing to rotate

TRUNDLER   *n* pl. -S one that trundles

TRUNK   *n* pl. -S the main stem of a tree **TRUNKED** *adj*

TRUNKFUL	*n* pl. -S as much as a trunk (a storage box) can hold
TRUNNEL	*n* pl. -S treenail
TRUNNION	*n* pl. -S a pin or pivot on which something can be rotated
TRUSS	*v* -ED, -ING, -ES to secure tightly
TRUSSER	*n* pl. -S one that trusses
TRUSSING	*n* pl. -S the framework of a structure
TRUST	*v* -ED, -ING, -S to place confidence in
TRUSTEE	*v* -TEED, -TEEING, -TEES to commit to the care of an administrator
TRUSTER	*n* pl. -S one that trusts
TRUSTFUL	*adj* inclined to trust
TRUSTOR	*n* pl. -S one that trustees his property
TRUSTY	*adj* TRUSTIER, TRUSTIEST worthy of trust **TRUSTILY** *adv*
TRUSTY	*n* pl. TRUSTIES one worthy of trust
TRUTH	*n* pl. -S conformity to fact or reality
TRUTHFUL	*adj* telling the truth
TRY	*v* TRIED, TRYING, TRIES to attempt
TRYINGLY	*adv* in a distressing manner
TRYMA	*n* pl. -MATA a type of nut
TRYOUT	*n* pl. -S a test of ability
TRYPSIN	*n* pl. -S an enzyme **TRYPTIC** *adj*
TRYSAIL	*n* pl. -S a type of sail
TRYST	*v* -ED, -ING, -S to agree to meet
TRYSTE	*n* pl. -S a market
TRYSTER	*n* pl. -S one that trysts
TRYWORKS	*n/pl* a type of furnace
TSADE	*n* pl. -S sade
TSADI	*n* pl. -S sade
TSAR	*n* pl. -S czar
TSARDOM	*n* pl. -S czardom
TSAREVNA	*n* pl. -S czarevna
TSARINA	*n* pl. -S czarina
TSARISM	*n* pl. -S czarism
TSARIST	*n* pl. -S czarist
TSARITZA	*n* pl. -S czaritza
TSETSE	*n* pl. -S an African fly
TSIMMES	*n* pl. TSIMMES tzimmes
TSK	*v* -ED, -ING, -S to utter an exclamation of annoyance
TSKTSK	*v* -ED, -ING, -S to tsk
TSOORIS	*n* pl. TSOORIS tsuris
TSORES	*n* pl. TSORES tsuris
TSORIS	*n* pl. TSORIS tsuris
TSORRISS	*n* pl. TSORRISS tsuris
TSUBA	*n* pl. TSUBA a part of a Japanese sword
TSUNAMI	*n* pl. -S a very large ocean wave **TSUNAMIC** *adj*
TSURIS	*n* pl. TSURIS a series of misfortunes
TUATARA	*n* pl. -S a large reptile
TUATERA	*n* pl. -S tuatara
TUB	*v* TUBBED, TUBBING, TUBS to wash in a tub (a round, open vessel)
TUBA	*n* pl. -BAS or -BAE a brass wind instrument
TUBAIST	*n* pl. -S a tuba player
TUBAL	*adj* pertaining to a tube
TUBATE	*adj* tubular
TUBBABLE	*adj* suitable for washing in a tub
TUBBED	past tense of tub
TUBBER	*n* pl. -S one that tubs
TUBBING	present participle of tub
TUBBY	*adj* -BIER, -BIEST short and fat
TUBE	*v* TUBED, TUBING, TUBES to provide with a tube (a long, hollow cylinder)
TUBELESS	*adj* having no tube
TUBELIKE	*adj* resembling a tube
TUBENOSE	*n* pl. -S a bird having tubular nostrils
TUBER	*n* pl. -S a thick underground stem
TUBERCLE	*n* pl. -S a small, rounded swelling
TUBEROID	*adj* pertaining to a tuber
TUBEROSE	*n* pl. -S a Mexican herb
TUBEROUS	*adj* pertaining to a tuber
TUBEWORK	*n* pl. -S tubing
TUBFUL	*n* pl. -S as much as a tub will hold
TUBIFEX	*n* pl. -ES an aquatic worm
TUBIFORM	*adj* tubular
TUBING	*n* pl. -S material in the form of a tube
TUBIST	*n* pl. -S a tubaist

TUBLIKE	*adj* resembling a tub	**TUMBLE**	*v* -BLED, -BLING, -BLES to fall or roll end over end
TUBULAR	*adj* shaped like a tube	**TUMBLER**	*n* pl. -S one that tumbles
TUBULATE	*v* -LATED, -LATING, -LATES to form into a tube	**TUMBLING**	*n* pl. -S the sport of gymnastics
TUBULE	*n* pl. -S a small tube	**TUMBREL**	*n* pl. -S a type of cart
TUBULIN	*n* pl. -S a protein that polymerizes to form tiny tubules	**TUMBRIL**	*n* pl. -S tumbrel
		TUMEFY	*v* -FIED, -FYING, -FIES to swell
TUBULOSE	*adj* tubular	**TUMID**	*adj* swollen **TUMIDLY** *adv*
TUBULOUS	*adj* tubular	**TUMIDITY**	*n* pl. -TIES the quality or state of being tumid
TUBULURE	*n* pl. -S a short tubular opening		
TUCHUN	*n* pl. -S a Chinese military governor	**TUMMLER**	*n* pl. -S an entertainer who encourages audience participation
TUCK	*v* -ED, -ING, -S to fold under	**TUMMY**	*n* pl. -MIES the stomach
TUCKAHOE	*n* pl. -S the edible root of certain arums	**TUMOR**	*n* pl. -S an abnormal swelling **TUMORAL, TUMOROUS** *adj*
TUCKER	*v* -ED, -ING, -S to weary	**TUMOUR**	*n* pl. -S tumor
TUCKET	*n* pl. -S a trumpet fanfare	**TUMP**	*v* -ED, -ING, -S to tip over
TUCKSHOP	*n* pl. -S a confectioner's shop	**TUMPLINE**	*n* pl. -S a strap for supporting a load on the back
TUFA	*n* pl. -S a porous limestone		
TUFF	*n* pl. -S a volcanic rock	**TUMULAR**	*adj* having the form of a mound
TUFFET	*n* pl. -S a clump of grass	**TUMULI**	a pl. of tumulus
TUFOLI	*n* pl. TUFOLI a large macaroni shell	**TUMULOSE**	*adj* full of mounds
		TUMULOUS	*adj* tumulose
TUFT	*v* -ED, -ING, -S to form into tufts (clusters of flexible outgrowths attached at the base)	**TUMULT**	*n* pl. -S a great din and commotion
		TUMULUS	*n* pl. -LI or -LUSES a mound over a grave
TUFTER	*n* pl. -S one that tufts		
TUFTY	*adj* TUFTIER, TUFTIEST abounding in tufts **TUFTILY** *adv*	**TUN**	*v* TUNNED, TUNNING, TUNS to store in a large cask
TUG	*v* TUGGED, TUGGING, TUGS to pull with force	**TUNA**	*n* pl. -S a marine food fish
		TUNABLE	*adj* capable of being tuned **TUNABLY** *adv*
TUGBOAT	*n* pl. -S a boat built for towing	**TUNDISH**	*n* pl. -ES a receptacle for molten metal
TUGGER	*n* pl. -S one that tugs		
TUGGING	present participle of tug	**TUNDRA**	*n* pl. -S a level, treeless expanse of arctic land
TUGHRIK	*n* pl. -S tugrik		
TUGLESS	*adj* being without a rope or chain with which to pull	**TUNE**	*v* TUNED, TUNING, TUNES to put into the proper pitch
TUGRIK	*n* pl. -S a monetary unit of Mongolia	**TUNEABLE**	*adj* tunable **TUNEABLY** *adv*
		TUNEFUL	*adj* melodious
TUI	*n* pl. -S a bird of New Zealand	**TUNELESS**	*adj* not tuneful
TUILLE	*n* pl. -S a tasset	**TUNER**	*n* pl. -S one that tunes
TUITION	*n* pl. -S a fee for instruction	**TUNEUP**	*n* pl. -S an adjustment to insure efficient operation
TULADI	*n* pl. -S a freshwater fish		
TULE	*n* pl. -S a tall marsh plant	**TUNG**	*n* pl. -S a Chinese tree
TULIP	*n* pl. -S a flowering plant	**TUNGSTEN**	*n* pl. -S a metallic element **TUNGSTIC** *adj*
TULLE	*n* pl. -S a silk material		
TULLIBEE	*n* pl. -S a freshwater fish	**TUNIC**	*n* pl. -S a loose-fitting garment

TUNICA *n* pl. -CAE an enveloping membrane or layer of body tissue

TUNICATE *n* pl. -S a small marine animal

TUNICLE *n* pl. -S a type of vestment

TUNING present participle of tune

TUNNAGE *n* pl. -S tonnage

TUNNED past tense of tun

TUNNEL *v* -NELED, -NELING, -NELS or -NELLED, -NELLING, -NELS to dig a tunnel (an underground passageway)

TUNNELER *n* pl. -S one that tunnels

TUNNING present participle of tun

TUNNY *n* pl. -NIES a tuna

TUP *v* TUPPED, TUPPING, TUPS to copulate with a ewe

TUPELO *n* pl. -LOS a softwood tree

TUPIK *n* pl. -S an Eskimo tent

TUPPED past tense of tup

TUPPENCE *n* pl. -S twopence

TUPPENNY *adj* twopenny

TUPPING present participle of tup

TUQUE *n* pl. -S a knitted woolen cap

TURACO *n* pl. -COS touraco

TURACOU *n* pl. -S touraco

TURBAN *n* pl. -S a head covering worn by Muslims **TURBANED** *adj*

TURBARY *n* pl. -RIES a place where peat can be dug

TURBETH *n* pl. -S turpeth

TURBID *adj* thick or opaque with roiled sediment **TURBIDLY** *adv*

TURBINAL *n* pl. -S a bone of the nasal passage

TURBINE *n* pl. -S a type of engine

TURBIT *n* pl. -S a domestic pigeon

TURBITH *n* pl. -S turpeth

TURBO *n* pl. -BOS a turbine

TURBOCAR *n* pl. -S an auto powered by a gas turbine

TURBOFAN *n* pl. -S a type of jet engine

TURBOJET *n* pl. -S a type of jet engine

TURBOT *n* pl. -S a European flatfish

TURDINE *adj* belonging to a large family of singing birds

TUREEN *n* pl. -S a large, deep bowl

TURF *n* pl. TURFS or TURVES a surface layer of earth containing a dense growth of grass

TURF *v* -ED, -ING, -S to cover with turf

TURFIER comparative of turfy

TURFIEST superlative of turfy

TURFLESS *adj* having no turf

TURFLIKE *adj* resembling turf

TURFMAN *n* pl. -MEN a person who is devoted to horse racing

TURFSKI *n* pl. -S a type of ski

TURFY *adj* TURFIER, TURFIEST covered with turf

TURGENCY *n* pl. -CIES turgor

TURGENT *adj* turgid

TURGID *adj* swollen **TURGIDLY** *adv*

TURGITE *n* pl. -S an iron ore

TURGOR *n* pl. -S the quality or state of being turgid

TURISTA *n* pl. -S intestinal sickness affecting a tourist in a foreign country

TURK *n* pl. -S one who eagerly advocates change

TURKEY *n* pl. -KEYS a large American bird

TURKOIS *n* pl. -ES turquois

TURMERIC *n* pl. -S an East Indian herb

TURMOIL *v* -ED, -ING, -S to throw into an uproar

TURN *v* -ED, -ING, -S to move around a central point **TURNABLE** *adj*

TURNCOAT *n* pl. -S a traitor

TURNDOWN *n* pl. -S a rejection

TURNER *n* pl. -S one that turns

TURNERY *n* pl. -ERIES the process of shaping articles on a lathe

TURNHALL *n* pl. -S a building where gymnasts practice

TURNING *n* pl. -S a rotation about an axis

TURNIP *n* pl. -S an edible plant root

TURNKEY *n* pl. -KEYS a person who has charge of a prison's keys

TURNOFF *n* pl. -S a road that branches off from a larger one

TURNOUT *n* pl. -S an assemblage of people

TURNOVER *n* pl. -S an upset or overthrow

TURNPIKE *n* pl. -S a toll road

TURNSOLE *n* pl. -S a plant that turns with the sun

TURNSPIT *n* pl. -S one that turns a roasting spit

TURNUP *n* pl. -S a part of a garment that is turned up

TURPETH *n* pl. -S a medicinal plant root

TURPS *n* pl. TURPS turpentine

TURQUOIS *n* pl. -ES a greenish blue gem

TURRET *n* pl. -S a small tower **TURRETED** *adj*

TURRICAL *adj* resembling a turret

TURTLE *v* -TLED, -TLING, -TLES to catch turtles (tortoises)

TURTLER *n* pl. -S one that turtles

TURTLING *n* pl. -S the act of one that turtles

TURVES a pl. of turf

TUSCHE *n* pl. -S a liquid used in lithography

TUSH *v* -ED, -ING, -ES to tusk

TUSHIE *n* pl. -S the buttocks

TUSHY *n* pl. TUSHIES tushie

TUSK *v* -ED, -ING, -S to gore with a tusk (a long, pointed tooth extending outside of the mouth)

TUSKER *n* pl. -S an animal with tusks

TUSKLESS *adj* having no tusk

TUSKLIKE *adj* resembling a tusk

TUSSAH *n* pl. -S an Asian silkworm

TUSSAL *adj* pertaining to a cough

TUSSAR *n* pl. -S tussah

TUSSEH *n* pl. -S tussah

TUSSER *n* pl. -S tussah

TUSSIS *n* pl. -SISES a cough **TUSSIVE** *adj*

TUSSLE *v* -SLED, -SLING, -SLES to struggle

TUSSOCK *n* pl. -S a clump of grass **TUSSOCKY** *adj*

TUSSOR *n* pl. -S tussah

TUSSORE *n* pl. -S tussah

TUSSUCK *n* pl. -S tussock

TUSSUR *n* pl. -S tussah

TUT *v* TUTTED, TUTTING, TUTS to utter an exclamation of impatience

TUTEE *n* pl. -S one who is being tutored

TUTELAGE *n* pl. -S the act of tutoring

TUTELAR *n* pl. -S a tutelary

TUTELARY *n* pl. -LARIES one who has the power to protect

TUTOR *v* -ED, -ING, -S to instruct privately

TUTORAGE *n* pl. -S tutelage

TUTORESS *n* pl. -ES a female who tutors

TUTORIAL *n* pl. -S a session of tutoring

TUTOYER *v* -TOYERED or -TOYED, -TOYERING, -TOYERS to address familiarly

TUTTED past tense of tut

TUTTI *n* pl. -S a musical passage performed by all the performers

TUTTING present participle of tut

TUTTY *n* pl. -TIES an impure zinc oxide

TUTU *n* pl. -S a short ballet skirt

TUX *n* pl. -ES a tuxedo

TUXEDO *n* pl. -DOES or -DOS a man's semiformal dinner coat **TUXEDOED** *adj*

TUYER *n* pl. -S tuyere

TUYERE *n* pl. -S a pipe through which air is forced into a blast furnace

TWA *n* pl. -S two

TWADDLE *v* -DLED, -DLING, -DLES to talk foolishly

TWADDLER *n* pl. -S one that twaddles

TWAE *n* pl. -S two

TWAIN *n* pl. -S a set of two

TWANG *v* -ED, -ING, -S to make a sharp, vibrating sound

TWANGER *n* pl. -S one that twangs

TWANGIER comparative of twangy

TWANGIEST superlative of twangy

TWANGLE *v* -GLED, -GLING, -GLES to twang

TWANGLER *n* pl. -S one that twangles

TWANGY *adj* TWANGIER, TWANGIEST twanging

TWANKY *n* pl. -KIES a variety of green tea

TWASOME *n* pl. -S twosome

TWATTLE *v* -TLED, -TLING, -TLES to twaddle

TWEAK *v* -ED, -ING, -S to pinch and twist sharply

TWEAKY *adj* TWEAKIER, TWEAKIEST twitchy

TWEE *adj* affectedly cute or dainty

TWEED *n* pl. -S a coarse woolen fabric

TWEEDLE   *v* -DLED, -DLING, -DLES to perform casually on a musical instrument

TWEEDY   *adj* TWEEDIER, TWEEDIEST resembling tweed

TWEEN   *prep* between

TWEENY   *n* pl. TWEENIES a housemaid

TWEET   *v* -ED, -ING, -S to chirp

TWEETER   *n* pl. -S a loudspeaker designed to reproduce high-pitched sounds

TWEEZE   *v* TWEEZED, TWEEZING, TWEEZES to pluck with a tweezer

TWEEZER   *n* pl. -S a pincerlike tool

TWELFTH   *n* pl. -S the number twelve in a series

TWELVE   *n* pl. -S a number

TWELVEMO   *n* pl. -MOS a page size

TWENTY   *n* pl. -TIES a number

TWERP   *n* pl. -S a small, impudent person

TWIBIL   *n* pl. -S a battle-ax with two cutting edges

TWIBILL   *n* pl. -S twibil

TWICE   *adv* two times

TWIDDLE   *v* -DLED, -DLING, -DLES to play idly with something

TWIDDLER   *n* pl. -S one that twiddles

TWIDDLY   *adj* -DLIER, -DLIEST having many turns

TWIER   *n* pl. -S tuyere

TWIG   *v* TWIGGED, TWIGGING, TWIGS to observe

TWIGGEN   *adj* made of twigs (small branches)

TWIGGY   *adj* -GIER, -GIEST twiglike

TWIGLESS   *adj* having no twigs

TWIGLIKE   *adj* resembling a twig

TWILIGHT   *n* pl. -S the early evening light

TWILIT   *adj* lighted by twilight

TWILL   *v* -ED, -ING, -S to weave so as to produce a diagonal pattern

TWILLING   *n* pl. -S a twilled fabric

TWIN   *v* TWINNED, TWINNING, TWINS to bring together in close association

TWINBORN   *adj* born at the same birth

TWINE   *v* TWINED, TWINING, TWINES to twist together

TWINER   *n* pl. -S one that twines

TWINGE   *v* TWINGED, TWINGING or TWINGEING, TWINGES to affect with a sharp pain

TWINIER   comparative of twiny

TWINIEST   superlative of twiny

TWINIGHT   *adj* pertaining to a baseball doubleheader that begins in the late afternoon

TWINING   present participle of twine

TWINJET   *n* pl. -S an aircraft with two jet engines

TWINKLE   *v* -KLED, -KLING, -KLES to shine with a flickering or sparkling light

TWINKLER   *n* pl. -S one that twinkles

TWINKLY   *adj* twinkling

TWINNED   past tense of twin

TWINNING   *n* pl. -S the bearing of two children at the same birth

TWINSET   *n* pl. -S a matching pair of sweaters to be worn together

TWINSHIP   *n* pl. -S close similarity or association

TWINY   *adj* TWINIER, TWINIEST resembling twine (a strong string)

TWIRL   *v* -ED, -ING, -S to rotate rapidly

TWIRLER   *n* pl. -S one that twirls

TWIRLY   *adj* TWIRLIER, TWIRLIEST curved

TWIRP   *n* pl. -S twerp

TWIST   *v* -ED, -ING, -S to combine by winding together

TWISTER   *n* pl. -S one that twists

TWISTING   *n* pl. -S a form of trickery used in selling life insurance

TWISTY   *adj* TWISTIER, TWISTIEST full of curves

TWIT   *v* TWITTED, TWITTING, TWITS to ridicule

TWITCH   *v* -ED, -ING, -ES to move or pull with a sudden motion

TWITCHER   *n* pl. -S one that twitches

TWITCHY   *adj* TWITCHIER, TWITCHIEST fidgety

TWITTED   past tense of twit

TWITTER   *v* -ED, -ING, -S to utter a succession of chirping sounds

TWITTERY   *adj* nervously agitated

TWITTING   present participle of twit

TWIXT   *prep* between

TWO   *n* pl. TWOS a number

TWOFER   *n* pl. -S something sold at the rate of two for the price of one

TWOFOLD   *n* pl. -S an amount twice as great as a given unit

TWOPENCE   *n* pl. -S a British coin worth two pennies

TWOPENNY   *adj* worth twopence

TWOSOME   *n* pl. -S a group of two

TWYER   *n* pl. -S tuyere

TYCOON   *n* pl. -S a wealthy and powerful business person

TYE   *n* pl. -S a chain on a ship

TYEE   *n* pl. -S a food fish

TYER   *n* pl. -S one that ties

TYING   a present participle of tie

TYKE   *n* pl. -S a small child

TYLOSIN   *n* pl. -S an antibiotic

TYMBAL   *n* pl. -S timbal

TYMPAN   *n* pl. -S a drum

TYMPANA   a pl. of tympanum

TYMPANAL   *adj* tympanic

TYMPANIC   *adj* pertaining to the tympanum

TYMPANO   *n* pl. -NI timpano

TYMPANUM   *n* pl. -NA or -NUMS the middle ear

TYMPANY   *n* pl. -NIES a swelling of the abdomen

TYNE   *v* TYNED, TYNING, TYNES to tine

TYPAL   *adj* typical

TYPE   *v* TYPED, TYPING, TYPES to write with a typewriter **TYPABLE, TYPEABLE** *adj*

TYPEBAR   *n* pl. -S a part of a typewriter

TYPECASE   *n* pl. -S a tray for holding printing type

TYPECAST   *v* -CAST, -CASTING, -CASTS to cast in an acting role befitting one's own nature

TYPED   past tense of type

TYPEFACE   *n* pl. -S the face of printing type

TYPESET   *v* -SET, -SETTING, -SETS to set in type

TYPEY   *adj* TYPIER, TYPIEST typy

TYPHOID   *n* pl. -S an infectious disease

TYPHON   *n* pl. -S a type of signal horn

TYPHOON   *n* pl. -S a tropical hurricane **TYPHONIC** *adj*

TYPHOSE   *adj* pertaining to typhoid

TYPHUS   *n* pl. -ES an infectious disease **TYPHOUS** *adj*

TYPIC   *adj* typical

TYPICAL   *adj* having the nature of a representative specimen

TYPIER   comparative of typey and typy

TYPIEST   superlative of typey and typy

TYPIFIER   *n* pl. -S one that typifies

TYPIFY   *v* -FIED, -FYING, -FIES to serve as a typical example of

TYPING   present participle of type

TYPIST   *n* pl. -S one who types

TYPO   *n* pl. -POS a typographical error

TYPOLOGY   *n* pl. -GIES the study of classification according to common characteristics

TYPP   *n* pl. -S a unit of yarn size

TYPY   *adj* TYPIER, TYPIEST characterized by strict conformance to the characteristics of a group

TYRAMINE   *n* pl. -S a chemical compound

TYRANNIC   *adj* characteristic of a tyrant

TYRANNY   *n* pl. -NIES the rule of a tyrant

TYRANT   *n* pl. -S an absolute ruler

TYRE   *v* TYRED, TYRING, TYRES to furnish with a covering for a wheel

TYRO   *n* pl. -ROS a beginner **TYRONIC** *adj*

TYROSINE   *n* pl. -S an amino acid

TYTHE   *v* TYTHED, TYTHING, TYTHES to tithe

TZADDIK   *n* pl. -DIKIM zaddik

TZAR   *n* pl. -S czar

TZARDOM   *n* pl. -S czardom

TZAREVNA   *n* pl. -S czarevna

TZARINA   *n* pl. -S czarina

TZARISM   *n* pl. -S czarism

TZARIST   *n* pl. -S czarist

TZARITZA   *n* pl. -S czaritza

TZETZE   *n* pl. -S tsetse

TZIGANE   *n* pl. -S a gypsy

TZIMMES   *n* pl. TZIMMES a vegetable stew

TZITZIS   *n/pl* zizith

TZITZIT   *n/pl* zizith

TZITZITH   *n/pl* zizith

TZURIS   *n* pl. TZURIS tsuris

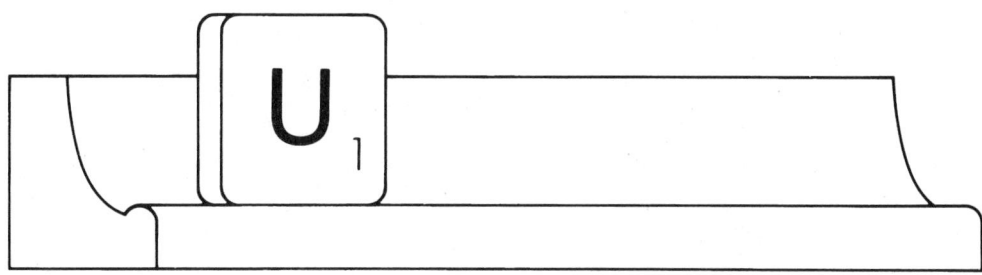

UBIETY   *n* pl. -ETIES the state of having a definite location

UBIQUE   *adv* everywhere

UBIQUITY   *n* pl. -TIES the state of being everywhere at the same time

UDDER   *n* pl. -S a mammary gland

UDO   *n* pl. UDOS a Japanese herb

UDOMETER   *n* pl. -S a rain gauge

UDOMETRY   *n* pl. -TRIES the measurement of rain

UFOLOGY   *n* pl. -GIES the study of unidentified flying objects

UGH   *n* pl. -S the sound of a cough or grunt

UGLIER   comparative of ugly

UGLIES   pl. of ugly

UGLIEST   superlative of ugly

UGLIFIER   *n* pl. -S one that uglifies

UGLIFY   *v* -FIED, -FYING, -FIES to make ugly

UGLINESS   *n* pl. -ES the state of being ugly

UGLY   *adj* -LIER, -LIEST displeasing to the sight **UGLILY** *adv*

UGLY   *n* pl. -LIES one that is ugly

UGSOME   *adj* disgusting

UH   *interj* — used to express hesitation

UHLAN   *n* pl. -S one of a body of Prussian cavalry

UINTAITE   *n* pl. -S a variety of asphalt

UKASE   *n* pl. -S an edict

UKE   *n* pl. -S ukelele

UKELELE   *n* pl. -S ukulele

UKULELE   *n* pl. -S a small guitar-like instrument

ULAMA   *n* pl. -S ulema

ULAN   *n* pl. -S uhlan

ULCER   *v* -ED, -ING, -S to affect with an ulcer (a type of lesion)

ULCERATE   *v* -ATED, -ATING, -ATES to ulcer

ULCEROUS   *adj* being or affected with an ulcer

ULEMA   *n* pl. -S a Muslim scholar

ULEXITE   *n* pl. -S a mineral

ULLAGE   *n* pl. -S the amount that a container lacks of being full **ULLAGED** *adj*

ULNA   *n* pl. -NAE or -NAS a bone of the forearm **ULNAR** *adj*

ULNAD   *adv* toward the ulna

ULPAN   *n* pl. -PANIM a school in Israel for teaching Hebrew

ULSTER   *n* pl. -S a long, loose overcoat

ULTERIOR   *adj* more remote

ULTIMA   *n* pl. -S the last syllable of a word

ULTIMACY   *n* pl. -CIES an ultimate

ULTIMATA   *n/pl* final proposals

ULTIMATE   *v* -MATED, -MATING, -MATES to come to an end

ULTIMO   *adj* of or occurring in the preceding month

ULTRA   *n* pl. -S an ultraist

ULTRADRY   *adj* extremely dry

ULTRAHIP   *adj* extremely hip

ULTRAHOT   *adj* extremely hot

ULTRAISM   *n* pl. -S advocacy of extreme measures

ULTRAIST   *n* pl. -S an advocate of extreme measures

ULTRALOW   *adj* extremely low

ULTRARED   *n* pl. -S infrared

ULU   *n* pl. -S an Eskimo knife

ULULANT   *adj* howling

ULULATE   *v* -LATED, -LATING, -LATES to howl

ULVA   *n* pl. -S an edible seaweed

UM   *interj* — used to indicate hesitation

UMANGITE   *n* pl. -S a mineral consisting of copper selenide

UMBEL   *n* pl. -S a type of flower cluster **UMBELED, UMBELLAR, UMBELLED** *adj*

UMBELLET   *n* pl. -S a small umbel

UMBER   *v* -ED, -ING, -S to color with a brown pigment

UMBILICI   *n/pl* navels

UMBLES   *n/pl* the entrails of a deer

UMBO   *n* pl. -BONES or -BOS the rounded elevation at the center of a shield **UMBONAL, UMBONATE, UMBONIC** *adj*

UMBRA   *n* pl. -BRAE or -BRAS a dark area **UMBRAL** *adj*

UMBRAGE   *n* pl. -S resentment

UMBRELLA   *v* -ED, -ING, -S to provide with an umbrella (a portable cover for protection from rain or sun)

UMBRETTE   *n* pl. -S a wading bird

UMIAC   *n* pl. -S umiak

UMIACK   *n* pl. -S umiak

UMIAK   *n* pl. -S an open Eskimo boat

UMIAQ   *n* pl. -S umiak

UMLAUT   *v* -ED, -ING, -S to modify a vowel sound by partial assimilation to a succeeding sound

UMM   *interj* um

UMP   *v* -ED, -ING, -S to umpire

UMPIRAGE   *n* pl. -S the function of an umpire

UMPIRE   *v* -PIRED, -PIRING, -PIRES to act as umpire (a person appointed to rule on the plays in a game)

UMPTEEN   *adj* indefinitely numerous

UMTEENTH   *adj* being the last in an indefinitely numerous series

UN   *pron* pl. -S one

Following is a list of self-explanatory adjectives and adverbs containing the prefix UN- (not):

UNABATED	*adj*
UNABLE	*adj*
UNABUSED	*adj*
UNACTED	*adj*
UNADULT	*adj*
UNAFRAID	*adj*
UNAGED	*adj*
UNAGEING	*adj*
UNAGILE	*adj*
UNAGING	*adj*
UNAIDED	*adj*
UNAIMED	*adj*
UNAIRED	*adj*
UNAKIN	*adj*
UNALIKE	*adj*
UNALLIED	*adj*
UNAMUSED	*adj*
UNANELED	*adj*
UNAPT	*adj*
UNAPTLY	*adv*
UNARGUED	*adj*
UNARTFUL	*adj*
UNASKED	*adj*
UNATONED	*adj*
UNAVOWED	*adj*
UNAWAKED	*adj*
UNAWARE	*adj*
UNAWED	*adj*
UNBACKED	*adj*
UNBAKED	*adj*
UNBANNED	*adj*
UNBARBED	*adj*
UNBASED	*adj*
UNBATHED	*adj*
UNBEATEN	*adj*
UNBENIGN	*adj*
UNBIASED	*adj*
UNBILLED	*adj*
UNBITTED	*adj*
UNBITTEN	*adj*
UNBITTER	*adj*
UNBLAMED	*adj*
UNBLEST	*adj*
UNBLOODY	*adj*
UNBONED	*adj*
UNBORN	*adj*
UNBOUGHT	*adj*
UNBOUNCY	*adj*
UNBOWED	*adj*
UNBRED	*adj*
UNBRIGHT	*adj*
UNBROKE	*adj*
UNBROKEN	*adj*
UNBULKY	*adj*

UNBURIED	*adj*	**UNDUBBED**	*adj*
UNBURNED	*adj*	**UNDULLED**	*adj*
UNBURNT	*adj*	**UNDYED**	*adj*
UNBUSTED	*adj*	**UNEAGER**	*adj*
UNBUSY	*adj*	**UNEARNED**	*adj*
UNCALLED	*adj*	**UNEATEN**	*adj*
UNCANDID	*adj*	**UNEDIBLE**	*adj*
UNCARING	*adj*	**UNEDITED**	*adj*
UNCASHED	*adj*	**UNENDED**	*adj*
UNCASKED	*adj*	**UNENDING**	*adj*
UNCATCHY	*adj*	**UNENVIED**	*adj*
UNCAUGHT	*adj*	**UNERASED**	*adj*
UNCAUSED	*adj*	**UNEROTIC**	*adj*
UNCHARY	*adj*	**UNERRING**	*adj*
UNCHASTE	*adj*	**UNEVADED**	*adj*
UNCHEWED	*adj*	**UNEVEN**	*adj* -EVENER, -EVENEST
UNCHIC	*adj*	**UNEVENLY**	*adv*
UNCHICLY	*adv*	**UNEXOTIC**	*adj*
UNCHOSEN	*adj*	**UNEXPERT**	*adj*
UNCIVIL	*adj*	**UNFADED**	*adj*
UNCLEAN	*adj* -CLEANER, -CLEANEST	**UNFADING**	*adj*
UNCLEAR	*adj* -CLEARER, -CLEAREST	**UNFAIR**	*adj* -FAIRER, -FAIREST
UNCLOYED	*adj*	**UNFAIRLY**	*adv*
UNCOATED	*adj*	**UNFAKED**	*adj*
UNCODED	*adj*	**UNFALLEN**	*adj*
UNCOINED	*adj*	**UNFAMOUS**	*adj*
UNCOMBED	*adj*	**UNFANCY**	*adj*
UNCOMELY	*adj*	**UNFAZED**	*adj*
UNCOMIC	*adj*	**UNFEARED**	*adj*
UNCOMMON	*adj* -MONER, -MONEST	**UNFED**	*adj*
UNCOOKED	*adj*	**UNFELT**	*adj*
UNCOOL	*adj*	**UNFILIAL**	*adj*
UNCOOLED	*adj*	**UNFILLED**	*adj*
UNCOUTH	*adj*	**UNFILMED**	*adj*
UNCOY	*adj*	**UNFIRED**	*adj*
UNCRAZY	*adj*	**UNFISHED**	*adj*
UNCUFFED	*adj*	**UNFLASHY**	*adj*
UNCURED	*adj*	**UNFLEXED**	*adj*
UNCURSED	*adj*	**UNFOILED**	*adj*
UNCUT	*adj*	**UNFOND**	*adj*
UNCUTE	*adj*	**UNFORCED**	*adj*
UNDAMPED	*adj*	**UNFORGED**	*adj*
UNDARING	*adj*	**UNFORKED**	*adj*
UNDATED	*adj*	**UNFORMED**	*adj*
UNDECKED	*adj*	**UNFOUGHT**	*adj*
UNDENIED	*adj*	**UNFOUND**	*adj*
UNDEVOUT	*adj*	**UNFRAMED**	*adj*
UNDIMMED	*adj*	**UNFUNDED**	*adj*
UNDOABLE	*adj*	**UNFUNNY**	*adj*
UNDOCILE	*adj*	**UNFUSED**	*adj*
UNDOTTED	*adj*	**UNFUSSY**	*adj*
UNDREAMT	*adj*	**UNGALLED**	*adj*
UNDRIED	*adj*	**UNGENIAL**	*adj*

UNGENTLE	adj	UNLIKE	adj
UNGENTLY	adv	UNLIKELY	adj -LIER, -LIEST
UNGIFTED	adj	UNLINED	adj
UNGLAZED	adj	UNLISTED	adj
UNGOWNED	adj	UNLIT	adj
UNGRACED	adj	UNLIVELY	adj
UNGRADED	adj	UNLOBED	adj
UNGREEDY	adj	UNLOVED	adj
UNGROUND	adj	UNLOVELY	adj -LIER, -LIEST
UNGUIDED	adj	UNLOVING	adj
UNHAILED	adj	UNLUCKY	adj -LUCKIER, -LUCKIEST
UNHALVED	adj	UNMACHO	adj
UNHAPPY	adj -PIER, -PIEST	UNMANFUL	adj
UNHARMED	adj	UNMANLY	adj
UNHASTY	adj	UNMAPPED	adj
UNHEALED	adj	UNMARKED	adj
UNHEARD	adj	UNMARRED	adj
UNHEATED	adj	UNMATED	adj
UNHEDGED	adj	UNMATTED	adj
UNHEEDED	adj	UNMEANT	adj
UNHELPED	adj	UNMELLOW	adj
UNHEROIC	adj	UNMELTED	adj
UNHEWN	adj	UNMENDED	adj
UNHIP	adj	UNMERRY	adj
UNHIRED	adj	UNMET	adj
UNHOLILY	adv	UNMILLED	adj
UNHOLY	adj -LIER, -LIEST	UNMINED	adj
UNHUMAN	adj	UNMIXED	adj
UNHUNG	adj	UNMIXT	adj
UNHURT	adj	UNMODISH	adj
UNIDEAL	adj	UNMOLTEN	adj
UNIMBUED	adj	UNMOVED	adj
UNIRONED	adj	UNMOVING	adj
UNISSUED	adj	UNMOWN	adj
UNJADED	adj	UNNAMED	adj
UNJOINED	adj	UNNEEDED	adj
UNJOYFUL	adj	UNNOISY	adj
UNJUDGED	adj	UNNOTED	adj
UNJUST	adj	UNOILED	adj
UNJUSTLY	adv	UNOPEN	adj
UNKEPT	adj	UNOPENED	adj
UNKIND	adj -KINDER, -KINDEST	UNORNATE	adj
UNKINDLY	adv -LIER, -LIEST	UNOWNED	adj
UNKINGLY	adj	UNPAID	adj
UNKISSED	adj	UNPAIRED	adj
UNKOSHER	adj	UNPARTED	adj
UNLAWFUL	adj	UNPAVED	adj
UNLEASED	adj	UNPAYING	adj
UNLED	adj	UNPEELED	adj
UNLETHAL	adj	UNPITIED	adj
UNLETTED	adj	UNPLACED	adj
UNLEVIED	adj	UNPLAYED	adj
UNLICKED	adj	UNPLIANT	adj

UNPLOWED	adj		UNSEEMLY	adj -LIER, -LIEST
UNPOETIC	adj		UNSEEN	adj
UNPOISED	adj		UNSEIZED	adj
UNPOLITE	adj		UNSENT	adj
UNPOLLED	adj		UNSERVED	adj
UNPOSED	adj		UNSEXUAL	adj
UNPOSTED	adj		UNSEXY	adj
UNPOTTED	adj		UNSHADED	adj
UNPRETTY	adj		UNSHAKEN	adj
UNPRICED	adj		UNSHAMED	adj
UNPRIMED	adj		UNSHAPED	adj
UNPRIZED	adj		UNSHAPEN	adj
UNPROBED	adj		UNSHARED	adj
UNPROVED	adj		UNSHARP	adj
UNPROVEN	adj		UNSHAVED	adj
UNPRUNED	adj		UNSHAVEN	adj
UNPURE	adj		UNSHED	adj
UNPURGED	adj		UNSHOD	adj
UNQUIET	adj -ETER, -ETEST		UNSHORN	adj
UNRAISED	adj		UNSHOWY	adj
UNRAKED	adj		UNSHRUNK	adj
UNRANKED	adj		UNSHUT	adj
UNRATED	adj		UNSIFTED	adj
UNRAZED	adj		UNSIGNED	adj
UNREAD	adj		UNSILENT	adj
UNREADY	adj -READIER, -READIEST		UNSINFUL	adj
UNREAL	adj		UNSIZED	adj
UNREALLY	adv		UNSLAKED	adj
UNRENTED	adj		UNSLICED	adj
UNREPAID	adj		UNSMART	adj
UNRESTED	adj		UNSMOKED	adj
UNRHYMED	adj		UNSOAKED	adj
UNRIFLED	adj		UNSOBER	adj
UNRIMED	adj		UNSOCIAL	adj
UNRINSED	adj		UNSOILED	adj
UNRISEN	adj		UNSOLD	adj
UNROPED	adj		UNSOLID	adj
UNROUGH	adj		UNSOLVED	adj
UNRULED	adj		UNSORTED	adj
UNRUSHED	adj		UNSOUGHT	adj
UNRUSTED	adj		UNSOUND	adj -SOUNDER, -SOUNDEST
UNSAFE	adj		UNSOURED	adj
UNSAFELY	adv		UNSOWED	adj
UNSALTED	adj		UNSOWN	adj
UNSATED	adj		UNSPENT	adj
UNSAVED	adj		UNSPILT	adj
UNSAVORY	adj		UNSPLIT	adj
UNSAWED	adj		UNSPOILT	adj
UNSAWN	adj		UNSPRUNG	adj
UNSCALED	adj		UNSPUN	adj
UNSEARED	adj		UNSTABLE	adj -BLER, -BLEST
UNSEEDED	adj		UNSTABLY	adv
UNSEEING	adj		UNSTEADY	adj -STEADIER, -STEADIEST

UNSTONED	adj	UNVEXT	adj
UNSTUFFY	adj	UNVIABLE	adj
UNSTUNG	adj	UNVOCAL	adj
UNSUBTLE	adj	UNWALLED	adj
UNSUBTLY	adv	UNWANING	adj
UNSUITED	adj	UNWANTED	adj
UNSUNG	adj	UNWARIER	comparative of unwary
UNSUNK	adj	UNWARIEST	superlative of unwary
UNSURE	adj	UNWARILY	adv
UNSURELY	adv	UNWARMED	adj
UNSWAYED	adj	UNWARNED	adj
UNSWEPT	adj	UNWARPED	adj
UNTAGGED	adj	UNWARY	adj -WARIER, -WARIEST
UNTAKEN	adj	UNWASTED	adj
UNTAME	adj	UNWAXED	adj
UNTAMED	adj	UNWEANED	adj
UNTANNED	adj	UNWEARY	adj
UNTAPPED	adj	UNWED	adj
UNTASTED	adj	UNWEDDED	adj
UNTAXED	adj	UNWEEDED	adj
UNTENDED	adj	UNWELDED	adj
UNTESTED	adj	UNWELL	adj
UNTHAWED	adj	UNWEPT	adj
UNTIDILY	adv	UNWETTED	adj
UNTIDY	adj -DIER, -DIEST	UNWHITE	adj
UNTILLED	adj	UNWIELDY	adj -WIELDIER, -WIELDIEST
UNTILTED	adj	UNWIFELY	adj
UNTIMELY	adj -LIER, -LIEST	UNWILLED	adj
UNTINGED	adj	UNWISE	adj -WISER, -WISEST
UNTIPPED	adj	UNWISELY	adv
UNTIRED	adj	UNWON	adj
UNTIRING	adj	UNWOODED	adj
UNTITLED	adj	UNWOOED	adj
UNTOLD	adj	UNWORKED	adj
UNTORN	adj	UNWORN	adj
UNTRACED	adj	UNWORTHY	adj -THIER, -THIEST
UNTRENDY	adj	UNWRUNG	adj
UNTRIED	adj	UNYOUNG	adj
UNTRUE	adj -TRUER, -TRUEST	UNZONED	adj
UNTRULY	adv		
UNTRUSTY	adj		
UNTUFTED	adj		
UNTURNED	adj		
UNUNITED	adj		
UNURGED	adj	UNAI	n pl. -S unau
UNUSABLE	adj	UNAKITE	n pl. -S an igneous rock
UNUSED	adj	UNANCHOR	v -ED, -ING, -S to loosen from an anchor
UNUSUAL	adj		
UNVALUED	adj	UNARM	v -ED, -ING, -S to disarm
UNVARIED	adj	UNARY	adj consisting of a single element
UNVEINED	adj		
UNVERSED	adj	UNAU	n pl. -S a two-toed sloth
UNVEXED	adj	UNAWARES	adv without warning

UNBAN   *v* -BANNED, -BANNING, -BANS to remove a prohibition against

UNBAR   *v* -BARRED, -BARRING, -BARS to remove a bar from

UNBATED   *adj* unabated

UNBE   *v* to cease to have being — UNBE is the only accepted form of this verb; it cannot be conjugated

UNBEAR   *v* -BEARED, -BEARING, -BEARS to free from the pressure of a rein

UNBELIEF   *n* pl. -S lack of belief

UNBELT   *v* -ED, -ING, -S to remove the belt of

UNBEND   *v* -BENT or -BENDED, -BENDING, -BENDS to make or allow to become straight

UNBID   *adj* unbidden

UNBIDDEN   *adj* not invited

UNBIND   *v* -BOUND, -BINDING, -BINDS to free from bindings

UNBLOCK   *v* -ED, -ING, -S to free from being blocked

UNBODIED   *adj* having no body

UNBOLT   *v* -ED, -ING, -S to open by withdrawing a bolt (a metal bar)

UNBONNET   *v* -ED, -ING, -S to uncover the head

UNBOSOM   *v* -ED, -ING, -S to reveal

UNBOUND   past tense of unbind

UNBOX   *v* -ED, -ING, -ES to remove from a box

UNBRACE   *v* -BRACED, -BRACING, -BRACES to free from braces

UNBRAID   *v* -ED, -ING, -S to separate the strands of

UNBRAKE   *v* -BRAKED, -BRAKING, -BRAKES to release a brake

UNBREECH   *v* -ED, -ING, -ES to remove the breeches of

UNBRIDLE   *v* -DLED, -DLING, -DLES to set loose

UNBUCKLE   *v* -LED, -LING, -LES to loosen a buckle

UNBUILD   *v* -BUILT, -BUILDING, -BUILDS to demolish

UNBUNDLE   *v* -DLED, -DLING, -DLES to price separately

UNBURDEN   *v* -ED, -ING, -S to free from a burden

UNBUTTON   *v* -ED, -ING, -S to unfasten the buttons of

UNCAGE   *v* -CAGED, -CAGING, -CAGES to release from a cage

UNCAKE   *v* -CAKED, -CAKING, -CAKES to break up a cake (a block of compacted matter)

UNCANNY   *adj* -NIER, -NIEST strange and inexplicable

UNCAP   *v* -CAPPED, -CAPPING, -CAPS to remove the cap from

UNCASE   *v* -CASED, -CASING, -CASES to remove from a case

UNCHAIN   *v* -ED, -ING, -S to free by removing a chain

UNCHANCY   *adj* unlucky

UNCHARGE   *v* -CHARGED, -CHARGING, -CHARGES to acquit

UNCHOKE   *v* -CHOKED, -CHOKING, -CHOKES to free from obstruction

UNCHURCH   *v* -ED, -ING, -ES to expel from a church

UNCI   pl. of uncus

UNCIA   *n* pl. -CIAE a coin of ancient Rome

UNCIAL   *n* pl. -S a style of writing

UNCIALLY   *adv* in the uncial style

UNCIFORM   *n* pl. -S a bone of the wrist

UNCINAL   *adj* uncinate

UNCINATE   *adj* bent at the end like a hook

UNCINUS   *n* pl. -NI an uncinate structure

UNCLAD   a past tense of unclothe

UNCLAMP   *v* -ED, -ING, -S to free from a clamp

UNCLASP   *v* -ED, -ING, -S to free from a clasp

UNCLE   *n* pl. -S the brother of one's father or mother

UNCLENCH   *v* -ED, -ING, -ES to open from a clenched position

UNCLINCH   *v* -ED, -ING, -ES to unclench

UNCLIP   *v* -CLIPPED, -CLIPPING, -CLIPS to remove a clip (a fastening device) from

UNCLOAK   *v* -ED, -ING, -S to remove a cloak from

UNCLOG   *v* -CLOGGED, -CLOGGING, -CLOGS to free from a difficulty or obstruction

UNCLOSE   *v* -CLOSED, -CLOSING, -CLOSES to open

UNCLOTHE *v* -CLOTHED or -CLAD, -CLOTHING, -CLOTHES to divest of clothing

UNCLOUD *v* -ED, -ING, -S to free from clouds

UNCO *n* pl. -COS a stranger

UNCOCK *v* -ED, -ING, -S to remove from a cocked position

UNCOFFIN *v* -ED, -ING, -S to remove from a coffin

UNCOIL *v* -ED, -ING, -S to release from a coiled position

UNCORK *v* -ED, -ING, -S to draw the cork

UNCOUPLE *v* -PLED, -PLING, -PLES to disconnect

UNCOVER *v* -ED, -ING, -S to remove the covering from

UNCRATE *v* -CRATED, -CRATING, -CRATES to remove from a crate

UNCREATE *v* -ATED, -ATING, -ATES to deprive of existence

UNCROSS *v* -ED, -ING, -ES to change from a crossed position

UNCROWN *v* -ED, -ING, -S to deprive of a crown

UNCTION *n* pl. -S the act of anointing

UNCTUOUS *adj* greasy

UNCUFF *v* -ED, -ING, -S to remove handcuffs from

UNCURB *v* -ED, -ING, -S to remove restraints from

UNCURL *v* -ED, -ING, -S to straighten the curls of

UNCUS *n* pl. -CI a hook-shaped anatomical part

UNDE *adj* wavy

UNDEAD *n* pl. UNDEAD a vampire

UNDEE *adj* unde

UNDER *prep* in a lower position than

UNDERACT *v* -ED, -ING, -S to act subtly and with restraint

UNDERAGE *n* pl. -S a shortage

UNDERARM *n* pl. -S the armpit

UNDERATE past tense of undereat

UNDERBID *v* -BID, -BIDDING, -BIDS to bid lower than

UNDERBUD *v* -BUDDED, -BUDDING, -BUDS to bud from beneath

UNDERBUY *v* -BOUGHT, -BUYING, -BUYS to buy at a lower price than

UNDERCUT *v* -CUT, -CUTTING, -CUTS to cut under

UNDERDO *v* -DID, -DONE, -DOING, -DOES to do insufficiently

UNDERDOG *n* pl. -S one who is expected to lose

UNDEREAT *v* -ATE, -EATEN, -EATING, -EATS to eat an insufficient amount

UNDERFED *adj* fed an insufficient amount

UNDERFUR *n* pl. -S the thick, soft fur beneath the outer coat of certain mammals

UNDERGO *v* -WENT, -GONE, -GOING, -GOES to be subjected to

UNDERGOD *n* pl. -S a lesser god

UNDERJAW *n* pl. -S the lower jaw

UNDERLAID past tense of underlay

UNDERLAIN past participle of underlie

UNDERLAP *v* -LAPPED, -LAPPING, -LAPS to extend partly under

UNDERLAY *v* -LAID, -LAYING, -LAYS to place under

UNDERLET *v* -LET, -LETTING, -LETS to lease at less than the usual value

UNDERLIE *v* -LAY, -LAIN, -LYING, -LIES to lie under

UNDERLIP *n* pl. -S the lower lip

UNDERLIT *adj* lacking adequate light

UNDERLYING present participle of underlie

UNDERPAY *v* -PAID, -PAYING, -PAYS to pay less than is deserved

UNDERPIN *v* -PINNED, -PINNING, -PINS to support from below

UNDERRUN *v* -RAN, -RUNNING, -RUNS to pass or extend under

UNDERSEA *adv* beneath the surface of the sea

UNDERSET *n* pl. -S a current below the surface of the ocean

UNDERTAX *v* -ED, -ING, -ES to tax less than the usual amount

UNDERTOW *n* pl. -S the seaward pull of receding waves breaking on a shore

UNDERWAY *adv* in progress

UNDERWENT past tense of undergo

UNDID past tense of undo

UNDIES *n/pl* underwear

UNDINE *n* pl. -S a female water spirit**

UNDO *v* -DID, -DONE, -DOING, -DOES to bring to ruin

UNDOCK *v* -ED, -ING, -S to move away from a dock

UNDOER *n* pl. -S one that undoes

UNDOING *n* pl. -S a cause of ruin

UNDONE past participle of undo

UNDOUBLE *v* -BLED, -BLING, -BLES to unfold

UNDRAPE *v* -DRAPED, -DRAPING, -DRAPES to strip of drapery

UNDRAW *v* -DREW, -DRAWN, -DRAWING, -DRAWS to draw open

UNDRESS *v* -DRESSED or -DREST, -DRESSING, -DRESSES to remove one's clothing

UNDRUNK *adj* not swallowed

UNDUE *adj* exceeding what is appropriate or normal

UNDULANT *adj* undulating

UNDULAR *adj* undulating

UNDULATE *v* -LATED, -LATING, -LATES to move with a wavelike motion

UNDULY *adv* in an undue manner

UNDY *adj* unde

UNDYING *adj* not subject to death

UNEARTH *v* -ED, -ING, -S to dig up

UNEASE *n* pl. -S mental or physical discomfort

UNEASY *adj* -EASIER, -EASIEST marked by mental or physical discomfort **UNEASILY** *adv*

UNEQUAL *n* pl. -S one that is not equal to another

UNFAITH *n* pl. -S lack of faith

UNFASTEN *v* -ED, -ING, -S to release from fastenings

UNFENCE *v* -FENCED, -FENCING, -FENCES to remove a fence from

UNFETTER *v* -ED, -ING, -S to free from fetters

UNFIT *v* -FITTED, -FITTING, -FITS to make unsuitable

UNFITLY *adv* in an unsuitable manner

UNFIX *v* -FIXED or -FIXT, -FIXING, -FIXES to unfasten

UNFOLD *v* -ED, -ING, -S to open something that is folded

UNFOLDER *n* pl. -S one that unfolds

UNFORGOT *adj* not forgotten

UNFREE *v* -FREED, -FREEING, -FREES to deprive of freedom

UNFREEZE *v* -FROZE, -FROZEN, -FREEZING, -FREEZES to cause to thaw

UNFROCK *v* -ED, -ING, -S to divest of ecclesiastical authority

UNFURL *v* -ED, -ING, -S to unroll

UNGAINLY *adj* -LIER, -LIEST awkward

UNGIRD *v* -GIRDED or -GIRT, -GIRDING, -GIRDS to remove a belt from

UNGLOVE *v* -GLOVED, -GLOVING, -GLOVES to uncover by removing a glove

UNGLUE *v* -GLUED, -GLUING, -GLUES to disjoin

UNGODLY *adj* -LIER, -LIEST impious

UNGOT *adj* ungotten

UNGOTTEN *adj* not obtained

UNGUAL *adj* pertaining to an unguis

UNGUARD *v* -ED, -ING, -S to leave unprotected

UNGUENT *n* pl. -S an ointment

UNGUENTA *n/pl* ointments

UNGUIS *n* pl. -GUES a nail, claw, or hoof

UNGULA *n* pl. -LAE an unguis **UNGULAR** *adj*

UNGULATE *n* pl. -S a hoofed mammal

UNHAIR *v* -ED, -ING, -S to remove the hair from

UNHALLOW *v* -ED, -ING, -S to profane

UNHAND *v* -ED, -ING, -S to remove the hand from

UNHANDY *adj* -HANDIER, -HANDIEST difficult to handle

UNHANG *v* -HUNG or -HANGED, -HANGING, -HANGS to detach from a hanging support

UNHAT *v* -HATTED, -HATTING, -HATS to remove one's hat

UNHELM *v* -ED, -ING, -S to remove the helmet of

UNHINGE *v* -HINGED, -HINGING, -HINGES to remove from hinges

UNHITCH *v* -ED, -ING, -ES to free from being hitched

UNHOOD *v* -ED, -ING, -S to remove a hood from

UNHOOK *v* -ED, -ING, -S to remove from a hook

UNHOPED *adj* not hoped for or expected

UNHORSE *v* -HORSED, -HORSING, -HORSES to cause to fall from a horse

UNHOUSE *v* -HOUSED, -HOUSING, -HOUSES to deprive of a protective shelter

UNHUSK *v* -ED, -ING, -S to remove the husk from

UNIALGAL *adj* pertaining to a single algal cell

UNIAXIAL *adj* having one axis

UNICOLOR *adj* of one color

UNICORN *n* pl. -S a mythical horselike creature

UNICYCLE *n* pl. -S a one-wheeled vehicle

UNIDEAED *adj* lacking ideas

UNIFACE *n* pl. -S a coin having a design on only one side

UNIFIC *adj* unifying

UNIFIED past tense of unify

UNIFIER *n* pl. -S one that unifies

UNIFIES present 3d person sing. of unify

UNIFILAR *adj* having only one thread, wire, or fiber

UNIFORM *adj* -FORMER, -FORMEST unchanging

UNIFORM *v* -ED, -ING, -S to make uniform

UNIFY *v* -FIED, -FYING, -FIES to make into a coherent whole

UNILOBED *adj* having one lobe

UNION *n* pl. -S a number of persons, parties, or political entities united for a common purpose

UNIONISE *v* -ISED, -ISING, -ISES to unionize

UNIONISM *n* pl. -S the principle of forming a union

UNIONIST *n* pl. -S an advocate of unionism

UNIONIZE *v* -IZED, -IZING, -IZES to form into a union

UNIPOD *n* pl. -S a one-legged support

UNIPOLAR *adj* showing only one kind of polarity

UNIQUE *adj* UNIQUER, UNIQUEST existing as the only one of its kind; very unusual **UNIQUELY** *adv*

UNIQUE *n* pl. -S something that is unique

UNISEX *n* pl. -ES the condition of not being distinguishable as to sex

UNISON *n* pl. -S complete agreement **UNISONAL** *adj*

UNIT *n* pl. -S a specific quantity used as a standard of measurement

UNITAGE *n* pl. -S amount in units

UNITARD *n* pl. -S a leotard that also covers the legs

UNITARY *adj* pertaining to a unit

UNITE *v* UNITED, UNITING, UNITES to bring together so as to form a whole **UNITEDLY** *adv*

UNITER *n* pl. -S one that unites

UNITIES pl. of unity

UNITING present participle of unite

UNITIVE *adj* serving to unite

UNITIZE *v* -IZED, -IZING, -IZES to divide into units

UNITIZER *n* pl. -S one that unitizes

UNITRUST *n* pl. -S a type of annuity trust

UNITY *n* pl. -TIES the state of being one single entity

UNIVALVE *n* pl. -S a mollusk having a single shell

UNIVERSE *n* pl. -S the totality of all existing things

UNIVOCAL *n* pl. -S a word having only one meaning

UNJOINT *v* -ED, -ING, -S to separate at a juncture

UNKEMPT *adj* untidy

UNKEND *adj* unkenned

UNKENNED *adj* not known or recognized

UNKENNEL *v* -NELED, -NELING, -NELS or -NELLED, -NELLING, -NELS to release from a kennel

UNKENT *adj* unkenned

UNKINK *v* -ED, -ING, -S to remove curls from

UNKNIT *v* -KNITTED, -KNITTING, -KNITS to unravel

UNKNOT *v* -KNOTTED, -KNOTTING, -KNOTS to undo a knot in

UNKNOWN *n* pl. -S one that is not known

UNLACE *v* -LACED, -LACING, -LACES to unfasten the laces of

UNLADE *v* -LADED, -LADEN, -LADING, -LADES to unload

UNLAID past tense of unlay

UNLASH *v* -ED, -ING, -ES to untie the lashing (a type of binding) of

UNLATCH	*v* -ED, -ING, -ES to open by lifting the latch (a fastening device)
UNLAY	*v* -LAID, -LAYING, -LAYS to untwist
UNLEAD	*v* -ED, -ING, -S to remove the lead from
UNLEARN	*v* -LEARNED or -LEARNT, -LEARNING, -LEARNS to put out of one's knowledge or memory
UNLEASH	*v* -ED, -ING, -ES to free from a leash
UNLESS	*conj* except on the condition that
UNLET	*adj* not rented
UNLEVEL	*v* -ELED, -ELING, -ELS or -ELLED, -ELLING, -ELS to make uneven
UNLIMBER	*v* -ED, -ING, -S to prepare for action
UNLINK	*v* -ED, -ING, -S to unfasten the links (connecting devices) of
UNLIVE	*v* -LIVED, -LIVING, -LIVES to live so as to make amends for
UNLOAD	*v* -ED, -ING, -S to remove the load or cargo from
UNLOADER	*n* pl. -S one that unloads
UNLOCK	*v* -ED, -ING, -S to unfasten the lock of
UNLOOSE	*v* -LOOSED, -LOOSING, -LOOSES to set free
UNLOOSEN	*v* -ED, -ING, -S to unloose
UNMAKE	*v* -MADE, -MAKING, -MAKES to destroy
UNMAKER	*n* pl. -S one that unmakes
UNMAN	*v* -MANNED, -MANNING, -MANS to deprive of courage
UNMASK	*v* -ED, -ING, -S to remove a mask from
UNMASKER	*n* pl. -S one that unmasks
UNMEET	*adj* improper **UNMEETLY** *adv*
UNMESH	*v* -ED, -ING, -ES to disentangle
UNMEW	*v* -ED, -ING, -S to set free
UNMINGLE	*v* -GLED, -GLING, -GLES to separate things that are mixed
UNMITER	*v* -ED, -ING, -S to depose from the rank of bishop
UNMITRE	*v* -TRED, -TRING, -TRES to unmiter
UNMIX	*v* -MIXED or -MIXT, -MIXING, -MIXES to separate from a mixture
UNMOLD	*v* -ED, -ING, -S to remove from a mold
UNMOOR	*v* -ED, -ING, -S to release from moorings
UNMORAL	*adj* amoral
UNMUFFLE	*v* -FLED, -FLING, -FLES to free from something that muffles
UNMUZZLE	*v* -ZLED, -ZLING, -ZLES to remove a muzzle from
UNNAIL	*v* -ED, -ING, -S to remove the nails from
UNNERVE	*v* -NERVED, -NERVING, -NERVES to deprive of courage
UNPACK	*v* -ED, -ING, -S to remove the contents of
UNPACKER	*n* pl. -S one that unpacks
UNPAGED	*adj* having no page numbers
UNPEG	*v* -PEGGED, -PEGGING, -PEGS to remove the pegs from
UNPEN	*v* -PENNED or -PENT, -PENNING, -PENS to release from confinement
UNPEOPLE	*v* -PLED, -PLING, -PLES to remove people from
UNPERSON	*n* pl. -S one who is removed completely from recognition
UNPICK	*v* -ED, -ING, -S to remove the stitches from
UNPILE	*v* -PILED, -PILING, -PILES to take or disentangle from a pile
UNPIN	*v* -PINNED, -PINNING, -PINS to remove the pins from
UNPLAIT	*v* -ED, -ING, -S to undo the plaits of
UNPLUG	*v* -PLUGGED, -PLUGGING, -PLUGS to take a plug out of
UNPUCKER	*v* -ED, -ING, -S to remove the wrinkles from
UNPUZZLE	*v* -ZLED, -ZLING, -ZLES to work out the obscured meaning of
UNQUIET	*n* pl. -S a state of unrest
UNQUOTE	*v* -QUOTED, -QUOTING, -QUOTES to close a quotation
UNRAVEL	*v* -ELED, -ELING, -ELS or -ELLED, -ELLING, -ELS to separate the threads of
UNREASON	*v* -ED, -ING, -S to disrupt the sanity of
UNREEL	*v* -ED, -ING, -S to unwind from a reel
UNREELER	*n* pl. -S one that unreels

UNREEVE   *v* -REEVED or -ROVE, -ROVEN, -REEVING, -REEVES to withdraw a rope from an opening

UNRENT   *adj* not torn

UNREPAIR   *n* pl. -S lack of repair

UNREST   *n* pl. -S a disturbed or uneasy state

UNRIDDLE   *v* -DLED, -DLING, -DLES to solve

UNRIG   *v* -RIGGED, -RIGGING, -RIGS to divest of rigging

UNRIP   *v* -RIPPED, -RIPPING, -RIPS to rip open

UNRIPE   *adj* -RIPER, -RIPEST not ripe
UNRIPELY *adv*

UNROBE   *v* -ROBED, -ROBING, -ROBES to undress

UNROLL   *v* -ED, -ING, -S to open something that is rolled up

UNROOF   *v* -ED, -ING, -S to strip off the roof of

UNROOT   *v* -ED, -ING, -S to uproot

UNROUND   *v* -ED, -ING, -S to articulate without rounding the lips

UNROVE   a past tense of unreeve

UNROVEN   a past participle of unreeve

UNRULY   *adj* -LIER, -LIEST difficult to control

UNSADDLE   *v* -DLED, -DLING, -DLES to remove the saddle from

UNSAFETY   *n* pl. -TIES lack of safety

UNSAY   *v* -SAID, -SAYING, -SAYS to retract something said

UNSCREW   *v* -ED, -ING, -S to remove the screws from

UNSEAL   *v* -ED, -ING, -S to remove the seal of

UNSEAM   *v* -ED, -ING, -S to open the seams of

UNSEAT   *v* -ED, -ING, -S to remove from a seat

UNSET   *v* -SET, -SETTING, -SETS to unsettle

UNSETTLE   *v* -TLED, -TLING, -TLES to make unstable

UNSEW   *v* -SEWED, -SEWN, -SEWING, -SEWS to undo the sewing of

UNSEX   *v* -ED, -ING, -ES to deprive of sexual power

UNSHELL   *v* -ED, -ING, -S to remove the shell from

UNSHIFT   *v* -ED, -ING, -S to release the shift key on a typewriter

UNSHIP   *v* -SHIPPED, -SHIPPING, -SHIPS to unload from a ship

UNSICKER   *adj* unreliable

UNSIGHT   *v* -ED, -ING, -S to prevent from seeing

UNSLING   *v* -SLUNG, -SLINGING, -SLINGS to remove from a slung position

UNSNAP   *v* -SNAPPED, -SNAPPING, -SNAPS to undo the snaps of

UNSNARL   *v* -ED, -ING, -S to untangle

UNSOLDER   *v* -ED, -ING, -S to separate

UNSONCY   *adj* unsonsie

UNSONSIE   *adj* unlucky

UNSONSY   *adj* unsonsie

UNSPEAK   *v* -SPOKE, -SPOKEN, -SPEAKING, -SPEAKS to unsay

UNSPHERE   *v* -SPHERED, -SPHERING, -SPHERES to remove from a sphere

UNSTACK   *v* -ED, -ING, -S to remove from a stack

UNSTATE   *v* -STATED, -STATING, -STATES to deprive of status

UNSTAYED   *adj* not secured with ropes or wires

UNSTEADY   *v* -STEADIED, -STEADYING, -STEADIES to make unsteady

UNSTEEL   *v* -ED, -ING, -S to make soft

UNSTEP   *v* -STEPPED, -STEPPING, -STEPS to remove from a socket

UNSTICK   *v* -STUCK, -STICKING, -STICKS to disjoin

UNSTITCH   *v* -ED, -ING, -ES to remove the stitches from

UNSTOP   *v* -STOPPED, -STOPPING, -STOPS to remove a stopper from

UNSTRAP   *v* -STRAPPED, -STRAPPING, -STRAPS to remove a strap from

UNSTRESS   *n* pl. -ES a syllable having relatively weak stress

UNSTRING   *v* -STRUNG, -STRINGING, -STRINGS to remove from a string

UNSTUCK   past tense of unstick

UNSWATHE   *v* -SWATHED, -SWATHING, -SWATHES to unbind

UNSWEAR   *v* -SWORE, -SWORN, -SWEARING, -SWEARS to retract something sworn

UNTACK   *v* -ED, -ING, -S to remove a tack from

UNTANGLE   *v* -GLED, -GLING, -GLES to free from tangles

UNTEACH   *v* -TAUGHT, -TEACHING, -TEACHES to cause to unlearn something

UNTENTED   *adj* not probed or attended to

UNTETHER   *v* -ED, -ING, -S to free from a tether

UNTHINK   *v* -THOUGHT, -THINKING, -THINKS to dismiss from the mind

UNTHREAD   *v* -ED, -ING, -S to remove the thread from

UNTHRONE   *v* -THRONED, -THRONING, -THRONES to remove from a throne

UNTIDY   *v* -DIED, -DYING, -DIES to make untidy

UNTIE   *v* -TIED, -TYING, -TIES to free from something that ties

UNTIL   *prep* up to the time of

UNTO   *prep* to

UNTOWARD   *adj* unruly

UNTREAD   *v* -TROD, -TRODDEN, -TREADING, -TREADS to retrace

UNTRIM   *v* -TRIMMED, -TRIMMING, -TRIMS to strip of trimming

UNTRUSS   *v* -ED, -ING, -ES to free from a truss

UNTRUTH   *n* pl. -S something that is untrue

UNTUCK   *v* -ED, -ING, -S to release from being tucked up

UNTUNE   *v* -TUNED, -TUNING, -TUNES to put out of tune

UNTWINE   *v* -TWINED, -TWINING, -TWINES to separate the twisted or tangled parts of

UNTWIST   *v* -ED, -ING, -S to untwine

UNTYING   present participle of untie

UNVEIL   *v* -ED, -ING, -S to remove a covering from

UNVOICE   *v* -VOICED, -VOICING, -VOICES to deprive of voice or vocal quality

UNWASHED   *n* pl. -S an ignorant or underprivileged group

UNWEAVE   *v* -WOVE, -WOVEN, -WEAVING, -WEAVES to undo something woven

UNWEIGHT   *v* -ED, -ING, -S to reduce the weight of

UNWIND   *v* -WOUND, -WINDING, -WINDS to reverse the winding of

UNWINDER   *n* pl. -S one that unwinds

UNWISDOM   *n* pl. -S lack of wisdom

UNWISH   *v* -ED, -ING, -ES to cease to wish for

UNWIT   *v* -WITTED, -WITTING, -WITS to make insane

UNWONTED   *adj* unusual

UNWORTHY   *n* pl. -THIES an unworthy person

UNWOUND   past tense of unwind

UNWOVE   past tense of unweave

UNWOVEN   past participle of unweave

UNWRAP   *v* -WRAPPED, -WRAPPING, -WRAPS to remove the wrapping from

UNYEANED   *adj* unborn

UNYOKE   *v* -YOKED, -YOKING, -YOKES to free from a yoke

UNZIP   *v* -ZIPPED, -ZIPPING, -ZIPS to open the zipper of

UP   *v* UPPED, UPPING, UPS to raise

UPAS   *n* pl. -ES an Asian tree

UPBEAR   *v* -BORE, -BORNE, -BEARING, -BEARS to raise aloft

UPBEARER   *n* pl. -S one that upbears

UPBEAT   *n* pl. -S an unaccented beat in a musical measure

UPBIND   *v* -BOUND, -BINDING, -BINDS to bind completely

UPBOIL   *v* -ED, -ING, -S to boil up

UPBORE   past tense of upbear

UPBORNE   past participle of upbear

UPBOUND   past tense of upbind

UPBOW   *n* pl. -S a type of stroke in playing a bowed instrument

UPBRAID   *v* -ED, -ING, -S to reproach severely

UPBUILD   *v* -BUILT, -BUILDING, -BUILDS to build up

UPBY   *adv* upbye

UPBYE   *adv* a little farther on

UPCAST   *v* -CAST, -CASTING, -CASTS to cast up

UPCHUCK   *v* -ED, -ING, -S to vomit

UPCLIMB   *v* -ED, -ING, -S to climb up

UPCOAST   *adv* up the coast

UPCOIL   *v* -ED, -ING, -S to coil up

UPCOMING   *adj* about to happen or appear

UPCURL	*v* -ED, -ING, -S to curl up
UPCURVE	*v* -CURVED, -CURVING, -CURVES to curve upward
UPDART	*v* -ED, -ING, -S to dart up
UPDATE	*v* -DATED, -DATING, -DATES to bring up to date
UPDATER	*n* pl. -S one that updates
UPDIVE	*v* -DIVED or -DOVE, -DIVING, -DIVES to spring upward
UPDO	*n* pl. -DOS an upswept hairdo
UPDRAFT	*n* pl. -S an upward movement of air
UPDRY	*v* -DRIED, -DRYING, -DRIES to dry completely
UPEND	*v* -ED, -ING, -S to set or stand on end
UPFIELD	*adv* into the part of the field toward which the offensive team is going
UPFLING	*v* -FLUNG, -FLINGING, -FLINGS to fling up
UPFLOW	*v* -ED, -ING, -S to flow up
UPFOLD	*v* -ED, -ING, -S to fold up
UPFRONT	*adj* honest; candid
UPGATHER	*v* -ED, -ING, -S to gather up
UPGAZE	*v* -GAZED, -GAZING, -GAZES to gaze up
UPGIRD	*v* -GIRDED or -GIRT, -GIRDING, -GIRDS to gird completely
UPGOING	*adj* going up
UPGRADE	*v* -GRADED, -GRADING, -GRADES to raise to a higher grade or standard
UPGROW	*v* -GREW, -GROWN, -GROWING, -GROWS to grow up
UPGROWTH	*n* pl. -S the process of growing up
UPHEAP	*v* -ED, -ING, -S to heap up
UPHEAVAL	*n* pl. -S the act of upheaving
UPHEAVE	*v* -HEAVED or -HOVE, -HEAVING, -HEAVES to heave up
UPHEAVER	*n* pl. -S one that upheaves
UPHELD	past tense of uphold
UPHILL	*n* pl. -S an upward slope
UPHOARD	*v* -ED, -ING, -S to hoard up
UPHOLD	*v* -HELD, -HOLDING, -HOLDS to hold aloft
UPHOLDER	*n* pl. -S one that upholds
UPHOVE	a past tense of upheave
UPHROE	*n* pl. -S euphroe
UPKEEP	*n* pl. -S the cost of maintaining something in good condition
UPLAND	*n* pl. -S the higher land of a region
UPLANDER	*n* pl. -S an inhabitant of an upland
UPLEAP	*v* -LEAPED or -LEAPT, -LEAPING, -LEAPS to leap up
UPLIFT	*v* -ED, -ING, -S to lift up
UPLIFTER	*n* pl. -S one that uplifts
UPLIGHT	*v* -LIGHTED or -LIT, -LIGHTING, -LIGHTS to light to a higher degree
UPLINK	*n* pl. -S a communications channel to a spacecraft
UPLOAD	*v* -ED, -ING, -S to transfer information from a small computer to a larger computer
UPMARKET	*adj* upscale
UPMOST	*adj* highest
UPO	*prep* upon
UPON	*prep* on
UPPED	past tense of up
UPPER	*n* pl. -S the part of a boot or shoe above the sole
UPPERCUT	*v* -CUT, -CUTTING, -CUTS to strike an upward blow
UPPILE	*v* -PILED, -PILING, -PILES to pile up
UPPING	*n* pl. -S the process of marking young swans for identification purposes
UPPISH	*adj* uppity **UPPISHLY** *adv*
UPPITY	*adj* tending to be snobbish and arrogant
UPPROP	*v* -PROPPED, -PROPPING, -PROPS to prop up
UPRAISE	*v* -RAISED, -RAISING, -RAISES to raise up
UPRAISER	*n* pl. -S one that upraises
UPRATE	*v* -RATED, -RATING, -RATES to improve the power output of an engine
UPREACH	*v* -ED, -ING, -ES to reach up
UPREAR	*v* -ED, -ING, -S to upraise
UPRIGHT	*v* -ED, -ING, -S to make vertical
UPRISE	*v* -ROSE, -RISEN, -RISING, -RISES to rise up
UPRISER	*n* pl. -S one that uprises
UPRISING	*n* pl. -S a revolt

UPRIVER *n* pl. -S an area lying toward the source of a river

UPROAR *n* pl. -S a state of noisy excitement and confusion

UPROOT *v* -ED, -ING, -S to pull up by the roots

UPROOTAL *n* pl. -S the act of uprooting

UPROOTER *n* pl. -S one that uproots

UPROSE past tense of uprise

UPROUSE *v* -ROUSED, -ROUSING, -ROUSES to rouse up

UPRUSH *v* -ED, -ING, -ES to rush up

UPSCALE *v* -SCALED, -SCALING, -SCALES to make appealing to affluent consumers

UPSEND *v* -SENT, -SENDING, -SENDS to send upward

UPSET *v* -SET, -SETTING, -SETS to overturn

UPSETTER *n* pl. -S one that upsets

UPSHIFT *v* -ED, -ING, -S to shift into a higher gear

UPSHOOT *v* -SHOT, -SHOOTING, -SHOOTS to shoot upward

UPSHOT *n* pl. -S the final result

UPSIDE *n* pl. -S a positive aspect

UPSILON *n* pl. -S a Greek letter

UPSOAR *v* -ED, -ING, -S to soar upward

UPSPRING *v* -SPRANG or -SPRUNG, -SPRINGING, -SPRINGS to spring up

UPSTAGE *v* -STAGED, -STAGING, -STAGES to outdo theatrically

UPSTAIR *adj* pertaining to an upper floor

UPSTAIRS *adv* up the stairs

UPSTAND *v* -STOOD, -STANDING, -STANDS to stand up on one's feet

UPSTARE *v* -STARED, -STARING, -STARES to stare upward

UPSTART *v* -ED, -ING, -S to spring up suddenly

UPSTATE *n* pl. -S the northern region of a state

UPSTATER *n* pl. -S an inhabitant of an upstate region

UPSTEP *v* -STEPPED, -STEPPING, -STEPS to step up

UPSTIR *v* -STIRRED, -STIRRING, -STIRS to stir up

UPSTOOD past tense of upstand

UPSTREAM *adv* toward the source of a stream

UPSTROKE *n* pl. -S an upward stroke

UPSURGE *v* -SURGED, -SURGING, -SURGES to surge up

UPSWEEP *v* -SWEPT, -SWEEPING, -SWEEPS to sweep upward

UPSWELL *v* -SWELLED, -SWOLLEN, -SWELLING, -SWELLS to swell up

UPSWING *v* -SWUNG, -SWINGING, -SWINGS to swing upward

UPTAKE *n* pl. -S an upward ventilating shaft

UPTEAR *v* -TORE, -TORN, -TEARING, -TEARS to tear out by the roots

UPTHROW *v* -THREW, -THROWN, -THROWING, -THROWS to throw upward

UPTHRUST *v* -THRUST, -THRUSTING, -THRUSTS to thrust up

UPTICK *n* pl. -S an increase or rise

UPTIGHT *adj* nervous

UPTILT *v* -ED, -ING, -S to tilt upward

UPTIME *n* pl. -S the time during which machinery is functioning

UPTORE past tense of uptear

UPTORN past participle of uptear

UPTOSS *v* -ED, -ING, -ES to toss upward

UPTOWN *n* pl. -S the upper part of a city

UPTOWNER *n* pl. -S one that lives uptown

UPTREND *n* pl. -S a tendency upward or toward growth

UPTURN *v* -ED, -ING, -S to turn up or over

UPWAFT *v* -ED, -ING, -S to waft upward

UPWARD *adv* toward a higher place or position **UPWARDLY** *adv*

UPWARDS *adv* upward

UPWELL *v* -ED, -ING, -S to well up

UPWIND *n* pl. -S a wind that blows against one's course

URACIL *n* pl. -S a chemical compound

URAEMIA *n* pl. -S uremia **URAEMIC** *adj*

URAEUS *n* pl. URAEI or URAEUSES the figure of the sacred serpent on the headdress of ancient Egyptian rulers

URALITE *n* pl. -S a mineral **URALITIC** *adj*

URANIA *n* pl. -S uranium dioxide

URANIC *adj* pertaining to uranium

URANIDE *n* pl. -S uranium

URANISM *n* pl. -S homosexuality

URANITE *n* pl. -S a mineral **URANITIC** *adj*

URANIUM *n* pl. -S a radioactive element

URANOUS *adj* pertaining to uranium

URANYL *n* pl. -S a bivalent radical **URANYLIC** *adj*

URARE *n* pl. -S curare

URARI *n* pl. -S curare

URASE *n* pl. -S urease

URATE *n* pl. -S a chemical salt **URATIC** *adj*

URB *n* pl. -S an urban area

URBAN *adj* pertaining to a city

URBANE *adj* -BANER, -BANEST refined and elegant **URBANELY** *adv*

URBANISE *v* -ISED, -ISING, -ISES to urbanize

URBANISM *n* pl. -S the lifestyle of city dwellers

URBANIST *n* pl. -S a specialist in city planning

URBANITE *n* pl. -S one who lives in a city

URBANITY *n* pl. -TIES the quality of being urbane

URBANIZE *v* -IZED, -IZING, -IZES to cause to take on urban characteristics

URBIA *n* pl. -S cities collectively

URCHIN *n* pl. -S a mischievous boy

URD *n* pl. -S an annual bean grown in India

UREA *n* pl. -S a chemical compound **UREAL** *adj*

UREASE *n* pl. -S an enzyme

UREDIA pl. of uredium

UREDIAL *adj* pertaining to a uredium

UREDINIA *n/pl* uredia

UREDIUM *n* pl. -DIA a spore-producing organ of certain fungi

UREDO *n* pl. -DOS a skin irritation

UREIC *adj* pertaining to urea

UREIDE *n* pl. -S a chemical compound

UREMIA *n* pl. -S an abnormal condition of the blood **UREMIC** *adj*

URETER *n* pl. -S the duct that conveys urine from the kidney to the bladder **URETERAL, URETERIC** *adj*

URETHAN *n* pl. -S urethane

URETHANE *n* pl. -S a chemical compound

URETHRA *n* pl. -THRAE or -THRAS the duct through which urine is discharged from the bladder **URETHRAL** *adj*

URETIC *adj* pertaining to urine

URGE *v* URGED, URGING, URGES to force forward

URGENCY *n* pl. -CIES the quality of being urgent

URGENT *adj* requiring immediate attention **URGENTLY** *adv*

URGER *n* pl. -S one that urges

URGING present participle of urge

URGINGLY *adv* in an urging manner

URIAL *n* pl. -S a wild Asian sheep

URIC *adj* pertaining to urine

URIDINE *n* pl. -S a chemical compound

URINAL *n* pl. -S a fixture used for urinating

URINARY *n* pl. -NARIES a urinal

URINATE *v* -NATED, -NATING, -NATES to discharge urine

URINE *n* pl. -S a liquid containing body wastes

URINEMIA *n* pl. -S uremia **URINEMIC** *adj*

URINOSE *adj* pertaining to urine

URINOUS *adj* pertaining to urine

URN *n* pl. -S a type of vase **URNLIKE** *adj*

UROCHORD *n* pl. -S a rodlike structure in certain lower vertebrates

URODELE *n* pl. -S a type of amphibian

UROLITH *n* pl. -S a concretion in the urinary tract

UROLOGY *n* pl. -GIES the branch of medicine dealing with the urinary tract **UROLOGIC** *adj*

UROPOD *n* pl. -S an abdominal limb of an arthropod **UROPODAL** *adj*

UROPYGIA *n/pl* the humps from which birds' tail feathers grow

UROSCOPY *n* pl. -PIES analysis of the urine as a means of diagnosis

UROSTYLE *n* pl. -S a part of the vertebral column of frogs and toads

URSA *n* pl. -SAE a female bear

URSIFORM *adj* having the form of a bear

URSINE *adj* pertaining to a bear

URTEXT *n* pl. -S the original text

URTICANT   *n* pl. -S an urticating substance

URTICATE   *v* -CATED, -CATING, -CATES to cause itching or stinging

URUS   *n* pl. -ES an extinct European ox

URUSHIOL   *n* pl. -S a toxic liquid

US   *pron* the objective case of the pronoun we

USABLE   *adj* capable of being used **USABLY** *adv*

USAGE   *n* pl. -S a firmly established and generally accepted practice or procedure

USANCE   *n* pl. -S usage

USAUNCE   *n* pl. -S usance

USE   *v* USED, USING, USES to put into service

USEABLE   *adj* usable **USEABLY** *adv*

USEFUL   *adj* serving a purpose **USEFULLY** *adv*

USELESS   *adj* serving no purpose

USER   *n* pl. -S one that uses

USHER   *v* -ED, -ING, -S to conduct to a place

USING   present participle of use

USNEA   *n* pl. -S any of a genus of lichens

USQUABAE   *n* pl. -S usquebae

USQUE   *n* pl. -S usquebae

USQUEBAE   *n* pl. -S whiskey

USTULATE   *adj* scorched

USUAL   *n* pl. -S something that is usual (ordinary)

USUALLY   *adv* ordinarily

USUFRUCT   *n* pl. -S the legal right to use another's property so long as it is not damaged or altered

USURER   *n* pl. -S one that practices usury

USURIES   pl. of usury

USURIOUS   *adj* practicing usury

USURP   *v* -ED, -ING, -S to seize and hold without legal authority

USURPER   *n* pl. -S one that usurps

USURY   *n* pl. -RIES the lending of money at an exorbitant interest rate

UT   *n* pl. -S the musical tone C in the French solmization system now replaced by do

UTA   *n* pl. -S any of a genus of large lizards

UTENSIL   *n* pl. -S a useful implement

UTERUS   *n* pl. UTERI or UTERUSES an organ of female mammals **UTERINE** *adj*

UTILE   *adj* useful

UTILIDOR   *n* pl. -S an insulated system of pipes for use in arctic regions

UTILISE   *v* -LISED, -LISING, -LISES to utilize

UTILISER   *n* pl. -S utilizer

UTILITY   *n* pl. -TIES the quality of being useful

UTILIZE   *v* -LIZED, -LIZING, -LIZES to make use of

UTILIZER   *n* pl. -S one that utilizes

UTMOST   *n* pl. -S the greatest degree or amount

UTOPIA   *n* pl. -S a place of ideal perfection

UTOPIAN   *n* pl. -S one who believes in the perfectibility of human society

UTOPISM   *n* pl. -S the body of ideals or principles of a utopian

UTOPIST   *n* pl. -S a utopian

UTRICLE   *n* pl. -S a saclike cavity in the inner ear

UTRICULI   *n/pl* utricles

UTTER   *v* -ED, -ING, -S to give audible expression to

UTTERER   *n* pl. -S one that utters

UTTERLY   *adv* totally

UVEA   *n* pl. -S a layer of the eye **UVEAL** *adj*

UVEITIS   *n* pl. -ITISES inflammation of the uvea **UVEITIC** *adj*

UVEOUS   *adj* pertaining to the uvea

UVULA   *n* pl. -LAE or -LAS the pendent, fleshy portion of the soft palate

UVULAR   *n* pl. -S a uvularly produced sound

UVULARLY   *adv* with the use of the uvula

UVULITIS   *n* pl. -TISES inflammation of the uvula

UXORIAL   *adj* pertaining to a wife

UXORIOUS   *adj* excessively submissive or devoted to one's wife

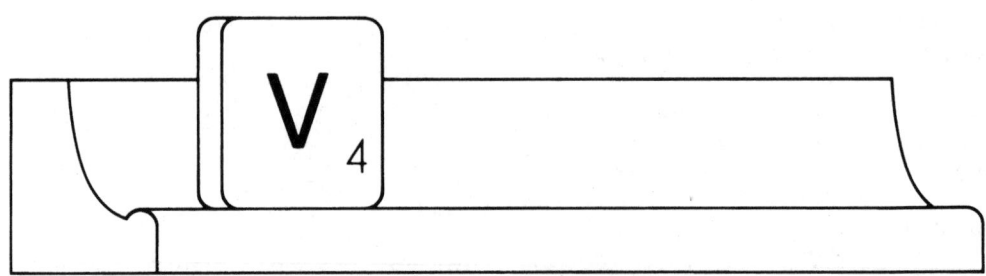

VAC   n pl. -S a vacuum cleaner

VACANCY   n pl. -CIES the quality or state of being vacant

VACANT   adj empty **VACANTLY** adv

VACATE   v -CATED, -CATING, -CATES to make vacant

VACATION   v -ED, -ING, -S to take a vacation (a period of time devoted to rest and relaxation)

VACCINA   n pl. -S vaccinia

VACCINE   n pl. -S a preparation given to produce immunity to a specific disease **VACCINAL** adj

VACCINEE   n pl. -S one that is vaccinated

VACCINIA   n pl. -S cowpox

VACUA   a pl. of vacuum

VACUITY   n pl. -ITIES an empty space

VACUOLE   n pl. -S a small cavity in organic tissue **VACUOLAR** adj

VACUOUS   adj empty

VACUUM   n pl. VACUUMS or VACUA a space entirely devoid of matter

VACUUM   v -ED, -ING, -S to use a device that cleans by suction

VADOSE   adj located above the permanent groundwater level

VAGABOND   v -ED, -ING, -S to live like a vagabond (a vagrant)

VAGAL   adj pertaining to the vagus nerve **VAGALLY** adv

VAGARY   n pl. -RIES a whim

VAGI   pl. of vagus

VAGILE   adj free to move about

VAGILITY   n pl. -TIES freedom of movement

VAGINA   n pl. -NAE or -NAS the passage leading from the uterus to the vulva **VAGINAL** adj

VAGINATE   adj enclosed in a sheath

VAGOTOMY   n pl. -MIES surgical division of the vagus nerve

VAGRANCY   n pl. -CIES the state of being a vagrant

VAGRANT   n pl. -S a wanderer with no apparent means of support

VAGROM   adj wandering

VAGUE   adj VAGUER, VAGUEST not clearly expressed or understood **VAGUELY** adv

VAGUS   n pl. -GI a cranial nerve

VAHINE   n pl. -S wahine

VAIL   v -ED, -ING, -S to lower

VAIN   adj VAINER, VAINEST filled with undue admiration for oneself **VAINLY** adv

VAINNESS   n pl. -ES the quality or state of being vain

VAIR   n pl. -S a fur used for lining and trimming medieval garments

VAKEEL   n pl. -S a native lawyer in India

VAKIL   n pl. -S vakeel

VALANCE   v -LANCED, -LANCING, -LANCES to furnish with a short drapery

VALE   n pl. -S a valley

VALENCE   n pl. -S the degree of combining power of an element or radical

VALENCIA   n pl. -S a woven fabric

VALENCY   n pl. -CIES valence

VALERATE   n pl. -S a chemical salt

VALERIAN   n pl. -S a perennial herb **VALERIC** adj

VALET   v -ED, -ING, -S to act as a personal servant to

VALGUS   n pl. -ES the position of a joint that is abnormally turned outward **VALGOID** adj

VALIANCE   n pl. -S valor

VALIANCY   n pl. -CIES valor

VALIANT   *n* pl. -S a courageous person

VALID   *adj* based on evidence that can be supported

VALIDATE   *v* -DATED, -DATING, -DATES to give legal force to

VALIDITY   *n* pl. -TIES the quality or state of being valid

VALIDLY   *adv* in a valid manner

VALINE   *n* pl. -S an amino acid

VALISE   *n* pl. -S a small piece of hand luggage

VALKYR   *n* pl. -S valkyrie

VALKYRIE   *n* pl. -S a maiden in Norse mythology

VALLATE   *adj* bordered by a raised edge

VALLEY   *n* pl. -LEYS a depression of the earth's surface

VALONIA   *n* pl. -S a substance obtained from dried acorn cups and used in tanning and dyeing

VALOR   *n* pl. -S courage

VALORISE   *v* -ISED, -ISING, -ISES to valorize

VALORIZE   *v* -IZED, -IZING, -IZES to establish and maintain the price of by governmental action

VALOROUS   *adj* courageous

VALOUR   *n* pl. -S valor

VALSE   *n* pl. -S a concert waltz

VALUABLE   *n* pl. -S a possession of value

VALUABLY   *adv* with value

VALUATE   *v* -ATED, -ATING, -ATES to appraise

VALUATOR   *n* pl. -S one that valuates

VALUE   *v* -UED, -UING, -UES to estimate the value (the quality that renders a thing useful or desirable) of

VALUER   *n* pl. -S one that values

VALUTA   *n* pl. -S the agreed or exchange value of a currency

VALVAL   *adj* resembling or pertaining to a valve

VALVAR   *adj* valval

VALVATE   *adj* having valves or parts resembling valves

VALVE   *v* VALVED, VALVING, VALVES to provide with a valve (a device for controlling the flow of a liquid or gas)

VALVELET   *n* pl. -S a small valve

VALVULA   *n* pl. -LAE valvule

VALVULAR   *adj* pertaining to a valve

VALVULE   *n* pl. -S a small valve

VAMBRACE   *n* pl. -S a piece of armor for the forearm

VAMOOSE   *v* -MOOSED, -MOOSING, -MOOSES to leave quickly

VAMOSE   *v* -MOSED, -MOSING, -MOSES to vamoose

VAMP   *v* -ED, -ING, -S to repair or patch

VAMPER   *n* pl. -S one that vamps

VAMPIRE   *n* pl. -S a reanimated corpse believed to feed on sleeping persons' blood **VAMPIRIC** *adj*

VAMPISH   *adj* seductive

VAN   *v* VANNED, VANNING, VANS to transport in a van (a type of motor vehicle)

VANADATE   *n* pl. -S a chemical salt

VANADIUM   *n* pl. -S a metallic element **VANADIC, VANADOUS** *adj*

VANDA   *n* pl. -S a tropical orchid

VANDAL   *n* pl. -S one who willfully destroys or defaces property **VANDALIC** *adj*

VANDYKE   *n* pl. -S a short, pointed beard **VANDYKED** *adj*

VANE   *n* pl. -S a device for showing the direction of the wind **VANED** *adj*

VANG   *n* pl. -S a rope on a ship

VANGUARD   *n* pl. -S the forefront of a movement

VANILLA   *n* pl. -S a flavoring extract **VANILLIC** *adj*

VANILLIN   *n* pl. -S a chemical compound used in flavoring

VANISH   *v* -ED, -ING, -ES to disappear

VANISHER   *n* pl. -S one that vanishes

VANITORY   *n* pl. -RIES a combined dressing table and basin

VANITY   *n* pl. -TIES inflated pride in oneself **VANITIED** *adj*

VANMAN   *n* pl. -MEN a person who drives a van

VANNED   past tense of van

VANNER   *n* pl. -S a person who owns a van

VANNING   present participle of van

VANPOOL   *n* pl. -S an arrangement whereby several commuters travel in one van

VANQUISH *v* -ED, -ING, -ES to defeat in battle

VANTAGE *n* pl. -S superiority over a competitor

VANWARD *adv* toward the front

VAPID *adj* insipid **VAPIDLY** *adv*

VAPIDITY *n* pl. -TIES the quality or state of being vapid

VAPOR *v* -ED, -ING, -S to emit vapor (visible floating moisture)

VAPORER *n* pl. -S one that vapors

VAPORING *n* pl. -S boastful talk

VAPORISE *v* -ISED, -ISING, -ISES to vaporize

VAPORISH *adj* resembling vapor

VAPORIZE *v* -IZED, -IZING, -IZES to convert into vapor

VAPOROUS *adj* vaporish

VAPORY *adj* vaporish

VAPOUR *v* -ED, -ING, -S to vapor

VAPOURER *n* pl. -S vaporer

VAPOURY *adj* vapory

VAQUERO *n* pl. -ROS a cowboy

VAR *n* pl. -S a unit of reactive power

VARA *n* pl. -S a Spanish unit of length

VARACTOR *n* pl. -S a capacitor with variable capacitance

VARIA *n/pl* a collection of various literary works

VARIABLE *n* pl. -S something that varies

VARIABLY *adv* in a varying manner

VARIANCE *n* pl. -S a license to perform an act contrary to the usual rule

VARIANT *n* pl. -S a variable

VARIATE *v* -ATED, -ATING, -ATES to vary

VARICES pl. of varix

VARICOSE *adj* abnormally swollen or dilated

VARIED past tense of vary

VARIEDLY *adv* in a varied manner

VARIER *n* pl. -S one that varies

VARIES present 3d person sing. of vary

VARIETAL *n* pl. -S a wine designated by the variety of grape

VARIETY *n* pl. -ETIES something differing from others of the same general kind

VARIFORM *adj* having various forms

VARIOLA *n* pl. -S smallpox **VARIOLAR** *adj*

VARIOLE *n* pl. -S a foveola

VARIORUM *n* pl. -S an edition containing various versions of a text

VARIOUS *adj* of diverse kinds

VARISTOR *n* pl. -S a type of electrical resistor

VARIX *n* pl. VARICES a varicose vein

VARLET *n* pl. -S a knave

VARLETRY *n* pl. -RIES a group of common people

VARMENT *n* pl. -S varmint

VARMINT *n* pl. -S an animal considered to be a pest

VARNA *n* pl. -S any of the four main Hindu social classes

VARNISH *v* -ED, -ING, -ES to give a glossy appearance to

VARNISHY *adj* glossy

VAROOM *v* -ED, -ING, -S to vroom

VARSITY *n* pl. -TIES the principal team representing a university, college, or school in any activity

VARUS *n* pl. -ES a malformation of a bone or joint

VARVE *n* pl. -S a deposit of sedimentary material **VARVED** *adj*

VARY *v* VARIED, VARYING, VARIES to become or make different

VAS *n* pl. VASA an anatomical duct **VASAL** *adj*

VASCULAR *adj* pertaining to ducts that convey body fluids

VASCULUM *n* pl. -LA or -LUMS a box used to hold plant specimens

VASE *n* pl. -S a rounded, decorative container **VASELIKE** *adj*

VASIFORM *adj* having the form of a vase

VASOTOMY *n* pl. -MIES a surgical cutting of the vas deferens

VASSAL *n* pl. -S a person granted the use of land by a feudal lord in return for homage and allegiance

VAST *adj* VASTER, VASTEST of great extent or size

VAST *n* pl. -S a vast space

VASTIER comparative of vasty

VASTIEST superlative of vasty

VASTITY *n* pl. -TIES vastness

VASTLY *adv* to a vast extent or degree

VASTNESS *n* pl. -ES the quality or state of being vast

VASTY	*adj* VASTIER, VASTIEST vast
VAT	*v* VATTED, VATTING, VATS to put into a vat (a large container for holding liquids)
VATFUL	*n* pl. -S as much as a vat can hold
VATIC	*adj* pertaining to a prophet
VATICAL	*adj* vatic
VATICIDE	*n* pl. -S the killing of a prophet
VATTED	past tense of vat
VATTING	present participle of vat
VATU	*n* pl. -S a monetary unit of Vanuatu
VAU	*n* pl. -S vav
VAULT	*v* -ED, -ING, -S to provide with a vault (an arched ceiling)
VAULTER	*n* pl. -S one that leaps
VAULTING	*n* pl. -S the structure forming a vault
VAULTY	*adj* VAULTIER, VAULTIEST resembling a vault
VAUNT	*v* -ED, -ING, -S to brag
VAUNTER	*n* pl. -S one that vaunts
VAUNTFUL	*adj* boastful
VAUNTIE	*adj* boastful
VAUNTY	*adj* vauntie
VAV	*n* pl. -S a Hebrew letter
VAVASOR	*n* pl. -S a high-ranking vassal
VAVASOUR	*n* pl. -S vavasor
VAVASSOR	*n* pl. -S vavasor
VAW	*n* pl. -S vav
VAWARD	*n* pl. -S the foremost part
VAWNTIE	*adj* vaunty
VEAL	*v* -ED, -ING, -S to kill and prepare a calf for food
VEALER	*n* pl. -S a calf raised for food
VEALY	*adj* VEALIER, VEALIEST immature
VECTOR	*v* -ED, -ING, -S to guide in flight by means of radioed directions
VEDALIA	*n* pl. -S an Australian ladybug
VEDETTE	*n* pl. -S a small boat used for scouting
VEE	*n* pl. -S the letter V
VEEJAY	*n* pl. -JAYS an announcer on a program of music videos
VEENA	*n* pl. -S vina
VEEP	*n* pl. -S a vice president

VEEPEE	*n* pl. -S veep
VEER	*v* -ED, -ING, -S to change direction
VEERY	*n* pl. -RIES a songbird
VEG	*n* pl. VEG a vegetable
VEGAN	*n* pl. -S one that eats only plant products
VEGANISM	*n* pl. -S the practice of eating only plant products
VEGETAL	*adj* pertaining to plants
VEGETANT	*adj* characteristic of plant life
VEGETATE	*v* -TATED, -TATING, -TATES to grow in the manner of a plant
VEGETE	*adj* healthy
VEGETIST	*n* pl. -S one that eats only plant products
VEGETIVE	*adj* growing or capable of growing
VEGGIE	*n* pl. -S a vegetable
VEGIE	*n* pl. -S veggie
VEHEMENT	*adj* ardent
VEHICLE	*n* pl. -S a device used as a means of conveyance
VEIL	*v* -ED, -ING, -S to provide with a veil (a piece of sheer fabric worn over the face)
VEILEDLY	*adv* in a disguised manner
VEILER	*n* pl. -S one that veils
VEILING	*n* pl. -S a veil
VEILLIKE	*adj* resembling a veil
VEIN	*v* -ED, -ING, -S to fill with veins (tubular blood vessels)
VEINAL	*adj* of or pertaining to the veins
VEINER	*n* pl. -S a tool used in wood carving
VEINIER	comparative of veiny
VEINIEST	superlative of veiny
VEINING	*n* pl. -S a network of veins
VEINLESS	*adj* having no veins
VEINLET	*n* pl. -S a small vein
VEINLIKE	*adj* resembling a vein
VEINULE	*n* pl. -S venule
VEINULET	*n* pl. -S venule
VEINY	*adj* VEINIER, VEINIEST full of veins
VELA	pl. of velum
VELAMEN	*n* pl. -MINA a velum
VELAR	*n* pl. -S a kind of speech sound

VELARIUM	*n* pl. -IA an awning over an ancient Roman theater
VELARIZE	*v* -IZED, -IZING, -IZES to pronounce with the back of the tongue touching the soft palate
VELATE	*adj* having a velum
VELD	*n* pl. -S veldt
VELDT	*n* pl. -S a grassland of southern Africa
VELIGER	*n* pl. -S a larval stage of certain mollusks
VELITES	*n/pl* foot soldiers of ancient Rome
VELLEITY	*n* pl. -ITIES a very low degree of desire
VELLUM	*n* pl. -S a fine parchment
VELOCE	*adv* rapidly — used as a musical direction
VELOCITY	*n* pl. -TIES rapidity of motion
VELOUR	*n* pl. -S a fabric resembling velvet
VELOUTE	*n* pl. -S a type of sauce
VELUM	*n* pl. -LA a thin membranous covering or partition
VELURE	*v* -LURED, -LURING, -LURES to smooth with a velvet or silk pad, as a hat
VELVERET	*n* pl. -S a fabric resembling velvet
VELVET	*n* pl. -S a soft, smooth fabric **VELVETED, VELVETY** *adj*
VENA	*n* pl. -NAE a vein
VENAL	*adj* open to bribery **VENALLY** *adv*
VENALITY	*n* pl. -TIES the quality or state of being venal
VENATIC	*adj* pertaining to hunting
VENATION	*n* pl. -S an arrangement of veins
VEND	*v* -ED, -ING, -S to sell **VENDABLE** *adj*
VENDACE	*n* pl. -S a European fish
VENDEE	*n* pl. -S a buyer
VENDER	*n* pl. -S vendor
VENDETTA	*n* pl. -S a feud between two families
VENDEUSE	*n* pl. -S a saleswoman
VENDIBLE	*n* pl. -S a salable article
VENDIBLY	*adv* salably
VENDOR	*n* pl. -S a seller
VENDUE	*n* pl. -S a public sale
VENEER	*v* -ED, -ING, -S to overlay with thin layers of material
VENEERER	*n* pl. -S one that veneers
VENENATE	*v* -NATED, -NATING, -NATES to poison
VENENOSE	*adj* poisonous
VENERATE	*v* -ATED, -ATING, -ATES to revere
VENEREAL	*adj* involving the genital organs
VENERY	*n* pl. -ERIES sexual intercourse
VENETIAN	*n* pl. -S a flexible window screen
VENGE	*v* VENGED, VENGING, VENGES to avenge
VENGEFUL	*adj* seeking to avenge
VENIAL	*adj* easily excused or forgiven **VENIALLY** *adv*
VENIN	*n* pl. -S a toxin found in snake venom
VENINE	*n* pl. -S venin
VENIRE	*n* pl. -S a type of judicial writ
VENISON	*n* pl. -S the edible flesh of a deer
VENOGRAM	*n* pl. -S a roentgenogram of a vein
VENOM	*v* -ED, -ING, -S to inject with venom (a poisonous secretion of certain animals)
VENOMER	*n* pl. -S one that venoms
VENOMOUS	*adj* poisonous
VENOSE	*adj* venous
VENOSITY	*n* pl. -TIES the quality or state of being venous
VENOUS	*adj* full of veins **VENOUSLY** *adv*
VENT	*v* -ED, -ING, -S to provide with a vent (an opening for the escape of gas or liquid)
VENTAGE	*n* pl. -S a small opening
VENTAIL	*n* pl. -S the adjustable front of a medieval helmet
VENTER	*n* pl. -S the abdomen
VENTLESS	*adj* having no vent
VENTRAL	*n* pl. -S a fin located on the underside of a fish
VENTURE	*v* -TURED, -TURING, -TURES to risk
VENTURER	*n* pl. -S one that ventures
VENTURI	*n* pl. -S a device for measuring the flow of a fluid
VENTURING	present participle of venture
VENUE	*n* pl. -S the locale of an event

VENULE	*n* pl. -S a small vein **VENULAR, VENULOSE, VENULOUS** *adj*
VERA	*adj* very
VERACITY	*n* pl. -TIES conformity to truth
VERANDA	*n* pl. -S a type of porch
VERANDAH	*n* pl. -S veranda
VERATRIA	*n* pl. -S veratrin
VERATRIN	*n* pl. -S a poisonous mixture of alkaloids
VERATRUM	*n* pl. -S a poisonous herb
VERB	*n* pl. -S a word used to express an act, occurrence, or mode of being
VERBAL	*n* pl. -S a word derived from a verb
VERBALLY	*adv* in a spoken manner
VERBATIM	*adv* word for word
VERBENA	*n* pl. -S a flowering plant
VERBIAGE	*n* pl. -S an excess of words
VERBID	*n* pl. -S a verbal
VERBIFY	*v* -FIED, -FYING, -FIES to use as a verb
VERBILE	*n* pl. -S one whose mental imagery consists of words
VERBLESS	*adj* lacking a verb
VERBOSE	*adj* wordy
VERBOTEN	*adj* forbidden
VERDANCY	*n* pl. -CIES the quality or state of being verdant
VERDANT	*adj* green with vegetation
VERDERER	*n* pl. -S an officer in charge of the royal forests of England
VERDEROR	*n* pl. -S verderer
VERDICT	*n* pl. -S the decision of a jury at the end of a legal proceeding
VERDIN	*n* pl. -S a small bird
VERDITER	*n* pl. -S a blue or green pigment
VERDURE	*n* pl. -S green vegetation **VERDURED** *adj*
VERECUND	*adj* shy
VERGE	*v* VERGED, VERGING, VERGES to come near
VERGENCE	*n* pl. -S a movement of one eye in relation to the other
VERGER	*n* pl. -S a church official
VERGING	present participle of verge
VERGLAS	*n* pl. -ES a thin coating of ice on rock
VERIDIC	*adj* truthful
VERIER	comparative of very
VERIEST	superlative of very
VERIFIER	*n* pl. -S one that verifies
VERIFY	*v* -FIED, -FYING, -FIES to prove to be true
VERILY	*adv* in truth
VERISM	*n* pl. -S realism in art or literature
VERISMO	*n* pl. -MOS verism
VERIST	*n* pl. -S one who practices verism **VERISTIC** *adj*
VERITAS	*n* pl. -TATES truth
VERITE	*n* pl. -S the technique of filming so as to convey candid realism
VERITY	*n* pl. -TIES truth
VERJUICE	*n* pl. -S the juice of sour or unripe fruit
VERMEIL	*n* pl. -S a red color
VERMES	pl. of vermis
VERMIAN	*adj* pertaining to worms
VERMIN	*n* pl. VERMIN small, common, harmful, or objectionable animals
VERMIS	*n* pl. -MES a part of the brain
VERMOULU	*adj* eaten by worms
VERMOUTH	*n* pl. -S a liqueur
VERMUTH	*n* pl. -S vermouth
VERNACLE	*n* pl. -S vernicle
VERNAL	*adj* pertaining to spring **VERNALLY** *adv*
VERNICLE	*n* pl. -S veronica
VERNIER	*n* pl. -S an auxiliary scale used with a main scale to obtain fine measurements
VERNIX	*n* pl. -ES a fatty substance covering the skin of a fetus
VERONICA	*n* pl. -S a handkerchief bearing the image of Christ's face
VERRUCA	*n* pl. -CAE a wart
VERSAL	*adj* entire
VERSANT	*n* pl. -S the slope of a mountain or mountain chain
VERSE	*v* VERSED, VERSING, VERSES to versify
VERSEMAN	*n* pl. -MEN one who versifies
VERSER	*n* pl. -S a verseman
VERSET	*n* pl. -S a versicle
VERSICLE	*n* pl. -S a short line of metrical writing

VERSIFY   *v* -FIED, -FYING, -FIES to change from prose into metrical form

VERSINE   *n* pl. -S a trigonometric function of an angle

VERSING   present participle of verse

VERSION   *n* pl. -S an account or description from a particular point of view

VERSO   *n* pl. -SOS a left-hand page of a book

VERST   *n* pl. -S a Russian measure of distance

VERSTE   *n* pl. -S verst

VERSUS   *prep* against

VERT   *n* pl. -S the heraldic color green

VERTEBRA   *n* pl. -BRAE or -BRAS any of the bones or segments forming the spinal column

VERTEX   *n* pl. -TEXES or -TICES the highest point of something

VERTICAL   *n* pl. -S something that is vertical (extending up and down)

VERTICIL   *n* pl. -S a circular arrangement, as of flowers or leaves, about a point on an axis

VERTIGO   *n* pl. -GOES, -GOS, or -GINES a disordered state in which the individual or his surroundings seem to whirl dizzily

VERTU   *n* pl. -S virtu

VERVAIN   *n* pl. -S a flowering plant

VERVE   *n* pl. -S vivacity

VERVET   *n* pl. -S an African monkey

VERY   *adj* VERIER, VERIEST absolute

VESICA   *n* pl. -CAE a bladder **VESICAL** *adj*

VESICANT   *n* pl. -S a chemical warfare agent that induces blistering

VESICATE   *v* -CATED, -CATING, -CATES to blister

VESICLE   *n* pl. -S a small bladder

VESICULA   *n* pl. -LAE a vesicle

VESPER   *n* pl. -S an evening service, prayer, or song

VESPERAL   *n* pl. -S a covering for an altar cloth

VESPIARY   *n* pl. -ARIES a nest of wasps

VESPID   *n* pl. -S a wasp

VESPINE   *adj* pertaining to wasps

VESSEL   *n* pl. -S a craft for traveling on water **VESSELED** *adj*

VEST   *v* -ED, -ING, -S to place in the control of

VESTA   *n* pl. -S a short friction match

VESTAL   *n* pl. -S a chaste woman

VESTALLY   *adv* chastely

VESTEE   *n* pl. -S a garment worn under a woman's jacket or blouse

VESTIARY   *n* pl. -ARIES a dressing room

VESTIGE   *n* pl. -S a visible sign of something that is no longer in existence

VESTIGIA   *n/pl* vestiges

VESTING   *n* pl. -S the right of an employee to share in and withdraw from a pension fund without penalty

VESTLESS   *adj* being without a vest

VESTLIKE   *adj* resembling a vest (a short, sleeveless garment)

VESTMENT   *n* pl. -S one of the ceremonial garments of the clergy

VESTRY   *n* pl. -TRIES a room in which vestments are kept **VESTRAL** *adj*

VESTURAL   *adj* pertaining to clothing

VESTURE   *v* -TURED, -TURING, -TURES to clothe

VESUVIAN   *n* pl. -S a mineral

VET   *v* VETTED, VETTING, VETS to treat animals medically

VETCH   *n* pl. -ES a climbing plant

VETERAN   *n* pl. -S a former member of the armed forces

VETIVER   *n* pl. -S an Asian grass

VETIVERT   *n* pl. -S the essential oil of the vetiver

VETO   *v* -ED, -ING, -ES to forbid or prevent authoritatively

VETOER   *n* pl. -S one that vetoes

VETTED   past tense of vet

VETTING   present participle of vet

VEX   *v* VEXED or VEXT, VEXING, VEXES to annoy

VEXATION   *n* pl. -S a cause of trouble

VEXEDLY   *adv* in a vexed manner

VEXER   *n* pl. -S one that vexes

VEXIL   *n* pl. -S vexillum

VEXILLUM   *n* pl. -LA the web or vane of a feather **VEXILLAR** *adj*

VEXINGLY   *adv* in a vexing manner

VEXT   a past tense of vex

VIA	*prep* by way of	**VICINAGE**	*n* pl. -S vicinity
VIABLE	*adj* capable of living **VIABLY** *adv*	**VICINAL**	*adj* nearby
VIADUCT	*n* pl. -S a type of bridge	**VICING**	present participle of vice
VIAL	*v* VIALED, VIALING, VIALS or VIALLED, VIALLING, VIALS to put in a vial (a small container for liquids)	**VICINITY**	*n* pl. -TIES the region near or about a place
		VICIOUS	*adj* dangerously aggressive
VIAND	*n* pl. -S an article of food	**VICOMTE**	*n* pl. -S a French nobleman
VIATIC	*adj* pertaining to traveling	**VICTIM**	*n* pl. -S one who suffers from a destructive or injurious action
VIATICAL	*adj* viatic	**VICTOR**	*n* pl. -S one who defeats an adversary
VIATICUM	*n* pl. -CA or -CUMS an allowance for traveling expenses		
VIATOR	*n* pl. -ES or -S a traveler	**VICTORIA**	*n* pl. -S a light carriage
VIBE	*n* pl. -S a vibration	**VICTORY**	*n* pl. -RIES a successful outcome in a contest or struggle
VIBIST	*n* pl. -S one who plays the vibraphone	**VICTRESS**	*n* pl. -ES a female victor
VIBRANCE	*n* pl. -S vibrancy	**VICTUAL**	*v* -UALED, -UALING, -UALS or -UALLED, -UALLING, -UALS to provide with food
VIBRANCY	*n* pl. -CIES the quality or state of being vibrant		
VIBRANT	*n* pl. -S a sonant	**VICUGNA**	*n* pl. -S vicuna
VIBRATE	*v* -BRATED, -BRATING, -BRATES to move back and forth rapidly	**VICUNA**	*n* pl. -S a ruminant mammal
		VIDE	*v* see — used to direct a reader to another item; VIDE is the only form of this verb; it cannot be conjugated
VIBRATO	*n* pl. -TOS a tremulous or pulsating musical effect		
VIBRATOR	*n* pl. -S something that vibrates		
VIBRIO	*n* pl. -RIOS any of a genus of bacteria shaped like a comma **VIBRIOID** *adj*	**VIDEO**	*n* pl. -EOS television
		VIDEOTEX	*n* pl. -ES an electronic system for transmitting data to a subscriber's video screen
VIBRION	*n* pl. -S vibrio		
VIBRISSA	*n* pl. -SAE one of the stiff hairs growing about the mouth of certain mammals	**VIDETTE**	*n* pl. -S vedette
		VIDICON	*n* pl. -S a type of television camera tube
VIBRONIC	*adj* pertaining to changes in molecular energy states resulting from vibrational energy	**VIDUITY**	*n* pl. -ITIES the quality or state of being a widow
		VIE	*v* VIED, VYING, VIES to strive for superiority
VIBURNUM	*n* pl. -S a flowering shrub		
VICAR	*n* pl. -S a church official	**VIER**	*n* pl. -S one that vies
VICARAGE	*n* pl. -S the office of a vicar	**VIEW**	*v* -ED, -ING, -S to look at **VIEWABLE** *adj*
VICARATE	*n* pl. -S vicarage		
VICARIAL	*adj* pertaining to a vicar	**VIEWDATA**	*n* pl. VIEWDATA a videotex
VICARLY	*adj* vicarial	**VIEWER**	*n* pl. -S one that views
VICE	*v* VICED, VICING, VICES to vise	**VIEWIER**	comparative of viewy
		VIEWIEST	superlative of viewy
VICELESS	*adj* having no immoral habits	**VIEWING**	*n* pl. -S an act of seeing, watching, or looking
VICENARY	*adj* pertaining to the number twenty		
		VIEWLESS	*adj* having no opinions
VICEROY	*n* pl. -ROYS one who rules as the representative of a sovereign	**VIEWY**	*adj* VIEWIER, VIEWIEST showy
		VIG	*n* pl. -S a vigorish
VICHY	*n* pl. -CHIES a type of mineral water	**VIGA**	*n* pl. -S a ceiling beam in Spanish architecture

VIGIL   *n* pl. -S a period of watchfulness maintained during normal sleeping hours

VIGILANT   *adj* watchful

VIGNERON   *n* pl. -S a winegrower

VIGNETTE   *v* -GNETTED, -GNETTING, -GNETTES to describe briefly

VIGOR   *n* pl. -S active strength or force

VIGORISH   *n* pl. -ES a charge paid to a bookie on a bet

VIGOROSO   *adv* with emphasis and spirit — used as a musical direction

VIGOROUS   *adj* full of vigor

VIGOUR   *n* pl. -S vigor

VIKING   *n* pl. -S a Scandinavian pirate

VILAYET   *n* pl. -S an administrative division of Turkey

VILE   *adj* VILER, VILEST morally despicable or physically repulsive **VILELY** *adv*

VILENESS   *n* pl. -ES the state of being vile

VILIFIER   *n* pl. -S one that vilifies

VILIFY   *v* -FIED, -FYING, -FIES to defame

VILIPEND   *v* -ED, -ING, -S to vilify

VILL   *n* pl. -S a village

VILLA   *n* pl. -LAE or -LAS an agricultural estate of ancient Rome

VILLADOM   *n* pl. -S the world constituted by suburban residences and their occupants

VILLAGE   *n* pl. -S a small community in a rural area

VILLAGER   *n* pl. -S one who lives in a village

VILLAIN   *n* pl. -S a cruelly malicious person

VILLAINY   *n* pl. -LAINIES conduct characteristic of a villain

VILLATIC   *adj* rural

VILLEIN   *n* pl. -S a type of serf

VILLUS   *n* pl. -LI one of the hairlike projections found on certain membranes **VILLOSE, VILLOUS** *adj*

VIM   *n* pl. -S energy

VIMEN   *n* pl. -MINA a long, flexible branch of a plant **VIMINAL** *adj*

VINA   *n* pl. -S a stringed instrument of India

VINAL   *n* pl. -S a synthetic textile fiber

VINASSE   *n* pl. -S a residue left after the distillation of liquor

VINCA   *n* pl. -S a flowering plant

VINCIBLE   *adj* capable of being conquered **VINCIBLY** *adv*

VINCULUM   *n* pl. -LA or -LUMS a unifying bond

VINDALOO   *n* pl. -LOOS a curried dish made with meat, garlic, and wine

VINE   *v* VINED, VINING, VINES to grow like a vine (a climbing plant)

VINEAL   *adj* vinous

VINEGAR   *n* pl. -S a sour liquid used as a condiment or preservative **VINEGARY** *adj*

VINERY   *n* pl. -ERIES a place in which grapevines are grown

VINEYARD   *n* pl. -S an area planted with grapevines

VINIC   *adj* derived from wine

VINIER   comparative of viny

VINIEST   superlative of viny

VINIFERA   *n* pl. -S a European grape

VINIFY   *v* -FIED, -FYING, -FIES to convert into wine by fermentation

VINING   present participle of vine

VINO   *n* pl. -NOS wine

VINOSITY   *n* pl. -TIES the character of a wine

VINOUS   *adj* pertaining to wine **VINOUSLY** *adv*

VINTAGE   *n* pl. -S a season's yield of wine from a vineyard

VINTAGER   *n* pl. -S one that harvests wine grapes

VINTNER   *n* pl. -S a wine merchant

VINY   *adj* VINIER, VINIEST covered with vines

VINYL   *n* pl. -S a type of plastic **VINYLIC** *adj*

VIOL   *n* pl. -S a stringed instrument

VIOLA   *n* pl. -S a stringed instrument

VIOLABLE   *adj* capable of being violated **VIOLABLY** *adv*

VIOLATE   *v* -LATED, -LATING, -LATES to break or disregard the terms or requirements of

VIOLATER   *n* pl. -S violator

VIOLATOR   *n* pl. -S one that violates

VIOLENCE   *n* pl. -S violent action

VIOLENT *adj* marked by intense physical force or roughness

VIOLET *n* pl. -S a flowering plant

VIOLIN *n* pl. -S a stringed instrument

VIOLIST *n* pl. -S one who plays the viol or viola

VIOLONE *n* pl. -S a stringed instrument

VIOMYCIN *n* pl. -S an antibiotic

VIPER *n* pl. -S a venomous snake **VIPERINE, VIPERISH, VIPEROUS** *adj*

VIRAGO *n* pl. -GOES or -GOS a noisy, domineering woman

VIRAL *adj* pertaining to or caused by a virus **VIRALLY** *adv*

VIRELAI *n* pl. -S virelay

VIRELAY *n* pl. -LAYS a medieval French verse form

VIREMIA *n* pl. -S the presence of a virus in the blood **VIREMIC** *adj*

VIREO *n* pl. -EOS a small bird

VIRES pl. of vis

VIRGA *n* pl. -S wisps of precipitation evaporating before reaching ground

VIRGATE *n* pl. -S an early English measure of land area

VIRGIN *n* pl. -S a person who has never had sexual intercourse

VIRGINAL *n* pl. -S a musical instrument

VIRGULE *n* pl. -S a diagonal printing mark used to separate alternatives

VIRICIDE *n* pl. -S a substance that destroys viruses

VIRID *adj* verdant

VIRIDIAN *n* pl. -S a bluish-green pigment

VIRIDITY *n* pl. -TIES verdancy

VIRILE *adj* having masculine vigor **VIRILELY** *adv*

VIRILISM *n* pl. -S the development of male secondary sex characteristics in a female

VIRILITY *n* pl. -TIES the quality or state of being virile

VIRION *n* pl. -S a virus particle

VIRL *n* pl. -S a metal ring or cap put around a shaft to prevent splitting

VIROID *n* pl. -S a viruslike plant pathogen

VIROLOGY *n* pl. -GIES the study of viruses

VIROSIS *n* pl. -ROSES infection with a virus

VIRTU *n* pl. -S a love or taste for the fine arts

VIRTUAL *adj* having the effect but not the actual form of what is specified

VIRTUE *n* pl. -S moral excellence

VIRTUOSA *n* pl. -SAS or -SE a female virtuoso

VIRTUOSO *n* pl. -SOS or -SI a highly skilled artistic performer

VIRTUOUS *adj* characterized by virtue

VIRUCIDE *n* pl. -S viricide

VIRULENT *adj* extremely poisonous

VIRUS *n* pl. -ES any of a class of submicroscopic pathogens

VIS *n* pl. VIRES force or power

VISA *v* -ED, -ING, -S to put an official endorsement on, as a passport

VISAGE *n* pl. -S the face or facial expression of a person **VISAGED** *adj*

VISARD *n* pl. -S vizard

VISCACHA *n* pl. -S a burrowing rodent

VISCERA pl. of viscus

VISCERAL *adj* pertaining to the internal organs

VISCID *adj* thick and adhesive **VISCIDLY** *adv*

VISCOID *adj* somewhat viscid

VISCOSE *n* pl. -S a viscous solution

VISCOUNT *n* pl. -S a British nobleman

VISCOUS *adj* having relatively high resistance to flow

VISCUS *n* pl. -CERA an internal organ

VISE *v* VISED, VISING, VISES to hold in a vise (a clamping device)

VISE *v* VISEED, VISEING, VISES to visa

VISELIKE *adj* resembling a vise

VISIBLE *adj* capable of being seen **VISIBLY** *adv*

VISING present participle of vise

VISION *v* -ED, -ING, -S to imagine

VISIONAL *adj* imaginary

VISIT *v* -ED, -ING, -S to go or come to see someone or something

VISITANT *n* pl. -S a visitor

VISITER *n* pl. -S visitor

VISITOR   *n* pl. -S one that visits

VISIVE   *adj* visible

VISOR   *v* -ED, -ING, -S to provide with a visor (a projecting brim)

VISTA   *n* pl. -S a distant view **VISTAED** *adj*

VISUAL   *n* pl. -S something that illustrates by pictures or diagrams

VISUALLY   *adv* with regard to sight

VITA   *n* pl. -TAE a brief, autobiographical sketch

VITAL   *adj* necessary to life

VITALISE   *v* -ISED, -ISING, -ISES to vitalize

VITALISM   *n* pl. -S a philosophical doctrine

VITALIST   *n* pl. -S an advocate of vitalism

VITALITY   *n* pl. -TIES exuberant physical strength or mental vigor

VITALIZE   *v* -IZED, -IZING, -IZES to give life to

VITALLY   *adv* in a vital manner

VITALS   *n/pl* vital organs

VITAMER   *n* pl. -S a type of chemical compound

VITAMIN   *n* pl. -S any of various organic substances essential to proper nutrition

VITAMINE   *n* pl. -S vitamin

VITELLIN   *n* pl. -S a protein found in egg yolk

VITELLUS   *n* pl. -ES the yolk of an egg

VITESSE   *n* pl. -S speed

VITIATE   *v* -ATED, -ATING, -ATES to impair the value or quality of **VITIABLE** *adj*

VITIATOR   *n* pl. -S one that vitiates

VITILIGO   *n* pl. -GOS a skin disease

VITRAIN   *n* pl. -S the material in the vitreous layers of banded bituminous coal

VITREOUS   *n* pl. -ES the jelly that fills the eyeball

VITRIC   *adj* pertaining to glass

VITRICS   *n/pl* the art of making or decorating glass articles

VITRIFY   *v* -FIED, -FYING, -FIES to convert into glass

VITRINE   *n* pl. -S a glass showcase for art objects

VITRIOL   *v* -OLED, -OLING, -OLS or -OLLED, -OLLING, -OLS to treat with sulfuric acid

VITTA   *n* pl. -TAE a streak or band of color **VITTATE** *adj*

VITTLE   *v* -TLED, -TLING, -TLES to victual

VITULINE   *adj* pertaining to a calf

VIVA   *n* pl. -S a shout or cry used to express approval

VIVACE   *n* pl. -S a musical passage played in a brisk spirited manner

VIVACITY   *n* pl. -TIES the quality or state of being lively

VIVARIUM   *n* pl. -IA or -IUMS a place for raising and keeping live animals

VIVARY   *n* pl. -RIES vivarium

VIVE   *interj* — used as an exclamation of approval

VIVERRID   *n* pl. -S any of a family of small carnivorous mammals

VIVERS   *n/pl* food

VIVID   *adj* -IDER, -IDEST strikingly bright or intense **VIVIDLY** *adv*

VIVIFIC   *adj* vivifying

VIVIFIER   *n* pl. -S one that vivifies

VIVIFY   *v* -FIED, -FYING, -FIES to give life to

VIVIPARA   *n/pl* animals that bring forth living young

VIVISECT   *v* -ED, -ING, -S to dissect the living body of

VIXEN   *n* pl. -S a shrewish woman **VIXENISH, VIXENLY** *adj*

VIZARD   *n* pl. -S a mask **VIZARDED** *adj*

VIZCACHA   *n* pl. -S viscacha

VIZIER   *n* pl. -S a high official in some Muslim countries

VIZIR   *n* pl. -S vizier **VIZIRIAL** *adj*

VIZIRATE   *n* pl. -S the office of a vizir

VIZOR   *v* -ED, -ING, -S to visor

VIZSLA   *n* pl. -S a Hungarian breed of dog

VOCABLE   *n* pl. -S a word

VOCABLY   *adv* in a manner that may be voiced aloud

VOCAL   *n* pl. -S a sound produced with the voice

VOCALIC   *n* pl. -S a vowel sound

VOCALISE   *v* -ISED, -ISING, -ISES to vocalize

VOCALISM   *n* pl. -S the act of vocalizing

VOCALIST   *n* pl. -S a singer

VOCALITY   *n* pl. -TIES possession or exercise of vocal powers

VOCALIZE   *v* -IZED, -IZING, -IZES to produce with the voice

VOCALLY   *adv* with the voice

VOCATION   *n* pl. -S the work in which a person is regularly employed

VOCATIVE   *n* pl. -S a grammatical case used in some languages

VOCES   pl. of vox

VOCODER   *n* pl. -S an electronic device used in transmitting speech signals

VODKA   *n* pl. -S a liquor

VODOUN   *n* pl. -S vodun

VODUN   *n* pl. -S a primitive religion of the West Indies

VOE   *n* pl. -S a small bay, creek, or inlet

VOGIE   *adj* vain

VOGUE   *v* VOGUED, VOGUING or VOGUEING, VOGUES to imitate poses of fashion models

VOGUISH   *adj* fashionable

VOICE   *v* VOICED, VOICING, VOICES to express or utter

VOICEFUL   *adj* sonorous

VOICER   *n* pl. -S one that voices

VOICING   present participle of voice

VOID   *v* -ED, -ING, -S to make void (of no legal force or effect) **VOIDABLE** *adj*

VOIDANCE   *n* pl. -S the act or process of voiding

VOIDER   *n* pl. -S one that voids

VOIDNESS   *n* pl. -ES the quality or state of being void

VOILA   *interj* — used to call attention to something

VOILE   *n* pl. -S a sheer fabric

VOLANT   *adj* flying or capable of flying

VOLANTE   *adj* moving with light rapidity — used as a musical direction

VOLAR   *adj* pertaining to flight

VOLATILE   *n* pl. -S a winged creature

VOLCANIC   *n* pl. -S a rock produced by a volcano

VOLCANO   *n* pl. -NOES or -NOS an opening in the earth's crust through which molten rock and gases are ejected

VOLE   *v* VOLED, VOLING, VOLES to win all the tricks in a card game

VOLERY   *n* pl. -ERIES a large birdcage

VOLITANT   *adj* volant

VOLITION   *n* pl. -S the power of choosing or determining

VOLITIVE   *adj* pertaining to volition

VOLLEY   *v* -ED, -ING, -S to return a tennis ball before it touches the ground

VOLLEYER   *n* pl. -S one that volleys

VOLOST   *n* pl. -S an administrative district in Russia

VOLPLANE   *v* -PLANED, -PLANING, -PLANES to glide in an airplane

VOLT   *n* pl. -S a unit of electromotive force

VOLTA   *n* pl. -TE a turning

VOLTAGE   *n* pl. -S electromotive force expressed in volts

VOLTAISM   *n* pl. -S electricity produced by chemical action **VOLTAIC** *adj*

VOLTE   *n* pl. -S a fencing movement

VOLTI   *interj* — used to direct musicians to turn the page

VOLUBLE   *adj* talkative **VOLUBLY** *adv*

VOLUME   *v* -UMED, -UMING, -UMES to send or give out in large quantities

VOLUTE   *n* pl. -S a spiral architectural ornament **VOLUTED** *adj*

VOLUTIN   *n* pl. -S a granular substance that is common in microorganisms

VOLUTION   *n* pl. -S a spiral

VOLVA   *n* pl. -S a membranous sac that encloses certain immature mushrooms **VOLVATE** *adj*

VOLVOX   *n* pl. -ES any of a genus of freshwater protozoa

VOLVULUS   *n* pl. -LI or -LUSES a twisting of the intestine that causes obstruction

VOMER   *n* pl. -S a bone of the skull **VOMERINE** *adj*

VOMICA   *n* pl. -CAE a cavity in the body containing pus

VOMIT   *v* -ED, -ING, -S to eject the contents of the stomach through the mouth

VOMITER   *n* pl. -S one that vomits

VOMITIVE   *n* pl. -S an emetic

VOMITO   *n* pl. -TOS the black vomit of yellow fever

VOMITORY	*n* pl. -RIES an emetic
VOMITOUS	*adj* pertaining to vomiting
VOMITUS	*n* pl. -ES vomited matter
VOODOO	*v* -ED, -ING, -S to hex
VORACITY	*n* pl. -TIES the quality or state of being ravenous
VORLAGE	*n* pl. -S a position in skiing
VORTEX	*n* pl. -TEXES or -TICES a whirling mass of fluid **VORTICAL** *adj*
VOTABLE	*adj* capable of being voted on
VOTARESS	*n* pl. -ES a female votary
VOTARIST	*n* pl. -S a votary
VOTARY	*n* pl. -RIES a person who is bound by religious vows
VOTE	*v* VOTED, VOTING, VOTES to cast a vote (a formal expression of will or opinion)
VOTEABLE	*adj* votable
VOTELESS	*adj* having no vote
VOTER	*n* pl. -S one that votes
VOTING	present participle of vote
VOTIVE	*adj* performed in fulfillment of a vow **VOTIVELY** *adv*
VOTRESS	*n* pl. -ES votaress
VOUCH	*v* -ED, -ING, -ES to give one's personal assurance or guarantee
VOUCHEE	*n* pl. -S one for whom another vouches
VOUCHER	*v* -ED, -ING, -S to establish the authenticity of
VOUSSOIR	*n* pl. -S a wedge-shaped building stone
VOUVRAY	*n* pl. -VRAYS a French white wine
VOW	*v* -ED, -ING, -S to make a vow (a solemn promise)
VOWEL	*n* pl. -S a type of speech sound
VOWELIZE	*v* -IZED, -IZING, -IZES to provide with symbols used·to indicate vowels
VOWER	*n* pl. -S one that vows
VOWLESS	*adj* having made no vow
VOX	*n* pl. VOCES voice
VOYAGE	*v* -AGED, -AGING, -AGES to travel
VOYAGER	*n* pl. -S one that voyages
VOYAGEUR	*n* pl. -S a person employed by a fur company to transport goods between distant stations
VOYEUR	*n* pl. -S one who is sexually gratified by looking at sexual objects or acts
VROOM	*v* -ED, -ING, -S to run an engine at high speed
VROUW	*n* pl. -S a Dutch woman
VROW	*n* pl. -S vrouw
VUG	*n* pl. -S a small cavity in a rock or lode
VUGG	*n* pl. -S vug
VUGGY	*adj* -GIER, -GIEST abounding in vugs
VUGH	*n* pl. -S vug
VULCANIC	*adj* pertaining to a volcano
VULGAR	*adj* -GARER, -GAREST crude **VULGARLY** *adv*
VULGAR	*n* pl. -S a common person
VULGATE	*n* pl. -S the common speech of a people
VULGO	*adv* commonly
VULGUS	*n* pl. -ES an exercise in Latin formerly required of pupils in some English public schools
VULPINE	*adj* pertaining to a fox
VULTURE	*n* pl. -S a bird of prey
VULVA	*n* pl. -VAE or -VAS the external genital organs of a female **VULVAL, VULVAR, VULVATE** *adj*
VULVITIS	*n* pl. -TISES inflammation of the vulva
VYING	present participle of vie
VYINGLY	*adv* in a vying manner

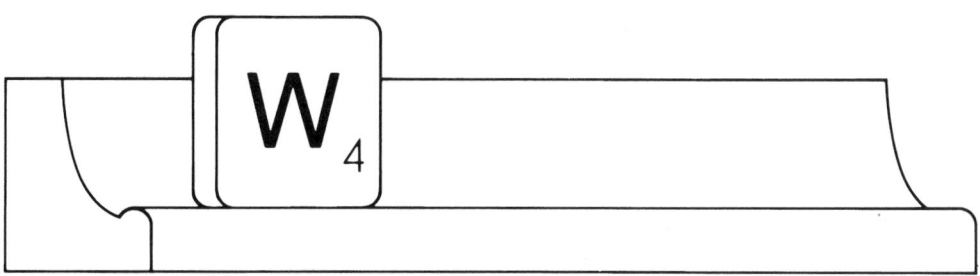

WAB	*n* pl. -S a web		**WADMEL**	*n* pl. -S wadmal
WABBLE	*v* -BLED, -BLING, -BLES to wobble		**WADMOL**	*n* pl. -S wadmal
			WADMOLL	*n* pl. -S wadmal
WABBLER	*n* pl. -S one that wabbles		**WADSET**	*v* -SETTED, -SETTING, -SETS to mortgage
WABBLY	*adj* -BLIER, -BLIEST wobbly		**WADY**	*n* pl. -DIES wadi
WACK	*n* pl. -S a wacky person		**WAE**	*n* pl. -S woe
WACKE	*n* pl. -S a type of basaltic rock		**WAEFUL**	*adj* woeful
WACKO	*n* pl. WACKOS a person who is wacky		**WAENESS**	*n* pl. -ES woeness
WACKY	*adj* WACKIER, WACKIEST very irrational **WACKILY** *adv*		**WAESUCK**	*interj* waesucks
			WAESUCKS	*interj* — used to express pity
WAD	*v* WADDED, WADDING, WADS to form into a wad (a small mass of soft material)		**WAFER**	*v* -ED, -ING, -S to seal with an adhesive disk
WADABLE	*adj* wadeable		**WAFERY**	*adj* resembling a wafer (a thin, crisp biscuit)
WADDER	*n* pl. -S one that wads		**WAFF**	*v* -ED, -ING, -S to wave
WADDIE	*n* pl. -S a cowboy		**WAFFIE**	*n* pl. -S a vagabond
WADDIED	past tense of waddy		**WAFFLE**	*v* -FLED, -FLING, -FLES to talk vaguely or indecisively
WADDIES	present 3d person sing. of waddy		**WAFFLER**	*n* pl. -S one that waffles
WADDING	*n* pl. -S a wad		**WAFFLING**	*n* pl. -S an indecisive statement or position
WADDLE	*v* -DLED, -DLING, -DLES to walk with short, swaying steps		**WAFT**	*v* -ED, -ING, -S to carry lightly over air or water
WADDLER	*n* pl. -S one that waddles		**WAFTAGE**	*n* pl. -S the act of wafting
WADDLY	*adj* having or being a waddling gait		**WAFTER**	*n* pl. -S one that wafts
WADDY	*v* -DIED, -DYING, -DIES to strike with a thick club		**WAFTURE**	*n* pl. -S waftage
			WAG	*v* WAGGED, WAGGING, WAGS to move briskly up and down or to and fro
WADE	*v* WADED, WADING, WADES to walk through water		**WAGE**	*v* WAGED, WAGING, WAGES to engage in or carry on
WADEABLE	*adj* capable of being passed through by wading		**WAGELESS**	*adj* unpaid
WADER	*n* pl. -S one that wades		**WAGER**	*v* -ED, -ING, -S to risk on an uncertain outcome
WADI	*n* pl. -S the bed of a usually dry watercourse		**WAGERER**	*n* pl. -S one that wagers
WADIES	pl. of wady		**WAGGED**	past tense of wag
WADING	present participle of wade		**WAGGER**	*n* pl. -S one that wags
WADMAAL	*n* pl. -S wadmal			
WADMAL	*n* pl. -S a thick woolen fabric			

WAGGERY *n* pl. -GERIES waggish behavior

WAGGING present participle of wag

WAGGISH *adj* playfully humorous

WAGGLE *v* -GLED, -GLING, -GLES to wag

WAGGLY *adj* waggling

WAGGON *v* -ED, -ING, -S to wagon

WAGGONER *n* pl. -S wagoner

WAGING present participle of wage

WAGON *v* -ED, -ING, -S to convey by wagon (a four-wheeled, horse-drawn vehicle)

WAGONAGE *n* pl. -S conveyance by wagon

WAGONER *n* pl. -S one who drives a wagon

WAGSOME *adj* waggish

WAGTAIL *n* pl. -S a songbird

WAHCONDA *n* pl. -S wakanda

WAHINE *n* pl. -S a Hawaiian woman

WAHOO *n* pl. -HOOS a flowering shrub

WAIF *v* -ED, -ING, -S to throw away

WAIFLIKE *adj* resembling a waif (a homeless child)

WAIL *v* -ED, -ING, -S to utter a long, mournful cry

WAILER *n* pl. -S one that wails

WAILFUL *adj* mournful

WAILSOME *adj* wailful

WAIN *n* pl. -S a large, open wagon

WAINSCOT *v* -SCOTED, -SCOTING, -SCOTS or -SCOTTED, -SCOTTING, -SCOTS to line the walls of with wooden paneling

WAIR *v* -ED, -ING, -S to spend

WAIST *n* pl. -S the part of the body between the ribs and the hips **WAISTED** *adj*

WAISTER *n* pl. -S a seaman stationed in the middle section of a ship

WAISTING *n* pl. -S a type of dressmaking material

WAIT *v* -ED, -ING, -S to stay in expectation of

WAITER *n* pl. -S one who serves food in a restaurant

WAITING *n* pl. -S the act of one who waits

WAITRESS *v* -ED, -ING, -ES to work as a female server in a restaurant

WAIVE *v* WAIVED, WAIVING, WAIVES to give up intentionally

WAIVER *n* pl. -S the act of waiving something

WAKANDA *n* pl. -S a supernatural force in Sioux beliefs

WAKE *v* WAKED or WOKE, WOKEN, WAKING, WAKES to rouse from sleep

WAKEFUL *adj* not sleeping or able to sleep

WAKELESS *adj* unbroken — used of sleep

WAKEN *v* -ED, -ING, -S to wake

WAKENER *n* pl. -S one that wakens

WAKENING *n* pl. -S the act of one that wakens

WAKER *n* pl. -S one that wakes

WAKERIFE *adj* wakeful

WAKIKI *n* pl. -S shell money of the South Sea Islands

WAKING present participle of wake

WALE *v* WALED, WALING, WALES to mark with welts

WALER *n* pl. -S an Australian-bred saddle horse

WALIES pl. of waly

WALING present participle of wale

WALK *v* -ED, -ING, -S to advance on foot **WALKABLE** *adj*

WALKAWAY *n* pl. -AWAYS an easy victory

WALKER *n* pl. -S one that walks

WALKING *n* pl. -S the act of one that walks

WALKOUT *n* pl. -S a strike by workers

WALKOVER *n* pl. -S a walkaway

WALKUP *n* pl. -S an apartment house having no elevator

WALKWAY *n* pl. -WAYS a passage for walking

WALKYRIE *n* pl. -S valkyrie

WALL *v* -ED, -ING, -S to provide with a wall (an upright structure built to enclose an area)

WALLA *n* pl. -S wallah

WALLABY *n* pl. -BIES a small kangaroo

WALLAH *n* pl. -S a person engaged in a particular occupation or activity

WALLAROO *n* pl. -ROOS a large kangaroo

WALLET *n* pl. -S a flat folding case

WALLEYE *n* pl. -S an eye having a white cornea **WALLEYED** *adj*

WALLIE *n* pl. -S a valet

WALLIES pl. of wally

WALLOP	*v* -ED, -ING, -S to beat soundly
WALLOPER	*n* pl. -S one that wallops
WALLOW	*v* -ED, -ING, -S to roll about
WALLOWER	*n* pl. -S one that wallows
WALLY	*n* pl. -LIES waly
WALNUT	*n* pl. -S an edible nut
WALRUS	*n* pl. -ES a marine mammal
WALTZ	*v* -ED, -ING, -ES to perform a ballroom dance
WALTZER	*n* pl. -S one that waltzes
WALY	*n* pl. WALIES something visually pleasing
WAMBLE	*v* -BLED, -BLING, -BLES to move unsteadily
WAMBLY	*adj* -BLIER, -BLIEST unsteady
WAME	*n* pl. -S the belly
WAMEFOU	*n* pl. -S a bellyful
WAMEFUL	*n* pl. -S wamefou
WAMMUS	*n* pl. -ES wamus
WAMPISH	*v* -ED, -ING, -ES to throw about
WAMPUM	*n* pl. -S a form of currency formerly used by North American Indians
WAMPUS	*n* pl. -ES wamus
WAMUS	*n* pl. -ES a heavy outer jacket
WAN	*adj* WANNER, WANNEST unnaturally pale
WAN	*v* WANNED, WANNING, WANS to become wan
WAND	*n* pl. -S a slender rod
WANDER	*v* -ED, -ING, -S to move about with no destination or purpose
WANDERER	*n* pl. -S one that wanders
WANDEROO	*n* pl. -ROOS an Asian monkey
WANDLE	*adj* supple
WANE	*v* WANED, WANING, WANES to decrease in size or extent
WANEY	*adj* WANIER, WANIEST wany
WANGAN	*n* pl. -S wanigan
WANGLE	*v* -GLED, -GLING, -GLES to obtain or accomplish by contrivance
WANGLER	*n* pl. -S one that wangles
WANGUN	*n* pl. -S wanigan
WANIER	comparative of waney and wany
WANIEST	superlative of waney and wany
WANIGAN	*n* pl. -S a supply chest used in a logging camp

WANING	present participle of wane
WANION	*n* pl. -S vengeance
WANLY	*adv* in a wan manner
WANNED	past tense of wan
WANNER	comparative of wan
WANNESS	*n* pl. -ES the quality of being wan
WANNEST	superlative of wan
WANNIGAN	*n* pl. -S wanigan
WANNING	present participle of wan
WANT	*v* -ED, -ING, -S to have a desire for
WANTAGE	*n* pl. -S something that is lacking
WANTER	*n* pl. -S one that wants
WANTON	*v* -ED, -ING, -S to behave immorally
WANTONER	*n* pl. -S one that wantons
WANTONLY	*adv* immorally
WANY	*adj* WANIER, WANIEST waning in some parts
WAP	*v* WAPPED, WAPPING, WAPS to wrap
WAPITI	*n* pl. -S a large deer
WAR	*v* WARRED, WARRING, WARS to engage in war (a state of open, armed conflict)
WARBLE	*v* -BLED, -BLING, -BLES to sing with melodic embellishments
WARBLER	*n* pl. -S one that warbles
WARCRAFT	*n* pl. -S the art of war
WARD	*v* -ED, -ING, -S to turn aside
WARDEN	*n* pl. -S the chief officer of a prison
WARDENRY	*n* pl. -RIES the office of a warden
WARDER	*n* pl. -S a person who guards something
WARDRESS	*n* pl. -ES a female warden
WARDROBE	*n* pl. -S a collection of garments
WARDROOM	*n* pl. -S a dining area for officers on a warship
WARDSHIP	*n* pl. -S the state of being under a guardian
WARE	*v* WARED, WARING, WARES to beware of
WAREROOM	*n* pl. -S a room in which goods are displayed for sale
WARFARE	*n* pl. -S the act of engaging in war
WARFARIN	*n* pl. -S a chemical compound

WARHEAD *n* pl. -S the front part of a missile containing the explosive

WARHORSE *n* pl. -S a musical or dramatic work that has been performed to excess

WARIER comparative of wary

WARIEST superlative of wary

WARILY *adv* in a wary manner

WARINESS *n* pl. -ES the state of being wary

WARING present participle of ware

WARISON *n* pl. -S a call to attack

WARK *v* -ED, -ING, -S to endure pain

WARLESS *adj* free from war

WARLIKE *adj* disposed to engage in war

WARLOCK *n* pl. -S a sorcerer

WARLORD *n* pl. -S a military leader of a warlike nation

WARM *adj* WARMER, WARMEST moderately hot

WARM *v* -ED, -ING, -S to make warm

WARMAKER *n* pl. -S one that wars

WARMER *n* pl. -S one that warms

WARMISH *adj* somewhat warm

WARMLY *adv* in a warm manner

WARMNESS *n* pl. -ES the state of being warm

WARMOUTH *n* pl. -S a freshwater fish

WARMTH *n* pl. -S warmness

WARMUP *n* pl. -S a preparatory exercise or procedure

WARN *v* -ED, -ING, -S to make aware of impending or possible danger

WARNER *n* pl. -S one that warns

WARNING *n* pl. -S something that warns

WARP *v* -ED, -ING, -S to turn or twist out of shape

WARPAGE *n* pl. -S the act of warping

WARPATH *n* pl. -S the route taken by attacking American Indians

WARPER *n* pl. -S one that warps

WARPLANE *n* pl. -S an airplane armed for combat

WARPOWER *n* pl. -S the power to make war

WARPWISE *adv* in a vertical direction

WARRAGAL *n* pl. -S warrigal

WARRANT *v* -ED, -ING, -S to give authority to

WARRANTY *n* pl. -TIES the act of warranting

WARRED past tense of war

WARREN *n* pl. -S a place where rabbits live and breed

WARRENER *n* pl. -S the keeper of a warren

WARRIGAL *n* pl. -S a dingo

WARRING present participle of war

WARRIOR *n* pl. -S one engaged or experienced in warfare

WARSAW *n* pl. -S a marine fish

WARSHIP *n* pl. -S a ship armed for combat

WARSLE *v* -SLED, -SLING, -SLES to wrestle

WARSLER *n* pl. -S a wrestler

WARSTLE *v* -TLED, -TLING, -TLES to wrestle

WARSTLER *n* pl. -S a wrestler

WART *n* pl. -S a protuberance on the skin **WARTED** *adj*

WARTHOG *n* pl. -S an African wild hog

WARTIER comparative of warty

WARTIEST superlative of warty

WARTIME *n* pl. -S a time of war

WARTLESS *adj* having no warts

WARTLIKE *adj* resembling a wart

WARTY *adj* WARTIER, WARTIEST covered with warts

WARWORK *n* pl. -S work done during a war

WARWORN *adj* showing the effects of war

WARY *adj* WARIER, WARIEST watchful

WAS 1st and 3d person sing. past indicative of be

WASABI *n* pl. -S a pungent herb

WASH *v* -ED, -ING, -ES to cleanse by immersing in or applying a liquid

WASHABLE *n* pl. -S something that can be washed without damage

WASHBOWL *n* pl. -S a bowl used for washing oneself

WASHDAY *n* pl. -DAYS a day set aside for washing clothes

WASHER *n* pl. -S one that washes

WASHIER comparative of washy

WASHIEST superlative of washy

WASHING *n* pl. -S articles washed or to be washed

WASHOUT *n* pl. -S an erosion of earth by the action of water

WASHRAG *n* pl. -S a small cloth used for washing oneself

WASHROOM *n* pl. -S a lavatory

WASHTUB	*n* pl. -S a tub used for washing clothes
WASHUP	*n* pl. -S the act of washing clean
WASHY	*adj* WASHIER, WASHIEST overly diluted
WASP	*n* pl. -S a stinging insect **WASPISH, WASPLIKE** *adj*
WASPY	*adj* WASPIER, WASPIEST resembling a wasp **WASPILY** *adv*
WASSAIL	*v* -ED, -ING, -S to drink to the health of
WAST	*n* pl. -S west
WASTABLE	*adj* capable of being wasted
WASTAGE	*n* pl. -S something that is wasted
WASTE	*v* WASTED, WASTING, WASTES to use thoughtlessly
WASTEFUL	*adj* tending to waste
WASTELOT	*n* pl. -S a vacant lot
WASTER	*n* pl. -S one that wastes
WASTERIE	*n* pl. -S wastry
WASTERY	*n* pl. -RIES wastry
WASTEWAY	*n* pl. -WAYS a channel for excess water
WASTING	present participle of waste
WASTREL	*n* pl. -S one that wastes
WASTRIE	*n* pl. -S wastry
WASTRY	*n* pl. -RIES reckless extravagance
WAT	*adj* WATTER, WATTEST wet
WAT	*n* pl. -S a hare
WATAP	*n* pl. -S a thread made from the roots of various trees
WATAPE	*n* pl. -S watap
WATCH	*v* -ED, -ING, -ES to observe carefully
WATCHCRY	*n* pl. -CRIES a password
WATCHDOG	*v* -DOGGED, -DOGGING, -DOGS to act as a guardian for
WATCHER	*n* pl. -S one that watches
WATCHEYE	*n* pl. -S a walleye
WATCHFUL	*adj* closely observant or alert
WATCHMAN	*n* pl. -MEN a man employed to stand guard
WATCHOUT	*n* pl. -S the act of looking out for something
WATER	*v* -ED, -ING, -S to sprinkle with water (a transparent, odorless, tasteless liquid)
WATERAGE	*n* pl. -S the conveyance of goods by water
WATERBED	*n* pl. -S a bed whose mattress is a plastic bag filled with water
WATERDOG	*n* pl. -S a large salamander
WATERER	*n* pl. -S one that waters
WATERIER	comparative of watery
WATERIEST	superlative of watery
WATERILY	*adv* in a watery manner
WATERING	*n* pl. -S the act of one that waters
WATERISH	*adj* watery
WATERLOG	*v* -LOGGED, -LOGGING, -LOGS to soak with water
WATERLOO	*n* pl. -LOOS a decisive defeat
WATERMAN	*n* pl. -MEN a boatman
WATERWAY	*n* pl. -WAYS a navigable body of water
WATERY	*adj* -TERIER, -TERIEST containing water
WATT	*n* pl. -S a unit of power
WATTAGE	*n* pl. -S an amount of power in terms of watts
WATTAPE	*n* pl. -S watap
WATTER	comparative of wat
WATTEST	superlative of wat
WATTHOUR	*n* pl. -S a unit of energy
WATTLE	*v* -TLED, -TLING, -TLES to weave into a network
WATTLESS	*adj* denoting a type of electric current
WAUCHT	*v* -ED, -ING, -S to waught
WAUGH	*adj* damp
WAUGHT	*v* -ED, -ING, -S to drink deeply
WAUK	*v* -ED, -ING, -S to wake
WAUL	*v* -ED, -ING, -S to cry like a cat
WAUR	*adj* worse
WAVE	*v* WAVED, WAVING, WAVES to move freely back and forth or up and down
WAVEBAND	*n* pl. -S a range of radio frequencies
WAVEFORM	*n* pl. -S a type of mathematical graph
WAVELESS	*adj* having no waves (moving ridges on the surface of a liquid)
WAVELET	*n* pl. -S a small wave
WAVELIKE	*adj* resembling a wave

WAVEOFF	*n* pl. -S the act of denying landing permission to an approaching aircraft
WAVER	*v* -ED, -ING, -S to move back and forth
WAVERER	*n* pl. -S one that wavers
WAVERY	*adj* wavering
WAVEY	*n* pl. -VEYS the snow goose
WAVIER	comparative of wavy
WAVIES	pl. of wavy
WAVIEST	superlative of wavy
WAVILY	*adv* in a wavy manner
WAVINESS	*n* pl. -ES the state of being wavy
WAVING	present participle of wave
WAVY	*adj* WAVIER, WAVIEST having waves
WAVY	*n* pl. -VIES wavey
WAW	*n* pl. -S vav
WAWL	*v* -ED, -ING, -S to waul
WAX	*v* -ED, -ING, -ES to coat with wax (a natural, heat-sensitive substance)
WAXBERRY	*n* pl. -RIES a berry with a waxy coating
WAXBILL	*n* pl. -S a tropical bird
WAXEN	*adj* covered with wax
WAXER	*n* pl. -S one that waxes
WAXIER	comparative of waxy
WAXIEST	superlative of waxy
WAXILY	*adv* in a waxy manner
WAXINESS	*n* pl. -ES the quality of being waxy
WAXING	*n* pl. -S the act of one that waxes
WAXLIKE	*adj* resembling wax
WAXPLANT	*n* pl. -S a tropical plant
WAXWEED	*n* pl. -S an annual herb
WAXWING	*n* pl. -S a type of passerine bird
WAXWORK	*n* pl. -S an effigy made of wax
WAXWORM	*n* pl. -S a moth that infests beehives
WAXY	*adj* WAXIER, WAXIEST resembling wax
WAY	*n* pl. WAYS a method of doing something
WAYBILL	*n* pl. -S a list of goods relative to a shipment
WAYFARER	*n* pl. -S a traveler
WAYGOING	*n* pl. -S the act of leaving
WAYLAY	*v* -LAID, -LAYING, -LAYS to ambush
WAYLAYER	*n* pl. -S one that waylays
WAYLESS	*adj* having no road or path
WAYSIDE	*n* pl. -S the side of a road
WAYWARD	*adj* willful
WAYWORN	*adj* fatigued by travel
WE	*pron* 1st person pl. pronoun in the nominative case
WEAK	*adj* WEAKER, WEAKEST lacking strength
WEAKEN	*v* -ED, -ING, -S to make weak
WEAKENER	*n* pl. -S one that weakens
WEAKFISH	*n* pl. -ES a marine fish
WEAKISH	*adj* somewhat weak
WEAKLING	*n* pl. -S a weak person
WEAKLY	*adj* -LIER, -LIEST weak and sickly
WEAKNESS	*n* pl. -ES the state of being weak
WEAKSIDE	*n* pl. -S the side of a basketball court with fewer players
WEAL	*n* pl. -S a welt
WEALD	*n* pl. -S a woodland
WEALTH	*n* pl. -S a great quantity of valuable material
WEALTHY	*adj* WEALTHIER, WEALTHIEST having wealth
WEAN	*v* -ED, -ING, -S to withhold mother's milk from and substitute other nourishment
WEANER	*n* pl. -S one that weans
WEANLING	*n* pl. -S a recently weaned child or animal
WEAPON	*v* -ED, -ING, -S to supply with a weapon (an instrument used in combat)
WEAPONRY	*n* pl. -RIES an aggregate of weapons
WEAR	*v* WORE, WORN, WEARING, WEARS to have on one's person
WEARABLE	*n* pl. -S a garment
WEARER	*n* pl. -S one that wears something
WEARIED	past tense of weary
WEARIER	comparative of weary
WEARIES	present 3d person sing. of weary
WEARIEST	superlative of weary
WEARIFUL	*adj* tiresome
WEARISH	*adj* tasteless

WEARY *adj* -RIER, -RIEST tired
WEARILY *adv*

WEARY *v* -RIED, -RYING, -RIES to make or become weary

WEASAND *n* pl. -S the throat

WEASEL *v* -SELED, -SELING, -SELS or -SELLED, -SELLING, -SELS to act evasively

WEASELLY *adj* resembling a weasel (a small carnivorous mammal)

WEASELY *adj* weaselly

WEASON *n* pl. -S weasand

WEATHER *v* -ED, -ING, -S to expose to atmospheric conditions

WEAVE *v* WOVE or WEAVED, WOVEN, WEAVING, WEAVES to form by interlacing threads

WEAVER *n* pl. -S one that weaves

WEAZAND *n* pl. -S weasand

WEB *v* WEBBED, WEBBING, WEBS to provide with a web (an interlaced fabric or structure)

WEBBING *n* pl. -S a woven strip of fiber

WEBBY *adj* -BIER, -BIEST weblike

WEBER *n* pl. -S a unit of magnetic flux

WEBFED *adj* designed to print a continuous roll of paper

WEBFOOT *n* pl. -FEET a foot having the toes joined by a membrane

WEBLESS *adj* having no webs

WEBLIKE *adj* resembling a web

WEBSTER *n* pl. -S a weaver

WEBWORK *n* pl. -S a weblike pattern or structure

WEBWORM *n* pl. -S a web-spinning caterpillar

WECHT *n* pl. -S weight

WED *v* WEDDED, WEDDING, WEDS to marry

WEDDER *n* pl. -S one that weds

WEDDING *n* pl. -S a marriage ceremony

WEDEL *v* -ED, -ING, -S to perform a wedeln

WEDELN *n* pl. -S a skiing technique

WEDGE *v* WEDGED, WEDGING, WEDGES to force apart with a wedge (a tapering piece of wood or metal)

WEDGIE *n* pl. -S a type of woman's shoe

WEDGY *adj* WEDGIER, WEDGIEST resembling a wedge

WEDLOCK *n* pl. -S the state of being married

WEE *adj* WEER, WEEST very small

WEE *n* pl. -S a short time

WEED *v* -ED, -ING, -S to remove weeds (undesirable plants)

WEEDER *n* pl. -S one that weeds

WEEDIER comparative of weedy

WEEDIEST superlative of weedy

WEEDILY *adv* in a weedy manner

WEEDLESS *adj* having no weeds

WEEDLIKE *adj* resembling a weed

WEEDY *adj* WEEDIER, WEEDIEST resembling a weed

WEEK *n* pl. -S a period of seven days

WEEKDAY *n* pl. -DAYS any day of the week except Sunday

WEEKEND *v* -ED, -ING, -S to spend the weekend (the end of the week)

WEEKLONG *adj* continuing for a week

WEEKLY *n* pl. -LIES a publication issued once a week

WEEL *adj* well

WEEN *v* -ED, -ING, -S to suppose

WEENIE *n* pl. -S a wiener

WEENSY *adj* -SIER, -SIEST tiny

WEENY *adj* -NIER, -NIEST tiny

WEEP *v* WEPT, WEEPING, WEEPS to express sorrow by shedding tears

WEEPER *n* pl. -S one that weeps

WEEPIE *n* pl. -S a very maudlin movie

WEEPING *n* pl. -S the act of one that weeps

WEEPY *adj* WEEPIER, WEEPIEST tending to weep

WEER comparative of wee

WEEST superlative of wee

WEET *v* -ED, -ING, -S to know

WEEVER *n* pl. -S a marine fish

WEEVIL *n* pl. -S a small beetle
WEEVILED, WEEVILLY, WEEVILY *adj*

WEEWEE *v* -WEED, -WEEING, -WEES to urinate

WEFT *n* pl. -S a woven fabric or garment

WEFTWISE *adv* in a horizontal direction

WEIGELA *n* pl. -S a flowering shrub

WEIGELIA *n* pl. -S weigela

WEIGH	*v* -ED, -ING, -S to determine the weight of
WEIGHER	*n* pl. -S one that weighs
WEIGHMAN	*n* pl. -MEN one whose occupation is weighing goods
WEIGHT	*v* -ED, -ING, -S to add weight (heaviness) to
WEIGHTER	*n* pl. -S one that weights
WEIGHTY	*adj* WEIGHTIER, WEIGHTIEST having great weight
WEINER	*n* pl. -S wiener
WEIR	*n* pl. -S a fence placed in a stream to catch fish
WEIRD	*adj* WEIRDER, WEIRDEST mysteriously strange
WEIRD	*n* pl. -S destiny
WEIRDIE	*n* pl. -S a very strange person
WEIRDIES	pl. of weirdy
WEIRDLY	*adv* in a weird manner
WEIRDO	*n* pl. WEIRDOES or WEIRDOS a weirdie
WEIRDY	*n* pl. WEIRDIES weirdie
WEKA	*n* pl. -S a flightless bird
WELCH	*v* -ED, -ING, -ES to welsh
WELCHER	*n* pl. -S one that welshes
WELCOME	*v* -COMED, -COMING, -COMES to greet cordially
WELCOMER	*n* pl. -S one that welcomes
WELD	*v* -ED, -ING, -S to join by applying heat **WELDABLE** *adj*
WELDER	*n* pl. -S one that welds
WELDLESS	*adj* having no welded joints
WELDMENT	*n* pl. -S a unit composed of welded pieces
WELDOR	*n* pl. -S welder
WELFARE	*n* pl. -S general well-being
WELKIN	*n* pl. -S the sky
WELL	*v* -ED, -ING, -S to rise to the surface and flow forth
WELLADAY	*n* pl. -DAYS wellaway
WELLAWAY	*n* pl. -WAYS an expression of sorrow
WELLBORN	*adj* of good birth or ancestry
WELLCURB	*n* pl. -S the stone ring around a well (a hole dug in the ground to obtain water)
WELLDOER	*n* pl. -S a doer of good deeds
WELLHEAD	*n* pl. -S the source of a spring or stream
WELLHOLE	*n* pl. -S the shaft of a well
WELLIE	*n* pl. -S a Wellington boot
WELLIES	pl. of welly
WELLNESS	*n* pl. -ES the state of being healthy
WELLSITE	*n* pl. -S a mineral
WELLY	*n* pl. -LIES wellie
WELSH	*v* -ED, -ING, -ES to fail to pay a debt
WELSHER	*n* pl. -S one that welshes
WELT	*v* -ED, -ING, -S to mark with welts (ridges or lumps raised on the skin)
WELTER	*v* -ED, -ING, -S to roll about
WELTING	*n* pl. -S a cord or strip used to reinforce a seam
WEN	*n* pl. -S a benign tumor of the skin
WENCH	*v* -ED, -ING, -ES to consort with prostitutes
WENCHER	*n* pl. -S one that wenches
WEND	*v* -ED, -ING, -S to proceed along
WENDIGO	*n* pl. -GOS windigo
WENNISH	*adj* wenny
WENNY	*adj* -NIER, -NIEST resembling a wen
WENT	past tense of go
WEPT	past tense of weep
WERE	a pl. and 2d person sing. past indicative, and past subjunctive of be
WEREGILD	*n* pl. -S wergeld
WEREWOLF	*n* pl. -WOLVES a person capable of assuming the form of a wolf
WERGELD	*n* pl. -S a price paid for the taking of a man's life in Anglo-Saxon law
WERGELT	*n* pl. -S wergeld
WERGILD	*n* pl. -S wergeld
WERT	a 2d person sing. past tense of be
WERWOLF	*n* pl. -WOLVES werewolf
WESKIT	*n* pl. -S a vest
WESSAND	*n* pl. -S weasand
WEST	*n* pl. -S a cardinal point of the compass
WESTER	*v* -ED, -ING, -S to move toward the west
WESTERLY	*n* pl. -LIES a wind from the west
WESTERN	*n* pl. -S one who lives in the west

WESTING   *n* pl. -S a shifting west

WESTMOST   *adj* farthest west

WESTWARD   *n* pl. -S a direction toward the west

WET   *adj* WETTER, WETTEST covered or saturated with a liquid

WET   *v* WETTED, WETTING, WETS to make wet

WETHER   *n* pl. -S a gelded male sheep

WETLAND   *n* pl. -S land containing much soil moisture

WETLY   *adv* in a wet manner

WETNESS   *n* pl. -ES the state of being wet

WETPROOF   *adj* waterproof

WETTABLE   *adj* capable of being wetted

WETTED   past tense of wet

WETTER   *n* pl. -S one that wets

WETTEST   superlative of wet

WETTING   *n* pl. -S a liquid used in moistening something

WETTISH   *adj* somewhat wet

WHA   *pron* who

WHACK   *v* -ED, -ING, -S to strike sharply

WHACKER   *n* pl. -S one that whacks

WHACKO   *n* pl. WHACKOS wacko

WHACKY   *adj* WHACKIER, WHACKIEST wacky

WHALE   *v* WHALED, WHALING, WHALES to engage in the hunting of whales (large marine mammals)

WHALEMAN   *n* pl. -MEN a whaler

WHALER   *n* pl. -S a person engaged in whaling

WHALING   *n* pl. -S the industry of hunting and processing whales

WHAM   *v* WHAMMED, WHAMMING, WHAMS to hit with a loud impact

WHAMMO   *interj* — used to indicate a startling event

WHAMMY   *n* pl. -MIES a supernatural spell bringing bad luck

WHAMO   *interj* whammo

WHANG   *v* -ED, -ING, -S to beat with a whip

WHANGEE   *n* pl. -S an Asian grass

WHAP   *v* WHAPPED, WHAPPING, WHAPS to whop

WHAPPER   *n* pl. -S whopper

WHARF   *v* -ED, -ING, -S to moor to a wharf (a docking place for vessels)

WHARFAGE   *n* pl. -S the use of a wharf

WHARVE   *n* pl. -S a round piece of wood used in spinning thread

WHAT   *n* pl. -S the true nature of something

WHATEVER   *adj* being what or who it may be

WHATNESS   *n* pl. -ES the true nature of something

WHATNOT   *n* pl. -S an ornamental set of shelves

WHATSIS   *n* pl. -SISES whatsit

WHATSIT   *n* pl. -S something whose name is unknown or forgotten

WHAUP   *n* pl. -S a European bird

WHEAL   *n* pl. -S a welt

WHEAT   *n* pl. -S a cereal grass

WHEATEAR   *n* pl. -S a small bird of northern regions

WHEATEN   *n* pl. -S a pale yellowish color

WHEE   *interj* — used to express delight

WHEEDLE   *v* -DLED, -DLING, -DLES to attempt to persuade by flattery

WHEEDLER   *n* pl. -S one that wheedles

WHEEL   *v* -ED, -ING, -S to convey on wheels (circular frames designed to turn on an axis)

WHEELER   *n* pl. -S one that wheels

WHEELIE   *n* pl. -S a maneuver made on a wheeled vehicle

WHEELING   *n* pl. -S the condition of a road for vehicles

WHEELMAN   *n* pl. -MEN a helmsman

WHEEN   *n* pl. -S a fairly large amount

WHEEP   *v* -ED, -ING, -S to wheeple

WHEEPLE   *v* -PLED, -PLING, -PLES to give forth a prolonged whistle

WHEEZE   *v* WHEEZED, WHEEZING, WHEEZES to breathe with a whistling sound

WHEEZER   *n* pl. -S one that wheezes

WHEEZY   *adj* WHEEZIER, WHEEZIEST characterized by wheezing **WHEEZILY** *adv*

WHELK   *n* pl. -S a pustule

WHELKY   *adj* WHELKIER, WHELKIEST marked with whelks

WHELM   *v* -ED, -ING, -S to cover with water

WHELP	*v* -ED, -ING, -S to give birth to
WHEN	*n* pl. -S the time in which something is done or occurs
WHENAS	*conj* at which time
WHENCE	*adv* from what place
WHENEVER	*adv* at whatever time
WHERE	*n* pl. -S the place at or in which something is located or occurs
WHEREAS	*n* pl. -ES an introductory statement of a formal document
WHEREAT	*adv* at what
WHEREBY	*adv* by what
WHEREIN	*adv* in what
WHEREOF	*adv* of what
WHEREON	*adv* on what
WHERETO	*adv* to what
WHEREVER	*adv* in or to whatever place
WHERRY	*v* -RIED, -RYING, -RIES to transport in a light rowboat
WHERVE	*n* pl. -S wharve
WHET	*v* WHETTED, WHETTING, WHETS to sharpen by friction
WHETHER	*conj* if it be the case that
WHETTER	*n* pl. -S one that whets
WHETTING	present participle of whet
WHEW	*n* pl. -S a whistling sound
WHEY	*n* pl. WHEYS the watery part of milk **WHEYEY, WHEYISH** *adj*
WHEYFACE	*n* pl. -S a pale, sallow face
WHEYLIKE	*adj* resembling whey
WHICH	*pron* what particular one or ones
WHICKER	*v* -ED, -ING, -S to whinny
WHID	*v* WHIDDED, WHIDDING, WHIDS to move rapidly and quietly
WHIDAH	*n* pl. -S whydah
WHIFF	*v* -ED, -ING, -S to blow or convey with slight gusts of air
WHIFFER	*n* pl. -S one that whiffs
WHIFFET	*n* pl. -S an insignificant person
WHIFFLE	*v* -FLED, -FLING, -FLES to move or think erratically
WHIFFLER	*n* pl. -S one that whiffles
WHIG	*n* pl. -S one who interprets history as a continuing victory of progress over reactionary forces
WHILE	*v* WHILED, WHILING, WHILES to cause to pass pleasantly
WHILOM	*adv* formerly
WHILST	*conj* during the time that
WHIM	*n* pl. -S an impulsive idea
WHIMBREL	*n* pl. -S a shore bird
WHIMPER	*v* -ED, -ING, -S to cry with plaintive, broken sounds
WHIMSEY	*n* pl. -SEYS whimsy
WHIMSY	*n* pl. -SIES a whim **WHIMSIED** *adj*
WHIN	*n* pl. -S furze
WHINCHAT	*n* pl. -S a songbird
WHINE	*v* WHINED, WHINING, WHINES to utter a plaintive, high-pitched sound
WHINER	*n* pl. -S one that whines
WHINEY	*adj* WHINIER, WHINIEST whiny
WHINGE	*v* WHINGED, WHINGEING or WHINGING, WHINGES to whine
WHINIER	comparative of whiny
WHINIEST	superlative of whiny
WHINING	present participle of whine
WHINNY	*v* -NIED, -NYING, -NIES to neigh in a low or gentle manner
WHINNY	*adj* -NIER, -NIEST abounding in whin
WHINY	*adj* WHINIER, WHINIEST tending to whine
WHIP	*v* WHIPPED or WHIPT, WHIPPING, WHIPS to strike with a whip (an instrument for administering corporal punishment)
WHIPCORD	*n* pl. -S a strong, twisted cord
WHIPLASH	*n* pl. -ES the lash of a whip
WHIPLIKE	*adj* resembling a whip
WHIPPED	a past tense of whip
WHIPPER	*n* pl. -S one that whips
WHIPPET	*n* pl. -S a small, swift dog
WHIPPIER	comparative of whippy
WHIPPIEST	superlative of whippy
WHIPPING	*n* pl. -S material used to whip
WHIPPY	*adj* -PIER, -PIEST pertaining to or resembling a whip
WHIPRAY	*n* pl. -RAYS a stingray
WHIPSAW	*v* -SAWED, -SAWN, -SAWING, -SAWS to cut with a narrow, tapering saw
WHIPT	a past tense of whip

WHIPTAIL	*n* pl. -S a lizard having a long, slender tail
WHIPWORM	*n* pl. -S a parasitic worm
WHIR	*v* WHIRRED, WHIRRING, WHIRS to move with a buzzing sound
WHIRL	*v* -ED, -ING, -S to revolve rapidly
WHIRLER	*n* pl. -S one that whirls
WHIRLY	*adj* WHIRLIER, WHIRLIEST marked by a whirling motion
WHIRLY	*n* pl. WHIRLIES a small tornado
WHIRR	*v* -ED, -ING, -S to whir
WHIRRED	past tense of whir
WHIRRING	present participle of whir
WHIRRY	*v* -RIED, -RYING, -RIES to hurry
WHISH	*v* -ED, -ING, -ES to move with a hissing sound
WHISHT	*v* -ED, -ING, -S to hush
WHISK	*v* -ED, -ING, -S to move briskly
WHISKER	*n* pl. -S a hair on a man's face **WHISKERY** *adj*
WHISKEY	*n* pl. -KEYS a liquor
WHISKY	*n* pl. -KIES whiskey
WHISPER	*v* -ED, -ING, -S to speak softly
WHISPERY	*adj* resembling a whisper
WHIST	*v* -ED, -ING, -S to hush
WHISTLE	*v* -TLED, -TLING, -TLES to make a shrill, clear musical sound
WHISTLER	*n* pl. -S one that whistles
WHIT	*n* pl. -S a particle
WHITE	*adj* WHITER, WHITEST of the color of pure snow
WHITE	*v* WHITED, WHITING, WHITES to whiten
WHITECAP	*n* pl. -S a wave with a crest of foam
WHITEFLY	*n* pl. -FLIES a small whitish insect
WHITELY	*adv* in a white manner
WHITEN	*v* -ED, -ING, -S to make white
WHITENER	*n* pl. -S one that whitens
WHITEOUT	*n* pl. -S an arctic weather condition
WHITER	comparative of white
WHITEST	superlative of white
WHITEY	*adj* whity
WHITHER	*adv* to what place
WHITIER	comparative of whity
WHITIEST	superlative of whity
WHITING	*n* pl. -S a marine food fish
WHITISH	*adj* somewhat white
WHITLOW	*n* pl. -S an inflammation of the finger or toe
WHITRACK	*n* pl. -S a weasel
WHITTER	*n* pl. -S a large draft of liquor
WHITTLE	*v* -TLED, -TLING, -TLES to cut or shave bits from
WHITTLER	*n* pl. -S one that whittles
WHITTRET	*n* pl. -S a weasel
WHITY	*adj* WHITIER, WHITIEST whitish
WHIZ	*v* WHIZZED, WHIZZING, WHIZZES to move with a buzzing or hissing sound
WHIZBANG	*n* pl. -S a type of explosive shell
WHIZZ	*v* -ED, -ING, -ES to whiz
WHIZZED	past tense of whiz
WHIZZER	*n* pl. -S one that whizzes
WHIZZES	present 3d person sing. of whiz
WHIZZING	present participle of whiz
WHO	*pron* what or which person or persons
WHOA	*interj* — used to command an animal to stop
WHODUNIT	*n* pl. -S a mystery story
WHOEVER	*pron* whatever person
WHOLE	*n* pl. -S all the parts or elements entering into and making up a thing
WHOLISM	*n* pl. -S holism
WHOLLY	*adv* totally
WHOM	*pron* the objective case of who
WHOMEVER	*pron* the objective case of whoever
WHOMP	*v* -ED, -ING, -S to defeat decisively
WHOMSO	*pron* the objective case of whoso
WHOOF	*v* -ED, -ING, -S to make a deep snorting sound
WHOOP	*v* -ED, -ING, -S to utter loud cries
WHOOPEE	*n* pl. -S boisterous fun
WHOOPER	*n* pl. -S one that whoops
WHOOPLA	*n* pl. -S a noisy commotion
WHOOSH	*v* -ED, -ING, -ES to move with a hissing sound
WHOOSIS	*n* pl. -SISES an object or person whose name is not known

WHOP	v WHOPPED, WHOPPING, WHOPS to strike forcibly	**WIDEBAND**	adj operating over a wide band of frequencies
WHOPPER	n pl. -S something unusually large	**WIDEN**	v -ED, -ING, -S to make wide or wider
WHORE	v WHORED, WHORING, WHORES to consort with prostitutes	**WIDENER**	n pl. -S one that widens
		WIDENESS	n pl. -ES the state of being wide
WHOREDOM	n pl. -S prostitution	**WIDEOUT**	n pl. -S a receiver in football
WHORESON	n pl. -S a bastard	**WIDER**	comparative of wide
WHORING	present participle of whore	**WIDEST**	superlative of wide
WHORISH	adj lewd	**WIDGEON**	n pl. -S a river duck
WHORL	n pl. -S a circular arrangement of similar parts **WHORLED** adj	**WIDGET**	n pl. -S a gadget
		WIDISH	adj somewhat wide
WHORT	n pl. -S an edible berry	**WIDOW**	v -ED, -ING, -S to deprive of a husband
WHORTLE	n pl. -S whort		
WHOSE	pron the possessive case of who	**WIDOWER**	n pl. -S a man whose wife has died and who has not remarried
WHOSEVER	pron the possessive case of whoever		
		WIDTH	n pl. -S extent from side to side
WHOSIS	n pl. -SISES whoosis	**WIDTHWAY**	adv from side to side
WHOSO	pron whoever	**WIELD**	v -ED, -ING, -S to handle or use effectively
WHUMP	v -ED, -ING, -S to thump		
WHY	n pl. WHYS the reason or cause of something	**WIELDER**	n pl. -S one that wields
		WIELDY	adj WIELDIER, WIELDIEST easily wielded
WHYDAH	n pl. -S an African bird		
WICH	n pl. -ES wych	**WIENER**	n pl. -S a frankfurter
WICK	n pl. -S a bundle of loosely twisted fibers in a candle or oil lamp	**WIENIE**	n pl. -S a wiener
		WIFE	n pl. WIVES a woman married to a man
WICKAPE	n pl. -S wicopy	**WIFE**	v WIFED, WIFING, WIFES to wive
WICKED	adj -EDER, -EDEST evil **WICKEDLY** adv	**WIFEDOM**	n pl. -S the status or function of a wife
WICKER	n pl. -S a slender, pliant twig or branch	**WIFEHOOD**	n pl. -S the state of being a wife
		WIFELESS	adj having no wife
WICKET	n pl. -S a small door or gate	**WIFELIKE**	adj wifely
WICKING	n pl. -S material for wicks	**WIFELY**	adj -LIER, -LIEST of or befitting a wife
WICKIUP	n pl. -S an American Indian hut		
WICKYUP	n pl. -S wickiup	**WIFING**	present participle of wife
WICOPY	n pl. -PIES a flowering shrub	**WIFTY**	adj -TIER, -TIEST ditsy
WIDDER	n pl. -S a widow	**WIG**	v WIGGED, WIGGING, WIGS to provide with a wig (an artificial covering of hair for the head)
WIDDIE	n pl. -S widdy		
WIDDLE	v -DLED, -DLING, -DLES to wriggle	**WIGAN**	n pl. -S a stiff fabric
		WIGEON	n pl. -S widgeon
WIDDY	n pl. -DIES a hangman's noose	**WIGGED**	past tense of wig
WIDE	adj WIDER, WIDEST having great extent from side to side **WIDELY** adv	**WIGGERY**	n pl. -GERIES a wig
		WIGGIER	comparative of wiggy
		WIGGIEST	superlative of wiggy
WIDE	n pl. -S a type of bowled ball in cricket	**WIGGING**	n pl. -S a scolding

WIGGLE	v -GLED, -GLING, -GLES to move with short, quick movements from side to side
WIGGLER	n pl. -S one that wiggles
WIGGLY	adj -GLIER, -GLIEST tending to wiggle
WIGGY	adj -GIER, -GIEST crazy
WIGHT	n pl. -S a living being
WIGLESS	adj having no wig
WIGLET	n pl. -S a small wig
WIGLIKE	adj resembling a wig
WIGMAKER	n pl. -S one that makes wigs
WIGWAG	v -WAGGED, -WAGGING, -WAGS to move back and forth
WIGWAM	n pl. -S an American Indian dwelling
WIKIUP	n pl. -S wickiup
WILCO	interj — used to indicate that a message received will be complied with
WILD	adj WILDER, WILDEST living in a natural state
WILD	n pl. -S an uninhabited or uncultivated area
WILDCAT	v -CATTED, -CATTING, -CATS to search for oil in an area of doubtful productivity
WILDER	v -ED, -ING, -S to bewilder
WILDFIRE	n pl. -S a raging, destructive fire
WILDFOWL	n pl. -S a wild game bird
WILDING	n pl. -S a wild plant or animal
WILDISH	adj somewhat wild
WILDLAND	n pl. -S uncultivated land
WILDLIFE	n pl. WILDLIFE wild animals and vegetation
WILDLING	n pl. -S a wilding
WILDLY	adv in a wild manner
WILDNESS	n pl. -ES the state of being wild
WILDWOOD	n pl. -S natural forest land
WILE	v WILED, WILING, WILES to entice
WILFUL	adj willful **WILFULLY** adv
WILIER	comparative of wily
WILIEST	superlative of wily
WILILY	adv in a wily manner
WILINESS	n pl. -ES the quality of being wily
WILING	present participle of wile
WILL	v -ED, -ING, -S to decide upon **WILLABLE** adj

WILL	v past sing. 2d person WOULD, WOULDEST, or WOULDST — used as an auxiliary followed by a simple infinitive to express futurity, inclination, likelihood, or requirement
WILLER	n pl. -S one that wills
WILLET	n pl. -S a shore bird
WILLFUL	adj bent on having one's own way
WILLIED	past tense of willy
WILLIES	present 3d person sing. of willy
WILLING	adj -INGER, -INGEST inclined or favorably disposed in mind
WILLIWAU	n pl. -S williwaw
WILLIWAW	n pl. -S a violent gust of cold wind
WILLOW	v -ED, -ING, -S to clean textile fibers with a certain machine
WILLOWER	n pl. -S one that willows
WILLOWY	adj -LOWIER, -LOWIEST pliant
WILLY	v -LIED, -LYING, -LIES to willow
WILLYARD	adj willful
WILLYART	adj willyard
WILLYWAW	n pl. -S williwaw
WILT	v -ED, -ING, -S to become limp
WILY	adj WILIER, WILIEST crafty
WIMBLE	v -BLED, -BLING, -BLES to bore with a hand tool
WIMP	n pl. -S a weak or ineffectual person
WIMPISH	adj wimpy
WIMPLE	v -PLED, -PLING, -PLES to pleat
WIMPY	adj WIMPIER, WIMPIEST weak, ineffectual
WIN	v WON or WAN, WINNING, WINS to be victorious
WIN	v WINNED, WINNING, WINS to winnow
WINCE	v WINCED, WINCING, WINCES to flinch
WINCER	n pl. -S one that winces
WINCEY	n pl. -CEYS a type of fabric
WINCH	v -ED, -ING, -ES to raise with a winch (a hoisting machine)
WINCHER	n pl. -S one that winches
WINCING	present participle of wince

WIND	*v* WOUND or WINDED, WINDING, WINDS to pass around an object or fixed center **WINDABLE** *adj*
WINDAGE	*n* pl. -S the effect of the wind (air in natural motion) on a projectile
WINDBAG	*n* pl. -S a talkative person
WINDBURN	*v* -BURNED or -BURNT, -BURNING, -BURNS to be affected with skin irritation caused by exposure to the wind
WINDER	*n* pl. -S one that winds
WINDFALL	*n* pl. -S a sudden and unexpected gain
WINDFLAW	*n* pl. -S a gust of wind
WINDGALL	*n* pl. -S a swelling on a horse's leg
WINDIER	comparative of windy
WINDIEST	superlative of windy
WINDIGO	*n* pl. -GOS an evil demon in Algonquian mythology
WINDILY	*adv* in a windy manner
WINDING	*n* pl. -S material wound about an object
WINDLASS	*v* -ED, -ING, -ES to raise with a windlass (a hoisting machine)
WINDLE	*v* -DLED, -DLING, -DLES to wind
WINDLESS	*adj* being without wind
WINDLING	*n* pl. -S a bundle of straw
WINDMILL	*v* -ED, -ING, -S to rotate solely under the force of a passing airstream
WINDOW	*v* -ED, -ING, -S to provide with a window (an opening in a wall to admit light and air)
WINDPIPE	*n* pl. -S the trachea
WINDROW	*v* -ED, -ING, -S to arrange in long rows, as hay or grain
WINDSOCK	*n* pl. -S a device used to indicate wind direction
WINDSURF	*v* -ED, -ING, -S to sail on a sailboard
WINDUP	*n* pl. -S a conclusion
WINDWARD	*n* pl. -S the direction from which the wind blows
WINDWAY	*n* pl. -WAYS a passage for air
WINDY	*adj* WINDIER, WINDIEST marked by strong wind
WINE	*v* WINED, WINING, WINES to provide with wine (the fermented juice of the grape)
WINELESS	*adj* having no wine
WINERY	*n* pl. -ERIES an establishment for making wine
WINESHOP	*n* pl. -S a shop where wine is sold
WINESKIN	*n* pl. -S a goatskin bag for holding wine
WINESOP	*n* pl. -S a food sopped in wine
WINEY	*adj* WINIER, WINIEST winy
WING	*v* -ED, -ING, -S to travel by means of wings (organs of flight)
WINGBACK	*n* pl. -S a certain player in football
WINGBOW	*n* pl. -S a mark on the wing of a domestic fowl
WINGDING	*n* pl. -S a lively party
WINGEDLY	*adv* swiftly
WINGER	*n* pl. -S a certain player in soccer
WINGIER	comparative of wingy
WINGIEST	superlative of wingy
WINGLESS	*adj* having no wings
WINGLET	*n* pl. -S a small wing
WINGLIKE	*adj* resembling a wing
WINGMAN	*n* pl. -MEN a pilot behind the leader of a flying formation
WINGOVER	*n* pl. -S a flight maneuver
WINGSPAN	*n* pl. -S the distance from the tip of one of a pair of wings to that of the other
WINGTIP	*n* pl. -S a type of man's shoe
WINGY	*adj* WINGIER, WINGIEST swift
WINIER	comparative of winey and winy
WINIEST	superlative of winey and winy
WINING	present participle of wine
WINISH	*adj* winy
WINK	*v* -ED, -ING, -S to close and open one eye quickly
WINKER	*n* pl. -S one that winks
WINKLE	*v* -KLED, -KLING, -KLES to displace, extract, or evict from a position
WINLESS	*adj* having no wins
WINNABLE	*adj* able to be won
WINNED	past tense of win (to winnow)
WINNER	*n* pl. -S one that wins
WINNING	*n* pl. -S money won in a game or competition
WINNOCK	*n* pl. -S a window
WINNOW	*v* -ED, -ING, -S to free grain from impurities

WINNOWER *n* pl. -S one that winnows

WINO *n* pl. WINOES or WINOS one who is habitually drunk on wine

WINSOME *adj* -SOMER, -SOMEST charming

WINTER *v* -ED, -ING, -S to pass the winter (the coldest season of the year)

WINTERER *n* pl. -S one that winters

WINTERLY *adj* wintry

WINTERY *adj* -TERIER, -TERIEST wintry

WINTLE *v* -TLED, -TLING, -TLES to stagger

WINTRY *adj* -TRIER, -TRIEST characteristic of winter
WINTRILY *adv*

WINY *adj* WINIER, WINIEST having the taste or qualities of wine

WINZE *n* pl. -S a steeply inclined mine shaft

WIPE *v* WIPED, WIPING, WIPES to rub lightly in order to clean or dry

WIPEOUT *n* pl. -S a fall from a surfboard

WIPER *n* pl. -S one that wipes

WIPING present participle of wipe

WIRE *v* WIRED, WIRING, WIRES to fasten with wire (a slender rod, strand, or thread of ductile metal)
WIRABLE *adj*

WIREDRAW *v* -DREW, -DRAWN, -DRAWING, -DRAWS to draw into wire

WIREHAIR *n* pl. -S a dog having a wiry coat

WIRELESS *v* -ED, -ING, -ES to radio

WIRELIKE *adj* resembling wire

WIREMAN *n* pl. -MEN one who makes or works with wire

WIRER *n* pl. -S one that wires

WIRETAP *v* -TAPPED, -TAPPING, -TAPS to intercept messages by means of a concealed monitoring device

WIREWAY *n* pl. -WAYS a tube for protecting electric wires

WIREWORK *n* pl. -S an article made of wire

WIREWORM *n* pl. -S a wirelike worm

WIRIER comparative of wiry

WIRIEST superlative of wiry

WIRILY *adv* in a wiry manner

WIRINESS *n* pl. -ES the quality of being wiry

WIRING *n* pl. -S a system of electric wires

WIRRA *interj* — used to express sorrow

WIRY *adj* WIRIER, WIRIEST resembling wire

WIS *v* past tense WIST to know — WIS and WIST are the only accepted forms of this verb; it cannot be conjugated further

WISDOM *n* pl. -S the power of true and right discernment

WISE *v* WISED, WISING, WISES to become aware or informed

WISE *adj* WISER, WISEST having wisdom

WISEACRE *n* pl. -S a pretentiously wise person

WISEASS *n* pl. -ES a wiseacre

WISED past tense of wise

WISELY *adv* -LIER, -LIEST in a wise manner

WISENESS *n* pl. -ES wisdom

WISENT *n* pl. -S a European bison

WISER comparative of wise

WISEST superlative of wise

WISH *v* -ED, -ING, -ES to feel an impulse toward attainment or possession of something

WISHA *interj* — used to express surprise

WISHBONE *n* pl. -S a forked bone in front of a bird's breastbone

WISHER *n* pl. -S one that wishes

WISHFUL *adj* desirous

WISHLESS *adj* not wishful

WISING present participle of wise

WISP *v* -ED, -ING, -S to twist into a wisp (a small bunch or bundle)

WISPIER comparative of wispy

WISPIEST superlative of wispy

WISPILY *adv* in a wispy manner

WISPISH *adj* wispy

WISPLIKE *adj* wispy

WISPY *adj* WISPIER, WISPIEST resembling a wisp

WISS *v* -ED, -ING, -ES to wish

WIST *v* -ED, -ING, -S to know

WISTARIA *n* pl. -S wisteria

WISTERIA *n* pl. -S a flowering shrub

WISTFUL *adj* yearning

WIT *n* pl. -S intelligence

WIT *v* WIST, WITING or WITTING, present sing. 1st person WOT, 2d WOST, 3d WOT, present pl. WITE to know

WITAN *n/pl* the members of a national council in Anglo-Saxon England

WITCH *v* -ED, -ING, -ES to bewitch

WITCHERY *n* pl. -ERIES sorcery

WITCHING *n* pl. -S sorcery

WITCHY *adj* WITCHIER, WITCHIEST malicious

WITE *v* WITED, WITING, WITES to blame

WITH *prep* in the company of

WITHAL *adv* in addition

WITHDRAW *v* -DREW, -DRAWN, -DRAWING, -DRAWS to move back or away

WITHE *v* WITHED, WITHING, WITHES to bind with flexible twigs

WITHER *v* -ED, -ING, -S to dry up and wilt

WITHERER *n* pl. -S one that withers

WITHHOLD *v* -HELD, -HOLDING, -HOLDS to hold back

WITHIER comparative of withy

WITHIES pl. of withy

WITHIEST superlative of withy

WITHIN *n* pl. -S an interior place or area

WITHING present participle of withe

WITHOUT *n* pl. -S an exterior place or area

WITHY *n* pl. WITHIES a flexible twig

WITHY *adj* WITHIER, WITHIEST flexible and tough

WITING present participle of wit and wite

WITLESS *adj* lacking intelligence

WITLING *n* pl. -S one who considers himself witty

WITLOOF *n* pl. -S chicory

WITNESS *v* -ED, -ING, -ES to see or know by personal experience

WITNEY *n* pl. -NEYS a heavy woolen fabric

WITTED *adj* having intelligence

WITTIER comparative of witty

WITTIEST superlative of witty

WITTILY *adv* in a witty manner

WITTING *n* pl. -S knowledge

WITTOL *n* pl. -S a man who tolerates his wife's infidelity

WITTY *adj* -TIER, -TIEST humorously clever

WIVE *v* WIVED, WIVING, WIVES to marry a woman

WIVER *n* pl. -S wivern

WIVERN *n* pl. -S a two-legged dragon

WIVES pl. of wife

WIVING present participle of wive

WIZ *n* pl. -ES a very clever or skillful person

WIZARD *n* pl. -S a sorcerer **WIZARDLY** *adj*

WIZARDRY *n* pl. -RIES sorcery

WIZEN *v* -ED, -ING, -S to shrivel

WIZZEN *n* pl. -S weasand

WO *n* pl. WOS woe

WOAD *n* pl. -S a blue dye **WOADED** *adj*

WOADWAX *n* pl. -ES an ornamental shrub

WOALD *n* pl. -S a yellow pigment

WOBBLE *v* -BLED, -BLING, -BLES to move unsteadily

WOBBLER *n* pl. -S one that wobbles

WOBBLY *adj* -BLIER, -BLIEST unsteady

WOBBLY *n* pl. -BLIES a member of the Industrial Workers of the World

WOBEGONE *adj* affected with woe

WODGE *n* pl. -S a chunk of something

WOE *n* pl. -S tremendous grief

WOEFUL *adj* -FULLER, -FULLEST full of woe **WOEFULLY** *adv*

WOENESS *n* pl. -ES sadness

WOESOME *adj* woeful

WOFUL *adj* woeful **WOFULLY** *adv*

WOK *n* pl. -S a cooking utensil

WOKE a past tense of wake

WOKEN a past participle of wake

WOLD *n* pl. -S an elevated tract of open land

WOLF *n* pl. WOLVES a carnivorous mammal

WOLF *v* -ED, -ING, -S to devour voraciously

WOLFER *n* pl. -S one who hunts wolves

WOLFFISH *n* pl. -ES a marine fish

WOLFISH *adj* wolflike

WOLFLIKE *adj* resembling a wolf

WOLFRAM *n* pl. -S tungsten

WOLVER *n* pl. -S wolfer

WOLVES pl. of wolf

WOMAN *n* pl. WOMEN an adult human female

WOMAN *v* -ED, -ING, -S to play the part of a woman

WOMANISE *v* -ISED, -ISING, -ISES to womanize

WOMANISH *adj* characteristic of a woman

WOMANIZE *v* -IZED, -IZING, -IZES to make effeminate

WOMANLY *adj* -LIER, -LIEST having the qualities of a woman

WOMB *n* pl. -S the uterus **WOMBED** *adj*

WOMBAT *n* pl. -S a nocturnal mammal

WOMBY *adj* WOMBIER, WOMBIEST hollow

WOMEN pl. of woman

WOMERA *n* pl. -S a device used to propel spears

WOMMERA *n* pl. -S womera

WON *v* WONNED, WONNING, WONS to dwell

WONDER *v* -ED, -ING, -S to have a feeling of curiosity or doubt

WONDERER *n* pl. -S one that wonders

WONDROUS *adj* marvelous

WONK *n* pl. -S an overly studious student

WONKY *adj* -KIER, -KIEST unsteady

WONNED past tense of won

WONNER *n* pl. -S a prodigy

WONNING present participle of won

WONT *v* -ED, -ING, -S to make accustomed to

WONTEDLY *adv* in a usual manner

WONTON *n* pl. -S a pork-filled dumpling used in Chinese cooking

WOO *v* -ED, -ING, -S to seek the affection of

WOOD *v* -ED, -ING, -S to furnish with wood (the hard, fibrous substance beneath the bark of a tree or shrub)

WOODBIN *n* pl. -S a bin for holding firewood

WOODBIND *n* pl. -S woodbine

WOODBINE *n* pl. -S a European shrub

WOODBOX *n* pl. -ES a woodbin

WOODCHAT *n* pl. -S a European shrike

WOODCOCK *n* pl. -S a game bird

WOODCUT *n* pl. -S an engraved block of wood

WOODEN *adj* -ENER, -ENEST resembling wood in stiffness **WOODENLY** *adv*

WOODHEN *n* pl. -S the weka

WOODIE *n* pl. -S woody

WOODIER comparative of woody

WOODIES pl. of woody

WOODIEST superlative of woody

WOODLAND *n* pl. -S land covered with trees

WOODLARK *n* pl. -S a songbird

WOODLESS *adj* having no wood

WOODLORE *n* pl. -S knowledge of the forest

WOODLOT *n* pl. -S an area restricted to the growing of forest trees

WOODMAN *n* pl. -MEN woodsman

WOODNOTE *n* pl. -S a song or call of a forest bird

WOODPILE *n* pl. -S a pile of wood

WOODRUFF *n* pl. -S an aromatic herb

WOODSHED *v* -SHEDDED, -SHEDDING, -SHEDS to practice on a musical instrument

WOODSIA *n* pl. -S a small fern

WOODSMAN *n* pl. -MEN one who works or lives in the forest

WOODSY *adj* WOODSIER, WOODSIEST suggestive of a forest

WOODWAX *n* pl. -ES woadwax

WOODWIND *n* pl. -S a musical wind instrument

WOODWORK *n* pl. -S work made of wood

WOODWORM *n* pl. -S a wood-boring worm

WOODY *adj* WOODIER, WOODIEST containing or resembling wood

WOODY *n* pl. WOODIES a wood-paneled station wagon

WOOER *n* pl. -S one that woos

WOOF *v* -ED, -ING, -S to utter a gruff barking sound

WOOFER *n* pl. -S a loudspeaker designed to reproduce low-pitched sounds

WOOINGLY *adv* attractively

WOOL *n* pl. -S the dense, soft hair forming the coat of certain mammals

WOOLED *adj* having wool of a specified kind

WOOLEN *n* pl. -S a fabric made of wool

WOOLER *n* pl. -S a domestic animal raised for its wool

WOOLFELL *n* pl. -S woolskin

WOOLHAT *n* pl. -S one who works a small farm

WOOLIE *n* pl. -S a woolly

WOOLIER comparative of wooly

WOOLIES pl. of wooly

WOOLIEST superlative of wooly

WOOLLED *adj* wooled

WOOLLEN *n* pl. -S woolen

WOOLLIER comparative of woolly

WOOLLIES pl. of woolly

WOOLLIKE *adj* resembling wool

WOOLLY *adj* -LIER, -LIEST consisting of or resembling wool **WOOLLILY** *adv*

WOOLLY *n* pl. -LIES a garment made of wool

WOOLMAN *n* pl. -MEN a dealer in wool

WOOLPACK *n* pl. -S a bag for packing a bale of wool

WOOLSACK *n* pl. -S a sack of wool

WOOLSHED *n* pl. -S a building in which sheep are sheared

WOOLSKIN *n* pl. -S a sheepskin with the wool still on it

WOOLWORK *n* pl. -S needlework

WOOLY *adj* WOOLIER, WOOLIEST woolly

WOOLY *n* pl. WOOLIES a woolly

WOOMERA *n* pl. -S womera

WOOPS *v* -ED, -ING, -ES to vomit

WOORALI *n* pl. -S curare

WOORARI *n* pl. -S curare

WOOSH *v* -ED, -ING, -ES to whoosh

WOOZY *adj* -ZIER, -ZIEST dazed **WOOZILY** *adv*

WORD *v* -ED, -ING, -S to express in words (speech sounds that communicate meaning)

WORDAGE *n* pl. -S the number of words used

WORDBOOK *n* pl. -S a dictionary

WORDIER comparative of wordy

WORDIEST superlative of wordy

WORDILY *adv* in a wordy manner

WORDING *n* pl. -S the act or style of expressing in words

WORDLESS *adj* being without words

WORDPLAY *n* pl. -PLAYS a witty exchange of words

WORDY *adj* WORDIER, WORDIEST using many or too many words

WORE past tense of wear

WORK *v* WORKED or WROUGHT, WORKING, WORKS to exert one's powers of body or mind for some purpose

WORKABLE *adj* capable of being done

WORKADAY *adj* everyday

WORKBAG *n* pl. -S a bag for holding work instuments and materials

WORKBOAT *n* pl. -S a boat used for commercial purposes

WORKBOOK *n* pl. -S an exercise book for a student

WORKBOX *n* pl. -ES a box for holding work instruments and materials

WORKDAY *n* pl. -DAYS a day on which work is done

WORKER *n* pl. -S one that works

WORKFARE *n* pl. -S a welfare program that requires recipients to perform public-service work

WORKFOLK *n/pl* manual laborers

WORKING *n* pl. -S a mining excavation

WORKLESS *adj* unemployed

WORKLOAD *n* pl. -S the amount of work assigned to an employee

WORKMAN *n* pl. -MEN a male worker

WORKMATE *n* pl. -S a fellow worker

WORKOUT *n* pl. -S a period of physical exercise

WORKROOM pl. -S a room in which work is done

WORKSHOP *n* pl. -S a workroom

WORKUP *n* pl. -S an intensive diagnostic study

WORKWEEK *n* pl. -S the number of hours worked in a week

WORLD *n* pl. -S the earth and all its inhabitants

WORLDLY *adj* -LIER, -LIEST pertaining to the world

WORM *v* -ED, -ING, -S to rid of worms (small, limbless invertebrates)

WORMER *n* pl. -S one that worms

WORMHOLE *n* pl. -S a hole made by a burrowing worm

WORMIER comparative of wormy

WORMIEST superlative of wormy

WORMIL *n* pl. -S a lump in the skin of an animal's back

WORMISH *adj* wormlike

WORMLIKE *adj* resembling a worm

WORMROOT *n* pl. -S pinkroot

WORMSEED *n* pl. -S a tropical plant

WORMWOOD *n* pl. -S a European herb

WORMY *adj* WORMIER, WORMIEST infested with worms

WORN *adj* affected by wear or use

WORNNESS *n* pl. -ES the state of being worn

WORRIED past tense of worry

WORRIER *n* pl. -S one that worries

WORRIT *v* -ED, -ING, -S to worry

WORRY *v* -RIED, -RYING, -RIES to feel anxious and uneasy about something

WORSE *n* pl. -S something that is worse (bad in a greater degree)

WORSEN *v* -ED, -ING, -S to make or become worse

WORSER *adj* worse

WORSET *n* pl. -S worsted

WORSHIP *v* -SHIPED, -SHIPING, -SHIPS or -SHIPPED, -SHIPPING, -SHIPS to honor and love as a divine being

WORST *v* -ED, -ING, -S to defeat

WORSTED *n* pl. -S a woolen yarn

WORT *n* pl. -S a plant, herb, or vegetable

WORTH *v* -ED, -ING, -S to befall

WORTHFUL *adj* worthy

WORTHY *adj* -THIER, -THIEST having value or merit **WORTHILY** *adv*

WORTHY *n* pl. -THIES a worthy person

WOST a present 2d person sing. of wit

WOT *v* WOTTED, WOTTING, WOTS to know

WOULD past tense of will

WOULDEST a 2d person sing. past tense of will

WOULDST a 2d person sing. past tense of will

WOUND *v* -ED, -ING, -S to inflict an injury upon

WOVE a past tense of weave

WOVEN *n* pl. -S a woven fabric

WOW *v* -ED, -ING, -S to excite to enthusiastic approval

WOWSER *n* pl. -S a puritanical person

WRACK *v* -ED, -ING, -S to wreck

WRACKFUL *adj* destructive

WRAITH *n* pl. -S a ghost

WRANG *n* pl. -S a wrong

WRANGLE *v* -GLED, -GLING, -GLES to argue noisily

WRANGLER *n* pl. -S one that wrangles

WRAP *v* WRAPPED or WRAPT, WRAPPING, WRAPS to enclose in something wound or folded about

WRAPPER *n* pl. -S one that wraps

WRAPPING *n* pl. -S the material in which something is wrapped

WRAPT a past tense of wrap

WRASSE *n* pl. -S a marine fish

WRASSLE *v* -SLED, -SLING, -SLES to wrastle

WRASTLE *v* -TLED, -TLING, -TLES to wrestle

WRATH *v* -ED, -ING, -S to make wrathful

WRATHFUL *adj* extremely angry

WRATHY *adj* WRATHIER, WRATHIEST wrathful **WRATHILY** *adv*

WREAK *v* -ED, -ING, -S to inflict

WREAKER *n* pl. -S one that wreaks

WREATH *n* pl. -S a band of flowers **WREATHY** *adj*

WREATHE *v* WREATHED, WREATHEN, WREATHING, WREATHES to shape into a wreath

WRECK *v* -ED, -ING, -S to cause the ruin of

WRECKAGE *n* pl. -S the act of wrecking

WRECKER *n* pl. -S one that wrecks

WRECKFUL *adj* destructive

WRECKING *n* pl. -S the occupation of salvaging wrecked objects

WREN *n* pl. -S a small songbird

WRENCH *v* -ED, -ING, -ES to twist suddenly and forcibly

WREST *v* -ED, -ING, -S to take away by force

WRESTER	*n* pl. -S one that wrests	**WRITHER**	*n* pl. -S one that writhes
WRESTLE	*v* -TLED, -TLING, -TLES to engage in a type of hand-to-hand contest	**WRITHING**	present participle of writhe
		WRITING	*n* pl. -S a written composition
		WRITTEN	past participle of write
WRESTLER	*n* pl. -S one that wrestles	**WRONG**	*adj* WRONGER, WRONGEST not according to what is right, proper, or correct
WRETCH	*n* pl. -ES a wretched person		
WRETCHED	*adj* -EDER, -EDEST extremely unhappy		
		WRONG	*v* -ED, -ING, -S to treat injuriously or unjustly
WRICK	*v* -ED, -ING, -S to wrench		
WRIED	past tense of wry	**WRONGER**	*n* pl. -S one that wrongs
WRIER	a comparative of wry	**WRONGFUL**	*adj* wrong
WRIES	present 3d person sing. of wry	**WRONGLY**	*adv* in a wrong manner
WRIEST	a superlative of wry	**WROTE**	past tense of write
WRIGGLE	*v* -GLED, -GLING, -GLES to turn or twist in a sinuous manner	**WROTH**	*adj* very angry
		WROTHFUL	*adj* wroth
WRIGGLER	*n* pl. -S one that wriggles	**WROUGHT**	a past tense of work
WRIGGLY	*adj* -GLIER, -GLIEST wriggling	**WRUNG**	a past tense of wring
WRIGHT	*n* pl. -S one who constructs or creates	**WRY**	*adj* WRIER, WRIEST or WRYER, WRYEST contorted **WRYLY** *adv*
WRING	*v* WRUNG or WRINGED, WRINGING, WRINGS to twist so as to compress	**WRY**	*v* WRIED, WRYING, WRIES to contort
		WRYNECK	*n* pl. -S a European bird
WRINGER	*n* pl. -S one that wrings	**WRYNESS**	*n* pl. -ES the state of being wry
WRINKLE	*v* -KLED, -KLING, -KLES to make wrinkles (small ridges or furrows) in	**WUD**	*adj* insane
		WURST	*n* pl. -S sausage
		WURZEL	*n* pl. -S a variety of beet
WRINKLY	*adj* -KLIER, -KLIEST having wrinkles	**WUSS**	*n* pl. -ES a wimp
		WUSSY	*n* pl. -SIES a wuss
WRIST	*n* pl. -S the junction between the hand and forearm	**WUSSY**	*adj* WUSSIER, WUSSIEST wimpy
WRISTLET	*n* pl. -S a band worn around the wrist		
		WUTHER	*v* -ED, -ING, -S to blow with a dull roaring sound
WRISTY	*adj* WRISTIER, WRISTIEST using much wrist action	**WYCH**	*n* pl. -ES a European elm
		WYE	*n* pl. -S the letter Y
WRIT	*n* pl. -S a written legal order	**WYLE**	*v* WYLED, WYLING, WYLES to beguile
WRITE	*v* WROTE, WRITTEN, WRITING, WRITES to form characters or symbols on a surface with an instrument **WRITABLE** *adj*		
		WYN	*n* pl. -S wynn
		WYND	*n* pl. -S a narrow street
WRITER	*n* pl. -S one that writes	**WYNN**	*n* pl. -S the rune for W
WRITERLY	*adj* characteristic of a writer	**WYTE**	*v* WYTED, WYTING, WYTES to wite
WRITHE	*v* WRITHED, WRITHING, WRITHES to squirm or twist in pain		
		WYVERN	*n* pl. -S wivern
WRITHEN	*adj* twisted		

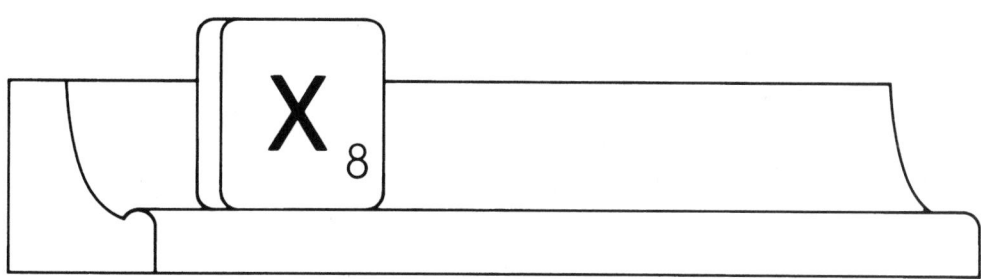

XANTHAN *n* pl. -S a gum produced by bacterial fermentation

XANTHATE *n* pl. -S a chemical salt

XANTHEIN *n* pl. -S the water-soluble part of the coloring matter in yellow flowers

XANTHENE *n* pl. -S a chemical compound

XANTHIC *adj* tending to have a yellow color

XANTHIN *n* pl. -S a yellow pigment

XANTHINE *n* pl. -S a chemical compound

XANTHOMA *n* pl. -MAS or -MATA a skin disease

XANTHONE *n* pl. -S a chemical compound

XANTHOUS *adj* yellow

XEBEC *n* pl. -S a Mediterranean sailing vessel

XENIA *n* pl. -S the effect of pollen on certain plant structures **XENIAL** *adj*

XENIC *adj* pertaining to a type of culture medium

XENOGAMY *n* pl. -MIES the transfer of pollen from one plant to another

XENOGENY *n* pl. -NIES the supposed production of offspring totally different from the parent

XENOLITH *n* pl. -S a rock fragment included in another rock

XENON *n* pl. -S a gaseous element

XERARCH *adj* developing in a dry area

XERIC *adj* requiring only a small amount of moisture

XEROSERE *n* pl. -S a dry-land sere

XEROSIS *n* pl. -ROSES abnormal dryness of a body part or tissue **XEROTIC** *adj*

XEROX *v* -ED, -ING, -ES to copy on a xerographic copier

XERUS *n* pl. -ES an African ground squirrel

XI *n* pl. -S a Greek letter

XIPHOID *n* pl. -S a part of the sternum

XU *n* pl. XU a monetary unit of Vietnam

XYLAN *n* pl. -S a substance found in cell walls of plants

XYLEM *n* pl. -S a complex plant tissue

XYLENE *n* pl. -S a flammable hydrocarbon

XYLIDIN *n* pl. -S xylidine

XYLIDINE *n* pl. -S a chemical compound

XYLITOL *n* pl. -S an alcohol

XYLOCARP *n* pl. -S a hard, woody fruit

XYLOID *adj* resembling wood

XYLOL *n* pl. -S xylene

XYLOSE *n* pl. -S a type of sugar

XYLOTOMY *n* pl. -MIES the preparation of sections of wood for microscopic examination

XYLYL *n* pl. -S a univalent radical

XYST *n* pl. -S xystus

XYSTER *n* pl. -S a surgical instrument for scraping bones

XYSTOS *n* pl. -TOI xystus

XYSTUS *n* pl. -TI a roofed area where athletes trained in ancient Greece

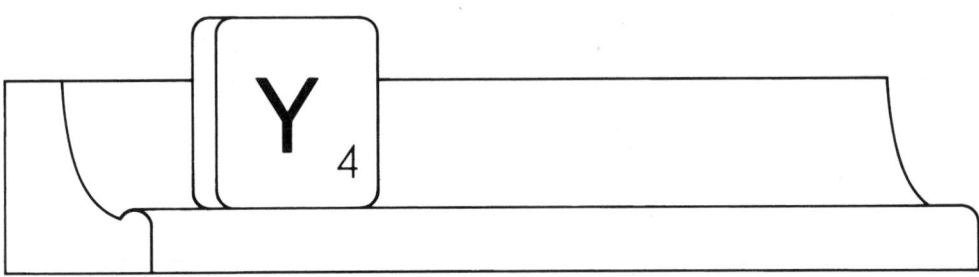

YA	*pron* you	**YANG**	*n* pl. -S the masculine active principle in Chinese cosmology
YABBER	*v* -ED, -ING, -S to jabber	**YANK**	*v* -ED, -ING, -S to pull suddenly
YACHT	*v* -ED, -ING, -S to sail in a yacht (a vessel used for pleasure cruising or racing)	**YANQUI**	*n* pl. -S a United States citizen
YACHTER	*n* pl. -S one who sails a yacht	**YANTRA**	*n* pl. -S a geometrical diagram used in meditation
YACHTING	*n* pl. -S the sport of sailing in yachts	**YAP**	*v* YAPPED, YAPPING, YAPS to bark shrilly
YACHTMAN	*n* pl. -MEN a yachter	**YAPOCK**	*n* pl. -S an aquatic mammal
YACK	*v* -ED, -ING, -S to yak	**YAPOK**	*n* pl. -S yapock
YAFF	*v* -ED, -ING, -S to bark	**YAPON**	*n* pl. -S yaupon
YAGER	*n* pl. -S jaeger	**YAPPED**	past tense of yap
YAGI	*n* pl. -S a type of shortwave antenna	**YAPPER**	*n* pl. -S one that yaps
		YAPPING	present participle oi ρ
YAH	*interj* — used as an exclamation of disgust	**YAR**	*adj* yare
YAHOO	*n* pl. -HOOS a coarse, uncouth person	**YARD**	*v* -ED, -ING, -S to put in a yard (a tract of ground adjacent to a building)
YAHOOISM	*n* pl. -S coarse, uncouth behavior	**YARDAGE**	*n* pl. -S the use of an enclosure for livestock at a railroad station
YAHRZEIT	*n* pl. -S an anniversary of the death of a family member observed by Jews	**YARDARM**	*n* pl. -S either end of a ship's spar
YAIRD	*n* pl. -S a garden	**YARDBIRD**	*n* pl. -S an army recruit
YAK	*v* YAKKED, YAKKING, YAKS to chatter	**YARDLAND**	*n* pl. -S an old English unit of land measure
YAKITORI	*n* pl. -S marinated chicken pieces on skewers	**YARDMAN**	*n* pl. -MEN a man employed to do outdoor work
YAKKER	*n* pl. -S one that yaks	**YARDWAND**	*n* pl. -S a measuring stick
YALD	*adj* yauld	**YARDWORK**	*n* pl. -S the work of caring for a lawn
YAM	*n* pl. -S a plant having an edible root	**YARE**	*adj* YARER, YAREST nimble **YARELY** *adv*
YAMALKA	*n* pl. -S yarmulke		
YAMEN	*n* pl. -S the residence of a Chinese public official	**YARMELKE**	*n* pl. -S yarmulke
		YARMULKE	*n* pl. -S a skullcap worn by Jewish males
YAMMER	*v* -ED, -ING, -S to whine or complain peevishly	**YARN**	*v* -ED, -ING, -S to tell a long story
YAMMERER	*n* pl. -S one that yammers	**YARNER**	*n* pl. -S one that yarns
YAMULKA	*n* pl. -S yarmulke	**YARROW**	*n* pl. -S a perennial herb
YAMUN	*n* pl. -S yamen		

YASHMAC	*n* pl. -S yashmak	**YEARN**	*v* -ED, -ING, -S to have a strong or deep desire
YASHMAK	*n* pl. -S a veil worn by Muslim women	**YEARNER**	*n* pl. -S one that yearns
YASMAK	*n* pl. -S yashmak	**YEARNING**	*n* pl. -S a strong or deep desire
YATAGAN	*n* pl. -S yataghan	**YEASAYER**	*n* pl. -S one that affirms something
YATAGHAN	*n* pl. -S a Turkish sword	**YEAST**	*v* -ED, -ING, -S to foam
YATTER	*v* -ED, -ING, -S to talk idly	**YEASTY**	*adj* YEASTIER, YEASTIEST foamy **YEASTILY** *adv*
YAUD	*n* pl. -S an old mare	
YAULD	*adj* vigorous	**YECCH**	*n* pl. -S something disgusting
YAUP	*v* -ED, -ING, -S to yawp	**YECH**	*n* pl. -S yecch
YAUPER	*n* pl. -S one that yaups	**YECHY**	*adj* disgusting
YAUPON	*n* pl. -S an evergreen shrub	**YEELIN**	*n* pl. -S yealing
YAUTIA	*n* pl. -S a tropical plant	**YEGG**	*n* pl. -S a burglar
YAW	*v* -ED, -ING, -S to deviate from an intended course	**YEGGMAN**	*n* pl. -MEN a yegg
		YEH	*adv* yeah
YAWL	*v* -ED, -ING, -S to yowl	**YELD**	*adj* not giving milk
YAWMETER	*n* pl. -S an instrument in an aircraft	**YELK**	*n* pl. -S yolk
		YELL	*v* -ED, -ING, -S to cry out loudly
YAWN	*v* -ED, -ING, -S to open the mouth wide with a deep inhalation of air	**YELLER**	*n* pl. -S one that yells
		YELLOW	*adj* -LOWER, -LOWEST of a bright color like that of ripe lemons **YELLOWLY** *adv*
YAWNER	*n* pl. -S one that yawns	
YAWP	*v* -ED, -ING, -S to utter a loud, harsh cry	**YELLOW**	*v* -ED, -ING, -S to make or become yellow
YAWPER	*n* pl. -S one that yawps	**YELLOWY**	*adj* somewhat yellow
YAWPING	*n* pl. -S a loud, harsh cry	**YELP**	*v* -ED, -ING, -S to utter a sharp, shrill cry
YAY	*n* pl. YAYS yea	
YCLEPED	*adj* yclept	**YELPER**	*n* pl. -S one that yelps
YCLEPT	*adj* called; named	**YEN**	*v* YENNED, YENNING, YENS to yearn
YE	*pron* you	
YEA	*n* pl. -S an affirmative vote	**YENTA**	*n* pl. -S a gossipy woman
YEAH	*adv* yes	**YENTE**	*n* pl. -S yenta
YEALING	*n* pl. -S a person of the same age	**YEOMAN**	*n* pl. -MEN an independent farmer **YEOMANLY** *adj*
YEAN	*v* -ED, -ING, -S to bear young	
YEANLING	*n* pl. -S the young of a sheep or goat	**YEOMANRY**	*n* pl. -RIES the collective body of yeomen
		YEP	*adv* yes
YEAR	*n* pl. -S a period of time consisting of 365 or 366 days	**YERBA**	*n* pl. -S a South American beverage resembling tea
YEARBOOK	*n* pl. -S a book published each year by a graduating class	**YERK**	*v* -ED, -ING, -S to beat vigorously
YEAREND	*n* pl. -S the end of a year	**YES**	*v* YESSED, YESSING, YESSES or YESES to give an affirmative reply to
YEARLIES	pl. of yearly	
YEARLING	*n* pl. -S an animal past its first year and not yet two years old	**YESHIVA**	*n* pl. -VAS, -VOT, or -VOTH an orthodox Jewish school
YEARLONG	*adj* lasting through a year	**YESHIVAH**	*n* pl. -S yeshiva
YEARLY	*n* pl. -LIES a publication appearing once a year	**YESSED**	past tense of yes

YESSES	a 3d person sing. of yes
YESSING	present participle of yes
YESTER	*adj* pertaining to yesterday
YESTERN	*adj* yester
YESTREEN	*n* pl. -S the previous evening
YET	*adv* up to now
YETI	*n* pl. -S the abominable snowman
YETT	*n* pl. -S a gate
YEUK	*v* -ED, -ING, -S to itch
YEUKY	*adj* itchy
YEW	*n* pl. -S an evergreen tree or shrub
YIELD	*v* -ED, -ING, -S to give up
YIELDER	*n* pl. -S one that yields
YIKES	*interj* — used to express fear or pain
YILL	*n* pl. -S ale
YIN	*n* pl. -S the feminine passive principle in Chinese cosmology
YINCE	*adv* once
YIP	*v* YIPPED, YIPPING, YIPS to yelp
YIPE	*interj* — used to express fear or surprise
YIPES	*interj* yipe
YIPPED	past tense of yip
YIPPEE	*interj* — used to express joy
YIPPIE	*n* pl. -S a politically radical hippie
YIPPING	present participle of yip
YIRD	*n* pl. -S earth
YIRR	*v* -ED, -ING, -S to snarl
YIRTH	*n* pl. -S yird
YLEM	*n* pl. -S hypothetical matter from which the elements are derived
YO	*interj* —used to call attention or to express affirmation
YOB	*n* pl. -S a hooligan
YOBBO	*n* pl. -BOS or -BOES a yob
YOCK	*v* -ED, -ING, -S to laugh boisterously
YOD	*n* pl. -S a Hebrew letter
YODEL	*v* -DELED, -DELING, -DELS or -DELLED, -DELLING, -DELS to sing with a fluctuating voice
YODELER	*n* pl. -S one that yodels
YODELLER	*n* pl. -S yodeler
YODELLING	a present participle of yodel
YODH	*n* pl. -S yod
YODLE	*v* -DLED, -DLING, -DLES to yodel
YODLER	*n* pl. -S yodeler
YOGA	*n* pl. -S a Hindu philosophy involving physical and mental disciplines
YOGEE	*n* pl. -S yogi
YOGH	*n* pl. -S a Middle English letter
YOGHOURT	*n* pl. -S yogurt
YOGHURT	*n* pl. -S yogurt
YOGI	*n* pl. -S a person who practices yoga
YOGIC	*adj* pertaining to yoga
YOGIN	*n* pl. -S yogi
YOGINI	*n* pl. -S a female yogi
YOGURT	*n* pl. -S a food made from milk
YOICKS	*interj* — used to encourage hunting hounds
YOK	*n* pl. -S a boisterous laugh
YOKE	*v* YOKED, YOKING, YOKES to fit with a yoke (a wooden frame for joining together draft animals)
YOKEL	*n* pl. -S a naive or gullible rustic
YOKELESS	*adj* having no yoke
YOKELISH	*adj* resembling a yokel
YOKEMATE	*n* pl. -S a companion in work
YOKING	present participle of yoke
YOKOZUNA	*n* pl. -S a champion sumo wrestler
YOLK	*n* pl. -S the yellow portion of an egg **YOLKED** *adj*
YOLKY	*adj* YOLKIER, YOLKIEST resembling a yolk
YOM	*n* pl. YOMIM day
YON	*adv* yonder
YOND	*adv* yonder
YONDER	*adv* over there
YONI	*n* pl. -S a symbol for the vulva in Hindu religion **YONIC** *adj*
YONKER	*n* pl. -S younker
YORE	*n* pl. -S time past
YOU	*pron* the 2d person sing. or pl. pronoun
YOUNG	*adj* YOUNGER, YOUNGEST being in the early period of life or growth
YOUNG	*n* pl. -S offspring
YOUNGER	*n* pl. -S an inferior in age

YOUNGISH	*adj* somewhat young	**YTTRIUM**	*n* pl. -S a metallic element
YOUNKER	*n* pl. -S a young gentleman	**YTTRIC** *adj*	
YOUPON	*n* pl. -S yaupon	**YUAN**	*n* pl. -S a monetary unit of China
YOUR	*adj* a possessive form of the pronoun you	**YUCA**	*n* pl. -S yucca
		YUCCA	*n* pl. -S a tropical plant
YOURN	*pron* yours	**YUCCH**	*interj* — used to express disgust
YOURS	*pron* a possessive form of the pronoun you	**YUCH**	*interj* yucch
		YUCK	*v* -ED, -ING, -S to yuk
YOURSELF	*pron* pl. -SELVES a form of the 2d person pronoun	**YUCKY**	*adj* YUCKIER, YUCKIEST disgusting
YOUSE	*pron* you	**YUGA**	*n* pl. -S an age of time in Hinduism
YOUTH	*n* pl. -S a young person	**YUK**	*v* YUKKED, YUKKING, YUKS to laugh loudly
YOUTHEN	*v* -ED, -ING, -S to make youthful		
YOUTHFUL	*adj* young	**YULAN**	*n* pl. -S a Chinese tree
YOW	*v* -ED, -ING, -S to yowl	**YULE**	*n* pl. -S Christmas time
YOWE	*n* pl. -S a ewe	**YULETIDE**	*n* pl. -S yule
YOWIE	*n* pl. -S a small ewe	**YUM**	*interj* — used to express pleasurable satisfaction
YOWL	*v* -ED, -ING, -S to utter a loud, long, mournful cry	**YUMMY**	*adj* -MIER, -MIEST delicious
YOWLER	*n* pl. -S one that yowls	**YUMMY**	*n* pl. -MIES something delicious
YPERITE	*n* pl. -S a poisonous gas	**YUP**	*n* pl. -S a yuppie
YTTERBIA	*n* pl. -S a chemical compound	**YUPON**	*n* pl. -S yaupon
YTTERBIC *adj*		**YUPPIE**	*n* pl. -S a young professional person working in a city
YTTRIA	*n* pl. -S a chemical compound	**YURT**	*n* pl. YURTA or YURTS a portable tent
		YWIS	*adv* iwis

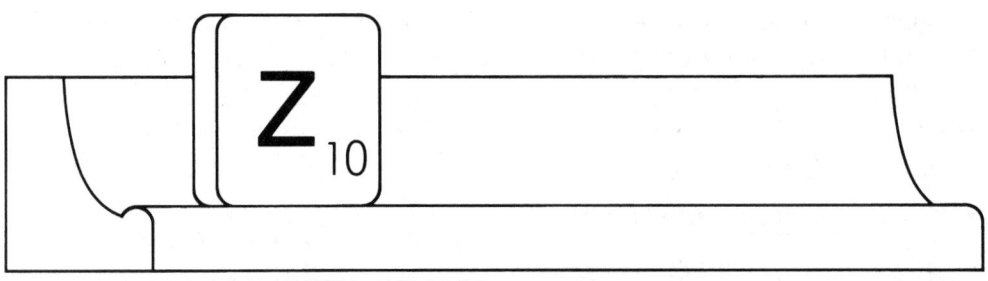

ZABAIONE *n* pl. -S a dessert resembling custard

ZABAJONE *n* pl. -S zabaione

ZACATON *n* pl. -S a Mexican grass

ZADDICK *n* pl. -DIKIM zaddik

ZADDIK *n* pl. -DIKIM a virtuous person by Jewish religious standards

ZAFFAR *n* pl. -S zaffer

ZAFFER *n* pl. -S a blue ceramic coloring

ZAFFIR *n* pl. -S zaffer

ZAFFRE *n* pl. -S zaffer

ZAFTIG *adj* full-bosomed

ZAG *v* ZAGGED, ZAGGING, ZAGS to turn sharply

ZAIBATSU *n* pl. ZAIBATSU a powerful family combine in Japan

ZAIKAI *n* pl. -S the business community of Japan

ZAIRE *n* pl. -S a monetary unit of Zaire

ZAMARRA *n* pl. -S a sheepskin coat

ZAMARRO *n* pl. -ROS zamarra

ZAMIA *n* pl. -S a tropical plant

ZAMINDAR *n* pl. -S a tax collector in precolonial India

ZANANA *n* pl. -S zenana

ZANDER *n* pl. -S a freshwater fish

ZANIER comparative of zany

ZANIES pl. of zany

ZANINESS *n* pl. -ES the quality or state of being zany

ZANY *adj* ZANIER, ZANIEST ludicrously comical **ZANILY** *adv*

ZANY *n* pl. -NIES a zany person

ZANYISH *adj* somewhat zany

ZANZA *n* pl. -S an African musical instrument

ZAP *v* ZAPPED, ZAPPING, ZAPS to kill or destroy instantaneously

ZAPATEO *n* pl. -TEOS a Spanish dance

ZAPPER *n* pl. -S a device that zaps

ZAPPY *adj* -PIER, -PIEST zippy

ZAPTIAH *n* pl. -S a Turkish policeman

ZAPTIEH *n* pl. -S zaptiah

ZARATITE *n* pl. -S a chemical compound

ZAREBA *n* pl. -S an improvised stockade

ZAREEBA *n* pl. -S zareba

ZARF *n* pl. -S a metal holder for a coffee cup

ZARIBA *n* pl. -S zareba

ZARZUELA *n* pl. -S a Spanish operetta

ZASTRUGA *n* pl. -GI sastruga

ZAX *n* pl. -ES a tool for cutting roof slates

ZAYIN *n* pl. -S a Hebrew letter

ZAZEN *n* pl. -S meditation in Zen Buddhism

ZEAL *n* pl. -S enthusiastic devotion

ZEALOT *n* pl. -S one who is zealous

ZEALOTRY *n* pl. -RIES excessive zeal

ZEALOUS *adj* filled with zeal

ZEATIN *n* pl. -S a chemical compound found in maize

ZEBEC *n* pl. -S xebec

ZEBECK *n* pl. -S xebec

ZEBRA *n* pl. -S an African mammal that is related to the horse **ZEBRAIC** *adj*

ZEBRASS *n* pl. -ES the offspring of a zebra and an ass

ZEBRINE *adj* pertaining to a zebra

ZEBROID *adj* zebrine

ZEBU *n* pl. -S an Asian ox

ZECCHIN *n* pl. -S zecchino

ZECCHINO *n* pl. -NI or -NOS a former gold coin of Italy

ZECHIN	*n* pl. -S zecchino
ZED	*n* pl. -S the letter Z
ZEDOARY	*n* pl. -ARIES the medicinal root of a tropical plant
ZEE	*n* pl. -S the letter Z
ZEIN	*n* pl. -S a simple protein
ZEK	*n* pl. -S an inmate in a Soviet labor camp
ZELKOVA	*n* pl. -S a Japanese tree
ZEMINDAR	*n* pl. -S zamindar
ZEMSTVO	*n* pl. -VOS or -VA an elective council in czarist Russia
ZENAIDA	*n* pl. -S a wild dove
ZENANA	*n* pl. -S the section of a house in India reserved for women
ZENITH	*n* pl. -S the highest point **ZENITHAL** *adj*
ZEOLITE	*n* pl. -S a mineral **ZEOLITIC** *adj*
ZEPHYR	*n* pl. -S a gentle breeze
ZEPPELIN	*n* pl. -S a long, rigid airship
ZERK	*n* pl. -S a grease fitting
ZERO	*v* -ED, -ING, -ES or -S to aim at the exact center of a target
ZEROTH	*adj* being numbered zero in a series
ZEST	*v* -ED, -ING, -S to fill with zest (invigorating excitement)
ZESTER	*n* pl. -S a utensil for peeling citrus rind
ZESTFUL	*adj* full of zest
ZESTLESS	*adj* lacking zest
ZESTY	*adj* ZESTIER, ZESTIEST marked by zest
ZETA	*n* pl. -S a Greek letter
ZEUGMA	*n* pl. -S the use of a word to modify or govern two or more words, while applying to each in a different sense
ZIBELINE	*n* pl. -S a soft fabric
ZIBET	*n* pl. -S an Asian civet
ZIBETH	*n* pl. -S zibet
ZIG	*v* ZIGGED, ZIGGING, ZIGS to turn sharply
ZIGGURAT	*n* pl. -S an ancient Babylonian temple tower
ZIGZAG	*v* -ZAGGED, -ZAGGING, -ZAGS to proceed on a course marked by sharp turns
ZIKKURAT	*n* pl. -S ziggurat
ZIKURAT	*n* pl. -S ziggurat
ZILCH	*n* pl. -ES nothing
ZILL	*n* pl. -S one of a pair of finger cymbals
ZILLAH	*n* pl. -S an administrative district in India
ZILLION	*n* pl. -S an indeterminately large number
ZIN	*n* pl. -S a dry red wine
ZINC	*v* ZINCED, ZINCING, ZINCS or ZINCKED, ZINCKING, ZINCS to coat with zinc (a metallic element)
ZINCATE	*n* pl. -S a chemical salt
ZINCIC	*adj* pertaining to zinc
ZINCIFY	*v* -FIED, -FYING, -FIES to coat with zinc
ZINCITE	*n* pl. -S an ore of zinc
ZINCKED	a past tense of zinc
ZINCKING	a present participle of zinc
ZINCKY	*adj* resembling zinc
ZINCOID	*adj* zincic
ZINCOUS	*adj* zincic
ZINCY	*adj* zincky
ZINEB	*n* pl. -S an insecticide
ZING	*v* -ED, -ING, -S to move with a high-pitched humming sound
ZINGANO	*n* pl. -NI zingaro
ZINGARA	*n* pl. -RE a female gypsy
ZINGARO	*n* pl. -RI a gypsy
ZINGER	*n* pl. -S a pointed witty retort or remark
ZINGY	*adj* ZINGIER, ZINGIEST enjoyably exciting
ZINKIFY	*v* -FIED, -FYING, -FIES to zincify
ZINKY	*adj* zincky
ZINNIA	*n* pl. -S a tropical plant
ZIP	*v* ZIPPED, ZIPPING, ZIPS to move with speed and vigor
ZIPLESS	*adj* lacking vigor or energy
ZIPPER	*v* -ED, -ING, -S to fasten with a zipper (a fastener consisting of two rows of interlocking teeth)
ZIPPING	present participle of zip
ZIPPY	*adj* -PIER, -PIEST full of energy
ZIRAM	*n* pl. -S a chemical salt
ZIRCON	*n* pl. -S a mineral
ZIRCONIA	*n* pl. -S a chemical compound
ZIRCONIC	*adj* pertaining to a certain metallic element

ZIT	*n* pl. -S a pimple
ZITHER	*n* pl. -S a stringed instrument
ZITHERN	*n* pl. -S zither
ZITI	*n* pl. -S a tubular pasta
ZIZIT	*n/pl* zizith
ZIZITH	*n/pl* the tassels on the four corners of a Jewish prayer shawl
ZIZZLE	*v* -ZLED, -ZLING, -ZLES to sizzle
ZLOTY	*n* pl. ZLOTYS, ZLOTE, ZLOTIES, or ZLOTYCH a monetary unit of Poland
ZOA	a pl. of zoon
ZOARIUM	*n* pl. -IA a colony of bryozoans **ZOARIAL** *adj*
ZODIAC	*n* pl. -S an imaginary belt encircling the celestial sphere **ZODIACAL** *adj*
ZOEA	*n* pl. ZOEAE or ZOEAS a larval form of certain crustaceans **ZOEAL** *adj*
ZOECIUM	*n* pl. -CIA zooecium
ZOFTIG	*adj* zaftig
ZOIC	*adj* pertaining to animals or animal life
ZOISITE	*n* pl. -S a mineral
ZOMBI	*n* pl. -S zombie
ZOMBIE	*n* pl. -S a will-less human capable only of automatic movement
ZOMBIFY	*v* -FIED, -FYING, -FIES to turn into a zombie
ZOMBIISM	*n* pl. -S the system of beliefs connected with a West African snake god
ZONAL	*adj* pertaining to a zone **ZONALLY** *adv*
ZONARY	*adj* zonal
ZONATE	*adj* arranged in zones
ZONATED	*adj* zonate
ZONATION	*n* pl. -S arrangement in zones
ZONE	*v* ZONED, ZONING, ZONES to arrange in zones (areas distinguished from other adjacent areas)
ZONELESS	*adj* having no zone or belt
ZONER	*n* pl. -S one that zones
ZONETIME	*n* pl. -S standard time used at sea
ZONING	present participle of zone
ZONK	*v* -ED, -ING, -S to stupefy
ZONULA	*n* pl. -LAE or -LAS zonule
ZONULE	*n* pl. -S a small zone **ZONULAR** *adj*
ZOO	*n* pl. ZOOS a place where animals are kept for public exhibition
ZOOCHORE	*n* pl. -S a plant dispersed by animals
ZOOECIUM	*n* pl. -CIA a sac secreted and lived in by an aquatic organism
ZOOGENIC	*adj* caused by animals or their activities
ZOOGLEA	*n* pl. -GLEAE or -GLEAS a jellylike mass of bacteria **ZOOGLEAL** *adj*
ZOOGLOEA	*n* pl. -GLOEAE or -GLOEAS zooglea
ZOOID	*n* pl. -S an organic cell or body capable of independent movement **ZOOIDAL** *adj*
ZOOKS	*interj* — used as a mild oath
ZOOLATER	*n* pl. -S one that worships animals
ZOOLATRY	*n* pl. -TRIES the worship of animals
ZOOLOGY	*n* pl. -GIES the science that deals with animals **ZOOLOGIC** *adj*
ZOOM	*v* -ED, -ING, -S to move with a loud humming sound
ZOOMANIA	*n* pl. -S an excessive interest in animals
ZOOMETRY	*n* pl. -TRIES the measurement of animals or animal parts
ZOOMORPH	*n* pl. -S something in the form of an animal
ZOON	*n* pl. ZOA or ZOONS the whole product of one fertilized egg **ZOONAL** *adj*
ZOONOSIS	*n* pl. -NOSES a disease that can be transmitted from animals to man **ZOONOTIC** *adj*
ZOOPHILE	*n* pl. -S a lover of animals
ZOOPHILY	*n* pl. -LIES a love of animals
ZOOPHOBE	*n* pl. -S one who fears or hates animals
ZOOPHYTE	*n* pl. -S an invertebrate animal
ZOOSPERM	*n* pl. -S the male fertilizing element of an animal
ZOOSPORE	*n* pl. -S a type of spore
ZOOTOMY	*n* pl. -MIES the dissection of animals **ZOOTOMIC** *adj*

ZOOTY   *adj* ZOOTIER, ZOOTIEST flashy in manner or style

ZORI   *n* pl. ZORI or ZORIS a type of sandal

ZORIL   *n* pl. -S a small African mammal

ZORILLA   *n* pl. -S zoril

ZORILLE   *n* pl. -S zoril

ZORILLO   *n* pl. -LOS zoril

ZOSTER   *n* pl. -S a virus disease

ZOUAVE   *n* pl. -S a French infantryman

ZOUNDS   *interj* — used as a mild oath

ZOWIE   *interj* — used to express surprise or pleasure

ZOYSIA   *n* pl. -S a perennial grass

ZUCCHINI   *n* pl. -S a vegetable

ZWIEBACK   *n* pl. -S a sweetened bread

ZYDECO   *n* pl. -COS popular music of southern Louisiana

ZYGOID   *adj* pertaining to a zygote

ZYGOMA   *n* pl. -MAS or -MATA the cheekbone

ZYGOSIS   *n* pl. -GOSES the union of two gametes **ZYGOSE** *adj*

ZYGOSITY   *n* pl. -TIES the makeup of a particular zygote

ZYGOTE   *n* pl. -S a cell formed by the union of two gametes **ZYGOTIC** *adj*

ZYGOTENE   *n* pl. -S a stage in meiosis

ZYMASE   *n* pl. -S an enzyme

ZYME   *n* pl. -S an enzyme

ZYMOGEN   *n* pl. -S a substance that develops into an enzyme when suitably activated

ZYMOGENE   *n* pl. -S zymogen

ZYMOGRAM   *n* pl. -S a record of separated proteins after electrophoresis

ZYMOLOGY   *n* pl. -GIES the science of fermentation

ZYMOSAN   *n* pl. -S an insoluble fraction of yeast cell walls

ZYMOSIS   *n* pl. -MOSES fermentation **ZYMOTIC** *adj*

ZYMURGY   *n* pl. -GIES a branch of chemistry dealing with fermentation

ZYZZYVA   *n* pl. -S a tropical weevil